METAPHYSICAL
BIBLE DICTIONARY

Unity School of Christianity

Unity Village, Mo.

The Metaphysical Bible Dictionary was compiled and published in 1931. It is one of the basic books containing Charles Fillmore's inspired thinking and teaching, which we regard as a vital part of our spiritual heritage.

Charles Fillmore was an innovative thinker, a pioneer in metaphysical thought at a time when most religious thought in America was entirely orthodox. He was a lifelong advocate of the open, inquiring mind, and he took pride in keeping abreast of the latest scientific and educational discoveries and theories. Many years ago he wrote, "What you think today may not be the measure for your thought tomorrow"; and it seems likely that were he to compile this book today, he might use different metaphors, different scientific references, and so on.

Truth is changeless. Those who knew Charles Fillmore best believe that he would like to be able to rephrase some of his observations for today's readers, thus giving them the added effectiveness of contemporary thought. But the ideas themselves—the core of Charles Fillmore's writing—are as timeless now (and will be tomorrow) as when they were first published.

If I speak with the tongues of men and of angels, but have not love, I am become sounding brass, or a clanging cymbal. And if I have *the gift of* prophecy, and know all mysteries and all knowledge; and if I have all faith, so as to remove mountains, but have not love, I am nothing. And if I bestow all my goods to feed *the poor,* and if I give my body to be burned, but have not love, it profiteth me nothing. Love suffereth long, *and* is kind; love envieth not; love vaunteth not itself, is not puffed up, doth not behave itself unseemly, seeketh not its own, is not provoked, taketh not account of evil; rejoiceth not in unrighteousness, but rejoiceth with the truth; beareth all things, believeth all things, hopeth all things, endureth all things. Love never faileth: but whether *there be* prophecies, they shall be done away; whether *there be* tongues, they shall cease; whether *there be* knowledge, it shall be done away. For we know in part, and we prophesy in part; but when that which is perfect is come, that which is in part shall be done away. When I was a child, I spake as a child, I felt as a child, I thought as a child: now that I am become a man, I have put away childish things. For now we see in a mirror, darkly; but then face to face: now I know in part; but then shall I know fully even as also I was fully known. But now abideth faith, hope, love, these three: and the greatest of these is love.—*I Cor. 13.*

KEY TO SIGNS USED IN THIS DICTIONARY

The pronunciation adopted in this Metaphysical Bible Dictionary, and the diacritical marks used to express it, are based on Nelson's American Standard Version of the Bible, teachers' edition.

Syllables are indicated by a hyphen (-), while those on which stress has to be laid are marked with an accent ('). In compound names, accent of each name is given where necessary, and component parts separated by a double hyphen (–).

ā *as in* dāy.	ê *as in* êvent.	oi *as in* oil.
å " senåte.	ĕ " ĕnd.	ș " z (Moșeș).
ă " ădd.	ē " tērm.	th " t (thyme).
ă " ăccount.	ġ " ġentle.	ū " ūse.
â " câre.	ḡ " ḡet.	û " ûnite.
ä " fär.	ī " tīme.	ŭ " ŭs.
å " låst.	î " îdea.	û " tûrn.
a " sofa.	ĭ " ĭll.	ų " rųde.
ą " fąll.	ī " fīrm.	x " gz (Alexandria).
āi " aid.	į " y (Christįan).	ȳ " defȳ.
e " cane.	ō " ōld.	y̆ " pity̆.
ç " s (Sadduçees).	ô " ôbey.	ci)
ch " chord.	ŏ " nŏt.	si } = sh	shi
ē " mēte.	ô " lôrd.	ti)

ci
si } = sh
ti)
{ Cilicia.
Persia.
Egyptian.

ABBREVIATIONS

Arab. . . . Arabic	Gal. . . . . Galatians	N. T. Gk. . . New Testament Greek
Aram. . . . Aramaic	Gen. . . . . Genesis	
A. S. V. . . American Standard Version	Gk. . . . . Greek	Num. . . . . Numbers
	Hab. . . . . Habakkuk	Obad. . . . Obadiah
Assyr. . . . Assyrian	Hag. . . . . Haggai	Pers. . . . . Persian
A. V. . . . . Authorized (King James) Version	Heb. . . . . Hebrew	Pet. . . . . Peter
	Heb. . . . . Hebrews	Phil. . . . . Philippians
Bab. . . . . Babylonian	Hos. . . . . Hosea	Philem. . . . Philemon
Chald. . . . Chaldean	i. e. . . . . that is	Prov. . . . . Proverbs
Chron. . . . Chronicles	Isa. . . . . Isaiah	Rev. . . . . Revelation
Col. . . . . Colossians	Jer. . . . . Jeremiah	Rom. . . . . Romans
Cor. . . . . Corinthians	Josh. . . . . Joshua	R. V. . . . . Revised Version
Dan. . . . . Daniel	Judg. . . . . Judges	
Deut. . . . Deuteronomy	Lam. . . . . Lamentations	Sam. . . . . Samuel
Eccles. . . . Ecclesiastes		Skr. . . . . Sanskrit
Egypt. . . . Egyptian	Lat. . . . . Latin	Song of Sol. . Song of Solomon
Eph. . . . . Ephesians	Lev. . . . . Leviticus	
Esth. . . . . Esther	Mal. . . . . Malachi	Syr. . . . . Syriac
Ethiop. . . . Ephesians	Matt. . . . Matthew	Thess. . . . Thessalonians
e. g. . . . . for example	*Meta.* . . . . Metaphysical Interpretation	
etc. . . . . and so on		Tim. . . . . Timothy
Exod. . . . Exodus	Mic. . . . . Micah	viz. . . . . namely
Ezek. . . . Ezekiel	Nah. . . . . Nahum	Zech. . . . . Zechariah
fr. . . . . from	Neh. . . . . Nehemiah	Zeph. . . . . Zephaniah

PREFACE

This Metaphysical Bible Dictionary is offered by the Unity School of Christianity to meet a very definite demand, on the part of Bible students and of metaphysicians generally, for a work setting forth in simple language the inner, esoteric meanings of Scriptural names.

Apart from its being a book of great historical and biographical interest, the Bible is, from Genesis to Revelation, in its inner or spiritual meaning, a record of the experiences and the development of the human soul and of the whole being of man; also it is a treatise on man's relation to God, the Creator and Father. Therefore we are confident that this dictionary will prove very beneficial to Bible students. By opening up new avenues of thought it will inspire a greater understanding and interest in studying the Scriptures, and will aid its readers much in solving life's problems.

The metaphysical interpretations given in this dictionary are based on the practical teachings of Jesus Christ, as understood and taught by the Unity School of Christianity under the direction of Charles Fillmore and Myrtle Fillmore, its founders. In this dictionary, Mr. Fillmore's interpretations, which have appeared in *Unity* magazine and in other Unity literature from time to time, have been used. The Bible names that had not appeared in the lessons published in Unity literature have been interpreted (with Mr. Fillmore's approval) by Theodosia DeWitt Schobert, who was formerly employed in the Unity Editoral Department and in the Society of Silent Unity.

The names with their pronunciations are taken from Nelson's American Standard Version of the Bible, teachers' edition. Wherever this version gives a spelling different from that set forth in the King James, or Authorized, Version, both are given. The American Standard Version spelling is shown first, and is followed by that of the Authorized Ver-

sion in parentheses, thus: **Zerubbabel** (A. V., Zorobabel). Following these the name is syllabified and marked for pronunciation, thus: zĕ-rŭb′-bă-bĕl. The diacritical marks employed are those used in the American Standard Version. Following the pronunciation of each name, the tongue from which it originated is indicated: (Heb.) for Hebrew, (Aram.) for Aramaic, (Gk.) for Greek, and so on.

In the compilation of the word definitions, which go far in forming the foundations for the metaphysical interpretations, great care has been exercised. Many authorities and lexicons have been consulted in the preparation of this part of the work. Wherever a divergence of opinion between authorities of equal weight was found, the most reasonable etymology was followed.

So far as possible, except where the etymology has become lost, the definitions have been traced back to their original root ideas. These simple ideas, out of which more or less complex expressions have often developed, have been given first; in each case definitions that have developed out of the root idea are given in sequence. This feature is an innovation, and should make for greater clarity in the deeper understanding of the Scriptures.

Many of the Hebrew words that form the basis of proper names derive from pure abstractions, and thus have acceptations that may be either good or bad. Take for instance the word Cain, which comes from the root idea of centralized power, accretion, or accumulation. On the one hand this name could be an expression for benign rulership, kingly qualities, lawful possession, and the like; on the other hand it could stand for despotism, usurpation, extreme selfishness. This peculiarity of the Hebrew tongue has been a source of confusion to many Bible students, and has not been explained in many Bible helps that have been published. This is also a reason for much apparent disparity among the authors of Bible helps wherein only a one-word definition is given: some have taken one acceptation while others have adopted another. In this dictionary the aim has been to clarify. The large number of definitions selected in giving the meaning of names will help the student to feel his way into many bypaths of metaphysical deduction.

One can also gather from the differences and similarities in name definitions something that we have found to be a fact in our experience in studying the Scriptures. This fact is that Scripture names cannot be limited to any one interpretation; no one can truthfully say that a certain text means such or such a thing and nothing else. A dozen persons may get inspiration in a dozen different ways from one Scripture text.

Following the definitions given for each name will be found a brief sketch of the individual, or place, with references telling where the name can be found in the Bible. Unless some particular incident warrants calling attention to it elsewhere, only one reference is given. This reference is either to the place where the name first appears, to that which explains most clearly the historical facts regarding the person or place for whom or which the name stands, or to the passage discussed in the metaphysical interpretation. Wherever the name of an individual is spelled differently in other texts, where another name is used, or where there are several persons bearing the same name, note is made of such fact. In a few cases we have found two names alike, apparently, but separated and having entirely different meanings. This is due to the spelling in translations, which cannot or does not convey the differences in the Hebrew spelling. An instance of this kind is found in Abel, second son of Adam, which should be spelled Hebel, and Abel, the name of several villages. In the Hebrew the two names are spelled with entirely different letters of the alphabet.

Following the biographical sketch of a name comes the metaphysical interpretation. This interpretation is headed *Meta.*, an abbreviation of "metaphysical."

By "metaphysical" we refer to the inner or esoteric meaning of the name defined, as it applies to every unfolding individual and to his relation to God.

We have found in interpreting Bible names that there are varying phases or shades of meaning connected with some of them, beyond that conveyed in the strict definition of the name word. Who the individual was, who his father or mother was, what his occupation was, who his associates were—all these things are modifying factors that we must consider in working out the true character definitions and the metaphysical interpretations as they relate to man generally. Thus we may have two or more men with identical names, each of whom may relate to a different line of thought and develop very different characteristics. These character indexes, which we call names, might therefore be symbolic of divers phases of Truth or error, and different applications of it. For instance, suppose that we have an Israelite and a Gentile with the same name. These two men would symbolize different planes of consciousness in the individual. The Israelite would relate to the religious tendencies, either intellectual or spiritual; the Gentile would relate to some phase of the outer man—perhaps to the carnal, sensual, or purely material if he were an enemy of the Israelites.

Furthermore the social status of the individual whose name is being analyzed and interpreted has to be considered. Whether he was a king, a prince, a priest, a governor, a freeman, or a slave makes a difference in the importance or influence of the idea that he represents. His occupation is also taken into consideration. If he were a shepherd, the significance would differ from what it would be were he a warrior, a hunter, or a tiller of the soil.

The student will find the foregoing methods of analysis worked out in the metaphysical interpretations. We do not wish to convey the impression, however, that the reader will find herein presented the beginning and the end of all Bible symbology and of the phases of Truth that may be developed from it. The interpretations given are suggestions, by no means final. Each may be worked out more fully and comprehensively. An entire volume could easily be devoted to one name, in many cases. If the reader will trust to his own indwelling Spirit of truth for light, he will find in these suggestions a guide to endless inspiration in the understanding of Truth.

The Scriptures veil their metaphysical meaning under the names of towns, rivers, seas, and so forth, and the acts of men in connection therewith. The name of each person and of everything in the Scriptures has an inner meaning, a clew to which may be found in any teachers' Bible under such a head as "Names and Their Meanings." For instance, Bethlehem means *"house of bread,"* and indicates the nerve center at the pit of the stomach, through which universal substance joins the refined or spiritualized chemical products of the body metabolism. Through this center are gradually generated the elements that go to make up the spiritualized body of the Christ man. Jesus was born in Bethlehem of Judea.

All is mind, and all material forms are pictures of ideas. By studying a picture we may get a concept of the idea that it represents. The Statue of Liberty at the entrance to New York Harbor, showing the goddess as enlightening the world, is the picture of an idea that nearly everybody understands. It was made by a man as an embodiment of his idea of American freedom and its majesty. Divine Mind has ideas, and they become embodied through natural processes. The Hebrew Scriptures give a series of pictures representing those ideas.

The product of the first day's creation is recorded in Genesis as being "heaven," "earth," and "light." Heaven represents spiritual ideas. Earth represents material thoughts. Light represents understanding.

The firmament in the midst of the waters is an idea of confidence or faith in the invisible. Waters represent changing conditions, which are a necessary part of creation; but when faith establishes itself and separates what is above (spiritual) from what is below (material) the result is harmony or heaven.

The dry land is the thought form, or substance concept, in which the seed of propagation or increase is implanted.

The lights in the firmament, one to rule the day and the other to rule the night, are ideas of intelligent action (lights) in both the conscious and subconscious realms of mind.

The abundant bringing forth of the waters is the fecundity of the mind, which great fishes symbolize. In order to bring forth great results the mind must realize its innate thinking capacity to be great.

After the idea of unlimited capacity follows the image and likeness of God, the ideal or divine man. Then appears the man idea in its developing or evolution phase. As Adam and Eve, the man idea is the innocent child of nature, just entering experience. As Cain and Abel it is developing the idea of self-preservation from the standpoint of personality. Noah is the thought of obedience and of the safety that follows.

Abraham is a partially developed photograph of the faith idea, which is more fully brought out in Peter. Jacob is the accumulative idea in process of development under divine guidance.

The New Testament is a veiled textbook for the initiate who is seeking degrees in the inner life. It gives rules for working out every mental state that may be found in the mind. It is like a textbook on mathematics, a textbook in which are acted out by living figures all the rules for working every problem that may come up in human life.

The key to the mystical theme of the New Testament is found in the spiritual nature of its star character, Jesus Christ. *Christ* is the Greek form of the Hebrew *Messiah,* and the Messiah is the anointed of God, or God identified as perfect man. This perfect man was the image and likeness of Elohim, described in the 1st chapter of Genesis. The perfect-man idea or I AM of Elohim appears in the 2d chapter of Genesis as Jehovah God, or I AM God. Throughout the Old Testament, up to the advent of Jesus Christ, Jehovah is concerned with the evolution of man. The Christ, or Jehovah, in Jesus affirmed its Mosaic antecedent in the statement,

"Before Abraham was born, I am." The Christ claimed also that Moses wrote of Him, again identifying Jehovah and Christ. Jesus represented the external consciousness, or Adam, the man that the Christ or Jehovah formed (in the Edenic allegory) out of the dust of the ground, or elemental substance.

Jesus worked out step by step in His three years' ministry spiritual and mental formulas that we all can apply and thus be healed of our sins and ills of mind and body; by following Him as Guide, Teacher, and Helper we can finally attain the perfect expression of the divine-ideal man imaged by Elohim in the 1st chapter of Genesis. Interpreters of Jesus have given slight value to the part that the body plays in the redemption of man, but Jesus Christ plainly teaches that the whole man—spirit, soul, and body—must be redeemed from the effects of sin. He overcame death and saved His body from the grave. He promised that all those who followed Him in the regeneration would do likewise. Question arises as to how this doctrine was, and is, applied to the restoration of man's body. The various processes in raising the body to wholeness are symbolized in the many healings wrought by Jesus. Every so-called miracle of His points to the transformation of some function of the body consciousness. For example, consider His changing of water to wine at Cana of Galilee: Cana means *"place of reeds"* (the larynx); and Galilee means *"rolling energy, rolling, turning,"* or, as we say in modern terms, "vibration." So we understand that the first miracle of Jesus (the I AM), the turning of water into wine in Cana of Galilee, represents the change that goes on in the waters of life, or the nerve fluids, as they are brought into vibration by a spiritually quickened man or woman. The waters of life are thus changed into wine, or are given elements of greater stimulating, life-giving power than they possessed before they passed through the vibration of the voice. The whole organism may be invigorated and stimulated through the vibratory thrill of the voice. In connection with this miracle there is a still more interior meaning. The six waterpots indicate that, when the six great nerve centers in the body are purified, "after the Jews' manner of purifying," the vibratory power of the voice will become so great that by the spoken word a vessel filled with water may be changed into wine. The means by which this purification can be accomplished and the power thus acquired are also explained in the symbolism of the Old Testament.

We could go on thus through all the Bible, but the foregoing is enough to show how we see in the Bible symbolical pictures showing the growth and unfoldment of the latent spiritual power in man up to the time when he comes into manifestation of the perfect "image" and "likeness" in which he was created.

In presenting these methods of interpretation we have endeavored to give with each one sufficient explanation to enable the student to get an idea as to how and why we arrive at given metaphysical conclusions. By reasoning along the same lines the student can develop the inner interpretation of the Scriptures for himself. Our real aim is to assist in leading the student into the inner or spiritual interpretation of the Bible, that he may apply it in the very best and most practical way in his own life. If he does not wish to accept our interpretations, but would rather do his own thinking, entirely apart from our suggestions, we fully recognize his right to do so. We are always pleased when any one learns to go within and get his inspiration direct from his own indwelling Lord or Spirit of truth. By doing this a person will come to appreciate, as he can in no other way, the patient, faithful effort that culminates in the production of such books as this one.

As stated before, this book is not final in the field that it covers; at best it is only a stepping-stone to the higher realm of spiritual consciousness, toward attainment of the mind "which was also in Christ Jesus."

To all mankind, and for the highest spiritual attainment and good of every individual, this volume is lovingly and prayerfully dedicated.

UNITY SCHOOL OF CHRISTIANITY

AARON

Aaron, aâr'-ŏn (Heb.)—*illumined; enlightener; mountaineer (very lofty).*

Brother of Moses; of the Israelitish tribe of Levi, and first high priest of Israel (Exod. 6:20; 28:1-4).

Meta. Executive power of divine law. Aaron, the first high priest of Israel and the bearer of intellectual light to the Israelites, signifies the ruling power of the intellectual consciousness. The making of the "molten calf" by Aaron (Exod. 32:1-8) signifies the false states of thought (idols) that man builds into his consciousness when he perceives the Truth but does not carry his spiritual ideals into execution, choosing instead to let his thoughts function in a lower plane of consciousness.

In Exodus 40:12, 13, Aaron and his sons typify spiritual strength, which becomes the presiding, directive power of a new state of consciousness. Through spiritual strength there is set up an abiding thought action that contributes to the building of the holy Temple (redeemed body). Bringing Aaron and his sons to the door of the tent of meeting and washing them with water means that we should declare spiritual strength to be the presiding, directive power of this new state of consciousness—not a mere animal strength, but a strength purified from all grossness of sense. This declaration of strength is absolutely necessary to the permanency of the body tabernacle. Through it is set up an abiding thought action that continues while one's attention is elsewhere: Aaron continues to minister in his priestly office.

Abaddon, ă-băd'-dŏn (Heb.) — *destroyer; destruction.*

Called Apollyon, in the Greek tongue. Said to be king over the great army of locusts that came out from the abyss to destroy (Rev. 9:2-11).

Meta. That this name has reference

ABAGTHA

to a very destructive belief of man's is evident from the meaning of the name and from the 9th chapter of Revelation. From Exodus 10:14, 15 and Joel 2:3-10 (compare these texts with their references and you will see that they all are speaking of the same thing) one can get an idea of the destructiveness of the locusts of Palestine and the surrounding countries. They quite commonly came up like great armies and ate every living plant in their path; also, the leaves and the branches of the trees. So Abaddon must stand for the error belief in utter destruction of life and form.

The true life principle can never be destroyed; only the outer form of man's belief in materiality is destructible. So long as man believes in materiality or destruction, the outer destruction of forms will take place. It is very necessary, therefore, that the thought of the possibility of life's being destructible, or in any way limited, be erased entirely from the consciousness. "There is only one Presence and one Power in the universe —the Good omnipotent." Life is omnipresent, eternal, sure; life cannot be destroyed, because it is God Himself.

Abagtha, ă-băg'-thá (Pers.)—*happy; prosperous.*

One of the seven eunuchs, or chamberlains, who served in the palace of Ahasuerus, king of Persia (Esther 1:10).

Meta. A eunuch, in consciousness, represents a thought from which the capacity to increase life and its forms has been eliminated. The chamberlain, in this instance, is a keeper of the king's bedchamber. Abagtha therefore represents a pure, *happy, prosperous* thought guarding and ministering to the king (the will). This thought is not spiritual (Abagtha was not of Israel), but it is of the outer realm, or realm of phenomena. The Medes and Persians are thought to have been descended from Japheth (one of the sons of Noah), who typifies the intellect or reason. The thoughts that they signify therefore belong to the mental and the psychic in man. Seven signifies perfection or fullness on the natural plane of consciousness.

Abanah (A. V., Abana), ăb′-ă-năh (Heb.)—*permanent; enduring; perennial; a rock, a stone; stony.*

A river in Syria (II Kings 5:12). This river flows through Damascus, which is one of the oldest known cities of the world.

Meta. The name symbolizes something constantly renewing, therefore permanent and enduring. From its setting, however, the river Abanah signifies intellectual thoughts and reasonings about life. A river represents a current of thought. The thoughts of the intellectual domain (Syria) apart from the real life current in the organism (the Jordan symbolizes this current in the instance of the healing of Naaman the Syrian, who thought that he could just as well wash in the rivers Abanah and Pharpar of Syria as in the Jordan) and apart from the loving, spiritual power of the I AM (Elisha) have no healing potency. Intellectual thoughts become permanent only when the intellect is quickened by Spirit and becomes transmuted into spiritual consciousness.

Abarim, ăb′-ă-rĭm (Heb.)—*regions beyond; passages; fords; crossings.*

A range of mountains in the country of Moab, opposite Jericho (Num. 33:47, 48; Deut. 32:49).

Meta. The Moabites were descended from Lot, whose name means *hidden, a covering, dark colored.* Lot's domain is the flesh, the part of man's consciousness that is still in darkness. Mountains are high places in consciousness. Among the peaks in this range of mountains (Abarim) are Nebo, Pisgah, and Peor. It was from the top of one of these mountain peaks that Moses was shown the land of Canaan, which was to be possessed by the Israelites. It was there that Moses died, that the Moses consciousness or understanding of divine law was merged into the I AM (Joshua), positive expression of the law. Abarim,

therefore, though situated in Moab (the flesh or carnal consciousness) represents high, inspiring thoughts that look away from error over into the Promised Land; that see the possibility of the elevation of the whole man, spirit, soul, and body, to spiritual consciousness.

Abba, ăb′-bà (Aram.)—*father.*

A word of endearment signifying *my father* (Mark 14:36; Rom. 8:15; Gal. 4:6).

Meta. In olden times a slave or menial servant was not allowed to call his master (the lord or head of the house) Abba. Only the children of the family could do this, or some one in close relationship or association, because it was an indication of the tenderest affection. When Abba is used in the Bible the word Father follows it and therefore gives emphasis to the term. It is only as we come to know our sonship, our true relation to God, that we enter into the consciousness of love and tender affiliation with Spirit that is signified by the word Abba.

Abda, ăb′-dà (Aram.)—*servant; a servant of God* is implied; also *slave; worshiper; worshiper of God.*

a Father of Adoniram, one of the princes of King Solomon who "was over the men subject to taskwork" (I Kings 4:6). **b** Son of Shammua, a Levite who returned from the Babylonian captivity (Neh. 11:17).

Meta. The idea of spiritual work or service, but containing a thought of bondage (*servant, slave, worshiper*). This idea of service was lifted to a higher level in the son, Adoniram, meaning *my lord is high, my lord is exalted,* or *lord of heights.*

Abdeel, ăb′-dĕ-ĕl (Heb.)—*servant of God.*

Father of Shelemiah, who was one of those whom the king of Judah, Jehoiakim, sent to take Jeremiah after he (the king) had burned the roll that contained the law of God (Jer. 36:26).

Meta. A thought of service to God (*servant of God*), but dominated by the ignorant, disbelieving will (Jehoiakim, the king). Jehoiakim, the king (the will), has the capacity to establish God in consciousness, since the name Jehoiakim means *whom Jehovah hath set up, Jah establishes,* and the will in man has the power to accept or to reject Truth. Jehoiakim, however, represents a ruling state of mind that does not reverence or obey the higher law and is not receptive to new ideas; therefore Abdeel signifies a thought of service to God that is in bondage to old established religious ideas that persecute man's inner spiritual faith and discernment (the prophet Jeremiah). Jeremiah also signifies the exalted state of thought that connects us with Divine Mind and demands that all our religious thoughts (Israelites) be faithful in observance of divine law.

Abdi, ăb′-dī (Heb.)—*my servant; servant of Jah.*

a Son of Malluch (I Chron. 6:44) and father of Kish, of the Levites (II Chron. 29:12). **b** A son of Elam (Ezra 10:26).

Meta. Thoughts that serve Jehovah or are subject to Jehovah (*my servant, servant of Jah*). The first mentioned Abdi signifies a thought that springs from counseling with Spirit and meditating on divine law. The father of this Abdi was named Malluch, which means *counselor.*

Abdi, the son of Elam, represents a thought of service to God that is established in an idea of youth and strength (Elam means *fully developed, a young man*) but is united to a physical or carnal soul quality (he was married to a foreign wife). This carnal idea has to be given up. The Israelites had to separate themselves from their foreign wives and from the children (mixed thoughts) that had come of union with them.

Abdiel, ăb′-dĭ-ĕl (Heb.)—*servant of God.*

A Gadite, who lived in Gilead in Bashan (I Chron. 5:15, 16).

Meta. Gad means *fortune,* or *fortunate;* also, a *troop,* and refers to the power faculty in individual consciousness. (See GAD.) Gilead means *enduring rock,* and Bashan means *smooth, fertile soil, fruitful.* So it is quite evident that the thought of service that Abdiel (*servant of God*) typifies has reference to the expression of power and strength in relation to bountiful supply and increase of good.

Abdon, ăb′-dŏn (Heb.)—*servile; service; a servant.*

a A judge of Israel. He had "forty sons and thirty sons' sons, that rode on threescore and ten ass colts: and he judged Israel eight years" (Judg. 12:13-15). **b** The name of a city in Asher that was given to "the children of Gershon, of the families of the Levites" (Josh. 21:30).

Meta. A phase of the judging, discerning faculty in man. Abdon served Israel as judge. The forty sons imply a thought of completeness, and the seventy ass colts refer to the animal part of man as expressed through the seven senses, seventy being a multiple of seven and showing a tenfold increase of the expression of this animal phase of consciousness, which was held in dominion by the thoughts for which Abdon's sons and sons' sons stand. The riding of Abdon's sons and sons' sons on seventy asses shows that in thought the animal phase of man symbolized by the ass (meekness, stubbornness, persistency, and endurance) is in subjection. (One meaning of *servile* is *held in subjection.*)

"And Abdon . . . died, and was buried in Pirathon in the land of Ephraim, in the hill-country of the Amalekites" (Judg. 12:15). This means that, as the thought of good judgment, service, and dominion over the animal phase of man (symbolized by Abdon and by the riding of his sons and sons' sons on the asses) sinks deeper into the consciousness, a fuller uplifting of the animal forces, appetites, and passions (Amalekites) may be accomplished.

The city of Abdon symbolizes a happy (Asher), fixed state of consciousness, or an aggregation of thoughts of judgment and service utilized by the natural religious tendencies (Levites) of the individual, from which opposite thoughts of error have been expelled. (Gershon means *expulsion.*)

Abed–nego, ă-bĕd′–nĕ-gō (Aram.)—*servant of Nego* or *Nebo.*

A friend of Daniel's, by the name of Azariah, to whom the name Abed–nego was given by the prince of the eunuchs of King Nebuchadnezzar of Babylon (Dan. 1:7). He was of the tribe of Judah, of royal blood, and was skilled in all wisdom (Dan. 1:3, 4, 6). He was one of the three (Abed–nego, Meshach, and Shadrach) who came out of the fiery furnace unharmed (Dan. 3:12-30).

Meta. Light, understanding. Nebo was a Babylonian and Assyrian deity who represented the planet Mercury. Nebo was worshiped as the god of wisdom, and was believed to be the scribe and interpreter of the gods. The name Nebo, according to The New International Encyclopædia, means *announcer, proclaimer.*

Abel, ā'-bĕl (in Hebrew, *heh-bel*)— *breath* or *vanity; transitoriness; a breath; vapor.*

Second son of Adam and Eve, killed by his brother Cain (Gen. 4:2-8).

Meta. Abel means *breath,* which places him in the air, or the mental realm. He represents not the spiritual mind but the mind that controls the animal functions—he was a sheep raiser. The mental is more closely related to the spiritual consciousness than the physical (Cain) is, and its offerings are more acceptable to Spirit than are those of the physical. In Hindu metaphysics, Abel would be termed the *animal soul.* Paul would call him the *creature.*

Abel, ā'-bĕl (in Hebrew, *aw-bali*)— *meadow; fresh; grassy; a grassy place.*

A great stone "in the field of Joshua the Bethshemite," "whereon they set down the ark of Jehovah" (I Sam. 6:18, see marginal note also).

Meta. A very firm, abiding realization of substance in consciousness.

Abel–beth–maacah, ā'-bĕl-bĕth-mā'-ă-căh (Heb.)—*meadow of the house of Maacah; meadow of the house of oppression.*

A city of Naphtali (I Kings 15:20; II Kings 15:29); in II Chronicles 16:4 it is called Abel–maim.

Meta. Abel means *meadow.* A meadow is a grassland, and is generally used to provide grass and hay for do-mestic animals, principally horses, cattle, and sheep. These animals symbolize the physical strength and the natural vital forces of the human organism. Abel therefore stands for a substance state of consciousness by which the animal forces of the body are sustained.

Naphtali refers to the strength center in man. This center is located in the region of the kidneys, whose office is to eliminate certain watery elements from the blood.

Beth means *house,* and Maacah means *oppression, depression,* or *pressed down, worn.* Abel–beth–maacah, *meadow of the house of oppression,* a city of Naphtali, therefore. signifies the weighed-down, worn-out feeling that we experience when our strength (Naphtali) has been given over to the physical and our substance has been dissipated through sense activity. When this condition obtains, the whole vitality is lowered; the depression usually strikes first at the pit of the stomach, the substance center in consciousness.

Abel–beth–maacah also was called Abel–maim, *meadow of waters.* Waters symbolize an unstable, changing element in consciousness; waters often stand for a cleansing quality also. So the substance in our organism must be cleansed, uplifted, and transmuted (changed) into its original spiritual essence before it becomes stable, abiding.

Abel–cheramim, ā'-bĕl-ĕhĕ-rā'-mĭm (Heb.)—*plain of the vineyards; meadow of the vineyards.*

A small town to the east of the Jordan (Judg. 11:33).

Meta. A fixed state of thought in which the idea of the substance of life predominates. Abel, or *meadow,* stands for substance, while a *vineyard* (grapes) always suggests life.

Abel – meholah, ā'-bĕl – mĕ-hō'-lăh (Heb.)—*meadow of the dance; dance-meadow.*

A town that is mentioned in connection with Gideon's victory over the host of Midian (Judg. 7:22; see also I Kings 4:12; 19:16). This town is supposed to have been in the Jordan valley.

Meta. An aggregation of joyous, harmonious thoughts of substance activity, or of the activity of substance.

Abel – mizraim, ā′-bĕl – mĭz′-ră-ĭm (Heb.)—*mourning of Egypt* or *Egyptians; mourning* or *meadow of distress.*

The name was given by the Canaanites to the threshing floor of Atad, because it was there that Joseph, his brothers, and the Egyptians who were with them mourned seven days for Jacob, while they were on their way to bury him in the cave of the field of Machpelah, where Abraham and Isaac were buried (Gen. 50:11).

Meta. The feeling of sorrow and loss, in the sense man, that often accompanies the letting go of some good idea in consciousness after it has finished its work. Man's tendency is to cling to the old ideas that have been helpful to him. But when their work is done in the individual for the time being, these old ideas, no matter how well they have served, must be released from consciousness, that other and higher ideas may take their place. In the Bible a threshing floor always typifies a process of judgment, a sifting of ideas and thoughts in consciousness, a letting go of the chaff and a laying hold of the wheat.

Abel-shittim, ā′-bĕl–shĭt′-tĭm (Heb.)—*meadow of the acacias; place of acacias.*

A town "in the plains of Moab" (Num. 33:49). It is more often called Shittim. (See SHITTIM.)

Meta. A perception, or conception, of the substance, reality, and resurrecting power of the inner spiritual life. (Acacias refer to resurrection, life, and a meadow refers to substance).

Abi, ā′-bī (Heb.)—*Jah is father; founder;* an old form of *father of,* which forms the first part of several Hebrew proper names; *progenitor.*

Daughter of Zechariah, and mother of Hezekiah, king of Judah (II Kings 18:2). In II Chronicles 29:1 she is called Abijah.

Meta. The inner conception, in the soul, of Jehovah as Father, or source of being (*Jah is father*). This comprehension of Truth, held in mind (see AHAZ—meaning *to lay hold of*—husband of Abi), is the mother of, or brings to pass in consciousness, that which Hezekiah, king

of Judah, represents—faith in God, or the expression of spiritual strength.

Abi–albon, ā′-bĭ–ăl′-bŏn (Heb.)—*father of strength; father of valiance; father of prevailing.*

One of David's mighty men (II Sam. 23:31); he is called Abiel in I Chronicles 11:32.

Meta. A mighty thought of conquest.

Abiasaph, ă-bī′-ă-săph (Heb.)—*father of gathering.*

A descendant of Levi (Exod. 6:24). He is called Ebiasaph in I Chronicles 6:37.

Meta. A thought in consciousness, of a kind that gathers together, or draws together (*father of gathering*). Such thoughts belong to the love (Levi) nature in man. They are of a harmonizing character and they help to hold the organism together.

Abiathar, ă-bī′-ă-thär (Heb.)—*the great one is father; father of abundance.*

Fourth high priest in descent from Eli. He was high priest during David's reign and at the beginning of Solomon's reign (I Kings 2:26).

Meta. A ruling religious belief that abundant good comes from recognition of God as Father (*the great one is father, father of abundance*) and of David (love) as king (the directive or guiding quality of the will). Though excellent, the intellectual thought represented by Abiathar has in the end to take a lowly position, and his place is taken by Zadok, the true high priest, who represents a spiritual quality. Zadok was a descendant of Aaron, through Aaron's eldest son, Eleazar.

Abib, ā′-bĭb (Heb.)—*month of green ears; sprouting; budding; to fructify,* properly, *an ear of grain; green fruits.*

The first month of the ecclesiastical, and seventh of the civil, year of the Hebrews; it corresponded to parts of our March and April (Exod. 13:4; 23:15; Deut. 16:1). It is called Nisan in Nehemiah 2:1 and in Esther 3:7.

Meta. In Spirit there is no time; there are only growth and steps in unfoldment of consciousness. In the spiritual realm the days, months, and years by which man counts time represent degrees or steps in growth and attainment. Considered in a spiritual light, Abib symbolizes a period of resurrection out of the old (it was on the fifteenth of this month that Israel left Egypt) and a bringing forth of fruit to newness of life. (See NISAN.)

Abida, ă-bī′-dȧ (Heb.)—*father of knowledge,* i. e., *knowing; father of wisdom; father of understanding.*

Son of Midian (Gen. 25:4).

Meta. The belief that knowledge comes through the senses (*father of knowledge,* i. e., *knowing*). The Midianites, descendants of Midian, were enemies of the Israelites. They represent contentious thoughts, and judgment or discrimination in sense consciousness. The judgment of the senses, based on outer appearances, produces discordant thoughts, jealousies, and so forth.

Abidan, ăb′-ĭ-dăn (Heb.)—*father of judgment,* i. e., *a judge.*

A Benjamite who was chosen by Jehovah a prince over the tribe of Benjamin, in the wilderness (Num. 1:11).

Meta. Abidan's father was Gideoni, meaning *like Gideon, destroyer* of error; *warlike.* Benjamin (*son of the right hand*) means dexterous, skillful, expert, quick. Abidan (*father of judgment, a judge*) therefore stands in consciousness for a strong, influential thought of righteous discrimination, or justice, with power to execute its decisions. Abidan was first appointed chief man over the Benjamites, in accordance with Jehovah's command to Moses, for the purpose of numbering the people, to find out how many men of the tribe were above twenty years of age and able to go to war.

Abiel, ă-bī′-ĕl (Heb.)—*God is father; father of might; father of strength; my father is God.*

a Father of Kish and grandfather of Saul (I Sam. 9:1; 14:51). **b** "The Arbathite," one of David's mighty men (I Chron. 11:32); this Abiel is called Abi-albon in II Sam. 23:31.

Meta. A mighty thought, a thought of great power and strength, which has its source in God (*God is father, father of might, father of strength, my father is*

God). (See ABI–ALBON.)

Abiezer, ă-bĭ-ē′-zẽr (Heb.)—*father of help; succoring father.*

A man of Manasseh, from whom Gideon was descended (Josh. 17:2; Judg. 6:11, 15). In Numbers 26:30 he is called Iezer. (Iezer means *he will help; he will succor.*)

Meta. The acknowledgment that God (Spirit) is the source of understanding and of all true help (*father of help; succoring father;* a man of Manasseh).

Abigail, ăb′-ĭ-gāil (Heb.)—*father of joy; source of exultation* or *cause of delight.*

a A Carmelitess (See I Chron. 3:1) who was David's wife (I Sam. 25:3, 42). **b** David's sister (I Chron. 2:16).

Meta. The idea back of this name and of its association with David is that joy comes from God and should go with his love (David). A Carmelitess signifies abundance. Thus we see that joy and abundance are closely connected. (See AHINOAM.)

Abihail, ăb-ĭ-hā′-ĭl (Heb.)—*father of might; father of strength; father of brilliance; father of splendor.*

A name given to both men and women of the Bible (Num. 3:35; II Chron. 11:18; Esth. 2:15).

Meta. The idea that power, strength, honor, and glory originate in God and are spiritual in their true character (*father of might, father of strength, father of brilliance, father of splendor*).

Abihu, ă-bī′-hū (Heb.)—*father is (he who is) God; whom he (God) is father of; he who is (my) father; God is father.*

One of the sons of Aaron. With his father and his brothers, he was set apart for the priesthood (Exod. 6:23; 28:1; Lev. 10:1, 2).

Meta. The priesthood points to the Christ, sonship. The Christ, the Son of God, was perfectly demonstrated in Jesus Christ, and must be demonstrated in all men. Abihu stands for an idea of divine sonship (*father is God; God is father*).

Abihud, ă-bī′-hŭd (Heb.)—*father of majesty; father of vigor, youth; father of praise.*

Grandson of Benjamin (I Chron. 8:3).

Meta. The idea that true authority, praise, wholeness, and might have their inception in, and come from, God (Spirit).

Abijah (in A. V., I Chron. 2:24; 7:8; Matt. 1:7; Luke 1:5, name is given as Abiah and Abia), ă-bī'-jăh (Heb.)— *whose father Jehovah is; (my) father is Jah; (my) father is Jehovah.*

The Bible mentions several persons of this name (I Sam. 8:2; I Chron. 3:10).

Meta. Abijah refers to manifest man as being the offspring of the Christ, or Jehovah God (*whose father Jehovah is.* See Genesis, 2d and 3d chapters). Though this is a true, spiritual idea, not all the Biblical characters named Abijah carried out the Christ principle in their lives. Some were of the priesthood, and lived according to the Christ principle to a greater or less extent, while others, though Israelites, wandered far from the ideal that the name Abijah signifies. For instance, we are told that Abijah, king of Judah (called Abijam in I Kings 15:1-8), walked in all the sins of his father, Rehoboam. (See I Kings 15:3.)

Abijam. See ABIJAH.

Abilene, ăb-ĭ-lē'-nĕ (Gr.)—*a plain; region of Abila;* fr. Abila, *land of meadows.*

A rich, fertile Syrian district or tetrarchy, governed by Lysanias at the time of the beginning of the ministry of John the Baptist (Luke 3:1-3). Its name was taken from its capital city, Abila.

Meta. Assyria, the Syrians, and John the Baptist all refer to various phases of the intellect and its activities. Abilene therefore represents a richness and a fertility of intellectual capacity through which Spirit can work to bring about in the individual a perception and acceptance of Truth.

Abimael, ă-bĭm'-ă-ĕl (Heb.)—*a father from God; (my) father from God; father of Mael* or *father of abundance.*

Son of Joktan, a descendant of Shem, one of Noah's sons, and supposed to have been the founder of an Arabian tribe (Gen. 10:28).

Meta. A thought of man as being de-scended from God; also a thought of abundance as coming from God (*a father from God, father of abundance*). The thought that the name *Abimael* signifies, however, at this stage of man's unfoldment, is not established in consciousness with enough positiveness to produce spiritual results. Arabia means *barren, sterile, wild;* and in consciousness Arabians represent unproductive thoughts.

Abimelech, ă-bĭm'-ĕ-lĕch (Heb.)—*father of the king; Melek (the king) is father; a royal father.*

a Kings of Gerar in the time of Abraham and Isaac (Gen. 20:2-18; 26:1). Abimelech was the name of a line of Philistine kings. **b** A son of Gideon, or Jerubbaal, by his concubine in Shechem (Judg. 8:31; 9:1). This Abimelech slew all his brothers, except one who escaped, and made himself ruler after his father's death. **c** A priest in the time of David (I Chron. 18:16).

Meta. The will. Most of the Bible characters of this name stand for some phase of the unregenerate will, but Abimelech of I Chronicles 18:16, a priest of Israel in David's time, is an exception. In his case spiritual rulership is suggested, or at least a higher form of intellectual rulership than that of the unregenerate will. This Abimelech stands for the intellectual thought or tendency that accepts and acknowledges God as the supreme ruler in man's consciousness.

Abinadab, ă-bĭn'-ă-dăb (Heb.)—*father of generous abundance; father of liberality; (my) father is noble.*

The name of several men who are mentioned in the Bible (I Sam. 7:1; 16:8; 31:2).

Meta. The Abinadab spoken of in I Samuel 7:1 and II Samuel 6:3, 4 represents the realm of unlimited mind. It was in his house, "in the hill" (super-consciousness), that the Ark of the Covenant was kept for many years.

Abinadab, brother of David (I Sam. 16:8), represents an extreme in consciousness. He stands for very high aspirations (*my father is noble*). High aspirations alone, however, do not fit one for kingship. David's faithful service in the humble walks of life seems to have been an important factor in preparing him for his greater ministry. "He that is faithful in a very little is faithful also in much" (Luke 16:10).

Abinadab, son of Saul (I Sam. 31:2), represents a phase of the physical will in its control of body. Abinadab and his brothers met death in battle, at the hands of the Philistines; their father, Saul, died by his own hand in the same battle, to avoid being captured. This incident symbolizes the dissolution of the whole organism, the result of disobedience to the Lord, or law of Being.

Abinoam, ă-bĭn'-ō-ăm (Heb.)—*father of pleasantness; father of delight; father of graciousness.*

An Israelite, of the tribe of Naphtali, and father of Barak the judge, who, with Deborah the prophetess, delivered Israel (Judg. 4:6; 5:1).

Meta. The strength (Naphtali) of beautiful, pleasant, gracious thoughts, whose true origin is God—Divine Mind (*father of pleasantness, father of graciousness, father of delight*).

This name seems to suggest the thought that delight, pleasantness, sweetness, and beauty are the result of giving oneself over to the expression of sense in the physical. This is a mistake that mortal man has always made, but he must rise to the understanding that all real joy and grace come from Spirit and are the result of high, pure, spiritual thinking.

Abiram, ă-bī'-răm (Heb.)—*father of elevation; father of altitude,* i. e., *high or proud; the exalted (one) is (my) father; high father.*

a Son of Eliab, one of those who conspired against Moses and Aaron and was swallowed up by the earth (Num. 16:1-33). **b** The eldest son of Hiel the Bethelite, who rebuilt Jericho (I Kings 16:34).

Meta. This name can denote either the arrogance of pride or the nobility of true spiritual exaltation. Abiram, the son of Eliab, signifies presumptuous, arrogant, and rebellious thoughts or tendencies that are caused by spiritual pride (*father of altitude,* i. e., *high or proud*).

The Abiram of I Kings 16:34 symbolizes a lofty thought, or spiritual ideal (*the exalted one is my father*).

Abishag, ăb'-ĭ-shăg (Heb.)—*father of error; father (cause) of wandering; father of ignorance.*

A Shunammite woman, very beautiful and young, who became the wife of David and ministered to him (I Kings 1:1-4).

Meta. The meaning of Abishag, with the history of her as given in the Bible, reveals her as being representative of the ignorant, error, limited belief that spiritually unawakened man holds in regard to life. Life is divine and its source is God, Spirit. It does not emanate from the soul; it is not a psychic or a purely mental quality, nor does it spring from the physical. It is spiritual, and one can be truly quickened with new life and vitalized in soul and in body only by consciously contacting Spirit.

Abishai, ă-bī'-shāi (Heb.)—*father (source) of precious gifts; source of wealth; (my) father gives.*

Son of David's sister, Zeruiah, and brother of Joab and Asahel. He was with David during David's conflict with Saul and his wars with the Philistines. He was a chief, a warrior, and a mighty man (II Sam. 2:18; 21:17; I Chron. 2:16).

Meta. The inherited law of destruction to the enemies of the natural man. Before the light and all-sufficiency of the Father's presence (*father or source of precious gifts, source of wealth, my father gives*), all seeming errors sink into nothingness; they cannot withstand the almightiness, omnipresence, and omniscience of the one Good, active.

Abishalom, ă-bĭsh'-ă-lŏm (Heb.)—*father of peace; father (source) of salvation.*

Grandfather of Abijam, king of Judah, according to I Kings 15:2. In II Chronicles 11:20, 21, he is called Absalom and is mentioned as father-in-law of Rehoboam.

Meta. An idea of peace, or an idea of spiritual unity, wholeness, order, soundness, and completeness that gives peace (*father of peace*). This peace idea must have degenerated to a very sensual plane in the consciousness of the individual, however; otherwise the thoughts emanating from it would have been different. Maacah, Abishalom's daughter, signifies *oppression*, or *depression*. Abijam, king of Judah, "walked in all the sins of his father, which he had done before him." Rehoboam, the son-in-law of Abishalom, is that in man's consciousness which exalts the senses instead of the spirit.

Abishua, ăb-ĭ-shū′-à (Heb.)—*father of deliverance; father (source) of abundance; (my) father is opulence; my father is rescue.*

Third in descent from Aaron, and high priest of Israel (I Chron. 6:4, 50); grandson of Benjamin (I Chron. 8:4).

Meta. A ruling thought of God as being the source of deliverance and abundance (*father of deliverance, my father is opulence*).

Abishur, ă-bī′-shŭr (Heb.)—*father of a strong wall; father of fortitude; (my) father is a wall of strength.*

A man of the tribe of Judah; son of Shammai (I Chron. 2:28).

Meta. A perception, or recognition, of God as a wall of strength and of protection about one and within one; a stronghold; a fortification against error and seeming weakness (*father of a strong wall, father of fortitude, my father is a wall of strength*).

Abital, ăb′-ĭ-tăl (Heb.) — *father (source) of the dew; father of freshness; (my) father is bedewing freshness.*

One of David's wives, and mother of Shephatiah (II Sam. 3:4).

Meta. The idea, entertained by the soul, that all renewing and refreshing of mind and body come from God (*father, or source, of the dew; my father is bedewing freshness; a woman, one of David's wives*). This idea is united to love (David); love makes harmony and peace, and opens the consciousness to receive the dews of God's grace, which one cannot enjoy while one is in a restless or inharmonious state of mind. Dew falls only on a still night.

Abitub, ăb′-ĭ-tŭb (Heb.) — *father (source) of good; my father is goodness.*

A Benjamite, son of Shaharaim and Hushim (I Chron. 8:11).

Meta. The idea that God is good and that all goodness is from God and is divine and that the Father is bountiful in goodness (*father, or source, of good; my father is goodness*). Thoughts of wholeness and bounty enter into the significance of the meaning of this name.

Abiud, ă-bī′-ŭd (Heb.)—*father of majesty; father of praise.*

A Judahite named in the genealogy of Jesus (Matt. 1:13). Abiud is a form of the name Abihud.

Meta. The significance is virtually the same as that of Abihud: Praise and dominion, also true power and might, are spiritual in their character, and spring from God (*father of majesty, father of praise*).

Abner, ăb′-nēr (Heb.)—*father of light, i. e., enlightener; father of enlightenment.*

Captain of Saul's army (II Sam. 2:8).

Meta. The meaning of the name Abner is *father of enlightenment*, denoting the transmission of light from the principle of light (God). As the captain of Saul's army, Abner signifies illumined reasoning or the intellect's having received some enlightenment from Spirit. It is to this power that the undeveloped will (Saul) must look for protection and safety. When Abner (illumined reasoning) fails in the trust that has been given him, he is considered worthy of death; in other words, just as the illumined intellect, represented by John the Baptist, must be merged with the Christ, so illumined reasoning, represented by Abner, must be absorbed by the all-knowing Mind. (See I Sam. 26:7-17.)

Abraham, ā′-brà-hăm (Heb.)—*father (source, founder) of a multitude.*

Abram, son of Terah, of Ur of the Chaldees, and the father of the Hebrew nation (Gen. 11:27-31; 17:5).

Meta. The power of the mind to reproduce its ideas in unlimited expression. This ability of the mind to make substance out of ideas is called faith. When told by Jehovah that he was henceforth to be Abraham, Abram was told also that he was to be the *father of a multitude.* This means that one is to express faith by bringing the faith of God into the multitude of manifested thoughts and acts.

The first step in spiritual development is the awakening of faith (represented by Abraham). We must have faith in the reality of the power of the realms invisible. Abraham, inspired by the Lord, went forth into another country, where his progeny, or manifestations, increased tremendously.

Through faithful obedience to the inner urge of Spirit, we gradually develop communication with the supermind; then in various ways we receive the assurance that we are guided by Spirit.

The early growth of faith is not very deeply rooted. Abraham lived in a tent, which illustrates that faith has not yet become an abiding quality of the consciousness. Through certain experiences and movements of the mind, faith takes a firmer hold; it establishes the firmament mentioned in the 1st chapter of Genesis.

In Matthew 3:9 Abraham represents a certain phase of consciousness in the development of the Adam man, who was formed out of the "dust of the ground." "God is able of these stones to raise up children unto Abraham." What we want is a baptism of mind that will free us from all the limitations of the Adam man and open our eyes to the Christ state, with its New Jerusalem environment, now forming in the heavens all about us.

Abram, ā'-bram (Heb.)—*father of height; father of exaltation; exalted father.*

Known as Abram, before God changed his name to Abraham (Gen. 11:26; 12:1; 17:5).

Meta. Abram is the name that the author of Genesis gave to the quality through which man has faith in the forces invisible. When this faith is concentrated upon the one God, a God consciousness is established and man intuitively knows that he is in communication with the ever living source of all existence. It was in this way that Jehovah communicated with Abram (Gen. 12:1).

When high ideals begin to possess the mind (when the Lord, or inner spiritual impulse, begins pressing forth to religious activity), Abram, the lofty one, is father. Faith in the unseen God and in divine guidance becomes part of the consciousness without special effort when man is obedient to Spirit. It may seem blind faith to those who depend upon sense evidence, but it works out beautifully in the lives of those who are true to it. So we discern Abram as a historical type of faith because he acted in faith, following obediently his spiritual inspirations; consequently we conclude that he is a type of faith that may be studied profitably by all persons who aspire to the attainment of the higher life.

The Bible speaks repeatedly of Abraham's faith. He believed God, we are told, and his faith was counted to him for righteousness. He represents faith in its early establishment in the consciousness, and in his life we see portrayed the different movements of the faith faculty on the various planes of human action. In order to understand the lessons in Abram's life one must have a certain familiarity with each plane of consciousness.

A person does not have to change his residence in order to enter a new country. "The land that I will show thee" is a new concept of substance. When we deny our attachment to matter and material conditions, and affirm our unity with spiritual substance, we enter the new consciousness of real substance. Substance is not confined to matter; it is the idea that is the firm foundation of all that we conceive to be permanent.

Absalom, ăb'-să-lŏm (Heb.)—*father (source) of peace; father of salvation.*

Third son of David, by Maacah the daughter of Talmai, king of Geshur (II Sam. 3:3, and 13th to 19th chapters). This name is a contracted form of the name ABISHALOM, which see.

Meta. That which is implied in the meaning of this name was not borne out in the life of the man who bore the name. The quality of true peace might have worked out in unlimited good had it been applied to the inner man instead of to the physical only.

Absalom represents physical beauty, without corresponding beauty of the soul. David's love for physical beauty, without spiritual understanding as a foundation, is illustrated in Absalom. He was so absorbed in that state of consciousness that he gave himself up to it without realizing its character. When Absalom marched against Jerusalem with an army, David fled, and the usurper took possession of the capital. Likewise we let our affection for the physical forms of life engross our attention, to the exclusion of the spiritual. Parents frequently give up everything to a selfish child. A parallel to this is found in the individual when some cherished idea takes complete possession of him to the exclusion of good judgment.

When we give excessive love to a thing on the sense plane, there is a reaction, and an adjustment takes place under the working of what may be termed the law of nature. In a measure the subjective consciousness is self-regulating. We may transgress the law of nature up to a certain degree; then all at once we seem to lose command; the mind and the body are in a state of chemicalization —a war is on between the thoughts of Truth and the thoughts of error. Some cherished ideal that has been ruling on the physical plane must be deposed, and the rightful king must be restored to dominion. This movement may appear to the individual as an illness of which he does not understand the cause; its explanation is below the line of conscious mind.

Joab led the army that defeated Absalom, and Joab and his armor-bearers slew Absalom. Joab represents the inner center that preserves the unity and integrity of soul and body, the individual will. This is the focal point around which all the forces of the organism, objective and subjective, adjust themselves.

Yet the conscious love does not want to give up its cherished ideal, no matter how great its error. When the messengers brought the tidings of Absalom's death, David cried: "O my son Absalom, my son, my son Absalom! would I had died for thee, O Absalom, my son, my son!" This illustrates the absorbing love that the affections feel for the realm of sense when they are not balanced by understanding.

Absalom was a son by a heathen wife (there was no redeeming spirituality in the thought, and the soul forces were cemented to it as a material reality). This is why it is so hard for us to give up our material possessions, whether they be in the form of our children or in the form of money. If we love our children with an earthly love, without the understanding that they are the children of God, the very substance of our soul goes out to them. So, when the soul loves money, it becomes saturated with materiality. Jesus saw this when He said, "How hard is it for them that trust in riches to enter into the kingdom of God!"

Accad, ăc'-eăd (Heb.)—*a castle; fortress; vantage point; highland.*

A city built by Nimrod in the land of Shinar (Gen. 10:10).

Meta. A fixed state of thought that believes in protection, great strength, exaltation, superiority, to be attained through the intellectual and the physical alone (*a castle, fortress, vantage point, highland;* a city built by Nimrod; Nimrod pertains to the personal will ruling in the animal forces of the organism, also to a material belief in courage and might).

Acco (A. V., Accho), ăc'-eô (Heb.)— *sandy compression; heated sand.*

A town on the Mediterranean coast in Palestine. The inhabitants of this city were some of the enemies that Asher had failed to drive out of the land of Canaan (Judg. 1:31).

Meta. An aggregation of thoughts in the sense or carnal consciousness of man that believe in suppression, limitation, irritation, bondage (*compression, heated sand*). These thoughts are so material in their concepts that they cannot believe in the overcoming power and strength of Spirit; it takes something more than the happy, joyous state of mind that Asher represents to bring them under control and to transmute their energies into constructive thoughts and uses.

Achaia, ă-chā´-ĭà (Gk.)—*land of Achaicus; trouble.*

A part of, or a province in, Greece (Acts 18:12; 19:21).

Meta. Greece represents the intellect of man, and so Achaia pertains to the intellect. The reasonings of the intellect, apart from the inspiration and guidance of the Holy Spirit, lead to *trouble.* Divine Mind, not human consciousness, is the one source of true joy and good.

Achan, ā´-chăn (Heb.)—*trouble; troublesome; troubler.*

A man of Judah who sinned in that he saved for himself "a goodly Babylonish mantle, and two hundred shekels of silver, and a wedge of gold of fifty shekels weight," when Jehovah had said that the silver, gold, brass, and iron were to be holy to Him, and all else was to be destroyed. This incident occurred at the taking of Jericho, after the Israelites had first entered the Promised Land to possess it. But Achan coveted these things and took them for himself, and hid them in the earth in the midst of his tent. "And Joshua said, Why hast thou troubled us?" (See Joshua, 7th chapter.)

Meta. In the outer consciousness Achan represents covetousness, which always results in much trouble and sorrow to those who let it dominate their thoughts and acts. Achan was an Israelite, however, and the Israelites stand for the religious thoughts of man. True Israel is spiritual consciousness. The great troubler of the spiritual thoughts in us, which go to make up our spiritual consciousness, is the notion that certain sense beliefs and habits that appear to be good should be held indefinitely. The truth is that all that pertains to the sense mind of man must be given up. Our old ideas of the comforts and things of sense, which have seemed to us to be so good and necessary, represented by the "goodly Babylonish mantle," must be denied away, while all the gold, silver, brass, and iron (earthly wisdom, substance, and life and strength activities) must be dedicated to God and transmuted into their true spiritual essence.

Achbor, ăch´-bôr (Heb.)—*a mouse; gnawing mouse; a rat.*

a Father of Baal–hanan, a king of Edom (Gen. 36:38). b A son of Micaiah, an Israelite. He was sent by Josiah, king of Judah, to inquire of Jehovah concerning the words of the book of the law that had been found (II Kings 22:12). In II Chronicles 34:20 he is called Abdon the son of Micah.

Meta. The Edomites were descended from Esau (*hairy*), who represents the body, or physical vigor. The Edomites therefore represent thoughts pertaining to the outer body consciousness. Achbor represents a gnawing, fretting, destructive belief in evil, in the human consciousness, a belief that tends to weaken and to tear down the body (*mouse, rat, gnawing*). Rats and mice represent a belief that evil is working underhandedly against one.

The Achbor of II Kings 22:12 represents in consciousness a thought of spiritual service sent by the king (will) to search out the Truth. This Achbor is also called Abdon, and one meaning of Abdon is *a servant.*

Achim, ā´-chĭm (Gk.)—Greek phonetic equivalent of the Hebrew name Iachin (*he whom God makes firm*), which in turn is a contraction of Jehoiachin (*whom Jehovah establishes*).

Son of Sadoc, named in the genealogy of Jesus Christ (Matt. 1:14).

Meta. The work of the just and righteous (Sadoc) law in us in preparing the way for the establishing of the Christ or spiritual consciousness in our mind and our body.

Achish, ā´-chĭsh (Heb.)—*angry; serpent-charmer.*

King of Gath of the Philistines (I Sam. 21:10-15).

Meta. A phase of the unregenerate will in which a consuming, destructive thought is uppermost. The Philistines represent the outer sense consciousness, with its lawless, rebellious thoughts and tendencies. Achish was friendly toward David and trusted him; however, the "lords of the Philistines" (the ruling thoughts of the five senses) instinctively felt that David was not one of them. David is symbolical of love, in consciousness, and was a forerunner of Jesus

Christ, who brought to light the truth about life.

Achish suggests the sense man's mistaken idea that the life forces in the body can be controlled and brought under subjection by the power of the personal will (*serpent-charmer*), apart from any real discipline of the emotions or uplifting of one's desires.

Achmetha, ăch'-mĕ-thá (Heb.)—*station or fortress; a walled place; a place of horses.*

Supposed to be the same as Ecbatana, a city in Media (Ezra 6:2). Some writers, however, think that the word "Achmetha" should be translated, "in a coffer," and that it does not refer to a city. Fallows says: "The derivation of the name is doubtful; but Major Rawlinson (Geographical Journal, x:134) has left little question that the title was applied exclusively to cities having a fortress for the protection of the royal treasures." It was at "Achmetha, in the palace," that the record of the decree of Cyrus concerning the rebuilding of the house of God in Jerusalem was found. Some of the enemies of the Israelites, who did not want Jerusalem or the Temple rebuilt, professed to believe that the Jews had never been authorized by Cyrus to do this work. They therefore hindered the work for some time by appealing to the governor and having him order that the work cease. Then a letter was sent to the king of Media and Persia, and he caused a search to be made to learn whether Cyrus had ever made a decree giving the Israelites the right to rebuild the Temple in Jerusalem and to make use of all the vessels of the Temple. The record of such a decree was found at Achmetha, and the rebuilding of Jerusalem's wall and Temple was allowed to proceed.

Meta. The foregoing explanation, with the meaning of the name, infers that the symbology of Achmetha is as follows: Deep within the very life forces of the organism of man, even though they may be governed by the unregenerate will (a heathen king), there is preserved the truth that man is in reality a spiritual being. This truth, upon being brought

to light in the consciousness, silences the sense beliefs of limited life and a material body. Then the work of renewing the whole man—spirit, soul, and body—proceeds through the medium of the spiritual thoughts (Israelites).

Achor, ā'-chôr (Heb.)—*affliction; trouble; sorrow.*

A valley near Jericho, where Achan, with all that he had, was destroyed because of the trouble that he had brought upon Israel by his sin (Josh. 7:24-26).

Meta. Trouble, sorrow. In Isaiah 65: 10 we read of the valley of Achor, in the redeemed earth (spiritualized body), as being "a place for herds [the animal forces of the organism] to lie down in." This means that all the inner activities of man will come into harmony and peace because they will have been lifted from material to spiritual expression.

In Hosea 2:15 Israel is promised that the valley of Achor shall become a "door of hope." This is a true experience in almost every individual who comes into the Truth. His darkest and most sorrowful problems are the very conditions that cause him to turn away from his errors and look to God for deliverance. Thus the valley of Achor becomes a door of hope to him, since in seeking a way of escape from his troubles he learns to know God as the one source of his being and as his one true love, life, and joy.

Achsah (in A. V., I Chron. 2:49, Achsa), ăch'-säh (Heb.)—*anklet; an amulet; a charm; a charmer; serpent-charmer.*

Caleb's daughter (Josh. 15:16-19).

Meta. An Israelitish woman, and therefore belonging to the higher, or more spiritual, phase of the soul of man. Her father, Caleb, symbolizes spiritual faith and enthusiasm. These qualities naturally would bring forth a soul quality pertaining to the directing of the life forces into true ways (Achsah—*an amulet; a charm; serpent-charmer*). A serpent-charmer is one who has power over serpents, usually by a kind of personal dominion, assurance, and magnetism. Serpents refer to the animal or sense life, or to sensation, in man; also to the seeming wisdom that is gained through the senses.

Caleb gave his daughter, Achsah, a south land for her inheritance. In Scriptural symbology, south means below. This suggests the lower part of the organism, wherein is the life center. In consciousness south refers to the subconscious realm. Because Achsah had been given "the land of the South," she asked her father to give her also springs of water, and he gave her the upper and the nether springs. Upper means higher, superior; nether means situated down or below, lying beneath. So these springs of water represent both the seemingly material life fount in man and the higher, or true, spiritual consciousness of divine life. Jesus said, "The water that I shall give him shall become in him a well of water springing up unto eternal life" (John 4:14). Achsah therefore symbolizes the inner soul consciousness of spiritual life as being the directive and controlling power to lift up all life; or, the unity of all life and substance, since there is in reality but one source of life and substance, and only one life and one substance: God.

Achshaph, ăch'-shăph (Heb.)—*dedicated speech; fascination; incantation; delusion.*

A Canaanitish city that was allotted to the tribe of Asher when the Israelites took possession of the land of Canaan (Josh. 11:1; 12:20; 19:24, 25).

Meta. Achshaph was the capital city of one of the Canaanitish kings. These kings represent the ruling thoughts in the subconscious realm of mind in man; Canaan means *lowland* and refers to the subconsciousness. This aggregation of thoughts (city of Achshaph), which to a certain extent rules over the elemental forces in the subconsciousness, is of a misleading and destructive nature under the old sense or carnal belief (*incantation, delusion*), but when it is *dedicated* to the Lord it comes under a higher law (Achshaph was taken by the Israelites). Then these thoughts are elevated to the place of true prayer and worship of God, thus becoming a powerful influence for good in man's mind and body.

Achzib, ăch'-zĭb (Heb.)—*deceit; false-*

hood; lies; a dried-up water course; a winter brook.

a A city of Canaan that was on the border of the land allotted to Asher (Josh. 19:29). **b** A city in the lowland of Judah (Josh. 15:44). The Asherites never succeeded in overcoming the Canaanitish inhabitants of the city of Achzib (Judg. 1:31).

Meta. False, lying, deceptive groups of thoughts in consciousness (*falsehood, lies, deceit;* two Canaanitish cities).

Adah, ā'-dăh (Heb.)—*beauty; comeliness; adornment; ornament; pleasure.*

a Wife of Lamech; Lamech was fifth in descent from Cain (Gen. 4:19). **b** A wife of Esau's (Gen. 36:2).

Meta. A phase of the human soul, or love nature. Love, even in the limited, personal consciousness and expression, has its pleasing aspect (*pleasure*). Expression of it adorns one with a certain beauty of character and a grace and comeliness that are lacking in persons who are wanting in love (*ornament, beauty*).

Adaiah, ă-dā'-iăh (Heb.)—*whom Jehovah adorns; pleasing to Jah.*

The name of several Israelitish men mentioned in the Bible (II Kings 22:1; I Chron. 6:41; 8:21; 9:12).

Meta. An awakening to, and acceptance of, spiritual Truth. Such an awakening is *pleasing to Jehovah*, and it gives adorning grace to the individual (*whom Jehovah adorns*).

The two men named Adaiah who took foreign wives (Ezra 10:29, 39) signify a seeking to unify spiritual ideals with carnal affection. Such an attempt can bring only trouble. It must be given up before the individual can be blessed truly and permanently.

Adalia, ă-dā'-lĭ-à (Heb. fr. Pers.)—*a sun god; fire god.*

One of the sons of Haman (Esth. 9:8, 10). Haman and his sons were put to death because of having sought to destroy the Jews.

Meta. The adverse belief that heat, warmth, and life are produced and kept in expression in man by the activities of his animal nature—passions and appetites. It was from Shushan, the palace (meaning *lily* and symbolizing pure thought unadulterated by error belief), that the command was issued for the destruction of the sons of Haman, the Jews' enemy. (See ARIDAI, another of Haman's sons.)

Adam, ăd'-ăm (Heb.)—*red; ruddy; reddish; firm.*

a The name of the first man of the human race, according to the Bible (Gen. 5:1-5). b A city (Josh. 3:16).

Meta. The first movement of mind in its contact with life and substance. Adam also represents the generic man, or the whole human race epitomized in an individual-man idea. Eve is the feminine aspect of generic man, outwardly manifest: "male and female created he them."

If the ego, or will, which is man, has adhered to wisdom faithfully and has carried out in its work the plans that are idealized in wisdom, it has created a harmonious consciousness. Adam in the Garden of Eden is symbolical of that consciousness.

Adam in his original creation was in spiritual illumination. Spirit breathed into him continually the necessary inspiration and knowledge to give him superior understanding. But he began eating, or appropriating, ideas of two powers—God and not God, or good and evil. The result, so the allegory relates, was that he fell away from spiritual life and all that it involves.

Man is Spirit, absolute and unconditioned; but man forms an Adamic consciousness into which he breathes the breath of life; this, in its perfect expression, is the Son of man, an expression of the divine idea. This Adam is all of what we term soul, intellect, and body. We are continually at work with this Adam; we can breathe into his nostrils the breath of life, inspiring him with the idea of life in all its unlimited fullness. We can lift up this Adam by infusing into him these sublime ideas, and in no other way.

Adamah, ăd'-ă-măh (Heb.)—*ground; red earth.*

A fortified city of Naphtali (Josh. 19:36; also verses 32 and 35).

Meta. A group of thoughts in consciousness, or a thought center, that is quite firmly established in a belief in material or physical strength (*ground, red earth;* a fortified city of Naphtali, Naphtali referring to the strength faculty in man).

Adar, ā'-där (Heb.)—*eclipsed* (in the sense of outshining and not of covering up); *large; eminent; the returning sun; fire god.*

Twelfth month of the Jewish ecclesiastical year (Esth. 3:7); it corresponds to parts of our February and March.

Meta. A phase of our progress in which we appear to face the complete destruction of our true, higher ideals (see Esth. 3:13), but in which we eventually unfold spiritually to a degree that outshines all of our former realizations and demonstrations (see Ezra 6:15). In giving up phases of the sensual that greater good may come into expression, we sometimes appear, to the outer consciousness, to be losing all; but eventually we find that we have gained all instead. This truth was exemplified in its fullness in the crucifixion and the resurrection of Jesus Christ.

Adbeel, ăd'-bĕ-ĕl (Heb.)—*yearning for God; languishing for God; disciplined of (for) God; miracle of God.*

Son of Ishmael, and the founder of an Arabian tribe (Gen. 25:13).

Meta. A thought that seemingly springs from the sense or flesh mind, but in reality is inspired by Spirit. It longs for God, for something higher and better than it has heretofore experienced (*yearning for God; languishing for God*). This yearning will bring forth fruit in time, when it has been subjected to the necessary education and training (*disciplined of,* or *for, God*). Though not always recognized as coming from God, this discipline is brought about by the working of the divine law.

Addar (A. V., Josh. 15:3, Adar), ăd'-där (Heb.)—*large; ample; a wide-open space; a threshing floor; height; honor; mighty.*

a An Israelite, son of Bela and grandson of Benjamin (I Chron. 8:3); he is called Ard, in Genesis 46:21. b

A city in the south of Judah (Josh. 15: 3).

Meta. The uplifting, strength-giving power and might that comes to a person when he makes room in his life for the good and separates it from the error—from that which is no longer useful in his progress from sense to Spirit (*height, honor, mighty, threshing floor, a wide-open space*). A threshing floor always suggests a sifting, separating process in consciousness.

Addi, ăd′-dī (Heb.) — *ornament; adorned.*

A man named in the genealogy of Jesus Christ (Luke 3:28).

Meta. The thought that the Spirit of truth is the ornament that enriches the soul of man, giving him true grace and beauty, is suggested in this name (*ornament, adorned*).

Addon, ăd′-dŏn (Heb.) — *strong; powerful; a foundation stone; low* (in the sense of being humble but of great strength).

Evidently a place in Babylonia whence some Jews who could not prove their Israelitish origin returned to Jerusalem from the Captivity (Neh. 7:61); called Addan in Ezra 2:59.

Meta. An aggregation of thoughts of great power and strength in consciousness (*strong, powerful*). These thoughts have their foundation in humility (*low, a foundation stone*), and they lead to freedom from sense confusion (Babylon). However, at a certain stage of his unfoldment the individual needs a clearer realization of his spiritual identity: the Jews who returned to Jerusalem from Addon could not prove their Israelitish origin.

Adiel, ā′-dī-ĕl (Heb.)—*an ornament of God; adornment of God; witness of God.*

a A chief, or prince, of the tribe of Simeon (I Chron. 4:36). **b** A man of the Israelitish priesthood (I Chron. 9:12). **c** Father of Azmaveth, who was over King David's treasures (I Chron. 27:25).

Meta. The adorning, beautifying quality of spiritual thoughts that bear witness in consciousness to Truth (*an ornament of God, adornment of God, witness*

of God; men of Israel).

Adin, ă′-dĭn (Heb.)—*voluptuous one; ornament; effeminate; dainty.*

a The head man of one or more Israelitish families that returned to Jerusalem from the Babylonian captivity (Ezra 2:15; Neh. 7:20). **b** An Israelite who joined Nehemiah in sealing the covenant (Neh. 10:16).

Meta. A somewhat negative (*effeminate*) thought in consciousness. While this thought is of a refined, spiritual origin, it is taken captive into Babylon. It enters a state of confusion because of its having given its substance to the belief in pleasure through the senses (*voluptuous one*). But out of its foundation in Truth come ideas (the descendants of Adin) that become free from the confusion of the sense mind (Babylon) and reënter Jerusalem (the consciousness of peace and of Spirit) and do a part in reëstablishing the consciousness in spiritual understanding (*ornament;* one of the men named Adin joined Nehemiah in sealing the covenant).

Adina, ăd′-ĭ-nà (Heb.)—*ornament; slender; delicate.*

Son of Shiza the Reubenite; a chief of the Reubenites, and one of David's captains (I Chron. 11:42).

Meta. A perceptive, discerning, seeing thought of the mind (*ornament, slender;* a chief man of the Reubenites, and Reuben refers to the sense of sight). This thought is of a harmonizing, attracting nature because the loving idea (Shiza) is back of it.

Adino, ăd′-ĭ-nō (Heb.)—*his ornament; his pleasure.*

"The Eznite," one of David's mighty men, and "chief of the captains" (II Sam. 23:8); Josheb–basshebeth or Jashobeam, a Tahchemonite, and Adino are the same man. He is called Jashobeam in I Chronicles 11:11.

Meta. See JASHOBEAM and EZNITE.

Adlai, ăd′-lāi (Heb.)—*justice of God; Jehovah's justice; my witness; lax; weary.*

An Israelite; father of Shaphat (I Chron. 27:29).

Meta. A just, discerning thought in consciousness, which is based on divine justice (*justice of God, Jehovah's justice*). *Lax, weary,* suggests a need of a more definite purpose on the part of this thought.

Admah, ăd'-măh (Heb.)—*dumb; silent; unrelenting; unmerciful; menacing; a fortress; a tomb.*

One of "the cities of the Plain." Its king, and later the city itself, were destroyed (Gen. 10:19; 14:2, 8; Deut. 29: 23).

Meta. The seeming strength and merciless sureness of the death thought and condition that enter into man's experience as the result of his carnal, material, adverse thoughts and activities. (See SODOM and GOMORRAH.)

Adnah, ăd'-năh (Heb.) — *delight; pleasure; rest.*

a An Israelite of the tribe of Manasseh (I Chron. 12:20). **b** An Israelite of the tribe of Judah (II Chron. 17:14).

Meta. The understanding that true overcoming, joy, and peace (*pleasure, delight, rest*) are the products of love, good judgment, and praise; they are not brought about by personal will. (Both men named Adnah were captains of thousands, and mighty men of valor. Adnah, the Manassite, was a captain under Saul first, but he left Saul and went to David. The other Adnah was one of Jehoshaphat's captains. Manasseh symbolizes understanding; Saul—personal will; David —love; Jehoshaphat—the development in consciousness of the idea of judgment; Judah—praise.)

Adoni-bezek, ă-dŏn'-ĭ-bē'-zĕk (Heb.)— *lord of Bezek; lord of lightning.*

A heathen king of the Canaanites and Perizzites. He was captured by Judah and his kingdom was overthrown (Judg. 1:5-7).

Meta. Bezek means lightning. Lightning is a force that gathers and then explodes and dissipates its energy, because it is not in harmony with universal equilibrium. This illustrates well the mind of the individual who believes himself to be an independent and unrelated creation. When this kind of thought is allowed full sway in man's consciousness, man becomes so egotistical and self-opinionated that he destroys himself. Thus error is its own destruction.

Adoni-bezek represents the ruling ego of this force in consciousness, which is symbolized by lightning. In its original purity this force is good, but, by its being used in sense instead of in spiritual ways, many of the natural forces of the organism that had not been lifted to true understanding have been bereft by this ruling sense thought (Adoni-bezek) of the power or executive ability (thumbs) and understanding (great toes) wherewith they had been endowed by nature to carry on their activities in the organism. In fact, a complete reversal of the right uses of the natural forces of the individual takes place, as is evidenced by the number of kings (seventy) that Adoni-bezek rendered incapable of any real service by cutting off their thumbs and their great toes. He allowed them only such food as they could gather under his table (could glean from his darkened understanding and from whatever energy might be left after he had wasted all that he desired to waste).

Adoni-bezek in turn had his own thumbs and great toes cut off (his darkened and adverse understanding and his executive power were taken away from him). He was taken to Jerusalem, where he died. This means that by praise (Judah) the error use of the force that Adoni-bezek represents is put away, and the thoughts about it are changed by the declaration that it is spiritual and not material. Then the force itself is transmuted, and its expression is lifted to a higher activity, one in harmony with the law of man's true being. Thus conservation is established in consciousness, instead of waste and dissipation, and conservation leads to life eternal.

Adonijah, ăd-ŏ-nī'-jäh (Heb.)—*Jehovah is Lord; (my) lord is Jehovah.*

a Fourth son of David. His mother was Haggith, and he was born in Hebron (II Sam. 3:4; I Kings 1:11-53; 2:13-25). **b** A Levite (II Chron. 17:8). **c** A chief of the people, who joined Nehemiah in sealing the covenant (Neh. 10:14-16).

Meta. Hebron symbolizes the front brain, the seat of conscious thought. David at Hebron represents the love of the heart center in the act of becoming unified with understanding, or working in coöperation with it, in the head. While the thought that Adonijah symbolizes is good, it is a thought that tends more to service than to rulership. He may serve as a Levite, or as a chief of the people. He may not become king, however, because the idea for which he stands savors too much of the outer, or intellectual, and is not closely enough allied to the inner assurance and peace of heart, to the feeling of sonship, that is the true off-spring of love (David).

Adonikam, ă-dŏn'-ĭ-kăm (Heb.)— *whom the Lord establishes; the Lord stands (firm); (my) Lord is raised; lord of the enemy.*

An Israelite whose descendants, to the number of six hundred and sixty-six, returned from the Babylonian captivity (Ezra 2:13).

Meta. A resurrecting, uplifting, firmly based spiritual belief (*whom the Lord establishes, my Lord is raised, the Lord stands*) that, even though it resided in sense confusion (Babylon), brought forth a company of thoughts (the descendants of Adonikam) that returned to spiritual consciousness (Jerusalem), their true abiding place. Every true thought in man aids in the resurrection of the whole man into a consciousness of life and wholeness.

Adoniram, ăd-ŏ-nī'-răm (Heb.)—*my lord is exalted; my lord is high; lord of height,* i. e., *high lord; lord of heights.*

He was "over the men subject to task-work" ("over the tribute," A. V.), in Solomon's reign (I Kings 4:6; 5:14). He is the same person as Adoram of II Samuel 20:23 and I Kings 12:18, whom the people stoned to death when King Rehoboam sent him to carry out his work of receiving tribute after they had asked to have their yoke made lighter.

Meta. An exalted thought of service to the Lord (*my Lord is exalted;* Adoniram, or Adoram, served in the same office under both David and Solomon). This thought, while it concerns spiritual service, is more intellectual than spiritual in its nature and origin. It is high to begin with, but it makes a slave of the in-

dividual in the end. By our use of the intellect we put ourselves in bondage to set religious rules and tasks, which sometimes become so burdensome and so hard that we are glad to throw away apparently all religious observances for a time, until we find our balance again. The "yoke" of Christ is easy, and His "burden is light." True spiritual service and worship tend to give freedom to body and soul; they take away all sense of burden instead of adding to it.

Adoni–zedek, ă-dŏn'-ĭ-zē'-dĕk (Heb.)— *lord of righteousness; lord of justice,* i. e., *just lord; lord of Zedek.*

A Canaanitish or Amoritish king of Jerusalem. He was defeated and slain by the Israelites under Joshua, when they began to take possession of the Promised Land (Josh. 10:1-27).

Meta. The sensual or carnal idea of what is just and right having dominion over the life forces of the individual and ruling according to carnal affections and desires. Adoni–zedek cannot represent spiritual justice and righteousness, since he was not an Israelite but was an enemy to the Israelites. Though he was king of Jerusalem—the spiritual center in consciousness—he was an Amorite, and the Amorites symbolize carnal, sensual thoughts and desires.

Adoraim, ăd-ŏ-rā'-ĭm (Heb.)—*mounds, or dwellings; double mounds; double strength; double honor; strength of the sea.*

One of the cities of Judah that Rehoboam fortified (II Chron. 11:9). The text reads as though Rehoboam built the cities mentioned in II Chronicles 11:6-9, but since most of these cities are mentioned in the Bible as having existed long before Rehoboam's time, it is evident that he only fortified them.

Meta. Adoraim was close to Hebron— the seat of conscious thought. The idea that is conveyed by the meaning of Adoraim (*double mounds, double honor, mounds or dwellings*) is double-mindedness. When the conscious thoughts of man are guided and ruled by a high, spiritual idea, honor and strength are given to the things of Spirit; but when the city is fortified by Rehoboam, who represents that in man's consciousness which exalts the senses, the animal man is lifted up in place of the true understanding of God and His righteousness. Thus the strength of this state of consciousness, which the city of Adoraim signifies, is as the *strength of the sea* —it is unstable and shifting, until the sense man becomes fully subject to the spiritual. Then all its forces will become stabilized, and constructive only.

Adrammelech, ă-drăm'-mė-lĕch (Heb.) —*the majesty of the king; honor of the king; splendor of the king; splendor of Moloch* (fire god).

a Son of Sennacherib, king of Assyria (II Kings 19:37; Isa. 37:38). **b** A god of Sepharvaim (II Kings 17:31).

Meta. A fiery, consuming thought in man. This fiery thought is the offspring of, and destroys, Sennacherib (*bramble of destruction*), the head of the realm of psychic sense thought, which is represented by the Assyrians. (Adrammelech and his brother Sharezer killed their father, Sennacherib.)

Adrammelech the idol, worship of which was introduced into Samaria by the Sepharites, represents the belief that God (symbolized by the sun) can be discerned and worshiped through the senses; it is the mistaken idea that the psychic, or purely mental soul plane of consciousness, is the source of spiritual understanding and power. Those who hold this belief bring upon themselves fiery trials and experiences, and many of their good and true newborn thoughts (children) are given over to the destroying power of this wrong belief. (Those who worshiped this idol sacrificed their children to it.)

Adramyttium, ăd-ră-mỹt'-tĭ-ŭm (Gk.) —*court of death.*

A seaport town in Mysia, Asia Minor (Acts 27:2); its inhabitants were Athenians.

Meta. Mysia means *criminal, abominable.* The Athenians symbolize purely intellectual thoughts, Athens representing the intellectual center in consciousness.

When Paul appealed to Cæsar (who symbolizes the tyrannical rule of the personal will through the reason, unmodified by spiritual love, mercy, and justice), he was taken to Rome, the head, or center from which the will rules. In being taken to Rome, Paul embarked in a ship of Adramyttium. This means that when we, under stress because of the condemnation of the Jews (our old fixed religious ideas), appeal to the outer personal will for protection instead of fully trusting in Spirit, the word of Truth in us (which Paul represents here) is subjected to the judgments of the unawakened intellect as well as to the personal sense man (Cæsar).

Adramyttium symbolizes one of the intellectual states of consciousness that believe in death and error (*court of death*) and would aid in destroying the Truth in us were such a thing possible.

Adria, ā'-drĭ-ȧ (Gk.)

Adria, or the Adriatic Sea (Acts 27:27), in the time of Paul included all of the part of the Mediterranean Sea that lies between Crete and Sicily. It was much more than what is now known as the Adriatic Sea.

Meta. The great flood of sense reasonings that the word of Truth (Paul) has to pass over in going from Jerusalem to Rome—from the heart or spiritual center in consciousness, to the head or domain of the personal will (Cæsar at Rome).

Adriel, ā'-drĭ-ĕl (Heb.)—*flock of God; host of God; my help is God.*

Son of Barzillai the Meholathite. Saul gave his daughter Merab to Adriel to wife after he had promised her to David (I Sam. 18:19; II Sam. 21:8, 9).

Meta. Merab refers to increase. The true thoughts of life and substance (*flock of God*) and the thoughts of increase that Adriel and Merab signify, one in the soul consciousness and the other in the outer intellectual realm, are closely related to the personal will (Saul). Therefore, though these thoughts and their activities may have been helped by God (*my help is God*), and seem to be good and true, they are of the personal consciousness and are limited; they need to be raised to a higher and more spiritual plane. David (love) gave the five sons of Adriel and Merab over to the Gibeonites, who hanged them. Gibeon represents a high place in consciousness, where man lets go of personal ideas and desires and seeks the presence of God only. It is here, at this place of sacrifice, that the thoughts of personality are lifted and transmuted into spiritual energy and substance. This transmutation is suggested by the Gibeonites' putting Adriel's sons to death.

Adullam, ă-dŭl'-lăm (Heb.)—*justice of the people; equity of the people.*

a A city of Judah, which had formerly been one of the royal cities of the Canaanites (Josh. 12:15; 15:35); it was one of the cities that Rehoboam fortified (II Chron. 11:7). **b** A cave to which David escaped (I Sam. 22:1).

Meta. A phase of prayer, or a state of poise and discernment, in the individual. Being in the valley, it would not refer to a high, exalted state of mind in prayer, but would be more of an established equilibrium and adjustment in the body consciousness (*equity of the people, justice of the people*). The cave of Adullam, to which David (love) fled to get away from Saul (the adverse personal will attempts to destroy the love consciousness, which is destined to rule), would especially be deep within the subjective life forces of the organism.

Adummim, ă-dŭm'-mĭm (Heb.)—*the Edomites; place of the red ones; place of blood; red places.*

A steep pass on the road from Jericho to Jerusalem (Josh. 15:7). It was a very dangerous place because of robbers, and was the setting of Jesus' parable of the good Samaritan.

Meta. On the road from Jericho (the external consciousness, or realm of reflected thought) up to Jerusalem (spiritual consciousness) there are dangerous places through which we have to pass. The thieves and robbers that we have to meet are thoughts of error that would turn us aside from the real Truth and would dissipate the life substance of mind and body in outer ways. "The thief cometh not, but that he may steal, and kill, and destroy: I came that they may have life, and may have *it* abundantly"

(John 10:10). The greatest robber with which the race has to deal is the lie of the serpent: "Ye shall not surely die." This turns millions aside from the true seeking after life through the one source and giver of life—the indwelling Christ —to a multitude of error religious ideas, which exalt death as the way to heaven and to spiritual realization. This leads people to the grave and away from life eternal. We can find the life eternal only by a daily resurrection into life here and now, and not by letting go of the consciousness of life—which each one does who dies. The pure, unadulterated Christ Truth alone leads to life.

Adummim symbolizes the place in man's consciousness where the foregoing error thought is most likely to enter. This thought, if properly met, makes "the ascent of Adummim" the place, or state, of going up to life; but to those who fall into the hands of the robbers that infest the way (error, limited thoughts regarding life), it becomes a *red place*—a place of returning to sense consciousness and its results: death and the grave.

Æneas, æ'-nĕ-ăs (Gk.)—*praise; laudable.*

A man of Lydda; he had been paralyzed for eight years, and was healed by Jesus Christ, through Peter (Acts 9:33-35).

Meta. Lydda means *strife*. Peter symbolizes faith in the power of Spirit, which has been quickened in us by the example of Jesus Christ. The mission of this faith is to renew the whole consciousness, of which the body is part. Thought is the oversoul of every bodily function. If there is a part of the consciousness that has not been exercised rightly in harmonious thought, the bodily organ of which it is the oversoul will become paralyzed. Praising, giving thanks, and bestowing gratitude are natural to the normal consciousness. Lydda (*strife*) symbolizes the center of bodily action of which the liver is the focal point. Persons who pray much are seldom troubled with torpid livers. When you are throwing your positive thought to every part of the system, the electric life of the body is generated in every cell, and all forms of inertia disappear.

Æneas (*praise, laudable*, that which is praiseworthy, full of thankfulness, and gratitude), when no longer bound by cross currents of criticism, faultfinding, and weakness, arises and in the name of Jesus Christ proclaims life, health, and freedom; all strife is turned into constructive, spiritual activity; all desert places in consciousness receive the redeeming power of the living word.

Ænon, æ'-nŏn (Gk.)—*springs; (natural) fountains.*

A place where John the Baptist was baptizing, "because there was much water there" (John 3:23).

Meta. John the Baptist represents the intellectual concept of Truth. His baptism symbolizes a mental cleansing through the word of denial. Water represents cleansing. A spring of water refers to a natural rising, in consciousness, of the cleansing, life-giving power of the thought and word of purification and life. Ænon was near Salim (*peace*), and so represents a purifying phase of thought that, while seemingly belonging to the natural, or outer, intellectual man, is closely associated with spiritual life and peace.

Agabus, ăg'-ă-bŭs (Gk.)—*to breathe out; to desire ardently; to love; locust.*

One who prophesied famine, and also foretold Paul's afflictions (Acts 11:28; 21:10, 11).

Meta. That in us which perceives the different forces working in the soul, the point at which these forces are likely to clash, and the evident outcome. This ability to perceive is known in man's consciousness as the power of prophecy. Agabus prophesied of error things, hence the thought of *locust*, which infers something very destructive in its nature. Prophecy, however, may be of good results that are to manifest in one's experiences; in such prophecies the idea of *love* is in evidence. Prophecy apparently deals with both destruction of error and establishment of good.

Agag, ā'-găg (Heb.)—*violent; high; warlike; flame.*

King of the Amalekites (I Sam. 15:8-33).

Meta. The Adversary—the ruling ego of the adverse, carnal consciousness in man (*violent, warlike, flame*).

Agagite, ā'-găg-īte (Heb.)—*belonging to Agag.*

Same as Amalekite; "Haman the Agagite" (Esth. 8:3).

Meta. See AGAG and AMALEKITE.

Agee, ăg'-ĕ-ē (Heb.)—*fugitive.*

A Hararite (II Sam. 23:11).

Meta. A thought in consciousness that is high and uplifting (Hararite means *mountaineer*), but is not strong enough to stand its ground against the Philistines (outer, rebellious, sense thoughts). This high idea therefore flees from the seeming strength of error, and becomes a *fugitive;* however, it brings forth a son, Shammah (*fame, renown*), who becomes one of David's (love's) mighty men of valor and aids effectually in defeating the Philistines.

Agrippa, ă-grĭp'-pȧ (Gk.)—*one who causes pain at birth;* perhaps *wild-horse tamer.*

Son of the Herod of Acts 12:1-23 and king over several united tetrarchies (Acts 25:13—26:32).

Meta. As Festus, in Acts 26:19-32, represents the transient joys of the external life, his brother-in-law, Agrippa, shows the close association that this sort of pleasure has with pain. So long as we are enjoying ourselves in the sense life, our ears are usually dull to Truth: Festus was not moved by Paul's eloquent appeal. But pain brings us very close to an acceptance of the higher way: Agrippa was almost persuaded to believe. Most of those who are now studying Truth became interested because of an urgent need for physical healing, for release from inharmony.

Agur, ā'-gŭr (Heb.) — *gathered; scraped together; small money; profit; tax money; a hireling; a stranger.*

Son of Jakeh (Prov. 30:1).

Meta. Outer understanding—man's intellectual consciousness — gathering knowledge and substance for personal advancement and gain. This is not the true, spiritual understanding and substance, but is *a hireling, a stranger*, so far as concerns the getting of good by waiting on the inner teacher, the Spirit of truth, and then carrying out its instructions. The spiritual way of gaining wisdom and supply is easy, but the way of the outer man, of the intellect, is hard work (*scraped together, small money*).

Ahab, ā'-hăb (Heb.) — *father's brother; uncle.*

a Son of Omri; became king of Israel after his father's death (I Kings 16:29-33); **b** A son of Kolaiah (Jer. 29:21-23).

Meta. Error states of consciousness based on false intellectual reasoning, or the intellect that has dropped to the level of sense worship. Ahab married Jezebel, who represents the counterpart, in bodily sensations and desires, of the false intellectual concepts; she is the animal soul of unbridled passions and desires. When this union of forces takes place the whole man is involved in error.

Omri and Ahab passed away in the resurrection of man from this retrogression; the intellectual man cannot bear the coarser expressions of the senses. Jezebel met with a violent death; passion and appetite burn themselves out. Elijah destroys the prophets of Baal; the quickening, fiery word of Truth sets up its activity, revealing the higher principle of man's being and erasing the thoughts of error. Harmony in mind and in body results.

In I Kings 21:1-20, King Ahab represents the will dominated by covetousness. Inordinate acquisitiveness ruled the mind and took possession of the man. When this trait throws its influence over man he develops an insatiable desire to possess things. Ahab built himself a splendid summer palace and inlaid it with ivory. Extravagance grows: Ahab's palace of ivory must have additional gardens. The vineyard of Naboth best suited him, and it was acquired by foul means. Covetousness has no wisdom, and when a man gives up to its demands he does most foolish things to get possession of coveted objects. Seemingly subtle plans, like Jezebel's plan to have the innocent Naboth stoned to death, are always exposed eventually.

There is no escape from justice. It overtakes men when they think that they are secure in ill-gotten gains, and they have to give up everything. The man who takes advantage of another's necessity to enrich himself must in due season restore fourfold, as did Zacchæus. Acquisitiveness is a legitimate faculty of the mind, but covetousness is a Judas. When acquisitiveness acts within the law it builds up the consciousness, but when it oversteps the law it is a destroyer.

Ahab and Omri represent discordant activities of the mind. Disregard of the laws of life draws the vital force of the organism away from the life center, and the life currents run low. This condition is called drought (I Kings 17).

Aharah, ă-hăr'-ăh (Heb.)—*after the brother.*

Son of Benjamin (I Chron. 8:1.) He is called Ahiram, Aher, and Ehi in other places in the Bible; see Numbers 26:38; I Chronicles 7:12; Genesis 46:21.

Meta. That in man's spiritually awakening consciousness which follows after lofty, kindly, brotherly, constructive ideals (*after the brother;* a Benjamite).

Aharhel, ă-här'-hĕl (Heb.)—*behind the intrenchment; behind the breastwork; after might.*

Son of Harum, a descendant of Judah (I Chron. 4:8).

Meta. A belief in protection and might as coming from God and not emanating from the outer man.

Ahasbai, ă-hăs'-bāi (Heb.)—*I have taken refuge in Jehovah.*

Father of one of David's mighty men, a Maacathite (II Sam. 23:34).

Meta. An idea of faith and trust in Jehovah, the true, inner spiritual I AM (*I have taken refuge in Jehovah*).

Ahasuerus, ă-hăs-û-ē'-rŭs (Heb. fr. Pers.)—*lion; king.*

King of Persia (Esth. 1:1 to end of book).

Meta. The will puffed up by its conquests and dominated by ambition. It is the function of the will to rule, and when man is more ambitious than wise he often makes a spectacle of himself.

The edict to destroy the Jews, which King Ahasuerus sent forth at the instigation of Haman, represents one of those foolish and unreasoning laws that we lay down when we are influenced by sense consciousness. Queen Esther, in her relation to King Ahasuerus, represents the power of love to win the will from self. The fast held by the Jews signifies a denial of all selfishness in the expression of love. The golden scepter symbolizes wisdom.

Ahava, ă-hā'-và (Heb.)—*stream; water.*

A river, beside which the Jewish captives gathered when returning to Jerusalem under Ezra (Ezra 8:15).

Meta. A current of cleansing thought (*stream*) where the waters of denial (fasting, see Ezra 8:21) wash away fearful thoughts and material beliefs, thus enabling our religious thoughts (Jews) to proceed on their way to Jerusalem (spiritual consciousness) in safety.

Ahaz, ā'-hăz (Heb.)—*possessor; possessing; to lay hold of; to grasp.*

Son of Jotham, and King of Judah (II Kings 16).

Meta. The will given over to Baal worship, or materiality—the will that grasps things of sense and gives the substance of mind and body to them (*to lay hold of, to grasp, possessor*).

Ahaziah, ă-hă-zī'-ăh (Heb.)—*Jehovah hath grasped; Jah holds, possesses; whom Jehovah sustains; Jehovah sustains.*

a King of Israel and son of Ahab and Jezebel (I Kings 22:40). **b** A king of Judah, son of Joram and Athaliah. (Athaliah was a daughter of Ahab and Jezebel. See II Kings 8:24—9:28.)

Meta. Although both these kings were idolatrous, and were directed in their reigns by the selfishness of the sense man, yet they represent the continuity of the inner spiritual will of man (*whom Jehovah sustains, Jah holds, possesses*), which selfishness cannot kill out.

In the case of Ahaziah, king of Judah, this idea is carried out quite clearly by the saving (hiding) of his son Joash, or Jehoash, from being destroyed by Athaliah. Later this son was given the throne, and he proved to be a good king.

(See II Kings 11:1-17.)

Ahban, äh'-băn (Heb.)—*brother of intelligence; brother of understanding,* i. e., *wise, discreet.*

Son of Abishur by Abihail; a Judahite (I Chron. 2:29).

Meta. The uniting (in consciousness) of strength and might to intelligence, or wisdom (*brother of intelligence, wise, discreet*). Abishur, father of Ahban, symbolizes a consciousness of strength brought about by uprightness and praise (Judah) while Abihail, mother of Ahban, signifies the idea that power and strength come from God and are spiritual qualities. When strength and power are unified with and express through wisdom, true wisdom being one with love, the individual grows in discretion and in strength of character; thus he is enabled more perfectly to avoid error and discern and express the good.

Aher, ā'-hēr (Heb.)—*after; behind; following.*

A Benjamite (I Chron. 7:12). He is called Aharah in I Chronicles 8:1, and Ahiram in Numbers 26:38.

Meta. See AHARAH.

Ahi, ā'-hī (Heb.)—*my brother; my friend; brotherly.*

a A chief of the tribe of Asher (I Chron. 7:34). **b** A man of the tribe of Gad (I Chron. 5:15).

Meta. An established thought of the brotherhood of man. This thought springs from the understanding that God is the one Father and that all men are brothers (*my brother, my friend, brotherly*).

Ahiam, ă-hī'-ăm (Heb.)—*brother of mother; mother's brother; uncle.* Some commentators think that this name should have been written Ahiab, "father's brother."

A captain in David's army (II Sam. 23:33).

Meta. A sense of the close union that n Truth exists between all men, universal relationship (*father's brother, mother's brother, uncle*). This feeling of universal relationship is always in evidence where love (David) is, and it aids greatly in preparing the way for love (David) to rule in consciousness. It also helps to sustain the rule of love after it is established.

Ahian, ă-hī'-ăn (Heb.)—*brotherly.*

Son of Shemida, a Manassite (I Chron. 7:19).

Meta. The significance here is that true understanding expressing in the consciousness of an individual establishes a sense of union with and *brotherly* kindness toward all mankind and all creation. (Shemida, father of Ahian, is interpreted *splendor of wisdom, renowned knowledge,* while Manasseh refers to the understanding faculty in man, from the negative standpoint, the standpoint of denial.)

Ahiezer, ā-hī-ē'-zēr (Heb.)—*helping brother; brother of help,* i. e., *helpful; (my) brother is help.*

a Son of Ammishaddai, and a prince of the tribe of Dan (Num. 1:12; 7:66). **b** A chief and warrior of the Danites who came to David at Ziklag when David was in hiding from Saul (I Chron. 12:3). In the text this latter Ahiezer appears to be a Benjamite, but both Young and Fallows say that he was a Danite chief.

Meta. Good judgment (Dan refers to the judgment faculty in man), even if it be of the intellectual consciousness, acknowledges God as the source of all might, and love (David) as the true king of Israel. Being positive in its nature, good judgment is very helpful (*helping brother, helpful;* Ammishaddai, father of Ahiezer, means *people of the Almighty*) in guiding the true thoughts of the consciousness from the bondage of sense to the realm of spiritual understanding and realization (the Israelites in their journey from Egypt to Canaan). Later, good judgment helps to bring about a right adjustment so that love (David) may become the ruling power in consciousness, instead of the will directed by the limitations of the personal self (Saul).

Ahihud, ă-hī'-hŭd (Heb.)—*brother of majesty; brother of honor; brother of renown.*

a A prince of the tribe of Asher; he helped in dividing the Promised Land among the twelve tribes of Israel (Num. 34:27). **b** One of the heads of the family of Ehud (I Chron. 8:7).

Meta. The exaltation of joy, and its unifying power (*brother of honor, majesty, renown;* a prince of Asher, Asher meaning *happy*).

The Ahihud of I Chronicles 8:7 was of the tribe of Benjamin, and was one of the heads of the family of Ehud. This name is different in the Hebrew from the other Ahihud. It means *brother of mystery; brother of a riddle,* i. e., *mysterious.* This Ahihud symbolizes the working of faith (Benjamin), which is a mystery to the consciousness that has not been awakened spiritually.

Ahijah, ă-hī'-jäh (Heb.) *brother of Jehovah; Jah is brother; Jehovah's friend.*

The name of several prominent Israelitish men: **a** a prophet (I Kings 14:2-18); **b** a high priest (I Sam. 14:3), one of David's mighty men (I Chron. 11:36); **c** a Levite who during David's reign "was over the treasures of the house of God" (I Chron. 26:20).

Meta. The establishing, in consciousness, of the close relationship that exists between man and the Christ—Jehovah (*brother of Jehovah, Jehovah's friend*).

Ahikam, ă-hī'-kăm (Heb.)—*my brother has arisen; brother of rising,* i. e., *standing; brother who rises and stands.*

Son of Shaphan the scribe. Ahikam was sent with several others to the prophetess Huldah to learn more about the book of the law that had been found (II Kings 22:12); he took Jeremiah's part, and protected him (Jer. 26:24; 39:14). Gedaliah was his son.

Meta. A certain spiritual awakening, an elevation and stabilization of thought, and a revivifying of soul that take place in the consciousness of man (*my brother has arisen, brother of rising,* i. e., *standing, brother who rises and stands*) and cause him to search earnestly to learn more about the great law of Being, that he may harmonize himself with it and so escape having to reap the disastrous results of error.

Ahilud, ă-hī'-lŭd (Heb.)—*brother of a son,* i. e., *of one who is already born; a brother born; brother of one born or brother of the Lydian.*

Father of Jehoshaphat, who was recorder for both David and Solomon (II Sam. 8:16; I Kings 4:3).

Meta. A *brother born* capacity for fairness; also a protective, brotherly love toward and unity with one's own inner functions, faculties, and powers, and toward all persons in the outer, which enables one to bring forth good judgment—Jehovah judgment. (Jehoshaphat, the son of Ahilud, means *judgment of Jehovah.*)

Ahimaaz, ă-hĭm′-ă-ăz (Heb.)—*brother of travail; brother of power,* i. e., *powerful effort; brother of wrath; brother of anger,* i. e., *irascible; (my) brother is anger.*

a Son of Zadok the priest and a messenger of David's (II Sam. 15:36). He was a very fast runner. On one occasion David said of him, "He is a good man, and cometh with good tidings" (II Sam. 18:27). He was very tactful and kind in breaking the news of Absalom's death to David. **b** The father of Ahinoam, the wife of King Saul (I Sam. 14:50); **c** Ahimaaz of Naphtali was the husband of Basemath, a daughter of Solomon (I Kings 4:15).

Meta. Ahimaaz does not stand in man's consciousness for anything pertaining to our present day idea of wrath, anger, or touchiness. Ahimaaz the son of Zadok represents an inner quickness of thought, an intuition that is of Spirit and is governed by love and brotherly kindness. This intuition will warn one when one is in danger of erring, and will do much toward showing one the right path to choose if one will but listen. The thought that Ahimaaz signifies also urges one to persevere in the effort to break through the seeming denseness of error to the full light of Truth (*brother of power;* i. e., *powerful effort*).

Ahiman, ă-hī′-măn (Heb.)—*brother of a portion; brother of allotment; brother of a gift,* i. e., *liberality.*

One of the three sons of Anak (Num. 13:22). Anak and his sons were giants in the land of Canaan; they were driven out by Caleb, and were finally killed by the Judahites (Josh. 15:14; Judg. 1:10).

Meta. Anak and his sons lived in Hebron. (Hebron signifies the front brain, or seat of conscious thought.) They represent certain strongly intrenched intellectual reasonings that derive their energy from the elemental life forces of the subconscious mind (Canaanites), because they have become such a deeply established part of the inherited race thought.

The person who is a great reasoner from the purely human standpoint finds it more difficult than other persons really to accept the spiritual Truth and to understand it and put it into practice. Such a one can reason away every truth that is presented to him, and can do it in a seemingly logical way. To the carnal reasoning mind the most precious truths of Spirit are foolishness. (See I Cor. 2:14.) Over and over again we fail to put into practice the spiritual inspirations that come to us from the Great Teacher within us, because the giants of established worldly reasoning take up their warfare against the ideas of Spirit.

The phase of reasoning that Ahiman symbolizes is seemingly very liberal in its views (*brother of a gift,* i. e., *liberality*). It can give apparently logical reasons why one should be guided by the established views of the world, by the understanding of highly educated men, by the decisions of ministers of the Gospel, and by tradition, instead of giving oneself over to the new, different, spiritual thoughts that appear to the natural man to be foolish fads. This line of reasoning for which Ahiman stands is very subtle, hence powerful, because there is usually a grain of Truth in it (*brother of a portion*), and half truths are harder to recognize and combat successfully than out-and-out falsehoods. Only by spiritual faith, enthusiasm, loyalty to Truth (Caleb), and use of praise and prayer (Judah) can this form of reasoning be overcome entirely.

Ahimelech, ă-hĭm′-ĕ-lĕch (Heb.)—*brother of Melek; brother of the king,* i. e., *the king's friend; my brother is king.*

A high priest in the city of Nob, in the allotment of Benjamin; he gave David "holy bread" when David was fleeing from Saul (I Sam. 21:1-9). This act so enraged Saul that he caused Ahimelech and all the other priests of Nob to be killed, except one who escaped (I Sam. 22:9-23).

Meta. A high ideal of the intellectual consciousness that ministers to the religious thoughts of man (Israelites), especially to the thoughts pertaining to faith (Benjamin). Ahimelech is a brother and a friend of the true king, Spirit, which is the one source of all true intelligence and ruling power (*brother of the king, the king's friend;* the illumined intellect is closely related to Spirit, since it reflects the light or understanding of Spirit), yet because of his timidity and fearfulness, the result of believing in the inability of the flesh or outer consciousness to be lifted up and established in Truth (Doeg the Edomite), Ahimelech comes under the adverse dominion of the ignorant personal will (Saul) and is slain. The very fearfulness (Doeg) that is responsible for Ahimelech's coming under the adverse power of Saul (personal will) is appointed to slay him. The king's guards first were commanded to kill Ahimelech and the other priests who were with him, but the guards would not do it because they recognized the high, consecrated position of the priests. Doeg the Edomite, however, did not hesitate to kill them; he represents purely material belief, which cannot discern anything of a nature higher than itself.

Thus may our high aspirations be brought into a state of inactivity if we allow fear to possess our mind and if we are afraid of the consequences of giving our holy bread (spiritual substance) over to the sustaining of David (love) before Saul (personal will) has come under the abiding rule of Spirit. If we see the apparent weakness and inability of the flesh, instead of being always strong and bold in the consciousness of God in us as our overcoming power and our all-sufficiency in all things, our high, illumined thoughts (priests) will not be protected as they should be.

Ahimoth, ă-hī'-mŏth (Heb.)—*my brother is death; brother of death.*

Son of Elkanah, of the Israelitish tribe of Levi (I Chron. 6:25). Mahath of I Chronicles 6:35 and Ahimoth of Luke 3:26 are thought by some authorities to be the same person.

Meta. That phase of life which pertains to the breaking up and passing away of the "old man," or mortal thoughts and states of consciousness (*breaking in pieces, dissolution,* are meanings of Mahath). Paul said, "I die daily." In order to keep on living, in order to attain eternal life, one must attain a right balance between the letting go of false ideas and of corresponding body cells and the laying hold of true, vital ones.

"Why, we all have to die sometime," commented one to whom the "life" subject was new. A Truth student answered: "Yes, every one has to die; but there are two ways to die: God's way and the Devil's way. The way of the Adversary is to let the body go to corruption in the grave, because of our holding to carnality. God's way is to deny the lesser self, as Jesus taught. In His way we 'die daily' to that which pertains to the carnal mind and to the limitations of the personal man. If we die in His way and by our thoughts daily lay hold of and appropriate the resurrection or Christ life, our whole being will be renewed, revitalized, and spiritualized, and we shall demonstrate eternal life. Thus we shall be saved alive and entire, and shall escape the grave."

So Ahimoth represents the phase of life that seems to the sense man to be closely akin to death—the dissolving of error states of consciousness and of thoughts that have served their purpose in us and will become detrimental to our progress if we retain them longer. They must be released, and the corresponding dead cells in our bodies must pass away in order that we may realize new ideas and new life and substance.

Ahinadab, ă-hĭn'-ă-dăb (Heb.)— *brother of liberality; liberal brother; (my) brother is noble.*

One of the twelve men appointed by Solomon to gather provisions for the king and his household. He was to gather the supplies from the part of the land of Israel called Mahanaim. For one month in every twelve this portion of the country had to supply the royal household with food, and Ahinadab was commissioned to collect the food (I Kings 4:14).

Meta. Mahanaim was the name that Jacob gave to the place where the angels of God met him when he was returning from Laban to become unified with Esau. Mahanaim means *two hosts* or *companies*. These refer to the angels of God (spiritual ideas) and to Jacob and his company, his wives, children, and possessions (the mentality of man). Esau, to whom Jacob was going, represents the body. By the mind we get into conscious touch with Spirit so that we may receive and appropriate its substance and life ideas (spiritual food), which become the very life and substance of the whole organism. Thus we are truly fed. Through the medium of the mind, also, we make conscious union with our body.

Ahinadab represents a phase of thought that helps to make the union between the spiritual and the seemingly material, in order that the ruling peace and wisdom, with the immediate thoughts pertaining to them (Solomon and his household), may be sustained. Ahinadab stands for a high, liberal spirit, tendency, or characteristic (*brother of liberality, my brother is noble*) in the religious and spiritual thoughts of men (Israelites), which makes them willing to give of their substance for the sustaining of peace and poise (Solomon and his household) in consciousness.

Ahinoam, ă-hĭn'-ŏ-ăm (Heb.)—*my brother is delight; pleasant brother; brother of grace; gracious.*

a Saul's wife (I Sam. 14:50). b A wife of David's (I Sam. 25:43).

Meta. The ruling idea in mind represented by David's wife, Ahinoam, is activity without discord (*my brother is delight, pleasant brother, gracious*). The wives of David represent the substance side of thought, which must enter into the demonstration of our rule in divine love. The first step is obedience to the Lord; the second is to go up into our highest spiritual realization and there concentrate all our thoughts. (See II Sam. 2:2.)

Ahio, ă-hī'-ŏ (Heb.)—*brotherly; his brother.*

a Son of Abinadab (II Sam. 6:3, 4). b Two Benjamites (I Chron. 8:14, 31).

Meta. A comprehension of the close relationship that exists between God and the true self of man. Man attains this understanding by going up in his thoughts (praying) and communing with Spirit. (See ABINADAB, father of Ahio, who lived in the "hill" and represents the superconscious mind in the individual.) Understanding of the close relationship that exists between the superconscious mind and the man himself must engender a kindly, compassionate spirit, which aids in removing the Ark of the Covenant from Abinadab's home in the hill to the city of David—from the superconsciousness in the top head to the heart center—that all Israel (the religious and spiritual thoughts and states of consciousness in man) may be blessed.

Ahira, ă-hī'-rå (Heb.)—*brother of evil,* i. e., *unlucky.* In a good sense: *brother of nourishment; brother shepherd.*

Son of Enan, and prince over the tribe of Naphtali while the Israelites were in the wilderness under Moses' jurisdiction (Num. 1:15).

Meta. The central controlling thought, at a certain period of man's unfoldment, of the strength faculty (Naphtali) in consciousness. This very influential thought, in leading the individual to give his strength to material thinking, brings about error conditions such as weakness, disease, and inharmony. Thus it becomes a *brother of evil,* and the individual believes himself to be *unlucky.* On the other hand, when the thought that Ahira signifies gives its sustaining strength to spiritual thinking, it becomes a *brother shepherd;* it becomes akin to the Christ principle of life and good. The Christ is the true shepherd of the sheep (man's life thoughts; see John 10).

Ahiram, ă-hī'-răm (Heb.)—*brother of height,* i. e., *high, lofty; exalted brother; (my) brother is high.*

Grandson of Benjamin and son of Bela

(Num. 25:38). This name is the same as Aher and Aharah.

Meta. See AHARAH.

Ahisamach, ă-hĭs'-ă-măch (Heb.)— *brother of support, i. e., helpful, aiding; supporting brother; my brother is supporting.*

Father of Oholiah, of the tribe of Dan (Ex. 31:6; 35:34).

Meta. A helpful, sustaining attitude of mind that is based on good judgment (*supporting brother, aiding, helpful; a Danite, Dan meaning judge*). This attitude of mind tends to build up and maintain the body temple in poise and harmony. The tabernacle in the wilderness refers to the outer physical body; Oholiah, son of Ahisamach, was one of the wise workmen employed in making this tabernacle and its furnishings.

Ahishahar, ă-hĭsh'-ă-här (Heb.)— *brother of dawn; brother of the dawn, i. e., early.*

A Benjamite warrior, son of Bilhan (I Chron. 7:10).

Meta. The breaking forth of new light into consciousness (*brother of dawn— that which is unified with light, understanding*).

Ahishar, ă-hī'-shär (Heb.)—*brother of song; (my) brother is song; brother of the upright, i. e., righteousness.*

A prince over Solomon's household (I Kings 4:6).

Meta. The harmony and order (*brother of song, brother of the upright, i. e., righteousness*) that prevail in the consciousness when peace has been established by the union of wisdom and love, or, the blending of love (David) into wisdom (Solomon).

Ahithophel, ă-hĭth'-ŏ-phĕl (Heb.)— *foolish brother; brother of foolishness, i. e., foolish; brother of folly.*

A counselor of King David's, a very wise man, who foolishly joined himself to Absalom when Absalom tried to seize his father's throne. When David heard of it he said: "O Jehovah, I pray thee, turn the counsel of Ahithophel into foolishness" (II Sam. 15:12, 31-34; 17:1-23).

Meta. The history of Ahithophel as given in the Bible, together with the meaning of the name, shows him to be a good example of the utter foolishness of the highest worldly or intellectual wisdom when it is compared with true spiritual understanding. In his ill treatment of David and in his suicide which followed, Ahithophel suggests Judas and his relation to Jesus Christ (Psalms 41:9; Matt. 27:5).

Ahitub, ă-hī'-tŭb (Heb.)—*brother of goodness,* or *benignity, i. e., benign.*

a Father of Ahijah, a high priest who was descended from Eli (I Sam. 14:3). **b** Father of Ahimelech, the priest who was slain at Saul's command for having befriended David (I Sam. 22:9-20). **c** Father of Zadoc, a priest (II Sam. 8:17).

Meta. A conception of the truth that God (Spirit) is good only and that He expresses in individual consciousness as kindness and goodness (*brother of goodness, benignity, benign*).

Ahlab, äh'-lăb (Heb.)—*fat; fruitful place; fertile.*

A city of Canaan that was allotted to the tribe of Asher. Asher, however, failed to drive the Canaanites from this place, and so lived among them (Judg. 1:31).

Meta. Rich possibilities to be attained by man when he gains dominion over the elemental life forces (Canaanites) in his body consciousness (Canaan), and raises them to righteous and full expression (*fruitful place, fatness, i. e., fertile*).

Ahlai, äh'-lāi (Heb.)—*Oh that! would God! an intense wish; ornamental.*

Daughter of Sheshan. Sheshan had no sons; his lineage was preserved through his daughters (I Chron. 2:31-35). The Ahlai of I Chronicles 11:41 may have been this same woman, since in I Chronicles 2:36 we see that Zabad was descended from Ahlai the daughter of Sheshan.

Meta. An inner or soul desire for a more positive (masculine) expression of truth (*Oh that! would God! an intense wish; ornamental;* an Israelitish woman). This desire was realized in due time. Attai, the son of Ahlai, means *timely, opportune, seasonable.*

Ahoah, ă-hō'-äh (Heb.)—*brother's reed; brotherly; living brother; brother,*

i. e., *friend of Jah.*

A descendant of Benjamin through his son Bela (I Chron. 8:4). He is called Ahijah in I Chronicles 8:7. Ahi and Ahiah are also different forms of the same name.

Meta. See AHI and AHIJAH.

Ahumai, ă-hū'-māi (Heb.)—*heated by Jah; brother of water; water reeds; cowardly; indolent.*

Son of Jahath and descendant of Judah (I Chron. 4:2).

Meta. A negative state of mind caused by too much denial, a letting go and a letting down in thought (*brother of water, cowardly, indolent*). Courage is needed, and greater enthusiasm (*heated by Jah*), that a positive laying hold of good may lift the consciousness to spiritual activity and accomplishment.

Ahuzzam (A. V., Ahuzam), ă-hŭz'-zăm (Heb.)—*their possession; holding fast; possessions.*

Son of Ashhur and Naarah, of the tribe of Judah (I Chron. 4:6).

Meta. The ability to perceive, acquire, and possess (*their possession, holding fast, possessions*), belonging to the Judah faculty of mind.

Ahzai (A. V., Ahasai), äh'-zāi (Heb.) —*my holder; protector; whom Jehovah holds; whom Jehovah upholds.*

A priest of Israel (Neh. 11:13); a form of the name Ahaziah.

Meta. The Israelitish priests represent our so-called "natural religious tendencies." Some of these may be spiritual, and others may be simply of the intellect. Ahzai signifies just what the name means—that Jehovah upholds, sustains, and protects the true religious nature of man as it is unfolding into spiritual consciousness. (See AHAZIAH.)

Ahuzzath, ă-hŭz'-zăth (Heb.)—*holding fast; a possession; possessions.*

A friend of Abimelech, who was a Philistine king (Gen. 26:26).

Meta. The selfishness of the unregenerate will (Abimelech) in its belief that it is the rightful ruler of man and that the substance and the forces of man's being are for its own sense desires. Having witnessed the ever increasing power and possessions of Isaac (who is

a symbol of the divine sonship), Abimelech fears that he will lose his own rule and possessions, and so with Ahuzzath, his friend, he goes to Isaac and makes a covenant with him in order to protect himself, his people, and their goods.

The divine son, Christ, does not destroy, but saves. Error eventually brings about its own destruction, but there is a period of development when the wheat and the tares must be allowed to grow together until the harvest—when the error seems to flourish along with the good. The harvest time of the Philistines came when the Israelites under Joshua took possession of the Promised Land. In our own individual body consciousness we begin the redemption of our body when we begin the real overcoming of the thoughts that are in opposition to the laws of our being (the Philistines).

Ai, ā'-ī (Heb.)—*the heap; a heap of rubbish; heap of ruins.*

A city east of Bethel; it is now a hill of stones. In Scripture history, Ai (eye), or Hai, was a royal city of the Canaanites (Josh. 7:2-5; 8:9-28; Ezra 2:28). The Aiath of Isaiah 10:28 is a form of Ai.

Meta. Ai is mentioned in the Bible with Bethel. In Joshua 8, much is written about the utter destruction of Ai, but nothing is said about Bethel's being destroyed, though both at that time were cities of the Canaanites. We are told that Jacob named Bethel *house of God,* when he had the dream that caused him to exclaim: "Surely Jehovah is in this place; and I knew it not" (Gen. 28: 10-22). Abraham also built an altar between Bethel and Ai (Gen. 12:8). Abraham signifies faith in God as awakening in the human consciousness. This faith is inner spiritual sight, that in man which perceives the divine presence and man's oneness with it (Bethel). Ai must refer to egotism and self-confidence without recognition of Spirit. These are counterfeits of faith; they are destructive (*heap of ruins*) to the building of a truly spiritual character and must be put away that the individual may come into a knowledge of his unity with God.

Real, practical faith in God, in the unseen yet almighty, omnipresent, omniscient Spirit of truth, is *a heap of rubbish* to the state of thought that is built up in self. The ruling idea of egotism and skepticism in the sense consciousness (the King of Ai) must be overcome by the I AM (Joshua), that faith in God may be established and that the individual may come into a realization of his true relation to God.

Aiah (in A. V., Gen. 36:24, Ajah), ā'-jäh (Heb.)—*a cry; a clamor; a hawk; a vulture.*

a Father of Saul's concubine, Rizpah, whose sons were delivered by David to the Gibeonites to be hanged (II Sam. 3:7; 21:8). **b** A descendant of Seir the Horite (Gen. 36:24).

Meta. Destructive, devouring thoughts pertaining to the animal consciousness and to what should be the higher thought realm in the individual (*a cry, a clamor, a hawk, a vulture;* an Israelite and a Horite).

Aijalon (in A. V., Joshua 10:12 and in II Chronicles 28:18, Ajalon), āi'-jà-lŏn (Heb.)—*place of deer; place of oaks; a strong place.*

a A valley and a city in the portion of Canaan that was allotted to the tribe of Dan (Josh. 10:12; 19:42). **b** A place belonging to the tribe of Zebulun (Judg. 12:12). (See I Chron. 6:69; II Chron. 11:10.)

Meta. Dan and Zebulun refer to phases of order, judgment, and intelligent discrimination in the consciousness. Joshua commanded the moon to stand still in the Valley of Aijalon while the Israelites completed their destruction of the Amorites. Aijalon therefore has to do with intellectual or reflected thought: the moon borrows its light from the sun, and the intellect reflects its understanding from the one Intelligence, Spirit.

Aijalon represents the fleetness (*deer*) of thought and the strength and protection (*place of oaks, a strong place*) inherent in the true thoughts that meet and overcome error (Ammonites) when these thoughts are established in Spirit and directed by I AM, Joshua.

Ain, ā'-in (Heb.)—*eye; a (natural) fountain; a fountain,* literally, *an eye.*

A city on the eastern boundary line of Canaan (Num. 34:11). First it seems to have been a city of Judah, and then of Simeon (Josh. 15:32; 19:7). It was one of the places that were given over to the Levites, or priesthood (Josh. 21:16).

Meta. Praise (Judah) of our natural religious tendencies (Levites) and hearing of, or obedience (Simeon) to, them open the way for discernment (*eye*) of spiritual Truth. Light, love, and Truth enter a person's consciousness and become in him *a fountain* (Ain) of living water. "The water that I shall give him shall become in him a well of water springing up unto eternal life," said Jesus.

Akan, ā'-kăn (Heb.)—*keen; acute; twisted; warped; perverted; keen of vision.*

A chief of the Horites, grandson of Seir (Gen. 36:27); in I Chronicles 1:42 he is called Jaakan.

Meta. A ruling thought, or at least a very strong, influential thought, in the sense consciousness. This thought aids in diverting the individual from the Truth, and causes much trouble in the flesh. It is *acute,* and is quick to perceive (*keen*) on the sense plane, but is blind (*warped, twisted*) to the real truth of man's being.

The Horites were closely associated with the Edomites, the descendants of Esau. They were inhabitants of the land of Seir before they were overcome by Esau. After that they lived in the land along with the Edomites. Horites means *cave dwellers;* Seir means *rough, hairy.* Considered metaphysically, the Horites, like the Edomites, have their seat of action in the physical organism. The Horites refer more especially to deep-seated (*cave dwellers*) error, fleshly tendencies, and activities of the physical in man than the Edomites do, though both symbolize phases of the body consciousness.

Akeldama (A. V., Aceldama), ă-kĕl'-dă-mȧ (Gk. fr. Aram.)—*field of blood; portion of blood.*

A field not far from Jerusalem that was bought with the money that Judas received for betraying Jesus. In Matthew 27:7, 8, it is called "the potter's field," and seemingly it was bought by the Jewish priests and elders who were instrumental in having Jesus crucified, after Judas returned the thirty pieces of silver to them. In Acts 1:17-19, however, it is inferred that Judas himself bought the field and then, falling headlong in it, "burst asunder in the midst, and all his bowels gushed out."

Meta. Judas carried the bag from which the disciples drew the funds to meet their physical needs. A portion of the substance that supports our organism is extracted in a very intricate manner from the food that we eat. From mouth to stomach, to blood, to nerve fluid it is refined step by step to the highest degree, where Spirit can reach it and use it at the nerve endings in magnetic vibration.

The stomach stands for the meditative faculty of the mind—its ability to receive ideas, turn them over and over, and get mental pabulum out of them. On his plane, Judas (the animal) does much of his thinking in the stomach; and after he had sacrificed everything to material ends (so states Peter, the real thinker), he went out into the field and his bowels gushed out, showing that there must be an end to that way of thinking.

Akeldama was the field into which Judas went. It symbolizes a certain element in thought substance that receives the blood (life) of the Judas (sense) man, and the essence of all errors (Akeldama was a field bought as a burial ground for the bodies of deceased strangers) that have to do with the stomach, bowels, and generative center, and eliminates these errors from the consciousness and from the body.

Akkub, ăk'-kŭb (Heb.)—*to take by the heel; to lie in wait; cunning; insidious.*

There were several Israelitish men by this name; most of them were of the tribe of Levi and served as porters in the Temple and as priests who helped to teach the people out of the law (I Chron. 3:24; 9:17; Ezra 2:45; Neh. 8:7). Akkub is a form of the name Jacob.

Meta. Akkub, though it suggests deceit and craftiness (*to take by the heel;*

cunning; to lie in wait; insidious), has reference, like Jacob, to the subtle working of sense mind in the progression of the individual toward spiritual consciousness.

Akrabbim, ă-krăb'-bĭm (Heb.)—*scorpions; scourges; wounds the heel; the going up,* in sense of *a pass.*

A range of mountains or hills, or a pass of steep ascent, in a mountain range that formed a part of the southern boundary of the Promised Land (Num. 34:4).

Meta. South always means below, in Biblical symbology, and often refers to the subconscious. Akrabbim, in Judges 1:36, is said to have been a border of the territory of the Amorites. It represents the passing up, in consciousness, out of the realm of the Amorites (the error race belief in and exaltation of generation, through sex) into the land of Judea—the higher ideals of the Israelites, or true thoughts about life (*the going up,* in sense of *a pass*). *Scorpions, scourges,* refer to the stinging experiences that beset one who has given way to the sensations of the flesh; they goad him on to seek a higher expression of his creative forces, that he may enter an abiding consciousness of life, health, peace, and harmony—the Promised Land.

Alemeth, ăl'-ĕ-mĕth (Heb.)—*place of concealment; hiding place; covering,* otherwise *adolescence.*

a Son of Becher and grandson of Benjamin (I Chron. 7:8). **b** A Benjamite who was descended from Saul and Jonathan (I Chron. 8:36).

Meta. True faith thoughts (Benjamites) developing within the consciousness; an inner unfoldment, or soul progression, that the outer man does not realize (*hiding place, adolescence*). (See ALLEMETH.)

Alexander, ăl-ĕx-ăn'-dĕr (Gk.)—*man defender; helper of man; helper of men; defender of men.*

The name of several different men (Mark 15:21; Acts 4:6; 19:33; I Tim. 1:20). Some of these men worked against Paul and some helped him.

Meta. Alexander refers more to the

outer belief in positive mental and physical force (*man defender, helper of man*) than it does to the true, inner overcoming power of divine love. The thought that he represents, therefore, is as likely to work against the real, spiritual good of man as it is to act for that good.

The Alexander of Acts 19:33 worked constructively to help quiet the riot at Ephesus and to bring about peace and poise. He symbolizes a certain righteous expression of justice and mastery, and a broadness of comprehension that succeeded in quieting the people and showing them the proper way to adjust their grievances. In consciousness this refers to quieting the raging mind, and instilling into it a right sense of adjustment and balance. (See DEMETRIUS.)

Alexandria, ăl-ĕx-ăn'-drĭ-ȧ (Gk.)—*of Alexander; from Alexander.*

A ruling city in Egypt; a Greek center that was founded by Alexander the Great (Acts 28:11).

Meta. Alexandria denotes a phase of the intellect that rules the body consciousness at a certain stage of man's unfoldment, until the position of rulership is given over to the rightful ruler in man, his spiritual I AM, or Christ. In this phase of the intellectual realm, which Alexandria signifies, there are Egyptians, Greeks, Jews, and Christians—all classes and kinds of thoughts have room until the intellect becomes quickened and guided by the true understanding of spiritual Truth. Then all error thoughts and ideas are gradually weeded out. Among the Alexandrians, therefore, we find powerful thoughts and thought forces working for and against the Christ word in us in its work of redeeming our body.

The Alexandrian of Acts 18:24-28 was a Jew who believed; he did much toward spreading the gospel of Christ. He represents a religious intellectual thought that has been quickened by Spirit to an understanding of the Christ Truth, and then gives itself over to the work of establishing this Truth further in the consciousness.

The Alexandrians of Acts 6:9 represent fixed states of thought in the realm of sense that rise up and oppose the further progress of spiritual ideas. They are stirred up by the arguments of Stephen (the illumined reason).

(There were many Jews in the city of Alexandria in Egypt, as well as people of other nationalities. It was a noted city of learning. It had a wonderful library that was very famous, and it was the seat of commerce, science, and education of the then known world.)

Allammelech (A. V., Alammelech), ăl-lăm'-mĕ-lĕch (Heb.)—*king's oak.*

A place in Asher (Josh. 19:26).

Meta. A state of consciousness in man that realizes that "the joy of Jehovah" is his fortress and strength (*the king's oak;* a place in Asher, Asher meaning *happy*). An oak tree stands for something very strong and protective; it signifies the defense of the Almighty.

Allemeth (in A. V., Alemeth), ăl'-lĕ-mĕth (Heb.)—*place of concealment; hiding place; covering,* otherwise *adolescence.*

A city of the Levites in the allotment of Benjamin—a city of refuge (I Chron. 6:60). This city is called Almon in Joshua 21:18.

Meta. An inner development, or soul progression. The outer man does not know that this development is going on in him (*adolescence*), but it becomes a "city of refuge" in his consciousness— a stronghold of true justice (*covering, hiding place*) wherein there is release and protection from all consciousness of sin and from all condemnation for past errors of mind or of body. True justice delivers the individual from error and its results; it does not condemn or destroy. Man must learn that God is lifting up and redeeming, or saving, His creation and making it perfect. As the realization of this truth dawns upon man and grows strong in his consciousness, he is lifted out of mortality into Godlikeness.

Allon, ăl'-lŏn (Heb.)—*oak; an oak.*

An Israelite, descended from Simeon (I Chron. 4:37). The "oak" of Joshua 19:33 is called Allon in the Authorized Version.

Meta. A realization of protection and strength (*oak*).

Allon–bacuth, ăl′-lŏn–băc′-ŭth (Heb.)
—*oak of weeping.*

The oak tree under which Rebekah's nurse, Deborah, was buried (Gen. 35:8).

Meta. Weeping is an expression of emotion, a negative condition, a letting go throughout the organism. Rebekah's nurse, Deborah (*a bee*), represents a very active, serving, sustaining soul quality. Her death and burial symbolize a ceasing of the activity of this soul quality in serving and sustaining the outer expression of beauty (Rebekah), and a sinking back into the secret place of the Most High deep within the center of one's being. She was buried below Bethel (*house of God,* near the heart center in man), under the oak (the protection of Spirit).

Allon–bacuth (*oak of weeping*) therefore signifies an inner strengthening of the true man, which comes when, in trying to serve, one lets go of outer, personal activities and goes within to the source of all strength and true energy, and rests there in God. When one does this, though the outer man may mourn at first, since one seems to have lost one's personal, mortal hold on strength, yet God works in and through one to will and to do His good pleasure, and one's every thought and act counts for real spiritual good to the whole man.

Almodad, ăl-mō′-dăd (Heb.)—*incommensurate; immeasurable; measure of God; agitated; the agitator.*

Son of Joktan, who was descended from Shem, son of Noah (Gen. 10:26).

Meta. A certain discernment of the boundless possibilities that are open to man if he makes practical application of Truth (*immeasurable, measure of God*). This understanding, however, proves to be a disturbing element (*agitated*) in the consciousness because it is not definite enough or held strongly enough to bring about the real change of mind that is necessary to establish peace and order and to bring forth spiritual fruit. (Almodad was the ancestor of an Arabian tribe, and Arabians represent unsettled, wandering, unproductive thoughts in man.)

Almon, ăl′-mŏn (Heb.)—*hiding place; hidden.*

A city of refuge in the allotment of Benjamin (Josh. 21:18); it is the same city as Allemeth (I Chron. 6:60).

Meta. See ALLEMETH.

Almon–diblathaim, ăl′-mŏn–dĭb-lă-thā′-ĭm (Heb.)—*hiding of two fig cakes; hiding of troubles.*

The last camping place of the Israelites in the wilderness before they reached the mountains of Abarim, from whose heights Moses was shown the Promised Land (Num. 33:46, 47).

Meta. Figs, or fig trees, are a symbol of prosperity. Figs are also representative of the seed of man. This seed in its original essence is mind energy, and when ideas are related purely to Divine Mind the seed of man is the life stream in its original purity. Man's original sin is the misappropriation of ideas, which leads to sensation. Almon–diblathaim represents spiritual life and substance, which increase steadily in man from the time that he leaves the darkness of sense (Egypt) and begins his journey toward spiritual consciousness and redemption of the body (the Promised Land). Man does not realize the richness of the Christ possibilities that are unfolding within him, however, until he begins uplifting and spiritualizing his entire being (symbolized by the Israelites' taking possession of Canaan). Until then the inner riches are concealed from him (*hiding of two fig cakes*). If the inner substance and the life that are all the time increasing in consciousness are misappropriated by the individual in fulfillment of carnal desire, inharmonies result (*hiding of troubles*).

Alpha, ăl′-phȧ (Gk.).

a The first letter of the Greek alphabet. **b** A title applied to Christ (Rev. 1:8; 21:6; 22:13).

Meta. Christ, the word of God, or idea of Divine Mind, as the "beginning" or the "first-born" of all creation. "And he that sitteth on the throne said . . . I am the Alpha and the Omega, the beginning and the end."

Alphæus, ăl-phæ′-ŭs (Gk.)—*a successor; a supplanter; a leader; a chief.*

a Father of Matthew (Levi), who became a disciple of Jesus Christ (Mark 2:14). **b** Another Alphæus was the father of James the Less, a disciple of Jesus, and husband of Mary, a sister of Jesus' mother (Mark 3:18). The Clopas of John 19:25 is believed to be the same person. Compare this text with Luke 24:10 and Matthew 10:3.

Meta. The true spiritual man in us, the Father, in which the will (Matthew) and the faculty of order (James, the son of Alphæus) had their inception. Our outer man, with all his faculties and powers, his soul qualities and his possibilities, is the child, or product, of spiritual man—the Son, Jehovah God, or Christ who was made in the image and likeness of the great principle of Being —the Father-Mother Mind. So both of these men named Alphæus represent in a measure the Jehovah God, or Christ, in us who is our spiritual parent, and our *leader,* or *chief.* When we recognize this truth, by means of the will (Matthew) we give up our mortal ideas and consecrate ourselves with all our faculties to spiritual expression; then Spirit in us supplants and succeeds the sensual. We are in truth spiritual, and we function naturally only when we function spiritually. (See CLOPAS.)

altar, al'-tar (Lat.).

Meta. The place in consciousness where we are willing to give up the lower to the higher, the personal to the impersonal, the animal to the divine.

The golden altar for incense, the altar of the burnt offerings, and so forth (Ex. 40:5, 6) symbolize the establishing of permanent resolutions of purity and covenants of conformity with the higher law of obedience, though it cause daily sacrifice.

The brazen altar that was used in the Temple worship (I Kings 8:64) represents the generative life.

The altar that is mentioned in Revelation 11:1 symbolizes the consciousness of full consecration that takes place first in the temple of worship. "Present your bodies a living sacrifice, holy, acceptable to God, *which is* your spiritual service" (Rom. 12:1). "Them that worship therein" represent our true spiritual thoughts that love and worship God.

The altar of I Kings 18:30 represents

the solar plexus, or the centralization of all the nervous energy in body consciousness.

Alush, a'-lŭsh (Heb.)—*wild place; desolation; crowd.*

One of the camping places of the Israelites in the wilderness (Num. 33:13).

Meta. A worldly active, undisciplined phase of the mentality (wilderness, *wild place, crowd*) that has to be met and overcome by the children of Israel (true thoughts) before the Promised Land can be entered. If allowed to continue its ignorant activities, the state of mind that Alush represents will bring more and more *desolation* to the whole consciousness.

Alvah, ăl'-văh (Heb.)—*sublimation (of evil); sublimity; twisted; pervert; wicked; evil.*

A chief of Edom, descended from Esau (Gen. 36:40); in I Chronicles 1:51 he is called Aliah.

Meta. The animal nature in man exalting itself (*sublimation of evil*). This is evil in the sight of Truth, since true sublimity and exaltation come only by one's unifying the entire being with the spiritual or Christ consciousness.

Alvan, ăl'-văn (Heb.)—*sublime; tall.*

Son of Shobal, a descendant of Seir the Horite (Gen. 36:23); in I Chronicles 1: 40 he is called Alian.

Meta. A lofty concept, of man's seemingly material consciousness, concerning the apparently sensual or physical phase of his organism—a glimpse of the truth that even the outer man has his origin in Spirit. (See SHOBAL.)

Amad, a'-măd (Heb.)—*people of duration; enduring; a station.*

A border town in the allotment of Asher near Allammelech (Josh. 19:26).

Meta. An aggregation of thoughts of an established, enduring, sustaining character, founded in Truth principles (*a station, people of duration, enduring*).

Amal, a'-măl (Heb.)—*labor; laboring; toil.*

A descendant of Asher, in the land of Canaan (I Chron. 7:35). His father was Helem.

Meta. A belief that the exertion of one's strength (Helem, the father, signifies strength) is hard work and is accompanied by fatigue (*laboring, toil*). This belief really belongs to the old carnal thoughts, but if we are not watchful it finds its way into what we intend to make "spiritual service." All one's use of strength and faculties should be joyful, to increase one's powers and to give loving service.

Amalek, ăm'-ă-lĕk (Heb.)—*warlike; dweller in the vale; valley dweller; that licks up.*

Son of Eliphaz by his concubine, Timna, and grandson of Esau (Gen. 36: 12).

Meta. Esau represents the body consciousness. From him the Amalekites were descended. Amalek (*warlike, dweller in the vale, that licks up,* or consumes) signifies lust, that base desire which, when established in the animal forces of the subconscious mind of man, is the begetter of destructive, rebellious, perverted appetites and passions. Amalek's father was Eliphaz, meaning *God is strength, God is fine gold.* Thus desire at its origin is good and is of God; but when it is misinterpreted by the carnal man it becomes lust (Amalek).

Amalekites, ăm'-ă-lĕk-ītes (Heb.)—*belonging to Amalek.*

Descendants of Amalek, grandson of Esau (Gen. 14:7; I Sam. 15:6-8; 30: 1-18). They are usually called "Amalek."

Meta. The base desires of the individual. To those in spiritual understanding it is clear that the vale (*valley dweller*) represents that great realm of mind called the subconscious. The Amalekites symbolize the animal forces, appetites, and passions. They are *warlike,* and are destructive in their nature. They must be cleansed completely out of consciousness by denial (see I Sam. 15).

Disobedience has many forms; the most stubborn is that which absolutely refuses to obey. It stands up for its rights. It tells us that certain things are good for us, that the race has always indulged in them, and that such indulgence is necessary. Such ideas as these are the Amalekites down in the vale. They have become fixed in consciousness and refuse to abdicate. They are

not receptive to the illumination of Spirit; they crave self-gratification and are determined to have it. They must be taken up in prayer and denied place in consciousness. If we do not destroy these errors that God commands us to destroy, sooner or later they will obtain command to such an extent that they will endeavor to destroy us. Obedience to the Lord (divine law) insures peace and joy and leads into the paths of pleasantness and abundant prosperity.

Amam, ā'-măm (Heb.)—*gathering place.*

A city of Judah in the land of Canaan (Josh. 15:26); it was in the extreme south, toward the border of Edom.

Meta. A fixed state of thought in the subconscious mind, and very close to the body consciousness. (Edom refers to the body, or flesh. The south always means below; it usually pertains to the subconsciousness.) It is an assembling place (*gathering place*) in which a certain phase of subconscious thought force prepares to work out in the body. (Amam is spoken of in connection with Shema —*hearing, rumor,* and Moladah—*birth, generation.*) As this thought center is given over to praise and prayer (the city came into the possession of Judah) it is raised to higher and more spiritual expression. Then, instead of working out the results of error in the body, it causes life, health, and good to manifest.

Amana, ăm'-ă-nå (Heb.)—*constant; permanent; integrity; a seal of verity; a covenant.*

A high mount, or summit, of the Antilibanus range (Song of Sol. 4:8).

Meta. A high place in consciousness where we enter into the realization of a deeper union with our indwelling Christ —our bridegroom—than we have known before. We get a clearer understanding of His promises (*covenant,*) and the Christ becomes to us such a source of constancy and integrity (*constant, permanent, integrity, a seal of verity*) that we experience the joy and the rapture that are symbolized in the 4th chapter of the Song of Solomon.

Amariah, ăm-ă-rī'-ăh (Heb.)—*Jah says; word of Jehovah; Jehovah en-*

lightens.

A descendant of Aaron, by his eldest son, Eleazar. He lived during the time that Eli and his sons were in possession of the priesthood, before it reverted to the rightful line of high priests—the descendants of Aaron through his eldest son (I Chron. 6:7, 52). There are others by this name also.

Meta. An inner assurance of sonship, of oneness with God and dependence upon His word (*Jah says, word of Jehovah*), which stays with one when one seems incapable of outer spiritual expression for the time being; it is the light and assurance of the inner Word with its creative power to bring forth fruit in due season.

Amasa, ăm'-ă-sȧ (Heb.)—*burden; burden-bearer; sparing the people.*

A nephew of David's, and a cousin to Joab, the commander of David's army. Absalom made Amasa the head of his troops when he rebelled against his father, David. David afterward gave Amasa command of his army in place of Joab, but Amasa was slow in carrying out David's orders, and so Abishai and Joab had to take the lead. He was slain by Joab (II Sam. 17:25; 19:13; 20:9-12).

Meta. A negativeness or uncertainty of the will (the executive power of the mind) that arises when one's love (David) is divided between the outer and the inner, when one is of a double mind and desires to please and to save the thoughts (people) of the physical-sense man and yet wishes to serve the true king—to be loyal to Truth. This places a heavy *burden* upon one, and such a state of mind must be destroyed by Joab (the positive power of the will) before one's love (David) may again become fully centered in Spirit.

Amasai, ăm'-ă-sāi (Heb.)—*burden-bearer; burdensome.*

The name of several men who were of the Levites, or priesthood (I Chron. 6:25; 12:18; 15:24; II Chron. 29:12).

Meta. The thought of great responsibility or burden (*burdensome, burden-bearer*) that comes to one who feels very strongly the necessity for following set rules in keeping the letter of the law. Priests and Levites represent our "natural religious tendencies." They typify religious thoughts, but not necessarily spiritual thoughts. When they are of the intellect rather than of Spirit, they become the basis of a formal religion wherein rites and ceremonies take the place of true spirituality. Thus they make one's religious experience a burden instead of a blessing. The Truth makes one free.

Amashsai (A. V., Amashai), ă-măsh'-să-ī (Heb.)—*carrying a load; burdensome.*

A priest of Nehemiah's time, who returned to Jerusalem from the Babylonian captivity (Neh. 11:13).

Meta. A religious tendency in man that, because of its multiplicity of thoughts not established in divine wisdom, leads to confusion (Babylon). (Amashsai was of the family of Immer, the name Immer meaning *talkative.*) "And the burden of Jehovah shall ye mention no more: for every man's own word shall be his burden" (Jer. 23:36). The "word" here relates to thought. Man's thoughts build his burdens, his responsibilities, his cares. (The meaning of Amashsai is *carrying a load; burdensome.*) Yet this religious tendency, which Amashsai symbolizes in us, has laid hold of something of the true word, by the power of which it has been set free to return to the spiritual center in consciousness (Jerusalem), bringing with it the good that it has gained (*carrying spoil* is suggested by one authority as a meaning of Amashsai) in the experience through which it has passed.

"I rejoice at thy word,
    As one that findeth great spoil"
(Psalms 119:162).

Amasiah, ăm-ă-sī'-ăh (Heb.)—*Jehovah bears; Jah has strength (to bear); whom Jehovah bears.*

Son of Zichri, "who willingly offered himself unto Jehovah" (II Chron. 17:16). He was captain over "two hundred thousand mighty men of valor" during Jehoshaphat's reign.

Meta. Sustaining strength, through the inner Christ (*whom Jehovah bears,*

Jah has strength to bear). Amasiah was of the tribe of Judah. By means of praise (Judah) our strength is increased and all our inner faculties and powers are greatly increased in consciousness.

Amaziah, ăm-ă-zī'-ăh (Heb.)—*Jehovah makes mighty; the Lord protects; strength of Jehovah.*

a A king of Judah. He began his reign well, but after he had, by obedience to spiritual guidance, gained a victory over Edom, or Seir (the outer flesh consciousness), he set up the gods of Seir in his own land and worshiped them. Then the hand of the Lord, which had been with him, was turned against him. The remainder of his reign was troublesome, and finally he was killed by his subjects (II Kings 12:21; 14:1-20; II Chron. 25). **b** A priest of Bethel in the time of Jeroboam, king of Israel (Amos 7:10).

Meta. The overcoming strength that inheres in the will when it is established in Jehovah (Christ), when man's trust is in the Lord (*strength of Jehovah*). When the will admits into consciousness the error belief that strength and power are physical instead of spiritual, and begins to trust in the flesh instead of trusting in God, its strength begins to weaken and soon its reign comes to an end. The kingdom of Judah represents the inner life forces of man's organism, and its king, the will, should not utilize the inner vitality in outer sense ways. When it utilizes this inner vitality wrongly, it is setting up the gods of Seir and worshiping them.

Amittai, ă-mĭt'-tāi (Heb.)—*truthful; true.*

Father of Jonah (II Kings 14:25; Jonah 1:1).

Meta. The tendency in us to adhere very closely to that which we believe to be true (*truthful, true*). This tendency is good, but if it is of the intellect alone, rather than of the spiritual consciousness, we are likely to become narrow and condemnatory in our dealings with ourselves and with others. Amittai signifies in us that intellectual adherence to truthfulness which lacks the love and the mercy that cover a multitude of shortcomings. The Amittai thought demands

an eye for an eye and a tooth for a tooth. This attitude causes an inner condemnation and a fearfulness that are destructive (Jonah) because as yet no man has attained that perfect state wherein he needs no longer to be dealt with forgivingly and mercifully. All hard judgment, even though it may be truthfully given so far as the outer man is concerned, comes back to one in the same measure in which it has been sent out.

Ammah, ăm'-măh (Heb.)—*a (natural measure) cubit; a (natural) maternal nation; a metropolis; a people.*

A hill "that lieth before Giah by the way of the wilderness of Gibeon" (II Sam. 2:24).

Meta. A place of agreement, in consciousness, between the executive power of love (Joab, David's commander) and the conclusions of the somewhat spiritually enlightened intellect (Abner, captain of Saul's host). This agreement is based upon the innate knowing that all intelligence, whether of the heart or of the head, has a common source, Divine Mind (*maternal nation, a metropolis; a hill in Israel*).

(Abner, captain of Saul's host, represents the intellect, spiritually quickened in some degree. Joab, David's commander, is the inner pivotal center that preserves the unity and integrity of soul and body, the individual will. Abishai stands for the inherited law of destruction to all the enemies of the natural man. Saul had been defeated and killed, and Abner was fleeing from Joab and Abishai. They met at the hill of Ammah. There Abner convinced Joab that he and Abishai and their men should not follow him further with intent to kill. The intellect must not be destroyed, even though it is functioning in unison with the ignorant, personal will—Saul. It must be raised to a higher plane of action and must learn to reason entirely from a spiritual instead of a material standpoint.)

Ammi, ăm'-mī (Heb.)—*my people; my flock; my troop; my servants.*

A symbolical name given to the redeemed people of Israel (Hos. 2:1).

Meta. The acknowledgment by Jehovah, the Christ or true self in us, that our Israel thoughts have become obedient to the true ideas of the mind of Spirit (*my people*). Formerly, they had given themselves over to belief in a formal religion, to belief in materiality.

Ammiel, ăm'-mĭ-ĕl (Heb.)—*people of God; servants of God; my kinsman is God; my people is strong.*

The name of four Israelitish men; one of them was of the tribe of Dan, and was one of the twelve who were sent to spy out the land of Canaan (Num. 13:12; II Sam. 9:4; I Chron. 3:5; 26:5).

Meta. Spiritual thoughts in consciousness (*people of God*). These thoughts are related closely to the divine (*my kinsman is God*), and potentially they are strong (*my people is strong*). But not all the men named Ammiel recognized the unfailingness of spiritual strength; some of them attributed strength to error (see Num. 13:31-33). Our spiritual thoughts, also, are not always conscious of their overcoming power; or perhaps it would be more correct to say that we are not always conscious of the overcoming power of our spiritual thoughts.

Ammihud, ăm-mĭ'-hŭd (Heb.)—*people of excellence; my kinsman is majesty; people of glory; people of praise; my people is honorable.*

The name of four different men; all were Israelites except one (Num. 1:10; 34:20; I Chron. 9:4). The name is spelled Ammihur in II Samuel 13:37.

Meta. Ideas pertaining to the honor, authority, high moral integrity, and worth of true spiritual thoughts in consciousness; also the high esteem in which such thoughts should be held by the individual (*people of excellence, people of glory, people of praise, my kinsman is majesty, my people is honorable*).

Amminadab, ăm-mĭn'-ă-dăb (Heb.)—*people of liberality; people of willing generosity; my people is abundance.*

The name of several Israelitish men (Exod. 6:23; Num. 1:7; I Chron. 6:22; 15:10; Matt. 1:4).

Meta. The broad-mindedness and generosity of true spiritual thoughts in man (*people of liberality, people of willing generosity, my people is abundance*).

Although the Israelites of old may not have lived up to what their names imply, yet the names show the possibilities that lie in the mind of God for man. "Ye therefore shall be perfect, as your heavenly Father is perfect."

Ammishaddai, ăm-mĭ-shăd'-dāi (Heb.) —*people of the Almighty; people of Providence; my kinsman is the Almighty.*

Father of Ahiezer. Jehovah chose Ahiezer, through Moses, to be leader of the tribe of Dan at the time of the numbering of the Israelites in the wilderness (Num. 1:12).

Meta. The efficiency and the power of which man becomes conscious when he recognizes his unity with omnipotent God (*people of the Almighty, my kinsman is the Almighty*); also the assurance of divine oversight and supply (*people of Providence*).

Ammizabad, ăm-mĭz'-ă-băd (Heb.)—*people of endowment; people of the giving; my people is endowed; kindred of the giver.*

Son of Benaiah, who was a mighty man during David's reign (I Chron. 27:6).

Meta. The idea of God as the source of all, and man as the receiver and expresser of the faculties and powers of Being (*people of endowment, my people is endowed, kindred of the giver*).

Ammon, ăm'-mŏn (Heb.)—*a great people; an extensive people; a fellow countryman.*

From Ben–ammi, son of the younger daughter of Lot (Gen. 19:38). The Ammonites were descended from him.

Meta. The central dominating thought of that which the Ammonites symbolize in consciousness—the belief in carnality; also the extensiveness of this line of thought in mortal man. (See AMMONITES.)

Ammonites, ăm'-mŏn-ītes.

Descendants of Ben–ammi, son of Lot, and enemies of the Israelites (Deut. 23:3; I Sam. 11:11; I Kings 11:5).

Meta. Popular opinion; also the wild, uncultivated states of consciousness that thoughts of sensuality, sin, and ignorance have formed in the outer world. Careless, disorderly thinking weakens the positive, upbuilding power of the mind and opens the way for invasions of error thoughts. Thoughts of similar character congregate and form states of consciousness, just as people who think along similar lines congregate and form organizations. When the central thought is of the power of good, a constructive center in consciousness is formed; when the prevailing thought is evil, a destructive center is formed. There is a constant push and pull between these two states of consciousness, each one striving for supremacy, and the result is weakness in mind and body.

In II Chron. 26:8 the Ammonites refer to the generative region. "The Ammonites gave tribute to Uzziah." Uzziah symbolizes strength. (See UZZIAH.) The strength center in the body, which is at the small of the back, is connected directly with the physical forces, and when this center is dominant it draws upon all the region below the diaphragm.

Amnon, ăm'-nŏn (Heb.)—*faithful; upbringing; tutelage.*

David's eldest son, who was killed by his half-brother, Absalom, because of his conduct toward Absalom's sister, Tamar (II Sam. 3:2; 13:1-39).

Meta. A mental quality in man, under discipline or in process of education. When completed this training will bring about faithfulness (*upbringing, tutelage, faithful*). From the Bible history of Amnon, the faithful attitude of thought and action was yet to be attained by him.

Amon, ā'-mŏn (Heb.)—*master workman; workman; builder.*

This word in its primitive purity referred to the universal Mother, and designated the basic wisdom of God, the architect of the universe. Pliny renders this word as *"artifex omnium natura,"* the universal artificer, creator, of nature. From these developed the ideas of master craftsman, an architect, a builder, a mason. The Egyptians knew and understood this truth, but their priestcraft allowed it to degenerate into idolatry and nature worship. Amon of No, the Egyptian god, signifies the unmanifest, the uncreated, the mysterious.

a An Egyptian god (Jer. 46:25). **b** An idolatrous king of Judah (II Kings 21:18-26). **c** A governor of the city of Samaria at the time that Ahab was king of Israel (I Kings 22:26). **d** There were others by this name.

Meta. Egypt is the realm of substance and life in body consciousness. To the unregenerate soul it is the land of mystery and darkness, yet it is essential to the continuation of the body. When the individual looks upon his body as material and believes that the substance and the life that sustain it are material, a fleshly inheritance, instead of recognizing their true source in Spirit, that individual is worshiping the Egyptian god Amon.

When the will (king) is guided by material belief concerning the body, the will does not become a true builder of the body temple in spiritual substance and life, but decides according to the outer letter, or shadow of the real, a decision that leads to death. The will is a *master builder* when established in Truth, but not otherwise.

Amon, governor of Samaria, signifies a ruling thought of the intellect. This ruling intellectual thought is also a *workman* necessary to body building. But in order to do its proper work in building a perfect body, the intellect must be set free from confused mortal reasonings: The Samaritans must come into an understanding of the Christ Truth—the intellect must be illumined by Spirit, that it may base its reasonings on the real instead of the unreal.

Amorites, ăm'-ôr-ītes (Heb.)—*dwellers of the summits; mountaineers; highlanders.*

One of the strongest and most eminent of the Canaanitish tribes, or nations (Gen. 14:7; Deut. 3:2; Josh. 10:6-12). The Amorites were descended from a son of Canaan, grandson of Noah (Gen. 10:16).

Meta. A race inheritance; the Amorites' seat of action is the generative function. They can be overcome only by purification of the consciousness within and without—that is, in thought and deed—with the "flaming torch" of Spirit. (See

Gen. 15:16-21.) Generation is very strongly rooted in man's consciousness, and has been elevated by man in personal thought to the very heights (*highlanders, mountaineers, dwellers of the summits*). But it must be put away, that one may be regenerated in mind and body.

Amos, ā'-mŏs (Heb.)—*burden; load; borne up; sustained; carried.*

The writer of the book of Amos. He was a shepherd (Amos 1:1; 7:10-14).

Meta. Conscience, which shepherds the natural forces of mind and body. (Sheep represent thoughts that are obedient to the natural law; they also represent the pure natural life of the body.) Amos in us warns us when we have transgressed the divine law.

Amoz, ā'-mŏz (Heb.)—*vigorous; strong; courageous; quick.*

Father of Isaiah the prophet (Isa. 1:1).

Meta. A firm, active trust in God, which is an encouragement and protection to the individual and is the forerunner of salvation (*strong, vigorous,* father of Isaiah—*salvation of Jehovah,* or *God saves*).

Amphipolis, ăm-phĭp'-ŏ-lĭs (Gk.)—*around the city; about the city; surrounded city.*

A Macedonian city through which Paul and Silas passed while Paul was on one of his missionary journeys (Acts 17:1).

Meta. Truth passes through several stages in entering the mind: doubt, then examination, then great desire for the Truth, then acceptance. These are represented by the Gentile cities, Amphipolis, Apollonia, and Thessalonica, through which Paul passed, and Berœa, where "he received the word with all readiness of mind."

Ampliatus (A. V., Amplias), ăm'-plĭ-ă-tŭs (Lat.)—*large; full; ample.*

A Christian friend of Paul's at Rome (Rom. 16:8).

Meta. A very great capacity to comprehend Truth (*large, full, ample*).

Amram, ăm'-răm (Heb.)—*kindred of the lofty One, i. e., of God; exalted people; high people.*

a Father of Moses and of Aaron (Exod. 6:20). **b** A son of Bani (Ezra 10:34).

Meta. A very high conception of oneness with God and of the true thoughts of man's consciousness as being emanations from the ideas of the one Mind (*kindred of the lofty One,* i. e., *of God, exalted people*).

Amramites, ăm'-răm-ītes (Heb.)—*belonging to Amram.*

Descendants of Amram, of the Kohathite Levites (Num. 3:27).

Meta. Thoughts springing from and of character like that in consciousness which Amram signifies. See AMRAM.

Amraphel, ăm'-rä-phĕl (Heb.)—*keeper of the gods; keeper of the treasures; or, speaker of mysteries; enlightener of secrets.*

A heathen king of Shinar, in Abraham's time (Gen. 14:1, 9).

Meta. The belief of unawakened man that in generation, physical reproduction, he is fulfilling the creative law of Being. The truth is that the command to be fruitful and multiply and to replenish the earth and subdue it includes the bringing forth and expressing of the ideas of the one Mind. The Word is the creative power of God, and it will transform men into spiritual beings. By the Word every man can build for himself a spiritual body, incorruptible and immortal.

Amzi, ăm'-zī (Heb.)—*strong.*

Son of Bani (I Chron. 6:46).

Meta. Strength.

Anab, ā'-năb (Heb.)—*cluster of grapes; grape town.*

A city in the hill country of Judah (Josh. 15:50). It was formerly a city of the Anakim, who were overcome by Joshua (Josh. 11:21).

Meta. A state of thought that magnifies the life idea in man, thus increasing his consciousness of life and making union with the one Source of all life. *Grapes* suggest wine, and wine symbolizes life; Judah (*praise*) gives the thought of increase of life. A *cluster* of grapes bespeaks a conjunction, a grouping, or joining of that which grapes suggest. Anab was a city in the hill country of Judah, and hills represent high, exalted states of mind.

Anah, ā'-näh (Heb.)—*answering*.

a A chief or prince of the Horites, son of Seir (Gen. 36:20, 29). **b** The son of Zibeon the Hivite, and parent of Esau's wife, Oholibamah (Gen. 36:2, 14, 18, 25). Authorities agree that this latter Anah was a son of Zibeon, not a daughter.

Meta. Error tendencies, or strongly influencing thoughts, deep within the subjective life forces in individual consciousness, which cause these life forces to respond to the desires of the flesh or sense man (*answering*) instead of listening to Spirit. (The Hivites and the Horites were descendants of Canaan, son of Ham; they were hostile to the Israelites in the Promised Land, and they had to be destroyed.)

Anaharath, ăn-ă-hā'-răth (Heb.)—*a way of groaning; a narrow way; a gorge*.

A border city in the allotment of Issachar (Josh. 19:19).

Meta. A fixed place in consciousness where man feels instinctively and knows that trustworthiness, uprightness, and honesty are the passageway that leads to real success in all the affairs of life (a city in the allotment of Issachar, Issachar referring to substance of earth, supply, prosperity). This way may seem narrow, winding, troublous (*a way of groaning*), and even dangerous and rocky (*a gorge*) at times to the sense man, yet it is the only way that leads safely through "mountains of difficulties" to true peace and supply.

Anaiah, ă-nā'-įăh (Heb.)—*Jah answers; Jah has answered; whom Jehovah answers*.

a A priest who stood at the right hand of Ezra the scribe when Ezra read the book of the law to the people of Israel (Neh. 8:4). **b** One who joined Nehemiah in sealing the covenant (Neh. 10:22).

Meta. A positive assurance in the consciousness of awakened man that God hears and answers when man seeks to understand and obey the divine law (*Jah answers, Jah has answered*).

Anak, ā'-năk (Heb.)—*long-necked; giant; collar*.

Son of Arba, a giant (Josh. 21:11).

Meta. The home of Anak and his three sons was in Hebron (the front brain or seat of conscious thought). Anak symbolizes the belief that the intellect functioning in material thought is the seat of power and the source of Truth. This belief is very strongly intrenched (*giant*) in the mind of him who is unawakened spiritually, and it causes him to be very bold and brazen (*long-necked*) in exalting his personality; he thinks that the meekness and humility of spiritual Truth are foolish and weak. In the end, however, Truth always triumphs over error. Adherence to the true God overcomes all seemingly intellectual giants in our Promised Land. (See AHIMAN.)

Anakim (A. V., Anakims), ăn'-ă-kĭm (Heb.)—*the long-necked; giants*.

Descendants of Arba, through Anak (Deut. 9:2). They were a race of giants, in southern Canaan (Josh. 11:21).

Meta. The intellectual thoughts and states of consciousness in man that believe that the outer, formed world, with its customs and teachings, is real and is the source of man's strength, power, and good, instead of seeing that the outer manifestation is but an expression of man's inner thought and word and of itself has no sustaining power. (See ANAK.)

Anamim, ăn'-ă-mĭm (Heb.)—*statues; rockmen; fountains*.

Son of Mizraim, son of Ham (Gen. 10:13); his descendants are supposed to have inhabited a portion of Egypt. The name Mizraim in the Bible is in meaning identical with Egypt.

Meta. Hard, material thoughts (*rockmen*) about life (*fountains*). Material thoughts about life aid in building corruptible bodies, mere *statues* in so far as being truly alive through union with the Source of all life is concerned.

Anammelech, ă-năm'-mě-lěch (Heb.)—*king's statue; king's rock; kingly image*.

The companion god of Adrammelech in the heathen worship of the Sepharites, and introduced into Samaria by them (II Kings 17:31).

Meta. See ADRAMMELECH.

Anan, ă´-năn (Heb.)—*a covering; a cloud; beclouded.*

A chief man of the Israelites, who signed the covenant with Nehemiah (Neh. 10:26).

Meta. A high spiritual thought of consecration to God. This thought aids the true consciousness (Israel) to make an agreement with God to serve Him and be loyal to Him. Yet the thought that Anan signifies is obscured, or clouded (*cloud, beclouded*) to some extent by a belief in sin and evil as a power that holds man in servitude and bondage. (The Israelites still were servants to Gentile kings and princes, even though they were dwelling again in their own land; they were bowed down and grieved because of their former sins that had brought all their troubles upon them. See Neh. 9:32-38.)

Ananiah, ăn-ă-nī´-ăh (Heb.)—*covered by Jehovah; protected by Jehovah.*

a Grandfather of Azariah, who helped Nehemiah to rebuild the wall of Jerusalem (Neh. 3:23). **b** The name of a Benjamite town in the land of Canaan (Neh. 11:32).

Meta. A thought of divine protection, of the inner Christ or Father as one's refuge and defense (*covered by Jehovah, protected by Jehovah*).

The Benjamite town of Ananiah symbolizes an aggregation of thoughts in consciousness, thoughts of faith in Jehovah, I AM, or Christ as one's protection and shield.

Ananias, ăn-ă-nī´-ăs (Gk. fr. Heb.)—*graciousness of Jah; mercy of Jehovah; compassion of Jehovah.*

a A man of the early Christians who, with his wife Sapphira, tried to deceive the apostles by keeping back part of the price of the property that they had sold, while professing to be giving it all. According to the Bible text, they met instant death because of their deception (Acts 5:1-5). **b** Another Ananias was a godly man who was sent to Paul to restore his sight after his conversion (Acts 9:10; 22:12). **c** Still another Ananias was a high priest of the Jews and was opposed to the followers of Je-

sus Christ (Acts 23:2).

Meta. There is a lurking belief in the mind that we can join the great school of spiritual development and at the same time retain our hold upon worldly thoughts. This belief represents Ananias of Acts 5:1-5, deception. Such deception of the mind is a very subtle error and causes the would-be disciple much misery. The best way to handle it is to uncover the whole inner consciousness to Spirit and to ask to be thoroughly purified and cleansed.

This liar and deceiver has two sides in the mind. Outwardly, or in conscious thought, it is Ananias; in the subconscious thought it appears as Sapphira. Both of these must die before the spiritual thoughts (church) will increase in numbers and in power. The best and quickest way to dissolve these errors is to face them boldly and accuse them of holding back part of the price of salvation.

Some persons, when the redemptive process begins, are so wrapped up in material possessions that they do not give up wholly to Spirit; they retain a part of the price. Man must be cleansed thoroughly before he can come into the full light. Once he truly discerns Spirit, material thoughts give way; when the false is destroyed the good is more and more manifest. This is true of every man's spiritual development. If you give yourself wholly to God He will destroy all the devils that have become part of you. You must give spirit, soul, and body to God. God is everywhere. You can hide nothing from this universal eye (I).

The Ananias of Acts 9:10 represents a different attitude of thought from that represented by the foregoing Ananias. Those who look to the Holy Spirit for guidance find that its instruction is given to all who believe in Christ, and they are drawn together often by the direction of the inner voice, or by a dream, or by a vision. Paul needed help to restore his sight. The brightness, or high potency, of Jesus' glorified presence had confused his intellectual consciousness, and this brought about blindness. He needed the harmonious, peace-giving power of one who understood the inner life, and this power was found in Ananias, a disciple living at Damascus. Ananias was receptive and obedient; doubtless he had received this sort of guidance many times. From the text we readily discern his spiritual harmony. He knew the reputation of Paul and protested against meeting him, but the Lord explained the situation and assured him that it would be right for him to go, and so it turned out to be.

The high priest Ananias symbolizes a still different phase of character in man. He represents the hypocrisy that inheres in the intellectual, religious, ruling mind in man when it is governed by the letter of the word, outer forms, and ceremonies, instead of being given over to real spiritual Truth.

Anath, ā'-năth (Heb.)—*shouting; answering; oppressed; afflicted; humbled.*

Father of Shamgar, who was a judge of Israel (Judg. 3:31).

Meta. The Spirit's response to the cry of the soul for deliverance from opposing thoughts. The *answer,* in the case mentioned in Judges 3:31, came through the son of Anath, Shamgar, "who smote of the Philistines six hundred men" and saved Israel. (The Philistines are typical of lawless, rebellious thoughts.)

Anathoth, ăn'-ă-thŏth (Heb.)—*shoutings; answers; answers, i. e., to prayer; chants; afflictions; poverty.*

A city in the allotment of Benjamin that was given over to the Levites (Josh. 21:18; I Kings 2:26; Jer. 1:1).

Meta. In Isaiah 10:30 we read, "O thou poor Anathoth!" This comment was inspired by the Lord's having sent the Assyrians (reasonings and thoughts of the sense mind plane that do not recognize Spirit) against Anathoth and other places in Israel because of their sins.

Solomon told Abiathar the priest, "Get thee to Anathoth, unto thine own fields; for thou art worthy of death." Thus Abiathar was taken away from the high-priesthood and was sent to his own place. Abiathar represents a ruling religious belief that great and abundant good comes from the recognition of God as Father and love (David) as king. (See ABIATHAR.) But he was of the intellectual consciousness and was not founded consciously in the realm of spiritual thought, whence the true priests come. Therefore he did not hold fast to Truth, but took sides against Solomon (the consciousness of wisdom and peace); and so he was sent to Anathoth, to his own fields. In other words, he fell from the abundance of rich thought to a belief in trouble and lack (*poverty, afflictions*).

Anathoth represents the negative side of *answers to prayer*: the working of the law to fulfill thoughts of lack and of error rather than positive thoughts of good. The law works both ways for us, according to the trend of our thinking. Our negative prayers (thoughts and acts that tend to limitation and inharmony) are answered, as well as our positive prayers (thoughts and words of wholeness and plenty).

Andrew, ăn'-drew (Gk.)—*strong; a strong man; manly.*

A disciple of Jesus Christ, and brother of Simon Peter (Matt. 10:2).

Meta. The strength of the mind (*a strong man, manly*) that is rejoiced greatly when it finds the inexhaustible Source of all strength, and exclaims, "We have found the Messiah" (John 1:41). Andrew symbolizes the strength, while Simon Peter symbolizes the faith capacity, of the mind. When strength finds faith, and they are brothers consciously in the mind, a bond of unity is established that carries one along, even though one may encounter the most adverse experiences.

Andronicus, ăn-drŏ-nī'-cŭs (Gk.)— *man of victory; conquering man; a conqueror.*

A kinsman of Paul's, and a fellow prisoner (Rom. 16:7).

Meta. Paul's statement that Andronicus was "of note among the apostles," and was "in Christ before me," means that man was ideally perfect in the Christ mind from the beginning, before he ever exercised his free will in a perverse way; also that he is inherently perfect before his will is finally converted to Truth

(Paul signifying here the converted will). Andronicus stands for knowledge of this Truth, a knowledge that makes us "more than conquerors" in all things pertaining to our overcoming error and our putting on Christ (*man of victory*).

Anem, ā′-nĕm (Heb.)—*double fountain; two fountains; two springs.*

A Levitical city in the allotment of Issachar (I Chron. 6:73).

Meta. A springing up of life and substance for both the spiritual and the seemingly material phases of man's being (*double fountain*). Levites pertain to the mental and spiritual of man; Issachar (*bearing hire, reward, tribute*) refers more to the earthly, or body consciousness. His are "the hidden treasures of the sand," substance (Deut. 33:19; see Gen. 49:14, 15, also). A belief in separation is suggested (*two fountains, two springs*) as though the body received its sustenance from an earthly or physical source while soul and spirit were nourished from a different one. The truth is that there is but one life and one substance for the whole man and for all creation; there is but one source of both the manifest and the unmanifest, of all being, and that source is spiritual. Even the apparently physical body of man must be nourished with words of Truth, since "man shall not live by bread alone, but by every word that proceedeth out of the mouth of God."

Aner, ā′-nĕr (Heb.)—*a boy; adolescent youth; a young sprout; shaken off; an exile.*

a An Amorite, or Canaanite, "confederate with Abram" (Gen. 14:13). He helped Abram to overcome the heathen kings who had taken Lot and his household prisoners and had carried away their goods. **b** A Levitical city in the allotment of Manasseh (I Chron. 6:70).

Meta. A refreshing, renewing thought —new life springing into consciousness (*a boy, youth, a young sprout*; the Canaanites are the elemental life forces in the subconsciousness, and the Amorites are erroneous thoughts and desires that have their seat of action in the generative function). Under the old thought, sex desire in man and generation are always connected with the idea of renewal of life. Back of the belief in sex and generation are the life forces, which are a very necessary factor in man's constant renewal and upbuilding; and these life forces are friends to the higher concepts of the individual and to his faith in God (Abram). They yield substance and strength to the building up of the spiritual man, even while they are yet dominated to a certain extent by error ideas of sex—the Amorites—and they aid in putting away (*shaken off*) his seeming bondage to carnality. This situation is symbolized by Aner and his brothers (Amorites) in their kindly and helpful relations with Abram, especially in helping Abram to free Lot.

Aner, the Levitical city in the allotment of Manasseh, represents a certain consciousness of youth and renewal of life that is based on understanding (Manasseh) and love (Levi).

angel, ān′-ġĕl (Gk.)—*messenger; messengers of God.*

Meta. Thought of the Lord (Luke 1:11). Our angels are our spiritual perceptive faculties, which ever dwell in the presence of the Father (Matt. 13:49).

"Their angels do always behold the face of my Father who is in heaven" (Matt. 18:10). These angels of our childlike, spiritual thoughts, "these little ones," are the thoughts that understand spiritual principles. The office of the angels is to guard and guide and direct the natural forces of mind and body, which have in them the future of the whole man.

The "two angels in white sitting, one at the head, and one at the feet, where the body of Jesus had lain" are affirmation and denial. It is by the use of these messengers of the I AM that the body is taken out and away from the tomb of matter and flesh (John 20:12).

The angel mentioned in Exodus 3:2 symbolizes a *messenger;* it is the projection into consciousness of a spiritual idea direct from the fountainhead, Jehovah.

Aniam, ā′-nĭ-ăm (Heb.)—*sighing; groaning; mourning; lamentation of the people.*

Son of Shemida, a descendant of Manasseh (I Chron. 7:19).

Meta. Manasseh refers to the understanding faculty in man, but more to an intellectual and negative phase of it that is not yet spiritually enlightened. Shemida means *name of wisdom, fame of wisdom;* but the understanding that is of the outer mentality alone, and is negative in its nature, cannot give true joy and satisfaction. So this exaltation and pride of knowing (Shemida) that comes of intellectual wisdom brings forth Aniam—a *sighing* and *mourning* of the religious thoughts of the consciousness (people of Israel) for true, positive, spiritual understanding. Such understanding alone can take sorrow from our thought people and can satisfy the desire of the soul.

Anim, ā'-nĭm (Heb.)—*fountains; natural springs; (weeping) eyes.*

A city in the hill-country of Judah (Josh. 15:50).

Meta. New life, from the one unfailing Source of all life, springing into consciousness (*fountains*). Mountains symbolize high places in consciousness, exalted states of mind, and Judah symbolizes praise. By practicing praise and prayer we come into a realization of the truth of Jesus Christ's words, "The water that I shall give him shall become in him a well of water springing up unto eternal life."

Unless the individual has been quite fully awakened to spiritual understanding and thought, the outer man looks upon his renewal of vitality and strength as having a natural, or physical, cause (*natural springs*); thus he brings about a negative expression of life (*weeping eyes*).

Anna, ăn'-nȧ (Gk.)—*grace; gracious.*

Daughter of Phanuel, of the tribe of Asher, a prophetess in the Temple at the time of Jesus' birth (Luke 2:36).

Meta. A certain conservation of spiritual life, which has been built up by devotion and faithfulness. This spiritual life is transmitted through many incarnations and becomes an inheritance of the soul; it is of great importance in the formation of the Christ body. Nothing is lost in the evolution of the soul.

Annas, ăn'-năs (Gk. fr. Heb.)—*gra-ciousness; grace of Jah.*

Father-in-law of Caiaphas, who was high priest at the time of the ministry and the crucifixion of Jesus and during the persecution of the disciples a little later. He held a high position among the Jews, and was a leading factor in these persecutions (Luke 3:2; John 18: 13-24; Acts 4:6).

Meta. A very influential religious thought of the intellect, that is given over to rites and ceremonies—the outer letter of the word, or form of religion, without the inner spiritual Truth. The Bible history of Annas shows how a merely formal religion will persecute and attempt to kill the inner Christ Spirit and all that pertains to it. A purely intellectual understanding and practice of religion cannot comprehend the deep inspirations of the heart and the loving, forgiving informality and nonresistance of the inner Spirit of truth. Formal religion, apart from the real spirit, is that in man which, when he asks bread, will give him a stone. There is nothing in it truly to satisfy the soul.

anointed ones, (Lat.) — *greased; smeared* or *rubbed with oil.* The term has the same sense as the Greek Chrio, from which the word Christ is derived, and the Hebrew Mashah, from which the word Messiah is drawn.

Meta. The "two anointed ones" (sons of oil), "that stand by the Lord of the whole earth" (Zech. 4:14) are the avenues through which the oil of the Spirit of life is brought into the body consciousness. In Revelation 11:3, 4 they are called "my two witnesses" and "the two olive trees." In Zechariah 4:6 we read, in answer to the question, "What are these, my lord?": "This is the word of Jehovah unto Zerubbabel, saying, Not by might, nor by power, but by my Spirit, saith Jehovah of hosts." Zerubbabel is one who restores the worship of God. And so these two anointed ones, or witnesses, keep declaring the word of God in faith and power, from the heart center (Jerusalem), to the uttermost parts of our body (the whole earth). Just below the heart we find the judgment center; the two witnesses have power to discern and to judge the thoughts and intents of the heart and to cause a drought to come upon the earth (carnal consciousness). They also have power to send plagues of different kinds, as well as fire, to purify the thoughts, and to destroy the thoughts that continue to oppose the Truth. (See WITNESSES.)

Anthothijah (A. V., Antothijah), ăn-thŏ-thī′-jăh (Heb.)—*answers of Jah; answers from Jehovah.*

Of the tribe of Benjamin (I Chron. 8:24). He was one of the men who "were heads of fathers' *houses* throughout their generations, chief men," and they "dwelt in Jerusalem" (I Chron. 8:28).

Meta. The truth that Jehovah, the Christ or Father in us, always responds (*answers of Jah*) to our faith when it is centered in the one true principle of Being, God the All-Good. The answers, or fulfillment of our faith, are ever present in Jerusalem, our own inner spiritual consciousness.

antichrist, ăn′-tĭ-chrīst (Gk.)—*against Christ; opposed to Christ; instead of Christ.*

That which does not confess that Jesus Christ is come in the flesh (I John 4:2, 3; II John 7; see also I John 2: 18-22).

Meta. That which denies or opposes the idea that the Christ dwells in and is the true self of each individual (*against Christ;* the meaning of *anti* is *opposite, against, contrary to*).

Those who make the indwelling Spirit of truth their guide and authority will not be deceived by false claims made either by individuals or by institutions. The way to safety is to trust the Spirit of truth continually for protection from false ideas. The "man of sin" is the carnal mind in each individual, and it always opposes and misrepresents the Truth; sometimes it poses as an angel of light and Truth. Every one who overcomes this inner adversary will be saved from all deception that may be practiced by anybody or anything that claims the place of the Lord Jesus Christ. The overthrow of the "man of sin" is promised; to obtain fulfillment of that promise we

have only to keep ourselves one with the Spirit of truth.

As an instance of the work of antichrist, we see in the world a very active effort to exalt death and to delude men into believing that death is the way to eternal life in heaven. Such a thought is opposed to Christ, because Jesus came to deliver the human race from death and to fulfill in man God's perfect will: abundant life. Those who are guided by the Spirit of truth understand the life teaching, and are not led astray by any philosophy that makes death and the grave necessary factors in spiritual growth.

Antioch, ăn′-tĭ-ŏch (Gk.)—*withstanding; lasting; speedy as a chariot.*

a The capital of Syria until Syria was overcome by the Romans and made a Roman province. **b** A city in Pisidia of Asia Minor (Acts 11:19; 13:1, 14).

Meta. Formulated theology. This state of mind must be Christianized thoroughly. Our ideas of God and of man's relation to God must undergo a great change before we can begin uplifting and unifying the whole man— spirit, soul, and body—in life. The apostles did much teaching and preaching in Antioch (Acts 11:26).

In Acts 14:8-20 the formulated theology that Antioch represents takes on a spirit of antagonism and opposition. (See LYSTRA for a further explanation of this text.)

Speedy as a chariot implies swiftness and a capacity for carrying.

Antipas, ăn′-tĭ-păs (Gk.)—*against one's native country; against all.*

A faithful follower of Jesus Christ; he was martyred at Pergamum (Rev. 2:13).

Meta. Faithfulness to Truth ideals, even to the point of becoming *against all* that does not measure up to these ideals. This resistant attitude of mind leads to martyrdom. Jesus said that we should "resist not him that is evil" (Matt. 5:39). We do not need to resist evil, since it has no power of itself. By our being fully assured of this truth, and then remaining positive in the good, all error will fall away from our life. We must keep Jesus' word if we would escape death. (See John 8:51.)

Anub, ā'-nūb (Heb.)—*strong* or *high; bound together; joined; confederated.*

Son of Hakkoz, a descendant of Judah (I Chron. 4:8).

Meta. A thought of unity, in consciousness (*bound together, joined, confederated*), a man of Judah.

Apelles, ă-pĕl'-lēṣ (Gk.)—*called; set apart.*

A Christian friend of Paul's at Rome, whom Paul wrote of as being "the approved in Christ" (Rom. 16:10).

Meta. That in man which follows the inner leading of Spirit onward and upward (*called, set apart*) to the exclusion of lesser, sense promptings and desires. This brings about a realization of the approval of the inner Christ: "The Father approves of what I do."

Apharsathchites, ă-phär'-săth-chītes (Heb.)—*the breakers-up; the renders.*

Nomads from Assyria who settled in Samaria (Ezra 4:9).

Meta. Wandering thoughts and reasonings of the sense plane of thought in man that have no settled or fixed place in his consciousness. They are of a tearing apart, disagreeing nature (*the breakers-up, the renders*).

Aphek, ā'-phĕk (Heb.)—*strong; holding firm; tenacious; fortress.*

The name of three or four fortified cities in Israel (Josh. 13:4; 19:30; I Kings 20:26; II Kings 13:17). They were places that belonged to the enemies of the Israelites, or where these enemies —the Assyrians, Philistines, and others —encamped against Israel in battle, time after time.

Meta. The apparent ability of error states of consciousness in man to stay with him. From a sense standpoint the thoughts and states of consciousness that comprise the carnal mind are very deep-seated and are strongly fortified. It is only by the positive power of the I AM or Christ dominion that they can be overcome.

Aphekah, ă-phē'-kăh (Heb.)—*the fortress; the strong city.*

A city of Judah (Josh. 15:53). It is thought to be the same place as the Aphek of Joshua 12:18.

Meta. See APHEK.

Aphiah, ă-phī'-ăh (Heb.)—*blowing; breathing; uttering; refreshing; revivifying; panting; striving.*

A Benjamite from whom Saul was descended (I Sam. 9:1).

Meta. The renewing, reanimating work of faith in consciousness (*blowing, breathing, refreshing, revivifying,* a Benjamite).

Aphik, ā'-phĭk (Heb.)—*a fortress; a strong place.*

A city in Canaan belonging to the Israelitish tribe of Asher, but from which the Asherites failed to drive the Canaanites (Judg. 1:31). Aphek is the same name.

Meta. See APHEK.

Apollonia, ăp-ŏl-lō'-nĭ-à (Gk.)—*city of Apollo; place of Apollo; destruction.*

According to Greek mythology, Apollo was the god of light who resided in the sun. He was the healer, the purifier, the bane of evil; since light and heat are not always beneficial, he was also the sender of pestilence and destruction. Sunlight without water will burn up crops and bring pestilence. The thought of "destruction" is taken from this latter phase of Apollo's nature.

A Macedonian city situated between Amphipolis and Thessalonica (Acts 17:1).

Meta. Examination or investigation into Truth. Truth passes through several stages in entering the mind: first doubt, then examination, then a great desire for the Truth, then acceptance. These are represented by the Gentile cities—Amphipolis, Apollonia, and Thessalonica—through which Paul passed, and Berœa where "they received the word with all readiness of mind." The critical, investigating state of mind represented by Apollonia is of a destructive nature (*destruction*) while under carnal thought; but it is willing to examine into Truth, and as it becomes more and more guided by wisdom and love it becomes a great help in the spiritual life of the individual.

Apollos, ă-pŏl'-lŏs (Gk.)—*belonging to Apollo; destroyer; the sun,* i. e., *as laying waste.* (See APOLLONIA. This name should not be confused with Apollyon. See ABADDON.)

A very learned man, a Jew of Alexandria (Acts 18:24-28); he first taught the John the Baptist doctrine, but later was instructed in "the way of God more accurately" by Priscilla and Aquila, at Ephesus.

Meta. While one has but an intellectual concept of Truth (the John the Baptist doctrine) one is very likely to be hard and destructive in judgments (*destroyer, laying waste*), because of a zeal to get rid of error; but when the Christ understanding enters the consciousness, love predominates. Then a true purifying and uplifting takes place.

In I Corinthians 3:6 Paul says: "I planted, Apollos watered; but God gave the increase." Paul symbolizes the converted will sowing the word of Truth (seed) in all parts of the body. Apollos, who waters the growing Truth in consciousness, stands for *the sun*, as light, understanding—a true, practical understanding of faith and of love and of the other faculties of the mind, and an understanding of how to apply these faculties as they are needed to refresh, encourage, and aid the new Truth thoughts into fruition. The increasing power of Truth is Spirit.

Apollyon, ă-pŏl'-lў-ŏn (Gk.)—*destruction; destroyer.*

The same as Abaddon (Rev. 9:11).

Meta. See ABADDON.

Appaim, ăp'-pă-ĭm (Heb.)—*breathing places; two nostrils; countenance; face; presence; two persons; comprehension; apprehension; passion; anger.*

Son of Nadab, and a descendant of Jerahmeel, who was the head of an important family of the tribe of Judah (I Chron. 2:30, 31).

Meta. The ability to *face* apparent facts and conditions squarely, and to originate (*nostrils,* nose—initiative capacity of the mind) or inaugurate new thoughts and modes of conduct, new rules of action, in order to bring about better conditions.

Appaim also signifies the ability to detect, discern, or comprehend (*breathing places, nostrils, comprehension*) the di-

vine *presence* and understanding (*face, countenance,* referring to understanding).

In the significance of Appaim there is a thought of duality (*two nostrils, two persons*). This suggests an outer as well as an inner source of discernment and knowledge. When man trusts to the outer senses for his information, he is under the dominion of the sense mind, wherein *apprehension, passion,* and *anger* find place and darken his true understanding.

Apphia, ăp'-phĭ-á (Gk.)—*productive.*

A Christian woman whom Paul addressed along with Philemon and Archippus (Philem. 2). She is supposed to have been Philemon's wife.

Meta. Philemon means *loving;* he was a friend to Truth. Archippus means *chief of the horses, master of horses,* which suggests dominion over the vital forces of the organism and ability to care for them wisely. These qualities represented by Philemon and Archippus bring about a soul productiveness or fertility (*productive,* Apphia) that enables the individual to bring forth abundantly of the fruits of the Spirit.

Appius (A. V., Appii forum), ăp'-pĭ-ŭs (Lat.).

A town in Italy, on the Appian Way, or great road, which connects Rome with the Bay of Naples. It was at the market of Appius that some Christians (brethren from Rome) met Paul as he was being taken to Rome to appear before Cæsar for trial. When Paul saw these Christians "he thanked God, and took courage" (Acts 28:15).

Meta. A market is a place where provisions and other things are bought and sold. The forum or market place in ancient cities was the open space before the gates in which were transacted all civic activities as well as trade. The Greek *phoron* and the Latin *forum* are identical in meaning.

The root meaning is to speak, to utter one's thoughts, to exchange ideas. The market of Appius represents an exchange of ideas, or a comparison of ideas, in intellectual consciousness. The word of Truth, which is being taken to the head, or ruling power of the intellect, for trial (Paul was a prisoner on the way to Rome; Rome represents the head, from which the will rules, while Paul here symbolizes the word of Truth) is encouraged at this place to see that even in the region of the will, and among the outer thoughts of the intellect, the Truth is gaining a foothold.

Aquila, ăq'-uĭ-là (Lat.)—*eagle.*

A Jewish Christian, a native of Pontus, a tentmaker by trade. Aquila, with his wife, Priscilla, became associated with Paul at Corinth (Acts 18:1-3) and was of great help to him.

Meta. By misunderstanding himself and his relation to the one Mind, man in his unregenerate state is constantly tearing down his organism. The heart center and the solar plexus, instead of being pervaded by thoughts of peace and harmony, and a just appreciation of divine law, are perverted to the basest thoughts and most violent passions. But the patient, sustaining power within man is not wholly thwarted. When the body is lacerated, this power sets its builders to work and they repair the damage. We call this the healing force of nature. In every part of the organism are these patient building forces that constantly repair the ravages of the ignorant man. They are called the positive and the negative forces of life. They are introduced to us in Acts 18:1-3 under the names of Aquila and Priscilla, born in Pontus and "lately come from Italy." Pontus means *the sea* (universal Mind), and Italy signifies strength.

Ar, är (Heb.)—*a city* (especially *a fortified city*); *a strong city; to excite, arouse, an enemy.*

The chief city and capital of Moab. It often stands for the whole of Moab (Num. 21:28).

Meta. An aggregation of strongly established thoughts (*a strong city*) in the carnal mind (Moab). It is the seat of the activities of the carnal mind—of the seemingly inherent baseness and depravity in one who has given himself over to sensuality (*to excite, arouse, an enemy*). When an individual is awakened to the understanding that he is a son of God, that his body is God's temple, and that he is inherently good instead of evil, the overthrow of Ar of Moab is at hand. (See Isa. 15:1.)

Arab, ā'-răb (Heb.)—*ambuscade; a lurking place; a snare; ambush.*

A city of Judah, in the hill country (Josh. 15:52).

Meta. The reasoning faculty (this city was near Hebron, in the hill country of Judah, and belongs therefore to the front brain, or seat of conscious thought— see HEBRON) in man used as *a snare* to entangle (*ambuscade*) the enemies (error thoughts and beliefs) of Judah (praise) and Israel (true thoughts).

Arabah, är'-ȧ-băh, (Heb.)—*an arid tract; a sterile region; a desert; burnt up.* (In A. V., II Kings 14:25, sea of the plain; Amos 6:14, wilderness; Deut. 1:1, 2:8, plain; Deut. 11:30, champaign; Ezek. 47:8, desert.)

A place in Palestine on the border of the allotment of Benjamin (Josh. 18:18).

Meta. The empty, barren phases of thought and feeling that arise from the earthly ideas of substance in man, which have been separated from the indwelling vitality (*an arid tract; a desert*).

Arabia, ȧ-rā'-bĭ-ȧ (Heb.)—*darkened; toward the west; a stranger; uncultivated; unproductive; barren; sterile; wild.*

A very large tract of country comprising the southwestern part of Asia (Isa. 21:13; Gal. 4:25). It is the home of many wandering tribes, and in Bible times was in close touch with the Hebrews through commerce; through Ishmael the Arabians were related to the Hebrews.

Meta. An outer, or Gentile, state of consciousness that in its wild, ignorant, undisciplined, and unsettled nature is destructive in its tendency and is unproductive of good (*darkened, toward the west, uncultivated, barren, wild*). It must, however, be redeemed.

Arabians, ȧ-rā'-bĭ-ăns (Heb.).

Inhabitants of Arabia (Isa. 13:20; Acts 2:11).

Meta. Unproductiveness. When you begin the work of rebuilding your body walls (Neh. 4:6-9) you will meet with opposition. The various ignorant, barbaric, undisciplined thoughts that have not come within your civilization (the Arabians, the Ammonites, and the Ashdodites) will offer subtle resistance. They will even invade your dreams, and try to make you think that the rebuilding cannot be accomplished.

Arad, ā'-răd (Heb.)—*fleeing; a fugitive; a wild ass.*

a A city of the Canaanites, whose king came out against Israel while the Israelites were in the wilderness on their way from Egypt to the Promised Land (Num. 21:1). This king of Arad took some of the Israelites captive. Then "Israel vowed a vow unto Jehovah, and said, If thou wilt indeed deliver this people into my hand, then I will utterly destroy their cities. And Jehovah hearkened to the voice of Israel, and delivered up the Canaanites; and they utterly destroyed them and their cities: and the name of the place was called Hormah" —*utter destruction, extermination* (Num. 21:2, 3; see also Josh. 12:14 and Judg. 1:16). **b** A Benjamite, son of Beriah (I Chron. 8:15).

Meta. An aggregation of ignorant, destructive subconscious thoughts about life; they are in opposition to the true, upbuilding thoughts and understanding of man—children of Israel—and so must be overcome (*fleeing, a fugitive, a wild ass;* a city whose inhabitants fought against Israel). Arad was "in the South," meaning the subconsciousness, and the Canaanites signify in man the elemental life forces in the subconscious mind.

The Arad who was a Benjamite was the son of Beriah (*misfortune, evil*) and lived in Jerusalem. He represents a negative belief in peace; this negative thought, because of not being positive in knowing the unreality and nothingness of apparent evil, flees from error (*fleeing, a fugitive*) instead of overcoming it.

Arah, ā'-răh (Heb.)—*to go; to walk; to be on the way; a traveler; a wayfarer; a wanderer; the way one goes; a way.*

a An Asherite (I Chron. 7:39). **b** The head man of a large family that returned from the Babylonian captivity (Ezra 2:5). **c** A man of Judah whose granddaughter was married to Tobiah the Ammonite, who did all that he could to hinder Nehemiah from having the wall of Jerusalem rebuilt (Neh. 6:18).

Meta. An unstable thought in man's consciousness, or a tendency to digress from Truth (*a way,* but not *the* way). This thought is not established but is of a roaming, uncertain nature—*a wanderer.* There is, in these thoughts that the men named Arah signify, that which is moving toward a higher and more stable and true understanding (*to go; to be on the way, a traveler*). A large number of the descendants of one of these men returned to Jerusalem from Babylon.

Aram, ā'-răm (Heb.)—*highlands; high; exalted.* "Aram is used in the Hebrew to denote the nation of which *Aram,* son of Shem, was the founder . . . In such cases the English Version has it always rendered *Syrians,*" says Young.

a Son of Shem (Gen. 10:22). **b** A country (Num. 23:7). Aram and Syria are the same nation. (See SYRIA and SYRIANS.) The Bible mentions other men named Aram (Gen. 22:21; I Chron. 7:34); in Luke 3:33, Arni.

Meta. Aram refers to the intellect. The intellect has its foundation in Spirit, but in unawakened man it has linked itself so entirely with the outer or seemingly material realm that it reasons from the base of the senses instead of acknowledging Divine Mind as the source of all intelligence. The intellect is very necessary to man, and it becomes truly *high* and *exalted* when it is illumined by Spirit. Men in personal consciousness exalt it even above the wisdom of Spirit, but such exaltation cannot last; intellectual understanding must give way to spiritual knowing.

Aram–maacah (A. V., Syria–maachah), ā'-răm–mā'-ă-căh (Heb.)—*high pressure; high compression; exalted oppression; high exhaustion; high depression.*

A country to the north of Israel (I Chron. 19:6). This name is applied to the part of Syria that is hemmed in by mountains.

Meta. A much depressed state of consciousness that is the outcome of oppressing, tyrannical thoughts. These thoughts work against the spiritual good of the individual; they aid the wild, uncultivated, undisciplined, and sensuous thoughts (Ammonites) in an attempt to overcome the true spiritual thoughts (Israelites) and so gain dominion over the whole man (Aram and Syria symbolize thoughts of the intellectual realm that have no understanding of the real, Israel). Maacah means *compressed, depressed, worn,* and signifies thoughts of an oppressing and depressing character. The children of Ammon, when they "saw that they had made themselves odious to David," hired chariots and horsemen out of Aram–maacah to fight against Israel.

Aram–naharaim, ā'-ram-nā'-ha-rā'-im (Heb.)—*Aram of the two rivers; highlands of two rivers.*

Mesopotamia, the country between the Tigris and the Euphrates rivers (Gen. 24:10, margin; Psalms 60, title).

Meta. The Tigris is the river Hiddekel of Genesis 2:14, and symbolizes the nervous system. The Euphrates symbolizes the circulation of the blood in physical man. The circulatory system is closely connected with the outer physical, or seemingly material, organism of man, and the nervous system is more the organ of the mental and spiritual. The circulation of the blood symbolizes the flow of divine life throughout the body, and true, spiritual life is the real vitalizing element in both the outer and the inner phases of man. But Aram-naharaim refers to the belief of the spiritually unawakened intellect that the purely physical blood is the life of man, that which keeps the whole organism alive; this belief takes no account of the interior and spiritual phase of life, but thinks the outer to be all-sufficient.

There are persons who think that when one takes up the study of spiritual things one becomes queer and unbalanced. Sometimes those who are in the overcoming life are confronted with just such ideas, and the thought presents itself to them that they had better be content with the generally established ideas of the world regarding life and existence. These are some of the people from Aram–naharaim; they are of the intellect, governed by the sense man, or carnal mind.

Aram–zobah, ā'-ram-zō'-bah (Heb.)—*high warriors; highland warriors; Aram of Tsobah.*

A part of Syria, though a separate kingdom at the time of David and Solomon; it spent much time fighting against Israel (Psalms 60, title).

Meta. The assembling of the warring thoughts of the intellect (see ZOBAH and ARAM), thoughts that believe in the enforcement of personal rights, thus stirring up strife and inharmony. These thoughts intend to stay in the consciousness; they encamp; they make man believe that he cannot get along in the world without fighting his way. But Solomon (peace and wisdom) captured the capital of Zobah, or Aram-zobah, Hamath, and the country became subject to Israel.

Aran, ā'-răn (Heb.)—*active; nimble; a wild goat; firmness.*

Son of Dishon, a Horite descended from Seir (Gen. 36:28).

Meta. Aggressiveness, and a firmness or obstinacy of thought that is untrained and undisciplined and is guided, not by understanding, but by outer desires (a *wild goat, firmness,* a Horite). This makes a place of refuge for many of the sense ideas of man that should be overcome.

Ararat (A. V., Armenia, II Kings 19:37 and Isa. 37:38), ăr'-ă-răt (Heb.)—*sacred land; holy land; light's effluence; wilderness; accursed terror.* The last two definitions are accepted by a certain group of commentators, but do not accord with the Sanskrit, or the true Hebraic root. The first three are the most accurate.

According to the Bible, Ararat was a country, not a mountain as has been commonly supposed. The ark of Noah, at the time of the flood, rested "upon the mountains of Ararat" (Gen. 8:4). Other Bible texts refer very clearly to Ararat as a land, and so we are led to believe that the ark rested upon some mountains in the country of Ararat, and not on a mountain by the name of Ararat. Sennacherib, king of Assyria, was murdered by his sons, who then fled to the land of Ararat (II Kings 19:37). In Jeremiah 51:27 we find that Ararat was one of the powers that Jehovah was going to send against Babylon and Chaldea. History is not decided as to where this land of Ararat was, but it is thought to have been Armenia of the present day, or a part of it.

Meta. From the lack of decision on the part of historians as to where and what Ararat really was, and the diversity of meanings attributed to the name, we infer that it represents that which to the spiritually unawakened man is unknown. This "unknown" may to one individual be sacred, high, holy, and filled with creative power (*sacred land, holy land, light's effluence*), and to another it may be a chaotic wilderness or something fearful and terrible (*wilderness, accursed terror*), according to the trend of each person's thought and belief.

The rivers Euphrates and Tigris (Hiddekel) rise in Armenia, which is supposed to be the land of Ararat of Bible history. The Hiddekel symbolizes the great nervous system in man; the Euphrates symbolizes the circulatory system of man. The nervous system lies very close to the mental and spiritual; the circulatory system is more in the region of the physical. Thus the realm of which Ararat is symbolical (the unknown) is the source of both the mental and the physical of man. We should call this source the realm of Spirit; it is a savior of life unto life, or of death unto death, according to whether the laws of Spirit are recognized and obeyed, or are unacknowledged in thought and act.

Araunah, ă-rạu′-năh (Heb.)—*pine of Jah; Jehovah is firm; a strong one; a hero.*

It was at the threshing floor of Araunah the Jebusite that the angel's hand was stayed, at the command of Jehovah, from destroying Jerusalem. David bought this threshing floor from Araunah, and offered sacrifices there for the children of Israel (II Sam. 24:16, 24).

The name is Ornan in I Chronicles 21:15-28.

Meta. A threshing floor is symbolical of judgment; threshing out grain and separating it from the straw or chaff symbolizes a discriminating between good and apparent error in consciousness and a letting go of the error. At first this process may seem hard, and one may see only the unyielding firmness and strength of Spirit in these judgments, apart from anything of a loving or merciful nature (*Jehovah is firm, a strong one*). When divine love, represented here by David, begins to express consciously, a real refining process takes place (David offered sacrifices after building an altar to Jehovah); then the seeming destructiveness of judgment disappears, and harmony is established.

Araunah represents judgment, or separation of good from error, as it appears to the error side, which is being destroyed. David symbolizes the realization of divine love, which changes one's attitude toward this judgment or segregating of error and putting it away from the consciousness. Thus Araunah (the firm determination of Jehovah—the I AM in us—to put away seeming error) becomes a preserving quality, since we can be saved alive and entire only as we rise above all limitation and error. As we so overcome, the forces and powers within us work constructively instead of destructively (the destroying angel stayed his hand).

Arba, är′-bà (Heb.) — *a giant; strength; a cube; four.* Arba is the name of the number four, symbol of great strength and stability, characterized in the square and the cube.

Father of Anak (Josh. 15:13). "Now the name of Hebron beforetime was Kiriath-arba; which Arba was the greatest man among the Anakim" (Josh. 14:15). Hebron "became the inheritance of Caleb . . . because that he wholly followed Jehovah, the God of Israel" (Josh. 14:14).

Meta. The reasoning of the sense mind in man, which attributes power and reality to the outer formed world instead of knowing that all power and reality exist in Spirit—the unformed ideas of the one Mind. (See ANAK, also.) Sense reasoning, which is based on sense observations, is very firmly established in the spiritually unawakened individual, and it has its place of action in Hebron —the seat of conscious thought. This line of reasoning can be overcome only by that which Caleb, the faithful Israelite, signifies: spiritual faith. Truth is first perceived and accepted by faith; then it becomes the basis of one's conscious thinking (Hebron.)

Arbathite, är'-băth-īte (Heb.)—*belonging to Arabah; of the sterile region; of the desert.*

a An inhabitant of the Arabah or a native of the city of Arab. A designation of Abi–albon, or Abiel, one of David's mighty men (II Sam. 23:31; I Chron. 11:32).

Meta. See ARABAH and ARAB.

When Abiel, or Abi–albon, the Arbathite, one of David's mighty men of valor (a strong, mighty thought that has its source in God), arises in consciousness, the restoring of these desert places (Arabah) to fruitfulness begins.

Archelaus, är-chĕ-lā'-ŭs (Gk.)—*people's chief; ruler of the people.*

Son of Herod the Great, and his successor as ruler of Judea (Matt. 2:22).

Meta. A phase of the sense will, or ruling power in sense consciousness.

Archevites, är'-chĕ-vītes (Chald.)—*belonging to Erech.*

Supposed to have been inhabitants of Erech, a city of the kingdom founded by Nimrod in the land of Shinar (Ezra 4:9).

Meta. Thoughts belonging to the state of consciousness that Erech signifies. (See ERECH.)

Archippus, är-chĭp'-pŭs (Gk.)—*master of the horse; chief of the horses; ruler of horses.*

Addressed by Paul as "our fellow-soldier" (Philem. 2).

Meta. Dominion over the vital forces of the organism, and the wisdom and ability to train and care for these forces wisely (*master of the horse, chief of the horses, ruler of horses;* horses refer to the vitality, or vital forces). In

Colossians 4:17 Paul admonishes Archippus: "Take heed to the ministry which thou hast received in the Lord, that thou fulfil it."

Archite, är'-chīte (Heb.)—*a man of Erech; prolonged; lengthened; extended; adapted.*

Hushai, a friend of David's (II Sam. 15:32; I Chron. 27:33). Archite and Archevite are supposed to be the same.

Meta. See ARCHEVITES and HUSHAI.

Ard, ärd (Heb.)—*fugitive; to flee; wild ass.*

Another name for Addar, son of Bela and grandson of Benjamin (Gen. 46:21; Num. 26:40).

Meta. The thought that Ard signifies belongs to the outer or animal phase of consciousness, where fear enters and one runs away (*to flee*) from seeming evil, or resists it wildly and stubbornly (*wild ass*), as the case may be, because one fears it. In this phase of consciousness one does not understand that evil is unreal and has no power of itself; when one realizes the truth about seeming evil, one will no longer fear it and it will be dissolved from one's world. (See BELA and ADDAR.)

Ardon, är'-dŏn (Heb.)—*fugitive; one wandering about; bewildered.* Strictly speaking, *fugitive* does not express the true significance of this word; a better definition is *becoming lost, having lost one's sense of location.*

Son of Caleb (I Chron. 2:18).

Meta. A bewildered state of mind. A stirring up of one's thoughts and a somewhat "lost" feeling are very apt to follow bold, zealous, impetuous denials of error and declarations of Truth by faith (Caleb —faith, *bold, impetuous, fearless,* father of Ardon). The reason for this is that the individual is changing his base. He has become released from certain errors that he had trusted in formerly, but he has not yet entered into spiritual understanding and become established in the Christ consciousness, or consciousness of Truth. Thus he becomes, for the time being, like a ship without a rudder; he scarcely knows what to think or do.

Areli, ă-rē'-lī (Heb.)—*lionlike; valiant; heroic.*

Son of Gad and grandson of Jacob (Gen. 46:16).

Meta. Courage to abide by that which one believes to be right and best; also boldness and fearlessness in making one's ideas practical (*lionlike, valiant, heroic*).

Areopagite, ăr-ĕ-ŏp'-ä-ġīte (Gk.)— *of the Areopagus.*

A member of the court of Areopagus (Acts 17:34). This court, at Mars' Hill, Athens, was the oldest and most honored court of justice in the whole known world at that time. It existed throughout many centuries. Even foreign countries sought its decisions because of their value and equity.

Meta. The court of Areopagus represents the highest understanding and rendering of justice in the intellectual domain, and is very close to the spiritual. An Areopagite symbolizes one of the thoughts or qualities of justice and fairness and discernment that comprise this court in consciousness. (See AREOPAGUS.)

Areopagus, ăr-ĕ-ŏp'-ä-gŭs (Gk.)— *Mars' Hill; the hill of Ares or Mars.*

Areopagus, or Mars' Hill, was a rocky hill in Athens, near the center of the city; on this hill the court of justice was held (Acts 17:19-34; see margin also).

Meta. A hill always represents a high place in consciousness, and in this instance it symbolizes the intellectual phase of thought in man, since Athens was the center of intellectual learning in the then known world. The council of Areopagus was also known as "the Council on Mars' Hill," or the "Upper Council." This court of justice represents the place in consciousness where the different aggregations of thought forces receive a hearing and (according to the light manifested in consciousness) righteous judgment. (See AREOPAGITE.)

Aretas, ăr'-ĕ-tăs (Gk.)--*excellence; virtue; power; purity.*

An Arabian king, or chief, who was in possession of Damascus at the time that the occurrence that Paul mentions in II Corinthians 11:32, 33 took place. He was father-in-law of Herod Antipas. The title, Aretas, was applied to many Arabian kings.

Meta. A certain natural love of virtue, merit, and goodness inherent in the outer man, although he does not appreciate the spiritual word in its work throughout the body consciousness (Paul and his ministry). Even the outer man, however, is inherently good. The physical is not of itself evil; the body is an obedient servant. Carnal thought incites man to unwise expression—evil deeds.

Argob, är'-gŏb (Heb.)—*a heap of stones; to stone any one; stony; hard; durable; strong.*

A rocky territory in Bashan. It comprised "threescore great cities with walls and brazen bars." It was under the dominion of Og, king of Bashan, an Ammonitish ruler, until he was defeated by the Israelites (Deut. 3:4). Then Argob became a part of the possessions of the half tribe of Manasseh (I Kings 4:13).

Meta. Judging from its meaning, as well as from its fortified cities, its rocky location, and the cliffs that bordered it, Argob must symbolize a very strong defensive state of consciousness in man. This, when controlled by the sense or carnal mind (when under the rule of Og, the Ammonitish king), would be hard, quarrelsome, and resistant. But when it is taken over and lifted up by the Israelites (spiritual or religious thoughts seeking truer expression), Argob becomes a firm, positive, and invincible factor in the establishment of the consciousness in Truth.

Aridai, ă-rī'-dāi (Heb., Pers. origin)— *strong; worthy; deserving.*

One of the sons of Haman, "the Jews' enemy" (Esth. 9:9, 10). Haman was an Agagite, or Amalekite.

Meta. The Agagites or Amalekites were descended from Agag, who represents the Adversary in man's consciousness. The Agagites symbolize the animal forces, the appetites and passions. They are warlike, rebellious, and destructive, and are very detrimental to man's spiritual growth. Aridai (*strong, worthy, deserving,* son of Haman, an Agagite) represents a belief that the unrestrained animal activities in man, his appetites and carnal desires, are necessary to his well-being and should be sustained by him; also that they are too deeply rooted in his consciousness to be overcome. This thought must be destroyed and its substance must be given over to strengthening the true thoughts of man.

Aridatha, ă-rĭd′-ă-thȧ (Heb., Pers. origin)—*strength; worthy; deserving.*

One of Haman's sons, who was hanged with his brothers (Esth. 9:8, 13, 14).

Meta. The darkened thought in man that calls evil good and that attributes strength to error. The truth is that error has no strength or power except that which man gives to it temporarily by believing in it. (See ARIDAI.)

Arieh, ă-rī′-ĕh (Heb.)—*lion; the lion; strength; valor; fierceness; cruelty.*

A prince in Israel who was slain with King Pekahiah (II Kings 15:25).

Meta. A bold, courageous, conquering phase (*lion*) of the ruling power of the outer consciousness pertaining to Israel (the religious thoughts struggling toward perfection, of which not all are spiritual). The will has its origin in Spirit. It is a spiritual faculty, even though it is often directed by intellectual reasonings and by sense desires instead of true spiritual understanding. (King Pekahiah represents the will. He was a king of Israel and was a wicked ruler. Arieh, who was killed with the king, also must have been in error.) While the thoughts and states of consciousness that the Israelites and Jews signify have their inception in Truth, yet in their expression some of them seem far from spiritual, because of their having been influenced by adverse and untrue thoughts from the carnal mind.

Ariel, ā′-rĭ-ĕl (Heb.)—*lion of God; strength of God; burning place of God; altar of God.*

Fallows says of the name Ariel (II Sam. 23:20) that "it was applied as an epithet of distinction to bold and warlike persons, as among the Arabians, who surnamed Ali 'The Lion of God.'"

Meta. Ariel of Moab signifies a bold, warlike tendency pertaining to the carnal mind of man. The Ariel of Ezra 8:16, who was a chief man among those who returned from the Babylonian captivity,

also stands for a bold, conquering thought quality in man, but of a higher nature than that symbolized by Ariel of Moab.

The Ariel of Isaiah 29:1-7 refers to Jerusalem and suggests an interpretation according to other meanings given to the name—*altar, burning place of God.* The altar as located in the body is the solar plexus, through which the soul connects with the outer or physical organism. Just above the solar plexus, at the heart center, we find the place that Jerusalem symbolizes, and it is in the spiritual consciousness, which Jerusalem represents, that full consecration can be made to God. It is at this place in consciousness that we become willing to give up the lower for the higher, the personal for the impersonal, the animal for the Godlike, and a transmutation takes place. (See ALTAR.)

Arimathæa, ăr-ĭ-mā-thē′-ȧ (Gk.)—*the height; high place; highland.*

The birthplace and home of Joseph, a wealthy man and a follower of Jesus Christ. Joseph took the body of Jesus down from the cross and put it in his own tomb (Matt. 27:57-60). Arimathæa is thought to have been the same place as Ramah of the Old Testament.

Meta. An aggregation of thoughts of a lofty character—a high state of consciousness in man (*the height*). (See RAMAH.)

Arioch, ā′-rĭ-ŏch (Gk.)—*lionlike; venerable.*

a King of Ellasar, one of the four kings who took Lot captive but were defeated and destroyed by Abraham (Gen. 14:1). **b** Captain of the king of Babylon's guard (Dan. 2:14).

Meta. The Arioch of Genesis 14:1 represents the seeming power, strength, and dominion (*lionlike*) that sex lust has over man; also, the belief so prevalent among all peoples that the secret desires and habits pertaining to the sex life must be good and must have been ordained of God because of ages of acceptance and practice. Therefore they are regarded as sacred (*venerable*). It is natural to man to accept, as true and unchangeable, ideas and habits that have been universally believed and acted upon for ages.

The Arioch of Babylon refers more to the power and veneration that sense man attributes to worldly wisdom and to the psychic realm.

Arisai, ă-rī'-sāi (Pers.)—*arrow of Ariæ; arrow of Vishnii; excellence.*

One of the ten sons of Haman the Agagite; he was hanged with his brothers (Esth. 9:9).

Meta. The significance is virtually the same as that of Aridai and Aridatha, which see. Arisai also bespeaks the swiftness of the *arrow* and its ability to pierce, to penetrate. These qualities are attributed to the errors that this name signifies.

Aristarchus, ăr-ĭs-tär'-chŭs (Gk.)— *best ruling; the best ruler; best leader; supreme beginning; first principle.*

A Christian man from Thessalonica, a city in Macedonia. He was a companion of Paul's on missionary journeys, and was Paul's fellow prisoner at Rome (Acts 19:29; Col. 4:10).

Meta. Spiritual power, authority, and soul fervor—the very Christ of God or Divine Mind itself (*best ruler, best leader, supreme beginning, first principle;* a Christian man who accompanied Paul on his missionary journeys and was a prisoner at Rome with him), which must accompany the word of Truth (Paul) in its redeeming work throughout the body in order to make the word operative in consciousness.

Aristobulus, ăr-ĭs-tŏ-bū'-lŭs (Gk.)— *best deliberating; best advising; best counsel; supreme deliberation (with oneself).*

The household of Aristobulus was in Rome (Rom. 16:10).

Meta. The Holy Spirit as counselor and adviser in man (*best advising, best counsel, supreme deliberation with oneself).* The Holy Spirit is not confined to one place in man, but is active throughout his whole consciousness—everywhere present. The ideas and the inspirations of Spirit (household of Aristobulus), however, are received by and abide in the understanding faculty, which is located in the head (Rome).

ark, ärk (Lat.)—*a holy abode; a sanctuary; a tabernacle; any vessel for preservation; a sphere; a coffer; receptacle; depository; treasury; coffer; corporeity of light; body of light.*

a Noah's ark (Gen. 6:14-16; 7:13). **b** The basket in which Moses was hidden (Exod. 2:3). **c** The Ark of the Covenant (Exod. 25:10-22).

Meta. Noah's ark symbolizes the spiritual part of oneself, built in the midst of the flood of error. One builds one's ark on the scientific understanding of the wisdom, presence, and power of God. The ark is built upon the affirmations of what one is in Spirit.

One takes into the ark one's wife, one's sons, and their wives (spiritual principles inhering in the soul), "and of every living thing of all flesh, two of every sort" ("male and female," the positive and the negative activities of life in the organism); that is, one affirms Spirit as all in all, as primal essence.

The Ark of the Covenant, sacred ark, or ark of the testimony, represents the original spark of divinity in man's being. It is a covenant, or agreement, of the Father with the son that He shall inherit all that the Father has. "All things whatsoever the Father hath are mine" (John 16:15).

This original spiritual spark is a very sacred, holy thing, because upon its development depends man's immortality. It is represented as occupying the most holy place in the temple and as being protected and cared for with great devotion. All that man is has been brought forth from this central spark, yet the sense-conscious man often neglects it and ignores its very existence. The attention is taken up with the things of sense to the exclusion of Spirit.

In individual consciousness, when the ark of the covenant is removed from the heart center (city of Jerusalem) the spiritual forces are scattered. Because of lack of a substantial basis from which to operate, no definite spiritual unfoldment can take place. It was therefore necessary to establish this holy meeting place, as David (love) well knew (II Sam. 6:1-19).

After David had fully learned that working with divine law always brings good, and that disobedience is the cause of destruction, he brought the Ark of the Covenant back to its proper place in Jerusalem. Its presence there insured to the Israelites a peace and a harmony and a spiritual progress that they had not known during the absence of the Ark.

Arkite, ärk'-īte (Heb.)—*fugitive; blind passions; brutish appetites; a tusk.*

A member of a family or tribe descended from Canaan, son of Ham (Gen. 10:17).

Meta. A thought pertaining to the carnal consciousness in man.

Armoni, är-mō'-nī (Heb.)—*palace-born; of the palace; of a fortress.*

Son of Saul by his concubine, Rizpah (II Sam. 21:8).

Meta. A seemingly strongly fortified belief in the human consciousness that the personal will (Saul) is inherently the rightful ruling power in man (*of a fortress, palace-born*). Armoni was one of the seven sons and grandsons of Saul who were given over to the Gibeonites by David and were put to death by them; that is, this error belief relating to the personal will is discerned and is overcome, or adjusted, by spiritual thoughts attained through prayer. (See GIBEON.)

Arnan, är'-năn (Heb.)—*active; nimble; strong.*

An Israelite mentioned in the genealogy of Zerubbabel (I Chron. 3:21).

Meta. A constructive, restoring, upbuilding thought in consciousness—a thought that is powerful, vigorous, alert, resourceful, and *active* in its nature (*strong, nimble*); it might be named a belief in efficiency.

Arni, är'-nī (Gk., from Heb.)—*Aram.*

Same as Aram (Luke 3:33).

Meta. Refers to the intellect. (See ARAM.)

Arnon, är'-nŏn (Heb.)—*swift; roaring; rushing stream; a murmur; noisy; rejoicing.*

A river on the boundary between Moab and the land of the Amorites; later between Moab and Israel (Num. 21:13; Josh. 12:1).

Meta. The life current in man, which is tumultuous (*swift, roaring, noisy, rushing stream*) under the dominion of carnal thought (Moab and the Amorites), but is a *rejoicing* of the whole man when possessed and guided by Israel, the real and the true.

Arod, ā'-rŏd (Heb.)—*fleeing; a wild ass.*

Son of Gad and grandson of Jacob (Num. 26:17); in Genesis 46:16 he is called Arodi.

Meta. Arod and his descendants, the Arodites, represent the phase of the animal nature in man that is characterized by the *ass*—meekness, stubbornness, persistency, and endurance. These qualities are good when they are directed by the true I AM, but are destructive when given over to sense rule.

Aroer, är'-ŏ-ēr (Heb.)—*ruins; desolation; barren; bare; naked; inclosed.*

The name of three or four cities and towns in Palestine (Num. 32:34; Josh. 13:16; I Sam. 30:28). One of these towns had been taken from the Amorites; it was situated on the north side of the river Arnon (Deut. 4:48).

Meta. Those seemingly empty, waste, despairing states of thought into which one gets occasionally, states wherein everything looks dark and bare and there appears to be no way to the fulfillment of the good that one is seeking to demonstrate (*ruins, desolation, naked*). In such a time one needs more than ever to be strong and of good courage. One should hold faithfully to the abundant substance, strength, joy, and overcoming power of Spirit, so that the thought aggregations represented by the cities named Aroer may be built up and established in Truth.

Aroerite, är'-ŏ-ēr-īte (Heb.)—*of Aroer.*

A native of Aroer (I Chron. 11:44).

Meta. A thought belonging to that in consciousness which Aroer signifies. (See AROER.)

Arpachshad (A. V., Arphaxad), är-păchs'-hăd (Heb.)—*providential regeneration; realm of astrology; limits of Chaldea.*

Son of Shem (Gen. 10:22); called Arphaxad in Luke 3:36.

Meta. A belief in man that his good depends wholly upon something outside of himself—his ruling star, fate, providence—instead of knowing that he holds in his own thoughts the power to establish within himself and his world what he wills.

Arpad (in A. V., Isa. 36:19, Arphad), är'-păd (Heb.)—*spread out a bed; a couch; strong; supporting; resting; refreshing; light's redemption.* The latter is not affiliated with the former sense, but is a distinct development.

A very idolatrous Syrian city. It is mentioned along with Hamath (II Kings 18:34; Jer. 49:23).

Meta. A settled belief (*a couch, spread out a bed, resting*) that material reasonings of the intellect, rather than trust in God and in the wisdom of Spirit, are the source and power of man's true enlightenment and redemption (*strong, supporting, refreshing, light's redemption*). (See SYRIA.)

Artaxerxes, är-tăx-ērx'-ēṣ (Pers.)— *mighty shah; great king; mighty warrior.*

King of Persia, and title of various Persian kings (Ezra 4:7). The accounts of King Artaxerxes given in Ezra 4 and 7 may have belonged to two different kings, one of whom was influenced by the Jews' enemies to sign a decree forbidding further work on the wall of Jerusalem and the Temple, while the other Artaxerxes, by the influence of Nehemiah, not only consented to the continuance of the work at Jerusalem but also furnished supplies with which to carry it on.

Meta. The will (*great king*) ruling in sense consciousness but open to both error and spiritual thought and acting according to whichever appeals most strongly to it at the time.

Artemas, är'-tĕ-măs (Gk.)—*gift of Artemis; gift of perfection; gift of wholeness.*

A follower of Jesus Christ, whom Paul was thinking of sending to Crete to take the place of Titus, so that Titus could come to Paul at Nicopolis (Tit. 3:12).

Meta. Crete means *carnal*, while Tychicus, whom Paul considered sending to Crete to relieve Titus instead of send-

ing Artemas, represents a belief in fate. Paul seems to have been undecided as to whether it would be best to leave this carnal state of consciousness (Crete) to its fate (Tychicus) for a time, or to send Artemas to it; that is, to seek at that time, through a further use of true, sound words of wholeness and perfection (*gift of perfection, gift of wholeness*), to lift this carnal state of mind to the spiritual plane.

Artemis, är'-te-mis (Gk.)—*Diana; huntress; goddess of night.*

Artemis is another name for the goddess Diana of the Ephesians (Acts 19:24, margin). Fallows says: "The Diana of the Romans is a goddess known under various modifications, and with almost incompatible attributes. As the tutelary divinity of Ephesus, in which character alone she concerns us here, she was undoubtedly a representative of the same power presiding over conception and birth that was adored in Palestine under the name of *Ashtoreth*. She is therefore related to all the cognate deities of that Asiatic Juno-Venus, and partakes, at least, of their connection with the *moon* . . . The Arabic version of the Acts renders Artemis, in the chapter cited, by *Az Zuharat*, which is the Arabic name for the planet Venus."

Meta. See DIANA and ASHTORETH.

Arubboth (A. V., Aruboth), är-ŭb'- bŏth (Heb.)—*fourfold forces; lattice works; windows; courts; sluice gates.* These are the floodgates that were opened in the deluge referred to in Gen. 7:11 and 8:2. A channel or opening through which any force or principle may fully emanate to the created world.

A district in Israel from which Ben-hesed gathered victuals for King Solomon's household for one month of each year (I Kings 4:10). Arubboth is thought to have been a rich corn-growing country belonging to the tribe of Judah.

Meta. The increasing of substance (a rich corn-growing country) through praise (Judah), its entrance into consciousness (*windows, sluice gates*) and its adjustment in mind (*courts*), that a certain portion of this substance may be appropriated for the sustenance of the peace consciousness in man (Solomon and his household). Benhesed, pertaining to *mercy* and *kindness*, is needed to attend to the adjustment and distribution of substance.

Arumah, ā-ru̯′-măh (Heb.)—*height; exalted; elevated; on high.*

A place near Shechem; it was the home of Abimelech, son of Gideon, for a time during his rule over Israel (Judg. 9:41).

Meta. The lifting up of the personal will and desire for leadership (*height, exalted*), guided by a destructive tendency without being directed by good judgment. (Gideon means *destroyer;* he was a destroyer of error and a deliverer of Israel. Abimelech, however, represents this destructive tendency without the good judgment that characterized his father, Gideon. Therefore, he destroyed his own brethren as well as some of Israel's enemies.)

Arvad, är′-văd (Heb.)—*refuge; pirates' den; place of fugitives; plundering rovers; wanderers.*

A small island not far from the seaport of Tyre (Ezek. 27:8).

Meta. A retreat (*refuge*) in the mixed, confused, ever changing sense consciousness of man (the sea) for unstable, erring, destructive thoughts (*place of fugitives, plundering rovers, wanderers*). These thoughts are unreal, though they are warriors and boast great conquering ability. They are of the carnal mind and will fade away with the overthrow of that which Tyre signifies. (See TYRE.)

Arvadite, är′-văd-īte (Heb.)—*avarice; plunder; piracy.*

An inhabitant of Arvad (Gen. 10:18). The Arvadites were descended from Canaan, son of Ham.

Meta. A thought belonging to the Arvad phase of consciousness. (See ARVAD.)

Arza, är′-zȧ (Heb.)—*earth; land; domain; firm; low; inferior; terminated.*

A man who was over King Elah's household in Tirzah (I Kings 16:9).

Meta. That phase of man's thought which predominates when the will (king) allows the individual to give himself over to the appetites and desires of the flesh (*earth; low; inferior; terminated;* the king was "drinking himself drunk in the house of Arza" when he was slain). Giving up entirely to carnal appetites and desires leads to a breaking up of the whole consciousness: Elah the king and all his relatives and friends were killed.

Asa, ā′-sȧ (Heb.)—*physician; healer; binding up; making whole.*

King of Judah (I Kings 15:8, 14; II Chron. 14-16:14).

Meta. The will working constructively. In body consciousness the work of Asa is the rebuilding process that goes on in the subconscious mind, directed by the will to be well.

When the natural life in the organism is acknowledged as God life, when it is quickened, purified, and regenerated with words of Truth, it is transmuted into divine life and its harmonious relation to Divine Mind is established. When this right relation is established in consciousness between the subjective vitality and Divine Mind, a harmonious expression follows, and continuous rebuilding of the tissues goes on in the organism. Asa is the dominant healing force in the inner life of the organism.

Asahel, ā′-sȧ-hĕl (Heb.)—*whom God created; whom God constituted; whom God has made; God's creature; God is doer.*

Son of David's sister, Zeruiah, and brother of Joab and Abishai (I Chron. 2:16). He was very active in David's service. He was a very swift runner; it is said of him that he was "as light of foot as a wild roe" (II Sam. 2:18).

Meta. The swiftness of the activity of the creative word in man's consciousness when love (David) is the ruling power (king). Before the intellect (Abner, captain of Saul's host) gives way fully to the new spiritual rulership, there is sometimes such keen competition between the two that the word of Truth is hindered in its expression and its effects are seemingly denied any place in consciousness for a time. (Abner killed Asahel in self-defense.)

Asaiah (A. V., II Kings 22:12, 14,

Asahiah), ă-sā'-ĭăh (Heb.)—*whom Jah constituted; Jehovah has made; Jah is doer; whom the Lord made.*

The name of at least four different Israelitish men (I Chron. 4:36; 6:30; 9:5; 15:6, 11).

Meta. The innate truth of man's being, that he is spiritual, he came forth from God (*whom Jah constituted, Jah is doer, Jehovah has made*).

Asaph, ā'-săph (Heb.)—*collector; gatherer; harvester; assembler.*

The name of several Israelitish men. Most of them were men of note; some were Levites (I Chron. 9:15; 26:1; Neh. 2:8); one of them was the man whom David and Solomon appointed to oversee the song services in the Temple worship (I Chron. 6:39; Psalms 50 and 73 to 83 are attributed to him); another was a recorder in Hezekiah's reign (II Kings 18:18).

Meta. The Asaph who had charge of the song services in the Temple worship represents the gathering together (*collector, gatherer, assembler*) of the thoughts and forces of man through his concentrating in I AM, the spiritual center and true directive power, thus establishing harmony and all the healing, rejoicing, uplifting elements of constructive music.

Asaph the recorder refers to the memory, or subjective consciousness, wherein all the records of past thought processes and experiences are assembled and kept.

The other men named Asaph represent the gathering together of the thoughts and forces for harmonizing and upbuilding purposes.

Asarel (A. V., Asareel), ăs'-ă-rĕl (Heb.)—*whom God has bound; vow with God; fettered by God; oath-bound.*

Son of Jehallelel, of the tribe of Judah (I Chron. 4:16).

Meta. A certain restriction of error in consciousness, of the purely selfish and personal; this is the result of consecration to God (*vow with God, oath-bound, fettered by God*).

Asenath, ăs'-ĕ-năth (Egypt.)—*she is of Neith; dedicated to Neith; favorite of Neith.*

Daughter of Potiphera, Egyptian priest of On (Gen. 41:45, 50).

Meta. The feminine or love side of the natural man. She was Joseph's wife, and mother of his two sons, Ephraim and Manasseh (will and understanding). These two sons of Joseph (imagination) inherited his allotment in the Promised Land (the perfected body). The front brain is the field of operation for these closely related faculties: imagination, understanding, will.

The twin forces of the mind, will and understanding, are dominant in the race because they are necessary in the soul's free development. If the imagination were wholly in command it would indulge in a riot of daydreams or fanciful schemes that could not be worked out successfully in a world where natural law is inexorable. It is this dreamy state that the mind considers, and brings forth in sequence the two sons, will and understanding.

Ashan, ā'-shăn (Heb.)—*smoke.*

a A Levitical city of Judah (Josh. 15:42; I Chron. 6:59). **b** A city of Simeon in Judah (Josh. 19:7, 1).

Meta. In almost every instance where smoke is mentioned in the Bible it is connected with the anger, wrath, or jealousy of Jehovah. Otherwise it is used in connection with the passing away of the results of evil. This shows the unreality and transitoriness of that which is not founded in God—good. When Truth is discerned in consciousness man enters into a judgment or sifting process, wherein the Truth reveals certain errors or limitations of thought, and if the individual remains firm in the Truth that he has discerned, the seeming error is overcome. But during the process wherein the law is working to destroy all that is unlike God, there is likely to be confusion in mind and body according to whether the error is deep-seated, also according to whether it is given up fully or held to by the personal will. This confusion is the smoke of the Lord's anger (see Psa. 74:1 and Psa. 18:8 with margin), the anger and wrath of Jehovah being symbolical of the divine law in man in its work of revealing and erasing error from the consciousness. So Ashan refers to this phase of Spirit's work in man—the work of breaking up and casting out seeming error.

Asharelah (A. V., Asarelah), ăsh-ă-rē'-lăh (Heb.)—*upright toward God; happiness of God; blessedness of God.*

Son of Asaph, and one of those who were set apart by David and the captains of his host to "prophesy with harps, and psalteries, and with cymbals" (I Chron. 25:2); in verse 14, Jesharelah.

Meta. Uprightness of thought—the "upward look" and attention—also the joy and blessedness that come from God to those whose thoughts are stayed on Him (*upright toward God, happiness of God, blessedness*). These activities, expressing through love (Asharelah was of the Israelitish tribe of Levi), do their part in keeping man's mind and body "in tune with the Infinite," that the consciousness may be open to the revelation and clear understanding of Truth (prophesy).

Ashbea, ăsh-bē'-à (Heb.)—*I adjure; I swear; an adjuration; an oath; man of Baal.*

Either a man of Judah or a place in Judah (I Chron. 4:21).

Meta. The *I,* in man's spiritually awakening consciousness, appealing earnestly and solemnly to God, the All-Good, and declaring its highest concept of Truth.

Man of Baal is a possible interpretation of the name Ashbea, but a doubtful one. If this interpretation stands, the significance of Ashbea takes on the nature of an outer or formal prayer—that of beseeching and supplicating a personal God. (Baal refers to a belief in the outer formed world as real, hence an outer God with personal form. See BAAL.)

When an individual knows the Truth he ceases to pray to a far-away personal God; instead he acknowledges the spiritual reality that lies back of all manifestation, and he affirms his own good joyously. Thus he demonstrates abundantly.

Ashbel, ăsh'-bĕl (Heb.)—*man of Baal; reproof of God; judgment of God.*

Son of Benjamin, and head of the family of Ashbelites (Gen. 46:21; Num.

26:38).

Meta. The admonition of Spirit (*reproof of God*) in man's consciousness against looking upon as real (and thus giving power to) the material thought about outer formed things (*man of Baal*). The inharmonious result of worshiping Baal—looking upon the outer world as real and as the source of life, understanding, and existence, instead of seeing formless Spirit (Divine Mind) as the true God and as the one reality standing back of all manifestation—is suggested in *judgment of God.*

Ashdod, ăsh'-dŏd (Heb.)—*stronghold; fortress; castle; an oppressor; despoiler; ravager; theft.*

A Philistine city, a seat of Dagon worship, that was allotted to Judah, but a long time passed before the men of Judah really conquered the inhabitants of Ashdod (Josh. 15:47; I Sam. 5:1-7; II Chron. 26:6; also prophesied of in Isaiah, Jeremiah, Amos, Zephaniah, and Zechariah); called Azotus in Acts 8:40.

Meta. A strongly fortified aggregation of rebellious, oppressing, thieving, destroying thoughts in man's consciousness (*stronghold, fortress, an oppressor, despoiler, ravager, theft*). (See PHILISTINES and ASHDODITES.)

Ashdodites, ăsh'-dŏd-ītes (Heb.).

Inhabitants of Ashdod (Josh. 13:3; Neh. 4:7).

Meta. All-around thieves, or thieving thoughts, in man's consciousness. The state of consciousness that they represent utilizes the substance and energy of the organism that should be given over fully to building up and sustaining true thoughts and true ideas, which establish both soul and body in eternal life.

Asher (A. V., Luke 2:36, Aser), ăsh'-ēr (Heb.)—*straight; straightforward; prosperous; happiness; blessedness.*

Jacob's second son by Zilpah, Leah's handmaid, and the name of one of the twelve tribes of Israel (Gen. 35:26; Josh. 19:24). "And Zilpah Leah's handmaid bare Jacob a second son. And Leah said, Happy am I! for the daughters will call me happy: and she called his name

Asher" (Gen. 30:12, 13). In blessing his sons, Jacob said of Asher:

"Out of Asher his bread shall be fat,
    And he shall yield royal dainties" (Gen. 49:20). Moses said, in blessing the tribes of Israel (Deut. 33:24):

"Blessed be Asher with children;
    (above sons, margin)
Let him be acceptable unto his brethren,
And let him dip his foot in oil."

Meta. The meaning of the name and the blessings given to Asher point both to understanding and to substance, which are attendant upon uprightness of character. In Proverbs 3:13-18 we are told of the happiness that comes to one who gains wisdom and understanding, and the priceless value of these qualities. "Out of Asher his bread shall be fat, and he shall yield royal dainties," bespeaks the substance of true ideas—true spiritual bread, the word of Truth. Both Jacob and Moses, in blessing Asher, were surely prophesying of the time when man should learn that all his faculties and powers are spiritual, and not carnal and material. "Blessed be Asher above sons," refers to bringing forth spiritual ideas, for this is the fruitfulness that is above physical generation. Wisdom and true understanding, with the oil of Spirit (love), make the various states of consciousness in man harmonize: "Let him be acceptable unto his brethren, And let him dip his foot in oil" means that Spirit should be taken into all one's understanding, even into the consideration of outer conditions (understanding is represented by the foot). It is not true that spiritual understanding is for religion only and is impractical in one's everyday outer affairs and business relations. When man takes spiritual understanding conscientiously into all the affairs of life, he does far better than he ever has done theretofore. The fact that Leah said at the birth of Asher, "the daughters will call me happy," shows that the quality that is signified by Asher is established first in the soul.

Asherah, ă-shē'-răh (Heb.)—*straight; upright; a pillar; fortune; happiness.*

Asherah is thought to be the same as Ashtoreth. In many places in the Bible, Asherah seems to relate directly to the groves wherein Ashtoreth was worshiped, and to the images themselves. Asherah and Ashtoreth are usually mentioned in connection with Baal (Deut. 16:21; Judg. 6:25-28; II Kings 21:7).

Meta. Asherah suggests merely an outer form or show of honor, uprightness, and stability; it also suggests outer worldly pleasures and possessions as constituting true happiness and prosperity. (See ASHTORETH, BAAL, and ASHERIM.)

Asherim, ă-shē'-rĭm (Heb.)—*Asherahs; pillars; columns; groves; symbols of the goddess Asherah.*

Heathen, idolatrous goddesses or worship (Exod. 34:13; I Kings 14:23).

Meta. Human love with its animal propensities. Through Jehoshaphat's allegiance to Jehovah, the inner forces (Judah) are purified. "He took away . . . the Asherim out of Judah" (II Chron. 17:6).

Asherites, ăsh'-ĕr-ītes (Heb.).

Men belonging to the tribe of Asher (Judg. 1:32). They were descendants of Asher, one of the sons of Jacob.

Meta. Thoughts relating to uprightness, understanding, substance, and happiness. (See ASHER.)

Asheroth, ă-shē'-rŏth (Heb.)—*Asherahs; pillars; columns; groves; groves (a shrine of the goddess Asherah).*

The temples and *groves* of Asheroth were the sacred shrines where worship of the Phœnician Venus was practiced in licentious ways (Judg. 3:7; II Chron. 33:3). Eadie's Biblical Cyclopedia says: "Originally she was an Arcadian goddess, the mother and bride of Adonis. In Canaan, however, she became the mere reflection of the sun god, and was as such identified with the moon, the symbol in this case being the cow, whose horns resemble the crescent moon lying on its back."

Meta. Human love, with its animal propensities. It requires fine discrimination to distinguish between human love and divine love. In its origin all love is divine, but in passing through the lens of man's mind it is apparently broken into many colors. Yet, like the ray of white light, it ever remains pure. Man's province is to make love's manifestations in his life as pure as its origin. This requires painstaking discrimination and good judgment.

Ashhur (A. V., Ashur), ăsh'-hŭr (Heb.)—*blackness; black; aurora; the dawn; morning; break forth; become free; a freeman; successful.*

A Judahite, and the father or founder of Tekoa (I Chron. 2:24; 4:5).

Meta. Tekoa means *confirming, settling, securing, fixing (of tents)*, and represents the establishing, in the individual, of a more firm and abiding idea regarding his body. This is accomplished by Ashhur, founder of Tekoa, who typifies recognition that the entire man, spirit, soul, and body, is free, of spiritual origin, and not bound by the limitations of matter (*freeman*).

Ashima, ăsh'-ĭ-mȧ (Heb.)—*heaven; offense; transgression.* Ashima is doubtful in its etymology. It may be the Hebrew form of the Persian *asuman*, heaven; or it may be a Hebrew development of the two latter named definitions.

An idol worshiped by the people of Hamath whom Shalmaneser, king of Assyria, caused to settle in Samaria after he had carried the Israelites away captive (II Kings 17:30). This idol was in the form of a goat.

Meta. Hamath signifies confidence in material conditions rather than trust in God. This, with the meanings of Ashima, signifies that though the sense mind may promise much peace and harmony (*heaven*), yet resistance and strife (*goat*) are always the result of looking to the outer for guidance, understanding, protection, and salvation. Thoughts of the sense mind are an *offense* to Spirit because they lead man away from Truth.

Ashkelon, ăsh'-kĕ-lŏn (Heb.)—*migration; sojourn; stranger; weight; fire of infamy.*

A Philistine city, and a center of worship of the goddess Ashtoreth (Judg. 1:18; Zeph. 2:4).

Meta. The changeableness and uncertainty of man's sense beliefs and activities; also their foreignness to spiritual understanding (*migration, sojourn,* *stranger;* the Philistines refer to sense thoughts in man).

Sense thoughts and beliefs lead to sensuality, which becomes a heavy burden (*weight*) to the whole consciousness until it is overcome and is replaced by praise to God (tribe of Judah) and abundant increase of true substance and good. Man's every misuse of vital energy sets the currents of life into inharmonious action and starts a fire that burns out the nerve centers and consumes the substance of the organism (*fire of infamy*).

Ashkenaz (A. V., Jer. 51:27, Ashchenaz), ăsh'-kĕ-năz (Heb.)—*fire that spreads; latent fire; hidden fire.*

a Grandson of Japheth, Noah's son (Gen. 10:3). **b** A tribe descended from Ashkenaz, and a State in Armenia where these people lived. Ashkenaz was named with Ararat and Minni as kingdoms whose inhabitants the Lord was going to send against Babylon to overthrow it (Jer. 51:27).

Meta. Babylon signifies confusion. The *fire that spreads* to assist in doing away with the confused state of mind that Babylon represents is the life thought founded in Spirit (Ashkenaz). When this thought is taken up consciously by man it extends quickly to the whole consciousness and overthrows sense confusion and its inharmonies (Babylon). Fire is generally used in the Bible as a symbol of the destruction of evil and error. It stands for cleansing and purification. In its real, true essence, it is the fire of Spirit, or the divine energy, which never ceases its life-giving, purifying glow; but when its cleansing work is completed in man's mind and body, there is no more error to be consumed and it then manifests in purified man as his eternal life.

Ashnah, ăsh'-năh (Heb.)—*hard; strong; firm; robust; change; transform; shining; bright.*

Two different towns of Judah (Josh. 15:33, 43).

Meta. A *change* is continually taking place in man's organism. An adjustment in thought is constantly going on; cells of the body are each moment passing away to make room for new ones. When this change is brought about by praise and thanksgiving, founded in spiritual understanding and substance (the true Judah), a real transformation is the result; the individual grows more firmly fortified (*hard, strong, firm, robust, transform, shining, bright*) in life and Truth day by day. This is what Ashnah symbolizes.

Ashpenaz, ăsh'-pĕ-năz (Pers.)—*nose of the horse; horse's nose.*

Master of the eunuchs in the palace of Nebuchadnezzar, king of Babylon (Dan. 1:3).

Meta. Ashpenaz listened to the advice of Daniel (spiritual judgment) in regard to the kind of food that Daniel desired to eat, and was quick to note the good effects of the change of diet. The nose is the organ of smell, and smelling suggests a certain power to perceive, detect, or get an inkling of things. A horse always represents vitality, the vital forces. Ashpenaz (*horse's nose*), the master of the eunuchs, would signify a keen and quick perception of the importance of the vital forces in man, but without recognition of one's innate power and ability to utilize these forces to build up one's true spiritual being.

Ashtaroth, ăsh'-tă-rŏth (Heb. from Pers.)—*statues of Astarte; stars; riches; abundance; love; good fortune.* Ashtaroth is the plural form of Ashtoreth.

a Idols, mentioned with the Baalim, as being worshiped by the Israelites when they turned away from the true God (I Sam. 12:10). **b** A city of Og of Bashan that was given to the half tribe of Manasseh (Deut. 1:4; I Chron. 6:71).

Meta. After Joshua died the children of Israel "forsook Jehovah, and served Baal and the Ashtaroth. And the anger of Jehovah was kindled against Israel, and he delivered them into the hands of spoilers that despoiled them" (Judg. 2: 13, 14). If we would avoid the condition that overcame the children of Israel, we must daily transmute our creative power, as we become conscious of it, into harmony with our spiritual consciousness. If we follow this plan the goal of spiritual attainment is ever within our reach and becomes a great stabilizing influence in our life. After we discover our spiritual powers, however, if we use them in an ignorant, material way (the worship of Baal), we are swept back into darkness. The only light that is left us then is the flicker of purely intellectual perception, which previously has guided us. (Ashtaroth means *stars*. Ashtaroth is said to refer to the worship of the moon also. The moon shines by light borrowed from the sun, and in man represents purely intellectual understanding.)

Ashterathite, ăsh'-tĕ-răth-īte (Heb. fr. Pers.)—*of Ashtaroth.*

One whose home was in the city of Ashtaroth (I Chron. 11:44).

Meta. A thought pertaining to intellectual perception devoid of spiritual understanding. (See ASHTAROTH.)

Ashteroth–karnaim, ăsh'-tĕ-rŏth–kär-nā'-ĭm (Heb.)—*horned Ashteroth; Astarte of the two horns; Ashteroth of two peaks.*

A city of Bashan (Gen. 14:5), the home of the Rephaim, or giants. Og, king of Bashan, was the last of these giants to be overcome.

Meta. A state of consciousness in man that attributes double honor, authority, exaltation, and power to purely intellectual understanding and capacity. In this state of thought man does not recognize that God instead of intellect is the source of intelligence. The intellect borrows all its real light from Spirit, just as the moon, which has no light of its own, reflects light from the sun. (Ashteroth refers to the moon, or intellect, while karnaim—*two horns or peaks*—suggests exaltation and power.)

Ashtoreth, ăsh'-tŏ-rĕth (Heb. fr. Pers.)—*the goddess Astarte; a star; riches; abundance; love; good fortune.*

The principal Phœnician or Sidonian goddess (I Kings 11:5).

Meta. Inasmuch as Ashtoreth relates to the moon and stars, it seems to refer to the rule of the intellect instead of the rule of Spirit. Since lustful practices formed the chief part of her worship, Ashtoreth also stands for sensuality, which man in carnal mind cultivates in the belief that it is essential to his well-being, instead of lifting his thoughts and acts to the Christ standard of purity. (See ASHERIM, ASHEROTH, ASHTAROTH, and ASHERAH.)

Ashurites, ăsh'-ŭr-ītes (Heb.)—*belonging to Ashhur* or *Ashur*.

A people who occupied the district of the plain of Esdraelon. They are named among those over whom Abner set Ishbosheth, son of Saul, as king (II Sam. 2:9); they were descendants of Ashur, no doubt.

Meta. Thoughts brought forth by the state of mind that Ashhur represents. (See ASHHUR.)

Ashvath, ăsh'-văth (Heb.)—*forged; labored; smoothed; wrought; bright; polished; shining; thinking; purposing.*

Son of Japhlet and descendant of Asher, Jacob's son (I Chron. 7:33).

Meta. Ashvath suggests the process by which man brings the wholeness and perfection of Spirit into expression in his mind, body, and affairs. Realization and manifestation of completeness are not accomplished in an instant, nor by one great faith step. Moment by moment, day after day, and year after year one must work patiently, faithfully, and understandingly toward the goal of Christlikeness. This perfecting work is emphasized in the meaning of Ashvath (*forged, labored, wrought, smoothed; polished, bright, shining, thinking, purposing*); also in many Bible texts, such as Malachi 3:1-3; Philippians 3:12-14; I Corinthians 9:24, 25, and Isaiah 28:10. "But the path of the righteous is as the dawning light,

That shineth more and more unto the perfect day."

(Prov. 4:18.)

Asia (in A. V., Rom. 16:5, Achaia), ā'-si̯-à (Lat. from Gk.)—*unique continent; unique land; central land; Orient; the East; aurora.*

The country of Asia Minor (Acts 19:10).

Meta. In Acts 16:6 Asia refers to a state of consciousness impregnated by old, decayed, worn-out, material ideas that should have been left behind long ago by the one who would progress spiritually.

The foregoing symbology no doubt enters into the metaphysical interpretation of Asia as given in other texts in the Bible. As the name stands for itself, however, in its reference simply to the Eastern Hemisphere, the meanings, *unique continent, unique land, central land, Orient, the East, aurora,* bring out a significance that should not be overlooked. The East always refers to the within, the hidden, the spiritual, and *aurora* means "rise, dawn, beginning." These meanings, coupled with the fact that Palestine is in Asia and that Asia is supposed to be the site of the Garden of Eden and the birthplace of man, all point to the within, to the spiritual in man, to the Source of all.

All religions had their first impetus in Asia. Asia therefore must signify the inner, the spiritual, in individual consciousness, wherein lay the beginning of man's conscious existence, and wherein lies the dawn, or rise, of the light and wisdom of his new day of spiritual understanding and realization.

Asiarchs, ā'-si-ärchs̟ (Lat.)—*chief of Asia.*

Men in the Roman province of Asia who were chosen to preside over the religious ceremonies that were held in honor of their gods and of the Roman emperor (Acts 19:31). These ceremonies were in the nature of very formal sacred games and festivals that took place in the theater; their expense was borne by the Asiarchs. An Asiarch held office for one year only.

Meta. A ruling tendency in man to pay homage to power, whether it is expressed by some individual who has acquired great fame and position and makes a great show of it (the Roman emperor), or whether it is displayed by nature and the elements (the gods of the Romans and of the unenlightened countries ruled by them). Some of the Asiarchs were friends of Paul's. The tendency in man that they represent is quick to recognize and respect anything that is out of the ordinary in the way of power, ability, or character.

Asiel, ă'-sĭ-ĕl (Heb.)—*creation of God; made by God; God is doer.*

A Simeonite, a great-grandparent of Jehu (I Chron. 4:35).

Meta. The inner revelation that man is in reality spiritual and came forth from God (*creation of God; made by God; God is doer; emanation of God*). Simeon means "hearing" and signifies the state of mind that listens and is obedient. By listening to God in the silence and heeding the voice of Spirit within him, man is led into the knowledge that he is truly spiritual, that he has his origin in God and is an expression of the divine.

Asnah, ăs'-năh (Heb.)—*bramble; dweller in the thorn bush; thorn bush.*

A man whose children belonged to the Nethinim, who came up from the captivity with Zerubbabel (Ezra 2:50). The Nethinim were servants in the Temple. They were set apart to wait on the priests and to do the menial work in the Temple and in the Temple worship. After their return from the captivity their position was regarded as more honorable than it had been before.

Meta. The belief in servitude to God; a belief that, when it dominates the mind of a Christian, makes him really a slave. The life of such a one is full of trials and harassing experiences and hard places (*bramble, thorn bush, dweller in the thorn bush*). His path is thorny indeed, until he recognizes that he is a son of God, free-born; then he enters into the joy and the freedom of sonship. His Christian life is no longer a burden, nor is his service given from the standpoint of duty. He lovingly and happily expresses his spiritual faculties and powers in serving God and his fellow men; even the most lowly service is a joy to him.

Aspatha, ăs-pā'-thȧ (Heb. from Pers.) —*horse; horse-given.*

One of the ten sons of Haman, the Jews' enemy. He was put to death by the Jews (Esth. 9:7, 10).

Meta. Aspatha refers to the vital forces in man (horses always relate to vitality). Being of an adverse consciousness (Aspatha was descended from Agag, meaning adversary) he symbolizes the life activities swayed or influenced adversely by carnal beliefs and desires.

Asriel (A. V., I Chron. 7:14, Ashriel), ăs'-rĭ-ĕl (Heb.)—*joining of God; God has bound together; vow of God.*

Son of Gilead, and great-grandson of Manasseh and his concubine the Aramitess (Num. 26:31).

Meta. A unifying thought in consciousness (*joining of God*); man's awakening to the truth that there can be no real understanding, whether intellectual or otherwise, apart from God. (Manasseh relates to the understanding in its negative aspect, and Aram means the same as Syria, which refers to the intellect in man.) When man consciously unifies his understanding faculty with Divine Mind, the one source of all intelligence, he enters into a realization of his oneness with Spirit; he also realizes the vastness and sureness of the divine promises to man, or the divine operation in man (*God has bound together, vow of God*).

Asshur, ăssh'-ŭr (Heb.)—*a step; level ongoing; straightforward; observation of laws; harmonious; gracious; happy; a level place; a plain; a steppe; mighty one; a hero.*

a Son of Shem (Gen. 10:22). **b** The country of Assyria (Num. 24:22; Ezek. 27:23). (See ASSYRIA.)

Meta. The intellectual, or mental reasoning, plane in man (Assyria) in its progress toward the spiritual, or, in its upliftment and union with true spiritual understanding (*a step, level ongoing, straightforward, observation of laws,* and so on). In Isaiah 19:23-25 we read that Egypt, Assyria, and Israel shall all worship the true God together and shall be a blessing in the midst of the earth. These three represent the trinity in man —body, soul or mental realm, and spirit —all unified in Truth and redeemed so as to express spiritually for the good of the entire man. Egypt refers to the body; Assyria to the mental realm or intellect, and Israel to the spirit.

Asshurim, ăs-shu'-rĭm (Heb.)— *mighty ones; dwellers of the plain; liers in wait.*

Son of Dedan, and great-grandson of Abraham (Gen. 25:3).

Meta. Abraham represents the faith (the power of the mind to bring forth ideas into unlimited expression) that reproduces on the sense-mind plane as well as in spirit. Abraham's seed was counted through Isaac, the son of Sarah; Isaac represents divine sonship. But Abraham had seven sons who had been begotten in personal consciousness. They pertain to the body in its animal thought and seeming. The outer man must be sustained as he is until such time as the inner man shall have grown strong enough in consciousness to change the outer into spiritual expression and manifestation. Asshurim was descended from Abraham in the outer personal way. He refers to the reasoning sense side of this power of faith to reproduce ideas, which Abraham represents. The reasoning of the intellect, guided by the senses, may seem almost invincible at times (*mighty ones*), but it does not endure. (Nothing is really known of Asshurim's descendants, although his father, Dedan, is supposed to have been the founder of Idumean or Arabian tribes.) Only spiritual ideas and their manifestations are truly strong, powerful, and abiding.

Assir, ăs'-sĭr (Heb.)—*captive; prisoner.*

A Levite, son of Korah (Exod. 6:24). Korah was one of those who headed the rebellion against Moses and Aaron. These malcontents were not willing to acknowledge the positions of Moses and Aaron as above their own, but thought that they could fill the places of leadership and high-priesthood just as rightly and as capably as did those whom God had chosen for these places (Num. 16). Korah and the others who rebelled with him, with their families, were destroyed by the earth's opening beneath them and swallowing them.

Meta. Moses represents the divine law and Aaron represents the executive power of divine law. Korah springs from love (Levi), as do Moses and Aaron, but Korah means *bald, ice.* This infers the opposite of love—a state in which one is cold and unproductive of life and good

because of unwillingness to be guided in one's love faculty by the law of God. This is love expressing in personality, and it brings forth Assir (*captive, prisoner*), who represents bondage, generation, sorrow, and death. Love in its divine purity is the key to life, harmony, and peace, but when love is exercised in the selfishness of the personal consciousness it leads one into bondage and makes one a *prisoner* to sense. Thus one becomes swallowed up in the earthly life, in sensuality and materiality.

Assos (also called Apollonia), ăs'-sŏs (Gk.)—*approaching.*

A Roman town and seaport in Mysia, Asia, not far from Troas and Mitylene (Acts 20:13).

Meta. An intellectual state of consciousness that is willing to examine into the truth (Apollonia), and is therefore drawing near to (*approaching*) an understanding of it.

Assyria (A. V., in some places Assur), ăs-sўr'-ĭ-à (Gk., Assyria; Heb., Asshur)—*country of Asshur.* The definitions are the same as those for Asshur.

At one time a very mighty empire. It was overthrown by the Babylonians and Medes about 600 B. C., after it had been in existence for some 1,200 years. Nineveh was the capital of ancient Assyria. At the time of its greatest power, Assyria included many of the countries that we read about in the Bible: Babylonia, Media, Chaldea, Armenia, Syria, Palestine, Phœnicia, Idumea, and others, besides Assyria proper (Gen. 25:18; II Kings 17:3-6; Zeph. 2:13).

Meta. The reasonings, philosophical and psychical, that do not recognize the spiritual Head of the universe, but are based upon sense observation, upon the formed instead of the formless. Such thoughts are destructive and undisciplined. If man keeps his attention fixed on Spirit he is protected from the materialism that is constantly encroaching upon his consciousness; but if he worships the mysterious and the occult, or if he reasons wholly from the appearances of the senses or outer world, he defeats the protective action of the higher law and falls into the hands of the Assyrians. To pay tribute to the Assyrians (II Kings 15:19, 20) is to make concessions to the unregenerate, material realm of consciousness in us that they represent. When spiritual understanding predominates in one, the mental realm that Assyria signifies is redeemed. (See ASSHUR.)

Asyncritus, ă-sўn'-erĭ-tŭs (Lat. from Gk.)—*unlike; incomparable.*

A Christian friend of Paul's at Rome (Rom. 16:14).

Meta. The understanding that spiritual Truth is so superior to worldly wisdom as to be beyond comparison with it (*unlike, incomparable*).

Atad, ā'-tăd (Heb.)—*bramble; thorn bush; a thorn.*

At the threshing floor of Atad, Joseph and his brethren mourned seven days for their father Jacob, when they were on their way to bury his body (Gen. 50:10). (See ABEL–MIZRAIM.)

Meta. A threshing floor infers a place of judgment or separation, a letting go of that which it is no longer needful to express in consciousness. Atad (*bramble, thorn bush, a thorn*) represents the belief that vexations trials, and sorrows are real. It is that unredeemed thought or belief in man which causes him to experience deep grief and tribulation in letting go of the personal hold on old ideas and objects that are due to be released from his mind and affairs. This unredeemed belief sees and dwells on the trial phase of the process rather than the blessing side of it. If entertained it makes one's path very thorny.

Atarah, ăt'-ă-răh (Heb.)—*crown; diadem; head ornament.*

Wife of Jerahmeel, a man of Judah, and mother of Onam (I Chron. 2:26).

Meta. When one learns to know God as a loving, merciful, kind, compassionate Father, Husband, and Friend (Jerahmeel, husband of Atarah, means *whom God loveth, on whom God hath mercy* or *compassion*), not as an angry and revengeful deity, great rejoicing crowns the soul (*crown, diadem, head ornament*) and adorns the whole consciousness of the individual. This rejoicing makes one strong (Onam *strong*). "The joy of

Jehovah is your strength" (Neh. 8:10).

Ataroth, ăt'-ă-rŏth (Heb.)—*crowns.*

The name of several towns that belonged to different Israelitish tribes (Josh. 16:2, 7). Some of these towns were in Palestine, and at least one of them was on the other side of the Jordan. This town was one of the cities that were given to Gad and Reuben on condition that they should send all their fighting men into Canaan with the other tribes of Israel to help drive out the enemies there. The land of Jazer, or Gilead, where this city of Ataroth was located, was "a place for cattle," and the children of Reuben and Gad had a great many cattle (Num. 32:3, 34).

Meta. Crowns symbolize victory, reward, authority, honor. Ataroth (*crowns*) here is representative of victory or dominion over, and intelligent direction of, animal strength (cattle) in individual consciousness; also of the reward that follows this victory, which is an increase of spiritual strength and power. Each individual, as he learns to express and to direct aright the inner forces of his being, becomes clothed with righteousness and is given a crown of life; this is in store for all persons who love and serve God.

The other towns named Ataroth also typify dominion gained over various phases of the earth-life or sense reasonings, and the spiritual uplift and good that are experienced thereby.

Ataroth–addar, ăt'-ă-rŏth–ăd'-där (Heb.)—*crowns of addar.*

A town on the eastern border of Ephraim (Josh. 16:5); some think that it is the same town as the Ataroth of Joshua 16:2, 7.

Meta. See ATAROTH and ADDAR.

Ater, ā'-tĕr (Heb.)—*bound; shut up; dumb; tongue-tied; impeded; left-handed.*

a and b The name of the heads of two Israelitish families who returned from the Babylonian captivity (Ezra 2:16, 42). c A man by this name joined Nehemiah in sealing the covenant (Neh. 10:17).

Meta. A binding, limiting, suppressing thought, or group of thoughts, in individual consciousness (*bound, shut up, dumb, tongue-tied, impeded, left-handed*). These thought families belong to the religious phase of man's being (they are Israelites), but because of their limiting nature they have entered into Babylon (confusion). They aspire to Truth, however, and are brought back to their own land. These limiting beliefs may begin in our mental realm by seeking to oppress and cast out that which appears to be evil; if binding thoughts are allowed to increase, sooner or later they will react on the spiritual and will bring limitation, confusion, and bondage to our true thoughts also, even though they may be directed against apparent error. Our aim in overcoming must not be to oppress, bind, and silence that which seems to be evil; it must be to give righteous expression to the forces that are back of these apparent evils. That end having been accomplished, the error manifestations will drop away of themselves.

Athach, ā'-thăch (Heb.)—*lodging; inn; stopping place.*

A place in Judah "where David himself and his men were wont to haunt" (I Sam. 30:30, 31). It was one of the places to which David sent a portion of the spoil that he had seized from the Amalekites after defeating them and regaining what they had taken from him and his friends at Ziklag.

Meta. A fixed state of consciousness, or aggregation of thoughts of abidingness in Truth and of trust in the great Source of all, in the inner life forces of the subconscious in man. Love (David) often finds there a temporary abode (*lodging, inn, stopping place*) while hiding from the personal will (Saul). The personal will (Saul) would kill love (David), the rightful ruling power in man, and so love, until it becomes strong enough in consciousness to take that which is rightfully its own, and until the outer opposition of the personal will (Saul) is removed, must often retire to the hidden strongholds of the subjective consciousness. But while it is there it is not idle; much overcoming is being done that is not apparent at first to the outer man.

Athaiah, ăth-ă-ī'-ăh (Heb.)—*created of Jah; whom Jehovah made; time of Jah; Jehovah's opportunity.*

A prince of Judah who lived in Jerusalem after the return from the Babylonian captivity (Neh. 11:4).

Meta. The attitude of mind in which man acknowledges Jehovah as the source of his existence (*created of Jah, whom Jehovah made*). This attitude of mind is trusting, and it believes in the working of the divine law (*time of Jah, Jehovah's opportunity*). Jehovah's time is measured by steps in overcoming in consciousness, by the orderly working out of the law of God; it has nothing to do with days and years as man reckons time.

Athaliah, ăth-ă-lī'-ăh (Heb.)—*Jehovah suspends; Jah constrains; distress of Jehovah; affliction of Jah; Jehovah is exalted.*

a Daughter of Ahab and granddaughter of Omri, kings of Israel. She became the wife of Jehoram and mother of Ahaziah, kings of Judah (II Chron. 22:2-4). **b** Two Israelitish men (I Chron. 8:26; Ezra 8:7).

Meta. The feminine or love nature in man wholly given to selfishness. This is the *distress of Jehovah.* Its dominant ambition is to rule, and it destroys everything that stands in the way of its attaining this ambition (II Kings 11:1-16). The selfishness of Athaliah was engendered through love for her son, and when he was slain it centered upon self. A selfish affection for children and a human ambition for them often bring about a separation of the soul from the higher law, and a consequent elimination of the unlawful condition from consciousness, as is symbolized in the overthrow of Athaliah and her removal from the throne by death. After selfish love has ruled in the consciousness for a time, the higher thoughts bring their forces to bear and put it out.

Although selfish ambition causes discord for a season, there are forces at work in man that restore the rightful king, represented by Joash (*Jehovah supports*). Then the *distress of Jehovah* (Athaliah, love dominated wholly by personal selfishness) is erased from consciousness; Athaliah was allowed to pass out by the way that the horses came in, and was then slain. This means that affectional selfishness is to be relegated to the rear—where the vital or animal forces originate—and then eliminated. It is a fact of experience among metaphysicians that when a selfish thought is broken up in consciousness and allowed to pass away there is unusual activity in the functions of elimination—the bowels and the kidneys. This demonstrates that thoughts are things and that they can be broken up and passed out of the system (house) through this back door, in their material symbols (refuse matter).

The meaning, *Jehovah is exalted,* refers particularly to the two men named Athaliah. However, the working of the law in a seemingly adverse way is seen in the life of the one whose descendants returned from the captivity in Babylon, in that the thought for which he stands, spiritual might, is taken captive and utilized, or wasted, by the outer mortal phase of mind in man (Babylon). This thought, however, being of spiritual origin, is the forerunner of an idea of divine helpfulness, which takes its rightful place in the consciousness (Athaliah's son Jeshaiah, meaning *Jah is help,* was delivered from Babylon and returned to Jerusalem). The love and power that are symbolized by Athaliah, queen of Judah, are divine too; but in this case they are used for selfish ends entirely, to their final destruction, or rather to the destruction of the selfish ruling thought that dominates them.

Atharim, ăth′-ă-rĭm (Heb.)—*regions; places.* "By the way of Atharim" is translated "by the way of the spies," in the Authorized Version. Doubtless the place was infested with spies, hence that manner of translation. The correct rendering, however, is that of the American Standard Version, "by the way of Atharim."

A place in the southern part of Palestine that was on the route by which the Israelites made their way from Egypt to the land of Canaan (Num. 21:1). When the Canaanitish king of Arad ("who dwelt in the South") learned that the Israelites were coming that way he fought against them and took some of them captive.

Meta. "By the way of Atharim" refers to the indefinite, little known *regions* or realms of the subconsciousness ("the South") in man. It refers especially to the parts relating to the rudimentary life forces (Canaanites) in the subconscious phase of man's being.

Athens, ăth′-ĕns (Gk.)—*city of Athene* (named after the goddess Athene, corresponding to the Latin Minerva); *virtue; firmness; strength.* A satisfactory meaning for Athene has never been developed. Her prototype in Minerva gives a clew that the virtue represented by Athene has to do with Spirit, mind, intellect, thought, and so forth.

Capital of Greece, and a very celebrated city (Acts 17:16). It was the birthplace of Plato, and was widely noted for its citizens' intellectual attainments.

Meta. The intellectual center in man. Paul's going from Athens to Corinth (Acts 18:1) signifies the withdrawal of the power of the divine word from the intellectual center (Athens) to the love center (Corinth).

Acts 17:16-31 shows in symbols how the word of Truth (Paul) commends the intellect's attempts at religious worship, yet proclaims its shortcomings. The intellectual concept of God is always relative. The Athenians were purely intellectual; the more than three thousand images and statues of gods and of demigods or heroes in the city testified to their material concepts of the Deity. Such conceptions are typical of the mind that is not enlightened as to the true character of God. Yet, notwithstanding all these concrete concepts of God, there is a yearning to know the unrevealed Spirit, and the mind is ever reaching out for a fuller realization of its source. This yearning is symbolized by the altar with the inscription, "To an Unknown God."

Paul did not call the Athenians ignorant; he said to them: "What therefore ye worship in ignorance (not understanding its name, attributes, and nature), this I set forth unto you." When Truth has been declared and has been received by the intellect, a new state of consciousness is set up. A day, or open state of mind, has been established. When Truth becomes active in our mind, the seed germ of our being, which is the Christ of God, is resurrected; then we have within us the assurance that this uplift is for the whole of our being—spirit, soul, and body—"all men," "all things," "all life." (See verses 24, 25, 26, 31.)

The thoughts of the intellect do not all fall into line with Truth at once; some mock, and others defer the acceptance to another time. But there are the elect few that form the nucleus of a strong church—a new state of consciousness where spiritual thoughts gather.

Athlai, ăth′-lāi (Heb.)—contracted form of Athaliah. (See ATHALIAH for definitions.)

An Israelite who had returned from the Babylonian captivity and had taken a foreign wife. He gave up this wife later, in response to Ezra's command (Ezra 10:28).

Meta. A thought of spiritual exaltation, uplift. The history of Athlai reveals how the substance and energy of spiritual thought can be given over to sense affection (a foreign wife). Then through the activity of divine law they are restored to constructive use. (Athlai gave up his foreign wife, at the command of Ezra, and returned to the true worship of God.)

The law of Being is always working for man's ultimate good, though in the process, because of his ignorance and disobedience, man sometimes passes through bitter experiences. Then he thinks that God afflicts him (*affliction of Jah*), when the truth of the matter is that he has brought his troubles upon himself by living out of harmony with, and often in direct opposition to, the law of existence—God's law. Thus the very law that was intended to give life and peace is an afflicting and disintegrating power to those who work against it.

atonement, the.

Meta. By reading the letter of the Bible and accepting it as authority, men have formed erroneous ideas regarding the atonement. The Spirit of truth alone can reveal the true meaning of Jesus Christ's mission and work. The atonement as it has been understood by Christian people in the past has not taken sin, suffering, and death from the world; therefore it must be that their understanding has fallen short of the Truth. Spiritual understanding of the atonement shows the way to deliverance from sin and consequently from all the effects of sin. In proportion as people understand and have faith in Jesus Christ as their actual Savior from sin, they are set free from appetite, passion, jealousy, prejudice, and all selfishness; wholeness of mind and body is the result. The ultimate of this knowledge and of daily practice in overcoming (even as Jesus Himself overcame) will be a new race that will demonstrate eternal life—the lifting up of the whole man—spirit, soul, and body—into the Christ consciousness of oneness with the Father. By means of the atonement—reconciliation, or at-one-ment—that Jesus Christ reëstablished between God and man, we can regain our original estate as sons of God, here upon earth. "Ye therefore shall be perfect, as your heavenly Father is perfect" (Matt. 5:48).

"To comprehend the atonement requires a deeper insight into creative processes than the average man and the average woman have attained; not because they lack the ability to understand, but because they have submerged their thinking power in a grosser thought stratum. So only those who study Being from the standpoint of pure mind can come into an understanding of the atonement and the part that Jesus played in opening the way for humanity to enter into the glory that was theirs before the world was formed." (See the tract, "Jesus Christ's Atonement," by Charles Fillmore.)

Atroth–beth–joab (A. V., Ataroth, the house of Joab), ăt′-rŏth-bĕth-jō′-ăb (Heb.)—*crowns of the house of Jehovah-father.* Atroth and Ataroth are the same word, meaning *crowns; head ornaments.* (See ATAROTH.)

Named among the descendants of Caleb

(I Chron. 2:54).

Meta. Atroth, or Ataroth, means *crowns,* and beth means *house;* therefore Atroth–beth–joab means *crowns of the house of Joab.* Joab (*Jehovah is father*) led David's army that defeated and slew Absalom. Joab represents the executive power of love—the pivotal center within man that preserves the unity and integrity of soul and body—the individual will acknowledging Jehovah God as its source and inspiration. Atroth–beth–joab signifies the honor and glory (*crowns*) that belong to the substance-clothed ideas (*house*) that are generated in consciousness by that for which Joab stands; also the victory, the dominion, and the results of good that are realized by the individual who entertains and sustains these ideas (victory, dominion, and reward are other symbolic meanings of a *crown*).

Atroth–shophan (A. V., Atroth, Shophan), ăt′-rŏth–shō′-phăn (Heb.)—Shophan: *covered; concealed; hidden* (especially *under ground*); *crafty; cunning.* Atroth: *crowns.* Atroth–shophan: *crowns of craftiness.*

A city on the east of Jordan that was given to the tribe of Gad after the Amorites had been defeated (Num. 32:35); the Gadites fortified it and made it a fold for sheep.

Meta. The subtle, underhanded, deceitful way by which the thoughts, beliefs, and activities that are symbolized by the Amorites (see AMORITES) work to retain their hold in man's consciousness and life. But Atroph–shophan, after the Israelitish conquest of the Amorites, was given over to the Israelitish tribe of Gad (*fortune, seer*), who fortified it and made it a fold for sheep. Thus this thought center that Atroth–shophan signifies is cleansed by truer, purer, more understanding, and more honorable intents and becomes a shelter for pure, natural, obedient life thoughts and forces (a fold for sheep).

Attai, ăt′-tāi (Heb.)—*timely; opportune; seasonable; fit; in time; ready; my time.*

The name of three different Israelitish men (I Chron. 2:35; 12:11; II Chron. 11:20).

Meta. Attai symbolizes what the meanings of the name infer—that there is an *opportune* or *seasonable* time for all fruition of thought. This time has no reference to man's outer way of counting time in minutes, hours, days, and so forth. It refers to certain steps in consciousness that must be taken in order to bring about the expression and demonstration of that which is being held in mind. The time is always *ready;* the hour of fulfillment is in the keeping of the individual himself (*my time*), since demonstrations are always made just as soon as the necessary conditions are met by the individual.

Attalia, ăt-tă-lī′-à (Gk.)—*that increases.*

A seaport town in Pamphylia (Acts 14:25).

Meta. Pamphylia means *mixture of nations* and signifies mixed thoughts and states of consciousness. Attalia represents an aggregation of thoughts in the outer consciousness, on the border of the sea of mortal thought. This aggregation of thoughts pertains to increase, growth, enlargement, multiplication (*that increases*). Under the dominion of the carnal mind the increase is in materiality, sense, and their consequent limitations. But the going of Paul and Barnabas (the word of Truth, and inspiration) to Attalia denotes an increase of action in that which is spiritual.

Augustus, äu-gŭs′-tŭs (Lat.)—*sacred; kingly; venerable; augmented.*

Part of a title taken by the Roman emperor next after Julius Cæsar (Luke 2:1); he was called Augustus Cæsar, or Cæsar Augustus. He was emperor of Rome at the time of the birth of Jesus Christ. At that time the Roman empire extended over the greater part of the then known world.

Meta. The worship of the will ruling in selfishness and directed by human reason (*sacred, kingly, venerable;* a Roman emperor). When one is in this state of consciousness the intellect is his god, and he believes that his good can be increased (*augmented*) and that his dominion, power, and honor can be extended through his setting up the sense consciousness. He proclaims self as the rightful ruler in his entire being, instead of denying self and acknowledging God (Divine Mind) as the one source of all authority and of all existence. (See CÆSAR.)

Aven, ā'-vĕn (Heb.)—*vanity; nothingness; trouble; calamity; evil; debilitated; fruitless.*

a The "valley of Aven," mentioned in Amos 1:5, is a plain or valley the identity of which has not been established. The Aven of Hosea 10:8 is no doubt the Beth-aven of Hosea 4:15, and both probably refer to the valley of Aven, or Baal, where the sun was worshiped in a great temple that was built there for that purpose. This "valley of Aven" is thought to be the same as the "Plain of Cœle-Syria," which means much in helping to determine its metaphysical import, since Syria pertains to the intellect in man under the rule of sense rather than under spiritual direction. **b** In Ezekiel 30:17 Aven refers to the city of On, city of the sun, in Egypt.

Meta. The *nothingness* and *vanity,* or vainness, of Baal worship. (See BAAL.) When man thinks that the intellect is the source of true understanding, he believes the outer world of phenomena to be real in itself. He forms his conclusions from appearances, and he builds up the idea that he is ruled over by the sun and the planets. He thinks that circumstances and conditions master him; thus he becomes a slave to appearances and to inharmony (*trouble, calamity, evil*), and becomes weak and inefficient (*debilitated, fruitless*) instead of exercising the dominion over all things that was given him in the beginning. When his eyes become opened to spiritual Truth he learns the emptiness of his former belief; he then realizes the nothingness of error seemings, and as he puts his trust in the spiritual reality that is at the back of all manifestation he regains his rightful dominion and inheritance as a son of God.

Avith, ā'-vĭth (Heb.)—*ruins; overthrown; overturned; perverted; perverse.* A city of Hadad, an Edomitish king

(Gen. 36:35).

Meta. The perverted, corruptible, and destructive character (*ruins, overthrown, overturned, perverted, perverse*) of a line of thought that helps to make up and rule the body consciousness in man before man's natural religious tendencies, founded in Spirit, come into any appreciable degree of influence or dominion within him ("before there reigned any king over the children of Israel.")

Edom refers to the body and to the external conditions of life. The rule of the outer or sense man is opposed to Spirit and to the real good of the individual; it brings about a ruinous situation in the body, eventually even its disintegration, unless a higher impulse sets into action the power of Spirit to redeem and preserve the whole man.

Since in thought man wandered away from God, he has seemed always to be conscious first of the body, the outer formed phase of himself. He has to grow into consciousness of the spiritual. "That is not first which is spiritual, but that which is natural; then that which is spiritual" (I Cor. 15:46). This seems to be true of man now, but it was not so in the beginning, since the inner spiritual man made in God's image and likeness was created first, and the outer consciousness and body came into existence later.

Avva (A. V., Ava), ăv'-vȧ (Heb.)—*ruin; overthrown; overturned; perverted; perverse; iniquity.*

A small country under Assyrian rule. After the Assyrian king had conquered Hoshea, king of Israel, and had carried the Israelites as captives into Assyria he took men from Avva to settle in Samaria (II Kings 17:24).

Meta. The unrighteousness (*iniquity*) that works in the consciousness of man when he allows intellectual reasonings based upon sense observation (Assyrians) to direct his will and to rule in his life. They take away his sense of safety (Hoshea, king of Israel). They take away his true thoughts founded in Spirit (the Israelites) and in place of them put erroneous ideas that are perverted and devastating (people of Avva

—ruin, perverse, overturned, overthrown) because they are founded upon a belief in evil instead of being founded upon faith in the living God, good.

Avvim (A. V., Avim, Avims, Avites), ăv'-vĭm (Heb.)—*the Avites; ruins; perversions; iniquities.*

a A rude, uncultivated people descended from Canaan, a people who for a long while lived in a portion of Palestine (Deut. 2:23; Josh. 13:3). **b** A city of Benjamin (Josh. 18:23). **c** The people that the king of Assyria sent from Avva to live in Samaria in place of the Israelites, whom he had taken away (II Kings 17:31, Avvites).

Meta. The most primitive, unenlightened ideas of the carnal man regarding his life forces and functions. These ideas cause man to look upon himself as purely physical and to place himself on a plane with animals—the dog and the ass, symbolized by the gods Nibhaz and Tartak, whose worship the Avvim, or Avvites, introduced into Samaria (II Kings 17:31). It is needless to point out that such thoughts (people) are very erroneous in their character (*iniquities, perversions*) and are decidedly inimical (*ruins*) to the spiritual good of the individual. They work against Truth, which alone can set man free from materiality and bring him into his true birthright of abiding life and good.

Azaliah, ăz-ă-lī'-ăh (Heb.)—*Jehovah reserves; whom Jah has separated; beside Jehovah; Jah is noble.*

Father of Shaphan, the scribe, whom Josiah, king of Judah, sent to help repair the house of God (II Chron. 34:8).

Meta. A thought of consecration and of nearness to that which Jehovah implies (*Jehovah reserves, whom Jah has separated, beside Jehovah, Jah is noble*). This thought works very strongly in our consciousness and our organism when loyalty to Truth (Josiah) is dominating our thoughts and we are seeking earnestly to make at-one-ment with God. (See JOSIAH.)

Azaniah, ăz-ă-nī'-ăh (Heb.)—*Jehovah hears; whom Jehovah hears; hearing Jah; hearing the Lord.*

Father of Jeshua, a Levite (Neh. 10:9).

Meta. A natural religious tendency in man that is receptive and obedient to spiritual Truth and guidance (*hearing Jah, hearing the Lord*). This spirit of receptivity and obedience to Jehovah and the divine law is recognized by the true I AM in consciousness, the Christ, or Jehovah (*whom Jehovah hears*); and from it springs a perception of salvation (Jeshua, a form of Joshua, and meaning *savior, Jehovah is help,* or *salvation*).

Azarel (A. V., Azareel and Azarael), ăz'-är-ĕl (Heb.)—*help of God; whom God succors; God hath helped.*

The name of several Israelitish men (I Chron. 12:6; 25:18; 27:22; Ezra 10:41; Neh. 12:36).

Meta. The attitude of mind in which the would-be overcomer recognizes and acknowledges God, Spirit, as his strength and his assistance in every kind of need (*whom God succors*).

Azariah, ăz-ă-rī'-ăh (Heb.)—*help of Jehovah; whom Jah succors; whom Jehovah hath helped; whom Jehovah aids.*

Twenty-eight different persons of this name are mentioned in the Old Testament. In II Kings 15:1, Uzziah, king of Judah, see margin.

Meta. That in man which realizes Jehovah as a very present and efficient deliverer and help at all times, whatever the need may be (*help of Jehovah, whom Jah succors, whom Jehovah aids*). In II Chronicles 26:8-21 Azariah signifies the spiritual quality of strength. (See UZZIAH.) In II Chronicles 31:13 the clause, "and Azariah the ruler of the house of God," refers to the I AM dominion within man, the Christ.

Azaz, ā'-zăz (Heb.)—*strong; mighty; powerful.*

An Israelite of the tribe of Reuben (I Chron. 5:8).

Meta. A realization and expression of strength and power (*strong, mighty, powerful*). Strength and power are of spiritual origin. They can, however, be exercised either constructively or destructively, according to whether the thought held over them by the individual is spiritual or purely material and physical.

Azazel, ă-zā'-zĕl (Heb.)—*removal; scapegoat; a goat for going away.*

"And Aaron . . . shall take the two goats, and set them before Jehovah at the door of the tent of meeting. And Aaron shall cast lots upon the two goats; one lot for Jehovah, and the other lot for Azazel. And Aaron shall present the goat upon which the lot fell for Jehovah, and offer him for a sin-offering. But the goat, on which the lot fell for Azazel, shall be set alive before Jehovah, to make atonement for him, to send him away for Azazel into the wilderness" (Lev. 16:6-10, 26).

Meta. The two goats of Leviticus 16 signify the twofold operation in consciousness that attends the putting away of sin. Sacrificing one goat as a sin offering to Jehovah signifies the process of uplifting and refining the energies that lie back of all action and have been used to do evil. These energies are good and must be refined and elevated to spiritual expression in the consciousness and organism of man, that he may become perfect even as the Father is perfect. (See Matt. 5:48.)

Sending the other goat (Azazel—*removed, separated, sent away*) out into the wilderness bespeaks denial of error, putting away sin, or releasing from the consciousness all belief in and thought of sin and evil, and all condemnation for sin.

"As far as the east is from the west,
So far hath he removed our transgressions from us" (Psa. 103:12).

"For I will forgive their iniquity, and their sin will I remember no more" (Jer. 31:34). (See GOAT.)

Azaziah, ăz-ă-zī'-ăh (Heb.)—*Jehovah is mighty; Jah is strong; strengthened by Jehovah; strength of the Lord.*

a A Levite who was a musician during David's reign (I Chron. 15:21). He was appointed as one of those who were to play musical instruments while the Ark of the Covenant was being brought to Jerusalem from the house of Obed-edom. **b** An Ephraimite, a chief, and father of Hoshea (I Chron. 27:20). **c** A Levite, one of those who had charge of the tithes and so forth in the Temple during Hezekiah's reign (II Chron. 31: 13).

Meta. The *strength of the Lord* expressed in and through man (*strengthened by Jehovah*) as harmony (music) and as a conserver of spiritual substance in the body temple; also as an aid to the salvation (Hoshea) of the whole man.

Azbuk, ăz'-bŭk (Heb.)—*strong devastation; mighty desolation.*

Father of Nehemiah, ruler of half the district of Beth-zur (Neh. 3:16).

Meta. Strong denial of error (*strong devastation, mighty desolation*). Error, in thought and deed, must be dissolved by denial, that the consciousness and the organism may be built up in Truth. (Azbuk was the father of Nehemiah, who helped to rebuild the walls of Jerusalem after the return from the Babylonian captivity.)

Azekah, ă-zē'-kăh (Heb.)—*dug over; harrowed; tilled; broken up; loosened.*

a A city of Judah in the land of Canaan. It was a place where the Amorites were slain by Joshua and by great stones that Jehovah cast down from heaven upon them. More Amorites were slain by the hailstones than by the Israelites, we are told (Josh. 10:10, 11). (See also I Sam. 17:1 and Jer. 34:7.)

Meta. A certain degree of cultivation or refinement of thought (*dug over, harrowed, tilled*) that has taken place in the individual. This refinement of thought opens the way for a purification in consciousness, which in turn brings about a disruption of amicable relations with the carnal thoughts (Amorites) that were hitherto in control there; it also makes possible the casting out and destroying of these error thoughts, all the way from Gibeon (*hill, height,* a high, illumined state of consciousness) to Azekah (to the degree of cultivation, refinement, and purification, hence spiritualization, of thought that Azekah symbolizes).

The great stones that Jehovah cast down from heaven upon the Amorites symbolize the working of the divine law (Jehovah, or Lord) in bringing about very hard conditions. While the law is of heaven, of righteousness and harmony, and brings life and peace to those who live in accord with it, it reacts destructively upon thoughts, desires, and practices that are adverse to the real good of the individual. Error really brings destruction upon itself; by recognizing and using our I AM authority and dominion (represented by Joshua) we assist in cleansing from our consciousness the errors that hinder us from reaching the goal of perfection that is our divine inheritance.

Azel (A. V., Zech. 14:5, Azal), ā'-zĕl (Heb.)—*reserved; separated; noble.*

a A Benjamite who was descended from Saul through Jonathan (I Chron. 8:37). **b** A place near Jerusalem (Zech. 14:5).

Meta. Thoughts of conservation (*reserved*) and consecration (*separated*), exalted thoughts (*noble*) that are active, in man's higher, religious, or spiritual nature (a Benjamite; also a place in Israel, near Jerusalem).

Azgad, ăz'-găd (Heb.)—*Gad is mighty; strong troop; strong, organized body; strong fortune; the mighty god of fortune* (*Gad,* sometimes called *Baal*); *worship; supplication.*

a A Judahite whose "children," to the number of 1,222, returned to their own land from the Babylonian captivity (Ezra 2:12). **b** One of those who joined Nehemiah in sealing the covenant (Neh. 10:15).

Meta. Azgad, with his family, signifies a well-balanced mind in a well-balanced body (*strong, organized troop* or *body*). The thought of might, as well as that of sustenance and abundance, is also contained in that which Azgad signifies.

Aziel, ā'-zĭ-ĕl (Heb.)—*strength of God; might of God; power of God.*

A musician in David's reign (I Chron. 15:20); he is called Jaaziel in verse 18.

Meta. A thought of spiritual strength and power. (See JAAZIEL.)

Aziza, ă-zī'-zà (Heb.)—*robust; strong.*

An Israelite who had married a foreign wife but put her away at the command of Ezra (Ezra 10:27).

Meta. A belief in physical strength and energy (*robust, strong*). This belief in individual consciousness is very likely to link itself with sensuous affections (a foreign wife) if it is not kept consciously centered in Spirit, the origin and sustaining power of all true vigor and strength.

Azmaveth, ăz'-mă-vĕth (Heb.)—*strong as death; strength of death; strong unto death.*

a A Benjamite town (Ezra 2:24; Neh. 12:9; in Neh. 7:28, Beth–azmaveth). **b** The name of several Benjamite men (II Sam. 23:31; I Chron. 8:36; 12:3; 27:25). Some of these men were descended from Saul, and others were among David's valiant men and over his treasures.

Meta. Faith active in man's consciousness to bring results. Love (David) recognizes the value of faith (Benjamin or Benjamites) and uses it. To man in sense consciousness death is about as strong and sure a thing as can be named. We are learning today that death of itself has no power and is not real, because only that which is of God (life) is real; that death can no longer enter the experience of an individual when he once gives all the power of his thought and faith to the good, to life and peace.

But even as death seems so very strong to mortal man (*strong as death*), faith is strong and sure to bring results for good when it is established firmly in one's consciousness; that is, when one believes strongly in good as one's birthright. On the other hand, if one's faith is centered in a belief in error or in a fear of error, one's experiences will be inharmonious and of a destructive character.

Faith is a power in itself because it is one of the attributes of God. It works in man for good or for apparent ill according to the way he directs it by his thoughts; hence the injunction: "Have faith in God."

Azmon, ăz'-mŏn (Heb.)—*strong of bone; strong of muscle; robust of body; numerous; strong in mass* or *number; a fortress.*

A town at the south border of Judah and of Canaan (Num. 34:4; Josh. 15:4); it was near the "brook of Egypt," and so was near the western extremity of the south boundary line of Canaan.

Meta. Strength, firmness, vigor—the result of the many thoughts of strength that have been entertained in consciousness (*strong of bone, strong of muscle, robust of body, numerous, strong in mass* or *number, a fortress*). Strength is necessary to fortify one in the good when one has learned to discern what belongs to the Promised Land (spiritual consciousness and the redeemed body) and what belongs to the unreal, to the enemies—doubt, fear, and carnality—that are ever seeking to utilize one's soul and body substance in their unrighteous expression. It takes firmness of purpose and strength of mind to know Truth and to abide in it while one's life forces are being lifted out of sense thought and changed into spiritual expression and manifestation.

Aznoth–tabor, ăz'-nŏth–tā'-bôr (Heb.) —*peaks of Tabor; ears or peaks of Tabor; summits of Tabor.*

A place on the western border of Naphtali (Josh. 19:34), evidently a mountain or mountains.

Meta. A twofold realization (*peaks of Tabor,* two mountain peaks; a mountain always represents a high plane of consciousness or a state of spiritual exaltation and realization) of strength (Naphtali) through the recognition that all strength is spiritual. When the material thought is removed from the strength faculty (which Naphtali signifies) it becomes more than doubled in consciousness in the knowledge that it is founded in Spirit, God, and does not have its source or its sustaining power in the physical. There is therefore no limit to one's strength.

Azor, ā'-zôr (Gk.)—*helper.*

Son of Eliakim, and father of Sadoc, in the genealogy of Jesus (Matt. 1:13).

Meta. The God-inspired idea that man's true and all-efficient *helper* in all things pertaining to his life and wellbeing is Spirit. When man looks without for assistance, he looks away from the true Source of all his strength, understanding, life, love, substance, and good, which Source is within him. The Christ will never be born in us until we learn

to turn within to the Holy Spirit for light, guidance, and overcoming power.

Azotus, ă-zō'-tŭs (Gk.)—*fortress; castle.*

The Greek rendering of Ashdod. Philip, after having baptized the eunuch who was on his way from Jerusalem to Gaza, was caught away by Spirit, and was found at Azotus (Acts 8:40).

Meta. The apparently deceiving, destructive, sense or carnal state of consciousness that Ashdod symbolizes, lifted to a higher intellectual realm (Azotus of the Greeks) and being imbued with spiritual power (Philip) to a still further resurrection into constructive spiritual expression.

Azriel, ăz'-rĭ-ĕl (Heb.)—*my help is God; God is helper; help of God.*

a A head man of the half tribe of Manasseh (I Chron. 5:24). **b** Father of Jeremoth, a chief man over the tribe of Naphtali (I Chron. 27:19). **c** Father of Seraiah, one of the officers of Jehoiakim, king of Judah (Jer. 36:26).

Meta. That in us which perceives and acknowledges spiritual assistance in all the activities of life (*my help is God*). This thought of God as helper, as deliverer from mortal errors, darkness, and difficulties, as our spiritual guide in all things, as our understanding, strength, and power, brings great executive ability and wonderful success in all that is good and true.

Azrikam, ăz'-rĭ-kăm (Heb.)—*my help has risen; my help is firmly established; my help rises and stands firm; help against the enemy; defending help; avenging help.*

The name of several Israelitish men (I Chron. 3:23; 8:38; 9:14; II Chron. 28:7; Neh. 11:15).

Meta. Firmness in standing for Truth, resulting from lifting up in consciousness thoughts of the reality and power of Spirit as one's sure helper and sustainer.

Azubah, ă-zū'-băh (Heb.)—*deserted; forsaken; ruins.*

a Wife of Caleb (I Chron. 2:18). **b** Mother of Jehoshaphat, king of Judah (I Kings 22:42).

Meta. The soul, or feeling, feminine

side of man's being, which has been functioning on the emotional plane where animal desires and sensations rule. When man begins to lay hold of Truth, he refuses to let his old thoughts and feelings dominate him. He walks by faith (Caleb), and brings forth good judgment (Jehoshaphat). Thus his inner soul sense, feelings, and desires (the emotional phase of his nature) seem to be *deserted, forsaken,* and *in ruins.* In gaining control of his emotions and feelings the individual may appear for a while to be hard-hearted and the soul may feel that it is allowed no expression at all. By holding steadily to Truth, however, by holding in faith to the Christ judgment and dominion, the individual lifts his soul into constructive, temperate, peaceful expression; it will then bring forth on the spiritual plane instead of on the mortal. It thus becomes a saving power that conveys good to the whole man, whereas before it was destructive in that it led to dissipation of substance and life through its lack of balance and self-control.

Azzan, ăz'-zăn (Heb.)—*very strong; sharp; a thorn.*

A man of the Israelitish tribe of Issachar. He was father of Paltiel, who was chosen by Jehovah as prince over this tribe when the land of Canaan was divided among the Israelites (Num. 34: 26).

Meta. The attitude of mind in us that is definite, unwavering, and to the point. Both *strong* and *sharp,* it does not quibble over sense feelings or appearances; it is keen in its discernment, comes quickly to a well-defined decision, and abides by it.

Azzur, ăz'-zŭr (Heb.)—*helper.*

a One who joined Nehemiah in sealing the covenant that the returned Israelites made to God, in which they promised to serve Him and keep His statutes (Neh. 10:17). **b** Father of a false

prophet in Jeremiah's time (Jer. 28:1). **c** The father of Jaazaniah, whom Ezekiel saw in a vision standing at the east of Jehovah's house, looking eastward, devising iniquity and giving evil counsel. Ezekiel was told, by the Spirit that showed him the vision, to prophesy against this Jaazaniah, son of Azzur (Ezek. 11:1).

Meta. A certain perception of the truth that our help is spiritual (*helper*). This should assist in our true service to God and to man, and in our real overcoming in ourselves. This interpretation seems to be true of the first Azzur that we have mentioned. In the two latter instances where Azzur is spoken of, however, the individual is seeking to apply spiritual truths to the exaltation of the personal self and is claiming the blessings of God without putting away carnal beliefs, desires, and activities. This always brings trouble in the end, since the blessings of God are to His obedient children and not to the willful and disobedient.

The true prophet of God in one discriminates between that which is of the absolute good and that which is of the lesser self and knows that the limitations of sense must be denied or crucified. The true prophet is not loved by the carnal mind. When the king (will) gives himself over to personal selfishness and to the rule of the senses, the true spiritual helper is almost silenced, because false thoughts (prophets) arise in consciousness. These false thoughts pervert the Truth that has been gained, and seek to apply it to the building up of the personal man. Man likes to think that he can have everything good that he desires, without giving up any of his personal selfishness in order to get this good. The false thoughts and beliefs in him (false prophets) tell him that he can; but they do not tell him the truth, and in the end he will realize this.

B

Baal, bā'-ăl (Heb.)—*lord; master; possessor; owner; guardian; a husband; Jove; Jupiter; the sun.* . . . a generic term for God in many of the Syro-Arabian languages.

Chief male deity of the Phœnicians and Canaanites, as Ashtoreth was their principal female deity (Judg. 2:13). The worship of Baal was directed to Jovis, Jupiter, or the Sun as the guardian and giver of good fortune, prosperity, and abundance.

Meta. Baal means *lord,* and it was the besetting sin of the ancient Hebrews to apply this title to things formed instead of the formless. This tendency is still prevalent, and not merely among the Hebrews.

All concepts of God as less than universal mind are Baal. Those who believe in a personal god are Baal worshipers, because they make an image of that which is "without body, parts, or passions." They should learn to go back of the realm of things, that they may come in touch with God, who is Spirit, mind, cause, omnipresence.

Baal worship was a form of nature worship. All people who study materiality and seek to find in it the source of existence are sacrificing to Baal. This is strictly intellectual. But there are those on the soul plane who think that they are spiritual because they feel the throb of nature and join in all her moods. They are closely allied to the whirling dervish, and dissipate their soul substance in the various forces of nature with which they are in love. Such persons must do away with this Baal worship and call upon the life-fire of the Spirit to consume every material phase of sacrifice.

Baalim and Asheroth represent nature in its various sensuous aspects. "All the host of heaven" (see Deut. 4:19 and 17:3) are the sun, moon, and stars and the twelve signs of the zodiac. When we fall into the evils of Manasseh (II Chron. 33:1-13) we think that the planets and stars rule over us and that it is necessary to pay them a certain degree of homage or worship because of their influence. Some people in this day have great faith in their "ruling planets," and think that they are bound to certain traits of character because they were born when those sidereal bodies were in the ascendancy. They are forgetful of the God power within them, and so are brought into condemnation.

The Manasseh mentality usually goes from one step of Baalim worship to another, until it exhausts them all. Luck, chance, sorcery, familiar spirits, and wizardry are some of the avenues through which the Manasseh mind attempts to regulate its life. Astrology, palmistry, the guidance of spirits, mesmerism, hypnotism, are some of the many modern forms of denial of God. Indulged in for a time they lead the negative mind into deeper and deeper bondage, until the transgressed law reacts upon the transgressor and he is put "in chains" and bound "with fetters" and carried to Babylon, or utter confusion. The way of escape is through prayer to God and return to His "city of peace" within the soul, Jerusalem.

Baalah, bā'-ăl-ăh (Heb.)—*lady; mistress; possessor; guardian; sorceress; citizenship; a citizen.*

A border town of Judah. Kiriath-jearim is another name for this city (Josh. 15:9).

Meta. An innate consciousness of authority and ownership in man, a consciousness that pertains to the feminine or affectional nature, the soul (*mistress, possessor*), and is expressed in the psychic and material to the point of idolatry. (See BAAL.)

Baalath, bā'-ăl-ăth (Heb.)—*citizens; subjects; possessions; belonging to Baal; mistresses.*

a A town of the tribe of Dan (Josh. 19:44). **b** A town that Solomon rebuilt after he married the daughter of the king of Egypt (I Kings 9:18). This latter was perhaps the same place as the previously named town of the tribe of Dan.

Meta. Baal means *lord, master, possessor,* and pertains to the attributing of power and authority to the outer world of phenomena instead of recognizing Spirit as the one true source of all existence and of all prosperity and supply. Baalath represents the belief of the spiritually unawakened soul in man that his possessions, his privileges, and the good that he enjoys have their source in the outer, the material.

Baalath—beer, bā'-ăl-ăth-bē'-ĕr (Heb.) —*city of the well; place of the well; lady of the well; mistress of the well; subjects of the pit.*

A city of Canaan that was allotted to the Israelitish tribe of Simeon (Josh. 19:8); Baal of I Chronicles 4:33 may be the same city.

Meta. Baalath—beer, meaning *city of the well, place of the well, lady of the well,* pertains to the waters of life, which lie deep within the subjective vital forces of man. Under material thought the life forces in man are expressed in sense ways until they have become a snare, a pit, to trap and to destroy (*subjects of the pit*). By listening to and obeying the voice of Truth (Baalath—beer was taken over by the Israelitish tribe of Simeon, Simeon meaning *hearing, obedience*) the seeming pitfall of ignorance concerning life is subjected to the enlightenment of Spirit. Thus the individual becomes conscious of the truth about life, and the waters of life spring up in his mind and body in their original purity and abundance, giving him eternal life.

Baal—berith (A. V., Judges 9:46, "the god Berith"), bā'-ăl-bē'-rĭth (Heb.)— *Baal of the covenant; lord of the covenant; guardian of the covenant; lord Berith.*

a The god Berith, a deity of a form of Baal worship that was taken up by Israel after the death of Gideon (Judg. 8:33; 9:4). **b** El-berith in Judges 9:46.

Meta. This idol was known as the *lord of the covenant,* or *guardian of the covenant,* meaning the power that defends and guards agreements or compacts. Baal—berith symbolizes the belief that is so current in the world today— the belief that mortal man can make outer laws and enter agreements that will insure safety and protection to the people of the earth and will bring about peace at home and abroad. But mortal man has no such power. The law of God, which is the law of unselfishness and love, must be established in the minds and the hearts of mankind, to bring absolute security.

Baale—judah, bā'-ăl-ē-jū'-dăh (Heb.)— *lords of Judah; Baale of Judah; a citizen of Judea.*

A city belonging to the tribe of Judah (II Sam. 6:2). The same place as Baalah and Kiriath—jearim.

Meta. See BAALAH, KIRIATH—BAAL, and KIRIATH—JEARIM.

Baal—gad, bā'-ăl-găd (Heb.)—*Gad is lord; the god of fortune is lord; lord of fortunes; possessor of fortune; lord of troops; troop of Baal.* Gad is the ancient god of plenty and prosperity.

A city on the northern border of that part of Palestine which was conquered by the Israelites under Joshua; it was "in the valley of Lebanon under mount Hermon" (Josh. 11:17).

Meta. Lebanon means *white,* and represents pure thoughts. Mount Hermon (*lofty, prominent, sacred mountain*) indicates a high, sublime state of mind. Baal—gad (*Gad is lord, the god of fortune is lord, lord of fortunes*), a city in the valley of Lebanon under Mount Hermon, signifies a realization of substance and bounty, but with a strong tendency toward the belief that the source of this good is in the outer formed or psychic world instead of in the inner formless Spirit. (See BAAL.)

Baal—hamon, bā'-ăl-hā'-mŏn (Heb.)— *possessor of plenty; place of the multitude; lord of the multitude; place of Jupiter Ammon.*

A place where Solomon had a vineyard (Song of Sol. 8:11). It is thought by some to be the same place as Baal—gad.

Meta. The significance is much the same as that of Baal–gad, though Solomon's vineyard gives the added thought of abundant life. While both life and all increase of substance and supply come from Spirit, Baal gives a suggestion of the mistaken belief that is still so prevalent among people today, the belief that the source of life and substance is in the outer world of form and activity. Man needs to learn that the true source of all people, as well as the source of all supply and of every real expression and manifestation, is unformed Spirit; having learned that, he will get away from Baal worship entirely. (See BAAL.)

Baal–hanan, bā'-ăl-hā'-năn (Heb.)— *Baal is gracious; possessor of compassion; lord of mercy.*

a King of Edom (Gen. 36:38). **b** A Gederite who was "over the olive-trees and the sycomore-trees that were in the lowland" during David's reign over Israel (I Chron. 27:28).

Meta. Grace, mercy, and kindliness as belonging to and being expressed by the outer man (*Baal is gracious, possessor of compassion, lord of mercy*). All these God qualities are expressed in measure by the outer physical and mental man, even before their true origin is understood to be spiritual. Until man learns the Truth, he usually takes to himself all the honor and glory resulting from any good that he does, instead of ascribing all honor and glory to God—Divine Mind.

Baal–hazor, bā'-ăl-hā'-zôr (Heb.)— *Baal's village; lord of the village; possessor of the inclosure; lord of the castle.*

The place where Absalom held his sheep-shearing feast at the time that he killed his half-brother Amnon (II Sam. 13:23).

Meta. A place in the apparently higher or religious consciousness of man where material thought still prevails.

Absalom represents physical beauty without the corresponding beauty of soul. Amnon symbolizes a mental quality in man in process of education, a quality that, when its education is completed, will bring about faithfulness. Material thought blinds the individual to the good that is in process of coming to light and causes him to judge according to the senses. This manner of judging is common to unawakened man; the thoughts in his consciousness that approve of it are many (*Baal's village*). It is this outer form of judging that upholds that which looks so well to the eye of the physical (Absalom), and destroys, or limits in its expression, the inner qualities that would bring about faithfulness to Truth if allowed full awakening. This in time would change the whole man into spiritual expression and manifestation. But the flesh is always warring against the spiritual.

Baal–hermon, bā'-ăl-hēr'-mŏn (Heb.) —*Baal of the mountain; lord of the high place; lord of devotion; lord of consecration.*

A place near Mount Hermon (I Chron. 5:23). It is supposed by some to be the same place as Baal–gad.

Meta. See BAAL–GAD. Mount Baal–hermon (Judg. 3:3) seems to refer to a peak of this mountain itself—a peak of Hermon. As such it would symbolize the exalting of the formed and manifest world (the wonderful and sublime works of nature) above the unformed mind of Spirit.

Baalis, bā'-ă-lĭs (Heb.)—this word has nothing to do with Baal; it is a contracted form of Ben–alis (*son of exultation; son of joy; in exultation; in a state of joy*). In a negative sense Baalis means *proudly exulting; insolently joyous.*

A king of the children of Ammon who was accessory to the killing of Gedaliah, a ruler of the Jews who were not carried captive to Babylon (Jer. 40:14).

Meta. The ruling thought of the error state of consciousness that the Ammonites typify. Baalis refers especially to the exultation and rejoicing that take place in the sense consciousness of man when it seems to be in the ascendancy (*in exultation, proudly exulting, insolently joyous*); when for the time being it appears to have gained dominion over the truer thoughts (Jews) of the mind. But joy and elation of that sort are short-lived, since the good is destined to increase and to rule and to overcome all its enemies.

Baal-meon, bā'-ăl-mē'-ŏn (Heb.)—*lord of habitations; place of dwellings; possessor of houses; lord of dwellings.*

A city of the Reubenites; it was built by them in the land that had been taken from Sihon, king of the Amorites, and Og, king of Bashan (Num. 32:38).

Meta. Reuben means *behold a son, vision of a son,* and signifies understanding. Baal-meon (*lord of habitations, possessor of the houses, lord of dwellings*), a city of Reuben, represents understanding centered in the outer consciousness, understanding that still looks upon the manifest world and outer possessions as being real and true of themselves; this limited understanding does not see back of the manifest to spiritual reality.

Baal-peor, bā'-ăl-pē'-ôr (Heb.)—*lord of the chasm; yawning place; lord of the opening.*

a Baal of Peor, or a form of Baal worship practiced in Peor (Num. 25:3-18); sometimes called only Peor, as in Joshua 22:17. b Baal-peor was an idol of the Moabites and the Midianites, and is said to have been worshiped in obscene ceremonies.

Meta. The exalting of sensuality.

Baal-perazim, bā'-ăl-pĕr'-ă-zĭm (Heb.) —*lord of breaches; place of dispersions; place of sunderings; lord of destructions.*

A place where David gained a victory over the Philistines. "And David came to Baal-perazim, and David smote them there; and he said, Jehovah hath broken mine enemies before me, like the breach of waters. Therefore he called the name of that place Baal-perazim," that is, "the place of breakings forth" (II Sam. 5:20 and margin).

Meta. The understanding that Baal (trust in the outer things of sense) is at the head of all divisions, separations, and disruptions in consciousness (*lord of breaches, place of dispersions, lord of destructions*). When love (David) unified with I AM (Jehovah) comes to this place of comprehension, the Philistines (lawless, rebellious thoughts and beliefs of the sense consciousness in man) are

defeated.

Baal-shalishah, bā'-ăl-shăl'-ĭ-shăh (Heb.)—*lord of Shalishah; place of the triad; lord of the three.*

A city in the district of Shalishah (II Kings 4:42).

Meta. A thought center in the individual that exalts the outer man as prince or ruler (*lord of Shalishah;* Baal is that in man which looks upon outer forms and appearances as real and true, while Shalishah means *third, triangular, threefold, triad, trinity*). Triangular relates to a triangle, a three-sided figure or something comprising three parts, elements, or the like. Three suggests the trinity, and man is the third in the trinity composed of God, Christ, divine man. This man, however, is manifest man in his perfect state, and not mortal man subject to corruption, as he so generally appears to be today. Baal-shalishah is that in man's consciousness which gives precedence to the outer, the manifest, above the true inner spiritual self (the Christ), and above the one Source of all—God, the Father.

Baal-tamar, bā'-ăl-tā-mär (Heb.)—*lord of the palms; place of palm trees; lord of the columns.*

A place in Benjamin where the other tribes of Israel fought against the Benjamites and killed 25,100 of them because of the lewdness of certain Benjamites in Gibeah, and because the Benjamites would not destroy the ones who acted so wickedly (Judg. 20:33).

Meta. Tamar means *palm,* or *palm-tree,* and Baal is *lord* as applied to the outer formed world instead of formless Spirit. In olden times palm branches were carried before conquerors in celebration of their triumphs. Palms denote victory and resurrection. The palms in the hands of the multitude (Rev. 7:9) signify victory over all error and its results. Baal-tamar (*lord of the palms*) represents the attributing of conquering power to outer efforts instead of to the Christ within one.

Baal-zebub, bā'-ăl-zē'-bŭb (Heb.)—*lord of flies; place infested with flies; possessed of flies.*

The god of Ekron, one of the five

principal cities of the Philistines. Ahaziah, king of Israel, sent to inquire of this god whether he would recover from his sickness (II Kings 1:2-16). Baalzebub was supposed to be prince of all moral impurities, or of evil spirits. (See BEELZEBUB, the New Testament form of Baal–zebub.)

Meta. Man's belief in a personal devil. Baal–zebub, or Beelzebub, prince of demons, is not an adversary with outer form; evil is not originated by a personal devil, nor are evils thrust upon man from without, as so many people seem to think; Baal–zebub signifies the adverse belief in man that man has built up himself because of his mistaken idea that he is separate from God, a belief that gives rise to multitudes of thoughts in opposition to Truth. These rebellious, opposing thoughts are the demons or the evil spirits over which Baal-zebub is prince, or the central, controlling thought.

Baal–zephon, bā′-ăl-zē′-phŏn (Heb.)— *lord of Typhon; evil spirit of the Egyptians; place sacred to Typhon; lord of the north; lord of the north wind, i. e., winter.*

A place by the Red Sea, in Egypt. The Israelites, when fleeing from the Egyptians, camped at this place just before they passed through the Red Sea (Exod. 14:2, 9).

Meta. Typhon is mythical, and means a monster. It is said that Phœnician sailors of old used to seek to pacify the god of the north wind whenever they began a trip down the Gulf of Suez. Baalzephon (*lord of Typhon, evil spirit of the Egyptians, lord of the north wind,* i. e., *winter,* a place in Egypt) signifies the darkened belief that some outer personal god or power rules the elements and that he creates the cold, the storms, and monsters of evil to destroy people, apart from any direct thought or cause on their part.

Baana, bā′-ă-nà (Heb.)—*son of affliction; son of wretchedness; son of oppression; son of humility; patient.*

a Two men, officers of King Solomon's, who were commissioned to gather victuals for the king's household (I Kings 4:12, 16). **b** Father of Zadok; Zadok worked with Nehemiah in rebuilding the wall of Jerusalem after the Babylonian captivity (Neh. 3:4).

Meta. An enduring attitude of mind —that which causes one to "let patience have *its* perfect work," even while inharmony and error seem to abound in one's life and affairs (*son of affliction, son of humility, patient;* the name of Israelitish men who did constructive work). This attitude of mind is the result of a spirit of fairness (Ahilud, father of one of the men named Baana) that realizes that the apparent evil is the outpicturing of some past error sowing that has been done by the individual himself, and in that realization is confident that good is all-powerful and will triumph in the end.

Patient continuance in knowing the Truth, regardless of appearances, establishes substance in mind and thus aids in sustaining the peace consciousness in the individual (gathers victuals for King Solomon's household). It also brings forth Zadok (*righteous,* a strong belief in the right relation of things), and this belief does its part in healing the soul and the body—rebuilding the wall of Jerusalem.

Baanah, bā′-ă-năh (Heb.)—*son of affliction; son of grief.*

There were different men by this name (II Sam. 4:2; 23:29; Ezra 2:2); it is a form of Baana.

Meta. From the Bible history of the men named Baanah, we are shown how giving way to seeming affliction and sorrow works out greater evil in one's life, as in the case of the Baanah of II Samuel 4, who with his brother killed Ishbosheth the son of Saul, and was slain himself because of this act. On the other hand we can cause even suffering, and that which appears evil, to work out for our good; we can become more firmly established in strength, love, and Truth by refusing to be daunted by seeming error conditions and by rising out of them through exercise of the Christ power in ourselves. (One of the men named Baanah was a mighty man of David's; another was an officer of King Solomon's; still another was one of those who returned with Zerubbabel from the Babylonian captivity.)

Baara, bā'-ă-rȧ (Heb.)—*brutish; stupid; consumed with fire; burned up.*

Wife of Shaharaim, a Benjamite (I Chron. 8:8).

Meta. A putting away of coarseness and dullness from the soul consciousness; this takes place when the light of faith arises within one (Baara—*brutish, stupid*—was the wife of Shaharaim—*two dawns, double morning*—a Benjamite, Benjamites signifying faith). *Consumed with fire, burned up,* bespeak destruction of the error characteristics symbolized by *brutish* and *stupid;* also a certain transmutation that always occurs when the darkness of error gives way to the light of Truth.

Baaseiah, bā'-ă-sē-ịah (Heb.)—*work of Jehovah; Jehovah's creation; labor of Jah.*

A Levite from whom Asaph was descended (I Chron. 6:40).

Meta. The knowledge of Jehovah as king (Malchijah, father of Baaseiah) brings forth the *work of Jehovah,* which Baaseiah represents, love's pressing or blending together thoughts of Truth (Baaseiah was of the Israelitish tribe of Levi, and Levi refers to the love faculty in man), resulting in a Godlike or perfect state of being (Michael, Baaseiah's son).

Baasha, bā'-ă-shȧ (Heb.)—*boldness; offensiveness; bad; vile; loathsome.*

King of Israel, and a son of Ahijah, of the house of Issachar. He killed Nadab, son of Jeroboam, and all the rest of the house of Jeroboam, thus fulfilling the prophecy regarding this wicked king (I Kings 15:27-33). But Baasha too was a wicked king, and all his descendants were destroyed later (I Kings 16:3).

Meta. A phase of the will in man (a king always relates to the will) that is aggressive and daring (*boldness;* of the tribe of Issachar, referring to active zeal). This phase of the will that Baasha represents seeks greater dominion and authority, but, because of being guided by sense consciousness instead of listening to and obeying the voice of the Spirit of wisdom and love, it is offen-

sive, vile, and destructive instead of constructive.

Babel, bā'-bĕl (Heb.)—*Babylonia; gate of Bel; court of Baal; confusion; chaos; vanity; nothingness.*

a A city in the land of Shinar, or Chaldea, built by Nimrod, great-grandson of Noah (Gen. 10:10). **b** A tower that was built with the city, the intention being to make the tower so high that it would reach to heaven; it was here that a confusion of tongues took place, and men began to speak in different languages, according to Bible history (Gen. 11:1-9).

Meta. Babel signifies what the name means—*confusion.* When man thinks that in outer, or purely mental and psychic, ways he can comprehend and contact the divine, confusion is always the outcome. It is only through the inner Spirit of truth that he can come in touch with and gain spiritual Truth and perfection of poise, peace, power, all good—the kingdom of heaven.

Babylon, băb'-ỹ-lŏn (Gk.) — from Babel; *gate of Bel* (Bel was the supreme deity in the Babylonian pantheon). See BABEL for definitions.

Capital of the Babylonian Empire, and founded by the followers of Nimrod (II Kings 25; Isa. 13:19).

Meta. Confusion or mixture, outer confusion, sense confusion, mental confusion, a chaotic condition. There are times when we find ourselves in the confusion of the sense consciousness, and its thoughts are so strong that they seem to have us in complete subjugation. Such cases symbolize captivity in Babylon.

In Daniel 3:1 we read, "the king made an image of gold." The Babylon state of consciousness worships gold, and unless you accept its commercial customs it will put you in the fiery furnace of persecution.

The Babylonians symbolize the mixed, confused thoughts of the material consciousness.

A city is an aggregation of thoughts. The city of Babylon, of Revelation 17 and 18, signifies the aggregation of the states of mind of the people of the earth. The kings of the earth are the ruling egos of the people of the earth, of the thoughts of people's minds.

The great harlot is the mental phase or psychic condition of the sensuality of sex. The judgment, verse 1, is that the whole race, all the people (many waters), are coming to judgment; they have to account for their thoughts and their acts. This chapter reveals a coming to judgment of sensuality and of all the conditions symbolized in the preceding chapters in Revelation by the beast, and so forth.

The scarlet-colored beast is the beastly nature in man; it also represents the bodily, or outer, phase of the individual. The woman, or the psychical, mental, feeling plane, must have a base of activity, and the body is this base of activity. Thus the woman was sitting upon the beast (verse 3).

This "mystery" woman, city of Babylon, verse 5, is the mother of life, sensuality, confusion of mind under sense law. She represents a phase of the universal race thought. The "harlot" is an adulterated state of mind, symbolical of the psychical realm in its occult, mystical, mental phase. Scarlet and red represent life. By lack of understanding of life we have brought confusion into the race thought. Revelation 17 tells of the woman on the beast who comes up out of the bottomless pit, who was, is to be, yet is not. The beast comes up out of the abyss and goes to perdition; that is, it has no real resting place, no foundation. The abyss, or bottomless pit, is negation. Thus all confusion of thought and its results are really without foundation in Truth; not having any reality, they must pass away.

Baharumite, bă-hā'-rŭm-īte (from Heb.).

A native of Bahurim. "Azmaveth the Baharumite" was one of David's mighty men (I Chron. 11:33); he is called Barhumite in II Samuel 23:31.

Meta. Baharumite pertains to fearlessness, enthusiasm, and strength. (See BARHUMITE; also BAHURIM.)

Bahurim, bă-hū'-rĭm (Heb.)—*young men's village; choice young men; prime of manhood; young warriors; choice;*

select; excellent.

A Benjamite town near Jerusalem, on the road to the Jordan (II Sam. 3:16). It was there that Shimei, of the family of Saul, cursed David and threw stones and dust at him when he was fleeing from Absalom (II Sam. 16:5-8); it was in that place that a woman hid in a well the messengers (Jonathan and Ahimaaz) of David, who were being pursued while they were on their way to David to tell him of Absalom's plans (II Sam. 17:18).

Meta. A consciousness of physical strength and power (*choice young men, young warriors*). Such a consciousness is *excellent,* but if it is not established in love and wisdom the result is strife and a tendency to do unwise things, for which one repents afterward; this is typified in the case of Shimei. One may also do noble acts (saving David's messengers by hiding them in a well).

Bakbakkar, băk-băk'-kär (Heb.)—*diligent searcher; exceedingly pleasing.* Due to the doubling of characters, the word has the force of a superlative.

A Levite, one of those who "dwelt in the villages of the Netophathites" after the return from the Babylonian captivity (I Chron. 9:15).

Meta. A thought belonging to the natural religious tendencies of man (a Levite), that is, of a character exceedingly investigating, examining, penetrating, seeking (*diligent searcher*). This thought activity is founded in love (the Levites were descended from Levi, who represents the love faculty in individual consciousness) and therefore is not of a contentious nature. It is harmonious, though faithful in its search after Truth; thus it brings great joy and satisfaction to the person who entertains it and gives it substance.

Bakbuk, băk'-bŭk (Heb.)—*empty; poured out; wasted; hollow; a bottle; a flask.*

A man of the Nethinim whose children returned from the Babylonian captivity (Ezra 2:51).

Meta. Many professing Christians are like this belief that Bakbuk, of the Nethinim, signifies. Their lives are as empty bottles, waste and hollow (*empty, poured out, wasted, hollow, a bottle*), because while they have cleansed their minds and their body temples, to some degree at least, they have never laid hold of the Holy Spirit in faith, and so have not been filled with the consciousness of the abundant sufficiency and joy of Spirit. They look upon their spiritual service and their daily duties as crosses, or heavy burdens, to be borne "for Christ's sake." (The Nethinim were set apart to wait on the priests and do the menial work in the Temple and Temple worship; many of them were virtually slaves.) But all this will change when they once get a vision of their divine sonship. They will then be servants no longer, but friends and sons, and will be shown all that the Christ in them has received of the Father (Gal. 4:6; John 15:15). They will then radiate Truth joyfully, and their service will to them be opportunities to express their own innate possibilities and to show their love to God and to man.

Bakbukiah, băk-bû-kī′-ăh (Heb.)— *pouring out (wasting) from Jehovah; wasted by Jah; emptying, i. e., wasting, of Jehovah; destruction by Jehovah.*

A Levite who had an office of responsibility in the Temple worship. He was "the second among his brethren" (Neh. 11:17). He was one of the "porters keeping the watch at the storehouses of the gates" (Neh. 12:25).

Meta. A thought of service to and worship of God. It is one of the thoughts that help to guard the consciousness against error (he was a porter who kept watch at the gates). It is of a destructive character, tearing down and casting out (*emptying, wasting of Jehovah, destruction by Jehovah*); it watches for evil and the results of evil, that it may rid the consciousness of them. To be on the constructive side, this thought that Bakbukiah represents would have to be watching for good only that it might aid in establishing the good. It is necessary in its place, however, for that which falls short of the divine perfection must be discerned, at least enough to be cast out. But error appearances should not be magnified and destructive thoughts should not be built up.

Balaam, bā′-lăam (Heb.)—*lord of the people; destruction of the people; a pilgrim; a foreigner; a stranger.*

Son of Beor, a native of Pethor in Mesopotamia. He was a prophet, or soothsayer, of the Midianites. He was hired by Balak, king of Moab, to curse the Israelites; instead he obeyed the voice of Jehovah and blessed them (Num. 22:5—24:25). Though Balaam could not curse Israel, he counseled with Balak to lead the Israelites into idolatry and fornication, that they might forsake God and be destroyed. (See Rev. 2:14; Num. 25 and 31:16.)

Meta. Balaam belongs to the mental sense plane in man. He is *a foreigner*, in so far as the true Israelitish consciousness is concerned. Yet he represents that in our contentious, sense nature (Midian) which, though ever striving for the ascendancy, discerns the superiority of Spirit and cannot fight openly against the Truth. This discernment that Balaam represents, however, being of the sense man and reaching no higher in its expression than the phase of the psychical that is governed by the sense mind, is deceptive. It seeks in subtle ways to undermine, adulterate, and destroy the Israelitish thoughts that are continually struggling to gain a more perfect comprehension, realization, and expression of Truth. In the end, all of sense is overcome and its powers of discernment are lifted to a higher plane of activity. (The Moabites and Midianites were defeated, and Balaam, who was fighting with them against the Hebrews, was slain. See Numbers 31:8).

Baladan, băl′-ă-dăn (Bab.)—*Baal is his lord; worshiper of Bel; having power.*

A Chaldean, father of Berodach–baladan, or Merodach–baladan, king of Babylon (II Kings 20:12).

Meta. The Chaldeans belong to the psychical realm of consciousness in man. Babylon symbolizes confusion. Baladan (*having power*) signifies a certain psychical (Chaldean) power in man's consciousness; it lacks true spiritual judgment (*Baal is his lord; worshiper of*

Bel), though it reflects some borrowed light and force. It brings forth a thought that for a time rules the state of mental confusion that is known as Babylon. (His son, Merodach–baladan, was king of Babylon.)

Balah, bā'-lăh (Heb.)—*trembling; terrified; withered; worn out; exhausted; decayed; old.*

A city allotted to the Israelitish tribe of Simeon, in Canaan (Josh. 19:3). Balah is a short form of Baalah.

Meta. A group of thoughts in man that is formed by the belief that evil is real and is powerful, and that life is limited. Fear, weakness, old age, and decay are the result of this error belief (*trembling, terrified, exhausted, withered, old*); it must be redeemed by the thoughts that hear and obey the voice of Truth (Simeonites). By listening and obeying one becomes fully assured that only the good is true, that life is limitless and abiding, and that it can be demonstrated in eternal youth and vigor.

Balak, bā'-lăk (Heb.) — *emptier; waster; spoiler; devastator; destroyer.*

A king of Moab who was frightened because of Israel's victories. He fought against Israel and tried to hire Balaam to curse the men of Israel that he might defeat them (Num. 22:2—24:25).

Meta. An empty, void, destructive, wasting thought (*emptier, devastator, waster, spoiler, destroyer*) that rules the carnal mind (Moab).

Bamah, bā'-măh (Heb.)—*high place; height; stronghold; hill-chapel; tabernacle; place of worship.*

A word that is used figuratively by Ezekiel as the name of places in which Israel offered sacrifices to idols (Ezek. 20:29).

Meta. The mentality, or intellect, of man given over to exaltation (*high place, height, stronghold, place of worship*) of the world of sense and materiality.

Bamoth, bā'-mŏth (Heb.) — *high places; heights; sepulchral mound; hill-chapels.*

A place in which the Israelites camped while they were on their way to the Promised Land (Num. 21:19). It was a city of the Moabites, situated on the river Arnon, or near it, and was allotted to the tribe of Reuben; it is called Bamoth–baal in Joshua 13:17, and "the high places of the Arnon" in Numbers 21:28. (See margin also.)

Meta. Arnon refers to the life current in man, and Bamoth, or Bamoth–baal (the height or sanctuary of Baal) signifies the exaltation of carnality. In other words, Bamoth symbolizes the honor and the veneration (worship) that the carnal mind (Moab) gives to the life forces for use in sensuality. No idol is served more persistently by man in sense consciousness than this one. Bamah must be lifted up and redeemed by Reuben, who represents sight, the seeing or perceiving mind. This clear seeing reveals the truth about life and its right functioning in man for his eternal good.

Bamoth–baal, bā'-mŏth–bā'-ăl (Heb.) —*heights of Baal; temples of Baal.*

The same place as Bamoth (Josh. 13:17).

Meta. See BAMOTH.

Bani, bā'-nī (Heb.)—*built; begotten; emanated; a son; posterity.*

The name of several Israelitish men (II Sam. 23:36; I Chron. 6:46; 9:4; Ezra 2:10); called Binnui in Nehemiah 7:15.

Meta. Constructive thoughts in consciousness (*built*; the name of Israelitish men). These thoughts are of God, of Truth (*begotten, emanated, a son*), and, because of the spiritual qualities of love, praise, discernment, wisdom, substance, bounty, and strength that enter into them, they build and preserve to the furthest generation (*posterity*). One of the men named Bani was a Judahite (Judah means *praise*). Another was a Levite (Levi pertains to *love*). Another was a Gadite (Gad means *fortune, a troop, seer*). Another is mentioned with his son and his father: The son, Amzi, means *strong,* and the father, Shemer, means *guard, watch, shepherding.*

baptism (Gk.).

Meta. The "baptism of repentance unto remission of sins" (Luke 3:3), which the church has made an outward form, is in fact a simple matter of thought training. The Greek word *metanoia* is translated "repentance," and repentance has been interpreted to mean an admission to God of sorrow for past sin and a resolve to be good in the future. It has been supposed that the field of action for that which is goodness in the sight of God is in conduct. Virtually the whole Christian world has in a measure failed to discern the teaching of the New Testament about mental laws. A proper translation of the mission of John the Baptist is, "He came into all the region round about Jordan preaching immersion in mentation for the doing away with shortcoming." W. Lyman Abbott says that it is plain that the mission of John was to bring about a change of mind. The fundamental idea taught by the Scriptures is not that man must know sorrow, but rather that he must undergo a change, a change not merely of conduct but of the thinking and immortal part of him.

So water baptism symbolizes a cleansing process, the letting go of error. It is the first step in the realization of Truth. It is the process of pouring into consciousness the dissolving power of the Word, which breaks up and washes away all thoughts of materiality. This is the Word in the form of denial. Water baptism indicates a letting-go attitude of thought, denial. Spiritual baptism is positive, a taking on, an affirmation. All growth takes place through these two attitudes—a letting go and a taking hold, or denial and affirmation. First we let go of old material concepts; we cannot get into a new consciousness until we let go of the old.

The Holy Ghost is the same as the Holy Spirit or Spirit of truth. When we have received a concept of the relation that we as spiritual beings have to God, the old state of thought is easily dissolved and washed away by that of which water baptism is symbolical—denial. Then there come into our mind ideas direct from the Fountainhead, and we see everything in a new light. This baptism of the Holy Spirit quickens the whole man. When the mind has received words of Truth the way is open for the healing power, which is called the Holy Spirit, or the Spirit of wholeness, to descend further into the body consciousness. This outpouring, or inpouring, of the Holy Spirit is the second baptism.

Barabbas, bär-ăb'-băs (Gk. from Heb.) —*son of father; son of my father; father's son.*

A prisoner, charged with insurrection and murder, who was held at Jerusalem. The Jews demanded that he be released instead of Jesus (Matt. 27:16-26).

Meta. The adverse consciousness (rebellion and hatred) to which man gives himself when he allows himself to oppose the Christ. Man gives free rein to this adverse consciousness when he would destroy the Christ, or true spiritual I AM in himself, since it is through Christ alone that an overcoming can be gained over the Adversary. This adverse state of thought (Barabbas) is of its father—the Devil.

Barachel, bär'-ă-chĕl (Heb.)—*God doth bless; blessed of God; prospered of God; peace of God; whom God hath blessed; kneels before God; bows before God.* The primitive meaning back of this word is that of kneeling, one's prostration of self before another, self-abnegation—symbolized in the bended knee.

Father of Elihu the Buzite (Job 32:2).

Meta. A truly humble and obedient attitude of mind toward God (*kneels before God, bows before God*) that is always in divine favor (*blessed of God, prospered of God*).

Barachiah (A. V., Barachias), bär-ă-chī'-äh (Gk.)—*blessed of Jah; prospered of Jehovah; whom Jehovah hath blessed.*

Father of Zachariah, a Hebrew prophet who was slain by his own people in their blindness to the real Truth (Matt. 23:35).

Meta. A humbling or prostrating of the outer sense thoughts and activities that the inner Christ, or I AM, may be given first place in consciousness; a consecrated attitude of mind (*blessed of Jah;* father of an Israelitish prophet).

Barak, bā'-răk (Heb.)—*lightning flash; lightning; a thunderbolt; a flaming sword; a glittering sword; a gem.*

Son of Abinoam; he was called of God, through Deborah the prophetess, to deliver Israel (Judg. 4:6-16).

Meta. The fiery executiveness of an active will (*lightning;* the man who executed Deborah's command to deliver Israel). In an untrained state it leads men into all sorts of involved conditions. When we meet with apparent failure, it is not owing to the fact that the task is too great, but because we do not go at the work in the right way. When Barak was assigned the task of gaining a victory over the warlike hosts of Sisera, he refused to go unless Deborah accompanied him. Herein is hinted the first secret of success: The method used, or the manner in which we approach a situation, largely determines our success or failure. (See DEBORAH.)

barbarian (Gk.)—*foreign; strange; ignorant; rude; brutal* (Acts 28:2).

Meta. Barbarians symbolize the unillumined, uncultivated thoughts of man. They judge by man's law because they do not understand spiritual law. They are foreign to Spirit, and are totally lacking in true Christian love and refinement.

Barhumite, bär-hū'-mīte (from Heb.) —*belonging to young men.*

A native of Bahurim. Azmaveth the Barhumite was one of David's guard (II Sam. 23:31); called Baharumite in I Chronicles 11:33.

Meta. See BAHARUMITE.

Bariah, bä-rī'-äh (Heb.)—*fugitive.*

Son of Shemaiah, and descended from Solomon (I Chron. 3:22).

Meta. A quality of mind that is born into consciousness through the activity of divine inspiration (the name of his father, Shemaiah, means *Jehovah hears,* or *harkening unto Jah*), but is not established, as yet—it is transient (*fugitive*).

Bar–Jesus, bär-jē'-ṣus (Gk.)—*son of Jesus; son of Joshua.*

A Jewish man who was a sorcerer, a false prophet (Acts 13:6). He stood against Paul and Barnabas, and tried to turn the proconsul, Sergius Paulus, from the faith; he was smitten with blindness for a season, in consequence. His Arabic name was Elymas.

Meta. See ELYMAS.

Bar–Jonah (A. V., Bar–jona), bär-jō'-näh (Heb.)—*son of Jonah; son of Johanan; son of Jonas.*

Another name for Peter; a surname (Matt. 16:17).

Meta. The inner sight (faith) acting in consciousness through peace and love. (Peter represents the faith faculty in man; Jonah means a *dove,* which signifies peace; John stands for love. In John 21:15-17 Jesus said three times to Peter, "Simon, *son* of John," and John is a form of Johanan. See PETER.)

Barkos, bär'-kŏs (Heb.)—*party-col ored; paint with colors; a painter.*

His "children" were among the Nethinim who returned from the Babylonian captivity (Ezra 2:53).

Meta. The refinement of thought that enables one to comprehend the different shades of meaning in Truth, and the ability to apply these shades of meaning in quality and degree to meet the specific and varied needs of the consciousness (*party-colored; paint with colors; a painter;* party-colored means colored with different tints, variegated).

Barnabas, bär'-nă-băs (Gk. from Heb.) —*son of exhortation; son of divinely inspired speech,* (i. e., *excelling*); *son of prophecy; son of praise; son of consolation.*

A name given by the apostles to Joseph, a Jewish man of Cyprus, of the tribe of Levi, who was converted to Christianity. He did much to spread the Christ teaching (Acts 4:36; 12:25—15:41).

Meta. In Acts 4:36, 37, and 11:22-30, Joseph represents the imagination brought into expression through association with the word (Paul). The apostles renamed him Barnabas, which they interpret in the text to mean "Son of exhortation." As the imagination is the molder of the flexible substance of mind, so in the beginning of the Bible history of Barnabas are symbols that relate him to substance in its various forms. He was a Levite; the Levites had charge of the offerings. He had a field; he sold it and brought the money and laid it at the apostles' feet. The "field," the "money," the "feet," all refer to the substance side of Being.

Barnabas was a native of Cyprus, a large island in the northeastern portion of the Mediterranean. Cyprus means fairness, and in the individual consciousness it is in close touch with intellectual reasonings (the Greeks) and formulated theology (Antioch). The faculty of imagination is located in the front brain. It must become allied to wisdom, to fair, honest logic and reasoning, in order to become the *son of exhortation*. Barnabas "was a good man, and full of the Holy Spirit and of faith." We find him always broad-minded, big of heart, and generous of soul. He was the right companion for Paul, who represents the word of the Spirit of truth. Barnabas believed in Paul and persuaded the apostles at Jerusalem that his change of heart was sincere. Spiritual imagination and fairness of mind cause us to realize and acknowledge the changes that take place in our thoughts as we turn from the fighting, resisting attitude to one of receptivity to Truth.

The church at Jerusalem heard that the Greeks were turning to Christianity, and it sent Barnabas to Antioch to investigate. Barnabas, when he saw the "grace of God, was glad; and he exhorted them all, that with purpose of heart they would cleave unto the Lord." Spiritual imagination and foresight are always glad to see and to acknowledge the light reaching out to every avenue of man's being; they ever encourage the individual to adhere to the Lord, to hold fast to the good.

Barsabbas (A. V., Barsabas), bär′-săb-bäs (Gk. from Heb.)—*son of Saba; son of Sabas; son of return; son of restitution; son of restoration.*

A name of Joseph's, whose surname was Justus (Acts 1:23); also the surname of Judas (Acts 15:22). "Joseph called Barsabbas" was nominated with Matthias as an apostle to take the place of Judas Iscariot, but the lot fell to Matthias and so he was elected. Judas Barsabbas was chosen with Silas to accompany Paul and Barnabas to Antioch.

Meta. The return of the faculties of imagination (Joseph) and praise (Judas) to their true source, God (*son of return*); also the fruit of that return: a harvest of spiritual ideas that are given forth to the brethren—the true thoughts

in consciousness, those that are awakening to the right understanding of Christ and of God—for their exhortation and confirmation in Truth. "And Judas and Silas, being themselves also prophets, exhorted the brethren with many words, and confirmed them" (Acts 15:32).

Bartholomew, bär-thŏl′-ŏ-mew (Gk. from Heb.)—*son of Tolmai; son of the furrowed; son of the plowed,* i. e., *prepared for seed.*

One of the twelve apostles of Jesus Christ (Matt. 10:3).

Meta. The faculty of imagination. He is called Nathanael, in the 1st chapter of John, where Jesus saw him under the fig tree. The inference here is that Jesus discerned Nathanael's presence before the latter came into visibility.

Bartimæus, bär-tĭ-mæ′-ŭs (Gk. from Heb.)—*son of Timæus; son of pollution; son of the unclean; son of contamination.*

A blind beggar at Jericho. He was sitting by the wayside and was healed by Jesus (Mark 10:46).

Meta. A phase of the darkened mentality in man. This blinded, polluted, and poverty-stricken state of mind is the outcome of the race habit of attributing honor and precedence to old established beliefs and customs (Bartimæus was a Jew), to the exclusion of present spiritual inspiration. But this darkened, contaminated-with-error phase of the mentality is groping for light, which is realized through Jesus Christ, the Word of God expressed.

Baruch, bā′-rŭch (Heb.)—*blessed; prospered (of God); who is blessed.*

a Son of Neriah. He wrote down Jeremiah's prophecies for him and read them to the people (Jer. 36:4-32). **b** One who helped to repair the wall of Jerusalem after the return from Babylon (Neh. 3:20). **c** Father of Maaseiah, a Judahite who lived in Jerusalem after the return from the Babylonian captivity (Neh. 11:5).

Meta. Baruch means one upon whom blessings are poured. In man's consciousness he represents the thought or inner word of Spirit, which is transmitted from the spiritual consciousness, through the nerves, to the outer consciousness.

Barzillai, bär-zĭl'-lāi (Heb.)—*iron; man of iron; strong; transfixed; pierced; an iron tool to pierce.*

a A Gileadite who brought provisions for David and his followers when they were fleeing from Absalom (II Sam. 17:27). **b** Father of Saul's son-in-law, Adriel (II Sam. 21:8).

Meta. Physical strength (*strong*). There is a material aspect to the physical which, if held to and believed in, makes one hard and unyielding in one's strength (*man of iron*). Such a consciousness of strength becomes a tool that transfixes, pierces, and carries before it everything that in any way contacts it; this is very likely to lead to despicableness in the end. On the other hand, the outer man may impart the substance of his strength, or a share of it, to the positive spiritual love nature, which David represents, and thus bring good to the whole organism.

Basemath (A. V., Bashemath), băs'-ĕ-măth (Heb.)—*fragrant; aromatic; spicy; sweet; pleasant.*

a Wife of Esau (Gen. 26:34). **b** Daughter of Solomon and wife of Ahimaaz in Naphtali (I Kings 4:15).

Meta. The soul, or feminine, in man, in its fineness of ability to perceive, or to receive intuitively (*fragrant, aromatic, pleasant;* the sense of smell bespeaks perception, discrimination, intuition), spiritual understanding and guidance. Even the soul in its seemingly material aspect is intuitive, and is much quicker to feel instinctively and know the truth about things than is the outer reasoning quality, the masculine, in the individual.

Bashan, bā'-shăn (Heb.)—*light, sandy soil; smooth, fertile soil; fruitful.*

A district east of Jordan, the land of Og, who was the Amoritish king (Deut. 3:1-11). It was noted for its fruitfulness and its herds (Deut. 32:14).

Meta. Life and substance, inexhaustible and limitless (*smooth, fertile soil, fruitful*) when the animal forces (*herds*) are properly directed and handled by the understanding (half tribe of Manasseh to whom the land of Bashan was assigned).

baskets.

Meta. The twelve baskets of John 6:13 signify a fullness and completeness in consciousness.

Bath-rabbim, băth-răb'-bĭm (Heb.)—*daughter of many; daughter of a multitude; daughter of greatness; measure of greatness.*

A gate near the pools of Heshbon (Song of Sol. 7:4).

Meta.

"Thine eyes *as* the pools in Heshbon, By the gate of Bath-rabbim."
Solomon is speaking here to his beloved; the symbolism is of Christ and His bride, or the divine masculine (wisdom) in individual consciousness, in its attitude toward love (the true spiritual feminine).

In olden times gates were public meeting places as well as places to allow entrance to cities. Court and other meetings were often held in the gates. Bath-rabbim represents a place, in the phase of consciousness that Heshbon typifies, for the gathering together and guarding of the multitude of receptive soul thoughts (*daughter of many*) that belong to the feminine, or love, in man. This divine feminine (love, or the redeemed and purified soul) is very dear and beautiful to the masculine or wisdom, the Christ, which is the true bridegroom of the soul. "*Wisdom and love are lifted up together in me, and are unified in my consciousness,*" is a good thought to hold.

Bath-sheba, băth-shē'-bà (Heb.)—*daughter of the oath; seventh daughter; daughter of seven; measure of fullness.* The word Sheba is the ancient form of a Hebrew oath, "swear by the seven," whereby one declared that the thing promised would be fulfilled.

Wife of Uriah the Hittite. After his death she became David's wife (II Sam. 11:3-27). She was the mother of Solomon (II Sam. 12:24).

Meta. Fulfillment (*seventh daughter, daughter of the oath*). As David united to Bath-sheba brought forth Solomon, so love in its fulfillment, or completion, establishes peace. (Seven is the number that represents fulfillment and rest. God "rested on the seventh day from all his work which he had made," or fulfilled.)

Bath–shua, băth'-shụ-à (Heb.) — *daughter of opulence; daughter of riches; daughter of prosperity; measure of fulfillment.*

Another translation of Bath–sheba, David's wife and the mother of Solomon (I Chron. 3:5).

Meta. This form of the name Bath-sheba signifies that the fulfilling (accomplishing or carrying out in thought and practice) of love in consciousness is directly related to richly prosperous conditions in mind and affairs. Owing to the softening of the sounds, Bath–shua takes on a more spiritual quality than Bath–sheba. Where *sheba* signifies an oath of fulfillment, *shua* represents its accomplishment.

Bavvai (A. V., Bavai), băv'-vāi (Heb. from Pers.)—*desires; wishes; with the desire of God.*

Son of Henadad, a Levite (Neh. 3:18). He was one of those who helped to rebuild Jerusalem's wall after the return from the Babylonian captivity.

Meta. Desire for the good and the true (*wisher, wishes;* an Israelite). Such desires aid in building soul and body into higher and more spiritual expression and manifestation.

Bayith (A. V., Bajith), bā'-yĭth (Heb.) —*house; dwelling; temple.* It is only through association that this word takes on its negative or carnal aspect.

A temple of the gods of Moab (Isa. 15:2); in the margin it is translated "the temple."

Meta. The carnal mind's conception, or consciousness, of the body temple (*house;* a temple of the gods of Moab).

Bazlith, băz'-lĭth (Heb.)—*stripping; peeling; nakedness; asking.*

His "children" belonged to the Nethinim who returned from the Babylonian captivity with Zerubbabel (Neh. 7:54); he is called Bazluth, in Ezra 2:52.

Meta. Bazlith and his children belong to the letting-go or "denial" phase of the mind in its work of rebuilding soul and body in Truth (*stripping, nakedness, asking*). The rebuilding of the walls of Jerusalem and of the Temple by the returned Jews after the Babylonian captivity typifies the reconstruction of the body temple into spiritual expression and manifestation—immortality.

Bealiah, bē-ă-lī'-ăh (Heb.)—*whose Lord is Jehovah; Jehovah is Lord; Jah is Lord; Baal Jehovah; Jehovah is Baal.*

One of the men who "came to David to Ziklag" (I Chron. 12:5); a Benjamite.

Meta. Fallows says that the names of Baal and Jah are both contained in the name Bealiah. This denotes both the inner and the outer, the inner spiritual man Jehovah, or Christ, and the outer formed creation. Each is all right in its place. The outer formed world of phenomena, however, should be understood in its relation to the underlying Cause of all existence and should not be worshiped; that is, it should not be looked upon as the real and as the source. When the true Jehovah is understood and worshiped the Christ Spirit becomes expressed throughout every phase of creation, of the formed and manifest world as well as of invisible Spirit. The name Bealiah signifies putting Jehovah in His rightful place as Lord or ruler of the manifest; also it signifies the superiority of Jehovah over the material ideas (gods and idols) that have been given so great a place in man's consciousness (*Jehovah is Lord*).

Bealoth (A. V., I Kings 4:16, Aloth), bē'-ă-lŏth (Heb.)—*ladies; mistresses; citizens.*

A city of Judah "toward the border of Edom in the South" (Josh. 15:24).

Meta. A state of consciousness belonging to the subconscious realm of mind in the individual (a city of Judah "in the South" suggests this), and working toward expression in the body consciousness and the body (toward Edom, Edom representing the physical body and the phase of thought that belongs to it).

Bealoth signifies a state of thought that carries an idea of the right relation between soul and body. The soul has proprietary rights (suggested in the meaning of the name *mistresses*) over the body, in a way, since the body is the outpicturing of the soul. The body is formed and given its character by the soul, the consciousness. The soul also takes the place of a *citizen* in the body. The body is its home; it expresses in and through the body, and is protected by the laws that govern the body, just as a citizen of a country enjoys the privileges and the protection of citizenship. This right relation between soul and body is first discerned by the feminine or intuitive phase of the soul in man; thus the thought of "mistress" and "lady" instead of "master" and "man" is conveyed in the definitions of Bealoth.

Bear, the (A. V., Arcturus)—*group; crowd.*

The Bear (Job 9:9; 38:32) is a constellation or group of stars called Ursa Major but commonly known as the Great Bear. The Arcturus mentioned in the Authorized Version, one of the brightest stars in the northern heavens, is in the constellation Bootes.

Meta. The book of Job describes a man who has become very righteous in the outer or personal consciousness, and since he has prepared the way for the Lord (for a more internal revelation of Truth, a realization of the inner Christ, or true righteousness), this change takes place in him.

Man, we are told, is a universe in himself. Everything in the outside world has its counterpart in man. Stars represent high, noble, overcoming thoughts; sometimes they are symbolical of the faculties and powers of man. It is said of the saints that they will shine "as the stars for ever and ever," and Christ is called "the bright . . . morning star." Stars also represent revelations of Truth that are as yet remote. The human mind cannot conceive the wonders and immensity of the universe of stars. In the same way there are endless revelations of Truth that are beyond our present range of comprehension, but we shall understand them all in time. As we come into the true understanding of ourselves and of our own inner world, we become able to grasp more and more fully the phenomena of the outer world; and so we turn within for light.

Job 38:32, 33 says:

"Canst thou lead forth the Mazzaroth in their season?

Or canst thou guide the Bear with her train?

Knowest thou the ordinances of the heavens?

Canst thou establish the dominion thereof in the earth?"

As we progress and unfold in spiritual consciousness until our mind becomes capable of containing the remote revelations of Truth, which the stars here in Job stand for, we shall become able to comprehend all things and nothing will be impossible to us.

Bebai, bē'-bāi (Heb. from Pers.)—*fatherly.*

a A man whose descendants returned from the captivity with Zerubbabel (Ezra 2:11). **b** The father of a man named Zechariah, who came up from the Babylonian captivity with Ezra (Ezra 8:11). **c** The name of a man who joined Nehemiah in sealing the covenant (Neh. 10:15).

Meta. The *fatherly* quality that must have its place in every true spiritual thought in us that we would not have devoid of fruitfulness. In other words, that our true impulses and convictions may really bring forth fruit, we must recognize them as being our own children, the offspring of the Spirit of truth within us; we must not hold ourselves apart from them by thinking that some one else is responsible for them. For illustration: Some persons are always quoting others, in talking about Truth; they never speak the Truth out boldly, as Jesus Christ did, knowing that the Truth that they declare is the product of their own indwelling Christ and that they have the right to proclaim, "Thus saith the Lord within me."

The qualities in us that Zerubbabel, Ezra, and Nehemiah (with whom the men named Bebai were connected) represent cannot establish themselves in our consciousness very strongly or fruitfully until we recognize them as being spiritual and until we know that we, coöperating with the God within us, are the father or producer of them. Even though some teacher or healer on the outside may have spoken the quickening word for us many times and with great effect for our good, yet the good itself, the light, the healing, the help that we have received, has come always from our own indwelling Spirit of God, which responded to the spoken word, whether the word was declared by another or by us. Truth never becomes established firmly in us until we lay hold of our own divine sonship, our birthright, and take up for ourselves the responsibility and the joy of putting on Christ.

Becher, bē'-chĕr (Heb.)—*early; first fruits; first-born; birthright; youth; firstling; young camel.*

a Son of Benjamin (Gen. 46:21). **b** A son of Ephraim (Num. 26:35. In the margin Bered is suggested instead of Becher; this corresponds to I Chron. 7:20).

Meta. Faith's *first-born, first fruits,* or first bringing forth of positive, upbuilding thoughts. Benjamin stands for the quality of faith in man's consciousness. Bela, Benjamin's eldest son, signifies the destroying and letting go of error—denial—that precedes the affirming, or laying positive hold, of Truth. Ephraim signifies the will.

The camel signifies power of endurance, strength, and patient perseverance. Fallows says, of the figurative use of the camel: "Multitude of camels and dromedaries of Midian, Ephah, Shebah, and flocks of Kedar and Nebaioth (Isa. 60:6-8) most evidently refers to the future restoration of Israel, when 'they shall bring all your brethren out of all the nations for an oblation unto Jehovah, upon horses, and in chariots, and in litters, and upon mules, and upon dromedaries, to my holy mountain Jerusalem' (Isa. 66:20)." *Young camel,* therefore, in the meaning of the name Becher, signifies that this first bringing forth, by faith and will, of positive, uplifting thoughts in consciousness is of Jewish or Israelitish origin; that is, it belongs to the religious side of man's nature, that which is reaching after God, after the spiritual, and is growing in patience, perseverance, and strength.

It is thought that the Becher of the Benjamites and the Becher of the Ephraimites are the same, or are very closely related by intermarriage of this family of Benjamites with the other tribe. The will (Ephraim) is the executive power in man, and so in order that faith may bring forth the fruit of its positive ideas in outer corresponding conditions it has to make union with the will, since faith without works is dead—fruitless.

Becherites (A. V., Bachrites), bē'-chĕr-ītes (Heb.)—*belonging to Becher.*

Becher, or Bered, son of Ephraim, was the head of the family of the Becherites (Num. 26:35).

Meta. Thoughts belonging to the Becher consciousness. (See BECHER.)

Becorath (A. V., Bechorath), bĕ'-eō-răth (Heb.)—*first birth; first-born; seniority; primogeniture; birthright; first fruits.*

A Benjamite from whom Saul was descended (I Sam. 9:1).

Meta. A conception of sonship (*first birth, first-born, birthright, primogeniture*).

Bedad, bē'-dăd (Heb.)—*son of Adad; separation; alone.*

Father of Hadad, king of Edom (Gen. 36:35).

Meta. The belief in separation, or apartness, from God that exists in the sense man's thought of himself, and especially of his body (*separation, alone;* the Edomites were descendants of Esau; they pertain to the physical—the outer body consciousness).

Bedan, bē'-dăn (Heb.)—*son of Dan; son of judgment.*

a A judge of Israel (called Barak, in margin) who is named with Jerubbaal, Jephthah, and Samuel as a deliverer of Israel (I Sam. 12:11). **b** A Manassite (I Chron. 7:17).

Meta. A certain activity of the judgment faculty, in discrimination and understanding (*son of Dan, son of judgment, according to judgment;* a judge of Israel and a man of Manasseh), working to put error out of consciousness and to establish harmony, which is the reward of right doing.

Bedeiah, bĕ-dē'-ĭăh (Heb.)—*servant of Jehovah; servant of Jah.*

An Israelite who had a foreign wife after the return to Judea from the Babylonian captivity; he was "of the sons of Bani" (Ezra 10:35).

Meta. A thought of service to God (*servant of Jehovah*), but not yet set free in the full light of understanding. Until wisdom is completely unified to love in man's consciousness, man is likely to become carried away at times by his feelings, or emotions, or personal affections (a foreign wife), instead of always living and acting according to divine guidance.

Beeliada, bē-ĕ-lī′-ă-dȧ (Heb.)—*whom the Lord knows; the Lord knows; known of Baal.*

A son of David (I Chron. 14:7); he is called Eliada in II Samuel 5:16.

Meta. The idea that Baal (a personal god, or a being with form and shape) knows things and is the source of knowledge. The other form of the name, Eliada, comes nearer suggesting the truth. (See ELIADA.)

Beelzebub, bē-ĕl′-zĕ-bŭb (Gk. from Heb.)—*Baal of the flies; lord of the flies.*

Sovereign of evil spirits; a heathen deity, believed to be the head over evil spirits (Luke 11:15-19); the "prince of the powers of the air, of the spirit that now worketh in the sons of disobedience" (Eph. 2:2).

Meta. You are crying "Beelzebub" whenever you say "crank" of the one who has caught sight of the spiritual mountain tops now glistening in the sun of the new age, just as they called Jesus Beelzebub because He presented and demonstrated Truth ahead of the age in which He lived. (See BAAL–ZEBUB.)

Beelzebul, bē-ĕl′-zĕ-bŭl (Gk. from Heb.)—*Baal of filth; lord of filth,* i. e., *idolatry.*

Virtually the same as Beelzebub (Matt. 10:25, margin). These words are written sometimes one way and sometimes the other, but they are not strictly synonymous.

Meta. Impurity and uncleanness. See BEELZEBUB and BAAL–ZEBUB.

Beer, bē′-ĕr (Heb.)—*well; a dug well; ditch; pit; expounding; declaring; digging out.*

a A well to which the Israelites journeyed while in the wilderness. The Scriptures (Num. 21:16-18) speak of it thus: ". . . the well whereof Jehovah said unto Moses, Gather the people together, and I will give them water.

"Then sang Israel this song:
Spring up, O well; sing ye unto it:
The well, which the princes digged,
Which the nobles of the people delved,
With the sceptre, *and* with their staves."

b The name of a town to which Jothan fled from his brother Abimelech (Judg. 9:21).

Meta. The name Beer in the Bible, whenever used, whether in connection with some other name or not, denotes the presence of a well of water. Beer represents, therefore, the depths of life and of Truth in man's consciousness, which will spring up into everlasting life when he makes proper contact with it.

Beera, bĕ-ē′-rȧ, **Beerah** (Heb.)—*well; fountain; expounder; declarer; explainer.*

a Son of Zophah, an Asherite (I Chron. 7:37). **b** A Reubenite who was carried away captive by Tilgathpilneser, king of Assyria (I Chron. 5:6); the name here is Beerah.

Meta. That in us which interprets the truth about life (*expounder, a well*) and makes this truth clear to our consciousness.

Beer–elim, bē′-ĕr-ē′-lĭm (Heb.)—*well of trees; well of the gods; well of heroes; well of princes.*

A well to the south of Moab, or a place where there was a well (Isa. 15:8); it is the same place as Beer. (See BEER.)

Meta. The high esteem in which the deep reservoirs of life and Truth in us should be held; also our union in consciousness with the inexhaustible life of Spirit. This life is symbolized in *well of trees, well of the gods, well of heroes, well of princes;* trees represent the nerves, and the nerves are expressions of thoughts of unity. They connect thought centers. The nerves lie very close to the spiritual in man, also to the physical; so a *tree* represents the connecting link between heaven and earth, the formless and the formed. *Gods, heroes, and princes* suggest high rank and value, and *wells* denote inner sources of life.

Beeri, bĕ-ē′-rī (Heb.)—*my well; of a fountain,* i. e., *illustrious; of the principal cause; expounder.*

a A Hittite, father of Judith, Esau's wife (Gen. 26:34). b The prophet Hosea's father (Hos. 1:1).

Meta. Beeri, Hosea's father, symbolizes the magnifying of the great *well* or *fountain* of life and Truth in consciousness *(of a fountain,* i. e., *illustrious, of the principal cause, expounder),* and thus an aid in bringing about an understanding and realization of life and Truth.

In the case of Beeri the Hittite, *my well* signifies the limiting of the life and truth of Spirit—which are universal, or God qualities—to something personal for the use of the outer man in building up and sustaining the flesh consciousness.

Beer–lahai–roi (A. V., Gen. 24:62 and 25:11, the well Lahai–roi), bē'-ĕr-lå-hāi'-roi (Heb.)—*the well of the living one who seeth me; well of the living one that beholds me; the well of him that liveth and seeth me, or the well of the vision of life.*

A fountain of water in the wilderness (Gen. 16:7-14), "in the way to Shur," where the angel met Hagar when she fled from Sarai. Isaac lived by the same well later (Gen. 25:11).

Meta. The recognition by the individual that his life is divine, is spiritual *(the well of the living one who seeth me),* and is for the whole man. Even the outer or physical man and the human aspect of the soul are sustained by the life of God, *the living one.*

It was beside this well that the Lord met Hagar and instructed her to return to Sarai, and also blessed her son Ishmael who was to be born. Hagar represents the natural soul. Sarai represents the spiritual. Ishmael refers to the outer or flesh consciousness. Isaac symbolizes divine sonship (Isaac lived later by this well). When it is understood that there is but one life, and that it is always everywhere present in its fullness, the entire man will be lifted up into eternal life.

Beer–lahai–roi also denotes God as the guiding light of both the inner and the outer man *(the well of the vision of life),* thus leading man to a perfect understanding of the life idea.

Beeroth, bê-ē'-rŏth (Heb.)—*wells.*

Many think Beeroth to be the same place as Beer, only given in the plural. It was a city of the Hivites that was assigned to the Israelitish tribe of Benjamin (Josh. 9:17; 18:25).

Meta. A congregation of thoughts about life and its increase in spiritual consciousness *(wells,* a city). Under the Hivites this city, or group of thoughts in consciousness, would be of a material character, but it would be elevated to a higher level in passing into the possession of the Benjamites (active faith and illumination).

Beeroth Bene–jaakan (A. V., Beeroth of the children of Jaakan), bê-ē'-rŏth bĕn'-ē-jā'-ă-kăn (Heb.)—*wells of the children of Jaakan; wells of the children of the wrestler.*

A place where the children of Israel halted while journeying through the desert on their way to the Promised Land (Deut. 10:6). In Numbers 33:31 it is called Bene–jaakan.

Meta. Jaakan was a Horite. In unredeemed man the issues of life *(wells)* are actuated by carnal tendencies and desires that appear to be very deepseated. These are symbolized by the Horites, who were enemies of the Israelites. The Israelites typify true thoughts with their expression in the consciousness and body.

In that which Jaakan signifies there is a degree of intelligence that works in the sense plane and helps to open the way to a higher realm of thought, even the spiritual. By spiritual thinking (the children of Israel in their highest symbology) the inner forces of one's being are redeemed from material beliefs and practices, and they become in truth a source of unlimited, never failing, ever present life and wholeness. We are told in Proverbs 16:22 that "understanding is a wellspring of life unto him that hath it."

Beerothite, bê-ē'-rŏth-īte (from Heb.) —*belonging to Beeroth; belonging to the wells; a dweller of the wells.*

An inhabitant of the Benjamite city of Beeroth (II Sam. 4:2-9; 23:37); spelled Berothite in I Chronicles 11:38.

Meta. A thought belonging to the

Beeroth phase of consciousness, and of like character to it. (See BEEROTH.)

Beer–sheba, bē′-ĕr-shē′-bȧ (Heb.)— *well of the oath; well of the seven; well of fulfillment; seventh well.*

One of the oldest cities in southern Palestine (Gen. 22:19). It was named from the well that Abraham dug there and the oath that established the covenant made between Abraham and Abimelech (Gen. 21:27-34). It became a city of Judah, in the apportionment of the Promised Land.

Meta. Abraham represents the first activity of the faith faculty in man's consciousness. Abimelech signifies the will, which, though unregenerate at this phase of man's unfoldment, recognizes faith and its attainments (Abraham and his possessions). Abimelech fears that he and his kingdom will be overrun by Abraham and his ever increasing household and goods. On the other hand, Abimelech's servants have taken by force the well that Abraham had dug. This latter means that the life forces, which have been discovered and laid hold of by faith's activity, have been utilized and corrupted by the fleshly man instead of being retained for the use of the mental and spiritual. The covenant between Abraham and Abimelech denotes the establishing of a right relation in consciousness between the spiritual and the seemingly material. The outer man must have his place until such time as the spiritual shall have reached the degree of unfoldment wherein it can transmute the physical into spiritual thought and manifestation.

Beer–sheba represents the establishing of this agreement (*well of the oath*) between the inner and the outer, wherein faith and its adherents (the higher thoughts of consciousness) are given ample room in the organism and are allowed to retain possession of the well (reservoir of life) that they have been instrumental in bringing to light. On the other hand, the higher thoughts of faith realize that they must not harm or destroy the outer man (Abimelech and his kingdom).

Seventh well, well of the seven, well of

fulfillment, denotes the fulfillment of the agreement, or oath, that took place at the well—at the place of realization of life and Truth in the subconsciousness. To swear by the seven is to covenant that the thing promised will be fulfilled.

Be–eshterah (A. V., Beesh–terah), bĕ-ĕsh′-tĕ-räh (Heb.)—*house of Ashtoreth; house of Ashterah; house of Astarte.*

A city in Manasseh that was given to the Gershonite Levites (Josh. 21:27); it is the same as Ashtaroth of I Chronicles 6:71, and is a form of Beth–ashtaroth, meaning the "temple of Ashtoreth."

Meta. A state of consciousness in man that houses (shelters and protects) intellectual beliefs in the reality of the outer formed world, and in carnal sensations and pleasures. This city, being allotted to Manasseh (understanding) and given over to Levi (love), signifies that by means of an awakening to a degree of understanding of and love for Truth ideals the Be–eshterah state of thought is being lifted to a higher and truer level.

Being.

Meta. In its metaphysical sense, Being is composed of wisdom, will, and consciousness. It takes all of these to make what we term God, and man stands in this Godhead as will. Ideas exist eternally in wisdom; they are made manifest through will, and that manifestation is called consciousness. Thus, man being the faculty of will in the supreme Godhead, it is through him that the universe is brought into manifestation. That which is brought forth is consciousness, a thing made.

beka (A. V., bekah), bē′-kȧ (Heb.)— *portion; half; cleft; remnant; half shekel; half measure.*

One half of a shekel (Exod. 38:26). A shekel was a certain weight of either silver or gold. A gold shekel was worth about $5.50. A silver shekel was worth about 75 cents.

Meta. A degree of recognition (*portion, half, cleft*) of the rich and everywhere present substance of Spirit. (Money is a symbol of substance.)

Bel, bĕl (Heb.)—*lord.*

The Aramaic form of Baal (Isa. 46:1). Bel is mentioned in connection with Babylon, and refers to the Babylonish god (Jer. 50:2; 51:44). It is not certain whether it was the planet Jupiter or the sun that was worshiped under the name of Bel. Bel, however, is virtually the same name as Baal.

Meta. See BAAL and ASHTORETH.

Bela (A. V., Gen. 46:21, Belah), bē'-là (Heb.)—*swallow up; destroy; devour one's substance; utterly consume; vanish away; destruction.*

a The city called Zoar (Gen. 14:2). **b** A king of Edom (Gen. 36:32). **c** The eldest son of Benjamin (Gen. 46:21). **d** A son of Azaz—a Reubenite (I Chron. 5:8).

Meta. Destructive tendencies in consciousness (*destroy, utterly consume, destruction*). The city of Bela symbolizes a group of destroying, consuming thoughts. Bela, the eldest son of Benjamin, suggests the destroying or letting go of error by denial, an absorption (*swallow up*) of error by Truth, or of darkness by light, thus doing away with the error. (See BECHER, Bela's brother.)

Belial, bē'-lĭ-ăl (Heb.)—*worthlessness; badness; lawlessness; wickedness; evil; destruction; nothingness.*

Any man or woman who was considered wicked, worthless, lawless, or licentious might be called a son or daughter of Belial. (See Deut. 13:13; Judg. 19:22; I Sam. 1:16, and II Sam. 16:7; in these texts "Belial" is used in the A. V.) Belial is not the name of any individual, except that in the New Testament it is used as an appellative of Satan (II Cor. 6:15).

Meta. Belial refers to the Adversary, or (in our interpretation) to the adverse consciousness in man.

Belshazzar, bĕl'-shäz'-zär (Heb.)—*Bel, protect the king! the Lord's leader; prince of Bel.*

The last king of Babylon; during his reign Babylon was captured by the Medes and Persians (Dan. 5).

Meta. Mere sense judgment, or instinct. It is the "son" or bringing forth of the attempt to rule the consciousness without appealing to God for right judgment (signified by Nebuchadnezzar, who was the father of Belshazzar). That which Belshazzar signifies is a mere animal; it has no reverence or respect for holy things; it sensualizes all the "vessels" of the Lord and materializes everything. The vessels of the Lord refer to the various avenues of expression in the body. Instead of realizing their spiritual significance and use, mere sense judgment (Belshazzar) looks upon them as material and thinks that they are for pleasure and sensation, artificial stimulation (wine; see Dan. 5:1-5).

Belteshazzar, bĕl-tĕ-shäz'-zär (Heb.)—*Bel's prince; whom Bel protects; whom the Lord protects; the Lord's leader; Bel, protect him, i. e., his life.*

The name given by the prince of the eunuchs of Nebuchadnezzar, king of Babylon, to Daniel (Dan. 1:7). In olden times it was customary to change one's name when a change took place in one's life, especially when one's personal liberty was concerned.

Meta. Daniel represents spiritual judgment. When this true inner discernment of Spirit is transferred from its native place (Jerusalem, or spiritual consciousness in man) it appears to take on, for the time being, something of the material thought of the sense realm to which it has been removed. At least this outer realm of consciousness looks upon the true spiritual judgment from its own sense vision, and renames it accordingly. Bel (trust in the seeming powers of the outer material world) apparently rules over it. But spiritual judgment is always true to its own source, Spirit, and continues to work and to lay up treasure in secret until such time as it and its own thought people (the Jews) shall be restored to their rightful place of dominion. It also uses its clear vision, whenever it has opportunity, to warn and to serve its sensual environing thoughts and activities, to the upliftment and redemption of the whole man.

Ben, bĕn (Heb.)—*son; an emanation; a production; a grandson; a descendant; a pupil; a disciple; a follower.*

A Levite, one of the doorkeepers whom

David chose to assist in bringing the Ark to Jerusalem (I Chron. 15:18). Ben is a Hebrew word meaning *son*. In olden times people had no surnames; therefore, to distinguish one man from another, each one was always mentioned in conjunction with his father's name; thus: "John, the son of James." The word Ben was thus used as a prefix.

Meta. A positive, masculine thought in consciousness, that springs from whatever quality the name used with it indicates.

The Ben of I Chronicles 15:18 represents the idea of sonship, which idea aids greatly in returning the Ark of the Covenant (the original spark of divinity in man's being) to Jerusalem (the heart center), that it may express more perfectly in peace, harmony, and spiritual progression throughout the consciousness.

Ben – abinadab, bĕn – ă - bĭn'- ă - dăb (Heb.)—*son of Abinadab; son of the source of liberality; product of the source of generous outpouring; son of nobility; son of willingness.*

One of the twelve officers who gathered victuals for King Solomon and his household, and son-in-law of Solomon (I Kings 4:11).

Meta. The offspring of the very generous nature and high aspirations of the realm of thought that Abinadab signifies. (See ABINADAB.)

Benaiah, bĕ-nā'-ĭah (Heb.)—*son of Jah; whom Jehovah hath built up; produced by Jehovah; prospered of Jehovah; restored by Jah.*

One of the foremost of David's mighty men, and son of Jehoiada. He did many mighty deeds; among them was the slaying of the two sons of Ariel of Moab (II Sam. 23:20-23). He was appointed by Solomon, to whom he adhered after David's death, to kill Joab and Adonijah (I Kings 2:24-31).

Meta. Jehoiada, the father of Benaiah, represents the divine law of justice, which brings to retribution all who transgress it. It calls into action the forces that destroy error. Benaiah is one of these forces. He signifies a higher degree of intelligence and understanding than that of the carnal mind or of the intellectual (the two sons of Ariel of Moab, and Adonijah the half brother of King Solomon); he also supersedes the phase of the executive quality of the will that Joab signifies. This understanding force, which Benaiah signifies, is of the Lord, and is built up by Jehovah (*son of Jah; whom Jehovah hath built up; produced by Jehovah*); as it enters the consciousness it takes the place of all lesser and reflected understanding and executive power.

Ben–ammi, bĕn-ăm'-mī (Heb.)—*son of my people; son of my kindred; son of my tribe,* i. e., *my countryman; my tribesman.*

Son of Lot by his younger daughter (Gen. 19:38), and progenitor of the Ammonites.

Meta. The offspring of, and a ruling thought in, the darkened phase of consciousness in man that Lot signifies. (Lot means *dark-colored, hidden;* he represents the part of man's subjective consciousness that is still in darkness.)

Ben–deker (A. V., the son of Dekar). bĕn-dē'-kĕr (Heb.)—*son of Deker; son of thrusting through; son of piercing; son of stabbing;* i. e., *a lancer; a swordsman; a stabber.*

One of the commissary officers of King Solomon (I Kings 4:9).

Meta. The force or power of an active belief in omnipresent supply. This belief pierces error thoughts of limitation and the belief that the end of things (Makaz) is at hand. It destroys the sly thoughts of lack in consciousness (Shaalbim, meaning *place of foxes*). By the power of the true belief that it represents, the Ben–deker belief establishes *hope* (another meaning of Makaz), *strength, grace* (Elon–beth–hanan, and *light* (Beth–shemesh), that the household of Solomon (the consciousness of peace and wisdom) may be sustained. (Makaz, Shaalbim, Elon–beth–hanan, and Beth–shemesh were the places in Israel from which Ben–deker was to gather food for Solomon's household for one month in each year.)

Bene–berak, bĕn'-ĕ-bē'-răk (Heb.)—

sons of Berak; sons of lightning.

A city of Canaan that was allotted to Dan (Josh. 19:45).

Meta. A quick, fiery, active state of consciousness in executing judgment (*sons of lightning,* a city of Dan, Dan meaning *a judge*). Unless these thoughts are guided by reason and are balanced by some of the other faculties of the mind—love, order, and the like—they are likely to bring about disastrous results instead of the good ones desired. (See BARAK.)

Bene–jaakan (A. V., Deut. 10:6, Beeroth of the children of Jaakan), bĕn′-ĕ-jā′-ă-kăn (Heb.)—*sons or children of Jaakan; sons of the wrestler; children of the twister; children of the perverter,* i. e., *perverted.*

A place where the Israelites camped while on their way from Egypt to Canaan (Num. 33:31). In Deuteronomy 10:6 it is called Beeroth Bene–jaakan.

Meta. A group of thoughts belonging to the Horite phase of consciousness. Being on the sense plane and blind to the real truth of man's being (Jaakan was a Horite, and the Horites have their seat of action in the physical organism; they are *cave-dwellers,* and so refer especially to the deep-seated, error, carnal tendencies and activities of the physical man), the thoughts that Bene–jaakan signifies usually aid in leading the individual away from the true light of life (*children of the perverter,* i. e., *perverted*) instead of leading him to higher thought and activity; they turn, twist, and distort the Truth to suit their own error ends. The camping of the children of Israel at Bene–jaakan while on their way to the Promised Land bespeaks an adjusting of this seemingly perverted phase of consciousness by introducing the light of Truth into it.

Ben–geber, bĕn–gē′-bēr (Heb.)—*son of Geber; son of man; son of an illustrious one; son of a warrior; son of a strong man; son of a hero; son of a superman.*

One of Solomon's twelve commissaries (I Kings 4:13).

Meta. A realization of great strength, courage, nobility, and conquering power; a high spiritual thought; a thought of divine sonship.

Ben–hadad, bĕn–hā′-dăd (Heb.)—*son of Hadad; worshiper or follower of Hadad or Adad,* i. e., *chief divinity of the Syrians; son of vehemence; son of fierceness; son of sharpness.*

The name, or title, of several kings of southern Syria (I Kings 15:18-20; 20:1-43). Hadad was the Aramic name of the chief Syrian deity.

Meta. A ruling thought in the phase of intellect that is typified by the Syrians. In this phase of thought there is no understanding of the real and true in consciousness, the Israelites. It therefore works against man's spiritual development. It is destructive and undisciplined, and its dominating power (king) comprehends and seeks to attain the things of the sense life only.

Ben–hail, bĕn–hā′-ĭl (Heb.)—*son of strength; son of might; son of valor; son of integrity; son of virtue; son of ability; son of substance; son of riches.*

A prince of Jehoshaphat, king of Judah, whom the king sent to teach the book of the law of Jehovah to the people throughout the cities of Judah (II Chron. 17:7).

Meta. Ben–hail bespeaks the qualities of strength, might, courage, integrity, virtue, wisdom, and substance (*son of strength, son of might,* and so forth). The spoken word must contain these qualities, that its truth may be impressed upon and become established in man's thought people.

Ben–hanan, bĕn–hā′-năn (Heb.)—*son of kindness; very gracious; of one gracious; son of grace.*

A son of Shimon, a descendant of Judah (I Chron. 4:20).

Meta. The quality of graciousness and kindliness (*son of kindness, very gracious*), which is greatly strengthened in consciousness and is given freedom of expression through praise (Judah).

Ben–hesed, bĕn–hē′-sĕd (Heb.)—*son of zeal; son of benignity; son of lovingkindness; son of mercy.*

One of Solomon's commissary officers (I Kings 4:10).

Meta. The name means virtually the same as Ben–hanan, with perhaps more of a truly spiritual application. The expression in consciousness of this kindly, benevolent spirit (Ben-hesed—*son of loving-kindness, son of mercy*), is necessary, that the qualities needed to sustain peace and its associate thoughts (Solomon and his household) throughout one's being may be realized.

Ben-hur, bĕn'-hûr, (Heb.)—*son of Hur; son of whiteness; son of purity; son of nobility; son of splendor.* In a bad sense, *son of the hole; son of a prison.* (The idea of *a hole* is that of a burrowing animal; the idea of *a prison* is a filthy subterranean hole.)

One of Solomon's twelve commissary officers (I Kings 4:8); he gathered his share of provisions from the hill country of Ephraim.

Meta. A pure, uplifting, freeing idea in consciousness (*son of whiteness, son of purity, son of nobility*). This idea, working in an exalted, positive attitude of the will (the hill country of Ephraim), is sure to do its part in realizing substance for the sustenance of the Solomon consciousness in the individual who gives it place in mind. If such a one does not allow it expression in himself, he brings about darkened, limited experiences in both mind and body—makes *a prison* for himself.

Beninu, bĕn'-ĭ-nū (Heb.)—*our son; our production; our emanation; our posterity.*

A Levite who joined Nehemiah in sealing the covenant that the Jewish people made with God after their return from their captivity in Babylon (Neh. 10:13).

Meta. The true idea that love (Beninu was descended from Levi, who represents the love faculty in man), when it is acknowledged and is unified consciously with God, brings forth its fruit (*our son*) of good continuously, even to the farthest generation, to all future time (*our posterity*).

Benjamin, bĕn'-jă-mĭn (Heb.)—*son of the right hand; son of good fortune; son of prosperity; son of happiness; son of the south,* i. e., *productiveness.*

a The younger of the two sons of Rachel and Jacob: "And it came to pass, as her soul was departing (for she died),

that she called his name Benoni: but his father called him Benjamin" (Gen. 35:18). Jacob's blessing upon Benjamin was:

"Benjamin is a wolf that raveneth:
In the morning he shall devour the prey,
And at even he shall divide the spoil."

b Benjamin was also one of the tribes of Israel, and was composed of the descendants of Benjamin, the son of Jacob (Num. 1:37). In blessing this tribe, Moses said:

"The beloved of Jehovah shall dwell in safety by him;
He covereth him all the day long,
And he dwelleth between his shoulders."

c The name also of one of the gates of Jerusalem (Jer. 20:2; Zech. 14:10).

Meta. Faith—an active, accomplishing faith—in the consciousness of man. In II Chronicles 14:8 we see how praise (Judah) and faith (Benjamin) established in consciousness express as strong, courageous, and conquering thoughts ("mighty men of valor").

Benjamite. See BENJAMIN.

Beno, bē'-nô (Heb.)—*his son.*

A Levite, son of Jaaziah, and descended from Merari (I Chron. 24:27).

Meta. An idea of love (a Levite) that is working in man to bring about a realization of his divine sonship (*his son*). As yet, however, the individual has not made conscious union with this love idea or claimed his sonship. The inner forces of Spirit are working, though, to bring about the acknowledgment and consciousness of the truth of man's being. (Jaaziah, father of Beno, means *Jah will determine,* or *Jah will strengthen.*) Before he understands and realizes the fact of his divine sonship, man often has bitter experiences and is not centered in the poise, peace, and abidingness of Spirit. (Merari, the name of the Levite chief from whom Beno was descended, means *bitter, unhappy.*)

Ben-oni, bĕn-ō'-nī (Heb.)—*son of my sorrow.*

The name that Rachel gave to Benjamin at his birth; she died when he was born (Gen. 35:18), and Jacob changed his name to Benjamin (*son of the right hand*).

Meta. Rachel (*ewe, lamb*) stands for the pure, lamblike quality of the spiritual soul in its first stages of conscious unfoldment. It is untried and is without true understanding and guiding power. When it brings forth the active quality of faith (Benjamin) through its union with the mentality (Jacob), it experiences sorrow and dies. That is, it sinks back into seeming oblivion in the subconsciousness until a further understanding and development are attained. But the activity of faith (Benjamin), which for a period seems a Benoni (*son of my sorrow*) to the negative soul quality (Rachel), becomes strength and executive power (*son of the right hand*) to the more active mental side of the individual, which Jacob represents.

Ben–zoheth, bĕn–zō'-hĕth (Heb.)— *son of Zoheth; son of corpulence; son of strength.*

Son of Ishi, and descended from Judah (I Chron. 4:20).

Meta. The building up to excess and strengthening of the outer man (*son of corpulence, son of strength*), through a material aspect and use of the saving power (Ishi) of praise (Judah) and Truth.

Beon, bē'-ŏn (Heb.) — *habitation; dwelling; refuge.*

The same city as Baal–meon (Num. 32:3). In Hebrew, "b" and "m" have virtually the same sound and are often confused. Beon should have been rendered by the early Hebrew copyists as "Meon," a contraction of Baal–meon.

Meta. See BAAL–MEON.

Beor (A. V., II Peter 2:15, Bosor), bē'-ôr (Heb.)—*a torch; a lamp; consuming fire; an eating flame; consume by grazing; brutish; stupid; foolish; one who tends a flock; a shepherd.*

a Father of Bela, who was a king of Edom (Gen. 36:32). **b** The prophet Balaam's father (Num. 22:5).

Meta. An intuitive understanding belonging to the outer man of sense (*a torch, a lamp*). Since this light (understanding) is not established consciously in Spirit nor guided by Spirit, but by material beliefs and desires, it is not a true *shepherd* to the pure natural life of the organism (*a flock*); instead it works unwisely and destructively (*an eating flame, brutish, foolish*).

Bera, bē'-rȧ (Heb.)—*spontaneous gift; son of thought; son of desire; son of evil; son of wickedness.*

A king of Sodom, in Abraham's time (Gen. 14:2).

Meta. The directing thought and desire of the sensual state of consciousness that Sodom signifies. (See SODOM.)

Beracah (A. V., Berachah), bĕr'-ȧ-cȧh (Heb.)—*a blessing; a benediction; a gift; a present.*

a A valley between Bethlehem and Hebron, where the men of Judah, under Jehoshaphat, assembled to bless Jehovah for their victory over the Moabites and the Ammonites (II Chron. 20:26). **b** A Benjamite who came to David at Ziklag (I Chron. 12:3).

Meta. The true spirit of thanksgiving and *blessing* in man, which always adheres to the thoughts, tendencies, and powers in him that are in line with Truth—and thus aids in building up and strengthening in man's consciousness that which leads to his highest unfoldment and good.

Beraiah, bê-rā'-ĭah (Heb.)—*whom Jehovah created; begotten of Jah; brought forth of Jehovah; Jah is maker.*

A Benjamite, son of Shimei (I Chron. 8:21).

Meta. A perception of the truth that Jehovah, the Christ, is the true Father, or Maker, or Creator of manifest man. Man came forth from the Christ, the divine ideal man, which ever exists in the mind of God (*whom Jehovah created, begotten of Jah, brought forth of Jehovah, Jah is maker*). In spite of outer man's seeming direction of affairs, his apparent blunders and inharmonies, there ever remains in him the true guidance and activity of a higher light and understanding, even that of Spirit. Eventually there will be brought about a fulfillment of the good that from the beginning has been given to man, but which as yet he has so imperfectly realized and appropriated.

Berechiah (A. V., I Chron. 6:39, Berachiah), bĕr-ĕ-chī'-ȧh (Heb.)—*Jehovah* *blesses; Jah is blessing.*

Several prominent Israelitish men bore this name (I Chron. 9:16; 6:39; II Chron. 28:12; Zech. 1:1).

Meta. The meaning of Berechiah (*Jah is blessing, Jehovah blesses*), as well as the facts that are mentioned in the Bible concerning the men who bore this name, suggests the great significance and importance of becoming conscious of the blessing, or approval and good will, of God and of the divine law. The blessing of God is necessary, that a man may exercise his spiritual talents and gifts freely and fully in giving forth true service and in bringing about abundant good in his own life and in the lives of others.

Bered, bḗ'-rĕd (Heb.)—*strew; scatter; sprinkle; hail; seeding; spotted.*

A son or grandson of Ephraim (I Chron. 7:20). It seems to be another rendering of the name Becher (see BE-CHER). Bered was also the name of a place near Kadesh, in the southern part of Palestine (Gen. 16:14).

Meta. The seed is the word. The ideas and the thoughts that are accepted and appropriated by man are seeds that bear fruit in his life. Becher, a form of the name Bered, signifies a first bringing forth of positive, upbuilding thoughts in consciousness. Bered (*strew, scatter, seeding*) indicates the sowing of these ideas (seed thoughts) in the mind, that the individual may begin to act upon them consciously. *Hail* suggests a coldness and hardness with which these positive seed thoughts may "hit" the consciousness if the will (Ephraim) acts apart from love and praise, the harmonizing and multiplying attributes of mind. Love and praise sweeten, warm, mellow, and refresh the whole being of man; when his true thoughts and words are redolent with the influence of these qualities, they are received gladly, and they bring forth fruit a hundredfold.

Beri, bḗ'-rī (Heb.)—*well; fountain; expound; declare; my son; my productions.*

Son of Zophah, of the tribe of Asher (I Chron. 7:36).

Meta. A conception of the life idea and its constant activity in man (*well, fountain*). The thought of fruitfulness, of ability to perform, to do, to originate and bring forth, is also involved in the meaning of Beri (*my son, my productions*). Beri suggests too that understanding quality in man which interprets the truth about life and substance and makes this truth clear to his consciousness (*expound, declare*).

Beriah, bĕ-rī'-ăh (Heb.)—*evil; calamity; misfortune; in evil; a son of evil.*

a Son of Asher, and head of the Berites (Gen. 46:17). **b** A son of Ephraim. Ephraim named this son Beriah because of the evil that had come to his house in that several of his sons had been slain by the men of Gath and their cattle had been taken away from them (I Chron. 7:23). **c** Beriah was also the name of a Benjamite and of a Levite (I Chron. 8:13; 23:10). The Benjamite named Beriah helped to put to flight the inhabitants of Gath.

Meta. Gath means *wine press,* and Beriah suggests the seeming inharmony or *evil* that accompanies the sifting processes in consciousness that a wine press signifies. The little self, or personal man, who is limited and selfish in his thought and expression, experiences what appears to him to be evil when he is forced to let go his limitations that the individual may be raised to a higher level. But the crossing out of self results in good to the whole man, and man realizes this good after his faculties have gone through the cleansing process. The sons of Ephraim (the will) are overcome by the men of Gath, but the Benjamites drive them out. Thus faith, and not will power alone, must be exercised in overcoming the errors that the Philistines of Gath represent.

Beriites, bĕ-rī'-ītes (Heb.)—*misfortune.*

Descendants of Beriah, the son of Asher (Num. 26:44).

Meta. The thoughts that belong to the Beriah phase of consciousness. They suggest a belief in evil that causes one to behold the seeming error of an experience instead of the good that is attained in every instance wherein some of the self is crossed out that the spiritual may come into fuller and freer expression.

Bernice, bĕr-nī′-çĕ (Gk.)—*victorious; bringing victory.*

Eldest daughter of Herod Agrippa, and a sister of the Agrippa of Acts 25 and 26 (Acts 25:13).

Meta. Bernice, with Drusilla, the wife of Felix, represents the voluptuous side of the sense life. That is not true victory which is successful only in feeding and building up for a time the outer or sense man in his carnal state.

Berodach–baladan, bĕ-rō′-dăch-băl′-ă-dăn (Heb.)—*Merodach his lord; Mars has power; Merodach has given a son.*

A son of Baladan, and king of Babylon (II Kings 20:12). He is called Merodach–baladan in Isaiah 39:1. This king was a Chaldean by race. He sent messengers to King Hezekiah of Judah with a present and letters, because of Hezekiah's sickness and recovery. Hezekiah foolishly showed these messengers all his treasures, and later the Babylonians took them, and took the Jewish people captive to Babylon.

Meta. Merodach, or Berodach, meaning *war, death, slaughter,* was an idol of the Babylonians that was dedicated to the planet Mars; Mars was the Babylonian god of blood and slaughter, to whom they offered human sacrifices, and whom they worshiped as a star of evil omen. Baladan means *having power.* Berodach–baladan signifies the attributing of power to evil, the belief that war, strife, sin, and death are necessary and are inevitable. (See MERODACH–BALADAN.)

The Chaldeans represent psychic thoughts; they are not spiritual, but shine by borrowed light, or understanding. It is not wise to give the truths of Spirit and their substance and power over to the building up of the psychic realm of one's consciousness (represented in Hezekiah's showing the messengers of this king all his treasures and the treasures of the house of the Lord).

Berœa (A. V., Berea), bĕ-rœ′-à (Gk.) —*well watered; watered.*

A Macedonian city to which Paul and Silas went in order to get away from persecution such as they had suffered in Thessalonica (Acts 17:10). We read in Acts 17:11, 12, that the Jews of Berœa were more noble than those of Thessalonica in that they received the word readily and examined the Scriptures daily to see whether the things that Paul taught them were true, and many of them believed, also many of the Greeks, both men and women.

Meta. Macedonia stands for enthusiasm, the fervor of the soul in its desire for spiritual understanding and power. Thessalonica (ancient Thermæ, meaning *hot springs*), a city of Macedonia from which Paul was driven by persecution of the Jews there, represents the burning or heated zeal of the soul in its desire for Truth; however, it is without a sufficient thinking balance, in this instance, to give tolerance and wisdom. At Berœa, while there is the same desire for Truth, there is also a readiness to look into that which differs from the old established religious thought. So Berœa signifies the zeal of the soul in religious matters, tempered by good judgment, tolerance, and intelligent willingness to examine all thoughts presented to it, that the real Truth may be discerned and received into consciousness. By understanding is any phase of man's consciousness *watered* so that the Truth may take root and grow and bring forth fruit.

Berothai, bĕr′-ŏ-thāi (Heb.)—*wells; my wells; cypresses of Jah.*

A city of Hadadezer, king of Zobah, that was conquered by David (II Sam. 8:8). The Berothah of Ezekiel 47:16 is supposed to be the same city. Zobah was the portion of Syria that formed a separate empire at the time of David and Solomon.

Meta. Fallows says concerning the cypress, "It may have been the Syrian juniper, which grows wild upon Lebanon." This "tree . . . is a tall evergreen, the wood of which is heavy, aromatic, and remarkably durable . . . Coffins were made of it in the East, and the mummy-cases of Egypt are found at this day of the cypress-wood. The timber has been known to suffer no decay by the lapse of 1100 years." The cypress therefore would stand for the changeless substance of Spirit. *Wells* always refer to contact with the wellspring of life within man; and the *cypresses of Jah* symbolize enduring spiritual substance. Berothai must represent this life and substance in our organism. That this city belonged to the Syrians indicates that the inner life and substance was under the dominion of the intellect, apart from any true understanding; in that situation it would be looked upon as limited and transitory, and would manifest accordingly. But when taken over by David, who stands for love in individual consciousness and is a type of Christ, this inner life and substance that Berothai signifies becomes in us manifestly what it really is in Truth: spiritual, abiding, and unlimited.

Besai, bē'-sāi (Heb.)—*treading under foot; trampling down; domineering oppression; ruthless victory; conqueror.*

His descendants were among the Nethinim who returned from the Babylonian captivity with Zerubbabel (Ezra 2:49).

Meta. An overcoming tendency, or power, in man that brings forth thoughts that become active in freeing and restoring the Truth in consciousness (*conqueror;* Besai's "children" returned to Jerusalem with Zerubbabel from the captivity in Babylon). There is a personal element in this overcoming thought or force, however, that needs further enlightenment and uplift.

Besodeiah, bĕs-ō-dē'-ĭah (Heb.)—*in the intimacy of Jah; in familiar converse with Jehovah; in the Lord's secret; in counsel with Jehovah; given in confidence to Jah.*

His son Meshullam helped to repair the walls of Jerusalem after returning from the Babylonian captivity (Neh. 3:6).

Meta. A knowledge of man's true being, of his spiritual nature and sonship. This is *the Lord's secret,* and that in us which perceives it is in close association with Jehovah (*in familiar converse with Jehovah, in the intimacy of Jah, in counsel with Jehovah*). This knowledge generates, in the individual who has entered into a consciousness of his oneness with the Christ within him, a de-

votion to spiritual things, a unification with Spirit, and a companionship with true ideas that does much toward rebuilding his mind and body in enduring life, substance, and Truth. (Rebuilding the walls of Jerusalem refers to the rebuilding of the organism into its true spiritual likeness and durability.)

Besor, bē'-sôr (Heb.)—*cool water; cool brook; cold; good news; joyful news; fairness; beauty; brightness; cheerfulness.*

A brook in the southern part of Judah (I Sam. 30:9).

Meta. The cooling, cleansing waters of denial of seeming error (*cool water, cool brook*). Denials are necessary when one has become very much wrought up, and weakened, by a struggle against seeming dominance of error thoughts and desires. (The Amalekites had stolen away the families and possessions of David and his men in their absence. While pursuing the Amalekites to defeat them and regain their families and possessions, two hundred of David's men had to stay behind at Besor because they were physically unable to go farther.) True words of denial of error cleanse the consciousness and open the way for renewed life and power to enter into all one's fainting, overwrought, worn-out thoughts that have been struggling for the good and the true, but because of a belief in evil as a power have been unsuccessful. Thus the individual gains a new sense of victory and dominion, of joy, harmony, and wholeness (*good news, joyful news, fairness, brightness,* and so forth): David caught up with the retreating Amalekites and regained all that had been lost.

Betah, bē'-tăh (Heb.)—*trust; confidence; security; fearlessness; tranquillity.*

A city of Zobah-Syria that David took from Hadadezer (II Sam. 8:8); in I Chronicles 18:8 it is called Tibhath. From this city "David took very much brass, wherewith Solomon made the brazen sea, and the pillars, and the vessels of brass," for the Temple.

Meta. Confidence and *trust.* The brass that was taken from this city by David represents boldness, strength, and substance. When all these qualities are under the dominion of David (who signifies love, and is a type of Christ), they are centered in God. Thus they greatly strengthen one's whole being in life and Truth.

Beten, bĕ'-tĕn (Heb.)—*belly; womb; the inmost part; a valley; a swelling; a protuberance; a hill.*

A border city of the tribe of Asher (Josh. 19:25).

Meta. Thoughts of generation, from a very low and carnal standpoint (*belly, womb, a valley*). *A swelling, a protuberance, a hill,* give the idea of pride, pride in the carnal thought or belief of generation. (*A hill,* in the meaning of Beten, does not refer to height, but to enlargement, swelling; and swelling bespeaks pride in a carnal sense.)

Beth–anath, bĕth–ā'–năth (Heb.)—*house of 'Anat; house of answers,* i. e., *to prayers; house of response; house of reply; house of echo; house of wailing cry; house of affliction.*

A city of Canaan that was allotted to Naphtali (Josh. 19:38). The men of Naphtali did not drive out the Canaanitish inhabitants of this city, but made servants of them (Judg. 1:33).

Meta. A thought center in man that, to a degree at least, realizes the response of Spirit to the cry of the soul (see ANATH) for a greater realization of strength (*house of answers,* i. e., *to prayers, house of reply;* Naphtali is the Israelitish tribe that represents strength).

Naphtali failed to overcome the Canaanitish inhabitants of Beth–anath completely, but made them subject to taskwork. This incident symbolizes a drawing on the elemental life forces of the organism (Canaanites) for increased strength and vigor, while retaining more or less the old material belief concerning these forces. We must know that life is spiritual, immortal, abiding, unlimited, unchanging, and pure, before we can realize and express it in its fullness.

Beth–anoth, bĕth–ā'–nŏth (Heb.)—*house of 'Anat; house of answers,* i. e., *to prayers; house of response; house of re-*ply; *house of echo; house of the wailing cry; house of affliction.*

A city in the hill country that was, with other towns, allotted to Judah (Josh. 15:59).

Meta. Beth–anoth has much the same significance as Beth–anath, only it does not pertain to the realization of strength specifically. 'Anat, or Anath, represents Spirit's response to the cry of the soul for deliverance from opposing thoughts. Beth–anoth, in the hill country of Judah, signifies a high state of thought, above seeming materiality; by offering prayer and praise (Judah), man can lift himself into this high state and into a realization of Spirit's omnipresence and allness.

Bethany (A. V., John 1:28, Bethabara), bĕth'–ā–nў (Gk. from Heb.)—*house of figs* (derived from the moaning, sighing, wailing sound of the foliage, and from the "tears," drops of gum, that exude from the fruit); *house of afflictions; house of distress; house of depression.* Bethany, or Bethabara, the place where John baptized, means *place of crossings; place where crossings are made; place of fords.*

a A town near Jerusalem, the home of Lazarus and his sisters, often visited by Jesus (John 11:1; Mark 11:1). **b** A place beyond Jordan where John the Baptist baptized (John 1:28).

Meta. Bethany means *wailing, lamentation, affliction;* and signifies the demonstration over these conditions. Whenever we make a mental demonstration we get a certain result in mind and body. In Bethany Jesus raised Lazarus from the dead, and thus overcame the sorrow, lamentation, and affliction of Mary and Martha.

Beth–arabah, bĕth–ăr'–ă–băh (Heb.)—*house of the desert; house of the barrenness; house of the sterility; house of blackness; house of depression.*

a A city in the wilderness, near the Dead Sea, on the border of Judah (Josh. 15:6, 61). **b** A city of the tribe of Benjamin (Josh. 18:22).

Meta. The "arabah" is the desert, or places in the earthly, physical ideas of substance that have been separated from the indwelling vitality. The cities of Beth–arabah represent places of this kind in consciousness, that need to be lifted into fruitfulness by means of faith (Benjamin) and praise (Judah).

Beth–arbel, bĕth–är'-bĕl (Heb.)— *house of God's ambush; house of God's lying-in-wait; house of God's watching; house of God's windows; house of God's court.*

A place that was destroyed by Shalman, or Shalmaneser, king of Assyria (Hos. 10:14). It was a fortified place, apparently, and belonged to the Israelites, but was overthrown because they did not remain true to their worship of the one God.

Meta. The working out of the divine law in a way seemingly adverse to the higher religious thoughts of the consciousness (Israelites), in that the light and joy of their oneness with God is lost to them for a time. (Beth–arbel was destroyed by Shalmaneser, king of Assyria; Shalmaneser signifies a very destructive tendency in man. A *court* is a place where justice is administered, and an *ambush* bespeaks an unseen peril or attack.)

Beth–aven, bĕth–ā'-vĕn (Heb.)—*house of vanity; house of iniquity; house of nothingness; house of calamity; house of trouble; house of idols.*

A city, or town, near Bethel (Josh. 7:2; Hos. 4:15; 10:5, 8). Bethel is also said to have been nicknamed Beth–aven after Jeroboam had made it the chief seat of the worship of the golden calf. (See I Kings 12:25—13:10.)

Meta. See AVEN for the significance of Beth–aven, since apparently they are the same place. Beth–aven, in the case of Bethel's being called by this name, refers to the vanity of worshiping gold, money, or the outer, material thought about substance.

Beth – azmaveth, bĕth – ăz'-mă-vĕth (Heb.)—*house of Azmaveth; house of death's strength.*

A town of Benjamin (Neh. 7:28); it is called Azmaveth in Ezra 2:24 and in Nehemiah 12:29.

Meta. See AZMAVETH.

Beth–barah, bĕth–bā'-răh (Heb.)— *house of the crossing over; house of crossings; house of fords.*

A ford of the river Jordan (Judg. 7:24); same place as Bethabara (A. V.), or Bethany, where John did much of his baptizing, and where he baptized Jesus.

Meta. The place in consciousness where, by discernment and denial of seeming error, we can cleanse our thoughts from error sufficiently to enable us to cross safely over (*house of the crossing over*) the flood of mortal, earthly race thoughts about life, that the river Jordan represents.

Gideon, who won the victory over the hosts of Midian, at or near Beth–barah (Judg. 7), represents judgment in process of development, and the destroying of error by denial. John's baptism also signifies cleansing of the consciousness by denial of error.

Beth–biri (A. V., Beth–birei), bĕth–bĭr'-ī (Heb.)—*house of my creation; house of my begetting; house of my coming forth; house of fatness; house of my Creator.*

A city of Simeon, in the land of Canaan (I Chron. 4:31).

Meta. The truth that man's consciousness and body, established in substance, are the product of his own inner, true I AM (*house of my creation, house of my begetting, house of fatness*); also the truth that man's consciousness and body constitute the house, or temple, in which his Christ self, Jehovah God, or true I AM dwells, and through which it expresses (*house of my coming forth, house of my Creator*). Man comes into an understanding of this truth by hearing and obeying the divine law of Being as revealed by the Spirit of truth within him. (Simeon is one who hears and obeys; hearing is another word for receptivity, or a listening attitude of mind.)

Beth–car, bĕth'-cär (Heb.)—*house of exultation; house of leaping about; house of lambs; house of lambs' pasture.*

A place where the children of Israel quit pursuing the Philistines after putting them to flight (I Sam. 7:11).

Meta. That place where we consciously abide and rejoice abundantly in the overcoming power of Spirit and in a realization of omnipresent substance and life (*house of exultation, house of leaping about, house of lambs, house of lambs' pasture*). This is a genuine milestone in our spiritual progress; we have conquered all the ground that our consciousness grasps of that which *is real* (Israel) in ourselves and in the universe as well.

Beth–dagon, bĕth–dā'-gŏn (Heb.)— *house of Dagon; house of the little fish; house of that which is abundantly propagated; house of abundant increase.*

a A town in the lowlands of Judah, close to the Philistines (Josh. 15:41). **b** A border town of Asher (Josh. 19:27).

Meta. Increase of ideas, but upon a sense plane rather than a spiritual plane. (Dagon was a national god of the Philistines; the meaning of the name is *abundant propagation, fish.*) There was a temple of Dagon at Beth–dagon before the Israelites took this town from the Philistines; no doubt the town derived its name from that fact. After coming into the possession of the Israelites (true thoughts in consciousness) this place of increase of ideas (which Beth–dagon represents) is raised to a higher level, and the error beliefs are gradually erased from it.

Beth–diblathaim, bĕth–dĭb-lă-thā'-ĭm (Heb.)—*house of Diblathaim; house of the two fig cakes; house of pressing together; house of assembly.*

A Moabitish town. It is thought to be the same place as Almon–diblathaim (Jer. 48:22).

Meta. An assemblage of thoughts of duality that have become established in man's consciousness; they are now ripe for judgment, or adjustment. (So we derive the meaning, *house of assembly, house of two fig cakes, house of pressing together. Two fig cakes* and *pressing together* give the suggestion that two kinds of thought, or a belief in both evil and good, are being carried in consciousness; and judgment is pronounced upon Beth–diblathaim, or this state of thought, by the prophet. See Jer. 48:21, 22). Moab stands for the carnal mind and the most external conditions of life, yet within man's inner consciousness the

true idea of life and substance always abides. (See ALMON–DIBLATHAIM.)

Beth–eden, bĕth–ē'-den (Heb.)—*house of pleasantness; house of delight; house of pleasure; house of temporal sensibility.*

It seems to have been the city of a wicked ruler who was threatened with destruction by Amos (Amos 1:5, margin).

Meta. Eden means a pleasant, productive state of consciousness, having all possibilities; it represents the consciousness of the divine in natural man. Beth–eden (*house of pleasure*) symbolizes the house, or established consciousness, of that which is pleasing and harmonious. But if the central, controlling thought of this state of consciousness is one of selfishness and error, the whole peace, bounty, and other possibilities of good that lie in this Eden are greatly hindered in their expression; therefore error must be destroyed from its borders.

Beth–el, bĕth'–ĕl (Heb.)—*house of God.*

This town originally was named Luz. It is situated a few miles north of Jerusalem (Gen. 28:19; 35:1-15).

Meta. Luz means *turning away, departing.* That which seemed separate and apart is brought into unity, and the name is then Beth–el. In the individual, Beth–el refers to a certain center near the heart, which is called the *house of God.* It seems material, at first sight. Jacob thought that it was material, when he lay down there with a stone for a pillow; but he found there a ladder reaching to heaven, and he exclaimed: "Surely Jehovah is in this place; and I knew it not" (Gen. 28:16-22). So Beth–el really symbolizes a consciousness of God, or conscious unity with God.

Beth–emek, bĕth–ē'-mĕk (Heb.)— *house of the deep; house of the unsearchable; house of the valley.*

A boundary city of Asher (Josh. 19:27).

Meta. The subconscious realm of mind in man, and the mistaken idea that the depths of the subconsciousness are past finding out (*house of the deep; house of the unsearchable*); also a depressed state of thought in the subconscious realm of man. This depressed state of mind can be built up and the nature of the thoughts in it can be changed to joy and gladness, strength and abundance, by the work of the Asher consciousness in their midst. (A *valley* always refers to a low place in consciousness—thoughts that need to be raised to a higher level.)

Bethesda, bĕ-thĕṣ'-dȧ (Heb.)—*house of mercy; house of benignity; house of loving-kindness; house of healing.*

A pool in Jerusalem, by the sheep gate (John 5:2); it had five porches, which sheltered constantly a multitude of sick folk who expected to receive benefit from the healing virtue that was believed to exist in the waters of this pool at certain periods.

Meta. The point in consciousness where we feel the flow of the cleansing life of Spirit. This "pool," or place in consciousness, is formed by the realization that our life is being constantly purified, healed, and made new by the activity of mind. Physically this is expressed in the purification and upbuilding wrought in the blood when it comes in contact with the oxygen in the lungs. The ebb and flow of the waters of the pool are constantly going on, and when mind is active all the depleted blood corpuscles are purified and renewed.

Sheep represent the natural, innocent expression of spiritual life, and the "sheep *gate*" is the channel through which this life flows into the organism.

The "five porches" represent the five-sense limitation, which does not realize the power of Spirit. The porches are filled with the multitude of those who are sick, blind, halt, and withered, or with unregenerate thoughts.

"When the water is troubled" typifies the dependence of unawakened man upon certain slow, natural healing processes, which he calls the work of nature. At this stage of man's unfoldment, the "multitude" of weak, sick, infirm thoughts and conditions within him have not received the swift healing power of spiritual I AM.

The healing of the man at the pool represents the power of the I AM (typi-

fied by Jesus) to restore the equilibrium of the organism through the activity of spiritual ideas in consciousness, independently of the healing methods utilized by the sense man. The true spiritual healing method is the word of authority, as spoken by Jesus, which must be set into activity. Through the power of the word, the "infirmity" gives place to perfect equalization and strength.

Beth-ezel, bĕth-ē'-zĕl (Heb.)—*house firmly rooted, i. e., a fixed dwelling; house of the firm seat; house of the right side; house of declivity; a neighbor's house.*

A place in Philistia, not far from Samaria. The exact site is not known (Mic. 1:11); it is thought to be identical with the Azel of Zechariah 14:5.

Meta. A perception of the firm foundation and established place that man has in Being (*house firmly rooted, i. e., a fixed dwelling; house of the firm seat*). But because the outer sense man (represented by Philistia) is using man's substance and life, his faculties and powers, to further the pleasures of the senses regardless of the welfare of the inner man, man does not manifest according to what he really is in Spirit. He seems rather to go down hill, or retrograde (*place of declivity*) at times.

The house, or established consciousness of good, that Beth-ezel signifies, belongs to the true, higher self of the individual, and not to his sense life. This true, higher self will be in deed and in truth a real *neighbor* to the outer man, when the outer acknowledges the rulership of the inner and gives him his rightful abiding place in the consciousness.

Beth-gader, bĕth-gā'-dĕr (Heb.)—*house of the wall, i. e., a walled house; an inclosure; a fortification; house of obstruction.*

A city of Judah (I Chron. 2:51). It is thought to be the same place as Geder. Geder was a very old city of the Canaanites that was captured by Joshua (Josh. 12:13).

Meta. A consciousness of protection, of defense, of unconquerable strength (*house of a wall, walled place,* signifying a strongly fortified place). This consciousness is very deep-seated, having been established in the subconscious, elemental life forces of the individual from the beginning of his existence. The truth of Being, protected all along the way and ultimately arriving at manifest perfection, is really innate in every person. Every one carries with him the belief that he will come out all right in the end. However, the thought of God, Spirit, as a wall round about one brings with it a sense of limitation (*an inclosure, house of obstruction*) to those persons who are still beset by sense beliefs and desires, yet have a degree of insight into Truth. Such persons are unable to express Truth freely; they are also held back from sense expression. Thus are they bound until they enter more whole-heartedly into the light and freedom of Spirit.

Beth-gamul, bĕth-gā'-mŭl (Heb.)— *house of recompense (good or evil); house of retribution; house of deeds; house of the weaned; camel house.*

A Moabitish city, in the plains country. Jeremiah prophesied concerning it (Jer. 48:23).

Meta. A state of thought in the carnal consciousness (Moab) in man that has run its course and is now ripe for judgment; the error results must be met, and an adjustment must be made (*house of recompense; house of retribution; house of deeds; house of the weaned; camel house;* a city of Moab). The central idea here is that there is no escape from the fruits of one's established thoughts and from one's deeds, whether they be good or ill. *Camel,* in the meaning of Beth-gamul, bespeaks a carrier, a conductor, a conduit, that which does not turn to the right hand or to the left, but leads or conducts unswervingly to an end.

Beth-haccherem (A. V., Beth-haccerem), bĕth-hăc'-che-rĕm (Heb.)—*house of the vineyard; house of the generous nature.*

A city or beacon station on a height between Jerusalem and Tekoa (Neh. 3:14). "Raise up a signal on Beth-haccherem; for evil looketh from the north, and a great destruction" (Jer. 6:1); this instruction was given to the Benjamites

who were to flee for safety.

Meta. An exalted consciousness of life and Truth. From this "high place" in man, error tendencies and their outcome are recognized. If they have gone so far that a general harvest of error reaping is unavoidable, the true thoughts and faculties (represented in this instance by Benjamin) are warned to flee; that is, to retire to some other part of the organism, or consciousness, possibly to some place deep within the subconsciousness, that they may not be destroyed by the error that is being directed against them from the north—the outer, intellectual man.

Beth-haram (A. V., Beth-aram), bĕth-hā'-răm (Heb.)—*house or place of the height; house of elevation; place of elation (of mind, i. e., pride); mountain house.*

A town given to Gad by Moses (Josh. 13:27). It was east of the Jordan, and is thought to be the same place as the Beth-haran of Numbers 32:36. It was situated "in the valley," and had belonged to Sihon, king of the Amorites, but was rebuilt by Gad after having been taken and destroyed by the children of Israel.

Meta. A lifting up, in consciousness, of the life idea. This process of upliftment is inferred in the definition, *house of the height, house of elevation, mountain house.* The Amorites have their seat of action in the generative functions and so refer to the life idea brought down to the sense plane. When purified and elevated to its rightful activity in man, his life force, or creative energy and ability, becomes a source of strength, illumination, and power to him.

Beth-haram also suggests a lifting up of the thoughts in pride (*place of elation*). Man must be watchful that he does not allow pride, because of his seeming achievements in overcoming, to find place in his consciousness.

Beth-haran, bĕth-hā'-răn (Heb.)— *house of might; house of strength; place of overcoming, i. e., getting the upper hand.* This can refer to the domination of either good or ill.

A fortified city that was built by the

Israelitish tribe of Gad, beyond the Jordan (Num. 32:36). It is thought to be the same city as Beth–haram.

Meta. A strong, dominating, conquering phase of thought (*house of might, house of strength, place of overcoming,* i. e., *getting the upper hand*).

Beth–hoglah (A. V., Josh. 15:6, Beth-hogla), bĕth–hŏg'-läh (Heb.)—*house of partridge; house of magpies; house of locusts.*

A city of Benjamin, on the border between Judah and Benjamin (Josh. 18: 19, 21).

Meta. Impulsiveness; faith (Benjamin) acting intermittently, on the impulse of the moment, not yet being firmly established in consciousness so as to express consistently at all times (*house of partridge, house of magpies, house of locusts*). Birds usually signify free, unattached thoughts. In Beth–hoglah, however, the reference is to the manner of locomotion, that which hops along like a bird, a man walking with his feet shackled, or any irregular jerking movement as compared with walking along rhythmically and steadily.

Beth–horon, bĕth–hŏ'-rŏn (Heb.)—*house of the cave; place of the hollows; house of the caverns; place of the holes.*

There were two places by this name; one was called Beth–horon the nether, and the other was called Beth–horon the upper (Josh. 16:3, 5; I Chron. 7:24). Fallows says, "The Nether Beth–horon lay in the northwest corner of Benjamin; and between the two places was a pass, called both the ascent and descent of Beth–horon, leading from the region of Gibeon (el–Jib) down to the western plain." Down this pass the Amorites were driven by Joshua (Josh. 10:11). The upper and lower towns were both fortified by Solomon (II Chron. 8:5).

Meta. A thought center deep within the consciousness where error is judged and cast out (*house of the caverns, place of the holes*). It is an avenue of thought by which the higher thoughts of justice and Truth may descend to the more subjective planes of consciousness in order to cleanse them from error.

Beth–jeshimoth, bĕth–jĕsh'-ĭ-mŏth

(Heb.)—*house of desolation; place of destruction; house of the strong death.*

A city of Moab. It was allotted to the Israelitish tribe of Reuben, but it seems to have come again into possession of the Moabites later on (Num. 33:49; Josh. 13:20; Ezek. 25:9).

Meta. A seemingly established consciousness of lack, of unproductiveness; thoughts that are very destructive, ruinous, and death-dealing in their character (*house of desolation, place of destruction, house of the strong death*). This state of thought needs to be lifted up and changed to productiveness of good and to constructiveness by the Reuben consciousness—by a seeing phase of mind, a phase that understands Truth.

Beth–lebaoth, bĕth–lĕb'-ă-ŏth (Heb.) —*house of lionesses; place of lionesses.*

A city in the land of Canaan that was allotted to the Israelitish tribe of Simeon (Josh. 19:6). It is called Lebaoth in Joshua 15:32.

Meta. A consciousness of conquering power (*house of lionesses*), governed by a willing, receptive, obedient spirit (Simeon).

Bethlehem, bĕth'-lĕ-hĕm (Heb.)—*house of bread; place of food; house of sustenance; house of living.*

a A town of Zebulun (Josh. 19:15). **b** A city of Judah, the birthplace of David (I Sam. 17:12) and of Jesus (Matt. 2:1); in Genesis 35:19 it is called Ephrath, and in Ruth 4:11, Ephrathah.

Meta. Bethlehem means *house of bread,* symbolizing the abiding place of substance. It indicates the nerve center at the pit of the stomach, through which universal substance joins the refined or spiritualized chemical products of the body substance. Through this center are gradually generated the elements that go to make up the electrical body of the Christ man. Jesus was born in Bethlehem of Judea.

Judea means *praise,* or spiritual recognition. The tribe of Judah symbolizes the aggregation of thoughts that has acknowledgment of spiritual things as the one and only thought reality. Thus the *substance* in which the Jesus man is born in us must be spiritual in character.

At Bethlehem, the substance center in man, a union of love and wisdom takes place, and the Christ is brought forth in substance.

In Ruth 1:22 "the beginning of barley harvest" symbolizes a renewal or a reunion of soul and body with true substance. The love of the soul in man (Ruth) must be established in the substance of Spirit before it can become productive of eternal satisfaction.

Beth–maacah (A. V., Beth–maachah), bĕth–mā'-ă-căh (Heb.)—*house of Maacah; house of oppression.*

The same place as Abel–beth–maacah (II Sam. 20:15).

Meta. See ABEL–BETH–MAACAH.

Beth–marcaboth, bĕth–mär'-că-bŏth (Heb.)—*house of chariots; place of chariots.*

A city in Canaan that was allotted to Simeon (Josh. 19:5). It is thought to have been a stopping-place used in the chariot trade between Jerusalem and Egypt.

Meta. A place in consciousness where the body activities meet, and give themselves over to the guiding, directing light of Spirit (*house* or *place of chariots*). Chariots represent the body activities, and Simeon, to whom this city of Beth-marcaboth was allotted, means one who listens and obeys.

Beth–meon, bĕth–mē'-ŏn (Heb.)—*Beth–baal–meon; house of habitation; place of dwelling.*

A town of Reuben. It seems to have been in the hands of Moab at the time mentioned in Jeremiah 48:23; it is the same place as Baal–meon.

Meta. See BAAL–MEON.

Beth–merhak, bĕth–mĕr'-hăk (Heb.)—*far house; place afar off; house set at a distance; a dwelling far off.*

Either a place or a house between Jerusalem and the Mount of Olives, near the brook Cedron. David tarried here when he left Jerusalem to escape from Absalom (II Sam. 15:17).

Meta. A consciousness of separateness from God (*far house, house set at a distance, place afar off*) which for a season possesses the one in Truth when he has given himself over to the love (David) of

external beauty (Absalom) apart from Spirit, and has come to the period of reaction, readjustment, or "judgment" because of his error.

Beth–nimrah, bĕth–nĭm'-răh (Heb.)—*house of spots; speckled house; house of leopard* (so-called because of his spots); *place of flowing pure water; house of limpid sweet water.*

A city of Gad that had been taken from the Amorites (Num. 32:36).

Meta. "Can the Ethiopian change his skin, or the leopard his spots? then may ye also do good, that are accustomed to do evil" (Jer. 13:23). Beth–nimrah (*house of spots, speckled house, house of leopard;* a city that had belonged to the Amorites) signifies a very iniquitous state of thought and activity in the Amoritish phase of man's consciousness. *Place of flowing pure water, house of limpid sweet water,* meanings that are also contained in the name, Beth–nimrah, bespeak the truly cleansing character of life, life being in reality spiritual and manifesting spiritually when it is directed by high, true, spiritual thinking. (Beth–nimrah was taken from the Amorites, destroyed, and rebuilt by the Israelitish tribe of Gad. It was fortified by them and was made a sheepfold; sheep refer to the pure, natural life in man.)

Beth–pazzez, bĕth–păz'-zĕz (Heb.)—*house of dispersion; place of complete disintegration; place of destruction.*

A city of Canaan that was allotted to the Israelitish tribe of Issachar (Josh. 19:21).

Meta. A belief in the materiality of body substance and life. Such beliefs sooner or later bring about a dispersion, or separation, of the various cells and parts of which the outer formed organism is composed, and the body goes to corruption—is destroyed (*house of dispersion, place of complete disintegration, place of destruction*).

Issachar means *who brings hire, he will bring reward.* In his blessing by Jacob his father, he is likened to "a strong ass, couching down between the sheepfolds . . . he bowed his shoulder to bear, and became a servant under taskwork" (Gen. 49:14, 15). This infers material thinking in regard to the pure natural life forces (sheep), which makes one's seeming tasks, or loads, heavy and hard to bear, and, if continued, leads to disintegration. Moses, in blessing the tribe of Issachar, said that Issachar would rejoice in his tents, and the hidden treasures of the sand would be his (Deut. 33:18, 19); this statement conveys thought of body substance, and infers that eventually its true quality as spiritual and immortal will be recognized.

Beth–pelet (A. V., Josh. 15:27, Beth-palet; Neh. 11:26, Beth–phelet), bĕth-pē'-lĕt (Heb.)—*house of flight; house of escape; place of complete deliverance.*

A city in the southern part of Judah (Josh. 15:27).

Meta. A subconscious (southern) *escape,* or *deliverance,* from a seemingly fixed error state of thought; in the presence of praise and thanksgiving (Judah), error flees (*house of flight*).

Beth–peor, bĕth-pē'-ôr (Heb.)—*house of opening; temple of Peor,* i. e., *Baal-peor.*

A Moabitish city that was allotted to the Israelitish tribe of Reuben (Josh. 13:20). This city was noted for its worship of Baal–peor. Moses was buried "in the valley in the land of Moab over against Beth–peor" (Deut. 34:6).

Meta. See BAAL–PEOR. Beth–peor represents a corresponding state of consciousness (*house of Peor*).

Bethphage, bĕth'-phă-ġē (Gk. from Heb.)—*house of figs; house of unripe figs.*

A small town, or village, near Bethany, at the Mount of Olives (Mark 11:1).

Meta. A place in consciousness where grace is realized. It is a place of unripe fruit (*house of figs,* or *house of unripe figs*).

Beth–rapha, bĕth-rā'-phȧ (Heb.)—*house of repairing; house of healing; place of relaxing; house of lengthening; house of giants,* i. e., *long; place of fear.*

The son of Eshton, a descendant of Judah (I Chron. 4:12).

Meta. With the exception of its application to a people of tallness, Beth–rapha in its various forms refers to healing, remission, upbuilding, restoring (*house of repairing, house of healing, place of relaxing*). All fearfulness (*place of fear*) can be overcome by the exercise of praise and thanksgiving (the Judah consciousness), established in true, abiding thoughts of wholeness.

Beth–rehob, bĕth-rē'-hŏb (Heb.)—*house of the open space; house of the forum; place of the market; house of the street; broad house; roomy place.*

A small kingdom, or province, of Syria (II Sam. 10:6). The children of Ammon hired men from this place to fight against David.

Meta. A state of consciousness, of an intellectual nature, that is too "broad" in a material-minded way to accept spiritual Truth (*broad house, roomy place, house of the open space, house of the forum, place of the market, house of the street;* Syria refers to the intellect that is unillumined spiritually). The wisdom of Spirit is foolishness to the natural man; and there are many people today who are so full of worldly wisdom that they have no room for Truth. They take great pride in thinking that they are so "broad-minded" that they could never narrow themselves to the acceptance of any particular religious ideal or doctrine. But we know that such is not the true broadness of vision, the truly charitable attitude of heart and soul, that characterize the spiritually illumined consciousness. It is an enemy to the real Christ or love (David) state of mind in man, and when it joins itself to the sense side of man (the Ammonites) it engages in active warfare against the real good of the individual.

Bethsaida, bĕth-sā'-ĭ-dȧ (Gk. from Heb.)—*house of fishing; place of hunting; place of nets; fishing town; hunting town.*

A fishing town on or near the Sea of Galilee (Mark 6:45; John 1:44). Probably there were two villages of this name, one on the east side of the Jordan where it enters the Sea of Galilee, and the other on the west side. Some think that it was one city built on both sides of the river. That part of the city to the west of Jordan was the birthplace of Philip,

Andrew, and Peter; it was near Beth-saida on the eastern side that Jesus fed the five thousand. This city was not far from Capernaum and Chorazin.

Meta. A consciousness of increase of ideas, of gathering substance; a state of thought that is continually searching after new ideas, and endeavors to gain knowledge, by every possible means (*house of fishing, place of hunting; place of nets; fishing town; hunting town*).

In Mark 8:22 Bethsaida signifies spiritual mindedness. The blind man represents a darkened mind. When we are exalted in consciousness, darkness disappears.

In Matthew 11:21 Bethsaida and Chorazin represent the state of mind that has a limited amount of Truth and believes that portion to be the full measure. This is the self-righteous phase of consciousness. The openly wanton and wicked cities of Tyre and Sidon stand a better chance in the day of judgment; that is, those who are wholly wrong will offer no excuse when their sins or short-comings bring them before the law of adjustment; they will admit their errors and repent. But those who have a lim-ited amount of Truth, which they hover over and declare to be the whole of Truth, are in danger of mental and spiritual crystallization.

Beth-shean, bĕth-shē'-ăn (Heb.)— *house of rest; house of tranquillity; dwelling in quiet; house of security.*

A city of Canaan that was allotted to Manasseh (Josh. 17:11). Later this town is named as being in one of the districts that supplied Solomon's house-hold with provisions for one month in each year (I Kings 4:12); in I Samuel 31:10, 12, it is called Beth-shan.

Meta. A restful, peaceful, confident attitude of mind (*house of rest, house of tranquillity, dwelling in quiet, house of security*). It is only in the quietness of our periods of conscious waiting on God that we find the inner sense of peace and security and conservation that builds up soul and body in endur-ing substance and life.

Beth-shemesh, bĕth-shē'-mĕsh (Heb.) *–house of the sun.*

a A border city of Judah, a city of the priests (Josh. 15:10; 21:16). **b** A city in Naphtali (Josh. 19:38). **c** A border city of Issachar (Josh. 19:22). The Beth-shemesh of Jeremiah 43:13 is the same as the city of On in Egypt. Ir-shemesh (Josh. 19:41) is supposed to be another name for Beth-shemesh. It was to Beth-shemesh in Judah that the milch kine took the Ark when the Philis-tines gave it into their keeping, and it was there that so many men were killed miraculously (according to I Samuel 6: 19) for looking into the Ark.

Meta. A sun consciousness (*house of the sun*). To the unregenerate man (Philistines and Egyptians), also to the unawakened intellect of man, this con-sists of thoughts pertaining to Baal wor-ship, or a looking wholly to the outer formed universe and to outer methods and ways, or to the psychic, to bring about understanding and good. But as the individual comes into an understand-ing of Truth he realizes that the central sun (or Son) of the universe and of him-self is not a formed, manifest thing; that it does not belong to the psychic, soul, or purely mental realm. It is an idea in the one Mind, God, an idea that comprises all true ideas and alone con-tains all possibility. He then looks to this inner, unmanifest spiritual Source for his light, his power, and his every good, and he is blessed accordingly.

Beth-shittah, bĕth-shĭt'-täh (Heb.)— *place of acacia; house of the acacia.*

A place that is mentioned in the ac-count of Gideon's overthrow and pursuit of the hosts of Midian (Judg. 7:22).

Meta. A consciousness of quickening, vitalizing life—a resurrection in con-sciousness (*house,* or *place, of acacia; acacias refers to resurrection or life*). (See SHITTIM and ABEL-SHITTIM.)

Beth-tappuah, bĕth-tăp'-pū-ăh (Heb.) —*house of apples; place of fruit trees.*

A city in the hill country of Judah (Josh. 15:53).

Meta. A consciousness of fruitfulness, or abundance—a rich, prosperous con-sciousness (*house of apples, place of fruit trees*).

Bethuel, bĕ-thū'-ĕl (Heb.)—*dweller in*

God; dweller in God or abode of God; filiation of God.

a A nephew of Abraham, and father of Rebecca, Isaac's wife (Gen. 22:22, 23); he was also the father of Laban, whose daughters became Jacob's wives (Gen. 28:2, 5). **b** A city of Simeon (I Chron. 4:30).

Meta. Unity with God; consciously abiding in Him (*dweller in God, abode of God*).

Bethul, bē'-thŭl (Heb.)—*dweller in God; house of God.*

A contracted form of Bethuel; a city of Simeon (Josh. 19:4); it is thought to have been the same place as the Bethel of Joshua 12:16.

Meta. See BETHEL and BETHUEL.

Beth–zur, bĕth'–zûr (Heb.)—*house of rock; house of refuge; house of shelter* (especially *of God*); *place of rocks.*

A city in the hill country of Judah, not far from Hebron (Josh. 15:58; I Chron. 2:45).

Meta. A firm, Truth foundation in consciousness—an established consciousness of protection, of safety (*house of rock, house of refuge, house of shelter,* especially *of God, place of rocks;* a city in the hill country of Judah, near Hebron; Hebron signifies the front brain —the seat of conscious thought).

Betonim, bĕt'-ŏ-nĭm (Heb.)—*pistachio nuts* (so called on account of their shape); *mounds; humps; bellies; hollows; the inmost parts,* i. e., *where one thinks and feels.*

A city of Canaan that was allotted to the Israelitish tribe of Gad (Josh. 13: 26).

Meta. Spasmodic attempts to lift up the consciousness (*pistachio nuts, mounds, humps*) guided by impulse, or by one's feelings, apart from real, orderly, consistent Truth thinking (*the inmost parts,* i. e., *where one thinks and feels, bellies, hollows*). A sense of order and power is gained from that which Gad signifies (this Canaanitish city was allotted to Gad). (See GAD.)

Beulah, beū'-lăh (Heb.)—*married.*

A name given by Isaiah to the land and nation of Israel, and signifying the perfect union with God to which the Israelites would return (Isa. 62:4).

Meta. The rich and happy state of the individual who has entered into conscious union with the Divine; or one in whom the marriage of the Lamb has taken place, the raising of the whole consciousness to a perfect and complete oneness with the central I AM or indwelling Christ. We also speak of the "marriage of the Lamb" as the lifting up and unifying of wisdom and love in individual consciousness. When this spiritual marriage has taken place, the condition of the individual is indeed blessed, rich, and full.

Bezai, bē'-zāi (Heb. from Pers.)— *shining; high; victory; conqueror.*

a A Jewish man whose descendants, to the number of three hundred and twenty-three, returned from the Babylonian captivity with Zerubbabel (Ezra 2:17). **b** One who joined Nehemiah in sealing the covenant (Neh. 10:18).

Meta. An assurance of light and power to overcome error and remain true to Spirit (*shining, high, victory, conqueror*).

Bezalel (A. V., Bezaleel) bĕ-zăl'-ĕl (Heb.)—*in the shadow of God; in the likeness of God; in the shelter of God; in the protection of God.* This word is formed from the same root as that used in Genesis 1:26, 27, which is rendered as "image" and "likeness."

Son of Uri and grandson of Hur, of the tribe of Judah. Jehovah filled him with wisdom, understanding, and skill, and he was one of those who were given charge of the construction of the tabernacle in the wilderness, and of the priests' garments, and of other similar work. This man's work was in gold, silver, brass, the cutting of stones for setting, the carving of wood, and in all skilled workmanship (Ex. 31:2-11).

Meta. The inner assurance of the guarding, guiding, protecting presence and power of Spirit; a conception of divine sonship, Godlikeness (*in the shadow of God, in the likeness of God, in the shelter of God, in the protection of God*). If we have this assurance and conception of being in truth like God, it clears the way for the inflow of divine light and wisdom, that we may know better how to handle the substance ideas in our consciousness and our body. These ideas are in various phases, or degrees, of materiality and spirituality; we need understanding and wisdom, as well as the ability and protection of Truth, in order to mold or build them into a more enduring structure (body temple) wherein God can be worshiped in spirit.

Bezek, bē'-zĕk (Heb.)—*lightning; glittering brightness; scattered; dispersed.*

a The city of Adonibezek, a heathen king of the Canaanites (Judg. 1:4-7). **b** A place where Saul numbered the men of Israel and sent them out to defeat the Ammonites (I Sam. 11:8).

Meta. Bezek means *lightning.* (See ADONIBEZEK for the significance of Bezek, the city of Adonibezek.)

The second Bezek, where Saul numbered the Israelites in sending them forth to defeat the Ammonites, symbolizes the fiery executiveness of an active will. Since Saul (the will) was inspired by God at that time, his action was good and he was successful. Likewise we are always victorious over all our error-thought enemies when we exercise our will against them in coöperation with the will and inspiration of Spirit.

Bezer, bē'-zēr (Heb.)—*cut off; inaccessible; restrained; a fortification; strong city; ore; silver ore; gold ore* (in the sense of being cut out and broken); *vine gathering* (cutting off).

a A son of Zophah of the Israelitish tribe of Asher (I Chron. 7:37). **b** A city of refuge in the wilderness, for the tribe of Reuben (Deut. 4:43).

Meta. Divine protection and strength, wherein no enemy of error can enter, but all error is *restrained, cut off (a fortification, strong city, inaccessible).* This consciousness of Truth is a city of refuge, a preserving, redeeming quality, in the individual who possesses it.

Bichri, bĭch'-rī (Heb.)—*youthful; youth; first-born.*

A Benjamite, father of Sheba, a base fellow who started a rebellion against David after Absalom had been defeated and killed (II Sam. 20:1-22).

Meta. An idea of life, force, and action that is new and young in con-

sciousness (*youthful, youth, first-born*), and has as yet no true concept of the value and power of love (David).

Bidkar, bĭd'-kär (Heb.)—*thrusting through; son of stabbing, i. e., a stabber; in pain.*

A captain of Jehu's, who aided Jehu and his men in destroying all of Ahab's house (II Kings 9:25).

Meta. A piercing, destructive thought in individual consciousness, a strong belief in retribution (*thrusting through, son of stabbing, a stabber*), without the saving power of true justice, which includes mercy.

Bigtha, bĭg'-thȧ (Heb. from Pers. or Sanskrit)—*gift of God; given of fortune; gift of the sun; a garden; a gardener.*

One of the seven chamberlains of King Ahasuerus. He was one of the two who conspired against the king, but was defeated in his purpose by the timely warning of Esther and Mordecai, and was hanged (Esth. 1:10). In Esther 2:21 he is called Bigthan, and in Esther 6:2, Bigthana.

Meta. A belief in luck, or chance (*given of fortune*), as a compelling force in man's life that cannot be withstood (*gift of God*). This belief, if held, would eventually detroy King Ahasuerus, the will.

Man needs his will. The natural man even needs his bigoted, personal will until he rises into a higher understanding, for the will is the executive power in man— he is nothing without it. So we find spiritual love (Esther) and the spiritual power working within the soul for its full redemption (Mordecai) using their influence to preserve the human will (king) and to reveal in its true light the erroneous, destructive belief that conditions in man's life come about by chance instead of by exact law, a law of thought that enables man to rule himself and all his affairs.

Bigthan or **Bigthana.** See BIGTHA.

Bigvai, bĭg'-vāi (Heb.)—*happy; fortunate; a husbandman; a gardener; of the people.*

a More than two thousand of his descendants returned from the Babylonian captivity with Zerubbabel, and later seventy more returned (Ezra 2:14; 8:14). **b** A man by this name also joined Nehemiah in sealing the covenant (Neh. 10:16).

Meta. The recognition by the individual that his own thought people (*of the people*) make or mar his life. This understanding that one's good or ill does not depend upon chance, upon other persons, or upon any one or anything outside of oneself, brings true happiness because it gives one a working basis for transforming oneself and one's world (*happy, fortunate, a husbandman*).

Bildad, bĭl′-dăd (Heb.)—*Bel has loved; lord Adad; son of contention; son of strife.*

One of Job's three friends who came to see him in his affliction and took up an argument against him, in an effort to help set him right (Job 2:11; 8:1).

Meta. The great desire of the partially awakened intellect to contend and strive (*son of contention, son of strife*) for that which appears right to it, its judgments and decisions being founded more in outer appearances than in Truth. *Bel* (lord) is the same as Baal, and refers to the attributing of power to the outer formed world. *Adad*, or Hadad, the chief deity of the Syrians, symbolizes setting up, as all-powerful, the intellect apart from true spiritual understanding. The intellectual thoughts for which the Syrians stand always war against the spiritual consciousness.

Bileam, bĭl′-ĕ-ăm (Heb.)—*lord of the people; Baal of the people; destruction of the people; a pilgrim; a foreigner; a stranger.*

A city of the half tribe of Manasseh, on the east of the Jordan, that was given over to the Kohathite Levites (I Chron. 6:70).

Meta. Bileam is the same word as Balaam; in Hebrew they are spelled exactly the same. The meaning is identical. The only difference is that Bileam is a city and Balaam is an individual. Thus Bileam signifies a group of thoughts of like character to that which Balaam signifies. (See BALAAM.) The fact that the city of Bileam came into the possession

of the half tribe of Manasseh, and then was given over to the Kohathite Levites, bespeaks a lifting up of this group of thoughts, or state of consciousness, to higher, truer expression.

Bilgah, bĭl′-gah (Heb.)—*cheerful; rejoicing; bursting forth of joy; the early dawn; first-born.*

a A priest in the Temple service in David's time (I Chron. 24:14). **b** A priest who returned from the Babylonian captivity (Neh. 12:5).

Meta. A springing forth of Truth (light and joy) into consciousness (*bursting forth of joy, the early dawn*). The Truth, while it has always existed in the face, or light, of God, is ever new. To the soul that receives it, it is the *first-born*, or first fruits, of renewed life (new, resurrecting thoughts and conditions). This renewal of life brings great *rejoicing* to the individual and brings about his release from Babylon (confusion).

Bilhah, bĭl′-hah (Heb.)—*bashfulness; timidity; tenderness.*

a Rachel's handmaid whom she gave to Jacob as his concubine; Bilhah became the mother of Dan and Naphtali (Gen. 30:3-8). **b** A town of Simeon (I Chron. 4:29).

Meta. A soul receptivity, or susceptibility, somewhat given to self-abasement (*tenderness, timidity, bashfulness;* a concubine of Jacob's), which, when unified with the I AM (Jacob) of the unfolding mentality in individual consciousness, brings forth judgment and strength (Dan and Naphtali). These qualities find expression first in the physical or more outer consciousness of man; but their true origin is Spirit, and their spiritual nature and spiritual activity are in due time established.

The town of Simeon, named Bilhah, is also called Baalah. (See BAALAH.)

Bilhan, bĭl′-hăn (Heb.) — *bashful; modest; confused; timid; weak; tender.*

a Son of Ezer, a Horite of the land of Seir (Gen. 36:27). **b** A son of Jediael, a Benjamite (I Chron. 7:10).

Meta. Jediael means *knowledge of God, known of God.* "The wisdom that is from above is first pure, then peaceable, gentle, easy to be entreated, full of mercy" (James 3:17); this is the consciousness that is signified by Bilhan, son of Jediael (*tender, modest*). It is compassionate, tender, modest—not bold, presumptuous, or hypocritical; it is born of a true *knowledge of God*.

The Bilhan who was a Horite partakes more of a confused state of mind (*confused*), and a lack of self-assertion (*weak*); these are products of a giving way to the fulfillment of the thoughts and desires of one's unredeemed subconsciousness.

Bilshan, bĭl′-shăn (Heb.)—*son of the tongue,* i. e., *eloquent; searcher.*

One who returned to Jerusalem with Zerubbabel from the Babylonian captivity (Ezra 2:2).

Meta. A thought activity that gives itself to a diligent searching out of Truth (*searcher*); also the ability to express Truth clearly when it has once been thoroughly investigated and comprehended (*eloquent*). Zerubbabel is one who restores the worship of God.

Bimhal, bĭm′-hăl (Heb.)—*son of circumcision,* i. e., *circumcised; one cut off from impurity.*

Son of Japhlet, of the Israelitish tribe of Asher (I Chron. 7:33).

Meta. A thought in consciousness that is purified from all that is contained in "the mind of the flesh" (Rom. 8:6), and keeps the precepts of the divine law (*circumcised*). (See CIRCUMCISION.)

Binea, bĭn′-ĕ-à (Heb.)—*gush forth copiously; break forth; a wanderer; a fountain; a gushing stream.* This word has a dual sense. It may be either good or bad; on the one hand, praise of God; on the other, to belch forth wickedness.

A Benjamite who was descended from Saul (I Chron. 8:37).

Meta. Faith in the fountain of spiritual life that springs up from within the very depths of man's being (*gush forth copiously, fountain; a Benjamite refers to faith*). This faith thought that Binea signifies may seem at first to be a *wanderer* in man's consciousness; it is not steady and reliable, but is exercised impulsively (*break forth*); it has not been given any abiding place in him

because he has always looked upon his life as a material quality and as coming from without, or from natural causes. He has not known that the source of all life is Spirit and is within. But this true idea (Binea) is of God. In due time it will become established in the individual, and will aid in bringing about the spiritualization of his whole being.

Binnui, bĭn′-nū-ī ′(Heb.)—*a construction; a building; a rebuilding; the building of posterity; familyship.*

The name of several different Israelitish men who returned from the Babylonian captivity (Ezra 8:33; 10:30, 38; Neh. 3:24; 7:15; 12:8).

Meta. Constructive, renewing, unifying thoughts in consciousness (*a construction, a building, a rebuilding, familyship*). Two of these men had taken foreign wives before their return to their own land. This shows that the unifying quality or love quality of the thoughts that are symbolized by the men named Binnui is still more or less material in its nature; it needs a thorough cleansing that it may be raised to a more perfect, spiritual basis. The constructiveness of the thoughts that are signified by the men named Binnui is abiding, is lasting in its character (*the building of posterity;* posterity means offspring to the furthest generation). One of these men named Binnui is called Bani in another place. The two names are much alike in their meaning and significance. (See BANI.)

Birsha, bĭr′-shȧ (Heb.)—*son of wickedness; son of impiety; son of godlessness; full of wickedness; fat with evil.*

King of Gomorrah in Abraham's time (Gen. 14:2).

Meta. Gomorrah means *material force, tyranny, oppression;* it signifies a state of mind that is adverse to the law of Spirit. This state of mind has to do with the submerged or hidden, subconscious, sensual phase of man's life. Birsha is the ruling thought in this error state of consciousness in the individual (*son of wickedness, son of godlessness, fat with evil, full of wickedness*).

Birzaith (A. V., Birzavith), bĭr′-zāith (Heb.)—*olive wells; holes; wounds.* The different meanings of this word are due to the different spellings: Birzaith, *olive wells;* and Birzavith, *holes* (holes made with a spear), *wōunds.* The word is spelled both ways in the old manuscripts.

A descendant of Asher (I Chron. 7: 31).

Meta. The peace and harmony, also the possibilities, of the inner life (a *well* represents an inward source of life, and *olives* signify peace, also fruitfulness). This life, in its spiritual quality, is rather obscure to the consciousness of man at first (Birzaith's genealogy is not given clearly), but, as man opens his mind more fully to the inspiration of Spirit, he learns to discern the omnipresence of the life within him, and the spiritual origin of all life. Then he endeavors to express his life and energy constructively, instead of expressing them destructively, unwisely, and thus tearing down his organism (*holes, wounds*).

Bishlam, bĭsh'-lăm (Heb.)—*son of peace* (?); *in peace.*

One of the men who wrote to Artaxerxes, king of Persia, attempting to prejudice him against the returned Jews (Ezra 4:7). He tried to induce the king to prevent the Jews from rebuilding the Temple and the city and the wall of Jerusalem.

Meta. A thought of peace in man (*in peace, son of peace*) that is carried to extremes—a tendency even to side with error in order to keep an outer semblance of peace. This tendency would not allow the individual to undertake any active work of reconstruction in his manner of thinking and in his organism, because he might thereby stir up many seeming inharmonies and thus disturb his equilibrium and peace of mind. This thought, or tendency, is an enemy to man, since abiding peace and good can become established in one only by one's being strong in the Truth and not compromising with error.

Bithiah, bĭ-thī'-ăh (Heb.)—*daughter of Jehovah; daughter of Jah; worshiper of Jehovah; daughter of the Lord.*

A daughter of Pharaoh who became the wife of a Jewish man (I Chron. 4: 18).

Meta. A phase of the soul consciousness that, though it belongs to the force that rules man in his material state (Pharaoh, king of Egypt) yet has set its love upon the Truth, and worships Jehovah; that is, it gives its substance to building up the real Christ self in the individual (*daughter of Jehovah; worshiper of Jehovah*).

Bithron, bĭth'-rŏn (Heb.)—*cleft or valley; broken* or *divided place; ravine.*

A place between the Jordan and Mahanaim, through which Abner passed when he was fleeing from Joab (II Sam. 2:29). Fallows says of Bithron: "It probably denotes a region of hills and valleys, and not any definite place."

Meta. Abner was captain of Saul's army; he refers to the intellect in man, somewhat illumined by Spirit. The meaning of Abner is *father of enlightenment.* Joab was the leader of David's army; he symbolizes the executive power of love. When Saul, the will ruling in personality, is slain, his captain, Abner (intellectual reasoning), has to give up control, or leadership, of the army of thoughts that has adhered to it. In this change that takes place when Abner gives way to Joab, and when Saul gives way to David —when the transition from personal dominance to the rule of love is accomplished—the intellect becomes "broken up" in thought (*broken* or *divided place*). Its old basis of reasoning is gone. It is divided (*cleft*) and cannot become centered in any one rule of action. It goes down to the very depths (*valley, ravine*), as is signified by the place named Bithron, before it finally comes to a clear recognition of its real foundation and willingly merges itself with the Christ or true, spiritual understanding.

Bithynia, bĭ-thy̆n'-ĭ-à (Greek)—*violent precipitation.*

A province of Asia Minor (I Pet. 1:1). When Paul and Silas "were come over against Mysia, they assayed to go into Bithynia; and the Spirit of Jesus suffered them not" (Acts 16:7).

Meta. Mysia means *criminal,* and Bithynia means *violent precipitation.* Under the guidance of the Lord the redeeming power of Spirit is not set into action in these dark states of consciousness until neighboring thought centers that are more or less awakened to Truth have been spiritually strengthened.

This dark state of consciousness that Bithynia represents is characterized by its strong tendency to act hastily and impulsively, in a headlong manner, without any forethought, with undue vehemence, force, and lack of reverence and respect (*violent precipitation*). Peter names the "elect" who are sojourners in Bithynia as some of those to whom his first epistle was written. This shows that later the Truth must have been preached in that place, or state of consciousness, and must have been accepted by some of its inhabitants (thought people).

Biziothiah (A. V., Bizjothjah), bĭz-ĭ-ŏ-thī'-ăh (Heb.)—*comtempt of Jah; despises Jehovah; place of Jah's olives.*

One of "the uttermost cities of . . . Judah toward the border of Edom in the South" (Josh. 15:21, 28).

Meta. An established thought center in the subconsciousness, and very close to the point of working out into the body consciousness (Edom). The meaning (*place of Jah's olives*) suggests that this thought center should be filled with the consciousness of the Christ peace, and it should be rich with spiritual reality. Its mission is to carry the consciousness of peace and Truth out into the very cells of the body, for the body is inherently just as spiritual and abiding as any other phase of man's being. Yet, because of error ideas concerning manifest man, the Biziothiah state of consciousness holds him in *contempt*—it esteems him as something vile and not worthy of redemption. Thus it helps to keep him seemingly material instead of aiding in establishing him in the truth of his being, and it despises Jehovah also, since manifest man is really the product of Jehovah God, or I AM. It will do its true work when it becomes awakened to its true ideals and its real mission by the Judah state of thought into whose possession it has come.

Biztha, bĭz'-thȧ (Heb. from Pers.)—*weak person* (sexually, incapable of re-

production); *eunuch.*

One of the seven chamberlains who ministered to King Ahasuerus of Media and Persia (Esth. 1:10).

Meta. In consciousness a eunuch represents a thought from which the capacity to increase life and its forms has been eliminated. King Ahasuerus represents the will dominated by ambition and puffed up by its conquests. Biztha is a thought, void of vital strength and power, that serves the puffed-up will, and because of its weakening character helps to bring about the downfall of the will.

"Pride *goeth* before destruction,
And a haughty spirit before a fall" (Prov. 16:18).

The personal of itself has no power to give or to sustain life and wholeness. Only that which is founded in Spirit and acknowledges God as the one power will stand the test.

blasphemy (Acts 6:11-14). The roots from which this word is derived signify *slowness, sluggishness, stupidity of speech:* hence, *speaking evil, reviling, slandering.*

Meta. One significance of blasphemy is the tendency in our own mind to fear that we can go too far in spiritualizing our thought and its environment.

Blastus, blăs'-tŭs (Gk.)—*shoot; a bud; sprout; that buds.*

A chamberlain of King Herod Agrippa's. He was a friend to "them of Tyre and Sidon" (Acts 12:20).

Meta. Sense man's belief that the mortal will, or the ruling ego of the sense man (Herod), causes life and its awakening ideas of good to germinate and to come to fruition in consciousness (*shoot, sprout, that buds*). This belief brings forth no fruit (Blastus was a eunuch) because it is a false one. God (unformed Spirit) alone is the origin of all life, understanding, growth, unfoldment, and attainment of good. The human will cannot attempt to put itself in the place of God without bringing about disastrous results. (Read Acts 12:21-23.)

blind beggar (John 9:1-41).

Meta. The blind beggar of John 9 represents one who has no perception of his own capacity, and no confidence in his power to rise superior to conditions in the material realm. The sin of omission is even greater than the sin of commission. There is some hope for the one who is an active sinner, but what can we expect of the one who makes no effort to do for himself, who simply drifts with the tide or looks to others for all things?

The world is full of people who are in this blind, beggarly state. They sit by the wayside and wait for the workers to give them pennies and crusts, when they themselves might be manifesters and producers. The key to the situation is the denial of material darkness, ignorance, and inability.

The putting of clay on the eyes of the blind man shows how a person makes his understanding opaque by affirming the power of material conditions to hamper and impede his spiritual and material growth. The washing away of this clay by the man himself shows how we must deny by our own volition and efforts the seeming mountains of environing material conditions.

blind eyes (Mark 8:22).

Meta. Blind understanding—a darkened consciousness. When we are exalted and illumined in our thoughts, darkness disappears.

blood of Christ.

Meta. In the 9th chapter of Hebrews Paul sets forth the life-giving power of the blood of Christ. It is doubtful if even our most enlightened metaphysicians can follow and fully interpret the subject that this author elucidates. We here and there catch glimpses of a great plan to purify and redeem the race by pouring into its life currents a new and purer stream through Christ, and we have the history of this plan plainly written in the Scriptures, but we do not get its full import because we have not entered into and become consciously a part of the movement. The explanation here given in Hebrews, read and interpreted in the letter, is an interminable tangle. The blood atonement has always been and ever will be a question beyond intellectual comprehension.

There is a mighty fact and living potency in the blood of Christ; but the red blood of flesh does not carry the power to "cleanse your conscience from dead works to serve the living God." It is the "blood of Christ . . . through the eternal Spirit," that cleanses. Christ is the Word of God, and the life of that Word must be a form of energy far transcending any life current that inheres in blood. Blood represents life; it is the vehicle that carries life through the avenues of the body, but it is not life itself.

So "blood" is used to express a spiritual principle that has been introduced into the race mind through the purified Jesus. It is a spiritual principle in that it rests upon pure ideals, yet it manifests in mind and body in concrete form when rightly appropriated. That it can be appropriated, and used to the purification of the mind and the healing of the body, thousands are proving in this day.

This Christ principle does not offer a partial salvation, Paul explains, "as the high priest entering into the holy place year by year with blood not his own," but it represents a complete conjunction with the Father. "Ye therefore shall be perfect, as your heavenly Father is perfect." This can mean nothing less than complete sanctification; those who have adopted this as their creed are not far wrong.

If we accept the Christ principle as our true spiritual self, the Son of God in whose image and likeness we are, we must cling to it with all our might, mind, and strength. We are spiritual beings; there is no sin in us in our spiritual estate, and that estate is the *real*. Through Jesus it has been demonstrated that this estate is capable of outward manifestation, and by following His methods and making mental conjunction with Him we may manifest with Him.

Rotherham translates thus the concluding verse of the 9th chapter of Hebrews: "Thus the Christ also

Once for all having been offered,

For the *bearing of the sins of many*

A second time apart from sin will appear

To them who for him are ardently waiting—

Unto salvation."

Boanerges, bō-ă-nēr'-gĕş (N. T. Gk.)
—*sons of tumult; sons of rage,* i. e., *soon angry; sons of thunder,* i. e., *fiery and destructive zeal.*

A surname that Jesus gave to two of His disciples, James and John the sons of Zebedee (Mark 3:17).

Meta. That which John and James signify belongs to the solar plexus, or central seat of vibratory activity in the organism, the great emotional center, which extends from the pit of the stomach to the region back of the heart. Jesus' coming is likened to "lightning" that shines from the east even to the west. When the light of the Son, the Christ, shines into man with a force likened to lightning, it sets up vibratory waves between the solar plexus and the cardiac plexus, where John and James have their seats of expression, and the power of both of these faculties, love and judgment, is greatly accelerated in consciousness (they are *sons of thunder*). I AM, Christ, is the light, or lightning, and the disciples, James and John, Boanerges, sons of thunder, are secondary activities of the I AM.

Upon the first mighty awakening of these two disciples, there is a tendency to hasty judgment and somewhat limited, bigoted love because of impulsive zeal apart from the balance wheel of true understanding and wisdom. One meaning of thunder is a startling or impressive utterance of threat, denunciation, censure, and so forth (see Mark 9:38 and Luke 9:54). So Boanerges may also signify the tendency of the newly awakened follower of Christ to be too zealous in trying to right outer things without understanding the inner law of love, nonresistance, and Truth, which sees good back of all and seeks to save and restore in its adjusting processes rather than to destroy. In the beginning of our active Christian life we are likely to waste much of our energy in zeal without wisdom; later we learn to conserve our substance and to think, speak, and act in love and understanding at all times.

boat (Matt. 14:22).

Meta. A positive thought—a conveyance that is able to float upon the water (the unstable mind), and to bear up the disciples (the faculties of mind). The multitudes are the numberless thoughts that are seeking light, strength, and healing.

Boaz (A. V., Booz, Matt. 1:5 and Luke 3:32), bō'-ăz (Heb.)—*alacrity; quickness; fleetness; in strength; in might; in power.*

a A very wealthy man of Bethlehem, of the tribe of Judah; he married Ruth and became the great-grandfather of David (Ruth 2:1). **b** The left pillar at the porch of the Temple (I Kings 7:21).

Meta. The cheerful willingness, promptness, and quickness of action, also richness and power of thought, and strength of character (*quickness, fleetness, alacrity, strength, lovely*), that when established in substance (Bethlehem, *house of bread*) and allied with the love of the natural man (Ruth) open the way for the birth of the Christ into consciousness. (David, the great-grandson of Boaz, is a type of Christ.)

Bocheru, bŏch'-ĕ-rų (Heb.)—*the first-born is he; he is youthful; he is early; he is in season.*

One of the six sons of Azel, a Benjamite descended from Saul (I Chron. 8:38).

Meta. The tendency to receive new ideas, Truth, in order, in season; the reference here may be to the Christ idea (*the first-born is he, he is youthful, he is early, he is in season*).

Bochim, bō'-chĭm (Heb.)—*weepers; weepings; place of weeping.*

The place where "the angel of Jehovah" told the Israelites that, because they had not hearkened to the voice of God but had made covenants with the inhabitants of Canaan—which thing God had forbidden them to do, God would not drive out their enemies before them, but would let these enemies become as thorns in their sides to trouble them. Then all the people wept, "and they called the name of that place Bochim," that is, *weepers* (Judg. 2:5 with marginal note).

Meta. A deep feeling and expression of sorrow on man's part for his failure to live up to the perfect law of God, but more especially because of his inharmonious reaping. This expression of sorrow does not include the thorough, positive turning away from error to Truth that would keep one from reaping the inharmonious results of having given way in measure to error thoughts, the enemies of the inner kingdom.

Bohan, bō'-hăn (Heb.) — *thumb; stumpy.*

"The son of Reuben"; the stone of Bohan was used as a mark on the boundary line between Judah and Benjamin, in Canaan (Josh. 15:6; 18:17).

Meta. Determination, strength of thought, firmness of purpose (*thumb, stumpy;* a stone).

book, of the law, or "roll" that the king burned (Jer. 36:13, 23).

Meta. The intuitive perception of the progressive trend of all things. The burning of the roll represents a denial of the spiritual thought that is working in consciousness.

booths (Lev. 23:39-43).

Meta. Temporary abiding places, as contrasted with permanent houses, or places of abode. When man comes out of Egypt (mental bondage) into the light of freedom, he should keep green in memory, by thought and act, the idea of liberty. Young persons like to camp in the woods. This liking is a natural result of innate desire for freedom from the restraints of fixed thoughts.

Bozez, bō'-zĕz (Heb.)—*shining; glittering; height.*

A rocky crag or tooth on one side of the pass by which Jonathan and his armor-bearer went over into the garrison of the Philistines and put them to flight (I Sam. 14:4).

Meta. "The formidable tooth, 'I cannot.' " (See SENEH, the name of the crag on the other side of the pass.)

Bozkath (A. V., II Kings 22:1, Boscath), bŏz'-kăth (Heb.)—*stony; height; craggy.*

A city in the lowlands of Judah (Josh. 15:39).

Meta. A group of thoughts which, though humble and lowly, is of an exalted nature (*height*), and firm and strong, though somewhat rugged in character (*stony, craggy*). Jedidah, mother of

Josiah—Josiah was a good king of Judah —and Adaiah, her father, were of Bozkath; they signify thoughts that belong to the Bozkath phase of consciousness. (See ADAIAH and JEDIDAH.)

Bozrah, bŏz'-räh (Heb.)—*restraint; sheepfold; fortification; stronghold.*

a A city of Edom (Gen. 36:33). b A city of Moab (Jer. 48:24). Bozrah of Edom was a very important city, but it seems to have been conquered by the Moabites later, and its destruction is prophesied by Jeremiah and by Amos. Micah speaks of its sheep.

Meta. The pure natural life of the organism (sheep, *sheepfold*), controlled by the "mind of the flesh" or carnal mind (Edom and Moab). Though strongly intrenched in materiality (*stronghold, fortification*), the dominion of the sense man will be taken away. Then the life thoughts and forces, which are naturally pure and obedient in themselves, will be set free in righteous expression in the body temple.

bread (John 6:7).

Meta. Universal substance.

breaking of bread, and prayers (Acts 2:42).

Meta. The stirring into action, in consciousness, of the inner substance of Spirit (bread) and the concentrating of mind upon it as the real possession. Then "they took their food with gladness and singleness of heart." All who have attained realization of the inner substance will testify to the gladness with which it is appropriated in the consciousness. All outward pleasures give way to the inner light of the Holy Spirit when it begins to shed its rays in the heart.

brethren, five (Luke 16:28).

Meta. The five seemingly material avenues of sense expression.

Bukki, bŭk'-kī (Heb.)—*mouth of Jah; waster; void.*

a A Levite named in the genealogy of Ezra (Ezra 7:4). b A prince of the tribe of Dan, who was chosen as one of the men to help decide where each tribe of Israel should locate in the land of Canaan (Num. 34:22).

Meta. A receptive, willing, obedient attitude of mind in man, coupled with love of the Truth and spiritual discernment, by which Jehovah, the indwelling Christ, is enabled to express Himself to man's consciousness (*mouth of Jah*). If the thought of either *void* or *waster* comes into the significance of this character, it refers to the putting away of the personal that one may become an open channel to receive and express the Truth. Man becomes the mouthpiece of God when he gives voice to spiritual Truth. God has no mouth, or avenue of expression, except His creation.

Bukkiah, bŭk-kī'-ăh (Heb.)—*proved of Jehovah; mouth of Jah; wasted by Jehovah; wasting; dispensation of the Lord.*

A musician who was appointed by David for service in the Temple (I Chron. 25:4, 13).

Meta. The meaning of *dispensation* as given in Webster's New International Dictionary includes the thought of "distribution of good and evil by God to man." The seemingly contradictory meanings attributed to the name Bukkiah suggest the same thing. The truth is, however, that God is good and only good can come to man from Him. If man experiences error and inharmony, these are not put upon him by God; he brings them upon himself by his failure to harmonize his thoughts, words, and acts with the Lord, or divine law.

There is a positive pole and a negative pole to every expression of God in His creation. The negative is not evil, however, but needs to be rightly balanced with the positive in order to bring about the perfect good. Bukkiah represents divine harmony in the consciousness of man, established by a right adjustment of his positive and negative planes of thought, thus balancing and equalizing his forces.

Bul, bŭl (Heb.)—*pouring forth copiously; rain; produce; increase; abundance; changing; change produced by rain.*

The eighth month of the Jewish sacred or ecclesiastical year (I Kings 6:38). Some think that it answers to October; some, to parts of October and November; and others, to parts of November and December.

Meta. In their inner spiritual meaning, months, days, and years do not refer to divisions of time but to stages or degrees of unfoldment in consciousness and steps in demonstration. Bul refers to abundant increase of good, abundant supply, prosperity, as the result of a generous outpouring of the Holy Spirit, or of Truth, into the consciousness (*pouring forth copiously, rain,* rain referring to Spirit, or Truth, *produce, increase, abundance, change produced by rain*). This Holy Spirit baptism, with its quickening, illumining power, comes to man whenever he reaches the degree of mental and spiritual unfoldment wherein he is ready for it.

bullock; burnt offerings.

Meta. The bullock represents the animal life of the organism; the wood represents the corporeal substance. Pouring the water upon these represents denial of the sense appearance in order that the real character may be uncovered (I Kings 18:33).

In the regeneration all the animal forces and their manifestations on the natural plane must be transmuted into spiritual consciousness. This is the inner meaning of the ceremonial offerings of the Children of Israel.

The burnt offering of I Samuel 7:9-10 signifies a transmutation process. The sensual propensities go through the refiner's fire, through which action the outer consciousness is lifted into the purity and the life of Spirit.

Solomon presented "burnt-offerings" to Jehovah; these burnt offerings to Jehovah denote a conscious giving up of the sense life, that the spiritual may be gained. The prayer for the things of Spirit and a willingness to give up all thoughts of carnality transmute or burn up the beasts of the body (I Kings 3:4).

Bunah, bū'-năh (Heb.)—*perception; discernment; understanding; knowing; discretion; prudence; building.*

Second son of Jerahmeel, who was the son of Hezron and great-grandson of Judah (I Chron. 2:25).

Meta. A practical wisdom, discernment, sensibleness, and judgment (*per-*

ception, discernment, prudence, discretion, understanding). These are always of a *building,* constructive character.

Bunni, bŭn'-nī (Heb.)—*my understanding; built; building me up.*

The name of three Levites (Neh. 9:4; 10:15; 11:15).

Meta. The intellectual man's understanding of Truth, or of religion (*my understanding*). This builds up the personal in the individual (*building me up, built*), but not the truly spiritual.

burning bush (Ex. 3:2).

Meta. The angel of Jehovah, the flame of fire, and the bush, are all within the consciousness of man. The bush is a nerve center through which the universal life energy runs like electricity over a wire, making a light but not consuming. In mental activity there is a vibratory process that uses up nerve tissue, but in the wisdom that comes from the heart this "bush" or tissue is not consumed. The light of intuition or flame of fire burns in the heart, yet there is no loss of substance. The angel is the presiding intelligence always present in every life action or function.

Man is first attracted by the phenomenal side of spiritual things; then, when he gives his attention for the purpose of knowing the cause, the Lord reveals Himself. When Moses began to investigate, he found that he was on holy ground. The forces of Spirit at the center of man's body are so intense that the outer consciousness cannot stand the current and hold itself together. Absolutely pure in essence, this inner fire must be

approached by pure spiritual thought. Removing the shoes is symbolical of taking from the understanding all material concepts.

Another explanation of the burning bush is: the burning bush, which was not consumed, represents spiritual life's contacting substance. Divine life, spiritual fire, does not consume; it purifies and renews substance.

Buz, bŭz (Heb.)—*despicable; contempt; despised.*

a Son of Nahor, the brother of Abraham (Gen. 22:21). **b** A man of the Israelitish tribe of Dan (I Chron. 5:14). **c** Jeremiah mentions Buz as a people upon whom tribulations and judgments are to come (Jer. 25:23); the people of Buz are mentioned with Tema and Dedan, Arab tribes.

Meta. A scornful, scoffing state of thought; this is *despicable* in the light of Truth, and it cannot be productive of good.

Buzi, bū'-zī (Heb.)—*contemned of Jah; despised; my contempt; to disrespect.*

Father of Ezekiel the prophet (Ezek. 1:3).

Meta. Contempt or scorn for that which does not measure up to the divine phase of justice and right (*contemned of Jah*).

Buzite, bŭz'-īte (Heb.)—*of Buz or Buzi.*

Elihu, the son of Barachel, who talked to Job because Job justified himself rather than God, was a Buzite (Job 32:2).

Meta. See BUZI.

C

Cabbon, căb'-bŏn (Heb.)—*encircled; bound about; a circle; a globe; a village; a hamlet; hilly; honored.*

A town in the lowlands of Judah (Josh. 15:40).

Meta. An aggregation of thoughts of life in the subconsciousness that is of a spiritual nature or tendency, or that is *bound about* (*encircled*) by a higher, truer understanding of life than the

purely sense comprehension; thus it is reclaimed from carnal expression (*a circle, a globe, a village, a hamlet, hilly, honored*). A circle is that which has neither beginning nor ending, and refers to the spiritual, to oneness or unity. Cities of Judah, in their highest sense, represent spiritual centers of life in consciousness. The "lowland" of Judah suggests the subconscious realm.

Cabul, cā'-bŭl (Heb.)—*something exhaled, as nothing; vain; sterile; worthless; dry and sandy; dissatisfying; displeasing.*

a A town that was allotted to Asher (Josh. 19:27). **b** The name that Hiram, king of Tyre, gave to the twenty cities in the land of Galilee that Solomon gave to him in return for the cedar and fir trees and the gold that Hiram furnished Solomon for building his house and the Temple. Hiram was not pleased with these cities, and he called them the land of Cabul (I Kings 9:11-13).

Meta. Denial—a letting-go phase of mind (*something exhaled, as nothing*). The Solomon or spiritual mind of peace and wisdom understands that in all true building up of the organism into eternal life and abidingness there must be a balance between the negative and the positive; there must be the release of that which has served its purpose, as well as a laying hold and a building in of life and substance. But to the Hiram-king-of-Tyre understanding the letting-go attitude of thought seems *worthless, vain,* even destructive, and is very *dissatisfying* and *displeasing.* The possessor of such an understanding sees no need of denials, but would hold only and always to the affirmative.

Hiram was a builder; he was not of the Israelites (the religious and spiritual thoughts in man), but he represents a constructive power in the reasoning faculty of the individual—a constructive power that is firmly established in substance and in a fineness of understanding. This power lends itself and the thoughts that belong to it to the building of Truth into the consciousness and the body.

Cæsar, çæ'-ṣär (Lat.)—*hairy; sharp; cutting edge; keen.*

A title belonging to several of the Roman emperors (Matt. 22:17).

Meta. In the individual consciousness rulership implies the joint activity of reason and will. Cæsar, the Roman emperor, therefore refers to the personal self's ruling, through reason and will (unmodified by spiritual love, mercy, and justice), both mind and body, as indicated by the "world" (Luke 2:1), and

forcing all the faculties and powers to pay tribute in slavish carnal service. This is the natural attitude of the unspiritualized or Adam consciousness.

In our individual consciousness we must learn to "render unto Cæsar the things that are Cæsar's, and unto God the things that are God's" (Luke 20:25). The outer man, as well as the inner, must be given proper attention and care. Each must have its share of the sustenance of life. We even must keep harmony with the unenlightened human will, until the spiritual grows wise enough, loving enough, and strong enough in our consciousness to take its rightful dominion throughout our entire being.

By the stamp that is upon them we always shall know the thoughts and tendencies in ourselves that belong to Cæsar, and those that belong to God. That which is but a symbol of the true substance, the outer reasoning husk of the sensate thought of life and its resources, goes to Cæsar. The real substance of life, love, understanding, and Truth, goes to build up and to sustain the spiritual consciousness in mind and body.

Cæsarea, çæs-ă-rē'-à (Gk.)—*in honor of Cæsar; for Cæsar.*

A principal city and seaport of Palestine; it was built by Herod the Great (Acts 8:40). Cæsarea was the political capital of Palestine during the time that the country was ruled by the Romans. The Roman ruler of Palestine—the head administrator for the Roman emperor—always lived at Cæsarea.

Meta. Cæsarea, dominant world power, symbolizes the intellect.

Cæsarea Philippi, çæs-ă-rē'-à phĭ-lĭp'-pī (Gk.)—*Cæsarea of Philip.*

A place in the northern part of Canaan. It was near the foot of Mount Hermon, and is thought to have been the place where the transfiguration of Jesus Christ took place (Matt. 16:13).

Meta. Conquest and dominion; the temporal power of personality with its false claims of reality. The phrase, "When Jesus came into the parts of Cæsarea Philippi," means: when the I AM came into the realms of power. In this positive realm in consciousness (Cæsarea

Philippi) the personality (which always seeks glory and dominion, and demands to know to what extent its fame has been spread abroad) is met and overcome by Spirit.

This work is accomplished by meditation and prayer; spiritual realization comes in a wordless message direct from God. By one's assimilating this spiritual light, the broader vision appears. Personality is transmuted into individuality; self-glory is changed into holy reverence for the things of Spirit.

"Who is this Son of man?" is the question that presents itself when we come into consciousness of spiritual dominion and power, though that consciousness be of even a temporal nature—as indicated by the name Cæsarea.

Jesus admonished His followers (Matt. 16:24), "If any man would come after me, let him deny himself, and take up his cross, and follow me." He was telling them that if they wished to find the kingdom they should deny that which seeks personal praise and gratification and become willing channels through which God can bring more and more of Himself into visibility.

Caiaphas, cā'-ĭă-phăs (Gk. from Heb.) —*hollowed out; a depression.*

High priest of the Jews during a period that included the ministry and crucifixion of Jesus (John 11:49). He was the son-in-law of Annas (John 18:13).

Meta. The significance of Caiaphas is much the same as that of Annas (see ANNAS). He represents a ruling religious thought force that is entirely intellectual. He belongs to the religious world of forms and ceremonies, the "letter" of the word, and has no conception of the inner mind of Spirit.

Cain, cāin (Heb.; more properly Kain) —*possession; acquisition; centralization; draws to itself; to its own center; selfishness; sharp; cutting; a lance.* Among some of the ancient authorities, Cain represents the genius of evil. That which Cain symbolizes is not all bad, however, since all ideas of rulership are derived from the idea of centralized power. The benevolent or the malevolent aspects of the name Cain are deter-

mined from that upon which the centering is directed.

Adam and Eve's eldest son, who killed his brother Abel (Gen. 4:1-25).

Meta. Cain means *possession, acquisition, centralization,* that which *draws to itself, selfishness.* Cain refers directly to that part of the human consciousness which strives to acquire and possess. He was a tiller of the soil, which places him in the earthly domain. In Hindu metaphysics he would be called the physical body. Paul would call him the flesh.

The killing, by the body-selfishness, of all human sympathy and love is represented by Cain's slaying of Abel. When the body demands possession of all the resources of mind and soul, and reduces existence to mere material living, it has slain Abel, and his blood, or life, continually cries from the earthly consciousness to the Lord for expression.

When the selfishness of the body has killed the finer impulses of the soul and has reduced to material existence all the higher aspirations, there is no longer pleasure in living. Without the soul the body is a machine, with but little sensation and no progress. Cain thus tills the ground, but it yields him no strength.

The body feels its degradation, and those who get into this degenerate condition are usually miserable. Cain's punishment is great, and he fears the vengeance of the other faculties, which condemn the body for its impotency. But the Lord, or divine law, has fixed a limit to this and we are warned not to destroy the body, no matter how great its sins. The sign that was appointed for Cain to keep him from being slain is the consciousness of his divine origin. No matter how deep in transgression the body may be, it still bears the stamp of God and should never be killed.

Cainan (more properly Kenan), câ-ī'-năn (Heb.)—*possessor; acquisitor; centralizer; one who fixes and establishes his center; acquisition.*

Named twice in the genealogy of Jesus Christ (Luke 3:36, 37); the second Cainan in this genealogy is called Kenan in Genesis 5:9.

Meta. Cainan, named in the genealogy

of Jesus Christ, and meaning *possessor, centralizer, one who fixes and establishes his center,* symbolizes the establishing of one's outer consciousness and organism in the truth that the whole man, even the body, is in essence spiritual. Thus does one prepare oneself for the new or Christ birth. Through this new birth, even the very outermost phase of man's organism undergoes a change from seeming material to spiritual expression and manifestation—the body takes on its real spiritual nature.

Calah, cā'-lăh (Assyr.)—*completed; finished; soundness; firmness; integrity; strength; balanced judgment; an ancient; an old man,* i. e., a man whom age and experience have brought to fullness of perfection.

A city in Assyria that was built either by Nimrod or Asshur (Gen. 10:11, with marginal note).

Meta. Calah belongs to the intellectual or mental reasoning plane in man (see ASSHUR and ASSYRIA). It signifies a state of consciousness that is built about the belief that age (as it relates to time) and experience bring *balanced judgment* and fullness, or perfection. Sense wisdom (the serpent in the garden of Eden) led man to take the way of experience in order to acquire knowledge, in order to become "as God." Because of this choice, man's road to perfection has been long, winding, and thorny; but experience has helped to bring him to the place, or degree of unfoldment, wherein he perceives and is willing to unify himself with his indwelling Spirit of truth, that he may enter into true spiritual understanding and Godlikeness.

Calcol, căl'-cŏl (Heb.)—*supporter; sustainer; sustenance; nourishment; nutriment; nourishing.*

a A man whom Solomon excelled in wisdom (I Kings 4:31). **b** A son of Zerah, a Judahite (I Chron. 2:6). This latter is probably the same man as the former, since the same brothers are named in both of the texts where he is mentioned.

Meta. A line of reasoning that sustains, supports, and adheres to intellectual understanding (*supporter, sus-*tainer). There is a certain spiritual illumination and inspiration in this reasoning quality; it is food (*nourishment, nutriment*) for man during a phase of his unfoldment toward conscious spiritual inspiration and realization, for it is of high origin (Calcol and his brothers were looked upon as very wise and great men in their time), but it does not possess the fullness of the Christ wisdom. The Christ wisdom, which Solomon represents here, surpasses by far any and all other wisdom.

Caleb, cā'-lĕb (Heb.)—*dog* (onomatopœia from the sound of barking); *bold; fearless; ferocious to enemies; impetuous.*

Son of Jephunneh, of the tribe of Judah (Num. 13:6); he was one of the men whom Moses sent to spy out the land of Canaan. Caleb was not discouraged because of the giants in the land, but insisted that the Israelites were able to go up and possess it (Num. 13:30). It is said of him that "he wholly followed Jehovah, the God of Israel" (Josh. 14:14).

Meta. Caleb—*bold, fearless, ferocious to enemies, impetuous*—a man who wholly followed Jehovah, signifies an unyielding, uncompromising power in man that is loyal to its highest ideals. In Caleb we recognize a seemingly invincible power that wars ceaselessly against error, gives no quarter, is fearless and very zealous. In a lower sense he signifies a warrior, and carries a destructive thought in putting away error, rather than the constructing, elevating, redeeming spirit of the Christ. In a higher, truer sense, Caleb gives the idea of spiritual faith and enthusiasm. True faith is a rock, an invincible power for good in the consciousness. Through faith the I AM is ready and willing to enter into the inner consciousness and possess the people (soul forces). This process of regeneration must be carried on under the divine law, else psychic forces (men of great stature) will be aroused and will strive for dominion.

Caleb–ephrathah, cā'-lĕb–ĕph'-ră-thăh (Heb.).

The place where Hezron died, according to the reading of the text (I Chron. 2:24), but the interpretation is thought to be wrong. Fallows says concerning this text: "The reading of Jerome's Hebrew Bible, 'Caleb came in unto Ephrath,' is probably the true one, as no such place is elsewhere heard of. Ephrath, or Ephrathah, was a second wife, married after Hezron's death."

Meta. Ephrathah means *fruitfulness, fertility, abundance.* The union of Caleb with Ephrathah therefore bespeaks faith's fruition—the abundance of spiritual riches that man realizes in his soul through an active faith in God—the omnipotent, ever present good.

Calneh, căl'-nĕh (Heb.)—*complete concentration; centralized ambition; a fortress.* A literal rendering of Calneh would be "all in self."

A city in the land of Shinar that was built by Nimrod (Gen. 10:10). It is mentioned in Amos 6:2 as a one-time powerful city that had been overthrown because of its trust in materiality.

Meta. Selfishness, a centering in self; also confidence in material conditions rather than trust in God. Calneh was destroyed because of evil; even so the state of thought that it represents will be overcome and its seeming power will be taken away from it because it is founded and built up in error, in materiality, in idolatry, instead of Truth.

Calno, căl'-nŏ (Heb.)—*his complete concentration; his centralized ambition; his selfishness; his fortress.*

The same place as Calneh (Isa. 10:9).

Meta. See CALNEH.

camel.

Meta. An explanation of John the Baptist's being clothed with "camel's hair" (Matt. 3:4) is given as follows: A camel symbolizes power of endurance, strength, and patient perseverance. Hair is symbolical of the power to equalize the inner and outer life forces.

He who sets himself to do the work of manifesting God must have (be clothed with) the power, patience, perseverance, and strength of Spirit. He must will to seek, to know, to understand God and to do His holy will; he must learn to discriminate between the thoughts, imagina-

tions, desires, of self and the visions and commands of God. He must have strength to receive the wisdom of Spirit, to equalize the flow of thought substance, and to harmonize the ideas of Spirit with the manifestations of the outer world. He must put into practical, everyday use the Truth of the absolute, uninfluenced by the praise or condemnation of man. He must put God before self. All this must be done before he can recognize the Christ, the Spirit of God in himself. You will see readily that the work cannot be done by the human self; it can be accomplished only through the power of Spirit.

A comparison to the camel may be made of the Jews. In their zeal for God, their religious worship, they had the camel's persistence and patient determination, to the point of seeming obstinacy. On the other hand, they were just as zealous in their pursuit of idols.

Camels are "appropriately called the ships of the desert," Fallows says. To the ability to go long distances without outer nourishment, "are added a lofty stature and great agility; eyes that discover minute objects at a distance; a sense of smelling of prodigious acuteness . . . a spirit, moreover, of patience, not the result of fear, but of forbearance, carried to the length of self-sacrifice in the practice of obedience. . . . Without the existence of the camel immense portions of the surface of the earth would be uninhabitable and even impassable. Surely the Arabs are right: 'Job's beast is a monument of God's mercy!'" The Arabs call the camel "Job's beast" in reference to its great patience and forbearance. The thought of these characteristics in the camel, and their great value, recalls to mind the words of the Master: "In your patience ye shall win your souls" (*lives,* margin; Luke 21:19).

Cana, cā'-nȧ (Gk. from Heb.)—*place of reeds; reed; cane; staff; spear; measuring rod; rule; balance; hollow tube.*

A town in Galilee where Jesus performed His first miracle by turning water into wine at the marriage feast (John 2:1-11).

Meta. Cana means *place of reeds, reed,*

measuring rod, rule, balance. In the body it is symbolized by the larynx. Cana of Galilee is the power center in consciousness. The larynx originates and measures the volume and character of the sounds of the voice. Galilee (*circle, a circuit, rolling energy*) furnishes the vibratory force that acts through the *place of reeds.*

Canaan, cā'-năan (Heb.)—*realized nothingness; material existence; traffic in materiality; a merchant; a pirate; low; inferior; lowland.*

a The land that was given to the Israelites by God for an everlasting possession (Gen. 17:8; Deut. 32:49; Josh. 14:1-5). **b** A son of Ham, one of Noah's three sons (Gen. 9:18).

Meta. Canaan means *lowland,* that is, the body consciousness. The redeemed body is the Promised Land, and when man rediscovers this lost domain all the promises of the Scriptures will be fulfilled. It is not a dream that man is to possess an immortal body; it is a solid fact. In order to redeem the body man must enter with his spiritual thoughts into his organism and teach it the saving Truth. This is the symbolic teaching of Joshua 1.

We also think of Canaan (*lowland*) as referring to the subconsciousness. Metaphysically it represents humbleness and receptivity. The land of Canaan, too, represents the unlimited elemental forces of Being in which man is placed and to which he gives character through faith in God as omnipresent Spirit. To mystics it is the name of the invisible substance that surrounds and interpenetrates all forms, of which it is the mother.

Canaan, the son of Ham, refers to the fleshly organism and tendencies of man; it refers to the physical and not to the spiritual.

Canaanite, cā'-năan-īte (Heb.)—*one who exists in and for material things; a merchant; a pirate; trafficker in materiality.*

An inhabitant of the land of Canaan at the time that the Israelites took possession of it and overcame the Canaanites (Josh. 9:1). The Canaanites were descendants of Canaan, the son of Ham. (Gen. 10:15-19).

Meta. The elemental life forces in the subconsciousness. Under sense thought and expression they are all that the meaning of Canaanite implies. The Canaanites are delivered by Jehovah into the hands of the Israelites, and by them are destroyed. "And the name of the place was called Hormah." Hormah is from the same root as *herem,* a devoted thing. (See Num. 21:1-3, with margin.) The significance of this is that through our I AM (Jehovah) we gain control of our subconscious elemental life forces. Then by means of high, spiritual thinking (Israelites) these life forces come under the law of Spirit, and are transmuted into spiritual energy. (See HORMAH.)

Canaanitess, cā'-năan-ĭ-tĕss (from Heb.).

A female inhabitant of Canaan (I Chron. 2:3).

Meta. The soul, or receptive, feminine side of that which Canaanite signifies. (See CANAANITE.)

Candace, căn-dā'-çē (Gk. from Ethiopic)—*queen of servants.*

A queen of the Ethiopians whose servant was taught the truth concerning Jesus Christ and was baptized by Philip (Acts 8:27). The Ethiopians, or Cushites, were descendants of Ham, a son of Noah.

Meta. Ham refers to the physical in man. Ethiopia is a state of consciousness wherein the darkness of materiality and sense dwells. Candace, queen of the Ethiopians, is the ruling thought of that which Ethiopia signifies. This person's being a queen, and not a king, denotes the fact that the will of one who dwells in sense consciousness is directed by the feelings, desires, and emotions of the unawakened soul, the feminine, rather than by the reasoning mind, the masculine.

candlestick (Exod. 25:31).

Meta. The candlestick of the Temple represents the intelligence in man.

The "seven golden candlesticks" of Revelation 1 are receptacles of spiritual light. They are the spiritual aspect of the seven churches, the spiritual wisdom and understanding side of the churches.

Canneh, căn′-nĕh (Heb.)—*set up; placed; distinguished.*

It is thought to be the same city as Calneh (Ezek. 27:23).

Meta. Canneh was *set up,* or built up, in material thought. Its seeming eminence (*distinguished*) is short-lived because it is not established in Spirit, through trust in God. (See CALNEH.)

Capernaum, că-pēr′-nă-ŭm (Gk. from Heb.)—*village of Nahum; village of consolation; shelter of comfort; covering of compassion; covering of repentance.*

A city on the northwest shore of the Sea of Galilee, "in the borders of Zebulun and Naphtali" (Matt. 4:13; John 4:46).

Meta. Nahum means *comfort* or *consolation.* Capernaum (*village of consolation, shelter of comfort, covering of compassion*) refers to an inner conviction of the abiding compassion and restoring power of Being. When one enters this state of consciousness a healing virtue pours out of the soul and transforms all discord to harmony. It is this great soul compassion and yearning to help humanity out of its errors that makes the so-called "natural healer." In man's body consciousness Capernaum is located in the abdominal region.

Capernaum also means *covering of repentance.* Thus it indicates a cleansing of the mind, both conscious and subconscious. In this repentant attitude the individual is ready to change his mind. Such a man has lived in the outer realms of consciousness where materiality reigns, but now he has come to realize that there is another realm where he becomes acquainted with spiritual Truth. This is entering the synagogue (Mark 1:21).

Capernaum, in Matthew 11:23, represents Christian sympathy, which has been exalted to heaven but shall be brought down to hell, or Hades, the abode of the dead; that is, the sympathy that pours its thought substance out to error shall be brought down to hell. That sympathy helps the sick along in their delusions by sympathizing with them. It mourns over the dead and adds the burden of death thought to death. It joins those who grieve, and grief wears its weeds of sorrow in every home, and every heart slows its beats to meet the measure of the mournful thought. Yet the praises of the "sympathetic tear" are sung by poets; orators eulogize it, and preachers enjoin it. Thus it is "exalted unto heaven." But when Truth is revealed by her works, and casts out the demons of sickness and raises the dead, then false sympathy is brought down to Hades—nothingness.

Caphtor, căph′-tôr (Heb.)—*converted; changed; covered and surrounded; covered with a crown; a covered cup; the cupped hands; sphere; buckle; hand; capital of a column; a sphere; an arena; a circlet or buckle.*

Caphtor is connected with Egypt, also with the Philistines (Deut. 2:23; Jer. 47:4); it is thought that its inhabitants came formerly from Egypt and were descendants of a son of Ham. Caphtor was primarily the country or principal seat of the Philistines, the Philistines being of the same race as the Caphtorim, or Mizraites.

Meta. The evolution (*converted, changed*) that is constantly taking place in the hidden depths (*covered and surrounded, a covered cup*) of man's seemingly physical being (the Caphtorites, being descendants of Ham, represent the physical in man). *A covered cup, covered and surrounded, the cupped hands,* also suggest the warmth, the tenderness, the brooding quality of God's love; the loving care of the Father extends even to the phase of man that he has named physical and mortal. The crowning point of man's unfoldment Godward (*covered with a crown, capital of a column*) is the lifting up and redeeming of his outer consciousness and body, which have hitherto been deemed unworthy of his higher thought, and impossible of spiritualization.

One meaning of *sphere* and *arena* is "circuit or range of action . . . place or scene of action, or existence." A *buckle* is something that fastens or holds together, while *circlet* suggests spiritual unity.

Caphtorim (in A. V., I Chronicles 1:12, Caphthorim), căph′-tŏ-rĭm (Heb.)

—*converters; converts.*

The inhabitants of Caphtor (Gen. 10: 14); they are supposed to have been Egyptians who were descended from Mizraim, son of Ham, and of the same race as the Philistines.

Meta. Changing, growing, unfolding thoughts that belong to the seemingly physical in man. (See CAPHTOR.)

Cappadocia, căp-pă-dō′-çi-à (Gk. from Pers.)—*fine horses.*

A province of Asia Minor (Acts 2:9; I Pet. 1:1). It was noted for its fine pasture lands and for its horses, cattle, asses, and sheep.

Meta. A union in consciousness with the substance (pastures) of life, whereby the life activities and forces, the strength and vitality of the organism (horses, cattle, and sheep), are sustained.

Carcas, cär′-căs (Heb. from Pers.)—*severe; lamb's covering.*

One of "the seven chamberlains that ministered in the presence of Ahasuerus the king" (Esth. 1:10).

Meta. A harsh, devouring, wolfish thought (*severe*) in sheep's clothing; that is, having outwardly an appearance of mildness and obedience (*lamb's covering*), thereby being of a deceptive character. This thought serves the puffed up, ambitious personal will (Ahasuerus).

Carchemish, cär′-che-mĭsh (Heb.)—*fortress of Chemosh; citadel of the vanquisher; the defense of concealment.*

A strongly fortified city of the Hittites, on or near the Euphrates River. It was taken by Neco, king of Egypt; later he was defeated by Nebuchadnezzar, king of Babylon (II Chron. 35:20; Jer. 46:2). (Chemosh means *subduer, vanquisher, concealed, evil, dark star,* and was a national god of the Moabites.)

Meta. A thought center that is strongly established (*fortress, citadel*) in an opposing, resistant, carnal attitude of mind (a city of the Hittites). This darkened, error attitude of mind apparently is so strong that it carries all before it (*citadel of the vanquisher*). Its seemingly great strength lies in concealment. It hides the material and carnal, and therefore the destructive aspect of what

it is, under the deceptive belief that its expressions are natural to man and are of God (*the defense of concealment*).

Carmel, cär′-mĕl (Heb.)—*expanse of a generous nature; garden; orchard; park; fruitful place.*

a A city in the hill country of Judah (Josh. 15:55). **b** A mountain, or range of hills, in Palestine, that was very fruitful and beautiful, whose soil was exceedingly rich. It was on Mount Carmel that Elijah called Israel together and destroyed the prophets of Baal (I Kings 18:19-42). In Song of Solomon 7:5 the head of the bride is likened to Carmel. In Isaiah 35:2 we read of the excellency of Carmel and Sharon.

Meta. A place in consciousness where we realize the fullness of our possibilities under the divine law (*expanse of a generous nature, garden, fruitful place*). It is the garden of God; Jesus called it "Paradise," freedom from sense.

Mount Carmel stands for the center of spirituality, which is located in man's body consciousness in the top of the head.

Carmelite, cär′-mĕl-īte (Heb.).

An inhabitant of the city of Carmel in the hill country of Judah (I Sam. 30:5).

Meta. A rich, opulent thought belonging to the Carmel consciousness.

Carmelitess, cär′-mĕl-ī-tĕss (from Heb.).

A woman native of Carmel (I Sam. 27:3); it refers here to Abigail, David's wife, who was a Carmelitess.

Meta. A thought of great abundance that springs from the soul, or feminine, in individual consciousness.

Carmi, cär′-mī (Heb.)—*vinedresser; generous; fruitful; noble; my vineyard.*

a A son of Reuben (Gen. 46:9). **b** A man of Judah (Josh. 7:1).

Meta. A very vital, prosperous, and fruitful attitude of mind in individual consciousness (*fruitful*). This state of thought is actuated by a spirit of gratitude and thanksgiving (Judah) and a clear vision (Reuben) of abundant spiritual life throughout one's being as one's own divine inheritance (*my vineyard*). One's high, *noble* aspirations are the *vinedresser;* they prune out of consciousness all lesser, limited thoughts of lack.

Carmites, cär'-mītes (Heb.).

Descendants of Carmi, son of Reuben (Num. 26:6).

Meta. Thoughts of the same character that is suggested by the Carmi attitude of mind. (See CARMI.)

Carpus, cär'-pŭs (Gk.)—*harvest, i. e., ingathering of crops; fruitfulness; products; fruits.*

A friend of Paul's at Troas, with whom Paul left his cloak and some of his books (II Tim. 4:13).

Meta. The good effect (*fruits*) of the word of Truth that has been declared (Paul's work) in the Troas consciousness in the individual. (See TROAS.)

Carshena, cär-shē'-nà (Heb. from Pers.)—*black; spoiler; lean; slender; distinguished.*

One of "the seven princes of Persia and Media, who saw the king's face, and sat first in the kingdom" (Esth. 1:14). He is the first-named of the seven, and was one of the wise men to whom King Ahasuerus turned for counsel as to what he should do to Queen Vashti because of her refusal to obey when he commanded that she be brought before him that he might show her beauty to the princes and to the people.

Meta. There were seven of these princes who were next to the king in the kingdom; they represent the seven creative principles that have been developed in the natural man. There are five more to be developed in the superman. The seven princes and seven chamberlains—that is, the number seven—indicate that this whole experience relating to King Ahasuerus takes place in the natural man. Carshena is one of the seven creative principles, or dominant ruling thoughts, in the mentality of the unawakened individual, and upholds the ambitious, self-exalted, personal will (King Ahasuerus) in its attempt to dominate the whole of man's being, even the affectional nature of the human soul (Queen Vashti), according to its pleasure.

Casiphia, cȧ-sĭph'-ĭ-ȧ (Heb.)—*pale; pallid; white; silver* (so called from its pale color); *money; shining.*

A place in or near Babylon where many of the captive Jews lived; Ezra sent word to Iddo at this place to get ministers for the house of God from among the Levites there, men who would be willing to accompany Ezra on his return from the captivity in Babylon to Jerusalem (Ezra 8:17).

Meta. A certain purity of thought (*white*) with a degree of understanding and realization of substance, but in need of more direct spiritual illumination, strength, and vitality (*pale, pallid, silver, money, shining*).

Casluhim, căs'-lu̧-hĭm (Heb.)—*tried for atonement; expiatory trials; forgiveness of sins; hopes of life; fortified.*

A people who were descended from Mizraim, son of Ham (Gen. 10:14).

Meta. The thought contained in Casluhim is that, by means of trials, testings, tribulation, experience, man's outer consciousness (that which constitutes the sensate or physical in him) evolves, unfolds Godward, is released from error, and is lifted to its true spiritual quality and expression; that man must prove his atonement, his release from sin and his oneness with God, in order to become established in eternal life (*tried for atonement, expiatory trials, forgiveness of sins, hopes of life, fortified*).

Cauda (A. V., Clauda), cau̧'-dà (Gk.) —*broken; lame; lamentable.*

A small island near Crete, which is named in the account of Paul's very hazardous trip across the Mediterranean Sea to Italy, whence he was taken to appear before Cæsar at Rome (Acts 27:16).

Meta. Sorrow (*lamentable, broken, lame*) because of the errors of the carnal consciousness (Crete—*carnal, fleshly*), but mostly because of the inharmonious experiences that these errors have brought upon one. While it is helpful to be sorry for one's error, this alone will not really save one. There must be a complete turning away from sin in both thought and act, and a positive thinking and doing of that which measures up to the Christ standard of right.

Cenchreæ (A. V., Cenchrea), çĕn'-çhrĕ-æ (Gk.)—*millet; milletlike; small grains; small beads.*

A harbor of Corinth (Acts 18:18).

There was a Christian assembly in the place, and Phoebe was a deaconess in this church (Rom. 16:1). In this place, too, either Paul or Aquila (the text is not quite clear) had "shorn his head . . . for he had a vow."

Meta. Cenchreæ (*small grains, like millet*) signifies, like the mustard seed of Jesus' parable, the fact that the Truth established in the consciousness of man is at first similar to a very tiny seed (the word is the seed). We should not therefore despise nor look upon as insignificant any beginning of light and Truth that comes to us or to others, no matter how small it may seem. We should always remember the wonderful power of the Christ Spirit to cause the seed of Truth to grow and increase in the consciousness of each individual who gives it place and welcomes its presence.

centurion (Matt. 8:5-13).

Meta. The will, whose servant, the body, is sick. Until man blends his will with the divine will, he is "grievously tormented" in many ways. But here the will recognizes and calls upon the higher law, the Christ, and asks that the Christ word may go forth with the same imperative command that it is in the habit of exercising in its control of the organism. Even the Christ is unprepared for this evidence of faith in its naked word, but—quickened to action by the zealous will—the word of Truth goes forth, and the body is made whole.

Cephas, çē'-phăs (Gk. from Chald.)—*hard; unyielding; a stone; rock; cliff.*

A name that Jesus gave to Simon: "Thou shalt be called Cephas (which is by interpretation, Peter)." "That is, *Rock* or *Stone*," (margin, John 1:42).

Meta. An unwavering faith in God. (See PETER.) When this faith is established firmly in individual consciousness, it becomes a *rock*, a sure foundation, unshakable, immovable, upon which one can build spiritually.

Chaldea, chăl-dē'-à (Gk.)—*savant; astrologer; magi.*

An Asiatic country lying on both sides of the Euphrates River (Jer. 50:10; Ezek. 11:24). It was a portion of Babylon and, in a general sense, included all of Babylonia.

Meta. The psychic realm in man (*savant, astrologer, magi*) posing as the true spiritual realm, thus deceiving the individual and robbing him of the spiritual contact and good that he is seeking.

Chaldeans, chăl-dē'-ăns (Gk.)—*savants; astrologers; occultists; magi.*

The people of Chaldea, of that country of which Babylon was the capital (II Kings 25:4-26). Boyd says that the Chaldeans were "that people of Chaldea proper who, by the time of the Captivity, constituted the learned classes, the philosophers, magicians, and advisers of Babylon, and whose language was impressed on Babylonish literature." (See Dan. 1:4, last clause, also Dan. 2:2-12.)

Meta. Psychic thoughts that connect the individual soul with the soul of the earth and the heavenly bodies. They are not spiritual, but shine by borrowed light.

Chaldees, chăl'-dēes.

The same people as the Chaldeans (Gen. 15:7).

Meta. See CHALDEANS.

chariots.

Meta. Chariots, in the Bible, represent the body activities.

Chebar, chē'-bär (Heb.)—*binding together; joining; plaiting; braiding; strength; magnitude; abundance; length.*

A river or canal of Babylon, or Chaldea, by which Ezekiel saw his visions (Ezek. 1:1). A colony of Jewish captives was settled along the banks of this river; Ezekiel, meaning *God strengtheneth, God is strong*, was one of them.

Meta. A current (river) of vital thought, which strengthens the religious thoughts of man (Jews) that have been reaching out for spiritual Truth but have become entangled in psychic forces (Chaldeans) and have fallen into sense confusion (Babylon). Spiritual revelation also comes to them here and tends to unify them with (*joining*) the one true Source of all inspiration and strength and of all true greatness and abundance (Spirit).

Chedorlaomer, chĕd-ôr-lā'-ŏ-mēr (Heb. of doubtful origin)—*sheaf band; handful of sheaves; roundness of a sheaf.*

King of Elam (Gen. 14:1, 17). He

was one of the four kings who made war against the kings of Sodom and Gomorrah in Abraham's time, and took Lot captive. Lot was released and these kings were destroyed by Abraham. Fallows says of Chedorlaomer: "His Elamite name would be Kudur–Lagamar, meaning the servant of the goddess Lagamar, who, perhaps, represented the Dawn."

Meta. The generative functions of the body given over to the expression of sex lust. The kings of Genesis 14:2, who served Chedorlaomer for twelve years and then rebelled, represent ruling thoughts in the hidden, sense consciousness of man. The substance of these ruling energies is given over to the use of the functions pertaining to generation to build them up and strengthen them in sense expression. In time, however, this constant waste of substance in sex ways causes a deterioration of the whole man, and even the desire for sex expression leaves him: the ruling tendencies in his sense nature (kings) rebel against Chedorlaomer. He is of course frightened then, and goes to war with these kings to restore his dominion over them; he believes that youth (Elam) and the renewal of life, represented by the "Dawn" (the goddess Lagamar), depend upon his vigor and strength, and the only way that he knows of judging this power and vigor is by the strength of sex desire. He does not understand that age and decrepitude are brought about largely by the waste of the body substance in sense ways. He needs to learn that in his conserving the substance of his body temple by overcoming lustful desires and practices, and by lifting his thoughts and acts to higher and more spiritual expression, his life will be renewed from day to day; thus he will find the fountain of eternal youth, vigor, and unfailing strength.

Chelal, chē'-lăl (Heb.)—*perfection; completion; whole; finished; crowned.*

An Israelite who had a foreign wife after the return from the Babylonian captivity (Ezra 10:30); he is named as one of the sons of Pahath-moab.

Meta. The *perfection* or *completion* that Chelal signifies cannot refer to spiritual wholeness and perfection; if it did, he could not have taken a foreign wife—made union with the unredeemed affectional soul nature. Chelal must refer more to the rounding out of the outer man preparatory to a higher spiritual understanding and attainment. He put away his foreign wife when his mistake was revealed to him by Ezra.

Cheluhi (A. V., Chelluh), chĕl'-û-hī (Heb.)—*completed; perfected; finished; full; robust; prepared; accomplished; fulfilled.*

An Israelite, of the sons of Bani, who had a foreign wife after his return from the Babylonian captivity (Ezra 10:35).

Meta. Perfection of vigor and strength in the natural man (*completed, perfected, full, robust;* an Israelite who had taken a foreign wife). This expression of vigor and strength needs to be unified with true understanding that it may become more spiritual.

Chelub, chē'-lŭb (Heb.)—*a trap cage; a bird cage; a basket.*

a A man of Judah, brother of Shuhah and father of Mehir (I Chron. 4:11). **b** The father of Ezri, who was "over them that did the work of the field for tillage of the ground," in David's reign (I Chron. 27:26).

Meta. A degree of executive power attained through praise (a man of Judah who had charge of the field laborers in David's reign). This consciousness of executive power is somewhat limited by narrow personal beliefs, but is seeking freer, fuller expression (*a trap cage, a bird cage, a basket,* with the thought of the sound of clapping and flapping).

Chelubai, chĕ-lū'-bāi (Heb.)—*clapper; barker; trapper; basket weaver.*

Son of Hezron, of the tribe of Judah (I Chron. 2:9); he is thought to be the same person as Caleb, who is mentioned in verses 18 and 42. (See CALEB.)

Meta. A thought activity that works in the consciousness to put away error and establish good. The destructive tendency must be eliminated from this thought and the cleansing, redeeming spirit of the Christ must be wholly accepted, that it may do perfect work. (See CALEB.)

Chemarim (in A. V., Zeph. 1:4, Chemarims), chĕm'-ă-rĭm, (Heb.)—*burners; scorchers; black-robed; blackeners; idol priests; ascetics; monks; priests.*

Priests other than those of the true worship. Zephaniah says, speaking for Jehovah, "I will cut off . . . the name of the Chemarim with the priests" (Zeph. 1:4). In II Kings 23:5 "idolatrous priests" is given in the text, and "*Chemarim*" in the margin. See Hosea 10:5, also, with margin.

Meta. The priests of the Old Testament symbolize our natural religious tendencies; they are not necessarily spiritual. The Chemarim (idolatrous priests) are the ruling thoughts in our religious nature that pass under the guise of Truth but that ever magnify, build up, and strengthen the material and personal in us rather than the spiritual. Isaiah 5:20 describes them: "Woe unto them that call evil good, . . . that put darkness for light"; they must be uncovered and put away out of consciousness.

Chemosh, chē'-mŏsh (Heb.)—*subduer; depressor; vanquisher; an incubus; concealed; yearning fire; a hearth; the planet Saturn* (evil, dark star).

A national god of the Moabites (I Kings 11:7, 33).

Meta. The seeming strength and subtlety of error, of the "mind of the flesh" in man. (See CARCHEMISH.)

Chenaanah, chĕ-nā'-ă-năh (Heb.)—*existing in* and *for material things; trafficker in material things; a merchant; the basis of things; low; inferior.*

a Son of Bilhan, of the tribe of Benjamin; he was one of the "heads of their fathers' *houses*," and a mighty man of valor (I Chron. 7:10, 11). b The father of Zedekiah, a false prophet (I Kings 22:11).

A humble and lowly phase of thought, one that is commercial in its tendencies (*low, a merchant*). It is willing to trade ideas with other states of mind, with other faculties and qualities in consciousness. This phase of thought, united to an active, accomplishing faith in God (Benjamin), makes "a mighty man of valor," a strong, brave, uplifting, and up-building force in man.

In the case of the other Chenaanah, who was the father of Zedekiah, a false prophet, the commercial thought that he signifies partakes of a baseness of character that tends to materialize the whole consciousness (*existing in* and *for material things; inferior; the basis of things,* that is, of materiality).

Chenani, chĕn'-ă-nī (Heb.)—*whom Jehovah has set; Jehovah has planted; Jah has established; Jehovah is firm; whom Jah protects; Jehovah covers.*

A Levite; he was one of those who led the Israelites in the devotional service that followed the reading of the law to them by Ezra (Neh. 9:4).

Meta. The belief in man's higher, religious, or spiritual thoughts that he is of God, has come into manifest existence by the will of God—through the action of Jehovah, the Lord God, or Christ—and is established in his rightful place by Jehovah, wherein he is divinely sustained and protected (*Jehovah has planted, Jah has established, whom Jah protects, Jehovah covers*). This understanding and this acknowledgment are a very necessary factor in all true worship and in the cleansing of the consciousness.

Chenaniah, chĕn-ă-nī'-ăh (Heb.)—*whom Jehovah has set; Jah has established; whom Jah protects; strength of the Lord.* Chenani is a contracted form of Chenaniah, and the definitions are identical.

a A chief of the Levites. He had charge of the musical services when David brought the Ark of the Covenant from the house of Obed–edom to Jerusalem (I Chron. 15:22, 27). b A Levite; he and his sons "were for the outward business over Israel, for officers and judges"; this was also during David's reign (I Chron. 26:29).

Meta. The interpretation is virtually the same as that of Chenani. (See CHENANI.) When this realization of divine protection springs up in man's consciousness and throughout his whole being, he is greatly strengthened (*strength of the Lord*); he also experiences joy and harmony (music) in his soul and he sings praises to the Divine. This realization also officiates for love (David) in the business of the kingdom of the Israelites (true thoughts) and in establishing justice and Truth. (See I Chron. 26:29.)

Chephar–ammoni (A. V., Chephar–haammonai), chĕ'-phär–ăm'-mŏ-nī (Heb.)—*village of the Ammonites.*

A city of the Benjamites, in the land of Canaan (Josh. 18:24).

Meta. A thought center in man that, though given over to the activity of faith (Benjamites), still retains some of its old Ammonitish tendencies and beliefs (*village of the Ammonites*). (See AMMONITES.)

Chephirah, chĕ-phī'-răh (Heb.)—*covered; overlaid; village; hamlet.*

A city of the Hivites, or Gibeonites. The men from this city were among those who deceived Joshua and the Israelites into making a covenant, contrary to the command of Jehovah (Josh. 9:17). The Hivites are said to have been of a peaceable character and were inclined to be tradesmen. Chephirah was allotted to Benjamin (Josh. 18:26); it is also mentioned in Ezra and Nehemiah as one of the cities of Palestine to which some inhabitants returned from the Babylonian captivity (Ezra 2:25; Neh. 7:29).

Meta. A subconscious realm of thought, of a lowly, common, deceptive nature (*covered, overlaid, village, hamlet*). It recognizes the superiority of the higher, truer, religious thoughts that the Israelites signify. By subtlety, and because of its willingness to exchange ideas (the Chephirahites were tradesmen), it induces the individual to compromise with error, which causes him much trouble in his overcoming. However, when the Chephirah phase of thought comes into the possession of the Benjamites, it becomes a harborer of higher faith ideals that work toward the individual's ultimate freedom from sense confusion (Babylon), and toward his full redemption.

Cheran, chĕ'-ran (Heb.)—*lyre; harp; a stringed instrument; united; a joyous shout.*

Son of Dishon, who was a Horite chief (Gen. 36:26).

Meta. A harmonious, unifying thought that is active in the depths of the physical being of man (*united, lyre; a Horite*). Since this thought is not consciously one with Spirit, though its origin and intent are good, it cannot bring about the perfect union of man with God, and the true spiritual harmony, that the meaning of the name might imply.

Cherethites, chĕr'-ĕ-thītes (Heb.)—*executioners; couriers; foot runners; headsmen.*

The Cherethites belonged to David's life guards, or bodyguards. Benaiah, the son of Jehoiada, was over them (II Sam. 8:18).

Meta. Activities of a high degree of understanding and justice, also of life energy and executive power (*executioners, headsmen,* and *foot runners*); these protect and serve, and execute the demands of, the love faculty in man when it is raised to the seat of power and dominion in consciousness (King David). (See BENAIAH and JEHOIADA.)

Cherith, chĕ'-rīth (Heb.)—*cutting; separating; dividing; slaying; a trench; a gorge; a wound.*

"The brook Cherith, that is before the Jordan" (I Kings 17:3); a place in Palestine—a brook, or river, where Elijah hid in obedience to the word of Jehovah, and was fed by ravens.

Meta. Subjective life currents in individual consciousness.

Cherub, chĕ'-rŭb (Heb.)—the singular form of cherubim. (See CHERUBIM for further definition.)

A Babylonian city, or place, from which people returned to Palestine from the captivity (Ezra 2:59). These persons who are mentioned as having come from Cherub with the returned Israelites "could not show their fathers' houses, and their seed, whether they were of Israel, . . . therefore were they deemed polluted and put from the priesthood."

Meta. An aggregation of thoughts in consciousness that have been held in confusion (Babylon) but are becoming free because of the seeds of Truth thoughts (Israelites) that are working in them. They are still so tainted with the Babylonish thought, however, that they cannot take a place among our natural religious tendencies (priests and Levites) in ministering to our true higher beliefs and ideals (Israelites).

cherubim, chĕr'-û-bĭm (Heb.)—*legion-like; augmentation; growth to infinity; grasped; held fast.*

Symbolical figures used in the Scriptures to represent the majesty and ruling power of God; also His attributes (Exod. 25:18-22).

Meta. The "cherubim" of I Kings 8:6-8 were symbolic figures representing the attributes and majesty of God. They stand for the unfettered truths of Being, which must always be present in the holy of holies within us. If we do not have this higher realization before us constantly, we shall drop down to the physical plane and our religion will become a mere phenomenal display. We are told that the cherubim spread their wings over the place of the Ark and covered it and its staves, yet they were "not seen without: and there they are unto this day." Here is a true description of the omnipresence of the principle of Being in the whole spiritual life of man.

At heart we have this holy place and these cherubim with their wings spread over the whole Ark. No matter how great a backslider you may be, the presence of the Spirit of God is not far away from your conscious mind. Right under your heart you will find a brain that in its depths treasures the memories of all religious experiences, engraved on the very substance of your being (two tables of stone).

The word "Cherubim" of Genesis 3:24 means protection, or sacred life. The inner spiritual life is protected from the outer, coarser consciousness. The "flame of a sword" is the divine idea or Word of God. Man unites with the inner Word, or sacred life, through spiritual thought, meditation, and prayer. The Word is made flesh, or is brought into manifestation, when we conform in idea to the ideas of Divine Mind and set up the activity of the divine will, which is perfect thought and corresponding perfect action. The "way of the tree of life" is the narrow path referred to by Jesus Christ; it is the way of unfolding divine consciousness by realizing the divine na-

ture of man.

Chesalon, chĕs'-ă-lŏn (Heb.)—*loin; fleshy; fat; strength; great hope; sure confidence; fertile.*

A place on the border of Judah, in the land of Canaan (Josh. 15:10). It is mentioned as being on "the side of mount Jearim on the north." Mount Jearim is a mountain on the north border of Judah, a few miles west of Jerusalem.

Meta. A consciousness of physical strength (*loin; fleshy; fat; strength*). Under the influence of the higher ideals that Judah signifies, this consciousness of strength will be raised to the understanding that all true strength is founded in Spirit and works out great good to the individual who realizes God as his unfailing, abiding strength (*great hope, pure confidence, fertile*).

Chesed, chē'-sĕd (Heb.)—*wisdom; a savant; an astrologer; a magi; an occultist.*

A son of Abraham's brother, Nahor, by his wife, Milcah (Gen. 22:22).

Meta. A degree of wisdom, a wisdom that is psychical in its nature, rather than spiritual (*a savant, an astrologer, a magi, an occultist*).

Chesil, chē'-sĭl (Heb.)—*loin; fleshy; fat; fleshly; carnal; fool; foolish; impious; ungodly.*

A city of Judah, "toward the border of Edom in the South" (Josh. 15:30).

Meta. The unwise, *ungodly* thoughts and activities that hold sway in man when he lives purely in the sense mind. (Edom—red—refers to the outer or physical, sensate organism of man.) The whole man is to be redeemed, however, and this ungodly state of consciousness (Chesil), having been allotted to Judah, will be transformed into spiritual expression by means of prayer and praise, the Judah consciousness. Then it will become truly *fat*, rich with the abundance of spiritual thought.

Chesulloth, chĕ-sŭl'-lŏth (Heb.)—*loins; fatness; flanks; great hopes; sure confidence.* Chesulloth is the plural form of Chesalon.

A city of Issachar, on the border (Josh. 19:18).

Meta. A group of thoughts whose central idea is life and strength (*loins*) and abundant substance (*fatness*). Issachar (active zeal) of the Israelites (true, real, and more spiritual thoughts of the consciousness), becoming active in this aggregation of thoughts that Chesulloth signifies, will remove from them all material beliefs and will lift them to a higher standard. (See CHESALON.)

Chezib, chē'-zĭb (Heb.)—*lying; false; fraudulent; deceitful; fallacious; false hopes,* i. e., *idols.*

The place where Judah's wife, Shua the daughter of the Canaanite, gave birth to their third son, Shelah (Gen. 38:5). It is thought to be the same place as Achzib.

Meta. See ACHZIB.

This deceptive state of thought that Achzib and Chezib signify (*deceitful, lying, false*) lies deep within the elemental life forces of the individual (it was a Canaanitish city; see CANAANITES). It must be cleansed thoroughly of its error and deception, its double-minded, idolatrous belief in a power of evil as well as one of good, in order that the truth of the one life and the one God, good, may be established within its depths.

Chidon, chī'-dŏn (Heb.)—*javelin; spear; calamity; war; destruction; ruin.*

At "the threshing-floor of Chidon" Uzza put out his hand to steady the Ark and was killed (I Chron. 13:9); in II Samuel 6:6 it is called "the threshing-floor of Nacon."

Meta. See NACON.

Chileab, chĭl'-ĕ-ăb (Heb.)—*like unto the father; totality of the father,* i. e., *perfection of all that the father is.*

A son of David, by Abigail, who had been the wife of Nabal the Carmelite (II Sam. 3:3). In I Chronicles 3:1 this son of David is called Daniel instead of Chileab.

Meta. Daniel signifies spiritual judgment. Chileab here refers to love (*like unto the father;* David symbolizing love) established in judgment.

Chilion, chĭl'-ĭ-ŏn (Heb.)—*pining; wasting away; sickly; consumption; destruction.*

One of the two sons of Naomi and Elimelech, Israelites of Bethlehem–judah (Ruth 1:2).

Meta. Elimelech means *God is king.* But Naomi (the soul) has let her desire run out to the sense consciousness, and has given her substance to it. Therefore the sons, or thought emanations, that come from the soul and its consciousness of God as king are not strong, positive, and vital; they are not filled with confidence and assurance as they should be.

Chilion represents a thought that has its inception in spiritual Truth, but has been deprived of its true nourishment; it has been forced to give of its power and substance to the carnal mind (Moab), and in the end makes a union with the soul in its unawakened and darkened state (he married a Moabitish woman). Thus the thought that Chilion signifies loses strength (*wasting away, consumption*) and constantly longs for its true spiritual sustenance (*pining*); it is never contented, healthy, or happy, because it is out of its proper environment (it is *sickly*). It finally dies childless—passes out of consciousness without having brought forth any definite fruit to eternal life and good.

Chilmad, chĭl'-măd (Heb.)—*inclosed; surrounded; closed.*

A place in Asia that is mentioned with Sheba and Asshur, and with Haran, Canneh, and Eden. It is supposed to have bordered on the Euphrates River. In the prophet's lamentation over Tyre, Chilmad is named among the "traffickers in choice wares, in wrappings of blue and broidered work, and in chests of rich apparel, bound with cords and made of cedar" (Ezek. 27:23, 24).

Meta. The picture of Tyre as given by Ezekiel shows it to symbolize sense consciousness puffed up with pride and self-sufficiency. Chilmad signifies an active state of thought of the same character as Tyre. It is apparently wholly taken up with sense. It is *surrounded* by error, and is *closed* against spiritual Truth; it traffics in materiality—carnal reasonings and sense pleasures—and it holds a high place in the esteem of the personal self in man.

Chimham, chĭm'-hăm (Heb.)—*pining; longing; desiring greatly; pale; faint.*

A servant of Barzillai's who went with David back to Jerusalem when David returned after Absalom was defeated and killed (II Sam. 19:37). (See Jer. 41:17.)

Meta. Barzillai represents physical strength, whose substance is used for the sustenance of love ruling in consciousness (David, the king). Chimham (*pining, longing*), who went with David to Gilgal (Gilgal means *rolling,* and refers to a total denial, or rolling away, of sense bondage), is the intense longing and aspiring of the individual to come into a more spiritual expression of strength, that a depletion of strength (*pale, faint*) may never be sensed. His great desire (*desiring greatly*) is that he may realize his strength as purely spiritual, and that it may be exercised only and always in love, to the upbuilding of his true, spiritual self. Through the ruling power of love (David) and the denying of all bondage to sense (going to Gilgal) this will be accomplished.

Chinnereth, chĭn'-nĕ-rĕth (Heb.)—*harp; lyre; harplike.*

a A fortified city of Naphtali (Josh. 19:35). **b** A name that was given in olden times to the Lake of Gennesaret, or Sea of Galilee (Num. 34:11); the city of Chinnereth was situated by this lake.

Meta. A sea of vitality, of life activity, or of nervous energy, in individual consciousness. (See SEA OF GALILEE; also, GENNESARET.) The city of Chinnereth is an active life consciousness. The name Chinnereth also gives the thought of music, harmony, as well as of life activity (*harp, lyre, harplike*); it would therefore be an orderly, harmonious state of thought.

Chinneroth, chĭn'-nĕ-rŏth (Heb.)—the plural form of Chinnereth.

The same as Chinnereth (Josh. 12:3; I Kings 15:20).

Meta. See CHINNERETH.

Chios, chī'-ŏs (Gk.)—*wine; fertility; open.*

An island in the Ægean Sea. Paul came "over against" this island while he was on one of his missionary jour-

neys (Acts 20:15).

Meta. An *open,* unobstructed, fertile attitude of thought; this thought relates closely to Spirit and life (*wine*). When man opens his intellectual reasoning mind so that the word of Truth (Paul) may find access, he is "over against" Chios.

Chislev (A. V., Chisleu), chĭs'-lĕv (Heb.)—*hopeful; confident; Mars; Orion; a hunter.* The three latter definitions are in dispute.

The third month of the Jewish civil year, and the ninth of their ecclesiastical year (Neh. 1:1; Zech. 7:1), beginning with the new moon in December. The name came from the Persian names of months, which the Jews used after their captivity in Babylon.

Meta. A hopeful, confident attitude of mind. In individual consciousness divisions of time refer to degrees of unfoldment. Things that are spiritual and eternal cannot be measured by days, months, and years, but by steps or degrees in unfoldment and attainment. (See TIME.)

Chislon, chĭs'-lŏn (Heb.)—*strength; hope; confidence; trust.* This name comes from the same root as Chesalon.

Father of Elidad, who was chosen from the tribe of Benjamin as one of the men who were to decide as to the division of the land of Canaan among the Israelites (Num. 34:21).

Meta. Strength and confidence established in faith (*strength, hope, confidence, trust;* a Benjamite). The hope of man's full redemption must be based upon God before man can enter in and take possession of his Promised Land (the consciousness and the body), and before he can utilize all his inner forces and powers in a right and wise manner.

Chisloth – tabor, chĭs'-lŏth – tā'-bôr (Heb.)—*loins of Tabor; strength of Tabor; hope of the heaped up,* i. e., *the high.*

A city of Israel, on the side of Mount Tabor (Josh. 19:12). It is called Tabor in verse 22, and is named as one of the cities of Issachar. It is the same city as Chesulloth.

Meta. The strength of high, exalted thoughts and ideals (*loins of Tabor;* loins refer to strength). (See TABOR and CHESULLOTH.)

Chloe, chlō'-ê (Gk.)—*tender shoot; tender growth; verdant herbage; green herb.*

From the *"household of Chloe"* Paul learned that there were contentions and divisions among the members of the church at Corinth (I Cor. 1:11).

Meta. A springing up into expression, or manifest growth, of the word of Truth that has been planted in the love center (Corinth) in individual consciousness. This word has taken root in substance and is springing up into life and peace.

The *"household of Chloe"* means spiritual thoughts of life and love that are budding and growing naturally and harmoniously. They are quick to sense cross currents of a divided or contentious attitude of mind that sometimes become active in the assembly of love thoughts (church at Corinth). They communicate the news of this inharmony to the word of Truth (Paul), that through the activity of the word the cross currents may be eliminated and the love consciousness again may become established in the harmony of the real Christ Spirit.

Chorazin, chŏ-rā'-zĭn (Gk. from Heb.) —*place of proclamations; place of heralds; secret.*

A town, or city, in Galilee, near Bethsaida and Capernaum (Matt. 11:21).

Meta. The people of Chorazin, with Bethsaida, witnessed the mighty works of Jesus, yet were not moved to change their ways and accept the Truth. They are types of minds that are fixed in their ideas of what is religiously proper, and do not open to the more interior phases of Truth. The openly wanton and wicked cities of Tyre and Sidon stand a better chance in the day of judgment. That is, those who are wholly wrong will offer no excuse when their sins, or shortcomings, bring them before the final law of adjustment; they will admit their errors and repent; but those who have a limited amount of Truth, which they hover over and declare to be the whole of Truth, are in danger of mental and spiritual crystallization.

chosen people.

Meta. Along with the doctrine of hell and eternal punishment, there came into the theological world a very warped idea of a "chosen people." In the minds of certain churchmen and their followers the belief became general that God chose certain people to be saved in heaven, and elected the remainder of the race to eternal damnation. There is not the slightest foundation in the Bible for such a belief.

There is, however, a beautiful teaching about a chosen people. In all the history of this race God has at different times chosen certain ones to do a certain work. Sometimes He made the choice of an individual, as Moses, Elijah, and Paul. Early in recorded history He chose Abraham, and then his family, and then the whole race of Abraham's descendants. This race of people were called Israelites and they were chosen for a special purpose in God's plan of blessing for all men. They have been watched over, kept, guarded, guided, and disciplined by the Most High in a marvelous way, that the seed of faith in the one true God might be kept alive and nourished in men and that a people might be prepared through whom His kingdom would be established upon the earth.

But the "chosen people" of the greatest importance are the class described by Peter in his first letter: "Ye are an elect race, a royal priesthood, a holy nation, a people for *God's* own possession, that ye may show forth the excellencies of him who called you out of darkness into his marvellous light."

The calling of Israel was justified when out of Israel came Jesus Christ, the world's deliverer and Savior. The ministry that He began in Palestine has been going on for two thousand years, and has not yet reached its completion. His great work of restitution calls for a company of tried and trained and spiritually developed people to work with Him in establishing His glorious kingdom of righteousness and peace upon the earth; these people are now being made ready. We are living in the times of restitution. Out of this generation the royal priesthood of those that are to reign as kings and priests (Rev. 1:5, 6; 5:10, A. V.) will come. These people will be the beginning of the holy nation that is to fill all the earth with its glory. They are now the light of the world, and their light will increase until all the dark places of the earth are lighted up. By overcoming they are incorporating into their own consciousness the attributes, the virtues, of God, and are therefore becoming more and more the living expression of His righteousness and glory. They make up the Christ body that is so wonderfully described by Paul. Through them the world is to receive its restitutional blessings, and Jesus Christ shall be glorified as the King of this whole earth.

In individual consciousness "people" represent thoughts. Our "chosen people" are our spiritually enlightened and obedient thoughts. As fast as the various states of consciousness and thoughts in us become awakened by the inner Christ light and change their activities to accord with Truth, they enter the ranks of the "chosen people."

Christ, christ (from Gk.)—*anointed; the anointed; the Messiah.*

A name, or title, applied to Jesus of Nazareth (Matt. 16:16; Acts 17:3). Jehovah of the Old Testament is the I AM, or Christ of God invisible; the Messiah is the promise of the visible manifestation of that I AM or Christ, and Jesus Christ is the fulfillment in man of that original spiritual I AM, or Jehovah.

Meta. Christ is the divine-idea man. Jesus is the name that represents an individual expression of the Christ idea. Jesus Christ is the form of the name that is commonly applied to the man of Galilee who demonstrated perfection. Christ Jesus is the idea that is being expressed by men as the result of their faith in and understanding of Truth.

Christ is the only begotten Son of God, or the one complete idea of perfect man in Divine Mind. He is the embodiment of all divine ideas, such as intelligence, life, love, substance, and strength. In the architect's mind there may be one masterpiece, but that masterpiece is the sum of all the beautiful ideas that have come to his mind. This Christ, or perfect-man idea existing eternally in Divine Mind, is the true, spiritual, higher self of every individual. Each of us has within him the Christ, just as Jesus had, and we must look within to recognize and realize our sonship, our divine origin and birth, even as He did. By continually unifying ourselves with the Highest by our thoughts and words, we too shall become sons of God, manifest.

The cosmic man, or grand man of the universe, often referred to by religious mystics, is the Christ, and the Christ is the higher self of man. Thus a seemingly great mystery is reduced to simple numbers. We do not realize the nearness of this cosmic man, because we have not found our real selves. Jesus Christ educated His followers to discern the real man. He taught that there is a power in man that gives him authority over the things of the world. This principle is the higher self, the spiritual man, the Christ. If we would succeed we must bring forth the principle; it gives dominion and mastery.

Spiritual perception reveals to us that we are not persons, but factors in the cosmic mind. Reveal yourself to yourself by affirming, "*I am the Christ, son of the living God.*" Look at yourself not as flesh and blood, but as Spirit. Jesus Christ affirmed His true self and the Father acknowledged Him. The reason for the limited comprehension and power of the ordinary man is found in the fact that he sees the world about him as under material law, and agreeing with it he makes himself part of it.

Christ is the cosmic man, the grand man of the universe, demonstrated, developed, brought out, in every man.

The birth of Christ in man is the bringing to consciousness of the spiritual idea of man—the Christ of God—through the quickening power of the word of Truth. It is the beginning in the inner realms of consciousness of a higher set of faculties that, when grown to full stature, save the whole man from ignorance and sin. It is a growth in man as tangible to those who reach certain stages as is that of the child to the mother. In its beginnings it is a mere quickening flutter, under the stomach, accompanied often by unusual sensitiveness in the emotional nature. We do not in the first stages of this process understand it, and sometimes are moved to put it away from us. This is the spiritual significance of the statement that Joseph was merely "betrothed" to Mary, yet she was "great with child." The soul is heavily charged with divine life, and so full that it cannot express itself intelligently, because no union has yet taken place between it and the understanding (Joseph).

church, the.

Meta. The true Christ church is not an outer sect, or religious denomination. First of all it is an aggregation of spiritual ideas in individual consciousness. To establish the church, or ecclesia, of God in man, a new state of consciousness must be formed. Man must gain an understanding of God as Spirit, and also must understand his own relation to Spirit. This is revealed by the Holy Ghost, which is an epitome of Divine Mind projected into human consciousness. The church of God begins its activity in man as a mental perception, which must go through certain processes before it is established in the whole consciousness. Its work is subjective first; that is, it is a silent interior planting of spiritual ideas, which do not make themselves manifest at once, but work like leaven, and in time transform the individual.

In its outer sense the church of Christ consists of all persons in whom the consciousness of Truth has become firmly established; whether or not they belong to a denominational church makes no difference. They comprise that great brotherhood which Jesus Christ established in Spirit. Men have read the Bible in the letter instead of the spirit, and their different interpretations of the Scriptures, together with their adherence to forms and creeds, are the cause of the varying sects or churches of today. The true church is not made of creeds and forms, nor is it contained in walls of wood and stone; the heart of man is its temple and the Spirit of truth is the one guide into all Truth. When men learn to turn within to the Spirit of truth, who is in each one for his light and inspiration, the differences between the churches of man will be eliminated, and the one church will be recognized.

Chuzas (A. V., Chuza), chū'-zăs (Gk.) *seer.*

Herod's steward (Luke 8:3). Chuzas' wife, Joanna, was one of the women followers of Jesus, "who ministered unto them of their substance."

Meta. Herod is the human will, or sense consciousness, in active control in the individual. But when Jesus has been born in one's consciousness, and the Christ Truth is being imparted to the whole man, the faculties of body and soul that have been given over to sense begin to wake up, and to recognize their true origin.

Chuzas (*seer*), who was the manager of Herod's domestic affairs (his steward), represents the ability to see, or to understand clearly; also to decide and adjust vital matters pertaining to the sense will and its activities. While this capacity seems to be of the intellect or outer wisdom only, it is more closely allied with the God-given soul quality of intuition and discernment (Joanna) than even it has realized, let alone the outer-sense man (Herod).

Cilicia, çĭ-lĭ'-çĭ-å (Gk.)—*treacherous; cruel; brutish.*

A portion of Asia Minor through which Paul and Silas went "confirming the churches" (Acts 15:41). Paul's birthplace was in Tarsus, a city of Cilicia (Acts 21:39).

Meta. Cilicia, meaning *treacherous, cruel,* Derbe, meaning *harsh, stinging,* and Lystra, meaning *that dissolves,* indicate that the work of Paul and Silas required great effort; it was not pleasant. Forceful thoughts often stir up opposition, especially if these thoughts have much of the "purely intellectual" in them, and are not thoroughly and wholly of Spirit; gentle thoughts bring a peaceful victory. "The wisdom that is from above is . . . peaceable, gentle, easy to be entreated" (James 3:17). It is pure also; that is, it is free from all dissimulation, all strife, all self-seeking, and all double-mindedness.

circumcision (Lat.)—*cutting off.*

Meta. Circumcision, as referred to in the Old Testament, is an external ceremony practiced by the Jews to indicate a certain conformity to the Mosaic law. It is symbolical of the cutting off of mortal tendencies, and is indicative of purification and cleanliness. Under the law of Jesus Christ, circumcision is fulfilled in its spiritual meaning—the purification of the individual from the law of sin and death. One is circumcised in the true inner significance of the word only by being thoroughly purified in soul. Then the glory of the inner soul cleansing and purifying works out into the outer consciousness and the body and sets one free from all sensual, corruptible thoughts and activities. Thus man becomes a new creature in Christ Jesus; he manifests wholeness and perfection throughout his being.

When one has entered into the realization of the spirit of divine law, the symbol is no longer necessary to soul growth. "Circumcision is that of the heart, in the spirit not in the letter" (Rom. 2:29). He who keeps the precepts of divine law, and seeks to embody the principles of Truth in mind, body, and affairs, is circumcised unto the Lord, which is the essential purification.

cities.

Meta. Fixed states of consciousness, or aggregations of thoughts in the various nerve centers of the body. The presiding or central thought-meaning of a city is found in the significance of its name, combined with that of the man, tribe, country, or nation with which it is mentioned.

In their highest significance, the "cities of Judah" (II Sam. 2:1) represent spiritual centers of life in consciousness.

"The city which hath the foundations, whose builder and maker is God" (Heb. 11:10) is the spiritual body. Its foundation is the ideal body created by Divine Mind. By faith we bring this ideal body into manifestation.

Claudia, clau'-dĭ-à (Lat.)—*broken; lame; lamentable.*

A Christian woman at Rome (II Tim. 4:21). She was a friend to Paul and Timothy.

Meta. A soul quality that loves the truth of man's divine sonship (believes on Jesus Christ); this soul quality is somewhat limited or hindered in its practical understanding and expression (*broken, lame*) because of its relation to the head in its sensate reasoning and carnal personal will (Rome and the Roman ruling powers). Claudia is supposed to have been a Briton by birth, and to have come to Rome with the wife of the Roman leader in Britain. She no doubt changed her name to a Roman one, since Claudia is the feminine form of Claudius. (See CLAUDIUS.)

Claudius, clau'-dĭ-ŭs (Lat.)—*broken; lame; lamentable.*

A Roman emperor, who forced all the Jews to leave Rome (Acts 18:2). The famine that was foretold by Agabus came to pass in the reign of this emperor (Acts 11:28).

Meta. Lameness usually refers to the legs and feet; the feet represent the phase of man's understanding that comes in touch with the outer world of affairs. Claudius (*broken, lame, lamentable*) points to a serious and deplorable defect in the practical understanding, which should enable one to express toward and coöperate rightly with others in the outer. This lack of a workable understanding (Claudius) is caused by one's depending altogether upon the outer senses and the outer world for light and guidance. The next step is to put away from one's domain all religious and spiritual thoughts and beliefs (Claudius expelled the Jews from Rome), with all belief in the inner Source of understanding and wisdom. Consequently there is a dearth (famine) in the land, a famine that reaches from Rome down into Judea (from the intellect to deep within the inner consciousness).

Claudius Lysias, clau'-dĭ-ŭs lўs'-ĭ-ăs (Lat.).

The same man as Lysias (Acts 23:26).

Meta. See LYSIAS.

clay (John 9:6).

Meta. Jesus anointed the blind man's

eyes with clay. This is to symbolize the specific idea that stands in the way of clear vision. Clay represents a belief in materiality; a belief that certain manifest substances are matter and are void of the inherent powers and qualities of Being, which are omnipresent. The false idea that there is a lack of life, substance, and intelligence anywhere must be denied away, since it puts the soul in bondage: "Go, wash in the pool of Siloam." (See SILOAM.)

Clement, clĕm'-ĕnt (Lat. from Gk.)—*tender; merciful; mild; kind.*

A fellow worker of Paul's, whom Paul mentioned in his Epistle to the Philippians (Phil. 4:3).

Meta. The gentle, soothing, releasing (*tender, merciful, mild, kind*) quality of the word in its calming, equalizing, healing activities in the consciousness. (Paul, in his missionary work, represents the word of Truth in its ministry to the whole of man's being.)

Cleopas, clē'-ŏ-păs (Gk.)—*glorious father; renowned father; father of praise.*

One of the followers of Jesus. He and a companion were on their way to Emmaus, when Jesus appeared to them in the way and "interpreted to them in all the scriptures the things concerning himself" (Luke 24:18, 27).

Meta. A faculty of mind not yet awakened fully to spiritual understanding. It has heard the Truth: Cleopas was a follower of Jesus; he had walked and talked with Him, but he had never affirmed as his own the Truth that Jesus taught. Through the blessing and breaking of bread his eyes were opened—his comprehension was cleared—and he realized the Truth as his own.

The bread represents the pure spiritual substance of the resurrected body, and it is appropriated by positive affirmations. When man, through his I AM, makes positive affirmations of his oneness with life and of his own divine sonship, all his inner faculties and states of consciousness are awakened; he thus comes into the blessedness of knowing the God within him as his *renowned father*, the source of all the good that he can conceive of or desire.

Clopas (Cleophas—Alphæus), clō'-păs (Gk.)—*glory to the father; glorious father;* otherwise the same as Alphæus.

Husband of Mary (John 19:25); he was also called Alphæus, and was the father of one of Jesus' disciples (Matt. 10:3).

Meta. See ALPHÆUS.

cloud, the, that filled the whole place (I Kings 8:10, 11).

Meta. The presence of the mind of God in spiritual visibility, which comes to us when we have dropped all formal religious exercises and are resting in the very consciousness of Deity. This brightness of understanding is so great that the priests cannot stand to minister because of it—there is no place for formal religious ceremony or thought exercise.

coat, of Jesus, without seam (John 19:23, 24).

Meta. The Truth in its harmonious expression and unchangeable perfection.

Regeneration forms a new mind and a new body consciousness, or, as symbolically expressed in the Scriptures, "new heavens and a new earth." The seamless coat of Jesus symbolizes a consciousness of the indestructible unity of life and substance in the body consciousness. This consciousness inheres in the executive department of mind in man (soldiers), and can be exercised by Spirit in body projection when so desired. Jesus now lives in the heavens of the mind and has power to project His body consciousness and to make it appear to those who are not developed to His plane of idealism.

coats of skins (Gen. 3:21)—the Hebrew word is *chithanoth*, which signifies not only *coats*, but *bodylike; an embodiment; expression of bodily form; assimilation of corporeal body.*

Meta. The body of flesh. Man was connected originally with the spiritual-body idea, but when he took on personal consciousness he was given "coats of skins," which, under divine law, corresponded with the quality of his thought world. When spiritual thought becomes supreme in consciousness, the coats of skins will give way to the manifestation of the spiritual body, which is the immortal body that was spoken of by Paul.

Corruptible flesh is the manifestation of corrupt ideas in mind. "Be ye transformed [changed in form] by the renewing of your mind."

Cnidus, cnĭ'-dŭs (Gk.) — *nettle; scratch; irritate; tickle.*

A seaport town on a peninsula of the same name, which Paul passed while on his voyage to Rome: "And when we had sailed slowly many days, and were come with difficulty over against Cnidus, the wind not further suffering us, we sailed under the lee of Crete, over against Salmone" (Acts 27:7).

Meta. Paul, the word of Truth, was being taken to Rome (Paul bound at Rome represents the word of Truth confined to the intellect) in bonds, and the voyage was very hazardous; it was beset by carnal thoughts and desires of the "mind of the flesh" (Crete means *carnal, fleshly*); also by the vexed, irritated (*nettle, irritate*) state of mind that always results from waste of substance in sense ways (*tickle,* referring to sensual pleasures). This state of mind is Cnidus. It contends with the Truth, which is seeking to establish throughout man's whole being the realization of perfection, abiding life, health, Truth, and spirituality.

Colhozeh, cŏl-hō'-zĕh (Heb.)—*all-seeing; wholly a seer,* i. e., *of God; all prophets.*

a Father of Shallun, who repaired the fountain gate and the wall of the pool of Shelah, or Shiloah, at the rebuilding of Jerusalem's wall after the Babylonian captivity (Neh. 3:15). Father of Baruch of the tribe of Judah (Neh. 11:5).

Meta. Divine intelligence, the *all-seeing,* all-knowing spiritual light and wisdom, which is God and embraces the true understanding of *all prophets;* for it is *wholly a seer,* i. e., *of God*—the source of all true perception and knowledge.

Colossæ (A. V., Colosse), cŏ-lŏs'-sæ (Gk.)—*punishment; correction; discipline,* i. e., *instruction; penalty,* i. e., *retributive punishment.*

A city of Phrygia in Asia Minor. The Epistle of Paul to the Colossians was written to the Christian assembly at this place (Col. 1:2). Colossæ was destroyed by an earthquake about 65 A. D., during the reign of Nero, and was rebuilt.

Meta. An aggregation of thoughts in man's consciousness that pertains to the activity of the law of sowing and reaping (*punishment, penalty,* i. e., *retributive punishment*) as it is set forth in Galatians 6:7: "Be not deceived; God is not mocked: for whatsoever a man soweth, that shall he also reap. For he that soweth unto his own flesh shall of the flesh reap corruption; but he that soweth unto the Spirit shall of the Spirit reap eternal life." As the Christ thought and the Christ Spirit are introduced more fully into this state of consciousness, the individual recognizes more of the corrective and instructive (*correction, discipline,* i. e., *instruction*) side of seeming punishments, which are the results of error. By his holding to the good, seeming error falls away and he becomes established in good only.

Colossians, cŏ-lŏs'-si-ănṣ (Gk.).

Inhabitants of Colossæ; the reference here is to the Christians at this place to whom Paul wrote his Epistle (Col. 1:2).

Meta. The thoughts that comprise the Colossæ state of consciousness (see COLOSSÆ). The Christian assembly at Colossæ are the awakened thoughts that see the truth regarding the goodness of God and the unreality of all seeming error with its inharmonious activities.

Conaniah (in A. V., II Chron. 31:12, Cononiah), cŏn-ă-nī'-ăh (Heb.)—*Jah is founding; Jehovah has appointed; Jah has made; made by Jehovah; Jah has sustained.*

a A Levite who was ruler over the tithes and dedicated things in the house of Jehovah during Hezekiah's reign (II Chron. 31:12). **b** A chief of the Levites in Josiah's reign; he, with some others, gave large numbers of cattle and oxen to the Levites for the Passover offerings (II Chron. 35:9).

Meta. Love (the men named Conaniah were of the tribe of Levi) expressed in worship and service. There can be no true worship or service apart from love, for love is established and sustained by Jehovah (*made by Jehovah, Jah has sus-*

tained). It is the very essence of Jehovah, for God is love, and love is the spiritual quality that is appointed of the Lord as the governing factor in man's consciousness that he releases to God, in all that he affirms and realizes to be spiritual (the tithes and dedicated things). In all sacrifices also (the giving up of one's lower thoughts and activities that they may be transmuted into spiritual energy, life, strength, and substance) love plays a very important part.

Coniah, cŏ-nī′-ăh (Heb.)—*Jah is founding; Jehovah is setting up,* i. e., *establishing; Jah is creating.*

A king of Judah who reigned about three months and was then taken captive to Babylon, while Zedekiah was made king in his stead (Jer. 37:1). Coniah was the son of Jehoiakim, and was an evil ruler, as his father had been before him.

Meta. Coniah is an abbreviated form of Jeconiah and Jehoiachim. (See JECONIAH and JEHOIACHIM.)

consciousness.

Meta. Consciousness is our knowing that we know; that phase of knowing by which we take cognizance of our existence and of our relation to what we call environment. Environment is made by ideas held in mind and objectified. The ideas that are held in mind are the basis of all consciousness. The nature of the ideas upon which consciousness is formed gives character to it.

The subconscious mind, or subjective consciousness, is the sum of all man's past thinking. It may be called memory. The subconscious sometimes acts separately from the conscious mind; for instance, in dreams and in its work of carrying on bodily functions, such as breathing and digestion. The subconscious mind has no power to do original thinking. It acts upon what is given it through the conscious or the superconscious mind. All our involuntary, or automatic, activities are of the subconscious mind; they are the result of our having trained ourselves by the conscious mind to form certain habits and do certain things without having to center our thought upon them consciously.

The superconscious mind, Christ consciousness or spiritual consciousness, is a state of consciousness that is based upon true ideas, upon an understanding and realization of spiritual Truth.

Personal consciousness is formed from limited, selfish ideas.

Sense consciousness is a mental state formed from believing in and acting through the senses. It is the serpent consciousness, deluded with sensation. Since an individual becomes attached to whatever he thinks about, the result of his forming sense consciousness is that he withdraws his consciousness from Spirit, and loses conscious connection with his Source. To bring one out of sense consciousness a realization of the need of conscious oneness with the Father is necessary; also the determination to return to that conscious oneness with God in which one decides, "I will arise and go to my father."

Material consciousness is much the same as personal and sense consciousness. It is a state of mind based upon belief in the reality of materiality, or in things as they appear. It is carnal mind expressing its disbelief in the omnipresence of God.

A state of consciousness is a certain phase of mind built up through thinking of some particular idea. As you go on in your expression of Divine Mind you will find that you have many phases of mind in yourself with which to deal. These we call "states of consciousness."

It is very important to understand our place of consciousness in spiritual growth because, while all divine ideas—such as love, life, substance, and intelligence—are eternal and omnipresent, they are not so to us until we incorporate them into our consciousness. Unless we know this we may be satisfied with an intellectual concept of them, or deceive ourselves with the thought that, because life is eternal, our consciousness or nonconsciousness of that fact can make no difference. Consciousness of eternal life places one in the stream of life that never fails. Without this consciousness, dissolution will result and spirit, soul, and body will be separated.

Man merges his consciousness with the Absolute through harmonizing all his ideas with the unlimited ideas of the Christ mind. This is accomplished by his understanding Divine Mind and its laws. The necessary food for man is the word of God. Without it there is no sustenance for spiritual consciousness, and soul and body perish with hunger.

In the study of things pertaining to religion we should keep in mind the three activities of consciousness: spiritual, psychical, and physical. The spiritual is the realm of absolute principles; the psychical is the realm of thought images; the physical is the realm of manifestation. The well-balanced, thoroughly developed man, of which Jesus is the type, comprehends and consciously adjusts his spirit, soul, and body as a whole, and thereby fulfills the law of his being. Those who are on the way to this attainment have various experiences, which are symbolically set forth in the Scriptures.

It is by thinking upon the ideas of Divine Mind that man becomes conscious of Divine Mind.

cords, scourge of (John 2:15); a rope or cord made of *rushes.*

Meta. The "scourge of small cords" (A. V.) signifies the formulated word or statement of denial. When we deny in general terms we erase or cleanse the whole consciousness, like taking a bath; but secret sins may lurk in the inner parts and remain. The words that reach these are not the great ones, such as *"I am one with Almightiness; my environment is God,"* but some small, definite statements, that cut into them like whipcords.

Corinth, eôr'-inth (Gk.)—*ornament; ornamentation; beauty.*

A city of Greece, where a Christian assembly was established. It was to this assembly that Paul wrote his two Epistles to the Corinthians (I Cor. 1:2; II Cor. 1:1).

Meta. Corinth (*ornament, beauty*), forty miles to the west of Athens, contained the Greek temple of Venus, which was dedicated to the worship of love. So we discern that it was at the love center

in consciousness that the Truth sought to do a work. Paul here is referred to as the word of Truth, and Corinth is the love center. Paul wrote his matchless poem on love to the Corinthians. But this center was largely given over to licentiousness. Under the guise of religion, more than a thousand courtesans were attached to the temple of Venus at Corinth as assistants, says secular history. So the need of purification, and of the lifting up of the affections here at the love center in human consciousness, is very great when the word of Truth first enters to do its redeeming work.

Paul's going from Athens to Corinth (Acts 18:1) signifies the withdrawal of the power of the word of Truth from the intellectual center (Athens) and its entrance into the love center (Corinth).

Corinthians, eô-rĭn'-thĭ-ăns *of or belonging to Corinth.*

People who lived in Corinth (Acts 18:8; II Cor. 6:11).

Meta. The thoughts that comprise the love center in consciousness.

Cornelius, eôr-nē'-lĭ-ŭs (Lat.)—*as a horn; horn-bearing; horny; unyielding.*

A centurion who lived in Cæsarea (Acts 10:1-48); he was a devout man, and was told in a vision by an angel to send for Peter to come and instruct him in the way of Truth more perfectly. Peter was shown by his dream or vision that he was to go to Cornelius even though the man was a Gentile, for God had cleansed him and he was therefore no more common or unclean. (The Jews thought all Gentiles vile, and unfit for God's kingdom.)

Meta. According to Bible history Cornelius was the first Gentile to accept Christianity through the ministry of the apostles; he was a man of high rank and authority. There are two phases to the significance that he has in individual consciousness; they are suggested in the following explanations:

First, the spiritual aspirant is constantly finding that phases of his living must be corrected—shifted from a material to a spiritual basis. Such a need of change is represented in Acts 10:30-48 by Cornelius, centurion, commander of one hundred soldiers. Cornelius represents pride of rank (*horn-bearing*) or power of position; also a naturally hard, unyielding nature (*as a horn, unyielding*).

The material man may attach great importance to his rank in life, as he compares it with the rank of those about him. He may also feel that his power depends upon the position that he occupies. You will remember that this very point came up with the disciples, when they were discussing who should be greatest in the kingdom of heaven. Jesus clearly showed them that service, rather than position or material power, was the thing to be desired.

The pride of rank and of position is not confined to outer things and people. We find the autocratic tendency cropping out in the manner in which we deal with ourselves, belittling some phases of our being and tyrannically dominating others. The Christ way is that of redemption and fulfillment; it is to serve the conditions of mind and body, as well as those of the outer life, with that great corrective ideal that lovingly wins all things into the righteousness of divine order. Power exerted to produce slavish obedience never brings the greatest return. The power of love brings rich results because it elicits loving and wholehearted response.

When Cornelius faced this matter in himself he began to fast and pray. Fasting in this instance refers to the giving up of the ideas and practices that have fed the ideas of personal advancement, and prayer is the communion with Spirit that improves the soul quality. These spiritual exercises naturally increase faith, which is pictured as Cornelius's sending for Peter. This work of Spirit in the personal ego portrays clearly the universality of divine principles, and faith proclaims, "Of a truth I perceive that God is no respecter of persons." Following this great step in spiritual progress comes the instruction in the Christ principles that finally results in an outpouring of the Holy Spirit and the baptism of the whole man into spiritual consciousness.

Second, Cornelius, the first known Gentile convert to the Jesus Christ method of redemption, represents that in consciousness which, no longer bound by outer show and formality, truly searches after God. Cornelius typifies that in us which communes with the Father (he was a devout man) and feeds the soul with divine light and love in order to live the spiritual life and to make practical in all ways the understanding of Truth thus gained.

The man who comes and stands before Cornelius is an angel of the Lord, or that high spiritual perceptive faculty within the soul which ever dwells in the presence of the Father; its mission is to bring us messages direct from God, when we have opened our mind to Spirit sufficiently to receive.

In this instance the message reveals to Cornelius (or that in us which is seeking a higher spiritual basis) how to open the way for the light of spiritual faith, here typified by his sending for "Simon, who is surnamed Peter." The *unyielding* attitude of mind is good when it is set upon the attainment of spiritual understanding and practice.

Cos (A. V., Coos), cŏs (Gk.)—*summit*.

A small island in the Ægean Sea, or Grecian Archipelago (Acts 21:1); Paul stopped there for a day while on one of his missionary journeys.

Meta. Cos means *summit*; Rhodes, *roses*; Phœnicia, *land of palm trees*; Cyprus, *fairness*. These places symbolize certain pleasant phases of consciousness in the individual who is seeking the highest, but they are not, strictly speaking, on the spiritual plane.

Cosam, cŏ'-săm (Gk. from Heb.)—*diviner; divination; divining; an oracle; a seer.*

Father of Addi and son of Elmadam, named in the genealogy of Jesus Christ (Luke 3:28).

Meta. Clear spiritual perception and insight into Truth (*a diviner, divining, an oracle, a seer*).

council (Acts 6:15).

Meta. The whole consciousness.

Cozeba (A. V., Chozeba), cŏ-zē'-bȧ (Heb.)—*lying; false; deceptive; delud-*

ing with false hope, i. e., *idols*.

The same place as Chezib and Achzib (I Chron. 4:22).

Meta. See CHEZIB and ACHZIB.

creation.

Meta. Creation presupposes a creator. The creator is God, Divine Mind. God creates by the power of His word: "God said . . . and it was so."

The Word of God is the divine *Logos*, the creative power of God expressed in the fiat, "Let there be," "and it was." The *Logos*, or Word, includes all the attributes of God.

The idea that a word contains gives it character and power.

The character of God's creation is "good" and "very good." There is no other creator than God. He made all that is. God's creation was in the realm of ideas, in the ideal, in mind. The universe and man are potentially perfect. The expression and manifestation of the perfect, ideal creation was left to man, and he has not been true to his trust, but has used his God-given power to express other than the divine ideals; this is what causes evil to appear, in the face of the truth that God made all that is and that all that He made was good.

There is no reality in the inharmonies brought about by man; they are simply a wrong relation of things, brought about by ignorance and false, limited concepts of God's creation. Only that which is created by God is real, enduring, and abiding. If the untrue were real, it could not be changed. Only spiritual things are eternal and real.

The inharmonies in the world can be eliminated by eliminating them from man's mind. This can be done by understanding that God's creation is all that there is and knowing it to be good. In this way the divine ideals are established in mind, and by the law of mind action they are expressed, thus bringing into manifestation the perfection that ever exists in the ideal.

The law of mind action may be described in three steps—mind, idea, manifestation. First, there must be mind; second, everything exists first as an idea in mind; third, the inherent power and intelligence in the idea causes it to act or express, and when it is expressed we have the manifestation.

Man's part in the creative process is to express the divine ideal. When he knows himself as the perfect offspring of Divine Mind, he expresses perfection. When he holds the thought of himself as sinful, and of the universe as imperfect, he expresses those untrue ideas and so brings into manifestation all the discords that appear. This is eating of the fruit of the tree of good and evil—duality of thought, believing that there is a power of evil as well as one of good, and building up error ideas in his thoughts.

Man accomplishes his great work of bringing things into manifestation by using the power of the word; he speaks the word audibly, or he speaks it silently as thought. Every man forms his own world; its character depends upon the character of his word. It is his privilege to cease using all untrue words and to use only the word of God, by which he will bring into manifestation the kingdom of God upon earth.

Crescens, crĕs'-çĕns (Lat.)—*growing; advancing; increasing; attaining honor*.

An assistant of Paul's, who left Paul and went to Galatia (II Tim. 4:10). The text is not clear as to whether he went to Galatia to preach the gospel there, or whether he, like Demas, forsook Paul because he loved the world better than the things of Spirit.

Meta. There were Christians in Galatia. Paul went there to preach, and his Epistle to the Galatians was written to the Christian assemblies throughout that country, or province. If Crescens went there at the request, or with the consent, of Paul, to help spread and establish Truth in that place, he signifies the increase and growth of true ideas in consciousness. On the other hand, if he went to Galatia in a selfish spirit, because he desired worldly activity instead of Truth, he would represent an increase in thought and deed of that which belongs to the sense, personal, and limited consciousness in man. (See DEMAS.)

Cretans (A. V., Cretes, and Cretians), crē'-tăns (Gk.)—*cut off; carnal; fleshly.*

Inhabitants of Crete (Acts 2:11). "One of themselves, a prophet of their own, said, Cretans are always liars, evil beasts, idle gluttons" (Tit. 1:12).

Meta. Carnal, deceitful, gluttonous thoughts; they belong to the carnal consciousness in the individual. (See CRETE.)

In Acts 2:11, however, we see these Cretans hearing in their own tongue, from the Spirit-filled apostles, of the mighty works of God. There must therefore be something in the apparently carnal nature of man that can comprehend the Christ Truth, and so be raised to spiritual understanding and expression.

Crete, crēte (Gk.)—*cut off; carnal; fleshly.*

A large island in the Mediterranean Sea; it is now called Candia. The boat in which Paul was being taken to Rome to appear before Cæsar sailed along close to this island for some time, and Paul wanted the managers of the boat to stay in Crete for the winter because of the perils of storms at that time of the year. But they would not listen to him (Acts 27:7-21).

Meta. The material, sensual, worldly consciousness in man, as opposed to the spiritual (*carnal, fleshly*).

Crispus, crĭs'-pŭs (Lat.)—*curled; curly-headed; wrinkled.*

A man at Corinth who was converted to Christianity and was baptized by Paul. He was ruler of the synagogue of Corinth (Acts 18:8; I Cor. 1:14).

Meta. Crispus (*curled*), the ruler of the synagogue, who believed with all his house, indicates that Truth really encompasses the whole man. The consolation and the encouragement that came from the Lord in a vision to Paul (Acts 18:9) indicate the fulfillment of the law in this movement of Truth in its work of regeneration.

cross (John 19:17).

Meta. The crystallization of two currents of thought—the state of consciousness termed sense mind. The perpendicular bar symbolizes the inner current of divine life; the horizontal bar symbolizes the cross current of human limitation. The latter symbolizes the "mind of the

flesh," also, and it burdens the body with its various erroneous beliefs. The center of action of this sense mind is in the brain, and there it has to be met in the final overcoming that the I AM undertakes: "The place called The place of a skull."

crucifixion, of Jesus.

Meta. The giving up of the whole personality.

Cub (A. V., Chub), cŭb (Heb.)—*thorn bush; a thorn.*

Probably a Nubian tribe. Ezekiel named it (with Ethiopia, Put, Lud, and other peoples) for destruction by the sword (Ezek. 30:5). "They . . . that uphold Egypt shall fall; and the pride of her power shall come down" (Ezek. 30:6).

Meta. A darkened, thorny state of thought that gives its substance to the upbuilding and sustaining of the Egypt consciousness. (See EGYPT.)

Cun (A. V., Chun), cŭn (Heb.)—*stand upright; set up; found; firmly establish; form; prepare; create.*

A Syrian city of Hadarezer, from which David took much brass that Solomon used later in building the Temple (I Chron. 18:8); in II Samuel 8:8, this city is called Berothai.

Meta. The building of divine life and substance into consciousness, preparatory to the establishment (*form, prepare, firmly establish*) of mind and body in enduring existence and perfection. The foundation for an immortal, incorruptible body structure is laid in an upright character (*stand upright*) and in an understanding and realization of the life and substance of one's being as spiritual, unchanging, eternal. Cun's passing into the hands of David signifies that one is coming into a better understanding of this truth. (See BEROTHAI.)

cup (John 18:11).

Meta. "The cup which the Father hath given me" is the consciousness of eternal life. This must be attained by an utter crossing out, or crucifixion, of the personal self, both on its objective and subjective planes of volition; hence "they led him away" (John 18:12, A. V.) that other processes of the divine law might be carried out.

"Father, if thou be willing, remove this cup from me: nevertheless not my will, but thine, be done" (Luke 22:42). This was the cup of new spiritual life, which in this same chapter Jesus is recorded as having given to His disciples. When man affirms spiritual life he must be prepared to incorporate that life into his soul and his body. This incorporation is not always an easy task, because of the indifference of the faculties to spiritual ideas. One is therefore sorely tempted at times, when the changes being undergone seem so hard to the human, to pray that one may be allowed, if possible, to go on under the old race thought instead of rising in soul and body to the place of actually putting on Christ (see Rom. 13:14; Gal. 3:27) in the fullness of what this term implies.

To drink of the cup (Matt. 20:22, 23) means to take in faith, believing, before one can fully understand. Only those who are prepared in the principle can understand the law of the principle. The working out of the just law places each one where he belongs.

Cush (in A. V., Gen. 2:13, Ethiopia), cŭsh (Heb.)—*firelike; burned; blackened; combustible; Ethiopia.*

a Eldest son of Ham. **b** The country where Ham's descendants settled— Ethiopia (Gen. 10:6; Psalms 7, title).

Meta. Ham typifies the physical in man, in its very biased, material, sensual expression. The physical has always been looked upon as something very material and as being void of intelligence and spirituality. It has been in darkness, and has been given over to ignorance and sensuality, with corruption as its ultimate state. Cush represents this darkened thought in which man has held his body and its activities—the seemingly mortal, physical part of himself. But this will all change as he perceives the Truth and holds in mind the perfect-body idea. Then darkness will disappear, and even the very cells of the body will shine in spiritual light and life.

Cushan, cŭ'-shăn (Heb.)—*blackness.*

Supposed to be the same person as Cushan-rishathaim, king of Mesopotamia

(Hab. 3:7).

Meta. See CUSHAN–RISHATHAIM.

Cushan–rishathaim (A. V., Chushan-rishathaim), cŭ-shăn – rĭsh-ă-thā'-ĭm (Heb.)—*blackness of injustice; brand; falsehood; wickedness; iniquity; ungodliness.*

A king of Mesopotamia, or Aram–naharaim, into whose hands the Lord gave the people of Israel because they served Balaam and Asheroth. This king oppressed the Israelites for several years, but he was finally overthrown and Israel was delivered by "Othniel, the son of Kenaz, Caleb's younger brother" (Judg. 3:8-10).

Meta. A central ruling thought in the error state of consciousness that Aram-naharaim signifies—the belief of the unawakened intellect in man that all his sustenance comes from the outer and that he has no need of spiritual understanding and Truth to sustain him in either body or soul. (See ARAM–NAHARAIM.)

Cushi, cŭ'-shī (Heb.) — *firelike; burned; black; combustible; an Ethiopian.*

a Father of the prophet Zephaniah (Zeph. 1:1). **b** The great-grandfather of Jehudi. Jehudi read the roll, written by Baruch as given him by Jeremiah, to King Jehoiakim, who burnt it (Jer. 36:14).

Meta. The darkness and denseness of material, sensual thought and belief (*firelike, burned, black, combustible, an Ethiopian*). The fact that the men by this name were Israelites shows that the religious tendencies and desires and the spiritual aspirations of the individual are piercing this darkness; the gloom is giving way to the light of Truth, which will establish spiritual thought and belief.

Cushite (in A. V., Num. 12:1, Ethiopian; in II Samuel 18:21, Cushi), cŭsh'-ite (Heb.)—same definitions as Cushi.

Moses' wife was a Cushite woman, and Miriam and Aaron spoke against Moses because he had married a woman of that race (Num. 12:1). It was a Cushite also whom Joab sent to David to tell him of the overthrow and death of Absalom (II Sam. 18:21). A Cushite was a native of the land of Cush, or Ethiopia.

Meta. A thought that belongs to the state of consciousness that Cush typifies. (See CUSH.)

Cuth, cŭth (Heb.)—*separating; cutting; shrinking; fear.*

A place in Asia, or in the interior of Media and Persia, whence the king of Assyria transplanted people to Samaria after he had taken the Israelites away captive (II Kings 17:24); here the name Cuthah is given. The men of Cuth made Nergal their god (II Kings 17:30). Nergal means *great hero* and pertained to the planet Mars. In olden times, among the Oriental peoples, Mars was the symbol of war and bloodshed.

Meta. Strife, anger, fear, and all the error, warring thoughts and emotions of the outer sensate consciousness; these burn out and destroy the very nerve cells of the organism, and work against the health, peace, and general welfare of the individual who gives them place.

Cyprus, çy′-prŭs (Gk.)—*a measure of corn; fairness.*

One of the largest islands in the Mediterranean Sea (Acts 13:4). Being very close to Egypt, Asia Minor, and Phœnicia, it was a great commercial center. Its land was very fertile; its forests abounded in lumber, and it was rich in minerals also. It was settled first by Phœnicians, but at this time many Jews were there, and people of other nationalities. Christianity was established there very early too.

Meta. A fair, frank, honest, just, unbiased state of mind (*fairness*) established in a degree of substance (*a measure of corn*); thus it draws to one very favorable and desirable conditions. This state of consciousness that Cyprus signifies is not truly spiritual, however; it needs to become established in Truth in order to bring forth fruit that is abiding. (See COS.) Barnabas was a native of Cyprus (Acts 4:36), and Cyprus in the individual consciousness is in close touch with intellectual reasonings (the Greeks) and formulated theology (Antioch). (See BARNABAS.)

Cyrene, çy-rē′-nê (Gk.)—*wall; coldness.*

A city in northern Africa (Mark 15:21; Acts 2:10). It was settled formerly by Greeks, but later the Jews formed a large percentage of its population. There were so many Cyrenian Jews in Jerusalem at the time of Jesus and the apostles that they had a synagogue of their own there.

Meta. A fixed (*wall*) state of thought that has been founded in intellectual reasonings (Greeks) and has been built up and strengthened further by old, established, formal religious ideas (Jews). This thought center pertains to the sensual rather than to the spiritual in us, and needs to be thoroughly imbued with the Christ understanding, love, and Truth, that all *coldness* and hardness may be overcome.

Cyrenians, çy-rē′-nĭ-ăns (from Gk.).

Inhabitants of Cyrene (Acts 6:9).

Meta. Fixed states of thought in the realm of sense, that rise up and oppose the further progress of spiritual ideas. They are stirred up by the arguments of Stephen, the illumined reason.

Cyrus, çy′-rŭs (Gk. from Pers.)—*the sun; rays of the sun;* perhaps *shepherd.*

King of Persia (II Chron. 36:22). Cyrus founded the Persian Empire, united Media to Persia, conquered Babylon, and liberated the Jews (Ezra 1; 5:13-17; Isa 44:28).

Meta. In Daniel, Cyrus' capture of the kingdom of Babylonia represents the return of man to a state of barbarism, since, compared with the Babylonians, Cyrus was a barbarian.

King Cyrus, who represents the will as ruling in sense consciousness, or the ruling idea in consciousness, was "stirred up" by the Lord, and he made a proclamation to the effect that he had been divinely appointed to build a house for the Lord at Jerusalem (Ezra 1:1, 2). Cyrus was a heathen king, yet the Lord "stirred up" his spirit, or inspired him (*rays of the sun*), to act in a way quite contrary to his usual custom. By this we discern that the Lord inspires men who are open to Truth, wherever they may be found. It may be that you are in the most material of occupations and your thoughts are utterly worldly; yet if you have been "stirred up" by the Lord you can commence immediately the movement toward Jerusalem (the spiritual center of consciousness).

There are periods when the thoughts turn to religious subjects as easily as sparks fly upward. The man immured in sense suddenly begins to study matters pertaining to the soul; he joins a church, or investigates Christian metaphysics. This is symbolized by the return of the Children of Israel to Jerusalem.

You sometime "came forth from that city," as stated by Paul in Hebrews, and now you are to return and take all the "vessels of silver, with gold, with goods, and with beasts, and with precious things" (Ezra 1:6), which represent the fruit of your experience in the sense consciousness. So we learn that no effort is wholly lost, though it be put forth in a field apparently barren. The vessels that were taken from the Temple at Jerusalem at the time of the Captivity were used in the worship of false gods in Babylon; but now they are returned to be used again in the worship of the true God. These vessels represent our capacity of appreciation—the ability to comprehend or measure life. The man who is getting pleasure out of the lusts of the flesh is measuring up life—the one life—before false gods, and is using his God-given capacity (vessels) in doing it. He is getting experience, generating forces that eventually he will have to master and return to the Temple at Jerusalem. Nothing is lost in the divine economy, and in due season man will refine his every thought and act and extract the gold from it—though he may find that getting rid of the dross is hot work.

The significance of King Cyrus's making a proclamation throughout all his kingdom telling that he was to build for the Lord a house in Jerusalem is that the will, ruling in sense, discerns Truth and desires to abide in the consciousness of Truth; therefore it seeks to establish a place where its true thoughts (Israelites) may worship and commune with the Christ mind (Jehovah).

D

Dabbesheth (A. V., Dabbasheth), dăb'-bĕ-shĕth (Heb.)—*hump; soft protuberance; hump of a camel; mass of honey.*

A border town of Zebulun, to the westward (Josh. 19:11).

Meta. An aggregation of thoughts belonging to the faculty of order in man (a city of Zebulun). These thoughts are rich with substance (*mass of honey*), and are capable of conserving it for future use in the organism (suggested by *hump of a camel*).

Daberath (A. V., Josh. 21:28, Dabareh), dăb'-ĕ-răth (Heb.)--*words; oracles; reasons; to speak after a mode; anything arranged in order; leading to pasture.*

A city of Issachar that was given over to "the children of Gershon, of the families of the Levites" (Josh. 21:28). In Joshua 19:12 it is mentioned as being on the border of Zebulun.

Meta. The understanding that orderly true thinking, speaking, and living (*word, oracles, reasons, to speak after a mode, anything arranged in order*) lead to realization and demonstration of substance, supply, prosperity (*leading to pasture; pasture* indicates substance in a form in which it can be utilized by the individual).

Dagon, dā'-gŏn (Heb.)—*fish; little fish; fish god; abundant propagation.*

A god of the Philistines (Judg. 16:23).

Meta. A great increase of thoughts (*fish, abundant propagation*). This thought increase is on an error, sense plane, however, and not on the spiritual plane. The Philistines symbolize states of consciousness established in the senses; they were enemies to the Israelites, who symbolize true thoughts. The thoughts that the Philistines represent in us are constantly inducing us to trust to our outer senses for guidance and understanding; they lead us away from spiritual Truth. Their god therefore pertains to outer sense reasonings and activities, and not to the spiritual and the true. (See BETH–DAGON.)

Dalmanutha, dăl-mă-nū'-thȧ (Gk)—*overhanging branch; bucket.*

The place on the west shore of the Sea of Galilee to which Jesus went with His disciples after the feeding of the multitude with the seven loaves and the few small fishes (Mark 8:10).

Meta. A faculty in consciousness (*overhanging branch*) that has only a limited understanding of, and capacity to contain, the waters of life (signified by *bucket*). Jesus and His disciples crossed the Sea of Galilee (life activity) in a boat in order to reach Dalmanutha. Jesus did not stay long in this place, because the Pharisees met Him at once and began to question Him and to aṣk for a sign: the I AM cannot remain in such a limiting, doubting condition of mind, but departs quickly "to the other side."

Dalmatia, dăl-mā'-ti-ȧ (Gk.)—*cloaked; covered; concealed; deceitful.*

A European province, on the eastern side of the Adriatic Sea, in what is now known as Turkey; it was to this place that Paul sent Titus to preach the gospel of Christ (II Tim. 4:10).

Meta. A double-minded, misleading, deceptive state of consciousness in the individual (*cloaked, covered, concealed, deceptive;* a province). If given way to, it causes one to reason falsely and to think and act without sincerity.

Dalphon, dăl'-phŏn (Heb.)—*dropping; dripping; leaking,* particularly from the roof; *flowing copiously; tears.*

One of the ten sons of Haman. He was killed by the Jews (Esth. 9:7).

Meta. Hanman, the Jews' enemy, was an Agagite. The Agagites were descendants of Agag, who represents the Adversary in individual consciousness. Dalphon signifies a thought tendency that is very leaky (*dropping, dripping, leaking*), and not at all steadfast; it is very sympathetic in its nature, with a weak, human sympathy (*flowing copiously, tears*) that is of a destructive character.

It belongs to the adverse, and it works against the higher or spiritual thoughts and activities of man's being (represented by the Jews).

Damaris, dăm'-ȧ-rĭs (Gk.)—*tamed; yoked together; joined; a wife; a spouse; a betrothed young woman; a heifer.*

A woman in Athens who accepted Paul's teaching at the Areopagus, or Mars' Hill (Acts 17:34).

Meta. The soul in its relation to the intellect (Athens symbolizes the intellect, and a woman refers to the soul). The soul is more closely unified (*wife, joined*) with our intellectual thoughts and activities than most persons realize. When we think that we have reasoned a thing out entirely with our head, and that we are acting altogether from a reasoning standpoint, it would surprise us if we could see how much we have been guided all along by the intuitions, affections, emotions, and desires of the soul. *Young woman* and *heifer* give the idea of inexperience. *Heifer* also signifies that Damaris here stands for the animal phase of the soul's strength, but, since it has become receptive to the Truth as taught by Paul, it will be raised to higher and more spiritual expression.

Damascenes, dăm-ȧ-sçēneṣ' (Gk. from Heb.)—*belonging to Damascus.*

Natives, or inhabitants, of Damascus (II Cor. 11:32).

Meta. Thoughts that belong to the Damascus consciousness. (See DAMASCUS.)

Damascus, dȧ-măs'-ĕŭs (Gk. from Heb. and Arabic)—*activity; alertness,* in respect to trade or possessions; *sack of blood; blood sack; red sackcloth.*

Chief city of Syria. It is very beautifully located, and is believed by some to be the oldest city in the world. It still has a street called "Straight" (Acts 9:11). A river, which is thought to be either the Abanah or the Pharpar of the Bible, flows through the plain of Damascus and makes it very fertile and beautiful (Gen. 15:2; II Sam. 8:6; II Kings 5:12).

Meta. Syria represents the intellectual sense domain, and the river Abanah represents a current of intellectual thoughts and reasonings about life. Damascus (meaning *sack of blood*) signifies a state of consciousness that is founded upon a material concept of life in the body; this concept has been sustained by the race from time immemorial. (It is not known when Damascus was first built, but the time was before Abraham. Abraham's steward, Eliezer, was of Damascus.) The truth is that this material concept of the body began with Adam and Eve in the Garden of Eden; it had its inception in the desire for sensation, and it brought about their expulsion from Eden.

Damascus, too, stands for body sensation, which is held by the race to be the oldest and the most beautiful and pleasurable of all experiences (by the people of the East, Damascus is called the paradise of the world). But the desire for and seeking after sensation have brought man into sensuality and lust; they have caused the body of man and the life in his organism to manifest very materially, and in the end lust burns up the cells and the tissues of the organism and destroys the body.

In Acts 9:2, Damascus (*activity, alertness*, in respect to trade or possessions), to which place Paul was going to persecute the Christians when he had the vision whereby he was converted, refers to the capacity of the intellect to engender strife and warring thoughts and conditions. The intellect of itself is selfish; when it is unsoftened by love and uninspired by spiritual Truth, it always stirs up strife because its reasonings are hard, sharp, and contentious; they are bigoted and are unmixed with Christian mercy and broadness of vision.

Dan, dăn (Heb.)—*a judge; rule of righteous judgment; a defender; an advocate.*

a Fifth son of Jacob; his mother was Bilhah, Rachel's handmaid. When he was born Rachel said, "God hath judged me, and hath also heard my voice, and hath given me a son: therefore called she his name Dan" (Gen. 30:6). In blessing this son, Jacob said (Gen. 49:16-18):

"Dan shall judge his people,

As one of the tribes of Israel.
Dan shall be a serpent in the way,
An adder in the path,
That biteth the horse's heels,
So that his rider falleth backward.
I have waited for thy salvation, O Jehovah."

b Dan was also the name of one of the twelve tribes of Israel; the people of this tribe were descended from Dan, the son of Jacob (Josh. 19:40-48).

Meta. The faculty of judgment in man, in its earliest expression, before it is lifted to the spiritual plane. The faculty of judgment, when expressed in sense consciousness, often makes one to be of a critical and backbiting disposition; one needs to understand this faculty and to balance it with love.

In blessing the tribe of Dan, Moses said (Deut. 33:22):

"Dan is a lion's whelp,

That leapeth forth from Bashan."
This shows the strength, the conquering power, and the fruitfulness (lion and Bashan) that lie back of good judgment righteously expressed.

Daniel, dăn'-jĕl (Heb.)—*God is my judge; God is judge; judgment of God.*

a A great prophet of the tribe of Judah, who was taken as a captive to Babylon; he was renamed Belteshazzar by the king of Babylon (Book of Daniel). **b** David's son (I Chron. 3:1). **c** One of the sons of Ithamar, who came back with Ezra from the Babylonian captivity (Ezra 8:2).

Meta. Spiritual judgment. Daniel signifies pure judgment, conscious integrity. He typifies the clear, penetrating insight of Spirit. Daniel humbled himself in the presence of the universal Mind, and thereby opened his understanding and made himself receptive to the cosmic consciousness. Daniel and his companions were superior in wisdom and understanding to all the native magicians and seers in the whole Babylonian realm. The Scripture says that God gave Daniel knowledge and skill in all learning and wisdom, and "Daniel had understanding in all visions and dreams." Cultivate purity of mind and body and you will open the way to the higher planes of thought, as did Daniel. He "purposed in his heart that he would not defile himself with the king's dainties, nor with the wine which he drank: therefore he requested of the prince of the eunuchs that he might not defile himself" (Dan. 1:8).

Danites, dăn'-ītes (from Heb.)—*of or belonging to Dan.*

Persons who were descended from Jacob's son Dan, and therefore belonged to the Israelitish tribe of Dan (Judg. 13:2).

Meta. Thoughts that belong to the judgment faculty in man.

Dan–jaan, dăn–jā'-ăn (Heb.)—*Dan of the forest; Dan of the woods.*

A place to which Joab and the captains of the host came when they were numbering Israel at David's command (II Sam. 24:6).

Meta. A group of thoughts of a rich, prosperous, redundant nature, expressing in conjunction with the judgment faculty (*Dan of the forest; Dan* signifies judgment in the beginning of its expression in individual consciousness and *forest,* in the meaning of *jaan,* is developed from the idea of redundance, exuberance, luxuriance).

Dannah, dăn'-näh (Heb.)—*depressed; low; humble; whispering; murmuring; judging.*

A city in the hill country of Judah (Josh. 15:49).

Meta. Judgment, exercised in humility and through praise.

Dara, dā'-rȧ (Heb.)—*pearl of wisdom; bearer; holder, i. e., the arm.*

A shortened form of Darda. He is called Darda in I Kings 4:31; he was a son of Zerah of the tribe of Judah (I Chron. 2:6).

Meta. The recognition by man that he is, or may become, the *holder* or *bearer* of true spiritual understanding— the Christ wisdom (*pearl of wisdom*). The idea of expressing wisdom also enters into the significance of Dara (*the arm* bespeaks execution, expression, doing). There is still something of the human or sensate in this thought, however; in the true Christ wisdom, which Solomon signifies, the limited sense belief is put away. See DARDA.

Darda, där'-dȧ (Heb.)—*pearl of knowledge; pearl of wisdom.*

A son of Mahol, but is no doubt the same person as Dara of I Chronicles 2:6. Darda was one of the wise men of Israel, but his wisdom was exceeded by that of Solomon (I Kings 4:31).

Meta. A perception by the individual of his true source of wisdom, Christ. As the realization is ahead of the perception of Truth, however, so Solomon exceeds Darda in that Solomon signifies the actual expressing and manifesting of the Christ wisdom. (See DARA.)

Darius, dä-rī'-ŭs (Gk. from Pers.)— *one who conserves; one who restrains; (old Pers.) upholding the good.*

The name of three different Median-Persian kings that are mentioned in the Bible (Ezra 4:5; Neh. 12:22; Dan. 5:31).

Meta. The will, or the central ruling ego of the sense consciousness. However, it recognizes the value of, and gives a high place in government to, spiritual judgment (symbolized by Daniel). So that which Darius signifies becomes a conserver of true substance in the consciousness and organism, a restrainer of error, and an upholder of good (*one who conserves, one who restrains, upholding the good*).

darkness, over the land from the sixth to the ninth hour (Matt. 27:45).

Meta. The failure to understand that settles upon the soul in times of great trial.

Darkon, där'-kŏn (Heb.)—*bearer; hastener; scatterer.*

His "children" returned with Zerubbabel from the Babylonian captivity (Ezra 2:56).

Meta. A thought that supports and maintains the real and the true in consciousness; this thought also tends to dispel and dissipate the confused and darkened beliefs and thoughts of the Babylonian state of mind.

Dathan, dā'-thăn (Heb.)—*cistern; fountain; spring; mandate; edict; decree; religious law.*

A Reubenite, son of Eliab; he was one of those who rebelled against Moses and

Aaron and was destroyed (Num. 16:1).

Meta. A leading thought in the religious consciousness of man that is established in the letter of the law as being the fount, or *spring*—the source, cause, or motive—of religious service and Truth.

This thought does not see back of outer ceremonies to true spiritual understanding and service. It cannot perceive why that which Moses and Aaron signify should be chosen of the Lord ahead of it; that is, it cannot understand why thoughts centered in the inner spirit of divine law should give better, truer worship than those that are centered upon outer rites and ceremonies alone. Consequently it rebels against those ruling thoughts in consciousness (Moses and Aaron) which see beyond the outer form of religion to the Spirit of truth and order their service and worship accordingly.

David, dā′-vid (Heb.)—*beloved; loved; well-beloved.*

Youngest son of Jesse the Bethlehemite. He was anointed king of Israel in Saul's stead, and he succeeded Saul as king (I Sam. 17:12 to I Kings 2:10; Matt. 1:1).

Meta. David is often referred to as a type of Christ. His life was a forerunner of that of the more perfect man, Jesus Christ, who was of the house of David.

David represents divine love individualized in human consciousness. Love in Being (God) is the idea of perfect unity in all existence. When this divine idea is focused in man it is the Christ love on its inner side and the Jesus love on its outer. When David in his youth and purity daily communed with God, he closely reflected divine love. When he developed his human character, as a king in dominion over men, he manifested the limitations of the human in larger degree.

The rulership is withdrawn from the head, or the will (King Saul), and is gradually transferred to the heart, or love (King David). David was spiritually anointed by Samuel long before he assumed the reins of government. Saul became melancholic and at times insane. Because of David's skill on the harp, he was summoned at the suggestion of Saul's attendants, for the purpose of soothing Saul with music. He at once won the affection of Saul, and his music proved so effective in quieting the frenzied monarch that he was sent for often. This illustrates the power of love to harmonize the discords set up by a willful, violent consciousness.

David's father was Jesse, whose name means *Jah is,* and represents eternal existence, I AM. Thus Jesse relates to Jesus the Christ. His home was in Bethlehem (*house of bread*), which symbolizes the substance center in the body.

Saul was rejected as king because he was egotistical and disobedient, and David was selected in his stead on account of his modesty and his childlike obedience and simplicity.

This whole lesson in I Samuel 16:4-13 points to the heart as the center through which Spirit rules, and to love (David) as the ruling intelligence, or king. "Jehovah looketh on the heart." David was "ruddy" (red). He was a shepherd, a keeper of the natural animal forces. These symbols all describe the subconscious life energies centering about the heart.

God is love and His kingdom is "within you." "Within" is not an abstraction, but a definite place in the interior or subconscious realms of mind and body.

When you find that your willful (Saul) rule is not proving harmonious, call upon the Spirit of the Lord for His anointing. You will receive the baptism of Spirit if you are sincere in your asking, and this spiritual anointing will prove to be the first step in setting up a new reign in which love will be king.

day.

Meta. Days and nights, in Scripture, are symbols describing degrees of unfoldment, *night* being ignorance, and *day* understanding.

The "last day" (John 6:39, 40) is the last degree of understanding.

"I [John] was in the Spirit on the Lord's day" (Rev. 1:10). "The Lord's day" here is a state of mind in which we have released our own personal thoughts and activities, and rest in the realization that we have touched the mind of Spirit. Getting into Spirit is getting into the consciousness that we can and do understand the things of Spirit—the revelations of Spirit. The Lord's day is the day of illumination.

The "three days" of John 2:19 are the three degrees or parts of man's consciousness: spirit, soul, body. When I AM has purified and mastered these three in a person, he is in that dominion proclaimed for him in the 1st chapter of Genesis; then the Scripture, or word of God, is fulfilled in him and his faculties (disciples) recognize and respond to it every time that the lifting up word (resurrection) is proclaimed.

day-star (Lat., Lucifer; Gk., phosphorus; Heb. Or)—*the principle of light; anything consisting of light; halo; aurora; power of illumination; a star.*

The passage in Isaiah regarding the day-star, or Lucifer (A. V.), is believed by many to refer to the fall from heaven of angels who had sinned against God; Lucifer, their leader, is supposed to be Satan. In so far as the outer is concerned, this is a mistake; the text has no such inference. It refers to the fall of the king of Babylon, who had ruled in such brilliance and greatness, in such pomp and splendor, that Isaiah likened him to the morning star (Isa. 14:12; II Pet. 1:19).

Meta. The text in Isaiah, "O day-star, son of the morning!" signifies man's uplifting of the ruling ego of the sense consciousness (represented here by the king of Babylon), and attributing to the outer sense man those qualities of light, understanding, and greatness that belong to God only. This is adverse, of course, and it comes under the Satanic phase of thought in the individual; it must be overthrown, cast down and out of consciousness. Metaphysically interpreted, therefore, this text in Isaiah does refer to Satan, to his self-exaltation and downfall. (See SATAN.)

In II Peter 1:19, "day-star" is symbolical of the Christ light's springing up in individual consciousness. The Christ mind is the true source of understanding, power, and all good; glory should be attributed to God only.

dead (I Pet. 4:5).

Meta. The "dead" in Scripture signifies those who are unconscious of Truth. (See DYING.)

deaf (Mark 7:32).

Meta. To be deaf denotes a state of mind unreceptive (not listening) to the revealing Spirit. To be dumb signifies inactivity in expressing Truth.

Debir, dē'-bĭr (Heb.)—*the innermost part of the temple; sanctuary; place of oracles; speech; oracle; word.*

a An Amoritish king of Eglon who was defeated and slain by Joshua (Josh. 10:3). **b** A city of Judah (Josh. 15:7) that is also called Kiriath-sannah (Josh. 15:49) and Kiriath-sepher (Judg. 1:11). **c** Another place by this name was allotted to Gad (Josh. 13:26).

Meta. Debir, in its highest significance, is the secret place within the very center of man's being, the holy of holies where God dwells, where we can commune with Him. It also refers to the Christ, or Christ mind, which is the Word and from which we receive our revelations of Truth. Kiriath-sepher means *city of instruction, city of books,* and so this city is a center of learning, a place where understanding is attained, and it is very sacred.

When the cities named Debir belong to the Canaanites, they signify that state of mind in which man is ignorant of the true Source of inspiration and Truth; when he is in this unawakened consciousness man deifies, as it were, human methods of learning—he worships the created instead of the Creator; outer effects and methods instead of the one Source.

Debir, king of Eglon, an Amoritish ruler, represents the central ruling thought of the sense mind in man regarding that which is most sacred, the creative power of the word. This thought brings the highest truths of Spirit to a very material basis.

Deborah, dĕb'-ŏ-räh (Heb.)—*bee; wasp; a leader of the flock; one of the followers.*

a Rebekah's nurse (Gen. 35:8). **b**

A prophetess of Israel who, with Barak, delivered Israel from Sisera and his host (Judg. 4:4-16).

Meta. Deborah means a *bee*. Bees are noted for their fine sense of discrimination, and for their great activity. Rebekah's nurse Deborah symbolizes a very active, sustaining soul quality. (See ALLON—BACUTH.)

The prophetess Deborah represents judgment based upon spiritual discrimination. There is in every one a fine sense of discrimination, a keener perception than is known to the five senses. When this faculty functions in its native state (under its own palm tree, in connection with wisdom, Lappidoth the husband of Deborah), marvelous results are obtainable. Deborah dwelt under the palm tree of Deborah, between Ramah (*height*) and Beth–el (*house of God*), in Mount Ephraim (*doubly fruitful*).

When the inner intuitive judgment and the directive power in understanding are rightly joined, victory over the enemies of the Children of Israel follows. The Children of Israel represent the real, enduring spiritual thoughts, and the enemies are the material, transitory thoughts. Barak (the executiveness of the will), the general of the armies of Israel, should not go into action without good judgment (Deborah). The only way to overcome the opposition of the adverse thought realm is to understand the law and to keep constantly unified with judgment based upon inner discrimination. This is represented by Deborah's accompanying Barak to battle. (See BARAK.) The victory belongs to the intuitive judgment, and not to the will.

In mixed states of consciousness, where to appearances error is strongest, it is by following the intuitive leadings of Spirit that the way to the light is opened. When we are confronted with a problem the very first thing to be done is to consult our inner discrimination or guidance. We also must affirm that this intuitional faculty is functioning in its native state in perfect unison with infinite wisdom. But this is not enough; we must insist that this same discerning spirit of divine wisdom accompany us every step of the way. When we first receive a spiritual inspiration as to how to meet a situation, we often feel assured of our ability to succeed. However, as the matter progresses, certain aspects change and new aspects develop. We must be in conscious contact with wise discrimination at every step of the way that we may attain complete success.

Decapolis, dĕ-căp'-ŏ-lĭs (Gk.)—*ten cities; ten cities* (collectively).

A Roman district, partly in Syria and partly in Palestine, that contained ten cities (Matt. 4:25).

Meta. Decapolis means *ten cities*. A city represents a group of thoughts, or a thought center in consciousness. Mark 7:31 says of Jesus, "And again he went out from the borders of Tyre, and came through Sidon unto the Sea of Galilee, through the midst of the borders of Decapolis." This journey was made just prior to His healing of a deaf man. Metaphysically interpreted the passage would mean that the I AM (Jesus) withdrew its attention from the outer centers (borders of Tyre) and concentrated upon the inner centers (the "midst" of the borders of Decapolis). These ten thought centers (Decapolis: *ten cities*) are of the soul, and when lined up by a developed mind exert great power.

Dedan, dē'-dăn (Heb.)—*mutual attraction; selective affinity; physical love; low.*

a A descendant of Cush, who was a son of Ham and grandson of Noah (Gen. 10:7). **b** A son of Jokshan, a son of Abraham by Keturah (I Chron. 1:32). The descendants of these two men named Dedan are supposed to have been Arabian or Idumean tribes. The overthrow of Dedan is prophesied by both Jeremiah and Ezekiel (Jer. 25:23; Ezek. 25:13).

Meta. Dedan (*mutual attraction, selective affinity, physical love, low*) refers to a phase of physical or animal attraction and affection. This must give way to true love, which is spiritual in its character and is unselfish and pure.

Dedanites (A. V., Dedanim), dē'-dănites (from Heb.)—*of* or *belonging to De-dan.*

Descendants of Dedan (Isa. 21:13).

Meta. The rights springing from and belonging to that in consciousness which Dedan signifies. (See DEDAN.)

Dehaites (A. V., Dehavites), dĕ-hā'-ītes (Heb. from Pers.)—*villagers.*

A Persian colony that was taken to Samaria and settled there after the Israelites were carried away captive (Ezra 4:9).

Meta. A psychical phase of consciousness in man that attempts to take the place of one's true religious and spiritual thoughts (Israelites) when the individual has given himself over to the rule of the intellect guided by sense (the Assyrians and their king).

Delaiah, dĕ-lā'-ịah (Heb.)—*that which Jehovah has drawn, i. e., that it may be poured out; Jah has delivered; freed by Jehovah.*

a A son of Elioenai, in descent from Solomon (I Chron. 3:24). **b** A Levite who belonged in the priesthood (I Chron. 24:18). **c** A man whose "children" were among the returned Jews who could not prove their lineage (Ezra 2:60). **d** The father of Shemaiah and son of Mehetabel (Neh. 6:10). **e** A Jewish man by this name is mentioned in Jeremiah 36:12.

Meta. Freedom of expression. The delivering, freeing Truth is given to man by Jehovah God; it comes from the depths of his being in response to his I AM declaration of his oneness with the Source of all understanding and power, that he may manifest it and radiate it freely to others.

Delilah, dĕ-lī'-läh (Heb.)—*poured out; exhausted; weak; pining with desire; lustful pining; languishing; longing.*

A Philistine woman of Sorek, whom Samson loved; she was instrumental in bringing about his downfall (Judg. 16:4-18).

Meta. Sensuality. (See SAMSON.)

Demas, dē'-măs (Gk.)—*popular; of the people.*

One who worked with Paul in the Truth but later forsook him, "having loved this **present world**" (II Tim. 4:10). (See Col. 4:14 and Philem. 24.)

Meta. While the work of regeneration is going on, many old ideas are eliminated. We find Demas, whose name means *popular, of the people,* forsaking Paul and going to Thessalonica. His love for the material world separated him from the consciousness of Truth. The thoughts in us that believe in the material world as the source of our happiness and well-being cannot follow us in our spiritual development. Love of popularity, love of the approval of the world, and the *popular* beliefs about life cause one to fall short of the Truth standard.

Demetrius, dĕ-mē'-trĭ-ŭs (Gk.)—*belonging to Demeter or Ceres, i. e., the goddess of agriculture and rural life; grain.*

a A silversmith at Ephesus who stirred up a great tumult against Paul and the doctrine of Christ. He did this because he feared that the Truth would take away his business and he would thus lose materially (Acts 19:24, 38). **b** A convert to Truth (III John 12).

Meta. Material thoughts make a material body. Spiritual thoughts make a spiritual body. All thoughts and ideas embody themselves according to their character. If you find yourself using a body in which the material prevails, you are safe in assuming that somewhere in your consciousness are material beliefs upon which its manufacture is based, and that this manufacture is being carried forward day by day. Your body in the form, shape, and general character of its visibility represents your beliefs about substance. Man can idealize the divine substance idea in any way that he wishes, and according to his thought of it his body will manifest. In order to build a spiritual body, he must spiritualize his thoughts and beliefs that continually have been manufacturing a material body. This process of spiritualization begins and is carried forward in the mind through the introduction of true ideas about God and man.

Paul preached the Truth of the Lord Jesus Christ at Ephesus until material ideas that were there making material images began to lose their hold. The master craftsman, or chief thought, is Demetrius (substance) the silversmith. Out of substance he and his fellow craftsmen have been making material images of Diana, the goddess of vitality. (See DIANA.)

Demetrius was materializing the pure ideal and was spreading broadcast little images made of bronze and silver.

In the stomach the food undergoes one of the most wonderful processes that occur in the chemistry of body building. Some metaphysicians say that every cell that passes from this center to the circulation bears the exact image of the whole body—it is a picture of the body in miniature.. Here we find Demetrius and his fellow craftsmen making images that build the body of flesh. Some new and higher ideals are beginning to prevail there, however. The mind has become saturated with the thought of a more substantial and more permanent body. The resurrection of Jesus, the I AM, from this death of matter is being proclaimed and it stirs up these makers of matter. You cannot change established states of thought without some commotion. This commotion is called chemicalization. It is not uncommon for the metaphysician to have a "riot" in his stomach after a denial of matter and a powerful affirmation of the purity and permanency of Spirit. Sometimes this confusion is so great with beginners that they think themselves seriously ill, when the trouble is merely a riot of the little workers who are opposing a change of ideas. This turmoil continues until poise is gained in the Alexander thought (Alexander "beckoned with the hand"), symbolical of the word of power and mastery. But the battle of Spirit against matter is not won without effort. After Alexander began to talk to the people in an effort to enlighten and quiet them the craftsmen "with one voice about the space of two hours cried out, Great is Diana of the Ephesians." An appeal to the law of justice and the right relation of things in the body politic restores harmony and gains a point that will have lasting effect in establishing a new and greater vitality in every part of the organism.

demons, dē'-mons (Gk.)—*a superior power (for good* or *for evil)*; *a god; a devil.* As a rule the New Testament usage refers to an evil spirit; that is, a ruling consciousness that dethrones the normal reason.

Meta. Demons, or evil spirits, are conditions of mind, or states of consciousness, that have been developed because the creative power of man has been used in an unwise or an ignorant way. If in thought or in word you are using your creative power in an ignorant way, you are bringing forth an ego or a personality of like character. The mind builds states of consciousness that become established in brain and body. Both good and evil are found in the unregenerate man, but in the new birth evil and all its works must be cast out. The work of every overcomer is to cast out of himself the demons of sin and evil, through the power and dominion of his indwelling Christ.

Obsessions, dual personalities, and all mental aberrations are the result of personal error thoughts' crystallizing around the will of man. This crystallization must be broken up with a focalized thought energy of greater power, such as is found in the Christ I AM. We are empowered by the name of Jesus Christ to "cast out demons" (Mark 16:17). To reach the place referred to as "my name," affirm your unity with the Christ I AM; then silently, or audibly if you are so moved, speak the word of rebuke directly to the false personality.

"Jesus rebuked him; and the demon went out of him" (Matt. 17:18). He "suffered not the demons to speak" (Mark 1:34). These texts mean that Jesus did not admit for a moment that demons have any power; nor did He allow them to affirm power, but with the "finger of God" (Luke 11:20) He cast them forth. He concentrated the dissolving power of Spirit upon them and their hold was broken.

Derbe, dẽr'-bẽ (Gk.)—*harsh; stinging; juniper.*

Derbe is mentioned with Lystra; they are both towns of Lycaonia in Asia

Minor. Paul and Barnabas fled to Lystra and Derbe because of persecution in Iconium (Acts 14:6, 20).

Meta. Wounded feelings, self-condemnation (the keen pricking of the conscience) and the acute suffering and distress of mind that one experiences under certain conditions. (See CILICIA and LYSTRA.)

desert places.

Meta. A "desert place" (Matt. 14:13 and Mark 6:31, 32) in the consciousness of man is a seeming lack of substance and life. In Truth desert places do not really exist. Where God is, there is His inexhaustible resource, and God is everywhere present. From the viewpoint of Spirit there is no such thing as lack. When man realizes the quickening power of life, love, and substance he makes the seeming "desert places" in his mind bloom like the rose and bring forth abundantly.

Deuel, deū'-ĕl (Heb.)—*knowledge of God; God knoweth; known of God.*

Father of Eliasaph of the tribe of Gad (Num. 1:14). In Numbers 2:14, he is called Reuel.

Meta. Spiritual perception and enlightenment—the inner or spiritual knowing.

Deuteronomy, deū'-tĕr-ŏn'-ŏ-mў (Gk.)—*repetition of the law; restatement of the law.*

The fifth book of the Bible, and supposed to have been written by Moses; authorities, however, disagree as to this. It is named Deuteronomy because it rehearses, or retells, the law.

Devil (see proper names: ABADDON, APOLLYON, BEELZEBUB, BELIAL, SATAN), called Abaddon and Apollyon, Rev. 9:11; Beelzebub, Matt. 12:24; Belial, II Cor. 6:15; Satan, Luke 10:18 (A. S. V.)—*false accuser; calumniator; slanderer; liar.*

Meta. Same as Satan, which see. The "devil" signifies the mass of thoughts that have been built up in consciousness through many generations of earthly experiences and crystallized into what may be termed human personality, or carnal mind. Another name of the "devil" is sense consciousness; all the thoughts in

one that fight against and are adverse to Truth belong to the state of mind that is known to metaphysicians as the Devil.

Diana, dī-ā'-nȧ (Lat.)—same as Greek Artemis; *heavenly; divine; luminous; moon goddess; virgin goddess; great mother.*

A heathen goddess at Ephesus (Acts 19:24, 35).

Meta. Describing this famous image at Ephesus, which was one of the seven wonders of the world, a writer says that she was an impersonation of the vitality and power of nature, of the reproductive power that keeps up the race of man and animals in an unbroken series of offspring, and of the nourishing power by which the earth tenders to the use of man and animals all that they require to keep them in life. The upper part of her body was covered with rows of breasts, symbolizing her as the universal mother of all life. Diana was the goddess of vitality, yet the idea of life at that time was held very low. She was worshiped with the vilest debaucheries, incorporating the lusts of the flesh in the very ritual of worship, we are told. Thus the ideal that stands back of all life activity and manifestation has been materialized and sensualized by man in his carnal, unawakened state until it has come to mean mere sex-traffic—this is Diana. (See DEMETRIUS.)

Diblah (A. V., Diblath), dĭb'-läh (Heb.)—*pressed together; a round mass; squeezed into a cake; fig cake.*

In prophesying of the Israelites Ezekiel says that because of their idolatry their land will be made more desolate than "the wilderness toward Diblah" (Ezek. 6:14, with marginal note). It is thought that Riblah is the correct name for this place that Ezekiel calls Diblah.

Meta. Compressed, belittled, confused ideas of substance and Truth (*pressed together, squeezed into a cake*) because of a selfish holding to possessions, to the manifest, and an ignoring of the source of all life and of the omnipresent, abundant supply for both the inner and the outer phases of man.

There is no desolation (wilderness)

more pronounced than that which is in close contrast with richness and fertility (toward Diblah or Riblah, Riblah meaning *fertility*). Even so, in consciousness, when one has consciously contacted spiritual substance and life throughout his being and then falls away from this inner reality because of allowing himself to become absorbed in the outer demonstrations that he has made, he comes into a place where he experiences great emptiness, barrenness, and confusion of thought. This is the metaphysical import of Ezekiel 6:14.

Diblaim, dĭb'-lä-ĭm (Heb.)—*double cakes; twin cakes; two fig cakes; cakes.*

A parent (whether mother or father is not known) of Hosea's wife (Hos. 1:3). The wife of Hosea was a prostitute; she was taken by Hosea at the command of Jehovah, to signify the adultery of the Jewish nation in departing from Jehovah.

Meta. Double-mindedness—trying to serve and love both God and Mammon, or worldliness—is the great adultery, or "whoredom" of professed followers of God. Diblaim (*double cakes, twin cakes, two fig cakes*) signifies this doubleminded thought in regard to substance and life. It is the belief that certain phases of life and substance are spiritual, and that other phases of these qualities are material. Man must become established in the truth of the one substance and one life, in order to become pure in mind and body and to serve God wholly and perfectly—to have the single eye, or an eye single to God and Truth.

Dibon, dī'-bŏn (Heb.)—*pining; wasting away; consumed; languished; river course,* i. e., *channel eroded by water.*

a A city of Moab that was taken and destroyed by the Israelites. It was in the territory that was allotted to Gad, and was rebuilt by that tribe (Num. 32:3, 34). **b** A town of Judah (Neh. 11:25).

Meta. A wasting away, or dissolution, of the carnal current of thought regarding life (*river course* suggests the life current in man, or a current of thought about life, and Moab stands for the carnal consciousness), that an understanding of

Truth may take its place. Thus the life current in the organism is raised to a higher level, and is directed aright that the true, spiritual man may be built up.

Dibon–gad, dī'-bŏn–găd (Heb.)—*Dibon of Gad.*

A camping place of the Israelites (Num. 33:45); it is the same place as the Dibon that was allotted to Gad.

Meta. See DIBON.

Dibri, dĭb'-rī (Heb.)—*fluent speech; eloquent; orator; discourse with reason.*

A man of the tribe of Dan (Lev. 24: 11). Dibri's daughter, Shelomith, became the wife of an Egyptian; her son cursed God and was stoned to death by the Israelites for the sin.

Meta. The intellectual ability to express oneself freely and forcibly, with conviction and power (*fluent speech, eloquent, orator, discourse with reason*).

The ability to express oneself freely and persuasively in thought and word that Dibri signifies is of the intellect. The exercise of that ability brings forth a soul quality (daughter) that becomes unified with the darkened thought for which an Egyptian stands, an unwise and destructive use of the ability to express oneself results; this is the son who blasphemed and was stoned to death. One must remain consciously unified with the Highest, that one's intellect may be illumined by Spirit and one's God-given faculties and powers may be used always in constructive ways.

Didymus, dĭd'-ў-mŭs (Gk.)—*twofold; double; twain; twin.*

The surname of the apostle Thomas (John 20:24). This name infers that Thomas was a twin; instead of Thomas Didymus, we would say, Thomas the twin.

Meta. Thomas, or Didymus, both names having the same meaning, was the disciple of Jesus Christ who represents the faculty of reason or intellectual understanding. He does not signify spiritual understanding, else he would have comprehended Jesus' teaching and would not have had to receive the outer assurances and explanations that he was always demanding. He would have known and would not have doubted, had he represented spiritual understanding instead of understanding from a more human and limited standpoint. (See THOMAS.)

Diklah, dĭk′-läh (Heb.)—*palm tree; palm grove; ethereal lightness.*

A son of Joktan, who was descended from Shem, one of Noah's three sons (Gen. 10:27).

Meta. Shem was the son of Noah, who typifies the spiritual in man. In the sons of Joktan we find many spiritual qualities suggested. Most of Shem's sons, however, were the heads of Arabian tribes, or are believed to have been. This shows that at the stage of man's development that the sons represent the spiritual is not established in consciousness firmly enough to bring forth fruit (Arabians stand for unproductive thoughts); yet the spiritual impulses and inner knowing of Truth are implanted in the depths of man's being from the beginning. Ultimately they will work out in his inner and his outer life.

Palms and palm trees denote victory and triumph; they are significant especially of the resurrection—of victory over the appearance of death and of the tomb. *Ethereal lightness* bespeaks illumination, fineness or purity of understanding; therefore Diklah, meaning *palm tree, palm grove, ethereal lightness,* denotes the inherent belief in man, in his inner spiritual or true self, that complete victory over all error and complete triumph in understanding and life are his heritage.

Dilean, dĭl′-ĕ-ăn (Heb.)—*gourd field; gourd; cucumber;* anything that is *oblong, tongue-shaped.*

A lowland city of Judah (Josh. 15:38).

Meta. The gourd that the Lord prepared to shelter Jonah came up in a night and perished in a night (Jonah 4:6, 10). The wild gourds of II Kings 4:39-41 were poisonous. According to the texts in Jonah and in II Kings, gourds refer to a quality in consciousness that is not established or permanent. They refer also to some quality that is not in harmony with man's body and is very poisonous. This quality is anger, no doubt, and an unpoised frame of mind, because Jonah was very angry with the Lord.

The prophets who gathered the wild gourds and partook of the pottage made from them were in an excited state of thought also, until Elisha healed the pottage with some meal—in other words, established peace and assurance in consciousness through love.

Dilean (*gourd field, gourd, cucumber, tongue-shaped,* a city in the low lands of Judah) symbolizes a state of thought in man that is of a changeable, excited, scornful character, and seemingly of little value. It does not understand the opulence of Spirit or the abidingness of all that is established in Spirit—even the outermost consciousness and organism of every individual will abide alive and entire when man is wholly unified with God. The state of thought that Dilean signifies needs to be lifted into Truth, through praise and prayer (Judah).

Dimnah, dĭm′-năh (Heb.)—*dung pit; manure; offal; refuse.*

A city of Zebulun that was given over to the Merari Levites (Josh. 21:35). It is thought to be the same place as Rimmono of I Chronicles 6:77.

Meta. In Philippians 3:8 Paul tells us that in suffering the loss of all things, he counted them "but refuse" that he might win Christ. In the Authorized Version the word "dung" is used instead of "refuse." Dimnah therefore (meaning *dung pit, manure, offal, refuse,* and being a city of Zebulun given over to the Levites) would stand for denial, a letting go of thoughts and possibly of certain substances in the organism that are no longer needed by the individual; but if retained would become refuse and would cause impurity, adulteration of thought and of body substance—dis-ease. (Dung, in eastern countries, in Palestine especially, is dried and used for fuel. This carries further the thought signified by Dimnah: that which is denied out of consciousness is fit only to be burned).

Dimon, dī′-mŏn (Heb.)—*pining; wasting away; consumed; languished; river course,* i. e., *channel eroded by water.*

Isaiah mentions the "waters of Dimon" (Isa. 15:9). Dimon is thought to be the same place as Dibon.

Meta. See DIBON.

Dimonah, dĭ-mō'-näh (Heb.)—*pining; wasting away; consumed; languished; river course,* i. e., *channel eroded by water.*

A southern city of Judah (Josh. 15: 22); it is thought to be the same place as the Dibon of Nehemiah 11:25.

Meta. The significance is much the same as that of Dibon; Dimonah refers to the denying, letting go, or wearing away of error beliefs, that one may become established in Truth ideals and practices. (See DIBON.)

Dinah, dī'-näh (Heb.)—*judged; justified; acquitted; avenged.*

Jacob's daughter, by Leah (Gen. 30: 21).

Meta. The soul side, or feminine quality, of the judgment faculty in man; it might be called intuition, the intuition of the natural man. The thought of vengeance that is suggested in the name always comes to the natural man in his idea of judgment; he is more likely to discern the error side of a proposition than the true side. This thought is carried out by the action of Simeon and Levi in taking vengeance, for Dinah, upon Shechem and his people. As man becomes more spiritual in his ideas of judgment, thoughts of vengeance, punishment, and evil are eliminated from his mind and he sees the love, mercy, and goodness of God instead.

Dinaites, dī'-nä-ītes (from Heb.)—*judgment, a cause.*

A tribe of Cuthæan or Assyrian people who were settled in Samaria by the Assyrian king after he had carried the Israelites away captive. The Dinaites were among those who sought to hinder the returned Jews from rebuilding the Temple and the wall of Jerusalem (Ezra 4:9).

Meta. The thoughts, judgments, and impulses of the outer, intellectual, carnal consciousness in man that is guided by the senses; they work against the establishing of the whole man in eternal life and peace.

Dinhabah, dĭn'-hä-bäh (Heb.)—*robbers' den; place of plundering.*

The capital city of Bela, the son of Beor, who reigned in Edom (Gen. 36:32).

Meta. Edom refers to the outer, physical man. Beor represents an intuitive understanding that belongs to the sense man. Bela signifies a destructive, consuming tendency in consciousness. Dinhabah signifies an aggregation of thoughts belonging to man's outer, carnal consciousness. These thoughts are error; they build up and sustain destructive sense tendencies that rob the real inner man of the substance that is rightly his. The error beliefs that are ruled over by that which Bela represents tear down the organism of the individual who gives them place; they rob him of his sustaining substance and life.

Dionysius, dī-ŏ-nўs'-ĭ-ŭs (Gk.)—*a devotee of Dionysus or Bacchus,* i. e., *the god of wine; one filled with new wine,* or, *one inspired by Spirit; divinely touched.*

An Areopagite; he was one of those who were converted to Christianity by Paul at Mars' Hill, or the Areopagus (Acts 17:34).

Meta. One of the most enlightened of the intellectual thoughts in consciousness that are represented by the Areopagus, or "court of justice," the highest form of good judgment that is known to the intellectual in man. (See AREOPAGUS.) The intellectual thought that Dionysius represents has been quickened and illumined by Spirit (*one filled with new wine,* or *one inspired by Spirit, divinely touched*) through the word of Truth (Paul). It is possible for the entire intellect in man to be thus illumined and raised to spiritual consciousness. In this way the intellect becomes a channel through which the Spirit of God can work.

Diotrephes, dī-ŏt'-rĕ-phĕs (Gk.)—*fostered by Zeus; nourished by Jupiter; trained by Zeus.*

A professed Christian; he is mentioned as one who loved prominence, and for this reason would receive neither John nor his letter into the church wherein he (Diotrephes) ministered (III John 9).

Meta. Personal exaltation active in consciousness; the desire of the personal to rule and to have first place. Jesus had to meet and overcome this in His temptation in the wilderness. After Jesus had realized His power through His divine sonship, the Devil (personality) showed Him all the kingdoms of the world and told Him that all authority over them and all the glory of them would be His if He would worship, or give first place in His life to, the Devil, personality. Every overcomer has to meet this same thing and gain the victory over it. When a person lets himself be carried away with the desire for outer place and power, this is Diotrephes active in him.

disciples.

Meta. The disciples of Jesus represent, in mind analysis, the faculties. After one has been illumined by Truth, one desires to express it, to go forth in its ministry. This does not necessarily imply that all secular employment should be abandoned, but it does imply that the mind should make the dissemination of Truth the most important object of life. The various faculties of the mind have been occupied almost wholly in secular ways; now they are to be turned to spiritual ways.

Some of the disciples of Jesus are represented as being fishermen; this implies a striving to catch living ideas (fish) in the thoughts of this material world (waters). In the lesson in Mark 3:7-19, the I AM, Jesus, sees the futility of this struggle with temporal things and sets its energies at work upon things eternal. The scattered faculties are drawn together and are brought to a recognition of the Master—I AM. This is the inner interpretation of Jesus' calling His disciples.

Material things are temporary; spiritual things are eternal. When the mind of man is focused on materiality, and on its objects and aims, the faculties are not developed along permanent lines. Truth reveals to us that every faculty must be used to spiritual ends in order that the law of Being may be fulfilled.

Dishan, dĭ'-shăn (Heb.) — *gazelle; antelope; leaping walk; fatness; opulence; fertile; ashes,* so called from their use as a fattener of the soil, fertilizer.

Son of Seir the Horite, and a chief of the Horites (Gen. 36:21).

Meta. A very active, rich, or fertile controlling thought belonging to the Horite consciousness in the individual. (See HORITES.)

Dishon, dĭ'-shŏn (Heb.) — *gazelle; antelope; leaping walk; fatness; opulence; fertile; ashes,* so called from their use as a fattener of the soil, fertilizer.

Son of Seir the Horite, and a chief of the Horites (Gen. 36:21).

Meta. Dishon is a form of Dishan and signifies virtually the same thing. (See DISHAN.) The richness and seeming fertility of this phase of thought would be on a sensate or physical instead of a spiritual plane.

Di-zahab (A. V., Dizahab), dĭ'-ză-hăb (Heb.)—*auriferous; place rich in gold; abundance of gold; golden.*

A place in the wilderness; it was near this place that Moses made one of his talks to the children of Israel (Deut. 1:1).

Meta. A realization of divine wisdom and substance in the wilderness phase of consciousness in man.

doctors, in the temple (Luke 2:46, margin).

Meta. The thoughts that preside over and regulate the various functions. Jesus, the wisdom of God individualized, gives these doctors a new understanding of the divine law, and all are amazed at the higher revelation.

Dodai, dō'-dāi (Heb.)—*loving; amatory; beloved of Jah; his beloved.*

An Ahohite, captain of David's course of twenty-four thousand men for the second month of each year (I Chron. 27:4). Dodai is believed to be the same name as Dodo.

Meta. The loving thought and act, which are very dear to Jehovah—the Christ or divine law that is fulfilled by love (David as king signifies love ruling in consciousness). (See DODO for the significance of *amatory,* one of the definitions of Dodai.)

Dodanim, dŏd'-ă-nĭm (Heb.)—*covenanters; confederates; the elect; civilized; lovable; beloved; sympathetic; pleasing.*

According to Genesis 10:4, a son of Javan and grandson of Japheth, Noah's son; he is called Rodanim in I Chronicles 1:7.

Meta. Unifying thoughts (*covenanters, confederates*) of a very excellent character (*the elect, civilized, pleasing*) that belong to the intellect in man. Japheth, the second son of Noah, typifies the intellect, or reason. (See JAPHETH.) Javan, the father of Dodanim, also belongs to the intellect. Fallows says of Javan, "The interest connected with his name arises from his being the supposed progenitor of the original settlers in Greece and its isles. . . . Javan was evidently the name given by the Hebrews to Greece." This name is connected in history with the Grecians and the Syrians, and these peoples are symbolical of different phases of the intellectual in man, in its spiritually unillumined state.

While the intellect is prized very highly (*beloved*) by one who is just rising above the purely physical, and is far in advance of that phase of consciousness, yet its greatest degree of comprehension is much less than spiritual understanding. This is because intellectual reasoning is based on outer seeming, while spiritual understanding is founded on Truth. When the intellect is quickened and illumined by Spirit, it expresses in the highest and truest way, since it reasons then from the standpoint of Divine Mind, Principle.

Dodavahu (A. V., Dodavah), dŏd-ăv'-ă-hū (Heb.)—*beloved of Jehovah; Jehovah is loving; Jehovah loves him.*

A man of Mareshah, whose son Eliezer "prophesied against Jehoshaphat, saying, Because thou hast joined thyself with Ahaziah, Jehovah hath destroyed thy works" (II Chron. 20:37; margin, "made a breach in").

Meta. The love of God in expression in individual consciousness (*Jehovah is loving*). Those who love God keep His commandments, and they are the *beloved of Jehovah*. They are blessed accordingly. The same may be said of that loving quality in us which Dodavahu signifies.

Dodo, dō'-dô (Heb.)—*amatory; loving.*

a A man of Issachar whose grandson Tola became a deliverer and judge of Israel after Abimelech (Judg. 10:1). b A man of Beth–lehem whose son Elhanan was one of David's thirty valiant men (II Sam. 23:24). c The Father of Eleazer the Ahohite, who was one of David's three mightiest men (I Chron. 11:12); he is called Dodai in II Samuel 23:9.

Meta. Dodo signifies much the same loving thought and act and close relationship to love ruling in consciousness (King David) that Dodai signifies. *Amatory,* one of the definitions of Dodo and Dodai, suggests a thought of love degenerated into sensual desire. This shows that the love quality expressing in the individual at this stage of his unfoldment is in need of further purification and upliftment.

Doeg, dō'-ĕg (Heb.)—*fearful; anxious; timid.*

A servant of King Saul's, one of his chief herdsmen (I Sam. 21:7). Doeg told Saul that Ahimelech the priest had befriended David, and he slew the priests at Saul's command (I Sam. 22:9, 18).

Meta. Fearfulness, anxiety, and timidity, in individual consciousness. This is a result of believing in the impossibility of lifting the physical or outer consciousness into spirituality and establishing it in the Truth. This belief, when in control of the vital forces in one (Doeg was Saul's chief herdsman) does much to destroy, or to bring into inactivity, one's spiritual qualities (Ahimelech and the other priests whom Doeg slew). See AHIMELECH.

door, of the Temple, which is called Beautiful (Acts 3:2).

Meta. The way which opens to spiritual illumination, to an understanding of how to lay hold of and to apply spiritual law.

The lame man here represents a disabled thought, one that for a long time has been incapable of activity—one that is inert in the expression of buoyancy, strength, and joyousness.

Dophkah, dŏph'-kăh (Heb.)—*thrust; drive; knock; drive hard, i. e., to overdrive a flock or herd; cattle driver.*

A place where the Israelites camped while on their way through the wilderness to the Promised Land (Num. 33:

12).

Meta. A phase of thought that is of a hard, driving nature (*thrust, knock, drive hard,* i. e., *to overdrive a flock or herd, cattle driver*); the tendency to go beyond one's strength, to overdo, and thus to dissipate one's vitality and inner substance (cattle, flocks, and herds refer to physical strength and vitality). This may be done by driving oneself to overwork, or by running after worldly pleasures to the point of excess, or by engaging in any outer activity that saps one's vital forces.

Dor, dôr (Heb.)—*moving around in a circle; dwelling; inhabiting; a circle; an age: a generation.*

"The heights of Dor" was a place in the land of Canaan that was allotted to the tribe of Manasseh, but from which they did not fully drive the Canaanites (Josh. 11:2; 17:11; Judg. 1:27).

Meta. The Canaanites symbolize man's elemental life forces given over to the dominion of sense. Dor, a royal city of the Canaanites that came into the possession of the Israelitish tribe of Manasseh, pertains to the ability of man to abide in life (*dwelling, inhabiting*). The fact that Manasseh did not drive the Canaanites entirely from Dor (with the thought of *an age, a generation*) shows that at the stage of man's unfoldment represented by Dor the life forces are not redeemed fully from mortal tendencies. The higher understanding of the individual (Manasseh) is not allied to pure spiritual knowing strongly enough as yet to clear out of consciousness entirely the old established belief in time and in generation and in the brevity of life. Therefore for a time the error and the true dwell together (the Canaanites lived among the Israelites) and the individual goes round and round in a circle, living out one span of physical life and entering another, and making little or no apparent advancement. Constantly new, truer, higher ideas are needed that one may progress rapidly toward one's divine heritage of perfection.

Dorcas, dôr'-căs (Gk.)—*gazelle; doe.*

A Christian woman at Joppa who was noted for her good works. She is called Tabitha also. She died, but was resurrected by the ministrations of Peter (Acts 9:36-40).

Meta. See TABITHA.

Dothan, dō'-thăn (Heb.)—*two wells; double cisterns; edicts; decrees; laws; customs; double feasts.*

a The place where Joseph found his brethren when his father sent him to see how they were faring, and where his brethren conspired against him and sold him into Egypt (Gen. 37:17-28). **b** The place where Elisha was when the Assyrians came to take him (II Kings 6:13). It was here at Dothan that the Spirit of the Lord, in response to Elisha's request, showed his servant the hosts of God that were defending them. Then the eyes of the Assyrians were blinded, and Elisha led them away into Samaria, where their eyes were opened again. This caused them to cease troubling Israel at that time.

Meta. The law of Being, compared to custom (*edicts, decrees, laws, customs*). *Two wells, double cisterns, double feasts,* denote the double standard of thought that man holds regarding his life and substance. The customary beliefs lead to limited, warped experiences, while an understanding of the true law of Being increases the activity of the power of God in one's life; understanding makes one conscious of that activity, also. The customary belief is exemplified in the significance of Joseph's brethren's conspiring against him and selling him into Egypt; the result of true understanding is shown in the deliverance of Elisha and his servant.

Drusilla, dru̱-sĭl'-lȧ (Gk.)—*bedewed; watered by dew.*

Wife of Felix, who was the Roman governor of Judea at the time that Paul was tried and was sent to Rome to appear before Cæsar (Acts 24:24).

Meta. The voluptuous side of the sense life. (See BERNICE.)

Dumah, dū'-măh (Heb.) — *mute; dumb; silence; land of silence,* i. e., *Sheol; a tomb.*

a A son of Ishmael (Gen. 25:14). **b** A city in the hill country of Judah

(Josh. 15:52). **c** A place that is mentioned in connection with Arabia (Isa. 21:11).

Meta. The condition that man calls death (*mute, dumb, land of silence,* i. e., *Sheol, a tomb*); also the state of man wherein he is dead through his trespasses and sins (see Eph. 2:1). This latter state leads to the death experience; one must be awakened out of his belief in limitation, sin, disease, inharmony, and death in order to become established in abiding, omnipresent life. The "hill country" of Judah signifies a high consciousness of praise and prayer. Through prayer, words of Truth, and praise of life and good based on the Christ, one is raised out of the sin-and-death consciousness.

Dura, dū′-rȧ (Heb.)—*circle; sphere; time; endurance; generation; dwelling; habitation.*

A plain in Babylon, wherein Nebuchadnezzar set up his image of gold that he commanded all the people to worship (Dan. 3:1).

Meta. Nebuchadnezzar signifies the human will backing itself up by the human intellect and human judgment as opposed to spiritual understanding and judgment (Daniel). The golden image signifies money, or gold, an outer manifestation of substance. The plain of Dura, where the king had the golden image set up for all his subjects to worship, is the belief of the Babylonish consciousness in man (sense confusion and mixture of thoughts) that money is the all-powerful thing in this world; it is the loving of money more than the loving of God, and the trusting in gold to deliver and to save instead of the putting of one's faith in God. It is the belief in outer wealth as that which sustains one and as eternal (*circle*), all-inclusive, the one thing most needful.

dying, death, second death (Rev. 2:11).

Meta. Dying is the name that we give to that state of negation in man's consciousness wherein he no longer can retain possession of his body. Death is always the result of a failure to recognize God as the source of wisdom and life. When the soul falls short in this respect, it sins and there is a physical dissolution that is but the outer symbol of mental negation or spiritual inertia.

This death or dissolution of the body is the "second death," over the meaning of which church people have so long contended. The first death is where the consciousness has lost sight of spiritual wisdom and sunk into the belief that God is absent from man and the universe. This belief is the being "dead through your trespasses and sins."

There can be no other explanation of the first and second death. Metaphysically we know that the body is the outer form of the thoughts, and it therefore could not die or disintegrate unless a similar process had first taken place on the mental plane.

If you allow yourself to go to sleep spiritually—that is, if you live in the senses and fail to recognize your spiritual selfhood and your relation to Being—you are already virtually dying or dead. The fact that you seem to live and to exercise a limited consciousness on the animal plane is no evidence that you are alive, because the senses fail you ere long; they will dissolve, and you will then experience the second death.

E

east.

Meta. In Scriptural symbology east represents the within. As used in Matthew 2:1 the word in the original is plural; the significance therefore is that from the regions of interior wisdom come thoughts of reverence and rich gifts of substance and understanding and every spiritual help for the holy Life, the Christ Child, that has begun its growth in the consciousness.

eating.

Meta. The eating of spiritual things is the affirmation of spiritual sustenance. The cake on the coals and the cruse of water at the head of Elijah (I Kings 19:6-8) represent the thoughts, or the words, that these things represent. When in the silence you affirm that you are sustained and nourished by Spirit, you are following the command of the angel and are eating the cake and drinking the water. These are "at the head," place of intelligence. This eating of the "hidden manna" is to be done the "second time." In fact, it should become a daily habit.

"The strength of that food" lasts "forty days and forty nights," which is symbolical of completeness.

Ebal, ē'-băl (Heb.)—*stripped of all covering; bare; naked; barren; stone.*

a Son of Shobal and grandson of Seir the Horite (Gen. 36:23). **b** A mountain in Samaria on the opposite side of a valley from Mount Gerizim. When the Israelites entered the Promised Land, half of the tribes stood on Mount Ebal and pronounced the curses that would come upon the Israelites if they disobeyed the law of God; the other half stood on Mount Gerizim and declared the blessings that would follow obedience (Deut. 11:29; 27:13).

Meta. The activity of the law, in an adverse way, in those who think and act out of harmony with divine principle. It is that in us which takes cognizance of the working out of error that results from ignorance and disobedience. This phase of the activity of the law always seems hard (*stone*) to the sense consciousness upon which it falls, and it surely makes *bare,* exposes the nothingness of, all that does not measure up to the spiritual.

Ebed, ē'-běd (Heb.)—*worker, i. e., one who works for another; laborer; servant; slave.*

a Father of Gaal; Gaal aided the men of Shechem in opposing Abimelech (Judg. 9:26-31). In order to become ruler, or judge, over Israel, Abimelech had slain all his brothers except the youngest one, who escaped. **b** An Ebed returned with Ezra from the captivity in Babylon (Ezra 8:6).

Meta. Gaal the son of Ebed means *abortion, miscarriage, rejection with loathing.* His fighting against Abimelech was very much like one error's opposing another.

Service is good but it should always be done freely in love to God and man; it should be prompted by the idea of divine sonship, rather than by the thought of servitude. If we get the thought of serving from the standpoint of a hired *laborer, servant,* or *slave,* our ministry becomes a burden and we are not blessed thereby. This is the Ebed type of service. When directed against error it does not come to fruition; it miscarries (Gaal); it does not lead to real overcoming.

The Ebed who returned with Ezra from the Babylonian captivity symbolizes the serving thought from a more spiritual standpoint.

Ebed–melech, ē'-běd–mē'-lěch (Heb.) —*king's laborer; servant of the king; slave of the king.*

A eunuch in the retinue of King Zedekiah of Judah (Jer. 38:7-16). He told the king that the prophet Jeremiah had been put in a dungeon to perish, and so he was the means of delivering Jeremiah.

Meta. The king's servant, or the king's thought, as it went out to help rescue Jeremiah. The natural forces, represented by this Ethiopian servant, Ebed–melech, will pull the body out again after a time, if given an opportunity. These forces are constantly doing constructive work, and they will repair the damage done by destructive thoughts and dissipation. But there is a limit to their endurance. If they are abused continually, they will finally give up and cease their work.

God has placed the stamp of perfection upon the spirit of man. This stimulates the natural forces of the body and urges them on toward perfection. The natural forces of the body are willing to cooperate with man in manifesting a perfect body, but man hinders them by his disobedience and unbelief. This saving and this renewing of the body are illustrated by Ebed–melech's aiding in getting Jeremiah out of the dungeon, when he had gained the consent of the king (the will) to do so.

Eben–ezer, ĕb′-ĕn–ē′-zẽr (Heb.)—*stone of the help; precious stone of succor; gem of help.*

"Then Samuel took a stone, and set it between Mizpah and Sh'en, and called the name of it Eben–ezer, saying, Hitherto hath Jehovah helped us" (I Sam. 7: 12). This was just after the Philistines had been overcome and put to rout by the Israelites (I Sam. 7:5-11).

Meta. Realization and acknowledgment of God's aid in gaining victory over the errors of sense (Philistines). This is the result of mental and spiritual work and becomes an abiding consciousness in the soul, typified in the Scripture as the rock of Christ. (See MIZPAH.)

The stone called Eben–ezer refers to the Christ, who is a rock of deliverance, a very present help in every time of need, in every individual who will acknowledge Him. This stone's being placed between Mizpah and Shen—the watchtower of prayer and the assimilating of true ideas gained through prayer—heralds the lifting up of the whole organism, the bringing of the ideal man into manifestation; this is the work of the Christ in every individual.

Eber, ē′-bẽr (Heb.)—*passed over; come over; overcome; on the other side; beyond; region beyond; beyond the world; ultramundane; a shoot.*

a A descendant of Shem's, and father of Peleg and Joktan (Gen. 10:21-25). b A Benjamite (I Chron. 8:12). c A priest in the days of Joiakim (Neh. 12:20).

Meta. Shem was a son of Noah; he typifies the spiritual in man. Eber, a great-grandson of Shem's, reveals the germination (*a shoot*) in man's consciousness of this spiritual phase of his being. *Beyond* signifies that the individual, at the period of his unfoldment that is suggested by Eber, has not yet come to full growth spiritually; the time when he can bring forth the perfect fruit of the Spirit to eternal life and wholeness is still in the future. However, he has *passed over, come over, on the other side,* his old conception of mortality, and has entered into a new per-

ception of Truth, of the possibility of limitless attainment.

The Eber who was a Benjamite denotes the quickening of the faith quality in man, and its growth in consciousness.

Eber the priest typifies still another way in which the spiritual is beginning to show itself in and through the individual.

Ebez (A. V., Abez), ē′-bĕz (Heb.)—*white; pure whiteness; bright; shining; brilliant; conspicuous.*

A city in the land of Canaan that was allotted to Issachar (Josh. 19:20).

Meta. A state of consciousness that stands out (*is conspicuous*) in the individual because of its high, pure, radiant character (*white, shining, pure whiteness, brilliant*); it takes a prominent place within one and is the means of gathering much Truth because of its close union with Spirit.

Ebiasaph, ē-bī′-ă-săph (Heb.)—*father of gathering; father of increase; father of adding; father who adds.*

A Levite who is named in the genealogy of Levi (I Chron. 6:23).

Meta. The love quality in man actively expressing itself in increase in his consciousness and life, attracting to him (*father of gathering, father of increase, father who adds*) much spiritual blessing and attainment. (Love is the magnet that draws to one abundance of good. "God is love." Levi, of the sons of Jacob and of the tribes of Israel, represents the love faculty in man. A Levite therefore is one of the thoughts that help to make up the love center in individual consciousness.)

Ecbatana, ec-băt′-a-nȧ (Gk.)—*egress; way of escape; fortress; stronghold; place of horses.*

A city in Media (Ezra 6:2, margin). It is called Achmetha in Ezra 6:2.

Meta. See ACHMETHA.

Ecclesiastes, ĕc-clē-sĭ-ăs′-tēṣ (Gk.)—*preacher; leader of a convocation; speaker before the congregation.*

A book of the Old Testament that is supposed to have been written by Solomon in his old age. This book tells of the vanity of the desires, sensations, pleasures, and attainments of the outer personal man, and it points the way to that which alone is worthy of consideration: remembrance of God.

Meta. Experience. Experience preaches very effectively; the fruit of experience is the most impressive sermon in life. Experience teaches us that it is impossible to find satisfaction and true lasting joy in sensual, earthly pleasures and in self-seeking. The only way to gain the realities of life that satisfy both soul and body is to turn within to God and become unified consciously with Him.

Ed, ĕd (Heb.)—*duration, i. e., of time or space; eternal; a witness; testament; an ornament; pleasant; beauty; delight; perfection.*

An altar that was built by the Israelitish tribes of Reuben and Gad, and the half tribe of Manasseh, who were left on the other side of the Jordan. They built this altar as a witness to the other tribes of Israel, who went over the Jordan and settled in Canaan proper, that they too believed in Jehovah. "And the children of Reuben and the children of Gad called the altar *Ed*: For, *said they,* it is a witness between us that Jehovah is God" (Josh. 22:34).

Meta. The established evidence of Spirit within us that Jehovah, our indwelling Christ, is the Lord of our whole being, the ideal which we worship and seek to become like in both mind and body. (An altar in consciousness is a state of thought wherein some definite truth is realized and acknowledged, and wherein lesser thoughts and activities are released to Spirit, that the substance, energy, and power that the individual has put into them may be transmuted and thus be utilized in working out in his life the higher ideals that have been revealed to him.)

Eden, ē'-den (Heb.)—*sensible duration; time; pleasure; delight; pleasantness.*

a The name of the place where, we are told, God put the first man and woman—Adam and Eve (Gen. 2:8; Isa. 51:3; Ezek. 28:13). **b** A place that is prophesied against (Amos 1:5; Ezek. 27:23; see II Kings 19:12 also). **c** A man named Eden, a Levite, is mentioned in II Chronicles 29:12.

The Hebrew *"Gan–heden"* commonly rendered Garden of Eden is a compound of surpassing greatness. The word *Gan* means any organized sphere of activity, a garden, a body, a world, a universe. The word *Heden,* Eden, means a *time,* a season, an age, an eternity, as well as beauty, *pleasure,* an ornament, a witness. Thus it can be seen that only the most limited and restricted material acceptation would bring this remarkable word down to a small, hedged-in inclosure, a small area somewhere in Asia where the human race first emerged from the dust of this planet.

Meta. A pleasant, harmonious, productive state of consciousness in which are all possibilities of growth. When man is expressing in harmony with Divine Mind, bringing forth the qualities of Being in divine order, he dwells in Eden, or in a state of bliss in a harmonious body.

The "garden" symbolizes the spiritual body in which man dwells when he brings forth his thoughts after the original divine ideas. This garden is the substance of God (Eden) or state of perfect relation of ideas to Being. The Garden of Eden is the divine consciousness. Having developed a consciousness apart from his divine nature, man must "till the ground from whence he was taken," that is, he must come into a realization of God as the source of his Being and must express ideas in harmony with Divine Mind. Wisdom and love are joined in God, and a perfect balance is struck in consciousness between knowing and feeling when man spiritualizes his thoughts.

Eder, ē'-dẽr (Heb.)—*troop; flock; drove; herd; any movable aggregation that is numbered, arrayed, mustered.*

a A tower beyond which Israel (Jacob) journeyed and spread his tent, after he had buried Rachel (Gen. 35:21). **b** A city of Judah "toward the border of Edom in the South" (Josh. 15:21). **c** A Benjamite (I Chron. 8:15). **d** A Levite (I Chron. 23:23).

Meta. A *flock* may relate to animals or to birds; even people are said sometimes to "flock together" when they gather in great numbers. Animals represent the animal forces in man, birds are free, unattached thoughts, and people stand for thoughts, faculties, and tendencies.

The Benjamite and the Levite named Eder denote the assembling of thoughts belonging to the faith and love centers of consciousness in man. Eder, a city of Judah "in the South," toward Edom, is a subconscious gathering of thoughts pertaining to the life forces and activities. The tower called Eder, beyond which Israel (Jacob) journeyed and spread his tent, denotes the gathering of thoughts of dominion and rulership (Israel means *rulership with God*) and raising them to a higher degree of understanding; lifting them to a spiritual level by realizing that power and dominion come from God.

Edom, ē'-dŏm (Heb.)—*red; reddish; ruddy.*

a The name that was given to Esau because of the red pottage for which he sold his birthright to Jacob (Gen. 25:30; 36:1-19). **b** The country where Esau's descendants lived (Gen. 36:16); this country is also called Mount Seir and Idumæa.

Meta. The outer man, the body, or the carnal, physical phase of man's consciousness and organism.

Edomites, ē'-dŏm-ītes (fr. Heb.).

Esau's descendants (Gen. 36:9). They lived in the southern part of Palestine, and later were enemies of the Israelites (Num. 20:18). They were conquered by David and became servants to him (II Sam. 8:14).

Meta. Thoughts and tendencies in man that belong to the Esau or Edom consciousness. (See EDOM and ESAU.)

Edrei, ĕd'-rē-ī (Heb.) — *strong; mighty; armed; fortified; sown; seeded.* (The idea of the definitions *sown* and *seeded* is from the broad, strong sweep of the arm in sowing.)

a A city of Bashan, where the remnant of the Rephaim lived; this place was conquered by the Israelites under Moses and was given to Manasseh for an inheritance (Josh. 12:4-6). **b** A fortified city of Canaan that was allotted to Naphtali (Josh. 19:37).

Meta. A fixed state of consciousness, or aggregation of nerve cells, established in life and substance (see BASHAN), whose dominant idea is strength and might.

Eglah, ĕg'-lăh (Heb.)—*heifer; calf; the embryo; young of any animal.*

A wife of David's, mother of Ithream who was born in Hebron (II Sam. 3:5).

Meta. A phase of the soul.

Eglaim, ĕg'-lă-im (Heb.)—*two ponds; double wells; two springs.*

A city of Moab (Isa. 15:8).

Meta. A double-minded belief about the wellspring of life (*double wells, two springs, two ponds*). This double-minded belief refers to the seeming "good" and "evil" that are experienced in human consciousness because of ignorance concerning life and an unwise use of life. This unwise use causes the life activities in the body to become like ponds of stagnant water instead of being like ever renewing and ever bubbling springs.

Eglon, ĕg'-lŏn (Heb.)—*young bullock; calflike; round; rolling; a threshing drag; an oxcart; a war chariot.*

a A king of Moab who, with the help of the Ammonites and the Amalekites, overcame the Israelites and held them in subjection for some years; this was because of Israel's sins in serving the gods of the heathen nations about them (Judg. 3:12-25). **b** The city of Debir, a king in Canaan who was defeated by Joshua (Josh. 10:3); this city was allotted to Judah (Josh. 15:39).

Meta. A ruling thought belonging to the animal phase of consciousness in the natural man, especially pertaining to physical strength. But this thought does not get the individual advancement, in so far as true unfoldment and growth are concerned. Sensate thought goes round and round aimlessly, drifting with the tide of race thought and belief, guided by the emotions, with no definite purpose (*young bullock, calflike, round, rolling, a threshing drag, an oxcart, a war chariot*).

The city of Eglon signifies a subconscious state of thought whose central idea is strength (see DEBIR, king of Eglon, in connection with this). A lifting up of the idea of strength takes place when this city comes into the possession of Judah.

Egypt, ē′-ġўpt (Gk.)—*Coptic land;* from the Hebrew name Mizraim, which means *shut in, restraint, misery, tribulation, distress.*

A country in the northeast of Africa, where the Israelites were held in bondage for many years (Gen. 12:10; 37:28; 42:1 to end of Exod. 14). Jesus was taken into Egypt when a babe, to save him from Herod (Matt. 2:13).

Meta. The realm of substance and life in the depths of the body consciousness. To the unregenerate soul it is the land of darkness and mystery, yet it is essential to the perpetuation of the body. Egypt signifies the darkness of ignorance, obscurity; it has a special significance in the body consciousness, and we often think of it as referring to the subjective or subconscious mind. We also refer to Egypt as the flesh consciousness, sense consciousness, or material consciousness.

This hidden realm within our organism is in an Egyptian or obscured state to most of us. Yet it is a great kingdom, and its king is Pharaoh, ruler of the sun, or that brain and nerve center which our physiologists have correctly named the solar plexus. They tell us that this is the brain of the body, and that it directs the circulation, digestion, assimilation, and so forth. Students of mind have discovered that the solar plexus is but the organ through which a ruling thought acts, and this ruling thought is typified by Pharaoh, he of the *hard heart,* who would not "let my people go." But we should not forget that it is down in Egypt that we find the "grain" or substance required to sustain the man.

Many workers in Truth think that it is useless to go into this obscure kingdom within each man. They are not willing that Joseph shall spend a part of his time down in Egypt making ready the storehouses and filling them with the vitality that will be needed when the outer man has exhausted his resources. These will find that they cannot have that joyous reunion of mind and body with all its brothers, or faculties, as set forth in

Genesis 42 to 46, unless they are willing to let the higher thought go *consciously* down into Egypt and rule there second to King Pharaoh himself.

Physically Egypt typifies that part of the body below the diaphragm. The various plagues brought upon the Egyptians by the Lord through Moses are symbolical representations of what occurs in this part of the organism when the presiding intelligence (Pharaoh) opposes the influx of the higher life.

Parallels to the bloody waters, frogs, lice, flies, murrain, boils, hail, locusts, darkness, and death of first-born may all be found in the various diseases of bowels, kidneys, and other organs of the body as named by doctors. A very large number of these ills result from mental resistance to spiritual consciousness, which is working widely in humanity.

The spiritual man, the true ego, is the only rightful heir to the divine inheritance: spiritual consciousness. We as individuals must awake from the dream of mortality, leave Egypt (the flesh consciousness) forever, cross the Red Sea (the boundary line where we sacrifice every tie that binds us to the past), thence go through the wilderness (a transitory state), through the waters of Jordan (the boundary line between the transitional and the permanent), and plant our feet on Canaan's land—our inheritance. Once there, we have thirty-one kings (usurping thought forces) to conquer before we can peaceably settle down in our inheritance. But Christ, the Captain of the army of the Lord of hosts, meets us (is revealed to conscious thought) on Canaan's shore and directs our battles: Truth becomes an active, irresistible power.

When the spiritual man awakens and finds that he is the possessor of the divine germ (the word of Truth), he begins at once to make use of it. The result is an influx of light. Mortality, which is synonymous with darkness, begins to fade from his conscious thought. As this light increases, mortality decreases, until, as Paul says, mortality is swallowed up in immortality, "death is swallowed up in victory" (I Cor. 15:

53, 54).

Egyptian, ē-ġў̆p′-t̲i̲ăn (Gk.)—a Copt; from the Hebrew word Mizraim, which means *shut in, restraint, misery, tribulation, distress.*

Natives or inhabitants of Egypt; descendants of Mizraim, son of Ham (I Sam. 30:11).

Meta. Egyptians signify sense thoughts, or thoughts that pertain to the subjective consciousness in its unawakened state. They belong to the Egypt consciousness. (See EGYPT.)

Ehi, ē′-hī (Heb.)—*union; united; unity; brother; brotherly; friend; friend of Jehovah.*

Son of Benjamin. In other places he is called Ahiram, Aher, and Aharah (Gen. 46:21).

Meta. See AHIRAM, AHER, AHARAH, and add to the suggestions applied to them the thought of *unity*—conscious oneness with God and with mankind; thus you will get the metaphysical import of Ehi.

Ehud, ē′-h̆ud (Heb.)—*union; united; strong.*

a "Son of Gera, the Benjamite, a man left-handed." Ehud killed Eglon, the king of Moab, and thus delivered Israel (Judg. 3:15-30). b A son of Bilhan, and a Benjamite (I Chron. 7:10).

Meta. Faith greatly strengthened by being unified consciously with Spirit, or with spiritual Truth. (Benjamites belong to the faith faculty in man.)

Eker, ē′-kẽr (Heb.)—*plucked up; uprooted; eradicated; rendered barren; useless; transplanted; foreign; foreigner,* i. e., *one transplanted to a foreign soil.*

Son of Ram, descended from Hezron grandson of Judah (I Chron. 2:27).

Meta. A thought or tendency that is a *foreigner;* it is alien in character to the true praise consciousness (Judah) with which it is identified. Ram, father of Eker, means *lifted up, made high, extolled,* and signifies the exalting of true understanding in consciousness. (See ARAM.) Eker, however, suggests an intellectual belief that is accepted by the individual as a true spiritual inspiration, but proves in the end to be *barren;* it brings forth no fruit to eternal life and

good, because it is not really founded in Spirit, but falls short of the Truth.

Ekron, ĕk′-rŏn (Heb.)—*rooting out; extermination; expatriation; migration; naturalization.*

One of the five cities, or states, of the Philistines in Canaan. It was taken by Judah and was allotted to Judah (Judg. 1:18). When the Ark of God was carried by the Philistines to this place, great consternation and trouble were caused (I Sam. 5:10-12).

Meta. The belief of the sense consciousness in man (the Philistines) that nothing is or can be abiding and eternal on earth. This aggregation of thoughts, which Ekron represents, judges according to the outer senses and decides that man is purely human and physical, something entirely unlike and apart from God. It thinks therefore that man must die and go to heaven (*migrate* from this earth), where he will become a citizen of the heavenly kingdom (by *naturalization* only, and not by right of birth). The average Christian does not recognize his divine origin and sonship; he thinks that when he is converted he becomes a child of God by adoption, but he does not seem to consider the fact that he was made in the image and likeness of God in the beginning, and has always been a son even while wasting his substance in "a far country."

When the outer sense man (Philistines) takes over the original spark of divinity in man (the Ark of God) and tries to handle it according to his limited ideas and beliefs, he gets himself into great trouble and affliction; he would be *exterminated* (the Philistines died in great numbers in every place where they took the Ark) if he did not send the Ark quickly from his realm of thought. Where Truth is established, sense beliefs and activities cannot remain; they are rooted out.

Ekronites, ĕk′-rŏn-ītes (Heb.)—*of or belonging to Ekron.*

Inhabitants of Ekron (Josh. 13:3).

Meta. Thoughts and beliefs belonging to the Ekron consciousness in man. (See EKRON.)

Elah, ē′-lăh (Heb.)—*terebinth; oak; so*

called from its strength, hardiness, and size.

a A valley in Judah, where Saul and the men of Israel encamped and fought against the Philistines at the time that David killed Goliath (I Sam. 17:2). **b** Son of Baasha and king of Israel, who was killed by Zimri while in the house of Arza drunk (I Kings 16:8-14). **c** A chief who was descended from Esau (Gen. 36:41). **d** Son of Caleb of the tribe of Judah (I Chron. 4:15). **e** A Benjamite (I Chron. 9:8).

Meta. A consciousness of strength and protection (an oak stands for something very strong and protective). When this thought of strength and protection is based on God, sense errors (the Philistines) are overcome and all is well. When it is based on material beliefs, however, as would be the case with Elah, the drunken king of Israel who was assassinated, and the Elah who was descended from Esau (Esau signifies the physical in man), this thought of strength and protection would be limited; it would be likely to fail one at the very time that one needed it most.

Elam, ē'-lăm (Heb.)—*hidden; concealed; remote time; eternal; everlasting; fully developed; a young man; puberty.*

a Son of Shem (Gen. 10:22). **b** A country, or a people that was descended from Shem (Gen. 14:1). Elam is mentioned in Isaiah 11:11 as a place whence the Lord "will set his hand again the second time to recover the remnant of his people." **c** A Levite (I Chron. 26:3). **d** A Benjamite (I Chron. 8:24). **e** A man whose "children" returned from the Babylonian captivity (Ezra 2:7). **f** A priest who helped praise and give thanks at the dedication of the Temple after it was rebuilt (Neh. 12:42). **g** A chief of the people who joined Nehemiah in sealing the covenant (Neh. 10:14).

Meta. Thoughts of the abidingness, resourcefulness, and creative power of Truth, of that which is of God—Spirit (*eternal, everlasting, fully developed, a young man, puberty*). The natural man may not know the Truth of his being;

it may be *hidden, concealed* under the *débris* of sense thought and belief. It will come to light in due time, however, and will bring forth its fruit of perfection in the life of every individual.

Elamites, ē'-lăm-ītes (Heb.)—*of or pertaining to Elam.*

Descendants of Shem, and inhabitants of the country of Elam, who were settled in Samaria by the Assyrian king after he had carried the Israelites away captive (Ezra 4:9; Acts 2:9).

Meta. Thoughts, beliefs, and activities belonging to the Elam consciousness in man, and dominated by error views concerning life and Truth. (See ELAM.)

Elasah, ĕl'-ä-săh (Heb.) — *God is maker; whom God has made; God is creator,* i. e., *produced from Himself.*

a Son of Pashhur, a priest who had a foreign wife after the return from the Babylonian captivity (Ezra 10:22). **b** The son of Shaphan, by whom Jeremiah sent a letter to the Jewish elders and priests whom Nebuchadnezzar had carried away captive to Babylon (Jer. 29:3).

Meta. The innate belief in the religious nature of man that God is the maker of the universe, in that the universe came forth from and is an expression of God; that God is guiding and directing all things; and that He will bring order out of confusion and peace and good out of seeming chaos and evil. This inner assurance that all is well, or will be well in the end, comforts and strengthens the religious thoughts of man when they are apparently bound in the darkness of sense: Elasah was sent by Jeremiah to the captive Jews in Babylon to encourage them to make the best of existing conditions and to go on increasing and multiplying, to the end that they should be released and brought again to their own land. (Jer. 29:1-14.)

Elath, ē'-lăth (Heb.)—*oak trees; terebinth trees; grove of strong trees; palm grove; aggregation of strength.*

A place that the Children of Israel passed while on their way from Egypt to Canaan (Deut. 2:8). It was a city of Edom, a port on an eastern gulf of the Red Sea. In II Samuel 8:14 we read that all the Edomites became subject to David.

Under Joram, Edom revolted from Judah and made a king for itself (II Kings 8:20). Elath was rebuilt and was restored to Judah by Azariah, or Uzziah, king of Judah (II Kings 14:22). Later it was captured by the Syrians; the Jews were driven from it "and the Syrians came to Elath, and dwelt there, unto this day" (II Kings 16:6).

Meta. A strengthening of the whole nervous system (*aggregation of strength, oak trees*). A tree is a connecting link between the heavens and the earth, the formless and the formed. The nervous system in man connects the spiritual and the physical; it is in very close union with the mental—thoughts, or their impressions, are carried over the nerves— and it is by means of thinking that we contact both the physical and the spiritual. By the inner assurance of victory through Christ over error (*palm grove;* palms denote victory) and faith in God as a strong, protecting power and abiding place (*oaks*), the children of Israel (our higher, religious thoughts and tendencies) are helped on their way toward the Promised Land (the redemption of the body).

When man's nervous system is vitalized and strengthened, a conflict sometimes follows between the physical, the mental, and the spiritual as to which is to profit most by this new inflow of life and energy. Elath belonged to Edom, the physical. (Man in his unawakened state looks upon the nervous system as mortal and corruptible, just as he does the remainder of his organism.) Elath was captured and rebuilt by Judah, who symbolizes praise and prayer. (The religious and spiritual nature lays hold of this new quickening life as its own, and utilizes it to its good.) Then the Syrians took Elath and possessed it (the Syrians belong to the sense mental realm in man).

El–berith (A. V., the god Berith), ĕl'–bē'–rĭth (Heb.)—*the mighty league; covenant god; unto the covenant; a covenant; a league.*

The god Berith (Judg. 9:46); the same as Baal–berith.

Meta. See BAAL–BERITH.

El–bethel, ĕl'–bĕth'–ĕl (Heb.)—*unto the house of God; toward Bethel; strength of the house of God; the God of Bethel.*

The name that Jacob called the place where he built an altar because God had been revealed to him there (Gen. 35:7); it was at Luz, or Bethel, that God appeared to him in a dream when he had fled from Esau.

Meta. The revelation from within that the true origin of man is spiritual, that God dwells in man and reveals Himself when man comes to the place in consciousness where he is willing to give up the lower to the higher, the personal to the impersonal, the animal to the divine (builds an altar to Jehovah). Man is the house (temple) of God, and he is greatly strengthened when he perceives this part of Truth.

Eldaah, ĕl-dā'-ăh (Heb.)—*whom God has called; invocation of God; knowledge of God; God of understanding; wisdom of God.*

Son of Midian and grandson of Abraham and Keturah (Gen. 25:4).

Meta. A central thought that, although it belongs to the sense phase of man's consciousness, responds in measure to the quickening presence of Spirit (*whom God has called*). It perceives that God is the source of understanding (*God of understanding, wisdom of God*), yet it does not bring forth definite fruit in consciousness. (Eldaah had no descendants, so far as is known.)

Eldad, ĕl'-dăd (Heb.)—*whom God loveth; loved of God; stirred by God; nourished by God.*

One of the seventy elders of Israel whom Moses chose, at the word of Jehovah, to help him "bear the burden of the people" (Num. 11:16, 17). Eldad did not go with Moses to the tent of meeting, but the Spirit of the Lord came upon him in the camp, and he prophesied there; whereupon Moses expressed a desire that all Jehovah's people (meaning the Israelites) might be prophets and that Jehovah would put His Spirit upon them all (Num. 11:26-29).

Meta. The love of God, or the perception of God as love. Belief in law (Moses) in its apparently hard aspect of cause and effect, and its outer "thou shalt," and "thou shalt not," is not sufficient to meet the needs of our thought people. A knowledge of God as love is necessary, that a right adjustment may be made in consciousness and that the individual may be *stirred by God,* caused to become loving and kind.

Love stays in the camp; it abides among the thought people, in the body consciousness, that are being lifted to higher ideals. Love is not supposed to be a prophet, an expounder of Truth. It is looked upon by man in his first awakening to spirituality as being a negative quality and as being something personal; but when it is perceived to be divine, universal, it pours out its rays of light and healing to the whole being, and Moses (the directive phase of the outworking of the law) recognizes its true worth and power. By the action of the law in union with love, a desire is awakened throughout the individual that all the divine qualities and the spiritual thoughts in him may perceive their rightful places in Spirit and actively aid in bringing about the spiritualization of the whole man.

elders (I Kings 8:1).

Meta. The assembling of the "elders of Israel, and all the heads of the tribes, the princes of the fathers' *houses* of the children of Israel, unto king Solomon in Jerusalem" signifies a drawing together in conscious unity of all the intelligent directive powers of the spiritual self, to the standard of peace and harmony.

This process may take place without the conscious mind's understanding its import. The whole consciousness is made up of objective and subjective thoughts and their results. Like a chemical solution, they go through changes on the subjective side that are observed in their outer appearance only, and but dimly understood.

Elead, ē'-lĕ-ăd (Heb.)—*duration of God; God's time; witness of God; testament of God; beauty of God; perfection of God; praise of God.*

A son, or descendant, of Ephraim. He was killed by the men of Gath, "because they came down to take away their cattle" (I Chron. 7:21).

Meta. The understanding that the will of man (Ephraim stands for the will) has its inception in God, is in truth spiritual, and in its true expression is perfect and enduring, even as God is perfect and enduring. In this phase of unfoldment the individual does not really comprehend the necessity for consciously unifying his will with the divine will that it may express spiritually; he applies the Truth as it is revealed to him to the human aspect of the will as directed by the personal man. The result is that, because of the warring of the senses (men of Gath—Philistines) against the better judgment of the will, the substance and strength (cattle) of the will are taken away from it and this phase of it, which is represented by Elead, dies —that is, it sinks back into the subconscious mind until further spiritual unfoldment in the individual makes possible its reappearance and its perfect development.

Eleadah, ē'-lĕ-ā'-dăh (Heb.)—*whom God puts on,* i. e., *fills and dons with Himself; whom God adorns,* i. e., *brings to time of fullness of perfection; eternity of God; precept of God; ordained of God; witness of God.*

A son, or descendant, of Ephraim (I Chron. 7:20).

Meta. The individual will (Ephraim signifies the will) fully unified with and expressing the divine, having the quality of Godlikeness, and being eternal even as God is eternal. (The name Eleadah is prophetic, as many of the names of the Old Testament are, inasmuch as the Truth for which it stands was not fulfilled then but is to be established perfectly in individual consciousness when man unfolds spiritually to the place where this is possible.)

Elealeh, ē-lĕ-ā'-lĕh (Heb.)—*whither God ascends; whereto God arises; ascent of God; God is exalted.*

A city of Moab that was rebuilt by the Reubenites and was retained by them as a portion of their inheritance (Num. 32:3, 37); it was on the east side of the Jordan. Elealeh is named in Isaiah 15:4, 16:9, and Jeremiah 48:34 in prophecies against Moab.

Meta. A state of consciousness that, though of Moab (carnal mind), exalts God, Spirit, Truth, and so passes into the possession of the Reubenites, who signify discernment, sight, faith. This state of consciousness is thus reëstablished on a higher basis.

It is the seemingly good in the carnal mind that causes us to mourn its downfall (see the prophecies in Isaiah and Jeremiah concerning Moab). But we should not be troubled to see the carnal mind go, since all really true thoughts and aspirations of every phase of our consciousness will be preserved and carried to higher planes of activity, even to the spiritual plane.

Eleasah, ē-lē'-ă-săh (Heb.)—*God is maker; whom God has made; God is creator.*

a Son of Helez, of the tribe of Judah (I Chron. 2:39). **b** A Benjamite, son of Raphah, in descent from Saul and Jonathan (I Chron. 8:37).

Meta. The recognition by the individual that God, Spirit, is the source of deliverance, strength, healing, and of true greatness in both the inner and the outer man (*God is maker, whom God has made, God is creator*). Helez signifies deliverance and strength through praise (Judah). Raphah gives the thought of a hero, tall, gigantic; also of healing.

Eleazar, ē-lē-ā'-zär (Heb.)—*God has surrounded; God succors; God is helper; whom God has helped; help of God.*

a Son of Aaron. He succeeded his father as high priest of Israel (Ex. 6:23; 20:25, 28). **b** There are several other Israelitish men by this name (I Sam. 7:1; II Sam. 23:9; I Chron. 23:21; Ezra 8:33; Neh. 12:42; Matt. 1:15).

Meta. Spiritual strength through the individual's recognition of God as his supporting, sustaining power (*God is helper*). This becomes the presiding, directive faculty of a new state of consciousness. (See AARON.)

El–Elohe–Israel, ĕl–ê–lō'–hĕ–ĭş'–rå-ĕl (Heb.)—*unto the God of Israel; Elohe (Elohim) God of Israel; mighty God of Israel; strength of the God of Israel; Elohim He of Israel.*

The name of an altar that Jacob built on the ground that he bought from the children of Hamor the father of Shechem (Gen. 33:20).

Meta. The children of Hamor pertain to the earthly, carnal consciousness in man. The altar symbolizes the giving up of the "mind of the flesh" in individual consciousness to the spiritual, that the spiritual may prevail throughout and God alone may be recognized. Thus Israel (the true, spiritual thoughts, beliefs, and faculties) may indeed become a prince, prevailing and ruling with God, having power with both God and man; that is, having power for good in every phase of the consciousness, from the very highest to the seemingly most material plane.

Eleph, ē'-lĕph (Heb.)—*union; power; strength; instruction; learning; one thousand, i. e., a very great number; an ox, i. e., one broken and trained,* symbol of directed strength.

A city of Benjamin (Josh. 18:28).

Meta. Union with infinite strength, through understanding and faith. (*An ox* stands for physical strength; Benjamin relates to an active faith; *learning* bespeaks understanding.)

Elhanan, ĕl-hā'-năn (Heb.)—*God is gracious; grace of God; whom God has bestowed; compassion of God; merciful God.*

a A Beth–lehemite warrior in the time of David (II Sam. 21:19; I Chron. 20:5). He killed the brother of Goliath the Gittite. **b** One of David's guard of thirty valiant men (II Sam. 23:24); he also was of Beth–lehem.

Meta. A gracious, kindly, loving attitude of mind that emanates from God, Spirit, and is established in substance (Beth–lehem). This gives courage and fearlessness in combating seeming error.

Eli, ē'-lī (Heb.)—*ascent; summit; apex; a going up; exaltation; supreme; highest; Most High; my God.*

a High priest of Israel at the time of Samuel's birth (I Sam. 1:9—4:18). Eli was not of the regular line of high-priesthood, but was descended from a younger son of Aaron, Ithamar. It is not known just why this change in the high-priesthood was made. When Solomon came to the throne the position of high priest was given over fully to Zadok, who was descended from Aaron through Eleazar, an older son. (See ABIATHAR.) **b** Eli, meaning *my God*, was an exclamation that Jesus uttered while on the cross (Matt. 27:46). In Mark 15:34, Eloi. (See ELOI.)

Meta. The intellect under spiritual discipline. Our first unfoldment is always through the intellect. We get an intellectual concept of Truth and in due season clothe it with substance and life. While Eli (meaning *going up, ascent*) is typical of the phase of man's consciousness that is always seeking spiritual progress, yet true progress cannot be made by a merely intellectual understanding of Truth. Eli's eyes waxed old; he did not perceive the true aspect of Truth. He was not really progressive. The progressive man is always looking for new aspects of Truth; he is expecting to get a fuller understanding of spiritual laws and of their application. He knows that he will grow, that he will unfold by applying the law, that he will reach the *summit,* and he is always eager and active in reforming his thoughts and his habits.

Eliab, ē-lī'-ăb (Heb.)—*God is Father; strength of the Father.*

a Son of Helon of the tribe of Zebulun. He was one of the men who helped Moses and Aaron to number Israel (Num. 1:9). **b** The father of Dathan and Abiram of the tribe of Reuben (Num. 16:1). **c** An elder brother of David's (I Sam. 16:6). **d** There were others by this name, also (I Chron. 6:27; 12:9; 15:20).

Meta. That in our religious and spiritual nature which takes cognizance of the Author of being (*God is Father*) as the source of strength (*strength of the Father*).

We are apt to think of outer manifestation rather than of inner spiritual capacities. Samuel thought that Eliab, the first son of Jesse and elder brother of David, would surely be the chosen of Jehovah because of his beautiful countenance and his great stature and kingly bearing, but the Lord told Samuel not to judge by appearances.

Eliada, ē-lī'-ă-då (Heb.)—*God knows; God of knowledge; power of understanding; known of God.*

a A son of David (II Sam. 5:16); he is called Beeliada in I Chronicles 14:7. **b** A Benjamite, a mighty man of valor in the reign of Jehoshaphat, king of Judah (II Chron. 17:17).

Meta. Man's awakening, through the consciousness of love and active faith (David and Benjamin), to the understanding that God, Divine Mind, is the source of all knowing, of all knowledge. The loving (David) thought in this awakening bespeaks the idea that God cares, as well as knows.

Eliahba, ē-lī'-ăh-bå (Heb.)—*God hides; whom God conceals; hidden by God.*

A Shaalbonite, a mighty warrior of David's (II Sam. 23:32).

Meta. The concealing of divine love in consciousness from its enemies, the sense thoughts, desires, and activities of the carnal mind. By the wisdom and cunning of the outer senses (Shaalbim, whence Eliahba came, and meaning *place of foxes*) we cannot search out God or come into an understanding of our divine qualities. Our divine qualities are *hidden by God*—by the very fact that they are spiritual and not material. This natural concealment of the spiritual from the material is one of divine love's strong, protective, conquering powers (Eliahba was one of David's mighty warriors).

Eliakim, ē-lī'-ă-kĭm (Heb.)—*God sets up; whom God has established; God of raising,* i. e., *in judgment; raised of God.*

There were several Israelites by this name (II Kings 23:34; Neh. 12:41; Isa. 22:20; Matt. 1:13; Luke 3:30).

Meta. The will (which is of God) taking command. This command may be of oneself or of others; also a rising from a negative attitude of thoughts and a becoming positive in one's judgment (*God sets up, God of raising,* i. e., *in judgment, raised of God, whom God has established*). All power to be or to do is of God; yet the individual may use his power for good or for ill, according to whether he acts from the sense or from true understanding. Eliakim, or Jehoiakim, king of Judah, used his executive power to promote error; he "did that which was evil in the sight of Jehovah" (II Kings 23:37).

In the subconsciousness there are both good and evil until the seeming evil has been cleansed away by the power of Spirit. Therefore we need to be thoroughly purified of selfishness and of every error tendency and become established in love and Truth, that we may be positive in the good and use the power and judgment of God within us in righteous, constructive ways only.

Eliam, ē-lī'-ăm (Heb.)—*God of the people; God's people; who are the people of God.*

a Father of Bathsheba, who was the wife of Uriah the Hittite. Bathsheba afterward became David's wife and the mother of Solomon (II Sam. 11:3). **b** One of David's mighty men, son of Ahithophel the Gilonite (II Sam. 23:34).

Meta. Our true thoughts are *God's people.* They are gathered together and established in consciousness by divine light and power.

Eliasaph, ē-lī'-ă-săph (Heb.)—*God adds; God increases; whom God enlarges,* i. e., *adds to; added of God; God gathers together,* i. e., *sweeps or scrapes together that which was formerly scattered.*

a Son of Reuel and prince of the children of Gad at the time that Moses and Aaron numbered the Israelites in the wilderness, on the way to Canaan (Num. 2:14). **b** Son of Lael, and "prince of the fathers' house of the Gershonites" (Num. 3:24).

Meta. God, Divine Mind, is the power that increases and multiplies true ideas in consciousness. Our ability, or power, to concentrate, to gather our ideas and centralize them, control them, also comes from the one Mind—God.

Eliashib, ē-lī'-ă-shĭb (Heb.)—*God restores; whom God restores; God of restitution; requited of God; restored of God.*

a A high priest at the time that the walls of Jerusalem and the Temple were rebuilt under Nehemiah (Neh. 3:1). **b** A priest in David's time (I Chron. 24:12). **c** Others of the same name (I Chron. 3:24; Ezra 10:6).

Meta. The men named Eliashib signify thoughts in the religious and spiritual nature of man that assure him of his ultimate return to the original sinless, whole, perfect state (*God restores, God of restitution*) in which he was created—idealized in the mind of the Father-Mother God. These men also signify the assurance that the law of compensation, the law of sowing and reaping, cause and effect, is divine (*requited of God*). Man should not look to man, but he should look to God, for all things, since in reality all comes from God—all things come about by exact law.

Eliathah, ē-lī'-ă-thăh (Heb.)—*God has come; God is come; to whom God comes.*

Son of Heman, a singer or musician during David's reign. He with his sons and brothers, twelve in number, had the twentieth course in serving in the house of God (I Chron. 25:4, 27).

Meta. A realization and expression of the presence of God as divine harmony (*God is come;* a musician or singer).

Elidad, ē-lī'-dăd (Heb.)—*God is love; God loves; loved of God; God's beloved; God nourishes.*

Son of Chislon, a Benjamite. He was the prince chosen from this tribe to help divide the land of Canaan among the Israelites (Num. 34:21).

Meta. A keen discrimination and insight into Truth, and into man's relation to the various phases of Truth. This spiritual insight is the product of an active faith (Benjamin) and love (*God is love, God loves*) working in unison in man's consciousness; it is a great factor in helping to establish in their rightful places in the land of Canaan (the body consciousness) the true Israelitish thoughts, aspirations, qualities, and powers through which the body is to be redeemed, raised to spiritual expression and manifestation.

Eliehoenai (A. V., Elihoenai), ĕl'-ĭē-hō-ē'-nā-i (Heb.)—*unto Jehovah are mine eyes; toward Jah are my eyes; to*

Jehovah are mine eyes.

An Israelite, a descendant of Pahathmoab. He returned under Ezra from the Babylonian captivity (Ezra 8:4).

Meta. The turning of the attention from the outer world of manifestation to Jehovah, the Christ, or Father within one, as the power that delivers from sense bondage and saves to the uttermost—brings again to the Promised Land.

Eliel, ē-lĭ′-ĕl (Heb.)—*my God is God; God of gods; power of God; exaltation of God.*

The name of several Israelitish men (I Chron. 5:24; 6:34; 8:20, 22; 11:46, 47; 12:11; 15:9; II Chron. 31:13).

Meta. The strength, the power, the almightiness of God.

Elienai, ē-lĭ-ē′-nā-i (Heb.)—*unto Jehovah are mine eyes; toward Jehovah are my eyes; to Jehovah are mine eyes.*

A chief man of Benjamin who lived in Jerusalem (I Chron. 8:20). This name is a shortened form of Eliehoenai.

Meta. The attention turned to Jehovah as the saving power of man. (See ELIEHOENAI.)

Eliezer, ē-lĭ-ē′-zēr (Heb.)—*God of help; God my help; God of succor; God is help.*

a Abraham's servant, or steward, Eliezer of Damascus (Gen. 15:2). **b** The name of several Israelitish men (I Chron. 7:8; 15:24; 27:16; II Chron. 20:37; Ezra 8:16; 10:18, 23, 31; Luke 3:29). The last mentioned was one given in the genealogy of Jesus. Lazarus is a form of this name.

Meta. A belief in God as one's sustaining power, as the power that relieves one in distress and assists one to better conditions and to higher attainments (*God my help, God is help;* see Exod. 18:4).

Elihoreph, ĕl-ĭ-hō′-rĕph (Heb.)—*autumn God; God of autumn; God of harvest; God my recompense.*

Son of Shisha (I Kings 4:3). He was a scribe in Solomon's reign over Israel.

Meta. God is the power that brings our thoughts to fruition. He is the source of our bountiful supply and the power by which our good is gathered to us—is made manifest for our use.

Elihu, ē-lĭ′-hū (Heb.)—*my God is that which is; whose God is He; my God is He; God is He,* i. e., *Jehovah.*

a Son of Barachel the Buzite, one of Job's friends (Job 32:2-6). **b** An ancestor of Samuel's (I Sam. 1:1). **c** The name of other Israelitish men (I Chron. 12:20; 26:7; 27:18).

Meta. Elihu of the book of Job represents the Holy Spirit. The name Elihu also signifies the recognition by man that his true inner self is Spirit.

Elijah (in A. V., Matt. 11:14 and 17:3, Elias), ē-lĭ′-jăh (Heb.)—*Jehovah is God; my God is Jah; God of Jehovah; Jehovah God.*

A great prophet of Israel (I Kings 17; 18; 19; II Kings 1:3—2:14; Mal. 4:5).

Meta. The spiritual I AM of man's consciousness. Elijah on Mount Carmel (I Kings 18:19) represents the I AM in realization of its unfettered power.

Elijah championed the cause of God with such enthusiasm that he became violent and destructive. This was the Jezebel side of his character. But he was willing to be instructed. He slowly learned the lesson that one must receive the kingdom of God as a little child. He started out with the roar of the whirlwind, and ended with the whisper of the "still small voice."

II Kings 2:1-11 signifies changes of consciousness in the individual in his development and regeneration. Elijah (the spiritual I AM) represents the guardian and administrator of the divine law.

Elijah was taken by a whirlwind into heaven: the positive or dominant element of the I AM (Elijah) must be taken by the Lord into a state of peace and harmony (heaven); the fiery or destructive tendency of Elijah must be blotted out by the mildness and sweet-tempered obedience of Elisha.

Elijah, with Elisha, went from Gilgal when he was to be taken up into heaven (II Kings 2:1). One meaning of Gilgal is *rolling away;* it signifies the total denial of sense bondage. Denial of sense bondage must be followed by positive affirmations of Truth, accompanied by obedience and the quiet resolution to go forward in spiritual development (symbolized by Elisha). This results in the permanent establishment of higher states of consciousness—as man demonstrates more of his inherent powers.

Elika, ĕl'-ĭ-kȧ (Heb.)—*God is rejecter; God his rejecter; rejected of God.*

A Harodite who belonged to David's guard, named in II Samuel 23:25. He is omitted in the same list of men given in I Chron. 11:26-47.

Meta. Elimination of fear (a Harodite is a native of Harod, or one belonging to Harod, and Harod means *fear, terror, trembling*). It is fear that is *rejected of God,* or in other words is eliminated by Truth.

Elim, ē'-lĭm (Heb.)—*terebinths; palm trees; trees; oaks.*

The second camping place of the Israelites after they crossed the Red Sea: "And they came to Elim, where were twelve springs of water, and threescore and ten palm trees: and they encamped there by the waters" (Exod. 15:27).

Meta. A realization of fullness of life, strength, and cleansing Truth for the whole man; also a realization of victory (twelve is a number representing fullness in the spiritual. Springs of water stand for life and cleansing; *oaks* signify strength and protection; and *palm trees* denote victory).

Elimelech, ē-lĭm'-ē-lĕch (Heb.)—*God is king; God the king; my God is king.*

An Israelite of Beth–lehem–judah, and husband of Naomi (Ruth 1:2). Because of a famine in the land of Judah he took his wife and two sons to live in the country of Moab, and he died there.

Meta. The consciousness of the soul (Naomi) that *God is king.* (See NAOMI and CHILION.)

Elioenai, ē-lĭ-ō-ē'-nāi (Heb.)—*to Jah are mine eyes; toward Jehovah are my eyes.*

a Son of Becher and grandson of Benjamin (I Chron. 7:8). **b** The name of other Israelites (I Chron. 3:23; 4:36); a form of Eliehoenai.

Meta. Thoughts of the religious or spiritual consciousness looking Godward —beholding Jehovah, Christ, within one.

"Look unto me, and be ye saved, all the ends of the earth; for I am God, and there is none else" (Isa. 45:22). "Thou wilt keep *him* in perfect peace, *whose* mind *is* stayed *on thee*" (Isa. 26:3).

Eliphal, ĕl'-ĭ-phăl (Heb.)—*whom God judges; judgment of God; God is my judge.*

Son of Ur (I Chron. 11:35). He was one of David's guard of valiant men, and is called Eliphelet the son of Ahasbai, in II Samuel 23:34.

Meta. The recognition by love (David) that God is the true judge of His people—that true judgment, discernment, discrimination, and justice are spiritual and lead to salvation always. (See ELIPHELET.)

Eliphaz, ĕl'-ĭ-phăz (Heb.)—*God is purification; God is dispenser; God of strength; whom God makes strong.*

a Son of Esau, by Adah, the daughter of Elon the Hittite (Gen. 36:4). **b** The Temanite, one of Job's three friends, and supposed to have been descended from the son of Esau by this name (Job 2:11).

Meta. Teman refers to the *southern quarter,* or subconscious realm in man. Eliphaz the Temanite signifies a thought of strength and of purification that springs from the subconsciousness. This thought, however, does not measure up to spiritual Truth: Eliphaz did not prove himself able to help Job. But the thought that Eliphaz represents realizes that true cleansing, as well as strength and supply to meet man's needs, come from God (*God is purification, God is dispenser, God of strength*). The Eliphaz thought is capable of unfolding into greater understanding and fruitfulness, and so we find that Job, after receiving the light, prayed for his friends.

Eliphelehu (A. V., Elipheleh), ē-lĭph'-ē-lĕh-ū (Heb.)—*whom God makes distinguished; distinguished by God; who is consecrated to God; a miracle of God.*

One who played the harp when David had the Ark brought up to Jerusalem from the house of Obed–edom (I Chron. 15:18, 21).

Meta. He *who is consecrated to God* in thought and act is in turn exalted by

God, is distinguished above his fellows. This is true also of our inner thoughts and activities that give their love and substance to the building up of our spiritual consciousness; they produce a harmony, a joy, and a melody that is heaven; they attain a high place within us in establishing the divine nature throughout our whole being—this is the significance of Eliphelehu.

Eliphelet (in A. V., II Sam. 5:16, Eliphalet), ē-lĭph'-ĕ-lĕt (Heb.)—*God is deliverance; God is escape; God of deliverance.*

a A son of David (II Sam. 5:16). b One of David's guard (II Sam. 23:34). c Other Israelitish men (I Chron. 3:6; 8:39; Ezra 8:13; 10:33).

Meta. Deliverance from error and its results—salvation—is from God; it is accomplished by the power of Spirit. It is not by personal might or power that we are enabled to obtain the good that is our divine birthright, "but by my Spirit, saith Jehovah of hosts" (Zech. 4:6).

Elisabeth, ē-lĭṣ'-ă-bĕth (Gk. from Heb.)—*my God is my oath,* i. e., *a worshiper of God; God of the seven; God of the oath; God's oath.*

Wife of Zacharias the priest, and mother of John the Baptist (Luke 1:5-57). Elisheba is the same name.

Meta. The soul in the feminine or love consciousness. (See ELISHEBA.)

Elisha (A. V., Luke 4:27, Eliseus), ē-lī'-shȧ (Heb.)—*God is a savior; to whom God gives salvation; God of deliverance; to whom God gives victory; God is rich.*

The man who was appointed prophet in Israel in Elijah's stead (II Kings 2 to 13).

Meta. Spiritual I AM.

The double portion of Elijah's spirit for which Elisha asked is the positive and negative, or "yes" and "no," of Truth. Elisha, the tender, retiring one, needs the ability to say yes and no with all the positiveness of Elijah. He can have this only by perceiving the true character of the change that is taking place in consciousness. Elijah is not taken away but is translated to a more interior plane.

There is opened to the one who goes through this change a conscious unity with spiritual energies of which he has been heretofore ignorant. The chariot and horses represent the vehicles and vital forces that attend the transformation (II Kings 2:11, 12).

Elisha is often referred to by Bible commentators as a forerunner of Jesus. His character and his marvelous works are easily recognized as proceeding from the same spirit that inspired Jesus, and his gentleness and simplicity are paralleled only in the Master.

It is not difficult to see in Elisha an incarnation of the Christ, and he was in a certain degree God manifest. Jesus was a fuller manifestation of the same spirit.

If we admit that Elisha is a type of Christ, that is, the Jehovah, or supreme I AM of man, it should be equally admissible to allow that the other characters in II Kings 5, relating to the healing of Naaman the Syrian, are types of various kinds common to all men. Elisha apparently took no part in the healing, simply directing Naaman to bathe in the Jordan seven times. But there was a deep undercurrent of spiritual power at work in Elisha. He represented the higher self of the Naaman consciousness, which had been quickened. Jesus referred to this in Luke 4:27: "There were many lepers in Israel in the time of Elisha the prophet; and none of them was cleansed, but only Naaman the Syrian."

Elisha's dwelling in Dothan means the spiritual I AM established in the understanding of divine law.

The servant of Elisha represents the outer activity actuated by the spiritual I AM. The servant (thought action, which had its origin in Spirit) became fearful. Our thoughts and words are propelled from the central I AM station, like the arrow from the bow. They are indued with intelligence and power, according to the sending capacity of the I AM. Jesus sent His word and healed the centurion's servant. When we judge by opposing appearances the result is fearfulness or timidity in execution.

Confidence is restored and all enmity is overcome through prayer and meditation. These make contact with the great I AM, Jehovah, and all thought realms are lighted up; the adverse intellect is captured and enlightened, "and the bands of Syria came no more into the land of Israel" (II Kings 6:8-23).

The truth revealed in II Kings 4:1-7 is the increasing power of Spirit. The increase of Spirit is realized in individual consciousness. It is brought about through turning the attention within and acknowledging the reality and power of Spirit.

Elisha (salvation of God) is man's spiritual I AM. The widow symbolizes the state of consciousness that believes in separation from God, or the source of being. The empty "vessels" are the life centers throughout the body consciousness that have been depleted through wrong use of mental powers and functions.

Bringing the vessels into the widow's house and shutting the door symbolizes concentration. Concentration is the result of denial and affirmation (the widow's sons), based upon understanding of man's true being. The "oil" symbolizes the oil of life, the vital fluid that renews and reanimates the body in the regeneration.

Elishah, ē-lī′-shäh (Heb.)—*God firmly establishes; God sets upright; uprightness of God; God saves; God who is a help.*

Son of Javan and grandson of Japheth, who was one of Noah's three sons (Gen. 10:4). In prophesying of the destruction of Tyre, Ezekiel says, "Blue and purple from the isles of Elishah was thine awning" (Ezek. 27:7).

Meta. Even the human reasoning in man acknowledges that God is the saving power of His people (Japheth refers to the intellect, or reason, in man). Javan means *clayey soil, productiveness,* as it relates to the physical and material. The intellectual powers of man are human and they are deceiving, yet they are productive on their own plane, and back of the intellect is that which knows God to be the one true, helping, sustaining, saving power in man. This knowing force is represented by Elishah.

Elishama, ē-lĭsh′-ȧ-má (Heb.)—*whom God hears; God of hearing,* i. e., *understanding; God is hearer.*

a A son of David (II Sam. 5:16).
b A priest during the reign of Jehoshaphat, king of Judah (II Chron. 17:8).
c The name of other Israelitish men (Num. 1:10; I Chron. 2:41).

Meta. The inner assurance that God hears and answers the true desires of His people, and that Spirit is the source of true understanding.

Elishaphat, ē-lĭsh′-ȧ-phăt (Heb.)—*God of judgment; whom God judges; whom God sets upright; God is defender.*

Son of Zichri; he was one of the captains of hundreds, who assisted Jehoiada the priest to dethrone Athaliah and to put Joash, the rightful king, on the throne of Judah (II Chron. 23:1).

Meta. Spiritual judgment and adjustment active in the inner life force of man's organism (the kingdom of Judah represents the inner life force, or vitality).

Elisheba, ē-lĭsh′-ĕ-bá (Heb.)—*my God is my oath,* i. e., *a worshiper of God; God of the seven; God of the oath; God of the covenant; God's oath.*

Aaron's wife, and daughter of Amminadab (Exod. 6:23). Elisabeth is the same name.

Meta. The full assurance in the soul or feminine, love consciousness, that God is a God of Truth and keeps His promises to man; in other words, the inner conviction of the soul that the working out of the law of life and Truth in man's consciousness is inevitable and sure.

Elishua, ĕl-ĭ-shṳ′-á (Heb.)—*God is a savior; to whom God gives salvation; God of deliverance; to whom God gives victory; God is rich.*

Son of David (II Sam. 5:15); he is called Elishama in I Chronicles 3:6.

Meta. The understanding of love (David) that true riches are from Spirit; also that deliverance from all error, and help of every kind that pertains to salvation, are from the same source. (See ELISHAMA.)

Eliud, ē-lī′-ŭd (Heb.)—*God of Judah;*

God of the Jews; God of majesty; God of celebration; God my praise.

Son of Achim and father of Eleazar, in the genealogy of Jesus (Matt. 1:14).

Meta. Praise and exaltation of God, Spirit, as being in authority, as being King of Kings and Lord of Lords. This attitude of mind is necessary that the Christ may be born into one's consciousness.

Elizaphan, ē-lĭz'-ă-phăn (Heb.)—*God of the left side, i. e., the north; God of the hidden; God of concealment; God is protector; hidden of God; protected of God.*

a Son of Uzziel, a prince of the Kohathites (Num. 3:30). **b** Son of Parnach and a prince of the tribe of Zebulun (Num. 34:25). **c** The father of Shimri and Jeuel, Levites who aided in cleansing the "house of Jehovah" (II Chron. 29:13, 15).

Meta. The inner assurance of divine protection and safety through putting away error and doing right (cleansing the Temple).

Elizur, ē-lī'-zŭr (Heb.)—*God is a rock; God is a refuge, i. e., stable, sure, a bulwark of strength.*

Son of Shedeur of the tribe of Reuben (Num. 1:5). He helped to number the Israelites while they were in the wilderness on their way to the Promised Land.

Meta. The spiritual insight that discerns God as a rock, a sure, immovable foundation of strength, protection, and Truth, upon which man builds his spiritual consciousness, to eternal life and peace. (Reuben is faith in its aspect of discernment, sight; Shedeur, father of Elizur, means *shedder of light*.)

Elkanah, ĕl'-kă-năh (Heb.)—*whom God has founded; God has created; possessed of God; ransomed by God.*

a A Levite, of the hill country of Ephraim, husband of Hannah and father of Samuel the prophet (I Sam. 1:1). **b** A son of Korah of the Levites (Exod. 6:24). **c** Three other Levites by this name are mentioned in I Chronicles 9:16; 12:6; 15:23. **d** Second to King Ahaz of Judah, and slain by Zichri, a mighty man of Ephraim (II Chron. 28:7).

Meta. The understanding by man that he is from God, that his inheritance is from God, that he does not selfishly own anything, but that God possesses all and all that the Father has is man's.

Elkoshite, ĕl'-kŏsh-īte (Heb.)—*bowed of God; my bow is God; inclined of God.*

A native of Elkosh (Nah. 1:1); "Nahum the Elkoshite."

Meta. My defense, might, power, are of God, Spirit (*my bow is God;* a bow represents the power of the will to act and to direct the consciousness). My willingness to do God's will is also the result of the activity of Spirit in my consciousness (*inclined of God*).

Ellasar, ĕl'-lă-sär (Heb.)—*strong rebellion; oath of Assyria; oak of Assyria.*

Either a city or a tract of country in Asia. It was ruled over by Arioch, one of the four kings who later took Lot captive and were defeated and slain by Abraham (Gen. 14:1).

Meta. A state of consciousness whose central, controlling thought and belief is that for which Arioch stands. (See ARIOCH.) It does not look to Spirit for its strength and power, but trusts in "the mind of the flesh."

Elmadam (A. V., Elmodam), ĕl-mā'-dăm (Gk. from Heb.)—*God's measure; power of extension; unlimited measure; measured of God.*

Son of Er and father of Sosam, in the genealogy of Jesus (Luke 3:28).

Meta. The enlarging of the consciousness so that it may comprehend something of the immeasurable greatness of God.

Elnaam, ĕl'-nă-ăm (Heb.)—*God is pleasant; sweetness of God; delight of God; beauty of God; grace of God.*

Father of Jeribai and Joshaviah, two of David's mighty warriors (I Chron. 11:46).

Meta. The spiritual joy, satisfaction, delight, and fair-minded judgment that adhere to the will ruling in love (David). These qualities of mind aid in supporting and protecting the ruling love idea in consciousness and in causing it to be victorious over opposing sense thoughts and activities.

Elnathan, ĕl-nā'-thăn (Heb.) — *bestowed of God; God gives; given of God; God's gift, i. e., conscience that God* *bestows.*

a Grandfather of Jehoiachin, king of Judah, and son of Achbor (II Kings 24:8). He "made intercession to the king that he would not burn the roll" that contained Jeremiah's prophecies, but the king would not listen to him (Jer. 36:12, 25). **b** There were other Israelitish men by this name also (Ezra 8:16).

Meta. The *conscience that God bestows*—the inner intuition, discrimination, and sense of judgment that are *given of God* to man to enable him to know the right course to pursue and also to know the result of willfulness and disobedience.

Eloi (in Heb., Elohi), ē-lō′-ī (Aram.)— *my God; God;* in Aramaic also a contraction of Elias, or Elijah.

Part of the exclamation that Jesus made on the cross, and meaning *my God* (Mark 15:34). In Matthew 27:46 the word is spelled Eli.

Meta. The soul in great stress crying out for God.

Elon, ē′-lŏn (Heb.)—*strong man; an oak; any embodiment of strength, power, or stability.*

a A Zebulunite who judged Israel for ten years (Judg. 12:11). **b** A city of Canaan that was allotted to Dan (Josh. 19:43). **c** A Hittite, father of one of Esau's wives (Gen. 26:34). **d** A son of Zebulun, who was Jacob's son (Gen. 46:14).

Meta. Thoughts of strength and power. In the case of Elon the Hittite, the thought of strength and power is very material and is not enduring. In the significance of Elon who was a judge of Israel, and the city of Elon that belonged to the Israelitish tribe of Dan, the quality of judgment is also present. (See DAN.)

Elon–beth–hanan, ē′-lŏn–bĕth–hā′-năn (Heb.)—*oak of the house of Hanan; strength of the house of grace; strength of the habitation of mercy.*

A place in Palestine that constituted part of one of the commissary districts of Solomon (I Kings 4:9). It is thought to be the same place as the Elon of Joshua 19:43.

Meta. Strength and grace established in consciousness. (See BEN–DEKER, the name of the officer who had charge of this district.)

Elonites, ē′-lŏn-ītes (Heb.)—*belonging to Elon.*

Descendants of Elon, who was a son of Zebulun and grandson of Jacob (Num. 26:26).

Meta. A powerful protective state of consciousness in man that is brought about by his fully trusting in God. (See ELON.)

Eloth, ē′-lŏth (Heb.)—*oak or terebinth grove; grove of strong trees.*

The same place as Elath (I Kings 9: 26; II Chron. 26:2).

Meta. See ELATH.

Elpaal, ĕl-pā′-ăl (Heb.)—*God works; God's work; wages of God; God's reward.*

A Benjamite. His mother's name was Hushim, and his father was Shaharaim (I Chron. 8:11).

Meta. The activity of faith greatly increased in consciousness, and its good results. (Benjamites represent the active faith quality in man, which is the work of God; the wages or reward is a great increase of faith and its activity, and the good that man experiences by acting upon his faith in God, the good.) "Jesus answered and said unto them, This is the work of God, that ye believe on him whom he hath sent" (John 6:29).

El–paran, ĕl-pā′-răn (Heb.)—*terebinth of Paran; oak of Paran; strength of Paran; oak of the region of the caves.*

"The Horites in their mount Seir, unto El–paran, which is by the wilderness" (Gen. 14:6) were defeated by Chedorlaomer, king of Elam. They had been serving him but had rebelled against him.

Meta. The seeming strength of the multitude of man's confused and undisciplined subconscious thoughts and energies, which Paran symbolizes, given over to the furtherance of sense expression. (See PARAN and CHEDORLAOMER.)

Elpelet (A. V., Elpalet), ĕl′-pĕ-lĕt (Heb.)—*God is escape; God is deliverance; deliverance of God.*

David's son (I Chron. 14:5). He is called Eliphelet in I Chronicles 3:6.

Meta. See ELIPHELET.

Elteke (A. V., Eltekeh), ĕl'-tĕ-kē (Heb.)—*observance of God; reverence of God; fear of God; God's observance,* i. e., *care.*

A city in Canaan that was allotted to the Israelitish tribe of Dan and was given over to the Levites of the children of Kohath (Josh. 21:23). The name is spelled Eltekeh in Joshua 19:44.

Meta. Judgment (signified by Dan) is often looked upon by the outer man as punishment sent to him by a personal God because of his sins; thus he fears God (*fear of God*). As man unfolds, however, and begins to understand judgment and justice in a clearer light, he reverences divine law and ceases to fear. This *reverence* and worship of the one Mind, Spirit, leads to a conception of the loving *care* of God for mankind. Thus the individual experiences more and more of grace and mercy in judgment, and less of seeming punishment.

Eltekon, ĕl'-tĕ-kŏn (Heb.)—*God makes straight; God sets upright,* i. e., *establishes in order; God's precept; founded by God.*

A city in the hill country of Judah (Josh. 15:59).

Meta. An aggregation of thoughts in consciousness that is based upon divine principle (*founded by God*). This group of thoughts is centered in the assurance that Principle, God, is perfectly upright, correct, just, unchangeable, and that Spirit constantly works in the universe and man to establish in order, to make straight, all persons, all things (*God makes straight, God sets upright,* i. e., *establishes in order*).

Eltolad, ĕl-tō'-lăd (Heb.)—*begotten of God; born of God; God's generation.*

A city of Judah, toward the border of Edom in the south (Josh. 15:30); later it was allotted to Simeon (Josh. 19:4).

Meta. "As many as received him, to them gave he the right to become children of God, *even* to them that believe on his name: who were born [begotten, margin], not of blood, nor of the will of the flesh, nor of the will of man, but of God" (John 1:12, 13). "Having been

begotten again, not of corruptible seed, but of incorruptible, through the word of God, which liveth and abideth" (I Pet. 1:23).

Through praise and prayer (Judah) a new spiritual state of consciousness is born in us. When new ideas of Truth are begotten in us by the creative power of the word of God, we become more closely unified with Spirit in our thoughts and the very cells of our organism are renewed accordingly. This is a step in the process of regeneration, the new birth, and it will continue until we become wholly new creatures in Christ Jesus, until even the flesh body is spiritualized and redeemed from all possibility of corruption. This is our being begotten and born of God, and this is the significance of the name Eltolad.

Elul, ē'-lŭl (Heb.)—*the gleaning month; vine; outcry.*

Sixth month of the Jewish sacred year, and twelfth month of their civil year (Neh. 6:15). It began in our September and lasted until the latter part of October, or into November. Authorities differ as to which of our months correspond to the Jewish months mentioned in the Bible.

Meta. A place of fruition in consciousness (*the gleaning month*); also the earnest desire of the soul for greater fruitfulness (*outcry*).

Eluzai, ē-lū'-zā-i (Heb.)—*God is my strength; God is my refuge; God is my place of safety.*

A Benjamite, a mighty man, who came to David at Ziklag when David was hiding there from Saul (I Chron. 12:5).

Meta. Faith in God as one's strength and as one's protection and vindication. This faith thought (Eluzai was a Benjamite) acts jointly with love (David) in consciousness, while the personal will (Saul) is still being dominated by the selfishness of sense and would kill out the spiritual quality of love if it could.

Elymas, ĕl'-ў̆-măs (Gk.)—*wise; powerful; a Magus; an astrologer; a magician.*

A Jewish man, a sorcerer, or false prophet, who opposed Paul and Barnabas and tried to turn the proconsul, Sergius Paulus, from the faith (Acts 13:8). He is also called Bar–Jesus; he was stricken with blindness for a season because of his wickedness.

Meta. The sense thought that tries to counterfeit the working of Spirit. Paul had just received a special baptism of the Holy Spirit, with power to express the word of God. When he perceived that sense thought was working in the personality in opposition to the true working of Spirit, he called it to account.

Mental resistance closes the doors and windows of the mind, and shuts out the light of Spirit. Then the darkness of ignorance pervades the consciousness, and there is dependence on external leadings. (Elymas "went about seeking some to lead him by the hand.")

Elzaphan, ĕl'-ză-phăn (Heb.)—*God of the left side*, i. e., *the north; God of the hidden; God of concealment; God is protector; hidden of God.*

Son of Uzziel, and grandson of Kohath, who was one of Levi's sons (Exod. 6:22). Elizaphan is the same name.

Meta. Thoughts of divine protection and safety. (See ELIZAPHAN.)

Emek–keziz (A. V., the valley of Keziz), ē'-mĕk–kē'-zĭz (Heb.)—*vale of Keziz; vale of the cut-off; deep of the separated.*

a A city of Benjamin. b Evidently a valley (Josh. 18:21).

Meta. A depressed state of consciousness, caused by a belief in separation from God, the good (*vale of the cut-off*). It needs to be built up and strengthened by the assurance of man's oneness with the Divine.

Emim (A. V., Emims), ē'-mĭm (Heb.)—*the terrible; formidable people; terrors; objects of terror*, i. e., *idols.*

A race of giants, like the Anakim (Gen. 14:5). They lived formerly in the land of Moab. "The Emim dwelt therein aforetime, a people great, and many, and tall, as the Anakim: these also are accounted Rephaim, as the Anakim; but the Moabites call them Emim" (Deut. 2:10, 11).

Meta. *Terrors; fears.* They are a race of giants in human consciousness. They are the product of man's believing in the outer formed world, and in the conditions that man has built up, as being real and true. In this way belief in a power of evil is established in consciousness and man fears and dreads many things.

One overcomes fear by knowing the one Presence and the one Power, the good omnipotent. By setting his love on God, man enters into good and becomes strong in the knowledge that in all God's universe there is nothing to fear. Thus he realizes the fearlessness and the courage that are necessary to his proper spiritual unfoldment.

Emmaus, ĕm-mā'-ŭs (Gk.)—*mineral springs; medicinal springs; baths.*

A village, "threescore furlongs from Jerusalem," to which Cleopas and another of Jesus' disciples were going when Jesus met them, after His resurrection, and taught them from the Scriptures all the things concerning Himself (Luke 24:13).

Meta. A place in consciousness where the healing, restoring love and life and Truth of Spirit spring up and flow freely through man's being.

Enam, ē'-năm (Heb.) — *two eyes; double springs; two fountains.*

A city in the lowlands of Judah (Josh. 15:34). The Enaim of Genesis 38:14, in whose gate Tamar sat, is supposed to be the same city.

Meta. The fountain of understanding and life in man that, because of doublemindedness (belief in good and evil, in materiality as well as spirituality), is dedicated to two purposes: generation and regeneration, sense and Spirit. Double-mindedness causes instability. Stability is needed that one may grow and develop spiritually as one should. One establishes stability of character by giving oneself up wholly to the regenerative law, in singleness of purpose.

Enan, ē'-năn (Heb.)—*flowing forth; eyed*, i. e., *having eyes; a natural spring; a fountain.*

Father of Ahira, of the tribe of Naphtali (Num. 1:15).

Meta. The great strength and energy of the cleansing Christ life in consciousness (Naphtali refers to strength, and *a fountain* and *flowing forth* suggest life and cleansing). This cleansing fountain of life is allied with divine intelligence, sight, understanding (*having eyes*).

end, of world. (See Matt. 13:49.)

Meta. The end of a state of consciousness—the place of unfoldment where the old is cast off and the way is opened for the incoming of the new.

The "end of all things is at hand" (I Pet. 4:7) is the dissolution in mind of the realm of thought that has been built up by a belief in the reality of seemingly material things and conditions.

En-dor, ĕn'-dôr (Heb.)—*fountain of Dor; fount of the dwelling; fount of the habitation; fount of the generation.*

A city of Manasseh from which the Manassites failed to drive the Canaanites (Josh. 17:11). This city was the home of the woman who had a familiar spirit, to whom Saul sent for advice (I Sam. 28:7). According to Psalms 83:9, 10, En-dor seems also to have been the seat of the overthrow of Sisera, and of Jabin, king of Canaan.

Meta. The life faculty in man unified with and activated by generative and psychic sense thought (*fount of the habitation, fount of the generation*, the home of a woman who had a familiar spirit). As the Israelites, the true, higher thoughts of the individual, grow stronger in the regenerative idea, the Canaanites are gradually driven out; the old beliefs, desires, and habits give up their substance to the establishing of the uplifting, purifying, and restorative ideas of the Christ mind.

En-eglaim, ĕn-ĕg'-lä-ĭm (Heb.)—*fountain of two calves; well of two calves;* perhaps *fountain of two pools.*

A place that is mentioned with En-gedi. From En-gedi to En-eglaim was to be "a place for the spreading of nets; their fish shall be after their kinds, as the fish of the great sea, exceeding many" (Ezek. 47:10).

Meta. A great increase of ideas (fish) of life and cleansing (*fountain, well*) in consciousness, but on the innocent, untried animal plane (*calves*).

En-gannim, ĕn-găn'-nĭm (Heb.)—*fountain of gardens; fount of organic inclosures; fountain of the hedged fields.*

a A city in the lowland of Judah (Josh. 15:34). **b** A city of Issachar (Josh. 19:21).

Meta. Spiritual life and fruitfulness, inherent in and restricted to the consciousness of the individual (*fountain of gardens, fount of organic inclosures, fountain of the hedged fields*); thus the expression and manifestation may be very limited or very broad and abundant.

En-gedi, ĕn-ḡē'-dī (Heb.)—*fount of the kid; kid's fountain; fountain of Gad; fountain of fortune.*

A city of Judah in the wilderness (Josh. 15:62). David lived in the strongholds of En-gedi (I Sam. 23:29) and in the wilderness of En-gedi (I Sam. 24:1) for a time while he was hiding from Saul. The vineyards of En-gedi are mentioned in Song of Solomon 1:14, and Ezekiel speaks of En-gedi in connection with En-eglaim as being a place where fishers shall stand and spread their nets and shall catch many fish after their kinds (Ezek. 47:10).

Meta. The individual love (David) consciousness, consecrating itself to Spirit and earnestly seeking after, and increasing its realization of, the cleansing, freeing, redeeming Truth of Spirit, water of life; also the joy and power that come to one from a realization of the springing up of the cleansing life of Spirit (*fountain*) in consciousness, and the great increase of true ideas with their fruition for good in both mind and body. (*Fount of the kid, fountain of Gad, fountain of fortune; Gad* and *kid* are closely related, in the meaning of En-gedi, and come from the same root. They come from the idea of cutting off, cropping, as in eating; making a decision, a determination of fortune, casting a lot.) "In that day there shall be a fountain opened to the house of David and to the inhabitants of Jerusalem, for sin and for uncleanness" (Zech. 13:1).

En-haddah, ĕn-hăd'-dăh (Heb.)—*swift fountain; fount of vehemence; sharp fountain; fountain of zeal.*

A city of Canaan that was allotted to Issachar (Josh. 19:21).

Meta. The springing up of life into consciousness, quickened into greater activity and energy, and lifted to a higher level by the influence of the faculty of zeal (Issachar).

En–hakkore, ĕn–hăk'-kŏ-rḕ (Heb.)— *fount of the crying aloud; the crier's fountain; fount of the proclamation; the caller's fount; fount of the invocation; fountain of the emphatic prayer.*

The place where God brought water out of the jawbone for Samson to drink, in response to Samson's prayer to Jehovah for water to quench his thirst (Judg. 15:19).

Meta. The positive affirmative prayer, or demand, that results in a quickening of new life in consciousness (*fount of the crying aloud, fountain of the emphatic prayer*), the effect of this quickening being renewed vitality, strength, wholeness, and inspiration.

The water that Samson drank sprang out of "the hollow place that is in Lehi" (*the jawbone,* margin). Samson had just used the jawbone of an ass to slay a thousand Philistines. The jawbone represents determination, endurance, strength. Determination, strength of purpose, and endurance enable one to overcome the rule of the senses in oneself, and if given over to the affirming of new life and Truth through Jehovah, the indwelling Christ, it brings about the desired quickening and restoring of the whole man.

En–hazor, ĕn–hā'-zôr (Heb.)—*fount of Hazor; inclosed fountain,* i. e., *walled in; fountain of the court; village fountain; fount of the verdant field; fount of the stronghold.*

A fortified city of Naphtali (Josh. 19:37).

Meta. Cleansing life—the stronghold and defense of the strength center (Naphtali) in man's consciousness. Purity increases strength; the fountain of divine life springing up in man's consciousness is a purifying quality as well as a resurrecting, revitalizing quality (see Zech. 13:1). Until man reaches a certain degree of unfoldment his life expression is seemingly limited (*inclosed fountain,* i. e., *walled in*) because of his narrow, ignorant views of life. However, as man gains greater and clearer understanding he comes forth into unlimited strength and fruitfulness of expression (*fount of the verdant field, fount of the stronghold*).

En–mishpat, ĕn–mĭsh'-păt (Heb.)— *fountain of judgment; fount of rectitude; fountain of right; fount of justice.*

The same place as Kadesh, or a fountain in the city of Kadesh. It was there that Chedorlaomer and the kings that were with him smote the Amalekites (Gen. 14:7).

Meta. The significance of En–mishpat (*fountain of judgment*) is that, under the great law of adjustment, when sense indulgence reaches a certain point in its expression it destroys the very error desires that keep it active in consciousness. These desires die for lack of fuel to keep them alive—evil is its own destruction (see CHEDORLAOMER and KADESH)—and uprightness, true justice, becomes manifest (*fount of rectitude, fountain of right, fount of justice*).

Enoch, ē'nŏch (Heb.)—*founder; centralizer; teacher; instructor; initiator; fixer; repentance; contrition.*

a A son of Cain. **b** A city that Cain built and named after his son (Gen. 4:17). **c** Son of Jared and father of Methuselah (Gen. 5:18-24). This latter Enoch was the man who walked with God and was translated, who did not die (Heb. 11:5).

Meta. Entrance into and instruction in a new state of thought, of understanding. In the case of the Enoch who walked with God, the new state of thought would be spiritual consciousness, the new life in Christ.

Enosh (A. V., Enos), ē'-nŏsh (Heb.)— *mutable being; transient man; corporeal man; mortal man; suffering man; miserable man.*

Son of Seth and grandson of Adam (Gen. 4:26).

Meta. The outer, or body consciousness, in its limited, material, corruptible concept of the organism. See SETH in conjunction with this name; the two must be studied together in order to get the full significance of this one.

En–rimmon, ĕn–rĭm'-mŏn (Heb.)— *fountain of Rimmon; fount of the pomegranates; fount of substance.*

A place in Palestine where some of the Israelites lived after their return from the Babylonian captivity (Neh. 11:29). It is thought to be the same place as Ain and Rimmon, of Joshua 15:32; 19:7, and I Chronicles 4:32.

Meta. The springing up in consciousness of new, abundant life and substance after a period of seeming dearth and inactivity. En–rimmon is mentioned as being reinhabited by some of the Jews who returned from the Captivity; this indicates that praise and prayer, Judah, again become active in the aggregation of thoughts and of nerve cells that are indicated by this city; thus a renewing, a revitalizing, and a fruitful substance-state of mind is established.

En–rogel, ĕn–rō'-gĕl (Heb.)—*foot fountain; well of the treading feet; fullers' fountain,* because at the well of En–rogel the fullers trod their clothes.

A very ancient well near Jerusalem (II Sam. 17:17; I Kings 1:9). It is one of the three sources from which Jerusalem is now supplied with water; some think it to be the same place as Bethesda.

Meta. The cleansing, healing life of Spirit springing up into consciousness (see BETHESDA also) and, activated and directed by the power of the word, doing an orderly, disciplinary, cleansing, purifying, adjusting work in the life of the individual.

En–shemesh, ĕn–shē'-mĕsh (Heb.)—*fountain of the sun; fount of glorious brilliance; fount of astonishment.*

A place on the border of Judah, "and the border passed along to the waters of En–shemesh" (Josh. 15:7). Fallows says, "It is usually identified with the 'well of the Apostles,' about a mile and a half below or east of Bethany, on the road to Jericho."

Meta. The almost stupefying effect that the first entrance of the true Christ life and light (*fountain of the sun, fount of glorious brilliance*) into consciousness has upon the individual. Up to this time the individual has lived in sensate thought, and the light of Spirit is blinding (*fount of astonishment*) to the sense mind, just as gazing on the sun in its brilliance causes momentary blindness.

En–tappuah, ĕn–tăp'-pū-ăh (Heb.)—*fount of the fragrant breath; fount of the apple region, i. e., fragrant fruits; fountain of Tappuah or Tappuach.*

A fountain, or spring, on the border of Manasseh (Josh. 17:7).

Meta. Tappuah means *apple,* or *fragrant fruit* of some kind; also *fragrant breath,* referring to inspiration and life. En–tappuah (*fountain of Tappuah*) refers to the inbreathing life, intuition, discrimination, discernment springing into fruitfulness in mind, body, and affairs; in other words, bringing forth abundant health, vitality, good judgment, understanding, and substance. (See BETH-TAPPUAH and TAPPUAH.)

Epænetus, ĕp-æ-nē'-tŭs (Gk.)—*approbation; commendation; praise; praiseworthy.*

A Christian at Rome. He was a very dear friend of Paul's: "Salute Epænetus my beloved, who is the firstfruits of Asia unto Christ" (Rom. 16:5).

Meta. The first acceptance of the Christ, or love teaching of the heart, by the hardened, seemingly material, warring thoughts of the head (Rome), in individual consciousness. This is very *praiseworthy* and it causes great rejoicing in the realm of the word of Truth (Paul).

Epaphras, ĕp'-ă-phrăs (Gk.)—*lovely; covered with foam, i. e., impassioned.*

A faithful minister of Christ to the Colossian church, and later a prisoner with Paul at Rome (Col. 1:7; Philem. 23).

Meta. The loving message of the Christ (*lovely*) and its action in the Colossæ and Rome states of mind.

God is love and His expressions toward man are purely peaceful and good. When these ideas are sown into the belief in punishment and retribution (Colossæ) and into heady states of mind (Rome) they cause a stirring up in consciousness greatly like the action of soda in sour milk or yeast in bread (*covered with foam*). As love goes on in its activity, it sweetens the whole consciousness and raises the individual to a higher level.

Epaphroditus, ē-păph-rŏ-dī'-tŭs (Gk.) —*lovely; charming; fascinating; filled* *with love.*

A fellow worker of Paul's in the ministry. He was a messenger sent to Paul with gifts from the Philippian church, and was sent by Paul with an encouraging message to the Philippians (Phil. 2:25; 4:18). Some authorities think that he was the same man as Epaphras and that Paul sent the Epistle to the Philippians and the Epistle to the Colossians by this man at the same time.

Meta. A message of love and peace that is sent by the word of Truth (Paul) to the enlightened thoughts of the states of mind that Philippi and Colossæ signify in individual consciousness. (See PHILIPPI and COLOSSÆ.)

Ephah, ē'-phăh (Heb.)—*covered,* as with the wings of a fowl; *brooded; overcast; obscured; darkened; gloom; weak; weary; languid; faint.*

a Son of Midian and grandson of Abraham (Gen. 25:4). **b** A place mentioned with Midian in Isaiah 60:6. **c** A concubine of Caleb's (I Chron. 2:46).

Meta. Darkened and obscure phases of thought and soul in which the Spirit of God is working—over which Spirit is brooding, as it were—that Truth may blossom forth and come to fruition in due time. The prophecy in Isaiah, wherein Ephah is mentioned, bespeaks the clearing up of the phases of mind that are symbolized by Ephah.

Ephai, ē'-phāi (Heb.)—*weary; languid; tired; obscuring; gloomy; darkening; birdlike,* i. e., *covering with wings.*

The Netophathite whose sons were left behind in Judah after the greater portion of the Jews had been carried away captive to Babylon (Jer. 40:8).

Meta. A thought of divine protection (*birdlike,* i. e., *covering with wings*) that bears fruit (Ephai had sons who were saved from being taken into Babylon). "When I am weak, then am I strong" (II Cor. 12:10), because when I recognize the weakness (*weary, languid, tired, gloomy*) and insufficiency of the carnal, I trust more fully in the strength and all-sufficiency of the Christ in me and I am made truly strong and efficient. "Hide me under the shadow of thy wings" (Psalms 17:8).

"He will cover thee with his pinions,
And under his wings shalt thou take
   refuge" (Psalms 91:4).

Epher, ē'-phĕr (Heb.)—*light; quick; ethereal; young hart; gazelle; young deer; young calf.*

a Son of Midian who was Abraham's son by Keturah (Gen. 25:4). **b** A descendant of Caleb's (I Chron. 4:17). **c** A chief man of Manasseh (I Chron. 5:24).

Meta. Thoughts on the animal plane of consciousness in man that are active, yet young and inexperienced (*young hart, young deer, young calf*). By partaking of understanding (Manasseh), and by being guided and impelled by enthusiasm, fearlessness, and faithfulness to principle (Caleb), that which Epher signifies becomes more and more enlightened, swift, active, spiritual (*light, quick, ethereal*), and effective for good in its work in the organism.

Ephes–dammim, ē'-phĕş–dăm'-mĭm (Heb.)—*end of bloodshed; limit of blood; boundary of blood.*

A place between Socoh and Azekah, where the Philistines gathered together to fight against Israel (I Sam. 17:1). It was there that Goliath was killed by David. Ephes–dammim is the same place as the Pas–dammim of I Chronicles 11: 13.

Meta. Ephes–dammim bespeaks the end of warring thoughts and beliefs, the end of thoughts of strife and bloodshed, and the end of the error idea that life is material and limited (*end of bloodshed, limit of blood, boundary of blood*). As the consciousness is thus purified, as it is set free from the hordes of sense beliefs, material thoughts and fears (Philistines that had gathered together in battle against the Israelites), it learns the truth that life is spiritual, unlimited, and always present in fullness.

Ephesians, ē-phē'-şĭănş (fr. the Gk.)—*belonging to Ephesus.*

Inhabitants of Ephesus (Acts 19:28; also the book of Ephesians).

Meta. Thoughts that belong to the Ephesus state of consciousness in man. The Ephesians to whom the Epistle of Paul was written signify the enlightened and partially enlightened thoughts that belong to this state of consciousness. (See EPHESUS.)

Ephesus, ĕph′-ĕ-sŭs (Gk.)—*desirable; appealing.*

A city of Asia Minor, and capital of Ionia (Acts 20:17; Rev. 2:1). Ephesus was at one time a center of learning, also of commerce. It was noted for its wonderful temple that was built for worship of the goddess Diana.

Meta. The central, building faculty of the consciousness called desire.

In its physical aspect Ephesus symbolizes the stomach. In its mental aspect it symbolizes the ganglionic center at the pit of the stomach, which controls and directs all the organs pertaining to digestion and assimilation.

Philosophers like Darwin and Spencer say that desire is the root of all body building. They claim that desire draws together the few protoplasmic cells that make the stomach of the most primitive life forms. Desire is but another name for constructive thought. The desire is the center from which goes forth the impetus that makes the form.

The cells that build the form are moved upon by ideas; hence the character of the form is determined by the prevailing ideas back of it. Ephesus was given up to idolatry, superstition, and general materialism. So we find in unregenerate man that the Ephesus center is given over to physical and sense ideas and must be raised to the spiritual by the impregnating power of the word; hence Paul spent three years preaching the gospel in Ephesus.

Ephlal, ĕph′-lăl (Heb.)—*judgment; equity; judging,* i. e., *coloring with one's thoughts.*

A descendant of Judah (I Chron. 2:37).

Meta. The dawning concept in the individual that he has power to name, or give character to, whatever within himself or his world of affairs he passes judgment upon (*judgment, judging,* i. e., *coloring with one's thoughts.* See Gen. 2:19, 20.) By right judgment, thinking the truth about himself and all that he contacts, man can establish *equity,* har-

mony, balance in his life.

Ephod, ē′-phŏd, ĕph′-ŏd (Heb.)—*gird; clothe,* as a priest; *to cover; overlay with gold,* as an idol; *oracular.*

a Father of Hanniel, a prince of Manasseh (Num. 34:23). **b** A short cloak without sleeves that was worn by the Israelitish priests (Exod. 28:6-12); in the front, over the breast, was hung the breastplate on which were engraved the names of the twelve tribes of Israel. The Urim and Thummim were established in this breastplate; by them the high priest could obtain direct from God the answer to any difficult case that came up for his consideration. (See URIM and THUMMIM.) **c** Ephods made of linen were worn by others besides the high priest (I Sam. 2:18; II Sam. 6:14). In **b** and **c** the pronunciation in ĕph′-ŏd.

Meta. (**a**) Ephod as the name of a man pertains to an image; the idea here is that of divine authority and power like that of the Creator or Source. God made man in His own image, or likeness, and gave him dominion. Ephod was the father of a prince of Manasseh and Manasseh was a tribe of Israel.

(**b** and **c**) Divine understanding, authority, and power (*oracular* pertains to an understanding, or wisdom, that is beyond that of sense man.) We must *clothe* ourselves with light (spiritual understanding) as with a garment (see Psalms 104:2). True understanding increases the expression of one's Christ power and authority.

ephphatha, ĕph′-phă-thà (Gk. fr. Aram.)—*be thou opened; be opened; be thou unbound,* i. e., *liberated.*

A word that was used by Jesus when He healed the man who was deaf and who had an impediment in his speech (Mark 7:34).

Meta. An inner freeing, healing thought or word of the Christ that releases all tension in consciousness and opens the mind and the body to spiritual receptivity and wholeness.

Ephraim, ē′-phră-ĭm (Heb.)—*doubly fruitful; very fruitful; productive.*

Second son of Joseph, and brother of Manasseh (Gen. 48:14).

Meta. The will.

In Genesis 41:50-52 it is stated that Joseph had two sons, Manasseh and Ephraim. "And Joseph called the name of the first-born Manasseh: For, *said he,* God hath made me forget all my toil, and all my father's house. And the name of the second called he Ephraim: For God hath made me fruitful in the land of my affliction."

It is very plain that Manasseh means the thought of forgetfulness, or denial, and Ephraim means the thought of adding to, or affirmation. We also perceive that these two sons represent the understanding and the will. The first step that a beginner in Truth takes is to set up a new and better state of consciousness, based upon the absolute. He forgets, or denies, the "not good," and brings into vivid remembrance the very good by affirming it to be the real.

These two sons of Joseph, the understanding and the will, are to be especially active in the one who would overcome and master the sensations of the body. Their allotment in the Promised Land was in joint ownership. This shows that they should go hand in hand. In all building of permanent character and body, the action of the will (Ephraim) must be based upon understanding (Manasseh).

"The crown of pride of the drunkards of Ephraim" see TIMNATH-HERES and foot" (Isa. 28:3) is the pride of personality. The egotist builds up false states of mind, the thought back of them being sense gratification.

The fruits that such states of mind bring forth are chaff and humiliation. The mind becomes confused and unstable, producing disease and weakness of body.

The true "crown of glory" and the "diadem of beauty" are the attainment of understanding of the principles of Truth, and the understanding of how to express these principles in mind, body, and affairs.

For information on "the hill-country of Ephraim" see TIMNATH-HERES and JOSHUA.

Ephraimite (A. V., Ephrathite), ē'-phră-ĭm-īte (fr. Heb.)—*of* or *belonging to Ephraim.*

A person who belonged to the Israelitish tribe of Ephraim (I Sam. 1:1).

Meta. A thought that belongs to the will faculty in man.

Ephrath, ĕph'-răth (Heb.)—*fruitfulness; fruitful; productive; abundant.*

The original name of the town of Beth-lehem (Gen. 35:19).

Meta. A realization of abundant substance; this increase of substance ideas in consciousness brings about a corresponding fruitfulness, abundance, throughout one's entire life and affairs.

Ephrathah (A. V., Ephratah), ĕph'-ră-thäh (Heb.)—*fertility; productiveness; fruitfulness; abundance.*

An ancient name for Beth-lehem-judah, the house of Naomi (Ruth 4:11; Mic. 5:2). (See I Chron. 4:4.)

Meta. See EPHRATH.

Ephron, ē'-phrŏn (Heb.)—*fawnlike; gazellelike; quick; volatile; spirited.*

a Son of Zohar, of the children of Heth, from whom Abraham bought the cave of Machpelah to bury Sarah in (Gen. 23:8). **b** A range of hills on the northern border of Judah, in Canaan (Josh. 15:9).

Meta. A phase of thought that is very impulsive, light, airy, and quick to change its thinking base (*gazellelike, quick, volatile, spirited*). When going through an inner experience wherein some much cherished soul quality or phase of thought that has finished its work for the time being must be released from consciousness, one may have a tendency to grieve and to hold to the good that seems to be becoming inactive in one's life. Then the thought activity that Ephron signifies comes to one's rescue. It aids one in making the necessary change and in letting go of the old. (Sarah died in Hebron, and it was in Hebron that Abraham bargained with Ephron for the cave of Machpelah in which to bury Sarah. Hebron signifies the front brain or seat of conscious thought; also a certain association or alliance of thought.) Abraham suggests the awakening of man's mind to higher ideals, and hills also signify high places in consciousness—lofty thoughts and ideals.

Epicurean, ĕp-ĭ-cū-rē'-ăn (Gk.)—*followers of Epicurus.*

A sect of philosophers, founded by Epicurus (Acts 17:18). These philosophers believed that the soul dies with the body and that there is no future, either good or bad, for man beyond death. Their doctrine was one of pleasure seeking and ease; very naturally it led to sensuality and error.

Meta. The character of the thoughts that Epicurean signifies is revealed in Jesus' parable of Luke 12:16-21; see the 19th verse, especially the last part of the verse.

Er, ēr (Heb.)—*awake; watchful; alert; watcher; watchman.*

a Eldest son of Judah (Gen. 38:3). He was wicked and Jehovah slew him, according to Genesis 38:7. b A man named in the genealogy of Jesus Christ (Luke 3:28).

Meta. Observant, attentive, vigilant thoughts.

It matters a great deal what one watches, or gives attention to. If one persists in recognizing that which appears to be evil and error, one cannot obtain abiding life and good. We are transformed into the Christ likeness by beholding Him, not by taking cognizance of the lesser self with its seeming limitations. "If thine eye be evil, thy whole body shall be full of darkness. If therefore the light that is in thee be darkness, how great is the darkness!" (Matt. 6:23).

Eran, ē'-răn (Heb.)—*more watchful; vigilant; attentive; watcher.*

An Ephraimite, son of Shuthelah, and head of the family of the Eranites (Num. 26:36).

Meta. The will attentive to the greatly increasing power of Truth in consciousness.

Eranites, ē'-răn-ītes (fr. Heb.)—*of or belonging to Eran.*

Descendants of Eran (Num. 26:36).

Meta. Thoughts belonging to the Eran consciousness. (See ERAN.)

Erastus, ē-răs'-tŭs (Gk.)—*beloved; amiable.*

a A native of Corinth, a Christian worker with Paul. Paul sent him with Timothy into Macedonia (Acts 19:22; II Tim. 4:20). b A treasurer of the city of Corinth, whence Paul's Epistle to the Romans was sent (Rom. 16:23). Though the texts that are given may all refer to the same man, authorities believe that there were two men by this name.

Meta. The harmonizing quality of love. (See CORINTH.)

Erech, ē'-rĕch (Heb.)—*long; length; extended; prolonged; attenuated; slack; dissolute; prostrate; prostitute;* in a good sense, *prolonged; lasting; relaxed; health.*

A city that Nimrod built in the land of Shinar (Gen. 10:10).

Meta. The truth about the natural, inherent wholeness and goodness of man (because of his being made in the likeness of God), reduced in his consciousness to material thinking and, because of *long* and *extended* material thinking, bringing about the disastrous results of error in his body and affairs. (See ARCHEVITES.)

Eri, ē'-rī (Heb.)—*my watcher; watching; worshiping Jah.*

Son of Gad and grandson of Jacob (Gen. 46:16).

Meta. An unfolding of the power faculty (Gad) in consciousness. Power seems to express first on the mortal or human plane. The true, spiritual quality in the power faculty, however, is constantly seeking expression, and in Eri it is attentive to the higher or divine law.

Erites, ē'-rītes (fr. Heb.)—*of or belonging to Eri; posterity of Eri.*

A family of people descended from Eri (Num. 26:16).

Meta. Thoughts belonging to the Eri consciousness. (See ERI.)

error.

Meta. Thoughts, with their corresponding words and acts, that are not in harmony with Divine Mind. Error thoughts have no foundation in absolute Truth. They originate in the intellect. Such thoughts are eliminated by one's denying their reality and power, and affirming the Truth of Being; then their outer expressions and manifestations disappear also.

In prayer, in communion with God in the secret place of the Most High, the mind lays hold of divine ideas and establishes them in consciousness. This is the place that prayer has in controlling thought. There is no presence or power of evil, in reality; there is only one Presence and one Power—the good omnipotent.

Esar–haddon, ĕ′-sär–hăd′-dŏn (Heb. fr. Assyr.)—*Ashur* (Assyria) *hath given a brother; victorious conqueror; gift of fire.*

Son of Sennacherib, king of Assyria. He became king upon the assassination of Sennacherib (II Kings 19:37).

Meta. A fiery thought of conquest and victory. This thought springs from Sennacherib, the head of the Assyria state of consciousness (see ASSYRIA and SENNACHERIB), and later becomes the ruling idea in this consciousness. Since it is wholly on the sense-reasoning plane, it is consuming and destructive in its nature and thus sets into activity forces that react upon it and bring about its downfall ultimately. The limited, sense thoughts and sense tendencies in man do not last long. After a period of seeming rule in consciousness they give way to other governing ideas.

Esau, ē′-saụ (Heb.)—*hairy; hirsute; rough; shaggy.*

Son of Isaac, and twin brother of Jacob (Gen. 25:25; 27:38-41).

Meta. The body, or physical vigor.

In the immature consciousness the natural man is moved by desire. Appetite and passion are satisfied regardless of the higher law. Esau sold his birthright for a mess of pottage.

The threat of Esau against Jacob's life represents the inward rebellion that we often feel when we change our modes of thought.

Esek, ē′-sĕk (Heb.) — *oppression; strife; violence; injury; distress; straits; contention.*

A well that Isaac's herdsmen dug in the valley. "And the herdsmen of Gerar strove with Isaac's herdsmen, saying, The water is ours: and he called the name of the well Esek, because they contended

with him" (Gen. 26:20).

Meta. A warring that takes place in the subconsciousness (valley) between the sense animal desires (the herdsmen of Gerar, a Philistine city) and the attempt of the awakening spiritual understanding (Isaac, a type of Christ,) to lift up the animal forces of the organism.

The digging of the well signifies the uncovering of, or coming into touch with, the hidden life force. This is accomplished by Isaac's herdsmen, the spiritual thoughts that have care of the forces in man that are represented by the animals. These thoughts desire to elevate these seemingly animal qualities to a spiritual basis of expression; but the energy and vigor of life that man gains by his conscious contact with Spirit are claimed at once by his sense desires to be used for their gratification and pleasure, for the strengthening of sense instead of the building up of his spiritual nature. Thus *contention* and *strife* (Esek) arise.

Eshan, ē′-shăn (Heb.)—*couch; support; prop.*

A city in the hill country of Judah, in Canaan (Josh. 15:52).

Meta. An aggregation of thoughts in consciousness that is of a supporting, sustaining, restful character (*couch, support*). This aggregation of strengthening, sustaining thoughts is the product of, and belongs to, the praise-and-prayer consciousness (Judah).

Eshbaal, ĕsh′-bā-ăl (Heb.)—*man of Baal; Baal's man; fire of Baal; will of the master; dominant will.*

Son of Saul (I Chron. 8:33); the same person as Ishbosheth.

Meta. Self-will and its disastrous end in the individual who gives way to it. (See ISHBOSHETH.)

Eshban, ĕsh′-băn (Heb.)—*man of understanding; thinking man; man of wisdom; wise man; son of fire.*

Son of Dishon, or Dishan, a chief of the Horites (Gen. 36:26).

Meta. The belief, held by the outer man, that wisdom and understanding come through the perception and reasonings of the senses. (If Eshban had been an Israelite instead of a Horite, the significance of the name would be that of true understanding.)

Eshcol, ĕsh'-cŏl (Heb.)—*cluster; cluster of grapes; a bunch; cluster,* especially of grapes.

a An Amorite who was "confederate with Abram" (Gen. 14:13). **b** A valley in the land of Canaan, where the spies cut the bunch of grapes that had to be carried on a staff by two men. "That place was called the valley of Eshcol, because of the cluster which the children of Israel cut down from thence" (Num. 13:24).

Meta. The life forces in the subconsciousness; also a realization of their great fruitfulness in consciousness, and man's abundant possibilities through them.

Eshek, ē'-shĕk (Heb.)—*oppression; violence; strife; injury; distress; straits.*

A Benjamite who was descended from Saul (I Chron. 8:39).

Meta. The activity of the faith (Benjamin) thought in man, but directed and influenced by the selfish, oppressive, contentious dominance of the personal will (Saul). This brings about a very destructive attitude of mind. Faith must work by love in order to establish harmony, true freedom, and peace in man.

Eshtaol, ĕsh'-tä-ŏl (Heb.)—*excavation; hollow way; searching out; petition; entreaty; supplication; interrogation.*

A city in the lowland of Judah (Josh. 15:33). Samson's home, when "the Spirit of Jehovah began to move him," was in Mahaneh–dan, the camp of Dan, between Zorah and Eshtaol (Judg. 13:25).

Meta. The earnest prayer or entreaty of the soul, the subconscious depths of man's being, for a way of escape from the dominance of sense (the Philistines).

The Israelites were seemingly under complete subjection to the Philistines at this time; in other words, the error thoughts and activities of the outer sense life in the individual are in dominion, and the true, spiritual thoughts and activities are being controlled by the senses. It is here at Eshtaol (the earnest cry of the soul for deliverance) that the Spirit of Jehovah begins to move Sam-

son, or begins to make us conscious of our innate spiritual strength, by which the sense thoughts and activities (Philistines) may be overcome. Thus we can become free from the dominance of the sense life and from the sorrow and bondage that result from it.

Eshtaolites (A. V., Eshtaulites), ĕsh'-tă-ŏl-ītes (fr. Heb.)—*belonging to Eshtaol.*

The inhabitants of the city of Eshtaol (I Chron. 2:53). They were of the tribe of Judah.

Meta. Thoughts belonging to the Eshtaol phase of consciousness. (See ESHTAOL.)

Eshtemoa, ĕsh-tĕ-mō'-à (Heb.)—*hearing; hearkening; understanding; obedience; submission.*

a A city of Judah that was given over to the priests (Josh. 21:14). **b** A man, a Judahite of the city of Maachah (I Chron. 4:19).

Meta. The spirit of receptivity, understanding, and obedience, which causes one to give attention to spiritual guidance and to obey its leadings.

Eshtemoh, ĕsh'-tĕ-mōh (Heb.)—*hearing; hearkening; understanding; obedience; submission.*

The same place as Eshtemoa (Josh. 15:50).

Meta. See ESHTEMOA.

Eshton, ĕsh'-tŏn (Heb.)—*womanish; uxorious; weak; restful.*

Son of Mehir, a Judahite (I Chron. 4:11).

Meta. A thought of or tendency toward love of ease; also a *weak,* or negative, submissiveness to the emotions and desires of the human soul (*uxorious* means "excessively or dotingly fond of, or submissive to, a wife").

Esli, ĕs'-lī (Gk. from Heb.)—*God has reserved; separated from God; reserved.*

A man named in the genealogy of Jesus Christ (Luke 3:25).

Meta. A strong thought of consecration to God and of nearness to or oneness with Him. This thought belongs to man's spiritual consciousness. It is through the spiritual consciousness, or superconsciousness, in man that he contacts God and that the ideas of the one Mind enter the consciousness of the individual.

Esther, ĕs'-thēr (Heb. fr. Pers.)—
star; the planet Venus; happiness; good fortune.

A beautiful Israelitish woman who became the queen of King Ahasuerus of Persia (Esth. 2:7—9:32). She, with her cousin Mordecai, was instrumental in saving the lives of the Jewish people in Persia.

Meta. The dissolving power of spiritual love; this is an antidote for a dictatorial will.

Queen Esther had all her relatives, the Jews (spiritual thoughts), join her in a fast. This means that we must deny all selfish desires out of our love before we use it in softening the imperious will. When this consciousness of love stands in the inner court of our being we cannot help acceding to its demands. Unselfish love is fearless, because of its forgetfulness of self. Will divides its dominion with love when approached in the right attitude, which is by touching the highest point of the understanding (top of the golden scepter). Understanding of divine law is the one necessary thing in all permanent unions. When we know the Truth we all are one and there is no separation whatsoever.

Etam, ē'-tăm (Heb.)—*aerie; numbers of rapacious birds; lair of ravenous beasts.*

a A village of Simeon (I Chron. 4:32). **b** A city of defense in Judah, built, or fortified, by Rehoboam (II Chron. 11:6; see I Chron. 4:3). **c** The rock where Samson went to live after he had destroyed the Philistines' crops and had killed many of their people (Judg. 15:8).

Meta. Aggregations of thoughts in consciousness given over to force, violence, greed. Some of these thoughts have the characteristics of birds (they are free, unattached), and others belong to the "beast" life in the organism. In other words, Etam signifies the beast life's running wild and having gained a degree of ascendancy over the religious and spiritual attitudes of thought that are represented by Simeon, Judah, and Samson.

Man needs to be watchful in his overcoming, that he may keep in the spirit of love and not give way to vengeful, fighting, warring states of mind in his conflicts with seeming error. Even in the overcoming life he can fall into the attitude of "beasts" in striving against apparent error, if he is not watchful always to magnify the good in his thoughts instead of looking at error until it becomes a mountain in his sight rather than the nothingness that it actually is in Truth.

Etham, ē'-thăm (Heb. fr. Egypt.)—*border of the sea; seabound; extremes of habitation; desolation; sign of them; their universal symbol.*

A place at the edge of the wilderness, where the Israelites camped after leaving Succoth and before crossing the Red Sea (Exod. 13:20).

Meta. An apparently negative phase of consciousness (*desolation*). When our highest, truest conscious ideals (Israelites) go beyond the old environment of race thought and understanding and lead us into new, untried experiences, we should keep our attention fixed on God, Spirit. If we allow ourselves to meditate on the "unknown future" from a sense point of view, we are likely to become fearful and negative; a state of mind that is akin to loneliness and gloom is apt to take hold of us. But there is always the *sign of them*: "Jehovah went before them by day in a pillar of cloud, to lead them the way, and by night in a pillar of fire, to give them light; that they might go by day and by night: the pillar of cloud by day, and the pillar of fire by night, departed not from before the people" (Ex. 13:21, 22). Thus God, Truth, is always with us to show us the way to go and to meet our every need, if we will but look to Him and not to seeming limitations.

Ethan, ē'-thăn (Heb.)—*ancient; perennial; perpetual; firm; strong; mighty.*

a The Ezrahite, one of the wise men of Solomon's time (I Kings 4:31). **b** One of David's musicians or singers (I Chron. 6:44). **c** An ancestor of Asaph, a singer (I Chron. 6:42).

Meta. The *firm, strong* root in consciousness that the old thoughts about God have gained because of the length of time that they have been kept alive in the race (*ancient* suggests this).

There is a marked tendency in mankind to accept as a fixed, unalterable law (this is suggested by *perpetual*) anything that has been almost universally believed for ages. Yet many of these beliefs are very limited, and are decidedly erroneous; one by one they are being overthrown as new and fuller light dawns on the race. The Christ wisdom (represented by Solomon) is far ahead of any belief that is held to just because one's parents, grandparents, and ancestors for generations back believed it. We should always hold ourselves receptive to our inner Christ wisdom, even if we have to let go of many fondly cherished race beliefs in order to do so.

Ethanim, ĕth'-ă-nĭm (Heb.)—*munificent gifts; perennial flowing; flowing brooks.* Fallows says of Ethanim that it is "the month of streaming rivers, which are filled during this month by the autumnal rains. It corresponds with our September-October."

The seventh month of the sacred year of the Israelites, and the first month of their civil year (I Kings 8:2). The Day of Atonement occurred in this month; also the Feast of Tabernacles.

Meta. The whole consciousness of man is made up of objective and subjective thoughts and their results. Like a chemical solution they go through changes on the subjective side that are observed in their outer appearance only and are but dimly understood. This feast in the seventh month, Ethanim, refers to a culmination each year of certain thought forces engendered on the natural plane. Seven here refers to material fulfillment; and twelve to spiritual.

The metaphysician by study and meditation learns to observe these inner changes in soul and body, and instead of calling a certain chemicalization in thought health or sickness, he says that it is a culmination of true or of error thinking. It is in reality just what this Ethanim feast represents, a celebration of a thought harvest. (Months, in Scripture, refer to degrees or steps in overcoming and unfoldment, and not to the outer idea of time.)

Ethbaal, ĕth'-bā-ăl (Heb.)—*with Baal,* i. e., *with the favor or help of Baal; Baal's similitude,* i. e., *likeness; selfsameness of Baal.*

King of the Sidonians, and father of Jezebel, the wife of Ahab, king of Israel (I Kings 16:31).

Meta. A belief that is wholly given over to materiality; it is the ruling, or central thought of the Sidon state of consciousness. (See SIDONIAN.)

Ether, ē'-thēr (Heb.)—*plenty; riches; abundance; fullness.*

A city in the lowland of Judah (Josh. 15:42).

Meta. Praise (Judah) in touch with the fullness of abundant substance in the subconsciousness (lowland).

Ethiopia, ē-thĭ-ō'-pĭ-à (fr. Gk.)—*burned faces; country of the burning.*

A country in Africa, to the south of Egypt (Acts 8:27). In the Hebrew it is called Cush (Gen. 2:13).

Meta. The darkened or material thought in which man has held his body and its activities—the seemingly mortal, physical part of himself—as opposed to the Truth; also the result in his body of this error thinking. (Cush explains this more fully; see CUSH.)

Ethiopians, ē-thĭ-ō'-pĭ-ăns (fr. Gk.).

Inhabitants of Ethiopia (Acts 8:27). They are also called Cushites and are descendants of Cush, the eldest son of Ham. Ham is the one of Noah's three sons who represents the physical in man.

Meta. The Ethiopians of II Chronicles 14:12, 13 represent the undisciplined and undeveloped thought forces in the subconsciousness. These forces are destructive but they cannot withstand the power of the Israelites directed by King Asa, the healer.

The Ethiopians, generally speaking, are the thoughts that belong to the Ethiopia state of consciousness in man. (See ETHIOPIA.)

Ethnan, ĕth'-năn (Heb.)—*gift; reward; hire.*

Son of Ashhur and Helah, of the tribe of Judah (I Chron. 4:7).

Meta. "The free gift of God is eternal life in Christ Jesus our Lord" (Rom. 6:23).

From the human viewpoint there may be a sense of *hire,* of earning one's good (see Matt. 20:1-16), in the attaining of life, since every man must work out his own salvation. Each individual, however, will come to the place, in the course of his overcoming, wherein he will perceive that it must be God who works in him both to will and to work for His good pleasure, if anything worth while is to be accomplished or attained (see Phil. 2:12, 13). The *reward* is for faithful continuance in well-doing (see Rom. 2:7).

Ethni, ĕth′-nī (Heb.)—*giving; munificence; generosity; liberality.*

A Levite, an ancestor of Asaph (I Chron. 6:41).

Meta. A thought of great liberality, generosity, and broad-mindedness.

Eubulus, eū-bū′-lŭs (Gk.)—*good counsel; prudent.*

A Christian man who was with Paul at Rome, and saluted Timothy in Paul's letter to Timothy (II Tim. 4:21).

Meta. Good judgment, discretion, wisdom (*prudent, good counsel*) belonging to the illumined intellect in man.

Eunice, eū′-nī-çĕ (Gk.)—*conquering well; happily conquering; good victory.*

Timothy's mother, a Jewish woman who believed. Her husband, Timothy's father, was a Greek (II Tim. 1:5; Acts 16:1).

Meta. A blending of our inner spiritual qualities of faith and love. Faith is the victory that overcomes the world, and love is the harmonizing influence in our life that brings us conscious joy and good (Paul writes of the unfeigned faith that dwelt in Eunice).

eunuch.

Meta. A thought from which the capacity to increase life and its forms has been eliminated.

"The prince of the eunuchs" (Dan. 1:10) is that which stands highest in rank in the pure, illuminating spiritual consciousness, from which thought of sex has been excluded.

Euodia (A. V., Euodias), eū-ō′-dĭ-à (Gk.)—*prosperous journey; prosperous course; good journey; fragrant; sweet-scented.*

A Christian woman of Philippi (Phil. 4:2).

Meta. The soul aspiring to that which is spiritual and high, to abundant good

(*fragrant* and *sweet-scented* refer to the sense of smell; smelling stands for aspiration in consciousness).

Euphrates, eū-phrā′-tēṣ (Gk. fr. Heb.) —*bursting forth; breaking out; fructifying; that which is the fructifying cause.*

One of the four rivers of Eden (Gen. 2:14). It is a large river in western Asia (II Sam. 8:3, with margin; II Kings 23:29; Rev. 16:12).

Meta. For the metaphysical interpretation of Euphrates see the Addenda.

Euraquilo (A. V., Euroclydon), eū-răq′-uĭ-lō (Gk.)—*northeast wind.*

A very strong and stormy northeast wind that is experienced at times in the eastern part of the Mediterranean Sea and countries that border on it. The storm that arose when the Roman soldiers were taking Paul to Rome to appear before Cæsar was called the Euraquilo (Acts 27:14).

Meta. The tempest or brain storm that sometimes arises in one's mind because of the introduction of the word of Truth (Paul) into the material thoughts and beliefs of the intellectual consciousness. (The countries of Bible times that bordered on the eastern, southeastern, and northeastern parts of the Mediterranean Sea refer, for the greater part, to the intellect or head in man.)

Eutychus, eū′-ty̆-chŭs (Gk.)—*fortunate.*

A young man at Troas. Because of his going to sleep during Paul's talk he fell from an upper-chamber window and was killed, but he was restored to life again by Paul (Acts 20:9).

Meta. The understanding that the youthful energies of the organism can be quickened into new life again even after they appear to be utterly dead, after such a renewal appears to be hopeless. Man is indeed *fortunate* in having the word of Truth (indicated here by Paul) always at hand, since by the word of Truth he can speak his whole being into newness and fullness of life at will.

Eve, ēve (Heb.)—*elementary life; life; living.*

The first woman: "And the man called his wife's name Eve; because she was the mother of all living" (Gen. 3:20).

Meta. Love, or feeling, in individual consciousness. The I AM (wisdom) puts feeling into what it thinks, and so "Eve" (feeling) becomes the "mother of all living." Feeling is Spirit, which quickens. Woman symbolizes the soul region of man and is the mother principle of God in expression. Back of the woman (feeling) is the pure life essence of God. Adam and Eve represent the I AM identified in life substance. They are the primal elemental forces of Being itself.

Eve is very closely identified, as elementary life, with absolute life, God.

The verb "Hoh," to-be being, luminous absolute life, which forms the basis of the name Ihoh, Jehovah, is the basis also of Eve; however, due to a slight change in characters and a hardening of the vowels, it no longer represents absolute life, but the struggle of elementary existence. This is the struggle of the soul to regain its perfect state of existence, of the Absolute, God.

Evi, ē'-vī (Heb.)—*desire; inclination; choice; the will; object of desire,* i. e., *where the will is centered.*

A king of Midian who was slain by the Israelites at the time that Balaam, son of Beor, was killed and the Midianites were defeated (Num. 31:8).

Meta. Unjust desire. All desire at its origin is good and is of God; but in interpreting itself to the human consciousness it takes on the dominant beliefs therein. This, in Evi's case, is the belief in materiality and sense, in rebellion against the true thoughts of Spirit (Israelites). Thus the desire expresses itself as a longing for thoughts and activities that would mean injustice to one's higher self and degradation to one's whole being.

Evil – merodach, ē'-vĭl – mĕ-rō'-dăch (Heb.)—*fool of Merodach; Merodach's fool,* i. e., *his foolish worshiper; fool of Mars; foolish oppression; fool's destruction; fool grinds bitterly.*

King of Babylon, son of Nebuchadnezzar (II Kings 25:27).

Meta. A central, ruling thought in the Babylon state of consciousness in man. This thought is foolish in that it looks upon worldly pride, pomp, and power as worthy of one's effort to attain; it also believes in outer, limited, error conditions as real. Persons who behold the outer constantly, and believe in error seemings, bring about strife and confusion in mind, body, and affairs; they are foolish, and *grind bitterly,* in the end, (See BABYLON, BERODACH–BALLADAN, and MERODACH.)

Exodus, ĕx'-ŏ-dŭs (Gk.)—*exit; departure; going out; decease.*

The second book of the Pentateuch and the second book of our Bible. It is supposed to have been written by Moses, but authorities disagree on this. It is called Exodus because it deals with the Children of Israel's leaving Egypt.

Meta. Exodus refers to the deliverance of man's highest religious and spiritual thoughts from the obscurity, darkness, and ignorance of the Egyptian consciousness, or "mind of the flesh." We make our exodus when we die to sin and are born anew to righteousness in Jesus Christ.

Ezbai, ĕz'-bāi (Heb.)—*shining; beautiful; hyssoplike,* i. e., *fragrant.*

Father of Naarai, who was one of David's warriors (I Chron. 11:37).

Meta. The light of Truth as *shining* into individual consciousness, graciously (*beautiful*) and with fragrance (*hyssoplike*), ever aspiring to higher and better things. (Anything good connected with the sense of smelling bespeaks aspiration.)

Ezbon, ĕz'-bŏn (Heb.)—*pushing to understanding; hastening to understand; splendor; bright.*

a Son of Gad (Gen. 46:16). He is called Ozni in Num. 26:16. **b** A son of Bela and grandson of Benjamin (I Chron. 7:7).

Meta. Thoughts that come into the light, into the brightness and glory of Truth, because of being attentive to the things of Spirit. Because these thoughts have a receptive ear to hear the Truth, they understand quickly. (See OZNI.)

Ezekiel, ē-zē'-kĭ-ĕl (Heb.) — *God strengthens; God is strong; God is powerful; whom God makes strong.*

One of the four major prophets. He was one of a colony of captive Jews by the river Chebar, in Babylon; it was there that he did his prophesying (The Book of Ezekiel).

Meta. That in us which relies on Spirit and encourages us to place our full trust in Jehovah, that the Lord Jehovah (the spiritual I AM in us) may become the keeper of our sheep (our spiritual thoughts). Ezekiel was an enthusiast. His mind was open and alive to things spiritual. He shows us how to demonstrate strength.

Ezekiel saw a vision (Ezek. 1:4-28) in which the glory and splendor of God were revealed to him. The power of God's presence threw him down upon his face, where he remained for a time. But God called him to stand up and commanded him to go to Israel and carry a message to the people there. God encouraged him and told him not to be afraid when trials came (Ezek. 2:1-6; 3:17-21).

Ezekiel means *God strengthens.* We may apply this story of Ezekiel's vision to our own development, for it is a symbol of what may happen in any one's spiritual growth. When we touch the God consciousness we realize the presence of a mighty power, and at first we fall down; that is, we become inactive, for we feel our insignificance and our inability to do anything but worship. We soon find, however, that we must go forth and carry the message to others. We must be busy. We do not always need to preach in order to carry the message. We may become living messages that will be more eloquent in God's cause than words could possibly be.

God strengthens the one who seeks Him in the inner chamber and finds Him there. God fills that one with an urge that he cannot suppress; he must go forth and carry the message of life to all living creatures.

There is a great work to be done among men. They must be shown that good is real and that evil is unreal. They must be taught that evil is an inharmonious state of mind, an unprofitable state of mind. Lasting health, happiness, and life eternal come only when one lives and thinks in harmony with the divine law of the universe.

There is a great work to be done among men, but there is a greater work to be done within man. Every thought of the mind and every organ and cell of the body must be taught and redeemed before heaven can be established in your earth.

The mind and the body must be taught and assured that they are filled with the life and substance of God. They must be redeemed from the old race thoughts of sin and sickness or they will die; if they die, their blood will be on your head because of your not telling them. God is life and He sends forth the message of life. It is for all who will accept it. An organ of the body that receives God's message is quickened and vitalized. All the cells and organs of the body must be taught the truth about themselves; they must be taught that they are a harmonious part of God's creation and that they are not subject to discord or sickness. Begin today. Find the Father within you and carry His message to every living creature.

Ezel, ē'-zĕl (Heb.)—*roll off rapidly; go away quickly; depart suddenly; separation.*

A stone just outside the city where Saul lived. David hid by this stone when Jonathan made known to him that he must flee from Saul since Saul had determined to kill him. It was by Ezel that David and Jonathan parted (I Sam. 20:19).

Meta. A sense of *separation* that the soul (Jonathan) feels very keenly when forced, seemingly, to part from the true love quality (David) because of the hardness of the adverse, personal will (Saul), which is intent upon killing love out of consciousness. Thus love has to go into hiding, as it were; it must cease its active ministrations in the presence of the will. To the human soul (Jonathan), which longs for close association with love (David), the feeling of separation seems acute. Love, however, knows only eternal union with all that is good and true, and so a deeper oneness is established at this time of apparent parting (see the 42d verse of I Samuel, 20; also the last clause of the 41st verse).

Ezem (A. V., Joshua 15:29 and 19:3, Azem), ē'-zĕm (Heb.)—*collective growth; bone; strength; might; power.*

One of "the uttermost cities of the tribe of the children of Judah toward the border of Edom in the South" (Josh. 15:21, 29). In Joshua 19:3 and I Chronicles 4:29 Ezem is named as a city of Simeon.

Meta. An aggregation of thoughts in consciousness that are unified in their development in *strength*, stability, and *power* (*collective growth* bespeaks unity in development and *bone* bespeaks stability).

Ezer (A. V., I Chron. 1:38, Ezar), ē'-zer (Heb.)—*surround; envelop; help; unite; succor; aid; treasure.*

a A chief of the Horites of the children of Seir (Gen. 36:21). **b** The name of several Israelites (I Chron. 4:4; 7:21; Neh. 3:19; 12:42).

Meta. Man's innate belief in a substance, a wisdom (*treasure*), an established oneness with All-Good (*unite*), and a power to aid and to protect (*surround, envelop, help*) that come from something higher, stronger, and more real and lasting than sense consciousness can give. This innate belief springs up throughout the whole man, the seemingly sense part of himself as well as the thoughts and tendencies that belong to his higher nature (the latter is symbolized by the Israelitish men, while the sense part is suggested by the Ezer who was a Horite of Seir).

Ezion-geber (A. V., Ezion-gaber), ē'-zĭ-ŏn-gē'-bēr (Heb.)—*backbone of a mighty one; backbone of superman; backbone of a demigod; giant's backbone.*

A place on the Red Sea, a camping place of the Israelites when they were wandering in the wilderness (Num. 33:35). It is mentioned in Deuteronomy 2:8 in connection with Elath.

Meta. The Children of Israel's encamping at Ezion-geber refers to a great building up and strengthening of firmness and moral principle in consciousness. This place called Ezion-geber belongs to the main trunk of the tree of life in man, the spinal column (*backbone* also bespeaks firmness and strength).

Eznite, ĕz'-nīte (fr. Heb.)—*strong; firm; sharp; a spear.*

Adino the Eznite is the first named of David's mighty warriors, as given in II Samuel 23:8.

Meta. A perceptive, discerning, piercing thought in man. This thought is very strong, steadfast, and active in consciousness, in its defense of the ruling love ego (David).

Ezra, ĕz'-rà (Heb.)—*help.*

A priest and scribe of the Jews who brought a large number of Jewish exiles back to Palestine from the Babylonian captivity. He did much to establish the Truth among the people and helped to rebuild the Temple and the wall of Jerusalem. He worked with Nehemiah (Neh. 8:1-13; Book of Ezra).

Meta. There is a faculty of the mind that receives and transcribes upon the tablets of memory every wave of mind that touches the consciousness, whether from the flesh or from Spirit. This faculty is Ezra the scribe. This faculty may be exalted to a point where it will receive impressions from the spiritual side only; then it reads out of the law and interprets the spiritual meaning to all the people, or thoughts of the consciousness. Thus in Nehemiah 8 we find Ezra representing a spiritual consciousness that expresses the law of Being in such a way that all the thoughts (men and women) may receive the law in understanding.

In Ezra, 7th to 10th chapters, we find in the man Ezra the thought of the spirit of loyalty to Truth: "For Ezra had set his heart to seek the law of Jehovah, and to do it" (Ezra 7:10).

Ezra is often called the Puritan of the Bible. Metaphysically, therefore, he represents order, the faculty of the mind that holds every thought and act strictly to the Truth of Being, regardless of circumstances or environments.

The Book of Ezra is supposed to be a historical description of the return of the Children of Israel to Jerusalem after their captivity in Babylon, and of the rebuilding of the Temple in Jerusalem, under the direction of Cyrus, king of Persia.

The history of this Scripture is that Esdras was its author; that it was written long after the time at which it was supposed to have been written. Ezra and Esdras are the same. In the Apocıypha, Esdras says that he was quickened of Spirit and remembered these things. We perceive, therefore, that he was spiritually quickened and saw the building of the body temple. The Book of Ezra, then, is a lesson in the building of the house that is "not made with hands." It really describes the building of our consciousness—a house for God.

Ezrahite, ĕz'-rā-hīte (fr. Heb.)—a *native,* i. e., in his own country, not a foreigner.

a Ethan the Ezrahite was a wise man in Solomon's time (I Kings 4:31).
b Heman the Ezrahite (Psalms 88, title).

Meta. Intellectual understanding, which is natural to man in his seemingly mortal state (*a native,* i. e., in his own country). One may become very brilliant in so far as education and the intellect are concerned, yet fall far short of the true spiritual wisdom and understanding that Solomon signifies.

Ezri, ĕz'-rī (Heb.)—*my help; help of Jehovah.*

"And over them that did the work of the field for tillage of the ground was Ezri the son of Chelub" (I Chron. 27:26). This was during David's reign over Israel.

Meta. By denials and affirmations we cultivate the soil of our mind and of our body consciousness (ground); thus we make both ready for the bringing forth of abundant realization of substance and Truth. These denials of error and affirmations of Truth are, or they reveal, the *help of Jehovah* to us. They assist in making ready the way of the Lord throughout our entire consciousness, that better conditions in every way may be established.

F

faculties.
Meta. The twelve faculties of mind in man, as symbolized by the twelve disciples of Jesus Christ, with their location in the body, are as follows:

Faith—Peter—center of head, pineal gland.

Strength—Andrew—small of back.

Judgment—James, son of Zebedee—in lower part of solar plexus.

Love—John—back of heart, cardiac center.

Power—Philip—root of tongue.

Imagination—Bartholomew, or Nathanael—between the eyes.

Understanding—Thomas—front brain.

Will—Matthew—center front brain.

Order—James, son of Alphæus—navel.

Zeal—Simon the Canaanite—lower back head, medulla.

Elimination, or renunciation—Thaddæus—lower part of back.

Appropriation or life conservation—Judas—generative function.

The names of these faculties are not arbitrary—they can be expanded or changed to suit a broader understanding of their full nature. For example, Philip, at the root of the tongue, governs taste; he also controls the action of the larynx, and all power vibrations. So the term *power* expresses but a small part of his official capacity.

false prophets (Matt. 7:15).
Meta. Deceptive thoughts that have been built up by error, selfish desires. Outwardly they present the appearance of being candid and open; inwardly they are ravenous for personal sensation and worldly gain. In order to attain their end they deceive even "the elect."

"By their fruits ye shall know them." Constructive, spiritual thoughts always yield a bountiful harvest of good; therefore the motive back of every thought should be watched prayerfully. Under the analysis of Truth all deception is brought into the light and the fact that the fruit is error reveals the motive to be error. The tree (motive) should be cut down and cast into the fire (denied).

fasting.
Meta. Denial; also abstinence from error thoughts, to the end that we may meditate upon spiritual truths and incorporate them into our consciousness of oneness with the Father.

fear.

Meta. The word fear as used in I Sam. 12:24 implies reverence or respect for the law of God. "All your heart" represents the whole of the inner consciousness or the inner source of life, which should be dedicated to the Lord.

feast.

Meta. Appropriation in a large measure; that is, laying hold of divine potentialities. Several of the miracles of Jesus were in connection with a feast of some kind. Eating is the outer representation of an inward fact, that fact being spiritual. Jesus used the outer symbol to represent the spiritual reality when He told His disciples to eat the bread as His body, and drink the wine as His blood. When we affirm with spiritual understanding the fact of omnipresent substance we are eating the body of Christ, and when we affirm the omnipresent energy and eternal life of Spirit we are drinking the blood of Christ. When we enter into this understanding the outer symbols are not necessary—we have the substance in mind and spirit (John. 5:1).

The real "marriage feast" is that which results from the union of man with the Spirit of God. When this union takes place, man may eat of the heavenly manna and drink of the living waters.

A thirsting for the things of Spirit is necessary before one can really come to the spiritual marriage feast. Great desire for the light and purity and justice of Spirit is the power that draws man to God.

The Feast of the Tabernacles (Lev. 23:33-44) is a festival of ingathering, like our Thanksgiving Day. It was also a commemoration of the deliverance of the Children of Israel from the forty years in the wilderness and their entrance into the Promised Land.

All the feasts and festivities of the Jews had their foundation in divine science, although the people may not have understood their significance.

These Jewish feasts represent the harvest and gathering, by Spirit, of the surplus energies of the soul and the body. The Feast of the Tabernacles typifies the "passing over" of the nervous energy from one plane of consciousness to another and the inflow of substance from objective to subjective centers. When this inflow is complete it is called the last day of the feast. Then another step is necessary to complete the upward trend of man's being, and that is union with Spirit. This union is brought about through faith or belief in Spirit and in the higher life. When the soul thirsts after Truth it can be satisfied only by drinking in this higher life.

It is the spiritual I AM in man that says to the full soul, "Come unto me and drink" (John 7:37).

feeding, the five thousand.

Meta. In the universal mind principle there is a substance that Jesus called the "Father," which is also the mother or seed of all visible substance. It is the only real substance because it is unchangeable, while visible substance is in constant transition.

The origin of all substance is the *idea* of substance. This substance idea is purely spiritual and can be apprehended only by the mind. It is never visible to the eye, nor can it be sensed by man through any of his bodily functions. When the attention has been centered upon this idea of substance long enough, and strongly enough, a consciousness of substance is generated and, by the powers of the various faculties of the mind in right relation, visible substance is formed. In this way Jesus brought into visibility the loaves and fishes to feed the five thousand.

feet.

Meta. That phase of our understanding which comes into contact with substance. Consequently we can take possession of all substance that we comprehend and understand, in the name of I AM. This is the meaning of Joshua 1:3: "Every place that the sole of your foot shall tread upon, to you have I given it, as I spake unto Moses."

The feet are the most willing and patient servants of the body. They go all day at the bidding of the mind, and upon them rests the burden of the thought of materiality. The more we believe in matter, the greater the burden laid upon the feet and the more tired they become.

The denial of materiality is illustrated

in the washing of the disciples' feet by Jesus (John 13:5-10). Even Peter, spiritual faith, must be cleansed from belief in the reality of material conditions. To wash the feet seems a menial thing, but in this humble way Jesus taught and exemplified the willingness of divine love to serve, that man may be redeemed from the pride of the flesh.

There had been contention among the disciples as to who should sit at the Master's right, and who at His left, in the kingdom. Jesus was putting an end to this strife by bringing home to His followers the truth that he who willingly performs lowly, humble service for others, with no thought for personal distinction, is greatest in God's kingdom.

Jesus signifies the I AM, and the feet represent that phase of the understanding which connects one with the outer, or manifest, world and reveals the right relationship toward worldly conditions in general. The washing of the disciples' feet by Jesus therefore typifies a cleansing process, or a denial of personality and materiality.

Felix, fē'-lix (Lat.)—*happy.*

A Roman administrator of affairs in Judea (Acts 23:26—24:27).

Meta. Transient prosperity and happiness; the thoroughly sense consciousness that believes the manifest world is the all of existence. It poses as judge and decides all matters from the standpoint of personality and personal profit. Felix listened to the exhortations of Paul, hoping to receive money. It is not uncommon to find people who hold to Truth hoping that they can in some way make money out of it.

Felix was terrified at the revelation of his shortcomings when Paul reasoned of righteousness, temperance, and the judgment to come, but he said to Paul, "Go thy way for this time; and when I have a convenient season, I will call thee unto me." Felix was not quite ready to give up the ambitions of personality.

One must be willing to give up the desires of the personal man in order to enter into the joys of the universal. This is a hard thing to do. The whole life has been devoted to worldly aims and sensual attainments, and the thoughts are welded to the material. Yet a renunciation of self must take place in man before he can realize the will of God. "Not what I will, but what thou wilt," said Jesus. If one does not give up willingly, divine law brings about that precipitation of error thoughts into the visible life which dissolves its temporal structures. The change usually results in tragedy, as in the case of Felix. His reign as governor of Judea was short; history says that he was deposed because of corruption in office and that he came near losing his life over it.

Felix also could be said to represent the twin faculties, will and understanding, functioning in sense consciousness. The word of Truth (Paul) did not move the will but disturbed the understanding, which was "terrified."

Festus, fĕs'-tŭs (Lat.)—*joyful.*

The Roman governor of Judea who succeeded Felix (Acts 24:27).

Meta. The transient joys of the external life, or festivity and joyfulness in the outer life.

When Truth has once entered the mind there is no getting rid of its work. It may seem to be bound and in a dungeon (as was Paul) and forgotten by the prosperous ruler (Festus), yet it is not inactive. There is an undercurrent of true thought that keeps up an incessant tapping at the door of conscience and justice, and eventually changes the whole character. The changes that come to us during this process are hardly discernible on the surface, and we are not always conscious of the transformations that are going on unless we compare the thoughts of today with those of a few years ago, or before we listened to the statements of Truth. It is common for us to think that there has not been progress, but a little retrospection shows that the divine light has brought about a whole new set of ideas and dissipated the darkness in ways beyond description.

Festus, signifying festive, *joyful,* succeeded Felix as governor of the province of Judea. Agrippa, his brother-in-law, and governor of a neighboring province, with his wife Bernice was visiting Festus. Paul was called before these persons and commanded to restate his case that they might determine what should be done with him.

Agrippa means one who causes pain at birth. As Festus represents the transient joys of the external life, his brother-in-law, Agrippa, shows the close association of this sort of pleasure with pain. Drusilla and Bernice represent the voluptuous side of the sense life. A change is taking place in consciousness; the Truth is finding its way to the surface. The man and his soul are communing. Yet the walls of sense are not all broken down. It took many journeys of the priests and people around Jericho, with their trumpets of true words, to shatter the walls. The Truth comes before us again and again before we finally accept it, if we are enamored of the sense life.

Paul recalled the former illumination that had come at midday near Damascus. Festus declared that he was a lunatic—that his study had unbalanced his mind. When the recollection of some great spiritual uplift comes to us as a memory, we are apt to consider it a delusion, especially if we are back in the sense consciousness. In order to realize the Truth of the superconscious mind we must keep up contact with it through frequent prayer and meditation. After we have lost the connection and are submerged in the intellectual and physical realms of thought, the higher seems so far away that we count it a dream, or insanity.

So long as we are enjoying ourselves in the sense life, our ears are usually dull to Truth. Festus was not moved by Paul's eloquent appeal. But Agrippa (pain, the "grippe") brings us very close to an acceptance of the higher way. He was almost persuaded to believe. He did not get there at the first appeal, nor do we always do so; often there is still some external remedy that we have not yet tried, and that we hope will do the work. Hence we put off turning wholeheartedly to God and His Truth, a turning that is the only way to abiding life and good.

fire.

Meta. Fire is generally used in the Bible as a symbol of destruction of evil and error. It stands for cleansing and purification. In its true essence it is the fire of Spirit, or the divine energy, which never ceases its life-giving, purifying glow; when its cleansing work is completed in man's mind and body there is no more error to be consumed, and it then manifests in purified man as his eternal life. "Our God is a consuming fire" (Heb. 12:29; see Deut. 4:24; 9:3, and Isa. 33:14-16). Besides being "a consuming fire," our God is Spirit, life, love, substance, power, intelligence, Truth.

Fire also represents the positive, affirmative state of mind, as opposed to the negative or watery state.

firmament (Gen. 1:7).

Meta. Faith in mind power—a firm, unwavering place in consciousness.

fish.

Meta. Ideas of multiplication, fecundity.

The reason why Jesus so often used fish to illustrate His teaching was that He was a living demonstration of ideas, and all that He did was in the realm of ideas rather than the realm of effects. Fish represent ideas in which there is great possibility of increase; Jesus used these ideas to represent the inexhaustible, everywhere present abundance.

Like all Scripture, the passage that tells of Jesus' eating fish should be read in the spirit and not in the letter. Jesus came to establish the reign of righteousness and to bring about the time when "they shall not hurt nor destroy in all my holy mountain." Therefore we must look back of the mere letter and find the spiritual significance of every act of His. There is evidence that the accounts in which Jesus figures as a party to fish eating are symbolical of the mental side of eating, which is the appropriation of ideas, fish representing ideas.

flaming sword, or "flame of a sword" (Gen. 3:24).

Meta. I AM is the gate through which the thinker comes forth from the invisible to the visible, and it is through this gate that he must go to get into the presence of Spirit. "I am the way, and the truth, and the life." Hence we take words and go to God. We came out from His presence through the I AM gate, and we must return the same way. On the inner side of the gate is the Garden of Eden, but "the Cherubim, and the flame of a sword" are there, "to keep the way of the tree of life." "The flame of a sword" is the inner motive that rules our thoughts and acts. It turns every way to guard the tree of life, for the tree of life is the precious substance of the Father.

flocks.

Meta. Our thoughts.

flood (Gen. 7 and 8).

Meta. Science teaches that man's body contains several of the elements that are found in the earth. Religion goes a step farther and proclaims that man is an epitome of Being; that he is like his Maker in spirit, soul, and body, the image and likeness of God. If man's body is of a character similar to the earth's, it must in some of its phases be like its prototype. The earth is about three-fourths water and one-fourth land. The body is about eighty per cent water. As the waters of the earth evaporate and surround it with clouds of mist, so the waters of life surround man's body. As the electrical forces move upon the earthly mists, so the mental forces cause the invisible ethers of the body to condense and flood it. The poet's, "A flood of thoughts came o'er me," is not a metaphor but a plain statement of fact. When mind and body reach a certain tense, strained condition the law of oneness forces a conjunction and a flood follows.

With these analogies we may reasonably assume that the lesson of the Flood is especially valuable to us in the light of its parallel in our mind and body.

Man is an epitome of all that exists in Being, even to the Spirit of God, which is inspired in him. But man is a free agent. He can open his mind to the divine intelligence and *know* the creative

law, or he can declare his independence and work out his character through blind experimentation. Our race is in its experimental stage. In our ignorance we transgress the divine law to the last limit, and a great reaction sets in. This is "the flood." Disease names express the general condition, which is negative to the point of dissolution. Then that in us which looks to God in extremity is awakened and we seek the divine law. This obedience is Noah, through whom a new state of consciousness is saved.

Fortunatus, fôr-tū-nā'-tŭs (Lat.)— *fortunate; lucky; happy; prospered.*

A Christian man of Corinth; he came to Paul at Ephesus, and he carried Paul's first letter to the Corinthian church (I Cor. 16:17).

Meta. The opening of the consciousness to the greater good that is in store for those who love and serve God. Those who keep the divine law of Truth realize and receive true, spiritual riches, as well as abundant supply in the outer. According to I Corinthians 2:9, God has prepared, for them that love Him, greater good than they have asked or thought. As they unfold spiritually day by day, this good is revealed to them more and more fully by Spirit. To the human or sensate thought these persons are *lucky,* but those in understanding know that all things come about according to law.

forty days and forty nights (I Kings 19:8).

Meta. Completeness — foursquare. "And the city lieth foursquare, and the length thereof is as great as the breadth . . . the length and the breadth and the height thereof are equal" (Rev. 21:16).

fruit of the vine (Matt. 26:29).

Meta. The "fruit of the vine" which man drinks anew in the Father's kingdom is the consciousness of spiritual life direct from the Fountainhead.

G

Gaal, gā'-ăl (Heb.)—*rejection with loathing; abhorrence; contempt; loathing; pollution; unclean; abortion; miscarriage.*

Son of Ebed (Judg. 9:26-41). Gaal helped the men of Shechem in opposing Abimelech.

Meta. Abhorrence of that which is

destructive, unjust, and tyrannical in the phase of the will that Abimelech signifies. (See ABIMELECH.) This thought or tendency for which Gaal stands contains so much of personal opposition that it does not lead to real overcoming.

Gaal's fighting against Abimelech was very much like one error's opposing another; Gaal was killed in the conflict. We too find that we cannot do away with seeming evil by fighting it, since in cultivating the resisting thought in ourselves we build up an error that will destroy us in the end. If we do not wish to be overcome by evil we must heed the injunction given in Romans 12:21, which is that we shall "overcome evil with good." We must be so strong in the good that evil will not be able to stand in our presence.

Gaash, gā'-ăsh (Heb.)—*pushed with a sudden impulse; an earthquake; shaking; quaking; agitating; commotion; staggering.*

A mountain in the hill country of Ephraim. Timnath–heres, where Joshua was buried, was on the north of the mountain of Gaash (Judg. 2:9). II Samuel 23:30 mentions "Hiddai of the brooks of Gaash."

Meta. As the individual, under the leadership of some central idea (here it is Joshua, the I AM), succeeds in bringing all his faculties and forces into subservience to this central idea, the ideal itself seems to die (Joshua died) or to be merged into the general activity of his being as a whole. This is the *portion of the sun,* or *portion of Heres* (Timnath–heres, where Joshua was buried). When the central idea is absorbed by the being, the individual becomes *doubly fruitful* (a meaning of Ephraim; Timnath–heres was in the hill country of Ephraim) and his creative forces are greatly increased. In this state it is not long before a great accumulation of new forces and powers becomes active in consciousness, and one is very likely to feel a *quaking,* a trembling, in both mind and body (this is represented by Gaash). One should not fear because of this inner *commotion;* by one's holding steadfastly to the Truth and to one's power, dominion, and guidance through the Christ, all will be well,

and spiritual progress will continue. (See JOSHUA.)

Gabbai, gă'-hāi (Heb.)—*organic ingathering; collective increase; taxgatherer; collector; my exaltation; my grandeur; my pride.*

Name of a Benjamite family, or of the head man of a family of Benjamites, who lived in Jerusalem after the return from the Babylonian captivity (Neh. 11:8).

Meta. A thought or group of thoughts that attracts. It attracts to itself, by its active exercise of faith (Benjamin), other thoughts of a faith character, as well as much substance and energy, that a harvest time of good may be brought about.

Gabbatha, găb'-bă-thà (Heb.)—*elevated place; arched; vaulted; domed; proud; a knoll.*

A place in Jerusalem called "The Pavement" (John 19:13). It was in this place, on the judgment seat, that Pilate sentenced Jesus to be crucified.

Meta. The place in the intellect (*elevated place, arched, vaulted, domed, proud;* The Pavement, a hard state of thought) where the carnal will, or ruling principle of sense consciousness (Pilate), passes sentence upon the spiritual manifestation of man (Jesus) and bars it from consciousness. In the end, however, it is only the sensual that can be killed out. Spiritual man and his manifestations cannot be destroyed; they simply rise to greater power as the sensual dies and so gives place to the divine.

Gabriel, gā'-brĭ-ĕl (Heb.)—*mighty man of God; hero of God; man of God; God is my strength.*

The angel who appeared to Daniel to interpret his vision to him (Dan. 8:16). This angel also appeared to Zacharias to tell him of the coming birth of John the Baptist (Luke 1:19), and to Mary, concerning the birth of Jesus (Luke 1:26). To Zacharias this angel said, "I am Gabriel, that stand in the presence of God."

Gabriel signifies man in realization and demonstration of his I AM power and might, unified with his inner faculties and elevated to conscious and manifest oneness with God. This man will rule the universe.

The name Gabriel, and the Gibborim, mighty men of renown, the offspring of the sons of God and the daughters of men, of Genesis 6:4, are very closely allied. In the latter, however, the consciousness of I AM power and might (sons of God) unified with the inner soul faculties (daughters of men) does not hold to God, the good—is not conscious of God, and so brings about great evil, which culminates in the Flood.

Gabriel could also be said to refer to the masculine or wisdom phase of the divine in man. The masculine contacts the love (feminine, soul, Mary) phase of man's spiritual nature, and causes man to become conscious of the Christ in himself, to the end that the individual may bring this Christ into expression and manifestation.

Gad, găd (Heb.)—*fortune; fortunate; good fortune; abundance; dispenser of fortune; lot; seer; organized division; assembly; troop; the god Jupiter.*

Seventh son of Jacob, and first of Zilpah, Leah's maid. "And Leah said, Fortunate! and she called his name Gad" (Gen. 30:11). Jacob's blessing to this son was (Gen. 49:19):
"Gad, a troop (a marauding band, margin) shall press upon him;
But he shall press upon their heel."
Moses' blessing to the tribe of Gad was (Deut. 33:20, 21):
"Blessed be he that enlargeth Gad:
He dwelleth as a lioness,
And teareth the arm, yea, the crown of the head.
And he provided the first part for himself,
For there was the lawgiver's portion (a ruler's portion, margin) reserved;
And he came *with* the heads of the people;
He executed the righteousness of Jehovah,
And his ordinances with Israel."
In the Fenton translation of the Bible, Moses' blessing is given in this way:
"Let the horseman, Gad, be blest.
Like a tiger he crouches down,
And tears with his arms and jaws!
But he thought at the first for himself,
So was granted a princely home,

And produced the leaders of men,
Who did the work of the LORD,
And first led My People right."
The Gadites were a warlike people.

Meta. The faculty of power ("Let the horseman, Gad, be blest"), but still mostly on the personal plane and not lifted to truly spiritual expression.

Of the disciples of Jesus, Philip, *a lover of horses*, represents the power faculty. (See PHILIP.)

Gadarenes (A. V., Gergesenes), găd-ă-rēneş' (Gk. fr. Heb.)—*fortunate; organized; assembled; trooped in; walled about; fortified.*

Inhabitants of Gadara (Matt. 8:28). Gadara means *walled.* Gerasenes is another name for the same people.

Meta. Strongly *organized* thoughts of energy and power in the subconscious realm of mind in man. When freed from carnal desires and warring tendencies, these thoughts will work mightily for the good of the individual, but in their unredeemed or error-possessed state they are very violent and destructive. (Upon coming into the land of the Gadarenes, Jesus was met by "two possessed with demons, coming forth out of the tombs, exceeding fierce, so that no man could pass by that way"—see Mark 5:1 also —and Jesus cast the demons out of the men and healed them.)

Gaddi, găd'-dī (Heb.)—*fortunate; of the fortunate; belonging to fortune, i. e., worshiper of Jupiter; of the organization; of the troop; my troop.*

Son of Susi (Num. 13:11). He was of the tribe of Manasseh, and was one of the twelve men whom Moses sent to spy out the land of Canaan.

Meta. The power (Susi, meaning *horseman,* and symbolizing power) of understanding (Manasseh) in individual consciousness, which enables one to perceive the fertility and productiveness of the Promised Land (the great possibilities of spiritual attainment that lie in man). At the Gaddi stage of its unfoldment, however, this understanding is still more intellectual in its nature than it is spiritual; it leads one to magnify the seeming errors that one has to overcome (the enemies in the land) in order to redeem his whole being. Thus it tends to discourage one from making the attempt.

Gaddiel, găd'-dĭ-ĕl (Heb.)—*God is my fortune; fortune of God; assembly of God; troop of God; organized of God.*

One of the twelve spies, a son of Sodi, of the tribe of Zebulun (Num. 13:10).

Meta. An understanding that all supply and all good, all orderly arrangement and demonstration of Truth in and for the individual, come from God. This understanding, or thought, belongs to the Zebulun, or order, consciousness. While it perceives the desirability of the Promised Land (of the attainment of perfection and immortality for the whole man), it is not yet spiritual enough in its nature, not active enough in consciousness, not sure enough of God's presence and power, to join fearlessly in attempting to reach the goal. Therefore it discourages the individual from trying to possess the land.

Gadi, gā'-dī (Heb.)—*fortunate; my fortune; of Gad,* i. e., *Jupiter; of the troop; organizer; assembler; a kid,* so called from its cropping the herbage.

Father of Menahem, who was an evil king over Israel. Menahem had killed Shallum, the former king, and taken the throne (II Kings 15:14).

Meta. A ruling thought in man that is of an organizing, assembling, drawing-together character; appropriation. Since this thought is directed by carnal, material ideas, and by belief in luck or chance, instead of a true love for and faith in the law of Spirit, it brings forth error instead of good. (See MENAHEM.)

Gadites, găd'-ītes (fr. Heb.)—*of Gad; posterity of Gad.*

Descendants of Gad, the son of Jacob (Deut. 3:12).

Meta. The assemblage of organized thoughts that belong to the power faculty in individual consciousness. These thoughts are presented as power because they are organized, assembled into troops or organs. The character "G" is the organic sign, associated with all organic ideas, conducting, leading, organizing.

Gaham, gā'-hăm (Heb.)—*flaming; burning; consuming; charring; blackness.*

Son of Abraham's brother Nahor, by his concubine Reumah (Gen. 22:24).

Meta. The heat of sense consciousness brought to a climax, a focus, and burning itself out. This is caused by the higher desires (Nahor and Reumah, parents of Gaham) that have been aroused by and accompany the awakening of faith (Abraham) in the individual. Thus a reaction sets in, the whole consciousness revolts against sense beliefs and activities, and a degree of purification is accomplished.

Gahar, gā'-här (Heb.)—*lurker; lurking place; hiding place; concealment; prostration.*

His children were of the Nethinim who returned from the Babylonian captivity (Ezra 2:47).

Meta. A hidden thought of deep lowliness and humility, which is carried to excess because of its being based on a feeling of servitude to God instead of being based on a realization of divine sonship. (The Nethinim were servants —many of them were slaves, virtually —who did the menial work in the Temple and the Temple worship.)

Gaius, gā'-ĭŭs (Gk.)—*of the earth; earthy man; exulting; rejoicing; gladness; Lord.*

Several Christian men by this name are mentioned in the New Testament. They all seem to have been friends of Paul's and workers with him. One was from Derbe (Acts 20:4); another one was of Corinth (I Cor. 1:14); another was of Macedonia (Acts 19:29). John's third Epistle was written to a Christian named Gaius, also.

Meta. The acceptance by the body consciousness (*of the earth, earthy man*) of the truth pertaining to the divine law, or *Lord.* This acceptance of Truth by the seemingly earthy phase of man's being works with Paul (the activity of the word of Truth) in bringing about the redemption of the body; great *gladness* and *rejoicing* are thus realized by the individual.

Galal, gā'-lăl (Heb.) — *rolling; weighty; massive; great; the force of momentum; a log; trunk; stone; prominent; an idol.*

Three Israelitish men by this name

are mentioned (I Chron. 9:15, 16; Neh. 11:17). They were all Levites who served in the Temple.

Meta. The great spiritual action (*rhythmic, rolling*) that takes place in consciousness while love thoughts (Levites) are establishing harmony, peace, and true worship of God. This work of love in man's being is very important (*weighty, great, prominent*), and increases as it proceeds (*the force of momentum;* the idea here is something that accumulates in size or power as it rolls along).

Galatia, gă-lā'-ti-à (fr. Gk.)—*Gallic Greece; land of the Gauls; white as milk.*

A province in Asia Minor where Paul did much teaching (Acts 16:6; 18:23).

Meta. Pure truths, but the simplest of truths, that belong to babes in Christ. In Acts 16:6 Galatia signifies a state of thought that is not yet ready for the operation of the word of Truth (Paul).

Galatians, gă-lā'-tĭăns (fr. Gk.)—*of or belonging to Galatia.*

People of Galatia, but here more especially the ones to whom Paul wrote his Epistle to the Galatians.

Meta. The thoughts that belong to the Galatia state of consciousness. (See GALATIA.)

The assembly of Christians at Galatia, to whom Paul wrote his Epistle, would be thoughts belonging to the Galatia consciousness; the word of Truth (Paul), doing its quickening work in the mind and the body of the individual, is awakening these thoughts to life and to an understanding of the things pertaining to Truth.

Galeed, gă̆l'-ĕ-ĕd (Heb.)—*massive witness; heap of witnesses; rock of time; great endurance.*

The heap of stones that Jacob and Laban gathered for a witness between them when Jacob with his wives, children, and possessions left Laban to return to Esau and to Jacob's own country. This heap of stones was also called Mizpah, and Jegar–saha–dutha (Gen. 31:47).

Meta. Laban said, "Jehovah watch between me and thee," and "God is witness betwixt me and thee" (verses 49 and 50). Mizpah symbolizes the watchtower of prayer, and Galeed signifies the witness that Spirit within man bears to the Truth. By following the true Jehovah Spirit in ourselves we shall always deal justly with every phase of our consciousness and of our entire organism; also, with other persons.

Galilæans, gă̆l-ĭ-læ'-ăns (Gk. fr. Heb.) —*of or belonging to Galilee; rolled; circle; circuit.*

Natives of Galilee (Acts 2:7). The text here refers especially to the disciples of Jesus who had just received the Holy Spirit baptism and were preaching the Gospel in "other tongues, as the Spirit gave them utterance."

Meta. Active life thoughts, illumined thoughts in the activity of life consciousness that exalt the Christ, they having received the Truth "at the feast" of spiritual communion and appropriation (John 4:45).

Galilee, gă̆l'-ĭ-lēe (Gk. fr. Heb.)—*rolling; turning; a ring; a circle; a band; a circuit; rolling energy,* i. e., *momentum.*

a One of the three main divisions of the country of Palestine. At one time it consisted of the circuit of twenty towns that Solomon gave to Hiram king of Tyre. At the time of Jesus Chirst it was a part of Palestine in which He did much of His ministry. The disciples were Galileans (Acts 2:7), and Nazareth, the home of Jesus, was in Galilee (Matt. 2:22; Isa. 9:1). **b** The name of a sea in Palestine (Matt. 4:18).

Meta. Energy of life; life activity; soul energy; power, force, energy, acting in conjunction with substance.

Jesus' entrance into Galilee (John 4:43-54) represents the increased activity that ensues when Truth comes down into the subconscious realm and brings about the realization of Christhood, after personality has been denied and praise of God has been set up.

When the illumined intellect (John the Baptist) is cut off from outer expression, the spiritual I AM (Jesus) withdraws into Galilee (consciousness of endless activity), in order to come into closer contact with God, the source of all energy. (See Matt. 4:12.)

"Galilee," associated with "mountain" (Matt. 28:16, 17), symbolizes a high consciousness of life. Science tells us that this Galilee consciousness exists everywhere as an interpenetrating ether. Jesus called it "the kingdom of the heavens." The disciples represent man's faculties. Our work is to call the attention of these faculties to this "kingdom of the heavens" within us. Some of them will appreciate and enter into it, while others will be unaffected, will be dubious.

Man has a dual nervous system. The nerves are the wires that conduct the messages of the mind to every part of the organism. The voluntary nervous system centers in the spinal cord. The involuntary, or sympathetic, nervous system centers in the solar plexus. A constant flow of nervous energy is making the circuit of this nervous system and carrying all kinds of messages from the mind. This sea of vitality is designated in the history of Jesus as the Sea of Galilee. John 6:1 means that I AM passed over the voluntary nervous energy to the involuntary, "to the other side," and concentrated at the solar plexus. The "great multitude" that followed are the legions of thoughts that swarm in the mind, seeking harmony. The "mountain" into which Jesus went is the high spiritual consciousness.

Gallim, găl'-lĭm (Heb.)—*heaps; rolling waters; rushing waters; fountains; springs.*

The home of Palti the son of Laish, to whom Saul gave Michal his daughter, David's wife (I Sam. 25:44). This place is thought to have been a town of Benjamin. Isaiah 10:30 also mentions a place called Gallim, against which the Assyrians were to come.

Meta. Thoughts about life. Because of the activity of the personal will (Saul) and the sense reasonings of the unillumined intellect (Assyrians), devitalizing thoughts are piled up (*heaps*) in consciousness, and for the time being they keep the *fountains* of life in a confused, tempestuous state (*rolling waters, rushing waters*) and keep life from being consciously realized in its purity and truth; therefore the individual is not revitalized and renewed.

Gallio, găl'-lĭ-ō (Gk.)—*one who lives on milk; white as milk.*

A Roman proconsul of Achaia. He paid no attention when the Jews who opposed Christianity beat Sosthenes, the ruler of the synagogue at Corinth, and would have nothing to do with religious matters and differences (Acts 18:12-17).

Meta. A ruling thought that is entirely intellectual. It has no spiritual illumination, and no desire for anything of a spiritual nature. (The metaphysical use of *gala* or *galactos,* milk, to designate the most simple and elemental of Christian truths would indicate that that which Gallio signifies is limited to the most elemental and material phases of consciousness.)

Gamaliel, gă-mā'-lĭ-ĕl (Heb.)—*led of God; God's recompense; reward of God; benefits of God.*

a A prince of the Israelitish tribe of Manasseh (Num. 2:20). **b** a Pharisee, a doctor of the Jewish law. He advised the council of Jews, who had taken Peter and other apostles prisoners, to be lenient with them and to let them prove by their fruits whether their doctrine was true or not (Acts 5:34; 22:3).

Meta. Gamaliel, the "doctor of the law" who advocates that Truth be tested by its fruits, was a leader among the most conservative Pharisees; he recommended common sense and reason. Prejudice and bigotry often blind us to real merit. There is in every one that spirit of fairness which will give every idea a chance to prove itself. "If this counsel or this work be of men, it will be overthrown: but if it is of God, ye will not be able to overthrow them" (Acts 5:38, 39). This is the conclusion of every well-balanced mind, and we should listen to every doctrine with this good judgment to the front.

Gamul, gā'-mŭl (Heb.)—*weaned, i. e., matured; render deserts; pay; recompense; reward; retribution.*

A priest to whom the twenty-second lot fell for service in the Temple (I Chron. 24:17). This was in David's reign, before the real Temple at Jerusalem was built.

Meta. A religious thought or tendency that is beginning to see something of the real law back of rites and ceremonies. This thought or tendency is *weaned,* as it were, from purely formal ideas of religion and is *matured* in the understanding of that which pertains to the natural man. It is now open to the spiritual. It has learned through the rule of David (love) that true, loving service in the Temple (body) brings about a sure compensation of abiding good.

Gareb, gā'-rĕb (Heb.) — *scratch; scrape; rough; scabby; mangy; scurf; scurvy; leprous; reviled; despised; unclean.*

a An Ithrite, one of David's thirty mighty warriors (II Sam. 23:38). **b** The name of a hill near Jerusalem. Some think this hill to be the same place as Golgotha (Jer. 31:39).

Meta. An Ithrite is a descendant of Jether, and both of these names refer to excellence, preëminence, superiority. Ideals of this kind may, however, while under the intellectual thought, aid in establishing love (David) in consciousness and in defending that which is good; yet they are apt to become very aggressive and resistant toward anything that appears to be evil or inferior. Such an idea scorns and disdains lower ideals than those for which it stands. This is Gareb, and unless this idea changes its attitude so as to conform more to the love that overcomes evil with good, it will cause itself to appear in a very mean light to the rest of the consciousness; this is suggested by the definitions of Gareb. It is very likely, too, to turn against spiritual ideals that are as yet beyond its comprehension. Jesus was reviled, smitten, and despised by those who thought that they were God's chosen people. When the high thoughts in man are really guided by Spirit, overcoming is accomplished in a much easier and better way and the results are then entirely good. The sense man, however, or the intellectual, which is suggested by Golgotha, gets so much of a fighting, reviling spirit into its attempts at reform that no real good is accomplished; moreover, much strife and much apparent foulness are stirred up.

Garmite, gär'-mīte (fr. Heb.)—*bony; strong.*

Keilah the Garmite, a man mentioned as being one of the descendants of Judah (I Chron. 4:19).

Meta. Man's innate belief in the truth that his organism is structurally strong and enduring.

Gashmu, găsh'-mu̧ (Heb.)—*rain; violent rainstorm; heavy downpour; bodylike; corporeal body; corporealness.*

An Arabian who opposed the Jews in the rebuilding of the Temple and the walls of Jerusalem (Neh. 6:6). Same as Geshem.

Meta. A leading factor in the Arabia state of consciousness in man. The Arabians signify unproductive thoughts and tendencies. The ruling tendency for which Gashmu stands believes firmly in the permanent materiality of man's outer consciousness and body. Gashmu signifies the error belief that every one who attempts to redeem and spiritualize his body has to deal with: the belief that it is utterly impossible to make the body immortal, and that it is foolish, and really a rebellion against nature and against God, to try to do so. (*Corporealness* refers to the body as material; the rebuilding of Jerusalem's wall signifies the renewing and eventually complete spiritualizing of the body.)

Gatam, gā'-tăm (Heb.)—*puny; thin; greatest fatigue; complete breath exhaustion; exhausted; burned field.*

Son of Eliphaz the eldest son of Esau, and a chief (Gen. 36:11).

Meta. The result of a belief in sense man that his strength is entirely material and not spiritual (Eliphaz, father of Gatam, stands for an active thought of strength). Strength is from God, though that which Eliphaz signifies is of the physical consciousness and does not lay hold of the truth about strength. Meanings attributed to Gatam—*puny, thin, greatest fatigue, exhausted, burned field*—clearly illustrate the outcome of believing in material strength. Until man realizes that his strength is spiritual, it cannot become abiding, unfailing, and enduring.

Gath, găth (Heb.)—*wine press; wine vat; fortune.*

A city of the Philistines (I Sam. 5:8; Amos 6:2).

Meta. A group of thoughts in the sense consciousness of man that believe in trial (*wine press*), and look upon all experiences from the standpoint of seeming trial and suffering. Thus it causes the one who gives heed to it to become conscious of that which appears to be evil, when he should be busy seeing and believing in good only and thus coming into a consciousness of the blessing aspect of all his overcoming.

Gath–hepher (A. V., Josh. 19:13, Gittah–hepher), găth–hē'-phĕr (Heb.)— *wine press of the pit; wine press of the well; wine press of the pitfall.*

A city of Zebulun (Josh. 19:13); it was the birthplace of the prophet Jonah (II Kings 14:25).

Meta. At every inflow of new life and Truth into consciousness there must be a letting go of old ideas and their accompanying habits, that the new may become established. To the sense mind of man this process of giving up his cherished beliefs is a sore trial (*wine press of the pit*). He sees only the trying aspect of the experience. This is what Gath–hepher stands for.

Gath–rimmon, găth–rĭm'-mŏn (Heb.) —*wine press of Rimmon; wine press of the height; wine press of the pomegranate.*

A city of Dan; it was given over to the Levites (Josh. 19:45; 21:24).

Meta. The lifting up of the "trial" idea in consciousness (*wine press of the height*) by seeing the fruitfulness of overcoming (*wine press of Rimmon, or of the pomegranate,* pomegranate signifying fruitfulness). As man comes into a true understanding of judgment (Dan) through love (Levites) he learns to rejoice in seeing trial because of the good that results from letting go of error and becoming established in Truth. Thus in time every vestige of the trial side of his overcoming will pass away.

Gaza, gā'-zȧ (Gk. from Heb. Azzah)— *strength; firmness; power; stronghold; fortified.*

A very old place—a border city of the Canaanites (Gen. 10:19), allotted to Judah (Josh. 15:47). It was one of the five cities of the Philistines (I Sam. 6:17). Samson did a great feat of strength in Gaza (Judg. 16:1-3). It was while he was on his way to Gaza ("the same is desert") that Philip was sent by Spirit to teach and baptize the Ethiopian eunuch (Acts 8:26). Jeremiah prophesied against the kings of Gaza (Jer. 25:20).

Meta. Strength on a purely sense or physical plane; it must become spiritual; that is, man must know God as the one source of his strength before his strength can become consciously abiding.

Gaza (Acts 8:26) means *strength,* whose center of action is in the loins, but it is "desert." Strength has departed from that part of the consciousness, and weakness and barrenness occupy its place. The Ethiopian eunuch represents the ignorance and impotency of the consciousness acting at this center. He is reading aloud the Scripture as he rides along in his chariot, but there is no understanding. This means that life is a mere sound of empty words to the transitory physical strength that journeys for a human lifetime in the vehicle of the body. An understanding of the power of the redemptive Christ life will change all this, however: "Philip . . . preached unto him Jesus."

Gazez, gā'-zĕz (Heb.)—*shearer; cut close; shaved; cut off.*

Son of Caleb by his concubine, Ephah (I Chron. 2:46). In this same text another is mentioned; he Gazez seems to be a son of Haran who was a son of Caleb and Ephah.

Meta. Caleb, in the highest, truest sense, represents spiritual faith and enthusiasm. He believed that the Israelites were able to go up and possess the Promised Land. Through faith the I AM is ready and willing to enter the inner consciousness and possess the people (soul forces). Ephah, Caleb's concubine, symbolizes the soul reaching out for Truth, though as yet darkened by sense beliefs. Gazez, the child of this union —meaning *shearer,* one who cuts off or severs something from an object—refers to the putting off of the seeming soul darkness of ignorance, that true light may shine throughout both mind and body.

Gazites, gā'-zītes (fr. Heb.).

Inhabitants of Gaza (Josh. 13:3).

Meta. Thoughts belonging to human-strength consciousness in man. (See

GAZA.)

Gazzam, găz′-zăm (Heb.)—*devouring; consuming.*

His children were of the Nethinim who returned from the Babylonian captivity (Ezra 2:48).

Meta. A *devouring, consuming,* destroying thought or belief that belongs to the religious consciousness in man. It comes from the destructive idea of killing out all that is ungodlike; it is of the "servant" class, because the sonship or Christ idea is to lift up and redeem. (The Nethinim were servants in the Temple; they served the priests and did all the menial work.)

Geba (A. V., Joshua 18:24, Ezra 2:26, and Nehemiah 7:30, Gaba), gē′-bȧ (Heb.) —*high; as a mountain; a hill.*

A city of Benjamin that was given over to the children of Aaron the priest (Josh. 21:17).

Meta. A high state of consciousness, the result of an active faith (Benjamin) combined with an executive, or practical, working understanding of divine law (Aaron).

Gebal, gē′-băl (Heb.)—*twisted cord for binding; a line; boundary line; boundary; border; limits; mountain,* i. e., *a natural boundary.*

A Phœnician city. It is mentioned with Edom, Moab, Ammon, and Amalek, in Psalms 83:6, 7, and with Tyre in Ezekiel 27:8, 9 (Tyre and Sidon were cities of Phoenicia). In Joshua 13:5 we read of the land of the Gebalites.

Meta. That in sense consciousness which marks the *limits,* the *boundary line,* of purely human conquest, capacity, and influence apart from the recognition and acknowledgment of God, Spirit, as the one source of all true dominion and power. (Phoenicia means *land of palm trees;* also *purple* and *red.* Palm trees refer to conquest, victory; purple signifies power; red typifies life activity.)

Gebim, gē′-bĭm (Heb.)—*reservoirs,* i. e., *water gatherers* or *collectors; cisterns; marshes; pits; ditches; trenches; springs,* i. e., *issuing out of the ground; locusts.* In Isaiah 33:4, "locusts"; in Jeremiah 14:3, "pits"; the A. S. V., Jeremiah 14:3, gives "cisterns" instead of "pits."

A Benjamite city near Jerusalem, and between Anathoth and Nob. "The inhabitants of Gebim flee for safety" from the Assyrians (Isa. 10:31).

Meta. Cisterns, reservoirs, and *ditches* are artificial places for containing water and for carrying away surplus water. *Trenches* here are the same as *ditches.* In Jeremiah 2:13 we read, "For my people have committed two evils: they have forsaken me, the fountain of living waters, and hewed them out cisterns, broken cisterns, that can hold no water." Water here represents life, and the "broken cisterns" are sense man's conception of a material and corruptible body, incapable of entering into immortality, abiding life. *Springs* suggest the natural springing up of abundant life into man's consciousness.

Gebim signifies the artificial and untrue thoughts about life that are held by the sense man; even his religious thoughts have a very limited concept of true, spiritual life, and what little they do comprehend is easily put to flight by the Assyrians (the false reasonings of sense).

Gedaliah, gĕd-ȧ-lī′-ăh (Heb.)—*whom Jah has made great; Jehovah is great; great things of Jehovah,* i. e., *wonders; Jehovah is my strength; my increase is from Jehovah.*

a Son of Ahikam, and governor of the Jewish people who were left in Judah after it was captured by Nebuchadnezzar, king of Babylon (II Kings 25:22). **b** A musician in the Temple during David's reign (I Chron. 25:3). **c** A priest who had a foreign wife after the return from the Babylonian captivity (Ezra 10:18). **d** Son of Pashhur (Jer. 38:1). **e** The grandfather of Zephaniah (Zeph. 1:1).

Meta. The recognition by the higher religious and spiritual thoughts of man that all true greatness and might are of God and that they express in and through man by Spirit (*whom Jah has made great, Jehovah is great, Jehovah is my strength, my increase is from Jehovah*).

Geder, gē′-dẽr (Heb.)—*surrounded; inclosed; a walled-in place; a garden; a court; a city; a fortification; protection; defense.*

A very old Canaanitish city that was captured by Joshua (Josh. 12:13).

Meta. The significance is the same as that of Beth–gader, which is believed to be the same city as Geder. (See BETH–GADER.)

Gederah (A. V., I Chronicles 4:23, hedges), gĕ-dē′-răh, (Heb.)—*a walled place; an inclosure; a protection; a fortification; a cote; a fold, for sheep or cattle; sheepfold; corral.* The final "h" in Gederah is the symbol of the breath, life, soul, spirit. This character, "he," while forming a feminine construction, emphasizes the expression to which it is attached.

A city in the lowlands of Judah (Josh. 15:36).

Meta. The metaphysical import of Gederah is virtually the same as that of Geder, except that Gederah refers more to the soul, or feminine, in man. When the soul is established in the consciousness that God is man's protection, defense, and unconquerable strength, it (the soul) becomes *a fold, for sheep or cattle,* a place where man's natural thoughts about life and strength can abide and be fed and protected.

Gederathite, gĕd′-ĕ-răth-īte (fr. the Heb.)—*of Gederah; a native of Gederah.*

Jozabad, the Gederathite, was one of David's thirty mighty warriors (I Chron. 12:4).

Meta. A strong, active, prominent thought belonging to the Gederah consciousness. (See GEDERAH.)

Gederite, gĕd′-ĕ-rīte (fr. Heb.)—*of or belonging to Geder; a native of Geder.*

Baal–hanan the Gederite was "over the olive-trees and the sycomore-trees that were in the lowland," during the reign of David (I Chron. 27:28).

Meta. A thought belonging to the Geder consciousness in man. (See GEDER and BETH–GADER.)

Gederoth, gĕ-dē′-rŏth (Heb.)—*inclosures; protections; sheepfolds; fortresses.*

A city in the lowlands of Judah (Josh. 15:41).

Meta. The plural form of Geder; it refers to the multiplying in consciousness of the assurance of Spirit as man's protection, defense, and unfailing strength. (See GEDER and GEDERAH.)

Gederothaim, gĕd-ĕ-rô-thā′-ĭm (Heb.) —*double walls; double inclosures; double protections; two fortifications; two folds.*

A city in the lowlands in the allotment of Judah; it is mentioned with Gederah (Josh. 15:36).

Meta. The Geder and Gederah consciousness doubled in strength. See GEDER and GEDERAH.) It is just possible, however, that this may refer rather to the double-minded attitude of man toward this Gederah consciousness—to his material concept of it as well as his spiritual understanding of it.

Gedor, gē′-dôr (Heb.)—*surrounding; enveloping; a wall; an inclosing protection; fold; fortification.*

a A city in the hill country of Judah (Josh. 15:58). **b** The Gedor of I Chronicles 4:39 is thought to be the same place as the Geder of Joshua 12:13. **c** A Benjamite town, the home of Jeroham, whose sons Joelah and Zebadiah joined David at Ziklag when David was in hiding from Saul (I Chron. 12:7). **d** An Israelitish man, a Benjamite (I Chron. 8:31; 9:37). **e** The name Gedor occurs in I Chronicles 4:4, 18 in the genealogy of Judah.

Meta. Man's innate yet exalted belief in divine strength and protection active in consciousness. (See GEDER and BETH–GADER.)

Gehazi, gĕ-hā′-zī (Heb.)—*valley of vision; valley of sight; depressed vision; diminished sight.*

The prophet Elisha's servant (II Kings 4:12).

Meta. Sight, or perception.

II Kings 5:20-25 shows that the sight that Gehazi symbolizes must be intellectual perception, since it cannot always be relied upon; here, it judges by appearances, and does not discern the inner work of the soul. The definitions of the name also point to physical sight rather than spiritual. Gehazi's theft and falsehoods were punished with leprosy.

Gehenna, gê-hĕnn-à (fr. Heb.)—*valley of Hinnom; valley of lamentation; valley of groaning* (because of the cries and groans of the victims).

A valley south of Jerusalem where the refuse of the city was burned. (The word Gehenna is not used in the American Standard Version, but it is the same as the Valley of Hinnom.)

Meta. The purifying fires of the soul are symbolized by the fires of Gehenna. (See HELL, and HINNOM, for further explanation.)

Geliloth, ġĕl'-ĭ-lŏth (Heb.)—*rings; bands; circles; circuits; regions.*

A place on the southern boundary of Benjamin (Josh. 18:17). It is believed to be the same place as Gilgal, and is called Gilgal in Joshua 15:7.

Meta. Unity of the inner thought and life (*rings, circles, circuits*). When sense bondage is rolled away (see GILGAL) one comes into spiritual unity and harmony, and becomes more alive and active.

Gemalli, ġĕ-măl'-lī (Heb.)—*of the camel; camel owner; camel rider; camel driver.*

Father of Ammiel, of the tribe of Dan (Num. 13:12). (See AMMIEL.)

Meta. Dominion over and direction of the nature in man that the "camel" represents—patience, persistence, determination, that tendency of thought which conducts unswervingly to an end. If directed by true understanding this tendency is very valuable; but when it is guided by error it often amounts to great obstinacy and a steadfast refusal to listen to true reason and wisdom. (See CAMEL and BETH–GAMUL.)

Gemariah, ġĕm-ȧ-rī'-ȧh (Heb.)—*whom Jehovah has perfected; Jehovah has accomplished; completed by Jehovah.*

a Son of Hilkiah. He was a messenger of King Zedekiah's to the king of Babylon. Jeremiah also sent a letter by him and by Elasah, the son of Shaphan, to the Jewish captives in Babylon; Jeremiah's message was to the effect that the captives should make the very best of their present state, do the very best that they could where they were, and not listen to false prophets who would prophesy a quick deliverance for them (Jer. 29:3). b Another Gemariah was the son of Shaphan the scribe, and father of Micaiah; his son Micaiah was one of those who listened to the reading of the roll by Baruch, and told the king about it (Jer. 36:10).

Meta. The innate belief, deep within the subjective religious nature of each individual, that God does, or will, accomplish the good that He has idealized, even the perfecting of man and the universe.

Genesis, ġĕn'-ĕ-sĭs (Gk.)—*source; origin; beginning; begetting; birth; lineage.*

The first book of the Bible; it begins with an account of creation, of the *beginning* of manifest man and the manifest universe; the Hebrew name is Sepher Berashith, *book of creations, book of first causes, book of unfolding* or *manifesting of elemental principles, book of emanations.*

Meta. Genesis points to the new birth, and to the perfection of man in the regeneration.

Gennesaret, ġĕn-nĕs'-ȧ-rĕt (Gk. fr. Heb.)—*garden of the prince; prince's garden; valley of riches.*

A lake in Palestine (Luke 5:1). The Sea of Galilee and Sea of Tiberias are other names for this lake; in the Old Testament it is called Chinnereth and Chinneroth.

Meta. Sea of divine life. We are related, both within the consciousness and without, to all creation through the universal life principle. When we recognize our unity with the one life, and with all life, we are on the way to true exaltation and rulership and abundant substance (*prince's garden, garden of riches*). (See GALILEE and CHINNERETH.)

Gentiles, ġĕn'-tīleṣ (Lat.)—*the nations; nations; peoples; all nations and peoples outside of a given body.*

The Gentiles of the Bible comprise all nations and peoples that were not of Israelitish origin and faith (Isa. 49:6; Acts 13:46).

Meta. Worldly thoughts—thoughts pertaining to the external, or thoughts that function through the senses. The Gentile is the unregenerate state of mind in us.

Genubath, ġĕ-nū'-băth (Heb.)—*theft; things stolen.*

Son of Hadad, a prince of Edom. Genubath's mother was a sister of Tahpenes, wife of the king of Egypt. Genubath was reared in Pharaoh's home **and became a member of Pharaoh's** household (I Kings 11:20).

Meta. The stealthy, thieving method that the sensate, earthly consciousness in man employs in combating his more religious and spiritual nature.

Gera, ḡē′-rȧ (Heb.)—*grain; kernel; scraping; rough; enmity; a pilgrimage; sojourn.*

The name of several Israelitish men of the tribe of Benjamin; one was a son of Benjamin (Gen. 46:21; Judg. 3:15; II Sam. 16:5).

Meta. Faith taking on substance, or working in substance (*grain*). Apart from true understanding, faith is likely to become aggressive and hard, and to hold *enmity* against that which is true and of God, as was the case when Shimei, the son of Gera, cursed David and threw stones at him when he was fleeing from Absalom (II Sam. 16:5-8). It does not wish to give way to love, but faith must work by love and must be established in spiritual understanding before it can be relied upon as a sure factor in always working to bring about man's good.

Gerar, ḡē′-rär (Heb.)—*a sojourn; a lodging place; an encampment; a halting place.*

A Philistine place, near Gaza (Gen. 10:19). Abraham sojourned in Gerar (Gen. 20:1), and Isaac also went to Gerar when there was a famine in the land where he had formerly lived. Both Abraham and Isaac at this place told that their wives were their sisters, and came near getting into serious trouble because of their deception. It was here that Isaac's herdsmen and the herdsmen of Gerar contended over the wells that Isaac's servants dug (Gen. 26).

Meta. Subjective substance and life. In the beginning of man's journey spiritward this substance and life are in the possession of the sense nature (Philistines), and the ruling ego of the sense nature lives in the region of this place (Isaac went to Abimelech, king of the Philistines, "unto Gerar"). The awakening intellectual and spiritual man must draw upon this substance and life for sustenance (faith, Abraham, must be established in substance) and sooner or later, when the spiritual in man has gained sufficient understanding, strength,

and power, it must take entire possession of this phase of man's being.

Gerasenes (A. V., Gadarenes), ḡĕr′-ȧ-sēneṣ (fr. Heb.)—*fortunate; organized; assembled; trooped in; walled about; fortified.*

Same as the Gadarenes or Gergesenes (Mark 5:1).

Meta. (See GADARENES.)

Gerizim, ḡĕr′-ĭ-zĭm (Heb.)—*shorn places; waste places; barren deserts; cutters; rocky places, i. e., cut up.*

The mount of blessing in the land of Canaan (Deut. 11:29; Josh. 8:33).

Meta. The working of the law in blessings and good to those who think and act in harmony with divine principle. It is that in us which takes cognizance of the working out of life, health, peace, joy, plenty, and every good in our life because of our understanding of and obedience to the law of God. This phase of the activity of the law builds up the seemingly *waste places;* it cuts out the error and establishes the good. (See EBAL, the mount of cursing.)

Gershom, ḡĕr′-shŏm (Heb.)—*thrusting out; driving off; expulsion; exile; a stranger there.*

a Son of Moses, by Zipporah, daughter of Reuel the Midianite. "And he called his name Gershom; for he said, I have been a sojourner in a foreign land" (Exod. 2:22). **b** A son of Levi (I Chron. 6:16). **c** Another Gershom is mentioned in Ezra 8:2.

Meta. The sense of strangeness and of isolation that comes over him who has been somewhat violent in his first great zeal to overcome error and to carry out the work that Spirit has told him to do. What he has sown in aggressively fighting evil (Moses killed the Egyptian who was oppressing an Israelite) he is now reaping in being cut off from his old accustomed thoughts and acts—and from former associates, perhaps, if his aggression has been expressed outwardly.

At this stage man has not yet established harmony in himself, nor has he really been fitted for the work that it is his to do. He is in a period of waiting, and of preparation—a "sojourner" in a strange land. He has left, or rather he sees the necessity for leaving, Egyptian darkness, but has not yet come into spiritual understanding. (Moses was forty years in the land of Midian. It was here, tending the sheep, that he was fitted for his work of delivering Israel from Egypt. He had to overcome all strife and contention in himself, just as each would-be overcomer must do before he can really find the deliverance that he is seeking. Midian means *strife* and *contention;* it also refers to a certain enlarging or extending of the senses, and belongs more to the mental realm than to the purely physical. There is some enlightenment in the Midian state of consciousness. Reuel, the grandfather of Gershom, means *friendship of God.*)

Gershon, gĕr'-shŏn (Heb.)—*thrusting out; driving off; expulsion; exile.*

Eldest son of Levi, who was one of Jacob's twelve sons (Gen. 46:11); he is called Gershom in I Chronicles 6:16.

Meta. See GERSHOM.

The love consciousness does not always dwell in or express love at the first; it sometimes acts quite contrary to a loving spirit. This is shown in Levi, who was the one of Jacob's sons who stands for the love faculty in man. See his violence as revealed by Jacob in blessing his sons (Gen. 49:5, 6). It is at this stage of individual unfoldment, before one has become established in divine love, which is always kind and true, that one experiences that for which Gershon stands.

Gershonites, gĕr'-shŏn-ītes (fr. Heb.) —*of Gershon.*

Descendants of Gershon, the son of Levi (Num. 4:24).

Meta. Thoughts belonging to the Gershon consciousness in man. (See GERSHON.)

Geshan (A. V., Gesham), gē'-shăn (Heb.)—*covered with dust or earth; unclean; filthy; dirty;* otherwise, *firm, strong.*

Son of Jahdi, a descendant of Caleb's (I Chron. 2:47).

Meta. Geshan suggests two conditions that can follow the uniting of that in consciousness for which Caleb and Ephah stand. If the Caleb thought predominates to the clearing up of the Ephah thought, greater *firmness* and *strength* will result. On the other hand, if the darkness and gloom of the sense soul thought (Ephah, the concubine of Caleb) remains in evidence and becomes strengthened in its sense darkness instead of being overcome by its union with faith, enthusiasm, and courage (Caleb), greater uncleanness and impurity (*unclean, filthy, dirty*) would be expressed than would have been expressed had the union not taken place.

A thought of deeper and more thorough cleansing and purification should be held at every fresh flow of new life, energy, and faith into consciousness; otherwise, errors are likely to become strengthened in one instead of being put out of consciousness.

Geshem, gē'-shĕm (Heb.)—*violent rainstorm; heavy downpour; bodylike; corporeal body; corporeality; corporealness.*

An Arabian who scoffed at the Jews and opposed them in the rebuilding of the Temple and of Jerusalem's walls. He is the same man as Gashmu (Neh. 2:19; 6:1).

Meta. See GASHMU.

Geshur, gē'-shŭr (Heb.)—*bridge; land of the bridge; bridge land.*

A province in Syria. Its king was Talmai, the father of one of David's wives and the grandfather of Absalom (II Sam. 3:3). Geshur was at the foot of Mount Hermon, at the border, or extending over the border, of Bashan. Its name comes from a bridge across the Jordan. The people of Geshur went in and out of the Holy Land, even within its borders, but were not subject to the Hebrew law.

Meta. Man's attempt, from an intellectual or sense-reasoning standpoint (Syria refers to the intellect), to *bridge* over the current of thought in consciousness that the River Jordan signifies. But one cannot really enter and dwell in the Promised Land by purely intellectual and outer means, though one may bring about much seeming good. True overcoming and entrance into spiritual perfection, however, come by spiritual quickening, guidance, and power.

Geshurites (in A. V., Deut. 3:14 Geshuri), gĕsh'-ū-rītes (fr. Heb.).

Inhabitants of Geshur (Josh. 12:5).

Meta. Thoughts belonging to the Geshur consciousness in man. (See GESHUR.)

Gether, ḡē'-thĕr (Heb.)—*abundance pressed out; reciprocal increase; vale of trial.*

Son of Aram, who was the son of Shem (Gen. 10:23).

Meta. Shem, son of Noah, stands for the spiritual in man. Aram, however, denotes the intellect. The intellect has its foundation in Spirit, yet in unawakened man it has linked itself so completely with the outer, material world that it reasons almost entirely from the senses instead of receiving its inspirations consciously from Spirit. For this reason man believes that much physical effort is needed to make a living and to acquire abundance; thus he experiences hard labor and many inharmonies (*vale of trial*). This is signified by Gether; the thought is expressed very clearly in Genesis 3:17 (latter part of verse) and 19 (first clause).

Gethsemane, ḡĕth-sĕm'-ă-nė (Gk. fr. Heb.)—*oil press; press for extracting unguents and ointments.*

A garden near Jerusalem, at the foot of the Mount of Olives; it was the scene of the agony and betrayal of Jesus (Matt. 26:36).

Meta. The struggle that takes place within the consciousness when Truth is realized as the one reality. All the good is pressed out and saved and the error is denied away. This is often agony—the suffering that the soul undergoes in giving up its cherished idols or in letting go of human consciousness.

The great work of every one is to incorporate the Christ mind in soul and body. The process of eliminating the old consciousness and entering into the new may be compared to Gethsemane, whose meaning is *oil press, press for extracting unguents and ointments;* a press is an emblem of trial, distress, agony, while oil points to Spirit and illumination.

Geuel, ḡe-ū'-ĕl (Heb.)—*majesty of God; exaltation of God; glory of God; God's lifting up,* i. e., *salvation, redemption.*

A prince, or ruler, of the tribe of Gad; he was the son of Machi, and was one of the twelve men who were sent by Moses to spy out the Promised Land (Num. 13:15).

Meta. A ruling thought in the Gad (power) consciousness in man. Though this thought activity is awakening to a perception of the might and power of God to uplift and redeem the whole organism of man, it is not yet firmly enough established in a consciousness of this truth to be unafraid when "enemies" in the land to be overcome are presented to it. It is still prone to magnify seeming evil and to think that the redemption of the body is too large and complicated a task for man to undertake at present. Some time in the future, after several more incarnations, he may do it, but not now, is the verdict of that which Geuel signifies when only partially awakened, as the case of Geuel indicates. (Geuel was one of those who did not think that the Israelites were able to go up and possess the land. See Numbers 13:31.)

Gezer (A. V., II Samuel 5:25, Gazer), ḡē'-zĕr (Heb.)—*sharply cut off; precipitous; steep; sharp; a precipice; a sentence; decree,* especially of destiny or fate.

An old Canaanitish city that was allotted to Ephraim, and by the Ephraimites was given over to the Levites. The children of Ephraim failed to drive the Canaanites entirely from this city (Josh. 16:10; 21:21).

Meta. The subjective life forces (Canaanites) given over to the domination and use of the senses become Gezer—*a precipice* to man, a very *steep* and dangerous place over which he is liable to pitch headlong to destruction if he gives himself over entirely to the desire for sensation.

In vain does the will (Ephraim) fight for victory against this phase of activity; in vain does the will pronounce *sentence* upon it and *decree* its overthrow. Sense activity is not overcome by condemnation and by repression through will power, especially since at this phase of his unfoldment the individual subconsciously still holds to the old race belief that man is destined to continue subject to sense so long as he lives on earth in a physical body. It takes the forgiving, harmonizing, cleansing, redeeming power of divine love (the Levites here suggest this) to make the necessary change in consciousness, that the life energy may be turned to good use and that all the forces of the mind and the body may be transmuted into spiritual substance and life.

Giah, gī'-ăh (Heb.)—*breaking forth; bursting forth; a birth; a spring; a fountain; a waterfall.*

A place in Palestine. "But Joab and Abishai pursued after Abner: and the sun went down when they were come to the hill of Ammah, that lieth before Giah by the way of the wilderness of Gibeon" (II Sam. 2:24).

Meta. Ammah (a *cubit*—natural measure; a *maternal nation*—natural; a hill in Israel) is symbolical of the idea that all intelligence, whether of the head or the heart, has a common source: Divine Mind. Here an agreement is reached between the executive power of love (Joab, David's commander) and the conclusions of the enlightened intellect (Abner, captain of Saul's host). (See AMMAH.) Gibeon represents the high point in the silence, which man reaches when he realizes his unity with Supreme Being. (See GIBEON.)

Giah refers to the *birth* or *breaking forth* of new life and cleansing in man's consciousness when a certain degree of illumination and realization is reached, through prayer and by declarations of Truth. Thus a greater purifying of the whole man takes place, and the individual becomes conscious of new health, vigor, vitality, and spiritual attainment.

Gibbar, gĭb'-băr (Heb.)—*mighty man; superior man; hero; archbaron; strong; mighty; powerful.*

A man whose descendants to the number of ninety-five returned from the Babylonian captivity (Ezra 2:20). His name is given as Gibeon in Nehemiah 7:25.

Meta. A highly illumined thought in consciousness; a realization of the truth of man's being and of his splendid possibilities, his inherent might and power. Jesus Christ fully understood and demonstrated the truth that is contained in the name Gibbar. (See GABRIEL in conjunc-

tion with this name; the meanings of the two are closely identified.)

Gibbethon, gĭb'-bĕ-thŏn (Heb.)—*height; eminence; a raised place; high; a high house.*

A city in Canaan that was allotted to the tribe of Dan and was given over to the Levites (Josh. 19:44; 21:23).

Meta. A group of highly illumined thoughts in consciousness, that belong to the judgment faculty (Dan).

Gibea, gĭb'-ĕ-à (Heb.)—*high; like a mountain; a hill; an eminence; a highlander.*

"Sheva the father of Machbena, and the father of Gibea" (I Chron. 2:49); either a man or city of Judah.

Meta. A *hill* always refers to a high, elevated thought, desire, aspiration, or state of consciousness. This may not always be spiritual; it may be of the intellect or of the soul, but it is an aspiring to higher things. The meaning of Gibea is virtually the same as that of Gibeah. (See GIBEAH.)

Gibeah, gĭb'-ĕ-ăh (Heb.)—*a height; as a mountain; a hill; a place on a high hill; an eminence.*

a A city in the hill country of Judah (Josh. 15:57). **b** A city of Benjamin (Judg. 19:12-16). Gibeah of Benjamin was the home of Saul (I Sam. 10:26).

Meta. At the time when Jonathan resolved to go over into the Philistine garrison, Saul was in Gibeah, which is Migron (I Sam. 14:2). Gibeah, meaning *a height, an eminence,* represents the spiritual aspiration inherent in every desire. Saul, the will, though undisciplined, aspired to high and lofty aims (symbolized by Gibeah).

Judges 19 and 20 tell the debasing story of what happens to the aspiring will when it is given over to sense desire; it sinks to the lowest degree of degradation (Migron—*cast down, overthrown*) and brings destruction both to the high aspirations and to the man himself.

Gibeath, gĭb'-ĕ-ăth (Heb.)—*heights; hills; eminences; distinctions.*

A town of Benjamin (Josh. 18:28). Gibeath is the plural form of the word Gibeah.

Meta. See GIBEAH.

Gibeathite, gĭb'-ĕ-ăth-īte (fr. Heb.)—

of or *belonging to Gibeah.*

A native or inhabitant of Gibeah; "the sons of Shemaah the Gibeathite" (I Chron. 12:3).

Meta. A thought belonging to the Gibeah consciousness. (See GIBEAH.)

Gibeon, gĭb'-ē-ŏn (Heb.)—*place of the hill; hill city,* i. e., *built on a hill; high hill.*

A royal city of the Canaanites (Josh. 10:2), whose inhabitants made peace with Israel. It was "upon Gibeon" that the sun stood still, in Joshua's great battle against the five kings of the Amorites. This city later was allotted to the tribe of Benjamin (Josh. 18:25) and was by them given over to the Levites (Josh. 21:17). At Gibeon Solomon went to sacrifice, and Jehovah appeared to him in a dream and told him to ask whatever he wanted and it would be given him. Solomon asked for an understanding heart, that he might judge the people righteously; this so pleased the Lord that He added riches and might to him, such as had never been known before (I Kings 3:4-15).

Meta. A high, illumined state of consciousness, that high point in the silence which man reaches when he realizes his unity with God.

Gibeon, the high point in spiritual consciousness, is called a place of sacrifice because it is here that man lets go of personal ideas and desires, and seeks only the presence of God. The essential steps that must be taken before man can enter Spirit are: First, there must be an earnest desire to know and feel the presence of God. Second, there must be willingness to eliminate sense thoughts from consciousness. This is accomplished through denying error expression, in thought and act, and affirming the substantial ideas of Spirit.

One must become as "a little child" when one desires to be taught by Spirit, because the childlike attitude is one of receptivity and obedience. This state of mind invites an inflow of spiritual ideas from the one Source of wisdom.

Gibeonites, gĭb'-ē-ŏn-ītes (fr. Heb.)— *of* or *belonging to Gibeon.*

The Gibeonites of II Samuel 21:1-9 refer to the Canaanitish inhabitants of Gibeon, with whom the Israelites made a covenant of peace; they do not refer to the Benjamites and Levites who later inhabited the city of Gibeon.

Meta. Thoughts of the sensate or carnal phase of the subjective consciousness that aspire to higher and more spiritual ideals and try to reach these ideals by making an alliance with man's real, true thoughts (Israel).

Giddalti, gĭd-dăl'-tī (Heb.)—*I magnify (God); I have magnified; I have made great; I have caused to grow; trained up,* i. e., *made to grow up.*

Son of Heman. He and his father and his brothers served as musicians in the "house of God" during the reign of David (I Chron. 25:4-6).

Meta. Love (Levite) magnifying God (spiritual Truth), thus producing rhythm and harmony in the body temple and bringing the organism into tune with the Infinite. This leads to true greatness and strength.

Giddel, gĭd'-dĕl (Heb.)—*very great; gigantic; greater magnitude,* i. e., *of size or number.*

a A man belonging to the Nethinim (Ezra 2:47). **b** A servant of Solomon's (Ezra 2:56). Descendants of both of these men returned from the Babylonian captivity under Zerubbabel.

Meta. The exaltation of service.

Gideon (A. V., Hebrews 11:32, Gedeon), gĭd'-ē-ŏn (Heb.)—*cutter-off; mutilator; destroyer; tree feller; impetuous warrior.*

An Israelitish man, son of Joash, of the tribe of Manasseh. He was a judge of Israel and was called Jerubbaal, meaning *contender with Baal* (Judg. 6:11— 8:35).

Meta. Denial.

Abraham "dwelt by the oaks of Mamre." Even so, "the angel of Jehovah" who came to Gideon "sat under the oak," and Gideon presented food to him there. An oak tree in itself stands for something very strong and protective; but in the Hebrew language it has a deeper significance than this. The word comes from the root from which is derived the word *Elohim.* The text, "He that dwelleth in the secret place of the Most High shall abide under the shadow of the Almighty," contains the spiritual interpretation of dwelling under an "oak."

Gideon, we read, was "beating out wheat" (dividing the true from the false) when "the angel of Jehovah appeared unto him" and said, "Jehovah is with thee." Gideon's answer to his heavenly visitor seems a natural one: "Oh, my lord, if Jehovah is with us, why then is all this befallen us?" It is what millions of hearts have asked since the days of Gideon. We read that "Jehovah looked upon him" (brought him into His own presence) and said to him: "Surely I will be with thee . . . Peace be unto thee; fear not: thou shalt not die." This reminds us of the wonderful words of the Hebrew blessing: "Jehovah lift up his countenance upon thee, and give thee peace." Only the peace that is of God can keep in man's heart and mind the knowledge of God's protective power.

God also said to Gideon, "Go in this thy might." The angel said to Mary, "The power of the Most High shall overshadow thee." That power, we know, was the Holy Spirit. "I can of myself do nothing," but "with God all things are possible."

The enemy against whom Gideon waged war was Midian, which means *strife* or *contention*. To many people there is no other enemy that is so difficult to kill. Petty quarrels, jealousies, uncharitable thoughts—how they come back again and again! They can never be overcome except by positive denial made in the realization that no error has any power or reality of itself. This form of denial, with an assurance of the power and love of God, will overcome all strife. The Midianites must be exterminated before we can possess the Promised Land in its entirety. We must "smite the Midianites as one man," as impersonal evil, and consider even that as a claim that never was and never shall be.

In Judges 2:16-18 and in Judges 7:2-8 is a lesson in the development of judgment. In these days many are worshiping or giving allegiance to materiality —to other gods than Jehovah; instead of being true to divine judgment, "they hearkened not unto their judges."

From thirty-two thousand men Gideon (*cutter-off*, *destroyer*, signifying denial) selected only three hundred with which to overcome the Midianites, because Gideon was working under the inspiration of divine judgment. Therefore it was revealed to him that the forces that he was to use must have the power of discrimination and judgment.

The act of getting down on the hands and knees and drinking from the brook indicates a lack of discrimination. People who are thus lacking mentally drink in everything that comes their way, and thereby load their minds with all sorts of thoughts—good, bad, and indifferent. Those who are represented as dipping the water up in their hands and drinking it use discrimination. They think about what they are doing, and are safe executives.

Dividing the three hundred into three companies represents the sending forth of the word in spirit, mind, and body. The trumpets represent the power of the word, and the torches concealed in the pitchers represent spiritual intelligence.

The trained metaphysician applies the law of denial by first meditating upon a central thought of spiritual judgment; then he realizes that spiritual judgment is throwing its spiritual light into his mind and dissipating all darkness and ignorance. He then speaks the word of victory, Truth destroys error, and Jehovah reigns.

Gideoni, ḡĭd-ĕ-ō′-nī (Heb.)—*of Gideon*, i. e., *having a likeness* or *quality of Gideon; warlike; impetuous; destructive.*

Father of Abidan. Abidan was the man whom God chose from the tribe of Benjamin to stand with Moses when Moses was numbering the men of Israel in the wilderness (Num. 1:11).

Meta. Denial, working through the activity of faith (a Benjamite) to destroy error and to bring about discrimination, good judgment (Abidan).

Gidom, ḡĭ′-dŏm (Heb.)—*severing; completely cutting off; destroying; laying waste; desolation.*

A place somewhere between Gibeah and the rock of Rimmon. The Israelites pursued and destroyed the Benjamites as far as Gidom because of their adulterous sin at Gibeah (Judg. 20:45).

Meta. A state of consciousness in which there is great activity during the *cutting off*, by denial, of impure thoughts and desires; also a sense of *desolation*, or emptiness, that comes over one when one has been very vigorous in the denial and putting away of some error that was strongly rooted in the consciousness, and has not as yet established positive Truth in its place.

gifts.

Meta. The gifts that the Wise Men of the East brought to Jesus represent qualities of mind given by divine wisdom. These Wise Men are bringing to us the consciousness of that which has been ideal. Gold represents the most precious substance. Gold is the standard of financial values between almost all civilized nations. Men are searching for gold the world over. It is not the most valuable of the metals, but it is the most universally accepted as representative of riches, of wealth. These wise thoughts from divine wisdom tell us that we have all riches; that the God-Mind in us has given us possession of the universal ether substance.

Gold is the concentration of an etheric essence. Gold grows from the invisible. It has its source in the universal thought substance. The gold that the Wise Men brought to the child Jesus was a consciousness of the omnipresent richness of infinite substance. To follow Jesus in prosperity we must charge our thoughts with wise and rich ideas.

Another of the presents brought by the Wise Men was frankincense. Frankincense is one of the richest of all perfumes. We are told that the sense of smell is allied very closely with the spiritual. Frankincense represents in man the transmutation of material things to spiritual essences. When the Christ mind begins its work in the body it has to meet many obstacles of material character, and a constant refining process is necessary. So wise metaphysicians select carefully the food that they eat, that it may be as spiritual as possible. They are careful about the air that they breathe, and especially watchful of the thought atmosphere with which they come in contact, for they know that they must raise every cell in their bodies to a higher consciousness.

Myrrh represents the power of love. God told Moses to take myrrh and a certain oil, and to anoint all the instruments used in worship in the tabernacle. The tabernacle represents the body, and through the wisdom of the mind we must anoint every part of the organism with myrrh, with the love of God. Daily we must give presents of love to the young Christ child. It lives upon love. Jesus, who represents the growth and full expression of the new man, the Christ child, laid down love as the highest of all the laws; He emphasized the fulfillment of the law of love as love of man for God and love of man for his neighbor.

Gihon, ḡī'-hŏn (Heb.)—*determining impulse; formative movement; a bursting forth; whirlpool; rapid stream.*

a A river of Eden (Gen. 2:13). **b** The name of a fountain, or a pool with springs, just outside the city of Jerusalem. David had Solomon taken there to be anointed king over Israel by Zadok the priest and Nathan the prophet (I Kings 1:33, 45; II Chron. 32:30).

Meta. Gihon means *formative movement*. It represents the deific breath of God inspiring man and purifying his blood in the lungs. It flows through the darkened consciousness (Cush).

The Gihon that was a fountain, or pool, with springs, just outside Jerusalem, indicates a *bursting forth* of joyous life and Truth. Substance and discrimination are also suggested by the "digestive system." Thus peace (Solomon) becomes the ruling factor of the heart and mind when abundant life, substance, and wisdom (discrimination) are realized.

Gilalai, ḡĭl'-ă-lāi (Heb.)—*rolling along; rolling together; weighty; dungy; like a ball; like a wheel; like a roll.*

A musician at the dedication of the wall of Jerusalem after the wall had been rebuilt under the direction of Nehemiah (Neh. 12:36).

Meta. A strong love thought in consciousness that realizes how important (*weighty*) it is to have coöperative, harmonious activity (*rolling along, rolling together*) in one's thoughts in order to increase one's substance, and to rebuild the seemingly mortal organism into a spiritual body.

Gilboa, ḡĭl-bō'-ȧ (Heb.) — *boiling springs; bubbling fountains; agitated pools; swelling with emotion.*

A mountain in Palestine. There Israel under Saul encamped against the Philistines, and there Saul and his three sons were slain (I Sam. 28:4; 31:8).

Meta. A great turmoil in consciousness, a great agitation of the life forces —it might be called chemicalization— brought about by the willful dominance of the personal will (Saul); if persisted in, it leads to disruption of the consciousness (Saul and his sons were slain in Gilboa, by the Philistines, and the Israelites were defeated and scattered for the time being). After an experience of this nature, only love (David) can restore peace and wholeness, and lead to victory over the error (Philistines).

Gilead, ḡĭl'-ĕ-ăd (Heb.)—*mound of witness; massive witness; enduring rock; rock of time; great endurance.*

a The mountain where Jacob encamped when he fled from his father-in-law, Laban. It was there that Laban overtook him, and that the covenant between them was made (Gen. 31:21, 23-55). The caravan of the Ishmaelites to whom Joseph was sold by his brothers was from Gilead (Gen. 37:25). It was on this mountain, too, that Gideon chose the men who went with him to defeat the Midianites (Judg. 7:3). **b** The name of an Israelitish man (I Chron. 5:14). **c** A city (Hos. 6:8).

Meta. The high place in consciousness where Spirit discerns and witnesses to what is true and to all man's thoughts and acts, that an adjustment may be made throughout mind and body. If we let our high ideals and standards become subject to sensate, error reasonings, our spiritual discernment becomes obscured and our Gilead becomes a city of them that work iniquity; it becomes stained with blood—works against our life and health (Hos. 6:8).

Gileadite, ḡĭl'-ĕ-ăd-īte (fr. Heb.)—*of* or *belonging to Gilead.*

A descendant of Gilead of the tribe of Manasseh (Num. 26:29). Jair and Jephthah, two of the judges of Israel, were Gileadites (Judg. 10:3; 11:1-40).

Meta. A discerning, discriminating, judging thought belonging to the Gilead consciousness in man. (See GILEAD.)

Gilgal, ḡĭl'-găl (Heb.)—*circle; rolling away; a wheel; a whirlwind; chaff; stubble.*

A place on the east border of Jericho, where the Israelites first encamped after entering the Promised Land (Josh. 4:19). At Gilgal Samuel sacrificed to the Lord; there Saul was made king over Israel (I Sam. 10:8; 11:15). Gilgal was the place where Elisha neutralized the poison in the pottage that the prophets were eating (II Kings 4:38-41). Elijah went from Gilgal to the place whence he was taken up in a chariot of fire (II Kings 2:1).

Meta. A total denial of sense bondage. In Joshua 5:9 it is written, "And Jehovah said unto Joshua, This day have I rolled away the reproach of Egypt from off you. Wherefore the name of that place was called Gilgal, unto this day." When we have, in the positive spirit of Elijah, rolled away the Egyptian darkness of sense thoughts, we are paving the way for a permanent ascent into a higher state of consciousness (II Kings 2:1).

Giloh, ḡī'-lōh (Heb.)—*welling up; rejoicing; uncovering; laying bare; revealing; making naked; migration; exile.*

A city in the hill country of Judah (Josh. 15:51). Ahithophel, David's counselor who joined Absalom in his conspiracy against David, was a native of Giloh (II Sam. 15:12).

Meta. Intellectual perception of Truth rejoicing because of its insight into spiritual things. It is not really spiritual in itself, however, and is an exile in so far as the kingdom of heaven is concerned, since the least of one's truly spiritual thoughts is greater than one's highest intellectual perceptions. Jesus said of John the Baptist, who represents the intellectual concept of Truth, that though there are none greater who are born of women, yet he that is but little in the kingdom is greater than John. (See

AHITHOPHEL.) Thus purely intellectual knowing is laid bare, is revealed in its real light, and must take a secondary place in consciousness as true spiritual understanding increases.

Gilonite, gī'-lō-nīte (fr. Heb.)—*of or belonging to Giloh.*

Ahithophel, a native of Giloh (II Sam. 15:12).

Meta. A thought belonging to the Giloh state of consciousness. (See GILOH.)

Gimzo, gĭm'-zŏ (Heb.)—*producing sycamores; place fertile in sycamores; one acute-minded; sagacious.*

A city in the south part of the lowland of Judah. The Philistines took this city from Judah and lived in it (II Chron. 28:18).

Meta. Sense shrewdness, subtleness, and wisdom (*one acute-minded, sagacious;* this city reverted to the Philistines). Jesus said in one of His parables: "The sons of this world are for their own generation wiser than the sons of the light" (Luke 16:8).

Ginath, gī'-năth (Heb.)—*garden; inclosure; protection.*

Father of Tibni. Part of the Israelites wanted Tibni to be their king instead of Omri, but Omri became king and Tibni was killed (I Kings 16:21, 22).

Meta. A thought of abundant sustenance (*garden*) and safety (*protection*) for the Israel consciousness in the individual. The fruit of this thought (Tibni, meaning *intelligence, building of Jehovah, knowing*) is endowed with a degree of spiritual insight or knowledge, and it aspires to rulership; but neither the thought nor its fruit is, at this stage of individual unfoldment, positive enough or well enough defined in character to overcome the aggressive, discordant ruling thought that Omri signifies here. Thus that which Ginath and Tibni represent is kept from further expression at this time; Tibni was killed, and Ginath is not mentioned elsewhere in the Bible.

Ginnethoi (A. V., Ginnetho and Ginnethon), gĭn'-nĕ-thōi (Heb.)—*gardener; great protection.*

One or more priests who returned from the Babylonian captivity (Neh. 12:4); called Ginnethon in Nehemiah 10:6; 12:16.

Meta. A strong assurance of divine *protection,* and that God the Father is caretaker, the power by which one is enabled to overcome that in one which falls short of perfection. (A *gardener* is one who tends a garden, sows the seed, prunes the vines, pulls the weeds, sees that the ground is well fertilized, watered, and worked. We are the garden of God: "My Father is the husbandman," Jesus said.)

Girgashite (A. V., Genesis 10:16, Girgasite), gĭr'-gă-shīte (fr. Heb.)—*of or belonging to that which is dense; condensed; palpable; marshy ground.*

A primitive Canaanitish tribe of which almost nothing is now known. This tribe was descended from Canaan, one of the three sons of Noah (Gen. 10:16), and was among the enemies, in the land of Canaan, that the Israelites were to drive out (Gen. 15:21; Josh. 3:10).

Meta. The very material (*dense, condensed*) state of thought that unawakened man holds concerning himself and especially concerning his seemingly material organism. He thus builds up a consciousness that cannot abide, because it is not established in Truth.

Girzites (A. V., Gezrites), gĭr'-zītes (fr. Heb.)—*of or belonging to Gezer.*

Inhabitants of Gezer (I Sam. 27:8).

Meta. Thoughts belonging to the consciousness in man that was symbolized by the city of Gezer while under the Canaanite, or error, dominion. (See GEZER.)

Gishpa (A. V., Gispa), gĭsh'-pà (Heb.)—*stroke; caress; fondle; flattery.*

An overseer of the Nethinim, who dwelt in Ophel after the return from the Babylonian captivity (Neh. 11:21).

Meta. Love for Truth or consideration of Truth, but directed more by sense thought than by spiritual thought.

Gittaim, gĭt'-tă-ĭm (Heb.)—*two wine presses; two vats; double fortune.* See GATH, of which Gittaim is the dual number.

A place that the Beerothites fled to and remained at; both Beeroth and Gittaim were cities of Benjamin (II Sam. 4:3). Gittaim was one of the places in which the Benjamites who returned from the Babylonian captivity lived (Neh. 11:33).

Meta. Trial doubled by a great influx of thoughts of life and increase (Beerothites) into consciousness, while one is still being governed to a great extent by the limited views of the personal man. Our sense consciousness sees and magnifies the seeming evil and the suffering phase of our experiences in unfoldment instead of understanding and rejoicing in Truth.

gittith, ḡĭt'-tith (Heb.)—*a stringed musical instrument; from* or *of Gath.*

Gittith is thought to have been a musical instrument made at Gath, or else the title of certain Psalms that were sung during the time of gathering grapes and making wine (Psalms 8; 81; 84, titles).

Meta. Soul refinement through seeming trial. The deep peace and harmony into which the soul enters after a seeming conflict has been experienced because of a flow of new life into consciousness, and the consequent quickening and resurrecting of all the forces of the organism into newness of life. (Grapes suggest life, and wine also stands for the life of Spirit with its renewing power. Whenever a great quickening takes place in man before error is fully overcome and the consciousness is thoroughly purified, he seems to be stimulated to unrighteousness as well as to good. This is where the apparent travail, or trial, comes in; it is in the overcoming and rising above the apparent limitations of sense. When this is accomplished, greater harmony and peace reign in the soul than it has known before, and the soul radiates this harmony to the whole organism; thus the soul really becomes a musical instrument for divine service and Truth.)

Gizonite, ḡĭ'-zō-nīte (fr. Heb.)—*cut or hewn stone; a quarry; ford; pass.*

I Chronicles 11:34 mentions the sons of Hashem the Gizonite as having been among David's mighty warriors. Nothing more is known of a place called Gizon.

Meta. A thought pertaining to the passing over (*ford, pass*) from a belief in lack to a consciousness of true spiritual riches; also the obtaining of a sure foundation (*cut or hewn stone, a quarry*) for one's supply of good within and without (Hashem means *shining, fat, wealthy,* thus suggesting riches).

Goah (A. V., Goath), gō'-ăh (Heb.)—*lowing; crying out; exclaiming.*

Mentioned with Gareb in Jeremiah 31:39; it was near Jerusalem, but nothing definite is known of it. (See GAREB.)

Meta. Physical strength in expression (*lowing, crying out, exclaiming.* A cow or an ox represents physical strength. This strength must be lifted up and transmuted into pure spiritual substance and life. (Jeremiah 31:38-40 prophesies of man's entire renewal in mind and his consequent transformation in body. See Romans 12:2 also. The whole of that which Jerusalem signifies—the heart center or subconscious mind; even the currents of confused and turbulent thoughts for which the brook Kidron stands; the seat of the conscious mind, the intellect; and the will—all these are to become holy to Jehovah, redeemed.)

goat.

Meta. The goat symbolizes resistance and opposition. It is a phase of personality. We resist Spirit on one hand, and we resist our fellows on the other. These two instances of resistance symbolize the two goats of Leviticus 16:5-22. They are both to be denied. Resistance to the Lord is to be killed out entirely and resistance to our fellows is to be sent into the wilderness—denied a place in consciousness.

This also illustrates the difference between sins toward God and sins toward man. There must be a complete and full union of the Father and child; every thought of obstruction and resistance must be done away with. It is very important that we make complete at-one-ment with the Father.

Resistance toward evil is not to be wholly destroyed, but consciousness of the nothingness of the thoughts of evil is to be dumped into the wilderness of sense. This is the scapegoat that carries away all the iniquities of the Children of Israel and loses them in the outer void.

Our relations to our fellow men are so complex that we are excused in a measure if we fall short in observing the law of nonresistance in its entirety.

Yet in superconsciousness we can rise with Jesus Christ and "resist not him that is evil"; we *must* do it before we can become like Him and see Him even as He is (I John 3:2).

Gob, gŏb (Heb.)—*hollowed out; a cistern; a pit.*

A place where battles were fought between the Philistines and the Israelites (II Sam. 21:18, 19). In I Chronicles 20:4 this place is called Gezer.

Meta. Sense rule deeply established in the subjective life forces of the organism. (See GEZER.) (At least two of the sons of the Philistine giant, Raphah, were slain at Gob by the Israelites.)

Gog, gŏg (Heb.)—*elastic; stretched out; extended; flat roof; plane top.*

a An Israelite, a descendant from Reuben (I Chron. 5:4). b A nation, or company of people, that was to come against Israel in battle and be defeated (Ezek. 38:2-18). c Symbolical of the satanic enemies of the saints (Rev. 20:8).

Meta. The satanic or selfish thought force in human consciousness, warring against the true thought force that is based upon the ideas taught and demonstrated by Jesus Christ.

Unity of purpose and effort is becoming widely recognized as the most potent means to attain any desired end. For instance, labor is proving its power to dictate terms to capital, through organized system in making its demands. Instead of many minds' pulling in many directions, labor speaks as one man and says in plain words what it will do if its terms are not granted. Something has to move when such unity of will obtains.

Sense wisdom is often resistant, however; the law of love is not observed. There arise antagonism, combativeness, war. What turmoil will result in this battle royal between the organized forces of man thought in the earth no one can tell. It is the battle of Gog and Magog, which will end only when the satanic or selfish thought is cast out of human consciousness. The push and the pull of these two forces are sure for a time to produce discord in the affairs of men. Those who are not organized against it will suffer—they will be ground between the millstones of material conditions un-

less they know how to rise above them.

But there is another organized thought force. It is based upon the ideas promulgated by Jesus Christ. It believes in love, reason, honesty, justice, unselfishness, nonresistance, and, above all, in the guidance and wisdom and power of a Mind that is higher than that of the present race consciousness. This organized thought of spiritual-minded men and women will, through the ideas planted in the race thought by Jesus Christ, make unity with Divine Mind and establish right here in earth conditions of peace and harmony. It will not be accomplished by any outside deity, but by inner forces' acting through the souls of those dwelling on earth.

Goiim, goi'-ĭm (Heb.)—*Gentiles; nations; peoples,* especially *foreign; bodies; corporealities.*

Tidal, king of Goiim, was one of the four kings who went to war with the kings of Sodom and Gomorrah, and defeated them. Later these four kings were overthrown and destroyed by Abraham (Gen. 14:1).

Meta. The carnal, material thoughts and state of consciousness that belong to the outer man (*Gentiles, nations*).

Golan, gō'-lăn (Heb.)—*circle; circuit; exultation; praise; overcome; led away; a captive; an exile.*

A city of refuge in Bashan, for the Manassites (Deut. 4:43); this city of Manasseh was given over to the Levites (Josh. 21:27).

Meta. Spiritual life activity (*circuit, circle, exultation, praise*) established in love (Levites) and understanding (Manasseh). Mistaken, limited thoughts in consciousness, upon awaking to greater light, may flee to this place and be forgiven and healed.

golden calf, the (Exod. 32:1-8).

Meta. The Scripture narrative is that Moses went up into the mountain again to get the Ten Commandments in more permanent form, written on tables of stone. This going up into the mountain to receive the divine law represents the high, exalted state of mind that one must attain before the inspiration of Spirit can be received. Every one who desires to grow in Spirit should make daily pilgrimages to the mountain of solitude.

To make this pilgrimage you need not go out of your room; simply go up in thought. Go into the silence; meditate; pray; affirm the presence and power of the omnipotent Good that is always with you. This is a necessary mental discipline.

But do not stay on the mountain top too long to the neglect of the thoughts below; for, if you do, they will seek another base of inspiration and make it, instead of Truth, their highest ideal. This is the meaning of the making of the golden calf by Aaron, who represents the high priest of the intellectual consciousness.

The ears represent the obedience and receptivity of the mind, and the giving to Aaron of the jewels of the ears means that the ideals were poured out upon the intellect and the intellect concentrated them into a state of consciousness on the natural (calf) plane. This is idol worship and results in the materialization of the whole body.

When the intellect is the center of consciousness, and all the jewels of the mind are poured into it, many golden calves, or material mental structures, are built up and worshiped. Around these the people eat and drink and play, often proclaiming, "These are thy gods, O Israel, which brought thee up out of the land of Egypt." There is a very widespread idea that it is through the power of money that man is developed from ignorance to wisdom. On every hand we hear people talking of the great good they could do to the race if they only had money to carry out their plans. This is worshiping the golden calf—making material things greater than spiritual. This idea must be ground to powder, as Moses ground the golden calf, before the true method will be put into action.

God is your sufficiency, and if you are willing to obey His law the way will open to you and all your plans will be worked out in just the right way; money will come to you as servant instead of master. People who are striving to get money and then go into the Lord's work are worshiping the golden calf. They are doubting God's providing capacity, and their

ideas along that line will be ground to powder. The great work of the Lord has always been done by those who were willing in the beginning to serve, as did Jesus, Paul, and the long line of reformers, whose only capital was the Spirit of God.

Golgotha, gŏl'-gŏ-thȧ (Gk. fr. Heb.)— *the skull; place of the skull,* i. e., *round, shaped like a head.*

The place just outside Jerusalem, a hill, where Jesus was crucified (Matt. 27:33). It is also called Calvary.

Meta. When we search the Scriptures to find the place where crucifixion takes place, we are introduced to a symbolism not hard to interpret. Golgotha, in the Aramaic-Jewish language, means *place of the skull.* The skull is the place where intellect is crossed out, that Spirit may win an eternal ascendancy. Jesus (the intellectual) was crucified at the *place of the skull,* that Christ (Truth) might become all in all.

The seat of the conscious mind is the front brain, and there the will has established its dominion. There all things affecting the body are either admitted or rejected. Even spiritual Truth has to be admitted through this door before it can become part of the consciousness. It is there that the human will must be crossed out, to give the divine will free expression.

Goliath, gȯ-lī'-ăth (Heb.)—*revealing; conspicuous; taken off; an exile; a soothsayer.*

A Philistine giant whom David killed with a stone thrown from his shepherd's sling (I Sam. 17).

Meta. Ideas are not all of the same importance. Some are large and strong, and some are weak and small. There are aggressive, domineering ideas, like Goliath, that parade themselves prominently, brag about their power, and with fearful threats of disaster keep us frightened into submission to their unrighteous reign.

These domineering ideas of error have one argument that they impress upon us at all times: fear of results should we dare to meet them openly and oppose their reign in consciousness. The fear of opposing prevailing ideas, although we know them to be erroneous, is woven into our whole mental fabric. This fear is portrayed by the spear of Goliath, and the narrative most aptly states, "And the staff of his spear was like a weaver's beam."

The "strong *man* fully armed," referred to by Jesus, is in the subconscious mind. In the natural man he manifests as physical strength, but in the regeneration he is overcome and his possessions are divided or given to the other faculties as a nucleus around which the higher forces gather. The "stronger than he," who takes away the "whole armor" in which the strong man trusted, is spiritual strength. The overcoming of Goliath by David illustrates this mastery of the spiritual over the material. Goliath trusted in his armor, which represents the protective power of matter and material conditions. David (spiritual strength) had no armor or material protection. His power was gained by trust in divine intelligence, through which David saw the weak place in the Goliath armor. Direct to this weak place, with the sling of his concentrated will, he sent a thought that shattered the forehead of the giant. This shows how easy it is to overcome any seemingly strong personal and material conditions, when the mind of Spirit is brought into action.

David was sure of himself, because he had slain the lion that killed his sheep. This lion symbolizes the beast in man; when overcome or, rather, transmuted to finer energy, it becomes a mighty soul strength.

The power of Goliath seems to have existed principally in his ability to frighten the Israelites. Their fear of him was induced by his great size and his pomp of outer display. Physical strength is prone to brag, and in the vanity that leads to boasting lies its utter weakness. Knowing this, David approached Goliath in a simple and inoffensive manner, which aroused the contempt of the giant and made him easy to defeat. Goliath stood for his own strength; David went forth with but one idea: to prove that there was a God in Israel. When one goes forth to prove his own strength he sooner or later comes to grief, but he who goes forth to prove the power of God is guided in every way and is the inevitable victor.

The story of David and Goliath is one of the most familiar of all Bible stories, and it is also one from which many practical lessons can be drawn. One lesson that may be considered is the individual's desire for both spiritual and worldly advancement. Side by side these desires are striving for supremacy, each in turn occupying a relative degree of importance in the mind. Even Jesus Christ had presented to His consideration the possibility of ruling over all the kingdoms of this world.

It does not take much of spiritual understanding to know the futility of so-called material advancement and power, but it does require very definite and well-directed activity really to correct one's tendencies in this direction. The lure of pomp and power is great to the one who does not fully realize the spiritual Truth that exists under all material manifestation.

The giant of outer splendor often looms up before the spiritual aspirant, but is not conquered by negative measures. The best means are always the simple, direct ones. To meet adversity with its own tactics but arouses it; to meet it with a direct declaration of Truth renders it an easy victim.

We are often scared, even terrified, at the gigantic proportions of some leading thought on the error side, represented by Goliath. Our Goliath may be different from that of our neighbor, but it boasts and brags daily of its strength and it intimidates us with its show of power. People who depend upon the resources of materiality, as Saul had come to do, often give up in despair when these thoughts of sense continue their bullying methods day and night. There is but one way to meet and subdue them, and that is through the power of love, represented by David, the ruddy-faced shepherd boy. Sympathetic love will not bring these results. Love must have the assurance of Truth and must be sent forth with confidence, courage, and power, in both thought and word.

Gomer, gŏ′-mĕr (Heb.)—*organic accumulation; organized aggregation; full* *and complete; finished; perfected; ended.*

a Son of Japheth, and grandson of Noah (Gen. 10:2). **b** In Ezekiel 38:6 we find a prophecy against "Gomer, and all his hordes"; evidently this Gomer was a nation hostile to Israel. **c** The adulterous wife of Hosea, the prophet (Hos. 1:3); she was the daughter of Diblaim.

Meta. Japheth, son of Noah, pertains to the intellect, or reasoning faculty, in man. Man cannot by intellectual reasoning understand or come in conscious touch with God, Spirit. Human reason in its greatest perfection and completion (Gomer) fails to reach spiritual wisdom and Truth. There is no real building, preserving quality in it; it is always destructive in the end. So human reason is an enemy to pure spiritual understanding; it is adulterous in that it looks to the outer and depends upon man-devised resources, even while proclaiming its perfect trust in God.

Gomorrah (A. V., Matthew 10:15; Rom. 9:29; II Pet. 2:6; Jude 7, Gomorrha), gŏ-mŏr'-räh (Heb.)—*overbearing; material force; tyranny; oppression.*

A city of the plain. With Sodom it was destroyed by fire and brimstone rained upon it by Jehovah out of heaven (Gen. 19:24).

Meta. A state of mind in man that is adverse to the law of Spirit. It is submerged in sense and is very tyrannical in its nature. (See SODOM.)

Goshen, gō'-shĕn (Heb.)—*drawing near.*

a A land in Egypt, where Joseph's father and brothers and their families settled when they first went down into Egypt for sustenance during the famine in Canaan (Gen. 45:10). It was on the east side of the Nile, and was not far from the Red Sea. **b** A district in Palestine, between Gaza and Gibeon (Josh. 10:41). **c** A city in the hill country of Judah (Josh. 15:51).

Meta. Unity.

The bringing of Jacob and the brothers of Joseph with their families and their flocks down into the land of Egypt symbolizes the unification of the I AM (Jacob) with all the faculties of the mind, the life energies, and the substance of the whole man. They dwelt "in the land of Goshen" (unity).

gospel.

Meta. Gospel is an Anglo-Saxon word derived from God (good) and spell (story, tidings). It is now universally identified with Jesus Christ's mission and the doctrine that has grown out of it. So when we speak of the gospel it is understood that we refer to religious beliefs that cluster about the teachings of Jesus of Nazareth.

The Holy Spirit is the only authorized interpreter of the gospel of Jesus Christ, and no man or woman can know what His doctrine is except the knowledge be obtained direct from this one and only Custodian. Whoever attempts to set forth His gospel from any other standpoint is acting in the letter, not the spirit. The writings of the New Testament, known as the four Gospels, are the most reliable external guide.

Gozan, gō'-zăn (Heb.)—*quarry; benefaction; dole; portion; fleece.*

A political division of Assyria, in Media (II Kings 17:6). It was one of the places to which the captive Israelites were taken by the king of Assyria.

Meta. The promise of the intellect to man's highest religious and spiritual thoughts (Israelites) that in the outer reasonings of the sense mind there is sufficient sustenance and good (*benefaction*) for the whole man, that Spirit is not needed. When man's higher ideals, however, are given over to the rule of the ego governing the outer sense reasonings (the Assyrian king), they are not really fed at all; they are instead stripped of their substance (*fleece*, one meaning of fleece being the wool shorn from sheep). Thus the sheep, the true thoughts of man, find that when they ask bread they are given a very unsatisfactory *portion*, a stone (*quarry* suggests stone). (See Matthew 7:9; also Jeremiah 23:1-4 and Ezekiel 34.)

Greece, grēeçe (fr. Lat.)—*hoary; old; fat; fertile; productive; going forward and upward; step; stage; degree; superiority; effervescent; spirituous.* These definitions are derived from the various names attached to Greece.

A country in the southeastern part

of Europe that is inhabited by Greeks (Acts 20:2; Dan. 8:21; Zech. 9:13). Greece was also called Javan and Achaia.

Meta. The intellect in man. Athens, the capital of Greece, and the birthplace of Plato, was a great center for learning throughout the then known world. In man's consciousness Athens refers to the intellectual center. (See ATHENS and ACHAIA.)

Greek, grēek (fr. Lat.).

a The language of Greece (Acts 21: 37). **b** Natives of Greece (John 12:20).

Meta. Intellectual reasonings.

In Acts 11:20-22 we find that the truth regarding the new teaching of Christ is beginning to reach the old reasonings of the intellect, and the wall of old ideas is being broken down. This change opens the way for the ministry of Paul to the Gentiles (the entire body consciousness), for the intellect must accept Truth before Truth can become life and redemption for the body.

(For an explanation of the Greek woman of Mark 7:26, see SYROPHŒNICIAN.)

Gudgodah, gŭd'-gŏ-däh (Heb.)—*incising; cutting; cleaving; pulsating; reverberating; thundering; fortunate; prosperous; happy; well of much water.*

A place in which the Israelites camped while in the wilderness, on their way to the Promised Land (Deut. 10:7).

Meta. A further *cutting,* or *cleaving* away from consciousness, of the remains of Egyptian darkness and ignorance, that more abundant vitality and wholeness (*well of much water,* signifying the life force) and happiness may be realized by the individual who has started out on his conscious journey toward perfection.

gulf, between Abraham and the rich man (Luke 16:26).

Meta. Every state of consciousness is formed by groups of ideas. Some dominant idea is the nucleus, and about this the ego builds a mental house. Thus are reared walls, or ideas of separation, that shut out the universal light, and the ego finds itself a prisoner in a dungeon of its own construction.

These mental houses are impregnable to light when there is a belief that the light does not shine. This darkness shuts them away from other groups of ideas, or states of consciousness, that would gladly reflect light into them. Abraham said to the rich man in torment, "Between us and you there is a great gulf fixed, that they that would pass from hence to you may not be able, and that none may cross over from thence to us." Then the rich man requested Abraham to send Lazarus to tell his brethren what the ideas they were cultivating would bring them to; but recognizing that they were in still another state of consciousness, a consciousness impregnable to ideas not of its order, Abraham told him that they would not heed even "if one rise from the dead."

Guni, gū'-nī (Heb.)—*colored; dyed; tinted; tinged; painted; overlaid; protected.*

a Son of Naphtali, who was one of Jacob's twelve sons (Gen. 46:24). **b** A Gadite, and father of Abdiel (I Chron. 5:15).

Meta. Colored, dyed, painted, tinged, all suggest a taking on of some foreign idea or substance. In this case the qualities of strength (Naphtali) and power (Gad) are involved. These qualities are inherently spiritual, but in coming into expression in the outer, physical, sense man who does not yet understand his inner spiritual origin and reality, these divine qualities become *tinged* with and *colored* by material ideas until they appear to be material, limited, transient, capable of error results as well as of good. Nevertheless, they are *protected* in individual consciousness by Spirit, until man awakens to the understanding that Spirit is the source and substance of all; then his strength and power, as well as all his other faculties of mind, become established in Spirit and express righteously and harmoniously only. Thus they become abiding, all-conquering.

Gunites, gū'-nītes (fr. Heb.)—*of or belonging to Guni.*

Descendants of Guni, of the tribe of Naphtali (Num. 26:48).

Meta. Thoughts belonging to the Guni phase of the strength (Naphtali) consciousness. (See GUNI.)

Gur, gûr (Heb.)—*turn aside; sojourn; dwell; stranger; foreigner; gather to-*

gether; assemble; suckling; whelp; cub.

A place near Ibleam, where Ahaziah, king of Judah, was smitten by the men of Jehu (II Kings 9:27).

Meta. "The ascent of Gur, which is by Ibleam," signifies a going up to victory (Ibleam means *victory of the people*). It was here that Ahaziah the wicked king of Judah was slain by Jehu's men. Jehu means *Jehovah is He*. The consciousness that I AM, Jehovah, eternally exists in us as our foundation Truth and overcoming power puts to naught the error rulings of the will guided by sense desires and by selfish, material thoughts, such as King Ahaziah suggests.

Gur represents a sojourning, or dwelling, abiding, in the truth that Jehovah is the one omnipresent king and ruling power. This is the place of overcoming realization, and it leads up to victory.

Gur-baal, gûr-bā'-ăl (Heb.)—*sojourn of Baal; dwelling of Baal; abode of Baal.*

A dwelling place of the Arabians who came under subjection to Uzziah, king of Judah (II Chron. 26:7).

Meta. A place in consciousness, or a state of consciousness, that had been given over to Baal, to material beliefs and worship. But the substance of these material beliefs and thoughts is now being used to uphold and sustain that in consciousness for which Uzziah stands, *Jehovah is my strength*. The Arabians that dwelt at Gur-baal were subject to Uzziah; "God helped him against" them.

H

Haahashtari, hā-ă-hăsh'-tă-rī (Heb. fr. Pers.)—*the muleteer; the mule driver; the courier; the messenger; the runner.*

Son of "Ashhur the father of Tekoa," by his wife Naarah (I Chron. 4:6).

Meta. That in us which bears our high ideals and revelations of Truth quickly to any of the various centers or parts of the organism to which the I AM wishes to transmit them—a swift messenger of the king.

Habakkuk, hă-băk'-kŭk (Heb.)—*embracing; infolding,* i. e., *with the hands or arms; a favorite; a lover; a wrestler; a struggler; an idler.*

One of the minor prophets. Little or nothing authentic is known of his life, though from the nature of his prophecies he must have lived in Jeremiah's time, during the reign of Jehoiakim, king of Judah. He must have written his prophecies just before the conquest of Judea by Nebuchadnezzar and the Chaldeans (Hab. 1:1).

Meta. The clearness of vision in us that, looking into the working of the thoughts of our consciousness, foresees their fruition and holds tightly to (*embraces*) that which is good and true, while it *wrestles,* or *struggles,* with the error in an attempt to purge it out.

Most of the old Jewish prophets emphasized the error side of things more than they did the good side. We find that our intellectual ideas of religion and Truth are prone to dwell on and magnify the results of evil, while the true Christ Spirit reveals and builds up the good, which alone can overcome seeming evil and injustice.

Habazziniah (A. V., Habaziniah), hăb-ăz-ĭ-nī'-ăh (Heb.)—*brightness of Jah; lamp of Jehovah; Jehovah's brilliance; light of Jehovah; whiteness, purity, shining, of Jehovah; glory of the Lord.*

A Rechabite (Jer. 35:3).

Meta. True, spiritual understanding. The Rechabites stand in consciousness for logical reasoning, level-headedness, good judgment, and the faithfulness of the intellect to that which one believes to be right. This opens the consciousness to spiritual thoughts; thus the true light, understanding, shines in and is recognized by the individual.

Habor, hā'-bôr (Heb.)—*joined together; united; confederated; allied; companion; cemented; bound by a spell; striped with a lash.*

Either a river in Media, a tributary of the Euphrates, or a place situated on that river (II Kings 17:6).

Meta. A forced seeming union made between the religious and spiritual thoughts of man (Israelites) and his intellectual sense reasonings (Assyrians). (The Israelites were taken captive by the Assyrians, and Habor was one of the places where they were placed.)

Hacaliah (A. V., Hachaliah), hăc-ă-lī'-äh (Heb.)—*wait (with confidence) upon Jehovah; whose eyes Jehovah brightens; darkness (flashing) of Jehovah.*

Father of Nehemiah (Neh. 1:1).

Meta. Light in seeming darkness; an inner attitude of prayer, of waiting on the Lord for light to dispel the seeming darkness that hides our good from us when our true (Israelitish) thoughts have become engulfed, apparently, in sense confusion (Babylon).

Hachilah, hăch'-ĭ-läh (Heb.)—*dark; darksome; brilliant; flashing eyes; waiting in confidence; drought.*

A hill in the wilderness of Ziph where David was in hiding from Saul, and where Saul encamped when he went to hunt for David (I Sam. 23:19; 26:3).

Meta. Hope, expectation of good, in the face of seeming darkness and lack; light, in the midst of apparent darkness.

Hachmoni, hăch'-mō-nī (Heb.)—*one who is wise; knowing; intelligent; skillful; dexterous; cunning.*

Father of Jehiel, who was with the king's sons in David's reign (I Chron. 27:32).

Meta. A thought that has its inception in the wisdom center in consciousness, situated at the top brain in the head, in the Christ mind in man.

Hachmonite, hăch'-mō-nīte (fr. Heb.) —*of or pertaining to Hachmoni.*

An Israelitish family to whom Jashobeam and Jehiel belonged (I Chron. 11:11; 27:32).

Meta. A thought belonging to the wisdom (Hachmoni) consciousness in man. (See HACHMONI.)

Hadad, hā'-dăd (Heb.)—*sharp; quick; vehement; might; force; power; majesty; glory; splendor; joyous; rejoicing.* Genesis 36:39 has another form of this name, Hadar, meaning *where one returns for rest; concealed inner chamber; hidden principle.*

a A king of Edom (Gen. 36:35).

b A son of Ishmael (Gen. 25:15). **c** Hadad was the name of the chief Syrian deity and was the title of several of their kings. **d** An Edomite prince in Solomon's time (I Kings 11:14).

Meta. The setting up, as all-powerful, of the intellect in its spiritually unawakened state. Back of the intellect, however, back of every expression of intelligence or understanding, there exists the *hidden principle* of all light, all wisdom, all knowledge—God, Spirit.

Hadadezer, hăd-ăd-ē'-zēr (Heb.)— *mighty is the help; powerful succor; Hadad or Adad is his help; joyous help.*

Son of Rehob and king of Zobah. Hadadezer was a seemingly powerful king defeated by David (II Sam. 8:3-12).

Meta. The ruling thought in the state of consciousness in man that believes that the intellect, directed by the senses, is man's greatest possible enlightener and help in all matters.

Hadadrimmon, hā - dăd - rĭm' - mŏn (Heb.)—*Hadad of Rimmon; Hadad of the pomegranate; joy of the pomegranate; rending of the pomegranate; joyous fruitfulness.*

A place in the valley of Megiddon where all Judah and Jerusalem mourned for King Josiah, who was slain in a battle with Neco, king of Egypt, in this valley (Zech. 12:11; see II Chron. 35: 20-26 also). Hadad and Rimmon are both names of Syrian deities.

Meta. Attributing joy, fruitfulness, abundance to the efforts of that which Hadad represents in man (see HADAD); or the putting away of true fruitfulness (*rending of the pomegranate*) from consciousness by ceasing to be loyal to spiritual Truth (Josiah, whose death was mourned at Hadadrimmon, is representative of loyalty to Truth) because of putting one's trust in and magnifying the outer or intellectual sense reasonings. (Syria pertains to the unawakened intellect, guided by the senses.)

Hadar. See HADAD.

Hadarezer, hăd-ăr-ē'-zēr (Heb.)—*Hadar or Adad is his help; Hadad's help.* (See HADADEZER.)

A Syrian king (II Sam. 10:16; I Chron. 18:3-10). He is called Hadadezer in II Samuel 8:3 and I Kings 11:23.

Meta. See HADADEZER.

Hadashah, hăd'-ă-shăh (Heb.)—*new; make new; make anew; repair; restore; renew.*

A city in the lowland of Judah, mentioned as between Zenan and Migdal-gad (Josh. 15:37).

Meta. A group of thoughts (city) in the subconscious mind (lowland of Judah) that is established in a power that works for perpetual youth (*new, make new, restore, renew*) in the individual. "If any man is in Christ, *he is* a new creature: the old things are passed away; behold, they are become new" (II Cor. 5:17). This group of thoughts, or state of consciousness, is closely associated with abundant substance, vitality, power, and clearness of vision (Zenan, *rich in flocks,* and Migdal-gad, *tower of Gad,* Gad referring to the power faculty in man and also meaning *seer*).

Hadassah, hä-dăs'-săh (Heb.)—*leaping; springing up; joy; gladness; myrtle.*

Esther's Hebrew name (Esth. 2:7).

Meta. The myrtle is a lovely evergreen shrub or moderate-sized tree, having white flowers. Both leaves and flowers give out a very pleasant odor. Among the ancient Greeks the myrtle was sacred to Venus as the symbol of youth and beauty; it was used extensively at festivals. It is symbolical of the life principle, ever vital and renewing. So Hadassah, the Jewish name of Esther, represents the joy, youthfulness, activity, and beauty of the soul established in a consciousness of the abidingness and potency of divine life and love. (See ESTHER.)

Hades (in A. V., the New Testament, hell), hā'-dēṣ (Gk.)—*not to be seen; not to be looked upon.*

Hades is a Greek word; the Hebrew word meaning the same thing is *sheol.* In the English version of the Bible (the King James or Authorized Version), in the New Testament especially, it is generally translated *hell.* It is supposed to refer to the unseen world, or the abode of the dead. In reality, however, the word has reference to the grave or the "pit." In the Authorized Version, in many places in the Old Testament *sheol* is interpreted grave or pit. For examples see Genesis 37:35; 42:38; I Samuel 2:6;

I Kings 2:6; Job 14:13; 17:13, 16, and there are others. In the American Standard Version the word *sheol* is used in these texts. Please compare the two, and then look up the places where the translation *hell* is given.

Meta. Hades refers to the outer darkness, the realm of sense, in contrast to the inner or luminously spiritual. To live in the outer is to live outside the body, as it were; hence Hades came to be considered the realm of discarnate souls. In individual consciousness it may be likened to the darkened and silenced condition of seeming error when we have withdrawn from it all the power and substance of our thoughts about it and beliefs in it, when we have denied it, put it away from mind and body. Hades denotes the burying out of sight, out of thought and mind, of that above which the overcomer has risen, of that which has become inactive in his consciousness.

Hades may also refer, like Gehenna, to a state of purification. (See GEHENNA and HINNOM.)

Hadid, hā'-dĭd (Heb.)—*one; unity; sharp; pointed; peak; pinnacle; quick; swift; alert; nimble; fierce; vehement.*

A Benjamite city. Some of the descendants of the former inhabitants of this city returned from the Babylonian captivity (Ezra 2:33; Neh. 11:34).

Meta. A group of thoughts in consciousness that are unified and high (*one, unity, peak*), to the point, clear, keen, active, discriminating, decisive, straightforward. They aid greatly in doing away with confusion and disorder in mind, body, and affairs, and in keeping the individual in an attitude of rejoicing.

Hadlai, hăd'-lāi (Heb.)—*lax; idle; resting; dissolute; keeping a holiday; forbearing; forsaking; ceasing; ceasing to be; languid; frail; dead.*

Father of Amasa, who was a chief among the children of Ephraim during the reign of Pekah, king of Israel. Amasa was one of those who objected to keeping the children of Judah captive (II Chron. 28:12).

Meta. A very negative thought in consciousness, which tends to lack of positiveness and of necessary self-discipline; thus it hinders one's realizing and demonstrating of good.

Hadoram, hă-dō'-răm (Heb.)—*Hadar is high; highly ornamental; powerful; pompous; majestic.*

a Son of Joktan (Gen. 10:27). **b** Son of Tou, king of Hamath, whom Tou sent to David to salute and bless him because David had defeated Hadarezer, king of Zobah (I Chron. 18:10). **c** An Israelite who was over the men subject to taskwork in David's, Solomon's, and Rehoboam's reigns. He was stoned to death by the Israelites when King Rehoboam sent him to collect tribute from them (II Chron. 10:18). This latter Hadoram is called Adoniram in I Kings 4:6, and Adoram in II Samuel 20:24.

Meta. The lifting up of the outer, sense mind of man, and the attributing of power and might to it as though it were man's highest source of light and good. This belief also held sway, to a certain extent at least, in the Hadoram who was an Israelite. It causes the thought for which he stands in our consciousness to become hard and exacting, and in consequence to become impotent.

Hadrach, hā'-drăeh (Heb.)—*periodical returning; over and over again; sun's returning; place to which one returns,* i. e., *a chamber,* especially *an inner one.*

A place in Syria, near Damascus (Zech. 9:1).

Meta. Man, in sense consciousness, moves in cycles. Over and over again (like the return of the sun, and of the seasons) he returns to, or goes through, almost precisely the same experiences. This is proved by history, which repeats itself. Each cycle may be on an almost imperceptibly higher plane than the preceding one. Thus very slowly man unfolds until he consciously touches the realm of spiritual inspiration and understanding. Then his progress becomes more rapid. Hadrach (*periodical returning, over and over again, sun's returning*) signifies this cyclic mode of development in the natural man. There is also, in that which Hadrach symbolizes, a thought of meditation, or prayer (*place to which one returns,* i. e., *a chamber,* especially *an inner one*), by means of which man's intellectual consciousness may receive spiritual inspiration and become awakened to true understanding.

Hagab, hā'-găb (Heb.)—*a locust; hiding; covering; leaping; bending.*

His descendants were among the Nethinim who returned from the Babylonian captivity (Ezra 2:46).

Meta. A serving thought in man's religious consciousness, but with a somewhat biased, darkening, and destructive (*locust*) tendency. (See Revelation 9:3-10 and Exodus 10:12-15 for an insight into the destructive thought force that locusts symbolize.) Likewise a strong belief in evil works destructively in one's consciousness, even if with the belief in evil or with fear of it there is a desire and a willingness to serve God.

To serve God (good) fully and fruitfully one must learn to give all of one's thought substance to the good; one must quit building a destructive current in oneself by magnifying evil through believing in it, or by thinking about it as having any power to perpetuate itself.

Hagaba, hăg'-ă-bà (Heb.)—*a locust.*

His descendants were of the Nethinim who returned from the Babylonian captivity (Neh. 7:48). The name is spelled Hagabah in Ezra 2:45.

Meta. This name signifies, like Hagab, a thought of service to God, in man's religious consciousness, yet with a destructive tendency. (The Nethinim were servants in the Temple.)

Hagar, hā'-gär (Heb.)—*flight; to flee one's country; fugitive; wanderer; stranger.*

Sarai's handmaid, the mother of Ishmael by Abraham (Gen. 16:1-16).

Meta. The natural soul. It is a *stranger* to the awakened spiritual phase of the soul, in that its thoughts and emotions are sensual and are likely to be selfish and unholy, thus producing fear and uncertainty (*wanderer*). The sensual must give way to the spiritual; it cannot stand in the presence of the Christ truth, but flees (*flight*). "Now we, brethren, as Isaac was, are children of promise. But as then he that was born after the flesh persecuted him *that was born* after the Spirit, so also it is now. Howbeit what saith the scripture? Cast out the handmaid and her son: for the son of the handmaid shall not inherit with the son of the freewoman. Wherefore, brethren, we are not children of a handmaid, but of the freewoman" (Gal. 4:28-31). (See also verses 21 to 27 of Galatians 4, and compare the metaphysical significance of Hagar and Ishmael with that of Sarah and Isaac.)

Haggai, hăg'-gă-ī (Heb.)—*festive; festal; feast; festival; joyous; rejoicing.*

One of the minor prophets, who prophesied at the time the Jews returned from the Babylonian captivity. (See Ezra 6: 14 and The Book of Haggai.)

Meta. A realization of good as taking the place of seeming evil. That spiritual insight in man which heralds joyous, full, free deliverance from oppression, and abundance of rich substance and life for mind and body; it feasts upon the Truth daily, and foresees and foretells the working out of good.

Haggi, hăg'-gī (Heb.)—*festive; festal; feast; festival; joyous; rejoicing.*

A son of Gad and grandson of Jacob (Gen. 46:16). Haggi is a form of the name Haggai.

Meta. See HAGGAI.

Haggiah, hăg-gī'-ăh (Heb.)—*Jehovah's feast; festival of Jehovah; feast of the Lord; joy of the Lord.*

A Levite, descended from Merari (I Chron. 6:30).

Meta. The Christ of God (Jehovah) feasting with man upon the joyous occasion of man's opening the door of his consciousness to the Christ rule of love. "Behold, I stand at the door and knock: if any man hear my voice and open the door, I will come in to him, and will sup with him, and he with me" (Rev. 3:20).

Haggites, hăg'-gītes (fr. Heb.)—*of or belonging to Haggi.*

Descendants of Haggi, the son of Gad (Num. 26:15).

Meta. Thoughts pertaining to the realization of good that Haggi stands for in consciousness; thoughts that spring from this realization. (See HAGGAI.)

Haggith, hăg'-gĭth (Heb.)—*festive; festal; feast; festival; joyous; rejoicing.*

One of David's wives, the mother of Adonijah (II Sam. 3:4).

Meta. The joyous activity of the soul

or feminine in man, unified with the ruling love faculty (David) in consciousness, drinking in, feasting upon, appropriating, substance and Truth.

Hagri (A. V., Haggeri), hăg'-rī (Heb.)—*fugitive; wanderer; stranger.*

Father of Mibhar, one of David's warriors (I Chron. 11:38). Mibhar, the son of Hagri, is thought to be the same person as Bani the Gadite, mentioned in II Samuel 23:36.

Meta. A roaming thought in consciousness. It is of the intellect, rather than of Spirit, but it has broken free from the realm of sense and is drifting spiritward, though it is not yet established in true understanding. But it chooses wisely in laying hold of the idea of never failing, ever renewing, divine life; thus it brings forth Mibhar, meaning *choice, youth*, who becomes a valuable aid to the ruling (David or love) faculty in the individual.

Hagrites (in A. V., I Chron. 5:10, Hagarites, and in I Chron. 27:31, Hagerite), hăg'-rītes (fr. Heb.)—*of or belonging to Hagar.*

Descendants of Hagar, a tribe of Ishmaelites (I Chron. 5:10; Psalms 83:6, margin; in text, Hagarenes). Jaziz the Hagrite was overseer of the flocks in David's reign (I Chron. 27:30).

Meta. Thoughts belonging to the Hagar and Ishmael phases of consciousness in man. (See HAGAR and ISHMAEL.)

Hakkatan, hăk'-kă-tăn (Heb.)—*the little one; the smaller; the lowly; the inferior; the younger; the junior.*

Father of Johanan, and descended from Azgad. Johanan with one hundred and ten other male descendants of Azgad returned with Ezra from the Babylonian captivity (Ezra 8:12).

Meta. The thought that Hakkatan symbolizes is clearly expressed in Jesus' words recorded in Matthew 18:3, "Except ye turn, and become as little children, ye shall in no wise enter into the kingdom of heaven," and in Mark 10:15, "Verily I say unto you, Whosoever shall not receive the kingdom of God as a little child, he shall in no wise enter therein." It is that humble, lowly attitude of mind and that youthful thought of the child —full of hope and willing to unfold and to learn new things, willing to change the mind and to accept the true Christ ideas—which will set one free from all sense bondage and confusion (Babylon).

Hakkoz (in A. V., I Chron. 4:8, Coz, and in Ezra 2:61, Koz), hăk'-kŏz (Heb.) —*the thorn; the thorn bush; the briar; the wounding; the cutting of fruits; the harvest; the summer; the nimble.*

a A Levite priest, to whom the seventh lot fell for service in the temple, in David's reign (I Chron. 24:10). **b** A Judahite, father of Anub (I Chron. 4:8). The children of the Hakkoz of Ezra 2:61 could not show their genealogy and so were put from the priesthood; this was after the return from the Babylonian captivity.

Meta. The quickness and lightness of the action of true thoughts in consciousness (*the nimble*); also *the harvest,* or time of reaping.

The thorn, the annoyance or cause of trouble, connected with this name, is a doubt on our part at times as to the truth of some new idea or experience that comes to us. This doubt is caused by our confusion of thought. Then we hesitate to accept the idea, or to see good in the experience; we may even go so far as to think it evil and cast it out of consciousness. This is symbolized by the Hakkoz whose descendants could not show their genealogy after their return from the Babylonian captivity, and so were expelled from the priesthood.

Hakupha, hă-kū'-phå (Heb.)—*bent; crooked; perverted; to incline; pervert; incite.*

His descendants were of the Nethinim who returned from the Captivity (Ezra 2:51).

Meta. A thought that incites or arouses one to give service to God. This thought is not really straightforward in its desire to serve, since it is biased by false ideas. It does not comprehend man's divine sonship, whereby he serves God in love and joy; it thinks that we must serve God in fear and trembling because our God is a God of wrath, one of hard-and-fast rules that we cannot possibly live up to. This form of service for which Hakupha stands is portrayed in Luke 19:20-24: "And another came, saying, Lord, behold, *here is* thy pound, which I kept laid up in a napkin: for I feared thee, because thou art an austere man: thou takest up that which thou layedst not down, and reapest that which thou didst not sow. He saith unto him, Out of thine own mouth will I judge thee, thou wicked servant. Thou knewest that I am an austere man, taking up that which I laid not down, and reaping that which I did not sow; then wherefore gavest thou not my money into the bank, and I at my coming should have required it with interest? And he said unto them that stood by, Take away from him the pound, and give it unto him that hath the ten pounds." Thus our God manifests to us just what we conceive Him to be.

Halah, hā'-lăh (Heb., doubtful origin) —*moist table; moist surface.*

A place in Assyria, where some of the Israelites were placed when they were carried away captive by the Assyrian king (II Kings 17:6).

Meta. A nervous state into which a portion of man's highest religious thoughts and beliefs (Israelites) are thrown when the reasonings of the sense intellect (Assyrians) gain the ascendancy over them. *Moist* suggests a nervous state of mind and body. Moist also gives the thought of an expression of sympathy. *Moist surface* would indicate that this is outer, human sympathy, which is on the surface only and sympathizes weakly with appearances. It is not the Christ compassion, which always points the way out of error and inharmony, and aids in lifting one above seeming limitations.

Halak, hā'-lăk (Heb.)—*smooth; bare; bald; bland; flattering; slippery; deceitful; false.*

"From mount Halak [*the bare mountain,* margin], that goeth up to Seir, even unto Baal–gad in the valley of Lebanon under mount Hermon: and all their kings he took, and smote them, and put them to death." Mount Halak was the scene of some of Joshua's conquests (Josh. 11:17; 12:7).

Meta. The deceitfulness of the sense consciousness, even though it seeks to exalt itself (Halak was a mountain).

Joshua's conquests at Mount Halak signify a going up in thought and aspiration, from the deceptiveness of sense belief and activity, to Seir (the ruling thought of the physical in man), to Baal-gad (a realization of substance, of bounty, and of power through clear seeing and good judgment, but with a strong tendency as yet toward the belief that the source of this good is in the outer formed world—Baal—instead of the inner formless Spirit). This aspiration, or overcoming power of the I AM (Joshua), goes still higher, to the valley of Lebanon under Mount Hermon. Lebanon means *whiteness*, and represents pure thoughts; Mount Hermon means *lofty, prominent, sacred mountain*, and signifies a high, sublime state of consciousness.

Halhul, hăl'-hŭl (Heb.)—*full of hollows, i. e., rolling depressions; pain; pang; travail; trembling; terror; fear; trepidation; grief.*

A city in the hill country of Judah (Josh. 15:58).

Meta. A group of thoughts belonging to the Judah or praise consciousness, and elevated to a higher plane than it really belongs to, since it is not so sincere and sound as it seems (*full of hollows*). Because of its insincerity, because it has not been wholly built up in Truth, this group of thoughts is sure to cause inner *fears, tremblings,* and sorrows (*grief*) that the individual may not be able to account for consciously. He should therefore be diligent in filling up all the weak places in mind and body with strong, true thoughts of praise and joy, of honor and strength, and with much real prayer and communion with God in the silence.

Hali, hā'-lī (Heb.)—*rubbed to brightness; polished; ornament; jewel; necklace; smooth; sweet; pleasant.*

A border town of Asher (Josh. 19:25).

Meta. The joy of an understanding heart (Asher means *happy*, and understanding and wisdom are the richest *jewels* with which an individual can *ornament* himself). *Rubbed to brightness,* and *polished,* suggest the wisdom and the excellent general characteristics that man grows into by daily use of his faculties and powers in coöperative association with his fellow men.

hallelujah (in A. V., Revelation 19:1, Alleluia), hăl-lĕ-lū'-jăh (Heb.)—*make a glad sound to Jehovah; praise ye Jehovah; rejoice in Jah; praise Jah.*

An expression of praise and joy that was commonly used in Hebrew worship. It stands at the beginning of many of the Psalms, in the form, "Praise ye Jehovah," with "hallelujah" given in the marginal notes. The Psalms were sung during worship in the Temple (Psalms 150, margin; Rev. 19:1).

Meta. The whole of man's religious and spiritual nature lifted up in thanksgiving and praise to Jehovah, the Christ, the Father within him.

Hallohesh (in A. V., Nehemiah 3:12, Halohesh), hăl-lō'-hĕsh (Heb.) — *the whisperer; the hisser; the enchanter; the conjurer; the charmer.*

a A chief of the returned Jews, who joined Nehemiah in sealing the covenant (Neh. 10:24). (b) A man whose son Shallum repaired a portion of the wall of Jerusalem, after the Babylonian captivity (Neh. 3:12).

Meta. A belief in the occult, the hidden, mysterious, or supernatural; it tends to superstition, but is very religious in its character. This belief gives its substance over to the building of a perfect consciousness and body (typified by the rebuilding of the Temple and Jerusalem's wall) by obedience to the law of God (signing the covenant).

Ham, hăm (Heb.)—*oblique; curved; inferior; hot; blackened.*

Son of Noah (Gen. 5:32).

Meta. The physical in man, given over to sensuality.

Haman, hā'-măn (Heb. fr. Pers.)—*magnificent; splendid; celebrated; famed; solely; only; the planet Mercury; noise; arrogance; tumult; inner commotion; trouble.*

Son of Hammedatha the Agagite. He was very high in the favor of King Ahasuerus of Persia and laid a plot for the destruction of all the Jews who were in that land. He was thwarted, however, by Mordecai and Esther, and was hanged on the gallows that he had built for Mordecai (Esth., 3d to 9th chapters).

Meta. Haman, "son of Hammedatha, the Jews' enemy" (Esth. 9:10), stands for the activity of the phase of the carnal consciousness in man (the Adversary) that gives itself up particularly to working against man's religious thoughts and tendencies, his highest spiritual beliefs and aspirations (the Jews).

Hamath, hā'-măth (Heb.)—*inclosed; held together; walled around; fortress; citadel; defense; heated; passionate; excited.*

A small Syrian kingdom on the northern border of Palestine (Num. 34:8).

Meta. Confidence in material conditions rather than trust in God; also the result of the material thought and belief —an unpoised, unbalanced state of mind. (See ASHIMA.)

Hamathite, hā'-măth-īte (fr. Heb.)— *of* or *belonging to Hamath.*

A descendant of Canaan the son of Ham (Gen. 10:18). It is thought that descendants of Canaan settled in Hamath; thus a Hamathite would also be an inhabitant of Hamath.

Meta. A thought or tendency in man that belongs to the body consciousness (Canaan), or to the Hamath consciousness (confidence in materiality, and its results).

Hamath – zobah, hā'-măth – zō'-băh (Heb.)—*fortress of Zobah; fortress of splendor; Hamath the great; encampment of Hamath.*

A place in Syria that Solomon captured (II Chron. 8:3). It is thought to be the same place as Hamath.

Meta. A state of consciousness that is fortified in outer, material, intellectual reasonings and in that which Hamath signifies. (See HAMATH.) It has to give way, however, before true spiritual wisdom (represented here by Solomon, who captured Hamath–zobah).

Hammath (in A. V., I Chronicles 2:55, Hemath), hăm'-măth (Heb.)—*hot places; hot springs; hot baths; physical heat; passion.*

a A fortified city of Naphtali (Josh. 19:35). Hammoth–dor of Joshua 21:32, and Hammon in I Chronicles 6:76, are thought to be the same place as Hammath. **b** A person or place given in the genealogy of Judah (I Chron. 2:55).

Meta. Strength (Naphtali) established (fortress) in the physical. (*Hot springs, hot places,* denote *physical heat, passion,* the "mind of the flesh" thought that is still active in the consciousness of the individual in his relation to life and strength, at this stage of his unfoldment.)

Hammedatha, hăm-mĕd'-ă-thȧ (Heb. fr. Pers.)—*who troubles the law; agitator of the law.*

An Agagite, father of "Haman son of Hammedatha, the Jews' enemy" (Esth. 9:10, 24).

Meta. Agag is the Adversary—the ruling ego of the adverse, carnal consciousness in man. Hammedatha, father of Haman, "the Jews' enemy," signifies a phase of the carnal, adverse consciousness (Adversary) in man, which works against the law of Being (*who troubles the law, agitator of the law*), more particularly as it relates to man's religious thoughts and tendencies, man's highest intellectual and spiritual beliefs and aspirations (the Jews). (See AGAG and HAMAN.)

Hammelech, hăm'-me-lech (Heb.)—*the king; the ruler; the counselor.*

The name of two different Israelites, seemingly; the name probably refers to King Jehoiakim and King Zedekiah (Jer. 36:26; 38:6, margin).

Meta. The will, or ruling ego, in man, expressing in opposition to the light of Truth, which is seeking to reveal the divine law. The will, impelled by the adverse, personal self, seeks to fight and destroy that which tries to make clear to it the bad results of its wicked, rebellious impulses (King Zedekiah wished to have Jeremiah the prophet out of the way), instead of conforming to the law and thus putting itself in the way to reap good.

The ancient idea of kingship was that of divided responsibility with the priesthood. The king ruled, not apart from, but by taking counsel of, the priests. Thus, when the will of man takes its counsel from the personal self and attempts to rule in its own right—that is, obstinately or arbitrarily, ignoring the guidance of man's higher, spiritual thoughts—the result is trouble.

Hammolecheth (A. V., Hammoleketh), hăm-mŏl'-ĕ-chĕth (Heb.)—*the queen*.

Daughter of Machir, and sister of Gilead. Her sons were Ishhod, Abiezer, and Mahlah (I Chron. 7:18). She was an Israelitess.

Meta. The soul, lifted up by prayer and spiritual thought. (Hammolecheth is particularly mentioned as being the sister of Gilead. See GILEAD.)

Hammon, hăm'-mŏn (Heb.)—*hot; torrid; heat of the sun; hot springs*.

a A city of Asher (Josh. 19:28).
b A city of Naphtali that was given over to the Levites of the family of Gershom (I Chron. 6:76). This latter Hammon is supposed to be the same place as Hammath of Joshua 19:35.

Meta. Joy, substance, understanding (Asher) and strength (Naphtali) established in the consciousness of life (springs).

Hammon of Naphtali was ceded to the Levites (thoughts belonging to the ruling intellectual religious consciousness in man). The idea of the sun connected with the thought of heat (*heat of the sun*) in a definition of Hammon suggests something of true spiritual understanding of life, though *hot, torrid, hot springs*, point to sensuality. (See HAMMATH.)

Hammoth–dor, hăm'-mŏth–dôr (Heb.) —*hot springs of Dor*.

A city of Naphtali that was given to the Gershonite Levites (Josh. 21:32). It is supposed to be the same place as Hammath of Joshua 19:35 and Hammon of I Chronicles 6:76.

Meta. See HAMMATH and DOR. Strength must be established in the never failing, inexhaustible life and love of God in order to become abiding and enduring. Man's thought of life must be cleansed from mortal beliefs.

Hammuel (A. V., Hamuel), hăm'-mū-ĕl (Heb.)—*warmth of God; enveloped by God; heat of God; wrath of God; burned of God*.

Son of Mishma, an Israelite of the tribe of Simeon (I Chron. 4:26).

Meta. Mishma and Simeon both refer to hearing and obeying. This receptive attitude of mind opens man's consciousness to inspiration; thus man comes to know something of God, Spirit. As yet, however, the individual has not gotten away from the old idea of two powers, one of evil as well as one of good; he believes in God as sometimes a God of anger, and sense prevails in his life (suggested by *heat of God, wrath of God, burned of God*).

Hamonah, hăm-ō'-năh (Heb.)—*host; multitude; noise; tumult; commotion of mind*.

The prophetic name of a city that is mentioned in conjunction with Hamon–gog: "And Hamonah shall also be the name of a city. Thus shall they cleanse the land" (Ezek. 39:16).

Meta. The great *multitude* of true thoughts that shall be established in man's consciousness in place of the hosts of error, selfish, warring thoughts that are being overcome and put entirely out of existence, in so far as the individual is concerned. (See GOG and HAMON–GOG.)

Hamon–gog, hā'-mŏn–gŏg (Heb.)— *multitude of Gog; tumult of Gog*.

The valley in which "Gog and all his multitude" are to be buried (Ezek. 39: 11).

Meta. Gog is to be given a place of burial in Israel. That is, the substance and force that have been used to promote and keep active the adverse, selfish, warring thoughts represented by Gog are to be preserved for use in building and strengthening the good and the true in man's consciousness.

Hamon–gog (*multitude of Gog, tumult of Gog*, a valley where the multitudes of Gog are to be buried) is a very low (that is, material), confused, depressed, subconscious state into which all the errors of Gog, after having been deprived of their substance and seeming power of activity, are buried—released completely from sight and thought—preparatory to their being taken entirely out of the organism by means of the eliminative functions. "Thus shall they cleanse the land" (Ezek. 39:16).

Hamor, hā'-môr (Heb.)—*ass; wild ass*, so called from its reddish color; *clay; loam; cement; heap; red; blushing; inflamed*.

A prince of the Hivites, from whom Jacob bought the land on which he built the altar El–Elohe–Israel (Gen. 33:19). Hamor was the father of Shechem, who defiled Jacob's daughter Dinah and wanted to marry her. Both father and son were slain by Jacob's sons, Simeon and Levi (Gen. 34:2-26).

Meta. The ruling or central thought in the Hivite state of consciousness in man (see HIVITE), stubborn foolishness and unreasonableness (*ass*); also the transitory and material (*clay*) character of man's sensual, worldly mind.

Hamul, hā′-mŭl (Heb.) — *spared; pitied; mildness; gentleness; compassion; sympathy; mercy.*

Son of Perez and grandson of Judah, by Tamar (Gen. 46:12).

Meta. Compassion, mercy, and forgiveness. These attitudes of mind are Godlike, and they pertain to the salvation of the individual who entertains them.

Hamulites, hā′-mŭl-ītes (fr. Heb.)— *of or belonging to Hamul.*

The family, or descendants, of Hamul of the tribe of Judah (Num. 26:21).

Meta. Thoughts belonging to the phase of mind in man that Hamul signifies. (See HAMUL.)

Hamutal, hă-mū′-tăl (Heb.)—*father-in-law of the dew; kinsman of the dew; affinity of the dew; like dew.*

Daughter of Jeremiah of Libnah, and wife of Josiah, king of Judah. Jehoahaz and Zedekiah, kings of Judah, were her sons (II Kings 23:31; Jer. 52:1).

Meta. The soul, constantly refreshed because of its recognizing divine grace as unfailing and as ever present to vitalize, invigorate, and renew.

Hanamel (A. V., Hanameel), hå-năm′-ĕl (Heb.)—*God's gift; gratuity of God; grace of God; compassion of God; mercy of God.*

Son of Shallum, and cousin of Jeremiah (Jer. 32:7-12).

Meta. A perception of God as full of grace and mercy, and the understanding that fullness of life and Truth is *God's gift* to the race. Faith (Jeremiah) lays hold of the substance of this understanding and establishes man in the assurance that he is to be wholly redeemed, even to his outer organism. (This is carried out in symbol by Jeremiah, who

bought Hanamel's field in Anathoth. Then Jeremiah put the deeds for the field in an earthern vessel, to stay there for many days, as a sign that houses, fields, and vineyards would again be bought in the land of Judah even if it was at that time desolate because of having been conquered by the king of Babylon, and its inhabitants carried away into captivity. See Jeremiah 32:14-25.)

Hanan, hā′-năn (Heb.)—*favorably disposed; gracious; merciful; compassionate.*

There were several Israelitish men by this name; some of them were men of note (I Chron. 8:23, 38; 11:43; Ezra 2:46; Neh. 8:7; 10:22, 26; 13:13; Jer. 35:4).

Meta. Kindness, forgiveness, compassion. The religious and spiritual consciousness of man (the Israelitish nation) abounds, or should abound, in thoughts of this character. Thoughts of fullness of the grace, or power and all-sufficiency, of the divine presence also belong to man's highest spiritual concepts (Israelites).

Hananel (A. V., Hananeel), hå-năn′-ĕl (Heb.)—*God has graciously given; God is gracious; favored of God; God's mercifulness; given of God.*

A tower on the wall of Jerusalem, and forming a portion of the wall (Neh. 3:1; Jer. 31:38).

Meta. The thought of mercy, and of the omnipotence of spiritual qualities, as belonging to man and established in his body consciousness through prayer and high spiritual aspirations.

Hanani, hă-nā′-nī (Heb.)—*gracious; merciful; compassionate.*

a A son of Heman (I Chron. 25:4). b A seer who rebuked King Asa of Judah because he relied on the king of Syria instead of Jehovah (II Chron. 16:7). c A priest who had taken a foreign wife (Ezra 10:20). d A brother to Nehemiah (Neh. 7:2). e A priest who helped at the dedication of Jerusalem's wall after it was rebuilt (Neh. 12:36).

Meta. The grace, or expressed power, of Divine Mind in man.

The outer thoughts crystallize about a center of which environment is the standard, while the inner thoughts see beyond into the realm of causes. Hanani signifies this inner soul consciousness, which perceives, and reports to Nehemiah, the outer, that all is not as it should be at the deeper spiritual center, Jerusalem (see Neh. 1:2, 3).

Hananiah, hăn-ă-nī'-ăh (Heb.)—*whom Jehovah has graciously given; Jah is gracious; mercy of Jehovah; compassion of Jah.*

There are several Israelitish men by this name (I Chron. 3:19 and Dan. 1:6 mention two of them).

Meta. The knowledge of Jehovah, the indwelling Christ, as love, mercy, goodness, and the channel of all power, wisdom, Truth, to the manifest man.

Not all the men of this name, however, understood that the goodness and free gifts of Spirit come to us by direct law, and that in order to receive them consciously and utilize them in our life we must observe the law of justice, of right and order, the law of the working out of Truth. The Hananiah of Jeremiah 28:1-17 typifies the persons of to-day, or that phase of thought in each of us, that would like to think—and some do deceive themselves into believing—that because God is love and mercy they may do anything they choose, regardless of the law of justice and right, and reap all the goodness of God just the same. Such beliefs are a mistake, for in order to experience the blessings of the grace of God we must put ourselves in line with them by cleansing our mind and heart and life, and by doing the will of the Father, thus keeping the divine law.

Hanes, hā'-nĕs (Heb.)—*the planet Mercury; banishment of grace; turning of favor.*

A place in Egypt that has not been identified; it is mentioned with Zoan (Isa. 30:4).

Meta. The belief that wisdom comes from the outer—the establishment of one's trust in stars, and so forth. This leads away from the grace of God (*banishment of grace*) and from consciousness of the divine presence and power in one's life.

Hannah, hăn'-nah (Heb.)—*grace; favor; compassion; defense.*

Wife of Elkanah of the hill country of Ephraim, and mother of Samuel (I Sam. 1:2 to 2:21).

Meta. The soul, because of its high aspirations, its consecration to God, and much earnest prayer, established in divine grace and favor. It receives that which it desires, the ability to hear the inner voice of Spirit, to perceive Truth. (Samuel represents the inner voice of Spirit, or divine inspiration and guidance; see SAMUEL.)

Hannathon, hăn'-nă-thŏn (Heb.)—*graciously regarded; favorably disposed; dedicated to grace; gift of grace.*

A city of Zebulun, on the northern boundary (Josh. 19:14).

Meta. A group of thoughts in which order (Zebulun) is the central idea. This group of thoughts is consecrated to the purpose of promoting, realizing, establishing a consciousness of the all-sufficiency of God, divine grace (*dedicated to grace*).

Hanniel (in A. V., I Chronicles 7:39, Haniel), hăn'-nĭ-ĕl (Heb.)—*favor of God; God is gracious; grace of God.*

a Son of Ephod, a prince of Manasseh. He was chosen by Jehovah to help divide the Promised Land among the twelve tribes of Israel (Num. 34:23). b A son of Ulla, an Asherite (I Chron. 7:39).

Meta. Divine grace, established in consciousness through understanding (Manasseh) and a realization of glad, joyous substance (Asher).

Hanoch, hā'-nŏch (Heb.)—*founded; centralized; arrested; straitened; agony of the soul; instructed; initiated; dedicated.*

a Son of Midian, who was one of Abraham's six sons by his second wife, Keturah (Gen. 25:4). b A son of Reuben and grandson of Jacob (Gen. 46:9). In Hebrew it is the same as Enoch.

Meta. Entrance into a higher consciousness than has been known and experienced before. (See ENOCH.)

Hanochites, hā'-nŏch-ītes (fr. Heb.)—*of or belonging to Chanok or Hanoch.*

The family, or descendants, of Hanoch the son of Reuben (Num. 26:5).

Meta. Thoughts that spring from and

belong to that in consciousness which Hanoch symbolizes. (See HANOCH.)

Hanun, hā'-nŭn (Heb.)—*favored; gracious; merciful; compassionate.*

a Son of Nahash and king of Ammon. He returned evil for good to David, then hired the Syrians to help him fight against Israel, but both the Ammonites and the Syrians were defeated and put to rout (II Sam. 10:1-4). **b** An Israelite who helped to repair the valley gate in the rebuilding of Jerusalem's wall (Neh. 3:13). **c** The sixth son of Zalaph, and who helped in rebuilding the wall of Jerusalem (Neh. 3:30).

Meta. The grace, mercy, and power of God, divine love, put to constructive use by man in the transforming of his thoughts and the rebuilding of his whole being, including his body, for eternal life.

Hanun, king of Ammon, shows how, in his ignorant, sinful, sensual state, man imposes on divine love and the saving power of God—or at least seeks to do so. He goes on in his old selfishness and error, and like a spoiled child expects to be saved fully and to gain eternal life by mercy alone, because of his belief that Jesus in an outer way atoned for his sins. He expects to be saved without any real, inner overcoming or change on his own part.

Hapharaim (A. V., Haphraim), hăph'-ā-rā'-ĭm (Heb.)—*double wells; two pits; diggings; excavations; searchings; explorations; plottings; spyings.*

A border city in Issachar (Josh. 19:19).

Meta. Hapharaim, in its definitions, shows how life can work destructively in consciousness as well as constructively, according to the use that man makes of it. If the life realization is doubly strong (*double wells*) because of a very active zeal (Issachar), and destructive sense thoughts rule the man, the pit, hell, inharmony, will be doubly in evidence (*two pits*). The idea of *searching, digging* into consciousness, for understanding and power, is also suggested in Hapharaim. This can also result in increased truth or error according to the purity and sincerity of the searching, or the selfishness and deceptiveness of the personal, which may yet rule the individual in degree.

Happizzez (A. V., Aphses), hăp'-pĭz-zĕz (Heb.)—*the dashing into pieces; the scattering; the dispersion.*

A Levite priest to whom was allotted the eighteenth course in Temple service, in David's reign (I Chron. 24:15).

Meta. The Levites, descendants of Levi, belong to the love consciousness in man. Love is an attracting, unifying power; it is not a quality that severs and scatters. In working through the religious intellect of man (many of the Israelitish priests typify this religious intellect; see AARON), a zealous love of the good is very likely to take on a warring attitude toward that which the intellect decides is not good. Thus a *dispersion* of the error takes place, and if the fighting spirit grows in the man and he does not overcome it, in time it will bring about the disintegration of his organism as well.

We cannot overcome seeming evil by hating and fighting it. The only way really to do away with it is to overcome it with good. We must dwell in the good so wholly that all the substance of our thoughts and of our being is given over to the promotion of the good. Then that which falls short of the perfect good will be no more in evidence.

Hara, hā'-rȧ (Heb.)—*mountainous land; region of the mountain; the mountain; strong peace.* The Chaldee Paraphrase renders Hara *mountains of darkness,* though *darkness* does not really enter into the meaning of the name.

One of the places to which Pul and Tilgath–pilneser, kings of Assyria, carried the Reubenites, Gadites, and the half tribe of Manasseh captive (I Chron. 5:26).

Meta. Darkness piles up like mountains before the religious thoughts of man (Israelites) when he gives himself over to the rule of the intellect guided by selfishness and sense (Assyria). He may think that true spiritual knowing and peace are to be attained through intellectual understanding and reason, but he is mistaken. True light comes only from Spirit.

Haradah, hăr'-ȧ-dăh (Heb.)—*excited; trembling; shaking; quaking; inclined with eagerness; hasten trembling; trepidation; fear; terror.* The original idea contained in the word Haradah was that of intense excitement or agitation, from any cause whatsoever. It could as well refer to the intensity of love as of fear, or any other cause. Later it became restricted to that of fear and terror. About the time that the translators got hold of the original, the idea had been quite thoroughly crystallized and restricted to that of fear, as we think of it today. When the translators saw this word in conjunction with God, the result was a catastrophe to humanity. Instead of rendering it the intense excitement, or intensity, of love, they thought it meant the fear of an adverse power over which we have no control. This helps to explain how the idea of fear of God got into our Bible.

A place where the children of Israel camped while in the wilderness, on their way to the Promised Land (Num. 33:24).

Meta. A state of anxiety and fearfulness, a trembling, which sometimes overtakes him who has left his old carnal, darkened beliefs (Egypt) but has not yet become firmly established in the new spiritual ideas and activities that he has taken up. He has not yet entered the Promised Land, but is wandering about in the wilderness of his thoughts, where he encounters many states of error thought that he cannot account for and does not know how to handle. He has to leave them and go on to other stopping places, until he shall grow in understanding, faith, and power to such an extent that he can meet boldly and overcome all the enemies of doubt and fear of every kind of seeming error.

Haran, hā'-răn (Heb.)—*strong; elevated; exalted; mountaineer.*

a Brother of Abram, and the father of Lot (Gen. 11:27). **b** A place where Abram and his father lived after they left Ur of the Chaldees to go into the land of Canaan (Gen. 11:31). It was here that Terah, Abram's father, died (Gen. 11:32). **c** A son of Shimei of the Gershonite Levites (I Chron. 23:9).

Meta. An exalted state of mind, wherein Truth is lifted up in consciousness and the individual is strengthened in his determination to go on toward fuller spiritual enlightenment and up-liftment.

Hararite, hā'-ră-rīte (Heb.)—*of or belonging to the mountain; a mountaineer; strong; elevated; exalted.*

Shammah, the son of Agee, a Hararite, was one of David's warriors (II Sam. 23:11). In I Chronicles 11:34, 35 two of David's mighty men are mentioned as being Hararites.

Meta. High aspirations; strong, noble, uplifting thoughts.

Harbonah, här-bō'-năh (Heb. fr. Pers.) —*ass driver; very warlike; destruction; desolation.*

One of the seven chamberlains of King Ahasuerus. He was the one who called the attention of the king to the gallows fifty cubits high that Haman had made to hang Mordecai on: "so they hanged Haman on the gallows that he had prepared for Mordecai" (Esth. 7:9, 10). In Esther 1:10 the name is spelled Harbona.

Meta. One of the seven senses of man's outer, carnal consciousness, under the dominion of the concerted, dominating, personal will (Ahasuerus the king). The stubborn, fighting, destructive attitude of this sense (*ass-driver, very warlike*) helps to get rid of the error in mind that Haman represents, when the will, because of its union with love (Esther), begins to see into and take sides with the Truth.

Hareph, hā'-rĕph (Heb.)—*rupture of elementary heat; interruption of elementary life; plucking off; picking off; autumn and winter; gathering of fruits; ripening; upbraiding; reproachful; lightly esteemed; early born.*

Son of Caleb, and founder of Beth-gader, a city of Judah (I Chron. 2:51).

Meta. The belief that man is limited in his life; that he exists only from the time of his physical conception and birth, and is under the dominion of age and seeming death. The truth is that he has existed with the Father always. At the very beginning of creation he was born into being through the Son, the Christ, the perfect, ideal man whom God made in His image and likeness (*early born*). Thus he is in truth infinite; all *reproach* is put away from him by his having a practical, working knowledge of this truth.

Harhaiah, här-hā'-ịah (Heb.)—*ardor of Jehovah; zeal of Jah; glowing of Jehovah; heat of the Lord; Jehovah's anger.*

Note: The root idea of the word Harhaiah comes from a verb meaning "to be kindled, to burn, to glow"; the meaning of the word has become restricted to anger. Primarily the idea is related to any burning ardor that fires one, or kindles to zeal over anything whatsoever.

Father of Uzziel, a goldsmith, who helped to repair Jerusalem's wall (Neh. 3:8).

Meta. Zeal.

There is still, at this phase of man's unfoldment, a belief in God as a God of wrath, as one who takes vengeance in a personal way on those who sin against Him. Truth students understand that all inharmony is the outworking of divine law in the lives of those persons who do not think and act in harmony with the law.

It means much for man to get entirely away from the thought that there is an *anger* side to God. Only a clear understanding that God is principle and not a person with outer shape like man, a knowledge of the great law that continually works in the affairs of men, will enable one fully to realize the truth.

Harhas, här'-häs (Heb.)—*glitter; splendor; glow of confidence; want; poverty; privation.*

Father of Tikvah and grandfather of Shallum, who was the husband of Huldah the prophetess (II Kings 22:14). In II Chronicles 34:22, Hasrah, thought to be the proper form of the name.

Meta. Zealously looking on the bright side of things; making a brilliant showing of light, truth, and bounty, in the face of seeming poverty and lack. By holding thus to the truth of one's being, and not giving way to appearances, one brings hope and strength (Tikvah, son of Harhas) into evidence. Then comes the compensation (Shallum, the grandson, means *recompense*).

Harhur, här'-hûr (Heb.)—*burning fever; parched; inflamed; intense ardor; free-born; noble; distinguished.*

His descendants were of the Nethinim who returned from the Babylonian captivity (Ezra 2:51).

Meta. The changeableness of the emotional state of one who thinks of himself as being a servant of God only, and does not know that he is a son of God by divine right, by reason of birth (see Galatians 4:6, 7, 21-31).

So long as we see ourselves as bond servants to God instead of sons of His, we shall be subject to all kinds of sensations in mind; destructive emotions of undue excitement and heat (*burning fever*) will express in and through us, as well as high and noble thoughts and feelings. But as we come to recognize our sonship more and more fully, we shall take our dominion and overcome all thoughts and emotions that are not constructive. We shall be zealous, but never unpoised; we shall be kind, loving, and compassionate, but not weakly sorrowful and sympathetic in a personal way.

Harim, hā'-rĭm (Heb.)—*drawn in; contracted; shut up; consecrated; dedicated; dried up; destroyed; snub-nosed; flat-nosed.*

a A priest who was given charge of the third division in the Temple worship, during David's reign (I Chron. 24: 8). **b** An Israelite whose descendants returned from the Captivity (Ezra 2:32). Some of his sons were among those who took foreign wives (Ezra 10:31). (c) Two men by this name joined Nehemiah in sealing the covenant (Neh. 10:5, 27).

Meta. The perceptive, discriminative, and initiative capacities of mind, somewhat dull in their expression, not so keen as they might be (*flat-nosed* or *snub-nosed, drawn in, contracted*), yet set apart for God's service, to be used for the promotion of the spiritual well-being of the individual (*consecrated, dedicated*). Spiritual use will quicken and enlarge these capacities to perfect and full expression. (The sense of smell, of which the nose is the organ, represents perception with a discriminative tendency, while the size of the nose has to do with initiativeness, aggressiveness.)

Hariph, hā'-rĭph (Heb.)—*autumn and winter; arrested life; plucking; early born; lightly esteemed; autumnal rains; ripened; fully developed.*

a "The children of Hariph, a hundred and twelve," returned from the Babylonian captivity (Neh. 7:24). **b** A man by this name joined Nehemiah in sealing the covenant (Neh. 10:19).

Meta. Omnipresent life and strength, established in the assurance of having always existed in Being (*early born*); also the fruition of this truth in consciousness (*autumn*), and the soul-refreshing showers that it brings, preparatory to a still further fruition (*autumnal rains*).

(No matter if *autumn* seems to bring a certain barrenness and a *plucking* away of some of the outer appearances of life, it is the time of harvest nevertheless, wherein abundance is in evidence everywhere. The rain that comes in the fall, too, especially after a comparatively dry summer, does much to insure the safety of vegetable life during the winter months, and helps to bring about good crops the following year.)

Harnepher, här'-nĕ-phĕr (Heb.)— *snoring; snorting; panting; hard breathing,* i. e., *through the nose.*

Son of Zophah, of the tribe of Asher (I Chron. 7:36).

Meta. Difficulty in realizing spiritual inspiration (breathing is symbolical of receiving inspiration, while *panting* is a shortened or labored breathing) because of the prevalence of outer activities of the personal and animal in consciousness (this latter is suggested in *snoring, snorting*).

Harod, hā'-rŏd (Heb.)—*excited; trembling; shaking; inclined with eagerness; hasten trembling; trepidation; fear; terror.* Harod relates to the heart or center of emotion. The idea in the name is that of trembling for any one, either in caring for him, loving him intensely and running toward him in greeting, or of running away from some one trembling because of fear and terror.

A spring beside which Gideon camped when he fought against and defeated the Midianites. It was there that he told all those of his army who were fearful and trembling to return to their homes (Judg. 7:1-3).

Meta. The enemy, *fear.* It must be met here and overcome before victory over the Midianites (strife and contention) can be gained. Perfect love casts out fear, and love establishes peace and unity in consciousness.

Harodite, hā'-rŏd-īte (fr. Heb.)—*of or belonging to Harod.*

Two of David's warriors were Harodites (II Sam. 23:25); there must have been a town named Harod in connection with the spring of Harod.

Meta. A thought belonging to the Harod consciousness in man. (See HAROD.) Shammah the Harodite bespeaks the *desolation* and *destruction* of fear, and Elika the Harodite symbolizes the elimination of fear. These two, therefore, do much toward keeping the ruling power of love (David) established in consciousness.

Haroeh, hăr'-ŏ-ēh (Heb.)—*the perceiver; the seer; the prophet.*

Son of Shobal, who was the "father" or founder of Kiriath–jearim. He was of the tribe of Judah (I Chron. 2:52).

Meta. Clear-seeing, spiritual understanding and insight into things; also a knowledge of the law of being and its working, thus enabling us to foresee the outcome of our thoughts, words, and acts.

Harorite, hā'-rō-rīte (Heb.)—*of or belonging to Harod.*

"Shammoth the Harorite" was one of David's mighty men (I Chron. 11:27). He is called Shammah the Harodite in II Samuel 23:25.

Meta. See HARODITE.

Harosheth, hă-rō'-shĕth (Heb.)—*a work; working,* i. e., *in wood* or *stone; engraving; place of workers; place of craft; magic; enchantment.*

"Harosheth of the Gentiles" was the city in which lived Sisera, captain of the hosts of Jabin, king of Canaan (Judg. 4:2).

Meta. A group of thoughts in consciousness that belong to the sense or seemingly mortal mind in man (Gentiles). By means of a phase of animal intelligence and instinct (Jabin) that rules in this group of thoughts, it is raised to a semblance of supernatural power (*magic, enchantment*) and to great skillfulness (*place of craft, working,* i. e., *in wood* or *stone, engraving, place of craft*). Its dominating, executive idea, however, is the intellectual aggressiveness that Sisera (meaning *battle array, ready for war*) signifies. Therefore this state of consciousness that Harosheth stands for is actively opposed to the more peaceful and true thoughts that the Israelites symbolize.

Harsha, här'-shȧ (Heb.)—*artificer; craftsman; worker; magician; enchanter; deaf; dumb; silent.*

He was of the Nethinim. His descendants returned from the Babylonian captivity (Ezra 2:52).

Meta. A religious thought in man that tends to the psychical yet seeks to serve God. It is not really receptive to spiritual Truth; it is *deaf*—meaning not receptive, not responsive. It works in the psychical, or soul, realm; thus it expresses much that seems to be occult, magical, supernatural (*magician, artificer, enchanter*). This thought belongs to the bond-servant class (Nethinim) in consciousness, and must give way to the true spiritual understanding that comes with the knowledge of divine sonship (see Gal. 4).

Harum, hä'-rŭm (Heb.)—*high; exalted; elevated; made great; overtopping.*

Named as a descendant of Hakkoz, in the genealogy of Judah (I Chron. 4:8).

Meta. A high, exalted thought in man's praise consciousness (Judah). It is descended from Hakkoz, symbolizing the quickness and lightness of the action of true thoughts in consciousness; "the families of Aharhel" are its offspring. Aharhel signifies a belief in protection and might as coming from God and not emanating from the outer man.

Harumaph, hȧ-rụ'-măph (Heb.)—*slit-nosed; flat-nosed; closed to perception; dulled understanding; mutilated apprehension.*

His son Jedaiah helped to repair Jerusalem's wall (Neh. 3:10).

Meta. A fruitful thought belonging to the perceptive capacity of mind (the sense of smell represents perception, with a keen and fine discriminating tendency). *Slit-nosed* indicates a severing of this sense of perception and discrimination for which Harumaph stands, a division

of thought. Since unity of thought and purpose is necessary for a right understanding, expression, and manifestation, a divided mind tends to the dulling and closing of the perception faculty and its expression.

Haruphite, hȧr'-ụ-phīte (fr. Heb.)—*of* or *belonging to Hariph;* patronymic for the natives of Hariph.

Shephatiah the Haruphite was among those who came to David at Ziklag, when David was hiding from Saul (I Chron. 12:5).

Meta. A thought belonging to that which Hariph signifies in consciousness. (See HARIPH.)

Haruz, hä'-rŭz (Heb.)—*cut-in; dug-out; entrenchment; sharpened; pointed; decided; careful; judicial; eager; acute; active; diligent; strenuous; industrious.*

"Haruz of Jotbah" was the father of Meshullemeth, who was the mother of Amon king of Judah (II Kings 21:19).

Meta. A thought that is active, analytical, persevering, serious, and vigilant in its character.

Hasadiah, hăs-ȧ-dī'-ăh (Heb.)—*whom Jah loves; love of Jehovah; zeal of Jehovah; compassion of Jehovah; mercy of the Lord.*

Son of Zerubbabel, of the royal line of David (I Chron. 3:20).

Meta. Compassion, forgiveness, love, as characteristic of Jehovah, the Lord, or law of Being.

Hashabiah, hăsh-ȧ-bī'-ăh (Heb.)—*thinking of Jehovah; whom Jehovah regards; regarded of Jehovah; with whom Jah is associated; purpose of Jehovah; estimation of the Lord.*

There are several Israelitish men by this name (I Chron. 6:45; 9:14; 25:3, and others).

Meta. The understanding that Jehovah, the Christ of God, is unified with man, is man's intimate friend and associate in working out divine law into expression and true manifestation. The Spirit of Christ is active everywhere, in the whole of creation, not alone in man and in every living thing. All are regarded by Him as worthy of and commanding His love and special, watchful care. God does not keep Himself separate from that which He has created, but is present everywhere and at all times, actively engaged in bringing about everlasting good.

Hashabnah, hă-shăb'-năh (Heb.)—*thinking of Jehovah; whom Jehovah regards; with whom Jah is associated; purpose of Jehovah; estimation of the Lord.*

One who joined Nehemiah in sealing the covenant (Neh. 10:25).

Meta. The meaning is the same as that of Hashabiah; that in us which knows Jehovah within us to be our friend who cares lovingly and watchfully for us. In our silent communion with God this truth is borne in upon our souls and we realize our oneness with the Christ.

Hashabneiah (A. V., Hashabniah), hăsh-ăb-neï'-ăh (Heb.)—*thinking of Jehovah; whom Jehovah regards; regarded of Jehovah; with whom Jah is associated; purpose of Jehovah; estimation of the Lord.*

a His son Hattush helped repair the wall of Jerusalem (Neh. 3:10). **b** A man by this name joined in praising and worshiping God in the fast at the time of the sealing of the covenant (Neh. 9:5).

Meta. See HASHABIAH and HASHABNAH.

Hashbaddanah (A. V., Hashbadana), hăsh-băd'-dā-năh, (Heb.)—*thought in judging; thoughtful judge; reason in judging; intelligent judgment; wise judge; judging with understanding.*

One of those who stood at Ezra's left hand and assisted him in reading the book of the law of Moses to the people (Neh. 8:4).

Meta. Discrimination, discernment, wisdom, love. These constitute good judgment, and they are very necessary to Ezra, who represents here the spiritual consciousness expressing the law of Being, in such a way that all our higher thoughts and aspirations (men and women of Israel) may receive the law in understanding.

Hashem, hă'-shĕm (Heb.)—*fat; opulent; rich; wealthy; the named; the upright; the shining.* The first four definitions of Hashem come from a construction and thought entirely different from the last three, and are preferable to the latter.

Hashem, the Gizonite. His sons were among the warriors who belonged to David's guard (I Chron. 11:34). In II Samuel 23:32 he is called Jashen.

Meta. A thought activity whose central characteristic is that of riches and opulence (*fat, opulent, rich, wealthy*).

Hashmonah, hăsh-mō'-năh (Heb.)—*fatness; fat soil; fruitfulness; opulence; riches; wealth.*

An encampment of the Israelites in the wilderness (Num. 33:29).

Meta. A place in consciousness where abundant riches and good are realized.

Hashubah, hă-shụ'-băh (Heb.) — *thought; esteemed; purposed; informed; comprehended; associated.*

A son of Zerubbabel, of royal lineage (I Chron. 3:20).

Meta. An inspiration, or enlightenment of thought, brought about by association with and a high estimation of true, spiritual ideals.

Hashum, hā'-shŭm (Heb.)—*fattened; enriched; fertile; opulent; distinguished, i. e., having many servants.*

a Two hundred and twenty-three of his descendants returned from the Babylonian captivity (Ezra 2:19). **b** A man by this name stood at Ezra's left hand when Ezra read the law of Moses to the people (Neh. 8:4). **c** A Hashum joined Nehemiah in sealing the covenant (Neh. 10:18).

Meta. Thoughts in consciousness that have been *enriched* by union with high ideals.

Hasrah, hăs'-răh (Heb.)—*glitter; splendor; glow of confidence; want; poverty; privation.*

The same person as Harhas of II Kings 22:14, which see (II Chron. 34:22).

Meta. See HARHAS.

Hassenaah, hăs-sĕ-nā'-ăh (Heb.)—*the thorny; the bristling; the thorn brush; the pointed.*

His sons built the fish gate in the repairing of the wall of Jerusalem (Neh. 3:3).

Meta. A thought activity whose substance and fruitfulness (sons) are used in the rebuilding of the body temple, especially the guarding and renewing of the avenue through which ideas of increase gain an entrance into consciousness (the fish gate, fish symbolizing ideas of increase).

To one who is not well established in divine love and wisdom, this task is likely to be a *thorny* one, beset with difficulties. This is the case with the thought that Hassenaah signifies; therefore this thought must be more intellectual than spiritual. Yet it is enlightened and true, and to the point, and so makes the way thorny also for the error ideas that it must eliminate and keep out.

Hassenuah (in A. V., Hasenuah in I Chronicles 9:7; Senuah in Nehemiah 11:9), hăs-sĕ-nū'-ăh (Heb.)—*the thorny; the bristling; the pointed; the violating; the hateful.*

a A Benjamite (I Chron. 9:7). **b** A man by this name is mentioned in Nehemiah 11:9. His son, Judah, was second over the city.

Meta. An active faith thought (Benjamite) in consciousness, which works direct to the point (*the pointed*) in seeking to establish the individual in Truth. But there must be a lack of love, the harmonizing element, in the activity of this thought; it is *thorny* and *bristling* in its manner, and is looked upon as *hateful* and harsh (*the violating*) by the thoughts, tendencies, and habits that are not in line with Truth.

Hasshub (A. V., Hashub, except I Chron. 9:14), hăs'-shŭb (Heb.)—*thinking; reasoning; apprehending with understanding; regarding; considering; comprehending; esteeming; associating; meditating; purposing; inventing; enlightening with intelligence.*

a A Levite (I Chron. 9:14). **b** The name of two men who helped repair the wall of Jerusalem (Neh. 3:11, 23). **c** One who joined Nehemiah in sealing the covenant (Neh. 10:23).

Meta. Its significance is much the same as Hashubah, which see. This trend of thought is highly esteemed in consciousness because of its intelligent association with spiritual ideals, and because of its kindly consideration of the other thoughts and ideas of the mind. It has partaken of that love essence which must impregnate the knowing qualities of mind that they may always act in the right spirit and so not stir up opposition.

Hassophereth (in A. V., Sophereth), hăs-sŏph'-ĕ-rĕth (Heb.)—*the engraver; the scribe; the writer; the enumerator; the recorder; the recounter; the narrator.*

A servant of Solomon's, whose descendants returned from the Babylonian captivity (Ezra 2:55). He is called Sophereth in Nehemiah 7:57.

Meta. That in man which inscribes, engraves, records, or establishes in his memory or subconscious mind all past understanding and events as he goes on to new ideas, new thoughts, and new experiences.

Hasupha (in A. V., Nehemiah 7:46, Hashupha), hă-sū'-phà (Heb.)—*stripped; uncovered; revealed; naked; bared; debased, i. e., a sacred truth laid bare.*

He was of the Nethinim. His descendants returned from the Babylonian captivity (Ezra 2:43).

Meta. The idea of service to God, stripped of its glory and true value; debased, as it were, by a sense of duty, with a belief in one's seemingly mortal, human inferiority, and with no true understanding of divine sonship. This makes one's service a sort of slavery, barren of the fruitfulness that belongs to true spiritual worship and to the service of a son to his Father and to his follow men.

The beauty, the glory, and the exaltation of service come in the spirit of divine sonship, and not in the material thought of baseness, and unworthiness. When one knows that one is a son of God and heir with Jesus Christ to all that the Father is and has, one serves gladly and joyously, with a true sense of power and dominion over all things. This is real humility, and brings a wonderful fruitage of good. (The Nethinim were servants in the Temple; many of them were virtually slaves, and they did all the menial work. This fact, with the definitions of Hasupha, suggests the foregoing ideas concerning the significance of the name.)

Hathach (A. V., Hatach), hā'-thăch (Heb. fr. Pers.)—*verity; of the inner part; the central court; who strikes; a gift.*

One of King Ahasuerus' chamberlains whom the king appointed to wait on Queen Esther. It was he who learned from Mordecai of the king's decree to destroy all the Jews, and told Esther of it (Esth. 4:5-10).

Meta. A sense of Truth (*verity*) in the seemingly mortal consciousness of man, which becomes a servant to divine love (Esther). Since this thought activity is really spiritual (*of the inner part*), it has access to the spiritual as well as the carnal in the individual. It reveals to the spiritual love quality the workings of the Adversary (Haman) to destroy the true thoughts and activities (the Jews). This thought for which Hathach stands, therefore, does its part in eliminating the Adversary and his functioning in consciousness; it becomes a real *gift* from God in defending and establishing the Truth.

Hathath, hā'-thăth (Heb.)—*broken; bruised; crushed; weakened; confounded; terrified; fear.* In Hathath the true idea of *fear* is given, in contrast to Harad—*excitement, agitation.*

Son of Othniel, of the tribe of Judah (I Chron. 4:13).

Meta. The natural result (which result is *terror, fear*) of believing in God as force, power, strength, apart from love and eternal goodness, mercy, and Truth (Othniel, the father of Hathath, means *God is strength, force of God, lion of God*).

Hatipha, hăt'-ĭ-phà (Heb.)—*taken; caught; seized; robbed; captivated; spoiled; injured.*

He was of the Nethinim. His descendants were among those who returned from the Babylonian captivity (Ezra 2:54).

Meta. An idea of service, apart from the realization of sonship with God. Many truly consecrated persons are *robbed* of the very substance of their lives, of their vitality, and come under subjection (are made *captive*) to weakness, illness, and even death, because in their spiritual zeal and service to God and man they fail to recognize God as their inherent, ever present, never failing fullness of life, energy, wholeness, strength, substance, power, and wisdom to keep them always in glad, joyous health. They do not know their inheritance here and now as sons of God, but they serve in the old error thought of inherent weakness and lack as being their portion in this world, with heaven and good to be gained only after they die. Not knowing God as omnipresent, they do not reap His good.

Hatita, hăt'-ĭ-tà (Heb.)—*digging; exploring; searching; inscribing; circumscribing; bending of sin; binding of sin.*

His descendants were among the Temple porters who returned from the captivity (Ezra 2:42).

Meta. A belief, or activity, that helps to guard our highest religious and spiritual thoughts (a porter in the Temple was a doorkeeper). By thorough *searching* after new ideas of Truth and impressing them in consciousness (*exploring, digging, inscribing*), the thought activity that Hatita signifies succeeds, to a certain extent at least, in binding and subduing much of that which is error in the individual (*bending of sin,* or *binding of sin*).

Hattil, hăt'-tĭl (Heb.)—*pendulous; going to and fro; loose; wavering; vacillating; uncertain; doubtful.*

His "children" were among the descendants of Solomon's servants who returned from the Captivity (Ezra 2:57).

Meta. A thought that, by serving the peace idea (which Solomon signifies here) in a negative way instead of being a strong factor in making and establishing peace in consciousness, has taken on a weak, changeable, wavering, doubtful tendency. This leads to decay and disintegration. (True peace and love are not weak qualities; they are strong, conquering, and enduring. One must be in dominion in order to obtain them consciously and to express them.)

Hattush, hăt'-tŭsh (Heb.)—*assembled one; gathered together; increased; extended; enlarged.*

a Son of Shemaiah, descended from David and Solomon (I Chron. 3:22). **b** Son of Hashabneiah. He helped in rebuilding Jerusalem's wall (Neh. 3:10). **c** One who joined Nehemiah in sealing the covenant (Neh. 10:4). **d** A priest who went up from the Captivity, with Zerubbabel (Neh. 12:2).

Meta. That in individual consciousness which seeks to maintain a high standard by assembling and increasing thoughts and ideas that are true, upright, and good, thus enlarging one's consciousness of Truth.

Hauran, hạu'-rän (Heb.) — *holed; caved; cave land; black hole; filthy prison;* by contrast: *enlightened; whiteness; fineness; purity; nobility; freedom; liberty.*

A place on the northeast border of the Promised Land (Ezek. 47:16).

Meta. A state of consciousness in man that belongs to the subconscious realm of mind, or has its root in and is sustained by the subconscious mind (*holed, caved, cave land*). It belongs to the seemingly mortal, material, limited, impure, and obscure (*black hole, filthy prison*), though it is close to the high place in consciousness that Gilead stands for (Ezekiel mentions Hauran with Gilead, as well as with Damascus). By holding to the light of Truth that shines upon it from Gilead, this thought can be made free from the seemingly material and corruptible (*liberty*) and established in true spiritual understanding and purity (*enlightened, whiteness*).

Havilah, hăv'-ĭ-lăh (Heb.) — *virtual travail; encompassed; surrounded; circular; struggle of elementary life; virtue born of trial; virtue born of courage; brings forth with effort,* i. e., *travail, suffering.*

a A land in the Garden of Eden around which the river Pishon flows (Gen. 2:11). **b** A son of Cush, who was Ham's son (Gen. 10:7). **c** A son of Joktan, who was descended from Shem (Gen. 10:29). **d** Ishmael and his immediate descendants "dwelt from Havilah unto Shur that is before Egypt, as thou goest toward Assyria" (Gen. 25:18). Saul smote the Amalekites in this same place (I Sam. 15:7), and disobeyed the Lord by saving alive some of them and some of the choicest of their animal possessions.

Meta. In the land of Havilah were gold and precious stones, according to the text in Genesis 2:11, 12. This, with the meaning of the word, bespeaks the effort, the travail, the trials, if you will, that are necessary to bring into manifestation the inner spiritual possibilities that lie back of and are wrapped up in the seemingly material organism.

Havvoth–jair (A. V., Havoth–jair), hăv'-vŏth–jā'-ĭr (Heb.) — *dwellings of Jair; habitation of his awakening; lives of his enlightenment; luminous lives; places of light; habitations of happiness; abodes of prosperity.*

The towns in Gilead that Jair, the son of Manasseh, took from the Amorites and named Havvoth–jair (Num. 32:41). (See Deuteronomy 3:14; Judges 10:4.)

Meta. Gilead is that high place in consciousness where spirit discerns and witnesses to the Truth. Manasseh is understanding, and Jair refers to enlightenment, illumination. Havvoth–jair, therefore (*dwellings of Jair,* towns in Gilead), signifies groups of high, illumined thoughts, which lead to happiness and abundance.

Hazael, hăz'-â-ĕl (Heb.) — *seen of God; seeing God; vision of God; favored of God; revelation of God; perception of God.*

An officer of Benhadad, king of Syria. Elijah was told by Jehovah to anoint Hazael as king of Syria (I Kings 19:15). Benhadad sent him to Elisha to find out whether he would recover from his sickness. Hazael murdered Benhadah and became king in his stead (II Kings 8: 7-15).

Meta. To anoint Hazael (all-seeing eye) king of Syria (confusion of thought) means to restore order in the confused consciousness.

Hazaiah, hă-zā'-ịah (Heb.) — *seen of Jah; seeing Jehovah; vision of Jah; favored of Jehovah; revelation of Jehovah; perception of Jah.*

The ancestor of a Judahite who dwelt in Jerusalem after the return from the Babylonian captivity (Neh. 11:5).

Meta. The all-seeing, all-knowing Christ Spirit or Spirit of truth in man. This Spirit knows and understands (beholds) God, is known of God, and makes God known to man. "But when the Comforter is come, whom I will send unto you from the Father, *even* the Spirit of truth, which proceedeth from the Father, he shall bear witness of me" (John 15: 26).

Hazar-addar, hā'-zär–ăd'-där (Heb.) — *village of Addar; court of the threshing floor; inclosure of ample area; im-*

prisoned greatness; inclosed verdant space.

A city on the southern border of the Promised Land (Num. 34:4).

Meta. It is no doubt the same city as the Addar of Joshua 15:3, and its significance is much the same. (See ADDAR.) Hazar–addar emphasizes the thought that the broadness and greatness that Addar signifies dwells in, is inclosed or imprisoned in, the unenlightened human consciousness and organism. Addar magnifies the uplifting, freeing power of Truth in the joy and good that are gained through its activity in man. Hazar, in this name, may refer to the Hezron that is named with Addar in Joshua 15:3. (See HEZRON.)

Hazar–enan, hā'-zär–ē'-năn (Heb.)— *village of fountains; court of the fountains; inclosure of natural springs.*

A place on the north border of the land of Canaan (Num. 34:9).

Meta. An abundant overflow of life (*village of fountains*) reaching to the objective, intellectual consciousness of the individual who accepts this spiritual life flow (the north means *above,* and refers to the highest thoughts of the intellectual or objective consciousness). *Court* and *inclosure, of the fountains,* suggest the confinement of the cleansing, renewing, vitalizing activities of the divine life to the human organism of man. The purpose of this would be the uplifting and redemption of the individual.

Hazar – gaddah, hā'-zär – găd'-däh (Heb.)—*village of Gad; court of fortune; court of troops.*

A southern city of Judah (Josh 15:27).

Meta. Strongly organized thoughts of abundant substance and power, in the subconsciousness (south means *below,* and here it represents the subconsciousness; *fortune* refers to abundant supply; *court of troops* bespeaks strongly organized thoughts, *Gad* suggests power).

Hazarmaveth, hä-zär-mā'-vĕth (Heb.) —*village of death; court of death.*

Son of Joktan, or a place in Arabia where some of Joktan's descendants settled (Gen. 10:26).

Meta. A central thought or group of thoughts belonging to the sense mind of man, having as its ruling idea a strong belief in death and in that which leads to disintegration, corruption. Its conception of justice (*court*) is always on the negative, condemnatory, and destructive side.

Hazar–shual, hā'-zär–shụ'-ăl (Heb.)— *village of foxes; court of jackals.*

A city in the southern part of Judah (Josh. 15:28).

Meta. A group of subconscious thoughts that, under the dominance of the sense mind, are destructive. However, the substance of that in these thoughts which has expressed in craftiness, slyness, cunning, and trickery (*fox*) can, when given over to the Judah (praise and prayer) consciousness, be transformed into true skill, wisdom, and ingenuity, for the bringing forth of abundant good fruits.

Hazar–susah, hā'-zär–sū'-săh (Heb.) —*village of the horse; court of the mare.* This name is feminine.

A city allotted to Simeon (Josh. 19:5).

Meta. A phase of the soul, or a group of thoughts in consciousness, whose central, dominating idea is activity, life, vital force, power (*village of the horse*). These thoughts are allotted to Simeon, are made receptive and obedient to the true light of Spirit (Simeon meaning receptivity, obedience, *hearing*).

Hazar–susim, hā'-zär–sū'-sĭm (Heb.) —*village of horses; court of cavalry.* This name is in the plural form.

A town of Simeon (I Chron. 4:31). Hazar–susah is the same place.

Meta. Its significance is the same as that of Hazar–susah, only increased, multiplied. (See HAZAR–SUSAH.)

Hazazon–tamar (in A. V., Genesis 14. 7, Hazezon–tamar), hăz'-ă-zŏn-tā'-mär (Heb.)—*a division of palms; pruning of the palms; felling of palms; victory divided; excellence cut in pieces; a column cut in pieces.*

The place where the Moabites and the Ammonites camped when they came to battle against Jehoshaphat, king of Judah (II Chron. 20:2).

Meta. A divided mind. This must be conquered before one can become fearless, and so gain a real victory over error. When the thoughts are divided, the results are divided, not satisfactory.

Hazer–hatticon (A. V., Hazar–hatticon), hā'-zĕr–hăt'-tĭ-cŏn (Heb.)—*the middle Hazer; the middle village; the central court; the innermost court.*

A place named by Ezekiel as being on the northern border of "the land" (Ezek. 47:16).

Meta. A meaning of middle is equally distant from given extremes. This clearly bespeaks temperance, equilibrium, balance, and poise in character. Hazer–hatticon therefore (*the middle village*) signifies a consciousness of adjustment, equableness, poise.

Hazeroth, hă-zē'-rŏth (Heb.)—feminine plural of Hazer; *villages; courts; inclosures; encampments.*

A camping place of the Children of Israel in the wilderness. It was there that Miriam and Aaron spoke against Moses because he had married a Cushite woman, and Miriam was smitten with leprosy. They remained in Hazeroth until she was healed (Num. 11:35 to 12:16).

Meta. A group of thoughts, belonging to the soul of man, that are of a unifying, coöperative, assembling character, though somewhat limited. The incident that is mentioned in the foregoing paragraph represents an adjustment that takes place in consciousness when our truest, highest, religious thoughts (Israelites) begin to recognize and declare divine unity.

Haziel, hā'-zĭ-ĕl (Heb.)—*vision of God; whom God sees; meditation of God; beholding of God.*

Son of Shimei, of the Gershonite Levites (I Chron. 23:9).

Meta. Spiritual seeing, seeing or understanding with the eye (or mind) of Spirit.

Hazo, hā'-zȯ (Heb.)—*vision; revelation; prophecy; league; covenant; agreement.*

Son of Abraham's brother Nahor (Gen. 22:22).

Meta. The arousing of a higher desire in man (Nahor) through the activity of faith (Abraham) causes the piercing of the darkness of material belief and opens the way for a new and clearer insight into Truth. This new insight is symbolized by Hazo, Nahor's son. This clearing of the understanding in man, at this stage of his unfoldment, is more mental and intellectual than spiritual, but it leads to a higher light, even to that of the Christ.

Hazor, hā'-zôr (Heb.)—*village; court; castle; fortification; habitation; encampment; pasture; verdant inclosure.*

a City of Jabin (Josh. 11:1). **b** A southern city of Judah (Josh. 15:23). **c** A place where Benjamites settled after their return from the Babylonian captivity (Neh. 11:33). **d** "The kingdoms of Hazor" are mentioned in Jeremiah 49:28.

Meta. A fortified state of thought in the subconscious mind of man; that which Jabin signifies is the central or dominating idea. (See JABIN.) When praise and prayer take dominion over this state of thought (the city of Jabin was allotted to Judah) a great change takes place in it; it is raised to a higher basis of spiritual understanding.

Hazor–hadattah (A. V., Hazor, Hadattah), hā'-zôr–hă-dăt'-tăh (Heb.)—*new village; new habitation; new encampment; repaired inclosure; renewed court.*

A city of Judah in the south (Josh. 15:25).

Meta. The character of the Hazor consciousness under the old thought, changed to a more spiritual, truer level (*new village, new habitation, repaired inclosure, renewed court*). "The old things are passed away; behold, they are become new" (II Cor. 5:17).

Hazzelelponi (A. V., Hazelelponi), hăz-zĕ-lĕl-pō'-nī (Heb.)—*the shadow looking back upon me; the shadow of my face,* i. e., *my reflected image; shadowed countenance, mine,* i. e., *sorrowful countenance; facing the approaching shades; protection of God looking on me.*

An Israelitish woman of the tribe of Judah (I Chron. 4:3).

Meta. The individual soul turning within to God (*the shadow—man—looking back upon me*—God). There is a suggestion of sorrow in the significance of this name, too, and it also suggests the truth that all sorrows disappear in the light of Spirit. Then the soul enters into the strength of abundant, joyous life and sunshine.

heaven, kingdom of.

Meta. The kingdom of heaven, or of the heavens, is a state of consciousness in which the soul and the body are in harmony with Divine Mind.

Teachers of metaphysics find that their most difficult work is getting students to recognize that heaven is a condition of mind. Jesus evidently experienced like difficulty in making Himself understood, which accounts for the numerous parables and comparisons that He gave of the kingdom. These were all illustrative of some condition pertaining to the kingdom, and never did He describe it as a place located in some distant realm.

In spite of these oft repeated illustrations by Jesus showing the kingdom of heaven to be a state of consciousness, the great mass of Christians are today teaching that it is a place, to which people who accept Jesus as their Savior will go when they die. There is no authority in the Bible for such doctrine. If such a place existed Jesus would certainly have described it plainly instead of giving parable after parable and illustration after illustration showing it to be a state of consciousness to be attained by man. In Matthew 13:31-33, 44-52, there are five short stories illustrating six different problems concerning this condition and our relation to it. Applying some of the laws of mind as we know them, we find that Jesus was talking about universal Truth and its expression.

The mustard-seed comparison is to show the capacity of the apparently small thought of Truth to develop in consciousness until it becomes the abiding place of a higher type of thoughts (birds of the air).

The "leaven" is the Truth, and the "woman" is the soul. When a word of Truth is apparently hidden in the inner mind it is not idle, but quietly spreads until the whole consciousness is light with Spirit. People who have for years had this hidden word of Truth at work in them are quick to respond to a larger exposition of the divine law, and we recognize that they are ripe for receiving Truth.

The treasure hid in the field is the logical truth that all that is belongs to Being and can be brought forth by one who gives up the outer and looks within for the real value.

The merchant is one who is seeking the jewel of the soul, or spiritual good, through exchange of thought, discussion, and argument. He also must give up all these so-called values for the inner pearl.

The net cast into the sea is the state of mind that seeks Truth in many places and gets much that has to be thrown away.

The "end of the world" is the point in consciousness where the true thoughts are in the majority and the error thoughts have lost their hold. This is the consummation of the regenerative process, and everything that has been stored up in consciousness is brought forth and becomes of visible, practical value to the man. This is the "householder" who brings forth his "things new and old."

"The kingdom of God is not eating and drinking [sensuous things], but righteousness and peace and joy in the Holy Spirit" (Rom. 14:17).

heaven and earth.

Meta. Two states of mind, the ideal and its manifestation. According to Revelation 21:1 we are to have new ideals, with manifestations in the earth to correspond.

God idealized two universal planes of consciousness, the heaven and the earth, or more properly, "the heavens and the earth." One is the realm of pure ideals; the other, of thought forms. God does not create the visible universe directly, as a man makes cement pavement, but He creates the *ideas,* which are used by His intelligent "image" and "likeness" to make the universe. Thus God's creations are always spiritual. Man's creations are both material and spiritual, according to his understanding.

It is important to know that heaven and earth, or spiritual and seemingly material planes, are states of mind primarily, and that we, as a race, are in the midst of their expression. The creative process has been going on for æons, and a great mass of thought force and mind force has been evolved. Man's body is the earthly side of an inner heaven, or mental realm. The *I* has fluctuated for ages between these two planes of consciousness. An incarnation in the body is followed by a vacation in the soul, and these two are gradually getting closer and closer together. When they are united the "new man" "in Christ Jesus" will step forth, and the weary round of incarnation and reincarnation will cease.

Heber, hē'-bēr (Heb.)—*that which passes further; on the other side; a passing over; a going beyond; ultramundane; beyond the terrestrial; not of this world; hidden from sense; occult.*

a Grandson of Asher (Gen. 46:17). **b** Heber the Kenite was the husband of Jael, who killed Sisera, captain of the hosts of Jabin, king of Canaan (Judg. 4:17). **c** A Judahite (I Chron. 4:18). **d** A Benjamite (I Chron. 8:17).

Meta. A *passing over* from the purely sensate, physical, earthly thought to a higher concept of religious Truth. This is the beginning of a conscious alliance with the mind of Spirit, and it will culminate in man and God's becoming companions, associates, friends, and, in a sense, equals: "Ye therefore shall be perfect, as your heavenly Father is perfect" (Matt. 5:48); "No longer do I call you servants . . . but I have called you friends" (John 15:15).

The names Heber and Eber in the Bible seem to be the same. (See EBER.) There is an idea held among the Jewish people that the term Hebrew is derived from the Eber of Genesis 10:24, who is believed to be an ancestor of Abraham (in the Authorized Version, in Luke 3:35, the name is written Heber).

Heberites, hē'-bēr-ītes (fr. Heb.)—*of or belonging to Heber or Eber.*

Descendants of Heber, of the tribe of Asher (Num. 26:45).

Meta. Thoughts and activities belonging to the Heber consciousness in man. (See HEBER.)

Hebrew, hē'-brew (fr. Heb.)—*belonging to Eber.*

a The descendants of Abraham (Gen. 14:13; Jer. 34:9). **b** The language of the Hebrew people (John 19:20). Con-

cerning the derivation of this name, Fallows tells us that some ascribe the origin of the word to Eber (Gen. 10:21). Eber is used as a national name in Numbers 24:24. "Others trace the name to the Hebrew *aw-bar*," says Fallows, meaning "to *pass over,* so that a Hebrew would mean the 'man from the region beyond,' and supposed to have been applied to Abraham, as having crossed the Euphrates to the westward. This last derivation is generally admitted. It seems to imply nothing more than that Abraham was an immigrant into Canaan—not a native."

Meta. See EBER and HEBER for ideas as to the symbology of Hebrew. The Hebrews surely represent the thoughts in man that have come up out of the purely material and passed over to a higher concept of God and of His laws, into a closer and clearer relationship with God. These thoughts are, however, still under law, the law of sin and death; for true freedom, spiritual understanding and realization, life and peace, come only by the still higher way—which is the Christ method, the way taught and demonstrated by Jesus Christ.

Hebrewess, hē'-brew-ess (fr. Heb.)—*a Jewess.*

A woman belonging to the Hebrew race (Jer. 34:9).

Meta. The soul, or feminine aspect of the thought for which Hebrew stands. (See HEBREW.)

Hebron, hē'-brŏn (Heb.)—*united; joined together; conjunction; cemented; welded; bound by a common bond; friendship; brotherhood; company; community; confederation; league; alliance.*

The place where Abram "dwelt by the oaks of Mamre" (Gen. 13:18). In the Promised Land Hebron became a city of Judah, having been given to "Caleb the son of Jephunneh for an inheritance" (Josh. 14:13). When David became king of Israel Jehovah told him to go up to Hebron (II Sam. 2:1). All the tribes of Israel came to David at Hebron to acknowledge him king (II Sam. 5:1-5).

Meta. An association of ideas; in other words, concentration. Hebron also means *friendship, brotherhood.* Spiritual unfoldment always causes one to give to God's children everywhere a kindly feeling that is constant, deep, tender. This is one of the indispensable requirements of every successful spiritual leader.

Hebron typifies the front brain, the seat of conscious thought. When the Lord told David to go up to the cities of Judah, and especially to Hebron, he was pointing the way to a harmonious co-operation between the indwelling love in the heart and the understanding in the head.

The gathering of the tribes of Israel at Hebron to acknowledge David as king represents the conscious recognition by all the thoughts that love shall reign supreme in consciousness. Love shall henceforth feed the thoughts (the people) and love shall be prince over Israel.

Hebronites, hē'-brŏn-ītes (fr. Heb.)—*of* or *belonging to Hebron; the confederated; the allied; the united.*

A family of Kohathite Levites (Num. 3:27).

Meta. Thoughts belonging to and springing from the Hebron consciousness unified with the love thought (Levi). (See HEBRON.)

Hegai (A. V., in Esth. 2:3, Hege), hē'-gāi (Heb. or Pers.)—*eunuch; separated; carried away; thought; meditation.*

A chamberlain of King Ahasuerus; he was "keeper of the women" for the king (Esth. 2:3).

Meta. A thought activity, belonging to the puffed-up personal will (King Ahasuerus), that has been intrusted by the will with the guardianship of the soul emotions and desires (the women of the king's harem). All capacity to increase life and its forms has been eliminated from this thought for which Hegai stands (*eunuch*); yet there is in it a certain power of contemplation, poise, and steadfastness (*meditation*) that makes it peculiarly fit for the place that it holds in one's consciousness.

heifer (Gen. 15:9).

Meta. The heifer, she-goat, ram, turtledove, and young pigeon that Abram was instructed to take represent ideas on the sense plane that must be sacrificed. The idea of physical strength must be given up, and its spiritual source must

be realized. The human will must be given up, that the divine will may work in one. All subconscious resistance to the working of the divine law must be denied away. One should let confidence and peace pervade the mind, yet know that swiftness (pigeon) is characteristic of all action in things spiritual. One should look for a swift fulfillment of all that one has had faith in. In all this process one is to drive away the "birds of prey" or carnal thoughts, as did Abram.

Helah, hē'-lăh (Heb.)—*worn away; scaled; rusted; sick; diseased; leprous; stroked; caressed; tenderness.*

Wife of "Ashhur the father of Tekoa" (I Chron. 4:5).

Meta. The kindly, sympathetic, and tender qualities of the human soul (*tenderness*). But this phase of the soul also suggests corrupting, deteriorating tendencies (*rusted, diseased*). The soul qualities must be raised to spiritual expression before they will work wholly for man's good.

Helam, hē'-lăm (Heb.) — *great strength; might; large army; fortress; great ability; substance; abundance; integrity; virtue.*

A place where David fought and defeated the Syrians (II Sam. 10:16).

Meta. A strongly fortified place in consciousness where there is much substance. It is a unification of the substance and strength ideas. The host of Hadarezer, with Shobach as their captain, came to this place to fight against Israel; they expected to utilize the substance and strength that Helam signifies, to build up and expand the sense consciousness (Syrians), that they might overcome what were, to them, foolish ideas of the true religious and spiritual beliefs (Israelites). The "host of Hadarezer," the Syrians, took it for granted that all the strength, power, and substance were on their side; but they were defeated and put to utter rout. They then made peace with the Israelites and served them. Thus even the sense reasonings of man (Syrians) may be used by his higher intelligence to serve him in constructive ways for the upbuilding of his hold on Truth when he reaches a stage of development wherein he realizes the power and richness of his true insight into spiritual things, through the inspiration of Spirit.

Helbah, hĕl'-băh (Heb.)—*fatness; richness; fertility; fertile region; rich country.*

A city of Asher, from which the Asherites did not drive the Canaanitish inhabitants (Judg. 1:31).

Meta. A place of great richness and substance (*fatness*) in man's consciousness However, the consciousness of rich substance and of the possibilities (*fertility*) that lie in it is not fully dedicated to the use of the higher and more religious and spiritual activities of the individual. The Canaanites, the error, sense tendencies of the subconscious life forces, still utilize a portion of this rich mind substance for the furtherance of carnal thoughts and desires.

Helbon, hĕl'-bŏn (Heb.)—*fat; fertile; fruitful; rich; fatness;* the negative aspects of the word are *thick; dull; indolent; stupid; unfeeling.*

The "wine of Helbon" is mentioned in Ezekiel 27:18.

Meta. The rich substance of life, with all its possibilities of unfoldment and fruitfulness.

Tyre and Damascus, places that are mentioned in conjunction with Helbon, belong in the realm of sensation and material thought, in individual consciousness; therefore the rich life substance that is signified by Helbon is being used for the promotion of the "mind of the flesh" instead of being utilized in spiritual ways to the uplift and regeneration of the whole man. The natural outcome of this waste of substance in sense ways is dullness, coarseness, and stupidity.

Heldai, hĕl'-dāi (Heb.) — *smooth; slippery; gliding away; fleeting; transitory existence; this world,* i. e., *the outer; changeable; temporal; worldly; worldliness.*

a The captain of 24,000 men who served King David during the twelfth month of each year (I Chron. 27:15). He was a Netophathite, of Othniel. **b** Zechariah mentions Heldai as one of those of the Captivity (Zech. 6:10).

Meta. The enduring essence of divine courage and strength. (Netophah means *distillation,* and one meaning of distillation is the essence of anything, obtained by a process of purification. Othniel means *lion of God, God is strength, force of God;* these words signify divine courage, strength, and conquering power.) But while in the ideal the qualities of courage, strength, and conquering power are infinite, and therefore enduring, in the case of Heldai the Netophathite the *worldly, transitory* thought or belief is still in evidence. This must be put away and the true spiritual standard must be recognized and maintained before the staying qualities, which are divine, can become really abiding in individual consciousness and experience.

Heleb, hē'-lĕb (Heb.)—*fat; fertile; fruitful; rich; the finest.*

Son of Baanah the Netophathite; one of David's guard (II Sam. 23:29). In I Chronicles 11:30, Heled.

Meta. Abundant substance (*fat, fertile, rich*) in essence, or ideal (Netophathite). This rich substance is spiritual. In Heled (see HELED), however, the subtle, worldly belief (*slippery, crafty, fleeting*) in the transitoriness of all things is actively expressing itself. This belief will bring about age, decay, lack, and disintegration instead of eternal life and abiding plenty; it must therefore be put away before the individual can come consciously into his true inheritance.

Heled, hē'-lĕd (Heb.)—*smooth; slippery; crafty; swift; fleeting; gliding away; transitory existence; this world; passing; changeable; temporal; worldly; worldliness.*

Son of Baanah the Netophathite, one of David's guard (I Chron. 11:30); in II Samuel 23:29, Heleb.

Meta. See HELEB.

Helek, hē'-lĕk (Heb.)—*a lot; portion; possession; distribution.*

The head of the family of Helekites, descended from Gilead, of the tribe of Manasseh (Num. 26:30).

Meta. A conception, by the individual, of his share in man's true inheritance (*portion, possession*). It is through high spiritual aspiration and discernment of Truth (Gilead of Manasseh) that the understanding of the individual is awakened to consciousness of his portion or allotment in the divine perfection, wholeness, abundance of every good, and life everlasting for spirit, soul, and body.

Helekites, hē′-lĕk-ītes (fr. Heb.)—*of* or *belonging to Helek.*

Descendants of Helek (Num. 26:30).

Meta. Thoughts springing from and belonging to the conception of Truth that Helek symbolizes. (See HELEK.)

Helem, hē′-lĕm (Heb.)—*full-grown; puberty; rounded; ripe; robust; strong; manly; dreaming; healing; recovering.*

An Asherite (I Chron. 7:35). Zechariah speaks of Helem as one for whom the crowns were to be made (Zech. 6:14); this Helem is evidently the same man as the Heldai of Zechariah 6:10.

Meta. The same as the Heldai of Zechariah 6:10, the enduring essence of divine courage, strength, and overcoming power of the full-grown and the fully rounded-out man.

In the Helem of Zechariah 6, there is no worldly belief to hinder the expression of the divine qualities in true visioning (*dreaming*) and in *healing*. Therefore a "crown" of life is given to the Helem thought, since it has been faithful to the death of all that is of the carnal, worldly belief (see Zechariah 6:14 and Revelation 2:10, last part).

Heleph, hē′-lĕph (Heb.)—*glide along; pass on; perish; disappear; change; exchange; renew; revive; flourish anew; place of renewing.*

A border city of Naphtali (Josh. 19:33).

Meta. A passing over from the belief that strength (Naphtali) is purely physical to the consciousness of Spirit as the source of one's strength; in other words, the *exchange* of one's material thought about strength for an understanding of the spirituality, the unfailingness, and the abidingness of strength in one who is established in the true knowledge of God as the one source and substance of all strength and of all life. Thus is one's conscious strength renewed.

The significance of this name is well outlined by Paul in Romans 6:1-11. Denials and affirmations aid in bringing about this change in consciousness from

the seemingly material to true spiritual thought and expression.

Helez, hē′-lĕz (Heb.)—*pull off encumbrances; strip; expedite; girded; armed; alert; ready; strong; free; delivered; vigorous; loin,* i. e., *seat of strength, where one girds oneself.*

a Helez the Paltite was one of David's guard of valiant men (II Sam. 23:26). b Son of Azariah and father of Eleasah, of the tribe of Judah (I Chron. 2:39).

Meta. Putting off human belief in limitation and weakness, and becoming established in divine energy, deliverance, and strength.

Heli, hē′-lī (Gk. fr. Heb.)—*lifted up; ascent; summit; supreme; highest; most high.*

Father of Joseph, the supposed father of Jesus (Luke 3:23).

Meta. A phase of man's consciousness that is always seeking spiritual progress, that is ever looking upward and onward to something higher and better. In its highest sense Heli refers to the Most High.

Helkai, hĕl′-kāi (Heb.)—*Jehovah is my lot; possessed of Jah; Jehovah his portion; apportioned; allotted.*

A priest, and head of the house of Meraioth (Neh. 12:15).

Meta. Meraioth means *revelations;* it also has directly opposing meanings, *rebellions* and *perversions.* This shows a divided mind, a consciousness that entertains both Truth and error, God and Devil. Helkai the priest, and head of the house of Meraioth, symbolizes a decision made in favor of Truth—a choosing of that which pertains to Spirit only (*Jehovah is my lot*).

Helkath, hĕl′-kăth (Heb.)—*smoothness; lot; portion; division; possession; territory; field.*

A border city of Asher (Josh. 19:25). It was given over to the "children of Gershon, of the family of the Levites" (Josh 21:31).

Meta. Conscious *possession* of substance (*field* signifying substance). Asher also pertains to the happiness associated with spiritual understanding and substance, but the Asher consciousness as symbolized in the city of Helkath lays hold of only a *portion* of the omnipresent, universal supply or spiritual substance.

In its outer expression and manifestation we have our part in the divine inheritance; yet we must know that all of Truth is at the disposal of every individual. The beauty of understanding the spiritual idea back of every expression and manifestation of the God qualities is that this understanding reveals to one how every individual may constantly use the fullness of God in every way and yet take nothing from Principle and nothing from any other individual, just as one using the principle of mathematics or of music could not possibly deplete these principles or in any way hinder another from having access to them. Thus "all" that the Father is and has is our inheritance.

Helkath–hazzurim, hĕl'-kăth–hăz'-zū-rĭm (Heb.)—*smoothness of the rocks; lot or portion of rocks; field of sharp-edged stones; division of sharp edges.*

A battlefield in Gibeon, where the servants of David defeated Abner and the Israelites who were with him (II Sam. 2:16).

Meta. The substance (*field*) of man's thoughts and words taking on the sharpness of sharp-edged stones and the hardness of rocks to defeat the intellect, or reason.

Abner signifies the light, the intelligence, of the illumined intellect, or reason. Gibeon is a high place in consciousness where man should let go of personal ideas and receive spiritual instruction. Abner was captain of Saul's host, and after Saul was slain Abner still sought to uphold Saul's house (the realm of personal will) against the rule of love (David). Thus to Abner and his followers (the intellect persistently upholding and seeking to exalt the personal will), Helkath–hazzurim in Gibeon would become a *field of sharp-edged stones*, or a *portion of rocks*. The substance of the Abner phase of intellectual consciousness would, when strengthened by the spiritual place (Gibeon) to which it has exalted itself without giving way to Spirit, naturally take on sharpness and hardness, and for that reason meet defeat.

hell, (marg. and A. V.)—Gehenna (Gk.)—*region of lamentations; place of purifying fires; place of defilement.* Ge Hinnom (Heb.)—*region of lamentations; place of groaning.* Hades (Gk.)—*not to be looked upon; outer darkness.* Sheol (Heb.)—*hollow; cavernous; empty; outer darkness; place of unquenchable, consuming desires.*

The Hebrew *sheol;* translated *grave* in I Samuel 2:6, *pit* in Numbers 16:30, and *hell* in Job 11:8, in the Old Testament, the Authorized Version; in the New Testament Hades and Gehenna are translated *hell* in Matthew 5:29. Gehenna, or Ge Hinnom, implies a place of fires and lamentation (Matt. 5:22, 29, in margin, and so forth), while Hades and Sheol give the thought of outer darkness, a place of consuming and unquenchable desires.

Meta. See HADES, HINNOM, and GEHENNA.

One does not have to die in order to go to hell, any more than one has to die to go to heaven. Both are states of mind, and conditions, which people experience as a direct outworking of their thoughts, beliefs, words, and acts. If one's mental processes are out of harmony with the law of man's being, they result in trouble and sorrow; mental as well as bodily anguish overtakes one, and this is hell.

The booklet, "The Bible and Eternal Punishment," by A. P. Barton, gives the following definition of the word "hell": "The English word *hell* is from the Saxon verb *helan,* 'to cover, or conceal,' and intrinsically contains no idea of a place of torment, and never did smell of fire and brimstone in its Saxon home."

Helon, hē'-lŏn (Heb.)—*strong; firm; stable; perseverance.*

His son Eliab, of the tribe of Zebulun, was chosen to stand with Moses and Aaron in the numbering of the men of the children of Israel (Num. 1:9).

Meta. Strength of character, courage, and perseverance established in the consciousness through order. (Zebulun represents the faculty of order. Of the disciples of Jesus Christ, James the son of Alphæus stands for order. Order, we are told, is heaven's first law. There can be no peace, harmony, or right relation of ideas without order. When "all things" are thought and done "decently and in order" in the individual, when divine order is established in him, his strength and courage are greatly increased.)

Heman, hē'-măn (Heb.)—*durable; lasting; faithful; trustworthy; sure; true.*

a A wise man in Solomon's time, but not so wise as Solomon (I Kings 4:31). b A singer, a Kohathite, in David's reign (I Chron. 6:33).

Meta. Thoughts full of faith and trust in God, thoughts that are honest, true, steadfast, accurate. Great wisdom and harmony are the result of these thoughts. In the case of the Heman of I Kings 4:31, however, these thoughts must be of the intellect, rather than of Spirit, since the wisdom of Solomon, spiritual wisdom, greatly excelled the wisdom of Heman. Solomon desired above all things to be given an "understanding heart" (I Kings 3:9). It is through the heart of man (symbolically), and not through his head, that the deep wisdom of God enters the consciousness.

Hemdan, hĕm'-dăn (Heb.)—*desirable; pleasant; grateful; precious.*

Son of Dishon, who was a son of Seir the Horite (Gen. 36:26); in I Chronicles 1:41, Hamran.

Meta. The seemingly *desirable* and *pleasant* aspect of the sense beliefs and activities of one that is not awakened spiritually. This pleasure, however, is but transitory and soon turns to dust and ashes, to vanity and vexation of spirit. (See DISHON, SEIR, and HORITE.)

Hen, hĕn (Heb.)—*grace; favor; kindness; beauty; elegance; restful.*

Son of Zephaniah. Hen was one of those for whom the crowns were to be made (Zech. 6:14).

Meta. Mercy, kindness (the margin gives, "for the kindness of the son," in place of, "to Hen the son of Zephaniah"). Hen therefore pertains to the kindly, charitable, merciful attitude of mind in man, which brings great reward, true peace (*restful*), and overcoming power (crown). "With the merciful thou wilt show thyself merciful" (Psalms 18:25). "With what measure ye mete, it shall be measured unto you" (Matt. 7:2).

"If ye forgive men their trespasses, your heavenly Father will also forgive you" (Matt. 6:14).

Hena, hē'-nȧ (Heb.)—*lowland; low ground; disquieting; troubling.*

A Mesopotamian city that was conquered by the Assyrians. Its gods are spoken of in II Kings 18:34 as being unable to deliver the city out of the hands of the Assyrians, and the king of Assyria takes this as proof that Judah's God cannot deliver Judah.

Meta. Low, very material thoughts and beliefs regarding substance (*lowland, low ground*), belonging to the sensual mind. They bring much unrest and trouble (*disquieting, troubling*) to the individual who harbors and cultivates them; it is well for this state of consciousness to be defeated by the Assyrians, who represent a somewhat higher phase of thought. The reasonings that the Assyrians symbolize, however, are also based upon sense observation, instead of Spirit; they are not therefore to be compared with true spiritual ideas and thoughts, which Israel and Judah in their highest significance represent.

Henadad, hĕn'-ȧ-dăd (Heb.)—*favor of Hadad; Hadad is gracious; grace is quickened,* i. e., *made sharp; vehement grace; grace of the beloved.*

a A Levite whose sons helped in the rebuilding of the Temple (Ezra 3:9). b An Israelite whose son Bavvai assisted in the rebuilding of Jerusalem's wall (Neh. 3:18).

Meta. Thoughts expressing a degree of the mercy, power, and divine qualities of Being (*grace of the beloved*), thus aiding in lifting the consciousness and the body to a higher and more abiding realization. (The rebuilding of the Temple and of Jerusalem's wall signifies the uplifting, renewing, and spiritualizing of the body.) The thoughts, however, are more intellectual than spiritual. They look without, to the material, for God and for power, instead of looking within (*favor of Hadad, Hadad is gracious*—Hadad, the name of a Syrian deity, and signifying the setting up of the intellect as all-powerful). The unilluminated intellect always bases its reasonings upon the testimony of the senses rather than upon the inspiration of Spirit.

Hepher, hē'-phĕr (Heb.)—*a digging; a well; an excavation; a pit; a search; an exploration; a spying out.*

a A man of the tribe of Manasseh, the head of the family of the Hepherites (Num. 26:32). **b** Son of Ashhur of the tribe of Judah (I Chron. 4:6). **c** One of David's guard (I Chron. 11:36). **d** A city of Canaan that was conquered by Joshua (Josh. 12:17).

Meta. Understanding, that which opens (*a digging, a well, a search*) the consciousness to recognition and realization of the great life forces of the organism. (See MANASSEH, GILEAD, and ASHHUR.)

Hepherites, hē'-phĕr-ītes (fr. Heb.)—*of* or *belonging to Hepher.*

The descendants of Hepher of Manasseh (Num. 26:32).

Meta. Thoughts of understanding and life, springing from that in consciousness for which Hepher stands.

Hephzi–bah, hĕph'-zĭ–bäh (Heb.)—*my delight is in her; my loving is in her; my willing mind is in that which is,* i. e:, *in reality.*

a Wife of Hezekiah and mother of Manasseh, kings of Judah (II Kings 21: 1). **b** A symbolical name that was to be applied to the restored Jerusalem (Isa. 62:4).

Meta. The joy and satisfaction of Jehovah, I AM, in the redeemed, spiritualized soul of man.

Heres, hē'-rĕṣ (Heb.)—*radiating orb of heat; the sun; hot; dry; baked; seared; scratched; rough; an earthen pot; potsherd.*

A mountain in the land of Canaan where the Amorites continued to dwell, "yet the hand of the house of Joseph prevailed, so that they became subject to taskwork" (Judg. 1:35).

Meta. A lifting up (mountain) of the life forces in individual consciousness.

The central sun in us, like the sun in the outer universe, radiates both light and heat; but, until the understanding unfolds sufficiently, life is known only in its phases of heat and force. When these are controlled by the Amorite thoughts, which have their seat of action in the generative function, sense impurities and excesses prevail in the individual. But through "the hand of the house of Joseph" (the power of the imaging faculty of the mind established in a degree of spiritual understanding), the Amorites are put under subjection and become subject to taskwork, become servants of the Israelites; that is, the substance and life that had formerly been utilized by these error thoughts and activities are turned to constructive use, to the building up and strengthening of the Truth, which in time will become the only actuating power of all of the man's thoughts and doings. Then the whole being will become established in abiding life and peace.

Heresh, hē'-rĕsh (Heb.)—*workman; artificer; craftsman; carpenter; worker in stone; magician; silent; secret; dumb.*

A Levite (I Chron. 9:15).

Meta. Love, active and passive (*workman, silent*). It is in the stillness, in passive waiting upon God, that strength and understanding are gained for greater activity; thus love becomes a skilled workman (*artificer*) in constructing anew the body temple (*carpenter,* one who plans and builds houses). The priests and Levites, in their activities connected with the worship of God, symbolize our so-called "natural religious tendencies," not necessarily spiritual. As the descendants of Levi, who represents the love faculty in individual consciousness, the Levites represent thoughts belonging to the love faculty.

Hereth (A. V., Hareth), hē'-rĕth (Heb.)—*thick wood; thicket; dense forest.*

A forest in the land of Judah where David went when he was hiding from Saul (I Sam. 22:5).

Meta. A state of mind that cannot be penetrated by error or force. By resorting to praise and prayer (Judah), love (David) builds up a state of spiritual thought to which the will functioning in the selfishness of personality (Saul) cannot possibly gain access. This is Hereth, a *thicket,* a dense growth of shrubbery and trees, in Judah, to which David fled from Saul.

Hermas, hĕr'-măs (Gk.)—*the planet*

Mercury; swift messenger; guide of the soul; interpreter.

A Christian friend of Paul's at Rome, to whom Paul sent his regards in his Epistle to the Romans (Rom. 16:14).

Meta. The ability of the spiritually awakened intellect in man to comprehend, and especially to explain, Truth. (Paul here represents the word of Truth, while Rome represents the head, the region of the intellect and will.)

Hermes, hĕr'-mēṣ (Gk.)—*Mercury; swift messenger of the gods; guide of the soul; interpreter; a cairn; monument; signpost.*

A Christian friend of Paul's at Rome, to whom Paul sent salutation in his epistle (Rom. 16:14).

Meta. Same as Hermas; the ability of the spiritually awakened intellect in man to interpret the Christ Truth. Hermes, the Greek Mercury, was the Mercurius of the Romans, and was believed by them to be the messenger of the gods, adroit of action and ready of speech. He was also supposed to be the attendant of Jupiter when he appeared on earth. Thus we can see why the inhabitants of Lystra (Acts 14:12), when they, in their limited understanding, believed that the gods had visited them in the likeness of men, discovered Hermes in Paul, because he was the chief speaker and accompanied Barnabas, who they thought was Jupiter.

Hermogenes, hĕr-mŏǧ'-ĕ-nēṣ (Gk.)—*born of Hermes; Mercury-born.*

A Christian in Asia who turned away from Paul (II Tim. 1:15).

Meta. The outer, verbal expression of one's Christian principles. This outer expression is very likely to be cut off for a time when the inner word of Truth (Paul) is limited in its activities by the dominating force of the unspiritualized will and intellect (is imprisoned in Rome). Firm establishment in Truth is necessary that one may remain faithful in one's outer thoughts, words, and acts when going through some serious conflict within oneself.

Hermon, hĕr'-mŏn (Heb.) — *sacred mountain; prominent mountain; high mountain; lofty; high; majestic; white.*

A mountain that marked the boundary

of the land beyond the Jordan that the Israelites took from the Amorites (Deut. 3:8; Josh. 12:1). Hermon is also mentioned in Psalms 89:12; 133:3, and Song of Solomon 4:8.

Meta. A high, sublime state of mind (*lofty, prominent, sacred mountain*).

Hermons (A. V., Hermonites), hĕr'-mŏnṣ (fr. Heb.)—*the peaks of Hermon.*

The three peaks of Mount Hermon (Psalms 42:6).

Meta. The exaltation of the triune God, the lifting up, in conscious recognition by man, of the three phases, or activities, of the Infinite—Father, Son, and Holy Spirit—mind, idea, expression.

Herod, hĕr'-ŏd (fr. Gk.)—*sprung from a hero; son of a hero; hero-born; heroic.*

The family name of several Roman rulers of Judea (Matt. 2:1; Mark 6:14).

Meta. The ruling will of the physical, the ego in the sense consciousness. This ruling ego is temporal because it does not understand man's true origin or the law of man's being. It is narrow, jealous, destructive. Under its rule man does not fulfill the law of his being, and another ego must supplant the ego of sense.

It would seem that we, knowing the wonderful glory that comes to a man when he develops his spiritual nature, should be earnestly seeking the inner illumination, that we should be willing to give up everything else to attain it. But it is not so. "For the flesh lusteth against the Spirit, and the Spirit against the flesh," wrote Paul. The man who lives in his appetites, in his passions, in his flesh, does not want anything but the flesh consciousness. When this is in the ascendancy he seeks the things of the world. He says: "If I have plenty of money in the bank I can get along all right. You can take your religion. I know nothing about a hereafter. I know nothing about another world. But I do know that if I have plenty of money I can get about anything I want." That is Herod. He is the ruler in the world mind, and if we do not watch him he will slay the Christ child.

We must be on our guard against this subtle sense mind and take tender care of the little, innocent, new idea that has been born deep down in the heart.

We must not give it over to the keeping of Herod. We must nurture it, care for it, and hide it away. If necessary we should take it down into Egypt (darkness) when Herod seeks to kill it. Jesus Christ said, "What I say unto you I say unto all, Watch." Watch what? Watch for this destroying thought, which is satisfied with the old, which is trying to carry the old conditions, the old world, and even flesh and blood into the kingdom of God. "Flesh and blood cannot inherit the kingdom of God." A new man is necessary—a new man, a new body, a new mind. "Be ye transformed by the renewing of your mind." Renew the mind and the body will follow as the day follows the night.

Herod, sense consciousness, rules on the plane of mortality. If allowed full rein he kills out the repentant and redemptive state of mind, represented by John the Baptist, which is beginning its ministry of change and purification in soul and body. The object of the Bible lesson about Herod and his killing of John the Baptist is to show the various steps leading up to the tragedy of sense dominion.

In regeneration there is a quickening of the whole man. The life flow is especially increased and every function connected with it is stimulated. This is represented in the lesson as Herod at a feast, at which he was evidently intoxicated. People who are naturally egotistical and domineering develop these qualities in a larger degree under the impulse of the new life current. Unless the meek and lowly frame of mind recommended by Jesus is adopted, such people lose their heads and go further in their rash egotism than they have anticipated.

If you are of haughty, domineering, self-sufficient will, you stand as Herod, the ruler in Judea. You are married to the passions of the human soul, Herodias. She leads you into sense gratifications so deep, so degrading, that you cut off the head of John, the conscience that would have turned you into the highway of the good. The reign of the sense man is short-lived, however. Your kingdom is taken away from you and you are banished from your native land. This

was the fate of Herod after he beheaded John the Baptist. This is the fate of every one who refuses to listen to the voice of his higher self.

Herodians, hĕ-rō'-dĭ-ăns (fr. Gk.)— Jewish political party.

A class of Jewish people who favored the Romans and Roman rulers. They were among those who sought to entrap and condemn Jesus (Matt. 22:16; Mark 3:6).

Meta. Thoughts that belong to man's old-established religious ideas, but in character are very selfish and material, even as Herod and the Romans were. They bitterly and actively oppose and seek to kill out of consciousness the higher Christ life and its ideals and activities.

Herodias, hĕ-rō'-dĭ-ăs (Gk.)—feminine of Herod.

Granddaughter of Herod the Great, and sister of Herod Agrippa I (Mark 6:17-22).

Meta. The passions of the human soul, the feminine side of sense thought. It resists the accusations of licentiousness made by John, the purifier, and schemes to have him put entirely out of consciousness. The daughter of this one, who dances before the king, is sex sensation. The king is so pleased with her dance that in his ecstasy he is willing to give her anything that she asks, even to the half of his kingdom. At the suggestion of her mother, she requests that the head of John the baptizer and purifier be brought to her on a platter. The king then sees what his giving up to lust ecstasy has done and he feels regret; but his oath, or thought-word, has gone forth and it cannot be broken. The next step is cutting off the head, or rather understanding, and its inanimate skull descends to the sensuous nature and is lost in carnality.

This is a true history of thousands who, immersed in the desires of sense lust, refuse to change their habits when the regenerative process begins. Generation and regeneration are opposites. Those who live under the law of generation give up their kingdom to their progeny, and die. Those who come out of this Egypt conserve their substance, and transmute it through thought to spiritual energy, which is the foundation of the new body in Christ. Through this conservation and control of the divine life and substance, they finally attain the kingdom of God, and sit on the right hand of the Father with Christ. This is not to be accomplished by an outside deity, but is a work that goes on in the individual. "To him that overcometh," is the oft repeated promise of the Holy One in Revelation. Strength and power and purity come to the soul through mastery of its passions and appetites, and in no other way.

Herodion, hĕ-rō'-dĭ-ŏn (Gk.)—*from Herod.*

Paul's kinsman (Rom. 16:11).

Meta. A central ruling thought of the outer or personality that has accepted the Christ Truth. (See HEROD.)

Heshbon, hĕsh'-bŏn (Heb.)—*power of thinking; reason; understanding; intelligence; purposing; inventing; arts; devices.*

The city of Sihon, king of the Amorites. It was taken and occupied by the Israelites (Num. 21:25-34). It belonged first to Moab and was taken by the Amorites, and in turn by the Israelites (Num. 21:26).

Meta. Sihon—*extreme boldness, a sweeping away,* as a warrior sweeps all before him—corresponds with the significance of the Amorites. The Amorites are a race inheritance that have their seat of action in the generative function. Sihon, the central ruling activity of this state of consciousness while man is under the dominion of the carnal mind, is the strong, seemingly unconquerable desire of the animal nature of man for sex sensation; also the almost ferocious determination with which he carries this desire into activity.

But Heshbon (purposeful, active intelligence, understanding, reason, which are naturally of a cleansing, constructive, uplifting character) cannot remain forever under the rule of sense and carnality. The day of truer purpose and understanding comes, and this intelligent life consciousness passes into the hands of the Israelites—the higher religious and spiritual thoughts in the individual.

Thus it becomes a great factor in the establishing of a consciousness of abiding life and Truth throughout the organism.

In Song of Solomon 7:4 the eyes of a loved one are likened to the "pools in Heshbon." This denotes great *intelligence,* light, and *understanding,* of which the eyes are the outer organs. The eyes shine in beauty and brilliance according to the depths of true spiritual sight, the very light of life, which is realized in consciousness and stands back of them.

Heshmon, hĕsh'-mŏn (Heb.)—*fatness; fat soil; fertile; fruitfulness; productive; rich.*

A city of Judah toward the border of Edom in the south (Josh. 15:27).

Meta. A group of thoughts of great richness, substance, and increase (*fatness, fertile, fruitfulness*) in the subconscious mind of the individual, working toward expression in the outer ("toward the border of Edom in the South," the south representing the subconscious mind and Edom referring to the physical or outer consciousness of man).

Heth, hĕth (Heb.)—*sundered; broken; weakened; destroyed; filled with fear; dismayed; terrified; confounded.*

Son of Canaan and grandson of Ham (Gen. 10:15). Ham, son of Noah, pertains to the physical in man. It was from the children of Heth that Abraham purchased a burial place for Sarah; these descendants of Heth were inhabitants of the land of Canaan at that time (Gen. 23:3-20). Esau took wives of the daughters of Heth, which was very displeasing to Isaac and Rebekah (Gen. 26:34, 35; 27:46).

Meta. A very active thought of fear, terror, dread, the result of thinking apart from Spirit (*sundered*). These errors are among man's greatest enemies; they belong to and dwell in the adverse, carnal consciousness. The Hittites, representing thoughts of opposition and resistance, were descendants of Heth. Resistance and opposition are the direct result of fearfulness; people fear many things and they set up a resistant state of mind, which expresses in their words and acts, as well as in their thoughts, and brings trouble. Like so many of man's internal enemies, fear springs from a belief in a power of evil. Only the love of God, and a firm belief in the one Presence and one Power, the good omnipotent, will eliminate fear from man's consciousness. Having won the victory over fear, he will dwell in safety and there will be nothing to molest him or to make him afraid (see Leviticus 26:6 and Zephaniah 3:13).

Hethlon, hĕth′-lŏn (Heb.)—*swathed, bound about; wrapped up; place of concealment; lurking place; stronghold.*

A place mentioned by Ezekiel as being on the north (Ezek. 47:15).

Meta. The strong tendency of intellectual man, through his highest sense reasonings, to keep the Truth *wrapped up* and hidden from view instead of clearing it up so that it can be comprehended in its fullness and reality. (Hethlon was on the north border of the land. North signifies above, in man's consciousness, and refers here to the reasonings of the intellect guided by outer observation and by the senses. Man can never, through reason alone, find God or come into an understanding of spiritual Truth. The understanding of Spirit springs from the indwelling Holy Spirit. Man receives this understanding by inspiration.)

Hezekiah (in A. V., Zephaniah 1:1, Hizkiah; Nehemiah 10:17, Hizkijah), hĕz-ĕ-kī′-äh (Heb.) — *Jehovah has strengthened; bound fast by Jah; girded of Jehovah; Jah has made firm; power of Jehovah.*

A king of Judah, who was healed by Jehovah. As a sign that the Lord would heal him, the shadow on the dial went back ten steps in response to the prayer of Isaiah (II Kings 20).

Meta. The expression of spiritual strength in the executive power of the mind.

The Scriptures recite that Hezekiah was a religious reformer among the Hebrews. He cleansed and repaired the Temple, restored the Temple services, and provided for the support of the Levites and for popular religious instruction from the books of the law, thus bringing about a great uprising against idolatry. Human strength is insufficient to carry out the necessary reforms, but there is a king who receives his strength from

God; and his name is Jehovah, the supreme I AM expressed in man (see Isa. 37:14-36 and II Chron. 29 to end of 32).

Hezion, hē′-zĭ-ŏn (Heb.) — *vision; transfixed with the eye; sight; revelation.*

Father of Tabrimmon and grandfather of Benhadad, king of Syria (I Kings 15:18).

Meta. Understanding, but on the sense intellectual plane, instead of true spiritual understanding.

Hezir, hē′-zīr (Heb.)—*returning; going about; intuitive; having small eyes; swine; having small seed; pomegranate.*

a The seventeenth course in Temple service, during David's reign, was allotted to him (I Chron. 24:15). **b** A man by this name joined Nehemiah in sealing the covenant (Neh. 10:20).

Meta. The thoughts that are signified by the men named Hezir may have been swinish (*swine*) when they belonged to the sense, animal plane, but they have now been elevated to a much higher phase of consciousness. *Returning, intuitive, pomegranate,* with the history of the men named Hezir, indicate a conception and a comprehension of the Truth of Being that restore these thoughts to their rightful place of understanding and fruitfulness in man's religious and spiritual nature.

Hezro (in A. V., II Samuel 23:35, Hezrai), hĕz′-rô (Heb.)—*surrounded; inclosed; walled in; verdant pasture; court.*

A Carmelite, one of David's guard (I Chron. 11:37).

Meta. A Carmelite signifies abundance—a rich, opulent thought belonging to the place in consciousness where we realize the fullness of the possibilities that are ours under divine law (Carmel). Hezro (*inclosed, verdant pasture*) symbolizes the spiritual essence or character of our divine possibilities. They are spiritual and are not material in their origin and composition—and "flesh and blood cannot inherit the kingdom of God." So these possibilities are protected (*surrounded, walled in*); they cannot be utilized by the thoughts of the carnal consciousness, but are ever open to the ruling love thought (David). Thus they bloom beautifully to true fruitfulness and supply for the beloved of the Lord.

Hezron, hĕz'-rŏn (Heb.)—*inclosed; shut in; verdant fields; green pasture; court.*

a Son of Reuben (Gen. 46:9). **b** A son of Perez, one of Judah's sons (Gen. 46:12). **c** The name of a place on the southern boundary of Judah, in the Promised Land (Josh. 15:3).

Meta. Single thoughts, and a group of thoughts, that belong to the seeing (Reuben) and the praise (or activity of life) and prayer (Judah) faculties of mind. These thoughts are not yet free in their expression in the consciousness and organism. They are *inclosed, shut in,* by the subconscious limiting error belief in man that all his faculties and powers are material and transient instead of spiritual and abiding.

In the case of the Hezron named in the genealogy of Jesus Christ (Luke 3:33), limiting beliefs are being thrown off and the truth that the name signifies is expressing itself more and more freely and fully.

Hezronites, hĕz'-rŏn-ītes (fr. Heb.)— *of* or *belonging to Hezron.*

Descendants of Hezron, son of Reuben (Num. 26:6); also the descendants of Hezron, grandson of Judah (Num. 26:21).

Meta. Thoughts springing from that in consciousness which Hezron represents. (See HEZRON.)

Hiddai, hĭd'-dāi (Heb.)—*mighty; vigorous; valiant; chief; rejoicing; praise; joyous shout.*

"Hiddai of the brooks of Gaash" was one of David's valiant men, a member of his guard (II Sam. 23:30). He is called Hurai in I Chronicles 11:32.

Meta. Gaash signifies the inner *quaking* or *commotion,* trembling in mind and body, that is likely to take place when one's creative forces and powers have been greatly increased by a new realization of divine life. The "brooks of Gaash" are the cleansing waters that clear from consciousness many errors if the individual keeps his trust firmly centered in Divine Mind and holds to its ideals.

Hiddai signifies the joy and *praise* that spring from within because of the realization of God's greatness and goodness, a realization that comes about by the cleansing and vitalizing experience that is signified by the "brooks of Gaash." This attitude of mind becomes a *mighty* and *chief* factor in guarding the ruling love quality (David) in consciousness.

Hiddekel, hĭd'-dĕ-kĕl (Heb.)—*swift propagator; universal generative fluid; quick flowing; rapid stream; rapid spiritous influx.*

One of the four rivers of the Garden of Eden. It is the same river as the Tigris (Gen. 2:14).

Meta. Hiddekel means *universal generative fluid, rapid stream, rapid spiritual influx.* The river Hiddekel symbolizes the spiritual nerve fluid that God is propelling throughout man's whole being continually, as the electro-magnetic center of every physically expressed atom. This wonderful stream of nerve fluid finds its way over all nerves in man's body temple, giving him the invigorating, steadying power of the Holy Spirit.

Assyria represents the psychic realm of the soul. The nerve fluid, the most attenuated and volatile fluid of the body, breaks into flares at the ends of the nerves, giving rise to various kinds of psychical and mental action, forming character of soul. The mind uses the nerve flares to express its ideas. The primal Spirit elements continually seek expression. Man ever cries out for a higher, fuller way of life and will continue to do so until his full redemption into spirituality is accomplished.

Hiel, hī'-ĕl (Heb.)—*God lives; God of the living; life of God; God is existence; God of animation.*

The Beth–elite, who rebuilt Jericho. "He laid the foundation thereof with the loss of Abiram his first-born, and set up the gates thereof with the loss of his youngest son Segub, according to the word of Jehovah, which he spake by Joshua the son of Nun" (I Kings 16:34).

Meta. The knowledge that all life, energy, existence, animation, is from and of God. This knowledge or realization brings one into conscious unity with God, or is the result of conscious unity with God (Hiel was a native of Beth–el, and Beth–el signifies a consciousness of God, or conscious unity with God).

Jericho, however, the city that Hiel rebuilt, refers to the intellect, a reflected state of consciousness. It is that in us which is not a source of light for itself, but simply reflects the light of Spirit. (See JERICHO.) So Hiel in rebuilding Jericho (in symbolic interpretation, man in putting his trust in the outer for understanding) of necessity draws away in degree from his oneness with the true light of Spirit. Thus the lofty thoughts and the strength that these exalted spiritual ideals (the eldest and youngest sons of Hiel) give become lost to him. Man cannot remain in conscious oneness with Spirit if he puts even a portion of his trust in outer intellectual avenues as being a source of true knowledge. He must keep his thought centered wholly in Spirit as the source of all, if he is to remain aware of his true identity and birthright.

Hierapolis, hī-ĕ-răp'-ŏ-lĭs (Gk.)— *mighty city; sacred city; consecrated city; holy city.*

A city of Phrygia, five or six miles north of Laodicea (Col. 4:13). Fallows says that Hierapolis was celebrated for, and probably looked upon as being sacred (*holy city*) because of, its very remarkable springs of mineral water, with the singular effects that these springs produced in the formation of stalactites and incrustations from their deposits.

Meta. The view, held by the natural man in his religious ideals, that life and substance are sacred. This permits true Christ ideals to gain an entrance into this state of consciousness (there was a Christian church established very early at Hierapolis, and Epaphras labored there: the loving message of the Christ was minister to this group of spiritually awakened thoughts).

Higgaion, hĭg-gā'-ĭŏn (Heb.)—*hum; murmur; a low, vibrant sound; chant; enchantment; meditate,* i. e., *to speak in a low voice to oneself; thought; deep reflection; contemplation.*

A word or name mentioned in Psalms 9:16. In the Authorized Version it is mentioned also in the margin of Psalms 92:3.

Meta. To think deeply along any specific line of Truth that has just been presented to consciousness; *contemplation;* meditation; also the bringing of the whole being into harmony with one's deep inner thought (*hum, murmur, a low vibrant sound*).

Hilen, hī'-lĕn (Heb.)—*strong place; mighty place; good place; place of virtue; a fortress; a sanctuary.*

A Levitical city of Judah (I Chron. 6:58). It is called Holon in Joshua 21:15.

Meta. A group of thoughts in individual consciousness that is strongly fortified (*strong place, fortress*) in goodness and Truth (*good place, place of virtue*) and in praise and prayer (Judah). These thoughts are given over to the Levites (one's natural religious and spiritual tendencies).

Hilkiah, hĭl-kī'-äh (Heb.)—*my portion is Jehovah; Jah is my lot; portion of Jehovah,* i. e., *especially set apart.*

a Father of Jeremiah (Jer. 1:1). b A high priest during Josiah's reign (II Kings 22:4-14). c There were several others by this name also (I Chron. 6:45; 26:11; Neh. 8:4; Isa. 22:20).

Meta. Consecration (*my portion is Jehovah, especially set apart*).

Hillel, hĭl'-lĕl (Heb.)—*praise; rejoice; celebrate; shout for joy; shine forth.*

A Pirathonite. His son Abdon was a judge of Israel (Judg. 12:13). He was of the tribe of Ephraim.

Meta. The action of the will (Ephraim) in praising and magnifying God—one's highest concept of Truth. (Pirathon means *peak, top, prince,* and Abdon represents a phase of the judging, discerning capacity in man, united to the activity of the will in establishing justice in consciousness.)

Hinnom, hĭn'-nŏm (Heb.)—*sorrow; groaning,* i. e., *of the afflicted; wailing; lamentation; purifying fires.*

The same place as Gehenna, a valley south of Jerusalem where the refuse of the city was burned. The fires there were kept going continually. Formerly it was in this valley that some idolatrous kings of Israel celebrated the terrible religious rites of Moloch in which their children were burned in the fire, sacrificed. Later this valley was used to burn refuse and filth from Jerusalem (Josh. 15:8; II Kings 23:10; II Chron. 28:3;

33:6). (See HELL.)

Meta. The purifying fires of the soul. Our God is a consuming fire, and when judgments, or times of separation of the true from the false, take place in our consciousness, the error is utterly consumed, swallowed up, by the love and perfection and Truth of Spirit. There will be no cessation of these cleansing, purifying processes until there is no more refuse to be burned; then this fire of God will express in us as eternal life. "Behold, I send my messenger, and he shall prepare the way before me: and the Lord, whom ye seek, will suddenly come to his temple; and the messenger of the covenant, whom ye desire, behold, he cometh, saith Jehovah of hosts. But who can abide the day of his coming? and who shall stand when he appeareth? for he is like a refiner's fire, and like fullers' soap: and he will sit as a refiner and purifier of silver, and he will purify the sons of Levi" (Mal. 3:1-3). Again, "Who among us can dwell with the devouring fire? who among us can dwell with everlasting burnings?" Not the wicked, but "he that walketh righteously, and speaketh uprightly" (Isa. 33:14-16).

Hirah, hī'-răh (Heb.)—*white; pure; noble; highborn; splendid; distinguished; freedom; liberty.*

An Adullamite, a friend of Judah's (Gen. 38:1).

Meta. An Adullamite, a native of Adullam, typifies a thought belonging to the Adullam consciousness in man. One meaning of Adullam is *justice of the people.* This indicates a sense of justice and right, an equilibrium and poise (see ADULLAM) that, awakened in the individual, even if at first in the seemingly material consciousness only, gives a *splendid, noble* quality to the man and leads toward true *liberty.* This is Hirah.

Hiram, hī'-răm (Heb.)—*whiteness; liberty; freedom; nobility; highborn; splendid.*

a King of Tyre, a friend of David's: "And Hiram king of Tyre sent messengers to David, and cedar-trees, and carpenters, and masons; and they built David a house" (II Sam. 5:11). He furnished Solomon with material and workers for building the Temple, also (I Kings 5:1-18). Solomon gave Hiram twenty cities in Galilee, but they did not please Hiram and he called them the "land of Cabul" (I Kings 9:10-14). **b** The son of a widow of the tribe of Naphtali. His father was a man of Tyre, a worker in brass. Solomon brought out of Tyre this Hiram, since he was a man filled with wisdom, understanding, and skill, to work all works in brass. He made the "molten sea" in the Temple, and did much of the fine work in it (I Kings 7:13-47).

Meta. Hiram was a builder; he was not of the Israelites (the religious and spiritual thoughts in man), at least not entirely, though the one Hiram was partly of Israelitish blood. He represents a constructive power in the reasoning faculty of the individual—a constructive power that is firmly established in substance and in an almost unlimited degree of fineness of discrimination, understanding. This power lends itself and its thoughts to the building of Truth in the consciousness and the body.

The skill of this Hiram thought is carried out in the affirmative, the positive, constructive attitude of building and doing. In order to spiritualize this ego, with the thought activities that belong in its domain, a balance between letting go and building up, denial and affirmation, must be established. For further suggestions along this line, and for an idea of the difference between the Solomon wisdom and the skill that Hiram signifies, see CABUL.

Hittites, hĭt'-tītes (fr. Heb.)—*broken in pieces; sundered; dismay; terror; dread.*

Descendants of Heth, who was a son of Canaan (Gen. 25:9, 10). They were a tribe, or nation, in the land of Canaan that the Israelites were to drive out and destroy (Exod. 23:28; Deut. 20:17).

Meta. Thoughts of opposition and resistance. (See HETH.)

Hivite, hī'-vīte (fr. Heb.)—*animation; physical existence; life born of effort; bestiality; wickedness; villager; midlander.*

Descendants of Canaan the son of Ham (Gen. 10:17). The Hivites were a nation in the land of Canaan that was to be overcome and destroyed by the Israelites (Exod. 3:8; Josh. 3:10).

Meta. Thoughts belonging to the carnal consciousness in man. The Hivites were descended from Canaan, son of Ham, and refer to the physical and carnal in the individual.

Hizkiah (A. V., Hezekiah), hĭz-kī'-ăh (Heb.)—*Jehovah strengthens; Jah is strong; power of Jehovah; force of Jah; strength of the Lord.*

A man mentioned among the descendants of Solomon (I Chron. 3:23). Hezekiah is the same name.

Meta. See HEZEKIAH.

Hobab, hō'-băb (Heb.)—*beloved; cherished; comforted.*

Brother-in-law of Moses (Num. 10:29).

Meta. The love of understanding. (Hobab, meaning *beloved;* Moses' remark to him, "Thou shalt be to us instead of eyes"; also Moses' great desire to have Hobab accompany him and the Israelites on their journey through the wilderness to the Promised Land, all signify this. See Numbers 10:29-32). Understanding and discrimination (one meaning of Midian being *judgment*) are much prized (*beloved*) by the awakening desire in man for the things of Spirit; and understanding pertains to peace, protection, wholeness, and. every good (*cherished, comforted*).

Hobah, hō'-băh (Heb.)—*hiding place; lurking place; place of concealment; hidden; concealed; covered; befriended; cherished.*

A place north of Damascus. It was to this place that Abram pursued those who took Lot captive (Gen. 14:15).

Meta. Natural man's belief that he is material. This belief is established deep within the subconscious mind, and is a *hiding place* or *lurking place* for the error thoughts and activities that are symbolized by the kings and their followers who took Lot captive and whom Abram pursued.

The sense life, with its carnal desires, can never be fully overcome until we put away all belief in materiality. We must know through and through that our whole being, including the body, is not material but is spiritual, before we can begin really to gain complete domin-

ion over the carnal in us, which tends to death and corruption. It is by sowing to Spirit that we reap eternal life.

Hobaiah (A. V., Habaiah), hŏ-bā'-jăh (Heb.)—*whom Jehovah hides; Jah is protection; Jehovah's concealment; beloved of Jehovah; the Lord covers.*

His "children" were among the priests who returned from the Babylonian captivity, but because they could not prove their genealogy they were deemed polluted and were put out of the priesthood (Neh. 7:63). In Ezra 2:61 he is called Habaiah.

Meta. Gaining spiritual protection for our higher ideals by hiding their true nature from the more established religious intellectual beliefs.

Our higher and more spiritual thoughts that really belong to the priesthood cannot, at a certain stage of our unfoldment, always make their spiritual origin (genealogy) understood by the more intellecual religious ruling thoughts that are established in ritualism and outer observance of the letter of the law; hence they are ignored by the ritualistic beliefs. This is really a protection to them and gives them an opportunity to grow in Truth unobserved until they become ready to take their true place as ministers to the more formal and intellectual religious thoughts (Jewish people) in the body (Temple).

Hod, hŏd (Heb.)—*vigorous; strong; splendor; majesty; glory; an acclamation; confession; a joyous shout; praise.*

An Asherite. He is named among those who were "heads of the fathers' houses, choice and mighty men of valor, chief of the princes" (I Chron. 7:37, 40).

Meta. A ruling, conquering thought in the Asher consciousness in man. (See ASHER.) It is the lifting up and exalting (*majesty, glory, splendor, praise*) of the joy of true spiritual understanding (see Prov. 3:13-18).

Hodaviah (in A. V., I Chronicles 3:24, Hodaiah), hŏd-ă-vī'-ăh (Heb.)—*praise ye Jehovah; glorify Jah; Jehovah is your strength; Jehovah is your majesty.*

a A man of Manasseh; one of those who were the "heads of their fathers' houses" (I Chron. 5:24). **b** A Benjamite of note (I Chron. 9:7). **c** A Levite whose descendants came up out of the Babylonian captivity with Zerubbabel (Ezra 2:40).

Meta. Leading thoughts (men who were "heads of their fathers' houses") from our understanding faculty (Manasseh), from our active faith consciousness (Benjamin), and from our love faculty (Levi) as expressed by our natural religious tendencies (Levites), giving praise and honor to Jehovah (the indwelling Christ or I AM) and being blessed and highly esteemed by Jehovah.

Hodesh, hō'-dĕsh (Heb.) — *polish; make shine; make new; renew; the new moon; day of the new moon,* i. e., *first of the month; month.*

Wife of Shaharaim, of the tribe of Benjamin (I Chron. 8:9).

Meta. Shaharaim (*double dawn, double morning*) represents the breaking of new light in consciousness, doubly strong. Hodesh (*new moon,* or *month, day of the new moon*) suggests the reflection of this light in the soul while it is being carried into the body consciousness, for its renewal (*make new*). (The moon symbolizes reflected understanding, since it shines by borrowed light.)

Hodevah, hō-dē'-văh (Heb.)—*praise of Jehovah; Jah is honor; strength of Jehovah; praise the Lord.*

A Levite. Seventy-four of his descendants came out of the Babylonian captivity (Neh. 7:43). In Ezra 2:40, Hodaviah.

Meta. Virtually the same as Hodaviah: thoughts and activities of the love consciousness as expressed by our natural religious tendencies (Levites), giving praise, honor, and glory to Jehovah (the indwelling Christ or I AM), and being blessed and highly esteemed by Jehovah.

Hodiah (in A. V., Nehemiah 8:7 and 10:18, Hodijah), hō-dī'-ăh (Heb.)—*my splendor is Jehovah; praise of the Lord; glory of Jah; majesty of Jehovah.*

a A descendant of Judah (I Chron. 4:19). **b** One who helped the people to understand the law when Ezra read it to them (Neh. 8:7). **c** One of those who joined Nehemiah in sealing the covenant (Neh. 10:18).

Meta. That in the religious and spiritual nature of man (Israelites) which

realizes that Jehovah (the indwelling Christ) is man's true splendor, might, power of dominion, joy, and praise—the source of all that is lasting and good to him.

Hoglah, hŏg'-läh (Heb.)—*hopping bird; partridge; quail; magpie.*

Daughter of Zelophehad the son of Hepher, of the tribe of Manasseh (Num. 26:33).

Meta. Zelophehad, father of Hoglah, signifies the denial or letting-go-of-error aspect of understanding (Manasseh). This that Zelophehad represents in the individual does not express as positive knowledge; it brings forth fruit in the soul consciousness only. (All Zelophehad's children were daughters, and they inherited their father's property as though they had been sons, the law having been altered for them).

Hoglah, daughter of Zelophehad, and meaning a *hopping bird, partridge, quail* (the idea is developed from an advance made in short hops, in contradistinction to walking freely, as, a hopping bird, a shackled man, or a hobbled animal), denotes progress in understanding, though the progress is still restricted. A greater freeing of thought is needed.

Hoham, hō'-hăm (Heb.)—*whom Jehovah stirs up; whom Jah impels; whom Jehovah incites; being of them; woe to them.*

King of Hebron who joined Adonizedek king of Jerusalem in an attack on the Israelites who had come into Canaan to possess the land. These kings were defeated and were hanged by Joshua (Josh. 10:3, 22-27).

Meta. As Adonizedek represents the sensate idea of justice, which in unredeemed man rules in Jerusalem, the heart center, so Hoham signifies a similar error idea ruling in the seat of conscious thought, Hebron, the front brain. If Hoham were an Israelite the significance would be good—life universal and true— but as he was a heathen king, the influence of the carnal mind is brought into play. Thus the life thought is materialized, degraded, and becomes the expression of a calamitous existence: woe, tribulation, misfortune (*woe to them*).

Holon, hō'-lŏn (Heb.)—*place of longevity; abundant; many days; sandy; rolling; phœnixlike,* or *the power of renewing life.*

a A city in the hill country of Judah (Josh. 15:51). It was given over to the Levites (Josh. 21:15). b A city in the plain country of Moab (Jer. 48:21).

Meta. A group of thoughts belonging to the intellect in man. When these thoughts are given over to the direction of the carnal mind (Moab) they are material and unstable, earthly, and they bring the individual to grief; but when they come under the dominion of Judah and the Levites (praise, prayer, love, and higher religious ideals), they become thoughts of true abundance and renewal of life and Truth.

holy ground (Exod. 3:5).

Meta. Substance in its spiritual wholeness; that is, the idea of substance in Divine Mind. When man approaches this he must remove from his understanding all limited thoughts of the Absolute —"Put off thy shoes from off thy feet." (See BURNING BUSH.)

Homam, hō'-măm (Heb.)—*destruction; blind; raging; riotous commotion; greatest consternation; rebellious rabble; noisy multitude.*

A descendant of Seir (I Chron. 1:39). In Genesis 36:22 he is called Heman.

Meta. Seir the Horite signifies the thought that rules in the deep-seated sense tendencies and activities of the physical in man. (See HORITES.) When sense desires, beliefs, and activities are allowed to prevail without restraint (*blind, raging*), they are very destructive and bring about desolation and ruin. Homam typifies such mental activities.

Hophni, hŏph'-nī (Heb.)—*pugnacious; strong; hard-fisted; a fighter.*

Son of Eli (I Sam. 1:3). He and Phineas his brother were priests of Israel. They were wicked men who desecrated their priestly office and brought destruction to themselves and caused the downfall of their father's house. "I will judge his house forever, for the iniquity which he knew, because his sons did bring a curse upon themselves, and he restrained them not" (I Sam. 3:13).

Meta. Eli means *a going up* and is typical of the phase of man's consciousness that is always seeking spiritual progress. The two sons of Eli represent the natural product of one's desire to grow spiritually. They represent spiritual strength and power. When these faculties begin to awaken, though they are priests in the Temple, there is great need for discipline and intelligent direction, lest they become selfish and act upon a purely material plane. In this state, Hophni becomes *pugnacious, a fighter,* and Phineas becomes *brazen-faced, a mouth of brass.* When one's spiritual strength becomes personalized, it seeks to accomplish its ends through combative measures, and this creates great resistance in the organism; it tries to gain its desires by means of brazen or bold speech. One's spiritual forces are disorganized by these methods, and so they become easy prey to the more material ideas. The material ideas are usually well trained, according to personal standards, and readily rally to the support of material leadership. When any great demand is made upon the material man, if he undertakes to meet it at all he throws into his task the full force of his material self.

This is just what happened to the Hebrews when the Ark of the Covenant was brought into their midst. When the vision of spiritual deliverance was presented to them they adopted the combative methods of the Philistines. The spiritual forces are never combative or boastful. One who seeks to exercise them in personal measures becomes unfit for success and is temporarily incapacitated. Spiritual man knows that his strength lies in his unity with God and that his power is his ability to speak the Truth. When he deviates from spiritual principles he soon becomes shorn of power and is taken captive by the organized forces of materiality (the Philistines).

This is a lesson that every Truth student should remember: As new forces and powers are awakened, they should be carefully trained in accordance with the true principles of Spirit. Such difficulties as befell the Hebrews (I Sam. 4:5-18) can be avoided if spiritual standards are always upheld in thought and act—no matter how seemingly trivial.

Hophra, hŏph'-rȧ (Heb. fr. Egypt.)—Pharaoh Hophra; *protector of Ra; priest of the sun.*

A king of Egypt against whom Jeremiah prophesied (Jer. 44:30).

Meta. The central ruling thought of the Egyptian consciousness in man. (See PHARAOH and EGYPT.)

Hor, hôr (Heb.)—*to be high; to conceive; to think; a height; a mountain;* Mount Hor—*the mountain of mountains.*

a A mountain in the wilderness, where Aaron died and where his son Eleazar was clothed with the priestly garments and became high priest of Israel (Num. 20:22-29). **b** A mountain on the northern border of the land of Canaan (Num. 34:7).

Meta. A much exalted state of thought in man. It is here that the ruling power of the intellectual consciousness (Aaron the first high priest of Israel), which has become the executive power of the divine law to the highest religious and spiritual thoughts of the individual (Israelites), ceases its activities, seemingly, and sinks back into the subconscious mind (Aaron died on Mount Hor). It is here, too, that spiritual strength, through the individual's recognition of God as his supporting, sustaining power (Eleazar takes the place of high priest), becomes the directive quality of the higher consciousness of divine law into which the individual is entering.

Horam, hō'-răm (Heb.)—*high; elevated; lofty; exalted; mountaineer.*

King of Gezer, who helped Lachish against the Israelites, but was overcome and destroyed, with all his people, by Joshua (Josh. 10:33).

Meta. The lifting up and exalting (*lofty, elevated, high*) in consciousness of the sense beliefs and activities that Gezer symbolizes. (See GEZER.)

Horeb, hō'-rĕb (Heb.) — *dryness; drought; heat; waste; desolation; desert; barren; solitude.*

A mountain or range of mountains that is mentioned many times in Scripture. It is called "the mountain of God" and is identical with Sinai (see Exodus 3:1; 17:6; Deuteronomy 4:15; 5:2; I Kings 19:8).

Meta. A state of high spiritual realization that we may attain by affirming the power and presence of the one inner, divine sustenance and nourishment. It is a high place in consciousness where we come into conscious union with the divine. (See REPHIDIM, also Exodus 17.) *Solitude,* as a meaning of Horeb, signifies that we have to go into the solitude of the inner mind and lead our flock of thoughts to the back of the wilderness, where dwells the Exalted One, the divine I AM, whose kingdom is good judgment. (See Exodus 3, and JETHRO.)

Horem, hō'-rĕm (Heb.)—*consecrated; sacred; devoted; set apart; shut off,* i. e., *removed from common use.*

A fortified city of Naphtali (Josh. 19:38).

Meta. Strength (Naphtali) dedicated to God (*consecrated*) or regarded as *sacred* and *devoted* to spiritual service and use. This truly becomes a fortress, a stronghold, in consciousness; strength cannot grow less when one realizes one's strength as from God and as divine; it ever grows stronger, surer, and more abiding when it is thus recognized.

Hor–haggidgad (A. V., Hor–hagidgad), hôr'–hăg-ḡĭd'-găd (Heb.)—*hole of the cleft; hole of the thunderings; hewn cavern; echoing cave.*

A place where the Israelites camped while they were in the wilderness, on the way to the Promised Land (Num. 33:32). It is probably the same place as the Gudgodah of Deuteronomy 10:7.

Meta. The same as Gudgodah, except that Hor–haggidgad refers more particularly to a work that is going on in the subconsciousness. (*Hole, cave, cavern,* bespeak the depths of the subconsciousness. The Hor in this name is spelled in Hebrew with a different "H" from that of Mount Hor, which causes it to refer to a hole or cavern instead of a hill or mountain.)

Hori, hō'-rī (Heb.)—*cave dweller; imprisoned; black; free; noble; white.*

a Son of Lotan of the Horites, and brother of Heman (Gen. 36:22). **b** An Israelite, of the tribe of Simeon, whose son Shaphat was one of the men whom Moses sent to spy out the land of Canaan (Num. 13:5).

Meta. Thoughts belonging to the depths of the subconsciousness (*cave dweller*). The one is wholly given over to the error beliefs signified by the Horites. The other, who is of the tribe of Simeon (one who listens and obeys), has become, through the dawning light of Spirit, higher and nobler, which tends to the ultimate freeing from the dominion of sense even of that in the individual which appears to be mortal and physical. The Horite and the Israelite named Hori represent the two extremes of this remarkable Hebrew word: one, *imprisoned, black;* the other, *free, noble, white.*

Horites (A. V., Genesis 36:30, Hori; Deuteronomy 2:12, Horims), hō'-rītes (fr. Heb.)—*troglodytes; cave dwellers; dwellers in black holes.*

The Horites were very closely connected with the Edomites, the descendants of Esau. They were the inhabitants of the land of Mount Seir, before they were overcome by Esau. After that they lived in the land with the Edomites (Gen. 14:6). (See also Genesis 36.)

Meta. The Horites, like the Edomites, have their seat of action in the physical organism. The Horites refer more especially to the deep-seated, subconscious (*cave dwellers*), error, fleshly tendencies and activities of the physical in man, while the Edomites refer more to the outer or body consciousness.

Hormah, hôr'-măh (Heb.)—*shut in; devoted; consecrated; dedicated; an asylum; a sanctuary; never to be redeemed; devoted to destruction; destroyed; laid waste; exterminated; a fortress.*

"And Jehovah hearkened to the voice of Israel, and delivered up the Canaanites; and they utterly destroyed them and their cities: and the name of the place was called Hormah" (Num. 21:3). In the margin, "devoted" is given in place of "utterly destroyed," and we are told that Hormah is from the same root as *herem*, a devoted thing. Hormah was also a city that Judah and Simeon took from the Canaanites, and it was allotted to Simeon (Judg. 1:17; Josh. 19:4). In Joshua 15:30 Hormah is mentioned as a city of Judah.

Meta. A seeming paradox in Christian overcoming: the letting go and utter destruction of error beliefs and ideas, and at the same time the devoting or dedicating, consecrating to God, to high and spiritual use, of all the energy, substance, power, faith, intelligence, and strength that have been given to promotion of error. When we give up old activities and deny them out of consciousness, it appears at first as though we were putting away our very life, our power of action, of accomplishment, of usefulness. This, however, is not the case. All the good, all the powers of Being, that in our ignorance we used to perpetuate the error, or the limitation, is preserved, and is set into constructive action to the upbuilding and spiritualizing of our . organism. Thus Hormah, this place of overcoming in us, becomes a *fortress* and a *sanctuary,* a place of retreat and seclusion (*an asylum*) for many of our inner thoughts during processes of adjustment in consciousness.

Horonaim, hŏr-ō-nā'-ĭm (Heb.)—*double caves; two caves; outbursts of anger; ragings.*

A place mentioned by both Isaiah and Jeremiah in their prophecies of the destruction of Moab (Isa. 15:5). "The sound of a cry from Horonaim, desolation and great destruction! . . . for at the descent of Horonaim they have heard the distress of the cry of destruction" (Jer. 48:3, 5).

Meta. Subconscious errors that are a part of the carnal mind. Great seeming distress and commotion often arise when these errors are being brought to the surface and denied away. At such a time a forsaken, desolate feeling sometimes takes hold of one, until the light of Truth fills in the seeming vacuum with renewed joy, thanksgiving, substance, and strength. (Moab here signifies the carnal mind, and when the individual enters into the overcoming life the carnal mind must be cast out, destroyed. See MOAB.)

Horonite, hŏr'-ō-nīte (fr. Heb.)—*cave; cavern; anger; indignation.*

A native of Horonaim or, according to the American Standard Version, of Beth-horon; Sanballat the Horonite was one of those who opposed Nehemiah's rebuilding of the wall about Jerusalem

(Neh. 2:10, 19).

Meta. A thought belonging to the Horonaim or Beth–horon state of consciousness and the opposing, fighting, resisting attitude that it takes while being dealt with in the overcoming of error. It must be, and finally will be, put entirely out of consciousness. (See Nehemiah 13:28-30; see also BETH–HORON and HORONAIM.)

Hosah, hō'-săh (Heb.)—*refuge; shelter; protection; trust; hope; confidence.*

a A city on the border of Asher (Josh. 19:29). **b** One of the doorkeepers of the Temple during David's reign (I Chron. 16:38); his place of watch was "westward, by the gate of Shallecheth" (I Chron. 26:16).

Meta. A trusting, hopeful spirit in man that becomes a true haven (*refuge*) to him at all times, and especially when he is passing through some overcoming experiences in which the error side of things appears to be triumphing over the true.

Hosanna, hŏ-săn'-nȧ (Gk. from Heb.) —*save now; deliver now; succor now; be propitious now.*

A word customarily acclaimed at the Feast of the Tabernacles. It was used by the multitude, in reference to Jesus (Matt. 21:9): "Hosanna to the son of David: Blessed is he that cometh in the name of the Lord; Hosanna in the highest." The meaning is, according to Fallows, "Lord, preserve this Son of David; heap favors and blessings on him!"

Meta. Worshipful prayer offered by the inner thoughts that are awakening spiritually, prayer for the preservation and safe growth of the Christ Spirit that is being formed and brought to birth in the soul and body of the individual. We desire every blessing and good for this true Christ ideal within us, that it may develop and take full possession to the complete putting on of the Christ, which means redemption for the whole man.

Hosea, hō-ṣē'-ȧ (Heb.)—*deliverance; safety; salvation; help.*

A prophet of Israel. He was the son of Beeri, and he prophesied "in the days of Uzziah, Jotham, Ahaz, and Hezekiah, kings of Judah, and in the days of Jeroboam the son of Joash, king of Israel" (Hosea 1:1).

Meta. I AM identity. It is by our recognition of our true I AM, or Christ identity, that we reap the benefits of our sonship and realize *deliverance* and *salvation.* We receive *help* from the Divine when we claim this help and affirm our birthright, through I AM.

Hoshaiah, hō-shā'-ĭȧh (Heb.)—*whom Jehovah delivers; help of Jah; safety of Jehovah; salvation of the Lord.*

a A prince of Judah who led one of the two companies of princes who gave thanks at the dedication of the newly rebuilt wall of Jerusalem (Neh. 12:32). **b** An Israelite, the father of Jezaniah, or Azariah (Jer. 42:1; 43:2).

Meta. The inner assurance that one has received one's needed help and salvation through I AM, or Jehovah.

Hoshama, hŏsh'-ȧ-mȧ (Heb.)—*whom Jehovah hears; hearken to Jah; understanding of Jehovah; obey the Lord.*

A man named among the descendants of Solomon (I Chron. 3:18).

Meta. The heeding, obedient attitude of mind in man, which opens the way to divine favor.

"The eyes of Jehovah are toward the righteous,
And his ears are *open* unto their cry."

Hoshea, hō-shē'-ȧ (Heb.)—*deliverance; safety; salvation; help.*

a Another name for Joshua (Deut. 32:44). **b** A son of Elah who killed Pekah, the king of Israel, and became king in his stead (II Kings 15:30). **c** One of those who joined Nehemiah in sealing the covenant (Neh. 10:23).

Meta. Hoshea means "save." Joshua and Jesus are variations of the same word, along with Jah and Jehovah. "Jehovah saves." Hoshea represents the saving grace of the inner I AM, Jehovah.

In II Kings 17:2 we are told that the king by this name, Hoshea, was not so bad as his predecessors. He was weak in his faith in the power of Spirit, however, for to the militant king of Assyria he gave presents and servile obedience. This shows how one with the saving grace of the I AM within him may weaken when attacked by materiality. The secret of this weakness is disobedience. Hoshea "did that which was evil in the sight of Jehovah." This "evil" is enumerated in II Kings 17:1-18 and is to be found in nearly all forms of worship. He and his people served many gods— calves, molten images, an Asherah; they set up pillars, and served Baal; in many ways they materialized the God idea. When they were reprimanded for all this they "hardened their neck"; obstinacy and self-will was their response.

History shows that all great religions were spiritual at their beginnings and became material with age. This tendency holds good in the evolution of the soul, and should be headed off by an increased devotion to Truth and the God of Spirit every time the tendency to drop into material ways of thought is observed.

This weakness of the soul for materialism is not in accordance with divine law, but pertains to a certain phase of soul evolution. The race is coming out of materialism, and the dominant thought is in that direction. Ample provision has been made for all who keep the eye of faith on the absolute good; the "gates of hell" shall not prevail against them.

host of heaven.

Meta. "All the host of heaven" (II Chron. 33:5) are the sun, moon, stars, and the twelve signs of the zodiac.

Hotham (A. V., I Chronicles 11:44, Hothan), hŏ'-thăm (Heb.)—*seal; a signet ring; closed; determined; fixed; ended.*

a Son of Heber. Heber was a grandson of Asher (I Chron. 7:32). **b** An Aroerite whose sons Shama and Jeiel were among David's valiant men (I Chron. 11:44).

Meta. The fixed resolution (*determined, seal*) of the spiritually awakened inner understanding and will of man to become consciously one with Spirit, to serve, obey, and magnify God, the good.

In Bible times, among certain nations, when a decree was sealed by the king it became irrevocable, unalterable; it had to be carried out and could not be changed even if the king himself became convinced that it was a mistake. (See Esth. 8:8.)

For an idea as to why this inner resolution that Hotham signifies is to serve God and become consciously one with Him, see the meaning of HEBER (the name of Hotham's father).

Hothir, hŏ'-thĭr (Heb.)—*the saved one; preserver; savior; excellence; fullness to overflowing; plenteousness; abundance.*

A son of Heman. He and his brothers were singers in the Temple worship (I Chron. 25:4).

Meta. A realization of abundant supply (*abundance, fullness to overflowing*) from the inner Spirit of harmony and wisdom. This fills the whole being and surpasses (*excellence*) anything that can be attained in outer intellectual or material searching. This inner knowledge of wisdom and Truth becomes the *preserver*, the source of sustenance, for the whole of man's organism.

house, Jehovah's (Mic. 4:1).

Meta. The body. "We are a temple of the living God" (II Cor. 6:16). The "mountains" are the higher brain centers, and the "top of the mountains" is the spiritual brain in the very apex of the cranium. When men cultivate spiritual thoughts this top brain is "exalted above the hills," and the whole consciousness or "peoples" shall flow to it. When this spiritual center is quickened it sends out a far-reaching thought energy, and the whole race consciousness is lifted up. This is represented as many nations going "up to the mountain of Jehovah."

The house that God builds and dwells in is man's body. "Know ye not that your body is a temple of the Holy Spirit?" (I Cor. 6:19). We worship God in the body temple by serving Him "day and night in his temple: and he that sitteth on the throne shall spread his tabernacle over them" (Rev. 7:15). The fruits of such service shall be: "They shall hunger no more, neither thirst any more; neither shall the sun strike upon them, nor any heat: for the Lamb that is in the midst of the throne shall be their shepherd, and shall guide them unto fountains of waters of life: and God shall wipe away every tear from their eyes" (Rev. 7:16, 17).

Hukkok, hŭk'-kŏk (Heb.)—*cut in; hew; engrave; carve; ordain; decree; ap-*

point; a ditch; a scribe; lawyer; judge; ruler.

A city on the western or southwestern border of Naphtali (Josh. 19:34).

Meta. The establishing of the idea of unfailing strength (Naphtali) in the mind and heart, engraving it in the very cells and fiber of the whole being. Divine Truth must be thus written (*engrave, cut in, a scribe*) in our inward parts, and all our thought and organism must become alive to the abidingness, unfailingness, and reality of strength, and of each of the faculties of mind. (See Hebrews 10:16 and Jeremiah 31:33.)

Hukok, hū'-kŏk (Heb.)—*cut in; hew; engrave; ordain; decree; appoint; a scribe; judge; ruler.*

A city out of the tribe of Asher. With its suburbs it was given over to the Gershomite Levites (I Chron. 6:75). In Joshua 21:31 it is called Helkath.

Meta. The same as Hukkok, except that this group of thoughts relates to Asher rather than Naphtali (see HUK-KOK), and to the understanding by man that he has his appointed part in the divine inheritance of all good. (See HEL-KATH.)

Hul, hŭl (Heb.)—*circle; circling; turning about; whirling; ecstasy; joy; attending; resolving; hoping; placing faith; turning away; dissolution; writhing; travail; childbirth; sorrow; pain; trembling; fear; terror.*

Son of Aram, who was a son of Shem and grandson of Noah (Gen. 10:23).

Meta. That in the intellect of man which seeks to conform to both the spiritual and the outer-sense ideas of wisdom and understanding. (A circle refers to the spiritual, to oneness, or unity, that which has no beginning or ending. *Pain, trembling, fear, sorrow,* exist in and are products of the "mind of the flesh" and its seemingly imperfect body manifestation.) Much can be drawn from the definitions of Hul.

Of the ancestors of Hul, Shem is a son of Noah, who pertains to the spiritual in man; Aram refers to the intellect, which has its foundation in Spirit. In the individuals who have not yet found their way back to the Father's house— to spiritual understanding, realization,

and manifestation, in some degree at least—the intellect has linked itself so firmly with the outer or seemingly material realm that it no longer acknowledges Spirit as the one source of understanding, and it is divided in its thoughts and reasonings.

Huldah, hŭl'-dăh (Heb.)—*smooth; gliding; fleeting; transient life, of this world, i. e., earthly, vain, fleeting; a mole; a weasel.*

"The prophetess, the wife of Shallum the son of Tikvah, the son of Harhas, keeper of the wardrobe (now she dwelt in Jerusalem in the second quarter)" (II Kings 22:14).

Meta. The intuitive perception of the "second" or subjective consciousness. The brain through which this divinity within us functions is between the breasts and is connected with the love nature. This is why it is designated as feminine.

Intuitive perception, or intuition, is something over which the outer personal man has no apparent control. It seems *fleeting, transient,* unreal to him; but it or its counterpart—spiritual inspiration —becomes abiding and real as the individual grows in true understanding and spirituality.

Humtah, hŭm'-tăh (Heb.)—*bow down; lie upon the ground; crawl upon the ground; grovel; lizard; snail; low earthwork; bulwark; fortress.*

A city in the hill country of Judah (Josh. 15:54).

Meta. Creeping thoughts (*lizard, snail*) of a *low* character, yet strong and fortifying (*fortress*), and due to be lifted to a higher level (a city in the hill country of Judah) by the ministry of praise and prayer (Judah).

Hupham, hū'-phăm (Heb.)—*coastman; seashore; bank; covered; under cover; veiled; protected; secret; covert.*

Son of Benjamin, and head of the family of the Huphamites (Num. 26:39).

Meta. A *coastman* is one who lives on or near the seashore; in all likelihood he is a fisherman, which symbolizes a gatherer of ideas, fish representing ideas, especially ideas of increase. This seeking out and gathering of true ideas of increase, together with an active faith (Benjamin) in the good only, becomes a protection to the individual.

Huphamites, hŭ′-phăm-ītes (fr. Heb.)
—*of* or *belonging to Hupham.*

Descendants of Hupham (Num. 26:
39).

Meta. Thoughts belonging to and
springing from that which Hupham signifies in consciousness. (See HUPHAM.)

Huppah, hŭp′-păh (Heb.)—*covering;*
protection; veil; canopy; curtain; covert;
sanctuary.

A priest in David's reign, on whom
the lot fell for the thirteenth course
in the Temple service (I Chron. 24:13).

Meta. The spiritual clothing (a *covering*) and defense, refuge, preservation,
protection, that love (David) and true
religious ideals (priests) are to the consciousness of man.

Huppim, hŭp′-pĭm (Heb.)—*coastman;*
seashore; bank; under cover; veiled;
protection; secret; covered; covert.

A Benjamite (I Chron. 7:12). In Numbers 26:39 he is called Hupham. He was
a son of Benjamin, according to Genesis
46:21.

Meta. Virtually the same as that of
Hupham. (See HUPHAM.)

Hur, hûr (Heb.)—*white; pure; brilliant; noble; liberty; freedom; hollowed
out; subterranean hole; black, filthy
prison; cavern.*

a The man who, with Aaron, held up
Moses' hands, so that Joshua and the
Israelites defeated the Amalekites (Exod. 17:10-13). Hur seemed to have been
a very influential man and very much
trusted and loved by Moses. He is
classed along with Aaron. When Moses
went up to the mount of God to receive
the law, he told the people to go to Aaron
and Hur if they had any important matters to decide (Exod. 24:14). According
to Fallows, Jewish tradition classes this
Hur as the son of Caleb, and husband of
Miriam, Moses' sister. Hur was the
father of Uri, whose son Bezalel was one
of the chief skilled workmen employed in
constructing the tabernacle (Exod. 31:2-
11). **b** There are other Israelites in the
Bible by this name, and one Midianite,
a king who was defeated and slain by the
Israelites (Num. 31:8).

Meta. Affirmative prayer, affirmation
of Truth; a strong, cleansing, freeing,
ennobling power whose activity in consciousness helps clear away the remaining darkness and obscurity (Egypt). It
also aids in keeping the attention fixed on
the divine executive power (he helped
hold up the hands of Moses while the
Israelites were fighting the Amalekites
under Joshua, and so long as Moses'
hands were held up the children of Israel prevailed), that the enemies of sense
may be overcome. This thought activity
that Hur signifies brings forth other
thoughts that do their part in building
up the body (tabernacle) and in overcoming the enemies in the land.

The Hur who was a king of the
Midianites shows the effect of introducing *strife* (a meaning of Midian) into
the freeing, cleansing, and ennobling
ideal for which the former Hur stands.
Strife and contention lead to great error,
limitation, and darkness (*subterranean
hole, black, filthy prison*). They must be
overcome and slain by man's true, higher
thoughts (Israelites) before Truth can
be realized in its purity and power. (The
definitions of error that are attributed
to the name Hur arise from perversion
of the good qualities for which the word
stands. Seeming evils come from perverted or adulterated good. Many, if not
all, of the Hebrew names have a negative
as well as a positive meaning.)

Hurai, hū′-rāi (Heb.)—*linen worker;*
*weaver of fine linen; bleacher of fine
linen; whitener; purifier; brilliant;
noble; splendid.*

"Hurai of the brooks of Gaash" was
one of David's mighty men (I Chron.
11:32). In II Samuel 23:30 he is called
Hiddai.

Meta. A freeing, ennobling power that
works in the spiritual qualities of discrimination, intuition, and love, to bring
about an orderly interblending of the
true thoughts and ideals in consciousness (*weaver of fine linen, linen worker,
whitener, purifier, splendid*); thus the
individual becomes purified and clothed
with the garment of light and wholeness.
(See Isaiah 52:1; 61:10; see HIDDAI.)

Huram, hū′-răm (Heb.)—*noble; free;*
highborn; pure; brilliant; white-robed.

a Son of Bela and grandson of Benjamin (I Chron. 8:5). **b** II Chronicles

2:3, 11-13, gives the name of Hiram, king of Tyre, as Huram. (See also II Chronicles 4:11, 16.)

Meta. See HIRAM.

The Huram who was a Benjamite signifies the activity of faith as a purifying, uplifting, constructive power in man's consciousness, to bring about true liberty and nobility. These building qualities in consciousness that Hiram or Huram represents are *noble, free,* and *highborn;* they are of spiritual origin.

Huri, hŭ'-rī—(Heb.)—*linen worker; weaver of fine linen; bleacher of fine linen; whitener; purifier; brilliant; noble; splendid.*

A man of the tribe of Gad (I Chron. 5:14).

Meta. The same word as Hurai. (See HURAI.)

Hushah, hū'-shäh (Heb.)—*haste; speed; vehemence; passion; eagerness; feverishness; lust; animal passion.*

A man of the tribe of Judah (I Chron. 4:4).

Meta. The swiftness and vehemence of unrepressed desire. In its expression this desire becomes good or evil according to the thoughts by which it is directed.

Hushai, hū'-shāi (Heb.) — *hasty; quick; rapid; vehement emotion; arduous passion; eager appetite; feverish lust; animal heat.*

"The Archite," a friend of David's, who went to Absalom when that young man had rebelled against his father David and was trying to take the throne. Hushai gave Absalom unwise counsel purposely to lead to his defeat, which it did (II Sam. 15:32; 16:16-18; 17:5-15).

Meta. At this time David's love for physical beauty without spiritual understanding, which was illustrated in Absalom, had brought him into trouble. Metaphysically interpreted, this would refer to a time when we let our affections for the physical forms of life take up our whole attention to the exclusion of Spirit and to a disregard of divine law. In order to get back into spiritual consciousness we sometimes enlist the help of our friends, or higher thoughts of the outer man. They can meet other thoughts on the physical plane in their own manner, and so make a way for love (David) to return to its own place of rulership. Hushai represents the swift activity with which one of these outer thoughts carries out instructions of the ruling love ego (David). (See HUSHAH.)

Husham, hū'-shăm (Heb.)—*hasting; quick; fleeting; vehement; passionate; ardorous.*

A king of Edom. He was "of the land of the Temanites" (Gen. 36:34).

Meta. The hurried attitude of mind, relating to physical desire. This belongs to the outer consciousness and tends to confusion and disorder.

Hushathite, hū'-shăth-īte (fr. Heb.)— name for the dwellers in Hushah.

Sibbecai the Hushathite was one of David's valiant men (II Sam. 21:18). He was appointed captain over twenty-four thousand who served King David in the eighth month of each year (I Chron. 27:11). In II Samuel 23:27 he is called Mebunnai; at least it is supposed that these two men are the same.

Meta. A thought belonging to and springing from the Hushah thought and attitude of mind. (See HUSHAH.)

Hushim, hū'-shĭm (Heb.)—*the hastening; hasters; hustlers; people of haste; vehement people; passionate people.*

a Son of Dan (Gen. 46:23). b A Benjamite (I Chron. 7:12). c The wife of Shaharaim, a Benjamite (I Chron. 8:8).

Meta. An acceleration of thought activity (*hasters, people of haste*) in the judgment faculty in man (Dan) and in the active faith faculty (Benjamin). In the former, this accelerating of thought activity takes place in the reasoning or masculine phase of the justice consciousness only (Hushim of Dan was a man), while the latter is of the soul, feminine, as well as of the masculine (one of the Hushims of Benjamin was a woman). In all three the tendency is toward the carnal or physical. A good antidote for a hurried thought is to be found in Isaiah 28:16: "He that believeth shall not be in haste."

Hymenæus, hȳ-mĕ-næ'-ŭs (Gk.)—*God of marriage; hymeneal; wedding song; nuptials.*

A professing Christian who had thrown aside his faith and good conscience, and whom Paul had "delivered unto Satan," along with Alexander, "that they might be taught not to blaspheme" (I Tim. 1:20). Hymenæus and Philetus, by their error, had succeeded in overthrowing the faith of some others (II Tim. 2:17).

Meta. A seemingly religious and spiritual thought activity in consciousness that unifies itself with worldly reasonings about spiritual truths, and with the thoughts and desires of the outer man. This is known as the marriage of the church with the world; it leads the individual away from the Christ Truth, into apostasy and adversity.

hypocrite (Gk.)—*answer; answering voice; echo; interpreter; imitator; play-actor; dissembler; pretender; impostor.*

Meta. Hypocrite, in classic Greek, means an actor in a theater; so the word came to mean any one who pretended to be one thing while really he was something far different.

Appearing to be lovingly thoughtful for others, while thinking only of self and reputation, is to deserve only the reward of a hypocrite. No wise man would seek the reward of empty applause, which might satisfy the boastful giver. A modest man asks the approval of Spirit only (see Matt. 6:1-18).

I

I AM.

Meta. I AM is God's name in man; it is Jehovah, the indwelling Christ, the true spiritual man whom God made in His image and likeness. The outer, manifest man is the offspring of the I AM, or inner spiritual man. By use of I AM we link ourselves with outer seemings—or we make conscious union with the Father, with Spirit, with abiding life, wisdom, love, peace, substance, strength, power, Truth, the kingdom of the heavens within us.

The I AM always assures us that the preponderance of power is with the spiritual. Fear throws dust in our eyes and hides the mighty spiritual forces that are always with us. Blessed are those who deny ignorance and fear, and affirm the presence and power of the I AM. They behold the "mountain" (exaltation) "full of horses" (powerful forces) and "chariots of fire" (life energies) round about "Elisha" (spiritual I AM). (See II Kings 6:8-23.)

The I AM can also be explained as the metaphysical name of the spiritual self, as distinguished from the sensate self. One is governed by God; the other, by self. Christ is the Scriptural name for spiritual I AM. Jesus called it the Father. It is the Father of the personal will, and a conscious unity between the two must finally be made to preserve the one-

ness of creation. That is what is meant by the phrase, "he that doeth the will of my Father." We must do the very will of God in our will, which is virtually to surrender the whole man to God.

Spiritual character is the rock foundation of being. Build yourself into God and you will find yourself in heaven right here on earth. Let go the little self and take hold of the big Self: "Not my will, but thine, be done." The I AM of each individual is the will in its highest aspect. The will may be said to be the man, because it is the directive power that decides the character formation—which makes what we call individuality. (See CHRIST, JESUS, JEHOVAH, and JOSHUA.)

Ibhar, ĭb'-här (Heb.)—*whom he chooses; he desires; he approves; He (God) delights; he selects; he elects.*

One of David's sons (II Sam. 5:15).

Meta. Desire and the thing desired. The root of this word refers to the object in which the will is centered and wherein it delights—the thing desired as well as the inner subjective force that sets the will in motion.

Ibleam, ĭb'-lĕ-ăm (Heb.)—*jubilation of the people; victory of the people; he consumes the people; he afflicts the people; not of the people, i. e., foreigners.*

A city of Manasseh, near Gur (II Kings 9:27).

Meta. Understanding (Manasseh) established in zeal (Issachar) and joyous substance (Asher) brings about victory over error (*victory of the people;* "And Manasseh had in Issachar and in Asher . . . Ibleam and its towns.") In a victory there is always the destroying aspect— since the enemies are defeated, cast out —as well as the conquering side of Truth.

In this symbol of victory (Ibleam), however, the overcoming is not complete. Manasseh did not drive out the Canaanitish inhabitants of Ibleam (*not of the people,* i. e., *foreigners*), "but the Canaanites would dwell in that land. And it came to pass, when Israel was waxed strong, that they put the Canaanites to taskwork, and did not utterly drive them out" (Judg. 1:27, 28). This reveals in man the tendency to compromise with generation and sense. A degree of dominion is exercised, but the "mind of the flesh" is not fully overcome—the life forces are not really lifted up and redeemed from sense. Many persons in process of overcoming today are right in this place; they are halting between two opinions. They feel that old thoughts and habits have a necessary place in consciousness; they fear that a complete eradication of sense might be detrimental to their physical well-being, and so they do not attain the good that they might have.

Ibneiah, ĭb-nē'-ĭah (Heb.)—*Jehovah will build; Jah will erect; Jehovah will construct; Jah will rebuild.*

Son of Jeroham, a Benjamite (I Chron. 9:8).

Meta. The understanding or belief that the I AM, *Jehovah,* the indwelling Christ, established in love (Jeroham, father of Ibneiah, meaning *he will cherish, he will love*) and an active faith (Ibneiah was a Benjamite), works constructively in man's consciousness and will build up his organism in full expression or manifestation of spiritual Truth.

Ibnijah, ĭb-nī'-jăh (Heb.)—*Jehovah will build; Jah is builder; Jehovah will reconstruct.*

Father of Reuel, a Benjamite (I Chron. 9:8).

Meta. Virtually the same as Ibneiah. Belief in the constructive activity of I AM, Jehovah, in man's consciousness

brings about a fellowship and association with the Divine, a consciousness of God as friend (Reuel, Ibnijah's son, meaning *friendship of God, companion of God*), that is very strengthening and precious to the individual who gives it place.

Ibri, ĭb'-rī (Heb.)—*a Hebrew; one who passes over; one from the other side; one not of this world; an occultist.*

Son of Merari, of the tribe of Levi (I Chron. 24:27).

Meta. A *passing over* from the bitter, unhappy frame of mind and conditions that result from love expressed negatively, to a true comprehension and expression of the love faculty. (Levi signifies love, and Merari, the father of Ibri and son of Levi, signifies the bitterness and sorrow that results when the power of love is not established in a right understanding of Truth, but is directed by false notions such as a belief in righteous indignation and wrath, "an eye for an eye, and a tooth for a tooth," and "love thy neighbor, and hate thine enemy.") (See HEBREW and MERARI. See HEBER and EBER also, since the word Ibri has virtually the same meaning.)

Ibzan, ĭb'-zăn (Heb.)—*white; shining; brilliant; splendid; famous; tin.*

A judge of Israel (Judg. 12:8, 10).

Meta. The excellence (*splendid, famous*) of true judgment in man, established in substance. It becomes a reflection of light, or, rather, it emits the true light of Spirit, to the whole consciousness. (Ibzan was a judge of Israel, a judge referring to the faculty of judgment and discernment in the individual. He was of Beth–lehem; and Beth–lehem, *house of bread,* is the substance center.)

Ibzan does not give the thought of inherent light, but a perfect reflecting medium, therefore it might be said to signify the highly illumined intellect, or the intellect lifted to a consciousness in which it knows and radiates Spirit.

Ichabod, ĭch'-ă-bŏd (Heb.)—*where is honor?; glory is departed; nonglorious; inglorious; impoverished.* Chabod (without the prefix where? where is? non, not, in) means *abundance, substance, riches, wealth, honor, glory, splendor, majesty,* all of which are interrelated and can be used as definitions.

Son of Phinehas, Eli's son. "And she named the child Ichabod, saying, The glory is departed from Israel; because the ark of God was taken, and because of her father-in-law and her husband" (I Sam. 4:21). In the margin the meaning of Ichabod is given as, "There is *no glory.*"

Meta. The sense of defeat, of ignominy, that comes over man when he becomes aware of the fact that he has let his awakening faculties, which are in reality spiritual, be influenced by the selfishness of the personal man to the extent that he has seemingly lost out spiritually, for a time at least. The soul (mother of Ichabod, in despair over the death of her husband, and of her father-in-law, Eli the high-priest, and over the taking of the Ark of God by the Philistines) brings forth this *inglorious* one, Ichabod, and then dies. This seems to infer a breaking up of the whole consciousness. For further light on the matter see ELI, PHINEHAS, and the Ark of the Covenant, under ARK.

Iconium, ī-cō'-nĭ-ŭm (Gk.)—*image-like; likeness; likely; yielding; retiring; giving away; breast of sheep.*

A city of Lycaonia, in Asia Minor. Paul and Barnabas taught there for some time, and then had to flee to other cities because of the persecutions that were stirred up by the unbelieving Jews (Acts 14:1), though a great multitude of both Jews and Greeks in this city believed.

Meta. A group of thoughts of an imaging and receptive (tending to negativeness) character, in the emotional nature. (Lycaonia, meaning *wolfland, she-wolf,* represents the emotional nature swayed by the undisciplined, devouring, unredeemed thoughts of the animal man. See LYCAONIA.) In this group of thoughts, Iconium, the true light is beginning to break. While it is of the natural animal affections and emotions (*breast of sheep*), and is open to both good and error, it is coming gradually into its true Christ light and dominion, despite the apparent commotion that still takes place there at times.

We should watch our emotional nature. We should not think that the spiritual uplift that comes to us, and the great demonstrations that we make through divine power, are miraculous; if we do we are likely to be carried away with feeling and with appearances instead of remaining in conscious oneness with the Spirit of truth, with divine understanding. We should see that only the good and the true—that which is wise and reasonable from the standpoint of Spirit—are impressed upon this emotional nature of ours. Stability and poise of soul must be cultivated, that we may not be unduly influenced by every wave of thought that sweeps through our consciousness.

Idalah, ĭd'-ă-läh (Heb.)—*the exalted One; He (God) is exalted; memorial.*

A city of Zebulun (Josh. 19:15).

Meta. A group of thoughts belonging to the faculty of order (Zebulun relates to order) in man, which serves to keep God—the creator and source of all power—in remembrance (*He is exalted, memorial*).

This group of thoughts must become more active in the consciousness, that one may become outwardly conscious always of God's presence, and become fully awake and alive to one's possibilities—to one's spiritual inheritance and good.

Idbash, ĭd'-băsh (Heb.)—*brown,* i. e., *honey-colored; honey; syrup; sweetness; kneadable; soft; fatty; corpulent.*

A descendant of Judah. He was a son of the "father," or founder, of Etam (I Chron. 4:3).

Meta. A thought of love (*honey, sweetness*), pliability (*kneadable*), and substance (*fatty, corpulent*), more of the physical than of spiritual consciousness.

Iddo, ĭd'-dō (Heb.)—*timely; seasonable; opportune; favorable; festal; full-formed; voluptuous; beautiful; lovable,* i. e., *desirable.*

There are several Israelites by this name (I Chron. 27:21; Zech. 1:1; I Kings 4:14; II Chron. 9:29, and others).

Meta. True ideas (Israelites) of the order and fitness of things; that in man's higher consciousness which works to keep his thoughts and inner activities orderly, that all may fit into their various places and times (*timely, seasonable, opportune, favorable, desirable*).

idol.

Meta. A material form representing an idea. It is not idolatry to make idols, and worship with them, if the heart understands their significance; but if the understanding is without love, mere intellectual perception, then man "knoweth not yet as he ought to know."

Those who have the love of God quickened in their heart are not disturbed by idols. It makes no difference to them how many representatives there are of God, because their inmost being, the very heart of their existence, is centered in the consciousness of the One.

The fact is that every form and shape in existence is representative of God.

The Jews thought Jesus a sinner because He healed the sick on the Sabbath day. They made an idol of the day; He said the day was for the convenience of man, and He went into the field and plucked grain regardless of the "bad example" of His acts.

The true disciple of Christ does not pay so much attention to the influence that his acts will have upon others as he does to the leading of Spirit. When we are always thinking and looking to the effect of our life on those with whom we associate we soon merge our individuality into theirs, and we lose sight of our identity with God.

Idumæa, ĭd-ū-mæ′-à (Gk. fr. Heb.)— territory of Edom.

The Greek name for Edom; Idumæa is the land of Edom (Mark 3:8). In the American Standard Version, Edom is given instead of Idumæa, in most places.

Meta. See EDOM.

Igal (in A. V., I Chronicles 3:22, Igeal), ī′-găl (Heb.)—*He (God) will redeem; He will ransom; deliverer; avenger; God will avenge.*

a Son of Joseph, of the tribe of Issachar, one of the twelve spies (Num. 13:7). b A son of Nathan of Zobah, one of David's mighty men (II Sam. 23:36). A descendant of David and Solomon (I Chron. 3:22).

Meta. An awakening of man to the thought of his full deliverance from sin and its results, through the power of Spirit (*He will redeem, deliverer*), but with belief in God as a God of wrath and vengeance. In believing that wrath and vengeance belong to God and are necessary at times, one gives power to evil as well as to good. This belief weakens one's faith in the truth that his full redemption can take place now; it causes one to hesitate about going up boldly to possess the Promised Land. (Igal was one of the spies who discouraged the Israelites from going over into Canaan. He was one of those who did not think that the Israelites were strong enough at that time to drive out the inhabitants of Canaan, and so the Israelites wandered about in the wilderness for forty years, when it was not at all necessary. There are many people today who are doing likewise. They expect to attain to the full lifting up of their whole being into spiritual perfection and life, but they do not think they can do it now. They put it off until some future incarnation. Their belief in the power of evil is still too strong for them to undertake the putting away of materiality.)

Igdaliah, ĭg-dă-lī′-ăh (Heb.)—*Jehovah will bind; Jah will make strong; Jehovah will make great; Jehovah will magnify.*

"The man of God" (Jer. 35:4).

Meta. Lifting up in consciousness and magnifying the I AM, Jehovah, or Christ —the ideal man whom God made in His image and likeness—as one's true self. Each individual who does this becomes "the man of God" in expression and becomes truly strong and great.

Iim, ī′-ĭm (Heb.)—*overthrown; subversions; heaps of ruins; heaps of rubbish.*

A city of Judah (Josh. 15:29). It is the same place as Iyim and Iye–abarim.

Meta. Overthrow and destruction of, and dominion over, some error seeming.

Ijon, ī′-jŏn (Heb.)—*ruin; rubbish; heap,* i. e., of a ruin.

A city of Naphtali that was smitten by Benhadad, king of Syria (I Kings 15:20).

Meta. The deterioration (*ruin*) that results in man's consciousness when the ruling intellectual thought, which works only for the outer things of the sense life (Benhadad, king of Syria), utilizes the strength of mind and body (Naphtali), which should be exercised only in spiritual ways to the uplifting of the organism to its highest good.

Ikkesh, ĭk'-kĕsh (Heb.)—*perverse; subtle; plotting; ensnaring; wicked.*

A Tekoite. His son Ira was one of David's mighty men (II Sam. 23:26); Ira was captain of the twenty-four thousand who served David in the sixth month of each year (I Chron. 27:9).

Meta. Tekoa (*confirming, securing, pitching a tent, fixing*) represents a firm and abiding idea regarding man's organism. Ikkesh the Tekoite (a thought activity belonging to the Tekoa consciousness in the individual) is of a discerning, penetrating, ingenious, visioning character (*subtle*), yet is inclined to perversity. He is obstinate in clinging to certain kinds of deception and error (*perverse, plotting, ensnaring, wicked*). This thought activity, however, brings forth some good fruit. Ira, the son of Ikkesh (meaning *watcher, watchful*), becomes a member of David's guard, a mighty man. The thought power that Ira stands for partakes of the rare discriminating quality of that which Ikkesh represents, and so is a strong factor in protecting the ruling love faculty (David) in consciousness.

Ilai, ĭ'-lāi (Heb.)—*elevated; exalted; supreme; uppermost; highest; most high.*

"The Ahohite," one of David's mighty men (I Chron. 11:29). In II Samuel 23:28 he is called Zalmon.

Meta. Ahoah, from whom the Ahohites were descended, means *friend of Jah, brotherly.* The understanding that God is the one Father and that all men are brothers is very uplifting and exalting when accepted by the individual (Ilai). It elevates the consciousness to a higher level, and does much toward bringing about that great realization of oneness which must ultimately exist consciously between God and the whole universe.

Illyricum, ĭl-lўr'-ĭ-cŭm (Gk.)—*joy; rejoicing; exultation; high.*

A country north of Macedonia and on the east shore of the Adriatic. Paul "fully preached the gospel of Christ" from Jerusalem to Illyricum (Rom. 15:19).

Meta. The joy, gladness, and upliftment of thought that takes possession of the whole man, even to his outer con-

sciousness, when the gospel of Christ, the word of Truth, has been taught and declared throughout the entire being, from Jerusalem, the inner spiritual center, to the outermost phases of thought.

image, graven (Exod. 20:4).

Meta. Graven images of God are made by mental pictures. The thought of God as a great king in a place called heaven makes just such a material image in our thought realms, and we grow to believe in and worship such an imaginary being, instead of the true God, who is Spirit.

We are not to make graven images of our God, for every established idea will sometime have to give way in order that we may receive the Holy (whole) Spirit of God. The whole is greater than any formed part thereof.

Imla, ĭm'-là (Heb.)—*He (God) will fill; He will make full; He will complete; He will satisfy; He will make abundant; He will make plenteous.*

Father of Micaiah, who was a true prophet in the reign of Ahab, king of Israel, and Jehoshaphat, king of Judah (II Chron. 18:7). In I Kings 22:8, the name is spelled Imlah.

Meta. A perception of the truth that true satisfaction, complete wholeness, and abundance of every good are of and from God.

Immanuel, ĭm-măn'-ū-ĕl (Heb.)—*God with us; God is with us.*

A prophetic name of Jesus Christ (Isa. 7:14; Matt. 1:23). The Greek form is Emmanuel.

Meta. The consciousness that *God is with us* and we are one with Him. The understanding of how the "Word became flesh" in Jesus Christ and is now being made flesh in us even as it was in Him. "We shall be like him; for we shall see him even as he is" (I John 3:2).

Immer, ĭm'-mĕr (Heb.)—*bearing forth; bringing to the light; projecting; commanding; eloquent; loquacious; talkative.*

The name of several different Hebrew priests (I Chron. 24:14; Ezra 2:37, 59; Neh. 3:29; Jer. 20:1).

Meta. That in our natural religious tendencies (priests) which causes us to delight in talking much about Truth, in making an outward show of our religion, in giving "lip service" to God, rather than in really making the saving Truth practical in our everyday living.

When this tendency to loquaciousness is lifted to spiritual expression, it becomes a great factor for good to us and to the race. Taken in the thought realm, the ability to think readily and clearly and abundantly, if guided aright, aids greatly in *projecting*, bringing to light and into manifestation, the good that we idealize in mind. In its very highest sense, Immer is used with reference to the utterances of God Himself, or the revelations of Spirit.

Imna, ĭm′-nȧ (Heb.)—*He (God) will restrain; He will withhold; He will keep back.*

Son of Helem, an Asherite (I Chron. 7:35).

Meta. The belief, which seems to be firmly fixed in our old established religious thoughts, that our good is withheld from us by God. When a person who is under the old thought experiences lack, instead of knowing that he needs to strengthen himself in the Truth and to change some of his ideas he immediately feels that his prosperity is being kept from him for some reason known only to "a wise Providence." If he realizes joy and good he is always holding thoughts of limitation regarding them. The fact is, of course, that there is no limit to the goodness and fullness of God that should be expressed and manifested in the lives and affairs of men. By his limited thoughts and beliefs, man invokes the only limiting influences that there really are in his world at any time to bar his spiritual unfoldment. Every good that man can possibly think of and desire is his as he understands Truth and is obedient to the laws of Being.

Imnah (in A. V., Genesis 46:17, Jimnah), ĭm′-năh (Heb.)—*good fortune; prosperity.*

a Son of Asher (I Chron. 7:30). **b** A Levite (II Chron. 31:14).

Meta. A strong belief in and realization of abundant prosperity and every good as being man's true inheritance and the Father's will for him. (Kore, the son of the second Imnah that is men-

tioned, "was over the freewill-offerings of God, to distribute the oblations of Jehovah, and the most holy things." This was in the Temple, in Hezekiah's reign.)

Imrah, ĭm′-răh (Heb.)—*he is perverse; he is refractory; he is stubborn; he is rebellious; he is boastful; he extols himself.*

Son of Zophah, of the tribe of Asher (I Chron. 7:36).

Meta. The Adversary, or personal ambition and selfishness, the determination (perhaps almost unconscious) to exalt self, working in man's higher religious understanding.

Imri, ĭm′-rī (Heb.)—*shedding light; projecting thought; eloquent; commanding; discoursing; talkative.*

a A descendant of Perez, son of Judah (I Chron. 9:4). **b** Zaccur, the son of another Imri, helped to rebuild Jerusalem's wall (Neh. 3:2).

Meta. The *projecting* of *thought* outwardly toward expression; the ability to express one's ideas of Truth forcefully and clearly (*shedding light, eloquent*). This always tends to a degree of talkativeness that, if given way to in the personal, tends to dissipation of one's substance and life force.

One who is inclined to be a great talker should perceive the real spiritual gift that is at the source of this trait of character, and should guard against a mere outer flow of words from habit, with no permanent good to result from it. Such a one needs a deep consecration of this talent to Spirit and the realization of his own Christ dominion over himself, over his every thought and word.

incense, burning of.

Meta. The symbology of the burning of incense (Luke 1:9) is transmutation. The finer essences of the body are transmuted to what may be termed the fourth or radiant dimension, and a firm foundation laid for an organism of permanent character. Paul calls it the "celestial" body. This process takes place whenever the I AM makes union in the body with the Lord, or higher Self.

Burning "incense upon the altar of incense" (II Chron. 26:16) is the most delicate, secret process that goes on in the body. It is a process of transmutation: the animal nature goes through a refinement and is changed; the corruptible puts on incorruption. This is typified by the offerings to the Lord, made by the Israelites through the priests. The priests only can take part in this, because it requires spiritual understanding.

India, ĭn'-dĭ-à (fr. Sanskrit)—*land of sindhu; praise; murmur; whisper; occult; law.*

A country east of Persia. In Esther 1:1 and 8:9 we are told that Ahasuerus reigned over all the provinces from India to Ethiopia, a hundred and twenty-seven provinces in all.

Meta. Man's seemingly inherent belief in the occult. India always suggests the occult. It is to the east of Persia; therefore it belongs more to the within, east meaning within. *Murmur, whisper,* makes us think of something mysterious, secret, hidden. It may bring to our mind the thought of "wizards, that chirp and that mutter" (Isa. 8:19), though the occult that India signifies comes nearer to spiritual Truth and power, or comprehension and practice of the divine law, than does the error that is suggested in Isaiah 8:19. *Praise* and *law,* definitions of India, suggest an understanding and adoration of that which is of Spirit, of the law of Being.

inn (Luke 10:34).

Meta. One's pure thought; the price of the care received there is paid through overcoming.

intellect.

Meta. The realm of reflected light, or the understanding of the five-sense man who judges by appearances and reasons in the bounds of their limitation. The unredeemed intellect, because of its limited concepts, cannot grasp absolute Truth. It forms its conclusions from observation and study of relative conditions; therefore it discerns only relative truths. "The natural man [intellectual man] receiveth not the things of the Spirit of God: for they are foolishness unto him; and he cannot know them, because they are spiritually judged" (I Cor. 2:14).

intellectual understanding, compared to spiritual understanding.

Meta. Intellectual understanding is understanding gained from teachers and books or from some outer source.

Spiritual understanding is understanding that comes from the quickening of the Spirit of truth within man.

" . . . There is a spirit in man,
And the breath of the Almighty giveth them understanding."

Intellectual understanding is not always false. It may be true in degree, but it is limited to the intellect, and intellect of itself does not grasp universal Truth. It follows the letter and not the spirit, and has no quickening power. When it deals with religion it makes religion materialistic and formal.

The Spirit of truth is the source of true understanding as revealed by Jesus. "When he, the Spirit of truth, is come he shall guide you into all the truth." The Bible is not the source of spiritual understanding; the truths in it can be understood only by one who is under the inspiration of Spirit within himself. The Bible should be studied with the Spirit of truth as guide and teacher. Spirit will lead us back of the letter to the principles of Being and will help us to see the application of those principles to our own individual development.

Many differing sects are formed because the Bible, instead of the indwelling Spirit of truth, is taken as authority, thus producing intellectual instead of spiritual understanding.

Intellectual understanding cannot bring about the redemption of man's body because it does not have in it the intelligent principle that lays hold of the flesh with quickening, life-giving, transforming power. Only spiritual understanding can do this and establish a spiritual state of consciousness that will clothe itself with substance, thus forming the imperishable spiritual body.

intuition.

Meta. There is a wisdom of the heart; it is called intuition. It is very much surer in guidance than the head. When one trusts Spirit and looks to it for understanding, a certain confidence in the invisible good develops in the soul. This faith awakens the so-called sixth sense, intuition or divine knowing.

Iphdeiah (A. V., Iphedeiah), ĭph-dē'-

iăh (Heb.)—*whom Jehovah sets free; Jah will liberate; whom Jah ransoms; Jehovah will redeem.*

Son of Shashak, of the tribe of Benjamin (I Chron. 8:25).

Meta. An active faith (Benjamite) in the power and willingness of Jehovah, I AM, the indwelling Christ, to redeem, liberate, set free from every limitation and error. This faith is born of an intense desire for and love of Truth. (Shashak, the name of the father of Iphdeiah, means *vehement desire, eagerness, longing, yearning.*)

Ir, īr (Heb.)—*confluence; flowing together; welding; kneading; cementing; metropolis; city; encampment; watcher; watchtower; vision; heat; anger; wrath.*

A Benjamite, father of Shuppim and Huppim (I Chron. 7:12). In verse 7, Iri.

Meta. The *flowing together* and unifying (*welding, cementing*) of thoughts that are similar in character, to form a consciousness (*city, metropolis*) of watchfulness, of waiting on God and keeping the mind's eye centered on that which is high and spiritual, that a keen insight into Truth may be realized (*watcher, watchtower, vision*). Jesus said, "Take ye heed, watch and pray: . . . And what I say unto you I say unto all, Watch" (Mark 13:33, 37).

By continually looking within to Spirit as our light, our all, the true Christ vision or insight into Truth is opened to us. Without this vision, without spiritual understanding, and a keen foresight into the workings of the law, the law is not kept and error results (*heat, anger, wrath*), hence there is no sure reaping of abiding good (see Prov. 29:19).

Ira, ī'-rà (Heb.)—*wakeful; watchful; watcher; citizen; archangel.*

a A Jairite who was chief minister to David (II Sam 20:26). **b** Son of Ikkesh the Tekoite (II Sam. 23:26). **c** Ira the Ithrite (II Sam. 23:38).

Meta. A positive, watchful, prayerful, overcoming attitude of mind. This is a great protection to the individual who cultivates it. (See IKKESH.)

Irad, ī'-răd (Heb.)—*excitative movement; self-leading passion; blind whirling; courser; fugitive; wild ass; dragon.*

Son of Enoch and grandson of Cain (Gen. 4:18). This was not the Enoch who walked with God.

Meta. Irad belongs to the outer physical consciousness and organism of man. He is the summing up of the stubborn, foolish, destructive, devouring—yet transitory and fleeting—emotions and desires that are the result of sense man's ignorant, confused thoughts and beliefs. (See ARAD; the two names seem to be identical, and the meanings are the same.)

Iram, ī'-răm (Heb.)—*urban; citywise; congregation; civic body.*

A chief of Edom (Gen. 36:43). The Edomites were descended from Esau (see 40th to 43d verses).

Meta. A thought of the outer physical or body consciousness (Edom) that pertains to coöperation, to wisdom in dwelling beside and harmonizing with other thoughts. While this thought is of a ruling and directive character (a chief), it cannot work alone; it belongs to a group of thoughts, a consciousness (*congregation, civic body*).

Iri, ī'-rī (Heb.)—*urbanite; heat of the mind; watchful; citizen; vigilance; sentient light; sentient fire.*

Son of Bela and grandson of Benjamin (I Chron. 7:7).

Meta. Watchfulness and a coöperative trend of thought, but evidently inclined more toward the physical, or outer sense seeming, than toward spiritual reality.

Irijah, ī-rī'-jăh (Heb.)—*whom Jehovah sees; Jah will look upon; apprehension of Jehovah; reverence of Jehovah; fear of Jehovah.*

A captain, son of Shelemiah (Jer. 37:13). He accused Jeremiah of being in sympathy with the Chaldeans, and was instrumental in having him imprisoned.

Meta. Reverence, awe, developed to the point of fearfulness because of being mixed with the sensate, personal thought of God. The *fear* of the Lord, as we understand fear, is not the beginning of wisdom. Fear always tends to superstition, narrow-mindedness, and ignorance. A great reverence and respect for God, however, and for all things spiritual, with a deep, all-absorbing love for and adherence to the divine qualities of life, love, peace, wisdom, and Truth, does lead to greater and greater light. But *fear of Jehovah* (Irijah) leads to imprisonment of faith (Jeremiah) and to the paralyzing of the spiritual activities of the organism.

Ir–nahash, ĭr–nā'–hăsh (Heb.)—*city of Nahash; city of the serpent; city of covetous passion; city of insidious desires; city of magic; city of incantations.* (Nahash is the same word that is rendered "serpent" in Genesis 3:1.)

A city of Judah (I Chron. 4:12); the margin says, "*the city of Nahash.*"

Meta. Ir means *city,* and Nahash means *serpent, oracle,* that which reveals or foretells, warns. Nahash was a leader, or king, of the Ammonites. Ir–nahash signifies a group of thoughts in the life center in man (*serpent* refers to sense life and the Ammonites have their seat of action in the generative functions) that believes in wisdom (*serpent* also pertains to a subtle sense wisdom in man) and revelation (*oracle*) to be attained by means of experience in sense. When Judah takes possession of this city, its ideals are elevated by praise and prayer to a higher level, even to that of true spiritual understanding.

Iron, ĭ'–rŏn (Heb.)—*place of vision; place of piety; place of reverence; place of apprehension; place of terror.*

A fortified city of Naphtali (Josh. 19:38).

Meta. A consciousness of strength (Naphtali), but one not yet established in love. We always have a deep respect (reverence) for strength. If, however, the love faculty has not been awakened in us to any appreciable degree, if we have not come to know God as love and to realize the value of love's working in unison with strength, our ideas of strength are hard; they build up fear in us. Thus our consciousness of strength (Iron) becomes a *place of terror* instead of being an assurance of protection and good only. (The definitions of Iron show clearly how the positive *vision* falls into *terror* on the negative side.)

Irpeel, ĭr'–pê–ĕl (Heb.)—*whom God will heal; health of God; God will repair; God will restore; God will allay.*

A city of Benjamin (Josh. 18:27).

Meta. The natural restoring forces of the organism. This healing power that constantly works in man is spiritual; its activity becomes greatly accelerated when the consciousness of omnipresent wholeness becomes centered in faith in God (when Irpeel becomes a city of Benjamin).

Ir–shemesh, ĭr'–shē'–mĕsh (Heb.)—*city of the sun.*

A border city of Dan (Josh. 19:41).

Meta. See BETH–SHEMESH.

Iru, ĭ'–rŭ (Heb.)—*citizen; watcher; flux; flowing together; heat of the mind; vigilance; wrath; anger.*

Son of Caleb (I Chron. 4:15).

Meta. A *citizen* of, or thought belonging to, the same consciousness as Ir. (See IR.) It is that in us which is ever attentive to and zealous for what it understands to be Truth (*watcher, heat of the mind, vigilance*). This zealousness might easily turn into *wrath* or *anger* if the personal is too much in evidence in one's zeal.

Isaac, ĭ'–sãae (Heb.)—*He (God) laughs; He will laugh; laughter; joy; singing; leaping.*

Son of Abraham and Sarah (Gen. 18:9-15; 21:1-7).

Meta. Divine sonship. Isaac, meaning *laughter,* signifies the joy of the new birth and the new life in Christ, which is the spiritual consciousness of relationship to God the Father. Man rejoices greatly in his privilege of expressing as the son of God.

According to the text, Isaac was born after Sarah was past the age for bringing forth. Besides, she was barren, so that there was no possibility of his conception under the natural course of things. So we, when born of Spirit, are born, "not . . . of the will of the flesh, nor of the will of man, but of God." The natural man has no power to bring forth "the new man" in Christ Jesus. So Hagar's son could not be the chosen seed and heir. The new man is a "new creature," begotten by the divine seed, the Word. An entirely new state of consciousness is formed, fulfilling the admonition, let "Christ be formed in you."

When Isaac was weaned, Ishmael, Hagar's son, mocked him. This is the experience of every one in the new birth.

The thoughts that are the fruit of the "mind of the flesh" rise up within and mock the new man. Here the overcomer has a work to do. Hagar, the bondmaid, and her son must be cast out. Abraham grieves at this. So we sometimes grieve over giving up the fruits that we have brought forth in the natural-man consciousness.

Isaac was not noted for his achievements; he represents the serenity, peace, and joy that man has when he accepts spiritual things as real, and lives "as seeing him who is invisible."

Isaiah, ĭ-ṣa'-ĭăh (Heb.)—*Jehovah is salvation; help of Jah; Jehovah succors; deliverance of Jehovah; welfare of Jah; prosperity of Jehovah.*

Son of Amoz; he was a prophet during the reign of Hezekiah, king of Judah (II Kings 19:20; II Kings 20; and The Book of Isaiah).

Meta. The higher self (*Jehovah is salvation*), that in us which discerns the reality, the real character, of spiritual man, and fearlessly proclaims it; spiritual understanding.

After the dominating physical strength has lost its hold on the organism (King Uzziah died), the higher self (Isaiah; *Jehovah is salvation*) begins the purification of the body (Isa. 6:1-8).

Isaiah also signifies understanding of the truth that deliverance, abundant supply, spirituality, and all other forms of good come to man through Jehovah, the Christ, his higher self or spiritual I AM.

Iscah, ĭs'-căh (Heb.)—*who looks upon; scans abroad; discerns; watchful.*

Daughter of Haran, who was the brother of Abram (Gen. 11:29). Some think that Iscah is the same person as Sarah, Abram's wife.

Meta. The soul attentive to the things of Spirit (*watchful, who looks upon*). (See SARAH.)

Iscariot, ĭs-căr'-ĭ-ŏt (Gk. fr. Heb.)— *man of Kerioth; man of the cities; man of hostile encounters; man of conveniences.*

The surname of Judas, the disciple of Jesus who betrayed Him (Matt. 10:4; 26:14).

Meta. Kerioth was a city of Moab against which Jeremiah prophesied (Jer.

48:24, 41). Moab is the carnal mind. Judas Iscariot was the disciple of Jesus Christ who refers to the life faculty in man. Iscariot (*man of Kerioth, man of hostile encounters*), as the surname of Judas, signifies that the life faculty at this phase of overcoming is not fully redeemed from carnal thought and desire. (See JUDAS ISCARIOT.)

Ishbah, ĭsh'-băh (Heb.)—*he will praise; he will laud; he will soothe; he will appease; he will still.*

"Father of Eshtemoa," of the tribe of Judah (I Chron. 4:17).

Meta. The activity of the spirit of praise in man's consciousness (*he will praise*). The habit of praising God in times of seeming stress or trial brings one into a calm and quiet state of mind very quickly and causes one to sense an inner peace and satisfaction (*he will appease, he will soothe, he will still*).

Ishbak, ĭsh'-băk (Heb.)—*leaving; forsaking; freeing; emptying; exhausting.*

Son of Abraham, by Keturah, and founder of an Arabian tribe (Gen. 25:2).

Meta. The transitoriness of human ambition and its results. The achievements attained by human ambition are not permanent; they will pass away. (A tribe of Arabians was descended from Ishbak; Arabians represent undisciplined, roaming, unproductive thoughts.)

The meanings of the names of the six sons of Abraham and Keturah point to divided thought; they are partly good and partly of the sense mind—limited. The descendants of these sons became enemies of the Israelites. While the trend of thought that they represent may be helpful in degree to the natural man at a certain stage of his unfoldment, the time comes when they must be released from one's mind, that the real, true thoughts and activities (Israelites) may have full sway in the consciousness.

Ishbi–benob, ĭsh'-bĭ–bē'-nŏb (Heb.)— *my dwelling place is in Nob; my seat is in Nob; my dwelling is on the prominence; my abiding place is in the height.*

A son of Raphah, the giant; he tried to kill David, and it looked as though he were going to succeed, but Abishai came to David's help and killed Ishbi–benob (II Sam. 21:16).

Meta. Personality, the man of sense, exalting himself—the outer man of sense taking to himself the high place in consciousness that belongs to the spiritual man only.

Ish–bosheth, ĭsh–bō′-shĕth (Heb.)—*man of shame; bashful man; man of confusion; naked man; man of vanity; idolatrous man.*

Son of Saul. He was made king over a portion of Israel by Abner, but his rule did not last long (II Sam. 2:8). He is called Esh–baal in I Chronicles 8:33.

Meta. A remembrance of past errors remaining as a subconscious remorse or shame in mind. He rules part of the consciousness, but he is a weakling and his kingdom is insignificant. We should always be on the alert to put down this accusing conscience and place divine love (David) in its stead.

Ishhod (A. V., Ishod), ĭsh′-hŏd (Heb.) —*man of strength; man of vigor; man of exuberance; man of splendor; man of majesty; comely man; man of renown.*

Son of Hammolecheth, of the tribe of Manasseh (I Chron. 7:18).

Meta. When the soul is lifted up by prayer and spiritual thought (Hammolecheth, mother of Ishhod), Jehovah, the Christ, is exalted in consciousness and is given due honor and authority (*man of renown, man of splendor, man of majesty*). By thinking and speaking of the greatness, the power, the goodness, and the allness of the Christ, of Spirit, the individual builds up for himself true spiritual comeliness—a strength and joy and beauty of character, and of outer form also—that is enduring because it is founded in Spirit. Such a one becomes a *comely man,* a *man of strength, of vigor, of exuberance.* It is a truth that one grows to be like that on which his thoughts and desires dwell.

Ishi, ĭsh′-ī (Heb.)—*my luminous principle; my man; my husband.* (See also the ISHI that follows this one.)

"And it shall be at that day, saith Jehovah, that thou shalt call me Ishi, and shalt call me no more Baali" (Hos. 2:16). In the margin, "*my husband*" is given in place of Ishi, and "*my master*" in place of Baali.

Meta. The foregoing text is prophetic of the time into which we are now coming, the time when we shall realize and demonstrate that we are no longer servants of God, but are His sons. This is the time when the marriage of the Lamb shall have taken place in our consciousness, and we shall have entered into the abiding realization of our oneness with God, our perfect union with the indwelling Christ, the time when wisdom and love shall have been made one in us. Spirit is then to us our positive illuminating principle, our wisdom, our *husband* (Ishi), and we no longer see in God and in Christ a *master* (Baali), for we "shall be sons of the Most High."

Ishi, ĭsh′-ī (Heb.)—*deliverance; help; saving; salvation; salutary; safety; welfare; prosperity.* This Ishi is in no way related to the preceding one, which is spelled differently in the Hebrew.

a Two men of Judah (I Chron. 2:31; 4:20). **b** A man of Simeon (I Chron. 4:42). **c** A man of Manasseh (I Chron. 5:24).

Meta. The inner acknowledgment of God, Spirit, as health for the whole man (*salutary* means "promoting health; wholesome; healthful"; salutary and healthy are synonyms). This understanding leads to true and full *deliverance, salvation.* By means of prayer and praise (Judah), attention and obedience to the things of Spirit (Simeon), and understanding (Manasseh) we come into a realization of the divine presence as wholeness, as supply (*prosperity*), as the source of our every good (*welfare*). (See also the ISHI that precedes this one.)

Ishma, ĭsh′-má (Heb.)—*high; elevated; upright; brilliant; marvelous; laid waste; desolation; ruin.*

A descendant of Judah (I Chron. 4:3). He was a son of the "father" or founder of Etam.

Meta. Ishma reveals the outcome of Truth expressed in one's consciousness and life; it also reveals the result of giving way to thoughts and activities such as those which are symbolized by Etam. (See ETAM.)

Ishmael, ĭsh′-má-ĕl (Heb.)—*whom God hears; understanding of God; whom God understands; who is obedient to God.*

Son of Abraham by Sarah's Egyptian handmaid, Hagar (Gen. 16:11).

Meta. The fruit of the thoughts of the natural man at work in the flesh. (See Paul's interpretation of the allegory concerning Abraham, Sarah, Isaac, Hagar, and Ishmael, in Galatians 4:21-31.) However, *God hears* even the outer, personal man, since he too must be redeemed from error and corruption (see Genesis 21:17).

Ishmael could also be said to signify the consciousness that recognizes God but, because of the seeming opposition of the outer world, does not express according to the highest standard. In other words Ishmael represents personality. Personality has its real source in I AM, but goes wrong in its activity. In its struggle to attain light, understanding, in contacting the outer or manifest world, it becomes involved in error.

Ishmaelites, ĭsh'-mà-ĕl-ītes (fr. Heb.) —*of* or *belonging to Ishmael.*

Descendants of Ishmael (Gen. 37:25).

Meta. Thoughts and states of consciousness belonging to that in man for which Ishmael stands. (See ISHMAEL.)

Ishmaiah (A. V., I Chronicles 12:4, Ismaiah), ĭsh-mā'-ĭǎh (Heb.)—*whom Jehovah hears; understanding of Jah; whom Jehovah understands; who is obedient to Jehovah; obeying the Lord.*

a Son of Obadiah. He was over the tribe of Zebulun, for service, in David's reign (I Chron. 27:19). b A Gibeonite who came to David at Ziklag, "a mighty man among the thirty" (I Chron. 12:4).

Meta. Active, controlling thoughts of serving and overcoming that are attentive and obedient to the inner spiritual ideals (*obeying the Lord*). They hear and heed the voice of Spirit, and are heard by Jehovah (*whom Jehovah hears*); their desires reach the heart of God and are fulfilled.

"The eyes of Jehovah are toward the righteous,
And his ears are *open* unto their cry."

Ishmerai, ĭsh'-mē-rāi (Heb.)—*whom Jehovah keeps; protection of Jah; preservation of Jehovah; preservative; observance.*

A chief man of Benjamin, one of those who were "heads of fathers' *houses*

throughout their generations" (I Chron. 8:18, 28).

Meta. Active, obedient faith (*observance;* a chief man of Benjamin) as a saving, protecting, sustaining quality (*preservative, whom Jehovah keeps*) in individual consciousness.

Ishpah (A. V., Ispah), ĭsh'-pǎh (Heb.) —*firm; strong; scratched; scraped; made smooth; polished; excellence; bald; bare,* i. e., *as a bone; jasper stone; worn; wasted; excess.*

A Benjamite chief (I Chron. 8:16, 28).

Meta. A leading faith thought in consciousness (a chief man of Benjamin) producing excellence, firmness, and strength (*firm, strong*). The working out of the definitions of Ishpah, however, show a wearing out tendency, or a tendency to dissipation, through use, instead of an increase of strength and all good. This is because the individual at this stage of his development does not comprehend clearly the omnipresent fullness of life, substance, and spiritual Truth. Life and good are abiding, and will increase daily in man's consciousness as he learns to abide in the inner truth of Being and quit throwing his forces to the outer, in his activities.

Ishpan, ĭsh'-pǎn (Heb.)—*firm; strong; scratched; scraped; made smooth; polished; excellence; bald; bare,* i. e., *as a bone; jasper stone; worn; wasted; excess.*

A chief of the tribe of Benjamin (I Chron. 8:22).

Meta. Faith (a Benjamite chief), a firm, unwavering place in consciousness, but tending to a belief in wearing out and dissipation of strength, through activity—the same as ISHPAH, which see.

Ishvah (A. V., Ishuah), ĭsh'-vǎh (Heb.)—*he will liken to; resembling (another); equal to; self-answering; self-satisfying; equality; plainness; bowed down; level; even; smooth; tranquil; quiet.*

Son of Asher (Gen. 46:17).

Meta. The highest significance is that true poise, peace, and equableness (*equality, level, smooth, tranquil, quiet*) come from within man's own true spiritual self when he realizes that he is made in the likeness of God (*resembling another, he will liken to*); when he comes to know that in truth he is one with the Divine, and becomes assured that he will manifest this in the outer in due time. "Ye therefore shall be perfect, as your heavenly Father is perfect" (Matt. 5:48). "We shall be like him; for we shall see him even as he is" (I John 3:2). We are no longer servants, but friends (John 15:15), and sons (Gal. 4:6).

The thought of *self-answering, self-satisfying*, is also brought out in this name. This suggests the truth that as we become conscious of the source of all understanding within us, which is Spirit, we find within ourselves the answer to all our questionings, the satisfaction of all our desires; we can draw on the Holy Spirit within us for all the understanding that we need and desire.

". . . There is a spirit in man,
And the breath of the Almighty giveth
        them understanding" (Job 32:8).
In the King James, or Authorized, Version, "inspiration" is given in place of "breath."

Ishvi (in A. V., Genesis 46:17, Isui; in Numbers 26:44, Jesui; in I Chronicles 7:30, Ishuai; in I Sam. 14:49, Ishui), ĭsh'-vī (Heb.)—*resemblance; likeness; equality; self-satisfaction; plainness; evenness; tranquillity; quietness.*

a Son of Asher (Gen. 46:17). **b** Son of Saul (I Sam. 14:49).

Meta. Virtually the same as ISHVAH, which see. As a son of Saul, Ishvi signifies a sense of equilibrium and poise (*evenness, tranquillity, quietness*) in man, but more personal and limited in its character than it is spiritual (Saul, father of Ishvi, and first king of Israel, represents the will's functioning in personality rather than in Spirit). *Self-satisfaction* in this name would tend to egotism.

Ismachiah, ĭs-mă-chī'-ăh (Heb.)—*whom Jehovah upholds; whom Jah sustains; refreshed by Jehovah; who lays hold of Jah; cleaving to the Lord.*

A Levite; he was an overseer in the Temple service, during the reign of Hezekiah (II Chron. 31:13). He was one of the overseers over the oblations, tithes, and dedicated things that were brought by the people of Judah to the Temple.

Meta. *Cleaving to the Lord*, joined to Spirit—man in his true, inner, spiritual consciousness sensing his oneness with the Divine and holding faithfully to God as his support and supply. "Man shall not live by bread alone, but by every word that proceedeth out of the mouth of God." Man is strengthened and sustained both within and without by spiritual substance and by the sustaining power, love, and Truth of Spirit. (See CONANIAH.)

Israel, ĭṣ'-rå-ĕl (Heb.)—*contending for God; striving for God; who prevails with God; a prince with God; dominion with God; rulership with God.* The idea is a development out of that of contending with and prevailing over anything whatever.

a Jacob's name was changed to Israel after he had wrestled with "a man" all night at "the ford of the Jabbok," and had succeeded in obtaining a blessing. "And he said, Thy name shall be called no more Jacob, but Israel: for thou hast striven with God and with men, and hast prevailed. . . . And he blessed him there" (Gen. 32:28, 29). **b** Israel is the nation that sprang from Abraham, Isaac, and Jacob, through Jacob's twelve sons (Gen. 49:28).

Meta. The significance of the changing of Jacob's name to Israel is this: The mind controls the body through the nerves, and a great nerve, the sciatic, runs down the leg through the hollow of the thigh. The will acts directly through this nerve and when the individual, through his mentality or understanding (Jacob), exercises his I AM power upon the natural man in an attempt to make unity between Spirit and the divine-natural, there is a letting go of human will (Jacob's thigh is out of joint). A great light of understanding breaks in the struggling soul when it discovers that there is a divine-natural body, and it clings to that inner life and strength and eventually brings it to the surface in perpetual vigor. This is the significance of the blessing and the new name, Israel (one who has power with God and man, spiritual and material).

If you are like Jacob (*supplanter*, one who is journeying from place to place to find satisfaction) counting the past and looking to the future, change your attitude to that symbolized by Israel, and find peace in the Lord's reality.

Israel as a nation, in its highest significance, symbolizes spiritual consciousness. The thoughts that have been wrought in Truth and righteousness make the spiritual mind, or spiritual consciousness (Israel).

In Numbers 21:1-3 Israel represents the reality of spiritual ideas in consciousness; the Canaanite represents the elemental life forces in subconsciousness. Through Israel the Canaanites are delivered unto Jehovah, or come under the law of Spirit and are transmuted into spiritual energy.

Isaiah 19:23, 25 symbolically describes the unification of seemingly material substance (Egypt) and the psychic forces (Assyria) under the control of spiritual thought (Israel).

"Israel" (a prince with God) is the real of man, that consciousness which is founded in God. It requires the story of Israel from Abraham to Jesus Christ to picture the growth and spiritualization of the whole man. The unfoldment and lifting into full spiritual consciousness includes the body of man, which must be unified with soul and spirit in Christ, that it may take on and manifest the true spiritual substance and character idealized of God in the beginning for man. In spirit, soul, and body each of us must come into the perfect expression of Godlikeness.

Faith is the foundation faculty or power in mind, through which spiritual man is brought forth. If you will read about Abraham, from whom the children of Israel are descended, you will see at once that he typifies faith.

Saul, the first king of Israel, represents the personal will. When the personal will does not recognize the right of I AM or Christ to rule, and does not make a union with wisdom and love, it becomes very obstinate and acts unwisely. Thus Saul brought great trouble to himself and his subjects, and had to give place to a higher phase of consciousness —was succeeded by David.

Animals represent certain physical qualities in the organism. Horses stand for vitality; oxen, for strength; and so forth. A mule typifies some very stubborn phase of the personal man. In the case of David it depicts the obstinacy of the personal will (Saul), over which David gained dominion.

David, who represents love (heart), makes a union with wisdom (top head). The human will is unified with the divine will and so is guided by love and wisdom. Thus David rides on, or has dominion over, the mule—the obstinacy of personal will. From this union of love and wisdom, the feminine and masculine principles within man, Solomon (peaceful, the wisdom consciousness) is brought forth into kingship. He reigns in peace, exercises wisdom, and builds the Temple— the body. He is the natural offspring or outcome of David's overcoming, and he judges wisely in ruling the people of Israel (the ideas that make up the real consciousness in man).

The uplifting and redeeming of the entire man is not complete until man is born of Spirit and Jesus Christ comes to perfection in and through him. The spiritual body, which is the perfect-idea body in each of us, enters into the very cells of the seemingly physical body until the physical man manifests the real spiritual substance, intelligence, and life that underlie every form. It is through Spirit within us, the Christ or real self, that the intellect is quickened and Truth is established in consciousness. Jesus Christ was of the house of David (love) and He brought the law of love to perfect fruition. He also quickened all His faculties and powers. This process is typified by the calling of the twelve disciples, who, individually, represent different spiritual qualities. The twelve sons of Jacob are the first or natural bringing forth of the faculties, which culminate in a higher expression in the twelve disciples of Jesus.

Israelites, ĭş′-rȧ-ĕl-ītes (fr. Heb.)— descendants of Jacob; belonging to one of the tribes of Israel.

Descendants of Jacob, or Israel (Exod. 9:7; II Kings 3:24; Rom. 11:1).

Meta. The illumined thoughts in consciousness, which are undergoing spiritual discipline. They are the total of our religious thoughts. In the beginning of our journey from sense consciousness to spiritual consciousness, from Egypt to the Promised Land, not all these religious thoughts are awake to spiritual Truth, but among them are the highly illumined ideas and faculties that the many inspired leaders, judges, prophets, and kings of Israel represent.

The Israelites represent the thoughts in us that belong to the Israel consciousness; they typify that in us which is always endeavoring to follow the inner leading of the divine law. They are our spiritual thoughts, the thoughts that pertain to the real and enduring ideas upon which man and the universe are founded.

The purpose of the spiritual thoughts in the body (Children of Israel down in Egypt) is to raise it up, gradually to infuse into it a more enduring life and substance. When you affirm the spirituality of your body and yearn for its release from bondage to material belief, you are making demands on Pharaoh, and in fear that he will all at once lose his hold on life he hardens his heart, and sometimes the Lord, the universal law of equilibrium, hardens it for him. Then there seems a failure to attain that which you have tried to demonstrate. But a step has been taken in the all-round evolution of the body, and you will find that you are gradually becoming stronger both physically and spiritually.

The Israelites in Egyptian slavery represent thoughts that once had the illumination of Spirit, but that have gone down into, and have become obscured by, matter and material conditions.

The army of the Israelites represents an aggregation of thoughts in the mind of every individual—thoughts that know Truth and strive to follow it. The army of Truth is made up of spiritual, invisible forces.

The strong point of the Israelites was their faith in the one God.

"The lost sheep of the house of Israel" (Matt. 10:6) are the spiritual thoughts unaware of their real character.

The disciples were instructed to go to the lost sheep of the house of Israel, and not to the Gentiles or to the Samaritans, because the thoughts and the people that have a knowledge of Spirit are the first to be redeemed and taught Truth. Here is where man's greatest spiritual power is first developed. Afterward he will find a way to redeem the Gentiles—his sense thoughts.

Israelitish, ĭş'-râ-ĕl-ĭ-tĭsh (fr. Heb.)—*of* or *pertaining to Israel.*

Pertaining to the Israelites; in Leviticus 24:10, a woman of Israel.

Meta. Pertaining to Israel, or to the Israelites; in this instance a religious thought activity that belongs to the soul in man.

Issachar, ĭs'-să-ehär (Heb.)—*he will bring reward; there is reward; who brings recompense; who brings hire,* i. e., *compensation.*

Son of Jacob and Leah (Gen. 30:17, 18). "And God hearkened unto Leah, and she conceived, and bare Jacob a fifth son. And Leah said, God hath given me my hire, because I gave my handmaid to my husband: and she called his name Issachar."

Jacob's blessing upon Issachar was (Gen. 49:14, 15):
"Issachar is a strong ass,
Couching down between the sheepfolds:
And he saw a resting-place that it was good,
And the land that it was pleasant;
And he bowed his shoulder to bear,
And became a servant under taskwork."
Moses' blessing upon this tribe was connected with the blessing that he gave to Zebulun; it reads (Deut. 33:18, 19):
"Rejoice, Zebulun, in thy going out;
And, Issachar, in thy tents.
They shall call the peoples unto the mountain;
There shall they offer sacrifices of righteousness:
For they shall suck the abundance of the seas,
And the hidden treasures of the sand."
Meta. Issachar (*hire, reward,* a strong ass, subject to taskwork, possess the hidden treasures of the sand, rejoice in thy tents) represents active zeal, substance of earth.

Isshiah (in A. V., I Chronicles 7:3, Ishiah), ĭs-shī'-ăh (Heb.)—*whom Jehovah lends; borrowed of Jah; Jehovah will lend.*

a A Levite chief, of the sons of Rehabiah (I Chron. 24:21). **b** Another Levite (I Chron. 24:25). **c** A chief man of Issachar (I Chron. 7:3).

Meta. That in our awakened consciousness which recognizes God, through Jehovah, I AM, as lending, or giving, Himself —love, life, intelligence, strength, power, substance, all the principles of Truth— to our use.

The thought suggested by Isshiah, that Jehovah only *lends* to us, also implies the truth that no one can ever really get something for nothing. Something must be given always in return. This is true even concerning our salvation. Life and all good are free gifts from God, yet in order that we may consciously make this good ours in its fullness, so that we can make practical use of it, we have a price to pay. This price is the complete giving up of the lesser self with all that pertains to it. To the degree that we actually let go of the limited, personal man in us we realize and demonstrate our inherent divine perfection, no more and no less.

Italian, ĭ-tăl′-ĭăn—*belonging to Italy.*

A native of Italy, a Roman citizen, no doubt, "Cornelius by name, a centurion of the band called the Italian *band*" (Acts 10:1).

Meta. A thought belonging to the state of consciousness in man that Italy stands for. (See ITALY.)

Italy, ĭt′-ă-lў—*kingdom of Italus; island of the fish,* or *of the lamb.*

A country in southern Europe (Acts 18:2).

Meta. Strength. Fish refer to increase of ideas, and lamb refers to the natural life of the organism. The strength that Italy signifies would be of both mind (intellect, or outer reason, here) and body. (Italy as mentioned in the New Testament is the Italy of the Roman period rather than Italy as it is today.)

Ithai, ĭ′-thāi (Heb.)—*nearness; companionate; with (God); being; existence; oneself; the same; selfsameness; reality.*

"Son of Ribai of Gibeah of the children of Benjamin," a mighty man of the armies, in David's reign (I Chron. 11:31). He is called Ittai in II Samuel 23:29.

Meta. Because God is, I am (*being, existence*). The awakening of man's inner consciousness to the understanding of his eternal existence in Being, to the knowledge that he has been *with God* from the beginning, "before the mountains were brought forth . . . even from everlasting to everlasting."

Ithamar, ĭth′-ă-mär (Heb.)—*island of palms; palm coast; palm island; land of palms; as the palm tree.*

Youngest son of Aaron (Exod. 6:23).

Meta. A consciousness of victory, triumph (palms being symbolical of victory and triumph, while a land or island refers to a state of consciousness).

Ithiel, ĭth′-ĭ-ĕl (Heb.)—*God is with me; God is; God is my being; God is reality; God is Himself; with God; God has arrived.*

a A Benjamite whose descendants returned from the Babylonian captivity (Neh. 11:7). **b** A name mentioned in Proverbs 30:1.

Meta. An awakening to the Christ consciousness of oneness with the Father: "Even as thou, Father, *art* in me, and I in thee, that they also may be in us" (John 17:21).

Ithmah, ĭth′-măh (Heb.)—*bereavement; orphanage; an orphan; fatherless; lonesome; alone.*

A Moabite who is mentioned as having been one of David's mighty warriors (I Chron. 11:46).

Meta. Moab represents the carnal mind. One meaning of *orphanage* is the state of being an orphan, and *an orphan* is a child who has lost its parents. *Bereavement* also refers to a state of being bereft of some near relative or dear friend by death. Ithmah, the Moabite, one of David's guard of mighty men, therefore would symbolize a positive love thought (David symbolizing love) in consciousness that has been made pure and has been separated from its old carnal beliefs and desires. It has been bereft of its carnal relatives and seeming sources of existence, and has been transplanted into different surroundings, has been given different expression. It now contributes its substance and strength to the guarding and building up of the real and the true.

Ithnan, ĭth'-năn (Heb.)—*constant; perennial; permanent; strong; firm; consistent; extended; excellent; bestowed; given.*

A city of Judah, "toward the border of Edom in the South" (Josh 15:23).

Meta. A group of thoughts of firm, steady, upright character (*strong, firm, consistent, constant, permanent*) in the subconscious mind, and working toward expression in the body consciousness ("toward the border of Edom in the South," south referring to the subconscious mind, and Edom to the outer, or the body). This group of thoughts is also broad and comprehensive (*extended*), thus giving to the individual a larger understanding of his true source and place in being, as well as giving him more strength and endurance. Thus it does its part in making the whole man, and especially the outer and seemingly physical, more abiding and spiritual.

Ithra, ĭth'-rȧ (Heb.)—*redundance; abundance; more than enough; excellence; preëminent; residue; that which is left over; surplus; ample.*

Father of Amasa. He was evidently an Ishmaelite, though in the text he is called an Israelite (II Sam. 17:25, see margin also); in I Chronicles 2:17 he is called "Jether the Ishmaelite."

Meta. Ishmaelites are descendants of Ishmael, and signify thoughts that are the fruit of the personal or mortal in man. Ithra, however, meaning *excellence, preëminent, redundance, surplus,* is a prominent thought belonging to the Ishmael consciousness in man, or springing from this consciousness seemingly; but because of its great superiority over its fellow thoughts, because of its excellence, its true worth, and abundant substance that even surpasses its need, it becomes classed with the true spiritual thoughts (Israelites). It enters into a union with the phase of the soul that signifies that joy comes from God; it enters into the realization of divine joy (Ithra married David's sister Abigail, meaning *father of joy*). Joy and abundance are always closely associated. The joyful soul is the abundantly wealthy soul, in the truest significance of substance and wealth.

Ithran, ĭth'-răn (Heb.)—*redundant; abundant; excellent; plenty; preëminent.*

a Son of Dishon, who was a chief of the Horites (Gen. 36:26). b A man of the Israelitish tribe of Asher (I Chron. 7:37). This latter Ithran is thought to be the same person as the Jether of I Chronicles 7:38.

Meta. Ideas of great *excellence* and of great value; thoughts that are superior to their fellows, working in both the seemingly deep-seated sense (Horite) consciousness in the individual and in his more spiritual phase of mind (the Israelites). These ideas have taken on abundant substance; they believe in bountiful supply, and they lead to *plenty.*

Ithream, ĭth'-rē-ăm (Heb.)—*abundance of the people; people of plenty; people of excellence; remnant of the people; residue of the people; survival of the people.*

A son of David, born in Hebron; his mother's name was Eglah (II Sam. 3:5).

Meta. There still survives in every individual an inherent belief that the power of that which is good and true far exceeds in value and worth all other seeming powers. (*People* symbolize thoughts, and *remnant,* or *residue,* refers to something that survives or remains. Even so, any one who will watch his inner thoughts will find an inherent belief in the good at work in his consciousness.)

Ithrite, ĭth'-rīte (fr. Heb.)—*of or belonging to Jether;* name applied to the descendants of Jether or Ithra.

Two men of David's guard were Ithrites, Ira and Gareb (II Sam. 23:38). (See I Chronicles 2:53.)

Meta. A thought springing from and resembling that in consciousness for which Jether stands. (See JETHER, ITHRA, and GAREB.)

Ittai, ĭt'-tāi (Heb.)—*nearness; companionate; with (God); being; existence; oneself; the same; selfsameness; reality.*

"The Gittite," a friend of King David's (II Sam. 15:19-22). David put him at the head of one third of the army that he sent out to fight Absalom (II Sam. 18:2). Another Ittai was "the son of Ribai of Gibeah of the children of Benjamin" (II Sam. 23:29); he was a member of David's guard, and is called Ithai in I Chronicles 11:31.

Meta. Like Ithai: the awakening of that within man which is ever conscious of his existence in Being, of his relationship to God. (See ITHAI.)

Ituræa, ĭt-û-ræ'-ȧ (Gk. fr. Heb.)— *land of Jetur.* See JETUR.

A province in the Northeast of Palestine, its name having been derived from Jetur, a son of Ishmael. Philip, brother of Herod, was tetrarch of this place when John the Baptist was preaching in Judea (Luke 3:1).

Meta. A state of consciousness, or group of thoughts, with its activities, that is of the Jetur character. (See JETUR.) It has high ideals but limits them in their growth and expression by encircling or inclosing them with narrow-minded rules and regulations. According to the belief of the sense mind in us, our high ideals should be well guarded, since, if too much freedom is given them to grow and express, we might become somewhat "queer" in the eyes of the world.

Ivvah (A. V., Ivah), ĭv'-vȧh (Heb.)— *overturning; useless; perversity; iniquity; turned upside down; the god Iva or Ava.*

The same as Avva, which see (II Kings 18:34; Isa. 37:13; in II Kings 17:24, Avva).

Meta. See AVVA.

Iye–abarim (A. V., Ije–abarim) ĭ'-yĕ-ȧb'-ȧ-rĭm (Heb.)—*ruins of Abarim.*

The same place as Iim and Iyim (Num. 33:44, 45).

Meta. See IIM and ABARIM.

Iyim (A. V., Iim), ĭ'-yĭm (Heb.)— *perverted; ruins; subverted; overthrown; heaps; rubbish.*

The same place as Iim (Num. 33:45).

Meta. See IIM.

Izhar (in A. V., Numbers 3:19, Izehar), ĭz'-här (Heb.)—*shine; glitter; come forth; become manifest; light; oil,* i. e., *latent light principle; anointed; high prosperity; happiness.*

Son of Kohath, who was one of Levi's sons (Exod. 6:18).

Meta. Spiritual understanding manifesting as true understanding in individual consciousness, and tending to happiness and prosperity, true riches.

Izharites (in A. V., Numbers 3:27, Izeharites), ĭz'-här-ītes (fr. Heb.).

Levites, descendants of Izhar (I Chron. 26:23). "Of the Izharites, Chenaniah and his sons were for the outward business over Israel, for officers and judges" (I Chron. 26:29); this was in David's reign.

Meta. Thoughts that spring from and belong to that in consciousness which Izhar represents. (See IZHAR.)

Izrahiah, ĭz-rȧ-hī'-ȧh (Heb.)—*whom Jehovah brings forth; Jehovah will rise as the sun; Jah will shine forth; Jehovah is the glory,* i. e., *of God; Jehovah is light.*

Son of Uzzi, of the tribe of Issachar (I Chron. 7:3).

Meta. The Christ mind, or spiritual understanding, shining brilliantly and clearly in and through the consciousness of the individual. This is made possible by an inner realization of divine strength (Uzzi, meaning *Jah is strong*) established in and actuated by a very active zeal (Issachar) for Truth, for the highest.

Izrahite, ĭz'-rȧ-hīte (fr. Heb.)—*of or belonging to Zerah.*

Shamhuth the Izrahite was captain of the course of twenty-four thousand that served King David in the fifth month of each year (I Chron. 27:8). An Izrahite was a descendant of Judah's son Zerah.

Meta. A thought springing from and belonging to that in consciousness which Zerah signifies. (See ZERAH and SHAMHUTH.)

Izri, ĭz'-rī (Heb.)—*forming; fashioning; framing; making; imagination; thought; purpose; create in form; Creator.*

Leader of the fourth course of singers for service in the Temple during David's reign (I Chron. 25:11; in the 3d verse of the same chapter he is called Zeri.)

Meta. Thought, imagination, based upon Principle (*Creator*), upon spiritual Truth and harmony, as the power that makes all forms, that brings the outer man into existence as a manifest being (*fashioning, framing, making;* thought is the formative power in man, and all thinking should be based upon Principle, Truth). (See ZERI.)

J

Jaakan (A. V., Jakan), jā'-ă-kăn (Heb.)—*keen; acute; wrestling; twisted; perverted; keen of vision; intelligent.*

Son of Ezer, a descendant of Seir (I Chron. 1:42). In Genesis 36:27 he is called Akan. He was the "father" of Bene–jaakan (Num. 33:1; Deut. 10:6).

Meta. See AKAN and see BENE–JAA-KAN.

Jaakobah, jā-ă-kō'-băh (Heb.)—*the Jacob; that Jacob;* another form of Jacob with the definite article: *the supplanter; the deceiver; the lier in wait.*

A prince of Simeon, an influential and prosperous man (I Chron. 4:36).

Meta. Jaakobah, like Jacob, pertains to the mental in man, which must supplant the animal, the fleshly, in consciousness, or, the spiritual, which must in turn take the place of the purely mental. (See JACOB.)

Jaala, jă-ā'-lă (Heb.)—*going up; ascending; surmounting; reaching the summit; wild mountain goat; ibex; grace; beauty.*

A servant of Solomon's, whose "children" or descendants returned from the Babylonian captivity with Zerubbabel (Neh. 7:58). In Ezra 2:56, Jaalah.

Meta. The lifting up (*going up, ascending*) of the adverse, reasoning, and animal phases in man to a higher and more spiritual phase of activity, wherein they can serve the Solomon rule (peace and wisdom) in consciousness.

When a ruler of Israel sinned, a male goat was made an offering for his sins, and when a common person sinned, a female goat was offered up (Lev. 4:22-31). In Jesus' parable of the sheep and the goats, the goats were put at the left hand and sent away into the fires of purification (Matt. 25:33, 41). A goat therefore pertains to the adverse, sinful nature in man. It must be given up to God and so be purified, that its substance may be transmuted into higher and more spiritual thought, activity, and manifestation; thus it will serve to promote the spiritual in the individual.

Jaare – oregim, jā-ă-rē – ŏr'-ĕ-ḡĭm (Heb.)—*weavers' forest; woods of the weavers; thicket of braids,* i. e., *closely woven together.*

Father of Elhanan the Beth–lehemite, who killed the brother of Goliath the giant (II Sam. 21:19; see margin, and I Chronicles 20:5).

Meta. Trees represent nerves, and nerves are expressions of thoughts of unity; they connect thought centers with one another. It is by means of the nervous system that our thoughts are transferred from point to point throughout the body. We can easily see, therefore, how a tree symbolizes a connecting link between the heavens and the earth—the formless and the formed—since thoughts in us bring us in touch with the divine, the heavenly or spiritual mind, which is God. And so we understand Jaare–oregim, meaning *weavers' forest, thicket of braids,* i. e., *closely woven together,* to represent networks of nerves, or interblending of thoughts of unity in consciousness, established in substance (Beth–lehem, *house of bread,* referring to the substance center in man, at the pit of the stomach) and in that which is real and true (Jaare–oregim was an Israelite). Beth–lehem was the birthplace of Elhanan, a name that means *grace of God.* (See ELHANAN.)

Jaareshiah (A. V., Jaresiah), jā'-ă-rĕ-shī'-ăh (Heb.)—*whom Jehovah makes fat; Jah will make full; whom Jah fosters; Jehovah will nourish; Jehovah overhangs; Jah will encouch; the Lord will rest.*

Son of Jeroham. He was a chief of the tribe of Benjamin (I Chron. 8:27) and lived in Jerusalem.

Meta. A resting in the assurance that God, omnipresent Spirit, through Jehovah, the Christ, is not only one's abundant supply and support, but is also the actual nourishment of one's soul and body. *Jah will encouch* and *the Lord will rest* denote resting in the assurance of some specific truth that Spirit has revealed and made real to the inner consciousness. *Jehovah will nourish, Jeho-*

vah makes fat, or full, pertains to supply and support and to the actual nourishing of one's being; it makes one think of the words of Jesus, "Man shall not live by bread alone, but by every word that proceedeth out of the mouth of God" (Matt. 4:4). In this trustful and restful assurance of God as all and in all, every belief in lack and fear of lack, as well as all outer manifestation of it, is removed.

Jaasiel, jå-ā'-sĭ-ĕl (Heb.)—*whom God has made; whom God has created; God's building; God's handiwork; God's working.*

Son of Abner. He was captain over the tribe of Benjamin, in David's reign (I Chron. 27:21). (See I Chronicles 11: 47.)

Meta. The illumined reason, or intellect (Abner, father of Jaasiel) awakening to the truth that man is the work of God; that God, Spirit, is the source of all intelligence, of all true understanding, and is also the creator and maker of the universe; that apart from Spirit nothing could come into expression and manifestation, and nothing could exist for a moment. Spirit is the keynote and the keystone of all that really is.

Jaasu (A. V., Jaasau), jā'-å-sū (Heb.) —*they will do; they will make; they will erect; they will build; they will create.*

An Israelite, son of Bani, who had taken a foreign wife (Ezra 10:37).

Meta. The idea here is that while Jehovah, or spiritual I AM, is the creator and sustaining power of the forward and upward movement in man and is the incentive to all true progress and freedom from thought bondage such as is signified by Babylon, from whose captivity Jaasu had been set free, yet Jehovah works in unison with, or by means of, the positive and negative poles of being in each individual, the masculine and feminine, wisdom and love, to bring about true and perfect expression and manifestation (*they will do, they will make, they will build*).

In the history of Jaasu, we also see the possibility all the way along that the life forces, strength, and vitality, which are constantly being accelerated and increased by conscious contact with Spirit,

are ever in danger, seemingly, of being attracted to a union with the animal soul, or the emotional nature under the dominion of carnal thought, which is always reaching out for expression in sensation. (This latter is suggested by Jaasu's marrying a foreign wife.) We must keep in constant touch with Ezra, the puritan, or ruling thought of purity within us, that our whole consciousness may be kept in order and chastity, undefiled by "foreign" or limited, error thoughts and desires.

Jaazaniah, jā-ăz-å-nī'-ăh (Heb.)— *whom Jehovah hears; Jah will hearken; Jehovah will listen; whom the Lord will hear.*

a Son of a Maacathite, one of those who came to Gedaliah at Mizpah (II Kings 25:23). **b** Son of Jeremiah of the Rechabites (Jer. 35:3). **c** Son of Shaphan, in Ezekiel's vision (Ezek. 8: 11). **d** A son of Azzur, a prince of the people, one whom Ezekiel was told to prophesy against because of the man's devising iniquity and giving wicked counsel (Ezek. 11:1).

Meta. Uplifting thoughts in consciousness, thoughts that are attentive and obedient to spiritual Truth. Thus they are recognized by Spirit (*whom Jehovah hears*) and are raised out of all depression and strife (one Jaazaniah was a Maacathite, a descendant of Maacah, who refers to oppression, depression, friction). See GEDALIAH and MIZPAH.)

The Jaazaniah of Ezekiel 11:1, who devised iniquity and gave wicked counsel, must refer to a deceptive thought in man that would cause him to believe that he can reap the blessings of divine favor without really becoming obedient to the law of God. Many persons today think that by faith in an outer Jesus they will be saved and taken to heaven, to enjoy spirituality and all the blessings of life and good, without really overcoming their sinful nature on this earth. They are mistaken, however. Those who teach such a doctrine are false prophets, for Jesus Christ came to save His people from their sins, not in them or in spite of them. Only those who actually put away sin here in the body will be able to enter the heavenly realm and be saved alive and entire.

Jaaziah, jā-ă-zī'-ăh (Heb.)—*whom Jehovah consoles; Jah will comfort; Jah will strengthen; Jah will determine; strength of the Lord.*

Son of Merari, of the tribe of Levi (I Chron. 24:26, 27).

Meta. The inner forces of Spirit strengthening, freeing, and lifting the consciousness out of the *bitter, unhappy* state of thought that Merari, father of Jaaziah, represents. This work of the inner forces of Spirit is to bring about in the individual a recognition and realization of the truth of his being, of his divine sonship. (This latter is suggested by Beno, son of Jaaziah, Beno meaning *his son.*)

Jaaziel, jȧ-ā'-zĭ-ĕl (Heb.)—*whom God consoles; God will comfort; God will strengthen; God will determine.*

A Levite of the second degree, appointed as one of the musicians who accompanied the priests that brought the Ark to Jerusalem, in David's reign (I Chron. 15:18).

Meta. The Spirit of God in the individual, working through love, harmony, life, joy, and all that pertains to music and to the love consciousness, to strengthen one in the knowledge of God's good will to man (*God will comfort, God will strengthen, God will determine*). This good will causes man to realize and demonstrate his inner spiritual perfection—the truth of his being. (The Ark symbolizes the inner spark of divinity that ever remains in each individual, and David's bringing the Ark to Jerusalem denotes one's giving this divine spark its rightful place in the consciousness.)

Jabal, jā'-băl (Heb.)—*flowing moisture; a welling up; flowing copiously; a stream; fertility; abundance; shouting with joy; jubilation; exultation; triumph.* The negative aspects of the word are: *flowing out; exhausting; passing away; wanderer; defeat; going out (death).*

Descendant of Cain. He was a son of Lamech by Adah. "And Adah bare Jabal: he was the father of such as dwell in tents and *have* cattle" (Gen. 4: 20).

Meta. The transitoriness of the outer, physical man of one who is dwelling in the animal-strength consciousness. (*Wanderer, passing away, going out,* and "dwell in tents" all show lack of permanence. Cattle refer to animal strength. *A stream* here means the life flow. Cain, from whom Jabal is descended, symbolizes the outer or physical man; Adah, Jabal's mother, is a phase of the animal soul in man; Lamech, father of Jabal, means *overthrower, a strong young man.* These all bear out the significance given to Jabal.)

Jabbok, jăb'-bŏk (Heb.)—*pouring out; emptying; flowing rapidly; effusing; diffusing; dissipating; pounding; beating down; pulverizing; covering with dust; wrestling.*

A tributary of the river Jordan; it was on the east side of the Jordan. Jacob wrestled with the angel at the ford of the Jabbok (Gen. 32:22). This river was at the border of the country inhabited by the children of Ammon (Num. 21:24), and became a boundary of the land allotted to the tribes of Reuben and Gad (Deut. 3:16).

Meta. The definitions of Jabbok point to an undue dissipation, effusion, pouring forth of the life force in man; they suggest a very swift and unrestrained flowing of this stream of life, with no intimation of conservation or of wise direction. This is because the life flow has been activated entirely by the "mind of the flesh"; the Jabbok river ran through the country of the Moabites, Amorites, and Ammonites. Israel smote Sihon, king of the Amorites, and possessed his land from the Arnon (see ARNON) to the Jabbok (Num. 21:24), even to the children of Ammon; for the Ammonite border was strong. (See AMORITES, MOABITES, and AMMONITES.) Thus the life stream is coming nearer to the dominion of the real, true thoughts and activities (Israelites) in the individual.

Jabbok ford (Gen. 32:22), where Jacob gives up and sends over his ideas of possessions when he is about to meet his brother Esau, means in the Hebrew evacuation or dissipation. At every forward move in his evolution, man gives up his present ideas that he may receive greater ones. The idea of struggle (*wrestling*), given in the meaning of this name, infers that it was hard for Jacob to put away all the things that he loved and alone enter the invisible and wrestle with the forces of the subjective consciousness in darkness. The individual does not like to undertake the struggle necessary to the overcoming of material habits.

Jabesh, jā'-bĕsh (Heb.)—*hot; glowing; dry; arid; parched; destitute of vitality; disappointment; shame; disgrace.*

a Father of the Shallum who conspired against, and killed, Zechariah (the son of Jeroboam and king of Israel) and reigned as king in his stead (II Kings 15:10). b A name for Jabesh–gilead, a city of Israel (I Sam. 11:1-10).

Meta. The individual's realization of the barrenness, joylessness, lifelessness, confusion, and shame that result from the will's ruling in idolatry and carnality instead of directing the activities of the organism according to the law of life and Truth (Jeroboam and his son Zechariah were two very wicked kings of Israel, and kings pertain to the will, the ruling faculty in man). This realization (Jabesh) begets Shallum, *retribution, recompenser,* who destroys the wicked rule of the will (kills Zechariah), and takes the governing power to himself. (See SHALLUM.)

See JABESH–GILEAD for the significance of the city of Jabesh.

Jabesh – gilead, jā'-bĕsh – g̈ĭl'-ĕ-ăd (Heb.)—*Jabesh of Gilead.*

A city of the half tribe of Manasseh, in the land of Gilead. All its inhabitants, except four hundred young virgins, were killed by the Israelites, presumably because they did not join in the fight against Benjamin, but really in order to get wives for the Benjamite men who survived the battle with Israel. Israel had fought against them because of their iniquity in Gibeah (Judg. 21:8-14). See I Samuel 11:1-11 and II Samuel 2:4, 5.

Meta. An extremely dry, barren phase of thought in man's higher consciousness. (See GILEAD.) It should be alive, but it is so permeated with negative ideas, so filled with a sense of shame, and so lacking in any element of true, positive understanding (which Manasseh should represent) that it does nothing toward helping to put out of consciousness that which the iniquity of the Benjamites of Gibeah signifies. It is therefore destroyed by the Israelites, all but the purity of the original soul quality (four hundred young virgins) that has placed it in the higher realm of thought in man's consciousness (Gilead).

In I Samuel 31:11-13 Jabesh–gilead represents the forces of nature that gather up and care for the dust and ashes of the organism. Nothing is lost in the divine economy, and that which is dissipated will in due course be gathered again and tried in the working of life's problem. When the personal will (Saul) has spent its force, the powers that Jabesh–gilead represents (*dry, parched, shame*) come forward and hide away all that remains of this Saul quality in consciousness. The way is then opened for a higher expression of the executive power to manifest under the banner of love (David).

Jabez, jā'-bĕz (Heb.)—*it causes travail; who causes pain; he causes sorrow.*

a A city in Judah (I Chron. 2:55). b The name of a man of Judah. "And Jabez was more honorable than his brethren: and his mother called his name Jabez, saying, Because I bare him with sorrow. And Jabez called on the God of Israel, saying, Oh that thou wouldest bless me indeed, and enlarge my border, and that thy hand might be with me, and that thou wouldest keep me from evil, that it be not to my sorrow! And God granted him that which he requested" (I Chron. 4:9, 10).

Meta. An awakening to the understanding that evil causes sorrow; also the earnest desire and prayer that the awakened individual directs toward God, inner Spirit, for deliverance from error that he may be blessed and may not reap error's results. In this awakening in man for which Jabez stands, there is a realization of victory, an inner assurance of the good that is so earnestly desired.

Jabin, jā'-bĭn (Heb.)—*perceiving; discerning; observing; intelligent; knowing; analysis; understanding.*

A Canaanitish king, of Hazor (Josh. 11:1; Judg. 4:2-24). There were evidently two kings of Canaan by this name, since the one mentioned in the first text given was overthrown and killed by Joshua (see verses 10-12 of Josh. 11).

Meta. A discernment and intelligence inherent in the elemental life forces of the organism (Canaanites). But in Jabin this intelligence is not subject to spiritual thought; it is centered in and activated by the "mind of the flesh." It takes Barak (the fiery executive of an active will), in coöperation with Deborah (a fine spiritual sense of discrimination), with ten thousand men of Naphtali and Zebulun (strength and order) to defeat Sisera, captain of the hosts of Jabin, king of Canaan, who reigned in Hazor.

Jabneel, jăb′-nē-ĕl (Heb.)—*whom God produces; God causes to build; building of God; posterity of God, i. e., sons of God.*

a A place on the northwest border of Judah (Josh. 15:11). **b** A border city of Naphtali (Josh. 19:33).

Meta. Abraham looked for "the city which hath the foundations, whose builder and maker is God" (Heb. 11:10). This is man's spiritual consciousness, Divine Mind or the Christ mind, expressed in and through man. Paul speaks of "a house not made with hands, eternal, in the heavens," which building we have from God (II Cor. 5:1); this is our perfected, spiritual body, which results from and is established in spiritual consciousness—the heavens. Jabneel signifies this Christ consciousness, in which is the perfect body consciousness (*building of God*).

Jabneh, jăb′-nĕh (Heb.)—*a building; a construction; a production; posterity.*

A city of the Philistines whose wall was broken down by Uzziah, king of Judah (II Chron. 26:6).

Meta. The outer-sense man's idea of himself, of man in general. (The Philistines signify the outer thoughts and activities of the senses established in the limited ideas of the personal man.) Uzziah, meaning *Jehovah is my strength, strength of Jehovah,* broke down the wall of Jabneh. In other words, through divine strength a victory is gained over carnal man's limited thought regarding himself, and the understanding is lifted to a higher, clearer, and more correct recognition of the entire organism as being founded in Spirit.

Jacan (A. V., Jachan), jā′-căn (Heb.) —*stirring up; making turbid; troubling; afflicting; oppressing.*

One of the head men of Gad, in the days of Jotham king of Judah, and Jeroboam king of Israel (I Chron. 5:13).

Meta. A chief thought in the power faculty (Gad), at an early stage of the individual's conscious development of this faculty. This thought (in its realization of power) is tyrannical and oppressive (*afflicting, oppressing*) in its dealings with the other thoughts and faculties of the consciousness. This leads to unrest, rebellion, and distress in mind and body (*stirring up, making turbid, troubling*).

Jachin, jā′-chĭn (Heb.)—*whom He (God) makes firm; He will set upright; He shall establish; founding; strengthening.*

a Son of Simeon (Gen. 46:10). **b** A pillar at the right side of the porch of the Temple (I Kings 7:21). **c** A priest who dwelt in Jerusalem after the Captivity (I Chron. 9:10). **d** A priest to whom was allotted the twenty-first course in Temple service, in David's reign (I Chron. 24:17). Simeon's son Jachin is called Jarib in I Chronicles 4:24.

Meta. The firmness, loyalty, steadfastness, and strength of character that result from the establishment of the consciousness in Truth—God, Spirit. The way is opened for this by a state of mind that is receptive and obedient to the things of Spirit (Simeon represents this receptive, obedient phase of mind).

Jachinites, jā′-chĭn-ītes (fr. Heb.)—*of or belonging to Jachin.*

Descendants of Jachin the son of Simeon (Num. 26:12).

Meta. Thoughts belonging to that in consciousness which Jachin signifies. (See JACHIN.)

Jacob, jā′-cob (Heb.)—*heel catcher; lier in wait; supplanter; leaving behind; bringing to an end; recompensing; rewarding.*

The younger of the twin sons of Isaac and Rebekah, but the one who obtained the birthright (Gen. 25:26-34; 27:11 to end of The Book of Genesis).

Meta. Jacob and Esau represent the mental and the animal consciousness within each of us. Esau, the hairy man, typifies the animal, which comes first into expression. Most of the human family let him rule in consciousness; but in the line of human unfoldment this man of nature, Esau, must be supplanted by a higher type, called Jacob, the *supplanter,* the mentality or understanding.

Jacob also represents an idea of the I AM identity, through which the faculties of the mind receive their original inspirations. Jacob had twelve sons, to each of whom he gave an office and each of whom he blessed, or inspired, with his spiritual wisdom.

The Bible narrative about Jacob and Esau has always been read historically, and theologians have had trouble trying to excuse Jacob and Rebekah for the apparent duplicity that they perpetrated upon Esau. When read in the light of spiritual understanding or considered as part of the history of the unfoldment of the individual soul, the incident loses its aspect of duplicity and we find that it is a description of the subtle working of the soul in spiritual evolution, under the guidance of Divine Mind. The soul is progressive. We must go forward. The soul must meet and overcome its limitations.

Esau was a hunter—he finds his pleasure in the realm of animal forces. The cravings of the lower nature are in the ascendancy—Esau gave his birthright to appease his hunger. The "red *pottage*" mentioned in the Scripture symbology refers to the life substance of the body. The natural man is first in man's evolution. First that which is natural, then that which is spiritual, says Paul. We all agree that a strong body is required to express a strong mind; that is the divine plan. The men of the new race will have robust bodies; they will not be weaklings mentally or physically. Healing of the body is fundamental in the outworking of God's perfect-man idea.

The natural man is not wise. Esau was a hunter, and he loved sport better than Spirit. He was not seeking development through soul culture, and in order to carry forward the whole man it was necessary to supplant and suppress him. This is the meaning of the deception by Jacob and Rebekah. The mental must gain the supremacy and the physical must lose prominence. This is what Jacob and Rebekah did. They got Isaac (I AM) to acknowledge the mind as first in consciousness. Jacob went to another country, which represents apparent separation.

An explanation of Genesis 28:10-22 is as follows: Jacob (the mental) went toward Haran (high place): the mind enters a higher state of consciousness.

At "a certain place" in consciousness the understanding is unillumined. "One of the stones of the place" that Jacob put "under his head" represents the contact of understanding with material conditions.

The "ladder" represents step-by-step realizations of Truth. These pure thoughts (angels of God) ascend and descend in consciousness. "Jehovah," the I AM (verses 13 and 14), occupies the highest place in consciousness. The spiritualized thoughts of the mind become the seed and bless all the earth (body consciousness).

The Lord is constantly in our midst, and we must eventually come into divine consciousness (verse 15). The mind is startled when it discovers God to be an omnipresent principle (verse 16). In verse 17 is represented the realization that the body (house) is the temple of God and that the mind is the gate to heaven (harmony).

In the light of understanding, "the morning" (verse 18), the things that have been our stepping-stones become holy and we anoint them with oil (love, joy, and gladness).

Beth-el signifies *house of God.* Luz means separation; that which has seemed separate and apart is brought into unity (verse 19).

Verses 20 to 22 represent the first attempt of the enlightened mind to covenant with God and trust Spirit for all things. Keeping the law of giving and receiving is recognized as a step in spiritual development.

Taking a wife symbolizes a unification of the I AM with the affections. Jacob was told to go to Paddan–aram (tableland) to the house of Bethuel (unity with God) and take a wife from the daughters of Laban (white, pure, shining) (Gen. 28:2-7). This points the way to a unification with the love principle in its higher aspects. Exalted ideas, divine aspirations, and pure motives are here designated as necessary to the union with the soul that the I AM is about to make.

In Genesis 33:1-15 we read of the reunion of Jacob and Esau. In the 1st and 2d verses Jacob (the mental) prepares to unite with Esau (physical expression). Mind and body must be joined before the divine law can be fulfilled.

Verses 3 and 4: The mind must be unified with the body in all the seven natural faculties. When the union between mind and body takes place a humility born of surrender of the self comes into expression.

Verses 5-7: The women and the children here represent the accumulations of the mind.

Verses 8 and 9: The mind is willing to share its accumulations, but the body (Esau) cannot receive the gift until it has been uplifted. In verses 10 and 11 we find that, after mind and body are reconciled and adjusted, they share alike the gifts of Spirit.

Verse 12: Jacob, the mind, should go before and direct the body (Esau).

Verse 13: The children, and the young animals in the flocks and herds, symbolize new ideas' being established in consciousness.

Verses 14 and 15: There is not necessarily enmity between the mind and body of man, but only a difference in states of consciousness. The body becomes an obedient servant of the mind when the two are unified in Divine Mind.

Jacob's well, jā'-cob's well.

A well near Sychar, a city of Samaria; it was at this well that Jesus met the Samaritan woman and talked to her about the true water of life (John 4:6).

Meta. Inspiration through the intellect alone. (See SYCHAR and SAMARIA.)

Jada, jā'-dȧ (Heb.)—*perceiving; learning; coming to know; knowing; wise.*

Son of Onam, and grandson of Jerahmeel, of the tribe of Judah (I Chron. 2:28).

Meta. The quality of perceiving, knowing, understanding, in man, which comes about by the individual's making a conscious union in his thoughts with the divine intelligence—the one all-knowing Mind, or wisdom, which is God.

Jaddua, jăd-dū'-ȧ (Heb.)—*skilled; adept; very knowing; wizard.*

a One who joined Nehemiah in sealing the covenant (Neh. 10:21). **b** A son of Jonathan of the Levites (Neh. 12:11).

Meta. Thoughts, belonging to our true Israelitish consciousness, established in wisdom, understanding, good judgment, and skill (*very knowing, skilled*). Such a thought unites with that in us which inspires us to higher and better things (Nehemiah), to aid us in keeping the spiritual law and so abiding in the blessings of God (one Jaddua joined Nehemiah in sealing the covenant).

Jadon, jā'-dŏn (Heb.)—*judge; administrator; executive.*

"The Meronothite," who assisted in the rebuilding of Jerusalem's wall (Neh. 3:7).

Meta. The ability to discern the inner thoughts of the mind and heart, and to discriminate as to their real intent; also to decide whether they shall remain or shall be put out of consciousness. This ability belongs to the restored Israelitish consciousness, or true, enlightened thoughts in man; it does much toward bringing about the reëstablishing of spiritual worship at the heart center (Jerusalem), and toward the spiritualizing of the entire organism. (Jadon helped in the rebuilding of Jerusalem's wall. The rebuilding of the wall and of the Temple, after the Captivity, signifies the uplifting and spiritualizing of the whole consciousness of man, especially his body.)

Jael, jā'-ĕl (Heb.)—*he will arise; he will go up; he will ascend; an ibex; a chamois; a wild mountain goat.*

Wife of Heber the Kenite. She received Sisera, captain of the army of

Jabin the king of Hazor, when he fled from the Israelites, and then killed him, while he slept in her tent, by driving a tent pin through his temples (Judg. 4:17-22). She was eulogized in song by Deborah and Barak for her deed (Judg. 5:24-27).

Meta. The human, seemingly animal (*a wild mountain goat*) phase of soul consciousness, lifting itself, by means of its kindly attitude toward and great desire for the real and true things of Spirit, to a higher level (*he will arise, he will ascend*). (See KENITES, HEBER, and MIDIANITES.)

Jagur, jā'-gŭr (Heb.)—*lodging place; place of sojourn; temporary dwelling; unsettled abode; dwelling by adoption.*

One of the "uttermost cities . . . of Judah toward the border of Edom in the South (Josh. 15:21).

Meta. Limited, transitory, human thoughts seeking to find a lodging place in the phase of the subconscious mind, in the individual, that should be *settled*, or inhabited, by true thoughts of praise, prayer, and permanency.

Jah, jäh (Heb.)—*unchangeable; eternal; everlasting; Lord; Jehovah; He.*

A shortened or poetical form of Jehovah (Psalms 68:4, margin). While Jah is accepted as a contraction of Jehovah, it is really one of the most ancient expressions attached to Deity.

Meta. See JEHOVAH.

Jahath, jā'-hăth (Heb.)—*becoming one; united; unity; conjunction; together; wholeness; revival; renewing; comfort.*

a A great-grandson of Judah (I Chron. 4:2). b A grandson of Gershom, the son of Levi (I Chron. 6:20). c The name of three other Levites, one an overseer in the work of repairing the Temple, in the reign of Josiah, king of Judah (I Chron. 23:10; 24:22; II Chron. 34:12).

Meta. The breaking down and the building up that constitute every true overcoming in man, and the accompanying realization of his eternal oneness with the Divine.

In every overcoming, in every realization of Truth, there must be first a letting go and dispersion of whatever limitation or error has been standing in the way of the higher good that is desired. Then the light of Spirit breaks into the consciousness of the individual and he realizes new life (*revival, renewing*), new understanding, and a new realization of God's presence.

Jahaz (in A. V., Joshua 13:18, Jahaza; Joshua 21:36, Jahazah), jā'-hăz (Heb.)—*trampled upon; a place trodden down; a threshing floor; contention; quarrel.*

The place in the wilderness where the Israelites, under Moses, fought against and defeated Sihon, king of the Amorites (Num. 21:23).

Meta. A place in the wilderness of man's undisciplined thoughts wherein he gains a decided victory over sense desire (see SIHON and AMORITES), while he is on his journey toward spiritual perfection in both mind and body (the Promised Land).

A threshing floor, a place trodden down, trampled upon, contention, and *quarrel* denote the seeming trial, inharmony, inner conflict, and positive affirmation of Truth that usually precede and aid in bringing about man's victories over error.

Jahaziel, jă-hā'-zĭ-ĕl (Heb.)—*whom God beholds; beholden of God; revelation of God; vision of God.*

a A Benjamite warrior who deserted Saul and came to David at Ziklag (I Chron. 12:4). b A priest who blew the trumpet before the Ark when David was having the Ark brought back to Jerusalem (I Chron. 16:6). c A Levite, descended from Kohath, through Moses (I Chron. 23:19). d A Levite, a descendant of Asaph, through whom the Spirit of Jehovah assured Jehoshaphat and the children of Judah that the battle that they were due to fight with the Ammonites and the multitudes from Syria was not theirs but the Lord's and that the Lord would defeat their enemies for them (II Chron. 20:14-30). e A man named Jahaziel is mentioned in Ezra 8:5. His son, with three hundred other men, returned from the Babylonian captivity with Ezra.

Meta. True spiritual inspiration and understanding; spiritual vision; a clear insight into Truth, into the things of God, the things that are eternal. This understanding is needed by man in ev-

ery avenue of his being, in every faculty and power. It comes to him when he makes the securing of this highest understanding the most vital thing in his life, when he gives his most earnest attention to Spirit. Proverbs 3:13-18 reveals the value of understanding and the earnestness with which it should be sought. The 15th verse reads:
"She is more precious than rubies:
And none of the things thou canst desire are to be compared unto her."

Jahdai, jäh'-dāi (Heb.)—*whom Jehovah directs; Jehovah leads aright; Jehovah shows the way; the Lord leads; of or belonging to Judah.*

A Judahite, descended from Caleb (I Chron. 2:47).

Meta. The consciousness of man awakening to divine guidance. It is by exercising faith (faithfulness to God and to the Truth that one has perceived) and enthusiasm (Caleb), coupled with praise and prayer (Judah), that man comes to realize his true inner leader and guide—Jehovah, the Christ Spirit. Thus he begins to receive conscious direction in his daily life and affairs, from the spiritual realm within him.

Jahdiel, jäh'-dĭ-ĕl (Heb.)—*whom God makes joyful; whom God makes glad; unity of God; united of God.*

A man of the half tribe of Manasseh, one of those who were "mighty men of valor, famous men, heads of their fathers' houses" (I Chron. 5:24).

Meta. The individual consciousness, coming through understanding (Manasseh) into a comprehension and realization of its oneness with God, Spirit, perfection. This gives much joy to those who receive it, and is the source of true greatness.

This name also suggests the truth that all real unity is of God—comes from Spirit within each individual—and cannot be attained by means of outer rules and regulations.

One authority suggests *revenge of God* as a possible meaning of Jahdiel. This suggests the old mistaken belief that God is divided into two powers, or aspects. The more accepted ideas regarding the meaning of Jahdiel do not include the thought of *revenge*, but of *unity* and *joy-*

ousness only. We see in the name, therefore, the truth that God is the one God, and that He is good. Spirit is not divided into two opposing factors such as good and evil signify. If it were it could not stand, since it would be a house divided against itself. The divided thought must therefore be put away and the truth that there is one God, one power, and one presence—the good omnipotent—must be established in its stead.

Jahdo, jäh'-dō (Heb.)—*his being one; his union; his oneness; his conjunction; his joining together; his wholeness.*

Son of Buz, of the tribe of Gad (I Chron. 5:14).

Meta. In giving the significance of Buz a Bible scholar remarks that the state of mind for which he stands "cannot be productive of good." (See BUZ.) This Buz, however, is the one whose descendants are classed by Jeremiah with Arabian tribes (Arabians signify unproductiveness). The contempt and scorn for which Buz of the tribe of Gad stands is directed against division and error, since out of it has come the thought of making union with Spirit by using the power of the *I* to connect oneself with that which is good and true (Jahdo, son of Buz of Gad; Gad signifying the power faculty in man, and Jahdo meaning *his union, his joining together, his wholeness*).

Jahleel, jäh'-lê-ĕl (Heb.)—*waiting on God; awaiting God; hoping in God; hope of God.*

Son of Zebulun (Gen. 46:14).

Meta. The significance of this name is revealed in Psalms 62:5:
"My soul, wait thou in silence for God only;
For my expectation is from him."

Jahleelites, jäh'-lê-ĕl-ītes (fr. Heb.). Descendants of Jahleel the son of Zebulun (Num. 26:26).

Meta. Thoughts in consciousness springing from and belonging to that which Jahleel signifies. (See JAHLEEL.)

Jahmai, jäh'-māi (Heb.)—*whom Jehovah guards; whom Jah protects; enveloped by Jehovah; joined in affinity of Jah; warmth of Jehovah; heat of Jah.*

Son of Tola and grandson of Issachar (I Chron. 7:2).

Meta. The heated condition that usually accompanies very active zeal (Issachar). Every person should guard and protect his zeal faculty by consciously dwelling in the I AM understanding, love, and power (*whom Jehovah guards, whom Jah protects*), that it may be directed aright and so caused to work always for one's highest good. One should see to it that one is always zealous in that which is constructive, uplifting, unifying, and good. When one's zeal is used to destroy, it becomes contentious and in the end reacts disastrously on one. This is the case even if one is zealously fighting against that which appears to be evil; hence the words of Jesus Christ, "Resist not him that is evil" (Matt. 5:39).

Jahzah (in A. V., Jeremiah 48:21, Jahazah), jäh′-zäh (Heb.)—*trampled upon; a place trodden down; a threshing floor; hard; compact; unrelenting; contentious; quarrelsome.*

A city of Reuben, on the east side of Jordan, that was given over to the Levites (I Chron. 6:78). It is the same city as Jahaz.

Meta. The same as Jahaz, only the thoughts that Jahzah typifies are in the phase of consciousness that Reuben signifies. (See JAHAZ and REUBEN.)

Jahzeel, jäh′-ze-ĕl (Heb.)—*whom God apportions; allotment of God.*

Son of Naphtali (Gen. 46:24). He is called Jahziel in I Chronicles 7:13.

The realization that strength (Naphtali signifies the strength faculty in man) is from God and that one receives it according to one's need (*whom God apportions, allotment of God*), or to the extent that one makes use of it. "As thy days, so shall thy strength be" (Deut. 33:25).

Jahzeelites, jäh′-ze-ĕl-ītes (fr. Heb.).

Descendants of Jahzeel, son of Naphtali (Num. 26:48).

Meta. Thoughts in man which pertain to the realization that his strength is from God. (See JAHZEEL.)

Jahzeiah (A. V., Jahaziah), jäh′-ze-iah (Heb.)—*whom Jehovah beholds; beholden of Jehovah; revelation of Jah; vision of Jehovah.*

Son of Tikvah; he was one of those who were appointed by Ezra to find out which of the returned Jews had taken foreign wives (Ezra 10:15).

Meta. Spiritual seeing, discernment, understanding, the inner perception of divine ideas and their right relation in consciousness, the upward vision. These come about by one's steadfastly beholding the Christ, by keeping one's thoughts on the things of Spirit, and by seeking above all else an understanding heart.

"Incline thine ear unto wisdom,
And apply thy heart to understanding;
. . . cry after discernment,
. . . lift up thy voice for understanding;
. . . seek her as silver,
. . . search for her as for hid treasures:
Then shalt thou understand . . .
And find the knowledge of God."
(See JAHAZIEL.)

Jahzerah, jäh′-ze-räh (Heb.)—*whom Jehovah leads back; Jah protects.*

Son of Meshullam, who was a grandson of Immer, of the priesthood (I Chron. 9:12).

Meta. Whom Jehovah leads back suggests the words that the prodigal son uttered "when he came to himself," "I will arise and go to my father" (Luke 15:17, 18). Then he started on his way back to his father's house, where there was plenty of every good thing. So we, when our eyes begin to open to the light of Truth, are led back by Spirit, step by step, to our original oneness with God. In this place of conscious union with our Father within us, who is our unfailing strength, power, wisdom, and resource, we are divinely protected (*Jah protects*) from the errors and inharmonies that trouble those individuals who live in the sense mind.

Jahziel, jäh′-zĭ-ĕl (Heb.)—*whom God apportions; allotment of God.*

Son of Naphtali (I Chron. 7:13). He is called Jahzeel in Genesis 46:24 and in Numbers 26:48.

Meta. See JAHZEEL.

jailor (Acts 16:27-34).

Meta. That in us which controls the body in its physical aspect. It wants to conform to the new relation and is open to the baptism of spiritual life, which is imparted by the word of Truth (Paul).

Jair, jä′-ĭr (Heb.)—*whom He (God) enlightens; He will make light; He will* *illuminate; instruction; enlightenment; prosperity; happiness; he shall shine.*

a Son of Manasseh; he "took all the region of Argob . . . and called them . . . Havvoth–jair" (Deut. 3:14). **b** A Gileadite, who judged Israel for twenty-two years. He had thirty sons, and these sons of his had thirty cities that were called Havvoth–jair; this Jair was no doubt a descendant of the former Jair, and the cities were the same (Judg. 10:3). See Joshua 13:30 and I Kings 4:13. **c** The father of Mordecai (Esth. 2:5).

Meta. The faculty of understanding (Manasseh) in the individual, receiving spiritual illumination, enlightenment, from God, Spirit. When we recognize Spirit as the source of all true understanding, Argob in us (the *hard, stony* aspect of our human reasonings) is transformed into Havvoth–jair—groups of rich, high, illumined thoughts. (See ARGOB and HAVVOTH–JAIR.)

Jairite, jā′-īr-īte (fr. Heb.).

Ira the Jairite was David's chief minister (II Sam. 20:26). A Jairite was one who was descended from Jair of Manasseh.

Meta. A thought springing from and belonging to that in consciousness which Jair signifies. (See JAIR.)

Jairus, jā-ī′-rŭs (Gk. fr. Heb.)—Greek form of Jair—*whom He (God) enlightens; he will illuminate; enlightenment; instruction; he shall shine; prosperity; happiness.*

A ruler of the synagogue; it was his daughter whom Jesus raised to life (Mark 5:22).

Meta. Much the same as Jair; a spiritually illumined, ruling thought belonging to the established religious ideas (Jews of the New Testament) in individual consciousness. When truly enlightened this thought becomes a radiating center of light (*he shall shine*).

Jakeh, jā′-kĕh (Heb.)—*hearkening; obedient; pious; venerating.*

Father of Agur (Prov. 30:1).

Meta. A faithful, attentive, receptive, reverent attitude of mind toward things spiritual.

Jakim, jā′-kĭm (Heb.)—*whom He (God) establishes; he will lift up; he will*

confirm; he will withstand.

a A chief man of Benjamin, who lived in Jerusalem (I Chron. 8:19). **b** A Levite on whom the twelfth lot fell for service in the Temple (I Chron. 24:12).

Meta. Active faith (Benjamin) and a natural religious tendency pertaining to spiritual service in the body temple (a Levite on whom the twelfth lot fell for service in the Temple) being raised to higher expression (*he will lift up*) and greatly strengthened, made more firm and stable (*whom He (God) establishes, he will confirm*) in consciousness.

Jalon, jā′-lŏn (Heb.)—*passing the night; tarrying; lodging; abiding; dwelling; persisting in a thing.*

Son of Ezrah, of the tribe of Judah (I Chron. 4:17).

Meta. The spiritual I AM, or indwelling Christ presence, becoming more and more an abiding consciousness. This results from perseverance in knowing Truth; it is the fruit of that which Ezra stands for in us. (See EZRA. Ezrah, or Ezra, was the father of Jalon.)

Jambres, jăm′-brēs (Gk. fr. Egypt.) —*wise man; magician; soothsayer; diviner.*

One of the "wise men" or "magicians" of Egypt, who withstood Moses by seeking to keep Pharaoh from letting the Israelites go (II Tim. 3:8; see also Exod. 7:11).

Meta. A perception, intuition, or semblance of wisdom, belonging to the consciousness in man that Egypt represents. (See EGYPT.) This partial wisdom works against man's real, true thoughts (Israelites). It perceives the immediate effect that will ensue if the Israelites are released from Egyptian slavery; it therefore withstands Moses (the upward expression of the evolutionary law of the soul) and counsels Pharaoh (the ruling ego of the Egypt phase of man's consciousness) not to let the Children of Israel go. It even seeks to counterfeit the workings of Spirit in order to blind Pharaoh's eyes and resist the progress of Truth.

James, jāmes (English form of Jacob) —*supplanter.*

a Son of Zebedee. This James was a disciple of Jesus Christ, and brother of

John (Matt. 4:21). **b** James the son of Alphæus was also a disciple of Jesus; to distinguish him from the other James, he is called "James the less" (Matt. 10: 3; Mark 15:40). **c** Mention is made of "James the Lord's brother" (Gal. 1:19). He was one of the apostles, and some think him to be the same person as James the Less.

Meta. James the son of Zebedee is that disciple of Jesus Christ who represents the faculty of judgment in individual consciousness. In the body this faculty has its central seat of activity in the lower part of the nerve center called the solar plexus. We also call this faculty justice, discrimination; it is that quality in us which carefully weighs a question and draws a conclusion. The prevailing tendency of judgment is toward caution, fearfulness, criticism, and condemnation, when it draws its conclusions from the effect side of existence. We should therefore faithfully affirm the spiritual aspect of this faculty and always seek the guidance and good judgment of spiritual light and understanding.

James the son of Alphæus signifies the faculty of order; the location of this faculty in the body is the navel.

Jamin, jā'-mĭn (Heb.)—*right hand; right place; proper; the south,* i. e., *on the right when facing the Orient; east; good fortune; productiveness; prosperity; happiness; dexterity.*

a One of Simeon's sons (Gen. 46:10). **b** Son of "Ram the first-born of Jerahmeel," of the tribe of Judah (I Chron. 2:27). **c** One of those who "caused the people to understand the law," when Ezra read it to them (Neh. 8:7).

Meta. Thoughts pertaining to divine order; also to executive ability, strength, power, skill (*right hand, right place, dexterity*). When such thoughts become active in consciousness they lead one to *happiness, prosperity,* abundant good.

Jaminites, jā'-mĭn-ītes (Heb.)—*of or belonging to Jamin.*

Descendants of Jamin, son of Simeon (Num. 26:12).

Meta. Thoughts springing from that in consciousness which Jamin signifies. (See JAMIN.)

Jamlech, jăm'-lĕch (Heb.)—*whom He (God) makes king; Jehovah rules; he reigns.*

A prince of Simeon (I Chron. 4:34).

Meta. A very prominent thought in the spiritually receptive, attentive, hearing attitude of mind in man (a prince of Simeon), which accepts the Christ, Jehovah, spiritual I AM, as the ruling light, intelligence, and power in consciousness (*Jehovah rules*).

Janim (A. V., Janum), jā'-nĭm (Heb.) —*slumber; a light sleep; lassitude; weariness; inactive; slothful.*

A city in the hill country of Judah (Josh. 15:53).

Meta. A group of thoughts of an innately high character (a city in the hill country of Judah), but lying dormant, *inactive,* asleep. These thoughts need to be awakened by praise and prayer (Judah) to true understanding and action.

Jannai (A. V., Janna), jăn-nå-ī (Gk.) —*oppression; suppression; affliction; humility; poverty.*

Named as son of Joseph and father of Melchi, in the genealogy of Jesus (Luke 3:24).

Meta. "Blessed are the poor in spirit: for theirs is the kingdom of heaven" (Matt. 5:3). Jannai signifies the humbling of the little or personal self, to the end that the true I AM of the individual may be exalted. (Jannai is named in the genealogy of Jesus Christ, and thus signifies a step that must be taken in the unfoldment of Truth in individual consciousness, that the Christ may be born in one, that one may accomplish the new birth.)

Jannes, jăn'-nĕṣ (Gk. fr. Egypt.)— *mockery; deception; poverty; rebellion.*

A man, supposedly an Egyptian magician, who opposed Moses when Moses was seeking from Pharaoh the release of the Israelites (II Tim. 3:8). This same adverse spirit worked in some of the professing Christians of Paul's day.

Meta. The significance is virtually the same as that of Jambres. The quality of seeming wisdom in consciousness for which these men stand is actuated and governed by the adverse, carnal mind, and cannot compare with the wisdom and power of true understanding. It is deceptive and is altogether lacking in reverence and respect for anything higher than itself. It cannot abide, therefore, but will be overthrown with the Egyptian obscurity and darkness to which it belongs.

Janoah, jă-nō'-ăh (Heb.)—*rest; quiet; peace; breathe; take a breath; resting place.*

a A place in Naphtali, that was taken by Tiglath–pileser, king of Assyria (II Kings 15:29). **b** A place on the eastern border of Ephraim (Josh. 16:6).

Meta. A group of thoughts (city) in close proximity to the will faculty (Ephraim). **b** A group of thoughts, belonging to the faculty of strength (Naphtali), that are inactive (*resting place, rest, quiet*). This inactive thought group of the strength faculty helps to lull the whole consciousness of strength into a quiescent, or dormant, attitude that allows the strength of the individual to be given over to the serving and sustenance of the more active, aggressive sense-reasoning plane of the consciousness. In other words, it opens the way for the king of Assyria to conquer and take captive the whole land of Naphtali.

Japheth, jā'-phĕth (Heb.)—*extended and wide; widespread; latitude; increase; expansion; unfoldment; absolute extension; infinite space; extends without limitation.*

One of Noah's three sons (Gen. 5:32).

Meta. The intellect or reason, the mental realm. To *extend without limitation* it would have to enter into the spiritual. Noah's three sons, Shem, Ham, and Japheth, refer to the spiritual, the physical, and the mental in man.

Japhia, jă-phī'-à (Heb.)—*bright; brilliant; gleaming; glowing; splendid.*

a King of Lachish, one of the kings who joined Adonizedek king of Jerusalem in fighting against Joshua, but was defeated and killed by the Israelites under Joshua (Josh. 10:3-27). **b** A place on the eastern border of Zebulun (Josh. 19:12). **c** A son of David's who was born in Jerusalem (II Sam. 5:15).

Meta. Light, intelligence, understanding.

In the two persons and the place named Japhia we discern intelligence increasing in consciousness and being raised to a higher level. Japhia king of Lachish signifies understanding expressing on a very low, carnal plane. By means of Joshua, I AM, this low phase of reason is cast out and the truer understanding that has taken its place grows to be a city, a group of thoughts, the central thought of which is an idea of order (Zebulun). Then in Japhia son of David, who was born to David in Jerusalem, light or understanding is lifted to the spiritual center in consciousness and is imbued with the qualities of love and peace. Thus our inner intelligence ever grows finer, purer, and more abundant until its light shines in greater and greater brilliance to every minutest phase of our being and lifts all into the very essence of that which is divine, perfect, whole, immortal.

Japhlet, jăph'-lĕt (Heb.)—*whom He (God) delivers; his complete deliverance; he will escape wholly; liberating; setting free.*

Son of Heber, who was a grandson of Asher (I Chron. 7:32).

Meta. Heber, father of Japhlet, signifies *a passing over* from a limited, earthly phase of thought to a higher concept of Truth. Japhlet, son of Heber, is a thought or concept of deliverance from (*his complete deliverance, whom He (God) delivers*), or victory over, the old error line of thinking and its results in mind and life. This comes about by means of the higher Truth that has been perceived and put into practice.

Japhletites (A. V., Japhleti), jăph'-lĕt-ītes (Heb.)—*of or belonging to Japhlet.*

Descendants of Japhlet (Josh. 16:3).

Meta. Thoughts belonging to the phase of overcoming that Japhlet signifies. (See JAPHLET.)

Jarah, jā'-răh (Heb.)—*exuberant; redundant; luxurious; overflowing; honey; dense thicket; forest; wood; pluck out; uncovered; unveiled; naked.*

A descendant of Saul (I Chron. 9:42). He is called Jehoaddah in I Chronicles 8:36.

Meta. A realization of abundant life and substance (*overflowing, exuberant, redundant*), with a suggestion of dissipation of nerve energy that leads to a reaction in the way of great depression, and so forth (*naked*). The Promised Land, we are told, was a land flowing with milk and honey—substance and Truth. But the consciousness of life and substance that comes to man when he realizes that his whole being is spiritual (enters into the Promised Land) must be conserved and used for the upbuilding of the spiritual and true in him. If he dissipates it in outer ways, through willfulness and sensuality (Jarah was a descendant of Saul, who represents the personal will), he comes into a consciousness of lack of strength, poise, and substance within and without.

Jareb, jā'-rĕb (Heb.)—*striver; contender; defender; advocate; avenger; adversary; revenger; enemy.*

A title given to the king of Assyria. "When Ephraim saw his sickness, and Judah *saw* his wound, then went Ephraim to Assyria, and sent to king Jareb [*a king that should contend*, margin]: but he is not able to heal you, neither will he cure you of your wound" (Hos. 5:13).

Meta. The intellect of man, when guided by the senses (Assyria), is given to contention, adversity, strife, "an eye for an eye, and a tooth for a tooth." This is Jareb (*striver, contender, avenger*). But true healing, overcoming, dominion, peace, and safety do not come from the warring attitude of mind that fights for its rights, that uses force to protect itself. They spring from love, from the power of Truth, from the divine wisdom that "is first pure, then peaceable, gentle, easy to be entreated, full of mercy and good fruits, without variance, without hypocrisy. And the fruit of righteousness is sown in peace for them that make peace" (James 3:17, 18; see also verses 14 to 16).

So long as an individual gives the power of his will (Ephraim) over to the furtherance of the outer-sense reasonings with their contentious, striving, warring, defensive attitude, and praises these things, his wound will never be healed; he will never know the enjoyment of abiding peace, happiness, safety, satisfaction, and bountiful supply for both the inner and the outer man.

Jared (in A. V., I Chronicles 1:2, Jered), jā'-rĕd (Heb.)—*descent; going down; descending; low country; declining.*

Son of Mahalalel, and father of Enoch (Gen. 5:15-20).

Meta. The *descent* of Spirit, through praise and acknowledgment of God (Mahalalel, father of Jared), into the seemingly earthly or physical in man (*low ground*), that man may be wholly lifted into spiritual consciousness (Enoch, son of Jared, signifying entrance into and instruction in spiritual consciousness, the new life in Christ.

Jarha, jär'-hà (Heb.)—*increasing moon; filling moon; adoption.*

A servant of Sheshan, an Israelite. Sheshan had no sons and so his genealogy was preserved through his daughter, who married Jarha (I Chron. 2:34, 35).

Meta. An obscure, darkened (Egyptian) thought force lifted to a degree of understanding of Truth that, though a reflected understanding (*increasing moon*, moon referring to the reflected light of the intellect), brings this seemingly obscure, darkened thought (Jarha) into the Israelite consciousness (*adoption*) and into union with an Israelitess, a true inner soul desire for a more positive expression of Truth (Ahlai, daughter of Sheshan). Through this union other steps are taken that lead to the full expression and demonstration of good that is desired. (See ATTAI, son of Jarha and Ahlai.)

Jarib, jā'-rĭb (Heb.)—*striver; contender; defender; avenger; adversary; enemy.*

a Son of Simeon (I Chron. 4:24). In Genesis 46:10 he is called Jachin. b A chief man of the Hebrews, whom Ezra sent for when he was getting a company of people together to return to Jerusalem from Babylon (Ezra 8:16). c The son of a priest, who had married a "foreign" wife but consented to put her away (Ezra 10:18).

Meta. The personal thought entering into the sincere desire of the individual for more light and for more freedom from seeming error.

When we let the personal element influence our earnest desire for Truth and good, a mental striving is set into action that is likely to result in contention, strife, and force. This is the *adversary* and does not belong to true spiritual understanding or to successful seeking for victory over error. Yet we are prone to let ourselves get into a contentious, adverse frame of mind by allowing the personal to dominate our zeal for that which is good and right. We must guard against this and must seek the love and the true Christ judgment and power that are ever gentle, yet firm, irresistible, and abiding.

Jarmuth, jär'-mŭth (Heb.)—*high; height; a high place; casting down death; deceiving death; downcast by death.*

a A place in Canaan that was captured by the Israelites under Joshua. Its king, Piram, was slain (Josh. 10:3). It became a city of Judah (Josh. 15:35). **b** A city of Issachar that was given over to the Levites (Josh. 21:29).

Meta. Under the Amorite king, Piram, Jarmuth signifies the exalting of death, the human belief that death is unconquerable.

Under the leadership of spiritual I AM (Joshua, *savior*) the true thoughts in us (Israelites) get a right vision of Truth and put away the belief in and fear of death; then death is cast down (*casting down death*) and life only is exalted—given the high place—in consciousness.

Jaroah, jă-rō'-äh (Heb.)—*pallor; moon; new moon; breathing; inspiring; exhaling; a sweet odor.*

A chief of the tribe of Gad (I Chron. 5:14).

Meta. A ruling intellectual thought belonging to the power faculty in man (Gad is the son of Jacob who represents power) that is being spiritually inspired, and to the refining influence of this inspiration. (The *moon* relates to the intellect, or a reflected state of thought. It shines by borrowed light. *Breathing* signifies inspiration; *a sweet odor* refers to the refining influence of true aspiration and inspiration.)

Jashar (A. V., Jasher), jă'-shär (Heb.)—*even; level; right; upright; uprightness; virtue; integrity; righteousness; Truth.*

A book (Josh. 10:13; II Sam. 1:18). Fallows says, "As the word Jasher signifies *just* or *upright*, by which word it is rendered in the margin of our Bibles, this book has been generally considered to have been so entitled as containing a history of *just men*."

Meta. The phase of our memory that retains thoughts that are just, righteous, and true.

Jashen, jā'-shĕn (Heb.)—*listless; weary; sleeping; dry; old,* i. e., *of former times, not new; quiet; tranquil; shining; brightness.*

His "sons" are mentioned as being among David's mighty men, and belonging to his guard (II Sam. 23:32). In I Chronicles 11:34 he is called Hashem the Gizonite.

Meta. A phase of seeming inactivity and rest (*sleeping*) into which the consciousness enters when it has attained a step in understanding of which it had not been conscious. This phase of apparent inactivity lasts until the inner urge of Spirit pushes the consciousness on to further steps in understanding and attainment. *Shining*, a meaning of Jashen, shows how Truth cannot be really inactive, but constantly radiates its light. (See HASHEM and GIZONITE.)

Jashobeam, jă-shō'-bĕ-ăm (Heb.)—*to whom the people turn; return of the people; who dwells among the people.*

a "The son of a Hachmonite, the chief of the thirty" of David's mighty men (I Chron. 11:11). **b** A Korahite who came to David at Ziklag (I Chron. 12:6). **c** The son of Zabdiel, who was over the first course for the first month, in serving King David (I Chron. 27:2).

Meta. Divine intelligence, omnipresent, permeating the thoughts (*who dwells among the people*) of those who look to the divine source for understanding, and the turning of one's thought people to Spirit for enlightenment (*to whom the people turn*).

(A Hachmonite signifies a thought belonging to the wisdom center in man; see HACHMONI and HACHMONITE. Zabdiel, the father of one of the men named Jashobeam, means *God is my gift, dowry of God.*)

Jashub, jăsh'-ŭb (Heb.)—*he returns;*

turning back; restoring; making restitution; replacing, i. e., *setting in a former place.*

a Son of Issachar and founder of the family of the Jashubites (Num. 26:24). **b** A son of Bani, who had taken a foreign wife (Ezra 10:29).

Meta. That in our higher thoughts (Israel) which causes us always to come back (*he returns*) to the unadulterated Truth, to God, even though we may at times be overtaken by sense affections and desires (take a foreign wife), or may err because of a very active zeal (Issachar) that is not established in wisdom and love.

Jashubi – lehem, jăsh'-ū-bī – lē'-hĕm (Heb.)—*returning of bread; restoration of sustenance; restitution of substance; turning back to Bethlehem; turning back for food.*

Either a person or a place mentioned in the genealogy of Judah (I Chron. 4:22). Fallows says that by some it is thought to refer to Naomi and Ruth, "who returned [from *jashubi,* 'to return'] to Bethlehem after the famine."

Meta. Bethlehem (*house of bread*) is the abiding place of substance in individual consciousness. (See BETHLEHEM.)

Jashubi–lehem (*turning back to Bethlehem*) indicates the individual's turning from the outer and centering his attention within on the substance center, in order to realize omnipresent spiritual substance as his true abiding sustenance and supply. (The substance center in the body is located at the pit of the stomach.)

Jashubites, jăsh'-ŭb-ītes (fr. Heb.)— *of* or *belonging to Jashub.*

Descendants of Jashub (Num. 26:24).

Meta. Thoughts springing from and belonging to that in consciousness for which Jashub stands. (See JASHUB.)

Jason, jā'-sŏn (Gk.)—*Greek form of Joshua; helper; deliverer; healer; he who succors; he who cures; Jehovah delivers.*

A Christian friend of Paul's, at Thessalonica. He was brought before the rulers of the city because of having received Paul and Silas in his home (Acts 17:5-9).

Meta. Jason means *deliverer, healer, he who cures, Jehovah delivers;* he represents the I AM in its first stages of growth in the higher law. He is hauled before the rulers and accused of setting up a new king in opposition to Cæsar. He is called upon to give security for the brethren; that is, he heals the breach between the opposing forces in the consciousness by making concessions for the time being. He sends away the fiery Paul and the psalm-singing Silas, and harmony is restored. We should not be too full of zeal in our spiritual ongoing. We are apt to become fanatical and disagreeable and make ourselves obnoxious. Pour oil on your troubled waters by now and then going into the silence and holding for harmony (slipping away in the night).

Jathniel, jăth'-nĭ-ĕl (Heb.)—*constancy of God; continued of God; God is permanent; God is everlasting; whom God bestows; God-given; gift of God.*

Son of Meshelemiah, who was a doorkeeper in the Temple and a descendant of Asaph (I Chron. 26:2).

Meta. Conscious acceptance of the truth that life comes from God and is continued by God (*gift of God, God is everlasting*), is everlasting because God —our life—is everlasting. "The free gift of God is eternal life in Christ Jesus our Lord" (Rom. 6:23). (A doorkeeper of the Temple signifies a thought that guards the door of our consciousness, admitting certain thoughts and ideas and refusing admittance to others.)

Jattir, jăt'-tīr (Heb.)—*excellent; preeminent; prominent; redundant; exceeding abundance; remnant,* i. e., *that which overflows, is excessive.*

A city in the hill country of Judah (Josh. 15:48).

Meta. A group of thoughts (city) belonging to the praise element, or positive pole of life (Judah), in man, which is very high, broad, and fruitful because of its insight into and constant eulogy of spiritual life and Truth (*excellent, preeminent, redundant*).

Javan, jā'-văn (Heb.)—*Greece; Ionia; the East; the dove; warmth; fertility; effervescence; productiveness; clayey soil; mud; mire; deception.*

a Son of Japheth, who was one of Noah's three sons (Gen. 10:2). **b** A Gentile country or place (Isa. 66:19; Ezek. 27:13). In Daniel 8:21, 10:20, and 11:2, Javan is given in the margin in place of "Greece," which is in the text.

Meta. Javan is a name that the Hebrews of old gave to Greece. The original inhabitants of Greece are supposed to have been descendants of Javan the son of Japheth. Javan therefore refers to the human or personal intellect in man, and to one of its governing characteristics, the deceptive, error belief (*clayey soil, deception*) that understanding is gained by the impressions of the senses in contacting the outer world, by books, teachers, and experiences, instead of its knowing that true understanding comes from the Spirit of God within the soul of man.

In its broadest sense Javan refers to the spiritual phase of intelligence, or to the illumined and inspired intellect; hence, the idea of *the East, fertility, productiveness.*

Jazer (in A. V., Numbers 21:32, Jaazer), jā'-zẽr (Heb.)—*whom He (God) helps; he will succor; helpful; shielding; aiding; protecting.*

A place east of the Jordan that the Israelites took from the Amorites (Num. 21:32). It is mentioned with the land of Gilead (Num. 32:1), and in David's reign some of his Hebronite mighty men of valor were found at Jazer of Gilead (I Chron. 26:31).

Meta. Gilead signifies a high place in consciousness where Spirit discerns and witnesses to Truth and to all of man's thoughts and acts, that perfect adjustment may be made throughout mind and body.

Hebron signifies the front brain, the seat of conscious thought.

Jazer represents the deliverance, strength, and sustenance (*help*) that come to each individual who consciously lays hold of spiritual Truth.

Jaziz, jā'-zĭz (Heb.)—*whom He (God) moves; movement; animation; life; abundance; an abundant breast, i. e., overflowing; brightness; brilliance; prominence; splendor.*

"The Hagrite," who was over the flocks of King David (I Chron. 27:30).

Meta. A Hagrite is a descendant of Hagar through Ishmael, or a thought belonging to the Hagar and Ishmael consciousness in man. Hagar is the natural soul. Ishmael signifies the thoughts that are the fruit of the personal; they belong to the outer, seemingly mortal man.

The flocks of King David are sheep, and they represent the pure, natural life thoughts and forces of the organism.

Jaziz the Hagrite, who had charge of these flocks, signifies the central thought or belief of the seemingly mortal man regarding life and its activities lifted to its highest and purest phase on the human plane; it is not yet raised to true spiritual understanding, though it recognizes Spirit as being back of all life action (*whom He moves; animation; life*) and back of all supply for man (*abundance; an abundant breast, i. e., overflowing*).

Jearim, jē'-ă-rĭm (Heb.)—*thickets; forests; woods; overflowing; honeycombs; abundances.*

A mountain on the northern border of Judah (Josh. 15:10). It was covered with woods.

Meta. Unifying thoughts in consciousness (*thickets, woods, forests*), raised to a high plane (mountain) of Truth realization, thus making union with Spirit mind; the result of this union with Spirit is a consciousness of abundance of good (*overflowing honeycombs, abundances*). (Trees represent the nervous system in man, and nerves are expressions of thoughts of unity. Trees signify connecting links between the heavens and the earth—the formless and the formed—and these connecting links are thoughts. It is through thought that we unify ourselves with God, Spirit, and with our outer organism and world.)

Jeatherai (A. V., Jeaterai), jē-ăth'-ĕ-rāi (Heb.)—*whom Jehovah will lead; following Jehovah; following the steps of Jehovah; steadfast; stepping; leading; following; searching.*

A Levite, son of Zerah and descended from Gershom (I Chron. 6:21). In verse 41 he is called Ethni.

Meta. The central significance of this

name is a steady progress in one's seeking after Truth (*stepping, following, searching*). This comes about by holding faithfully (*steadfast*) to the inner guidance of Spirit (*whom Jehovah will lead*) and by keeping one's eye single to the one good as taught and demonstrated by Jesus Christ (*following the steps of Jehovah*).

Jeberechiah, jē-bĕr-ĕ-chī′-ăh (Heb.)—*whom Jehovah blesses; blessed be Jehovah; whom Jah prospers; benediction of Jehovah; praised be Jehovah.*

Father of Zechariah (Isa. 8:2).

Meta. The significance is virtually the same as that of Berechiah. (See BERECHIAH.) As man reverences and praises Truth, gives earnest attention to that which is of Spirit, he becomes conscious of the divine blessings in his own life and world.

Jebus, jē′-bŭs (Heb.)—*trodden down; trampled under foot; a threshing floor; conquered; subjected; utterly subdued; laid waste; contemptuous; profaned; polluted.*

The original name of Jerusalem (Judg. 19:10; I Chron. 11:4).

Meta. The spiritual or peace center in consciousness (Jerusalem) under subjection to purely sense and carnal thoughts, beliefs, and desires (the Jebusites, who were enemies inhabiting Jerusalem and the country round about, and had to be cast out, destroyed, by the Israelites).

The higher impulses and inspirations are *trampled under foot* and scorned by the individual who has not yet experienced a real change of heart, who has not yet given this spiritual center (Jerusalem, the heart center in the organism) over to the control of his higher and more true and religious thoughts and desires (Israelites). When under one's error beliefs, Jerusalem is Jebus —*a threshing floor*—a place of contention and trial, of anything but the expression of peace and spirituality.

Jebusite (in A. V., Joshua 18:16, 28, Jebusi; Genesis 15:21, Jebusites), jĕb′-ū-sīte (fr. Heb. Jebusi)—*of or belonging to Jebus.*

a A name of the city Jebus (Josh. 18:16, 28). b A nation in Canaan, that built and inhabited the city Jebus, afterward called Jerusalem (Gen. 15:21; Josh. 3:10).

Meta. A Jebusite signifies a thought belonging to the state of consciousness that is symbolized by Jebus. (See JEBUS.)

Jechiliah (A. V., Jecoliah), jĕch-ĭ-lī′-ăh (Heb.)—*whom Jehovah makes able; able through Jah; strengthening of Jehovah; whom Jehovah overcomes; power of Jah; I can of Jehovah; enabled of Jah.*

Wife of Amaziah and mother of Uzziah, kings of Judah (II Chron. 26:3).

Meta. The soul established in divine strength, in the firm conviction that enables one to say, "I can do all things in him that strengtheneth me" (Phil. 4:13).

Jechoniah (A. V., Jechonias; the Greek form), jĕch-ō-nī′-ăh (Heb.)—*whom Jehovah has appointed; whom Jah has set upright; established by Jehovah; stability of Jah; Jehovah's creation.*

Son of Josiah, at the time of the carrying away of the Israelites to Babylon (Matt. 1:11).

Meta. The same as Jeconiah and Jehoiachin. (See JEHOIACHIN.)

Jecoliah (A. V., Jecholiah), jĕc-ō-lī′-ăh (Heb.)—*whom Jehovah makes able; able through Jah; strengthening of Jehovah; whom Jehovah overcomes; power of Jah; I can of Jehovah; enabled of Jah.*

Wife of Amaziah and mother of Azariah, or Uzziah, kings of Judah (II Kings 15:2). She is called Jechiliah in II Chronicles 26:3.

Meta. See JECHILIAH.

Jeconiah, jĕc-ō-nī′-ăh (Heb.)—*whom Jehovah has appointed; whom Jah has set upright; established by Jehovah; stability of Jah; Jehovah's creation.*

A king of Judah who was carried away captive to Babylon (I Chron. 3:16; Jer. 24:1). Jeconiah is a short form of Jehoiachin.

Meta. See JEHOIACHIN.

Jedaiah, jĕ-dā′-jăh (Heb.)—*praise Jehovah; celebrate Jah; profession of Jehovah; confess Jehovah; hand of Jehovah; executive power of Jehovah.*

a An Israelite of the tribe of Simeon (I Chron. 4:37). b Israelitish priests (I Chron. 9:10; 24:7; Neh. 11:10; 12:7).

c One who helped to rebuild Jerusalem's wall (Neh. 3:10).

Meta. The Israelitish men by this name signify one's high spiritual thoughts of greatly increased executive power, or the ability to decide matters and to do things, in the manifest as well as in the unmanifest or consciousness (*hand of Jehovah, executive power of Jehovah*), by acknowledgment of one's true, spiritual I AM, Jehovah, or Christ (*confess Jehovah, profession of Jehovah, praise Jehovah*).

Jediael, jě-dī'-ă-ĕl (Heb.)—*known of God; knowledge of God; perception of God; discernment of God; understanding of God.*

a Son of Benjamin (I Chron. 7:6). b Son of Shimri, one of David's mighty men (I Chron. 11:45). c A Manassite who came to David at Ziklag (I Chron. 12:20). d A son of Meshelemiah, a doorkeeper in the Temple (I Chron. 26:2).

Meta. The *knowledge of God*, spiritual knowing, becoming active in the awakening consciousness of the individual.

Jedidah, jě-dī'-dăh (Heb.)—*beloved; lovely one; delightful one; one dearly beloved.*

Daughter of Adaiah of Bozkath, and mother of Josiah king of Judah (II Kings 22:1).

Meta. The feminine aspect of the love faculty in the individual, or the soul established in the love of God. When the soul sets its love upon God it brings forth Josiah, meaning *Jehovah supports* and signifying in consciousness that which connects itself with Spirit and seeks to carry out the divine plan. (See JOSIAH.)

Jedidiah, jěd-ĭ-dī'-ăh (Heb.)—*beloved of Jehovah; Jehovah is the delightful one; friend of Jehovah; dearly loved of the Lord.*

The name that Nathan the prophet gave to Solomon (II Sam. 12:25).

Meta. Solomon means *peaceful*, and Jedidiah (*beloved of Jehovah, friend of Jehovah*) signifies the inner realization of divine love and the unifying quality of love in which alone true peace can be established.

Jeduthun, jě-dū'-thŭn (Heb.)—*prais-ing; celebrating; lauding; songs of love; love's celebration; full of songs of praise.*

One of the leaders among those who rendered the Temple music. His sons were doorkeepers "at the gate" (see I Chron. 16:38-42; 25:1-6; Psalms 39, 62, and 77, title).

Meta. The spirit of love, joy, and praise vibrating exultantly through the whole spiritual consciousness of man, and playing upon every center in his organism, establishing divine harmony (*full of songs of praise, praising, lauding, love's celebration*).

Jegar–sahadutha, jě'-gär-sā'-hă-dū'-thà (Heb.)—*heap of stones for a testimony; Jegar—a heap of stones; a stele; a cairn; Sahadutha—an eye witness; a testimony; a testimonial; a memorial.*

The Aramaic name of Galeed (Gen. 31:47). (See GALEED.)

Meta. See GALEED.

Jehallelel (in A. V., I Chronicles 4:16, Jehaleleel; II Chronicles 29:12, Jehalelel), jě-hăl'-lē-lĕl (Heb.)—*he shall praise God; who praises God; glorifying God; make a glad shout to God; shine forth God's glory.* (Our words "yell," and "hello," come from this ancient root, which means to make a great shout of rejoicing.)

a A man of Judah (I Chron. 4:16). b The father of Azariah, a Levite (II Chron. 29:12).

Meta. That in our religious nature, our higher and truer thoughts (Israel), which extols, magnifies, and worships God—the great principle of being, divine life, love, wisdom, Truth.

Jehdeiah, jĕh-dē'-ĭăh (Heb.)—*being one with Jehovah; whom Jehovah unites; unity of Jehovah; whom Jehovah makes joyful; Jehovah is their joy; gladness of Jah is theirs.*

a A Levite (I Chron. 24:20). b "The Meronothite," one who had charge of the asses, in David's reign (I Chron. 27:30).

Meta. Ideas of divine unity, or oneness with the inner Christ, Jehovah, the perfect-man idea in Divine Mind, or our true I AM. This gives joy, makes glad the heart, and enables us to direct aright, control, and care for even the stubborn animal nature in us that the word "asses" signifies.

Jehezkel (A. V., Jehezekel, Jehezkel, and Ezekiel are identical in Hebrew), jĕ-hĕz'-kĕl (Heb.)—*whom God makes strong; whom God holds fast; God will strengthen; cleave unto God.*

A priest to whom the twentieth lot fell for service in the Temple, in David's reign (I Chron. 24:16).

Meta. Like Ezekiel, Jehezkel signifies that in us which holds to Spirit and relies on Spirit as our all-sufficient strength. (See EZEKIEL.)

Jehiah, jĕ-hī'-āh (Heb.)—*Jehovah lives; Jah makes alive; Jehovah preserves alive; Jah restores to life; life of Jehovah.*

One of the doorkeepers for the Ark of the Covenant, when David had it brought back to Jerusalem (I Chron. 15:24). Jehiel of verse 18 is another form of the same name.

Meta. That in us which recognizes that life is of Spirit and comes from Spirit; that in Spirit there is no death or destruction. As Jesus said to the Sadducees, "God is not *the God* of the dead, but of the living" (Matt. 22:32). This recognition of life only, in regard to God and to His will for us, as expressed through our I AM, Jehovah, or indwelling Christ, helps to guard our inner divine spark, which the Ark of the Covenant signifies.

Jehiel, jĕ-hī'-ĕl (Heb.)—*God lives; God makes alive; God is the preserver of life; God restores life; life of God.*

The name of several Israelites, most of them Levites, of the priesthood (I Chron. 15:18; 23:8; 27:32; II Chron. 21:2; 31:13; 35:8; Ezra 8:9; 10:2, 21).

Meta. Much the same as Jehiah: the true thoughts (Israelites) in us that recognize God as life and the author of life for man. God is life, and He cannot will, or be the cause of, anything less than the fullness of eternal life to His offspring—mankind. Jehiel refers more to this truth; Jehiah, taking on the form of "Jehovah," signifies expression of the truth for which the name stands.

Jehieli, jĕ-hī'-ĕ-lī (Heb.)—*God of my life; my life is God.*

Son of Ladan (I Chron. 26:21). In I Chronicles 23:8 he is called Jehiel.

Meta. Individual understanding and acknowledgment of the thought that Jehiel signifies. (See JEHIEL.)

Jehizkiah, jē-hĭz-kī'-ăh (Heb.)—*whom Jehovah has strengthened; whom Jah has bound fast; Jah has made firm; whose power is Jehovah.* Jehizkiah is the same as Hezekiah except that it has the prefix of the pronoun.

Son of Shallum, one "of the heads of the children of Ephraim" who insisted that the Children of Israel should not keep as captives any of the people of Judah whom they had defeated in war, but should set them free (II Chron. 28:12).

Meta. The same as Hezekiah: the expression of spiritual strength in the executive power of the mind. (While Jehizkiah was not a king as Hezekiah was, he was one of the head men of the tribe of Ephraim, and Ephraim is the Israelitish tribe that represents the will faculty in man. The will is the executive power of the mind; kings also represent some phase of the action of the will.)

A realization of divine strength is needed in order to carry out necessary reforms in mind and body and to remain faithful to one's highest standards of truth and right. Only through Jehovah, the supreme I AM expressed in man, can this be done. Jehizkiah partakes of this quality of spiritual strength and faithfulness. (See HEZEKIAH.)

Jehoaddah (A. V., Jehoadah), jĕ-hŏ'-ăd-dăh (Heb.)—*whom Jehovah adorns; whom Jah makes eternal; whom Jehovah fully develops; beautifying of Jah; Jehovah reveals; testimonial of Jehovah.*

Son of Ahaz and father of Alemeth, a descendant of Saul (I Chron. 8:36). In I Chronicles 9:42 he is called Jarah.

Meta. The Spirit of Christ taking away obscurity and revealing Truth more clearly to our consciousness (*Jehovah reveals*). Thus error is put away, the Christ within us testifies to the new light that we have received (*testimonial of Jehovah*), and our adornment becomes not the outer adornment of the natural man but the inner grace and beauty of holiness and Truth (*whom Jehovah adorns*) that works out into the outer consciousness and life, transforming the whole being (*whom Jehovah fully develops*). "In that day will Jehovah of hosts become a crown of glory, and a diadem of beauty, unto the residue of his people" (Isa. 28:5). (See JARAH.)

Jehoaddin (A. V., Jehoaddan), jē-hō-ăd'-dĭn (Heb.)—feminine form of Jehoaddah—*whom Jehovah adorns; whom Jah makes eternal; whom Jehovah fully develops; beautifying of Jah; Jehovah reveals; testimonial of Jehovah.*

Wife of Joash and mother of Amaziah, kings of Judah (II Kings 14:2). She was "of Jerusalem."

Meta. The soul dwelling in peace (Jerusalem) and delighting in the things of Spirit. "I will greatly rejoice in Jehovah, my soul shall be joyful in my God; for he hath clothed me with the garments of salvation, he hath covered me with the robe of righteousness, as a bridegroom decketh himself with a garland, and as a bride adorneth herself with her jewels" (Isa. 61:10). The same as Jehoaddah. (See JEHOADDAH.)

Jehoahaz, jē-hō'-ă-hăz (Heb.)—*whom Jehovah upholds; Jah will sustain; whom Jehovah has joined; Jehovah possesses; Jah apprehends; Jehovah sees with the understanding.*

a Son of Jehu king of Israel, who succeeded his father on the throne (II Kings 10:35). b Son of Josiah, who succeeded his father on the throne of Judah (II Kings 23:30-34).

Meta. I AM, Jehovah, the indwelling Christ, as the sustaining, controlling, enlightening power of the will (*whom Jehovah upholds, Jah will sustain, Jah apprehends, possesses; kings stand for the will*).

Both of the kings by the name of Jehoahaz did evil in the sight of God; they were not true to that of which they are typical, and they brought trouble and destruction to themselves. Even so, when we are rebellious and disobedient, when we serve other gods by believing that our strength, our understanding, and our sustaining power are material and are built up and sustained by outer ways and means, we bring ourselves into bondage and trouble. The foundation faculties of our being can become abiding to us only as we understand and acknowl-

edge their spiritual nature.

Jehoash, jē-hō'-ăsh (Heb.)—*whom Jehovah has bestowed; given of Jehovah; whom Jah supports; Jehovah heals; fire of Jehovah; fire of the Lord.*

a Son of Ahaziah. He became ruler of Judah in place of his grandmother Athaliah (II Kings 11:21; 12:1). He is called Joash in II Kings 11:2, and 13:1. b King of Israel in Samaria (II Kings 13:10).

Meta. See JOASH.

Jehohanan, jē-hō-hā'-năn (Heb.)—*whom Jehovah bestows; Jehovah graciously gives; Jah is favorably inclined; compassion of Jah; mercy of Jehovah; grace of the Lord.*

There are several Israelites by this name (I Chron. 26:3; II Chron. 17:15; 23:1; Ezra 10:28; Neh. 6:18; 12:13, 42).

Meta. Love, mercy, and good will as qualities of Being and as becoming known to man and expressed in him through his spiritual I AM, or Jehovah (*whom Jehovah bestows, compassion of Jah, grace of the Lord*).

Jehoiachin, jē-hoi'-ă-chĭn (Heb.)—*whom Jehovah has appointed; whom Jah has set upright; established by Jehovah; stability of Jah; Jehovah's creation.*

Son of Jehoiakim, and next to the last king of Judah. He had reigned only a very short time when he was captured by Nebuchadnezzar and taken to Babylon (II Kings 24:6-15). Jeconiah and Coniah are contracted forms of Jehoiachin.

Meta. Jehovah, I AM, working in the consciousness of the individual to establish the will in spiritual uprightness, stability, assurance, faith.

Jehoiada, jē-hoi'-ă-dà (Heb.)—*whom Jehovah knows; whom Jah perceives; who knows Jehovah; who apprehends Jah, i. e., lays hold of; knowledge of Jah; understanding of Jehovah.*

a A priest who was instrumental in establishing Jehoash, or Joash, on the throne of Judah, and in putting away much of the idolatry of the people (II Kings 11:4 to 12:9). b There are other Israelites by this name also (II Sam. 8:18; Jer. 29:26).

Meta. Appropriation of spiritual, or true, understanding, i. e., the individual mind's laying hold of or apprehending

Truth, through I AM, Jehovah.

In II Kings 11 Jehoiada represents the divine law of justice, which brings to retribution all who transgress its law. He calls into action the forces that destroy error.

Jehoash, or Joash, king of Jerusalem, was a good king and did that which was right in the sight of God, so long as Jehoiada lived to guide him; after Jehoiada's death he did evil. This shows the necessity of the will's being guided by the inner Spirit of wisdom and justice.

Jehoiakim, jĕ-hoi'-ă-kĭm (Heb.)— *whom Jehovah has set up; Jah establishes; whom Jehovah constitutes; endurance of Jehovah.*

Son of Josiah. He was made king of Judah in place of his father, by Pharaoh-necoh king of Egypt, and had his name changed from Eliakim to Jehoiakim (II Kings 23:34-36).

Meta. The capacity to establish God in consciousness, through I AM, Jehovah. The king always represents the will.

Jehoiakim, the king, however, was not obedient to God, and so he represents a ruling state of mind that does not reverence or obey the higher law.

The burning of the book of the law, or the "roll" (see Jer. 36), represents the rejection of new and advanced ideas. New ideas are rejected because of the tendency of error thought to become fixed and crystallized. One may keep one's mind open to new revelations of Truth by denying the right and power of carnal mind to hold old ideas, and affirming the receptivity of the Christ mind.

The meaning of giving "another roll" is that the divine law persistently writes again in consciousness the words of Truth that have been rejected. No one escapes the divine law, although one may resist it temporarily.

Jehoiarib, jĕ-hoi'-ă-rĭb (Heb.)—*for whom Jehovah pleads; Jehovah intercedes; Jah contends; Jehovah defends; for whom Jah strives.*

a A priest of Israel (I Chron. 9:10). **b** Another priest, in David's reign (I Chron. 24:7).

Meta. The inner realization of Christ as our protection and defense.

Jehonadab, jĕ-hŏn'-ă-dăb (Heb.)— *whom Jehovah impels; Jehovah incites to follow freely; liberality of Jehovah; who gives voluntarily for Jah; munificence of Jehovah; freewill offering of Jah; abundance of Jehovah.*

Son of Rechab (II Kings 10:15). He is called Jonadab in Jeremiah 35:6.

Meta. The power (Rechab, meaning *horseman*) of true thoughts in us actuated by I AM (*whom Jehovah impels*). This leads to a consciousness of the munificence and generosity with which spiritual gifts of the Father are imparted to His children. (See RECHAB and JONADAB.)

Jehonathan, jĕ-hŏn'-ă-thăn (Heb.)— *whom Jehovah has given; Jehovah grants grace; yielding of Jah; whom Jehovah lets; whom Jah hinders; Jehovah donates.*

a One of the Levites whom Jehoshaphat king of Judah sent throughout all the cities of Judah to teach the people the book of the law of Jehovah (II Chron. 17:8). **b** A priest who went with Zerubbabel out of Babylon and back to Jerusalem (Neh. 12:18).

Meta. So far as God is concerned, all that He is and has, all the attributes of Being, have already been given to man freely and fully. All is ours to appropriate and use, as we conform to Truth, thus opening the way for the fullness of God—good—to come to us. Jehonathan (*whom Jehovah has given, Jehovah grants grace, yielding of Jah, whom Jah hinders, Jehovah donates*) signifies the entrance into man's consciousness, into his life and affairs, of either a limited or an unlimited measure of the divine blessings and good, according to man's realization of this good and his willing obedience to and coöperation with his true I AM, Jehovah, indwelling Christ mind.

Jehonathan helped to teach all the people throughout the cities of Judah the book of the law of Jehovah. This means that the Christ light, or understanding, penetrates every nerve and thought center (city) in the inner life consciousness (Judah) with power to open up to all the thoughts therein the true knowledge of how the divine principle works in establishing the consciousness of abiding life and wholeness in every phase of man's organism.

Jehoram, jĕ-hō'-răm (Heb.)—*whom Jehovah has exalted; whom Jah raises up; Jehovah makes high; elation of Jah; praise of Jehovah.*

a Son of Jehoshaphat king of Judah (I Kings 22:50). He became king upon the death of his father, but unlike his father he was a very wicked king (II Chron. 21:6). **b** A king of Israel. He was a son of Ahab and succeeded his brother Ahaziah on the throne (II Kings 1:17); called Joram in II Kings 8:16. **c** A priest in Jehoshaphat's reign (II Chron. 17:8).

Meta. The elevation of the individual, in character, in power, in joy, in true success and all good, because he has lifted up his spiritual I AM, Jehovah, the Christ, in his consciousness and life (*praise of Jehovah, whom Jehovah has exalted, whom Jah raises up.*)

Jehoshabeath, jē - hō - shăb' - ĕ - ăth (Heb.)—*whose oath Jehovah is; Jehovah has sworn; who worships Jehovah; fulfilling of Jah; fidelity of Jehovah; sevenfold Jehovah.*

The sister of Ahaziah king of Judah, who hid Joash from his grandmother Athaliah and kept him until he was made king (II Chron. 22:11). In II Kings 11:2 she is called Jehosheba. Jehoiada the priest was her husband.

Meta. See JEHOSHEBA.

Jehoshaphat, jĕ-hŏsh'-ă-phăt (Heb.)—*whom Jehovah has judged; judgment of Jehovah; rulership of Jah; government of Jehovah; whom Jah sets upright; rectitude of Jehovah.*

a Son of Asa, and fourth king of Judah (I Kings 15:24; II Chron. 17:1 to 21:1). **b** There were other Israelites by this name, some of them quite prominent men (II Sam. 8:16; I Kings 4:17; II Kings 9:2). Joel 3:2, 12 mentions the valley of Jehoshaphat, that is, "*Jehovah judgeth*" (margin). This valley of Jehoshaphat was a place where all nations were to be gathered for judgment.

Meta. The development, in consciousness, of the divine idea of judgment. Jehovah, I AM, gives forth its idea of judgment, which is incorporated in man's consciousness and called Jehoshaphat. Communication with Jehovah is established when man, by dwelling in thought upon divine ideas, harmonizes his thought realm with Divine Mind.

Divine judgment can be established in every function of our organism by our commanding that the various thought centers (cities) shall have a perpetual presiding thought of good judgment. This is the way to "set garrisons in the land" (II Chron. 17:2). False-judgment thoughts often infest the various centers through which the bodily functions are carried on. You will find that your stomach center has many arbitrary ideas as to what you should put into it. It may refuse to digest certain things that are good for your general health, and may cheerfully work on other things that are detrimental. No two people agree on what they can digest, yet there should be, and is, a divine law of harmony in this respect, as there is in all others. The kingdom must be established in good judgment; that having been done, the whole system, represented by Judah, will contribute to upbuilding in righteousness and Truth, and man will have "riches and honor in abundance" (verse 5).

Asherim typify human love with its animal propensities. Through Jehoshaphat's allegiance to Jehovah the inner forces (Judah) are purified. "He took away . . . the Asherim out of Judah" (II Chron. 17:6). Fine discrimination is required in order to distinguish between human and divine love. All love is divine in its origin, but in passing through the lens of man's mind it is apparently broken into many colors. Yet, like the ray of white light, it ever remains pure. Man's province is to make its manifestations in his life just as pure as its origin. This requires painstaking discrimination and good judgment.

We are warned not to help or love the ungodly desires and propensities. Under the Mosaic law of character cleansing, the most severe measures are recommended for accomplishing this result. Every enemy was slaughtered without mercy, and the most barbaric methods were adopted in exterminating those who opposed Israel. This is a parable: the enemies are false thoughts and error ways; they are to be utterly exterminated in thought and act.

The essential teaching of the lesson in II Chronicles 17 is that the establishment of judgment in the inner forces of the consciousness, through the I AM, overcomes all adverse ideas in the organism and contributes greatly toward peaceful and harmonious expression in both mind and body. "Mighty men of valor," that is, dominant ideas of power, strength, and judgment, are established in Jerusalem (verses 13 to 18), the dominant center of consciousness at the heart, through the reign of judgment founded in Principle.

Jehosheba, jĕ-hŏsh′-ĕ-bå (Heb.)—*whose oath Jehovah is; Jah is her oath; Jehovah has sworn; who worships Jah; fulfilling of Jah; fidelity of Jehovah; sevenfold Jehovah.*

Sister of Ahaziah. She protected Joash, heir to the throne, from being destroyed by his grandmother Athaliah (II Kings 11:2). In II Chronicles 22:11 she is called Jehoshabeath.

Meta. Jehosheba means *whose oath Jehovah is,* and represents the spiritual word of blessing that has been put upon the divine spark within man. This divine spark was typified in the Jewish religion as the sacred agreement contained in the Ark of the Covenant.

Jehosheba also signifies a certain fulfillment of faithfulness and Truth in the soul of the individual (*fulfilling of Jah, fidelity of Jehovah, sevenfold Jehovah*—seven denoting fulfillment), preparatory to the establishment of this faithfulness and Truth in the outer will and life. (This latter is suggested in protecting Joash and aiding in bringing him to the throne.)

Jehovah, jĕ-hō′-väh (Heb.)—*He-who-is—who-was—who-will-be manifest; the self-existent One; Ipseity; He who is eternal.* In "I AM THAT I AM," the absolute verb remains the same, but the prefix changes from manifestation to power, "he" to "I." The word-for-word rendering of the original would be: "I-am—I-was—I-will-be because I-am—I-was—I-will-be the power to be eternally I."

Jehovah is one of God's names as given in the Bible. In the Authorized Version it is improperly translated "the Lord." In the American Standard Version the name Jehovah is given where Jah occurs in the Hebrew text (see Ex. 6:2, 3 and Psalms 83:18).

Meta. Moses says in Exodus 3:14, 15 that Jehovah told him that His name means: "I AM THAT I AM." Hebrew students say that the original word is JHVH. which means the ever living male-and-female principle. Lee's Hebrew Lexicon identifies this name with Christ, as the manifestation of God that speaks to patriarchs and prophets. Jesus confirms this in Matthew 22:42-45, where He reveals that the Christ existed before David, whose son He was supposed to be. In the Old Testament the spiritual I AM is symbolically described as Jehovah; in the New Testament it is called Christ.

Creation originates and exists in Divine Mind, God. In the creative process Divine Mind first ideates itself. In the Scripture this ideal is named Jehovah, meaning I AM the ever living—*He who is eternal.* The creation is carried forward through the activity of the Holy Spirit.

The Hebrew Jehovah has been translated "Lord." Lord means an external ruler. Bible students say that Jehovah means *the self-existent One.* Then instead of reading "Lord" we should read I AM. It makes a great difference whether we think that I AM, self-existence, is within, or Lord, master, without. All Scripture shows that Jehovah means just what God told Moses it meant, I AM. "This is my name forever, and this is my memorial unto all generations." So whenever you read the word Lord in Scripture say I AM instead and you will get a clearer understanding of what Jehovah is. Jehovah–jireh means I AM the provider. If we expect to demonstrate prosperity from without we find it a slow process; but if we know that I AM is the provider we have the key to the inexhaustible resource. God was also known to the Israelites as Jehovah-shalom—"I AM peace." We can demonstrate peace of mind by holding the words, "I am peace," with the understanding that the real I AM is Jehovah within us. But if we start any demonstration and try to apply the I AM to personality we fall short. This is frequently the cause of failure to get the desired results from the laws that all metaphysicians recognize as fundamentally true. The mind does not always comprehend I AM in its highest, neither does it discern that the all-knowing, omnipotent One is within man. This recognition must be cultivated, and every one should become conscious of the I AM presence. This consciousness will come through prayer and meditation on Truth. In Truth there is but one I AM—Jehovah, the omnipotent I AM. If you take the word Jehovah–shalom into your mind and hold it with the thought of a mighty peace, you will feel a harmonizing stillness that no man can understand. It must be felt, realized, and acknowledged by your I AM before the supreme I AM can pour out its power. After experiencing it you know that you have touched a divine something, but you cannot explain to another just what it is, because you have gone beyond the realm of words and have made union with the cause side of existence. It is the quickening of your divinity through the power of the Word. This divine nature is in us all, waiting to be brought into expression through our recognition of the power and might of I AM.

Jehovah - jireh, jĕ-hō′-văh - jī′-rĕh (Heb.)—*Jehovah will see; Jehovah will behold; Jehovah will provide.*

A place on one of the mountains in the land of Moriah, where Abraham went to offer up Isaac. There he found a ram caught by its horns in the thicket, and he used it for a burnt offering in place of his son. "And Abraham called the name of that place Jehovah–jireh: as it is said to this day, In the mount of Jehovah it shall be provided [in margin, *he shall be seen*]" (Gen. 22:14).

Meta. Jehovah–jireh signifies "I AM the provider." If we expect to demonstrate prosperity from without we find it a slow process; but if we know that I AM is the provider we have the key to the inexhaustible resource. (See JEHOVAH.)

Jehovah - nissi, jĕ-hō′-văh - nĭs′-sī (Heb.)—*Jehovah is my high standard; Jehovah is my conspicuous sign; Jehovah is my banner; Jehovah is my admonisher.*

The name that Moses gave to the altar that he built on the hill where his hands were held up by Aaron and Hur so that Joshua and the Children of Israel might defeat the Amalekites. Jehovah here promised Moses, "I will utterly blot out the remembrance of Amalek from under heaven. And Moses built an altar, and called the name of it Jehovah–nissi; and he said, Jehovah hath sworn" (Exod. 17: 14, 15).

Meta. I AM, recognized by the individual as his standard of right, as his elevating and overcoming power, his defense from and victory over all error or lesser ideals than the one divine perfection (*Jehovah is my high standard, Jehovah is my banner,* "Jehovah hath sworn").

Jehovah–shalom, jĕ-hō′-văh–shā′-lŏm (Heb.)—*Jehovah is perfection; Jehovah is completely finished; Jehovah is equity; Jehovah is friendliness; Jehovah is peace; Jehovah is prosperity.*

The name that Gideon gave to an altar that he built in Ophrah after he had seen the angel of Jehovah face to face. "And Jehovah said unto him, Peace be upon thee; fear not: thou shalt not die" (Judg. 6:23, 24). The words Jerusalem and Salem come from the root word Shalom.

Meta. I am peace, perfection, wholeness, supply. We can demonstrate peace of mind by holding the words "I am peace," with the understanding that the real I AM is Jehovah within us. We can demonstrate any good by unifying our I AM with that good, in understanding and faith. (See JEHOVAH.)

Jehovah–shammah, jĕ-hō′-văh–shăm-mah (Heb.)—*Jehovah is there; Jehovah is high; Jehovah designates; Jehovah is the great name.*

The name of the city that Ezekiel saw in his vision; in the text it is called "Jehovah is there," and in the margin, "Jehovah–shammah" (Ezek. 48:35).

Meta. The realization, by the perfected individual, of the I AM presence throughout his faculties and powers, throughout his consciousness and organism. The twelve tribes of Israel (our real and true thoughts and activities) shall then have been lifted up into complete possession of the land (the body).

Jehozabad, jẽ-hŏz'-ă-băd (Heb.)— *whom Jehovah has given; Jehovah has bestowed; dowry of Jehovah; Jah has endowed; the Lord's presentation.*

a Son of Shomer, and one of the two servants of Joash, who killed him (II Kings 12:21). **b** Son of Obed–edom, a doorkeeper in the Temple during David's reign (I Chron. 26:4). **c** A captain of one hundred and eighty thousand men prepared for war, in Jehoshaphat's reign (II Chron. 17:18).

Meta. The awakening of the individual to the truth that Jehovah, I AM, the indwelling Christ, is the source of all the substance, overcoming power, strength, wisdom, guidance—of every quality that one can possibly need and utilize for good (*Jehovah has endowed, Jehovah has bestowed, the Lord's presentation*).

Jehozadak (A. V., Haggai 1:1, Josedech), jẽ-hŏz'-ă-dăk (Heb.)—*whom Jehovah makes just; Jah makes straight; righteousness of Jehovah; justification of Jah; Jah makes sincere; Truth of Jehovah; justice of the Lord.*

A priest who was taken into captivity by Nebuchadnezzar king of Babylon. He was the son of Seraiah (I Chron. 6:14, 15).

Meta. Justice and righteousness—divine order—established, or being established, in the consciousness of the individual through the exercise of his I AM —Jehovah, or Christ understanding— judgment and power.

Jehu, jē'-hū (Heb.)—*Jehovah is He; Jah is He; He is eternity of eternities; the life of life is He; the self-existent One is He.*

a Son of Hanani, a prophet. He was sent to Baasha king of Israel to tell him what would be the result of his sins (I Kings 16:1). He was also sent to reprove Jehoshaphat king of Judah for helping the wicked king of Israel in his war with the Assyrians (II Chron. 19:2; see II Chron. 20:34 also). **b** The son of Jehoshaphat the son of Nimshi. This Jehu was the one whom Elisha anointed king of Israel in place of Joram son of Ahab; Jehu destroyed the whole house

of Ahab (II Kings 9:2 to 10:36). **c** There were other Israelites by the name of Jehu (I Chron. 2:38; 4:35; 12:3).

Meta. Jehu the "seer," the son of Hanani, signifying the grace or expressed power of Divine Mind, signifies the monitor or inner guide that intuitively perceives the right.

Jehu, "son of Nimshi" (I Kings 19: 16), or grandson of Nimshi according to II Kings 9:2, signifies that error rule is to be put away and spiritual thoughts are to be affirmed and restored to supremacy through the consciousness of I AM, Jehovah, eternally existing in us as our foundation Truth and overcoming power (*Jehovah is He, the life of life is He, the self-existent One is He*).

Jehubbah, jẽ-hŭb'-băh (Heb.)—*he will conceal himself; he will be hidden; hiding; secreting; binding; respecting; reverencing.*

Son of Shemer, of the tribe of Asher (I Chron. 7:34).

Meta. A thought of watchfulness and caution (Shemer, father of Jehubbah) carried to such an extreme by the individual that it causes a fearfulness that tends to *hide* the newer and higher ideas of Spirit from his consciousness, and also *binds* or limits him in his expression of Truth.

Jehucal, jẽ-hū'-căl (Heb.)—*Jehovah is able; Jah is capable; Jehovah is mighty; prevailing; mastery; comprehending; superiority; Jehovah is I can.*

Son of Shelemiah. He was sent to Jeremiah the prophet, by Zedekiah king of Judah, to ask Jeremiah to pray for the people of Judah, to inquire of the Lord for them (Jer. 37:3); in Jeremiah 38:1 he is called Jucal.

Meta. The inherent belief of the will, or ruling ego of the awakening consciousness (Zedekiah the king), that the inner I AM, Jehovah, Christ, is mighty and is fully able to deliver the individual from the inharmonies into which he has fallen because of his not being loyal to Principle. The idea expressed in the name Jehucal is: I can do what I will to do because Jehovah, I AM, Christ in me, is able to do all things; in other words, I can because I AM (*Jehovah is able, Jehovah is I can*). The will has learned much through bitter experiences. Zedekiah the king had terrible reverses because he was not true to God. He knew the divine law, but he did not depend upon it for his defense. He made an alliance with Egypt (darkness) that weakened his hold on spiritual resources, and he was threatened with entire loss of his throne and dominion. In such times of deep trial (the result of depending on outer means of help instead of looking to God and doing His will) the inherent belief in the almightiness of Spirit to redeem and to save springs up in consciousness and is sent by the will (king, or executive power of mind) to Jeremiah (spiritual faith and sight) to inquire of the Lord—to seek a way out. But full deliverance cannot come until the will becomes centered in the will of the I AM and works in harmony with the divine law of right, of love, and of Truth.

Jehud, jē'-hŭd (Heb.)—*Judah; celebrated; lauded; praised; honored; acknowledged; confessed; thanksgiving.*

A city, or town, allotted to Dan (Josh. 19:45).

Meta. The attitude of praise and thanksgiving operative in and through the judgment faculty (Dan) in individual consciousness. Thus a higher and truer idea of divine justice is established.

Jehudi, jê-hū'-dī (Heb.)—*of Judah, i. e., land of Judea; a Jew; my celebration; my praise; my honor; my conferring; my thanksgiving.*

Son of Nethaniah; he was the one who was sent to read to the king the roll containing the words of Jehovah to Jeremiah; the king cut the roll with a penknife and burned it (Jer. 36:14-23).

Meta. A divine idea from the spiritual consciousness in the individual (a *Jew* here refers to a spiritual thought rather than to some old-established religious thought; see JEWS) to enlighten the will (king) with wise counsel and advice (*conferring*); this idea is born of the inner praise-and-prayer consciousness, and is for the upliftment (*my honor*) of the individual who gives it place. (See JEHOIAKIM for ideas as to the meaning of the burning of the roll.)

Jeiel, jê-ī'-ĕl (Heb.)—*God snatches away; God sweeps away, i. e., purifies,*

removes the refuge of lies; carried away of God; God collects, i. e., gathers together, unifies; treasure of God.

a A "chief" of the families of Reuben (I Chron. 5:7). **b** Father of Gibeon (I Chron. 9:35). **c** One of David's mighty men, son of Hotham the Aroerite (I Chron. 11:44). **d** There were others of the name, also.

Meta. God's treasure (*treasure of God*) is the man who was made in the image and likeness of the Father-Mother God (see Gen. 1:26). This is spiritual man, the Christ, or Son, the divine-ideal man, who is the true inner self of every individual. Jeiel signifies an awakening by man to his inner true self, to his divine sonship. Thus man is lifted by God out of human limitations and into spiritual consciousness and attainment (*God sweeps away, i. e., purifies, removes the refuge of lies; God collects, i. e., gathers together, unifies*).

Jekabzeel, jê-kăb'-zê-ĕl (Heb.)—*which God gathers; whom God collects; assemblage of God; whom God infolds; congregation of God; protection of God.*

A city in which some of the children of Judah lived after their return from the Babylonian captivity (Neh. 11:25). It is called Kabzeel in Joshua 15:21, and is a city in the extreme southern part of Judah.

Meta. Jekabzeel (the *congregation of God,* or that in us *which God gathers* together, *infolds,* and *protects,* takes special note of) typifies our highest, truest thoughts, our spiritual-thought people that make up our spiritual consciousness.

Jekameam, jĕk-ă-mē'-ăm (Heb.)—*heaping together of the people; gathering of the people; congregation of the people; rising of the people; standing of the people.*

Son of Hebron, of the Levites (I Chron. 23:19).

Meta. Jekameam (*congregation of the people*) comprises the thoughts of the intellectual, or purely mental, plane that are raised (*rising of the people*) to a higher standard (*standing of the people*) by the individual's consciously unifying himself (Hebron, father of Jekameam, means *alliance* and signifies the front brain or seat of conscious thought; see

HEBRON) with true spiritual ideals. This leads to abundant fruitfulness of good.

Jekamiah (in A. V., I Chronicles 3:18, Jecamiah), jĕk-ă-mī'-ăh (Heb.)—*Jehovah will heap together; gathering of Jah; congregation of Jehovah; rising of Jah; Jehovah will stand.*

a Father of Elishama and son of Shallum, in the genealogy of Judah (I Chron. 2:41). **b** Son of Jeconiah, born during the Captivity; Jeconiah is descended from Solomon (I Chron. 3:18).

Meta. The inner assurance of the spiritually awakening individual that regardless of present appearances the Jehovah, I AM, or Christ mind, will be lifted up in him (*rising of Jah*) and will bring him into conscious union with God (*gathering of Jah, congregation of Jehovah*), and into a realization of great stability (steadfastness, *Jehovah will stand*).

Jekuthiel, jē-kū'-thĭ-ĕl (Heb.)—*obedience toward God; piety toward God; hope of God; strength of God; mighty is God.*

Son of Ezrah, by "his wife the Jewess," and founder of Zanoah. He was of the tribe of Judah (I Chron. 4:18).

Meta. A thought belonging to the Judah (inner praise and life) consciousness that is very obedient and earnest in its devotion to Truth (*obedience toward God, piety toward God*). Its trust is in the divine law, in Spirit, as being its all-sufficient strength and might (*hope of God, strength of God, mighty is God*).

Jemimah (A. V., Jemima), jē-mī'-măh (Heb.)—*dove; purity; fruitfulness; fertility; love; desire; affection; brightness of the day; fullness of the seas.*

Eldest of the three daughters of Job who were born after his restoration to health, wealth, and power (Job 42:14).

Meta. The soul purified from fear, contention, and self-justification, and made gentle, peaceful, loving, fertile for greater acceptance and realization of good.

Jemuel, jĕm'-ū-ĕl (Heb.)—*God is light; day of God; infinite and universal luminous manifestation of God.*

Son of Simeon (Gen. 46:10). In Numbers 26:12 and I Chronicles 4:24 the name is Nemuel.

Meta. Jemuel (*God is light, day of God*) symbolizes the time in individual unfoldment when the light of Truth is accepted into consciousness and realized. The individual thus enters spiritual understanding, a comprehension of the light that is God (*infinite and universal luminous manifestation of God*). This comes about by the listening, attentive, obedient attitude of mind that Simeon, father of Jemuel, signifies.

Jephthah (in A. V., Hebrews 11:32, Jephthae), jĕph'-thăh (Heb.)—*whom He (Jehovah) sets free; he will open, i. e., as a door; he will loosen; he will unbind; He (Jehovah) is the open door; He (Jehovah) is the open way, i. e., to freedom.*

"The Gileadite," son of Gilead, but his mother was a harlot. He was driven from home by Gilead's legitimate sons, and lived in the land of Tob. Later he became a judge and deliverer of Israel. Because of a vow that he made to Jehovah, he sacrificed his daughter, his only child, or devoted her to the Lord, perhaps not to death but to a state of virginity and service in the Temple throughout her life (Judg. 11:1 to 12:7).

Meta. A very influential thought in the judgment faculty in man. Though cast out as evil by the more formal, established religious thoughts (his brethren), and denied inheritance with them, this Jephthah thought persists in holding to the good, to perfection. (Jephthah dwelt in the land of Tob, and Tob means *good;* the idea in the word is that all good and well-being come from the divine light within one.) Through Jehovah, the I AM (the open door to freedom when unified with the idea of wholeness, Truth, and understanding), the Jephthah thought becomes first a deliverer and then a judge of Israel (the true religious and spiritual thoughts of the consciousness). It even takes precedence over its brothers—which makes us think of Jesus' words to the effect that the publicans and harlots should enter the kingdom before self-righteous religious persons. This is because publicans and harlots believe and are cleansed when the Christ reveals Himself to the consciousness, while self-righteous persons, as well as self-righteous thoughts and ideals, are very likely to reject that which is truly spiritual (see Matthew 21:31, 32). So Jephthah, this ruling thought, having been given authority, leads the Israelites (true thoughts) to victory over the Ammonites (impure, ignorant, and disorderly thoughts), the soul is established in purity and Truth, and the land (body) has peace.

In fewer words, Jephthah could be said to be the judgment faculty *set free* from carnal thought and desire (his mother was a harlot) and restored to its rightful place in consciousness as the deliverer and judge of Israel.

Jephunneh, jĕ-phŭn'-nĕh (Heb.)— *which will be before his face; appearing; which holds attention; favorable-appearing; he will behold.*

a Father of Caleb, of the tribe of Judah (Num. 13:6). **b** Son of Jether, of the "children" of Asher (I Chron. 7:38, 40).

Meta. A thought in the Israelitish, or real, true, higher consciousness in man that, by attentively looking into (*he will behold, which holds attention*) the divine law and regarding it with favor, by seeking to promote the keeping of it (*which will be before his face, favorable-appearing*), brings to light in the consciousness spiritual faith and enthusiasm (Caleb, son of Jephunneh). Joyous life, praise, and prayer (Judah and Asher) do much to bring about the understanding of the law, as well as enthusiasm and faith in the possibility of keeping it, to the entire lifting up and spiritualizing of the whole organism (Caleb was one of the two spies who were sure that the Israelites were able to go in and possess the land).

Jerah, jē'-räh (Heb.)—*companionate radiation; radiating brother; he will breathe; he will become inspired; he will have sweet breath; moon; lunar month.*

Son of Joktan, a descendant of Shem, and the founder of an Arabian tribe (Gen. 10:26).

Meta. Jerah (*companionate radiation; he will breathe, he will become inspired, moon, lunar month*) refers to the light (understanding) of the inspired intellect, or to the fact that the intellect of man can and will become illumined by Spirit, and will radiate the light of Spirit—divine understanding.

Jerahmeel, jĕ-räh'-mĕ-ĕl (Heb.)— *whom God loves; on whom God has mercy; to whom God shows compassion; mother love of God.*

a Son of Hezron, who was a grandson of Judah (I Chron. 2:9). **b** Son of Kish, of the tribe of Levi (I Chron. 24:29). **c** "The king's son," one of those who were sent to arrest Baruch and Jeremiah (Jer. 36:26).

Meta. The true idea of God as a loving and compassionate father, mother, friend, and almighty resource, and not as an angry, revengeful deity. (When the personal man gets hold of this idea he is likely to carry it to an extreme by thinking that he can do anything that he wishes to do, even to the point of working directly against the divine law, and still reap only good.)

Jerahmeelites, jĕ-räh'-mĕ-ĕl-ītes (fr. Heb.)—*of or belonging to Jerahmeel.*

Descendants of Jerahmeel, son of Hezron of Judah (I Sam. 27:10).

Meta. Thoughts springing from and belonging to that in consciousness which Jerahmeel signifies. (See JERAHMEEL.)

Jered, jē'-rĕd (Heb.)—*going down, i. e., from a higher to a lower; descent; downcast; weeping; flowing down; flowing south; brought low; a mountain stream.*

Son of Ezrah (I Chron. 4:18). The same name as Jared.

Meta. Virtually the same meaning as Jared: the *descent* of the higher Truth thoughts into the subconsciousness (*flowing south*) and the body consciousness in one's seemingly mortal state (*brought low*), there to act as leaven and so to raise the whole of the individual to a higher, even to spiritual, understanding and demonstration. (See JARED.)

Jeremai, jĕr'-ĕ-māi (Heb.)—*of the heights; dwelling on high; dwelling on high places; mountaineer; set on high; Jah is high.*

One of the sons of Hashum who had taken a foreign wife (Ezra 10:33).

Meta. A high thought, or attitude of mind, in the consciousness of the spiritually awakening individual, but not entirely free from the influence of the lower emotions, affections, and desires of the phase of the soul that is given over to sense (he had taken a foreign wife).

Jeremiah (in A. V., Matthew 16:14, Jeremias; Matthew 2:17, Jeremy), jĕr-ĕ-mī'-ăh (Heb.)—*whom Jehovah sets up; whom Jah establishes; Jehovah will enthrone; Jah will set on high; exaltation of Jehovah.*

Besides the prophet Jeremiah there are several Israelitish men by this name in the Bible (I Chron. 5:24; 12:4, 10; II Kings 23:31, and others).

Meta. Spiritual faith demanding that all religious thoughts be true in observance of divine law.

The individual who has faith is very courageous spiritually, but in outer consciousness such a one may be timid and shrinking when directed by the Spirit of the Lord to testify to Truth, as was Jeremiah (see Jer. 1:4-10).

When ignorance and wickedness rule, faith is bound in the dungeon of materiality. When the extremity is great and the usual human aids are powerless, the ruling will (King Zedekiah) turns to submerged faith and asks the outcome.

Jeremiah is called the sorrowful prophet because he nearly always looked on the dark side and prophesied evil. When one's faith is pressed upon by thoughts of discouragement and condemnation one should deny belief in material bondage and affirm the living substance of Spirit as the one reality. King Zedekiah set Jeremiah free and gave him daily a loaf of bread, which represents denial and affirmation. Stimulate your faith in God by thinking of it and by using it. Faith is man's most marvelous faculty (*whom Jehovah sets up*), and if you have it in the very smallest degree (a grain of mustard seed) you can "remove mountains" (Jer. 37:4-21).

In Jeremiah 36 Jeremiah represents that exalted state of consciousness that connects us with Divine Mind (*exaltation of Jehovah*). He is that in us which intuitively discerns the divine law and seeks to impress it on the will (the king).

The meaning of Jeremiah's being shut up in the court of the guard so that he cannot go with his message into the house of Jehovah is that a separation in consciousness has been built up between the wisdom and the will; the will

has taken possession of the life in the organism, and has excluded the wisdom.

Jeremiah, in Jeremiah 26:8-16, represents spiritual consciousness' connecting us with Divine Mind. Spiritual consciousness sees the result of neglecting to make daily contact with God in prayer and in observance of divine law, and prophesies disaster like that which came to Shiloh (peace of mind).

Jeremoth, jĕr'-ĕ-mŏth (Heb.)—*elevations; heights; exaltations; terror of death; rejection of death.*

a A chief of Benjamin, who lived in Jerusalem (I Chron. 8:14). **b** Several other Israelitish men (I Chron. 23:23; 25:22; Ezra 10:26, 27).

Meta. Lofty, constructive thoughts in the true religious consciousness of man. Such thoughts aid in putting away death.

Jeriah, jē-rī'-ăh (Heb.)—*founded of Jehovah; constituted of Jah; Jehovah will throw, i. e., scatter as rain; Jah will sprinkle; Jehovah will point the way.*

A Kohathite Levite, son of Hebron, given a chief place by David in priestly service (I Chron. 23:19).

Meta. A strong religious tendency (Levite) that springs from the love faculty (Levi) and makes union with the outer conscious mind (Hebron, referring to the front brain, or seat of conscious thought). This religious tendency, or thought activity, has its inception in Spirit. It is based on Truth (*founded of Jehovah, constituted of Jah*) and it helps to water the germinating seeds of Truth throughout the consciousness and point the way to true worship of God, to true abidingness and wholeness (*Jehovah will throw, i. e., scatter as rain, Jehovah will point the way; Jeriah was given a chief place by David in priestly service in the Temple*).

Jeribai, jĕr'-ĭ-bāi (Heb.)—*for whom Jehovah pleads; whom Jehovah defends; for whom Jah strives; contention; strife; a quarrelsome adversary.*

One of David's mighty men (I Chron. 11:46), son of Elnaam.

Meta. The assurance of love (David) that our justice comes from the Lord and He will regulate all our affairs. When we know Truth and abide by it we do not have to contend with seeming adversaries within or without. We only need to turn them over to the Lord, the divine law of justice, and to declare the Truth, while Spirit adjusts our life and fights our battles for us.

Jericho, jĕr'-ĭ-eho (Heb.)—*place of fragrance; his sweet breath; his life; his animation; his soul; his mind; his spirit; his moon renewing.*

A city just over the Jordan in the land of Canaan. It was the first city that was taken and destroyed by the Israelites after their entering the Promised Land (Josh. 2:1; 6).

Meta. The definitions of Jericho express relative terms; that is, they stand in a state of dependence on the Absolute. The word expresses the elemental *soul, life, mind, spirit*—reflected breath and mind, the outer, intellectual—in contrast to the inner spirit. Jericho signifies the intellect, an external or reflected state of consciousness. The moon does not shine with its own light, but merely reflects the light of the sun. Before astronomy was a science men thought the moon emitted its own light. To the eye this is true today, but the scientific mind knows better. The relation of the moon to the sun is that of the intellect to Spirit. The intellect seems to express the light of understanding, but the science of Being reveals that it shines by reflected light.

Even as the moon is part of our planetary system, so the intellect has a legitimate place in consciousness. It is when intellect becomes egotistical, thinks that it originates its own light, and forms the adverse consciousness called Devil, or carnal mind, that it is out of harmony with the divine.

Luke 19:1 mentions that Jesus Christ (I AM) passed through Jericho (intellect) in His redemptive work.

Jericho is the opposite of Jerusalem. One represents the spiritual; the other, the material. We often start from Jerusalem with high spiritual resolves, but are robbed by outlaw thoughts on the way (Luke 10:30).

In II Kings 2:4, Jericho, the *moon* city, refers to the life center in the lower part of the abdomen. In verses 15 to 22 Jericho represents human consciousness in its relation to life. The "water" (verse 19) symbolizes the issues of life. The "land" signifies the body. When man is firmly established in his spiritual dominion, all his thoughts (men of the city) turn to the I AM (Elisha) for purification and healing. This is the explanation of Elisha's healing the waters (verses 19-22). Were men pure in thought, their bodies would be perfectly healthy and harmonious; but the issues of life (waters) have become polluted by error thoughts, and so the thoughts must be cleansed, made pure and healthful.

Jeriel, jē'-rĭ-ĕl (Heb.)—*founded by God; constituted by God; God points the way; vision of God; God scatters the early rain.*

Son of Tola, of the sons of Issachar. He was one of those who were "heads of their father's houses" (I Chron. 7:2).

Meta. A strong, spiritually enlightened, directive, cherishing (*vision of God, God points the way, God scatters the early rain*), ruling thought belonging to the zeal faculty in individual consciousness (a chief man of Issachar), that has its foundation in Spirit and receives its impetus from Spirit (*founded by God, constituted by God*).

Jerijah, jê-rī'-jäh (Heb.)—*founded of Jehovah; constituted of Jah; Jehovah will throw, i. e., scatter as rain; Jah will sprinkle; Jehovah will point the way.*

A "chief" of the Hebronites, in David's reign (I Chron. 26:31). Jeriah is the same name.

Meta. See JERIAH.

Jerimoth, jĕr'-ĭ-mŏth (Heb.)—*elevations; heights; exaltations; terror of death; rejection of death.*

The name of several prominent Israelites, some of the tribe of Benjamin, some Levites, and one a son of David, though not named in the general list of his sons (I Chron. 7:7; 12:5; 24:30; 25:4; II Chron. 11:18; 31:13).

Meta. High thoughts in the true religious consciousness of man—thoughts of faith and love (descendants of Benjamin and Levi) centered in the recognition of God as life, omnipresent and abiding in all its fullness. Thus the error idea of death is put away (*rejection of death*).

Jerioth, jē′-rĭ-ŏth (Heb.)—*veils; curtains; canopies; tents; tabernacles; tremulous; shakings; quakings; timidity.*

A wife of Caleb's, according to the reading of the text (I Chron. 2:18). Fallows says, "This seems to be contrary to the Hebrew text, and Jerioth was probably Caleb's daughter."

Meta. Fearfulness and lack of courage and positiveness (*tremulous, timidity*) that envelop the soul at times, so long as the individual still believes in a limited consciousness of life in the body (*tents, tabernacles*). Such thoughts cause obscurity of the inner vision, a certain darkness or lack of understanding (*veils, curtains*). Inner *shakings* and *quakings* may also be felt as reactions from too much vehemence and zeal, such as Caleb signifies, especially when the personal enters into one's zealous efforts to put away error and build up Truth.

Jeroboam, jĕr-ŏ-bō′-ăm (Heb.)—*whose people is many; many people; multiplying people; adverse people; hostile people; contentious people; the people's advocate; who pleads for the people.*

The first king of Israel after the ten tribes revolted and broke away from the rule of Rehoboam, Solomon's son (I Kings 12:20).

Meta. Jeroboam symbolizes what the name implies—the people are adverse (*adverse people, hostile people, contentious people*). The thoughts of man are his people.

The Rehoboam kingdom, called the kingdom of Judah, stands for the natural life forces of the organism, the subjective consciousness. The Jeroboam kingdom, the kingdom of Israel, signifies the intellect, or the objective consciousness. The division of the Israelites into two kingdoms represents the separation between the subjective and objective planes of consciousness. Jeroboam's withdrawal of the ten tribes of Israel from the kingdom of Rehoboam represents man's withdrawal into intellectual realms of consciousness, thus leaving the life forces to express the dominant ideas in body consciousness. This separation comes about as follows:

The memory of past experiences is stored in the subjective consciousness; also, the "book of the law" as given by Moses. By recognition of these stored-up treasures, and by constant looking to the one true God for help, man comes surely, step by step, into his Divine birthright: sonship with God. The intellect perceives powers and possibilities beyond its present demonstration, and endeavors to make a short cut in the attainment and use of these possessions.

After this separation in consciousness occurs, man lives in sense consciousness so long as he fails to unify the intellect and its activities with the wisdom of the subjective mind, wherein are also the life forces of the organism.

The ten tribes of Israel failed to prosper and grow spiritually under the leadership of Jeroboam because states of consciousness not founded on Principle must be broken up and reorganized. The ten tribes, faculties of mind, had withdrawn from Judah, representing the central faculty of consciousness. This faculty operates in body consciousness through the spinal cord and finds its outer expression through the life center, which, if unregenerated, is "Judas," who had a devil. When life is separated from the other faculties and endeavors to express without their coöperation man gives himself over to his animal nature.

But man works out his salvation even when he has broken the natural laws. His salvation comes through his remembering his innate spirituality. The Israelites are God's chosen people, and there is ever at the center of consciousness a divine urge to return to God and a sure feeling that the fullness of good is man's birthright. The Spirit of truth is ever present, seeking to reveal the Son to man, and man will receive the Word when he has convinced himself that sense efforts cannot set up a personal kingdom.

Jeroboam made false gods to worship because man is inherently religious and when he turns away mentally from Divine Mind he becomes restless. If he is being ruled by his intellect he naturally turns to the objective world and tries to deify some house of worship, a personality, material things, or an object of sense.

True worship is the recognition of God as omnipresent Spirit and the realization and identification of man as a spiritual being. When man takes up the study of Truth he begins to feel the quickening of Spirit. Spiritual understanding shows man that mind and body must' be united, and both thoughts and acts must come under the dominion of the spiritual I AM, the Christ mind. As the mind is opened to receive this Truth, it flows into consciousness, a cleansing, purifying, strengthening, illuminating stream of life and light (I Kings 12:6-33).

Jeroham, jĕr'-ŏ-hăm (Heb.)—*He (Jehovah) is compassionate; who finds mercy; he will cherish; he will love.*

a Father of Elkanah of the hill country of Ephraim, and grandfather of Samuel the prophet (I Sam. 1:1). **b** There were several other Israelites by this name (I Chron. 9:8, 12; 12:7; 27:22; Neh. 11:12).

Meta. Spiritual ideas of divine love, mercy, tender compassion, and support (*He is compassionate,· who finds mercy, he will cherish, he will love*) becoming active in the various faculties of individual consciousness that are represented by the tribes to which the Israelitish men by this name belonged: the will (Ephraim), faith (Benjamin), love (Levi), and judgment (Dan).

Jerubbaal, jĕr-ŭb-bā'-ăl (Heb.)—*with whom Baal contends; contender with Baal; Baal of strife; adverse Baal; Baal the adversary; who is to plead for Baal; let Baal defend himself.*

The name that Joash gave his son Gideon when Gideon had destroyed the altar of Baal and the Asherah, and had built an altar to Jehovah and offered up burnt offerings on it. The people wanted Joash to have Gideon put to death for cutting down the altar of Baal and the Asherah, but Joash said of Baal, "If he be a god, let him contend for himself, because one hath broken down his altar. Therefore on that day he called him Jerubbaal, saying, Let Baal contend against him" (Judg. 6:31, 32). Jerubbaal, or Gideon, defeated the Midianites, delivered Israel, and judged Israel for forty years (Judg. 7:1 to 8:32).

Meta. At this time the Israelites had so lost their consciousness of the one true God that they were worshiping Baal, or materiality. For them to be conducted out of darkness it was necessary that some capable leader be raised up. This leader was found in the person of Gideon or Jerubbaal. Jerubbaal is a family name, meaning *contender with Baal.* The name shows that he came from a family naturally opposed to the rule of materiality. This idea found its culmination in Gideon, which means *destroyer.* (See GIDEON.)

Jerubbesheth, jĕ-rŭb'-bĕ-shĕth (Heb.) —*who contends with idolatry; contender with shame; strife with ignominy; let the idol of disgrace defend itself.*

A name of Gideon, a form of the name Jerubbaal (II Sam. 11:21); in Judges 6:32, Jerubbaal.

Meta. See JERUBBAAL.

Jeruel, jĕ-rụ'-ĕl (Heb.)—*foundation of God; founded of God; God points the way; vision of God.*

A wilderness, where Jehoshaphat met and defeated the children of Ammon and Moab. This was the battle wherein Jehoshaphat was told that the battle was not his but God's and that he would not have to fight in it; he was simply to stand still, fearlessly, and see the salvation of Jehovah (II Chron. 20:16).

Meta. A firm trust in God—the mind stayed on God (*foundation of God, founded of God*)—even when one seems to be in a wilderness of conflicting, undisciplined thoughts. Thus spiritual inspiration (*God points the way, vision of God*) is realized and victory is gained over the carnal mind and the wild, uncultivated states of thought that are signified by Moab and Ammon.

Jerusalem, jĕ-rụ'-så-lĕm (Heb.)—*habitation of peace; dwelling place of peace; possession of peace; foundation of peace; constitution of harmony; vision of peace; abode of prosperity.*

The capital city of Palestine. In Abraham's time it was called Salem (Gen. 14:18). It was called Jebus later, when it was inhabited and ruled by the Jebusites (Judg. 19:10; I Chron. 1:4). The first time that it is mentioned in the Bible as Jerusalem is in Joshua 10:1. In Revelation 21:2 it is used symbolically to describe the redeemed state of man. *Meta.* Jerusalem means *habitation of peace.* In man it is the abiding consciousness of spiritual peace, which is the result of continuous realizations of spiritual power tempered with spiritual poise and confidence. Jerusalem is the "city of David," which symbolizes the great nerve center just back of the heart. From this point Spirit sends its radiance to all parts of the body.

The wall that Nehemiah's men (spiritual thoughts) were building around Jerusalem (Neh. 4:17) symbolizes in individual consciousness protecting spiritual substance, which limited error thoughts cannot penetrate. This wall is built by our realization of the enduring strength and stability of omnipresent Spirit substance. The rebuilding of the wall of Jerusalem under the direction of Nehemiah can also be said to symbolize the balancing of the negative and positive forces of the soul consciousness. This equalization will result in the renewing and spiritualizing of the whole organism.

A feast in Jerusalem (John 5:1) is a receptive state of mind toward all spiritual good. When we get deep down into the silent recesses of our soul we realize a stillness and a sweetness beyond expression. There is a great peace there, the "peace of God, which passeth all understanding" (Phil. 4:7) and fills the whole being with satisfaction. This is the point in consciousness where the inflow of original substance takes place. The substance center is physically a nerve center just back of the stomach; spiritually it is the soul's realization of the unfailing substance of Divine Mind.

The one way to Jerusalem, the city of peace, is the Christ way—perfect expression of all the mental faculties (disciples), under the dominion of the I AM (see Luke 17:11). We all long for the state in which we shall have peace. *Jeru,* the first part of Jerusalem, means *founding, constituting; Salem,* the latter part of the word, means *peace, quiet, safety, harmony, prosperity.* We are on the way to the attainment of peace when we identify ourselves with the Christ idea, originally called Jehovah, I AM.

Jesus' going up to Jerusalem (Matt. 20:17) means taking the last step in unfoldment preparatory to the final step, when the personality is entirely crucified and the Christ triumphs.

Jesus' riding out from near Bethphage into Jerusalem signifies progressive unfoldment, the fulfillment of the time when the spiritual I AM takes control and lifts all the animal forces of man into the spiritual plane of mastery, purity, and peace. It is the season for transmutation, transformation (Matt. 21:1-9).

Truth is first conceived in the heart of man, of which Jerusalem is the symbol, but because of intellectual dominance it drifts to the head, of which Rome is the symbol. Paul taken to Rome in chains is a fitting symbol of Truth captured by the intellect and confined to the bonds that it has placed upon itself (Acts 28:14-20).

Jerusalem, the Holy City (Matt. 23:37-39), represents the love center in consciousness. Physically it is the cardiac plexus. Its presiding genius is John the Mystic, who leaned his head on the Master's bosom. The loves and hates of the mind are precipitated to this ganglionic receptacle of thought and are crystallized there. Its substance is sensitive, tremulous, and volatile. What we love and what we hate here build cells of joy or of pain. In divine order it should be the abode of the good and the pure, but because of the error concepts of the mind it has become the habitation of wickedness. Jesus said, "Out of the heart come forth evil thoughts" (Matt. 15:18-20).

In the regeneration, Truth (symbolized by Paul, Acts 21:13 to 22:1) visits this holy place for the purpose of redeeming it. But Truth finds the very center of religious thought, the Temple, given over to bigotry and intolerance; a citadel of crystallized thoughts about religious matters. Truth must enter the Temple and speak the word that frees.

We all want Truth and the help that comes from it, but when it is presented to us we object to the broad, universal spirit that it proclaims. This is especially the case if our religious training has been narrow and pharisaical. The Jews were taught that they were the chosen people and that all others were barbarians. This is the foundation of the caste system. When man begins in thought to believe himself better than other men, he makes a place in his body that is the dwelling of this thought of superiority. Next this separation extends to environment. Separation in a physical sense follows. Temples are built with partitions, and whoever dares to transgress these walls meets opposition.

When Truth comes to one who is in this fixed state of mind, there is a tumult "in the temple." Fear that the rites and customs of the church will be interfered with is uppermost. The teachings of those in authority and the customs and beliefs of the past are of more weight than reason and logic. An innovation in methods of thought is resisted. The whole religious nature is moved. Thought runs to meet thought, and a concentration of resistance is set up in the mind that forces Truth right out and closes the doors, as described in the 30th verse.

Many people wonder why they do not develop divine love more quickly. Here is the reason: They make a wall of separation between the Jew and the Gentile, the religious and the secular, the good and the bad. Divine love sees no such difference between persons. It is Principle, and feels its own perfection everywhere. It feels the same in the heart of the sinner as in the heart of the saint. When we let this truth into our heart and pull down all walls of separation, we shall feel the flow of infinite love.

When we cast Truth from our heart and seek to kill it, the secular realms of thought also put it in bonds. The ruling intellect sees in it an assassin, who has been inciting a revolt against the intellectual authority. This ruler of the mind has little respect for religion but has a mighty awe of the rights of a Roman citizen. So when it learns that Truth (Paul) is both Jew and Gentile, common to both head and heart, it gives due respect, which goes to show that Truth is safer in the bonds of skepticism and infidelity than with the bigotry and fanaticism of ignorant religious zeal.

The "new Jerusalem" of Revelation 21:2 is spiritual consciousness, and it is founded on the twelve fundamental ideas in Divine Mind, each represented by one of these precious stones. It also represents an association of all people in peace, based on spiritual understanding, purity, and a willingness to be united with Christ —"made ready as a bride adorned for her husband."

Jerusha, jĕ-ru̇'-shȧ (Heb.)—*taking; seizing; possessing; possession; inheritance; heredity.*

Daughter of Zadok, also wife of Uzziah and mother of Jotham, kings of Judah (II Kings 15:33). She is called Jerushah in II Chronicles 27:1.

Meta. Man's *possession* by *inheritance*, his hereditary possession, is the soul, the whole consciousness, at one with the Christ mind and constantly open to ideas from the one Mind. The thought of *taking, seizing, possessing,* shows that man has work to do in order to enter into conscious oneness with Spirit, his divine inheritance. Thus Jerusha is a fitting daughter of Zadok, meaning *righteous,* and wife of Uzziah king of Judah, signifying *divine strength,* and mother of Jotham king of Judah, meaning *whom Jah makes perfect.*

Jeshaiah (in A. V., I Chronicles 3:21, Jesaiah), jĕ-shā'-ia̧h (Heb.)—*Jehovah is liberty; liberation of Jah; Jehovah delivers; Jah is help; safety of Jehovah; prosperity of Jah; Jehovah is opulent.*

There were several Israelites by this name (I Chron. 3:21; 25:3, 15; 26:25; Ezra 8:7, 19).

Meta. This name is virtually the same as Isaiah, and its symbology is the same: the higher self, *Jehovah delivers.* Spiritual understanding in us discerns the reality, or the real character, of spiritual man, I AM, Jehovah, and receives divine help in our daily overcoming.

Jeshanah, jĕsh'-a̧-nah (Heb.)—*sleeping; slumbering; inactive; dry; listless; old,* i. e., *not new.*

A place in Palestine whose cities were taken from Jeroboam by Abijah (II Chron. 13:19).

Meta. Inactivity; thoughts that are not open to new ideas, to the activity of spiritual life and youth, but cling to the old ways and old ideas. Such thoughts are at the root of old-age manifestations; the sleeping youth in each individual needs resurrecting, even as Jesus raised Lazarus, that true wakefulness, receptivity, and activity may be brought about.

Jesharelah, jĕ-shär′-ĕ-läh (Heb.)—*upright toward God; God is righteous; God's equity; plain way of God,* i. e., *not difficult; prospered of God.*

A Levite musician who had charge of those on whom the seventh lot fell for Temple service in music (I Chron. 25: 14). In verse 2 he is called Asharelah.

Meta. The significance is virtually the same as that of Asharelah: uprightness of thought, the upward look, the attention fixed on God, Spirit. This, with love, the joining, unifying quality in individual consciousness, does much toward keeping one's mind and body "in tune with the Infinite," in divine harmony. The way of Truth is clear, smooth, harmonious, to the one whose eye is single to the one Good (*plain way of God,* i. e., *not difficult*).

Jeshebeab, jĕ-shĕb′-ĕ-ăb (Heb.)— *seat of the father; sitting of the father,* i. e., *in judgment; abiding place of the father; temple of the Father (God).*

A priest in David's reign, who had charge of the fourteenth course in Temple service (I Chron. 24:13).

Meta. The fact that man is the dwelling place of God (*seat of the father, temple of the Father*). The individual awakening to the truth that the heavenly Father's *seat,* abiding place, or established place of rule, is within man.

Jesher, jē′-shĕr (Heb.)—*evenness; balance; plainness; straightness; uprightness; righteousness; integrity; tranquillity; radiating brightness; brilliant; joyous; harmonious.*

Son of Caleb by Azubah his wife (I Chron. 2:18).

Meta. Integrity and *uprightness* of thought and act, unbiased by error or prejudice. Such a life experiences and radiates light, peace, joy, and harmony.

Jeshishai, jĕ-shĭsh′-āi (Heb.)—*of or pertaining to age; son of venerable age; hoary; whiteness; purity; brilliance; tranquillity; wisdom.*

A man of the Israelitish tribe of Gad (I Chron. 5:14).

Meta. The idea that wisdom, peace, and true purity of thought and life come by age, experience, worship or great veneration of age, of that which is old: relics, thoughts and beliefs of ancestors, and so forth. Man must be watchful not to let this idea have place in his consciousness to the extent that his mind becomes closed to new ideas, since holding to the old hinders growth and is a direct cause of old age (*of* or *pertaining to age*).

Jeshohaiah, jĕsh-ŏ-hā′-ĭah (Heb.)— *whom Jehovah bows down; humbled by Jah; inclined toward Jehovah; of humble mind toward Jehovah; emptied for Jehovah; meditation of Jehovah.*

A man of the tribe of Simeon (I Chron. 4:36).

Meta. A humble, receptive state of thought. By meditating on the things of Spirit (*inclined toward Jehovah, meditation of Jehovah*) in a receptive attitude of mind (Simeon), one may be shown a shortcoming that one must put away, perhaps some outer word or act that must be corrected. This causes one to feel very humble, especially if one has really entered a consciousness of the inner divine presence of perfect purity, wisdom, life, and Truth (*humbled by Jah*). See James 4:10, in conjunction with this name, and enter a positive attitude of mind—a realization of your I AM power and dominion—which brings victory over all that falls short of the perfect law of God in your life; which raises your consciousness to its rightful place of oneness with God, with all wisdom, love, power, strength, and Truth.

Jeshua, jĕsh′-ū-å (Heb.)—*Jehovah is deliverance; Jehovah is help; Jehovah is salvation; Jah is freedom; safety is of Jehovah; opulence of Jah; abundance of Jehovah.*

a A priest on whom the ninth lot fell for Temple service, in David's reign (I Chron. 24:11). **b** A priest who was under Kore, the son of Imnah the Levite, in taking care of the freewill offerings in Hezekiah's reign (II Chron. 31:15). **c** One who came back from the Babylonian captivity with Zerubbabel (Ezra 2: 2). **d** A name for Joshua son of Nun, who led the Children of Israel into the Promised Land (Neh. 8:17).

Meta. Salvation or redemption through Jehovah, I AM. See JOSHUA.

Jeshurun (in A. V., Isaiah 44:2, Jesurun), jĕsh'-ū-rŭn (Heb.)—*rectitude; righteousness; justice; upright; the brilliant one; tranquillity; harmony; happiness; blessedness.*

A symbolical name applied to Israel (Deut. 32:15; 33:5, 26; Isa. 44:2).

Meta. The happy state (*blessedness*) of our real, religious thoughts (Israel), especially when they have become *upright* according to the true spiritual standard of righteousness, which includes love, mercy, good judgment, order, and the activity of all the faculties of the mind raised to spiritual consciousness.

Jesimiel, jĕ-sĭm'-ĭ-ĕl (Heb.)—*whom God has set up; constituted of God; whom God appoints; designation of God; naming of God; builded of God; God-made.*

A man named in the genealogy of Simeon (I Chron. 4:36), a chief, or prince.

Meta. An influential thought in the spiritually receptive, attentive, obedient attitude of mind in man (Simeon), which acknowledges God, Spirit, as the power that not only created man (*builded of God, God-made*), but that also establishes him in his rightful place in Being (*whom God has set up*), and gives him his true character (*naming of God*).

Jesse, jĕs'-sĕ (Heb.)—*upstanding; firm; strong; upright; he will give; Jah exists; Jah is; he who is.*

Son of Obed, grandson of Boaz and Ruth, and father of David (Ruth 4:22; I Sam. 16). He was an Ephrathite of Beth–lehem–judah (I Sam. 17:12).

Meta. In the Hebrew the root meaning of the word Jesse is Jah, Jehovah, or I AM, representing eternal existence (*Jah exists*). When man realizes the eternal existence of I AM, and is *firm* and *strong* in this realization, he is in the Jesse state of mind, and out of this state of mind will come God's idea of man, Christ. This is the "shoot," the "fruit" of the root idea that man is the ever living I AM of God (Isa. 11:1). (David, son of Jesse, is representative of the Christ, or of the spiritual seed whence came Jesus Christ, spiritual man expressed and demonstrated.)

Jesus, jē'-ṣŭs (Gk. fr. Heb. Jeshua or Joshua)—*whose help Jehovah is; deliverance; safety; salvation; Savior; Deliverer; helper; prosperer; deliverance through Jehovah.*

Jesus of Nazareth, son of Mary, and, according to the present-day Christian belief, the Savior of mankind. "Thou shalt call his name JESUS; for it is he that shall save his people from their sins" (Matt. 1:21).

Meta. The *I* in man, the self, the directive power, raised to divine understanding and power—the I AM identity.

Jesus represents God's idea of man in expression; Christ is that idea in the absolute. Jesus Christ was the type man, which includes all the mental phases through which man passes in demonstrating life's problems. So we find Jesus Christ passing through all the trials, temptations, and mental variations of each of us, "*yet* without sin," that is, not falling under the dominion of evil thoughts. The experiences of each individual are in miniature the experiences of all.

We may "put on the new man," that is, bring forth Jesus Christ in ourselves. First we must put away the "old man" of error and limitation through denial of his reality. The second step is to accept the truth of our being, in faith; then through understanding to begin diligently to live Truth in thought, word, and deed. The Christ is the man that God created, the perfect-idea man, and is the real self of all men; Jesus Christ is this Christ self brought forth into perfect expression and manifestation.

Jesus, the man of Nazareth, demonstrated that this attainment is possible to man, and as a consequence He is the type-man. We are exhorted to "have this mind in you, which was also in Christ Jesus," which implies that all may demonstrate as He did. To make this attainment requires careful training of the thoughts. The mind that was in Christ Jesus was the mind of God, so we know that we must be perfect even as the Father in heaven is perfect. This seems an almost superhuman attainment, and so it is. The human has to be put away and the divine established in its place.

The human is transient and fallible; the divine is permanent and infallible.

In the individual consciousness the meaning of Jesus' being born in Bethlehem of Judea is that the principles of Truth have laid hold of the intelligent substance of Spirit (Bethlehem), and through praise (Judea) have brought the Christ into manifestation.

It is wise to protect the newborn spiritual consciousness from contact with Herod, the personal ego. Herod seeks "the young child to destroy him," but under the guidance of Spirit no harm comes to the Child. He is taken down into Egypt (down into the protected places of the subconsciousness), to remain until the personal ego destroys itself; then the Christ child is free to come forth and to express.

Jesus in the Temple, at the age of twelve years, represents the growing consciousness within us that we are sons of God (Luke 2:40-52).

Jesus' going about all the cities and villages, teaching, preaching, and healing, represents the I AM in its universal capacity as a teacher and harmonizer of its own mental and bodily conditions (Matt. 9:35).

The "twelve" sent forth by Jesus (Matt. 10:5) typify the twelve faculties of mind in every man, functioning under the direction of I AM.

The *I* (Jesus) and His disciples (faculties) are always bidden to these unions of planes of consciousness (marriages; see John 2:2).

Jesus, in Luke 7:36-38, represents Divine Mind in its search for the motive rather than the outer act.

The temptation of Jesus (Matt. 4:1-11) took place within Himself. The place of overcoming is within the consciousness of man. When we follow Jesus we rise above the demands of the flesh-and-sense world. The forty days' fast is an all-round denial of sense demands. In fasting, we in our thoughts live above the material needs. We are "led up," and our appetites and passions are for a season in such an eclipse that we think that they will trouble no more. But "he afterward hungered." There is a return to sense consciousness.

The Devil is personality, the adverse consciousness that has been built up in ignorance and disregard of the divine law.

The temptation to turn stones into bread illustrates the thought of ignorance that deceives people with the belief that they can satisfy the soul with materiality, without looking for the bread that comes from heaven, the Word of God. We must feed our soul with new truths daily, that we may grow in spiritual ways.

The second temptation of Jesus means that no display of spiritual power for personal glory should be made. We cannot make a display of our spiritual power with safety.

To worship the Devil is to worship personality; to live in personal consciousness and give it the substance of our life and thought. When the temptation arises in our consciousness to use our God-attained spiritual faculties and powers for the building of our personal ambitions, we should know that under the divine law there is but one worthy of our worship and service, the Lord God. To serve God we must build up spirituality in mind, body, and affairs.

In Luke 4:16-30 Jesus represents the Spirit of truth declaring its mission and power in the place of its development, the common, everyday mind. The highest spiritual Truth may be flashed into your mind while you are performing the commonest duties of life. Nazareth is a type of inferiority; it was considered a community of commonplace, if not disreputable, people. "Can any good thing come out of Nazareth?" Yet in that mediocre village Jesus was reared—and in any one's mediocre mind the Christ Truth is expressed.

We know many of the trite statements of Truth so well that we find it hard to conceive that they are the mighty power that can relieve us from the bonds of sense. "Is not this Joseph's son?" But in no other place shall we find the Truth that sets free. The power that brings salvation from every ill is within us; it is in the gracious words of the indwelling Christ. "To-day hath this scripture been fulfilled in your ears." Every day our inner ears are filled full of this Truth. We know the right, we know the just, we know the pure. This is "this scripture" that is written on the heart.

Do you ask for a sign of power? Do you want miraculous healing without fulfilling the law of right thinking and right doing? Then you are not receiving the Christ Spirit rightly. You are seeking the temporal instead of the eternal, and if you let this superficial phase of mind rule, you will reject the Christ Spirit and cast it out of your midst.

Mark 9:2-13 tells us of the Transfiguration: Jesus went up into a mountain to pray, and was there transfigured. Prayer always brings about an exalted or rapid radiation of mental energy, and when it is accompanied by faith (Peter), love (John), and judgment (James) there is a lifting up of the soul that electrifies the body; the raiment (the aura surrounding the body) shines with glistening whiteness.

The presence of Moses and Elijah represents the two processes through which this picture of the purified man is to be objectified or demonstrated in real life. The first is the Mosaic or evolutionary process of nature through which there is a steady upward trend of all things. This evolutionary process is part of a spiritual plan for the redemption of the human race from its fallen state. The other is the ability of the prophet Elijah, or spiritual discerner of Truth, to make conditions change rapidly on the mental plane, to be in due season worked out in substance. Thus we are told in the lesson that Elijah must first come and restore all things. The mind must first be set right through spiritual understanding; then comes the demonstration.

Peter's proposing to erect three tabernacles carries out this idea of a substance manifestation for each; but Peter's ideas were vague as to the process, hence the accompanying voice out of the cloud, "This is my beloved Son: hear ye him."

To "tell no man what things they had seen, save when the Son of man should have risen again from the dead," means that we shall not consider these mental pictures as real, and so discuss them.

They represent ideas that can be understood only when they are demonstrated in the risen man. ("These mental pictures" refers to visions, dreams, and all that we see in our high moments of illumination.)

Jesus rode an ass into Jerusalem (Matt. 21:1-9). In Oriental countries, in Bible times, kings and rulers rode the ass, and this animal was the accepted bearer of royalty. In the man-consciousness, the animal part is typified by the ass, and its being ridden into Jerusalem by Jesus portrays the mastery by the I AM of the animal nature and its manifestation (colt). Jerusalem means *habitation of peace* and signifies spiritual consciousness.

"The Lord hath need of them." These forces of the so-called lower nature in man are necessary to his full expression. A man or woman with the animal nature asleep or suppressed is but partially alive. The vital fires are in this department of being, and it is in this purifying furnace that the material man is melted and the pure gold extracted.

Those who live on the plane of mere animal generation do not ride the ass into Jerusalem—they are not masters of their animal nature—but, like the beasts of the field, are mere slaves to animal desire.

In the regeneration these animal forces are turned inward; they become powers in a higher field of action. To fulfill this part of their mission they must be wholly weaned from animal habits. So long as the animal rules, the man is a slave. When the I AM man takes charge of the body, a new order of things is inaugurated. The vitality is no longer wasted in mere sense gratification. Through high and pure ideals the whole consciousness is raised to a higher standard. Through interior thought concentration the subtle essences of the organism are transmuted to vibratory energies and become important factors in building up that pure body which is to triumph over death.

Let not the one who is indulging the sense man in his animal ways think that he is on the royal road into Jerusalem. "Blessed *is* he that cometh in the name of the Lord." The Lord is the higher ruling principle in man; it is to be in supremacy, not the lower. There is much sophistry among a certain school of metaphysicians who love to live the life of the animal, and call it God. The Master metaphysician said, "That which is born of the flesh is flesh; and that which is born of the Spirit is spirit." Another said, "Be not deceived; God is not mocked: for whatsoever a man soweth, that shall he also reap. For he that soweth unto his own flesh shall of the flesh reap corruption; but he that soweth unto the Spirit shall of the Spirit reap eternal life."

The characteristics of the ass are meekness, stubbornness, persistency, and endurance. To ride these is to make them obedient to one's will. The outer thoughts, or people, recognize that some unusual movement of mind is going on, and they fall into line. Their cry, "Hosanna," means *save now*. A change of base from personal willfulness to meekness and obedience stirs the whole consciousness, or city, and there is questioning about the cause. Simply saying in the silence, "Not my will, but thine, be done," often stirs up a commotion, and then there is questioning as to the cause. The answer is, "This is the prophet [one who states the spiritual law], Jesus [the I AM], from Nazareth [place of development] of Galilee" (life activity). Rendered in modern metaphysical terms this would read, "This is the supreme I AM stating the law of Spirit in development of life action."

The betrayal of Jesus means, to individual consciousness, the appropriation and use in sense ways of the life and substance that the higher self imparts to us in our periods of exaltation. When we deny the bondage of sense and affirm our spiritual freedom, we set free in the organism an energy or vibratory force that goes through the nerves to every part. This is the eating of the Passover with our disciples. But these disciples, or faculties, are not all in understanding of the divine law and they do not use this spiritual force in right ways. This is shown by their desire to have first place (see Luke 9:46), implying

carnal ambition. Jesus demonstrated humility and a willingness to serve—which is always a sign of the true disciple—by washing their feet.

Judas represents the personal self of the body, whose center of consciousness is in the sex function. This consciousness is directly connected with appetite and feeling. This is indicated by the phrase, "He that dipped his hand with me in the dish, the same shall betray me." In body consciousness that which we eat is finally appropriated by this function and deposited in the seminal glands as a reserve supply for the whole nervous system. In this respect its office is good, and when its work is well done, physical harmony ensues.

Judas develops selfishness and sense desire, however. He steals the substance that should go to the upbuilding of the organism, and wastes it in sexual and other sense sensations. In this way he is a "thief" and is possessed of "a devil." When the new life from the spiritual fountain is poured into the body, Judas absorbs so much of it that its identity and power are lost in the consciousness, which is typified by the betrayal of the Christ. In the end Judas destroys himself, because he is ignorant of the constructive law.

There is, however, a feeding of all the faculties through descent of the divine life and substance, which is typified by the eating and drinking of the body and the blood of the Master. When we know the ways of Judas we are on our guard and we declare the law for him, and thus pave the way for his final redemption.

At the crucifixion of Jesus it was the human consciousness of a perishable body that died. "Our old man was crucified with *him*, that the body of sin might be done away, that so we should no longer be in bondage to sin." When the thoughts of sin and death are crossed out, the spiritual truth about life and its manifestation in the body takes form in consciousness. "The Spirit of him that raised up Jesus . . . shall give life also to your mortal bodies." This is pictured in the resurrection of Jesus as an angel of the Lord descending from heaven (the ruling spiritual kingdom) and rolling away the stone from the door of the tomb.

This angel in man's consciousness is the spiritual I AM. "I am the resurrection, and the life." The tomb represents the most negative phase of material thought or human ignorance. The descent of the spiritual ego into consciousness brings divine intelligence and power within and without. "His appearance was as lightning, and his raiment white as snow."

The first affirmation of the I AM for its body is that it is not under any limitation of material thought; that it is free with the freedom of Spirit. "He is not here: for he is risen." The second affirmation of the I AM for its body is a swift and universal proclamation of omnipresence and activity in all realms of consciousness. "Go quickly, and tell his disciples, He is risen . . . and . . . goeth before you into Galilee; there shall ye see him: lo, I have told you."

Jesus resurrected the body that was crucified; this is forcibly brought out in the Scripture account of the crucifixion. He did this by putting into the body the true state of consciousness. "Put on the new man, that after God hath been created in righteousness and holiness of truth."

We can resurrect our body just as Jesus resurrected His. "Follow me." We can overcome, and make our body like the body of Jesus. We must do this. "The law of the Spirit of life in Christ Jesus made me free from the law of sin and of death." We resurrect our body by putting a new mind into it—the mind of Spirit. "Be ye transformed by the renewing of your mind." Ignorance and sin kill the body; understanding and righteousness bring it to life.

The three days that Jesus was in the tomb represent the three movements of mind that are involved in overcoming error. First, nonresistance and humility; second, the taking on of the divine activity, or receiving the will of God; third, the assimilation and fulfillment of the divine will.

In individual consciousness the "Sabbath" is perfect rest in Spirit, after the cleansing of mind that follows the introduction and activity of Truth principles. Jesus arose "late on the Sabbath day."

In consciousness the two women, "Mary Magdalene and the other Mary," symbolize the feminine side of the soul forces of Jesus (manifest man). "Mary Magdalene" signifies love redeemed. "The other Mary" represents pure life thoughts welling up from the subconsciousness.

The "angel of the Lord" represents positive spiritual thought of the perfect law of life. The "watchers" at the tomb are the thoughts that tend to limit the activity of the body consciousness. The "disciples" represent ideas of Divine Mind that have centers of action in body consciousness.

The spiritual meaning of the two women's being sent to tell the disciples of the resurrection is that divine love and life must be felt in the centers of action in body consciousness as a result of spiritual thought (angel) before a demonstration or resurrection is complete (Matt. 28:1-10).

Jesus did not leave the planet, at His ascension; He simply entered the inner spiritual realms. He will become visible to those who "put on Christ" and manifest their incorruptible, undying bodies. Many are conscious of His presence in some degree, but they do not see Him as He is, because they have not brought their faculties of apprehension up to His standard. When we awake in His likeness (see Psa. 17:15) then we shall see Him as He is. This does not come about through the soul's leaving the body, but it is accomplished by refining, spiritualizing, and raising both soul and body to higher degrees of power.

Jesus exists in a realm of being where the limitations of form are dissolved. He lives in the body idea. When we have identified ourselves with the Father-Mind as Jesus identified Himself with it, we shall see Him face to face in His spiritual reality. But while we are in the consciousness of the physical body Jesus appears to us in that form. Those who see Jesus in these days as a man with form see a mental picture impressed upon their souls by Jesus. He "stood by" Paul in the same way. Many have seen Him in this mind mirage; but we shall not see Him as He is until we awake in His likeness. If the mind has grasped the capacity and power of spiritual ideas, then the appearance of Jesus will be understood.

Jether, jē′-thẽr (Heb.)—*to have a surplus; left over; redundant; abundant; preëminent; excellent; remainder; remnant,* i. e., *excess left over.*

a Father-in-law of Moses, called Jethro in the text, and Jether in margin (Exod. 4:18). **b** Eldest son of Gideon (Judg. 8:20). **c** "The Ishmaelite," father of Amasa (I Chron. 2:17). **d** Son of Jada of the tribe of Judah (I Chron. 2:32). **e** A son of Ezrah, a Judahite (I Chron. 4:17). In II Samuel 17:25, Amasa's father is called Ithra.

Meta. For the significance of Jether the Ishmaelite, the father of Amasa, see ITHRA; for the significance of Jether, priest of Midian and father-in-law of Moses, see JETHRO. The other men by this name also represent exalted thoughts in consciousness (*preëminent, excellent*) and thoughts of abundance (*to have a surplus, redundant*).

Jetheth, jē′-thĕth (Heb.) — *fixing firmly; securing; stability; subjection; subjugation; a tent peg; pin; nail.*

A chief, of Esau, in the land of Edom (Gen. 36:40).

Meta. A ruling thought in the outer and seemingly material consciousness of man (Esau and Edom refer to the physical) that believes in force, in compelling, driving, binding, suppressing (*subjugation, subjection, a tent peg, nail*) in order to keep one steadfast and in place. This of course is error, and leads to bondage instead of true freedom.

Jethro, jē′-thrō (Heb.)—*his abundance; his superiority; his preëminence; his excellence;˙his cords,* i. e., *nerves and tendons.*

Priest of Midian, and father-in-law of Moses (Exod. 3:1). He is called Jether in the margin of Exodus 4:18. See also Exodus 18:1-12.

Meta. Jethro means *his excellence, his superiority, his abundance.* Midian means *judgment,* and Horeb, *solitude.*

The metaphysical interpretation of Exodus 3:1 is that we have to go into the solitude of the inner and lead our flock of thoughts to the back of the wilderness, where dwells the exalted One, the divine I AM, whose kingdom is good judgment. There we are in training forty years, or until we arrive at a four-sided or balanced state of mind.

Jetur, jē′-tŭr (Heb.)—*inclosure; encircled; nomadic; encampment; border; fence; boundary; pillar; cairn; rock; mountain range; that which keeps within bounds,* i. e., *in good order.*

Son of Ishmael (Gen. 25:15).

Meta. An idea of order, solidity, strength (*that which keeps within bounds,* i. e., *in good order, a pillar, rock*), that has sprung from the carnal (Ishmael). This Jetur belief thinks that the individual can be kept in orderly existence only when limited to certain lines of thought and action, when his thoughts, beliefs, and acts are fenced in, as it were (*inclosure, encircled, boundary*). Sense man's way of making one better is always that of limiting one by means of outer rules and regulations; it knows nothing of true spiritual freedom and guidance, which alone can bring about real strength, unity, and adjustment in consciousness. Jetur is the central thought in the state of consciousness signified by Ituræa. (See ITURÆA.)

Jeuel (in A. V., Ezra 8:13, Jeiel), jeŭ′-ĕl (Heb.)—*God snatched away; God swept away,* i. e., *purified a refuge of lies; gathered up of God; treasured of God; collected by God,* i. e., *united.*

a Jeuel, son of Zerah, with six hundred and ninety of his brethren, lived in Jerusalem after returning from the Babylonian captivity (I Chron. 9:6). **b** Son of Adonikam. He returned with Ezra from the Babylonian captivity (Ezra 8:13).

Meta. The significance is very much like that of Jeiel. Zerah, father of one of the men named Jeuel, is man's first conscious awakening to the inner light of his being. Jeuel is a further awakening by man to his true self, to his divine sonship. Jeuel also signifies the treasuring, unifying, gathering together of this awakening consciousness by God, and its growth, further unfoldment, to the end that the individual may be wholly lifted out of limited, carnal thought into the fullness of the one Mind (*God snatched away, God swept away,* i. e., *purified a refuge of lies*). See ADONIKAM.

Jeush (in A. V., I Chronicles 8:39, Jehush), jĕ'-ŭsh (Heb.)—*to whom He (God) hastens; he will urge; he will make haste; he will collect; he will assemble; he will bring together.*

a Son of Esau by his wife Oholibamah (Gen. 36:5). **b** Son of Bilhan, a Benjamite (I Chron. 7:10). **c** son of Shimei of the Gershonite Levites (I Chron. 23:10). **d** A son of Rehoboam, Solomon's son (II Chron. 11:19).

Meta. Strong, unifying, attracting, accumulating thoughts in consciousness (*he will collect, he will assemble, he will bring together*). The thought of God, in the meaning of this name, *to whom He (God) hastens, he will make haste,* with the idea of bringing together, bespeaks the final lifting up and unifying of the entire man in spiritual life and wholeness.

Jeuz, jĕ'-ŭz (Heb.)—*advising; counseling; impressing; fertilizing.*

A Benjamite, one of those who were "heads of fathers' *houses*" (I Chron. 8:10).

Meta. An influential thought that is of a discriminating, guiding, counseling, enriching nature. It belongs to the Benjamite or active faith consciousness in the spiritually awakening individual. (Faith is the inner sight, which sees into spiritual realities and makes them very real to the consciousness of the individual, even before there is any outward sign or proof of them.)

Jew, jew (fr. Heb.)—*of* or *belonging to Judea.*

A man of the tribe of Judah; more broadly speaking, a Hebrew. Mordecai, the Jew (Esth. 2:5), was a Benjamite.

Meta. As a descendant of Judah, son of Jacob, and as a member of the tribe or kingdom of Judah, a Jew signifies a thought springing from and belonging to the praise and inner-life consciousness of the individual.

As a Hebrew, which a Jew is in the broader sense, the significance is the same

as that of HEBREW, which see.

For the symbology of Mordecai the Jew, see MORDECAI. See JEWS also.

jewels.

Meta. "Jewels of silver, and jewels of gold" (Exod. 12:35) represent wisdom and love in an external sense, which are to be asked or demanded by the Children of Israel (the word "borrowed," in the Authorized Version, is an error). This means that we are to affirm that all wisdom and all love, even in their most external manifestations, are spiritual. This puts Spirit in control both within and without, and does away with the external ruling power that is the "first-born in the land of Egypt." The "first-born" of every state of consciousness is the personal *I.* When the flood of light from the Universal is let in through our declaration of the one wisdom and one love, this *I* of every mortal state of consciousness is slain and there is a "great cry in Egypt; for there was not a house where there was not one dead."

Jewess, jew'-ess (fr. Heb.)—*a female Jew.*

A woman of the Hebrews (Acts 16:1).

Meta. The soul or feminine aspect of that in consciousness for which a Jew stands. (See JEW, JEWS, and HEBREW.)

Jewish, jew'-ish (fr. Heb.).

Pertaining to the Jews (Tit. 1:14).

Meta. Pertaining to that in consciousness for which a Jew stands. (See JEW and JEWS.)

Jews, jewş.

People belonging to the tribe and kingdom of Judah only, or to the Hebrew nation generally (II Kings 16:6; Matt. 2:2).

Meta. Jews in their highest aspect symbolize divine ideas, or spiritual consciousness. Each individual has his formless and his formed mind, and they seem in the present race consciousness to be hostile one to the other. In Scripture these are referred to as Jew and Gentile.

Mind has two broad aspects, the formless and the formed. In its formless aspect it is a unity; in its formed aspect it is a diversity. It might be compared in its first aspect to vapor, and in its second to that same vapor precipitated into crystals of snow. In the vapor aspect there is a homogeneous whole; in the snow each little crystal has form and character peculiarly its own. Raise these inanimate crystals to the plane of thought and free will and you have a parallel to the formed mind of humanity.

In the New Testament, Jews symbolize our established religious thoughts and systems of worship. The Jews were always the hardest to reach with the new thought. They were very set in their religion, and they usually refused even to listen to new teachings of Truth (see Acts 13:45). So we find in ourselves that our religious convictions frequently stand in the way of our accepting the new revelations of Truth that come to us. The orthodox church has a very large number of people who are truly spiritual and would quickly grasp the real import of Christianity were they free from the restraints of religious habits of thought and worship and from the established customs of the church.

The Jews symbolize our religious thoughts and the Gentiles symbolize our worldly thoughts. Paul was determined to reconcile the Jew and the Gentile (Acts 21:13, 19). We find that there is a separation between our religious thoughts and our worldly thoughts. We have built up a Sunday religion and thrown around it a wall of sacredness. In it are rites and ceremonies and sacrifices according to a standard fixed by some sect, whose teachings about God we have accepted as true. Then the broad Truth of the Holy Spirit enters the mind and begins to break down this wall of separation between the religious thoughts and the worldly thoughts. It perceives that the principles involved in the Fatherhood of God must go to the uttermost parts of the mind and the body and unify them in Spirit.

Fixed traditional religious thoughts, the Jews, that follow the letter of the law rather than the living Truth that seeks to unite in spiritual harmony both Jews and Gentiles, are the opposing force in Jerusalem (the religious consciousness) that would hinder the word, presented by Paul, from doing its work (Acts 21:11). But the living word of Truth cannot be killed. Paul's words of Truth were bound for a time, but they have filled the whole world. So it is with the living words of Truth now being sown in our consciousness: they will do their work of restoration throughout our being.

Jezaniah, jĕz-ă-nī'-ăh (Heb.)—*whom Jehovah hears; Jehovah understands; Jah balances; Jehovah determines; ear of Jehovah; implement of Jah; sharp weapon of Jehovah.*

a "The son of the Maacathite," who came to Gedaliah at Mizpah (Jer. 40:8). He is called Jaazaniah in II Kings 25:23. **b** Jezaniah son of Hoshaiah is the same person as the Azariah of Jeremiah 43:2. (See Jeremiah 42:1, both text and margin.)

Meta. An uplifting thought in consciousness, based on the divine will (*Jah determines*) and on the assurance that *Jehovah hears* us, perceives our true desires, and establishes them to us. The *sharp weapon of Jehovah* is the word of God (see Heb. 4:12). (See JAAZANIAH and AZARIAH.)

Jezebel, jĕz'-ĕ-bĕl (Heb.)—*intact; untouched; untouchable; unproductive; noncohabiting; without husband; chaste; virgin; adulterous; base; unexalted; licentious.*

a Daughter of Ethbaal king of the Sidonians, and wife of Ahab king of Israel (I Kings 16:31). **b** An adulterous prophetess mentioned in Revelation 2:20.

Meta. The animal soul, unbridled passions of sense consciousness. When the union of the ruling identity in the intellect (King Ahab) and the licentious desires of the body is complete, the whole man is involved in error. This is rearing "an altar for Baal in the house of Baal" (I Kings 16:32).

Jezebel could also be called the ruling emotions on the physical plane of consciousness. She met a violent death; passion and appetites burn themselves out (II Kings 9:30-37).

Jezer, jē'-zẽr (Heb.)—*formation; frame; image; imagination; thought; purpose; ideation; creation.*

Son of Naphtali (Gen. 46:24) and founder of the family of the Jezerites (Num. 26:49).

Meta. The forming (*formation*) faculty of the mind, the *imagination*, established in strength (Naphtali).

Jezerites, jē'-zēr-ītes (Heb.)—*of or belonging to Jezer.*

Descendants of Jezer son of Naphtali (Num. 26:49).

Meta. Thoughts and forces belonging to that in consciousness for which Jezer stands. (See JEZER.)

Jeziel, jē'-zĭ-ĕl (Heb.)—*whom God assembles; assembly of God; united of God; God unites; whom God sprinkles.*

Son of Azmaveth, a Benjamite who came to David at Ziklag (I Chron. 12:3).

Meta. Spiritual unity (*whom God assembles, united of God, assembly of God*) brought about by the activity of faith and love. (Azmaveth, father of Jeziel, a Benjamite who came to David at Ziklag, signifies faith's power to bring results; and David stands for love). These two working together in the consciousness of the individual accomplish a great unifying and harmonizing of his thoughts.

Jezrahiah, jĕz-rä-hī'-äh (Heb.)—*whom Jehovah brings forth; Jehovah shines forth; glory of the Lord; Jehovah arises, i. e., returns in splendor as the sun.*

An "overseer" of the singers at the dedication of Jerusalem's walls after they had been rebuilt, in the time of Nehemiah (Neh. 12:42).

Meta. The light of Truth shining forth, radiating in and from the redeemed consciousness of man (the rebuilding of Jerusalem's walls signifies the renewing and spiritualizing of man's organism).

Jezreel, jĕz'-rê-ĕl (Heb.)—*God scatters; whom God sows; seed of God; God's fruitfulness; virility of God; God's offspring; children of God.*

a A town in the hill country of Judah (Josh. 15:56). **b** A border town of the "children of Issachar" (Josh. 19:18). **c** A Judahite, son of the "father" or founder of Etam (I Chron. 4:3). **d** Son of the prophet Hosea by his wife Gomer (Hos. 1:4). **e** A valley (Hos. 1:5).

Meta. Words of Truth (*seed of God*) brought into man's conscious, thinking mind, or brought to his attention, by the inspiration of the Holy Spirit within him (*God scatters, whom God sows*).

Jezreelite, jĕz'-rê-ĕl-īte (fr. Heb.)—*of or belonging to Jezreel.*

Naboth the Jezreelite, a native of Jezreel. He was slain at the instigation of Jezebel so that Ahab king of Israel could obtain possession of his vineyard. The king coveted this vineyard, but Naboth would not sell it to him because of the law of inheritance that was kept so faithfully among the Israelites (I Kings 21:1-16).

Meta. A positive thought force belonging to the word-of-Truth consciousness for which Jezreel stands. (See JEZREEL.)

Jezreelitess, jĕz'-rê-ĕl-ĭ-tĕss (fr. Heb.) —*of or belonging to Jezreel.*

A woman inhabitant of Jezreel; here it is Ahinoam the Jezreelitess, one of David's wives (I Sam. 27:3).

Meta. Ahinoam the Jezreelitess symbolizes the harmonious activity (Ahinoam) of words of Truth in the soul or affectional phase of individual consciousness.

Jidlaph, jĭd'-lăph (Heb.)—*dropping; dripping; distilling; tearful; weeping; flowing out; wasting away.*

Son of Nahor, Abraham's brother (Gen. 22:22).

Meta. A very negative phase of thought in man.

Joab, jō'-ăb (Heb.)—*whose father Jehovah is; Jehovah is father.*

a Son of Zeruiah, sister of David, and captain of David's army (II Sam. 2:18; I Kings 11:15). **b** There were other Israelites by this name also (I Chron. 4:14; Ezra 2:6; 8:9).

Meta. The executive power of love. The pivotal center within man that preserves the unity and integrity of soul and body—the individual will. This is the focal point around which all the forces of the organism, objective and subjective, adjust themselves.

II Samuel 18:9-15 does not say that Joab killed Absalom, but that he ran three darts through his heart. He was afterward killed by the ten young armor-bearers of Joab. The three darts represent thoughts, which may be interpreted as life, love, Truth. The armor-bearers represent the most external forces of the will, or secondary movements of the mind, which bring about destruction of temporary forms of life.

Joah, jō'-ăh (Heb.)—*whose brother is Jehovah; Jah is brother; Jah is friend; confederated of Jehovah; likeness of Jehovah; the joining of the Lord.*

a Son of Asaph, the recorder, in the reign of Hezekiah king of Judah (II Kings 18:18). **b** A Gershomite Levite (I Chron. 6:21), called Ethan in verse 42. **c** Son of Obed–edom, of the Korathite Levites, doorkeepers (I Chron. 26:4). **d** A son of Joahaz the recorder, in Josiah's reign, who was sent to help repair the house of Jehovah (II Chron. 34:8).

Meta. Man's divine relationship to his I AM, or indwelling Christ (Jehovah); an awakening by man to his close friendship, kinship, fellowship, with his true, higher self—brotherhood, by right of divine origin, or birth. Man's conscious union with his true, inner, spiritual self.

Joahaz, jō'-ă-hăz (Heb.)—*who lays hold of Jehovah; Jehovah holds fast; who adheres to Jah; possession of Jehovah.*

"The recorder" in the reign of Josiah king of Judah, and the father of Joah, one of those who were sent to repair the house of Jehovah (II Chron. 34:8).

Meta. A phase of man's memory in his higher realm of consciousness, in which is kept a record of all true, helpful, spiritual thoughts and experiences (*who lays hold of Jehovah, who adheres to Jah*).

Joanan (A. V., Joanna), jō-ăn'-ăn (Gk. fr. Heb.)—*Jehovah has graciously given; to whom Jah is gracious.*

Father of Joda and son of Rhesa, in the genealogy of Jesus Christ (Luke 3:27).

Meta. Joanan (*Jehovah has graciously given*) symbolizes abundance of whatever is needed to meet every requirement of man. All of God is ever at man's disposal, and for his righteous use: all life, all love, all intelligence, all light, all faith, all power, all substance, all strength, all Truth, all that God is and has. These are free gifts with which the Creator and Source of all has endowed His creatures from the beginning. They all are ours, all the time. We have but to realize them and bring them forth into expression and manifestation by means of

our true thoughts and words, through I AM, Jehovah, our indwelling Christ mind. "My grace is sufficient for thee" (II Cor. 12:9). "By grace have ye been saved through faith; and that not of yourselves, it is the gift of God; not of works, that no man should glory" (Eph. 2:8, 9).

Joanna, jō-ăn'-nà (Gk. fr. Heb.)—*Jehovah has graciously given; grace of Jah.*

Wife of Chuzas Herod's steward, and a follower of Jesus Christ (Luke 8:3).

Meta. The soul quality of intuition, discernment, which perceives the Truth that is expressed in the metaphysical explanation given the name JOANAN, which see.

Joash, jō'-ăsh (Heb.)—*whom Jehovah has bestowed; given of Jehovah; whom Jah supports; Jehovah heals; fire of Jehovah; fire of the Lord.*

a Father of Gideon (Judg. 6:11, 29-31). **b** A king of Judah (II Kings 11:2). **c** There are others by this name (I Kings 22:26; I Chron. 4:22; 7:8; 12:3; 27:28). The name is a shortened form of Jehoash.

Meta. As a king of Judah, Joash signifies the will (king) animated and directed by Jehovah, I AM, indwelling Christ (*whom Jehovah has bestowed, fire of Jehovah*), and sustained by Spirit in its executive working (*whom Jah supports*).

Joash is the rightful king in consciousness. He is brought to the throne by certain changes in consciousness symbolized by the movements of the soldiers (II Kings 11:4-16).

When Joash, the rightful king, comes to the throne, Athaliah is overcome; that is, the states of consciousness that she represents are broken up and dissolved, and eliminated from mind and body.

Job, jōb (Heb.)—*persecuted; calamitous; afflicted; adversity; adverse desires; a coming back; restored to one's senses; penitent; converted.*

"A man in the land of Uz," the central figure of The Book of Job (Job 1:1; 2:3-7).

Meta. The transition of man from personal, formal righteousness, which is the basis of all self-righteousness, to a true **inner** change of heart and an entrance into the real Christ righteousness, which deals with the very thoughts and intents of the innermost consciousness instead of merely setting right a few outer acts.

In self-righteousness there is fear of evil; the things that Job feared came upon him (Job. 3:25, 26). Then along came his three friends to comfort him and to argue with him. These friends represent accusations against self and attempted self-justifications of the outer or personal consciousness.

Next came Elihu, the interpreter, or Holy Spirit, who opens man's eyes to the real righteousness. The self-righteousness of the outer man is based on outer acts only and does not bring about the reign of love and wisdom in the heart, in the thoughts, words, and the whole life; seeing this fact, the individual truly repents. Job said (Job 42:5, 6), after God had talked to him:

"I had heard of thee by the hearing of
   the ear;
But now mine eye seeth thee:
Wherefore I abhor *myself*,
And repent in dust and. ashes."

Then come forgiveness and healing. When Job turned to God and prayed for his friends, his captivity was put away, "and Jehovah gave Job twice as much as he had before" (Job 42:10). Thus when the awakened individual forgives, and seeks the cleansing, redeeming, transmuting Christ power for the uplift of his apparent failings and shortcomings, he enters into true peace, joy, and abundance.

Jobab, jō'-băb (Heb.)—*celestial jubilation; shout of joy; fullness of joy; welling shout of rejoicing; trumpet call of victory; desert; howling of wild beasts; wail of tribulation.*

a Son of Joktan, who was a descendant of Shem, Noah's son (Gen. 10:29). **b** Son of Zerah of Bozrah, and king of Edom (Gen. 36:33). **c** A king of Madon who joined Jabin king of Hazor against Israel (Josh. 11:1).

Meta. The noisy, contentious tumultuousness of the outer personal man while under the dominion of the "mind of the flesh" (*howling of wild beasts, wail of tribulation*).

In Jobab, the thirteenth son of Joktan

and the seventh generation from Noah, through Shem, we find a certain fulfillment of the seeming mortal and an entrance into that which the positive, spiritual meanings of the name signify—a realization of dominion over error and a rejoicing in Truth (*celestial jubilation, trumpet call of victory*).

Jochebed, jŏch'-ĕ-bĕd (Heb.)—*whose glory is Jehovah; Jah is honor; whom Jehovah multiplies; Jah makes great.*

Daughter of Levi, Jacob's son, wife of Amram, and mother of Moses, Aaron, and Miriam (Exod. 6:20; Num. 26:59).

Meta. The religious soul of man exalting, honoring, and glorifying Jehovah, Christ, I AM, by expressing the love (Levi, the love faculty) and Truth of Spirit. When man glorifies God and exalts Him in his thoughts, man in turn is exalted and enriched (*Jah makes great*).

Joda (A. V., Juda), jō'-dȧ (corruption of Gk., fr. Heb.)—*Judah; praise; celebration; lauding; praise Jah; Jehovah of praise.*

Father of Josech and son of Joanan, in the genealogy of Jesus Christ (Luke 3:26).

Meta. The growing tendency of the spiritually unfolding individual to *praise* God, to appreciate and hold to that which is good and true.

Joel, jō'-ĕl (Heb.)—*Jehovah God; Jah is his God; worshiper of God; he who desires; he who wills; he who fulfills every desire.*

a A son of Samuel (I Sam. 8:2). **b** Son of Pethuel, and prophet of Judah (Joel 1:1). **c** Also others (I Chron. 6:36; 7:3; 11:38; 15:7; 27:20).

Meta. Joel bespeaks the I AM in dominion in the individual (*Jah is his God, he who desires, he who wills, he who fulfills every desire*). In this consciousness all things are possible.

Joelah, jō-ē'-lăh (Heb.)—*whom Jehovah helps up; whom Jehovah raises; he who will stand upon the summit; lifting up; rising to eminence; profiting.*

Son of Jeroham of Gedor, and one of those who came to David at Ziklag (I Chron. 12:7).

Meta. A strong, uplifting, redeeming thought springing from the spiritual ideas of divine love, mercy, compassion, and support (Jeroham), and based on man's innate belief in divine protection (Gedor). This thought becomes a great help in establishing the dominion of love in the religious consciousness of the individual (in putting David on the throne of Israel).

Joezer, jŏ-ē′-zẽr (Heb.)—*whose help is Jehovah; Jehovah is help; succoring; helping; infolding; protecting; aiding.*

A Korahite who came to David at Ziklag (I Chron. 12:6).

Meta. I AM, Jehovah, the Christ, as our all-sufficient strength and support, an ever present help in every need.

Jogbehah, jŏg′-bĕ-hăh (Heb.)—*He shall be exalted; who will be elevated; who dwelleth on the heights; majesty; grandeur.*

A city on the east side of the Jordan that was rebuilt by Gad (Num. 32:35).

Meta. Exalting God in one's life; holding exalted thoughts (*He shall be exalted, who will be elevated, who dwelleth on the heights*) about life, in the inner or subjective phase of the power faculty (Gad) in individual consciousness. (This city was on the east of the Jordan. East signifies the within, and the Jordan here stands for the life currents in the organism.)

Jogli, jŏg′-lī (Heb.)—*carrying away; removing; passing over; uncovering; baring; disclosing; migrating; emigrating; exiling; revealing; making naked.*

Father of Bukki. Bukki was a prince of the tribe of Dan who was chosen to help divide the land of Canaan among the Children of Israel (Num. 34:22).

Meta. A thought, belonging to the judgment faculty of man (Dan), in transit (*passing over*) from Egyptian darkness to the wilderness experience— a partial discernment and comprehension of Truth. Jogli's son, Bukki, went on into the Promised Land—the clear light of spiritual understanding, realization, and substance.

Though to the unregenerate soul Egypt represents darkness and mystery, it is the realm of substance and life in the depths of the body consciousness. Much substance was there, and the Israelites who had lived in Egypt for a long period sadly missed this substance when they were wandering about in the wilderness, before coming into the Land of Promise, which flowed with milk and honey. They often felt as if they had been led into exile (*exiling*) instead of out of it. Even so our highest religious thoughts, which are seeking a clearer consciousness of Truth, sense a lack of substance and reality when they have left the old sense ideas of substance and Truth and have not yet reached an established realization of substance on its higher, more spiritual plane. There is often a great sense of lack in the wilderness experience of the soul (*baring, disclosing*) when it is being tried and purified and made fit to enter the Promised Land (true spiritual consciousness and bodily redemption). It is while one is in this wilderness experience, this state of transition from the lower plane of consciousness to the higher, that the feeling of being exiled is in evidence.

Joha, jō′-hȧ (Heb.)—*Jehovah lives; Jah enlivens; Jehovah perceives; alive; Jah gives life; Jehovah restores to life; Jehovah preserves alive.*

a Son of Beriah, a Benjamite (I Chron. 8:16). **b** Son of Shimri and brother of Jediael, one of David's mighty men (I Chron. 11:45).

Meta. The awakening individual's becoming conscious that life is spiritual and that life only is God's will for man and His gift to man, through I AM, Jehovah, the Christ. This leads to a putting away of the error belief that God—who is life and in whom there can be no death or error—has any part whatever in the death thought or experience. God is life and His will for man is only and always life. "For the wages of sin is death; but the free gift of God is eternal life in Christ Jesus our Lord" (Rom. 6:23).

Johanan, jŏ-hā′-năn (Heb.)—*Jehovah bestows mercy; Jah is gracious; Jehovah gives graciously; Jehovah with grace bestows; mercy and compassion of the Lord.*

There were several Israelites by this name, some of them men of note (I Chron. 3:15, 24; 6:10; 12:4, 12; Ezra 8:12; Jer. 40:8, 13-16).

Meta. The love, mercy, largeness, broadness, and generosity of Spirit. (See

JOHN, which is a contraction of this name.)

John, jŏhn (fr. Heb.)—*Jehovah bestows mercifully; Jah is gracious; grace and mercy of the Lord; dovelike; meekness; compassion; fertility; fruitfulness; love.*

a John the Baptist, son of Zacharias the priest and his wife Elisabeth, and the forerunner of Jesus Christ (Luke 1: 5-25, 57-66; Matt. 3:1-12). b A disciple of Jesus Christ, brother of James and son of Zebedee (Matt. 4:21). c John Mark (Acts 12:12). John is a contraction of Johanan and Jehohanan.

Meta. John the Baptist was the forerunner of Jesus Christ. He signifies a high intellectual perception of Truth, but one not yet quickened of Spirit. John represents that attitude of mind in which we are zealous for the rule of Spirit. This attitude is not spiritual, but a perception of spiritual possibilities and an activity in making conditions in which Spirit may rule. This John-the-Baptist perception of Truth leads us to strive with evil as a reality, not having discerned the truth about its transitory character.

John the Baptist may also be said to be that innate principle in us all which ever seeks to do right. Its origin cannot be located—it comes out of the wilderness. It is crude—it is like a voice in the wilderness crying for the right way. The whole human family is naturally true and honest, and this rugged reformer is a child of nature. Culture does not make people honest nor bring out their natural virtues. The inner soul consciousness that draws its nourishment from nature's storehouse opens the way for the advent of Spirit.

That which the baptism of John signifies is brought about by a process metaphysically known as "denial." This baptism symbolizes the getting rid of the limited thoughts that encumber and darken the understanding. It is found that to say mentally, *"I deny the belief in the reality of matter and material conditions,"* causes that aggregation of thoughts to scatter. This is a mental letting go that has to be applied to all departments of the mind. In Christian conversion the sinner lets go of his sins and there is a moral cleansing. The metaphysician finds it necessary to cleanse his mind from all moral iniquity, but he also finds that he must go further than this. The mind governs every part of the man, and a thorough reform requires that the baptism of John shall include a complete transformation of thought pertaining to things mental, moral, and physical.

Jesus said of John the Baptist, "He that is but little in the kingdom of God is greater than he" (Luke 7:28); and John said of Jesus, "He must increase, but I must decrease" (John 3:30). This means that the least of the spiritual thoughts in man is greater than the mightiest reasoning of the intellect, and that the intellectual concept of things must give way to the understanding that comes through the Holy Spirit.

The intellect is to prepare the way for the spiritual consciousness, the Christ. The alert intellect that has been working toward the fulfillment of a divine ideal recognizes the development of spiritual consciousness and acknowledges its very first appearance, as John the Baptist recognized Jesus Christ.

When the quickening by Spirit takes place in consciousness to the extent that the Christ is realized and felt and known, one depends on the inspiration of Spirit rather than on the reasonings of the intellectual man. Thus we are admonished, in Proverbs 3:5, 6:

"Trust in Jehovah with all thy heart,
And lean not upon thine own understanding:
In all thy ways acknowledge him,
And he will direct thy paths."

John the Baptist, the intellectual man, beholds the evils of civilization, condemns them, and advocates the punishment of the evildoers. This remedy leads to resistance and failure, as evidenced in the execution of John by Herod, the sinner. Man has to pass through the intellectual state of consciousness (which is the natural man), and his attempts at reform are evidences of the innate good within him, but his comprehension is narrowed to personal ends. The world today is in the throes of John-the-Baptist methods of reform. They all must fail because they lack a comprehension of the universal brotherhood of man and the great law laid down by Jesus Christ, which in essence is, "Whatsoever ye would that men should do unto you, even so do ye also unto them."

John the Baptist in prison represents the intellect hemmed in, imprisoned, because of its magnifying sin and evil and condemning them. Some persons see the evil in the world as a power so formidable that it paralyzes all their efforts, and they accomplish nothing in the service of Truth.

The death of John the Baptist, as described in Matthew 14:1-12, refers to the passing away of that first enthusiasm for character reform which possesses the disciple at the earthly stage of his experience. This John-the-Baptist phase is not the permanent state of consciousness, but is to be followed by one that is permanent. "He that cometh after me is mightier than I, whose shoes I am not worthy to bear: he shall baptize you in the Holy Spirit and *in* fire" (Matt. 3:11).

When the first enthusiasm wanes after spiritual enlightenment has occurred there is a certain barrenness of thought and action in mind, and we feel as if we should like to retire to a place where a complete rest and absence of effort could be had. When Jesus heard of the death of John "he withdrew . . . to a desert place apart." We cannot get away from our thoughts, however: the people followed Jesus into the desert place (Matt. 14:13).

Matthew 11:18, 19 may be explained as follows: The conscious mind is very chary of accepting the whole Truth. It comes "neither eating nor drinking." It does not eat the body (substance) of Christ, nor drink His blood (life). The result is that the adverse ego remains in the body, "He hath a demon." The Son of man comes and unites His life and substance with the appetites and passions of the subconsciousness, and He seems for a time to be of their kind. But "wisdom is justified by her works." The descent of the Spirit into one's body may stir up the Devil in one for a season, but his reign will be short if one is guided by the Spirit of truth, who will lead into all Truth. "Except those days had been shortened, no flesh would have been saved: but for the elect's sake those days shall be shortened" (Matt. 24:22).

The apostle John represents the spiritual faculty of love. He is known as the disciple whom Jesus loved, and love is the dominant theme of all his teachings and writings. In the outpicturing of Jesus' development, John signifies the faculty of love in its masculine or positive degree of action, while the various Marys of the New Testament characterize the different subjective activities of love.

For the metaphysical significance of John Mark, see MARK.

Joiada, joi'-ă-dȧ (Heb.)—*whom Jehovah knows; perception of Jah; knowledge of Jah; whom Jah acknowledges; praising Jehovah; whom Jah makes thankful.*

a Son of Eliashib, and his successor as high priest of Judah, under Nehemiah (Neh. 12:10). b A son of Paseah, one who repaired "the old gate," or "the gate of the old city," in the rebuilding of the wall of Jerusalem (Neh. 3:6 with margin). Joiada is a contraction of the name Jehoiada.

Meta. The inner spiritual knowing. (See JEHOIADA.)

Joiakim, joi'-ă-kĭm (Heb.)—*whom Jehovah has set up; Jehovah establishes; Jehovah rises, i. e., in judgment; whom Jah constitutes; Jehovah restores upright.*

Son of Jeshua, a high priest who returned from Babylon with Zerubbabel (Neh. 12:10). Joiakim is a contraction of the name Jehoiakim.

Meta. A ruling thought in man's religious or spiritual consciousness (high priest) that exalts Spirit, that perceives the possibility of establishing God in individual consciousness, and that works toward that end. (See JEHOIAKIM.)

Joiarib, joi'-ă-rĭb (Heb.)—*whom Jehovah defends; Jah will contend; for whom Jehovah pleads; Jehovah will increase; Jah will multiply.*

A teacher ("one who had understanding," margin) whom Ezra sent for while encamped by the river Ahava, that he might accompany him, and those with him, on their journey from Babylon to

Jerusalem (Ezra 8:16). (See Nehemiah 11:5, 10; 12:19.) Joiarib is short for Jehoiarib.

Meta. Like Jehoiarib, an inner realization of God, through Christ, Jehovah, I AM, as our protection and defense; also an idea of spiritual increase (*Jehovah will increase, Jah will multiply*).

Jokdeam, jŏk'-dĕ-ăm (Heb.)—*anger of the people; inflammation of the people; vehement burning of the people; possessed by the people; obsession of the people; perversion of the people.*

A city in the hill country of Judah (Josh. 15:56).

Meta. Wickedness in high places, and its result.

The hill country of Judah refers to the consciousness of life lifted to a high, exalted place through praise and prayer. In this high realm of consciousness, however, the seeds of strife and selfishness have not been wholly eliminated; and in Jokdeam we find certain thoughts, and their corresponding emotions, that are not of the single eye (see Luke 11:34). They do not see good only, but are perverse. (*Perversion of the people* carries this meaning. The word people refers to thoughts. A city also refers to a group of thoughts in consciousness, or a nerve center with the thoughts that act through it and belong to it.)

Thus irritation and antagonism are aroused (*anger of the people*). This of course brings about the reaction in a burning out of the cells and of the vitalizing element in the organism, corresponding in amount and degree to the intensity of the anger and irritation (*burning of the people*).

Jokim, jō'-kĭm (Heb.)—*Jehovah sets up; Jah establishes; Jehovah rises; Jah constitutes; Jehovah restores upright; righteousness of Jehovah.*

A man of Judah (I Chron. 4:22).

Meta. Jokim is one of those of whom it is said, "And the records are ancient. These were the potters, and the inhabitants of Netaim and Gederah: there they dwelt with the king for his work" (I Chron. 4:22, 23). In the margin, and in the Authorized Version, "those that dwelt among plantations and hedges" is given

in place of "the inhabitants of Netaim and Gederah."

The inference is that Jokim signifies an innate knowing that is established in the very foundation, or spiritual essence, of the cells of the organism and of the life forces. Potters represent body builders, cells, and atoms. Plantations and hedges refer to the seemingly earthly or physical in man and to substance. Jokim therefore symbolizes the inherent intelligence in every atom of man's organism, which knows that the essence of his whole being is Spirit and that God, Spirit, can and must be established in the entire consciousness as well as in its outer manifestation—the body itself. (See JOIAKIM.)

Jokmeam (in A. V., I Kings 4:12, Jokneam), jŏk'-mĕ-ăm (Heb.)—*gathering of the people; standing of the people; rising up of the people; the people will be raised up.*

A city of Ephraim that was given over to the Kohathite Levites (I Chron. 6:68).

Meta. A phase of the will (Ephraim) given over to religious thoughts and tendencies (Levites), thus indicating that the *standing of the people*, or the standard of the thoughts that comprise the city of Jokmeam in individual consciousness, is to be raised to a higher plane (*the people will be raised up*). The love thought (Levi, from whom the Levites, signifying love, were descended) aids greatly in drawing these thought people together into the harmony and the unification (*gathering of the people*) that are necessary in every true elevation of thought and activity.

Jokneam, jŏk'-nĕ-ăm (Heb.)—*let the people possess; possession of the people; foundation of the people; erection of the people; wailing of the people; the people will be lamented.*

A city in Carmel (Josh. 12:22). It was allotted to Zebulun and was given over to the Levites of the children of Merari (Josh. 19:11; 21:34).

Meta. Carmel means *fruitful place* and signifies abundance. It is a place in consciousness where we realize the fullness of our possibilities under the divine law. (See CARMEL.) Jokneam, a city in Carmel, typifies a group of established thoughts (*foundation of the people*) in the Carmel consciousness that are beginning to lay hold of the divine possibilities that Carmel signifies (*possession of the people, let the people possess*).

There is a tendency toward sorrow and grief in the lesser thoughts of the mind when old earthly ideas and conditions are released from consciousness that new and better ones may take their place (*the people will be lamented, wailing of the people*). But a real building, strengthening, and unifying of the true thoughts and activities always follow such a process (*erection of the people*).

Jokshan, jŏk'-shăn (Heb.)—*fowler; snarer; one who enmeshes; adversary; insidious; harsh; offensive; hard; difficult.*

Second son of Abraham by his wife Keturah (Gen. 25:2).

Meta. A sly, treacherous, deceitful tendency that often exists in the sense mind of man (*snarer, fowler, insidious*); also the results that follow the activity of this tendency (*offensive, hard*), and the *difficult* situations in which it places the individual who gives way to it. (See ISHBAK.)

Joktan, jŏk'-tăn (Heb.)—*extreme attenuation; that which is diminished; that which is made small; lessened; slight; thin; little; of little concern; a manifest lessening,* i. e., *of evil.*

Son of Eber, a descendant of Shem, one of Noah's three sons (Gen. 10:25). Several Arabian tribes are supposed to be descended from Joktan.

Meta. Peleg (*division*), the eldest son of Eber, in whose days the earth was divided, signifies a separation in man's consciousness between his apparently material thoughts and tendencies and his inner spiritual ideals. By one's recognition of the higher, or spiritual, it expands, grows, develops (the Hebrews, or Israelites, were descended from Peleg), and seeming evil becomes very small in comparison. Evil diminishes and will finally disappear, since the individual no longer gives it power by beholding it or by believing in it.

Joktan (*extreme attenuation, that which is made small, lessened, of little*

concern, a manifest lessening, i. e., of evil*), the youngest son of Eber, and brother of Peleg, signifies the lessening of error, to the vanishing point, in the consciousness and the life of the unfolding individual.

Joktheel, jŏk'-thĕ-ĕl (Heb.)—*subdued of God; protection of God; advantage of God; God's reward,* i. e., *for victory; veneration of God.*

a A city in the lowlands of Judah (Josh. 15:38). **b** A place in Edom called Sela, or the rock or cliff, a stronghold of Edom, that Amaziah, king of Judah, took and named Joktheel (II Kings 14:7).

Meta. Edom, or Esau, typifies the animal, physical, or sense consciousness in man. Sela, the rock or cliff, the capital of Edom, represents sense man's trust in physical strength and power. Amaziah's conquering this city and renaming it Joktheel signifies the transferring of one's faith and trust from outer personal strength and power to the inner spiritual ideas of strength and power. This brings about a consciousness of divine protection (*protection of God*), and a victory over error thoughts and activities. Thus the sensate comes into subjection to the spiritual (*subdued of God*), and great good for the whole man is the result (*God's reward,* i. e., *for victory*).

Jonadab, jŏn'-ă-dăb (Heb.)—*whom Jehovah impels; Jehovah is spontaneously liberal; Jah will impulsively give.*

a Son of Rechab, head of the Rechabites (Jer. 35:6-19). He is called Jehonadab in II Kings 10:15. **b** A very subtle man, a friend of Amnon, David's son (II Sam. 13:3).

Meta. The Rechabites, who were of the Children of Israel, were commanded to live in tents instead of houses (Jer. 35:7). This dwelling in tents symbolizes the progressive spiritual man who never allows his ideas to become crystallized, fixed, or final; who sees to it that they are receptive to new revelations and expressions. Spiritual progress is readily made when man is free from fixed ideas. This does not mean that he is to have an unstable consciousness. His mind is stable because it is established in the one infinite Principle, and his determination is that his life shall be a constant progression toward higher spiritual standards. He is always at home in the consciousness of ever present Spirit, which ever unfolds in him with new ideals of expression.

Therefore the edict of the Lord is that Jonadab (*whom Jehovah impels*), the son of Rechab (*horseman*, or power), "shall not want a man to stand before me forever." The Jehovah-impelled son of power will never lose the consciousness of the divine presence. (See JEHONADAB.)

The Jonadab who was a friend of Amnon, David's son, signifies the wisdom and the power that are gained through our Jehovah-impelled true thoughts, given over to deceptive, adverse, sense ways. (This Jonadab was a very subtle man; he gave Amnon advice that led Amnon to wrongdoing, and to death later). Even so, the power and the understanding that we gain through Spirit must be utilized only in true, honest, spiritual ways if we would reap an abiding consciousness of life, harmony, and good.

Jonah (in A. V., Matthew 12:39, Jonas), jō'-năh (Heb.)—*a dove; dovelike; warmth; affection; lovable; loving; fruitful; productive; fertile; effervescent; fermenting; passionate; oppressive; violent; intoxicating; destructive.*

Son of Amittai. He was the prophet who was sent to preach to Nineveh (Book of Jonah). He was of Gath–hepher (II Kings 14:25).

Meta. That prophetic state of mind which, if used without divine love, fixes man in bondage to belief in a law of cause and effect wherein error sowing cannot be redeemed or forgiven.

When error effects are revealed to one by the prophetic faculty of mind, which is open to receive the outpicturing of thought causes, one should fearlessly tear away the error and immediately proclaim the saving Truth, in the spirit of forgiving love. "Jonah" must be glad and must rejoice in omnipotent good.

The prophetic state of mind, on its highest plane, is *a dove*, a declarer of ultimate peace and good. When it functions on the intellectual or personal plane,

it becomes *oppressive, destructive*, in that it proclaims evil and disaster continuously, and when this belief in evil becomes intensified on the bodily plane it destroys itself.

Jonah signifies an error sense of justice and right in individual consciousness that prophesies evil to the evildoer and condemns him without mercy or saving grace, because love and mercy do not enter into its idea of justice and Truth. Unforgiving thoughts, which in one form or another are back of all evil prophecies, react on the thinker and cause him to have hard experiences.

Whoever expects failure, bad luck, or ill of any kind in body or affairs is a Jonah. Some persons are so mentally charged with thoughts of this character that they cast gloom and a feeling of failure all about them. Theatrical companies often detect a Jonah among their number and throw him overboard for the safety of the troupe. For this they are called superstitious, but it is not superstition; they live in a highly charged mental atmosphere that is very sensitive to adverse thoughts, and they feel more acutely than people in the more material states of mind.

There is a reaction to every prophecy of evil, because the fundamental law of Being is good, and the outcome of every thought and act under its law is a higher perception of that good. Therefore upon him who prophesies evil, or does evil, must be hurled back the force of his effort to defeat the supreme law of good. When Jonah felt this reaction coming upon him he tried to run away from it; but it so affected his field of thought that the equilibrium of nature was disturbed and storms ensued. Some people are so dense that they do not feel the reactions of evil; but Jonah represents one who is spiritually quickened and alive in both the conscious and the subconscious minds.

Jonah thought the people of Nineveh ought to be punished for their sins. One who believes that evil is punishment for infringement of divine law will have to meet hard conditions in mind and body. When the conscious mind casts out the evil thought it falls into the subconscious mind, the ocean or waters of life, where it is swallowed up by a great fish, or idea of increase. There Jonah was in hell with remorse and anguish. This realm also refuses to entertain him, and he is thrown upon the dry land (surface of the body).

The Lord does not desert those who have once given themselves to Him, so Jonah is watched over, in all his wanderings, by the infinite good. The people of Nineveh repent and are forgiven; therefore the evil that Jonah has prophesied upon them does not come to pass —and Jonah is angry. This shows another phase of the shortcomings of those who seek to follow the guidance of the Holy Spirit, yet are ambitious for the fulfilling of their prophecies. They call down upon the people the vengeance of God, and are angry if the people escape the threatened catastrophe. Jonah sulks in his childish pride. The Lord is tender, but firm, and He causes a gourd to grow so that it shall be a shadow over Jonah's head to deliver him from his grief. The word rendered gourd is "kikayon," the castor-oil plant, a native of Asia, now naturalized in America. The symbol is the pouring out upon him of God's compassion and healing love. "Thou hast loved righteousness, and hated iniquity; therefore God, thy God, hath anointed thee with the oil of gladness above thy fellows" (Heb. 1:9). "So Jonah was exceeding glad because of the gourd" (last clause of Jonah 4:6). Here again is the tendency of the personality to look to effects rather than causes. Jonah is glad to have the benefit of the gourd plant, but fails to acknowledge its source.

Again Jonah had to be reminded of God's wisdom and power. The "worm" smote the gourd and it withered, and the sun beat upon Jonah until he wished himself dead. He who works from a selfish standpoint is frequently disappointed in results and then is ready to abandon everything. The "worm" signifies conscience, the inner monitor that shows our selfishness in its true light— a withered plant. So he who is ambitious and zealous for his work in the Lord to bear fruit just as he has planned, and for his personal benefit, regardless of

the larger good that might come to humanity through other channels, will eventually find himself like Jonah, "angry, even unto death."

The true prophet must see as God sees —that only the good is true. Evil and all its effects pass away when men repent, and the compassion and love of God should always be proclaimed to the sinner. By asking, the suffering one may obtain forgiveness; and he who is soul-sick may receive the divine compassion.

"Should not I have regard for Nineveh, that great city, wherein are more than sixscore thousand persons that cannot discern between their right hand and their left hand, and also much cattle?" (Jon. 4:11). "If ye had known what this meaneth, I desire mercy, and not sacrifice, ye would not have condemned the guiltless" (Matt. 12:7).

Jonam (A. V., Jonan), jŏ'-năm (Gk. fr. Heb.)—Greek form of Johanan: *Jehovah bestows mercy; Jah is gracious; Jehovah gives graciously; mercy and compassion of the Lord.*

Son of Eliakim in the genealogy of Jesus Christ (Luke 3:30).

Meta. The Spirit of love, mercy, and peace becoming known and established in consciousness, through Jehovah, I AM.

Jonathan, jŏn'-a-thăn (Heb.)—*whom Jehovah gave; Jah has given; gift of Jehovah; Jah-given.*

There are several Israelites by this name, one a son of Saul and friend of David (I Sam. 14:49; 18:1; II Sam. 15:27; 21:21; Ezra 8:6; Neh. 12:35; Jer. 40:8).

Meta. The human or soul love of higher, more spiritual things.

In I Samuel 20:32-42 Jonathan typifies the soul substance that, in man's unfoldment, tries to unite will and love. He symbolizes that soul quality which, though the offspring of the will (Saul), turns yearningly toward love (David). Jonathan loved David as his own soul. The name Jonathan means *Jah-given, Jehovah has given,* that is, he came forth from Being. He may be termed human affection and desire set upon spiritual things, while David is divine love. These two are closely related in consciousness.

The shooting of arrows by Jonathan symbolizes the soul's darting forth loving, protecting thoughts toward that which it yearns to serve and to keep from all harm.

The boy who picked up the arrows symbolizes the outer activity in us that obeys and serves the executive power of the soul (Jonathan).

"David arose out of *a place* toward the South, and fell on his face to the ground, and bowed himself three times." This means that after love receives the protecting power of the soul it is able to come out of its hiding place in the subconsciousness (south) and make a closer union with the soul, as symbolized by David and Jonathan's kissing each other. David bowed three times in recognition of the supreme trinity, God, Christ, and man; or, mind, idea, and manifestation.

The spiritual meaning of Jonathan's parting words to David, 42d verse, is that through the deep understanding power of Spirit the soul is eternally unified with love.

In I Samuel 14:1-13, Jonathan, the son of Saul, represents desire in its spiritual aspect and clearly shows the spiritual method of overcoming. At the time when Jonathan resolved to go over into the Philistine garrison, Saul was in Gibeah, which is Migron (2d verse). Gibeah means *hill;* it represents the spiritual aspiration that is inherent in every desire. Jonathan, the awakened spiritual desire, recognizing that he has a definite mission in the redemption of man, resolves to enter upon his mission. Accompanied by his armor-bearer, he goes into the camp of the Philistines.

It will be noticed that Jonathan did not launch an aggressive campaign against the Philistines; he did not enter upon the work in his own wisdom, neither did he rely on the strength of Israel's fighting men. He went forth trusting in the guidance of God, and looked for His sign before undertaking the task. By following this guidance he was placed in a position of power and enabled to overcome the enemy.

One of the greatest reasons why we fail to overcome the difficulties of life is that we undertake this overcoming in our own wisdom and strength. Here is a valuable clew for us: we must first lay hold of spiritual wisdom and strength, and then we shall be guided into that position of power and authority where the Adversary is easily vanquished.

Jonathan's power was drawn from his obedience to Spirit. When desire is allowed to function independently of its spiritual significance man becomes more deeply involved in material complications; when desire is surrendered to Spirit it receives a cleansing that makes it a great liberating power.

The armor-bearer who accompanied Jonathan to the camp of the Philistines (sensualism) symbolizes that which wraps about the soul of the overcomer an atmosphere of unconquerable faith and confidence, wherewith one may scale insurmountable barriers and triumph over every difficulty.

When sensualism is faced by unconquerable spiritual desire clothed with omnipotent faith and confidence, such as Jonathan and his armor-bearer represent, sensualism falls; either the Philistines are delivered up into the hands of the Israelites, or they flee from the country, thus proving that one (true thought) shall chase a thousand (error thoughts), and two shall put ten thousand to flight.

Jonath elem rehokim (A. V., Jonath-elem-rechokim), jō'-nath ē'-lem re-hō'-kim (Heb.)—*the silent dove of those afar; a dumb dove of distant places.*

A name given in the title to Psalm 56. In the margin "The silent dove of them that are afar off" is given in place of the name.

Meta. Peace (*dove*) through the inner rhythm and melody of the soul and body attuned to Spirit. That which to the human sometimes seems afar off is brought close in the silence.

Joppa (in A. V., Joshua 19:46, Japho), jŏp'-på (Heb.) — *beauty; comeliness; good; excellence.*

A town in Palestine on the seacoast of the Mediterranean, about forty miles from Jerusalem; it was Jerusalem's seaport. It is now called Jaffa (II Chron. 2:16; Acts 9:36).

Meta. A group of thoughts in consciousness, or a nerve center, not far from the heart center (Jerusalem), in which a very exalted appreciation of *beauty* is the central or dominant characteristic.

Jorah, jō'-răh (Heb.)—*watering; sprinkling; first rains; autumn rain.*

One hundred and twelve of his descendants returned with Ezra from the Babylonian captivity (Ezra 2:18); in Nehemiah 7:24 Hariph is given in place of Jorah.

Meta. Jorah (*autumn rain, first rains, sprinkling*) is symbolical of the "early" rain, or beginning of the outpouring of Spirit upon all flesh (the entire consciousness), preceding the harvest time of the earth (body, and earthly consciousness). (See Joel 2:28 and Acts 2:17. See also Deuteronomy 11:14; Jeremiah 5:24; Joel 2:23, and James 5:7). Much is said in the Bible about the "early" or "former" and the "latter" rain.

Jorah also represents new and higher spiritual thoughts and activities that are born of one's harvest times of greater realizations of Spirit, preparatory to still further fruitions, or harvests, of spiritual understanding. See HARIPH.

Jorai, jō'-rāi (Heb.)—*whom Jehovah teaches; instructed of Jah; directed by Jehovah; Jah waters; Jehovah sprinkles; rain from Jehovah.*

A chief man of Gad (I Chron. 5:13).

Meta. A central thought of the power faculty (Gad) in individual consciousness, receiving spiritual inspiration, or spiritually inspired and guided (*whom Jehovah teaches, directed by Jehovah*).

Joram, jō'-răm (Heb.)—*whom Jehovah has set on high; Jehovah has exalted; Jehovah is exalted.*

a Son of Ahab king of Israel (II Kings 8:25). He was killed by Jehu (II Kings 9:24). **b** King of Judah (II Kings 8:20-24). These kings are also called Jehoram (II Chron. 22:1, 5).

Meta. See JEHORAM.

The kings, Jehoram of Judah, and Jehoram or Joram of Israel, in their individual characters and reigns, were not true to that which their name implies. Seeming evil came to them instead of the good that should have been their lot.

Jordan, jôr'-dan (Heb.)—*the de-scender; the descending one; the south flowing; flowing down abundantly; dispenser from above; flowing (river) of judgment.*

The largest and most noted river in Palestine (Gen. 13:10; 32:10; Josh. 3:17; Matt. 3:6).

Meta. There is a stream of thought constantly flowing through the subconsciousness (*the south flowing*), made up of thoughts good, bad, and indifferent, which is typified in Scripture by the river Jordan. In other words it is the life flow of thought through the organism from head to feet. In man's ignorant and unredeemed state it is muddy with sense concepts and turbulent with materiality.

This thought stream has to be crossed before the Children of Israel can go over into the Promised Land, before the true, real thoughts of the organism can enter into the divine substance and life in the subconsciousness. This stream of thought is also known as the adverse mind, or Adversary; when the adverse thought is removed it expresses as the life current. Adverse mind has spread itself over the underlying God consciousness and has dammed the free flow of divine energies in man, cutting off the divine expression. This adverse consciousness disturbs man as long as he believes in the presence or power of evil. The sooner the student of Truth comes to the conclusion that the subconscious realm of mind, which he is most concerned in bringing to light, is under control of Divine Mind, the more quickly will he set into activity in the body the inherent qualities of Spirit, and the sooner he will bear the fruits of Spirit in his flesh. Substance awaits the demands of the I AM man and shapes itself according to the play of thoughts and words upon it. As man consciously masters erroneous ideas, which suggest themselves from the external, he masters like ideas in consciousness, which have been the attracting magnet that drew the external experience to him; he clarifies his heart of the adverse thought until he comes to dwell in the poise and mastery of the Christ self, being master of ideas and their manifestation.

The Jordan (*flowing of judgment*) can also be said to represent that place in consciousness where we are willing to meet the results of our thoughts, face to face. When the divine law has been established in the consciousness and the Spirit of wisdom (savior, Joshua) is recognized as the "minister" of the law, we understandingly and courageously pass judgment on all thoughts. We command the sense thoughts (waters) to stand still afar off, to recede from consciousness, that the Israelites (positive thoughts of Truth) may pass over (stand in time of judgment) and come into possession of the Promised Land (realization of divine substance, the foundation of the new Christ body).

In II Kings 2:13, 14 the Jordan represents the universal race thought that flows through man's subjective mind. Overcoming of the limitations of race thought comes through positive I AM affirmations of the presence of God and His power to accomplish whatsoever is desired.

In the healing of Naaman (II Kings 5) the Jordan represents the life current. Naaman (will) was commanded to wash in the Jordan (life stream) because, as man's spiritual perception (the little Israelitish maiden) reveals to him the realities of life, he is convinced of the need of cleansing the personal will. Spiritual I AM (Elisha) commands the denial of material beliefs and limitations. When the will is under the direction of Spirit the mind and the body express their natural purity and perfection.

Seven is the number of completeness in the natural world, or in the body consciousness. The command to Naaman to wash in the Jordan seven times means that one must continue to bathe in this inner life stream until the body is wholly purified and completely healed.

Jorim, jō'-rĭm (Gk. fr. Heb.)—*whom Jehovah has set on high; Jehovah has exalted; Jehovah is exalted.*

Son of Matthat, in the genealogy of Jesus Christ (Luke 3:29). The name is the same as Joram.

Meta. See JEHORAM.

Jorkeam (A. V., Jorkoam), jôr'-kĕ-ăm (Heb.)—*the people is spread abroad; scattering of the people; spreading out of the people; verdure of the people; green fields of the people.*

Either a descendant of Caleb's or a place in Palestine that was founded by Raham, one of Caleb's descendants (I Chron. 2:44).

Meta. Jorkeam (*spreading out of the people, the people is spread abroad*) signifies the expanding of the faith-and-praise consciousness in us (Jorkeam was a descendant of Caleb, who signifies spiritual faith and enthusiasm, of the tribe of Judah, which signifies praise). This expansion is brought about by spreading praise and faith thoughts (people) throughout a greater area, or realm, of the consciousness, where they become as a leaven of Truth that continues its work until the entire consciousness will in time become awakened to enthusiasm over the true things of Spirit. This leads to abundant substance, supply, spiritual food, and the true Christ freedom (*green fields of the people;* this makes one think of the 23d Psalm).

Josech (A. V., Joseph), jō'-sĕch (Gk. fr. Heb.)—*whom Jehovah will add to; Jehovah shall increase; he shall increase progressively,* i. e., *to perfection.*

A man named in the genealogy of Jesus Christ (Luke 3:26).

Meta. The significance is the same as that of Joseph: the imagination, the imaging, increasing power of the mind.

Joseph, jō'-ṣeph (Heb.)—*whom Jehovah will add to; Jehovah shall increase; he shall increase progressively,* i. e., *from perfection unto perfection.*

a Son of Jacob, elder of the two borne to him by Rachel. "And she called his name Joseph, saying, Jehovah add to me another son" (Gen. 30:24; see also Genesis 37, 39, 41, 42, 46 to 50). Jacob's blessing of Joseph was (Gen. 49:22-26):
"Joseph is a fruitful bough,
A fruitful bough by a fountain;
His branches run over the wall.
The archers have sorely grieved him,
And shot at him, and persecuted him:
But his bow abode in strength,
And the arms of his hands were made strong,
By the hands of the Mighty One of Jacob

(From thence is the shepherd, the stone
of Israel),
Even by the God of thy father, who
shall help thee,
And by the Almighty, who shall bless
thee,
With blessings of heaven above,
Blessings of the deep that coucheth be-
neath,
Blessings of the breasts, and of the
womb.
The blessings of thy father
Have prevailed above the blessings of
my progenitors
Unto the utmost bound of the everlast-
ing hills:
They shall be on the head of Joseph,
And on the crown of the head of him
that was separate from his
brethren."
And Moses blessed the tribe of Joseph,
through his two sons, as follows (Deut.
33:13-17):
"Blessed of Jehovah be his land,
For the precious things of heaven, for
the dew,
And for the deep that coucheth beneath,
And for the precious things of the fruits
of the sun,
And for the precious things of the
growth of the moons,
And for the chief things of the ancient
mountains,
And for the precious things of the ever-
lasting hills,
And for the precious things of the earth
and the fulness thereof,
And the good will of him that dwelt in
the bush.
Let *the blessing* come upon the head of
Joseph,
And upon the crown of the head of him
that was separate from his breth-
ren.
The firstling of his herd, majesty is
his;
And his horns are the horns of the
wild-ox:
With them he shall push the peoples
all of them, *even* the ends of the
earth:
And they are the ten thousands of
Ephraim,
And they are the thousands of Manas-
seh."

In both Jacob's and Moses' blessings
upon Joseph, where the text says, "that
was separate from his brethren," the
margin gives, "that is prince among" his
brethren. b A follower of the Christian
doctrine, surnamed Barnabas by the
apostles. He was a companion of Paul's
in many missionary journeys (Acts 4:
36). c Husband of Mary the mother of
Jesus (Matt. 1:19). d Joseph of Arimathæa, a rich man and disciple of Jesus, who begged Jesus' body from Pilate
and buried it in his own tomb (Matt.
27:57-60). e Joseph called Barsabbas,
one of the two who were chosen to take
the place of Judas Iscariot, but the lot
fell to Matthias and not to Joseph Barsabbas (Acts 1:23).

Meta. The state of consciousness in
which we *increase* in character along all
lines; we not only grow into a broader
understanding but there is an increase
of vitality and substance. Joseph is
especially representative of the realm of
forms. He was clothed with a coat of
many colors; he was a dreamer and interpreter of dreams; the phenomenal was
his field of action. Among the primal
faculties of the mind Joseph represents
imagination. This faculty has the power
to throw onto the screen of visibility in
substance and life forms every idea that
the mind may conceive. While the imagination is a very necessary faculty and
is powerful and productive, yet it is
belittled and often derided and scorned
by the other faculties of the mind while
they are unawakened spiritually, while
they are functioning in intellectual consciousness instead of true spiritual understanding (Joseph's brothers persecuted him).

Joseph in Egypt symbolizes the word
of the imagination in subconsciousness,
or the involution of a high spiritual idea.
Joseph in Egypt could be said to represent also our highest perception of
Truth, dealing with the realm of forms
and bringing it into a more orderly state.

Joseph, our high ideal of Truth, comes
down into the Egyptian darkness of
sense consciousness, and under the law
will finally raise it into spiritual light.
In the process Joseph seems to die, but
his "bones" remain. The substance of

Truth is an abiding presence, though its form may be lost to sight.

How often we hear people say that they do not now seem to realize such uplift as came to them when they first began to understand Truth! Then they were so enthusiastic that they could think and talk of nothing else. They say that they even demonstrated for themselves and for others more easily than they demonstrate now. They think that they have somehow lost their grasp of Truth, because carnality seems so real to them. They are right in the place that was occupied by the Israelites after Joseph died. Truth, as a thing apart, a personality named Joseph, has disappeared, but it lives in his progeny in the land of Egypt, and these descendants are oppressed by Egyptians. We might say that the ideas that make up the statements of Truth that you have received have percolated through your mind; but the sense consciousness is ruling in you, and these "children of Israel" are oppressed. Instead of siding with Spirit in every thought, you side with the carnal, and you build up a ruling state of thought that remembers not the inspiring Truth. "Now there arose a new king over Egypt, who knew not Joseph" (Exod. 1:8).

But Truth cannot be destroyed, nor can true words and true thoughts ever be effaced from the mind that has willingly received them. The Children of Israel multiplied in the land of Egypt in spite of oppression; their power became a great source of concern to the Egyptians, who "made their lives bitter with hard service, in mortar and in brick" (material ways).

The several visits of Joseph's brothers to Egypt for corn, the bringing of Jacob and all the brothers of Joseph with their families and flocks down into Egypt, and the final reconciliation are a symbolical representation of the manner in which we make connection with the obscured vitality within the organism and bring all our faculties into conjunction with it. This symbolism depicts also the unification of the I AM (Jacob) with all the faculties of the mind, with the life energies, and with the substance of the whole man. They dwelt in the "land of Goshen" (unity). See Genesis 46 and 47.

Joseph as the imaging, increasing power of the mind refers to the imagination. For the significance of Joseph Barnabas, see BARNABAS.

Joseph and Mary, the parents of Jesus, represent wisdom and love, which have been ideas in mind but are now to bring forth a manifestation in substance (Luke 2:4, 5). Joseph might also be said to represent the Son of man and Mary the divine motherhood (Luke 2:40-52).

Joseph was merely betrothed to Mary, yet she was "great with child"; so Joseph "was minded to put her away privily." This means that we do not in the first stages of the birth of Christ in us understand the process, and sometimes are moved to put it away from us. The soul is heavily charged with divine life, and so full that it cannot express itself intelligently, because no union has yet taken place between it and the understanding (Joseph).

Joseph of Arimathæa signifies the imaging faculty functioning on a very high plane of consciousness (Arimathæa means a height).

For the significance of Joseph Barsabbas, see BARSABBAS.

Joshah, jō'-shäh (Heb.)—*whom Jehovah lets dwell; Jehovah establishes; Jehovah shall stand out; Jah exists in being.*

Son of Amaziah, a prince of the tribe of Simeon (I Chron. 4:34-41).

Meta. A ruling thought in the phase of the awakening consciousness of man that is attentive and receptive to higher spiritual ideals (Simeon). This thought, which belongs to the spiritually receptive phase of man's consciousness, is established by Jehovah (*Jehovah establishes*) in the deeper realms of substance and life (indicated by flocks and pasture) in the organism. Here it aids in overcoming the ignorant, carnal ideas of life and substance. (The descendants of Simeon overcame the Meunim and the descendants of Ham, and "dwelt in their stead; because there was pasture there for their flocks.")

Joshaphat, jŏsh'-ă-phăt (Heb.)—*whom*

Jehovah judges; whom Jah sustains; Jah defends.

One of David's mighty warriors, and a member of his guard (I Chron. 11:43). The name is a form of Jehoshaphat.

Meta. The significance is virtually the same as that of Jehoshaphat: the development in consciousness of the idea of judgment and of the sustaining power of I AM. (See JEHOSHAPHAT.)

Joshaviah, jŏsh-ȧ-vī'-ȧh (Heb.)—*Jehovah is equality; seat of Jehovah; throne of Jah; whom Jah enthrones; Jehovah is equity; sufficiency of Jah; Jah abides; dwelling of Jah.*

One of David's guard, son of Elnaam (I Chron. 11:46).

Meta. Establishing in consciousness (*seat of Jehovah, dwelling of Jah*) the spiritual idea of justice, fair-mindedness, equality (*Jehovah is equality*), and the all-sufficiency of God, Spirit, through I AM, Jehovah, to meet one's every need (*sufficiency of Jah*).

Joshbekashah, jŏsh-bĕk'-ȧ-shäh (Heb.) —*seated in hardness; abiding in harshness; eagerly seeking a habitation; diligently in search of a dwelling; beseeching a throne; requiring equity.*

Son of Heman, and head of the seventeenth course of Temple service in singing and music (I Chron. 25:4, 24).

Meta. A sense of the hardness of intellectual understanding (see HEMAN, father of Joshbekashah) when Spirit is not consciously recognized and acknowledged (*seated in hardness*); also a deep, inner soul yearning for conscious union with and an abiding place in true spiritual light and wisdom (*eagerly seeking a dwelling, beseeching a throne, requiring equity*).

Joshibiah (A. V., Josibiah), jŏsh-ĭ-bī'-ȧh (Heb.)—*seat of Jehovah; whom Jehovah causes to dwell; Jehovah enthrones; whom Jah causes to abide.*

A Simeonite, father of a prince of Simeon (I Chron. 4:35).

Meta. Obedience to, and therefore conscious oneness with, Jehovah, I AM, Christ (*seat of Jehovah, whom Jehovah causes to dwell, Jehovah enthrones*). Joshibiah, at this stage of individual unfoldment, simply signifies a recognition and inner acknowledgment of the Truth; it has not as yet been worked out in actuality.

Joshua (in A. V., Numbers 13:16 and I Chronicles 7:27, Jehoshua and Jehoshuah), jŏsh'-ū-ȧ (Heb.)—*Jehovah is salvation; Jah is savior; Jehovah is deliverer; whom Jehovah makes triumphant; Jehovah is the victory; Jah makes rich.*

Son of Nun, Moses' minister and the leader of Moses' army. Joshua was one of the two spies who gave a good report of the Promised Land. He took charge of the Israelites after Moses' death, and led them into the land of Canaan (Exod. 33:11; Num. 14:6-10, 38; Deut. 34:9; Josh. 1 to 23). He was of the tribe of Ephraim (Num. 13:8, 16).

Meta. Joshua means *Jah is savior, Jehovah is deliverer.* In the Hebrew the name is identical with the name Jesus. Both of these names are derived from the word Jehovah, meaning "I AM THAT I AM." The only difference between Joshua and Jesus is the extent of conscious realization of identity with the I AM. Under certain states of mind the I AM in man acquires greatly increased power. This power has its foundation in spiritual understanding. Joshua took the Children of Israel into the Promised Land. So it is through the power of our I AM or indwelling Christ that we lay hold of and attain the redemption of our life forces.

The leadership of the Israelites was given to Joshua because he had been under instruction and had acquired a proficiency that enabled him to perform his work with dispatch. (Joshua was of the tribe of Ephraim, typifying will, or executive faculty of mind.) When Joshua took command he notified the Children of Israel that they would pass over into the Promised Land in three days. This promptness of action is the result of confidence and power. When we know the law of spiritual demonstration and have the courage to act, we are Joshua. It is this state of mind that saves the whole mentality from its errors and brings it to a consciousness of its natural inheritance in Being.

In Joshua 3:5-17, Joshua (the I AM, which governs and controls the activity of thought in the inner realms) speaks to the Children of Israel and commands them, "Hear the words of Jehovah your God."

The priests symbolize our faith in the power of Spirit, through which understanding of mind action is established.

The "ark of the covenant" is the conscious realization that the spiritual nature in man is the real self.

One enters into the joys of the Promised Land (spiritual realization) by having faith in Spirit as the one reality active in man and by gaining an understanding of divine law. Established in understanding, man, through I AM (Joshua), commands his thought world to harmonize with divine standards, and thus sets up an entirely new state of consciousness of a spiritual character. This spiritual consciousness is the Promised Land.

Joshua's mission was to bring the Children of Israel into a realization of their inheritance in the Promised Land. After they had been brought up into this consciousness, they were sent forth actually to take possession of the land (Judges 2:6-16). At this time they were all servants of God and were unified in thought and purpose. Then Joshua died, and was buried "in the border of his inheritance in Timnath–heres" (*portion of the sun*, or *portion of Heres*, the meaning of Heres being given as *sun*) "in the hill-country of Ephraim" (*doubly fruitful*).

As the individual, under the leadership of some idea, succeeds in bringing all his faculties and forces into subservience to this idea, the idea itself seems to die, or to be merged into the general activity of his being as a whole. This is the *portion of Heres* or *portion of the sun*. When the central idea is absorbed by the being, the individual becomes *doubly fruitful;* his creative forces are greatly increased. In this state there is soon a great accumulation of new forces and powers, and unless they are definitely directed one encounters difficulties and is likely to be drawn back into materiality.

The individual should seek to avoid the condition that eventually overcame the Children of Israel. In order to do this

he daily must put his increasing creative power in harmony with his developing spiritual consciousness. By this plan the goal of spiritual attainment is ever within his reach, and remains a great stabilizing influence in his life.

On the other hand, when man discovers his spiritual powers and uses them in an ignorant way (the worship of Baal), he is swept back into Egypt, or darkness. The only light that is left to him is Ashtaroth, meaning *stars*, the intellectual perception that once had guided him.

The full light of Truth is available only to the one who constantly directs all the forces of his being in perfect harmony with the trend of his highest aspirations.

The death of Joshua and the falling away of the Children of Israel into idolatry after he died can be explained metaphysically as follows: As night follows the day, so, in the early religious experiences of the soul, a season of darkness always follows a high illumination. At this time the untried powers of the soul, also past sins and shortcomings, are brought into evidence; apparently disorder and confusion prevail. But in the light of Truth this experience is not a going back. It is only a letting go in order to get a better hold. The unalterable laws of God are constantly working to bring into expression the poise and serenity and joy of Divine Mind, to the final bringing forth of the perfect creation.

As in the winnowing process the grain is carefully separated from the chaff and stored away for future use, so the Lord preserves the "finest of the wheat" that springs up in an illumined mind and preserves it until such time as it can be best used in the soul unfoldment.

The final step into light out of this season of darkness is the dawning of a new day. When all human means of deliverance have failed, the only source of escape is to turn within to the one Helper. When Spirit is appealed to, the freeing power is set into activity and the path that leads into the light is made clear.

Under the Jesus Christ dispensation, in which we are living today, these experiences are not necessary. Though one may go down into the depths temporarily, the beacon light of spiritual illumination is not extinguished; those who have learned to trust the Lord, to keep their face turned toward the light regardless of appearances, are learning to pass from one state of consciousness to another (from glory to glory), with little or no disturbance. They have learned to make practical use of the divine law; to walk unafraid on the waters of untried seas of thought.

Josiah, jō-sī′-ăh (Heb.)—*whom Jehovah heals; Jehovah cures; whom Jehovah supports; Jah is a prop; fire of Jehovah.*

a A good king of Judah. His mother was Jedidah the daughter of Adaiah of Bozkath (II Kings 22). **b** A son of Zephaniah (Zech. 6:10).

Meta. Josiah (*whom Jehovah supports*) signifies that in consciousness which connects itself with Spirit and tries to carry out the divine plan, to substitute being for seeming. The significance of the fact that Josiah began his reign very young is that, in order to bring the whole man into harmony with Truth and demonstrate perfection, one must begin to act on and be loyal to one's first impressions and concepts of Truth.

When Josiah began to reign Israel had been taught to worship false gods. Man turns away from the one true God because the ruling faculties of mind have been allowed to set up sense laws; to give themselves over to sense consciousness, lascivious imaginations, physical sensations, and so forth. This causes the mind to cling to man-made creeds or organizations, or to spiritual leaders. As a result man loses sight of the one true God.

Jesus taught that God is Spirit. He denied the worship of personality when He said: "Be not ye called Rabbi: for one is your teacher, and all ye are brethren. And call no man your father on the earth: for one is your Father, *even* he who is in heaven" (Matt. 23:8, 9).

After man has denied personality, ignorance, and false worship he affirms his allegiance to Spirit, sets up true worship in the consciousness, affirms his spiritual power, life, and substance, and so builds anew his body temple.

The purging of Judah and Jerusalem (II Chron. 34:1-13) signifies a systematic denial of errors of thought and practice that have become habitual in both the objective and the subjective consciousness. After purging the mind of error, by denial, we should see to it that we put the builders to work upon "the temple." These builders are affirmations.

Josiah was king of Judah when the "book of the law" was found (II Chron. 34:14-28). Josiah here represents loyalty to Truth in man's consciousness, which is seeking to make at-one-ment with God. The "book of the law" is the Mosaic law, or the order of action proclaimed by the Lord (man's higher self) for the purification of the natural man. This purification enables him to receive Truth as proclaimed by Jesus Christ.

The "book of the law" was in "the house of Jehovah." This means that in the center of man's consciousness the law of the Lord is written, and that, as man begins to set his house in order, higher rules and standards of action are revealed. This revelation comes through the avenue of the subjective memory (Shaphan the scribe), which receives through the religious tendencies (Hilkiah) the impression of the higher standards of life as man consecrates himself to God and begins to use the energies of his mind and body (money in the house of Jehovah) in the restoration of his body temple.

The faculty that is brought to bear on this revelation of subconscious activities in order that man may rightly interpret and use the increased powers is the intuitive perception of the subjective consciousness; this faculty works through the love nature, illumining the thoughts and making man tender-hearted and nonresistant. This state of mind enables man to go through the transforming processes without hard experiences.

This transforming work is carried to completion through regeneration. We enter into the regeneration by letting the purifying fire of Spirit sweep through the body consciousness as we awake to Truth, and by then identifying ourselves with the Jesus Christ consciousness of strength, power, purity, life, and love.

Josiphiah, jŏs-ĭ-phī'-ăh (Heb.)—*whom Jehovah increases; increase of the Lord; Jehovah adds; enthroned with Jehovah; with whom Jah dwells.*

Josiphiah's son, with a hundred and sixty men, returned with Ezra from the Babylonian captivity (Ezra 8:10).

Meta. The increasing power of the mind—the faculty of imagination—established in I AM, Jehovah, Christ.

Jotbah, jŏt'-băh (Heb.)—*goodness; healthfulness; beauty; comeliness; pleasantness; excellence.*

The home of Haruz, father of Meshullemeth, the wife of Manasseh and mother of Amon, two kings of Judah (II Kings 21:19). Jotbah is thought to be the same place as Jotbathah of Numbers 33:33 and Deuteronomy 10:7.

Meta. A consciousness of the refreshing waters of life and Truth; this is indeed *pleasant* and *good* and *healthful.*

Jotbathah (in A. V., Deuteronomy 10:7, Jotbath), jŏt'-bă-thăh (Heb.)—*goodness; healthfulness; beauty; comeliness; pleasantness; excellence.*

A camping place of the Children of Israel in the wilderness, (Num. 33:33); "and from Gudgodah to Jotbathah, a land of brooks of water" (Deut. 10:7).

Meta. Like Jotbah, a place in consciousness where the waters of life and Truth flow in freely and refresh the whole consciousness of man, the soul. This excellent, healthful, and good experience is always realized after one goes through a period of letting go error and darkness, such as is symbolized by Gudgodah, from which place the Israelites journeyed to Jotbathah. (See GUDGODAH.)

Jotham, jō'-thăm (Heb.)—*Jehovah is upright; whom Jah makes perfect; Jehovah is perfection; Jah is solitude; Jehovah is alone.*

a Son of Uzziah, and a good king of Judah (II Kings 15:32). **b** Youngest son of Jerubbaal, or Gideon; he was the only one of Gideon's sons whom Abimelech, another son, did not kill (Judg. 9:5).

Meta. Jotham, king of Judah, is the individual will's laying hold of the idea of divine perfection, wholeness, upright-

ness, integrity, by means of the silence, true prayer.

Jotham, son of Gideon, or Zerubbaal, signifies that divine justice and uprightness (*Jehovah is upright, whom Jah makes perfect*) are being perceived and laid hold of by the understanding and judgment faculties of the individual. This Jotham was of the tribe of Manasseh (representing the understanding), and his father was one of Israel's great judges (a judge pertaining to the faculty of judgment). *Jah is solitude,* and *Jehovah is alone,* bespeak the inner place of stillness in each individual, where one comes in touch with the indwelling Christ Spirit.

Jozabad (in A. V., I Chronicles 12:4, Josabad), jŏz'-ă-băd (Heb.)—*whom Jehovah bestows; Jehovah endowed; Jehovah-given.*

a A Benjamite, who fell away from Saul and came to David at Ziklag (I Chron. 12:4). **b** A man of Manasseh, who came to David at Ziklag (I Chron. 12:20). **c** A Levite (Ezra 8:33). Jozabad is a contraction of Jehozabad.

Meta. See JEHOZABAD.

Jozacar (A. V., Jozachar), jŏz'-ă-cär (Heb.)—*whom Jehovah remembers; Jah is mindful; remembered by Jehovah; Jah recalls.*

Son of Shimeath. He was one of the two servants of Joash, king of Judah, who killed Joash (II Kings 12:21).

Meta. The divine something within man's consciousness that makes it impossible for anything really to pass out of memory until it is adjusted rightly (*Jah is mindful, remembered by Jehovah, Jah recalls*). The law of sowing and reaping exemplifies this. Every thought, word, and act brings about, or helps to bring about, like conditions in mind, body, and affairs. If our thoughts are out of divine order the results are not to our liking, and so an adjustment must be made. The error thoughts and habits must be forgiven—erased from consciousness—and truer thoughts and activities established in their place, that harmony, joy, peace, and good may express continuously. (Joash was a good king so long as Jehoiada the high priest lived to instruct him, but after Jehoiada died, Joash departed from the Lord and did evil; he had Jehoiada's son killed for trying to hold up the Truth before him. Later he was slain by his servants. See II Chronicles 24:15-26.)

Jozadak, jŏz'-ă-dăk (Heb.)—*whom Jehovah makes just; righteousness of Jah; innocence of Jehovah; Jah is great.*

His son Jeshua was one of those who joined Zerubbabel in building the altar of God in Jerusalem, and offering burnt offerings upon it (Ezra 3:2). This was after the return from the Babylonian captivity. Jozadak is a shortened form of Jehozadak.

Meta. The significance is virtually the same as that of Jehozadak: an inner perception of the greatness, the justice, the righteousness of the Christ, Jehovah, as inherently belonging to man and as being possible of expression in and through man. Through the son Jeshua (signifying the same as Joshua, I AM) these spiritual qualities of the Christ are established in the individual consciousness and become a part of one's character and life.

Jubal, jū'-băl (Heb.)—*principle of sound; source of joy; source of moral affections; source of happiness; cry of joy; jubilation; a constant stream; moral prosperity; harmony; melody; music.*

Son of Lamech by his wife Adah. Jubal "was the father of all such as handle the harp and pipe"; in other words, he represents a principle of harmony, which might find expression in musical instruments. Some suppose him to have been the inventor of the harp and the mouth organ (Gen. 4:21).

Meta. The natural rhythm, harmony, and joy of life (*a constant stream, music, source of joy*) that are experienced when the soul radiates grace, beauty of thought and character, and comeliness (Adah, mother of Jubal), and the body is healthy and strong. (This latter is suggested in the meaning of Lamech, the name of the father of Jubal.)

Jucal, jū'-căl (Heb.)—*Jehovah is capable; ability of Jah; strength of Jah; Jah will overcome; Jehovah is mastery; perfection of Jehovah; power of Jehovah.*

Son of Shelemiah, one of those who thought that Jeremiah was weakening the people by prophesying against them

and so complained of him to the king and had him put in the dungeon of Malchijah (Jer. 38:1). In Jeremiah 37:3 he is called Jehucal.

Meta. The significance is the same as that of Jehucal, with this exception: Jucal's misunderstanding of Jeremiah and his consequent attitude toward him show that, while the will (king) has the inherent belief that Jehovah is fully able to deliver, yet it lacks the understanding and the freedom from self-condemnation that would cause it to be firmly assured that God is *willing*, as well as *able*, to save, protect, and fully redeem. It cannot, therefore, comprehend the activities of that faith (Jeremiah) which combines belief in God's ability with the assurance of His willingness, and so would bring about results if not hindered and bound by the unbelieving and disobedient will. (The will, represented by the king, is the executive faculty of the mind, and none of the other faculties can work to a useful degree without the coöperation of the will.)

Judæa (in A. V., Luke 23:5 and John 7:1, Jewry), jū-dæ'-à (Gk. fr. Heb.)—*of Judah; praise Jehovah; celebration of Jehovah; laud Jehovah; confess Jah.*

The southern division of Palestine; the land or province of Judah (Matt. 2:1).

Meta. A reference to the interpretation of Scriptural names shows Judæa (now commonly spelled *Judea*) to mean "the praise of Jehovah." This then is a key to the mental attitude in which the Christ consciousness will be opened to us—while we are praising the Lord.

Judæa is the land of Judah. "Judah" means "*praise Jehovah, confession of Jah.*" In John 4:47 the I AM (Jesus) dwelling in "*praise of Jehovah*" (Judæa) identifies man with Christ thoughts and leads to greater expression of divine power. (See JUDAH, the tribe and kingdom.)

Judah, jū'-dăh (Heb.)—*praise Jehovah; celebration of Jehovah; laud Jehovah; confession of Jah.*

a Fourth son of Jacob and Leah (Gen. 29:35). "And she conceived again, and bare a son: and she said, This time will I praise Jehovah: therefore she called his name Judah; and she left off bearing." Jacob's blessing on Judah was (Gen. 49:8-12):

"Judah, thee shall thy brethren praise:
Thy hand shall be on the neck of thine enemies;
Thy father's sons shall bow down before thee.
Judah is a lion's whelp;
From the prey, my son, thou art gone up:
He stooped down, he couched as a lion,
And as a lioness; who shall rouse him up?
The sceptre shall not depart from Judah,
Nor the ruler's staff from between his feet,
Until Shiloh come;
And unto him shall the obedience of the peoples be.
Binding his foal unto the vine,
And his ass's colt unto the choice vine;
He hath washed his garments in wine,
And his vesture in the blood of grapes:
His eyes shall be red with wine,
And his teeth white with milk."

b The tribe of Judah was composed of the Israelites who were descended from Judah, the fourth son of Jacob. When the kingdom of Israel was divided, this tribe stayed with Rehoboam, Solomon's son, and became the kingdom of Judah (II Sam. 5:5; I Kings 12:20). At this time the tribe of Benjamin was with Judah (II Chron. 11:1). Moses' blessing on the tribe of Judah was (Deut. 33:7):

"And this is *the blessing* of Judah: and he said,
Hear, Jehovah, the voice of Judah,
And bring him in unto his people.
With his hands he contended for himself;
And thou shalt be a help against his adversaries."

Meta. The Hebrew meaning of the word Judah is *praise Jehovah*. It is evident that Judah represents the spiritual faculty that corresponds to accumulation or increase in the mental; this is prayer and praise. Prayer should be a jubilant thanksgiving instead of a supplication. It quickens the mind and makes it draw, like a magnet, that from the realm of causes which fulfills one's desires.

At the very apex of the brain is a ganglionic center that we may term the center of reverence or spirituality. It is there that man holds converse with the intelligence of Divine Mind. This brain center is the home or "house" of a spiritual consciousness, which is in Scripture designated as Judah, whose office it is to pray and praise. This faculty is also called the superconsciousness; that is, it is above the various states of mind, but not separate from them. It pervades every phase of thought as an elevating, inspiring quality. All lofty ideals come from this faculty; it is the inspiration of everything that elevates and idealizes in religion, poetry, art, in all things that are true and real.

This is one of the foundation faculties of the mind. It is that consciousness which relates man directly with the Father-Mind. It is quickened and enlarged through prayer and all other forms of religious thought and worship. When we pray we look up from within, not because God is off in the sky but because this spiritual center in the top of the head becomes active and our attention is naturally drawn to it.

One of the offices of the spiritual faculty is to gather ideas. Through it man can draw, from the universal Mind, God thoughts; that is, ideas absolutely true. Therefore prayer is accumulative; it accumulates spiritual substance, life, intelligence, and everything else necessary to man's highest expression. When we pray in spiritual understanding this highest realm of mind comes in touch with the universal and impersonal Mind, and the mind of man is joined to the very mind of God. Thus God answers our prayers in ideas, thoughts, words, which are translated into the outer realms of form, in due season.

Praise is closely related to prayer, and is an expression of spiritual consciousness. Whatever we praise, we increase, through law of mind.

Praise is the positive pole of life. Praise is the key to the increase of life activity. If you depreciate your life you decrease your consciousness of life. Thus we find that Judah, besides symbolizing the place in consciousness where we come into touch with the highest activities of Divine Mind, typifies also the central faculty of consciousness. It operates in body consciousness through the spinal cord, as well as in the top head, and finds its outer expression through the life center, which, unregenerated, is "Judas," who had a devil. When life is separated from the other faculties and endeavors to express without their cooperation, man gives himself over to his animals in human forms.

In Acts 3:2, the "door of the temple which is called Beautiful" signifies spiritual understanding. This door opens when we pray and praise. Among the twelve faculties of the mind, as typified by the twelve sons of Jacob, praise is *Judah*. When he was born Leah said, "This time will I praise Jehovah."

"Peter and John were going up into the temple at the hour of prayer." Some persons think that the understanding of the inner life can be attained without prayer, but they are mistaken. All who have reached heights in things spiritual have been noted for their devotions. Jesus was a striking illustration of this. He spent whole nights in prayer, and He seemed to be asking the Father and thanking Him in almost the same breath on every occasion where He did a great work or expounded a notable truth.

Judah means *praise Jehovah*. This tribe is often used to designate the whole Jewish nation, indicating that praise is an active principle in our spiritual thoughts and should be given first place in all our thanksgiving.
"Bless Jehovah, O my soul;
 And all that is within me, *bless* his
 holy name."

Praise keeps the soul fresh and pure and beautiful. It is the power that opens the inner portals of the soul to the full and free inflow of spiritual light and aspiration.

The tribe of Judah, which remained with Rehoboam when the kingdom of Israel was divided (I Kings 12), represents the central faculty of consciousness. It may be roughly described as the focal point of body organization. Its physical expression is the spinal cord, yet this is but the visible aspect of an invisible energy. This energy or mind substance at the very center of the man is susceptible of the highest and of the lowest. It is the serpent that may resist divine wisdom and crawl upon its belly in the dust of materiality, or it may be lifted up and exalted to the most high place among the faculties of man. When it is sensualized it becomes Judas, who had a devil. It is related in I Kings 12:20 that the only tribe that followed Rehoboam was Judah. Thus persistent sensuality vitiated the very core of the man, and he lost control of his other faculties. This is often observed in people who have lived on the sense plane until they are animal nature.

In II Sam. 2:1-6 the "cities of Judah" are aggregations of thoughts in the *praise* consciousness of man. Gratitude is another name for this state of mind, symbolically known here as Judah. Praise and thanksgiving multiply and increase everything that we center them on. Jesus gave thanks before He raised Lazarus. He gave thanks before He multiplied the loaves and fishes. Scientifically, He was increasing the thought stuff until it precipitated into the realm of visibility. "Go up into . . . the cities of Judah" and use the law as here stated, and you can bring forth whatever you set your heart on.

The kingdom of Judah, over which Asa was king (I Kings 15:9-24; II Chron. 14, 15, 16), metaphysically represents the inner life force of man's organism. We usually refer to this inner life force as the vitality. Those who are not students of mind have but slight comprehension of the real character of these subjective energies. They know that the heart beats and the blood circulates; that digestion and assimilation go on, and that the body is the most wonderful structure in existence; yet they are ignorant of the intelligent power that directs and sustains its intricate machinery. An intelligence transcending that of the intellect is manifest in this realm under the heart. Symbolically it may be said that another man presides there, who in these texts is designated as King Asa. (See ASA.)

The purging of Judah and Jerusalem (II Chron. 34:3) signifies systematic denial of errors of thought and practice, that have become habitual in both the objective and the subjective realms of consciousness.

"Asherim," or "groves," were symbols of the Phœnician Venus, the goddess of love, and were usually of a sensual character. Metaphysically, the "molten images" and the "graven images" mean the productions of the imagination that are first in a free state and then in a formed state of consciousness. The lascivious imagination is the "molten" state, the second step of which is the "graven image," or physical sensation. These are both to be purged and denied in mind and body. We thus dissolve or make "dust" of these conditions; they go back to the formless and inert.

The burning of the bones of the priests on the altars means the sacrificing or giving up of the material or gross forms of our religious ideas of God. You may have overcome sensuality, and changed your ideas about the personality of God, yet be clinging to some personal spiritual leader or priest. Burn these "bones" by vigorous denial of human foolishness and ignorance, and affirmations of divine wisdom. In ancient times it was (and today in some instances is) the habit of the devout to give special reverence to the priest or the spiritual leader and to call him father. Jesus commented on this man-worship in Matthew 23:8-9. "But be not ye called Rabbi: for one is your teacher, and all ye are brethren. And call no man your father on the earth: for one is your Father, even he who is in heaven."

After purging the mind of error by denial we should see to it that we put the builders to work upon "the temple." Denial is always destructive and leaves vacancies in the consciousness to be filled up with true statements. When vigorous denial is followed by a feeling of weakness, we may know that we have destroyed some thought structure on which we have been depending, and have built nothing in its place. The carpenters and builders are the universal constructive forces of Being. These are always at work in the organism when right thought is holding sway, but after a siege of error it is necessary to start them anew by using affirmations of substance based in Truth—"hewn stone"; the unity of good—"timber for couplings"; and the eternity of the *now*—"beams for the houses."

Judas, jū'-dăs (Gk. fr. Heb.)—Judah. See ISCARIOT for definitions of the surname of Judas Iscariot.

a The disciple of Jesus Christ who betrayed the Master and afterward went and hanged himself (Matt. 10:4; John 18:2-5; Matt. 27:5; Acts 1:18). **b** There were others by the name of Judas also (Acts 5:37; 9:11; 15:22).

Meta. Judas Iscariot—the custodian of life. This Judas represents the unredeemed life forces. He also typifies that in humanity which, though it has caught the higher vision of life, still resorts to underhanded methods in order to meet its obligations. Judas carried the money bag, and he betrayed Jesus for thirty pieces of silver.

The first step in our redeeming the Judas faculty is to assume a fearless attitude of mind, affirming our unity with the Spirit of purity. When we do this the Lord answers, "Thou hast said," and the redeeming, uplifting, transmuting forces are set into operation. When the Judas faculty reaches the spiritual standard of life it is known as Judah, whose office is praise and thanksgiving. Praise and thanksgiving call into activity greater expressions of spiritual substance and open larger avenues through which we may receive spiritual life. Praise radiates and gives glory to the latent powers of man.

Judas also symbolizes desire, appropriation, acquisitiveness. Acquisitiveness is a legitimate faculty of the mind, but covetousness is its Judas. When acquisitiveness acts within the law it builds up the consciousness. Exercised in its native realm, the free essences of Being, it draws to us the supplies of the universe and through it we enter into permanent possessions. But when it oversteps the law it is a destroyer. Judas was the treasurer of the disciples of Jesus, but he became covetous—he had a devil (John 6:70, 71), and his sin brought tragedy.

And so we find among our disciples, or faculties, this one whose tendency is such that through it we are brought into condemnation and suffering. It is known from the first; it is Judas, self-appropriation. While in its highest office it is Judah, spiritual appropriation through prayer and praise, yet introverted in human consciousness it becomes Judas, acquisitiveness overstepping the law, covetousness. It is through the exercising of this faculty that suffering and crucifixion are brought about. It is the faculty that draws to us the substance of things. While in its essence it is good, yet if one appropriates it in its personal sense "good were it for that man if he had not been born" (Matt. 26:24).

In our present state, however, Judas could not be excluded from the twelve. He carries the bag, he is the treasurer of our system, a thief also. He is selfish, proud, ambitious, tyrannical—but he cannot be spared. His faults must be overcome. They must be pointed out fearlessly: "Is it I?" "Thou hast said." Then the right relation is established by giving up absolutely the life and the substance that we have called our own: "Take, eat; this is my body." "Drink ye all of it; for this is my blood."

Let go of the idea that you can personally possess even the life and substance of your organism. They are of the Universal, and must be given up for the "remission of sins." When this place of absolute renunciation of all is attained, there rushes into consciousness a new power; the fruit of the vine of infinite life is drunk anew in every faculty "in my Father's kingdom" (Matt. 26:17-30).

In John 12:4-6, Judas Iscariot (sense consciousness) is incarnated selfishness and his every thought is to build up personality. When Mary (divine love) pours out her precious substance and diffuses its essence throughout the man, Judas protests and asks why it was not sold, that the proceeds might be given to the poor. This consciousness believes in poverty and has no understanding of the true law of relief. All that comes into consciousness is selfishly appropriated and dissipated by this thief, yet he produces nothing. He is the enigma of existence and in him is wrapped the mystery of individuality. Jesus knew that through this department of His being He would be betrayed, but He made no effort to defeat the act of Judas. Sense consciousness betrays man every day, yet it would be unwise wholly to destroy it before its time, because at its foundation it is good. It has simply gone wrong; it has a devil.

Judas is transformed and redeemed when all pertaining to personality is surrendered and the substance of divine love is poured into consciousness. Man is continually enriched as he gives up the things of sense and consecrates himself to purity of purpose.

Love is the faculty through which eternal life is demonstrated. Love overcomes all selfishness and transforms the sense man into his pure, original state. The quickening life of Spirit anoints the whole body and resurrects it into newness of life and substance, thus begetting the new creature in Christ Jesus.

Jude, jūde (Gk. fr. Heb.)—same as Judah and Judas; *praise Jehovah.*

Brother of James. He was an apostle of Jesus Christ; he was surnamed Thaddæus (Matt. 10:3; Luke 6:16; Jude 1).

Meta. Jude, or Thaddæus, among the twelve apostles of Jesus Christ represents the faculty of elimination. (See THADDÆUS.)

judge.

Meta. The judge in I Peter 4:5 represents Truth itself, with which every thought in consciousness must harmonize.

judgment.

Meta. The description of the Last Judgment, as given in the Gospels, has been used to terrify men and women and thus compel them to unite with the church; but in this day of enlightenment people are not so easily led or driven by fear. They ask for understanding. When they seek light concerning the judgment it is given, and they learn that the judgment is all a matter of divine law. They find that for every departure from this law they must suffer, not in some future time of great tribulation, not in a great judgment after death, but in this life—here and now.

What is the divine law? It is the universal something in us of which we all are conscious, that tells us when we are doing right and when we are doing wrong. It may be defined as the innate knowing of right and wrong, and this knowing may be quickened, cultivated. This quickening does not come by the study of material things, but by concentrating the mind on the Christ.

This brings us to the realization of what Jesus meant when He said, "The Son of man shall come in his glory . . . and he shall set the sheep on his right hand, but the goats on the left." The Son of man is the divine power in man. It is that in us which *knows*. The Son of man is not far away, and His "angels" are with Him. Angels are true concepts of the Absolute. Every man has within himself the sheep and the goats. The goats are thoughts of opposition, resistance, stubbornness. All of these must be separated from the true when the Son of man comes into the individual consciousness of the glory of the Father. The real man is the spiritual man, the I AM, and when it comes into dominion in any person a great judgment work, a great day of sifting and separation, goes on in the mind and the body and the outer world of that person.

The natural man is in a constant whirlpool of "yes" and "no." This is not dominion, and it is not true of the real man. He discerns the real from the unreal, the true from the false, and by his word of authority separates the sheep from the goats. The sheep are the meek, obedient, kind, tender, true, helpful thoughts. They are intelligent. In Oriental countries, where sheep are cared for by shepherds who love them, they show a remarkable intelligence. The "Lamb . . . that taketh away the sin of the world" is loving, intelligent obedience to the divine law.

Sin is always followed by suffering, the "hell of fire," unless you know the law and identify yourself with the Christ and His righteousness, and thus separate yourself from sin. If you get angry your blood will "boil"; your anger will cook the corpuscles. So with every departure from the law of love, a condition comes

that men have named disease. But there is no reality in the diseases that are described in the medical books, and no remedy can be found for them in the realm of materiality. They are all the outpicturing of error thoughts, and the only real healing power is in the Christ mind, where true ideas rule.

So the overcomer, the individual who consciously is in the overcoming process, knows that to him every day is a judgment day. Every day the act of separating the good and constructive thoughts (sheep) from the destructive ones (goats) is taking place in him; and the error states of consciousness, error thoughts (goats), are cast into the refiner's fire for purification, where they are refined, purified, and transmuted into helpful, upbuilding forces. (See Mal. 3:1-3 and Matt. 3:11, 12.)

Judith, jū′-dĭth (Heb.)—feminine form of Judah.

Wife of Esau and daughter of Beeri the Hittite (Gen. 26:34).

Meta. Judith, feminine of Judah, signifies the outer-sense soul (wife of Esau and daughter of Beeri the Hittite, both referring to the physical or sense man) or feminine aspect of praise-and-prayer thoughts in consciousness.

Julia, jū′-lĭ-à (Lat.)—*soft-haired; downy; curly; frizzled.*

Feminine of Julius. A Christian woman at Rome, whom Paul saluted in his Epistle to the Romans (Rom. 16:15). She is named with Philologus, and is thought by some to have been his wife or his sister.

Meta. The soul, or feminine aspect of that in consciousness for which Julius stands. (See JULIUS.) Julia's being a Christian and a friend of Paul's, worthy of his salutation, shows that this feminine aspect of the Julius thought in consciousness has not only perceived the great value of Truth but has accepted it as leader, teacher, and guide.

Julius, jū′-lĭ-ŭs (Lat.)—*soft-haired; downy; curly; frizzled.*

A centurion of the Augustan band, who had charge of Paul when he was taken as a prisoner to Rome; Julius treated Paul kindly on the way (Acts 27:1, 3).

Meta. A centurion, captain over one

hundred Roman soldiers, typifies a certain phase of the will. The soldiers here were of the "Augustan band." Augustus (*venerable, sacred*) signifies worship of the will that is ruling in selfishness and directed by human reason. The intellect is the god of the Augustus consciousness.

Julius (*soft-haired, curly*) was a centurion of the Augustan band; he conducted Paul as a prisoner to Rome, but treated him with consideration and kindness. He symbolizes the will directed by intellectual thought about the vital forces of the organism, yet lifted up and refined in degree by a perception, or comprehension, of Truth and its value in consciousness.

Junias (A. V., Junia), jū'-nĭ-ăs (Gk.) —*youthful; a youth.*

A "kinsman" of Paul's, at Rome, whom Paul saluted along with Andronicus (Rom. 16:7). Junias was not only a "kinsman" of Paul's, but his fellow prisoner also, a man of note among the disciples, and one whom Paul mentioned as having been "in Christ before me."

Meta. The inner, ever renewing vital force of the subjective mind. This vital force, along with the word of Truth (Paul), is held in bondage and is kept from doing its perfect renewing, vitalizing work in the organism of man, when man lets his spiritually unawakened intellect rule in consciousness instead of being open to and guided by the inspiration and understanding of the Christ.

Jupiter, jū'-pĭ-tẽr (Lat.)—*Zeus pater; Jove father; father of light; father of the ether; father of all living,* i. e., *gods and men.*

"The Latin form of the Greek name Zeus, the national god of the Greeks, and the supreme ruler of the heathen world," says Fallows. The people at Lystra called Paul Mercury, because he was the chief speaker, and Mercury was the god of eloquence; Barnabas, who was with Paul, they named Jupiter, the god whom they worshiped (Acts 14:12).

According to The New International Encyclopædia, Jupiter was the chief god of Latin mythology, identified by the Romans with the Greek Zeus. He was worshiped by the Greeks and the Romans as the god of light and the heavens, whence come the fructifying showers and also the destructive storms and deadly lightning. Especially was he looked on as the wielder of the thunderbolt. He was the god that all other gods had to obey because he was stronger than any of them. Thus he was the supreme god of both gods and men. Jupiter is a contraction of *Zeus pater,* or *Jove father.*

Meta. The great value that the man who is unawakened spiritua'ly puts on that which he can see with his outer eyes and conceive with his outer mind, or intellect, as "force," "power," "strength."

Jushab-hesed, jū'-shăb-hē'-sĕd (Heb.) —*whose love is returned; requited love; returner of kindness.*

Son of Zerubbabel, descended from David (I Chron. 3:20).

Meta. The individual consciousness, realizing and expressing toward God, toward itself and its fellow men, toward all creation, the same perfection of love and kindness that it has come to know exists in God toward man and toward all the universe.

Justus, jŭs'-tŭs (Lat.)—*just; upright; righteous.*

a "Joseph called Barsabbas, who was surnamed Justus" (Acts 1:23). **b** A Christian of Corinth named Titus Justus (Acts 18:7). **c** "Jesus that is called Justus," a friend of Paul's (Col. 4:11).

Meta. Justus means *just, upright.* One definition of "just" is "conforming to the spiritual law . . . righteous before God." Justus signifies that in man's religious consciousness which truly worships God, which conforms to divine law.

Jutah (A. V., Juttah), jū'-tăh (Heb.) —*extended; stretched out; measured; elongated; inclined; bowed; turned away; deflected; repulsed.*

A city in the hill country of Judah (Josh. 15:55).

Meta. A group of thoughts (city) in the higher praise and prayer consciousness of man (the hill country of Judah) turning away (*turned away, repulsed*) from set forms and creeds of religious belief, that are binding and limiting to the consciousness, and reaching out, broadening out (*extended*), to a more truly spiritual understanding and standard of thought and act.

K

Kabzeel, kăb'-zĕ-ĕl (Heb.)—*gathered by God; grasped of God; God assembles; assembly of God; congregation of God.*

A southern city of Judah, "toward the border of Edom" (Josh. 15:21). It is called Jekabzeel in Nehemiah 11:25.

Meta. The significance is the same as that of Jekabzeel: the *congregation of God,* or that in us which is *gathered by God,* i. e., our true thoughts, our spiritual thought people that make up our spiritual consciousness. This is the *assembly of God.*

Instead of being our whole spiritual consciousness, Kabzeel, a city in southern Judah, toward the border of Edom, would be an aggregation of spiritual thoughts in our subconsciousness, but belonging to our spiritual consciousness, since this higher realm of mind in us permeates both our subconscious and conscious minds, and also our body consciousness when a certain degree of spirituality is attained.

Kadesh, kā'-dĕsh (Heb.)—*clean; pure; bright; holy; sacred; sanctified; consecrated; a sanctuary.*

A very old place on the southeastern border of the land of Canaan, in the wilderness of Paran, or Zin. It is the same place as En–mishpat (Gen. 14:7), and Kadesh–barnea, a city on the southern border of Judah, and allotted to Judah (Josh. 15:3). Abraham "dwelt between Kadesh and Shur" (Gen. 20:1). The spies were sent out from Kadesh to investigate the Promised Land, and they returned to Moses at this place (Num. 13:26). Miriam died and was buried at Kadesh (Num. 20:1). Moses trespassed at the waters of Meribah of Kadesh, and so was not allowed to enter the Promised Land (Num. 20:10-13; Deut. 32:51). It was at Kadesh that the Children of Israel were twice turned back from entering Canaan, once at the beginning of their forty years' wandering in the wilderness because of their unbelief, as related in Numbers 13 and 14, and once later when the king of Edom refused to allow them

to pass through his country (Num. 20: 16-22).

Meta. The inherently pure, sinless, perfect, ideal state that exists in the depths of the consciousness of every individual. As the various thoughts of the consciousness come into the light of this *sacred* and *holy* phase of mind, they are measured up according to these high ideals, and a judgment, or adjustment, takes place, as signified by En–mishpat— *fountain of judgment*—one of the names of Kadesh. It is here that the carnal and personal, that which still falls short of the perfect law, is revealed to us, and a further cleansing of the consciousness is set into action. (Take note of the different, very important occurrences that took place at Kadesh and En–mishpat, all corresponding to experiences that we go through in putting off the "old man" of sin and putting on the Christ.)

Kadmiel, kăd'-mĭ-ĕl (Heb.)—*God aforetimes; primeval God; God of the east; before God,* i. e., *servant or minister; God of antiquity; God eternal.*

A Levite, who, with his "children," returned from the Babylonian captivity to Jerusalem and helped in rebuilding the Temple (Ezra 2:40; 3:9). A man by this name, possibly the same man, is mentioned several times in the book of Nehemiah; he joined in sealing the covenant (Neh. 10:9).

Meta. An inherently spiritual ideal in consciousness, founded on the innate knowledge of God, divine principle, as being from the beginning of time (*God aforetimes, primeval God*), serving God or ministering to the individual who gives it place (*before God,* i. e., *servant or minister*).

Since God is from everlasting to everlasting (*God eternal*), has always existed, and is the Source of all, man and the creation came from Him and are constantly being sustained and blessed by Him. Not only were all things made by Him but by Him all things continue to exist. The universe and man would pass quickly out of existence could they be separated in ever so small a degree from the omnipresent life, intelligence, and substance that are God, and with which man comes into conscious touch within his own soul (*God of the east*, east referring to the innermost of man's being).

Kadmonite, kăd'-mŏn-īte (Heb.)—*of the East; Oriental; primeval; prototype; ancient; eternal; unchangeable.*

A nation in Palestine at the time of Abraham (Gen. 15:19); ancient Canaanites.

Meta. The Canaanites signify the elemental life forces of man's organism. Kadmonite (*primeval, prototype, ancient, eternal, unchangeable*) refers to the very essence, source, beginning of all life, which is God, Spirit, the foundation principle of the life energy that animates man and the universe. *Of the East* points to the within, the center of man's being, where he comes into conscious touch with Spirit, with the inner life. Being named among the tribes in the land of Canaan, that later had to be overcome by the Israelites, the Kadmonites bespeak error, carnal thoughts about life.

Kain (A. V., the Kenite) kā'-ĭn (Heb.) —*the Kenites.*

Another name for the Kenites (Num. 24:22).

Meta. See KENITES. In Hebrew Kain is spelled the same as Cain, the son of Adam; therefore see CAIN also.

Kallai, kăl'-lāi (Heb.)—*Jehovah is light*, i. e., *not heavy; swift; fleet; swift messenger of Jehovah.*

A priest in the time of Jehoiakim (Neh. 12:20).

Meta. The swiftness, lightness, and power of spiritual thought emanating from the one Mind (God, Jehovah, Spirit) to the consciousness of man.

Kanah, kā'-năh (Heb.)—*place of reeds; reedlike; cane; hollow stem; rod; measuring beam; canal; stalk of grain.*

a A brook on the western border of Ephraim, in Palestine (Josh. 16:8). **b** A border city of Asher (Josh. 19:28).

Meta. The significance of Kanah is the same as that of Cana. (See CANA.) The city of Kanah, or Cana, symbolizes an aggregation of thoughts, or a nerve center, of power in individual conscious-

ness; the brook Kanah represents more nearly a current of power thoughts.

Kareah, kȧ-rē'-ăh (Heb.)—*smooth; bald; bare; glassy; crystal; ice; cold.*

Father of Johanan and Jonathan. These two sought to help avenge the killing of Gedeliah, whom the king of Babylon had left as governor of Judah (Jer. 40:8—43:5).

Meta. Bald and *bare* mean destitute of the natural or common covering; for instance, of hair on the top of the head. The common covering of sense man is personality, in which is found the carnal and adverse mind of sense. Kareah (*smooth, bald, bare, ice*), an Israelite of the kingdom of Judah, signifies a thought in the religious consciousness of man that is entirely removed from carnal, sense reasoning; that is poised and clear so far as the spiritual and true is concerned, and is fixedly cold toward all material, personal, limited thought. (Kareah's sons, Johanan—which is the same name as John—and Jonathan, both refer to the love faculty in man. The latter signifies the soul or human aspect of love, and the former refers more to love in its spiritual quality.)

Karka (A. V., Karkaa), kär'-kȧ (Heb.) —*foundation; bottom; ground floor; pavement; deep ground; bottom of the sea.*

A place mentioned as being on the south border of Judah (Josh. 15:3).

Meta. Karka (*ground floor, bottom*, a place on the south border of Judah) signifies a group of thoughts pertaining to the very bottom, or foundation principle, of man's subconscious life forces. This group of thoughts is deeply rooted in substance (*deep ground*).

Karkor, kär'-kôr (Heb.)—*foundation; excavation; deep floor; deep ground.*

A place on the east side of the Jordan where Zebah and Zalmunna, kings of Midian, camped with their armies, while fleeing from Gideon. Gideon overtook them there, and again defeated them and put them to rout (Judg. 8:10).

Meta. A group of thoughts, or state of consciousness, deeply rooted in substance (*deep ground*) and in the descending life flow of thought in the organism (to the east of the Jordan). It is the last stronghold of the phase of the sense mind that these two kings (Zalmunna and Zebah) and their armies symbolize, and is at the very *foundation* of this phase of consciousness. Here Zebah (*sacrifice*) and Zalmunna (*deprived of shade*), kings of Midian (*contention, strife*), with the remainder of their armies took refuge, thinking that they were secure in this place, or thought realm. But Gideon (*destroyer* of evil) found them and killed them with all their host.

This incident, with the meaning of the names connected with it, teaches that we must pursue error to its very beginning and root it out entirely. This can be done, since error is but a shadow and has no foundation in being (Zalmunna, *deprived of shade*). It must be wholly erased from consciousness, and the energy that has been utilized for its promotion must be transmuted into spiritual essence and use (Zebah, meaning *sacrifice*).

Kartah, kär'-täh (Heb.)—*city; meeting place; accessible; city; convenience; refuge.*

A city of Zebulun, that was given over to the Levites of the children of Merari (Josh. 21:34).

Meta. A group of unifying, protecting thoughts (*city, meeting place, refuge*), with its corresponding nerve center (belonging to Zebulun, the faculty of order) in man. This city's being given over to the Levites denotes a further quickening of these thoughts into religious love and Truth.

Kartan, kär'-tän (Heb.)—*double city; large city.*

A city of Naphtali that was given over to the Gershonite Levites (Josh. 21:32). It is believed to be the same city as Kiriathaim.

Meta. Kartan, like Kartah, represents a group of thoughts of a convening, cooperative nature, only doubly large in number, or two groups united in one (*double city*), and belonging to the Naphtali or strength center in consciousness. The strength of these thoughts is set apart for use in sustaining the natural religious tendencies (Levites) of the individual.

Kattath, kăt'-täth (Heb.)—*cut off;*
made smaller; reduced; small; smallness; little; littleness; very small; insignificant.

A border city of Zebulun (Josh, 19: 15). In Judges 1:30 it is called Kitron. Kattath is thought to be the same place as Kartah of Joshua 21:34.

Meta. The idea expressed in Kattath is that of cutting off, lessening, reducing to exceeding smallness and insignificance (*cut off, made smaller, very small, insignificant*). This no doubt refers to putting away error, the limitations of sense thought and belief. Kattath was a border city of Zebulun. The Zebulunites failed to drive out the Canaanitish inhabitants, but reduced them to slavery, made them "subject to taskwork" (Judg. 1:30).

Kedar, kē'-där (Heb.)—*turbid; dirty; dusky; dark-colored; dark-skinned; obscured; overcast; black; mournful; sorrowful.*

Son of Ishmael, and the name of an Arabian tribe that he founded (Gen. 25: 13; Ezek. 27:21; see also Psalms 120:5, and Song of Sol. 1:5).

Meta. A confused, unsettled, disturbed, obscure thought, yet one with a degree of power that belongs to the outer or sense phase of consciousness in man. This concept is darkened by materiality, yet for a time it brings forth substance. (From the Bible references to Kedar we gather that the tribe must have been both wealthy and powerful, though its downfall was prophesied. Only that which is of joy, gladness, and clearness of vision, that which is of God, that which is consciously founded in Spirit, will stand the test, will abide.)

Kedemah, kĕd'-ĕ-mäh (Heb.)—*eastern; toward the east; Orient; going before; precedence; the first; principle; ancient; eternal; immutable; that which exceeds all limits.*

Youngest son of Ishmael (Gen. 25:15).

Meta. The inner or true being of man, divine principle; that which exists from everlasting to everlasting, man's true spiritual or Christ self (*Orient, eastern, the first, principle, ancient, eternal*).

Ishmael represents the thoughts that are the fruit of the personal or carnal in man. Kedemah, the youngest of his twelve sons, bespeaks the individual's turning within to his inner or true being, which is spiritual, eternal (*toward the east*). This makes us think of Paul's words in I Corinthians 15:46, 47: "Howbeit that is not first which is spiritual, but that which is natural; then that which is spiritual. The first man is of the earth, earthy: the second man is of heaven." God, Spirit, and the Christ, who is man's true inner self, are first (*the first*); otherwise the outer man could not be. In outer expression and manifestation, however, the physical man appears to come first, and he seems to run the full gamut of experience in the outer consciousness before he finally turns about and begins to search within his own inner being to find God, Spirit, his true source and sustenance.

Kedemoth, kĕd'-ĕ-mŏth (Heb.)—*eastern districts; Orientals; Easterners; antiquities; ancients; beginnings; principles.*

a A city allotted to Reuben (Josh. 13:18). **b** A wilderness (Deut. 2:26). Kedemoth is the plural of Kedemah.

Meta. Each of the faculties of man has its foundation, its *beginnings*, in Spirit and is truly spiritual. To become conscious of the spiritual reality of those faculties, the individual must turn to his inner spiritual consciousness (*eastern districts, Easterners*). Kedemoth, a city allotted to Reuben, signifies thoughts relating to the foregoing truth; these thoughts belong to the faculty of faith in its aspect of discernment, or sight, for which Reuben stands.

Kedesh, kē'-dĕsh (Heb.)—*holy place; sacred; consecrated; sanctuary; holiness; cleanliness; purity.*

a A city of Judah, toward the border of Edom in the south (Josh. 15:23). **b** A city in Galilee, in the hill country of Naphtali, that was set apart for a city of refuge (Josh. 20:7). **c** A city of Issachar, that was given over to the Gershomite Levites (I Chron. 6:72). This city is thought to be the same place that is mentioned in Joshua 12:22. Kadesh is the same name.

Meta. The divine presence within the individual consciousness. (See KADESH.)

Kehelathah, kĕ-hĕl'-ă-thăh (Heb.)—*called together; convocation; assembly; gathering together; congregation; unification; entirety.*

A camping place of the Children of Israel in the wilderness (Num. 33:22).

Meta. Convocation means an assembly of persons summoned together. Kehelathah (*called together, convocation, assembly, congregation, unification*), a place in the wilderness where the Children of Israel camped while on their way to the Promised Land, typifies our gathering our true thoughts (Israelites) by the power of our word, or affirmations of Truth, to a definite place in consciousness wherein they become more unified, abiding, and sure. Here they are rested and strengthened for their next movement toward higher and more perfect realizations of spirituality.

Keilah, kēi'-läh (Heb.)—*carving; circular motion; inclosing; oppressing; citadel; fortress; castle; bow; sling.*

a A city in the lowlands of Judah (Josh. 15:44; I Sam. 23:1-13). **b** "The Garmite," a man of Judah (I Chron. 4:19). **c** The "district of Keilah" is mentioned in Nehemiah 3:17.

Meta. A thought, a group of thoughts, and a state of consciousness, belonging to the lower and more earthly phase of the Judah consciousness, that are firmly established, fortified, in that which Garmite symbolizes; namely: man's innate belief in the truth that his organism is structurally strong. (See GARMITE.)

This that Keilah signifies has its foundation in spiritual thought (*circular motion*). Because of the influence brought to bear on it by the personal or sense consciousness, it has crystallized into material thought, into the belief that strength and safety exist in the material, in outer expressions of force (*inclosing, oppressing, citadel, fortress, castle, bow, sling*).

Kelaiah, kĕ-lā'-ĭäh (Heb.)—*Jehovah is light; swift Jehovah; Jah is fleet.*

A Levite who had married a "foreign" wife (Ezra 10:23); "the same is Kelita."

Meta. The lightness, swiftness, fleetness, ethereality, of spiritual thought, going forth in the I AM or Christ consciousness and power (*Jehovah is light, swift Jehovah, Jah is fleet*).

When the personal prevails in one to the extent of causing one to give way to sense desires and to set love on the lesser things of life, the consciousness is always dwarfed and cannot grow so large, spiritual, broad, and truly useful as it must become in putting on the Christ likeness. (See KELITA.)

Kelita, kĕl'-ĭ-tå (Heb.)—*take into oneself; selfishness; shrink; contract; shrunken; dwarfed; insignificant; littleness; poverty; condensing; hardening.*

Another name for Kelaiah, a Levite who had taken a foreign wife (Ezra 10: 23). He was one of those who helped the people to understand the law (Neh. 8:7), and he also joined Nehemiah in sealing the covenant (Neh. 10:10).

Meta. Kelita shows the result of using the power of the I AM, the lightness and swiftness of Jehovah, which Kelaiah signifies, to bring about the fulfillment of selfish, sense desires (taking a foreign wife). This result is a lessening of one's good in mind, body, and affairs. Kelita also shows how wonderfully the divine intelligence and power works, through the thoughts that give it place, to enlighten our thought people and to unify them with Spirit. (Kelita helped the people to understand the law, and he joined Nehemiah in sealing the covenant.) Even when we give the light of Spirit only a small place in our consciousness, even when we restrict it by our poor, little, personal ideas (*poverty, dwarfed, shrunken*), the result for good is marvelous. What will it be, then, when we become perfect, open channels for expression of the one Mind.

Kemuel, kĕm'-ū-ĕl (Heb.) — *God stands; God's righteousness; God raises up; judgment of God; assembly of God; God's congregation.*

a Son of Nahor the brother of Abraham (Gen. 22:21). **b** Son of Shiphtan. This Kemuel was a prince who was chosen from the tribe of Ephraim to help divide the Promised Land among the Israelitish tribes (Num. 34:24). **c** Another Kemuel was a Levite. His son Hashabiah was captain of the tribe of Levi in David's reign (I Chron. 27:17).

Meta. The Spirit of God, divine righteousness and judgment, in the ascendancy in individual consciousness, growing and taking a firmer hold (*God stands, God's righteousness, judgment of God, God raises up*); also bringing about a closer union of the true, higher spiritual thoughts of the mind (*assembly of God*) in order to establish a further adjustment that is needed for the progress of the individual.

The faculties of faith, judgment, will, and love are especially quickened (*God raises up*) and unified in this new stand of Spirit in consciousness. (Shiphtan, father of Kemuel, the Ephraimite who helped to divide the Promised Land among the Israelites, means *righteous judgment, judicial,* while the tribe of Ephraim pertains to the will in man. The tribe of Levi pertains to the love faculty, and Abraham, brother of Nahor, represents faith. Nahor signifies the arousing of a higher desire in man through the activity of Abraham—faith—to the point of *piercing* the darkness of materiality, and aiding in bringing about a new line of thought in consciousness. One meaning of Milcah, Nahor's wife and mother of one of the men named Kemuel, is *counsel;* and Hashabiah, son of the Kemuel who was of the tribe of Levi, was captain of this tribe in David's reign.)

From the foregoing explanations one can see how the faculties of judgment, love, faith, and will are closely associated with that which Kemuel signifies. In fact, Kemuel represents the raising of these faculties to a higher and more spiritual standing, as well as the unifying of them in consciousness, that a further advancement of the individual into spiritual expression and realization may take place.

Kenan, kē'-năn (Heb.)—*self-centered one; fixed; ownership; central dominion; possession invading space; general usurpation; agglomeration; welding; smith; lancer; spearman.*

Son of Enosh. He is named fourth in descent from Adam (Gen. 5:9). He is the same person as Cainan (Luke 3:37).

Meta. Enosh (meaning *mortal man, mutable being, corporeal man*) refers to the outer or body consciousness, in its limited, material, corruptible concept of the organism; the unreality of the material is made evident by the higher, more spiritual thought (Seth) that has begun its work in the consciousness, to the end that it may be replaced by the spiritual concept and expression. Kenan, son of Enosh (meaning *self-centered one, fixed, ownership, general usurpation, welding*), signifies the seemingly established materiality of consciousness and organism. But the higher, more spiritual thought, found in Seth, is working, and the man, though seemingly established in materiality, is reaching out of the lesser self (*possession invading space*) and upward toward something more powerful to uplift, enlighten, heal, renew, and restore than is to be found in the material. Thus Kenan brings forth Mahalelel, meaning *praise of God*.

Kenath, kē'-năth (Heb.)—*possession; centralization; appropriation to self; self-seeking; substance; wealth.*

A place east of the Jordan that was taken by Nobah and was renamed after him (Num. 32:42). Later it was captured by Geshur and Aram (I Chron. 2:23).

Meta. A group of thoughts in consciousness whose central idea is that of *possession, appropriation to self.* This thought center belongs first to the Amoritish phase of consciousness in the individual. Carnal mind thinks that all the resources of man belong to it and are for its use exclusively. But upon awakening to a higher understanding (Manasseh) the individual begins to view things differently; he sees that his vitality and substance should be utilized more by the mental and not so much by the physical. So Kenath is taken by Nobah of Manasseh. Nobah, however (meaning *barking, prominent, vehement of voice*), is not really of spiritual understanding; he signifies the intellect's belief in using force and aggressive, personal means to attain its desires.

Aram and Geshur, who retook Kenath, also belong to the intellectual rather than to the spiritual. Therefore at this stage of his unfoldment the individual has not yet come into the true light, which is that his real inheritance is in and through Spirit, and that the resources of his organism should be directed by

Spirit and used to sustain the spiritual in him.

Kenaz, kē'-năz (Heb.)—*centralized strength; possessor; spear thrower; lancer; archer; hunter; loin; side; flank.*

a Son of Eliphaz, who was Esau's son (Gen. 36:11). Kenaz was a prince of Edom (see verses 15 and 16). **b** Brother of Caleb and father of Othniel (Josh. 15:17). **c** A descendant of Caleb (I Chron. 4:15).

Meta. Strength, centered in the physical (*centralized strength, possessor, hunter, loin*). A *hunter*, in the meaning of Kenaz, pertains to a thought that is connected with the animal forces of the organism. Esau was a hunter, and he symbolizes the body or physical vigor. Nimrod was "a mighty hunter before Jehovah." He also pertains to the strength of the animal forces in man, but under the observation or guiding light of Jehovah, since the physical in man has its foundation in Spirit and must ultimately be raised entirely to spiritual expression.

Kenaz therefore signifies the thought of man engrossed in the animal phase of his nature, in animal strength and activity (*spear thrower, lancer, archer,* are also definitions of Kenaz). Kenaz, brother of Caleb, and Kenaz, descendant of Caleb, point to the entrance of a higher motive power into the outer and seemingly purely physical consciousness of the individual, to do an uplifting and transforming work in it.

Kenites, kĕn'-ītes (fr. Heb.)—*of or belonging to Kain; possessions; acquisitions; purchases; forging; welding; a smith; spear; lance.*

The Kenites are thought to have been the same people as the Midianites, among whom Moses lived while he was being prepared for his work of leading the Israelites out of Egypt to the Promised Land. Some of the Midianites went with the Children of Israel to Canaan, and their descendants are supposed to have been the Kenites who were friendly with Israel and were protected by them. They were dwelling among the Amalekites when Saul sent them word to get away lest he destroy them with the Amalekites (I Sam. 15:6).

Meta. The Midianites signify thoughts

of contention and strife. The Kenites, who were of the Midianites, therefore have their place in the carnal consciousness of man, the enemies in the land. But they possess an element that the Canaanite nations that were to be utterly destroyed did not have. The thoughts that the Kenites of our text symbolize are distinguished from the thoughts that are in direct opposition to Spirit (Amalekites); they contain an element of good that must be saved.

The word Kenites means *possessions, acquisitions, forging, welding, a smith;* and one of the meanings of Midian is *judgment.* The thought of centralization of power, which is contained in the root word Kain, or Cain, can refer either to rulership or despotism, thrift or greed, a concentration on either good or error, personal or impersonal, a forging of strength or a driving to destruction, a central fire that radiates or consumes—all depending on how it is directed. In the Kenites we find thoughts that, though seemingly of the carnal or sense man, yet have and use a degree of judgment, discrimination, and activity for good that brings about their final upliftment into salvation.

Kenizzite (in A. V., Genesis 15:19, Kenizzites; Numbers 32:12, Kenezite), kĕn'-ĭz-zīte (fr. Heb.)—*of* or *belonging to Kenaz; centralized strength; possessor; spear thrower; lancer; archer; hunter; loin; side; flank.*

A Canaanitish tribe (Gen. 15:19). The Kenizzites are thought to have been a tribe that descended from Kenaz, grandson of Esau. Persons from this tribe became closely associated with the Israelites by marriage, and we find Jephunneh, the father of Caleb of the Israelitish tribe of Judah, called a Kenizzite (Num. 32:12). One of his sons and one of his descendants through Caleb are named Kenaz.

Meta. A thought springing from and belonging to that in consciousness which Kenaz represents. (See KENAZ.)

Keren–happuch, kĕr'-ĕn-hăp'-pŭch (Heb.)—*radiations of color; prismatic radiations; horn of beauty; horn for paint; paint horn; cosmetic box.*

Youngest daughter of Job; she was born to him after his possessions had been restored to him twofold (Job 42:14).

Meta. The elevating power of light, of spiritual beauty, of Truth, a beautiful soul, expressed in a beautiful character, also a beautiful exterior—beauty of face and form. (Keren–happuch means *radiations of color, prismatic radiations, horn of beauty;* a horn, while primarily an indication of defense, is used in the East as a token of eminence and high rank; it is symbolic of power, glory, dominion, authority, exaltation. Thus *horn of beauty* would signify the exalting power of beauty.) The daughters of Job represent the soul, or the feminine aspect of the individual character when it has passed through the Job experience and has come out refined and established in the true Christ righteousness; the thought of *paint* and *cosmetic box,* in the definitions of Keren–happuch that point to an outer or seemingly artificial beauty, is a very materialized aspect of the true meaning of the word.

Kerioth (in A. V., Amos 2:2, Kirioth), kē'-rĭ-ŏth (Heb.)—*meetings; conjunctions; cities; hamlets; buildings; communities; congregations.*

A city of Moab that Jeremiah named in his prophecies of the overthrow of Moab (Jer. 48:41). Amos also prophesied against this place (Amos 2:2).

Meta. Groups of thoughts (*meetings, conjunctions, cities, hamlets*), with their corresponding thought forms (*buildings*), belonging to and active in the Moab or carnal consciousness in the individual.

Kerioth–hezron (A. V., Kerioth, and Hezron), kē'-rĭ-ŏth-hĕz'-rŏn (Heb.)—*joining inclosures; adjoining pastures; cities of verdure; blooming congregations.*

A city of Judah, "toward the border of Edom in the South . . . (the same is Hazor)." (See Josh. 15:25.)

Meta. A central thought group, with the smaller groups of thoughts surrounding it (*joining inclosures; cities of verdure;* each of the cities of Judah named in the 15th chapter of Joshua had villages that belonged to it; see 32d, 36th, 41st verses), in the Judah, or praise-and-prayer, consciousness of the individual. The dominating characteristic of the thought groups that Kerioth–hezron signifies is that of thriving and growing, of vigor, freshness, substance, and beauty (*blooming, pastures, verdure*). Thus these thoughts tend toward renewing and keeping one ever in the realization of abundant life and youth. (See HAZOR, KERIOTH, and HEZRON.)

Keros, kē'-rŏs (Heb.)—*bent; curved; bowed; a weaver's comb; a curved joint; a hook; bowed down; contrition; collapse.*

One of the Nethinim whose "children" returned from the Babylonian captivity with Zerubbabel (Ezra 2:44).

Meta. An idea of service, in the religious phase of man's consciousness and body, that is *bowed down* under the thought of repentance (*contrition*), to the point of great negativeness (*collapse*). Thus this service idea, which is good inherently, is biased, turned away (*bent, curved*) from the positive purity, simplicity, and strength of Truth, and is kept from rising to a higher, freer state, even to that of sonship with God. (See NETHINIM.)

Keturah, kė-tū'-răh (Heb.)—*incense; fragrant smoke; fragrance; perfume; aloe-wood.*

The wife whom Abraham took after Sarah died (Gen. 25:1-4).

Meta. A phase of the soul consciousness that, though still in sense, aspires to higher things for the body. Through this sincere desire of the soul for higher and purer realizations of Truth, the animal nature is refined, and thus prepared for transmutation. (Burning of "incense" symbolizes the process of transmutation; *fragrance, perfume*, bespeaks aspiration.)

keys of the kingdom of heaven, given to man (Matt. 16:19).

Meta. Affirmation and denial.

Keziah (A. V., Kezia), kė-zī'-ăh (Heb.)—*cut off; stripped off; cassia bark; angular; acute; incisive; decisive; discrimination.*

The second of Job's three daughters who were born to him after his return to affluence and health (Job 42:14).

Meta. The purified soul expressing true perception and *discrimination*, thus aiding in the detection of all error, limited, human thoughts and ideals, that they may be put out of consciousness (*cut off, stripped off*). Spiritual perception and discrimination are great aids in cleansing the mind from thoughts and intents that are not really conducive to spiritual growth. By means of our perceptive and discriminative qualities of mind we distinguish between our true thoughts and our lesser thoughts that are no longer necessary to us. Then by the dissolving light and love of Spirit they are purged out of our consciousness, thus making us free to go on toward manifest perfection.

Kibroth–hattaavah, kĭb'-rŏth–hăt-tā'-ă-văh (Heb.)—*graves of lust; graves of the longing; burial places of appetite; sepulcher of willful desires; sepulchers of self-will.*

A camping place of the Children of Israel in the wilderness. It was given this name because in this place the people were buried who had died as a result of lusting after flesh to eat (Num. 11:34).

Meta. The result of intense, unrestrained, willful, sense desire. When man gives way completely to the appetites and desires of the flesh, he soon brings about a breaking up of his consciousness, known as death.

Kibzaim, kĭb'-ză-ĭm (Heb.)—*grasping with both hands; folding in the arms,* i. e., *as a shepherd or reaper; two gatherings; double congregations; two heaps.*

A city of Ephraim that was given over to the Kohathite Levites (Josh. 21:22). In I Chronicles 6:68, Jokmeam is given in place of Kibzaim.

Meta. A group, or assembly, of thoughts of unification, of appropriation, of fruition. This group is doubly large and strong and comprehensive (*two gatherings, double congregations; grasping with both hands, folding in the arms,* i. e., *as a shepherd or reaper*) because it is activated by and unified with both will and love. (This city was allotted to Ephraim, who represents the will; and it was given over to the descendants of Levi; Levi represents love.) (See JOKMEAM.)

Kidron, kĭd'-rŏn (Heb.) — *turbid stream; muddy; foul; dirty; dingy; dark; obscured; overcast; shadowed; mournful; gloomy; sad; sorrowful.*

A brook near Jerusalem that David and his followers passed over when David was fleeing from Absalom (II Sam. 15: 23). Jesus also passed over this brook with His disciples, just before He entered the garden where He was betrayed by Judas (John 18:1).

Meta. The current of confused thoughts that sometimes pours in upon us when we try to go into the silence. The "garden" locates it in the world of universal thought. But this is a small matter compared to that great personal self in the subjective consciousness, Judas, who "knew the place," and took advantage of its darkness to capture the I AM. He came with a "band" (combative thoughts) and "officers from the chief priests and the Pharisees" (the ideas of priestly authority and religious guidance from the standpoint of the letter), bearing "lanterns and torches and weapons" (light of intellect, torch of reason, and force of circumstances).

When Jesus went "over the brook Kidron" and entered the garden of Gethsemane, He passed in his own consciousness from the without to the within. David also had to pass over the confusion of the carnal to a more peaceful, trusting state of mind in order to escape from Absalom and gain the required victory.

Kinah, kĭ'-năh (Heb.)—*beating; striking; pulsating; smithy; musical instrument; strident sound; chant; elegy; dirge; lamentation; agglomeration; possession.*

A city of Judah, "toward the border of Edom in the South" (Josh. 15:22).

Meta. Inner expressions of sorrow (*dirge, elegy, lamentation*) of the human consciousness or natural man at having to give up its notion as to the desirability of personal *possession;* man must even give up the belief that he owns his body to do with as his sense mind pleases.

A *smithy* is the workshop of a smith; and a smith is one who works in metals. Metals signify the various faculties established in substance; for instance, gold stands for wisdom, iron for strength, and so forth. The idea here is that when this city of Kinah, or group of thoughts in individual consciousness, comes into the hands of Judah (praise and prayer), man receives a revelation of the truth that the outer organism is not an instrument given him for the purpose of carrying out his own sense pleasures; it is not for the convenience of the carnal man. The truth is revealed that his body is a temple of God, and must be kept holy (see I Cor. 3:16, 17; 6:15-20). Since the body is an emanation of Spirit and has been formed as a vehicle through which God, Spirit, might express, the carnal man must be brought under restraint, and finally cast out. The attempt to eliminate the carnal brings sorrow and lamentation to the individual at first, since he knows only human methods of obtaining pleasure and satisfaction. His sorrow, however, is soon turned into joy by the light and the power of Spirit, which are multiplied in his consciousness when the appetites and desires of the flesh no longer rule in him to the exclusion of spiritual things. Then he truly becomes a *musical instrument* to express the harmony and joy of Truth.

kingdom, of God, of heaven.

Meta. When in His teaching Jesus likened the "kingdom of the heavens" (see Emphatic Diaglott) to various conditions in the earth, He was explaining, in terms that the outer man could grasp, the various laws and relations of the spiritual realm, or the "kingdom of the heavens."

The kingdom of heaven is the orderly adjustment of divine ideas in man's mind and body.

Jesus definitely located the kingdom of God (heaven) when He said, "The kingdom of God cometh not with observation: neither shall they say, Lo, here! or, There! for lo, the kingdom of God is within you" (Luke 17:20, 21).

In order to find this kingdom, man must become conscious of Divine Mind and its realm of divine ideas, and be willing to adjust his thoughts to the divine standard.

Man adjusts his thought world to the kingdom of divine ideas through a process of denial by which he eliminates from consciousness all inharmonious ideas, and through affirmations of Truth by which he establishes himself in harmony with divine ideas.

Heaven is not confined to man's consciousness. It is everywhere present.

When man's mind and body are in harmonious relation to divine ideas, his true thoughts flow into the realm of manifestation and bring forth the kingdom in the earth "as in heaven."

Jesus likened the kingdom to a seed because a seed has unexpressed capacities, and needs to be planted in the soil best suited to its growth. The word of Truth is the seed, and when planted in a receptive mind it brings forth the fruits of Spirit. The life of the word is the spiritual idea that it contains.

The kingdom of heaven is attained, first, by one's establishing in one's mind the consciousness of the truth of Being; second, by one's adjusting one's outer life to Truth.

Jesus used many commonplace things to illustrate the establishing of the kingdom of heaven in consciousness in order that we might the more easily adjust all our thoughts and acts in harmony with the ideas that make heaven.

Jesus likened heaven to a man that sowed good seed in his field, but when he slept an enemy sowed tares there (Matt. 13:24-30). The explanation of this is: The field is consciousness; the good seed are our true thoughts, which are sown when we express our mind positively. The tares are the error thoughts that drift in when the consciousness is negative or ignorant. These subconscious errors should be left alone until the harvest, because man does not know enough about their subtle character to handle them wisely until he has the light of Spirit, or until the time of harvest, which is a day of judgment. The idea in this parable is that we shall be wise in using the law of affirmation and denial.

In the parable of the mustard seed (Matt. 13:31, 32) is taught the law of thought increase; from a very small idea (mustard seed) a thought grows until it becomes an abiding place for thoughts of a higher realm (birds of heaven).

Jesus, in "another parable," "The kingdom of heaven is like unto leaven, which a woman took, and hid in three measures of meal, till it was all leavened" (Matt. 13:33), illustrates how the word of Truth penetrates the three states of consciousness, spirit, soul, body. (See HEAVEN.)

Kir, kīr (Heb.)—*a digging; an earthwork; a wall; walled place; city; fortress; citadel.*

A place to which the king of Assyria carried the people of Damascus captive, at the time of Ahaz, king of Judah (II Kings 16:9). Prophecies concerning Kir are to be found in Amos 1:5; 9:7; Isaiah 22:6. Isaiah 15:1 speaks of Kir of Moab.

Meta. A group of thoughts that are strongly established in carnal belief (*fortress, a digging, an earthwork*).

Kir-hareseth (in A. V., II Kings 3:25, Kir-haraseth), kīr-hăr'-ĕ-sĕth (Heb.)—*pottery wall; brick fortress.*

A citadel, or stronghold, of Moab (II Kings 3:25; see Isaiah 15:1 and 16:7 also).

Meta. Moab signifies the carnal mind in man. Kir-hareseth, a citadel or stronghold of Moab, is first of all the almost universal belief that man is inherently and irrevocably separate from and inferior to God, at least while living in the body on earth. Second, it is the accompanying error belief of the race that man's outer organism is inherently and irrevocably earthly and corruptible; that it is not God's plan that man's outer organism should express Spirit and manifest immortality. Therefore the conclusion naturally is that there is no need or use for man to try to overcome the appetites and desires of the flesh, since he cannot lift himself above them while in the body, but will be free only after he gives up his body to corruption in the grave. This is what the carnal mind (Moab) in man is based on, and it is all lies; it is of the Devil, who, according to Jesus, is a liar from the beginning.

The truth is that man is inherently and irrevocably a spiritual being. Spiritual, immortal, incorruptible life, love, power, substance, intelligence, strength, wholeness, and perfection are innate in man, and must be expressed throughout his entire being—spirit, soul, and body—ere he really becomes that which he was created to be, and which he is all the time in the real inner truth of his being.

Kir-heres (in A. V., Isaiah 16:11, Kir-haresh), kīr-hē'-rĕş (Heb.)—*pottery wall; brick fortress.*

The same place as Kir of Moab and Kir–hareseth (Jer. 48:31, 36).

Meta. The significance is similar to that of KIR and KIR–HARESETH, which see. "Brick" and "pottery," in the meaning of Kir–heres and Kir–hareseth, bespeak something artificial, something that is put together, made by the outer personal man, and not real.

Kiriathaim (A. V., Kirjathaim), kĭr´-ĭ-ă-thā´-ĭm (Heb.)—*double meeting; double joining; double city; large city.*

a A city east of the Jordan that Moses gave to the tribe of Reuben (Josh. 13:19). b A city of Naphtali that was given over to the Gershomite Levites (I Chron. 6:76). This city is thought to be the same place as Kartan.

Meta. Kiriathaim of the tribe of Reuben would belong to the seeing, discerning faculty in individual consciousness, instead of the strength faculty. (See KARTAN.)

Kiriath (A. V., Kirjath), kĭr´-ĭ-ăth (Heb.) — *meeting; joining; uniting; building; city; town.*

A city of Benjamin (Josh. 18:28).

Meta. A city represents a group of thoughts, or a thought and nerve center, in the individual consciousness and body. Kiriath (meaning *meeting, uniting, joining, building, city,* and being a city of Benjamin) signifies a group of attracting, unifying, constructive thoughts whose central and dominating idea is an active, accomplishing faith (Benjamin).

Kiriath–arba (A. V., Kirjath–arba), kĭr´-ĭ-ăth-är´-bá (Heb.)—*city of Arba; city foursquare; four city; fourfold city; city of perfection; city of greatness; great city.*

The old name of Hebron; it was called Kiriath–arba after Arba, who was the greatest man among the Anakim (Gen. 23:2; Josh. 14:15 with marginal note).

Meta. Attributing to carnal reason the perfection that belongs to and comes forth from spiritual understanding only; attributing strength, power, knowledge, and greatness to the outer formed world, instead of knowing that all power and reality exist in Spirit—in the unformed ideas of the one Mind. (See ARBA; see HEBRON also.)

Kiriath–arim (A. V., Kirjath–arim),

kīr´-ĭ-ăth-ā´-rĭm (Heb.)—*city of redundant growths; city of dense thickets; city of forests.*

The same place as Kiriath–jearim (Ezra 2:25).

Meta. See KIRIATH–JEARIM.

Kiriath–baal (A. V., Kirjath–baal), kīr´-ĭ-ăth-bā´-ăl (Heb.)—*city of Baal; city of the lord; city of the master; city of dominion; city of possession.*

The same place as Kiriath–jearim, a city in the hill country of Judah (Josh. 15:60).

Meta. In Kiriath–baal the idea is given that, at this particular phase of unfoldment in the individual, this group of thoughts of *dominion* and abundance in consciousness still attributes power to things formed instead of understanding that all power and all reality exist in formless Spirit. (See BAAL; see KIRIATH–JEARIM also.)

Kiriath–huzoth (A. V., Kirjath–huzoth), kīr´-ĭ-ăth-hū´-zŏth (Heb.)—*city of divisions; city of streets; middle city; city of two parts.*

A city of Moab, where Balak brought Balaam and offered up oxen and sheep as sacrifices, when he wanted Balaam to curse Israel (Num. 22:39).

Meta. Divided thoughts, thoughts of good and evil, God and self (*city of divisions, city of two parts*), expressing in and through the psychic realm in individual consciousness (*middle city,* that which exists between the inner and the outer), that the carnal mind (Moab) would have one believe to be ways of Spirit. Thus the carnal mind would defeat the purpose of the real, true thoughts of the consciousness (Israelites), would bring the individual into deep trouble and confusion, and would perpetuate its own sensate activities.

Kiriath–jearim (A. V., Kirjath–jearim), kīr´-ĭ-ăth-jē´-ă-rĭm (Heb.)—*city of redundant growths; city of dense thickets; city of forests.*

A city of Gibeon (Josh. 9:17). The Ark remained in this city for twenty years after the Philistines sent it back to Israel, until David had it returned to its place in Jerusalem (I Sam. 7:1, 2).

Meta. A nerve center—a network of nerves—with its accompanying thoughts and thought activities (*city of forests; trees represent nerves, and it is over the nerves that the thoughts travel to every part of the body*). The aspirations of this thought center are of a high, rich, fruitful, spiritual character (*city of redundant growths*). (Kiriath–jearim was a city of Gibeon, and Gibeon signifies a very illumined state of consciousness. Then, too, the Ark remained in this city for many years, and that which it symbolizes could not find an abiding place in any but high ideals.)

Kiriath–sannah (A. V., Kirjath–sannah), kĭr'-ĭ-ăth–săn'-năh (Heb.)—*city of palm branch; city of palms; bristling city; city of broom; clean city.*

A city in the hill country of Judah. It is the same city as Debir (Josh. 15: 49) and Kiriath–sepher.

Meta. The central idea of the group of thoughts that Kiriath–sannah signifies is cleanliness, purity, victory over that which is impure and unclean, over that which is of a divided mind, by casting out the seeming error (*city of palm branch, city of broom, city of palms, bristling city*). (See KIRIATH–SEPHER and DEBIR.)

Kiriath–sepher (A. V., Kirjath–sepher), kĭr'-ĭ-ăth–sē'-phĕr (Heb.)—*city of engravings; city of scribes; city of the scrolls; city of books; city of numbers; city of writings; city of instruction; city of learning.*

A former name of the city of Debir (Josh. 15:15). Kiriath–sannah is the same place.

Meta. Thoughts relating to understanding. The central idea here seems to be that of storing up knowledge by the study of books, by memorizing, and so forth. The definitions of Kiriath–sepher point more to the outer than the inner. But man must rise to a comprehension of the truth that the source of true knowing is the Spirit of truth at the very center of his own being. (See DEBIR for further information regarding this secret inner place where man contacts divine wisdom.)

Kish, kĭsh (Heb.)—*curved; bent,* i. e., *as a bow; a bow; iris; bowman; archer; strength; power; rainbow; horny; harsh; stubborn; obdurate; difficult; severe.*

a A Benjamite, father of Saul, the first king of Israel (I Sam. 9:1, 2). **b** Two Levites (I Chron. 24:29; II Chron. 29: 12). **c** An ancestor of Mordecai, a Benjamite (Esther 2:5).

Meta. Endurance, strength, power (*a bow*), as definitions of Kish, in conjunction with the other definitions of the name, recall the text, "But his bow abode in strength." The steadfastness, power, and strength that Kish signifies may express in a carnal or in a spiritual way, according to whether it is established in and directed by self-will or understanding of and obedience to divine will.

Kishi, kĭsh'-ī (Heb.)—*bow of Jehovah; strength of Jah; power of Jehovah.*

Father of Ethan, who was one of the musicians in the tabernacle in David's reign (I Chron. 6:44). He is called Kushaiah in I Chronicles 15:17.

Meta. Kishi—*bow of Jehovah*—makes us think of the text in Genesis 49:24: "But his bow abode in strength,
And the arms of his hands were made strong (*active*, marg.),
By the hands of the Mighty One of Jacob."
Kishi represents divine strength, activity, and executive power.

Kishion, kĭsh'-ĭ-ŏn (Heb.)—*horny; hard; firm; inflexible; obdurate; difficult; stubborn.*

A city of Issachar (Josh. 19:20) that was given over to the Gershonite Levites (Josh. 21:28). In I Chronicles 6:72, Kedesh is named in place of Kishion.

Meta. Kedesh refers to the place within man where he communes with God and realizes the divine presence within himself. Thus light and strength are realized sufficient to put away error, limited, material ideas and conditions. Kishion (meaning *horny, hard, obdurate, difficult, stubborn*), a city of Issachar (active zeal), symbolizes the difficulty that the personal consciousness sometimes has in denying and putting away old, treasured material beliefs and conditions. Kishion refers also to the seeming hardness, stubbornness, and inharmoniousness of the error that is being put away.

Kishon, kī'-shŏn (Heb.) — *curved; winding; bent; crooked; hard; difficult; laborious.*

A river in Palestine, next in importance to the Jordan. It was at this river that the Israelites defeated Sisera, captain of the army of Jabin (Judg. 4:7, 13; 5:21). Elijah slew the prophets of Baal by "the brook Kishon" (I Kings 18:40).

Meta. The prophets of Baal that Elijah slew at "the brook Kishon" represent the many external impulses that sway the soul dominated by nature's elements. To cut off these emotions that have been counted so dear and have been treasured in song and prose is indeed an exceedingly *hard* process for some people; it is very *winding* and *laborious* to some, also.

Kitron, kĭt'-rŏn (Heb.)—*knotted; jointed; vertebrate; knotty,* i. e., *difficult of solution; parables; figurative; dwarfed; short; small; little.*

A city of Zebulun. The Zebulunites did not drive out its Canaanitish inhabitants, "but the Canaanites dwelt among them, and became subject to taskwork" (Judg. 1:30). This city is named Kattath in Joshua 19:15.

Meta. A group of thoughts in the Zebulun or order faculty in individual consciousness. Like Kattath, the ideas of this thought center are too small and savor too much of the belief in limitation (*little* and *short*); there is too little reality in them (*figurative*) and they believe the problem of putting away all error, sensate ideas (Canaanites) to be too *knotty* and hard a task for them to accomplish. They do not, therefore, at this phase of the unfoldment of the individual, make the attainment that they should. (See KATTATH.)

Kittim (in A. V., every instance except Genesis 10:4 and I Chronicles 1:7, Chittim), kĭt'-tĭm (Heb.)—*the cut off; the rejected; outsiders; islanders; schismatic; barbarous; uncivilized; terrible; gigantic; reprobate; damned.*

a Son of Javan and grandson of Japheth, Noah's son (Gen. 10:4). **b** Descendants of Javan; and their country, Cyprus, and islands and parts of the coast of the Mediterranean (Num. 24:24).

Meta. A phase of the outer, sense-reasoning mind in man, as opposed to the inner, true spiritual understanding. This phase of thought must be *cut off,* rejected, by the individual who would progress spiritually, since it is an outsider, uncivilized, and reprobate so far as Truth is concerned.

Koa, kō'-à (Heb.)—*cut off; cut out; selected; superior; a he-camel,* i. e., *one selected for breeding qualities; mounting; hoping; desiring; ruling; prince; noble.*

An eastern prince, or people, named with the Babylonians, Chaldeans, and Assyrians as enemies of Jerusalem (Ezek. 23:22, 23).

Meta. The ruling thought, or seemingly great power, of the animal nature in man, in its positive, determined, headstrong, actively aggressive aspect.

Kohath, kō'-hăth (Heb.)—*called together; convocation; assembly; one who obeys a call; an ally.*

Second son of Levi, who was one of Jacob's twelve sons (Gen. 46:11).

Meta. The attracting, unifying, gathering element in love, and the power of love (Levi is the son of Jacob who represents love, and love is unifying in its nature).

Kohathites, kō'-hăth-ītes (fr. Heb.)—*of* or *belonging to Kohath.*

Descendants of Kohath (Num. 3:27).

Meta. Thoughts springing from and belonging to that in consciousness which Kohath represents. (See KOHATH.)

Kolaiah, kō-lā'-iăh (Heb.)—*voice of Jehovah; listen to Jehovah; hearken to Jah; proclaim Jehovah.*

Two Israelites (Neh. 11:7; Jer. 29:21).

Meta. Spiritual inspiration with power to proclaim it (by means of the voice, ideas are expressed in audible words, and the seat of the voice—the throat—is the power center in man). The *voice of Jehovah,* however, is not an audible voice, but it signifies the power of spiritual inspiration, spiritual understanding, and knowing. Kolaiah also bespeaks the listening, obedient attitude of mind that is necessary to the receiving of spiritual inspiration.

Korah, kō'-răh (Heb.)—*bald; smooth; crystal; clear; ice; cold; bald-headed; without horns.*

a Son of Esau (Gen. 36:14, 16). **b** A son of Izhar, descended from Levi.

through Kohath. This Korah was one of those who rebelled against Moses and Aaron, and was destroyed by the earth's opening beneath him and swallowing him up (Num. 16).

Meta. Coldness and unproductiveness of life and good, because of one's not being willing to be guided in the love faculty (Korah was descended from Levi, who signifies the love faculty in individual consciousness) by the law of God. (See ASSIR, son of Korah.)

Korah, son of Esau, denotes the coldness, the crystallization (*ice*), and the barrenness (*bald*) of consciousness that result from dominance of the "mind of the flesh" (Esau) in the individual.

Korahites (in A. V., Num. 26:58, Korathites; Exod. 6:24, Korhites), kō'-räh-ītes (fr. Heb.)—*of* or *belonging to Korah.*

Levites descended from Korah, great-grandson of Levi (Exod. 6:24).

Meta. Thoughts springing from and belonging to that in consciousness which Korah, the great-grandson of Levi, signifies. (See KORAH.) *Clear, crystal,* definitions of Korah, bespeak a comprehen-sion that would aid in raising these Korah thoughts to the love and productiveness that belong to their true nature.

Kore, kō'-rĕ (Heb.)—*caller; crier; proclaimer; beseecher; convoker; reciter; a partridge; quail; any calling bird.*

a A Levite, a descendant of Korah (I Chron. 9:19). **b** A Levite, son of Imnah (II Chron. 31:14).

Meta. That in man's natural religious tendencies (Levites, in their office of ministering in the house of Jehovah) which insistently suggests and proclaims true ideas to man's inner consciousness and seeks to impress them on him. (The men named Kore belonged to the porters in the Temple. One of them "was over the freewill-offerings of God, to distribute the oblations of Jehovah, and the most holy things.")

Kushaiah, kŭsh-ā'-ịäh (Heb.)—*bow of Jehovah.*

Father of Ethan, a musician in the house of Jehovah during David's reign (I Chron. 15:17). He is called Kishi in I Chronicles 6:44.

Meta. See KISHI.

L

Laadah, lā'-ă-däh (Heb.)—*set to time; set in order; harmonious; adorned; to testify; to assemble; festive.*

Son of Shelah, who was a son of Judah. Laadah was the "father," or founder, of Mareshah (I Chron. 4:21).

Meta. A condition of harmony and order in the consciousness when one is ready to recognize the divine inner presence, and the answer to one's prayer. One's realizations and demonstrations come about in order, since order is heaven's first law and everything of Spirit is done according to the working of divine law. An inner rhythm, or harmony, a poise and peace (*set to time, set in order, harmonious*), must be attained in order to realize one's good. This inner state of mind and body is reached by the steps that one takes in going into the silence, by true prayer. Shelah, the father of Laadah, means *petition, prayer,* that which unites man with God and opens man's consciousness to receive the good that is his inheritance. Mareshah, the "son," or city, of Laadah, means *head, highest, summit, from the beginning, first principle, most precious,* and bespeaks Spirit, first principle, source of all that really is, of the good that is man's from the beginning and is now being made manifest. Laadah bespeaks the inner consciousness of man as receiving the realization from Spirit, testifying to the Truth, and rejoicing in his good (*to assemble, to testify, festive*).

Laban, lā'-băn (Heb.)—*white; clean; pure; gentle; clear; transparent; shining; glorious; noble.*

Son of Bethuel and grandson of Nahor. He was also the brother of Rebekah, Isaac's wife, and father of Rachel and Leah, Jacob's wives (Gen. 24:24, 29; 29:13); Laban's home was in Haran (see Gen. 29:4, 5).

Meta. Laban means *white, pure,*

clear, shining, gentle, noble; Haran means *exalted, mountain.* This clearly indicates that the attention shall be located in exalted states of mind and united with spiritual intelligence and nonresistance. Jacob grew rapidly in understanding and in possessions in the land of Laban, and his choice of location was a good one for the man developing to full stature in Christ Jesus.

In Genesis 28:2 we find Isaac charging Jacob to take a wife from the daughters of Laban. This points the way to a unification with the love principle in its higher aspects. Exalted ideas, divine aspirations, and pure motives are here designated as necessary to the union with the soul that the I AM (Jacob) is about to make.

Lachish, lā'-chĭsh (Heb.)—*adhering; strongly united; tenacious; unyielding; impregnable; persistent; striking; smiting; capturing.*

A city of the Amorites that was taken by the Israelites under Joshua, and was allotted to the tribe of Judah. It was in the lowland of Judah (Josh. 10:3-35; 15:39; see also II Kings 14:19 and 18:14).

Meta. The Amorites symbolize a race inheritance. They have their seat of action in the generative function. Lachish, a city of the Amorites, denotes carnal man's erroneous belief concerning his amorous sex impulses and desires. To the sensate, carnal mind of man, these are of God; they exist as a fundamental principle underlying the continuity of life in outer form and cannot be overcome (*impregnable, unyielding*).

We are now realizing, however, that all lusts of the flesh lead to sin and to corruption of the consciousness and body, and can be brought into subjection to the I AM (Joshua); the entire consciousness can be purified by means of the Spirit of God indwelling, which is as "a consuming fire" (see Mal. 3:1-3).

Ladan (A. V., Laadan), lā'-dăn (Heb.) —*set in order; festive; harmonious; pleasurable; delightful; adorned; for a witness.*

a An Ephraimite, from whom Joshua was descended (I Chron. 7:26). **b** Son of Gershon, of the Levites (I Chron. 23:

7). In I Chronicles 6:17 this latter Ladan is called Libni.

Meta. The individual will working constructively, with love and with the innate religious tendencies. (One Ladan was an Ephraimite, and Ephraim represents the will faculty in man. The other Ladan was a descendant of Levi, who signifies the love faculty; the Levites in their office of ministering spiritually to the people stand for the innate religious tendencies and activities of individual consciousness.) The Ladan attitude of mind always tends to bring about great joy and gladness (*festive, pleasurable, delightful*) by means of establishing harmony and order in the consciousness (*set in order, harmonious*). *Festive* also suggests feasting, an inner realization of substance. In thus entering a consciousness of Truth one becomes a witness to Truth (*for a witness*).

Lael, lā'-ĕl (Heb.)—*unto God; Godward; of God; belonging to God; consecrated to God; created by God.*

Father of Eliasaph, who was prince of the house of the Gershonites (Num. 3:24).

Meta. A ruling thought belonging to that phase of the love faculty in man for which Gershon, son of Levi, stands. (See GERSHON.) This thought is *of God,* is turned toward God (*Godward*), and is *consecrated to God;* thus it does its part in elevating the consciousness of the individual to a higher and more spiritual standard.

Lahad, lā'-hăd (Heb.)—*flaming; glowing; glittering; praising; bright; splendid; majestic; scorched; dark; oppression.*

Son of Jahath, of the tribe of Judah (I Chron. 4:2).

Meta. Jahath, father of Lahad, represents the tearing down and the building up that attend every true overcoming of error in individual consciousness. (See JAHATH.) Ahumai, Lahad's brother who is named with him, signifies a negative, denying, or letting-go state of thought, (See AHUMAI.) The negative meanings of Lahad (*scorched, dark, oppression*) do not belong to this man. He denotes the consciousness' coming up out of the seemingly negative attitude, into which it has been thrown in the process of putting away error, into a realization of conscious, joyous victory and strength (*praising, glowing, bright, splendid, majestic*).

Lahmam, läh'-măm (Heb.)—*toward noonday; toward noontime warmth; toward light; place of bread; place of food; universal assimilative substance.*

A city in the lowland of Judah (Josh. 15:40).

Meta. An increase of light, love, and substance (*toward noontime warmth, toward light, place of bread, universal assimilative substance*) in the subconscious mind (lowland of Judah).

Lahmi, läh'-mī (Heb.)—*Bethlehemite; of* or *belonging to bread; my bread; my substance.*

Brother of Goliath the Gittite, a Philistine warrior (I Chron. 20:5).

Meta. The mistaken belief of the sense mind (Philistines) in individual consciousness that substance, prosperity, man's bountiful supply, can be obtained only by personal ownership, by means of competition, oppression, defense, and by fighting for one's rights (*Bethlehemite, of* or *belonging to bread, my bread, my substance;* a Philistine warrior, brother of the giant Goliath).

Laish, lā'-ĭsh (Heb.)—*kneaded together; crushing; adhering; well-knit; firm; strong; courageous; a lion.*

a A man of Gallim, to whose son Saul gave his daughter Michal, David's wife (I Sam. 25:44). **b** A place in the northern part of Palestine that was conquered by the tribe of Dan and was included by them in their inheritance (Judg. 18:7, 29).

Meta. Courage, fearlessness, and strength (*lion, firm, strong, courageous*) brought about by a certain unification of thought (*kneaded together, adhering, well-knit*). Better judgment, however, is needed in the group of thoughts in consciousness that Laish represents, so that it may express constructively instead of destructively; thus it is conquered by the tribe of Dan (judgment) and comes into their possession.

Laishah (A. V., Laish), lā'-ĭsh-äh (Heb.)—same as Laish, used with the emphatic and designative article, a form used to designate a place or locality.

A place mentioned in Isaiah 10:30.

Meta. A *lion* signifies life (being of the cat family), as well as courage, aggressiveness, fearlessness, and strength. Gallim, the place mentioned with Laishah in Isaiah 10:30, also represents thoughts about life. (See GALLIM.) Because of failing to keep the courage, fearlessness, and strength of the Laishah consciousness centered in Spirit, God, they fail in the hour of greatest need; they fall a prey to the Assyrians (the destructive and undisciplined reasonings, philosophical and psychical, that do not recognize the spiritual Head of the universe but are based on sense observations, on the formed instead of the formless). (See ASSYRIA.)

Lakkum (A. V., Lakum), läk'-kŭm—(Heb.)—*stopping up; barring; barrier; for rising against; for rising in defense; for firmness; for establishing; fortification; castle; defense.*

A place on the border of Naphtali (Josh. 19:33).

Meta. Defensive, protective thoughts (*stopping up, barring, barrier, defense*); also firmness of purpose (*for firmness, for establishing*). These become a *fortification,* a *defense,* a stronghold, to protect one's strength (Naphtali—the faculty of strength in individual consciousness) from invasion by error beliefs of weakness, and to keep it alive and active.

Lamb of God.

Meta. The pure life and substance of Being. Jesus Christ, by His overcoming, restored to humanity the consciousness of this pure life and substance; hence He is called the Lamb of God (John 1:29, 36; Rev. 7:9-17).

In Scripture the divine life is termed the Lamb of God. This carries the symbology of its purity, innocence, and guilelessness. Its nature is to vivify, with perpetual life, all things that it touches. It knows only to give, to give unceasingly and eternally without restraint. It does not include wisdom, which is another quality of Being that man comprehends with a different part of his consciousness.

The pure life of God flows into man's consciousness through the spiritual body and is sensed by the physical at a point in the loins. This is the river of the "water of life" (mentioned in Rev. 22), bright as crystal, proceeding from the throne of God and the Lamb.

lame.

Meta. The "lame" of Matthew 11:5 are the impeded members of the body. The "lepers" are the stagnated fluids of the organism. These are liberated by Spirit, and the new activity strengthens and cleanses the whole man.

The subconsciousness, in most persons, is so benumbed by the neglect and ignorance of the conscious mind that it is seemingly deaf, dumb, blind, and dead. When the subconscious mind begins to receive the truth that the body is a living thing and that every cell is a conscious entity, there is a great awakening and resurrection of sleeping energies from the tomb of matter.

The "man that was lame from his mother's womb," who lay at the "door of the temple which is called Beautiful" and asked alms, is the one who has not affirmed his spiritual strength through the living Christ. The "door of the temple which is called Beautiful" is spiritual understanding. The door opens when we pray and praise.

Lamech, lā′-mĕch (Heb.) — *overthrown; leveler; arrester of dissolution; principle of law and order; a strong young man; strength; health; power.*

a Son of Methushael and father of Jabal, Jubal, Tubal-cain, and Naamah (Gen. 4:18-24). **b** Son of Methuselah, and father of Noah (Gen. 5:25-31).

Meta. The strength of youth; the vital something in us that overcomes thoughts and tendencies that lead to dissolution. The vital life principle constantly inspires us from within to keep on living. This thought of youth was in Lamech, the father of Noah, and it found expression in Noah. (See NOAH.) The thought of strength and youth that is symbolized by the Lamech descended from Cain is carnal and physical. The new line of descent from Adam, through Seth, that follows this Lamech introduces a higher, a more spiritual understanding.

Lamech signifies the principle of life, which not only tends to keep one alive

in the body but also brings about the building of a new body and reëntrance into manifest existence for each one who lets go of his consciousness of life in the body for a time, thus allowing his organism to disintegrate; in other words, for each one who goes through the experience that the world has named death.

Laodicea, lȧ-ŏd-ĭ-çē′-ȧ (Gk.)—*justice of the people; judgment of the people.*

A city of Phrygia, in Asia Minor, about forty miles from Ephesus. There was an assembly of Christians at Laodicea (Col. 2:1; Rev. 1:11).

Meta. A phase of the judgment faculty in the individual, expressing in the personal. It is that phase of judgment which bases its understanding, its decisions, on outer seemings and intellectual reasonings.

Laodiceans, lȧ-ŏd-ĭ-çē′-ăns (fr. Gk.)

People who lived in Laodicea. It was to the church in Laodicea that Paul and John wrote (Col. 4:16; Rev. 3:14).

Meta. Thoughts belonging to that in consciousness for which Laodicea stands. (See LAODICEA.)

Lappidoth (A. V., Lapidoth), lăp′-pī-dŏth (Heb.)—*light radiations; spreading abroad of lights; lamps; torches; flames; enlightened; enlighteners; instructors.*

Husband of the prophetess Deborah (Judg. 4:4).

Meta. Wisdom expressing, radiating (*light radiations, lamps, enlighteners*). (See DEBORAH.)

"Thy word is a lamp unto my feet,
    And light unto my path."
"The spirit of man is the lamp of Jehovah,
    Searching all his innermost parts."

Lasea, lȧ-sē′-ȧ (Gk.)—*thick; dense; hard; stony; wise.*

A city in Crete, near Fair Havens. It is mentioned in the account of Paul's dangerous and stormy voyage to Rome as a prisoner (Acts 27:8).

Meta. A group of thoughts signifying the wisdom (*wise*) of the material state of consciousness that Crete represents, or worldly wisdom. In the light of Spirit, worldly wisdom is very dense and is not at all clear in its attempted reasonings (*thick*). It is hard also (*stony*); it lacks the peaceable, gentle, and loving quality of the wisdom from above (Jas. 3:17).

Lasha, lā'-shȧ (Heb.)—*puncturing; bursting forth; cleaving; chasm; fountain; for looking upon; for anointing, i. e., the eyes.*

A place mentioned as being at the southern extremity of the border of Canaan (Gen. 10:19). It is thought to be identical with the hot springs of Callirrhoë, near the Dead Sea.

Meta. The cities that are mentioned in the text with Lasha, as being on the southern border of Canaan, are representative of the subconscious substance and life in man, ruled over and actuated by various phases of the subjective carnal, sensual mind.

Lasha signifies the *bursting forth* of this inner substance and life (*fountain*) into greater activity in consciousness. Lasha also points to a penetrating of the seemingly mortal and material state of the subjective substance and life in unawakened man (*puncturing, cleaving*) by higher ideals, truer understanding (*for anointing,* i. e., *the eyes; eyes* always point to understanding, and *anointing* bespeaks oil, which signifies Spirit) that the inner life and substance may become purified of the sensual and consecrated to spiritual expression and use.

Lassharon (A. V., Lasharon), lȧs-shȧr'-ŏn (Heb.)—*unto Sharon; according to Sharon; relating to Sharon; unto the plain; like the plain.*

A place in Canaan. Its king was killed by Joshua (Josh. 12:18).

Meta. A state of consciousness that is honest (*according to Sharon, like the plain*), frank, and open, and stands for just what it is. Here its king, or ruling thought, is one of the enemies in the land of Canaan (Canaan representing man's consciousness and body), and must be overthrown by Joshua—I AM. (See SHARON.)

Latin, lăt'-in (fr. Lat.)—*broad place; language of the Latini,* inhabitants of ancient Rome.

The native language of the ancient Romans. It is now a dead language, but is taught for educational purposes, since many of our modern words are derived from its roots. It was one of the three languages in which was written Pilate's superscription that hung over Jesus, on the cross (John 19:20).

Meta. The fact that the title, "JESUS OF NAZARETH, THE KING OF THE JEWS," was written in three languages signifies that the Jesus Christ Truth—life, perfection, immortality, expressed and demonstrated throughout man, even to his outer organism—must be recognized and acknowledged by man on all three planes of his consciousness. He must accept this Truth and the Christ must rule in his superconscious mind, his conscious mind, and his subconscious mind. The Hebrew language refers here to the spiritual, or superconscious phase of mind in man; Latin to the subconscious; and Greek to the conscious, reasoning mind.

law.

Meta. The law of God is the orderly working out of the principle of Being, or the divine ideals, into expression and manifestation throughout creation.

Only spiritual things are eternal and real. All inharmonies and seeming limitations in the world are the result of man's error beliefs and thoughts, and man can eliminate them by eliminating error from his mind. He can do this by understanding that God's creation is all that there is, and knowing it to be good. In this way divine ideals are established in mind, and by the law of mind action they are expressed, thus bringing into manifestation the perfection that ever exists in the ideal.

The law of mind action may be described in three steps: mind, idea, manifestation. First, there must be mind; second, everything exists first as an idea in mind; third, the inherent power and intelligence in the idea causes it to act or express, and when it is expressed we have the manifestation. (See CREATION.)

To serve the Lord is to keep the divine law, the law of right thought. It has come to be recognized as a law of mind action that men become like that which they behold; they manifest that which they mentally see. One who knew this law wrote, "Nothing foretells futurity like the thoughts over which we brood."

The "heart" is the subconsciousness of man. The laws of Jehovah are written on the heart by man's meditating on and realizing spiritual ideas as the reality of his being. (See Deut. 6:6-9; Heb. 8:10; 10:16.)

Lazarus, lăz'-ă-rŭs (Gk. fr. Heb.)— *whom God helps; succor of God; assistance of God; grace of God; not of help; without succor; helpless.* The true Hebrew derivation of Lazarus is disputed. Some consider it to be a form of Eleazer, meaning *whom God hath helped.* Others believe it to be derived from Loa–ezer, meaning "without help."

a The name of the "beggar" in one of Jesus' parables (Luke 16:20). **b** A friend of Jesus, and brother of Mary and Martha, whom Jesus raised from the dead (John 11:1-44).

Meta. Lazarus (*whom God helps, without succor*) refers to the part of the consciousness that is helped by the good, though apparently utterly neglected by the man himself.

In the parable (Luke 16:19-31) Jesus describes the states of consciousness of one who passes through the change called death. The rich man and Lazarus represent the outer and the inner consciousness of the average worldly-minded person. The outer consciousness appropriates the attributes of soul and body and expresses them through sense avenues. "He was clothed in purple and fine linen, faring sumptuously every day." This condition typifies carnal riches.

Material selfishness starves the inner man and devitalizes the true or spiritual phase of the soul and body, which is described in the sentence, "A certain beggar named Lazarus was laid at his gate, full of sores, and desiring to be fed with the *crumbs* that fell from the rich man's table." The higher soul life is put out of the consciousness and fed with the dogs.

When death overtakes such a one, both the inner and the outer change environment. The material avenues are lost to the outer, and the carnal phase of the soul finds self in a hell of animal desires without the flesh through which to express. "And in Hades he lifted up his eyes, being in torments."

Lazarus, the beggar, was "carried away by the angels into Abraham's bosom." The inner spiritual ego, drawn by its innate spiritual ideas, finds a haven or rest in the bosom of the Father, represented by Abraham.

(According to the best Bible authorities, "Abraham's bosom" represents a state of felicity, or celestial happiness. A good Bible translator also says that "Hades" means "the invisible land, the realm of the dead, including both Elysium and paradise for the good, and Tartarus, Gehenna, and hell for the wicked." We do not, however, understand that "Abraham's bosom" refers to a place called heaven, nor that "Hades" refers to a place called hell. The Teller of this allegory was striving, evidently, to depict the two states of consciousness in which the higher and the lower principles of the soul find themselves after the death of the body.)

When man loses the material avenues of expression and has not developed the spiritual, he is in torment. Appetite longs for satisfaction and, in its anguished desire for a cooling draft, calls to its spiritual counterpart (Lazarus). But the body consciousness, the place of union between all the attributes of man, has been removed, producing in the life consciousness a great gulf or chasm that cannot be crossed, except by man's incarnation in another body.

Then the sense man is contrite and would have his five brothers warned of the danger of sense life. These five brothers are the five senses. Abraham says: "They have Moses and the prophets; let them hear them"; that is, they understand the law (Moses) and they know what will follow its transgression (prophets). The rich man rejoins: "Nay, father Abraham: but if one go to them from the dead, they will repent." "And he said unto him, If they hear not Moses and the prophets, neither will they be persuaded, if one rise from the dead." The personal consciousness, which has been formed through material attachments, can be reached only through its own plane of consciousness. The phenomenal manifestations of spiritualism do not cause people to repent of their sins.

When one understands the disintegration that death produces in man, this parable is perceived to be rich in description of that process and of the new relation of the segregated parts of the complete man.

The raising of Lazarus, the brother of Mary and Martha, signifies the restoring to consciousness of the idea of youth, which is asleep in the subconsciousness, or tomb of the body. People grow old because they let the youth idea fall asleep. This idea is not dead, but is sleeping, and the understanding I AM (Jesus) goes to awaken it. This awakening of youthful energies is necessary to one in the regeneration. The body cannot be refined and made like its Creator, eternal, until all the thoughts necessary to its perpetuation are revived in it. Eternal youth is one of these God-given ideas that man loves. Jesus loved Lazarus.

The outer senses say that this vitalizing force is dead, that it has been dead for so long that it has gone into dissolution, decay, but the keener knowledge of the spiritual man proclaims, "Our friend Lazarus is fallen asleep; but I . . . awake him out of sleep."

Bringing this sleeping life to outer consciousness is no easy task. Jesus groaned in spirit and was troubled at the prospect. The higher must enter into sympathy and love with the lower to bring about the awakening—"Jesus wept." But there must be more than sympathy and love— "Take ye away the stone." The "stone" that holds the sleeping life in the tomb of matter in subconsciousness is the belief in the permanency of present material laws. This "stone" must be rolled away through faith. The man who wants the inner life to spring forth must believe in the reality of spiritual powers and must exercise his faith by invoking in prayer the presence of the invisible but omnipresent God. This reveals to consciousness the glory of Spirit, and the soul has witness in itself of a power that it knew not.

In Spirit all things are fulfilled now. The moment a concept enters the mind, that which is conceived is consummated, through the law that governs the action of ideas. The inventor mentally sees his machine doing the work designed, though he may be years short of making it do that work. The spiritual-minded take advantage of this law and affirm the completeness of the ideal, regardless of outer appearances. This stimulates the energy in the thought process and gives it power beyond estimate. This is the step that Jesus took when He lifted up His eyes and said, "Father, I thank thee that thou heardest me. And I knew that thou hearest me always." The sleeping life (Lazarus) does not awake, but the prayer of thanksgiving that is now in action gives the assurance that calls it at the next step to the surface—"Lazarus, come forth."

Jesus "cried with a loud voice." This emphasizes the necessity of working strenuously in vibrating the inner life to the surface. Neophytes find it easy, under proper instruction, to quicken the various life centers in the body and connect them as a vibrating body battery that, under the direction of the will, throws a current of energy to any desired place. A time comes when the outer flesh must be vitalized with this inner life; then arises the necessity of using the "loud voice," or powerful will vibrations in eye and ear; in fact, every function. This is removing the napkin from the face, which represents conscious intelligence.

Freedom from all trammels is necessary before the imprisoned life can find its natural channels in the constitution. "Loose him, and let him go" means unfettered life, expressing itself in joyous freedom of Spirit. The flesh would take this vital flood and use it in the old way, put new wine into old bottles, but Spirit guides those who trust it, and leads them in righteous ways if they listen patiently to the inner guide.

This raising of Lazarus is performed every day by those who are putting on the new Christ body.

"Lazarus . . . sat at meat" (John 12:2) means that this resurrected inner idea of life and youth abides as the vitalizing substance of the subconsciousness in the regeneration.

Leah, lē'-ăh (Heb.)—*weary; exhausted; faint; sluggish.*

Daughter of Laban, and wife of Jacob
(Gen. 29:16-32).

Meta. The human soul.

leaven.

Meta. The "leaven" of the Pharisees
and of Herod (Mark 8:15) represents
limited thoughts. When we attempt to
confine the divine law to the customary
avenues of expression, and scoff at anything beyond, we are letting the leaven
of the Pharisees work in us. When we
allow the finer forces of the body to go
to fulfill lust and appetite, we are letting
the leaven of Herod work to our undoing.
When the mind is raised up through affirmations of God's omnipresent substance and life, we are not only fed but
there is a surplus. This is the teaching
of Jesus, and it has always been exemplified by His faithful followers. It
is not the outward demonstration that
counts, but the increase of substance in
mind and body that always follows the
faithful application of the divine law.
(See Matthew 13:33 and I Corinthians
5:6, 7.) Whatever line of thought is received into consciousness goes on working
until it is rooted out by another line of
thinking or until it changes one's whole
consciousness and manifests fully in the
outer life.

Lebana, lĕb'-à-nà (Heb.)—*whiteness;
purity; brilliance; frankincense, i. e.,
from its whiteness; the moon.*

"The children of Lebana" were among
the Nethinim who returned with Zerubbabel from the Babylonian captivity
(Neh. 7:48). The name is spelled Leb-
anah in Ezra 2:45.

Meta. The purifying and altogether
lovely, refining effect that true service
and spiritual worship have on the character of the individual who renders them
(*whiteness, purity, brilliance, frankincense*). Even if such service and worship are of the intellect, as is suggested
by *the moon,* a definition of Lebana, they
are still very uplifting and good, if given
in wholeness and singleness of heart and
purpose.

Lebanon, lĕb'-à-nŏn (Heb.)—*white;
clean; pure; brilliant; snowy.*

A range of mountains in northern
Palestine (Deut. 3:25). It was noted
for its cedars (I Kings 5:6); also for

its beauty and grandeur of scenery, and
has been used much in symbol by sacred
writers.

Meta. Pure thoughts.

Lebaoth, lĕb'-à-ŏth (Heb.)—*roarings;
lowings; lions; lionesses.*

A city of southern Judah (Josh. 15:
32).

Meta. An inner consciousness of conquering power (*lions, roarings, lionesses*). (See BETH–LEBAOTH.)

Lebonah, lê-bō'-näh (Heb.)—*whiteness; purity; brilliance; frankincense;
the moon.*

A place north of Bethel and Shiloh
(Judg. 21:19).

Meta. Like Lebana, Lebonah signifies
the refining, beautifying effect of pure
thoughts, even though these thoughts
may be of the intellect, or partly so
(*frankincense, whiteness, purity, moon*).

Lecah, lē'-càh (Heb.)—*walking; going; progressing; living; a way; a
course; a journey; a promenade; speeding; hurrying.*

It is not certain whether Lecah was
a son of Er, or a place founded by Er
(I Chron. 4:21).

Meta. The life and unfoldment of
man is often likened to a *journey.* Lecah (*walking, going, progressing*) denotes the journey of life as it is taken
by every individual. The *course* of each
one is determined by his observing, attentive, vigilant thoughts, by that to
which he gives his attention (Er, father or founder of Lecah; see ER).

In this journey man enters into conditions and experiences that correspond
to the character of his thoughts; he becomes like that which he beholds, or
holds to in mind. If we wish our journey
to lead quickly (*speeding, hurrying*) to
the goal of perfection and of every real,
abiding good, we must be faithful and
constant in beholding the Christ; we
must dwell in mind on that which is
good, pure, and true only.

Lehabim, lē'-hà-bĭm (Heb.)—*inflamed
uprisings; blazing exhalations; fiery illusions; flaming; passionate; polished
swords; pointed weapons.*

Son of Mizraim, who was a son of Ham
and grandson of Noah (Gen. 10:13).

Meta. Ham, grandfather of Lehabim,

is one of Noah's three sons; he represents the physical in man. Mizraim, Lehabim's father, meaning *Egypt, tribulation,* refers to the carnal or earthly consciousness in the individual. Lehabim (*fiery illusions, inflamed uprisings, passionate, polished swords*) represents the life of the seemingly physical and material organism activated wholly by the tendencies and desires of the outer animal man. Thus this life, which is in essence spiritual and should always be of a vitalizing, harmonizing, and upbuilding character, becomes to the individual who is guided by material thought and desire a fire that burns up the organism and a sword that cuts and destroys.

Lehi, lē'-hī (Heb.)—*cheek; jaw; jawbone.*

A place in Judah where Samson killed a thousand Philistines with the jawbone of an ass (Judg. 15:9-19). Lehi also seems to have been a name given to the jawbone itself, which "God clave" and "there came water thereout," for Samson to drink, when he was about to die of thirst (see Judg. 15:17-19, and the marginal note concerning Lehi, of the 19th verse).

Meta. Determination, endurance, strength (*jawbone*). If the same determination, strength of purpose, and enduringness that result in overcoming sense consciousness (the Philistines) are used to affirm new life and Truth through Jehovah, the Christ, they will quicken and restore the whole man.

Lemuel, lĕm'-ū-ĕl (Heb.)—*for God; belonging to God; dedicated to God; unto God; Godward.*

A king, mentioned in Proverbs 31:1, 4; supposedly a symbolic name for Solomon.

Meta. The intelligent principle in man (*for God, belonging to God*) consecrated to the highest, or spiritual, service and use (*unto God, Godward, dedicated to God*). It radiates or transmits light (understanding) to the whole consciousness.

lepers.

Meta. The "ten men that were lepers" (Luke 17:12-19) typify the impure relation of life activities in one who has by his error thoughts about life separated his life expressions from the one Source of life. Leprosy here symbolizes substance so separated from the great central life Source that it has lost its vitality (stands afar off).

The life in man finds. expression through the avenue of the senses. Unless the senses are redeemed and uplifted there is a tendency to utilize the pure life of God in sense pleasure. A "leprous" or impure condition in the organism is the result.

The "priests" in verse 14 stand for the connecting link between carnal man and God—that point in consciousness where man exalts his thoughts and makes union with the healing power of God.

Everything resolves itself back to "one" as its starting point. All the avenues of expression in man are unified with God when one consciously lives in harmony with divine law. Thanksgiving follows in natural sequence (verse 15).

Leshem, lē'-shĕm (Heb.)—*firm; courageous; strong; fortress; precious gem,* i. e., *opal or amber.*

A place that the "children of Dan" conquered and possessed (Josh. 19:47). It is called Laish in Judg. 18:29.

Meta. Like Laish, a group of steadfast, *strong,* fearless, and *courageous* thoughts in consciousness. Coming into the possession of Dan, or becoming allied to and guided by the judgment faculty in the individual, this group of thoughts becomes a veritable *fortress,* a stronghold for the promotion of that which is good and true.

Letushim, lĕ-tū'-shĭm (Heb.)—*hammered; forged; sharpened; sharp; stern; oppressing; forbidding; threatening.*

Son of Dedan, who was a son of Jokshan. Jokshan was one of Abraham's sons by his second wife, Keturah (Gen. 25:3).

Meta. Dedan, father of Letushim, means *low, physical love,* and refers to the lower, seemingly physical and carnal mind in unredeemed man, especially as it relates to selfish loves and desires. Letushim signifies the friction, the sense of being oppressed and hard driven (*hammered, forged, sharpened, stern, oppressing, forbidding*), that all persons who are in this lower, earthly consciousness experience much of the time. Especially do they have these experiences if they have enough of the awakened thought that Abraham represents, and the soul desire for higher things that Keturah signifies, to give them the inner urge to better themselves and their conditions, but are unsuccessful in coming up out of the limitations of sensate belief and thought enough to "let" God work in and through them. In the Letushim consciousness, advancement is slow and is worked out by means of hard experiences.

Leummim, lĕ-ŭm′-mĭm (Heb.)—*peoples; nations; multitudes; no water; without water.*

Son of Dedan and great-grandson of Abraham and Keturah (Gen. 25:3). He founded an Arabian tribe.

Meta. Great increase and multiplication of thoughts in consciousness. Peoples, nations, multitudes, all refer to numerous thoughts and states of consciousness in the individual. Here, they would belong to the earthly, carnal phase of man's being, but with a tendency toward higher, better things. (See ABRAHAM and KETURAH, from whom Leummim was descended). However, as yet there is a dryness (*without water*), a lack of real spiritual quickening, so that this earthly phase of the individual consciousness is not at this stage of unfoldment brought to a higher level, to spiritual understanding and expression.

Levi, lē′-vī (Heb.)—*joining; clinging; wreathing; entwining; infolding; uniting; loving.*

Third son of Jacob by Leah. "And she conceived again, and bare a son; and said, Now this time will my husband be joined unto me, because I have borne him three sons: therefore was his name called Levi" (Gen. 29:34).

Jacob's blessing of his son Levi is given jointly with that of Simeon (Gen. 49:5-7):
"Simeon and Levi are brethren;
Weapons of violence are their swords.
O my soul, come not thou into their council;
Unto their assembly, my glory, be not thou united;
For in their anger they slew a man,

And in their self-will they hocked an ox.
Cursed be their anger, for it was fierce;
And their wrath, for it was cruel:
I will divide them in Jacob,
And scatter them in Israel.
Moses' blessing on the tribe of Levi was (Deut. 33:8-11):
"And of Levi he said,
Thy Thummim and thy Urim are with thy godly one [him whom thou lovest, margin],
Whom thou didst prove at Massah,
With whom thou didst strive at the waters of Meribah;
Who said of his father, and of his mother, I have not seen him;
Neither did he acknowledge his brethren,
Nor knew he his own children:
For they have observed thy word,
And keep thy covenant.
They shall teach Jacob thine ordinances,
And Israel thy law:
They shall put incense before thee,
And whole burnt-offering upon thine altar.
Bless, Jehovah, his substance,
And accept the work of his hands:
Smite through the loins of them that rise up against him,
And of them that hate him, that they rise not again."

Meta. The faculty of love in human consciousness. Love is the uniting, joining force of Divine Mind. When Leah (human soul) brought forth Levi, she said: "Now this time will my husband be joined unto me." We connect our forces with whatever we center our love on. If we love the things of sense, they become part of us and we lose the ability to enter into the realms of Spirit mind. This is why the Lord commanded Moses not to make any graven image of Him. Graven images are made by mental pictures. The thought that God is a great king in a place called heaven makes just such a mental image in one's thought realms, and one grows to believe in and worship such an imaginary being instead of the true God, who is Spirit.

Jacob's blessing on Levi, which seems more of a curse than a blessing, reveals how the strong emotions and feelings of man, before coming under the dominion of divine love, are often exercised in very adverse and destructive ways. Levi, meaning *joining* or *uniting*, signifies, in the body, feeling; in the soul, sympathy; in the spirit, love. Therefore when love is expressed through the body as feeling, apart from love's dominion, violence may result instead of kindness and unselfishness and an irresistible power for good.

Moses' blessing on the tribe of Levi reveals a great unfoldment and lifting up of the love faculty in consciousness. In this stage, however, it is still of the intellect and its true spiritual quality has not yet been realized, although a degree of perception of its perfection has been attained.

Levites, lē'-vītes (fr. Heb.)—*of or belonging to Levi.*

Descendants of Levi; the Israelitish tribe of Levi. The Levites who descended through Aaron became the priests of Israel, and the other Levites filled lower places in the religious worship and services of the Israelitish nation and in the Temple (Exod. 6:25; Num. 3:5 to 4:49).

Meta. The descendants of Levi represent thoughts that spring from and belong to the love faculty in individual consciousness. As ministers and priests in the Temple and in the Temple worship they signify our natural religious tendencies, not necessarily spiritual.

The priests and Levites of I Kings 8:4 symbolize our so-called natural religious tendencies. These officiate in the rites and ceremonies of the tent, or tabernacle, and when the more permanent structure is to be built they bring up all the "holy vessels" from that structure. We can thus understand why some persons are naturally of a religious turn of mind, though they may be born of worldly-minded parents. They carry over from a former tabernacle the results of exercising the mind in religious ways. Such results are symbolized by the priests and Levites. Thus the savage with his vague understanding of Deity may, by constantly repeating certain religious ceremonies, accumulate a religious tendency that will make him "naturally religious" when he attains a higher plane of expression. This also is the basis of the formal religion where rites and ceremonies take the place of true spirituality.

The priest and the Levite of Luke 10:31, 32 typify forms of religious thoughts in man that follow the set rule of the letter of the law, with little or no thought of its practical use, of its inner, spiritual import.

Leviticus, lĕ-vĭt'-ĭ-cŭs (fr. Heb.).

Third book of the Bible. It contains a summary of all the rules and ceremonies pertaining to the ministry of the Jewish priests and Levites, and pertaining to the activities of the Israelitish people. Not all the laws laid down in this book concern what we call religion; many of them are rules of health, social conduct, and so forth.

Meta. The real, inner spiritual law of life, of health, of peace, of plenty, and of true spiritual understanding and worship. Back of the outer letter of the law, back of the endless rules, restrictions, and ceremonies of an outer religion that binds and leads to death (see Rom. 7:9, 10), there is the real serving of God in Spirit, which leads to life, to all good (see II Cor. 3:6).

Libertines, lĭb'-ẽr-tĭnes (Lat.)—*freedmen.*

Libertines was a term that was applied by the Jews to persons who had not been born into the Jewish faith but had taken it up by adoption. The Libertines mentioned in Acts 6:9 are thought to have been Jews who had been made slaves by the Romans and, upon being set free afterward, returned to Jerusalem. In the Bible text they were cited among those who disputed with Stephen and stirred up the people against him, thus being instrumental in causing him to be stoned to death.

Meta. Fixed states of thought in the realm of sense, that rise up and oppose the progress of spiritual ideas.

Libnah, lĭb'-năh (Heb.)—*white; clean; pure; brilliant; clear; transparent.*

a A place where the Children of Israel camped while in the wilderness (Num. 33:20). b A city in Canaan that was taken by Joshua and became a city of Judah (Josh. 10:29; 15:42). It was given over to the Levites (Josh. 21:13).

Meta. Purity and clearness of thought.

Libni, lĭb'-nī (Heb.)—*whiteness; pu-*

rity; distinguished; unto the son mine; for building up.

a Son of Gershon, who was a son of Levi (Exod. 6:17). **b** A grandson of Merari, son of Levi (I Chron. 6:29). These two men are thought to be the same person, some error having been made in I Chron. 6:29.

Meta. Constructive thoughts (*for building up*), in the love consciousness (descendants of Levi) of the awakening individual, that are *distinguished* by their *purity, whiteness,* by their being unadulterated by personal, limited, carnal, and material ideas.

Libnites, lĭb'-nītes (fr. Heb.)—*of or belonging to Libni.*

Descendants of Libni, son of Gershon (Num. 3:21).

Meta. Thoughts that spring from that in consciousness which Libni signifies. (See LIBNI.)

light.

Meta. Light is a symbol of intelligence. We cannot affirm too often, "*I am intelligence—I am the light of my world.*"

Libyans, lĭb'-ў-ănṣ (fr. Heb.)—*land of the Lubim; dried; parched; thirsty.*

People of Libya (Dan. 11:43). Libya is that portion of Africa bordering on the Mediterranean Sea and lying west of Egypt. The Hebrew name for Libya is Put, or Phut, and the Libyans are thought to have been descendants of Put, the son of Ham. They are also identified with Lubim.

Meta. See PUT and LUBIM.

Likhi, lĭk'-hī (Heb.)—*taken; laid hold of; passed on; learned; known; a portion; doctrine of Jah.*

Son of Shemida, descended from Manasseh (I Chron. 7:19).

Meta. A grasping by the conscious thought, a laying hold, and a taking to oneself for use in a practical way, of the principles of Truth (*doctrine of Jah*—one definition of doctrine being "a principle, . . . or the body of principles, in any branch of knowledge"—*taken, laid hold of, passed on, learned, known*).

Linus, lĭ'-nŭs (Gk.)—*flaxen; linen; clothing; wick of a lamp; net; lionlike.*

A Christian friend of Paul's at Rome who sent salutation to Timothy (II Tim. 4:21).

Meta. Net suggests a fisherman, and a fisherman suggests a person who seeks to win others to the Christ Truth, or, that in each awakened individual which works with diligence to bring all his thoughts and the whole of his organism into subjection to and harmony with the Christ mind. Jesus, in calling two of His disciples—Simon Peter and Andrew—who were fishermen, said, "Come ye after me, and I will make you fishers of men. And they straightway left the nets, and followed him" (Matt. 4:19, 20).

Linus symbolizes the inner courage, fearlessness, initiative, life, and energy (*lionlike*) that are necessary in the teaching and training (the *clothing*) of our thought people, to the end that our entire being may be changed into the likeness of pure Spirit. "Be ye transformed by the renewing of your mind" (Rom. 12:2).

Lion (Rev. 5:5).

Meta. Courage, fearlessness, initiativeness, life.

We must have the courage to enter fearlessly into the overcoming life and into the understanding of things. But courage alone will not do. We must have reverence of spiritual things—a devotional attitude—in order to receive spiritual inspiration. The phrase, "of the tribe of Judah," bespeaks this reverential nature and attitude.

Jesus Christ purified His substance and His life and lifted them up until His life became a pure stream of divine life to cleanse us. The 5th chapter of Revelation reveals the full inner meaning of the atonement, of Jesus Christ's redeeming work on earth. If we understand it fully we shall understand the inner working of the divine principle in its redeeming work in our whole being.

The real spiritual life in race consciousness has been disregarded, put out of substance; so this Lamb of God—the original pure life and substance—appears to be slain in so far as the animal consciousness of man is concerned. But to our awakened and illumined thoughts, activities, and faculties it is the "Lion that is of the tribe of Judah"—a source of new life and substance—which we continually worship, praise, and love until we realize this new, all-conquering life more and more fully and perfectly. (The "Root of David" has reference to the love quality in its original purity. This is needed also. We must become rooted in love.)

The lions of Daniel 6:10-23 represent the savage thoughts that arise in us when we are accused wrongfully and know that we are innocent.

Lo–ammi, lŏ′–ăm′-mī (Heb.)—*not my people.*

A name that Hosea gave to his son to signify the casting off of Israel by Jehovah, because of its sins. "And *Jehovah* said, Call his name Lo–ammi; for ye are not my people, and I will not be your *God*" (Hos. 1:9).

Meta. The belief in and the sense of separation from God that come to every individual who allows his true, highest thoughts (Israelites) to become adulterated with the material, limited beliefs of the outer, personal, intellectual, sense man.

loaves and fishes (Matt. 15:32-38).

Meta. We get the practical lesson from the story of Jesus' increasing the loaves and fishes, by applying it within our own consciousness.

Eating symbolizes mental appropriation. The multitude to be fed is our thoughts. Man's food is the substance of Spirit. "Man shall not live by bread alone, but by every word that proceedeth out of the mouth of God." He partakes of the word of God by affirmation, and so eats of the sustaining substance of Spirit.

The "loaves" represent substance, and the "fishes" are ideas of increase.

Lod, lŏd (Heb.)—*division; conception; emanation; pregnancy; travail; nativity; birth; contest; cleavage; fissure; strife.*

A city of Benjamin (I Chron. 8:12). Its Greek name was Lydda. In the New Testament it is called Lydda.

Meta. The breaking up of an old group of thoughts, or thought habit in consciousness, that a renewal of the mind may be accomplished. In other words, the effort that the seemingly human mind expends in bringing forth new and higher ideas, or the strife and contention that

attend the breaking up of error that Truth may be brought to birth and take precedence (*division, conception, strife, travail, birth;* a city of Benjamin). (See Matthew 10:34. See LYDDA and ÆNEAS.)

Lo–debar, lō–dē′-bär (Heb.)—*without order; disorderly; no leader; not governed; rebellious; no shepherd; without pasture; no issue; barren; without speech; dumb; not the word or oracle; false; untrue.*

A city of Gilead to the east of the Jordan; it was the home of Machir the son of Ammiel. Machir cared for Jonathan's lame son, Mephibosheth, until David took him into his own house (II Sam. 9:4, 5; 17:27).

Meta. The *disorderly,* undisciplined, *barren,* substanceless (*without pasture*), and unillumined (*not the word or oracle*) state into which the consciousness of man comes when the personal will (Saul) has been exercised without restraint. (See MEPHIBOSHETH and MACHIR.)

Logos, lŏg′-ŏs, (Gk.).

Meta. "As used in John 1:1 it means the Word, symbolically referring to the creative law-giving, revealing activity of God," says Fallows.

In the Emphatic Diaglott, Logos is left unchanged in the first chapter of John where in other translations of the New Testament the term "Word" appears. The texts thus given read as follows: "In the Beginning was the Logos, and the Logos was with God, and the Logos was God. This was in the Beginning with God. Through it everything was done; and without it not even one thing was done, which has been done. In it was Life; and the LIFE was the LIGHT of MEN. . . . And the Logos became Flesh, and dwelt among us,—and we beheld his GLORY, a Glory as of an Only-begotten from a Father,—full of Favor and Truth" (John 1:1-4, 14).

Logos is the Christ, the Son, the divine light, the living Word, or Word of the Supreme, and it contains all potentiality; all things were made by it (Him). Man can appropriate all, or a part, as he chooses. Jesus expressed it in its fullness, and He became the Logos, or Word, made flesh. In other words, Jesus so unified Himself in thought, word, and deed with this inner Christ, Logos, Word, creative principle of God, in which are all the ideas in Divine Mind—life, substance, intelligence, wisdom, love, strength, power, that even His seemingly mortal or flesh body took on the divine nature and became immortal, was wholly transformed into Godlikeness, spirituality; thus throughout His entire being Jesus showed forth the glory and perfection of the Father. Those who follow Him can make this full attainment that He made, if they accept, as He did, the all-possibility of the Principle.

An understanding of the Logos reveals to us the law under which all things are brought forth—the law of mind action. The Divine Mind creates by thought, through ideas. Creation takes place through the operation of the Logos. God is thinking the universe into manifestation right now. The "beginning" is always now, since it has to do with the eternal, and not with time. The law of the divine creation is the order and harmony of perfect thought.

The Word, Logos, Thought of God, Son, or Christ, in which is the creative power of the Father-God, all-possibility, all-potentiality, the foundation principle, the true inner self of every individual, is ever associated with the Father in the glory of creating, and all men should "honor the Son even as they honor the Father," since the Father and the Son are one. This is just as true of the Logos, or Christ, in us as it was and is of the Logos, or Word, that became flesh in Jesus Christ. It is the idea of God, and the Father-Mind is always in its idea, just as the idea is in the Father-Mind. The mind that has begotten the idea, of course, is greater than the idea —"The Father is greater than I" (John 14:28, last clause), was the confession of the Christ in the perfected man, Jesus Christ. (See WORD.)

Lois, lō'-ĭs (Gk.)—*loosened; freed; agreeable; pleasing; better.*

Mother of Eunice, and grandmother of Timothy (II Tim. 1:5).

Meta. The very free, unbound, *pleasing* state, and high, superior quality (*better*), of the soul that is established in faith and Truth. (The "unfeigned faith" that Paul recognized in Timothy dwelt first in his grandmother Lois, and in his mother Eunice.)

Lo–ruhamah, lō–rụ'-hă-măh (Heb.)— *not soft; hardened; unsoothing; irritating; unloving; not merciful; without pity; not favored; not having found mercy.*

Hosea's daughter by his "wife of whoredom," Gomer. This daughter was symbolically named Lo–ruhamah to show that the Lord would not longer have mercy on the house of Israel, though He would still have mercy on the house of Judah (Hos. 1:6, 7).

Meta. The seemingly forsaken-by-God state of man's outer religious thoughts and activities (the house, or kingdom, of Israel here refers to the outer or conscious mind, while Judah refers to the inner or subjective consciousness) when man has, because of repeatedly breaking the law of God through willful disobedience, found himself apparently unable to lay hold of the saving, forgiving, healing, protecting, guiding power and presence of the Spirit of truth. When he gets into that state he must for the time being reap the result of his errors in sorrow and affliction—go into captivity.

Lord's Supper, the (Matt. 26:26-30).

Meta. God's covenant with mankind, through His perfect idea, Christ Jesus. This compact was completed through Jesus Christ's breaking the bread and blessing the cup. The bread symbolizes spiritual substance, or the body. The wine symbolizes the blood of Jesus Christ, or spiritual life.

By mentally eating the body of Jesus Christ and spiritually drinking His blood we appropriate in consciousness the imperishable substance and drink of the waters of eternal life.

We eat the body of Jesus Christ mentally, by affirming the one spiritual substance to be the substance of our body, and we drink His blood by affirming and realizing our oneness with the one divine, omnipresent life of Spirit.

Lot, lŏt (Heb.)—*covering; veiling; muffling; hidden; concealed; covert; secret; clandestine; black art; magic; sorcery; dark-colored; sad.*

Son of Haran, who was Abram's brother (Gen. 11:27, 31; 14:12).

Meta. The subjective or negative side of faith. Abram represents the expanding of faith in man's consciousness. When Abram went out to seek a new country in response to the call of Spirit, Lot went with him. Metaphysically interpreted this means that when faith expands in consciousness, begins to go out into a new country, its old subjective aspect goes with it and expands also.

When the division took place between Abram and Lot, Lot chose the "Plain of the Jordan, . . . like the land of Egypt, as thou goest unto Zoar" (Gen. 13:10). The Jordan here signifies equilibrium of forces, and Zoar means inferior. So we should beware how we link the I AM with faith that is established in the flesh. It is Lot, and is allied to the negative.

Lot, meaning *dark-colored, covering, hidden,* can also be said to symbolize the part of man's consciousness that is still in darkness—in other words, the natural or animal man.

It is related in Genesis 19:26 that when Lot's wife was fleeing from the destroyed cities of the plain, Sodom and Gomorrah, she looked back, and "became a pillar of salt." Salt is a preservative, corresponding to memory. When we remember the pleasures of the senses, and long for their return, we preserve the sense desire. This desire will manifest somewhere, sometime, unless the memory is dissolved through renunciation.

Lotan, lō'-tăn (Heb.) — *covered; wrapped up; hidden; secret; dark.*

Son of Seir the Horite (Gen. 36:20). He was a chief of the Horites, and his sister Timna was concubine to Eliphaz, Esau's son (see verses 12, 22, and 29 of the 36th chapter of Genesis).

Meta. A secret, hidden, ignorant ruling thought activity in the realm in man that the Horites symbolize. (See HORITES.)

love, divine, compared to personal love.

Meta. Love is a divine attribute; it is an idea in the one Mind. God is love and love is God, or a quality in Being. The difference between divine love and human love is that divine love is broad and unlimited, a universal and harmonizing power. Human love is based on personality and is selfish, lawless, and fickle.

In reality there is only one love; when man expresses divine love in limited ways he makes a separation in consciousness and his expression of love is personal instead of universal.

Divine love will establish one in fearlessness and courage, "For God gave us not a spirit of fearfulness; but of power and love and discipline."

By establishing ourselves in the consciousness of divine love and expressing that love at all times we are helped to fulfill the command, "Love your enemies, do good to them that hate you, bless them that curse you, pray for them that despitefully use you."

The development of divine love has its place in demonstrating supply. When love is established in the consciousness it will draw to us all that we require to make us happy and contented, all that really belongs to us.

We develop love in our heart by asking daily that the infinite love of the Father be poured out upon us; by praying, meditating, and affirming that we are one with and express at all times the perfect love of God.

Lubim, lū'-bĭm (Heb.)—*thirsty; dry; parched.*

A people who came with Shishak, king of Egypt, to fight against Jerusalem (II Chron. 12:3). Lubim is mentioned with the Ethiopians in II Chronicles 16:8, and with Egypt and the Ethiopians as helpers of Nineveh in Nahum 3:9. Lubim is identified with Lehabim and Libyans.

Meta. The *dry, thirsty, parched,* impoverished, feverish state of consciousness, body, and affairs that results from that which Lehabim signifies. (See LEHABIM.) A person must be very watchful that he does not give the substance of his higher, or spiritual, aspirations, thoughts, and desires (Israelites), to building up the material consciousness in himself. If he does, this great horde of darkened, ignorant, undisciplined thoughts and forces that Lubim and the Egyptians and Ethiopians signify will apparently spring up from everywhere and will bring him into bondage and affliction.

Lucius, lū'-ciŭs (Lat.)—*light; light bearer; illuminative; born of light.*

A prophet or teacher in the church at Antioch (Acts 13:1). In Romans 16:21 he is mentioned as being Paul's kinsman, and some think him to be the same person as Luke.

Meta. Lucius (*light, illuminative*) pertains to spiritual understanding and its expression in the awakening consciousness of man. The five prophets and teachers at Antioch, one of whom was Lucius of Cyrene, are the interpreters of Spirit to the outer or sense consciousness. (See LUKE.)

Lud, lŭd (Heb.)—*desire to bring forth; generative power; conception; pregnancy; travail; striving; emanating; bringing forth; creation; nativity; birth.*

Son of Shem, and grandson of Noah (Gen. 10:22; see also Isaiah 66:19 and Ezekiel 27:10). Lud is thought to have founded the kingdom of Lydia in Asia Minor; from him the Lydians get their name.

Meta. Shem is the son of Noah, who typifies the spiritual in man. Lud, son of Shem, is the beginning of man's concept of the truth that he is the offspring of God; that he came from Spirit instead of flesh (*nativity*). Thus a *desire to bring forth* on a higher plane is aroused within him. Because of his seemingly very material state, however, much *travail* of soul attends his efforts to bring to *birth* the higher ideals that have been conceived in him. In his first attempts to establish his higher, religious ideals he may strive and contend in a very material way. Later he learns the way of love and peace, and attains truer success.

Ludim (in A. V., Jer. 46:9, Lydians), lū'-dĭm (Heb.) — *travails; strivings; physical generation; conception; pregnancies; nativity; physical birth; childbirth.*

a Son of Mizraim, of the sons of Ham. b A people who were descended from Ludim (Gen. 10:13). The Ludim should not be identified with the Lydians, who were descended from Lud the son of Shem.

Meta. Man's material beliefs regarding his origination and the continuation of the race; also the expression of these beliefs. Such thoughts belong to the outer, mortal consciousness. (Ludim was a grandson of Ham, and Ham, one of Noah's three sons, signifies the physical in man.)

Luhith, lū'-hĭth (Heb.)—*polished; smoothed; made of slabs, i. e., of stone; made of planks, i. e., of wood; floored; tablet; table.*

An elevated place in Moab (Isa. 15:5; Jer. 48:5).

Meta. "For by the ascent of Luhith with continual weeping shall they go up; for at the descent of Horonaim they have heard the distress of the cry of destruction." Horonaim and Luhith both belong to carnal mind (Moab). Horonaim signifies a stirring up, by the power of the word of Truth, of man's deep-seated, subconscious errors regarding life and substance. Luhith bespeaks the bringing of these errors to the surface, or outer phase, of mind, that they may be eliminated from consciousness. Though this outer phase of consciousness (Luhith) has been disciplined in degree, brought into a degree of harmony (*polished, smoothed*), and so lifted up somewhat (an elevated place), it is still of the carnal mind (Moab) and must give way to true spiritual realization and expression.

Luke (in A. V., Philemon 24, Lucas), lūke (fr. Gk.)—*luminous; light-giving; enlightening; instructing.*

A Christian who traveled much with Paul in his ministry. Luke is called a "physician," and is thought to be the writer of the Gospel of Luke and The Book of Acts (Col. 4:14).

Meta. Luke means *luminous, light-giving.* When one ceases to cling to material things, the luminous state of mind becomes abiding. After the worldly ideals (represented by Demas, Titus, Dalmatia, Crescens, in II Timothy 4:10-12) have disappeared, the overcomer finds the one luminous Presence left with him. It is then that new mental qualities come to take the places of the old ideas that were dropped. Mark, the shining one, is called after Tychicus, whose name means *fate,* has been sent away. One who learns the divine law is not subject to fate. He makes his own destiny by the use of the law.

In Colossians 4:14 Paul refers to Luke as "the beloved physician." Metaphysically this would indicate that Luke belongs especially to that phase of the intelligence that has to do with keeping the body well. As a missionary Luke carries the healing message to all parts of the body. Paul and Luke working together symbolize the converted will and spiritual illumination united in presenting the healing ministry of Jesus Christ to the entire being.

There is but one way to attain healing, wholeness; that is the way of the spiritual man, mystically called Jesus Christ. Luke, the illumined healing intelligence in us, is ever seeking to impress this truth more and more deeply on our consciousness and on the very cells of our body.

Luz, lŭz (Heb.)—*bending; inclining; turning away; departing; perversion; wickedness; a shrub bearing nuts; almond tree; hazel tree; bone.*

a The original name of Beth–el (Gen. 28:19). b A place named Luz was built in the land of the Hittites, by a man of the city of Luz that was renamed Beth–el. This man, with his family, was spared by the Israelites when they conquered Beth–el and destroyed its Canaanitish inhabitants (Judg. 1:23-26).

Meta. Beth–el means *house of God.* Luz means *separation.* In Luz we also find an idea of substance and strength (*almond tree, a shrub bearing nuts, bone*), but of a more or less material character because of the belief that man and his qualities are something separate from Spirit (*bending, turning away, departing*). That which at first we conceived to be apart from God, however, we find to be His very abode. The stone that Jacob had for a pillow no doubt seemed very hard and material, with no suggestion, to the outer senses, of anything of a spiritual nature. But when Jacob awoke out of his sleep, he said: "Surely Jehovah is in this place; and I knew it not. And he was afraid, and said, How dreadful is this place! this is none other than the house of God, and

this is the gate of heaven" (Gen. 28:16, 17). When the consciousness is first being awakened to the divine presence, a fear sometimes comes over one after some deep, inner realization of Spirit. This is because of the carnal that cannot stand in the presence of God, but must decrease as the Christ increases in consciousness.

Lycaonia, lўc-ȧ-ō'-nĭ-ȧ (Gk.)—*place of wolves; wolfland; a wolf; she-wolf; greedy; rapacious; devouring; cruel; destructive.*

A region of Asia Minor. Paul and Barnabas went to Lystra and Derbe, cities of Lycaonia, and preached the gospel of Christ (Acts 14:6-11).

Meta. We sometimes find within ourselves states of consciousness that have been inherited from the human side of parentage; for example, the belief in inefficiency. This belief symbolizes the man who is "impotent in his feet, a cripple from his mother's womb, who never had walked." The inefficiency is described as in the "feet," the feet being typical of the understanding. The region in which the disciples are represented as preaching is the wild, uncultured Lycaonia, which means *wolfland.* The people were nature worshipers, passionate and emotional. When Paul healed the lame man by gazing at him steadily and telling him to stand upright on his feet, the people at once cried out that the gods had come down to earth in the form of men. Barnabas they called Jupiter, and Paul they called Mercury. They proceeded to prepare a sacrifice of oxen in honor of these two men.

In the subconscious region of our own nature we find these inherited conditions holding in abeyance some natural function; these, when released by the word of Truth, liberate waves of emotion, which are not always wise or stable. The emotions are not to be depended on. They pour out a flood of praise and adoration one moment, and a whirlwind of censure the next. When they are not trained and established in divine understanding they are moved by every passing thought. The Lycaonians wanted to offer sacrifices to Paul and Barnabas as gods from heaven, but when the jealous

Jews made charges against Paul and Barnabas the Lycaonians turned right about; they stoned Paul into insensibility and dragged his body out of the city.

The lesson is: Watch your emotional nature. Do not esteem as miraculous, nor as of the gods, the great uplifts that come to you in moments of spiritual illumination. You are simply developing the inherent powers of your own being. Cultivate stability and poise of soul. Do not be blown about by every wind of doctrine, but quietly and dispassionately weigh in the balance of your own higher understanding every wave of thought that sweeps through your soul. Do not attribute the powers of your own spirit to some outside Godlike source. "Why do ye these things? We also are men of like passions with you, and bring you good tidings, that ye should turn from these vain things unto a living God."

The "multitude . . . saying in the speech of Lycaonia" means that all the undisciplined, unredeemed, and unconverted thoughts of the consciousness believed that something had been accomplished outside of natural law, and desired to make gods of the personalities through which the work was done. When this thought presents itself, one should declare the Truth of Being. Give all credit to the divine life and intelligence manifest in heaven and earth through the divine-natural law.

Lycia, lў'-ci-à (Gk.)—*wild; uncultivated; rapacious; greedy; devouring; inflaming; heating; destroying; wolfish.*

A district in Asia Minor, part of it projecting into the Mediterranean Sea. Paul, while being taken to Rome as a prisoner, came to Myra, a city of Lycia (Acts 27:5).

Meta. A state of consciousness that is very intense, emotional, *wild,* and *devouring* in its nature (*wolfish, rapacious, inflaming, destroying*).

Lydda, lўd'-dà (Gk. fr. Heb.)—*travail; contention; strife; pregnancy; childbirth.*

A town near Joppa. It was at Lydda that Æneas, a palsied man, was healed (Acts 9:32-38). Lydda is the Greek name for Lod. It is called Lod in the Old Testament.

Meta. Lydda, like Lod, means *travail, strife, contention, childbirth,* and signifies the great effort of the seemingly mortal in man that attends the breaking up of error and bringing to birth of Truth ideals in consciousness. Lydda refers to the center of bodily action of which the liver is the focal point. (See ÆNEAS, and LOD.)

Lydia, lўd'-ĭ-à (Gk. fr. Heb.)—*travail; contention; strife; conception; pregnancy; childbirth; offspring.*

A woman of Thyatira. She was "a seller of purple," and lived in Philippi. She accepted Paul's teaching and was baptized. Paul and Silas abode in her house while they were teaching in that city (Acts 16:14, 15).

Meta. The *travail* that the soul undergoes in conceiving and giving birth to spiritual ideals. Spiritual understanding is developed in the feminine realm of the soul. This is pictured in the words, "And a certain woman named Lydia, a seller of purple, of the city of Thyatira, one that worshipped God, heard us: whose heart the Lord opened to give heed."

Thyatira means *burning incense;* it represents the soul's intense desire for the higher expressions of life. When this inner urge comes forth with power (seller of purple) the Lord opens the heart and, like the disciples who said one to another, "Was not our heart burning within us, while he spake to us in the way, while he opened to us the scriptures?" we receive the heavenly message.

Lysanias, lў-sā'-nĭ-ăs (Gk.)—*loosening of bonds; ending of sadness; driving away sorrow.*

Tetrarch of Abilene when John the Baptist began his preaching to prepare the way for Jesus Christ (Luke 3:1).

Meta. The ruling thought in that which Abilene signifies (see ABILENE), at the time of one's first, or intellectual (John the Baptist), understanding of the Christ Truth, when one seeks to cleanse one's thoughts and habits and to make oneself a fit conscious dwelling place for the Christ. Thus Lysanias becomes in one an aid to the ending of sadness and to the driving away of sorrow.

Lysias, lўs'-ĭ-ăs (Gk.)—*loosening; dis-*

solving; relaxing; breaking bonds; freeing; liberating.

Claudius Lysias was the chief captain of the Roman guard at Jerusalem. He took Paul from the mob of Jews who were trying to kill him because of his preaching the gospel of Christ. Lysias sent Paul to the Roman governor, Felix, at Cæsarea (Acts 23:26; 24:22).

Meta. A phase of the outer, intellectual, sense will (chief captain of the Roman guard in Jerusalem) in a *relaxing,* letting-go (*liberating, dissolving*) attitude. This comes about by the will's contact with the spiritual peace center in consciousness (Jerusalem). The result of this attitude of the outer will, which is seemingly in command here, is that the word of Truth (Paul) is released from one's old, fixed, formal, narrow religious thoughts that are seeking to put the real Truth out of consciousness (the Jews who were trying to kill Paul).

Lystra, lȳs'-trȧ (Gk.)—*that liberates; that dissolves; that frees.*

A city of Lycaonia, where Paul and Barnabas preached and where they healed the crippled man who was "impotent in his feet" (Acts 14:6, 8).

Meta. When one has received the spirit of peace and praise, and starts out in spiritual ministry with one's vision fixed on the idea of one Presence and one Power, adverse thoughts and conditions begin to disappear. In Acts 14:8-20 this dissolving influence is mentioned symbolically as Lystra. However, often in the dissolving process one may awaken antagonism, and therefore meet with opposition (Antioch). If one relinquishes one's steadfast vision of the one Presence and one Power, and becomes observant of opposition or adversity, one's growing spiritual consciousness seems to be stoned to death. But the spiritual consciousness cannot be destroyed. It revives at the first opportunity.

In meeting opposition, both within oneself and in the outer world, one should remember that Spirit does not arouse combativeness. Opposition comes from the personal. By one's keeping one's vision steadfastly in harmony with the one Presence and one Power, one can cause adversity to disappear in divine order, and the freedom of the whole man will result. As one's consciousness is thus clarified these same principles become effective in one's outer ministry.

Certain words in Acts 15:41 and 16:1 (Cilicia, meaning *treacherous;* Derbe, *harsh, stinging;* and Lystra, *that dissolves*) indicate that the work of Paul and Silas required great effort and that it was not altogether pleasant. We find that forceful thoughts often stir up opposition, while gentle thoughts bring a peaceful victory.

M

Maacah (A. V., in most instances, Maachah), mā'-ȧ-cȧh (Heb.) — *squeezed; compressed; depressed; emasculated; pressed down; worn.*

a Mother of Absalom, David's son. She was the daughter of Talmai, king of Geshur (II Sam. 3:3). **b** Daughter of Abishalom and mother of Asa, king of Judah. Asa removed her from her office as queen mother "because she had made an abominable image for an Asherah; and Asa cut down her image, and burnt it at the brook Kidron" (I Kings 15:10, 13). **c** Father of Achish, king of Gath (I Kings 2:39). **d** Father of Hanan, one of David's mighty men (I Chron. 11:43).

Meta. The women named Maacah symbolize very negative, depressed thoughts that belong to the sense consciousness in man. The men by this name take on more of an aggressively oppressive character. Maacah the father of Achish, king of Gath, a Philistine ruler, is of the outer-sense man. Maacah the father of Hanan, one of David's warriors, would relate to that in man which oppresses or takes authority over error thoughts, habits, and limitations.

Maacathites (in A. V., Deuteronomy 3:14, Maachathi), mȧ-ăc'-ȧ-thītes (Heb.) —*of* or *belonging to Maacah.*

Some of the Maacathites were people of Maacah, or Beth–maacah, of the tribe of Naphtali; others were enemies of Israel. According to Fallows these latter were the people of the kingdom of Maacah, or Syria (Deut. 3:14; Josh. 12:5; II Sam. 23:34; II Kings 25:23).

Meta. Thoughts (people) of oppression and depression, belonging to the states of consciousness in us represented by the city of Maacah in Naphtali, and the kingdom of Maacah in Syria.

Maadai, mā'-ă-dāi (Heb.) — *from adornment of Jehovah; Jah is ornament; ornament of Jehovah; precept of Jehovah; from the testimony of Jah.*

Son of Bani (Ezra 10:34).

Meta. The *ornament of Jehovah* is man established in and manifesting the Christ righteousness, grace, mercy, Truth. Maadai signifies the Christ righteousness and Truth as coming forth into expression in the individual consciousness from within. As we come into spiritual understanding and express the Christ Truth (*precept of Jehovah*) more and more fully in our life, our path becomes a path of pleasantness and peace; we become living testimony to this Truth that frees, testimony that can be seen and read by all men. "I will greatly rejoice in Jehovah, my soul shall be joyful in my God; for he hath clothed me with the garments of salvation, he hath covered me with the robe of righteousness, as a bridegroom decketh himself with a garland, and as a bride adorneth herself with her jewels" (Isa. 61:10).

Maadia¹ mā-ă-dī'-ăh (Heb.)—*from Jehovah's adornment; Jah is ornament; precept of Jehovah; from the testimony of Jah.*

A priest who returned with Zerubbabel from the Babylonian captivity (Neh. 12:5).

Meta. See MAADAI.

Maai, mā'-āi (Heb.)—*belly; bowels; womb; inmost part of a thing; heart; affection; mercy; Jah is compassionate.*

An Israelite, of the sons of the priests, one of the musicians who assisted at the dedication of the rebuilt wall of Jerusalem (Neh. 12:36).

Meta. Maai bespeaks the tender mercy and compassion of Jehovah (*Jah is com-*

passionate, merciful), the Christ or Father-Mind, expressing in man.

The *bowels* (*belly*) are closely associated with the idea of compassion and mercy. In I John 3:17 and in Colossians 3:12, in the Authorized, or King James, Version, we read of "bowels *of compassion*" and "bowels of mercies." (See also Philippians 1:8 and 2:1, in the Authorized Version.) Cruelty of some kind, or else weak, negative, human sympathy, is at the back of bowel troubles. Those who through affirmations of Truth and willingness to do the will of God fill themselves with strong, true, tender, Christ compassion, mercy, and love for all persons and all creatures, including themselves, never have bowel trouble.

Maarath, mā'-ă-răth (Heb.)—*blind; cavernous; darkness; denuded; naked; bared; opened; uncovered; empty; barren; waste.*

A city in the hill country of Judah (Josh. 15:59).

Meta. A sense of a lack of light, understanding, substance; a sense of emptiness, negativeness, and possibly of sadness or gloom (*blind, naked, bared, empty, barren, waste*), that one may sometimes feel if one is slow about affirming that which is good and true in order to fill the vacuum that has been made in consciousness by putting away some seemingly strongly intrenched error. Denials of error should be accompanied by affirmations of the desired good, and by much thanksgiving and praise to God, the good, that a right balance may be kept in consciousness. Then one will not experience anything of the nature of that which the city of Maarath represents.

Maasai (A. V., Maasiai), mā-ăs'-āi (Heb.)—*work of Jehovah; Jehovah's creation; fruits of Jah's labor.*

A priest of Israel, son of Adiel (I Chron. 9:12).

Meta. Maasai means *work of Jehovah.* The man was an Israelitish priest. The mission of the true, priestly thoughts in us is to carry out Jehovah's work. This work is to bring the God man in us into perfect expression; it is to finish, to perfect in manifestation, the man whom God made in His likeness—the spiritual or ideal man. We can work the works of God, Jesus tells us in John 6:29, by believing on Him whom He sent; in other words, by believing on the Christ, or Jehovah, who is the real, true, inner, ideal man or self of each of us. When we understand this and believe in our own indwelling Christ, who is our light and life, our "hope of glory," we open our consciousness and body to the activity of Spirit in and through us. Then Jehovah can accomplish His work of bringing forth into outer manifestation in us the perfect ideal man, the Christ.

Maaseiah, mā-ă-sē'-ïah (Heb.)—*work of Jehovah; Jehovah's creation; fruits of Jah's labor.*

There were several Israelites by this name. Among them were priests, chiefs, and princes (I Chron. 15:18, 20; II Chron. 23:1; 26:11; 28:7; 34:8; Ezra 10:18, 21; Neh. 11:5).

Meta. See MAASAI.

Maath, mā'-ăth (Gk. fr. Heb.)— *smooth; naked; polished; sharpened; removed; scraped off; scrap; small; little; few.*

Son of Mattathias, in the genealogy of Jesus Christ (Luke 3:26).

Meta. A refining process (*smooth, polished, sharpened*) in consciousness, by which seeming error, the personal and carnal in the individual, is *removed,* (*scraped off*) and becomes very *small,* very insignificant.

Maaz, mā'-ăz (Heb.)—*anger; wrath; counselor.*

Son of "Ram the first-born of Jerahmeel," of the tribe of Judah (I Chron. 2:27).

Meta. The name of Ram, father of Maaz, means *made high, elevated;* some identify the name with Aram. Aram (*high, exalted*) is the same as Syria, and refers to the intellect in man. While Ram and Aram are not the same name in the Hebrew, yet the *high, elevated* character of thought that Ram signifies must have something of the intellectual as well as the spiritual. Otherwise it could not bring forth in consciousness an idea corresponding to that which Maaz represents.

The advice, or teaching (*counselor*— Maaz) of intellectual thought leads to a divided mind, to a belief in the necessity of resistance, defense, and a fighting, warring attitude at times (*anger, wrath*), as well as love and peace. The intellect leads man to believe in the wrath and anger of God instead of knowing Him as God of love and good only. Spiritual understanding brings us to the singleness of heart and mind wherein we know the omnipresent and omnipotent God as nothing but good.

Maaziah, mā-ă-zī'-äh (Heb.)—*strength of Jehovah; fortitude of Jah; Jah is the bulwark; Jehovah's consolation.*

a A priest in the time of David who was allotted the twenty-fourth course in Temple service (I Chron. 24:18). **b** One of those who joined Nehemiah in sealing the covenant (Neh. 10:8).

Meta. Inherent religious tendencies of ours (priests; see LEVITES) that lay hold of, become unified with, our inner, spiritual strength, stability, endurance, and comforting power (*strength of Jehovah, fortitude of Jah, Jah is the bulwark, Jehovah's consolation*), and impart them to our consciousness.

Macedonia, măç-ĕ-dō'-nĭ-à (Gk.)—*extended; elevation; adoration; burning.*

A country north of Greece. At the time of Paul it was a Roman province. Paul did much preaching there (Acts 16:9; 20:1-3).

Meta. When the thoughts of man turn adoringly toward God, spiritual zeal and enthusiasm are awakened and these set the whole consciousness into constructive activity.

Fervor, intensity, and vehemence are required in order to carry the great and beautiful message of Truth over seeming hindrances to the different centers and states of consciousness (represented by the cities and nations through which Paul journeyed and preached). Macedonia signifies the enthusiasm and the energy of Spirit, which set the whole man aflame. It is necessary that this phase of the consciousness be cultivated, because without it a passivity sets in that makes one content with the battle only half won.

Man should stir up this fiery power when he finds himself getting into negative states of consciousness. The vision of the man imploring, "Come over into

Macedonia, and help us," is the discernment of the need of stirring up this inner fervor, this great consuming desire of the soul for spiritual understanding and power.

Macedonian, măç-ĕ-dō'-nĭ-ăn (fr. Gk.). An inhabitant or a native of Macedonia (Acts 27:2).

Meta. A thought belonging to the phase of consciousness that Macedonia symbolizes. (See MACEDONIA.)

Machbannai (A. V., Machbanai), măch'-băn-nāi (Heb.)—*what like my son?; stout; thick; fat; cloak of Jah; chain of Jah.*

A Gadite, a mighty man of valor, who joined David in his stronghold in the wilderness and became one of his captains (I Chron. 12:13).

Meta. A thought of power, in consciousness (a Gadite, a mighty man of valor). Though somewhat material in character as yet (*fat, thick*), it takes refuge in Jehovah, I AM, and is firm and strong (*cloak of Jah, stout, chain of Jah*). Thus turned to Truth, it unifies itself with love (David) and aids in establishing the dominion of love in consciousness. (Machbannai helped to protect David and to make him king of Israel.)

Machbena (A. V., Machbenah), măch'-bĕ-nà (Heb.)—*pallium; cloak; cowl; mantle; knob; lump; hump; hillock.*

Either a son of Sheva, of the tribe of Judah, or a place founded by him (I Chron. 2:49).

Meta. Ideas of substance somewhat exalted in character, but irregular, not equalized in consciousness or really established in right relation at this stage of individual unfoldment (*lump, knob, hump, hillock*). These ideas serve as a *cloak,* or covering to the consciousness, while true equilibrium, order, the perfect rounding out of substance and of Truth, is being established.

Machi, mā'-chī (Heb.)—*smiting; wounding; slaying; afflicting; decreasing; consuming of strength; pining away; poor.*

Father of Geuel of the tribe of Gad. Geuel was the man chosen from that tribe to aid in spying out the land of Canaan (Num. 13:15).

Meta. The natural reaction in man when his power faculty is used as a destructive force (Machi was of the tribe of Gad, and Gad refers to the power faculty in man). Man can never abide consciously in overcoming power, strength, and dominion until he develops true understanding, love, good judgment, and the other faculties of the mind, and expresses power in right relation to them. Having done that, he will be constructive in all of his activities, and his reaping will be good.

Machir, mā'-chĭr (Heb.)—*sold; purchased; acquired; gotten; enslaved.*

a The first-born son of Manasseh (Gen. 50:23; Josh. 17:1). b Son of Ammiel, in Lo–debar. He took care of Mephibosheth, the crippled son of Jonathan, until David took him to his home (II Sam. 9:4).

Meta. Machir (*sold, acquired,* imparting, receiving) represents the balance that must actively exist in us if we are abidingly to possess true understanding and strength. (Manasseh, father of one Machir, represents understanding; Ammiel, father of the other Machir, symbolizes the strength of spiritual ideas in consciousness.) There must be a balance in gaining both true understanding and strength; also in conscious increase of all the other spiritual qualities. We must both receive of Spirit within us, and give out, or use, what we have received, in building up our own soul and body in Truth, and in helping others. Thus a right balance is attained and we become firmly established in those qualities. If a proper balance is not maintained, a sense of limitation or bondage (*enslaved*) results.

Machirites, mā'-chĭr-ītes (fr. Heb.)—*of* or *belonging to Machir.*

Descendants of Machir the son of Manasseh (Num. 26:29).

Meta. Thoughts springing from and belonging to that in consciousness which Machir the son of Manasseh represents. (See MACHIR.)

Machnadebai, măch-nă-dē'-bāi (Heb.) —*gift of the noble; what is like the liberal?; what is like the spontaneous gift of Jehovah?*

An Israelite named as one "of the sons

of Bani"; he had taken a foreign wife, but put her away at the command of Ezra (Ezra 10:40).

Meta. The consciousness beginning to awaken to a perception of the liberality and nobility of Spirit; to the broadmindedness, generosity, bigness, and splendidness of spiritual understanding and Truth.

When man first begins to throw off the narrow restrictions and prejudices of the personal, he is liable to go to the other extreme and make a union with sense desires (Machnadebai married a foreign wife). But if he really has hold of Truth he willingly relinquishes all error desires, that he may make the greatest of all attainments—the putting on of the Christ. (Machnadebai gave up his foreign wife at the command of Ezra.)

Machpelah, măch-pē'-lăh (Heb.)— *double (cave); equally divided; double; twofold; manifold; folding; winding; spiral form; portion; part.*

A field, "before Mamre (the same is Hebron)," that Abraham bought from Ephron of the children of Heth. Abraham buried Sarah in a cave in this field; later he, Isaac, Rebekah, Leah, and Jacob were buried there (Gen. 23:19; 25: 9; 49:29—50:13).

Meta. Subconscious body substance (a field, in which there was a cave). Abraham and the others who were buried in this cave represent higher awakening thought activities in us. When these thoughts have done their work in the conscious realm of our mind, for the time being they give way to other succeeding activities of the mind, while they sink back into the subconsciousness. There they take deep root in substance and continue their work, which is not apparent to the outer, conscious, thinking phase of mind. They work out into the body consciousness, thus aiding in raising the whole organism to a higher plane of expression.

Madai, mā'-dāi (Heb.) — *Media; Medes; sufficiency; measurability; indefinite capacity; middle portion; medium.*

a Son, or descendants, of Japheth (Gen. 10:2). Madai refers to Media or the Medes.

Meta. The phase of being in man that lies between the outer or conscious thinking mind and the superconscious mind, or Spirit (*middle portion*); the psychic realm.

Madmannah, măd-măn'-năh (Heb.)— *dunghill; manure heap.*

A city of southern Judah (Josh. 15: 31; see I Chron. 2:49 also).

Meta. A thought center deep within the subconscious mind that receives from the conscious mind, preparatory to casting it entirely from the consciousness and the body, that which the individual has denied and has thus released from his thoughts as being no longer of value to him (*dunghill, manure heap;* Paul says, concerning those personal and sensate, carnal things of which he suffered the loss, that he counted them but refuse—A. V., dung—that he might gain Christ.

Madmen, măd'-měn (Heb.)—*dunghill; manure heap.*

A place in Moab that Jeremiah mentions in his prophecy of the destruction of Moab (Jer. 48:2).

Meta. The very low opinion (*dunghill*) that the carnal mind in man (Moab) entertains concerning man's true, higher, religious or spiritual, consciousness (Israel). This opinion must be cast out by the word of Truth (sword). "Thou also, O Madmen, shalt be brought to silence; the sword shall pursue thee."

Madmenah, măd-mē'-năh (Heb.)— *dunghill; manure heap.*

A town of Benjamin, north of Jerusalem. It is named as one of the towns that would be destroyed by the Assyrians in their march against Jerusalem (Isa. 10:31).

Meta. The significance is virtually the same as that of Madmen, except that Madmenah, a town of Benjamin, refers to the attitude that our active faith in God (Benjamin) has toward the lesser thoughts and activities of the personal, or outer, carnal man. When man allows the thoughts of the intellect guided by the senses (Assyrians) to possess the consciousness, he changes his attitude of mind toward both the personal and the spiritual. He then belittles that (the spiritual) which he cannot contact with the senses, and magnifies the things of the outer. Thus this Madmenah of Benjamin, near Jerusalem, becomes a "fugitive."

Madon, mā'-dŏn (Heb.)—*contention; quarrel; strife; from Dan; place of judgment; extension; measure; vestment; garment.*

A city of Canaan that was captured by Joshua. Its king was Jobab (Josh. 11:1; 12:19).

Meta. The established belief of the outer man that he must contend for his rights; that he will receive justice only by striving for it in a personal way (*contention, strife, quarrel, from Dan, place of judgment*). Madon's being conquered by Joshua bespeaks the introduction of a higher idea of justice into this thought realm, thus enlarging the vision and clothing the consciousness with true judgment (*extension, vestment, garment*).

Magadan (A. V., Magdala), măg'-ā-dăn (Gk. fr. Heb.)—*elevation; tower; fortress; castle; greatness.*

A village on the west shore of the Sea of Galilee (Matt. 15:39). It is thought to have been the birthplace of Mary Magdalene, and is probably the same place as Migdal–el, of Naphtali (Josh. 19:38).

Meta. Exalting and magnifying strength in consciousness (a village of Naphtali, and meaning *elevation, tower, castle, fortress, greatness*).

Magbish, măg'-bĭsh (Heb.)—*gathering; kneading together; agglutination; stiffening; amassing; a hump; a height.*

The "children," descendants, or inhabitants of Magbish, to the number of one hundred and fifty-six, returned with Zerubbabel from the Babylonian captivity (Ezra 2:30). Magbish is thought to have been a place rather than a person, a place in the Benjamite territory in Palestine.

Meta. That in man's higher consciousness which attracts, gathers together, unifies, conserves (*gathering, kneading together, amassing, a height*). This quality leads to one's being reëstablished in substance and Truth after having been entangled in sense confusicn (captured by the Babylonians).

Magdalene, măg-dă-lē'-nĕ (Gk. fr. Heb.)—*of* or *from Magadan* or *Migdal–el.*

The surname of one of the Marys who followed Jesus. The name no doubt indicates Magadan, where she was born and lived (Matt. 27:56; Luke 8:2).

Meta. A thought springing from and belonging to that in consciousness which Magadan signifies. (See MAGADAN.)

Mary Magdalene was the woman out of whom Jesus cast seven demons. She became one of His most devoted followers. A lifting up of power in consciousness, and letting this greatly increased faculty be guided by the emotions and desires of the human soul, may invite demons, or seemingly established error thought activities and habits, that need the power of the Christ word to dissolve their hold on the soul and set the individual free.

Magdiel, măg'-dĭ-ĕl (Heb.)—*excellence of God; most precious fruits of God; praise of God; God is renowned; God's most precious gift.*

A chief of Edom, descended from Esau (Gen. 36:43).

Meta. Esau and Edom signify the outer physical consciousness and organism of man. Magdiel indicates the truth about the outer and seemingly material phase of man's being. This truth is that even man's apparently physical body is the precious fruit of God. It has its origin in Spirit, and is innately spiritual. It must eventually express and manifest God, Spirit, thus giving all praise, honor, and glory to the Father-Mind through which it came into existence (*God is renowned*).

Magog, mā'-gŏg (Heb.)—*region of Gog; from the upper, i. e., north; elasticity; extreme extension; ample covering; enlargement.*

Son of Japheth, who was one of Noah's three sons (Gen. 10:2). A "land" or a nation against which Ezekiel prophesied (Ezek. 38:2). "Gog and Magog" are used symbolically in Revelation 20:8.

Meta. See GOG.

Magor-missabib, mā'-gôr-mĭs'-să-bĭb (Heb.)—*fear all round; fear everywhere; terror is about; terror on every side.*

A name that Jeremiah gave to Pashhur, who had smitten him and put him in the stocks (see Jer. 20:1-4).

Meta. "For thus saith Jehovah, Behold, I will make thee a terror to thyself, and to all thy friends; and they shall fall by the sword of their enemies, and thine eyes shall behold it" (Jer. 20:4).

Pashhur, whom Jeremiah renamed Magor–missabib, signifies that in man which perceives the goodness of God, and expects all good without conforming to the divine law. Pashhur means *liberation, freedom, prosperity round about.* When a man perceives the good and builds up his faith in receiving good, yet does not conform to the divine law of good in love, mercy, right living, obedience to Truth, the time comes when his faith will no longer work for him; the fruition of his error sowing overtakes him. Then great fear assails him, for, turn whichever way he may, he can see no way out of the seeming evil—this is Magor–missabib.

Magpiash, măg'-pĭ-ăsh (Heb.)—*collector of a star cluster; driven together in a cluster; plague of moths; moth-killer.*

One who joined Nehemiah in sealing the covenant (Neh. 10:20).

Meta. Stars signify truths that are as yet very dimly apprehended. Magpiash (*collector of a star cluster, driven together in a cluster, moth-killer*), a priest or chief of the Israelitish people, who joined Nehemiah in sealing the covenant, pertains to an innate Truth ideal in consciousness that grasps and attempts to unify itself with higher light than it can immediately assimilate. In the power that it gains through this light, however, the consciousness becomes more unified with Spirit by putting away the error thoughts that are destructive to man's actual living of the measure of Truth that he knows.

It is necessary that man should think, speak, and act according to his highest concepts of Truth; by doing this he weaves for himself a robe of righteousness—becomes clothed with light as with a garment. Moths eat garments, and so, by being a destroyer of those error, limited thought activities in the consciousness that tend to keep one from living in conformance with Truth, this high ideal that Magpiash represents can

be said to be a *moth-killer.*

Mahalaleel (A. V., Maleleel), mă-hă'-lă-lē-ĕl (Gk. fr. Heb.)—*mighty rising; glory of brightness; mighty exaltation; raise a joyous shout to God; praise of God; splendor of God.*

Father of Jared and son of Cainan, named in the genealogy of Jesus Christ (Luke 3:37).

Meta. Man expressing his innate tendency to praise God, to hold to the light, to the good. To exalt God in consciousness is very uplifting to the individual.

Mahalalel (A. V., Mahalaleel), mă-hă'-lă-lĕl (Heb.)—*mighty rising; glory of brightness; mighty exaltation; raise a joyous shout to God; praise of God; splendor of God.*

a Son of Kenan, and father of Jared (Gen. 5:12-17). b A man of Judah (Neh. 11:4).

Meta. Like Mahalaleel, Mahalalel signifies that in man which praises and blesses and glorifies God, the good. It is the higher Judah attitude, the attitude of praise and prayer in expression.

Mahalath, mă'-hă-lăth (Heb.)—*beautifully adorned; mild; smooth; pleasing to the touch; rhythmic movements; sweet, harmonious sounds; dancers; singers; cithara; harp; lyre.*

a Daughter of Ishmael, who became a wife of Esau (Gen. 28:9). b Daughter of Jerimoth, the son of David; she became Rehoboam's wife (II Chron. 11:18).

Meta. A peaceful, harmonious, light, rhythmically active, and tuneful attitude of the soul, expressing on the carnal or human plane of the soul consciousness, and also on a higher and more enlightened plane.

Mahanaim, mă-hă-nā'-ĭm (Heb.)—*two camps; two hosts; encampments; armies; hosts.*

a The place where the angels of God met Jacob when he was on his way to meet and be reconciled to his brother Esau (Gen. 32:1, 2). b A place in Israel from which Ahinadab was to gather provisions for Solomon's household for one month in each year (I Kings 4:14).

Meta. Mahanaim, in individual consciousness, pertains to spiritual ideas and the mental realm of man—*two hosts.* This significance is brought out very clearly in the naming of the place by Jacob: "And Jacob went on his way, and the angels of God met him. And Jacob said when he saw them, This is God's host: and he called the name of that place Mahanaim" ("That is, *Two hosts,* or, *Companies,*" margin). These refer to the angels of God (representing spiritual ideas) and to Jacob and his company, his wives, children, and possessions (signifying the mentality of man). Esau, to whom Jacob was going, symbolizes the body.

By means of thinking we get into conscious touch with Spirit so that we may receive and appropriate the ideas of substance and life—spiritual food—that become the very life and substance of the whole organism. Thus we are truly fed, since through our thoughts we also make conscious union with our body and declare Truth for it.

Mahaneh–dan, mā'-hă-nĕh-dăn (Heb.) —*encampment of Dan; camp of judgment; host of judgment; inclined unto judgment.*

A place just back of Kiriath–jearim, where the Danite warriors camped after they started out to take Laish (Judg. 18: 12).

Meta. The judgment faculty (Dan) in temporary session (*camp of judgment, inclined unto judgment*) in Kiriath-jearim of Judah, or illumination and praise, preparatory to a further establishment of the power of discernment and discrimination (*judgment*) throughout the consciousness.

Maharai, mā'-hă-rāi (Heb.)—*hasty; quick; swift; prompt; apt; skilled; impetuous; hurried; precipitate; rash; headlong.*

"The Netophathite," one of David's guard (II Sam. 23:28).

Meta. A quickness of thought and action, based on spiritual intelligence and ability (*quick, swift, prompt, apt, skilled*) but with a very human tendency, as yet, to rush *headlong,* without due deliberation (*impetuous, hasty, rash*).

Mahath, mā'-hăth (Heb.)—*taking; grasping; fire pan; censer; breaking in pieces; extinguishing; dissolution; destruction; ruin; consternation; terror; wiping out; erasing.*

Two Kohathite Levites (I Chron. 6:35; II Chron. 29:12). The Mahath of I Chronicles 6:35 is thought to be the same as Ahimoth of the 25th verse.

Meta. Like Ahimoth, breaking up and disorganizing seeming error in consciousness (*breaking in pieces, destruction, dissolution*); also mentally laying hold of higher ideals (*taking, grasping*). *Fire pan, censer,* definitions of Mahath, suggest transmutation too.

Mahavite, mā'-hă-vīte (fr. Heb.)— *live messenger; marrowy; preservation of life; living substance.*

Eliel the Mahavite was one of David's warriors (I Chron. 11:46).

Meta. A *messenger* is one who brings tidings; in consciousness a messenger is an enlightening thought.

Marrowy suggests one's most secret and innermost thoughts and tendencies, which can be discerned and brought to light only by Spirit through the spoken word (see Heb. 4:12). *Marrowy* also refers to the inner riches and substance upon which the soul may feed and be satisfied (Psalms 63:5); and abundant supply for the whole man (Isa. 25,:6). To "fear Jehovah, and depart from evil" is "marrow to thy bones" (Prov. 3:7, 8; "*refreshing, moistening,*" margin).

Mahavite, meaning *live messenger, marrowy, preservation of life, living substance,* signifies the enlightening idea of Spirit—man's all-sufficient life, inspiration, substance of supply—as entering into one's ruling love consciousness (Eliel the Mahavite was a warrior of David's, and David represents love as ruling in man).

Mahazioth, mă-hā'-zĭ-ŏth (Heb.)—*visions; oracles; prophecies; revelations; divine communications.*

Son of Heman and a musician in the Temple, in David's reign (I Chron. 25:4, 30).

Meta. Clear seeing, keenness of perception, of comprehension; spiritual inspiration, expressing as harmony, order, rhythm, music, in individual consciousness.

Maher–shalal–hash–baz, mā'-hĕr-shăl'-ăl-hăsh'-băz (Heb.) — *hastening spoiler will hush and tear in pieces.* Maher—*hastening; speeding; rushing* *headlong.* Shalal—*spoiler; plunderer.* Hash—*hushed; still; quiet; silenced.* Baz—*pulled in pieces; squandered; despoiled; dissipated.*

A name symbolical of the very short time that was to elapse before Damascus and Samaria would be taken captive by the king of Assyria. This name was given by Isaiah to his son, symbolizing the fact that before the child was old enough to call his parents Father and Mother the spoiling of Samaria and Damascus would take place (Isa. 8:1).

Meta. The rapidity with which the law of cause and effect works. The two phases of the law are virtually one, certain causes being followed almost immediately by their corresponding effects, or results.

Mahlah (in A. V., I Chronicles 7:18, Mahalah), mäh'-läh (Heb.)—*polished; smoothness; sweet; pleasing; caressing; mildness; worn down; wasted; infirmity; disease; sickness; hurtful; deadly.*

a Daughter of Zelophehad the son of Hepher, of the tribe of Manasseh (Num. 26:33). **b** A child of Hammolecheth sister of Gilead, of the tribe of Manasseh (I Chron. 7:18).

Meta. Zelophehad, father of one of the persons named Mahlah, means *firstborn, first fracture,* while Hammolecheth, mother of the other Mahlah, means *the queen* and signifies the soul lifted up by spiritual thought.

Mahlah is the child, or result, of the illumined soul (Hammolecheth) combined with the rather negative thought (Zelophehad) that at this stage of individual unfoldment still finds place in the consciousness. This result is twofold in its nature: it expresses in error and inharmony (*disease, infirmity*), which often come from negativeness, and in the harmony and the healing (*sweet, pleasing, mildness*) that radiate from the spiritually illumined soul. One in this state is continually having error experiences, and being delivered from them. In order that one may abide in wholeness and peace, fear must be eliminated entirely and the mind must be established in spiritual understanding.

Mahli (A. V., Mahali), mäh'-lī (Heb.) —*smooth; pleasing; caressing; sweet;* mild; worn; weak; infirm; sickly; diseased; pining.*

Son of Merari, who was one of Levi's sons (Exod. 6:19).

Meta. A negative, drooping, *pining, sickly* thought in consciousness, which is the result of the *bitter,* excited state of mind that Merari, father of Mahli, signifies.

(Merari was a son of Levi, and Levi was the son of Jacob that represents the love faculty in man. That which Merari and Mahli signify is the result of the mistaken ideas that many persons hold regarding love. While they think that love is *pleasing* and *sweet,* they also think that it is a negative quality, altogether lacking in power, strength, energy, the positive forces that give man overcoming ability. Love, when directed by the selfishness of the personal man, brings bitterness or lack of poise and harmony into one's experiences, instead of the abiding peace, strength, courage, fearlessness, and good that are always the result of true love's expressing in consciousness.)

Mahlon, mäh'-lŏn (Heb.)—*mild; weakness; disease; sickness; sickly; wasting; pining.*

Son of Elimelech and Naomi, Israelites of Beth–lehem–judah; he was the husband of either Ruth or Orpah of Moab (Ruth 1:2).

Meta. See CHILION.

Mahol, mā'-hŏl (Heb.)—*circling; whirling; dancing; twisting; wresting; writhing; shaking; shuddering; travail; infirmity.*

Father of some wise men of Solomon's time (I Kings 4:31).

Meta. The play of the intellect in man, guided by the senses, by outer seeming, in thinking out problems (*dancing, twisting, wresting*). The intellect of man, unless inspired and directed by Spirit, works in a circle (*circling, whirling*), never really getting anywhere but always coming back to the point that it started from and ending in fearfulness and error (*shaking, shuddering, travail, infirmity*). To get a satisfactory, complete, healthy, wholesome understanding of anything, man must base his logic on Truth, the one beginning and source of all. Then he can reach a definite conclusion that will not be ultimately overthrown by some other and altogether different idea, as is the case with worldly wisdom wherein newer ideas are always following the older ones and showing up their utter fallacy.

maid, in A. V., damsel, having a spirit of divination (Acts 16:16-18).

Meta. An intuitive force, partly in spiritual consciousness but still bound in the personal or serpent consciousness; hence the continual crying out, "These men are servants of the Most High God, who proclaim unto you the way of salvation." This mind force is brought under subjection to Spirit by the power of the converted will. When Paul spoke the word, the serpent consciousness dropped away and the intuitive force was free to operate in the light of Spirit.

maiden.

Meta. The "little maiden" who had been captured by the Syrians from the Israelites (II Kings 5:1-14) typifies an offshoot of intuition, which may be designated as spiritual perception. It reveals that the prophet in Israel can heal Naaman, and impresses this on the king until he sends a letter to Israel's king about the matter. This is a symbolical description of the manner in which we transfer the perceptions of Truth to the various departments of the consciousness, and of how they are received. Israel's king is not conscious of spiritual power, although ruling in a realm where power is unlimited. The orthodox religious world is in the place of this king, who "rent his clothes, and said, Am I God, to kill and to make alive?" Ostensibly the orthodox religious world rules in Israel, but when asked to demonstrate the privileges promised to all who believe in the power of God, it makes excuses and attributes evil intentions, as did Israel's king, to those who think such things possible.

Makaz, mā'-kăz (Heb.)—*end; termination; extremity; objective; aim; ambition; hope.*

A place in Israel. It is named in the portion of Israel from which Ben–deker gathered supplies for Solomon's household for one month in each year (I Kings 4:9).

Meta. The significance of Makaz is given under Ben–deker, since the two names are so closely related in the text. (See BEN–DEKER.)

Makheloth, măk-hē'-lŏth (Heb.)—*convocations; assemblies; meetings.*

A camping place of the Children of Israel in the wilderness (Num. 33:25).

Meta. An *assembling* of one's truest, highest thoughts (Israelites) in the great wilderness of one's undisciplined consciousness, that a certain centralization or poise may be gained.

Makkedah, măk-kē'-dăh (Heb.)—*pointing; marking; selecting, i. e., for excellence; place of shepherds; place of herdsmen; herdsmen's place.*

Five kings were fleeing from Joshua. They hid in the cave at Makkedah, and were killed and buried there by Joshua (Josh. 10:16-28).

Meta. The consciousness perceiving through discrimination, judgment, the true spiritual quality of man's inner life, strength, and substance (*marking, selecting, i. e., for excellence, place of herdsmen, place of shepherds*). Thus the subconscious life and strength, or seemingly animal forces, are lifted up by the I AM, and transmuted into higher and more spiritual expression, while the Carnal, error thoughts that have ruled them are put away (Joshua killed the five heathen kings and buried them in a cave at Makkedah).

Maktesh, măk'-tĕsh (Heb.)—*pounding; mashing; crushing; grinding; mortar; depression; tooth socket; hollow.*

A district in or near Jerusalem, possibly a valley lying near the city, a place where merchants traded (Zeph. 1:11).

Meta. "Wail, ye inhabitants of Maktesh ["*The mortar,*" margin]; for all the people of Canaan ["*the merchant people,*" margin] are undone; all they that were laden with silver are cut off."

Webster tells us that a mortar is a strong bowllike vessel in which substances are pounded or rubbed with a pestle; also any of various devices in which materials are brayed or crushed, as in a stamp battery, the box into which the ore is fed.

Maktesh (*pounding, mashing, crush-*

ing, grinding, a mortar), a valley just out of Jerusalem where merchants traded, signifies in individual consciousness a place where there is an exchange of ideas regarding substance, life, understanding, and all the kinds and shades of thought that these merchants' wares represent in consciousness. In this place in mind, or state of mind, these ideas are threshed out; they are turned over and over in thought, are affirmed, denied, and undergo a regular siege of beating on the one hand and upholding on the other, until there is seemingly nothing left of them but a broken, confused state of mind.

This trading of ideas and opinions between the higher, more spiritual activities of our consciousness (Israelites) and the lower and more earthly sensate thoughts, such as are symbolized by the nations round about Israel, does not always result in good. It rather brings *depression* and confusion, and so it must come to an end, as is signified by the text.

Truth must be taught to the lower states of consciousness in us by the higher ideals, through the ministry of the I AM, which must always be kept in conscious dominion. Thus the valleys, the low, depressed and empty places in mind, will be lifted up. But they will never be lifted up so long as we attempt to reason out Truth with these earthly, limited phases of consciousness on their own error, ignorant plane. Truth can be seen aright from the spiritual plane only. "Come now, and let us reason together, saith Jehovah" (Isa. 1:18).

Malachi, măl'-ă-chī (Heb.)—*one sent of Jehovah; messenger of Jehovah; angel of Jehovah; angel of the Lord; prophet of Jah; minister; servant.*

The last of the minor prophets. Nothing is really known of him aside from his writings, but it is thought that he lived in the time of Nehemiah (Mal. 1:1).

Meta. The voice of conscience in man calls his attention to his shortcomings and encourages him to do right. Conscience is symbolized by Malachi ("my messenger," margin of Mal. 1:1).

All real lasting wealth and happiness are based on unity with God. Malachi will tell you this, or you can prove it for yourself after you have spent years in material experiences.

Malcam (A. V., Malcham), măl'-căm (Heb.)—*their king; their ruler; their counseling.*

a Son of Shaharaim by Hodesh, a Benjamite (I Chron. 8:9). **b** The idol Molech (Zeph. 1:5, "*their king,*" margin).

Meta. Setting up the outer reasoning or thinking consciousness as *king,* thus giving it dominion in one's life. Especially does Malcam as referring to the idol Molech signify the worship of the intellect, or reason, directed entirely by the senses, by the prejudices, seemings, customs, and desires of the outer man. (See MOLECH.)

Malchiel, măl'-chĭ-ĕl (Heb.)—*rule of God; judgment of God; counsel of God; God is king; God's king, i. e., one appointed by Him; God's dominion.*

Son of Beriah and grandson of Asher (Gen. 46:17). He became head of the family of the Malchielites (Num. 26:45), and was the father or founder of Birzaith (I Chron. 7:31).

Meta. Man's acknowledgment of the supremacy of divine power and rulership; in other words, one's exalting God in consciousness and giving Him dominion, bowing to and obeying Truth. This in turn elevates the individual, and enables him through his I AM, or indwelling Christ, to obtain dominion over himself, to gain control of and to direct his thoughts, desires, words, and acts. Thus he becomes master in his whole life and affairs.

Malchielites, măl'-chĭ-ĕl-ītes (fr. Heb.)—*of* or *belonging to Malchiel.*

Descendants of Malchiel the grandson of Asher (Num. 26:45).

Meta. Thoughts springing from and belonging to that in consciousness which Malchiel represents. (See MALCHIEL.)

Malchijah (in A. V., I Chron. 6:40; Ezra 10:31; Neh. 3:14, 31; 8:4; 11:12; Jer. 38:1, Malchiah, and in Jer. 21:1, Melchiah), măl-chī'-jăh (Heb.)—*rule of Jehovah; counsel of Jah; Jehovah is king; Jehovah's king.*

There were many Israelites by this name. Most of them were priests (I Chron. 9:12; 24:9; Neh. 3:11; 10:3; 12:42).

Meta. The individual's acknowledgment of Jehovah, Christ, or I AM as king, as the ruling power in his consciousness and throughout his entire being. (The significance is virtually the same as that of Malchiel, except that Malchiel relates to the absolute principle of Being (God), while Malchijah relates to the principle or idea in expression (Jehovah).

Malchiram, măl-chī'-răm (Heb.)— *Melech is exalted; my king is exalted; high counselor; king of the heights; exalted rule.*

Son of Jeconiah (I Chron. 3:18).

Meta. Exalting the will in consciousness (*my king is exalted, king of the heights*), giving it a very high place, even attributing to it understanding and judgment (*high counselor*).

Malchi–shua, măl'-chĭ–shu̜'-á (Heb.) —*king of help; king of opulence; king of deliverance; king's help.*

Son of Saul (I Sam. 14:49). He was slain, with his father and brothers, by the Philistines in Mount Gilboa (I Sam. 31:2).

Meta. Help through the will, or one's trusting in will power to deliver and prosper one and to pull one through seeming error experiences.

The death of Saul and his three sons, Jonathan (human love), Abinadab (physical will or body control), and Malchi–shua (the will as king of health or physical vitality and supply), means the dissolution of the whole organism. This is the result of disobedience to the Lord, or law of Being, and of trusting in personal will and strength to carry one through.

By continued disregard of the divine law, man gets farther and farther away from the interior harmony that is perpetually fed from the spiritual springs of Being. The discordant realms of error, sense thought, represented by the undisciplined and savage Philistines, encroach on the sacred abiding places of the thoughts of Truth, which are represented by the Israelites. Gilboa means *boiling springs,* and represents a great turmoil in consciousness. It is there that the enemies of law and order, the Philistines, finally get one who has all his life followed the dictates of the personal will.

"So Saul died, and his three sons, and his armorbearer, and all his men, that same day together." The "armorbearer" signifies the soul's consciousness of its security in God; when that is withdrawn there is a complete loss of hope, and the whole personality gives up.

The undisciplined forces of error thought complete their work in the body by stripping it of all that gave it character—the object being to destroy it entirely.

But there is always a saving grace in the divine goodness; if we have ever done a kind act it has been preserved in the careful records of memory and will come forth when we need it most. In the beginning of his reign Saul had delivered the inhabitants of Jabesh–gilead from their enemies, the Amorites, who were about to put out their right eyes. In remembrance of the deed, the people of Jabesh–gilead took the bodies of Saul and his sons away from the Philistines, and gave them decent burial. Jabesh-gilead represents the forces of nature that gather up and care for the dust and ashes of the organism. Nothing is lost in the divine economy; that which is dissipated will in due course be gathered again, and another trial will be made in the working of life's problem.

Malchus, măl'-chŭs (Gk. fr. Heb.)— *ruler; counselor; judge; king.*

The high priest's servant, whose right ear Peter cut off with his sword, when the soldiers and the officials came out to take Jesus (John 18:10). Jesus rebuked Peter, and healed the man's ear (John 18:11; Luke 22:51).

Meta. The high priest represents the executive power of divine law. Here, the high priest symbolizes the executive power, or ruling thought, in the phase of man's consciousness that is established in old formal religious ideas and activities. It does not accept the Christ life and Truth, but attempts to deny them out of consciousness and crucify the Christ.

Malchus, the high priest's servant, meaning *ruler, counselor, judge, king,* signifies the limited understanding and judgment of the ruling power that the high priest represents. Though very limited and bigoted in its apprehension of spiritual things, and though it seemingly serves against the Christ, against the individual's highest spiritual good, one must not use one's word of faith (Peter's sword) against it destructively; such a proceeding would only serve to cut off its right ear, to limit still further the possibility that this phase of consciousness might perceive and lay hold of Truth. This limited understanding and judgment should be healed, illumined, and lifted up (Jesus' healing the man's ear) instead of being pushed still further into unreceptivity and darkness, if one's complete regeneration is to be accomplished.

Malchus, *counselor*, could also be interpreted as follows: Your faith (Peter) in the righteousness of your cause may lead you to combat the thoughts of the ruling religious powers, and in your impetuosity you resent their counsel (Malchus, *counselor*) and deny their capacity to receive Truth (cut of the right ear), but good judgment and a broad comprehension of the divine overcoming through which you are passing will cause you to adopt pacific means. "Put up the sword into the sheath."

malefactors, crucified with Jesus (Luke 23:32).

Meta. Duality—a belief in good and evil, past and future—comprising all the thought consciousness of opposites that has been built up since man began to eat, or enter into the conscious knowledge of, "good and evil."

Mallothi, măl'-lô-thī (Heb.)—*fullness; abundant; complete; perfection; splendid; consecration; circumcision.*

Son of Heman and a musician in the Temple, in David's reign (I Chron. 25:4).

Meta. The spiritual significance of circumcision is the purification of the individual from the law of sin and death. This is accomplished by the activity in consciousness of the Jehovah, or Christ word, the word of Truth, believed, affirmed, and accepted in its entirety. The accomplishment of this perfect purification is represented by Mallothi, meaning *fullness, complete, perfection, circumcision.*

Malluch, măl'-lŭch (Heb.)—*ruler; counselor; judge; king.*

A Merarite Levite whose great-grandson, Ethan, stood on the left hand of Heman the singer while ministering with song before the tabernacle of the tent of meeting, in David's reign (I Chron. 6:44). There were other Israelites and priests by this name also (Ezra 10:29, 32; Neh. 12:2).

Meta. The different men named Malluch signify thoughts belonging to our natural religious tendencies, and our highest religious and spiritual understanding (Levites, priests, and other Israelites), as *ruling* in consciousness and acting as *counselors* to us.

mammon, măm'-mon (Gk. fr. Heb.)—*treasure; wealth; riches; prop; stay; support.* The latter are derived from the sense of that which is of temporary or outer help only. The idea of treasure comes from that which is stored underground, hidden away, hoarded; that which is not placed in circulation, but is restricted in its use.

Mammon refers to outer riches and also to anything of the outer, formative world that one's affections desire to gather to him and to hoard, or treasure. Jesus used this word in Luke 16:9, 11, 13, and Matthew 6:24.

Meta. The material or worldly thought and belief regarding riches; money, possessions, and wealth, compared with the true inner riches of the mind—the understanding and the realization of the spiritual substance, life, and intelligence that lie back of every outer manifestation.

Mamre, măm'-rê (Heb.)—*fully assimilated; well-fed; abundantly supplied; fatness; firmness; virility; vigor; strength.*

Abram "dwelt by the oaks of Mamre, which are in Hebron" (Gen. 13:18). Mamre also seems to have been the name of an Amorite, who with two of his brothers was "confederate with Abram" (Gen. 14:13, 24; see also Gen. 23:17-19; 25:9; 35:27; 49:30; 50:13).

Meta. Mamre means *firmness, vigor, strength;* Hebron (*a community, alliance, company, friendship*) refers to the front brain, the seat of conscious thought. The lesson here is that faith in God (suggested by Abram) brings about the right relation among all the associated faculties, and withal an enduring *firmness, vigor,* and *strength. Fatness, abundantly supplied, well-fed,* definitions of Mamre, signify a consciousness of substance and riches also. The qualities that Mamre represents are not of the highest spiritual consciousness, or Christ mind, but they belong more to the spiritually awakening intellect of the individual.

Manaen, măn'-ă-ĕn (Gk. fr. Heb.)— *consoler; comforter.*

Foster brother of Herod the tetrarch. He was one of the five prophets and teachers in the church at Antioch (Acts 13:1).

Meta. The five prophets and teachers in the church at Antioch, mentioned in Acts 13:1, represent those who interpret Spirit to the outer consciousness. Manaen (*comforter, consoler*) refers especially to the activity of the Holy Spirit in individual consciousness in its rôle of comforter, giving consolation and cheer.

Manahath, mă-nā'-hăth (Heb.)—*resting; quieting; restoring; bequeathing; giving; forsaking; abandoning.*

a Son of Shobal, who was a son of Seir the Horite (Gen. 36:23). **b** A place, seemingly in Benjamin (I Chron 8:6). I Chronicles 2:54 gives the impression that half of the inhabitants of Manahath were descendants of Salma of the tribe of Judah.

Meta. A peaceful, restful thought and place in consciousness. A stillness and ceasing from outer activity, wherein both soul and body are renewed in strength and good, wherein something of error is forsaken and a degree of Truth is realized.

Manahathites (A. V., Manahethites), măn'-ă-hăth-ītes (fr. Heb.)—*of or belonging to Manahath.*

Inhabitants of Manahath that are named in the genealogy of Judah (I Chron. 2:54).

Meta. Thoughts springing from and belonging to that in consciousness which Manahath signifies. (See MANAHATH.)

Manasseh (in A. V., Matthew 1:10; Rev. 7:6, Manasses), mă-năs'-sĕh (Heb.) —*who makes to forget; causing forget-*

fulness; out of the forgotten; from oblivion.

a Eldest son of Joseph (Gen. 41:51). His descendants became one of the tribes of Israel (Num. 2:20). **b** A wicked king of Judah (II Kings 21:1).

Meta. The meaning of "Manasseh" is *who makes to forget.* The meaning of "Ephraim" is *doubly fruitful.* Manasseh represents understanding, and Ephraim stands for will. The understanding here denotes denial, the negative activity of mind. The will is the positive or affirmative quality, the affirmative attitude of mind.

Ephraim and Manasseh are brothers. When these two faculties express in harmony, divine order is established. Will and understanding have their centers of activity in the head and function through the front brain. When the understanding rules without the balancing force of will, Israel is led to worship false gods. Two of these false gods are "the Baalim and the Asheroth," which represent nature in its various sensuous aspects.

Man worships these false gods when he becomes so negative that he thinks that there are powers outside himself that regulate his life. He places his faith in the signs of the zodiac; believes in a "ruling planet"; trusts to "luck"; seeks guidance of "familiar spirits"; gives himself up to the influence of other minds, through hypnotism and suggestion; follows unquestioningly the advice given in the numerous sects and societies that have been set up for worship by man.

By this worship of false gods, man's mind is opened to the phenomenal and he places his faith in apparent powers outside his own spiritual consciousness. Thus he loses his I AM dominion. This is *forgetfulness* of the power of God within him, and it brings him into condemnation. It is then that the understanding, or ruling factor, is put "in chains," "bound . . . with fetters," and carried to Babylon, utter confusion.

The way of escape lies in the denial of the seeming (Manasseh "humbled himself"), and in seeking the real Source of wisdom and power, through prayer. When we open our mind to Spirit and declare the Truth, the understanding is established in harmony with divine standards. "Manasseh knew that Jehovah he was God" (II Chron. 33:1-13).

Manasseh's being twelve years of age when he began to reign (II Chron. 33:1) means that the negative mentality had involved all the twelve faculties. Hence all the thoughts were "evil in the sight of Jehovah."

Manassites, mă-năs'-sītes (fr. Heb.). Descendants of Manasseh the eldest son of Joseph, and members of the tribe of Manasseh (Deut. 29:8).

Meta. Thoughts springing from and belonging to the understanding faculty of mind in its outer, negative aspect. (See MANASSEH.)

manger (Luke 2:12, 16).
Meta. The animal life of the body in which the new life is first manifested.

Manoah, mă-nō'-ăh (Heb.)—*resting; quieting; restoring; giving; leaving; forsaking.*

Father of Samson. He was a man of Zorah, of the family of the Danites (Judg. 13:2-24).

Meta. The significance of Manoah is given in Isaiah 40:31: "They that wait for Jehovah shall renew their strength; they shall mount up with wings as eagles; they shall run, and not be weary; they shall walk, and not faint." In the Authorized Version the first clause reads, "They that wait upon the Lord shall renew *their* strength." Manoah—meaning *resting, restoring, forsaking,* and being the father of Samson, who represents strength—signifies this inner waiting upon the Lord, or resting in the consciousness of our oneness with the Father, Jehovah, within us. By this inner worship something of the limited in thought and belief is put away and a great increase in strength and might is experienced.

Maoch, mā'-ŏch (Heb.)—*pressed; oppressed; squeezed; emasculated; poor; breastband.*

Father of Achish, king of Gath, a Philistine (I Sam. 27:2).

Meta. The breast is the seat of the affectional nature. Maoch (*pressed, oppressed, emasculated, poor, breastband*) signifies in individual consciousness either a lack of natural affection or a being bound and limited by human, personal, sense loves and emotions. Either condition would cause one to be poor and oppressed in so far as the true inner riches and freedom of mind and heart are concerned.

Maon, mā'-ŏn (Heb.)—*habitation; dwelling; place of abode; refuge; sanctuary; temple; the place wherein one dwells; home.*

a A city in the hill country of Judah (Josh. 15:55). **b** Son of Shammai and founder of Beth-zur, of the tribe and cities of Judah (I Chron. 2:45).

Meta. A consciousness of abidingness, of stability, of continuity, of oneness with God, within the very center of one's being.

Maonites, mā'-ŏn-ītes (fr. Heb.)—*of or belonging to Maon.*

Mentioned with the Sidonians and the Amalekites as a people that oppressed Israel (Judg. 10:12). They are thought to be the same people as the Meunim of II Chronicles 26:7.

Meta. Carnal thoughts that believe in the reality and abidingness of error. (See MEUNIM, meaning *dwellings, homes, habitations.*)

marriage (John 2:1).
Meta. A union of two states of consciousness.

mansions, many (John 14:2).
Meta. Degrees of realization of the Truth of Being; the "place" prepared by Jesus is a definite state of realization of Truth into which may come all who faithfully take up the same denials and affirmations that He took up.

Those familiar with the power of man to establish in consciousness certain mental states easily perceive how it might be possible for one with the spiritual power of Jesus to fix right in our midst a place of harmony and peace (or heaven) into which may enter all who follow Him in mental discipline. "I go to prepare a place for you . . . that where I am, *there* ye may be also." This place can be entered right here and now, and to enter this state of consciousness is to become conscious of heaven.

Mara, mā'-rà (Heb.)—*bitter; acrid; galling; grief; misfortune; calamity.*

The symbolical name that Naomi gave

to herself because of losing her husband, sons, and home (Ruth 1:20).

Meta. The bitterness and distress that the partially awakened soul experiences when reaping the error result of some false step; this soul, not knowing enough of Truth to link cause with effect, lays the inharmony to God.

Naomi apparently blamed God for her losses and sorrows. Many professing Christians of today do likewise, not realizing that their troubles are the direct results of their own ignorant and unwise thinking and doing. They resort to worldly methods for their healing and sustenance; then they think that the resultant inharmonious experiences are sent on them by God. But we are learning better than this. We know that God is good and that only the good is true of God and of us as we unify ourselves with the one good and work harmoniously with the law of our being.

Marah, mā′-răh (Heb.)—*bitterness; grief; misfortune; calamity.*

A place in the desert to which the Israelites came after having crossed the Red Sea on their way out of Egypt. The water here was bitter, and Moses sweetened it, in obedience to the command of Jehovah, by casting a certain tree into the waters (Exod. 15:23; Num. 33:8).

Meta. The *bitterness,* the trouble, the sickness, and misery that those who pollute the waters of life with impure, rebellious, darkened, error thoughts and beliefs bring on themselves.

It was at Marah, after the sweetening of the waters so that the Israelites could drink, that Jehovah revealed this truth to them: "If thou wilt diligently hearken to the voice of Jehovah thy God, and wilt do that which is right in his eyes, and wilt give ear to his commandments, and keep all his statutes, I will put none of the diseases upon thee, which I have put upon the Egyptians: for I am Jehovah that healeth thee." Jehovah here represents the Lord, the divine law, the divine principle in action. It manifests in and through man according to his conception of it and of himself in relation to it, and according to the innermost thoughts and desires of his mind and heart.

Maralah, măr′-ă-lăh (Heb.)—*trem-bling; reeling; shaking; earthquake; declivity; depression; fear.*

A place on the western boundary of Zebulun (Josh. 19:11).

Meta. A quaking, or *trembling,* with possibly a feeling of weakness (*depression*), which sometimes takes place in the outer, earthly phase of man's consciousness, the body, when an inner realization of order has been attained and the outer has not yet fallen into line but is just beginning to sense the influence of this inner realization. (Zebulun represents order, and Maralah, meaning *earthquake, trembling, depression, fear,* was a city on the western boundary of Zebulun. West always refers to the outer, with reference to man.)

Marana tha, mär′-ăn-ā′ thà (Gk. fr. Chald.)—*our Lord is coming; our Lord will come; our Lord comes; our Lord has come.*

An expression that Paul used in closing his first Epistle to the Corinthians (I Cor. 16:22).

Meta. A recognition of the Christ presence, and its ultimate manifestation.

Jesus Christ is here. The Christ also lives in us and will come into perfect expression and manifestation in our life, even as it did in Jesus. We shall be like Him and shall see Him as He is.

Mareshah, mă-rē′-shăh (Heb.)—*head; highest; chief; summit; top of a hill; summit of a mountain; beginning; foremost; first principle; most precious.*

a A city in the lowland of Judah (Josh. 15:44). b "Father" of Hebron, in the genealogy of Judah (I Chron. 2:42). c Son of Laadah, of Judah (I Chron. 4:21).

Meta. Mareshah refers to Spirit, Divine Mind, *first principle,* the beginning or source of all that really is. Since Mareshah is the name of men and of a city, it bespeaks that in the individual consciousness which recognizes Spirit as one's true source and sustenance.

Mark, märk (Gk. fr. Lat.)—*brilliant; shining; polite.*

John Mark was the son of a woman named Mary. His home was in Jerusalem. He was the cause of such a sharp dispute between Paul and Barnabas that they ceased traveling together on their preaching tours (Acts 12:12, 25; 13:13;

15:37-39). In Colossians 4:10 he is called the cousin of Barnabas. He also wrote the Gospel named Mark.

Meta. John means *grace and mercy of the Lord*, "love working by faith." Mark means *brilliant, shining, polite.* John Mark had two natures: one, a polite and brilliant exterior that was affected by the people of the mixed state at Pamphylia; the other, a deep spiritual nature, which was called out and developed by the confidence that Barnabas placed in him.

Mark's mother was one of those Marys of the Bible who belong to the devotional, substance, and serving side of the soul. Mark was one of Peter's converts, though he possibly followed Jesus personally. Some authorities believe that his Gospel was written under Peter's direction. In I Peter 5:13 Peter refers to him as "my son." Born of Mary, the child of love, and begotten again into spiritual birth by the word of faith (Peter), the spiritual side of the quality that John Mark represents in us has a work to do that cannot be done by any other. When it comes to Perga (meaning *earthy*) in Pamphylia (*mixture of nations*) for the first time it feels that it cannot bear the materiality of the outer consciousness, and so returns to Jerusalem, its home, the heart or peace center. However, as faith becomes more firmly established in us and as love develops throughout the entire consciousness, a deep yearning to be of service in redeeming the organism inspires this quality again to activity. With the aid of tolerance and kindly, patient admonition (which Barnabas represents here), together with a spurring on by Paul, the zealous will, the necessary strength and courage are imparted to this spiritual quality in us to enable it to carry on its specific ministry boldly and successfully.

Mark served those whom he accompanied. He looked after the supplying of their daily needs while they preached and taught the people. Thus he also represents the substance idea in the overcomer and is very useful in many ways in ministering to our spiritual faculties in their redeeming work throughout our being. This Mark quality in us inspires us to obey the injunction of the text, "Whatsoever thy hand findeth to do, do *it* with thy might."

Another interpretation of John Mark is that he represents a combination of zeal and love. Mark means *shining*, and John, according to some authorities, means *God's gift*. God is love, and one of the shining activities of love is its zeal in giving. Paul did not think it wise to take John Mark with them again because he had deserted them before at Pamphylia. Paul discovered that enthusiasm and zeal have their reactions.

Zeal and enthusiasm are absolutely necessary to the success of any enduring work. When we find ourselves growing listless and indifferent, we should begin to affirm and to reach out for zeal, as Paul did in II Timothy 4:11: "Take Mark, and bring him with thee; for he is useful to me for ministering."

Maroth, mā'-rŏth (Heb.)—*acridness; bitterness; bitter herbs; bitter waters; unhappiness; sorrows; griefs.*

A city of Judah (Mic. 1:12).

Meta. "The inhabitant of Maroth waiteth anxiously for good, because evil is come down from Jehovah unto the gate of Jerusalem." The margin causes this text to read, "The inhabitress of Maroth is in travail for good."

Maroth (*bitterness, unhappiness, sorrows, griefs*) signifies the soul's working out its salvation and, in the midst of hard, trying, painful experiences that seem to reach the very "gate of Jerusalem" (the spiritual or innermost heart center), holding steadfastly to the good. (See Rev. 12:2; Gal. 4:19, and Isa. 53:11, first clause.)

Marsena, mär'-sĕ-nȧ (Heb. fr. Pers.) —*dignified man; man of nobility; worth while; worthy; honorable.*

One of the seven princes of Media and Persia who were next to the king and were his counselors, "who saw the king's face, and sat first in the kingdom" (Esth. 1:14).

Meta. One of the seven creative principles, or dominant ruling thoughts, that are developed in the natural man (seven is the number of the natural man). (See CARSHENA.) This foundation thought, which in its true essence is spiritual and of great value (*dignified man, worthy, honorable*) to the individual, is at this stage of its unfoldment ruled over by the puffed-up personal will (King Ahasuerus) and gives its substance to the building up and sustaining of the egotistical phase of the will.

Mars' Hill (in A. V., Mars' Hill; in A. S. V., Areopagus), märs hill.

A hill in Athens, with an open space, where the court of the Areopagus convened. It was there that Paul preached his sermon to the men of Athens, taking for his text the inscription that he found on one of their altars, "To an Unknown God" (Acts 17:22, 23).

Meta. See AREOPAGUS.

Martha, mär'-thá (Gk. fr. Heb.)— *mistress, i. e., of a family; wife; lady; governess; domestic; who becomes bitter; rebellious one.*

Sister of Mary and Lazarus. The three lived together at Bethany, and Jesus often visited at their home (Luke 10:38-42; John 11:1-39; 12:2).

Meta. In Luke 10:38-42 Martha and Mary represent the outer and the inner phases, respectively, of the soul's activity in welcoming the inner spiritual teacher. The soul, established in love, is always quick to discern the presence of true thoughts, and it welcomes the spiritual man, or teacher, who brings Truth. It is also in a receptive attitude toward understanding.

Martha represents the outer activity of the soul that is receiving the higher self; Mary represents the inner or soul receptivity. Martha desires to show her love by service; Mary shows hers by learning at Jesus' feet.

Both of these activities are necessary, but we should take heed that in our desire to serve we do not forget our times of communion with our indwelling Lord. We should not set greater value on active service than on quiet, loving receptivity to the Spirit of truth within us.

Mary at Jesus' feet represents the soul as learning the lessons of life from the higher self. When the learning of these lessons is given first place in consciousness, the activity or service that follows becomes simple and easy. But when Martha, the serving quality, is given precedence, anxiety and irritation result because there is a seeming separation from the Source of love and poise, and a lack is sensed in consciousness. Truly, "to obey is better than sacrifice." Understanding of Truth must precede all real and effective service.

Martha can also be said to represent the material consciousness, and Mary the spiritual.

Jesus is the visible head, representing the Christ (see Eph. 1:22; 4:15; Col. 1:18; 2:10).

It is Martha who satisfies the needs of the outer man and who wants the most assistance in carrying on her share of the work. She is most insistent in demanding that her duties be given first place. But the spiritual consciousness, Mary, "hath chosen the good part, which shall not be taken away from her," while Martha is "anxious and troubled about many things."

Martha can lighten her work and make it easy by doing all things "as unto the Lord," that is, by putting spiritual understanding and power into everything that she does, thus working out efficiency and ease in all the activities of the home.

Mary, mā'-ry (fr. Heb.)—*contradiction; rebellious outcry; bitter complaint; bitterness; myrrh; bitter waters; aromatic spirits.*

a Mother of Jesus (Matt. 1:18-22). **b** Mary Magdalene, out of whom Jesus cast seven demons, and who became one of His most devoted followers (Luke 8:2; John 20:1, 11-18). **c** Mary the sister of Martha and Lazarus (Luke 10:39; John 11:1, 2). **d** Mother of John Mark (Acts 12:12). **e** Other Marys are also mentioned (John 19:25; Rom. 16:6).

Meta. The feminine, the soul, the affectional and emotional phase of man's being, both when seemingly bound and limited by sensate thought, and in its freed, exalted state.

Mary, the mother of Jesus, represents the soul that magnifies the Lord "daily in the temple" and through its devotions prepares itself for the higher life. She signifies the divine motherhood of love. She can also be said to be intuition.

Jesus, the perfected-man manifestation, is conceived in the intuitive or soul nature, and is molded in its substance.

This coming of the Christ body into activity is the result of an exalted idea sown in the mind and matured by the soul (Mary). The soul is devout and expectant. It believes in the so-called miraculous as a possibility. Mary expected the birth of the Messiah, according to the promise of the Holy Spirit. She was overshadowed by that high idea; it formed in her mind the seed that quickened into the cell, and in due season there were aggregations of cells strong enough in their activity to attract the attention of the outer consciousness, and what is called the birth of Christ took place.

Mary, the soul, the mother of Jesus, as mentioned in Luke 2:34, 35, refers to the conservative, conventional principle that suffers when the new order of life and law is set up. The soul has been bound by race tradition and custom until it is atrophied. Now it is coming to life, and in its travail it reveals the Lord's body.

Mary the mother of Jesus, Mary Magdalene, Mary of Bethany, Martha, and the other women who were with Jesus and His disciples so much during His ministry, "who ministered unto them of their substance," all represent phases of the individual soul.

A wonderful lesson of constancy, gratitude, love, faithful attachment, and service is set before us in the glimpses of Mary Magdalene that are given in the Gospels. Wherever she is mentioned the power of love, devotion, and service is revealed. Her whole life and all that she had were apparently dedicated to the Christ.

The soul consciousness in each individual is capable of the strongest, deepest, and fullest allegiance to Truth. It is constantly seeking something that will satisfy. It can never be happy or at peace until the feelings are redeemed and harmonized by the Holy Spirit, until God's presence is known, felt, and fully realized throughout the individual being.

Through Jesus seven demons were cast out of Mary Magdalene. This means that the *I* in man, the directive will or higher self raised to divine understanding and power, releases the soul from the emotional errors that have their existence in the unregenerated feelings, and establishes peace and poise in the consciousness. As the soul is purified and lifted day by day out of the bondage of the errors (demons), it pours out upon the whole body consciousness more and more of its wealth of substance, life, and love. More especially are this devotion and service directed to the I AM in the individual—represented by Jesus—thus greatly aiding it in its ministry of Truth throughout the organism.

We may have been inclined to belittle the value of the feminine side of our nature. The feelings and affections, which are the seat of the emotions in our unredeemed state, belong to the soul. The purification of the soul and the wealth of its devoted, sustaining qualities are needed in the regeneration of the body, as much as is the quickening of the disciples, the twelve faculties of mind. Both soul and understanding (love and wisdom) must enter into our affirmations of Truth if those affirmations are really to become substance and life to us.

Without the depths of the "feeling" quality in soul consciousness, which Mary Magdalene seems especially to symbolize, we should be like one before whom a table is prepared as for a great feast: the table is laid with fine linen and silver, all the dishes and arrangements are perfect, but there is nothing to eat; or, if there should be something to eat, it would be as food without flavor or seasoning. A service rendered without depth of love and feeling, without the very substance of one's own being, is only a form, empty.

In Luke 8:1-3, John 19:25, and John 20:11-18 we find Mary Magdalene among those following Jesus from place to place, ministering to Him. We see her by the cross, and standing at the tomb weeping. Then the angels appear to her; next the risen Jesus reveals Himself to her, and she goes to tell the disciples the glad news. Thus the soul ever remains with the object of its devotion. When one's love is established in Truth, the soul stays closest to the Divine. When the human goes through crucifixion in dying to self the soul remains with it to befriend and help. When everything apparently is lost the purified soul is constant and true. When the resurrection light breaks in the consciousness the soul feels (perceives) the light first, and conveys the joyful tidings to the more outer faculties (the disciples).

Mary Magdalene can also be explained as representing the psychic realm of consciousness. This realm is demonized, and from it Jesus put forth seven devils (Luke 8:2). It is there that the emotions have their centers of action. It is the seat of desire. Its lower stratum is sensation, the serpent that tempted Eve to eat of the reserve life and substance of the generative nature, which is in the very center of the body—the fruit of the tree in the midst of the Garden of Eden. When the psyche tastes this animal sensation it becomes so infatuated with its new-found source of pleasure that it communicates its infatuation to the reason, and Adam also eats. Then trouble for man begins. Instead of an ascending, refining process in the consciousness, we have a descending, coarsening process. This proceeds to a point where the higher faculties separate from the lower, and "man is a god in ruins." This sin leads to sickness and death. The fires of lust and remorse burn in mind and body—hell is made.

But this "god in ruins" must be rebuilt. God sends His Christ into the soul sick of its fleeting lusts, and the process of again connecting Adam and Eve with the Father is completed in Jesus. Jesus is Adam resurrected in understanding; Mary Magdalene is Eve purified in desire.

In the narrative of the resurrection of Jesus, an element of human sympathy is pictured in the loving Mary who stooped and looked into the tomb for the Lord. He had risen, however, and she found Him walking in the garden. Beware the limitations of human love; look for your masterful I AM thought, Jesus, in the omnipresent living force and vitality of the one life that is penetrating and permeating every part of your body, which is the garden of God. Human sympathy holds us to material conditions when we think that we are

free. Those who are spiritualizing the consciousness are very apt to be pulled back into sense ways through their personal loves, when about to succeed. When Jesus said to Mary, "Touch me not; for I am not yet ascended unto the Father," He represented the wisdom of the I AM, which does not allow personal love to bind it on its upward way.

"Why seek ye the living among the dead? He is not here, but is risen." The weeping Mary and the sad disciples' stooping and looking into the tomb for their living Master suggest here the forgetfulness of sense consciousness. Jesus plainly taught that He would rise from the dead, yet His disciples forgot this and sought amongst the dead for the living. Christians who continue to think only about the crucified Jesus are looking into the tomb, trusting in death to save them, instead of looking up to the risen, glorified Christ who is life, wholeness, and Truth.

Mary of Bethany represents the devotional soul, and Martha represents the practical soul. Martha provides the material necessities and Mary the spiritual, while Lazarus sits at meat, or abides as the living substance of the subconsciousness.

Mary, the inner, devotional side of the soul, is grateful for the awakening of her brother Lazarus, because she depends for her manifestation on the subconscious life, which he represents.

Mary and Martha also represent two aspects of love: Martha the love that ministers to the physical, and Mary that which attends to the spiritual. Both are friends to Jesus, but He commends Mary above Martha (Luke 10:41, 42).

Martha does not consider that anything has been done unless there is external evidence, such as ministering to the body and its needs; but Mary sits at the feet of Jesus. John says that Mary poured the ointment upon Jesus' feet. Feet symbolize the understanding, and when Mary pours upon Jesus' feet the precious ointment she is symbolically bathing His understanding with the fragrance of love.

This lesson of John 12:1-8 and Matthew 26:6-13 is of great import to metaphysicians. The tendency is to concentrate on the understanding and to count its logic and cold reason as fulfillment of the law; but we learn by experience that the cold science of mind, without the warmth of the heart, is a very chilly doctrine. The floodgates of divine love must be opened in the soul and its precious, fragrant ointment must be poured out upon the understanding. This fills the whole house, or body, with a balm and an "odor" that heal and bless all.

Acquisitiveness (Judas) says that this precious substance should be sold, that the proceeds might be devoted to the poor; that is, the faculty of accumulation would not pour out so precious a thing as love without getting a money value in return, in order that the poor (thoughts of bodily need) might be supplied.

This Judas says to teachers of Truth: "It is better for people to pay promptly for all teaching and healing. You have temporal needs that have to be supplied. Don't be too liberal with this precious Truth; it is valuable and will bring money. Don't pour out your love and healing sympathy indiscriminately; make people pay a good round price, and they will appreciate what they get."

Remember, however, that this Judas is a thief, and a deceiver and betrayer of his own. He is deceiving the whole world today, and even metaphysicians who are free in all other ways are bound by his false reasoning.

The understanding has its days of darkness, but where love has been quickened and the whole consciousness has been flooded with its sympathy and compassion, there is always consolation. Jesus referred to this when He said, "Suffer her to keep it against the day of my burying."

Maschil, măs'-chil (Heb.)—*teaching circumspection; instructing in wisdom; inducing understanding; inducing piety; leading into piety.*

The title of several Psalms (Psalms 32; 42; 44; 53).

Meta. Spiritual inspiration, instruction—the inner understanding, or word of Truth—unfolding to the individual consciousness and inducing true understanding, wisdom, and godliness.

Mash, măsh (Heb.)—*pressing out by contractile force; pressing out of fruits; harvest of fruits.*

Son of Aram, who was a son of Shem, the eldest of Noah's three sons (Gen. 10:23). In I Chronicles 1:17, he is called Meshech.

Meta. Aram means *highlands.* Its significance is the same as that of Syria, the nation that was founded by Aram the son of Shem. Both Aram and Syria refer to phases of the mental or intellectual in man. The intellect has its foundation in Spirit (Shem represents the spiritual in man), and any true understanding that the intellect obtains comes from Spirit, since the intellect reflects the light of Spirit. In Mash, we see the intellect as obtaining knowledge. The intellect is not naturally receptive to spiritual understanding. It is aggressive in its nature, and it works very hard in the outer, seeking to obtain by force, by personal determination and much persistent study and research, the knowledge that it desires. And the very pressure of its outer seeking does open to it something of the inner light and intelligence of Spirit (*pressing out by contractile force, pressing out of fruits*), though in its ignorance of the one Source of all understanding it usually takes to itself the honor of having worked out the ideas that come to it from Spirit. However, fruit is realized (*harvest of fruits*) in increased knowledge, and the time will come when the whole man, even to his outermost intellectual consciousness, will perceive and glorify Spirit as his abiding and all-comprehensive intelligence.

Mashal, mā'-shăl (Heb.)—*proposition; likeness; parable; proverb; similitude; apothegm; fable; byword; government; rule; dominion; master; tyrant.*

A border city of Asher that was given over to the Gershomite Levites (I Chron. 6:74). In Joshua 19:26 and 21:30 it is called Mishal.

Meta. The truth of man's power and possibilities of dominion as the son of God, as made in the divine likeness, hidden under the common, everyday, apparent things of life (*likeness, parable, proverb, fable, byword, government, rule, dominion, master).* This truth is active, though because of a lack of true and full understanding it tends to adversity (*tyrant*). Man must understand that his dominion is over himself; then in unifying his power to rule with love and wisdom he will reap only good in his own life and will do good only to others.

Masrekah, măs'-rē-käh (Heb.)—*vineyard of noble (purple) vines; place of noble vines,* i. e., *bearing purple grapes; place of red streams.*

A place in Edom; the home of Samlah, a king of Edom (Gen. 36:36).

Meta. Currents of vital thoughts, of thoughts of power (*place of red streams, vineyard of noble (purple) vines, place of noble vines,* i. e., *bearing purple grapes;* a vineyard symbolizing life, streams representing currents of thoughts, and purple bespeaking power), that are active in the outer physical organism of man, and are dominated by sense beliefs and ideas. (Masrekah was a place in Edom and had Samlah, king of Edom, for its central ruling thought. Edom refers to man's outer, seemingly physical and mortal consciousness and body.)

Massa, măs'-sȧ (Heb.) — *burden bearer; porter; a lifting up,* i. e., *of the voice, of the soul; song; singing; divine declaration; oracle; prophecy; proverb; a speech; a discourse.*

Seventh of Ishmael's twelve sons (Gen. 25:14).

Meta. Ishmael, father of Massa, represents the fruit of the thoughts of the natural man at work in the flesh. Massa, seventh son of Ishmael (seven is the number of fulfillment in the natural man), ushers in a new element of thought regarding that in man which has hitherto been deemed by him to be wholly material, and doomed to death and dissolution. This new thought is a *prophecy* that the seemingly physical body will ultimately be lifted up and saved alive. Massa signifies a phase of thought that lays hold of, retains, and transports this truth (*divine declaration, burden bearer, a speech, a discourse,* from the idea of *lifting up* and carrying) into the outer organism, the seemingly mortal part of

the individual.

Massah (in A. V., Psalms 95:8, temptation), măs'-säh (Heb.)—*causing to flow; melting down; proving; temptation; trial; solution; dissolution; complaint; murmur; calamity; evil.*

The name of a place in the wilderness where the Israelites complained for want of water. "And he called the name of the place Massah [that is, *Tempting,* or *Proving,* margin], and Meribah [that is, *Chiding,* or *Strife,* margin], because of the striving of the children of Israel, and because they tempted Jehovah, saying, Is Jehovah among us, or not?" (Exod. 17:7; see also Deuteronomy 6:16; 9:22; 33:8).

Meta. The *trial* of faith, the *temptation,* that so often overtakes the would-be overcomer at the beginning of his awakening to the deeper truths of Spirit, at the beginning of his attempt to trust God fully for health, for supply, for all things. This temptation is to doubt God's guiding, protecting, restoring, sustaining, all-providing, all-sufficient, all-satisfying presence and power and willingness when one comes face to face with the seeming lack and hard conditions that are the result of one's former ignorant beliefs and thoughts. After his first great victory of healing, or whatever it may be, man feels that he is eligible for the Promised Land and is forever past all that pertains to error. But there are still many old unbeliefs and results of ignorant thoughts and doings to be straightened out before his life becomes a "grand, sweet song." It is while he is meeting these difficulties and overcoming them that his faith is tested; in such cases he sometimes finds himself very negative instead of remaining firm and steadfast in Truth (the meaning signified by Massah).

Matred, mä'-trĕd (Heb.)—*following continually; pursuing; thrusting forward; propelling; shoving; driving forth; a short spear; a goad; a wand; a scepter; a royal mace.*

Daughter of Mezahab, and mother of Mehetabel the wife of Hadar. This Hadar was king of Edom (Gen. 36:39).

Meta. Matred and Mehetabel, women of Edom, pertain to activities in the soul's progress toward spiritual perfection. Even the phase of the soul that pertains to Edom, or the outer physical man, has its impulses that are uplifting and are ever moving toward the more perfect understanding and expression of Being.

Mezahab, father of Matred, means *water of gold, emanations of the shining one,* and represents a wisdom that is of the one light, or sun, Spirit, though it may be somewhat negative, as suggested by *water, water of gold.* Matred signifies the pushing or urging forward of the soul (*thrusting forward, propelling, shoving, driving forth*), by means of this wisdom for which Mezahab stands, to still higher and clearer light and dominion (*a scepter, a royal mace*). Mehetabel the daughter of Matred, meaning *to whom God does good, God is the greatest good, God benefits,* bespeaks the further awakening of the human soul to the goodness of God.

Matrites (A. V., Matri), măt′-rītes (fr. Heb.)—*rain of Jehovah; Jah is the objective; Jehovah is the mark; Jah is a watchtower; Jah is watching.*

The family of the tribe of Benjamin to which Saul, the son of Kish, and first king of Israel, belonged (I Sam. 10:21).

Meta. Matrites (*rain of Jehovah*) pertains to showers of blessings, the result of working in harmony with divine law. Matrites also denotes a group of thoughts in the active faith consciousness in man (Benjamin) that is awake to the fact that Jehovah, the indwelling Christ or Father, is ever *watching* over, guarding, and caring for His own, is attentive to one's every need. This group of thoughts is seeking perfection through I AM (*Jehovah is the objective, Jehovah is the mark*).

Mattan, măt′-tăn (Heb.)—*strength; firmness; adult; a gift; present; death of them.*

a A priest of Baal who was slain before the altars of Baal in Jerusalem (II Kings 11:18). **b** Father of Shephatiah, an Israelite of note, who accused Jeremiah of treason, in the days of Zedekiah, king of Judah (Jer. 38:1).

Meta. Mattan bespeaks the fullness of strength and stability (*strength, firm-*

ness, adult) as being of and from Spirit (*a gift, present*).

The Mattan who was a priest of Baal signifies a ruling thought belonging to man's formal concepts of religion. It leads the truer thoughts of the consciousness (Israelites) into idolatry by causing them to look to an outer personal God, with form and shape, and therefore limited, as the source of their strength and good; it also leads them to believe the outer manifest world and conditions to be real. Thus it leads to death (*death of them*) instead of life, and must be put out of consciousness.

The Mattan who was the father of Shephatiah of Judah also refers to a religious thought that relies too much on outer appearances, instead of having cultivated the spiritual faith and intuition that enable one to look back of the seeming to the real inner guidance and endurance of Spirit. Thus this thought belongs to the truer consciousness of man, but for the time being it fails to work for the best good of the individual.

Mattanah, măt′-tă-năh (Heb.)—*gift; present; donation; gratuity.*

A place where the Israelites camped while in the wilderness (Num. 21:18).

Meta. A consciousness of the divine favor and blessing, of one's possibilities through Spirit, of eternal life through Christ the Son, which is God's *gift* of gifts to man.

Mattaniah, măt-tă-nī′-ăh (Heb.)—*gift of Jehovah; donation of Jah; present of Jehovah.*

a The former name of Zedekiah, king of Judah (II Kings 24:17). **b** There were several others by this name, mostly Levites (I Chron. 25:4; II Chron. 29:13; Ezra 10:26, 27, 30; Neh. 11:17).

Meta. The perception, by the ruling thought of the higher consciousness in man and by other thoughts in this consciousness (one who became king of Judah, and other Israelites), of the grace of God, or the possibilities of attainment that the individual has through Christ (*gift of Jehovah*).

At this Mattaniah, or Zedekiah, stage of unfoldment, the individual does not seem to understand the necessity for being obedient to divine law. He perceives and expects God's blessings, all good, but does not realize the necessity for his being obedient to the good in order to reap good. (This seemed to be the trouble with Zedekiah and the people of Judah in his time. They wanted prophets to prophesy good to them while they went on in their wicked and unbelieving ways; thus they became very bitter against Jeremiah, who tried to show them the inevitable result of their transgressions of divine law.)

Mattatha, măt'-tă-thà (Gk. fr. Heb.)— *gift of Jehovah; donation of Jah; present of Jehovah.*

Father of Menna and son of Nathan, in the genealogy of Jesus Christ (Luke 3:31).

Meta. Virtually the same as Mattaniah: the higher religious thoughts of man awakening to a realization of his divine possibilities of obtaining fullness of life and of all good, through Jehovah, I AM.

Mattathias, măt-tă-thī'-ăs (Gk. fr. Heb.)—*gift of Jehovah; donation of Jehovah; present of Jehovah.*

Two men named in the genealogy of Jesus (Luke 3:25, 26).

Meta. See MATTATHA and MATTANIAH.

Mattattah (A. V., Mattathah), măt'-tăt-tăh (Heb.)—*gift of Jehovah; gratuity of Jah; given wholly unto Jehovah.*

An Israelite, son of Hashum. He had taken a foreign wife, but put her away at the injunction of Ezra (Ezra 10:33).

Meta. A thought in the higher consciousness of man (an Israelite) that perceives the possibilities that man has through his true, or Christ, self—I AM, Jehovah. This thought is learning the necessity of eliminating all error and limitations of the soul in order to make these high attainments (he put away his foreign wife at the instigation of Ezra) and gain eternal life, which in its fullness is for the whole man—spirit, soul, and body.

Mattenai, măt-tĕ'-nāi (Heb.)—*liberality; generosity; gift of Jehovah; gift of Jah.*

a Two Israelites who had taken foreign wives after returning from the Babylonian captivity (Ezra 10:33, 37).

b A priest (Neh. 12:19).

Meta. The significance is almost the same as that of MATTATTAH, which see. In Mattenai there is also a thought of divine forgiveness—an erasing of error from consciousness (*liberality, generosity*)—which increases the individual's belief in the attainment of the good that he has perceived.

Matthan, măt'-thăn (Heb.)—*reaching out the hand; giving; presenting; a gift; a present; a donation; a gratuity.*

Son of Eleazer and father of Jacob, in the genealogy of Jesus (Matt. 1:15).

Meta. The activity of the law of giving and receiving in the consciousness and life of the spiritually unfolding individual. The symbol of Matthan is the open hand, both in giving and receiving, imparting and appropriating.

Matthat, măt'-thăt (Gk. fr. Heb.)—*gift; present; gratuity; gift (of God); (God's) gift.*

Two men named in the genealogy of Jesus (Luke 3:24, 29).

Meta. God's gift to man is encompassed in the word "grace." We understand the grace of God to include all to which man is heir through his divine inheritance, his spiritual sonship. This includes all things, unlimited attainment of spirituality and good. Thus these names meaning *gift, God's gift,* signify the all-possibility that man has through Spirit. Fullness of life, love, wisdom, power, every spiritual quality, belongs to man now and always, and is attainable by him at this present time.

Matthew, măt'-thew (Heb.)—*gift of Jehovah; gratuity of Jah; given wholly unto Jehovah.*

A tax collector, who became one of the disciples of Jesus, and writer of the Gospel of Matthew (Matt. 9:9; 10:3). He is called Levi the son of Alphaeus, in Mark 2:14.

Meta. Matthew is the disciple of Jesus Christ who represents the will faculty in man. In the body this faculty is located in the forehead.

In the regeneration, man controls, directs, teaches, and disciplines the faculties of his mind. To do this he must in a measure withdraw from the mercenary occupations and the material ambitions that have absorbed his time and attention. Levi, afterward called Matthew, willingly gave up his money-getting and followed Jesus.

The disciples of Jesus "left all and followed him" (*given wholly unto Jehovah*). Peter was afraid that they had made a mistake, and he received this assurance from Jesus: "Verily I say unto you, There is no man that hath left house, or brethren, or sisters, or mother, or father, or children, or lands, for my sake, and for the gospel's sake, but he shall receive a hundredfold now in this time, houses, and brethren, and sisters, and mothers, and children, and lands." This is a promise that is always fulfilled where there is a whole-hearted surrender of the old life and a full absorption into the new. No one ever hears a devoted Christian worker express disappointment or regret over anything that he has forsaken in the worldly life. On the contrary there is rejoicing as each human link is severed, because the new relation in Christ is deeper and stronger than the human relation and because love is increased and real possessions are multiplied.

The will always enters into man's decisions. The will makes the final choice to give up all and follow Jesus. This lesson on the surrendering of the old ideas and conditions, that the greater increase of good may come into one's life, is based on Matthew because Matthew represents the will. The will has been given over to the thought of accumulation by imposition on external resources (tax-gatherer). In the regeneration the will is converted, and is taught by prayer and meditation how to stabilize the universal substance. Under the spiritual law the will becomes a producer instead of a parasite. When the individual will has become a disciple of the Christ, spiritual I AM, the schooling of the man begins.

Matthias, măt-thĭ'-ăs (Gk. fr. Heb.)— *gift of Jehovah; gratuity of Jah; given wholly unto Jehovah.*

The man who was chosen as a disciple in place of Judas (Acts 1:23, 26). The name is equivalent to Matthew.

Meta. Judas Iscariot, the disciple of Jesus whom Matthias was chosen to re-

place, represents the acquisitive or life faculty in individual consciousness. Matthias signifies the lifting up of this faculty (*given wholly unto Jehovah*) that it may aid the individual in laying hold of his higher, spiritual attainments, even eternal life, through the power of his indwelling Christ, I AM, Jehovah.

Mattithiah, măt-tĭ-thĭ'-ăh (Heb.)— *gift of Jehovah; gracious gift of Jah.*

There are five Israelites mentioned by this name. At least three of them were Levites (I Chron. 9:31; 15:18; 25:3; Ezra 10:43; Neh. 8:4).

Meta. Man's high, true, spiritual thoughts (Israelites) awakening to his divine possibilities of attaining perfection, fullness of abiding life, wholeness, peace, and all good, through I AM, Jehovah.

Mazzaroth, măz'-ză-rŏth (Heb.)— *prognostications; forewarnings; constellations, i. e., the twelve signs of the zodiac; stellar influx; circle of places; diadems; crowns.*

A name given to the signs of the zodiac (Job 38:32; see margin also). The signs of the zodiac and the names of the greater stars reach so far into the past that no one knows for certain just where they originated. Josephus and the Jewish rabbis claim that the science of astronomy began with the immediate descendants of Seth, who was Adam's son.

The zodiac is the name given by people of old to an imaginary band passing around the heavens, wide enough to include the circuits of the sun and the planets Mercury, Venus, Mars, Jupiter, Neptune, and Saturn. It is just a convenient method of reference to the position of the stars. Animal figures and outlines were chosen to represent these stars, and their relative position in the heavens, for animistic reasons.

Meta. For ages man has believed that he is influenced by the stars for good or for ill, according to the planet under which he has been born, and entirely apart from his own volition. However, we are now awaking to the truth of Shakespeare's declaration, "The fault . . . is not in our stars, but in ourselves, that we are underlings," and to the truth of God's own word in Genesis, to the effect that He made man in His own image and likeness, and gave him dominion. This dominion is, first of all, over himself. Thus man becomes master of his own fate and can make his life what he will. In time he will rule even the elements and the stars, consciously.

The query, "Canst thou lead forth the Mazzaroth in their season?", means: Can you cause the sun and the planets to make their prescribed circuits, and to continue in them? Mazzaroth, meaning *prognostications* and referring to the signs of the zodiac, signifies metaphysically one's power to guide one's own life and to foretell the outcome of the thoughts and intents of one's own mind and heart.

Mearah, mĕ-ā'-răh (Heb.)—*excavation; pit; cave; cavern; empty eye socket; without sight; blind; making empty.*

A place at the north of Palestine belonging to the Sidonians (Josh. 13:4). It was a portion of the "very much land" that remained to be possessed by the Israelites (see Josh. 13:1-7).

Meta. A deep-seated, subconscious belief in lack of both understanding and substance (*cave, excavation, without sight, blind, making empty*).

Mebunnai, mĕ-bŭn'-nāi (Heb.)—*from my son; my posterity; building; structure; edifice; restoration; reconstruction; thicket of Jehovah,* i. e., *multitude of Jah's people; council of Jehovah.*

"The Hushathite," one of David's mighty men, one of his "guard," or "council," margin (II Sam. 23:27).

Meta. The true thought in individual consciousness that outer man is in reality the *building* of Jehovah, is *from the son* of God, the Christ, or Jehovah. Therefore even the outer man is not really carnal, but is spiritual. His true thoughts are Jah's people; that is, they are of the Christ mind. Recognition of this truth by man leads to the restoration of his entire being.

Mecherathite, mĕch'-ĕ-răth-īte (Heb.) —*of the sword; piercing; opening up; wounding; machinations; evil devices; compressions; oppressions.*

Hepher the Mecherathite was one of David's mighty men (I Chron. 11:36). It

is thought that the word should be Maachathite.

Meta. Hepher refers to the opening up of the consciousness to a recognition and realization of the great life forces of the organism, deep within the soul. Mecherathite symbolizes the power of the word, by which the consciousness of the individual is quickened to an understanding of Truth. (In Scriptural symbology a *sword* pertains to the word, either as a thought unexpressed or spoken. In Ephesians 6:17 we read of "the sword of the Spirit, which is the word of God," and in Psalms 57:4 the tongue is likened to a sharp sword. Again in Isaiah 49:2 we read, "And he hath made my mouth like a sharp sword." In Mecherathite the word (*sword*) that quickens to an understanding of Truth evidently reveals error to be overcome also (*evil devices, oppressions*).

Meconah (A. V., Mekonah), mĕ-cō'-năh (Heb.)—*basis; foundation; a place,* i. e., *the temple; base; pedestal; standing place.*

A place in Judah to which some of the Israelites returned after the Babylonian captivity (Neh. 11:28).

Meta. An established faith in God. This is a firm, steady, secure place in consciousness, an inner assurance on which the individual can stand and rest (*foundation, base,* or *standing place*).

Medad, mē'-dăd (Heb.)—*loving; beloved; highly esteemed; pleasant; delightful; divided; apportioned; measured.*

An Israelite who did not go with Moses to the tent of meeting; but the Spirit of the Lord came upon him in the camp and he prophesied there. This occurred in the wilderness (Num. 11:26).

Meta. The loving thought; that in us which perceives that God is love, and seeks to measure our experiences and conditions from this standpoint. (See ELDAD.)

Medan, mē'-dăn (Heb.)—*contention; striving; judgment; righteousness; greatly enlarged; fully extended.*

One of the six sons of Abraham by his second wife, Keturah (Gen. 25:2). His descendants helped to people the land of Midian.

Meta. See MIDIAN.

Medeba, mĕd'-ĕ-bå (Heb.)—*waters of quiet; waters of rest; gently flowing waters; waters of peace.*

A town and plain or table-land that originally belonged to Moab. It was in the inheritance that Moses and Joshua gave to the tribe of Reuben, on the east of the Jordan (Num. 21:30; Josh. 13:9, 16; Isa. 15:2).

Meta. A peaceful, restful attitude (*gently flowing waters, waters of quiet*) that always follows a victory over the carnal mind (Moab) and a fuller awakening to true spiritual understanding by the inner sight or discernment (Reuben) in the individual.

Medes, mēdeş (fr. Heb.)—*sufficiency; abounding; measure; the middle, midst; capacity; middle portion; in the midst.*

Inhabitants of Media (II Kings 17:6; Esth. 1:19; Dan. 5:28).

Meta. Thoughts springing from and belonging to that in consciousness which Madai, or Media, represents. (See MADAI and MEDIA.)

Media, mē'-dĭ-å (fr. Heb.)—*sufficiency; abounding; measure; capacity; middle portion; in the midst; midland.*

A country in Asia that is always mentioned with Persia in the Bible. The Medes were descended from Madai, son of Japheth (Esth. 1:3).

Meta. The idea of *sufficiency* enters into the significance of Media and Madai only as the psychical in man is raised to spiritual understanding and realization. (See MADAI.)

Megiddo, mĕ-ğĭd'-dô (Heb.)—*place of many organisms; place of troops, i. e., for predatory incursions; crowded place; rendezvous; place of great abundance; most fortunate place.*

A royal city of the Canaanites that was captured by Joshua (Josh. 12:21). It was in Taanach by the waters of Megiddo that Sisera was overthrown, according to Judges 5:19. It was at Megiddo that King Ahaziah of Judah died, after he had been smitten by Jehu (II Kings 9:27); and it was there that Pharaoh-necoh, king of Egypt, slew Josiah, king of Judah (II Kings 23:29).

Meta. The gathering together of the hordes of error thoughts in consciousness (which sometimes seem to be countless) to make war against the truer and higher thoughts and ideals of the individual (*place of many organisms, place of troops, i. e., for predatory incursions, rendezvous*). If the higher thoughts are not true to their spiritual ideals they are sometimes overcome by these errors, as is suggested by the metaphysical significance of the kings of Judah who were slain at Megiddo, yet it is really a *most fortunate place,* because it affords an excellent opportunity for the individual to obtain a great and sweeping victory over error (Sisera and his hosts were defeated there), and thus to bring forth precious fruit (*place of great abundance*) for growth in righteousness and Truth.

Megiddon, mĕ-ğĭd'-dŏn (Heb.)—*place of many organisms; place of troops, i. e., for predatory incursions; crowded place; rendezvous; place of great abundance; most fortunate place.*

A form of Megiddo. It is mentioned in Zechariah 12:11 as a valley, a place of mourning: "In that day shall there be a great mourning in Jerusalem, as the mourning of Hadad–rimmon in the valley of Megiddon."

Meta. See MEGIDDO for the significance. See HADAD–RIMMON also, and you will understand why in this particular instance Zechariah refers to the valley of Megiddon as a place of mourning. It is a place of mourning only when seeming error has for the time being apparently replaced one's higher ideals and aspirations.

Mehetabel (in A. V., Nehemiah 6:10, Mehetabeel), mĕ-hĕt'-å-bĕl (Heb.)—*to whom God does good; God benefits; bettered of God; God is the greatest good; the best part is God; God-favored; God is good.*

a Daughter of Matred, and wife of Hadar, king of Edom (Gen. 36:39). **b** Father of Delaiah; also grandfather of Shemaiah, a prophet who was hired by Tobiah and Sanballat to prophesy falsely to Nehemiah and thus cause him to fear, so that his work in rebuilding the wall of Jerusalem might be hindered (Neh. 6:10).

Meta. The symbology of Mehetabel is included with Matred. (See MATRED.)

The Mehetabel of Nehemiah 6:10 also symbolizes a belief in the grace and goodness of God toward man. This belief, however, is more of the intellect than of true spiritual understanding; thus it brings forth ideas (such as Shemaiah) that can be influenced by the secret error thoughts of the sense consciousness for which Tobiah and Sanballat stand.

Mehir, mē'-hĭr (Heb.)—*price; value; wage; reward; dowry; rapidity; ability; dexterity.*

Son of Chelub, and "father" or founder of Eshton. He was of Judah (I Chron. 4:11).

Meta. A quick, active, able thought (*dexterity, ability*) in the Judah or praise consciousness of man, but limited, in its true expression, by a belief in serving for *reward* and by looking to the seeming *price* that one must pay for one's growth in Truth. The price is to give up that which pertains to the carnal and sense phase of one's being, and to do all things freely, as to the Lord. When one does this, the reward, the divine blessing, is abundant and quick to manifest.

Meholathite, mē-hŏl'-ăth-īte (fr. Heb.) —*the dancing; the mirthful; the joyful.*

An inhabitant of Abel–meholah. Saul gave his elder daughter Merab as wife to Adriel the Meholathite. (I Sam. 18:19; see II Sam. 21:8 also.)

Meta. A thought springing from and belonging to that in consciousness which Abel–meholah signifies. (See ABEL–MEHOLAH.)

Mehujael, mē-hū'-jà-ĕl (Heb.)—*manifestation of strength; physical demonstration of power; smitten by God; manifestation of God; grief of God.*

Son of Irad and father of Methushael, descendants of Cain (Gen. 4:18).

Meta. The belief of the outer man that strength and power are purely physical. This belief leads to error manifestations and demonstrations of power and strength that always lead to trouble of some kind; and the outer, personal man usually attributes to God the afflictions and griefs that are the result of his own error activities.

Mehuman, mē-hū'-măn (Heb. fr. Pers.)—*faithful; trustworthy; true.*

The first mentioned of the seven chamberlains, or eunuchs, who ministered in the presence of Ahasuerus the king (Esth. 1:10).

Meta. A thought belonging to the outer mental realm in individual consciousness that ministers to the puffed up, personal will (Ahasuerus the king). This thought is faithful, loyal, true. (See ABAGTHA.)

Me–jarkon, mē-jär'-kŏn (Heb.)— *waters of greenness; verdant waters; yellowish waters; golden waters; pale waters; limpid waters; clear waters; transparent waters.* The ancients did not make so fine a distinction between colors as we do. The idea in Me–jarkon embraces a range of colors that extends from the greenness of grass to the yellow of gold, and gold itself. A thin sheet of gold held up to transmitted light is green. In reflected light it is yellow.

A city of Dan (Josh. 19:46).

Meta. Thoughts of wisdom, of understanding, and of rich substance. (Yellow is the color that represents wisdom; gold also symbolizes substance and wisdom. Green bespeaks verdure, substance. *Clear waters, transparent waters,* also bespeak a clear, clean keenness of understanding and of vision.)

Melatiah, mĕl-à-tī'-ăh (Heb.)—*whom Jehovah delivers; Jah is the way of escape; Jehovah hath delivered; salvation of Jehovah.*

"The Gibeonite" who helped in repairing the wall of Jerusalem, under Nehemiah (Neh. 3:7).

Meta. A high, aspiring thought in consciousness (Gibeonite), whose chief characteristic is a belief in man's full deliverance from all error and its results, through the Christ, or I AM—divine wisdom and power. Thus this thought becomes a helper in the reconstruction or transformation of the body temple from its seemingly physical and error state to spiritual perfection. (This latter is symbolized in the repairing of Jerusalem's wall.)

Melchi, mĕl'-chī (Heb.)—*my king; my ruler; my counsel; my judge; of or belonging to the king.*

Two men named in the genealogy of Jesus Christ (Luke 3:24, 28).

Meta. A phase of the will ruling in man (*my king, my ruler*); there is also a suggestion of understanding and good judgment, as well as dominion, in the meaning of this name (*my counsel, my judge*).

Melchizedek, mĕl-chĭz'-ĕ-dĕk (Heb.)—*king of righteousness; righteous rule; upright counselor; righteous judgment; king of justice.*

"King of Salem," and "priest of God Most High," who "brought forth bread and wine" for Abram on his return from the slaughter of the heathen kings who had taken Lot captive (Gen. 14:18; Heb. 7). Of Jesus Christ it was said that He should be a priest forever, after the order of Melchizedek (Psalms 110:4; Heb. 5:6).

Meta. The divine will established in man in righteousness, justice, and peace (*king of righteousness, king of justice,* king of Salem, Salem meaning peace). Melchizedek really refers to the Christ mind or superconsciousness, that which when ruling in man's consciousness establishes and maintains right doing, perfect adjustment, peace, and perfection.

Melea, mē'-lĕ-à (Gk. fr. Heb.)—*fullness; fully supplied; abundance; full measure; multitude.*

Son of Menna and father of Eliakim, in the genealogy of Jesus Christ (Luke 3:31).

Meta. An inner discernment of the all-sufficiency of Spirit (*fullness, fully supplied, full measure*).

Melech, mē'-lĕch (Heb.)—*king; ruler; counselor; judge.*

Son of Micah, a Benjamite, descended from Saul through Jonathan (I Chron. 8:35).

Meta. A thought that belongs to the will. It rules in the active faith faculty in the individual, and has become discriminative to the extent of being able to counsel and advise the other thoughts of the phase of consciousness to which it belongs. (*King* pertains to the will, or to a ruling thought; Benjamite refers to the active faith faculty in man; *counselor, judge,* suggests discrimination and judgment. Saul, from whom Melech was descended, signifies the will, since he was a king of Israel; Jonathan, his son, and an ancestor of Melech, represents a phase of love. When the will begins to recog-

nize love and to unify itself with the love thought, it becomes less dictatorial and more discriminating.)

Melita, mĕl'-ĭ-tà (Gk.)—*flowing with honey; honeysweet; sweetened with honey; yielding honey.*

The ancient name for Malta, an island in the Mediterranean Sea. Paul and his companions landed upon this island when they were shipwrecked, while on their voyage to Rome (Acts 28:1).

Meta. Here Melita refers to the sweetness (*honey*), joy, and agreeable, pleasant feeling that are sensed deeply by the individual when in his overcoming he has experienced some great deliverance from error and has entered into the peace, content, and satisfaction that follow such an experience in overcoming.

Memphis (in A. V., Isaiah 19:13 and Jeremiah 2:16, Noph), mĕm'-phĭs (fr. Egypt.)—*Moph* or *Noph* from *Ma-m-phtah; place of Vulcan; temple of the good god,* i. e., *Osiris; place of the good; abode of the good; gate of the blessed ones.*

An ancient city of Egypt (Hos. 9:6); the capital of a portion of that country.

Meta. Egypt represents the depths of the body consciousness, subjective mind. We have looked upon Egypt as a darkened, ignorant, and very material phase of our being. Physically Egypt refers to the obscured vitality of the organism. It represents, too, a combination of substance and life in the body consciousness. Substance and life are essential to the rounding out of man's perfection. A union of life and substance with imagination (Joseph), spiritual I AM (Jacob), and true thoughts (Joseph's brothers) takes away much of the seeming obscurity of this hidden realm (Egypt) and is very essential to the well-being of even our spiritual faculties. Without substance and life the higher faculties come to want—there is a famine in their land. And so, at the heart of this Egypt, or seemingly darkened and obscure phase of our organism, we find an abiding place of good (Memphis, *abode of the good*). In reality this place of substance and life is good; man cannot get along without it. It leads to great blessings when understood and rightly appropriated and used *(gate of the blessed ones).* When Jesus was a babe His parents took Him down into Egypt to preserve His life from the destructive Herod.

Memucan, mĕ-mū'-căn (Heb. fr. Pers.) —*upright; true; honorable; dignity; authority.*

One of the seven princes of Media and Persia, "who saw the king's face, and sat first in the kingdom" (Esth. 1:14, 16, 21). Memucan counseled the king as to what he should do to Queen Vashti for disobeying his orders.

Meta. Seven is the number of the natural man. Memucan represents one of the seven creative principles that have been developed in the natural man. At its root it is *honorable, upright, true,* and good.

Menahem, mĕn'-ă-hĕm (Heb.)—*comforter; consoler; compassionate; repentant; lamenting; grieving; sighing; avenging.*

A king of Israel. "And Menahem the son of Gadi went up from Tirzah, and came to Samaria, and smote Shallum the son of Jabesh . . . and reigned in his stead" (II Kings 15:14). He paid a thousand talents of silver to Pul, the king of Assyria, to save Israel from being invaded by Assyria.

Meta. Ambitious desire (the root idea of Menahem is that of breathing forcibly, panting, sighing, either from desire or from contentment because of having received the fulfillment of the desire) seeking rulership in consciousness, seeking to dominate and guide the will; also the mistaken thought that one can gain satisfaction by the fulfillment of one's human desires. When the human will is actuated by human desire, when it is not established in love, Truth, and divine understanding, but thinks that deliverance and dominion are gained by means of force and violence (*avenging,* a son of Gadi, Gadi meaning *of Gad* and referring to the power faculty in man), it falls far short of being a real ruler and *comforter.* The history of Menahem shows this.

mene, mē'-nĕ (Chald.)—*numbered; counted out; measured; meted; allotted; apportioned; appointed.*

The first word of the warning to King Belshazzar of Babylon. It appeared in the form of handwriting on the wall (Dan. 5:25, 26): "MENE; God hath numbered thy kingdom, and brought it to an end."

Meta. The assurance that the ruling error phase of will and consciousness that Belshazzar and his kingdom represent has been taken account of (*numbered*) by the divine judge, the Spirit of truth, and that its end is at hand.

Menna (A. V., Menan), mĕn'-nȧ (Gk. fr. Heb.)—*numbered; meted; rewarded.*

Father of Melea and son of Mattatha, in the genealogy of Jesus Christ (Luke 3:31).

Meta. That in man's higher consciousness (this name is mentioned in the genealogy of Jesus Christ) which perceives that the constantly growing and increasing good thoughts, tendencies, and desires of the individual are all taken account of (*numbered*) by the Father indwelling, and that the individual reaps greater and greater good accordingly (*meted, rewarded*).

Menuhoth (A. V., Manahethites), mĕnū'-hŏth (Heb.)—*resting; quieting; restoring; bequeathing; giving; forsaking; abandoning.*

The same people as the Manahathites. They were inhabitants of a place, half of whom were descended from Shobal, the founder of Kiriath–jearim, and half from Salma, who founded Beth–lehem (see I Chronicles 2:52, 54).

Meta. See MANAHATHITES and MANAHATH.

Meonenim, mê-ŏn'-ê-nĭm (Heb.)—*beclouded; covered over; covert; overcast; darkened; hidden; wizards; soothsayers; sorcerers; magicians; enchanters; occultists.*

A plain or place in Ephraim near Shechem. The "oak of Meonenim" is mentioned in Judges 9:37 as the way by which one of Abimelech's companies of men came down to fight against Shechem.

Meta. That in the consciousness of the individual which attributes great strength and power to divination, to the psychic ability to foretell events, to tell fortunes, and to predict things that are coming to pass (*soothsayers, wizards, enchanters*).

While education and true spiritual understanding are getting the race as a whole farther and farther away from belief in such things as sorcery, every one finds at a certain stage of his unfoldment that there is in his consciousness more or less of a superstitious belief in "fate," "luck," the power of some persons to predict things for others and even to place a curse upon others. This belief must be dealt with in the light of the Holy Spirit and put away, that one may become fully alive to the real truth, which is that man is not subject to any kind of fate, prediction, or error, but has the power through his own I AM dominion, his indwelling Christ, to make his life what he will and to change the course of events in it as he will.

Meonothai, mĕ-ŏn'-ô-thāi (Heb.)—*my dwellings; my habitations; Jah's abodes.*

A man named in the genealogy of Judah (I Chron. 4:14). He was the father of Ophrah.

Meta. A thought in the Judah consciousness, or praise-and-prayer consciousness, of the spiritually awakening individual that perceives and acknowledges that the habitations of man—the consciousness and the organism of each individual—are the abodes of Jehovah (*my dwellings, Jah's abodes*). Jehovah and man cannot be separated, since every man's higher self, or true I AM, is Jehovah, the Christ, and thence the outer man draws his life and existence.

Mephaath, mĕph'-ă-ăth (Heb.)— *height; lofty place; hill; shining; brilliant; illuminative; splendor; beauty.*

A city that Moses gave to the tribe of Reuben (Josh. 13:18). It was later given over to the Merarite Levites (Josh. 21:37). In Jeremiah's prophecy of the destruction of Moab, Mephaath is mentioned as a city of that nation (Jer. 48:21).

Meta. A group of exalted thoughts in consciousness (a city, *height*) whose central, ruling ideas and radiations are discernment (*illuminative, shining, brilliant,* a city of Reuben, Reuben referring to discernment or sight). But by the action of carnal thoughts (this city afterward came into the possession of Moab, and its destruction was prophesied by

Jeremiah) this group of thoughts or state of consciousness that Mephaath represents becomes impregnated with material beliefs that bring it under the law of dissolution; thus it passes away instead of remaining in Truth and bringing forth abiding good fruit.

Mephibosheth, mĕ-phĭb'-ô-shĕth (Heb.) —*breathing shame; blowing away confusion; scattering disgrace; dispersing ignominy; exterminating idolatry.*

Son of Jonathan, and grandson of Saul (II Sam. 4:4). He was lame in his feet, and was cared for by David after Saul and Jonathan were slain (II Sam. 9:5-13).

Meta. The faculty of mind that, though without full understanding of spiritual law as it relates to the manifest, symbolized by the crippled feet (feet stand for the phase of understanding that comes in touch with the world and outer conditions), has caught a glimpse of the divine pattern in the spiritual heavens of man's mind, and therefore endeavors to erase from consciousness all limited images and beliefs (*blowing away confusion, exterminating idolatry*).

The history of Mephibosheth shows us to what a destructive end an unrestrained exercise of the personal will can come. David found him in the house of Machir, which means *sold*, at the place called Lodebar, which means *barren.* The house of Saul was reduced to a barren, crippled state.

The invisible power that brought Mephibosheth into the house of David, where henceforth he was to eat bread at the king's table, was that love (David) sees perfection everywhere, and attracts forces of a character like its own. That which Mephibosheth symbolizes erases false images that have been formed in the mind by false thinking, and thus opens the way for the perfect to manifest. Therefore Mephibosheth is a servant of David (love) and is worthy to eat at his table.

Merab, mē'-răb (Heb.)—*increase; enlargement; greatness; greatly multiplied; myriad.*

Eldest daughter of Saul (I Sam. 14:49). Saul promised her to David for his wife, but gave her to Adriel the Meholathite instead (I Sam. 18:17, 19).

Meta. See ADRIEL.

Meraiah, mê-rā'-ĭăh (Heb.)—*vision of Jah; revelation of Jah; rebellion against Jehovah.*

A priest, of the house of Seraiah, in Joiakim's time (Neh. 12:12).

Meta. A natural religious tendency ruling in the higher thoughts of the consciousness of the awakening individual (a priest, of the "heads of fathers' *houses*"), that is open to the inspiration of the Christ mind (*vision of Jah, revelation of Jah*).

The thought of *rebellion against Jehovah,* which is suggested as a definition of Meraiah, shows that there is still something of the satanic characteristic in this religious tendency, and so a further lifting up or spiritualizing of it is in order.

Meraioth, mê-rā'-ĭŏth (Heb.)—*aspects; forms; visions; revelations; inversions; perversions; rebellions.*

a A man named in the genealogy of Levi (I Chron. 6:6). b A priest of Israel (I Chron. 9:11; Neh. 11:11).

Meta. The love faculty in man needs cleansing and lifting to a higher level, that all hatred, strife, jealousy, and the like may be removed. (Levi, a son of Jacob, symbolizes the love faculty in the natural man; priests refer to our natural, religious ruling tendencies in their varying degrees of understanding.) Meraioth, named in the genealogy of Levi and also named as a priest of Israel, and meaning *visions, revelations, perversions, rebellions,* reveals the foregoing truth.

The darkened, ignorant beliefs about God and about man that have permeated man's natural religious tendencies and governed them to a greater or less extent throughout the ages have so warped his love nature that, where all should be true understanding, kindness, forgiveness, joy, strength, and peace, with good will abounding, we find much bitterness, rebellion, and contention to be overcome. Love must rule in us fully, that true righteousness and wholeness may be established throughout our being.

Merari, mê-rā'-rī (Heb.)—*galling; bitter; unhappy; disobedient; rebellious.*

Son of Levi (Gen. 46:11).

Meta. A *bitter, rebellious,* inharmonious state of thought existing in the love consciousness of the natural man (Levi, father of Merari, was the son of Jacob who represents the love faculty in man). Merari signifies love directed by the ignorance and selfishness of the personal man; this gives a *bitter, disobedient* trend to one's thoughts and experiences, instead of the abiding peace, strength, and good that are always the result of true love's expressing in consciousness in union with wisdom. (See MAHLI and JAAZIAH, sons of Merari.)

Merarites, mê-rā'-rītes (fr. Heb.)—*of* or *belonging to Merari.*

Descendants of Merari the son of Levi (Num. 26:57).

Meta. Thoughts in consciousness springing from and belonging to that which Merari signifies. (See MERARI.)

Merathaim, mĕr-ă-thā'-ĭm (Heb.)—*double bitterness; double rebellion.*

A symbolical name given to Babylon on account of the double captivity to which the Israelites had been subjected by this country (Jer. 50:21).

Meta. The increasing resistance, strife, obstinacy (*double rebellion*), grief, distress, and all-round inharmony (*double bitterness*) that the higher consciousness of man (Israelites) experiences as his bondage to confused, error thoughts (Babylon) grows seemingly deeper and stronger while he allows himself to drift farther away from the Truth that frees.

Mercury (A. V., Mercurius), mĕr'-cū-rў (Lat.)—*Latin name for Hermes; swift messenger; reciprocal activity; commerce; trade; eloquence; oratory; interpretation.*

A name given to Paul in Lycaonia. Mercury was worshiped by the Greeks and Romans as the god of eloquence. The people of Lycaonia thought that the gods had come down to them in the persons of Paul and Barnabas. They called Paul Mercury because he was the chief speaker (Acts 14:12).

Meta. Worship of the intellect; the intellect in man attaining knowledge (*interpretation, oratory, eloquence*) from the outer material world and worshiping at this shrine instead of understanding that omnipresent Spirit is back of the manifest world, even of the stars, which represent remote and little understood ideas and powers. Spirit is the one source of all; therefore all homage, reverence, praise, honor, and worship should be given to God—Divine Mind, Spirit, Principle, Truth.

Mered, mē'-rĕd (Heb.)—*falling away; falling away from allegiance; rebellion; disobedient; perverse; rebellious; going down; cast down; subdued; descended.*

Son of Ezrah, in the genealogy of Judah (I Chron. 4:17).

Meta. Mered is closely associated with a high, exalted phase of consciousness in man, as is signified by his father Ezrah and his brothers Jalon, Jether, and Epher; also by the fact that he was an Israelite, of the tribe of Judah. But the definitions of the name that denote *falling away from allegiance, rebellious, perverse,* show that the adverse mind (Satan) has a foothold in the thought that Mered signifies. The adverse, rebellious phase of thought has not yet been fully cast out of the Judah, or the praise-and-prayer, life consciousness at this stage of the unfoldment of the individual. It seems that as the consciousness of man is lifted up the Adversary comes up with it. The Adversary will continue to express in higher and more deceptive ways until he shall finally be cast out of heaven entirely, and also out of the earth, heaven referring in a general way to the mind of man and the earth to his body. (See Rev. 12:7-10.)

Meremoth, mĕr'-ĕ-mŏth (Heb.)—*elevations; heights; elations; exaltations; powers; glories.*

a Son of Uriah the priest. Meremoth was given charge of the silver and gold and the vessels in the house of God, after the return from the Babylonian captivity (Ezra 8:33); he helped rebuild the wall of Jerusalem (Neh. 3:4, 21). **b** A man named Meremoth joined Nehemiah in sealing the covenant (Neh. 10:5).

Meta. Exalted spiritual thoughts, thoughts of power and might, in man's higher and truer realm of consciousness (Israelites). These thoughts minister in the house of God (body temple). They do much toward establishing the true worship of God in the consciousness of the individual who gives them place, and they work toward building the whole organism in Truth, that it may be renewed and become abiding.

Meres, mē'-rĕṣ (Heb. fr. Pers.)—*high; worthy; dignified; honorable; lofty.*

One of the seven princes of Persia and Media, in the reign of Ahasuerus (Esth. 1:14).

Meta. One of the seven creative principles, or dominant ruling thoughts, that are developed in the natural man; seven is the number of the natural man. This creative principle, or dominant ruling thought, is essentially of a *high, lofty, worthy* character; at its foundation it is spiritual. However, since it is expressing in the natural man, who is at this phase of his unfoldment ignorant of the truth of man's being and is under the dominion of the puffed-up, personal will (King Ahasuerus), error undoubtedly enters into it, and error always works in a nonspiritual way in the consciousness and the organism.

Meribah, mĕr'-ĭ-băh (Heb.)—*pleading; contention; strife; quarrel.*

A place in the wilderness where there was no water to drink, and the people "strove with Moses, and said, Give us water that we may drink." It was there that Moses smote the rock, at the command of Jehovah, and water came out of it for the people to drink (Exod. 17:7; Num. 27:14).

Meta. The seemingly ever present tendency in the carnal of us to murmur, complain, and doubt God every time we have an opportunity to prove Him true and to overcome some error in ourselves. So long as everything is going along smoothly we are happy and we think that we have abundant faith in God, the good. But just so soon as some apparent lack or inharmony descends upon us we begin to wonder why God ever let it come, and doubts and complaints creep in if we are not very watchful. (Jesus said to Peter, "Watch and pray, that ye enter not into temptation: the spirit indeed is willing, but the flesh is weak" Matt. 26:41.)

The tendency to complain diminishes as we progress in our understanding of Truth and in putting off the "old man" of sin and putting on Christ, until finally the tendency will disappear entirely. It is very apparent in virtually every one, however, at the beginning of his unfoldment Spiritward. It was because of giving way to this tendency of the carnal to doubt and complain that the Children of Israel who left Egypt, all but Joshua and Caleb, lost their bodies in the wilderness and failed to enter the Promised Land. We must fully overcome this tendency if we would enter God's sabbath of rest here and now, the perfection of life and good that is our divine inheritance (see Heb. 3:8-19; 4; see MASSAH, also).

Merib–baal, mĕr'-ĭb–bā'-ăl (Heb.)—*contender with Baal; striving with Baal; who resists Baal.*

Son of Jonathan; the same person as Mephibosheth (I Chron. 8:34).

Meta. See BAAL and MEPHIBOSHETH.

Merodach, mĕ-rō'-dăch (Heb.)—*Mars, i. e., god of blood and slaughter; war; death; slaughter; murder; bitter contrition; sacrifice.*

Mars, under the name of Merodach, was worshiped by the ancient Babylonians and Semites. Human sacrifices were offered to this god, hence Mars became the god of war, or of blood and slaughter. Merodach was also used as a title, or surname, of some of the kings of Babylon (Jer. 50:2).

Meta. The belief that war, fighting, evil, and death are necessary in man's existence, and are inevitable. To the extent that an individual believes any apparent evil or inharmony to be necessary or inevitable, and fears it, to that extent he worships the thought for which Merodach stands; he worships the Babylonian god Merodach and not the true God, in whom is good only. To the extent that one believes in evil of any kind, and magnifies it in one's consciousness by thinking about it, to that extent one remains in confusion (Babylon). (See BERODACH–BALADAN.)

Merom, mē'-rŏm (Heb.)—*height; altitude; elevation; elation; far above; the highest.*

A lake in Palestine, through which the Jordan River flows; it is above the Sea of Galilee. It was there that several of

the kings of the Canaanitish tribes encamped when they came up to fight against Israel; Joshua and the Israelites fought with them at Merom and defeated them (Josh. 11:5, 7).

Meta. The Sea of Galilee signifies a sea of vitality, or of life activity, of nerve energy. The Jordan River also refers to the life current, or life flow of thoughts in the body. Merom, a lake of the Jordan, in Palestine, above the Sea of Galilee, and meaning *elevation, height, far above, highest,* typifies one's lifting up the life energy to a very exalted place in consciousness. This results in a very great victory by Joshua and his Israelitish army (I AM, unified with the true thoughts of the consciousness) over the enemies in the land (one's lower, limited, error, carnal beliefs about life).

Meronothite, mē-rŏn'-ŏ-thīte (fr. Heb.)—*rejoicer; singer; crier; wailer; mourner.*

Jehdeiah the Meronothite had charge of the king's asses, in David's reign (I Chron. 27:30). Jadon the Meronothite is mentioned in Nehemiah 3:7, as one who helped in repairing Jerusalem's wall.

Meta. The harmony and the joy of mind that are realized by the individual when he learns to exercise good judgment (Jadon) and when he consciously unifies himself with Jehovah, the inner Christ. This idea of union is signified by Jehdeiah. (See JEHDEIAH and JADON.)

Meroz, mē'-rŏz (Heb.)—*contracting oneself; shrinking; becoming compact; firmly rooted; firm; stable; refuge; secret place; retreat.*

Curses were pronounced against Meroz because its inhabitants did not join Barak in fighting against Sisera and his hosts (Judg. 5:23). Evidently it was a place in Palestine belonging to the Israelites, though its location is unknown.

Meta. A phase of thought that receives Truth to itself but does not give out Truth. Thus, though it tends to make the consciousness stable and firm, it must learn to radiate its good, to assert itself positively in the expression and promulgation of the good, that it may aid actively in the progress of the unfolding individual and may not lack substance and vitality. The law of all growth and increase is that use must be made of what one already possesses. If man uses what he has, he gains more; but if he hides away his talents and does not use them, even that which he has will be taken away from him. Jesus taught this truth in His parables of the pounds and of the talents (Luke 19: 13-26; Matt. 25:15-30).

Mesha, mē'-shȧ (Heb.)—*harvest of spiritual fruits; heaped-up fullness of being; refuge; withdrawal; departure; deliverance; salvation; freedom.*

a A place named as being on the border of the land occupied by the descendants of Joktan (Gen. 10:30). **b** A king of Moab who was a sheepmaster and paid tribute to the king of Israel in great numbers of lambs, rams, and wool (II Kings 3:4, with marginal note). **c** The name of two Israelites, one of Judah and one of Benjamin (I Chron. 2:42; 8:9).

Meta. The freeing (*deliverance, freedom*) of the inner life forces of the organism from the dominion of carnal thought (Moab), by means of praise and prayer (Judah) and an active faith (Benjamin), thus raising them to higher and more spiritual expression (*salvation*).

Mesha, king of Moab, was a sheepmaster, and gave tribute to the king of Israel in sheep, rams, and wool. This shows that the inner meaning of this name has to do with the pure natural life forces of the organism (sheep); also with substance (wool) that has been under the dominion of the ruling thought of the carnal mind (king of Moab). The definitions of the name, and the fact that it belonged to a man of Judah and one of Benjamin, point to the upliftment and redemption of this state of consciousness and its abundant fruit of good (*harvest of spiritual fruits, heaped-up fullness of being*).

Meshach, mē'-shăch (Heb. fr. Pers.) —*guest of the king; guest of the shah; guest of the mighty one; withdrawn from the temple.*

A name given to Mishael, one of Daniel's three companions, by the prince of the eunuchs, in Babylon. Meshach was one of the three who were saved out of the fiery furnace (Dan. 1:7; 2:49; 3:12-30).

Meta. Love. Love is the *guest of the mighty one* that we all seek to entertain continuously throughout our being—the never failing love of God. Love is the attracting power of the universe; it is that which draws to us all good; it is irresistible.

Meshech (in A. V., Psalms 120:5, Mesech), mē'-shĕch (Heb.)—*perceptibility; perceptible cause,* i. e., distinguished from prime cause, which is not perceptible; *meditative conceptions; drawing out; deducting.*

a Son of Japheth (Gen. 10:2). **b** In I Chronicles 1:17, Mash the son of Aram is called Meshech. Meshech is mentioned in Ezekiel 27:13, with Tubal and Javan, two other sons of Japheth; there the names no doubt refer to countries or tribes of people descended from these men, and called by their name. (See Ezekiel 38:2, 3.)

Meta. Perception through the senses; judging according to appearances; the work of the mind in its drawing of conclusions and in conceiving ideas.

Meshelemiah, mē-shĕl-ē-mī'-ȧh (Heb.) —*whom Jehovah repays; whom Jehovah makes whole; Jehovah recompenses; Jah completes; friendship of Jah; peace of Jehovah.*

A Levite. His son Zechariah was porter of the door of the tent of meeting, in Saul's and David's reigns (I Chron. 9:21). He is named, with his sons, in Chronicles 26:1, 2, 9, also.

Meta. A natural religious tendency belonging to the love faculty and performing a definite work in the consciousness (a Levite who, with his sons and some other relatives, had charge of the east gate of the Temple in David's reign). This thought perceives the law of health and perfection (*whom Jehovah makes whole, Jah completes*), also the law of giving and receiving, sowing and reaping (*whom Jehovah repays, Jehovah recompenses*), and is in harmony with the indwelling Christ (*friendship of Jah*); it therefore experiences great peace (*peace of Jehovah*).

Meshezabel (A. V., Meshezabeel), mē-shĕz'-ȧ-bĕl (Heb.)—*whom God frees; God is deliverer; delivered by God.*

Named among Israelites who returned

from the Babylonian captivity (Neh. 3:
4; 10:21; 11:24).

Meta. That in man's high, true
thoughts (Israelites) which perceives
and accepts divine deliverance from the
confusion of mind signified by Babylon
(*God is deliverer, delivered by God*).

Meshillemoth, mĕ-shĭl'-lĕ-mŏth (Heb.)
—*retributions; recompenses; restorations; reconciliations; friendships; perfections.*

a His son Berechiah was one "of the
heads of the children of Ephraim," who
stood against the Israelites who had carried away captive their brethren of the
children of Judah, and induced them to
let the captives return to their own
homes (II Chron. 28:12). **b** Descendants of another Meshillemoth are named
among priests who returned from the
Babylonian captivity (Neh. 11:13).

Meta. That in man's natural religious
tendencies (a priest of Israel), and in
his executive faculty (Ephraim, signifying the will), which perceives the perfect
justice of, and equilibrium to be attained
by, the divine law of sowing and reaping
(*recompenses, retributions, restorations*).
Man reaps according to his sowing. By
means of this law, rightly understood
and based on the Christ Truth, all
debts can be repaid, and perfect reconciliation between man and God and between man and man can be attained; the
result will be peace and perfection of
spirit, soul, and body.

Meshobab, mĕ-shō'-băb (Heb.) —
*turned about; returned; restored; deliv-
ered; rewarded; rendered back.*

A prince of the Simeonites (I Chron.
4:34, 38).

Meta. Simeon, meaning *hearing*, refers to the listening, attentive, obedient
attitude of mind in man. Meshobab, a
prince of the Simeonites, and meaning
returned, restored, delivered, rewarded,
signifies a return by the individual to the
place of spiritual receptivity and obedience, with the great deliverance from
bondage and error that is the natural
result.

Meshullam, mĕ-shŭl'-lăm (Heb.)—*devoted; allied; associated; friend, i. e.,
of God; peaceful; pacified; perfected.*

a A Gadite (I Chron. 5:13). **b** One

who stood at the left hand of Ezra when
he read the book of the law to the people
(Neh. 8:4). **c** There were several other
Israelites by this name.

Meta. Thoughts in man's higher consciousness (Israelites) that are in accord with the Christ Spirit, with Truth
(*devoted*).

These thoughts are *friends* and *associates* of and are unified (*allied*) with Divine Mind; therefore that which is peaceable and perfect (*peaceful, perfected*)
is their keynote.

Meshullemeth, mĕ-shŭl'-lĕ-mĕth (Heb.)
—*devotee; ally; associate; friend, i. e.,
of God; peaceful; pacific; perfect.*

Wife of Manasseh, and mother of
Amon, kings of Judah. She was the
daughter of Haruz of Jotbah (II Kings
21:19).

Meta. The soul in harmony with the
Spirit of truth, or divine law (*friend,
i. e., of God*), and the *peaceful* state of
being that this alliance with Spirit produces.

Mesopotamia, mĕs-ŏ-pô-tā'-mĭ-à (Gk.)
*country between; middle region; middle
land.*

The country between the Tigris and
Euphrates rivers. Nahor, a city of Mesopotamia, was Rebekah's home (Gen.
24:10); in the margin Mesopotamia is
called "*Aram–naharaim; that is, Aram of
the two rivers.*" Aram is another word
for Syria, and so we find Rebekah's
brother Bethuel called the Syrian (Gen.
28:5). Mesopotamia is also mentioned
in Judges 3:8 and Acts 2:9. In Acts
7:2 we read that Abram was living in
Mesopotamia when God appeared to him
and told him to leave his own land and his
kindred and go to another country that
would be shown him.

Meta. See ARAM–NAHARAIM.

The state of consciousness that Mesopotamia represents lies close to the spiritual, at least close enough to be open
to the divine urge for higher light and
attainment. Otherwise it could not have
been the home of Rebekah and her
brother, nor of Abraham at the time that
he received from God the revelation directing him to come out from his people
into another country (to enter into a
higher and more spiritual phase of con-

sciousness) that he might possess his divine inheritance.

Messiah (A. V., Messias), mĕs-sī'-ăh (Heb.)—*anointed; consecrated by unction; constituted; appointed; consecrated; dedicated.*

The Hebrew equivalent for the Greek Christos, and referring in John 1:41; 4:25, 26 to Jesus Christ. The priests and kings of ancient Israel, and whoever and whatever were set apart for God's service, were anointed, under the old Jewish customs, and called the anointed of the Lord; but the word Messiah, *anointed,* has always referred especially to the advent of the Christ, that had been expected for ages. In Daniel 9:25, 26, where "the anointed one" is given in the American Standard Version, "the Messiah" (25th verse) or "Messiah" (26th verse) is given in the Authorized Version.

Meta. Set apart, *consecrated,* baptized of the Holy Spirit, illuminated, enlightened, endowed with a special mission. (See CHRIST, and JESUS CHRIST, for a fuller comprehension of the Messiah as referring to the Christ—the Savior of the world.)

Methushael (A. V., Methusael), mĕ-thū'-shå-ĕl (Heb.)—*man of God; extension of God; man who (is) of God; yawning gulf of death; extremity of death.*

A descendant of Cain's (Gen. 4:18).

Meta. The idea that man is a spiritual and perfect being is of God, and is inherent even in the body consciousness of man (Cain and his descendants refer to the outer or physical consciousness). Methushael refers also to the error idea of death, to disintegration of the outer organism, that unenlightened man thinks is desirable, inevitable, and of God. Thus unenlightened man is divided against himself, holds to both good and evil; as long as he does this he must reap accordingly.

Methuselah, mĕ-thū'-ṣé-lăh (Heb.)— *man of the sword; man of the dart; extension of the sword; swift hurled dart of death; sending forth of death; sting of death.*

Son of Enoch, of the line of descent from Adam through Seth. Methuselah has the record of having lived longer than any other man in the earthly body (Gen. 5:21-27).

Meta. A quick, piercing thought, or word (*man of the sword, man of the dart*) of life, power, and oneness with God which, while it causes a renewal of youth in degree, and serves to lengthen one's life in the body (*sending forth of death*), does not become abiding enough in the consciousness at the Methuselah stage of man's unfoldment to put away the appearance of death entirely (*sting of death*).

Meunim (in A. V., I Chronicles 4:41, habitations; in II Chronicles 26:7, Mehunims; in Ezra 2:50, Mehunim), mĕ-ū'-nĭm (Heb.)—*habitations; dwellings; homes; retreats; asylums; refuges; lairs; dens.*

A people who were enemies of the Israelites; the Lord helped Uzziah, king of Judah, against them (II Chron. 26:7). "The children of Meunim" who were among the returned Nethinim are believed to have been descendants of some of these people who were overcome by the Israelites (see I Chronicles 4:41 and Ezra 2:50).

Meta. An abiding place (*habitations, dwellings*) of substance and life in consciousness. This substance and life have been expressing on the animal plane, but are laid hold of by the higher and more spiritual thoughts and activities of the consciousness (Israelites) and are consecrated to the Lord, and thus are raised to higher expression and service.

The lifting up of this phase of seemingly material substance and life that the Meunim signify is revealed in the history of the Meunim as given in the Bible. They lived in a rich pasture country. They were conquered by the Simeonites (Simeonites refer to the seeing or perceiving faculty of mind), who destroyed them and dwelt in their country, making use of their pastures and flocks (see I Chron. 4:24-41). The margin, verse 41, says, "*devoted them*" in place of "destroyed them" as stated in the text. Then in the writings of Ezra and Nehemiah we find that later the descendants of these Meunim were serving as Nethinim in the Temple.

Me–zahab, mĕ–zā'–hăb (Heb.) —

water of gold; universal manifestation of light's glory; water of the golden light; water of purity; water of the sun, i. e., *light radiations; emanations of the shining one.*

An Edomite. Father of Matred, who was the mother of Mehetabel wife of Hadar, a king of Edom (Gen. 36:39).

Meta. A wisdom that, though expressing through the outer, earthly phase of man's consciousness (Me-zahab was an Edomite, and the Edomites refer to the physical in man), yet is of, or emanates from, the one light or sun, the Spirit of God—divine intelligence. This wisdom that Me-zahab signifies, while it is *emanations of the shining one—* God, is somewhat negative here in its expression by the outer man, as is suggested by "water," *water of gold.* (See MATRED.)

Mezobaite (A. V., Mesobaite), mē-zō'-bă-īte (Heb.)—*station of Jah,* i. e., *where He stands; the Lord's standing place; monument of Jehovah; pillar of Jah.*

A title given to Jaasiel. There is nothing known of any place from which this name could be taken (I Chron. 11: 47).

Meta. Jaasiel signifies the illumined reason or intellect (Abner, father of Jaasiel) awakening to the truth that God, Spirit, Divine Mind, is the source of all intelligence, of all true understanding, and is also the creator or maker (from definitions of Jaasiel) of the universe; that, separated from Spirit, nothing (man included) could come into being or could stay in existence for a moment. This understanding of God as omnipresent Spirit—life, substance, and intelligence—in whom and by whom all things exist, is *the Lord's standing place* (Mezobaite) in individual consciousness. It is the foundation truth in which Jehovah and man find a common meeting place.

Mibhar, mĭb'-här (Heb.)—*proved; examined; approved; chosen; choice; selected; best; delightful; excellent; youth,* i. e., *choice, in the prime of manhood, ripe, vigorous.*

Son of Hagri, and one of David's mighty men (I Chron. 11:38).

Meta. A new, high, discriminating, superior thought in consciousness (*approved, chosen, selected, best*); a thought of the vitality and vigor of *youth,* that allies itself to the ruling David, or love faculty, and becomes one of its strong supporters.

Mibsam, mĭb'-săm (Heb.)—*having good smell; aromatic; fragrant; sweet odor; delightful; pleasant.*

a Son of Ishmael (Gen. 25:13). **b** A son of Shallum, a Simeonite (I Chron. 4:25).

Meta. A perception or sensing of the joys and beauties of Spirit. This is possessed in degree both by a phase of the sense or carnal mind (son of Ishmael) and by a thought in the higher, more awakened and receptive mentality of the individual (a Simeonite). The sense of smell signifies the power to perceive, discriminate, detect, estimate; while the sweetness or fragrance of odor, given as the meaning of this name, suggest the joys of spiritual realities.

Mibzar, mĭb'-zär (Heb.)—*cut off; inaccessible; walled; lofty; impervious; fortified; difficult for assault; fortification.*

A chief of Edom, descended from Esau (Gen. 36:42).

Meta. A ruling belief of the carnal mind in man that the things of Spirit, of God, are hard to understand, that they are so far removed from the apparently finite mind of man that they are unattainable.

Mica (A. V., Micha), mī'-cȧ (Heb.)— *who is like Jehovah?; who can assimilate Jah?*

a Son of Mephibosheth, who was Jonathan's son (II Sam. 9:12). **b** One who joined Nehemiah in sealing the covenant (Neh. 10:11). **c** A Levite who is mentioned in Nehemiah 11:17, 22.

Meta. Thoughts in the high, true consciousness of man and among his natural religious tendencies (Israelites, and one a Levite) that have awakened to a perception of the magnitude and perfection, the love, greatness, and glory, of the Christ, of man's true, spiritual I AM, or Jehovah (*who is like Jehovah? who can assimilate Jah?*). When these revelations come to the human mind and soul, they cause man to seem very lowly and humble in his own eyes, since they expose the falsity of the personal that has hitherto been intent upon exalting itself. When one sees that the righteousness and glory of the outer personal self, apart from the true knowledge of God, are "as a polluted garment" (Isa. 64: 6), one can then see the necessity of putting on Christ.

Micah (in A. V., I Chronicles 24:24, Michah), mī'-eăh (Heb.)—*who is like unto Jehovah?; who can assimilate Jah?*

a A man of the hill country of Ephraim, who made a graven image, a molten image, an ephod, and a teraphim; he kept these in his house and had a Levite for his priest. This was in a time when "there was no king in Israel," but "every man did that which was right in his own eyes" (Judg. 17; 18). b The prophet Micah, the Morashtite, who lived in the days of Jotham, Ahaz, and Hezekiah, kings of Judah (Mic. 1:1). c There were other men by this name (I Chron. 5:5; 8:34; 24:24; II Chron. 34:20).

Meta. The individual's awakening to the truth of his real being, to the fact that in his real, true self he is spiritual, was made in the image and likeness of God, and is endowed with all the possibilities that can be attained through the use of his spiritual powers: life, love, wisdom, intelligence, faith, strength, power, substance, all that is contained in the Son, the Christ, Jehovah, I AM (*who is like unto Jehovah?*). This makes the individual both a prophet of God and a priest of God.

Micaiah, mī-eā'-ĭăh (Heb.)—*who is like Jah?; who can assimilate Jah?*

Son of Imlah, a true prophet of God in the days of Ahab, king of Israel, and Jehoshaphat, king of Judah (I Kings 22: 8).

Meta. The prophetic phase of man's higher consciousness, which perceives that the powers of Being are active in and through man, and foresees the end of all error activities in him even though for the time being the individual will is seemingly engaged in promoting these error activities. It also knows the futility of the personal will's trying in its own power to put away the inharmonious results of its idolatrous deeds. (Mi-

caiah told the wicked King Ahab of Israel what the outcome would be if he went up to fight against the king of Syria.)

Michael, mī'-ehå-ĕl (Heb.)—*who is like unto God?; who is like God; who is assimilated of God; Godlike; who is like expanding power.*

a "The archangel" (Jude 9), or "one of the chief princes" who came to help Daniel (Dan. 10:13). He is mentioned in Revelation 12:7 as the leader of the heavenly army that wars against the dragon. b There are several Israelites by this name mentioned in the Bible, too (Num. 13:13; I Chron. 5:13; 6:40; 7:3; 8:16; 12:20; 27:18).

Meta. Divine inspiration, and a realization of the all-conquering power of God; also a *Godlike* or perfect state of being.

Michal, mī'-ehăl (Heb.)—*brook; rivulet; shallow well; turbid stream; who is perfect; completion; perfection.*

Saul's youngest daughter, who loved David and became his wife (I Sam. 18:20, 27). Saul afterward gave Michal to Palti, or Paltiel, son of Laish, to be his wife (I Sam. 25:44), and later she was restored to David (II Sam. 3:12-14).

Meta. An intuitive quality active in the human soul, and becoming for the time being a cleansing, inspiring stream of pure thoughts and emotions to the preserving of the love thought (David); this thought has not, at this stage of the unfoldment of the individual, attained the ruling power in consciousness, because of the adverse activity of the personal will (Saul).

Michmas, mĭeh'-măs (Heb.)—*treasure house; place of concealment; something hidden; hidden treasure; place of Chemosh.*

A city of Benjamin (Ezra 2:27). It is called Michmash in I Samuel 13:5, Nehemiah 11:31, and Isaiah 10:28.

Meta. Chemosh was a national god of the Moabites, and signifies lustful desire. (See CHEMOSH.) It was at Michmash that the Philistines encamped when they came up to fight against Israel and Saul (I Sam. 13:5); and, according to Isaiah 10:28, the Assyrian stored his baggage at Michmash when he came against Israel. Michmas, or Michmash, therefore, *place of Chemosh*, a city of Benjamin, must represent a group of thoughts situated in the vital forces of the individual, its ruling quality being an active faith (Benjamin) or assurance that one can have whatever one desires. There the outer, unawakened intellectual and sense consciousness (the Assyrians and the Philistines) gather to bring about the fulfillment of the carnal and personal selfish desires of the individual in opposition to the higher and more spiritual requirements of the man (Israel).

From the foregoing, and from other definitions of Michmas, we perceive that the innate vital force in man, and his natural faith in all-possibility of good, which are at first secret and *hidden*, are a real *treasure house* to him as he learns to understand and use them for his true spiritual unfoldment and attainment.

Michmethath (A. V., Michmethah), mĭch'-mĕ-thăth (Heb.)—*hiding place; place of concealment; lurking place.*

A border city of Ephraim and Manasseh (Josh. 16:6; 17:7).

Meta. Michmethath, a border city between Ephraim and Manasseh, and meaning *hiding place, lurking place*, refers to a group of thoughts of indecision in consciousness. They lean to Truth, but are not positive enough in understanding (Manasseh) or will (Ephraim) to join either sufficiently to work boldly and constructively for the good of the individual. They belong to that attitude of mind in one that causes one never to be quite sure as to what one should do or what stand one should take in the daily problems that present themselves. Thus the individual in whom this state of thought prevails is continually bearing unnecessary burdens (Michmethath was "before Shechem," meaning *shoulder* and referring to the burden-bearing attitude of mind). He will continue to bear them until he lays hold of the hidden, lurking, indecisive thoughts that Michmethath symbolizes, and consciously unifies them with both will and understanding (Ephraim and Manasseh) until they become clear, active, wise, and decisive.

Michri, mĭch'-rī (Heb.)—*my price; price of Jehovah; dowry of Jah; Jah possesses*, i. e., *by purchase; value of Jah.*

Father of Uzzi, and grandfather of Elah, who was a chief man of Benjamin (I Chron. 9:8).

Meta. A wise and an understanding heart. Of understanding, it is said that "she is more precious than rubies." "The lips of knowledge are a precious jewel." "How precious also are thy thoughts unto me, O God!" (Prov. 3:15; 20:15; Psa. 139:17).

Knowledge and wisdom come from the Spirit of Christ within one (*Jah possesses, dowry of Jah, value of Jah*); and the *price* that one must pay for the conscious attainment of this divine and true understanding is the letting go of the personal self with its limited ideas.
"Trust in Jehovah with all thy heart,
And lean not upon thine own understanding:
In all thy ways acknowledge him,
And he will direct thy paths."
When the individual gives himself over to true, spiritual understanding, and has a strong, active faith in God (Michri was a Benjamite) he brings forth Uzzi (*Jah is strong, Jehovah is my strength*) and Elah (*oak*, signifying a consciousness of strength and protection).

Michtam, mĭch'-tam (Heb.)—*writing; prescript; poem; psalm; song; golden psalm; precious verse; epigram; preeminent inscription.*

A word mentioned in the titles of Psalms 16, 56, 57, 58, 59, and 60.

Meta. The entrance into consciousness of wise, inspiring, harmonious, uplifting thoughts of substance and Truth; and the inscribing of these Truth ideals in the memory. In the phrase, *golden psalm*, "golden" suggests wisdom and substance; *writing, precious verse*, "a poem intended to record memorable thoughts." *Writing* makes one think of something uplifting and inspiring, while both *poem* and *song* signify inspiration and rhythm or harmony.)

Middin, mĭd'-dĭn (Heb.)—*extended; lengthened; stretched out; meted; measured.*

A city in the wilderness of Judah (Josh. 15:61).

Meta. An extending or enlarging (*extended, lengthened, stretched out*) of one's inner spiritual capacity, in what seems to be the wilderness phase of one's Judah or praise consciousness, that all limitation (*meted, measured*) may be done away. "For he giveth not the Spirit by measure" (John 3:34).

Midian (in A .V., Acts 7:29, Madian), mĭd'-ĭ-ăn (Heb.)—*rule; government; judgment; subjugation; striving; contending; pleading; strife; contention.*

Fourth-mentioned son of Abraham by his second wife, Keturah (Gen. 25:2); from him the Midianites were descended. Moses went to the land of Midian and dwelt there when he fled from Pharaoh, king of Egypt (Exod. 2:15).

Meta. Midian pertains to *rule, government,* a certain sense of dominion in consciousness that comes about by the union of Abraham (the first activity of faith in human consciousness) and Keturah (a phase of soul consciousness that, though still in sense, aspires to higher things for the body; see KE- TURAH). This sense of dominion, while it includes and is founded in a degree of discrimination and understanding (*judgment*) even of God and of higher things, is full of *contention* and *strife.* It is not spiritual, but is opposed to real spiritual Truth. The Midianites, descendants of Midian, were enemies of the Israelites. They represent contentious thoughts, also judgment or discrimination in sense consciousness; judgment of the senses according to outer appearances produces discordant thoughts, jealousies, and the like.

Midianites mĭd'-ĭ-ăn-ītes (fr. Heb.)— *of* or *belonging to Midian.*

Descendants of Midian, Abraham's son by Keturah, and inhabitants of the land of Midian (Gen. 37:28; Num. 31:1).

Meta. Discrimination or judgment in sense consciousness; also strife, contention.

In Judges 7, the oppressors are represented by the Midianites, meaning *strife.* The Children of Israel had not fully followed the command, "Thou shalt not make unto thee a graven image." They were not strong enough to hold steady and let the divine imaging power do its perfect work. They tried to go ahead of the Lord, and false images, false stand-

ards, were established. This resulted in strife in both soul and environment, or within and without.

To many people there is no other enemy that is so difficult to eliminate as *strife.* Petty quarrels, jealousies, uncharitable thoughts—how they come back again and again! Nor can they ever be overcome except by divine love—the mind that was in Christ Jesus—"who, when he was reviled, reviled not again; when he suffered, threatened not; but committed *himself* to him that judgeth righteously." Strife and contention must be put wholly out of our life before we can entirely possess the Promised Land; we must "smite the Midianites as one man," impersonal evil, and that, even, as a claim that never was and never shall be.

Migdal–el, mĭg'-dăl–ĕl (Heb.)—*tower of God; from the great elevation of God; strength of God; who is bound of God.*

A fortified city of Naphtali (Josh. 19: 38).

Meta. The exaltation of divine strength in consciousness. Naphtali refers to the faculty of strength; a tower bespeaks something lofty and exalted, and in the nature of a stronghold or fortress. This *tower,* being *of God,* denotes divine strength. (See MAGADAN.)

Migdal–gad, mĭg'-dăl–găd (Heb.)— *tower of Gad; strength of Gad; who is bound by fortune; elevation of Gad; troop tower.*

A city in the lowland of Judah (Josh. 15:37).

Meta. Gad means *fortune, seer, troop.* "Let the horseman, Gad, be blest" (Deut. 33:20, Fenton translation). "Blessed be he that enlargeth Gad"—so runs the text in the American Standard Version. Blessed is he who enters into a greater power consciousness—Gad refers to the faculty of power in man, the power that results from organization (*troop*), an orderly consciousness. We also see in Gad a thought of understanding (*seer*) and abundance (*fortune*). Migdal–gad, therefore (meaning *tower of Gad, strength of Gad, troop tower, who is bound by fortune, elevation of Gad,* and being a city in the lowland of Judah), would indicate a group of thoughts in the subconsciousness of the individual that is lifted up and fortified in power, substance, and clear vision.

Migdol, mĭg′-dŏl (Heb.)—*bound together; strength; force; greatness; magnitude; elevation; great height; tower; watchtower; elevated stage; pulpit.*

A place near which the Children of Israel camped before they crossed the Red Sea on their way out of Egypt (Exod. 14:2). In Jeremiah 44:1 and 46:14 Migdol is mentioned as a city of Egypt.

Meta. The consciousness unified, in degree at least, built up, *strengthened,* and fortified in the idea of power.
"Thy neck is like the tower of David
Builded for an armory.
Whereon there hang a thousand bucklers,
All the shields of the mighty men."
The power center in man is in the throat. Migdol's being a city of Egypt where the Israelites camped while on their way out of Egypt shows that this consciousness of power here is seemingly of the carnal in man, yet is related to the freeing of his higher and more spiritual thoughts (Israelites).

Migron, mĭg′-rŏn (Heb.)—*cast down; overthrown; delivered; precipice; precipitate; fallen; landslide; level area.*

"Saul abode in the uttermost part of Gibeah under the pomegranate-tree which is in Migron," when Jonathan and his armor-bearer went over into the camp of the Philistines and put them to rout (I Sam. 14:2; see Isaiah 10:28 also).

Meta. Gibeah (*a height, an eminence*) signifies the spiritual aspiration inherent in every desire. Migron (*cast down, overthrown, fallen, landslide*) denotes the dangers that lie in receiving high spiritual inspirations and then giving them over to the command and direction of the uncultivated, selfish, personal will (Saul). Judges 19 and 20 tell the story of the debasement that results when the aspiring will and thought are given over to sense desire; it thus falls, or slips (Migron) to the lowest degree of degradation and brings about destruction both to the high aspirations and to the man himself.

Mijamin (in A. V., Ezra 10:25, Miamin), mĭj′-ă-mĭn (Heb.)—*from the right hand; on the right side; dexterous; fortunate; prosperous; happy; faithful; from the south.*

a A priest to whom the sixth course in Temple service was allotted, in David's reign (I Chron. 24:9). **b** An Israelite who had taken a foreign wife, but put her away at the instigation of Ezra (Ezra 10:25).

Meta. Man's knowing that executive ability, abundant supply, faithfulness, joy, all good, are his inheritance from God, and his receiving them consciously by exercising the divine power within himself (*from the right hand, from the south, fortunate, prosperous, happy, faithful*).

Mikloth, mĭk′-lŏth (Heb.)—*germinations; sprouts; twigs; sticks; rods; staves; divining rods,* i. e., *sticks used for deciding lots; punishments,* i. e., *smiting rods; walking sticks; shepherds' crooks.*

a A Benjamite (I Chron. 8:32). **b** The ruler of the course of twenty-four thousand who served King David in the second month (I Chron. 27:4).

Meta. "Thy rod and thy staff, they comfort me" (Psalms 23:4). *Rods* suggest correction, and *staves* denote something to lean upon. "He is in the way of life that heedeth correction" (Prov. 10:17). "Whoso loveth correction loveth knowledge" (Prov. 12:1).
"The eternal God is *thy* dwelling-place,
And underneath are the everlasting arms" (Deut. 33:27).
Divining rods and *sticks used for deciding lots* infer guidance by some higher intelligence than that of man's outer, personal self; they suggest that a power greater than man has realized is shaping his life. *Germinations, sprouts,* bespeak new understanding and a consciousness of new life. So Mikloth, a Benjamite, represents the awakening of the individual to the truths that are enumerated in this and in the foregoing paragraph. Fuller light, however, is needed, since at this stage of unfoldment the belief in *punishments* (*smiting rods*) and in the psychic seems to enter into man's thought of guidance and of God.

Mikneiah, mĭk-nē′-ĭăh (Heb.) — *founded in Jah; creation of Jehovah; conceived of Jah; begotten by Jehovah;*

acquired of Jah; Jehovah's purchase; possession of Jah.

A musician appointed by David, one who played the harp (I Chron. 15:18, 21).

Meta. That which is founded in Jehovah, that which is conceived in man and brought to light in his consciousness, made active in his life, by his higher, divine self—Jehovah, Christ, I AM, the Father. It may refer to spiritual understanding or to any of the other divine qualities. Mikneiah, as a musician appointed by David, stands for the activity in consciousness of a positive, harmonious love ideal that is in perfect accord with Truth (*possession of Jah*).

Milalai, mĭl′-ă-lāi (Heb.)—*elevated speech; high-spoken; eloquent; word of Jah; command of Jehovah; word of the Lord, i. e., His promise; great elevation of Jehovah.*

A musician of the Levites who was among those who gave thanks with Nehemiah on the wall of Jerusalem after it was rebuilt (Neh. 12:36).

Meta. An active, expressing (*eloquent*) thought of love and harmony, belonging to our natural religious tendencies (a musician of the Levites), in our true, higher consciousness, that magnifies Jehovah (*elevated speech, word of the Lord, great elevation of Jehovah*).

Milcah, mĭl′-căh (Heb.)—feminine of Melech, a king; *queen; rule; counsel; advice.*

a Wife of Nahor, Abraham's brother (Gen. 11:29). b A daughter of Zelophehad, who was the son of Hepher of the tribe of Manasseh (Num. 26:33).

Meta. The soul expressing dominion, wisdom, good judgment. The soul of man, in its feminine aspect, is intuitional, and often perceives or senses things that, while they do not appear to the outer or more active and positive phase of the individual consciousness, should be heeded by it.

Milcom, mĭl′-cŏm (Heb.)—*their king.*

A form of Molech, the god of the Ammonites. Solomon worshiped this god, along with gods of other heathen nations about Israel; therefore the kingdom was taken away from his descendants (I Kings 11:5). Josiah, a later king of Judah, tore down the high places that Solomon had built for the worship of Milcom, Chemosh, and Ashtoreth, the gods of the Ammonites, Moabites, and Sidonians (II Kings 23:13).

Meta. See MALCAM and MOLECH.

Miletus (in A. V., II Timothy 4:20, Miletum), mĭ-lē′-tŭs (Gk.)—*red; scarlet; purest wool.*

A seaport city of Ionia in Asia Minor (Acts 20:15).

Meta. Miletus, meaning *red, scarlet,* refers to the seemingly material life in the organism of the individual. *Purest wool,* from the fact that only the purest of wool could take the scarlet dye, points to the true substance of life as lying back of and existing in the apparently material and corruptible, which seem to be in the ascendancy at this stage of individual unfoldment: "Trophimus I left at Miletus sick," Paul said (II Tim. 4:20).

Millo, mĭl′-lŏ (Heb.)—*filling up; making full; fullness; abundant; mound, i. e., filled with earth or stones; rampart; fortress; castle.*

In Judges 9:6, 20 the fortress in or near Shechem is meant. In II Samuel 5:9 Millo is in the "city of David," or Jerusalem; it must therefore refer to a fortified part of the city of Jerusalem, or a fortification very near the city.

Meta. A building in of substance in consciousness (a *filling up, fullness*); also a strengthening and fortifying of oneself in the consciousness of substance (*abundant, fortress, castle*).

Mind.

Meta. By the term *Mind,* we mean God—the universal principle of causation, which includes all principles. Mathematics is a principle that in its field illustrates the exact and inexorable laws that are one with the manifestations of God, or Mind.

There is nothing but Mind and thought—Principle and its mode of expression. The things made, or externalized, are simply effects, and of themselves would quickly pass away; but Mind and thought are one and inseparable, self-existent and ever active, the cause of all that appears.

An understanding of God, or universal Mind, is a key to all scriptures and occult writings. In the story of creation as told by Moses, which is metaphysically correct, all things were brought forth by "God said"—Mind thought.

Miniamin, mĭ-nĭ'-ă-mĭn (Heb.)—*from the right side; on the right side; dexterous; fortunate; prosperous; faithful; true; happy.*

a A Levite in Hezekiah's reign, who helped Kore the son of Imnah in caring for and distributing the freewill offerings, the oblations, and the most holy things (II Chron. 31:15). b A priest who returned with Zerubbabel from the Captivity (Neh 12:17, 41).

Meta. Faithfulness, substance, fruitfulness, joy, skill, power to execute, active in the higher thoughts of man's consciousness and bearing fruit in his outer organism and life. There is that in every individual which causes him always to hope for and expect that which is good and true, and his very expectation causes the good to become active in his mind and life; this is one phase of the Miniamin thought, and is suggested by the definitions of the name and the history of the men who bore the name.

Minni, mĭn'-nī (Heb.)—*divided out; numbered; reckoned; meted; allotted; appointed; proceeding; issuing; emanating; source; origin; fate; fortune; destiny.*

Probably a part of Armenia. Jeremiah prophesied that the kingdom of Minni was to fight against Babylon (Jer. 51:27).

Meta. A day of reckoning, a period of judgment, for sense confusion (Babylon). The time always comes when one's thoughts and activities are taken into account, as it were, and one reaps according to that which one has sown. In fact man is every day reaping some of his past sowing, be it good or ill. Being unawakened spiritually, he is likely to look on his experiences, or reaping, as the working of *fate, destiny.* The truth, however, is that he makes his own life what he wills.

miracles.

Meta. The miracles or "signs" (John 7:31) that go so far in convincing one's unbelieving thoughts are the transformations that go on in the midst of one's unbelieving thoughts and are the result of one's true words. A woman once told her crossed eyes that they were not eyes of flesh but eyes of Spirit, and that they were of one mind, perfect and harmonious in every way. She was filled with joy to find that they, after a time, came into right relation—she was healed of that defect in thought. But more than this, she found that she perceived Truth much more clearly than she ever had before. Not only the eye as an organ of sight but that which stands back of the eye, spiritual perception, became clarified. The thoughts of sight became educated through the word of Truth sent forth by the I AM.

Miriam, mĭr'-ĭ-ăm (Heb.)—*contradiction; outcry; protest; rebellion; perversion; bitterness; grief; sorrow; amiable; aromatic; sweet-smelling; fragrant; height; altitude; elevation; exaltation.* Miriam and Mary both come from the same root word. There is no name that offers a wider range of seemingly conflicting ideas. Myrrh also comes from the same root, offering the same contradiction of bitterness to the taste and aroma to the smell. The taste, among the ancient sages, was always associated with sensuous desires, covetousness, whereas smell was associated with spirit, breath, understanding, inspiration.

a Sister of Moses and Aaron (Exod. 15:20). She accompanied them out of Egypt and on their journey through the wilderness toward the Promised Land; she was smitten by leprosy because of condemning Moses, and was healed again by means of Moses' prayer (Num. 12:10). Later she died at Kadesh (Num. 20:1). b Another Miriam is mentioned in I Chronicles 4:17.

Meta. The soul, or feminine side of the love quality that is active in man (Miriam was of the tribe of Levi—love) while he is struggling to free himself from the errors and selfishness of personality, that he may be fully released from all bondage to human limitations and enter wholly into the Promised Land of wholeness and Truth. At the Miriam stage of overcoming the soul has not yet been delivered from all its bitter, rebellious, sense tendencies or desires, though it has been awakened to its higher possibilities.

Miriam died at Kadesh; the feminine love quality experiences a higher revelation of Spirit and a deeper cleansing at this stage of unfoldment. (See KADESH.)

Mirmah (A. V., Mirma), mĭr'-măh (Heb.)—*deceit; fraud; perverse; full of guile; wicked; cast down; fallen; height; a high place, i. e., one consecrated to idolatry.*

Son of Shaharaim, a Benjamite, a chief (I Chron. 8:10).

Meta. In Ephesians 6:12 we read about "spiritual . . . wickedness in the heavenly *places*"—the higher realms of consciousness in man. Paul, in II Corinthians 11:13-15, speaks about "false apostles, deceitful workers, fashioning themselves into apostles of Christ." Then he goes on: "And no marvel; for even Satan fashioneth himself into an angel of light. It is no great thing therefore if his ministers also fashion themselves as ministers of righteousness, whose end shall be according to their works."

Mirmah refers to one of these wicked, or untrue, thoughts. It really belongs to the adverse or satanic phase of man's consciousness, but has gotten over into the higher state of mind in the individual and is posing there as a true ideal.

It seems that when new inspiration and illumination come to one, subconscious errors are apt to be revived, and apparently lifted up and glossed over by the light, along with the resurrection of good that takes place. It is thus in the case of the thought that Mirmah signifies. His parents, Shaharaim and Hodesh, bespeak a great illumination in consciousness that reaches to the very depths of the soul. Mirmah, meaning *deceit, fraud, height,* is a deceptive, error thought that has been raised to expression along with the good and the true ideals by this illumination, instead of being recognized and denied entirely out of consciousness.

Misgab, mĭs'-găb (Heb.)—*height; altitude; a high rock; refuge; security; an inaccessible place.*

A place in Moab that was to be "put to shame and broken down," according to Jeremiah 48:1.

Meta. The carnal mind, or limited, personal man (Moab), exalting itself and seeking to justify and fortify itself in its human and sense limitations.

Mishael, mĭsh'-ă-ĕl (Heb.)—*who is what God is?; who is like unto God?; what God is; from the likeness of God.*

a Son of Uzziel of the Kohathite Levites (Exod. 6:22). **b** One who stood at the left hand of Ezra when Ezra read the book of the law to the people (Neh. 8:4). **c** One of Daniel's three companions in Babylon, whose name was changed to Meshach (Dan. 1:6, 7). This latter Mishael was one of the three who were cast alive into the fiery furnace and came out without harm (Dan. 3:12-30).

Meta. Love, Godlikeness, that which is greatly desired and is prayed earnestly for by all persons who have in any degree been awakened to the Christ Truth. The inner self of every person, whether he recognizes it or not, ever seeks and longs to have the individual come into conscious oneness with his Source and into the full expression of his innate Godlikeness. This is the cause of all the unrest, dissatisfaction, and vain outer longings and seekings of man; he will never find peace and satisfaction until he returns to his Father's house, whence he has gone out to "a far country," even to sense consciousness.

Mishal (A. V., Joshua 19:26, Misheal), mĭ'-shăl (Heb.)—*digging out; hollowing out; searching; seeking; finding; questing; questioning; asking; beseeching; entreating; demanding; imploring; supplicating; begging; praying.*

A city of Asher that was given over to the Gershonite Levites (Josh. 21:30).

Meta. The central idea expressed in Mishal is prayer, an earnest seeking after God and Truth. By means of its great and sincere desire for light and overcoming, this group of thoughts (Mishal) comes to the Israelites (true, higher thoughts), and then is given over to the Levites, the natural religious tendencies of the individual, for further upliftment.

For any real elevating of the consciousness to take place in us, true religion must enter into our thoughts; spirituality must be recognized by us as the base of all our inner faculties and powers.

This is the significance of the fact that many cities of the various tribes of Israel were given over to the Levites who had no special possessions of their own in the Promised Land, but lived among the other Israelitish tribes.

Misham, mī'-shăm (Heb.)—*swift going; fleet; hasty; impetuous; quick; made clean; cleansed; purified.*

Son of Elpaal, a Benjamite (I Chron. 8:12).

Meta. One of the results of a great increase of the activity of faith in consciousness (a son of Elpaal; see ELPAAL). This result is a quick purification from error and an establishment of the good and true.

Mishma, mĭsh'-mȧ (Heb.)—*a hearing; hearkening; report; rumor; fame; call; declaration; summon; answering; obeying.*

a One of Ishmael's twelve sons (Gen. 25:14). b A descendant of Simeon (I Chron. 4:25).

Meta. A receptive, attentive, obedient attitude (*hearing, obeying*) in both the inner and the outer consciousness of the individual (Mishma, a descendant of Simeon, refers to the religious and spiritual realm of mind in man, while the other Mishma, a son of Ishmael, refers to the outer or sense consciousness); also the result of this attitude of mind, a result that is the receiving and expressing of a message, a revelation, a truth (*report, rumor, fame, declaration*).

Mishmannah, mĭsh-măn'-năh (Heb.)—*fatness; sumptuous; strength; vigor; fertility.*

A Gadite who came to David in his stronghold in the wilderness (I Chron. 12:10).

Meta. A strong, active thought of power, vitality, substance, strength, that allies itself to the love faculty (David) and aids it in coming into its rightful place of rulership in consciousness.

Mishraites, mĭsh'-rä-ītes (fr. Heb.)—*drawn out; extended; spread abroad; leaders; shepherds.*

A family of Kiriath–jearim (I Chron. 2:53).

Meta. High ideals being *extended, spread abroad*, throughout the consciousness of the individual, and becoming true

leaders and *shepherds* of his thoughts and forces. (See KIRIATH–JEARIM.)

Mispereth, mĭs'-pĕ-rĕth (Heb.)—*inscribing; engraving; writing; counting; tallying; scoring; numbering; enumerating; mustering; relating; narrating; declaring; telling.*

An Israelite who came up out of the Babylonian captivity with Zerubbabel (Neh. 7:7).

Meta. That in man which takes account of and places an estimate on his true spiritual values (*numbering*) and records them in the memory of the individual, upon the inner tablet of the heart (*engraving, inscribing, writing*). This Mispereth quality in man comes up out of Babylon (sense confusion) with Zerubbabel—one who restores the worship of God. Mispereth also bespeaks spiritual radiation, or the giving forth of Truth (*declaring, telling*).

Misrephoth–maim, mĭs'-rĕ-phŏth–mā'-ĭm (Heb.)—*burning waters; burning of waters; hot waters, i. e., hot baths; fiery waters; poisonous waters; venomous waters, i. e., venom of serpents.*

A place in the hill country of Palestine, near Sidon and Lebanon, or at least mentioned with these places (Josh. 11:8; 13:6). It is thought by some to be the same place as Zarephath.

Meta. The carrying away of impurities, errors, poisons, from the consciousness and organism by the cleansing waters of denial. During this process of cleansing, while errors and impurities are being thrown to the surface and eliminated, they may be much in evidence—the individual for a time may appear to be more sinful than he was before. This is suggested in the meanings *poisonous waters, venomous waters,* i. e., *venom of serpents.* The thought of fiery heat, in the meaning of Misrephoth-maim, also bespeaks a close association with the deeper purification of man's spirit by fire. (See ZAREPHATH.)

Mithkah (A. V., Mithcah), mĭth'-kăh (Heb.)—*relish; sweetness; pleasantness; sweet (well or fountain).*

An encampment of the Children of Israel in the wilderness (Num. 33:28).

Meta. A place, or condition, in the wilderness experience of one's truer thoughts (Israelites) that are on their way from the darkness of Egypt to the Promised Land, wherein an inflow of new substance and life is realized. This is indeed *sweetness* to one's higher consciousness. (*Well* or *fountain* points to the inner waters of life, or vitality, while the central idea in the name Mithkah is that of a child feeding with relish; thus substance and a feast are suggested.)

Mithnite, mĭth'-nīte (fr. Heb.)—*loin; strength; firmness; liberality; gift.*

Joshaphat the Mithnite was one of David's warriors (I Chron. 11:43).

Meta. The increase of strength, faithfulness, Truth, and broadness of vision in consciousness (*loin, strength, firmness, liberality;* "she girdeth her loins with strength"; "faithfulness the girdle of his loins"; "having girded your loins with truth." This great increase of good, or grace (*gift* of God), comes as the result of the development of the idea of judgment, or good judgment, clear discrimination, a quality in the Christ mind (Joshaphat, meaning *whom Jehovah judgeth*). "Wherefore girding up the loins of your mind . . . set your hope . . . on the grace that is to be brought unto you at the revelation of Jesus Christ" (I Pet. 1:13).

Mithredath, mĭth'-rĕ-dăth (Heb.)— *given by Mithra; gift of the sun god; mandate of Mithra; instructed in the laws; beholding the laws.*

a Treasurer of Cyrus, king of Persia (Ezra 1:8). **b** A man who wrote to the king of Persia in an attempt to keep the Israelites from rebuilding the wall of Jerusalem (Ezra 4:7).

Meta. Light, understanding, but more on the psychical than on the spiritual plane, because of one's *beholding the laws,* the secondary step in understanding as it comes forth into expression and manifestation, instead of keeping the attention fixed on the Source (*given by Mithra, gift of the sun god, mandate of Mithra*). Thus this understanding becomes mixed with fears and limitations, with outer reasonings according to appearances; so while the good in it is sometimes a help, its errors are at other times a hindrance to the establishing of

Truth in consciousness and body. (One man named Mithredath was the treasurer of Cyrus, king of Persia, through whom Cyrus returned to the Jews the vessels of the house of Jehovah, while the other man by this name was an enemy to the Jews.)

Mitylene, mĭt-ў-lē'-nĕ (Gk.)—*pressing; curtailing; cleansing; purifying.*

A seaport city in the island of Lesbos. Paul came to this place in one of his journeys (Acts 20:14).

Meta. A place in consciousness wherein the word of Truth (Paul) enters and does a much needed (*pressing,* meaning urgent) *cleansing* and *purifying;* thus error is diminished (*curtailing*) and the individual is made ready for the next step, which is signified by Chios, where Paul went from Mitylene. Chios means *open,* and is representative of an open, unobstructed attitude of mind.

Mizar, mī'-zär (Heb.)—*smallness; reduced; little; few; brought low; insignificant; despised; dishonored.*

A hill near the Hermons; *the little mountain,* margin (Psalms 42:6). It is thought to have been a summit of Lebanon.

Meta. Mount Hermon signifies a high, sublime state of mind. The Hermons, or three peaks of Hermon, bespeak the exaltation of the triune God; the lifting up, in conscious recognition, of the three phases or activities of the Infinite—Father, Son, and Holy Spirit, or mind, idea, and expression.

The mountains of Lebanon represent pure thoughts.

Mizar (meaning *little, smallness, brought low,* and believed to have been a summit of Lebanon, from which the writer of the 42d Psalm seems to have obtained a view of the Hermons) is representative of meekness, lowliness, humbleness of thought, which is one of the characteristics of the Christ mind; having let go of self-pride and self-seeking, the individual opens his consciousness to Truth. The mind of Christ, of divine love, "vaunteth not itself, is not puffed up . . . taketh not account of evil." Expressing in the individual, it makes him willing for the personal to be made very small, that God may be exalted; in the words of the hymn, "Content to fill a little space, if Thou be glorified."

Mizpah, mĭz'-păh (Heb.)—*looking about; scanning the horizon; watchtower; lofty place,* i. e., *giving increased vision; broad vision; seen from afar; speculation; observation; inquiry.*

a The place where Jacob and Laban met, and parted, after Jacob had taken his family and possessions and had stolen away from Laban, and Laban had come after him and overtaken him. They called the name of the place "Mizpah, for he said, Jehovah watch between me and thee, when we are absent [*hidden*, margin] one from another" (Gen. 31:49). This place became the site of a city of Israel (Judg. 10:17). b There were other places in Palestine by this name (Josh. 11:3; Neh. 3:15, and others).

Meta. Spiritual watching—being on guard against the encroachment of error. The great spiritual Teacher instructs us not only to pray, but to "take heed, watch and pray" (Mark 13:33).

The second step that Samuel took (I Sam. 7:2-12) in leading the Children of Israel out against the Philistines was to have the Israelites assemble at Mizpah, which means *watchtower.* In order to maintain consciousness of one's unity with God and to keep one's forces organized in singleness of thought and purpose, one must keep the attention steadily fixed in the direction of that to which one aspires. Samuel here is only carrying out the Scriptural injunction, "Look unto me, and be ye saved, all the ends of the earth." By looking away from the besetting forces of materiality and by maintaining the "high watch," the *broad vision,* one is enabled to discern the action of God in the various situations of life.

The stone called Ebenezer (I Sam. 7: 12) refers to the Christ, who is in every individual who will acknowledge Him, a rock of deliverance, a very present help in every time of need. This stone's being placed between Mizpah and Shen (the watchtower of prayer, and the assimilating of true ideas gained through prayer) heralds a lifting up of the whole organism and a bringing of the perfect, ideal man into manifestation. Such is the work of the Christ in every individual.

Mizpeh, mĭz'-pĕh (Heb.)—*watchtower;* same as Mizpah.

a A city in the lowlands of Judah (Josh. 15:38). b A valley (Josh. 11:8). c A town of Moab (I Sam. 22:3). d The Mizpeh of Joshua 18:26 is spelled Mizpah in other places (see Judg. 20:1; 21:1, and I Kings 15:22).

Meta. See MIZPAH.

Mizraim, mĭz'-râ-ĭm (Heb.)—*Egypt; Egyptians; circumscription; limitation; bondage; affliction; tribulation; straitness; distress.*

Son of Ham (Gen. 10:6).

Meta Ham, the father of Mizraim, typifies the physical in man, given over to sensuality. Mizraim signifies the sense belief that the life as well as the organism of man is bound in materiality, and that man is subject to sorrows and to all forms of errors that hinder him from receiving good (*limitation, bondage, tribulation*).

Mizzah, mĭz'-zăh (Heb.) — *flowing down; melting away; fear; terror; exhaustion; disintegration; dissolution.*

A son of Reuel, and grandson of Esau (Gen. 36:13).

Meta. A steady tearing down and wearing away of the consciousness and organism (*flowing down, melting away, disintegration, exhaustion, dissolution*). This is the result of *fear,* fear being one of the most subtle and destructive errors that the carnal mind in man contains. It is overcome by divine love, which knows only the good. "There is no fear in love: but perfect love casteth out fear, because fear hath punishment; and he that feareth is not made perfect in love" (I John 4:18).

Mnason, mnā'-sŏn—pronounced nā'-sŏn (Gk.)—*mindful; reminding; remembering; bringing to mind; exhorting; inspiring.*

A disciple, a resident of Cyprus, with whom Paul and his companions lodged at Jerusalem (Acts 21:16).

Meta. That in the spiritually awakening consciousness of the individual which causes him to *remember,* to be *mindful* of the word of Truth (Paul) and all the higher thoughts and ideals that pertain to the Christ mind. Mnason would be equivalent to the Holy Spirit, in significance.

Moab, mō'-ăb (Heb.)—*seed of the father; water of the water; flowing from the father; what of the father?; of his father.*

Son of Lot by his eldest daughter; from him the Moabites were descended (Gen. 19:37).

Meta. Moab seems to have two sides to its significance. Moab means *seed of the father, flowing from the father, of his father,* and while Moab represents the body and the most external conditions of life, there is something good in it, or at least a possibility of good. From the top of a mountain in Moab, "mount Nebo, to the top of Pisgah," Jehovah showed Moses the Promised Land (Deut. 34:1).

Ruth, who represents the love of the natural soul for God, and from whom David and Jesus were descended, was a Moabitess.

On the other hand, the text, "Cursed be he that doeth the work of Jehovah negligently; and cursed be he that keepeth back his sword from blood" (Jer. 48:10), accompanies a charge from the Lord to destroy Moab. Moab here signifies carnal mind, lust-born, turpitude; when the individual enters into the overcoming life he receives the commission to destroy—to cast out—the carnal mind or personal, limited self. This is the self to which Jesus referred when He said, "If any man would come after me, let him deny himself." When man takes up this work he must not be deceitful about it by keeping back part of the price, as Ananias and Sapphira did (Acts 5:1, 2), or by seeking to save some of the carnal self—the goodliest of it, as Achan did (see Joshua 7); for if he does these things he will be cursed, that is, he will not attain the happiness and the peace that come only to the whole-hearted and true. Nor may he be negligent in his work of dying to the carnal mind, for the lazy and slothful man will not win the prize that is set before him—eternal life, preservation of the entire man—spirit, soul, and body. The "sword" in this text (Jer. 48:10) represents the word of God.

Moabites, mō'-ăb-ītes (fr. Heb.)—*of or belonging to Moab.*

Descendants of Moab, son of Lot (Gen. 19:37).

Meta. Thoughts springing from and belonging to that in consciousness which Moab signifies. (See MOAB.)

Moabitess, mō'-ăb-ī-těss (fr. Heb.)—*of or belonging to Moab.*

A female descendant of Moab, the son of Lot. Ruth the Moabitess, who married Boaz, became the great-grandmother of David (Ruth 4:5, 10).

Meta. The carnal mind as it pertains to the soul of man. Ruth the Moabitess signifies human love raised to the divine because of its willingness to leave the love of the unreal. (See RUTH and MOAB.)

Moadiah, mō-ă-dī'-ăh (Heb.)—*appointed time of Jehovah; festival of Jah; ornament of Jehovah.*

A priest of Israel, mentioned among those who returned from the Captivity (Neh. 12:17). He is thought to be the same as Maadiah of the 5th verse.

Meta. See MAADIAH and MAADAI.

In the meaning of Moadiah the thought of feasting is emphasized (*festival of Jah*). A feast in the Scriptures is always symbolical of eating, or affirming, meditating on, and realizing, divine substance, spiritual ideas, words of Truth. The *appointed time of Jehovah* is whenever the individual unfolds to the place where he is ready for the next step forward, the next degree of realization and demonstration.

Moladah, mŏl'-ă-dăh (Heb.)—*begetting; conception; birth; nativity; offspring; progeny.*

A city of Judah (Josh. 15:26); also mentioned as a city of Simeon (Josh. 19:2); it is mentioned again after the return from the Babylonian captivity (Neh. 11:26).

Meta. New thoughts born into consciousness, thoughts of praise (Judah) and receptivity to Truth (Simeon).

Molech, mō'-lĕch (Heb.)—*king; ruler; counselor; judge.*

The national god of the Ammonites. Children were sacrificed in the fire to Molech (Lev. 18:21; 20:2-5; I Kings 11:7). Malcam is another name for this god.

Meta. The ruling of public opinion, and of the "mind of the flesh" in one's consciousness. Children's being sacrificed in the fire to this god signifies one's mentally burning and destroying new ideas by letting fear of or deep regard for what other persons may think (public opinion), with the prejudices, customs, and desires of the outer man of flesh, rule in one's life to the extent that one refuses or neglects to give place and expression to these new and higher ideals. (See MALCAM and AMMONITES.)

Molid, mō'-lĭd (Heb.)—*genitor; begetter,* i. e., *father; conceiver,* i. e., *mother; generation; conception; birth; nativity; progeny.*

Son of Abishur and Abihail, of the tribe of Judah (I Chron. 2:29).

Meta. Molid refers to the cause (*father*) and the reception (*mother*) of new ideas in consciousness, or that in the individual consciousness which opens the way for and causes new ideas to spring forth (*begetter, conceiver*). Both Abishur and Abihail, parents of Molid, signify strength and might brought into realization and expression through uprightness and praise. Praise and prayer (Judah) also enter into that which Molid signifies.

money changers (John 2:14-16).

Meta. Dishonest thoughts of materiality and greed. The consciousness must be cleansed from these if the body temple is to be kept pure and holy. That this cleansing of the Temple was intended for the individual is shown by the verses that follow. "But he spake of the temple of his body" (John 2:21).

So long as our body shows signs of decay it is evident that we have not cast out from the inner realms the thought butchers that kill doves, sheep, oxen, and goats for sacrifice. The allusion here is to the destructive thoughts that lie deep in the consciousness, at the very issues of life.

moon.

Meta. Personal intelligence, the intellect. Its light is supplied by the sun, symbol of spiritual intelligence. This influx of spiritual intelligence has regular periods of flooding the consciousness, and there is a definite relation between the body consciousness and the moon.

Morashtite (A. V., Morasthite), mō'-răsh-tīte (fr. Heb.)—*of* or *belonging to Moresheth–gath.*

An inhabitant of Moresheth–gath; here the name refers to Micah the prophet (Jer. 26:18; Mic. 1:1).

Meta. See MORESHETH–GATH and MICAH.

Mordecai, môr'-dĕ-cāi (Heb. fr. Pers.) —*little man; manikin; of Merodach; dedicated to Mars; crushed by rebellion; contrition.*

a Cousin of Esther (Esth. 2—10). **b** A man by this name is mentioned as having returned with Zerubbabel from the Babylonian captivity (Ezra 2:2).

Meta. Victorious for Truth, a spiritual power working within each soul for its full redemption. *Little man,* and *contrition,* definitions of the name Mordecai, signify that humbleness which always marks the truly great individual, or idea, and a repentance or turning away from error and a resolute turning to Truth. Mars, the Babylonian god of war, here indicates overcoming power. (See MERODACH.)

Moreh, mō'-rĕh (Heb.)—*teaching; a teacher; sage; prophet; imparter of wisdom.*

a An oak tree near Shechem where Abram came and built an altar to Jehovah, who appeared to him there (Gen. 12:6). It may have been a grove of oaks (Deut. 11:30). **b** A hill beside which the Midianites camped when Gideon went out against them (Judg. 7:1).

Meta. A state of mind receptive to Truth; a teachable state of mind. In a teachable state of mind the constructive methods that are always characteristic of the divine are revealed, and with this mind protection and strength (oak tree) are realized and victory is assured.

Moresheth–gath, mŏr'-ĕsh-ĕth-găth (Heb.)—*possession of Gath; possession of the wine press.*

A city of Judah; the birthplace of Micah the prophet (Mic. 1:14).

Meta Moresheth means *possession,* and Gath means *wine press.* Gath, *wine press,* a city of the Philistines, typifies a belief in trial, a looking at all experiences from the standpoint of seeming trial and suffering. Moresheth-gath, a city of Judah, signifies this error belief and habit as coming into the possession of and being acted on by the Judah consciousness in the individual (praise and prayer). Thus Micah the prophet—the individual consciousness awakening to the real truth of man's being—is brought forth, and the old belief that hard trials and tribulations are the lot of mankind gives way to the understanding that God is good and that He wills only good for His children.

Moriah, mô-rī'-ăh (Heb.)—*vision of Jehovah; revelation of Jah; chosen by Jehovah; Jah provides,* i. e., *makes the choice; the resisting of Jehovah; fortress of the Lord; bitterness of Jehovah.*

a A "land" to which Abraham was sent to offer up his son Isaac as a sacrifice to God (Gen. 22:2). **b** A mount in Jerusalem upon which Solomon built the Temple (II Chron. 3:1).

Meta. The "land of Moriah," to which Abraham was told to go to make his sacrifice, means *bitterness of Jehovah.* When changes take place in the consciousness there are sometimes very bitter experiences, and a stout faith is needed to believe that good will come out of them. But good always comes if there is a steadfast obedience and faith in the goodness of God.

Great power in spirit and in body grows out of this steadfast overcoming, this giving up of the old and entering into the new. The pleasures of sense are transitory, but the joys of Spirit endure forever. God provided (*Jah provides*) a sacrifice for Abraham. His son Isaac, who represents the Christ or new birth in individual consciousness, was restored to him and Abraham became the father of a multitude, "as the stars of the heavens, and as the sand which is upon the seashore." Thus in one's giving up self and holding firmly in faith to the higher good, multitudes of Truth ideals come to one (*vision of Jehovah, revelation of Jah*), until one's whole consciousness and life are transformed.

Moserah (A. V., Mosera), mô-sē'-răh (Heb.)—*bond; band; fetter; yoke; chain harness; correction; chastisement; dis-*cipline; admonition; reproof; example; precept; instruction; learning.*

A camping place of the Children of Israel in the wilderness. It was there that Aaron died and was buried, and his son Eleazar became high priest in his stead (Deut. 10:6).

Meta. The seeming trial (*chastisement*) and bondage (*bond, fetter*) in which the Christian remains so long as he has only an intellectual comprehension of divine law. To such a one, Hebrews 12:6 reads "whom the Lord loveth he chasteneth" instead of "whom the Lord loves, he disciplines." The latter is the correct rendering, according to the Emphatic Diaglott. Divine love must enter into man's idea of God and the divine law, and must fill his life, that he may find in all correction and discipline of Spirit only joy and delight, and that he may know sickness and sorrow to be the direct result of his own errors. Such unpleasant manifestations will pass away as soon as the errors that caused them are corrected; they are not chastisements sent by God, nor do they come from God. Thus Aaron, symbolizing the intellectual understanding and executive power of divine law, must give way to a higher and more spiritual comprehension of Truth.

Moseroth, mô-sē'-rŏth (Heb.)—*bonds; fetters; yokes; corrections; chastisements; reproofs; precepts; instructions.*

The same place as Moserah of Deuteronomy 10:6 (Num. 33:30).

Meta. See MOSERAH.

Moses, mō'-sĕs (Heb.)—*drawing out; drawer out; drawing forth; extracting,* i. e., *from the water; water-saved.*

Son of Amram and Jochebed, and brother of Aaron and Miriam, of the tribe of Levi (Exod. 2:1-10; 6:20; also all of Exodus, Numbers and Deuteronomy). He led the Israelites out of Egypt and through the wilderness preparatory to their entrance into the Promised Land.

Meta. Moses means *drawing out, extracting,* i. e., *from the water.* The birth of Moses represents man's development in consciousness of the law of his being, from the negative side. Water represents universal negation; but water also represents the great possibility. Out of seemingly negative conditions comes the new growth.

When we are in what seems Egyptian darkness, and weak as water, we are ripe for the higher understanding. The thoughts that rule in the darkness are bent upon putting out all the children of light, but if we are of the house of faith, as were Moses' parents, then our desire to bring forth the higher consciousness will find a protector.

We must care for the infant thought of Truth and surround it with the ark of love and trust, right in the midst of its seeming enemies. "Surely the wrath of man shall praise thee."

When we have arrived at a degree of understanding of Truth (represented by "when Moses was grown") we are zealous for our principles, to the point of destroying anything that interferes with their freedom. The thought that seeks to destroy those who oppose us reacts, and we find our own people in contention. This leads to self-examination and to the revelation that we have been in great error and tried to hide our sin in the deceptions of matter. This sin calls down on us the wrath of the moral law, and Truth is obscured from us for a season. But "he sat down by a well." The all-possibility is about to manifest from another viewpoint—the well of living water within the soul. (Exod. 2:1-15.)

Moses symbolizes this progressive or *drawing-out* process, which works from within outward; as applied to the universe, the upward trend of all things—the evolutionary law. In our interpretation we observe the working of the law in the individual, because it is there that we bring home the lesson, and through intelligent use of the hints given we apply it to ourselves with great profit.

Involution always precedes evolution. In Joseph down in Egypt (Gen. 37:23), we have portrayed the involution of a high spiritual idea.

In Exodus 2:15—4, Moses' fleeing to the wilderness represents the discipline that we must undergo when we have sought the exalted One. Horeb means *solitude;* that is, we have to go into the solitude of the within and lead our flock of thoughts to the back of the wilderness, where dwells the exalted One, the divine I AM, whose kingdom is good judgment. There we are in training forty years, or until we arrive at a four-sided or balanced state of mind. The light of intuition or flame of fire burns in our heart, yet it is not consumed—there is no loss of substance. In thinking there is a vibratory process that uses up nerve tissue, but in the wisdom that comes from the heart this "bush" or tissue is not consumed. This is "holy ground," or substance in Divine Mind. When man approaches this he must take off from his understanding all limited thoughts of the Absolute—"put off thy shoes from thy feet."

At this inner wisdom center, God proclaims Himself to be the Father of fathers, the God of Abraham, Isaac, and Jacob; thus our real Father is Spirit.

In our communion in the silence with the light within us, the bondage of the higher to the lower is made clear to us and the true way of release is indicated. We see the possibilities of man, and the goodness of that Promised Land to which we can raise our thought. But Moses was very meek: we feel our inability and say, "Who am I, that I should go unto Pharaoh, and that I should bring forth the children of Israel out of Egypt?" Then we have the assurance of God's power with us: "Certainly I will be with thee." It is in this recognition of the power and presence of God that all our strength and ability lie. Jesus said, "I speak not from myself: but the Father abiding in me doeth his works."

Death of Moses (Deut. 34:5-12). When we emphasize the observance of divine law we build that law in consciousness until it becomes the leader of all our spiritual thoughts. In the process of soul unfoldment every faculty must be rounded out. We find that the law (Moses) has given us the rule of action, but we must develop the acting ego (Joshua), which is very necessary to our possession of substance and life (the Promised Land). As the activity of the law wanes it is succeeded by I AM.

"No man knoweth of his sepulchre unto this day" means that the law (Moses) is carried along as the activity of a word of Truth in the subconsciousness (valley) as man unfolds in spiritual consciousness.

The idea of divine law is one of execution and activity, and unless the consciousness is purified through realizations of Truth, the law of the Lord is liberated in sense consciousness and destructive activities are set up in the organism. Purification of mind precedes regeneration of body.

When divine law is established in the subconscious realm of mind its activity is carried forward through "Joshua" (the Spirit of wisdom, I AM, Savior).

Moses, the law, ever urges man forward to greater expressions of inherent abilities, but the law requires adherence to certain principles, as it urges the children of the real to go forward. Moses, in Joshua 1:1, 2, represents the evolutionary force of new ideas that have grown in the subconsciousness until they have lifted Israel (our true, spiritual thoughts) out of the depths of sense (Egyptian) bondage into a higher life expression. He has led the new ideas safely through the wilderness of our untried and undisciplined mind to the border of Canaan; then he gives up his leadership to Joshua.

In Mark 7:10 Moses represents the phase of consciousness that is concerned with the moral law. This serves a purpose in disciplining the thoughts, but is only a preparation for the advent of the spiritual law.

In Luke 9:30 Moses represents the law, and Elijah the effect of the law; the association of the two means cause and effect.

mountain.
Meta. Exaltation, a high plane of consciousness, a state of spiritual realization.

Moza, mō'-zȧ (Heb.)—*going forth; origin; source; rising,* i. e., *of the sun; offspring; the east; outgoing; west; descend; exit; departure; exodus; words; language; fountain; springhead; gate; orifice; mouth; vein.* The name Moza relates to everything that goes forth from any source.

a Son of Caleb and his concubine Ephah (I Chron. 2:46). **b** Son of Zimri

and father of Binea, of the tribe of Benjamin (I Chron. 8:36, 37).

Meta. Thoughts belonging to the active faith (Benjamin) and praise (Judah) consciousness in man. These thoughts have their *origin* or *source* in Spirit (the two men named Moza were Israelites). They *go forth* throughout the organism of the individual as a bubbling *spring* or *fountain* of life and wholeness, of all good. "Whosoever drinketh of the water that I shall give him shall never thirst; but the water that I shall give him shall become in him a well of water springing up unto eternal life" (John 4:14).

Mozah, mō'-zăh (Heb.)—*outgoing; issuing; departing; source; origin; going out; exodus; fountain; springhead; mouth; bubbling waters; words; language.*

A city of Benjamin (Josh. 18:26).

Meta. The significance is virtually the same as that of Moza: the issuing forth of the waters of life, or thoughts of life and Truth, into the outer consciousness, the result of an active faith (Benjamin) that the one Source of all life (*springhead*) is the life of the outer man as well as of the inner man.

mule (I Kings 1:33).

Meta. Human will. When it is ridden and is obedient, it infers subjection of that faculty to the established order.

multitude.
Meta. The "great multitude" of John 6:5 is composed of our own hungry thoughts. They want an influx of the truths of Spirit into our consciousness. Man does not live by bread alone, but by every word proceeding out of the mouth of God.

Muppim, mŭp'-pĭm (Heb.)—*serpents; glidings; wavings; coverings; hiding under ground; obscurities; darkenings.*

Son of Benjamin (Gen. 46:21). He is also called Shephupham, Shephuphan, and Shuppim.

Meta. Human or sense wisdom (*serpents*) that is very subtle, and is unsteady and unsettled in its reasonings and deductions (*glidings, hiding under ground, wavings,* "tossed to and fro and carried about with every wind of doctrine") and is not clear therefore (*ob-*

scurities, darkenings), and does not lead the individual into the true light of spiritual understanding.

Muppim was a son of Benjamin the son of Jacob, and Benjamin represents an active faith quality in the spiritually awakening individual consciousness. At this stage of unfoldment these qualities that are innately spiritual are still expressing mostly on the natural or intellectual plane; the individual has not a clear recognition of his divine sonship, his spiritual reality.

Mushi, mū'-shī (Heb.)—*withdrawn; drawn out; letting go; taking away; deserting; departing; ceasing; feeling; touching; sensitive.*

Son of Merari, and grandson of Levi (Exod. 6:19).

Meta. A phase of the natural love in the human consciousness (a grandson of Levi; Levi signifies the first conscious development of the love faculty in man) that is very *sensitive,* susceptible, impressionable, touchy, quick to sense or feel conditions and to take offense. The individual who is dominated by this tendency of the love faculty expressing on the sense plane is likely to avoid direct contact with others (*withdrawn*) and to feel very negative and cut off from his associates, lonely and deserted, at times.

Mushites, mū'-shītes (fr. Heb.)—*of or belonging to Mushi.*

A "family" of Levites descended from Mushi son of Merari (Num. 3:33).

Meta. Thoughts springing from and belonging to that in consciousness which Mushi symbolizes. (See MUSHI.)

Muth–labben, mŭth'–lăb'-ben (Heb.) —*death of the son; even unto the death of the son; forever and forever; with virgin voice for boys.*

A word mentioned in the title of the 9th Psalm.

Meta. The overcoming power of a holy life, or of thoughts untainted by limiting and error beliefs and activities (*with virgin voice for boys,* voice relat-ing to power, and virgins to unadulterated Truth both in thought and in living). *Even unto the death of the son* here refers to the passing out from consciousness of thoughts and tendencies that connect one with the human limitations of generation. *Forever and forever* bespeaks the perpetuity of Truth.

Myra, mȳ'-rà (Gk. fr. Heb.)—*flowing; dripping; weeping; bitterness; grief; sadness; sorrow; ointments; unguents; bitters.*

A city of Lycia, in Asia Minor. The boat in which Paul was being taken to Rome stopped at this place (Acts 27:5).

Meta. Unrestrained emotion. *Ointments,* one definition of Myra, suggests something of a healing nature, but the other definitions, *weeping, dripping, flowing, bitterness, grief, sorrow,* all denote the emotional nature's expressing in a dissipating, destructive way. The emotions, expressing on the material plane, are usually of a destructive nature, though when lifted up and established in Truth, and directed by the I AM, or Christ mind of true love and wisdom, they become a power for good.

Mysia, mȳ'-ṣi-à (Gk. fr. Heb.)—*beyond bounds; beech land; border land; criminal; abominable.*

A district or province of Asia Minor by which Paul passed on one of his missionary journeys (Acts 16:7, 8).

Meta. The meaning of Mysia is *beyond bounds, criminal, abominable,* and the meaning of Bithynia, the place mentioned with Mysia, is *violent precipitation.* Under the guidance of the Lord the redeeming power of Spirit is not set into action in these dark states of consciousness until neighboring thought centers that are more or less awakened to Truth have been spiritually strengthened. (Spirit would not allow Paul to teach in these two places at this time. "When they were come over against Mysia, they assayed to go into Bithynia; and the Spirit of Jesus suffered them not.")

N

Naam, nā'-ăm (Heb.)—*comity; concord; amity; sociability; sweetness; pleasantness; delightfulness; abundant good.*

Son of Caleb (I Chron. 4:15).

Meta. Wisdom's ways are ways of pleasantness, and all her paths are peace. Naam (*comity, amity, pleasantness, sweetness, delightfulness,* and *abundant good*) signifies the joy and gladness, the harmony and satisfaction, that are the result of a true, faithful spirit, and of enthusiastic faith in God. Caleb, the father of Naam, represents faith and enthusiasm; he was a good man, and it was said of him that "he wholly followed Jehovah, the God of Israel" (Josh. 14:14). Naam represents the result of such a life; the result is set forth in Psalm 16:6:

"The lines are fallen unto me in pleasant places;

Yea, I have a goodly heritage."

Naamah, nā'-ă-măh (Heb.)—*comity; concord; amity; social unity; sweet; pleasant; grace; delight.*

a Daughter of Lamech and Zillah, and sister of Tubal–cain (Gen. 4:22). **b** An Ammonitess, wife of Solomon and mother of Rehoboam (I Kings 14:21). **c** A city in the lowland of Judah (Josh. 15:41).

Meta. The animal soul in *pleasing,* harmonious relationship with the youthful idea, even though this consciousness of strength and youth here is of the outer man (Lamech, father of the one Naamah, was descended from Cain, who represents the outer or the body; the other woman named Naamah was an Ammonitess, Ammonites referring to carnal thoughts). The lowland city of Judah named Naaman signifies a group of thoughts in the subconsciousness that are *pleasant* and agreeable, unifying, but need lifting to higher and more spiritual realization and expression; hence they have passed into the possession of Judah (prayer and praise). The central idea in Naamah is unity, the principle of unity as coming into activity.

Naaman, nā'-ă-măn (Heb.)—*sociable; agreeable; amiable; sweet; pleasant; graceful; good.*

a Son of Benjamin (Gen. 46:21); in Num. 26:40 this Naaman is mentioned as being a son of Bela, and grandson of Benjamin. **b** Captain of the host of the king of Syria. He was healed of leprosy through the ministrations of Elisha (II Kings 5:1-27).

Meta. The joy and *pleasant, agreeable,* harmonious, unifying result that ensues in consciousness when one's faith and will act in accord with one's highest Truth ideals. (One Naaman was a Benjamite, and Benjamites signify the faith quality in man actively executive, accomplishing results. Another Naaman was captain of the hosts of the king of Syria; a king always represents some phase of the will.)

Naaman of Syria represents the executive activity of the personal will. He is "captain of the host of the king of Syria"; symbolically he is the directive power of the intellectual realm of mind. Syria signifies the intellect; the king of Israel is the ruling lawgiver in the realm of spiritual thought, and the king of Syria is the same ruling power in the intellectual thought. The will is mighty, and when working under divine law is constructive. But if man allows himself to become attached, through the activity of the personal will, to the realm of flesh sensations, and bound by the belief that life is material, he becomes a leper, or unholy and unclean.

A complete cleansing process is necessary to restore man to his original purity. Seven stands for completeness, and the river Jordan represents the life current in the organism of man. When awakened to his spiritual possibilities, man begins cleansing his will from personal activities, ambitions, attainments, and sense attachments, and cultivates the childlike attitude of mind necessary to invite the inflow of the river of life (Jordan). When man has cleansed his mind through the baptism of spiritual thoughts, his body becomes clean, whole, and pure.

Naaman (executive activity of personal will) was commanded to wash in Jordan (life stream) because, as man's spiritual perception (maiden) reveals to him the realities of life, he is convinced of the need of cleansing the personal will. Spiritual I AM (Elisha) commands the denial of material beliefs and limitations. When the will is under the direction of Spirit, the mind and the body express their natural purity and perfection.

The servants of Naaman (II Kings 5: 13) are the thoughts that do most of the work, and they have learned by experience that the law is the same in both the great and the small. Meditating on this the mighty Naaman stoops to the simple denials of personal, material limitations in the seven departments of the formed man, and his flesh becomes "again like unto the flesh of a little child," and he is clean.

Naamathite, nā'-ă-mă-thīte (fr. Heb.) —*of* or *belonging to Naamah.*

Zophar the Naamathite was one of Job's three friends (Job 2:11).

Meta. A thought belonging to the group of thoughts that the town of Naamah signifies. (See NAAMAH.)

Naamites, nā'-ă-mītes (fr. Heb.)—*of* or *belonging to Naaman.*

The "family" that descended from Naaman, son of Bela and grandson of Benjamin (Num. 26:40).

Meta. Thoughts springing from and belonging to that in consciousness which Naaman, grandson of Benjamin, represents. (See NAAMAN.)

Naarah (in A. V., Joshua 16:7, Naarath), nā'-ă-răh (Heb.)—*girl; maiden; young virgin; youth; bride; handmaiden; servant; posterity; poured out; waterfall.*

a Wife of "Ashhur the father of Tekoa," of the tribe of Judah (I Chron. 4:5). b A town on the border of Ephraim (Josh. 16:7).

Meta. Ashhur represents the establishing of a more firm and abiding idea regarding the body of man. (See ASHHUR.) Naarah, wife of Ashhur (meaning *girl, young virgin, posterity, youth,*

poured out), refers to the soul's expressing the youthful, renewing thought that, unified with that which Ashhur signifies, aids in establishing this truth in the outer man.

The Naarah that was a border city of Ephraim signifies the will's (Ephraim) laying hold of and radiating the youth idea.

Naarai, nā'-ă-rāi (Heb.)—*of the young man; boyish; youthful; bridegroom; my young man; my youth.*

"The son of Ezbai," one of David's mighty men (I Chron. 11:37). In II Samuel 23:35 he is called Paarai the Arbite.

Meta. The youthful thought and ideal that are born anew into consciousness as a result of Truth's shining into the individual mind and creating aspirations for higher things (Ezbai, father of Naarai). (See PAARAI.)

Naaran, nā'-ă-răn (Heb.)—*boyish; youthful; juvenile; virgin; puerile; offshoot; descendant; waterfall.*

A town of Ephraim (I Chron. 7:28). In Joshua 16:7 it is called Naarah.

Meta. The significance is virtually the same as that of NAARAH and NAARAI, which see. The idea of youthfulness in these names is that of a fully developed youth, of marriageable age.

Nabal, nā'-băl (Heb.)—*empty; vain; stupid; foolish; abandoned; wicked; ungodly; an empty skin; a leather water bottle; carcass; a corpse.*

A wealthy man of Maon whose possessions were in Carmel. He refused to give assistance to David and his young men, when David was in hiding from Saul; a few days later Nabal died, having been smitten by Jehovah, according to the text, and Abigail his wife became the wife of David (I Sam. 25:2-42).

Meta. Maon, the home of Nabal, indicates a consciousness of abidingness, stability, or continuity. Carmel, where Nabal's possessions were, means *a garden, a fruitful place,* and refers to the center of spirituality in man, the garden of God, thoughts of great abundance of all good. Abigail, the wife of Nabal, symbolizes joy, cause or source of delight. She "was of good understanding, and of a beautiful countenance." Nabal, however, we are told, "was churlish and evil in his doings" (I Sam. 25:3). His name means *empty, vain, foolish, stupid, wicked.* He bespeaks an adverse thought —selfish, gluttonous, caring nothing for higher or spiritual things, and void of good judgment—that at this time is seemingly in possession of much of the good and beautiful of the soul and spirit, and is using this abundant good for its own selfish ends, for the gratifying of the fleshly appetites and desires (see 36th verse). But this thought is cast out by the joy and purity of soul, the good judgment and understanding, that Abigail represents, and by the love that David stands for in consciousness. Abigail intuitively discerns the Truth, and defends and helps David, the love that is at this time struggling for its existence and is destined to rule. She is rewarded by a union with David: joy and beauty and good understanding are unified with love.

Naboth, nā'-bŏth (Heb.)—*prominence; distinction; height; sprouting; flourishing; germinating; putting forth; produce; fruit; increase; words; utterances; prophecies; proverbs.*

A Jezreelite, whose vineyard in Jezreel was coveted by Ahab, king of Samaria, and who was murdered at the instigation of Ahab's wife, Jezebel, that Ahab might possess the vineyard (I Kings 21:1-19). Naboth's murder was duly avenged by Jehovah, meaning here the divine law (II Kings 9:26).

Meta. A word of Truth belonging to that in consciousness for which Jezreel stands (see JEZREEL), and pertaining to great *increase;* one that brings forth ideas of life and substance in abundance (*fruit, produce, prophecies, words*). This word of Truth has become so highly and widely recognized in consciousness (*prominence, distinction*), it is so elevated in its character, and its expressions and manifestations lie so near the domain of the will (the vineyard of Naboth that Ahab coveted was right beside the king's palace), that they have come to the notice of King Ahab, here representing the will dominated by covetousness. (See AHAB.) The will, in order to lay hold of this life and substance of

Spirit for its own selfish use, denies the word of Truth back of them out of consciousness (Naboth was stoned to death under false pretenses).

Nacon (A. V., Nachon), nā'-cŏn (Heb.) —*arranged; set in order; prepared; made ready; established; sure; beaten down; smitten; afflicted; stricken.*

At the threshing floor of Nacon (it is not certain whether Nacon was the name of the man who owned the floor, or the name of the floor itself) Uzzah died because of putting forth his hand to touch the Ark of God to steady it when the oxen stumbled (II Sam. 6:6).

Meta. The threshing floor of Nacon represents a place in which destruction rules. Nacon symbolizes that which has been *prepared* for destruction (*made ready, established, beaten down, smitten*), and the symbology is further strengthened by reference to the threshing floor.

Nadab, nā'-dăb (Heb.)—*impulsion; willing; spontaneous; voluntary; liberal; munificent; free gift; abundant gift; princely giving.*

a Son of Aaron (Exod. 6:23). He and his brother Abihu "offered strange fire before Jehovah," and were killed because of it, or by it (Lev. 10:1, 2). b Son of Jeroboam king of Israel. He became king after his father's death (I Kings 14:20; 15:25-31). He was a wicked king. c There are two other men by the name of Nadab in the Bible (I Chron. 2:28; 8:30).

Meta. Presumptuous ruling thoughts in the religious consciousness of the individual, and pertaining to the will (priest of Israel and king of Israel). They cause the individual to claim all good arrogantly for self, or to use divine law simply for the gratification of one's personal ambitions and desires. In this way one tempts or makes trial of God, which one should not do (see Matt. 4:7 and Luke 4:12).

It is disastrous, in the end, for one to attempt to demonstrate power, honor, place, position, and abundance for self, and then expect Spirit to protect and back one up in this. Self must be denied and the divine in the individual must be raised to dominion and power, that one may be kept safely and abide in blessings.

Naggai (A. V., Nagge), năg′-gå-ī (Heb.)—*giving light; shining; brilliant; illuminating; enlightening; luminous intelligence.*

A man named in the genealogy of Jesus Christ (Luke 3:25).

Meta. Light, understanding, active in the individual consciousness.

Nahalal (in A. V., Josh 19:15, Nahallal), nå-hăl′-ăl (Heb.)—*flowing forth; leading on; leading from afar; conducting; watering place; pasture; shepherding; protecting; sustaining.*

A city of Zebulun (Josh. 19:15). It was given over to the Levites of the family of Merari (Josh. 21:35).

Meta. A group of thoughts in the order faculty in individual consciousness (a city of Zebulun), pertaining to divine sustenance. (*Flowing forth* and *watering place* signify a place in consciousness wherein one is refreshed by the waters of life; *pasture* symbolizes substance; *leading on, conducting,* bespeak guidance; and *shepherding, protecting, sustaining,* refer to spiritual care and oversight in every way.)

Nahaliel, nå-hā′-lĭ-ĕl (Heb.)—*God flows forth; God leads on; God's torrent; pasture of God.*

A camping place of the Israelites, in the wilderness (Num. 21:19).

Meta. Nahaliel (meaning *God flows forth, God leads on, pasture of God,* and being a camping place of the Children of Israel in the wilderness) signifies an inner realization of vitality, substance, and guidance, of divine protection, and good. This is a source of uplift and encouragement to the true, higher thoughts of the consciousness that are struggling on toward the Promised Land—the full realization of life and Truth throughout the whole man. (*God's torrent,* one of the definitions of Nahaliel, suggests a very swift and abundant flowing of life and Truth into consciousness, with perhaps a belief in, or fear of, violence and undue force.)

Nahalol, nā′-hă-lŏl (Heb.)—the same name as Nahalal. (See NAHALAL.)

A city of Canaan. It was allotted to Zebulun, but the Zebulunites did not drive the Canaanites out of this city (Judg. 1:30).

Meta. The significance is the same as that of NAHALAL, which see. That the Zebulunites failed to drive the Canaanites out of Nahalol suggests a sense rule over the elemental life forces of the organism that has not at this stage of individual unfoldment been fully lifted up.

Naham, nā′-hăm (Heb.)—*panting; sighing; pity; compassion; comfort; consolation; solace; repentance.*

A brother of the wife of Hodiah, of the tribe of Judah (I Chron. 4:19).

Meta. The individual's becoming conscious of the Holy Spirit as comforter (*comfort, consolation, solace*) when he has whole-heartedly turned away from his errors in thought and act and has laid hold of Truth (repentance means a turning from error to Truth).

Nahamani, nå-hăm′-ă-nī (Heb.)—*compassionate; comforter; consoler.*

One of the twelve head men, or leaders, who returned with Zerubbabel from the Babylonian captivity (Neh. 7:7).

Meta. A comprehension of the Spirit of God as tender, merciful, long-suffering (*compassionate*), as comforter. (Many are now used to thinking of God and the Holy Spirit in this way, but it is a great step forward, for the individual who has believed in the "wrath of God," to come to a place in his development wherein he knows that God is good only and expresses only as love and good to man.) "Oh give thanks unto Jehovah; for he is good;

For his lovingkindness *endureth* for ever."

Naharai (in A. V., II Samuel 23:37, Nahari), nā′-hă-rāi (Heb.)—*snorter; snorer; one who breathes hard through the nose; eagerness; angry one; irascible; passionate.*

The Berothite, a mighty man of David's army and one of Joab's armorbearers (I Chron. 11:39).

Meta. Naharai (*snorer, snorter, one who breathes hard through the nose, eagerness, angry one, irascible, passionate*) signifies aspiration, a desire for something higher and better, but directed by personal effort (breathing and the nose bespeak aspiration, but the effort required to breathe, in this case, signifies the activity of the outer, limited personal self) and by the impulses and emotions of the natural man. These are usually destructive rather than constructive. (See JOAB; see the significance of his armor-bearers.) By serving love (David) that which Naharai signifies is raised to a more harmonious and true expression.

Nahash, nā'-hăsh (Heb.)—*hissing; whispering; insidious passion; muttering; witchcraft; incantation; enchantment; augury; omen; divination; prognostication; prophet; seer; oracle; a serpent; witch; charmer; brazen.*

a King of the Ammonites, who came up against Jabesh–gilead and was smitten by Israel under Saul's leadership (I Sam. 11:1; II Sam. 10:2). b The name of a parent of Abigal, sister of Zeruiah (II Sam. 17:25). This latter Nahash must have been the mother of Abigal and Zeruiah, since they were sisters to David, and Jesse was the name of David's father (see I Chron. 2:12-16).

Meta. Nahash, king of the Ammonites, represents a phase of sense wisdom (*serpent,* "Now the serpent was more subtle than any beast of the field which Jehovah God had made") and discernment (*oracle*) that exists in the Ammonite consciousness in the individual (see AMMONITES) and rules in this consciousness at a certain stage of his development.

Nahash, a parent of Abigal, supposedly her mother, denotes soul intuition and wisdom, that are not at this time fully redeemed from the sense or carnal realm of thought.

Nahath, nā'-hăth (Heb.)—*letting down; coming down; descending; reclining; resting; quieting; pressing down; leveling; sinking deep; lowness.*

a Son of Reuel, who was a son of Esau by Basemath; Nahath was a chief of Edom (Gen. 36:13, 17). b Son of Zophai, of the tribe of Levi (I Chron. 6:26). c A Levite who was an overseer over the oblations, tithes, and dedicated things in the house of Jehovah, in Hezekiah's reign (II Chron. 31:13).

Meta. A ruling thought in the Esau, Edom, or outer consciousness of man, the body (a chief of Edom). This thought is one of the prevailing beliefs of the outer man at a certain period of his unfoldment; it is restful, lulling, content (*resting, quieting*) in his seemingly material phase of expression (*lowness*). However, higher thoughts must be introduced into even the outer consciousness of man, that he may be aroused out of the false lethargy of the carnal and may be quickened throughout his whole spirit, soul, and body to the Truth of his being. Thus he enters into a truer peace and rest, signified by the other two men named Nahath.

Nahbi, näh'-bī (Heb.) — *covered; veiled; hidden; concealed; secret; secreted; protected; Jah is protection.*

Son of Vophsi, of the Israelitish tribe of Naphtali. He was one of the twelve men that Moses sent to spy out the land of Canaan, preparatory to the Israelites' going over and taking it (Num. 13:14).

Meta. A *hidden, secret,* innate belief in vigor and strength (a man of Naphtali, Naphtali referring to the strength faculty) and protection (*Jah is protection*) as man's birthright. This belief has its foundation in Truth, but at this stage of the unfoldment of the individual too many outer thoughts of fear and too great a belief in a power of evil as opposed to the good are expressing throughout even his truer ideals (Israelites). Therefore although this Nahbi thought sees the desirability of the Promised Land (eternal life and unlimited strength and youth) it does not believe that man is able now to make this attainment. (Nahbi was one of the spies who brought back a false report of the land; that is, he saw the goodliness of the land, but also saw the "giants" of seeming evil who lived there. And so he feared; he did not believe that the Israelites were able to go and overcome these giants and possess the land.)

Nahbi was very much like some of our higher thought people of today who see the possibility of lifting up and spiritualizing the whole man, even the body, but wish to put off the work until some future incarnation; they think the task too great and hard to be attempted at this time. We know, however, that now is the accepted time and today is our day of salvation. Let us therefore not harden our heart as these Israelites did, and so fail to enter into God's rest, the Land of Promise. Let us not permit our body to fall in the wilderness.

Nahor (in A. V., Joshua 24:2 and Luke 3:34, Nachor), nā'-hôr (Heb.)—*snorting; snoring; angry; passionate; eager; irascible; piercing; slaying.*

a Father of Terah, and grandfather of Abraham (Gen. 11:22-25). b A son of Terah, and grandson of the former Nahor (Gen. 11:26).

Meta. Nahor, grandfather of Abraham, signifies a *piercing* and breaking up (*slaying*) of the sense consciousness of the individual hitherto unpenetrated by Truth (this activity may be more subconscious than conscious), that a new line of thought action, even that of faith (Abraham), may be brought forth. Much commotion and inner excitement often accompany this inner first breaking up of lesser ideals, because so much effort of the outer, limited, personal, emotional self enters into it (*snorting, snoring, eager, passionate, irascible*).

Abraham's brother Nahor represents an arousing of a higher desire in man, through the activity of Abraham—faith —or accompanying the faith activity that Abraham signifies. This higher desire pierces the darkness of materiality and aids in bringing about a new line of thought in consciousness. (See CHESED, son of Nahor.)

Nahshon (in A. V., Exodus 6:23, Naashon; Matthew 1:4 and Luke 3:32, Naasson), näh'-shŏn (Heb.)—*hisser; whisperer; enchanter; incantator; oracle; diviner; prophet; seer; prognosticator; witch; brazen serpent.*

A prince of the children of Judah, and son of Amminadab. Boaz was his grandson (Num. 1:7; I Chron. 2:10).

Meta. The reception of divine wisdom and knowledge (*oracle*) into individual consciousness, and the imparting of this new light to man's true religious thoughts (Israelites). At this stage of the unfoldment of the individual there is still a superstitious belief in magic, as is evidenced by *enchanter, whisperer, witch*, definitions of Nahshon. We are learning, however, that there is a *prophet*,

a *seer*, in each of us, a Nahshon, who knows the natural outcome of our thought tendencies and so can foretell clearly what we are bringing to ourselves. Thus we can be shown whither error thought activities lead and can overcome them and replace them with the good and the true, so that our reaping may become all good (good being God's will for us).

Nahum (in A. V., Luke 3:25, Naum), nā'-hŭm (Heb.)—*panting; sighing; consolation; comfort; solace; ease; compassion; pity.*

a Father of Amos and son of Esli, named in the genealogy of Jesus Christ (Luke 3:25). b "The Elkoshite," one of the minor prophets of the Bible, writer of The Book of Nahum (Nah. 1:1).

Meta. The adjusting, soothing, healing effect of the Holy Spirit's presence in consciousness (*comfort, solace, ease*). Since one of the men named Nahum was a prophet, the thought of the Holy Spirit as teacher, as well as comforter and healer, is brought out.

Nain, nā'-ĭn (Gk. fr. Heb.)—*proper; suitable; becoming; decorous; comely; pleasant; beautiful; seat; dwelling; habitation; pasture.*

A city in Palestine, the place where Jesus raised the widow's son to life (Luke 7:11-17).

Meta. Man is the *proper* and *suitable* dwelling place for and the expresser of life and Truth and substance (*dwelling, seat, habitation, comely, pasture*; Truth is *beautiful*, and its ways are indeed *pleasant* to the consecrated soul). When the individual recognizes the abidingness of Truth, and acts on it by means of his I AM (Jesus), an inner quickening takes place and he is awakened to a newness of life and youth throughout his being. This is indicated by Jesus' raising the widow's son to life.

Naioth, nā'-ĭŏth (Heb.)—*habitations; dwellings.*

A place in Ramah, where Samuel lived and had his school of prophets. David fled there to Samuel when Saul was trying to take his life (I Sam. 19:18-20; 20:1).

Meta. Ramah means *the height.* Naioth, meaning *habitations, dwellings,* a place in Ramah, where Samuel lived and had his school of prophets, would signify the abiding place of the Most High in the man who is awakening to his inmost spiritual being. Samuel represents the inner voice, which lives in this inner place of Spirit and is the instructor of the higher and more receptive, intelligent thoughts of the individual (school of prophets).

name.

Meta. The "name" in Acts 4:12 ("Neither is there any other name under heaven, that is given among men, wherein we must be saved") means authority, or that which unites the right and the power of control. Jesus Christ, by taking upon Himself the sins of the flesh and demonstrating over them, instilled within the heart of the race both the understanding and the force that are today leading mankind out of sin and darkness and death into purity, light, and life everlasting.

Naomi, nå-ō′-mī (Heb.)—*my sweetness; my pleasantness; delight; my beloved; my delight; beauty.*

Wife of Elimelech, and mother of the first husband of Ruth the Moabitess. She was an Israelitish woman of Beth–lehem –judah. With her husband and sons she went to live in the country of Moab during a famine in their own country. In Moab her husband and sons died, and she came back to her own land a widow. (Ruth 1; 2; 3; 4).

Meta. The soul, when it has failed to unite itself with God. The soul feels that the "Almighty hath dealt very bitterly" with it, when it fails to express itself under the law of Jehovah.

Naomi, the soul, goes out from Jehovah charged with spiritual ideas. Man has free will in the exercise of spiritual ideas and may utilize his soul forces in the sense consciousness, but he is always brought back to his original spiritual starting point, no matter how far away from the Source of his being he may wander (Ruth 1:21).

The love nature of man is satisfied only as the soul is attached to thoughts of Spirit. Then love becomes a magnet to attract into one's experience only that which is uplifting and constructive. (See Ruth 1:14-22.)

Symbolically Naomi represents the outcome of the soul's experiences, when in its apparent lack it turns to the resources of sense instead of to God. This is going into a foreign land when apparent lack sets in at home. Prosperity may seem to express for a season in the new surroundings, but the ruling thought of sense is material; the apparent prosperity that it brings cannot be permanent. The love of the soul is for Spirit, and for the people (thoughts) of Spirit. When it is true to its highest wisdom it becomes a magnet to attract other souls, of like character, to the higher life.

Naomi (meaning *my pleasantness, my delight, my beloved*) may also be said to represent the divine feminine, or love. Her history illustrates the search of love for satisfaction in outer things when there seems a dearth in the inner. The result of leaving the true spiritual environment for what seems in the outer to be riches and honor is disappointment and lack; a return to the old home —the Father's house, Israel, the real—is necessary.

Ruth here means sweetness, beauty, firm will. She represents the symmetrical expression of the soul in form. Naomi loves the beautiful body, Ruth, but in her lack of spiritual sufficiency tries to deny it place in her life.

Ruth clung to Naomi; the spiritual quality of Naomi awakened the soul of her beautiful body, Ruth, and an indissoluble attachment was formed between them.

Beth–lehem means *"house of bread"*; the beginning of the barley harvest symbolizes a renewal, or a reunion of the soul and body with the true substance.

Naphish (in A. V., I Chronicles 5:19, Nephish), nā′-phĭsh (Heb.)—*recreated; refreshed; reinspired; animated; living; breathing; rational; soul; mind; spirit.*

a Son of Ishmael (Gen. 25:15); **b** also his descendants (I Chron. 5:19).

Meta. Naphish refers to the activity of the very breath of life by which every living creature is animated and inspired, either consciously or unconsciously.

Naphtali (in A. V., Matthew 4:13, 15, Nephthalim; Revelation 7:6, Nepthalim), năph'-tă-lī (Heb.)—*my wres-tling; mutual intertwining of Jah; wres-tling of Jehovah.*

a Sixth son of Jacob, and second son of Bilhah, Rachel's handmaid. "And Bilhah Rachel's handmaid conceived again, and bare Jacob a second son. And Rachel said, With mighty wrestlings [*wrestlings of God*, in margin] have I wrestled with my sister, and have prevailed: and she called his name Naphtali" (Gen. 30:7, 8). Jacob's blessing upon this son was:
"Naphtali is a hind let loose:
He giveth goodly words" (Gen. 49:21). Moses' blessing upon the tribe of Naphtali was (Deut. 33:23):
"O Naphtali, satisfied with favor,
And full with the blessing of Jehovah,
Possess thou the west and the south"
b Naphtali also refers to the tribe of people who were descended from the son of Jacob by this name, and **c** to the country in which they lived (Num. 1:43; Josh. 19:32-39; I Kings 15:20).

Meta. The brain in the small of the back (the kidneys), whose office is to direct the elimination of certain watery elements from the blood. This presiding genius is called strength, because it keeps up the positive tone of the circulating medium.

When we have been worshiping material things and filling our thoughts with worldly conditions to the exclusion of the spiritual, there is a deterioration of the soul quality, a gloom and a dimness of the mind prevail; one of the parts of the organism that this especially afflicts is Naphtali (kidneys; see Isa. 9:1).

When material thought has dimmed the eyes of the understanding, and shadows of carnal thought have gathered in consciousness, affecting the strength center in the back, the restorative power is the light of Spirit. The mind is opened to the light through prayer and spiritual meditation. The light increases from day to day, the soul grows into consciousness with the Christ mind, and one's whole being is thus purified and greatly increased in strength.

Naphtuhim, năph'-tu-hĭm (Heb. fr. Egypt.)—*they of Ptah; the opened; the hollow; the cavernous; the empty ones;*

the loosened; border people; bowmen.

A people who were descended from Mizraim, son of Ham (Gen. 10:13).

Meta. Empty thoughts, thoughts of lack (*the hollow, the empty ones*). Bowmen are archers, those who use bows and arrows. Shooting arrows signifies sending forth quick, darting thoughts. Mizraim, from whom the Naphtuhim were descended, represents the sense belief that the seemingly physical man is wholly material and is subject to all kinds of sorrows and errors that hinder him from receiving good. Naphtuhim, therefore, meaning *bowmen,* signifies the darting forth throughout the consciousness of the material ideas that spring from the Mizraim belief and lead to a consciousness of lack and of separateness from God. These must be denied and overcome, that the individual may get away from material to spiritual understanding and expression.

Narcissus, năr-çĭs'-sŭs (Gk.)—*daffodils; narcotic; illusion; stupefying.*

A man at Rome. Paul sent salutation to the members of his household, who were Christians (Rom. 16:11).

Meta. Mental inertia, or a thought tendency belonging to the intellect of man, the head (Rome), that tends to inertia of perhaps both mind and body (*narcotic, stupefying*). The family, or thoughts that lie nearest in relation to this cause of apathy and inaction, have been quickened and awakened by Truth (the household of Narcissus are "in the Lord"), thus the whole condition is in process of redemption.

Nathan, nā'-thăn (Heb.)—*reaching out the hand; giver; gift; given; give up; yield; grant grace; grant reward; instruct; requite.*

a A prophet during David's reign (II Sam. 7:2-17). **b** A son of David (II Sam 5:14). **c** Other men (II Sam. 23:36; I Kings 4:5; Ezra 8:16; 10:39).

Meta. Spiritual power and understanding in and back of words of Truth.

Nathan the prophet and Zadok the priest (I Kings 1:34, 38) are representatives of the spiritual kingdom. Solomon (peace and wisdom) is to be king in our heart, and we mentally anoint him in the name of the Lord. If we declare our word of authority without considering its spiritual relation in our thought, it will lack certain elements of stability and Truth, and instead of being related to the one inner Source it will be associated with some of the many man-made thought atmospheres; thus the spiritual qualities of power, foresight, understanding, and true Christ righteousness that Nathan and Zadok represent must be present and active in our true words, that those words may be alive and pregnant with success and all good.

Nathanael, nȧ-thăn'-ȧ-ĕl (Gk. fr. Heb.) —*given of God; gift of God; yielding of God; grace of God; honor to God; instructed of God; requited of God; rewarded by God.*

One whom Philip brought to Jesus (John 1:45-49). He is believed to be the same person as the apostle Bartholomew, since, in the Gospels of Matthew, Mark, and Luke, Philip and Bartholomew are always mentioned together when the names of the Twelve Apostles are given, and Nathanael is not mentioned. John says nothing of Bartholomew, but mentions Nathanael in connection with Philip. Bartholomew is thought to have been Nathanael's surname. His home was in Cana of Galilee (John 21:2).

Meta. The imaging power of the mind, the faculty of imagination. In the realm of the real (Israel) it is guileless—innocent of error images; it is open and receptive to the beauty and perfection of Being. This faculty makes the great artist, when the soul is lifted up with spiritual fervor. The guileless innocence of the Nathanael state of mind causes the religious enthusiast to believe all things about Spirit and the world invisible. Exercised without the Christ understanding, it is personal credulity. It is the image maker in the psychic, and the clairvoyant may be deceived to any extent by its conjuring power. It is not in itself error, but may, like all the other faculties, be used in erroneous ways. When the mind of Spirit uses it, as Jesus used it in discerning Nathanael when he was concealed under the fig tree, it is without guile. In the communication of God with man this faculty plays an important part. It receives divine ideas and reflects them in images into the soul in dreams and visions. This is the meaning of the passage, "Ye shall see the heaven opened, and the angels [thoughts] of God ascending and descending upon the Son of man."

Nathan – melech, nā'-thăn – mē'-lĕch (Heb.)—*king's gift; the king is giver; rewarded by the king; requited by the king.*

A chamberlain whose room, or place of dwelling, was "in the precincts," by "the entrance of the house of Jehovah" (II Kings 23:11). This was in the reign of Josiah, king of Judah.

Meta. Nathan signifies spiritual power and understanding in and back of words of Truth. Melech signifies the will, or a ruling thought pertaining to the will. Nathan–melech, the king's chamberlain, therefore would be this understanding and power of the word, ruled by the will. When the individual wills to do the will of God, as was the case with Josiah, the vital forces (horses) that have been given over to idolatrous use are taken away, are no longer given to that use; and the body activities (chariots) that are the result of this erroneous use of the vital forces are purified and lifted to higher expression ("he burned the chariots of the sun with fire").

Nazarene, năz-ȧ-rēne' (Gk. fr. Heb.)— patronymic for inhabitants of Nazareth.

An inhabitant of the town of Nazareth. Jesus and His followers were called Nazarenes, because Jesus' home was in Nazareth (Matt. 2:23; Acts 24:5).

Meta. A thought belonging to that in consciousness which Nazareth signifies. (See NAZARETH.)

Nazareth, năz'-ȧ-rĕth (Gk. fr. Heb.) —*branch; offshoot; sprout; verdant; shining; splendid; observed, i. e., as a covenant; watched; guarded; defended; preserved.* Nazareth should not be confused with Nazirite, since in the Hebrew the two names are quite different.

A town of Galilee; the boyhood home of Jesus (Matt. 2:23).

Meta. The meaning of Nazareth is *branch, offshoot, sprout, verdant, shining, watched, guarded.* A synagogue is a place of worship, and the Sabbath is a state of rest. Luke 4:16 runs, "And he came to Nazareth, where he had been brought up: and he entered, as his custom was, into the synagogue on the sabbath day, and stood up to read." This means that, when we begin to awaken to the truth that we are sons of God, branches of the one true vine, when we take the attitude of worship, of watching, of centering the mind's eye on the Christ Truth, and rest in that consciousness, we are receptive to the inspiration of Spirit.

Nazareth was a despised place (the things of the Spirit of God are considered foolish by the natural man; see I Cor. 2:14), and as such would be a type of inferiority. It was considered a community of commonplace, if not disreputable, people. "Can any good thing come out of Nazareth?" Yet in this commonplace village Jesus was reared; and in the seemingly mediocre mind the Christ Truth is received and expressed. Nazareth typifies the commonplace mind of man, but it is a place of development, through which the Christ comes into expression.

Nazirite (A. V., Nazarite), năz′-ĭ-rīte (fr. Heb.)—*separated; consecrated by vow; abstinence; set apart by choice; devotion.*

One chosen, or set apart; one consecrated to God by a vow (Num. 6:2-21). Samson was a Nazirite (Judg. 13:5, 24; 16:17; see Amos 2:11, 12, also).

Meta. A Nazirite signifies what the meaning of the word (*consecrated by vow, separated*) implies: the thoughts consecrated to Truth, to life, holy, sanctified, free from all worldliness and from belief in error, destruction, death. (One of the points relating to a Nazirite that is given more explicit directions than others is that he shall not come near a dead body, under any consideration. See Numbers 6:6-12. Even so, thoughts purified from error and given wholly to Truth are entirely separated from any belief or teaching relating to materiality and death, are separate from all destructive tendencies; they are fully centered in life, and in that which is uplifting and constructive.)

Neah, nē′-ăh (Heb.)—*moving; shaking; trembling; agitating; staggering;*

waving; wandering; disturbing; sifting; shaking down; settling.

A city of Zebulun, on the northeast border (Josh. 19:13).

Meta. A group of thoughts of a wandering, changeable, uncertain, unsettled, fearful tendency (*shaking, moving, trembling, agitating, disturbing*) coming under the dominion of the faculty of order (a city allotted to Zebulun, Zebulun representing the order faculty in man), that it may be made firm, steady, reliable, and become established (*shaking down, settling*).

Neapolis, nē-ăp′-ŏ-lĭs (Gk.)—*young city; youthful city; new city; restored city.*

A Macedonian seaport city, between Samothrace and Philippi. Paul came to this city on one of his missionary journeys (Acts 16:11).

Meta. The *new city,* or center of action. To make a straight course to Neapolis means that he who concentrates all his energies on the accomplishment of his purpose will surely achieve.

Neariah, nē-ă-rī′-ăh (Heb.)—*Jehovah shakes out,* i. e., *disperses; Jah drives out, casts forth; Jah shakes off,* i. e., *liberates; child of Jah; youth of Jehovah; Jah's bride; servant of Jehovah.*

a Son of Shemaiah, descended from David (I Chron. 3:22). **b** Son of Ishi, a captain of the five hundred Simeonites who went to Mount Seir and "smote the remnant of the Amalekites that escaped, and have dwelt there unto this day" (I Chron. 4:42, 43).

Meta. True thoughts in consciousness; thoughts that are born of God, the offspring of the divine idea of sonship; thoughts that serve Jehovah, the I AM, in the work of freeing the individual from sense errors and in unifying him consciously with spirit (*Jehovah shakes out,* i. e., *disperses, drives out, casts forth, liberates, child of Jah, servant of Jehovah, Jah's bride*).

Nebaioth (in A. V., Genesis 25:13, Nebajoth), nē-bā′-iŏth (Heb.)—*prominences; heights; cultivation of the soil; husbandry; fruitfulness; germinations; prophetic utterances; inspired words.*

a Eldest son of Ishmael (Gen. 25:13-16). **b** The name of the tribe of people that was descended from him, and the land in which these people lived (Isa. 60: 7).

Meta. The outer, sensate, or material consciousness, reflecting the light of the inner, true ideals that are born of Spirit (*heights*), and realizing the possibility of bringing forth abundant good (*cultivation of the soil, fruitfulness, germinations*) through the power of the word of understanding (*prophetic utterances, inspired words*).

Neballat, nĕ-băl'-lăt (Heb.)—*hardness; firmness; veiled prophecy; hidden germination; secret folly; hidden weakness; covered wickedness; foolishness; necromancy.*

A city of Palestine, to which some of the Benjamites returned from the Babylonian captivity (Neh. 11:34).

Meta. This group of thoughts embraces both good and seemingly error tendencies. There is a *firmness* and solidity about it that is good, yet tends to *hardness;* though seemingly hidden, Truth is working in it, giving promise of still better things (*veiled prophecy, hidden germination*). On the other hand it is the abode of secret sins, of foolish, concealed wickedness (*secret folly, hidden weakness, covered wickedness*) that needs to be uncovered and cleansed away by the power of an active faith in God (Benjamin).

"Who can discern *his* errors? Clear thou me from hidden *faults*" (Psalms 19:12).

Nebat, nē'-băt (Heb.)—*look; behold; regard; see; view; perceive, i. e., with the eye.*

Father of Jeroboam, of the tribe of Ephraim (I Kings 11:26).

Meta. A willing or determining to look into matters, to perceive or understand (*look, behold, regard, see, view, perceive, i. e., with the eye;* the eye, or seeing, beholding, always relates to understanding).

Nebat was of the tribe of Ephraim (the will), and his son Jeroboam became the first king of Israel after the nation of Israel was divided into two kingdoms, Judah and Israel. Israel, the part that Jeroboam ruled, represents the objective consciousness in the individual.

Nebo, nē'-bô (Heb.)—*planet Mercury; quick messenger; celestial scribe; interpreter, i. e., of the divine will; inspired speech; prophecies; prophet; oracle; height; distinguished; prominent.*

a A city in the land of Jazer, and of Gilead, that was allotted to Reuben and Gad, on the east of Jordan (Num. 32:3). b A mountain in Moab, from which Moses was shown the Promised Land, and where Moses is supposed to have died (Deut. 32:49; 34:1). (See also Isaiah 46:1; here the name relates to a Babylonian or Chaldean god.)

Meta. Divine inspiration, intuition, discernment, foresight, understanding (*celestial scribe, interpreter, i. e., of the divine will, inspired speech, prophecies, height*) expressing on the three planes of consciousness in man. The Nebo that was a city in the land of Jazer and Gilead, east of the Jordan, and was allotted to Reuben and Gad, is of the higher, spiritual consciousness. (See JAZER and GILEAD.) The Nebo that was a mountain of Moab, from which Moses was shown the Promised Land, pertains to a high place of understanding and perception expressing in the outer or sensate, material body consciousness. The Nebo of the Chaldeans is this power of discernment and understanding operative on the mental, psychic, or soul plane.

Nebuchadnezzar, nĕb-ū-chăd-nĕz'-zär (Heb. fr. Chald.)—*Nebo chief protector; Mercury fire of the gods; Nebo the lord of brightness; Nebo the original fire; may Nebo protect; great king of Mercury.*

King of Babylon, who conquered Judea and took the Jewish people, as a nation, captive to Babylon (Dan. 1:1; 2; 3; 4). He is called Nebuchadrezzar in the book of Jeremiah (see Jer. 52:28).

Meta. The word Nebuchadnezzar means *Nebo chief protector,* or *may Nebo protect.* Nebo was the Babylonian or Chaldean god of wisdom (*Nebo the lord of brightness*). Nebuchadnezzar represents in us the human will backing itself up by the human intellect; this brings about human judgment. A king always represents some function of the will. The will intrenched in intellectual learning, giving its full attention to material subjects, is very powerful up to a certain point. It feels itself to be all-powerful, but there comes a time when it realizes its weakness and inability, as Nebuchadnezzar learned.

The Hebrew developments from the word Nebuchadnezzar or Nebuchadrezzar are: *pouring out of restraining tribulation; outflowing of stored-up calamities; pouring forth of adverse treasures.* Take these in conjunction with the idea of "judgment" as explained in the former paragraph, and we perceive that Nebuchadnezzar also represents the emotional child of nature, who wants to fulfill all desires of the soul whether they be good for him or not. The world is full of these Nebuchadnezzar people. We call them psychics. They are loath to stand on their own judgment in any matter. When decision is required of them they fly to some oracle. It may be a friend whose good advice they ask, or a medium, or they may even resort to the tossing of a coin or the cutting of a deck of cards. They are willful and they rule arbitrarily. Refusing to bring forth their own good judgment, they become mendacious and tyrannical. The ultimate of this sort of action is a return to the animal-instinct plane of consciousness, as described in Daniel 5:21.

It is really a dangerous thing to neglect the development of judgment. If we go to our friends for advice we are weakened. If we act without judgment we fall short in our efforts; and if we trust to oracles and luck we become demoralized and animalized, and suffer the result.

Nebushazban (A. V., Nebushasban), nĕb-ū-shăz'-băn (Heb. fr. Chald.)—*Nebo saves me; favorable to Mercury; adherent of Nebo; whom interpretation sets free; favorable speech.*

One of the chief officers of the king of Babylon, who was sent to take Jeremiah out of prison (Jer. 39:13).

Meta. A degree of understanding (*Nebo saves me, favorable speech*) that acts as the executive power of the human will (king of Babylon) in setting free our spiritual faith (*whom interpretation sets free*), or that in us which intuitively discerns the divine law and seeks to have

it obeyed (Jeremiah). (See NEBO.)

Nebuzaradan, nĕb'-ū-zär-ā'-dăn (Heb. fr. Chald.)—*Nebo has given offspring; Nebo sends fruitfulness; chief whom Nebo favors; great lord of Mercury; prophetic; fruitfulness.*

"The captain of the guard, a servant of the king of Babylon" (II Kings 25:8; Jer. 39:9-13).

Meta. A thought activity that is the fruit of the purely mental, or soul, discernment and understanding that Nebo, the Babylonian god of learning, represents. (See NEBO.)

Neco (A. V., Necho), nē'-cô (Heb. fr. Egypt.)—*beaten; smitten; afflicted; smitten in the feet; lame.*

A king of Egypt at the time that Josiah was king of Judah. Josiah was killed in battle against this king (II Chron. 35:20-24).

Meta. A ruling thought of the Egyptian, or darkened, little understood phase of consciousness in man; it is greatly lacking in practical understanding (*smitten in the feet, lame*, the feet referring to the phase of the understanding that comes in touch with outer conditions).

Nedabiah, nĕd-ă-bī'-ăh (Heb.)—*whom Jehovah impels; Jehovah gives spontaneously; give willingly to Jehovah; freewill offering to Jah; largess of Jehovah.*

Son of Jeconiah the captive (I Chron. 3:18).

Meta. The fruit of the will activated by I AM (*whom Jehovah impels;* Jeconiah, father of Nedabiah, was a one-time king of Judah, and a king always represents a phase of the will or ruling power in individual consciousness). This fruit of the will impelled by I AM is insight into the largeness, broadness, nobility, and generosity of Spirit in its dealings with and expression in and through man (*Jehovah gives spontaneously, give willingly to Jehovah, largess of Jehovah*).

Nehelamite, nĕ-hĕl'-ă-mīte (fr. Heb.)—*dreamed; dreamer; dreaming; divine communication; healed; recovered; sound; strong; robust.*

Shemaiah the Nehelamite was a false prophet in the time of Jeremiah (Jer. 29:24, 31, 32).

Meta. The imagination (*dreamed,*

dreamer; Joseph, the son of Jacob, who represents the faculty of imagination in individual consciousness, was called a dreamer by his brothers, Gen. 37:19) directed by personal ambition and unbalanced by true understanding and good judgment (Shemaiah the Nehelamite was a false prophet). Directed by spiritual understanding, the imaging faculty leads to wholeness and soundness of mind and body (*healed, recovered, sound, strong*).

Nehemiah, ne̅-he̅-mī'-ăh (Heb.)—*Jehovah consoles; Jehovah comforts; repentance of Jehovah; compassion of Jah.*

a Son of Hacaliah, at one time cupbearer to the king of Persia, and a head man of the Jews who returned from the Captivity. He came back to Jerusalem by permission of the king, for the express purpose of rebuilding the walls of Jerusalem and getting things into better shape for the Jews who had returned from the Babylonian captivity (Neh. 1:1). **b** In Ezra 2:2 a Nehemiah is mentioned who returned with Zerubbabel from the Captivity. **c** In Nehemiah 3:16 we read of Nehemiah, the son of Azbuk, who helped to repair Jerusalem's wall.

Meta. In Nehemiah 1 Nehemiah represents one who has been carried away from spiritual peace (Jerusalem) into the confusion of sense (Babylon) and is desirous of again restoring the Holy City. Nehemiah has his representative in all those who have once realized the peace and joy of the spiritual life but have been captured and led away by the power of sense thought, because of laxity in keeping the divine law.

Nehemiah 1:11 shows the earnest faith and simplicity of this spiritual-minded man. He talked to God as if He were present and would give attentive ear to every request. This confidence in the power of God is what stirs the ethers of Mind and sets into action elements in soul and body that speed the consummation of every request. Divine Mind works through man; but it does great things only through the person who has absolute faith. Nehemiah was but a cupbearer slave to the king in Babylon; but his prayer lifted him into such courage and confidence in God and himself that he went to Jerusalem and inspired the poor, downtrodden remnant of Jews remaining there to rebuild the walls of that city.

The prophet Nehemiah (Neh. 4:1-20) is the faithful, persistent one within us that believes in this divine possibility for man: the rebuilding of the walls of Jerusalem, which is a symbolical description of the reconstruction of the soul consciousness so that it will keep out negative and error thoughts and conditions—this of course results in a renewed and spiritualized body.

Nehemiah can also be said to be that in us which inspires us to higher and better things. He represents, too, the boldness and the courage that set about the rebuilding of a character weakened by sin. We shall prove our victory over all seemingly opposing thoughts and forces by holding to that inner confidence of Truth represented by the words of Nehemiah 4:14: "Be not ye afraid of them: remember the Lord, who is great and terrible, and fight for your brethren, your sons, and your daughters, your wives, and your houses."

Nehiloth, ne̅'-hi-lŏth (Heb.)—*perforated instruments; wind instruments; pipes; flutes; tibiæ; the perforated; inheritance; possessions.*

A name mentioned in the title of the 5th Psalm; in the margin, *wind instruments* is given.

Meta. Man as a perfect channel for free, harmonious, rhythmical, tuneful expression (*wind instruments, pipes, flutes*).

Nehum, ne̅'-hŭm (Heb.)—*consolation; comfort; compassion.*

One who returned with Zerubbabel from the Babylonian captivity (Neh. 7:7).

Meta. The relief from distress, the strengthened hope and cheer, the good (*consolation, comfort*) that one experiences when one has been delivered from sense confusion (captivity in Babylon) and its results, and has entered into the peace of knowing one's oneness with God (returned to Jerusalem).

Nehushta, ne̅-hŭsh'-tä (Heb.)—*brass; brazen; brazen serpent; bright; basis; foundation; support.*

Daughter of Elnathan of Jerusalem,

and mother of Jehoiachin, king of Judah (II Kings 24:8).

Meta. A firmness, unyieldingness, and strength of purpose (*brass, brazen*), established in the soul. This is a *basis, foundation,* and *support* for the working of Jehovah, I AM, in individual consciousness to establish the will in spiritual strength, assurance, faith, and understanding. (See ELNATHAN, father of Nehushta, and JEHOIACHIN, her son.) Jehoiachin did not bear out in his acts that which his name implies. Even so, there is in that which Nehushta signifies a tendency to carnal-sense wisdom (*brazen serpent*), a suggestion of hardness, obstinacy, and presumption (*brass, brazen*) that must be eliminated before all the good that Nehushta stands for can be realized.

Nehushtan, nê-hŭsh'-tăn (Heb.)—*brazen; brass; copper; bright; brazen serpent; copper coin; fetter of brass; brazen thing; small brass object.*

The name that Hezekiah king of Judah gave to the brazen serpent that Moses had made, and that the children of Israel had converted into an idol (II Kings 18:4, in margin, *a piece of brass*).

Meta. The serpent is a symbol of elemental life. When the serpent elemental is lifted up, or spiritualized, it adds radiance to the whole man. The "brazen serpent" that Moses caused to be put up where all could see it, and by looking be healed, represents this elevation of the sense man to a higher consciousness. (See SERPENT.)

This by which the Israelites were healed, however, became to them later an idol, Nehushtan (*a small brass object, a fetter of brass, a brazen thing*). Even so it is possible for one to be lifted up in personal pride, because of a marked overcoming that has been accomplished, and to worship or become enamored of the fact that one has made this attainment, until one may become actually hardened, presumptuous, and obstinate in his pride and in his belief that he has in this one phase of overcoming gained the whole Truth. Thus he forgets the true God who is all-love, all-tenderness, all-compassion; the love that seeks not its own but always the good of others,

and is unselfish, humble, of good deportment, ever charitable toward all. To such an egotistic individual that which should be—and was in the beginning—a source of spiritual realization and attainment has become an idol that must be put away, that the individual may begin over again and really in all things put God first, instead of self, that he may become in all ways like Him.

Neiel, nê-ī'-ĕl (Heb.)—*God's dwelling place; habitation of God; dwelling place of the Most High.*

A border city of Asher in the Promised Land (Josh. 19:27).

Meta. A group of thoughts established in Truth, the abiding place of Spirit (*God's dwelling place*).

neighbor.

"Who is my neighbor?" (Luke 10:29).

Meta. Every soul that dwells upon the earth is your neighbor, "my neighbor." There is no such thing as distance in Spirit nor in the operation of spiritual laws. Through us must the law of divine love bind up and heal wounds, dissolve error, and restore light and order from out of chaos.

Your "neighbor" (Luke 10:25-37) refers to the outer forms in which life manifests, whether it be your own body, the bodies of other persons, or of animals.

To bind up the wounds (Luke 10:34) is to seek in every way to preserve the forms in which life manifests. Those who would lay hold on eternal life must do this. We all have life, and it is God's eternal life, but it does not become ours in reality until we consciously realize this fact. The one who enters into eternal life, as did Jesus, must lay hold on that life omnipresent and make it one with his body. This is the secret of inheriting "eternal life."

Have compassion on the life in the bodies of all living creatures, and especially in your own body. Declare life abiding perpetually in the organism of your body.

Nekoda, nê-kō'-dà (Heb.)—*pierced; marked; selected; separated; set apart; distinguished; celebrated; famous; shepherd; herdsman.*

a His "children" were among the Nethinim who returned to Jerusalem from the Captivity (Ezra 2:48). **b** Another Nekoda is mentioned in Ezra 2:60; six hundred and fifty-two of his descendants were among those who returned from the captivity but could not show their genealogy so as to prove that they were of Israel.

Meta. Thought activities, whose office in the organism is to *shepherd* the sheep—guide, protect, and feed one's thoughts—to care for the herds, or animal forces (*herdsman*). These thought activities are, or should be, of a high, devout, spiritual character (*selected, set apart, distinguished, famous*), but here they are more of the outer, somewhat inspired intellect than of Spirit (their descendants were Nethinim (bond servants in the Temple) and among those who could not show that they were of Israel—real, true, spiritual thoughts).

Nemuel, něm'-ū-ĕl (Heb.)—*God is spreading; sea of God; day of God; God's day; luminous manifestation of God.*

a Son of Eliab, who was a son of Pallu and grandson of Reuben (Num. 26:9). **b** A son of Simeon (Num. 26:12). In Genesis 46:10 and Exodus 6:15 this latter Nemuel is called Jemuel.

Meta. The significance is virtually the same as that of JEMUEL, which see. Nemuel also suggests an increase of light throughout the consciousness (*God is spreading, luminous manifestation of God*).

Nemuelites, něm'-ū-ĕl-ītes (fr. Heb.) —*of* or *belonging to Nemuel.*

The "family" or descendants, of Nemuel the son of Simeon (Num. 26:12).

Meta. Thoughts springing from and like to that in consciousness for which Nemuel stands. (See NEMUEL.)

Nepheg, ně'-phĕg (Heb.)—*coming forth; sprout; bud; emanation; breathe out; weak; faint; slack; expired.*

a Son of Izhar, who was a son of Kohath, and grandson of Levi (Ex. 6:21). **b** The name of one of David's sons who was born in Jerusalem (II Sam. 5:15).

Meta. A development in consciousness (*coming forth, bud*) of understanding (see IZHAR, father of Nepheg) in rela-

tion to the attracting, unifying quality of love that Kohath, father of Izhar and grandfather of Nepheg, represents. (David also represents love.) This development of understanding as it relates to love is not, at this stage of its unfoldment in the individual, so free from the limitations of the personal as it should be; therefore there is something of a dissipating and weakening character about the individual's expression of love, such as may be found in purely human sympathy (*emanation, breathe out, weak, faint, slack, expired*). Weak human sympathy leads to death and not to life; true love is strong, uplifting, and life-giving.

Nephisim (A. V., Nephusim), ně-phī'-sĭm (Heb.)—*expansions; deep inspirations; refreshing breaths.*

His "children" were among the Nethinim who returned to Judea with Zerubbabel, from the Babylonian captivity (Ezra 2:50). In Nehemiah 7:52, he is called Nephushesim.

Meta. A thought in consciousness that tends to expand, enlarge, and bring new inspiration and life into the serving idea. (*Expansions, deep inspirations, refreshing breaths,* are definitions of Nephisim; his "children" were among the returned Nethinim, the Nethinim being servants or virtual slaves in the Temple. True service, however, is glorified. Jesus said that the greatest of all should be the servant of all.)

Nephtoah, něph'-tŏ-ăh (Heb.)—*opening; loosening; unbinding; spring; entrance; insight; instruction; explanation.*

"The fountain of the waters of Nephtoah" was a place on the border between Judah and Benjamin (Josh. 15:9; 18:15).

Meta. Freeing the consciousness from one's obstructing thoughts and beliefs, through prayer, praise, and faith (Judah and Benjamin), so that the understanding may be renewed and the waters of life may spring up and flow in freely (*opening, loosening, unbinding, spring, entrance, insight, instruction*).

Nephushesim (A. V., Nephishesim), ně-phŭsh'-ĕ-sĭm (Heb.)—*expansions; inspiring breaths; refreshing breaths.*

The same as Nephisim of Ezra 2:50 (Neh. 7:52).

Meta. See NEPHISIM.

Ner, nĕr (Heb.)—*shining; spreading abroad light; a light; a torch; a lamp; fallow ground; newly tilled land.*

Grandfather of Saul (I Chron. 8:33). He was the father of Abner, Saul's uncle and captain of his host (I Sam. 14:50).

Meta. Ner, like Abner, signifies the illumined reason or intellect. (See ABNER.)

Nereus, nē'-reūs (Gk.)—*by the water; wet; god of water.*

A Christian at Rome. Paul sent salutations to him (Rom. 16:15).

Meta. A rather negative (*wet, god of water*) phase of thought that is of the head, or intellect (Rome), yet has access to the realm of unformed ideas (*by the water*) and has accepted the Christ Truth, which imparts true illumination and stability.

Nergal, nēr'-găl (Heb. fr. Pers.)—*planet Mars; great hero; fierce warrior; man-devourer; destruction; bloodshed; war.*

The god of the "men of Cuth" (II Kings 17:30).

Meta. Outer personal force, defense, oppression, war. Nergal, in its form *nare-gal,* is believed to be the same as the Zabian name for the planet Mars. This name of the planet, among both Zabians and Arabians, means *ill luck, misfortune;* and we understand that Mars, as worshiped by the ancients, is symbolical of bloodshed and war. Among the Zabians the planet Mars was typified by the figure of a man holding in one hand a drawn sword and in the other a human head just cut off; his garments were red, which, as well as the other ideas attached to this idol, were no doubt founded on the reddish hue that the body of the planet presents to the eye. Among the southern Arabs his temple was painted red. Bloodstained garments were offered to him, and a warrior (probably a prisoner) was cast into a pool as a part of the sacrificial ceremony.

Nergal-sharezer, nēr'-găl-shă-rē'-zĕr (Heb. fr. Pers.)—*Nergal prince of fire; Nergal save the king.*

A prince and chief officer of the king of Babylon. He helped rescue Jeremiah from the court of the guard (Jer. 39:3).

Meta. The error belief in outer force, in war, in fighting to defend one's rights and to increase one's possessions and power, exalted to an active, ruling place in consciousness. Though entirely of the outer, sense consciousness, and destructive in its character, this force is sometimes used for good, as is signified by the rescue of Jeremiah, in which Nergal-sharezer figured.

Neri, nē'-rī (Gk. fr. Heb.)—*Jehovah spreads light abroad; Jah is a light; lamp of Jehovah.*

Named in the genealogy of Jesus Christ (Luke 3:27); thought to be the same as Neriah.

Meta. Spiritual understanding quickened in individual consciousness (*Jehovah spreads light abroad, Jah is a light, lamp of Jehovah*).

Neriah, nĕ-rī'-äh (Heb.)—*Jehovah spreads light abroad; Jehovah is a lamp; Jah is light; Jehovah enlightens.*

Father of Baruch, to whom Jeremiah delivered the deed of the field in Anathoth that he bought from Hanamel his cousin (Jer. 32:12). Neriah is mentioned again, in Jeremiah 51:59, as the father of Seraiah.

Meta. The consciousness of the individual awakening to the truth that all true light or understanding is spiritual and exists in and radiates through the Christ mind in man, Jehovah (*Jah is light, Jehovah enlightens, Jehovah spreads light abroad*).

Nethanel (A. V., Nethaneel), nĕ-thăn'-ĕl (Heb.)—*given of God; God gives; gift of God.*

a Son of Zuar, and prince of the tribe of Issachar, while in the wilderness (Num. 1:18). **b** Fourth son of Jesse, and brother of David (I Chron. 2:14). **c** There were others by this name, also.

Meta. Zuar, father of one Nethanel, means *made little.* Jesse, the father of the second-named Nethanel, represents eternal existence (*Jah exists, Jah is, he who is*). *God gives* His grace to those who are small in their own eyes in so far as the lesser self is concerned. "God . . . giveth grace to the humble" (James. 4:6; I Pet. 5:5); "Whosoever shall humble himself shall be exalted" (Matt. 23:12); "Blessed are the meek: for they shall inherit the earth" (Matt. 5:5); "When I am weak, then am I strong" (II Cor. 12:10).

Nethanel signifies this grace of God, which is God's gift to His children (*gift of God*), to those who are not puffed up in personality and the lesser self, yet realize the eternal existence of their own indwelling Christ, or I AM, and are firm and strong in this realization (see JESSE), thus boldly and steadfastly laying hold of their good. To such persons especially applies the promise, "My grace is sufficient for thee" (II Cor. 12:9); whatever their need may be at any time —a greater consciousness of strength, vitality, love, joy, peace, power, faith, substance—God in them is their all-sufficiency in that thing and it comes quickly into expression.

Nethaniah, nĕth-ă-nī'-ăh (Heb.)— *given of Jehovah; Jehovah hath given; Jah gives.*

a Son of Asaph, and one of the singers in the Temple in David's reign (I Chron. 25:2, 6-12). **b** One of the Levites whom Jehoshaphat sent to teach the law throughout the cities of Judah (II Chron. 17:8). **c** Father of Jehudi, whom the princes sent to Baruch to invite him to come and read the "roll" of Jeremiah to them (Jer. 36:14). **d** The father of Ishmael, who killed Gedeliah, whom the king of Babylon had appointed governor over the cities of Judah (Jer. 41:1-3).

Meta. The individual consciousness awakening to the truth that all blessings, all harmony, all understanding, and all ability to express come from God, through the indwelling Christ, or I AM (*given of Jehovah, Jah gives*).

Nethinim (A. V., Nethinims), nĕth'-ĭ-nĭm (Heb.)—*the given; the devoted; those given; the consecrated; the offered; the dedicated.*

The Nethinim were servants in the Temple. They all were not Israelites. Many were Gibeonites, and others had been reduced to servitude and set apart for waiting on the priests and doing the menial work in the Temple and in the Temple worship. After the return from the Babylonian captivity their position was regarded as more honorable than it had been before (I Chron. 9:2; Ezra 2:43).

Meta. The belief in servitude to God, instead of sonship. To one who sees himself as a servant of God only, to one who sees in the Lord merely a master, the Christian life is a hard, thorny journey, with hopes that something better will come only after death. Such a person does what he believes to be right, from a standpoint of duty, with a repression of his inner desires rather than a change in them. Thus he is in bondage, and does not get much joy and satisfaction out of his religious experiences; but when he comes into a realization of his divine sonship, everything changes. Service then is lifted from duty to joyous opportunities of expressing his Godlikeness and spiritual powers for the good of himself and others. The very inner desires of his heart and mind undergo regeneration, and he does the will of God from his heart, because he loves to do it. He then knows his Lord not as a hard master, but as a loving and tender, yet all-powerful and wise, Father and friend.

Netophah, nĕ-tō'-phăh (Heb.)—*spontaneous dropping; distillation; falling in drops; resinous gum; speech; discourse; prophecy.*

A town in Judah, some of whose inhabitants returned from the Babylonian captivity (Ezra 2:22). It is named with Beth–lehem in Nehemiah 7:26.

Meta. Thoughts of Truth, from the ideal or Truth's primary essence, emanating from the inner source of one's being, little by little, as one is able to receive them (*spontaneous dropping, distillation, speech, discourse, prophecy*). "For it is precept upon precept, precept upon precept; line upon line, line upon line; here a little, there a little" (Isa. 28:10; in the margin "rule" is given in place of "line"; see HELDAI, the Netophathite).

Netophathites (in A. V., Nehemiah 12:28, Netophathi), nĕ-tŏph'-ă-thītes (fr. Heb.)—*of or belonging to Netophah.*

Inhabitants of Netophah (Neh. 12:28; Jer. 40:8). Two of David's warriors, Maharai, and Heleb the son of Baanah, were Netophathites (II Sam. 23:28, 29).

The Netophathites are mentioned in I Chronicles 2:54 as being "sons of Salma."

Meta. Thoughts in consciousness pertaining to that which Netophah indicates. (See NETOPHAH.)

new birth, the.

Meta. Nicodemus (John 3:1-15) was not acquainted with the power of Spirit, and had no understanding of regeneration, although he was a "teacher of Israel," Israel meaning thoughts pertaining to the religious department of the mind.

The new birth is a vague uncertainty to the intellectual Christian, hence there has gradually been evolved a popular belief in a change to come to the soul after death in those who have accepted the church creed and been counted Christians. But in his instructions to Nicodemus, Jesus makes no mention of a postmortem resurrection. He cites the blowing of the wind as an example of those who are born of Spirit. The new birth is a change that comes here and now. It has to do with the present man, the "Son of man," the real I AM in each of us. "And no one hath ascended into heaven, but he that descended out of heaven, *even* the Son of man, who is in heaven. And as Moses lifted up the serpent in the wilderness, even so must the Son of man be lifted up." This man in each of us is divine now, is in heaven now, but his manifestation is still in limbo. He must be lifted out of this condition into a spiritual one; this is being "born anew."

The two important factors in the new-birth process are to put away the old and to receive the new. Water is the natural and familiar symbol of cleansing from impurity, sin, and all its material filth. Spirit is the principle of the new life of harmony, the power from on high that puts in divine order both mind and body.

The Pharisees refused to be baptized by John. They did not consider that they needed the repentance that he demanded. They thought that they were good enough to take high places in the kingdom of God, because of their popularly accepted religious supremacy. Many people today refuse to deny their short-comings: they hold that they are now perfect in Divine Mind and that it is superfluous to deny that which has no existence. However, they are still subject to the appetites and passions of carnality, and will continue to be so until they are "born anew."

The new birth may be explained in a few words, as follows: It is the change from carnal to spiritual consciousness through the begetting and quickening power of the word of Truth. The begetting and quickening take place in man's inner consciousness, and the process of being born anew includes the whole of man—spirit, soul, and body. To be born again is to be made a "new creature," having "this mind in you, which was also in Christ Jesus," and a body like "the body of his glory."

new man (Eph. 4:21; Col. 3:10).

Meta. The "new man" is born of a divine idea through the overshadowing of the Holy Spirit. This idea is that man is a spiritual being. He is a "holy thing," as Mary (the soul) was informed.

Neziah, nĕ-zī'-ăh (Heb.)—*preëminent; illustrious; splendid; glorious; perfected; completed; sincerity; truth; eternity; not finite; perpetual.*

His "children" were among the Nethinim who returned from the Babylonian captivity (Ezra 2:54).

Meta. The idea of Christian service, lifted to its true, exalted place in consciousness (*preëminent, illustrious, perfected, not finite*). Neziah was one of the Nethinim, and they were servants in the Temple. (See NETHINIM.)

Nezib, nē'-zĭb (Heb.)—*set; placed; prefect; overseer; officer; military station; garrison; post; pillar; pedestal; base; statue; idol.*

A city in the lowland of Judah (Josh. 15:43).

Meta. A subconscious group of thoughts (a city in the lowland of Judah), founded in order, dominion, strength, and stability (*set, placed, overseer, garrison, pillar, pedestal, base*). This firm foundation is realized by means of praise and prayer (Judah); all that is of personal force and of a lifeless and idolatrous nature (*statue, idol*) is thus eliminated from the consciousness.

Nibhaz, nĭb'-hăz (Heb.)—*barker; striking; pulsating; conspicuous.*

An idol of the Avvites, or Avvim, and introduced into Samaria by them (II Kings 17:31). This idol is thought to have been in the form of a dog.

Meta. The prevailing tendency of the primitive, unenlightened thoughts of the sense mind in man to wrangle and dispute with and to accuse and attack upon any and every occasion (*barker, striking*) that which is good and true, that which is striving for the attainment of higher ideals. So long as this tendency exists in consciousness it is always in evidence (*pulsating, conspicuous;* see AVVA and AVVIM).

Nibshan, nĭb'-shăn (Heb.)—*heated; glowing; furnace; arid; dried; soft sand; light, sandy soil; light soil; fertile.*

A city in the wilderness of Judah (Josh. 15:62).

Meta. A group of thoughts, *fertile,* productive, capable of bringing forth much good, belonging to the wilderness or uncultivated and undisciplined phase of man's consciousness. This group of thoughts has come under the jurisdiction of the prayer-and-praise faculty (Judah) for further adjustment and upliftment. *Heated, glowing, furnace,* suggest the purifying light, life, and love of Spirit. (See Isaiah 33:14, latter half of verse, to 17.) "The refining pot is for silver, and the furnace for gold; and a man is *tried* by his praise" (margin, by "*that which he praiseth,* or, *that whereof he boasteth*"; Prov. 27:21). In Jeremiah 11:4 the land of Egypt, out of which the Children of Israel were brought, is likened to "the iron furnace."

Nicanor, nĭ-cā'-nôr (Gk.)—*overcomer; victor; victorious; conqueror; steadfast; constant; courageous.*

One of the seven men chosen by the Christians at Jerusalem to look after the distribution of provisions among the widows and others of the assembly there (Acts 6:5).

Meta. An inner realization of victory, of overcoming, especially as relating to substance and supply for the outer or intellectual phase of man's consciousness that is at this time partially established

in Truth. (Grecian widows symbolize half truths, of a somewhat negative character, pertaining to the intellect. They seem to have been neglected by the apostles, or spiritual faculties of mind, who were giving their greatest attention to the Hebrews—the higher thoughts of the inner consciousness that were consecrated to Truth). The central idea in Nicanor is that of overcoming victory through steadfastness; in conjunction with this see Luke 8:15 and 21:19, with marginal notes.

Nicodemus, nĭc-ŏ-dē'-mŭs (Gk. fr. Heb.)—*overcoming of the people; victor over the people; victory of the people; victorious among the people; innocent blood; pure blood; blood without blemish.*

A ruler of the Jews, who came to Jesus by night to inquire into His teaching. To Nicodemus Jesus emphasized man's need of a new or spiritual birth (John 3:1-9).

Meta. The popular idea of religion dominant in the consciousness, hence the esoteric meaning of his name, *victorious among the people, victor over the people, victory of the people.* He is pictured as a prominent Pharisee, one who believes in the strict letter of the Scripture, yet is open to conviction if a higher truth can be entertained safely. This pharisaical side of man's mind, in its faithfulness in the observance of religious form, becomes aware of the presence of divine power.

Nicodemus' coming to Jesus (spiritual I AM) "by night" (spiritual darkness) shows that intellectual learning counts for naught in the regeneration. Man must be born of Spirit in order to be redeemed.

When the pharisaical phase of the mind, which Nicodemus represents, becomes receptive to Truth, the spiritual I AM (Jesus) reveals the importance of man's coming into an understanding of "heavenly things." Man establishes the "heavenly things" (Truth) in mind, body, and affairs through denial of carnal beliefs and affirmation of spiritual realities.

To be "born of water" is to be cleansed of all impurity, sin, and materiality, through denial. To be "born of the

Spirit" is to come into the consciousness of divine law and to lift the whole man into a new life of harmony and order by affirmative prayer. A religion that is accepted just because our parents believed in it is a dark state, because there is no real understanding in it. This is the Nicodemus phase of mind. He was a Pharisee and a ruler of the Jews. He represents the pharisaical side of man's mind, which observes the external forms of religion without understanding their real meaning. We accept our inherited religious tendencies without giving much consideration to their origin. In olden times it was considered unfilial, and an evidence of disobedience, for children to join any church other than that to which their parents belonged. The Jews were especially rigid in the observance of this inherited religion, and they proudly referred to their forefathers—Abraham, Isaac, and Jacob—who were taught of God.

This ruling tendency of our surface religion is spiritual darkness; so it is represented as coming to Jesus (spiritual I AM) by night. But there is that in it which is pure (*pure blood*), is single in its desire to know Truth, and is seeking the light; when we begin to ask the cause of the works of healing that are being done on every hand by people who believe in Truth, we are acknowledging that there is evidence of divine power.

Nicolaitans (A. V., Nicolaitanes), nĭc-ŏ-lā´-ĭ-tăns (Gk.)—*followers of Nicolaus or Nicolas*. The Greek name Nicolaus coincides with the Hebrew name Balaam.

An apparently religious people whose teaching and works are condemned in Revelation 2:6, 15.

Meta. Mixed thoughts. In Revelation 2:14, 15 the teaching of the Nicolaitans is likened to that of Balaam, by which the Israelites were taught to eat things sacrificed to idols and to commit fornication. To commit fornication typifies the mixing of one's thoughts with error.

The "sword of my mouth," Revelation 2:16, is the word of absolute Truth. The word of Truth sets the law into action, and thus makes war against the Nicolaitans (mixed thoughts).

Unless we keep our eyes on our first love, Spirit, we are apt to make wrong combinations of thoughts. This is where the Adversary gets his power even when we do not like him. See Revelation 2:4-6.

Nicolaus (A. V., Nicolas), nĭc´-ŏ-lā´-ŭs (Gk.)—*conqueror of the people; victor of the people; victory of the people; overcoming the people; consuming the people; destruction of the people.*

"A proselyte of Antioch," one of the seven men who were appointed by the Christians at Jerusalem to attend to the daily apportionment of provisions, that none of the widows might be overlooked (Acts 6:5).

Meta. We understand Antioch to represent formulated theology. Nicolaus, a proselyte of Antioch, and meaning *conqueror of the people, victory of the people,* would have some such significance as Nicodemus. (See NICODEMUS.) While this popular and established formal idea of religion that has been dominant in the consciousness has, in Nicolaus, turned to the higher Christ faith and ideals, yet unless it gets fully away from its old, formal, inherited religious beliefs it could be the promulgator of mixed thoughts whose tendency is to consume and destroy (*consuming the people, destruction of the people*). It would all depend on how fully the thought that Nicolaus represents has been lifted into the true Christ understanding and expression. According to the text, Nicolaus was a man of good report, full of Spirit and of wisdom (Acts 6:3-6).

Nicopolis, nĭ-cŏp´-ŏ-lĭs (Gk.)—*city of victory.*

A city that is thought to have been on the boundary between Thrace and Macedonia. Paul told Titus to come to him at Nicopolis, since he intended to spend the winter there (Tit. 3:12).

Meta. A realization of victory for Truth, of triumph and mastery over lesser error thoughts and beliefs (*city of victory*). This conquering realization comes in the midst of a consuming desire of the soul for God, which desire awakens great enthusiasm and zeal (Macedonia signifies zeal, and Nicopolis was a city in or bordering on Macedonia).

Niger, nĭ´-ġĕr (Lat)—*black; dark;*

purplish; ill-omened; false; wicked.

"Symeon that was called Niger" was one of the "prophets and teachers" at Antioch (Acts 13:1).

Meta. The five prophets and teachers in the church at Antioch, mentioned in Acts 13:1, represent the interpreters of Spirit to the outer consciousness. Symeon, or Simeon, means *hearing*, and signifies a receptive, attentive attitude of mind. He was called Niger, meaning *black, dark, purplish, false*. This indicates that he lacked light, understanding, though possessed of an inherent power (*purplish*, purple being the color that stands for power) to cast out this darkness of ignorance and to come into the light. This casting out of darkness is accomplished, or at least is begun, by receptivity and attentiveness to the things of Spirit. The necessity of receptivity to spiritual Truth, that seeming darkness or lack of understanding may be overcome, is the burden of the work of the interpreter of Spirit (Symeon, who is called Niger) to the outer consciousness.

Nile, nīle (Gk. fr. Egypt.)—*leading; drawing; flowing; possessing; inheriting; a stream; a river; a brook; a torrent; a flood.* Other names by which the Nile is referred to are: Nachal Mizraim—*river of Egypt;* Narai Cush—*river of Cush, confluences of Cush, lights of Cush;* Narai Mizraim—*rivers of Egypt, lights of Egypt;* Yeor—*canal, channel, river;* Shihor or Sihor—*turbid, dark, black.* In A. V., Isaiah 19:7, brooks; Isaiah 23:3, 10, and Zechariah 10:11, river; Jeremiah 46:7, 8, flood.

A river of Egypt (Isa. 19:7). The Nile makes possible the fertility of Egypt. From the middle of June until the first of October, each year, the river overflows its banks and carries both moisture and sediment, which fertilize the ground of the adjacent valley. Thus the Nile has been and still is a source or channel of life and sustenance to the Egyptians. Were it not for the Nile, virtually the whole of Egypt would be a barren desert.

Meta. The Nile, which is one of the longest and greatest rivers in the world, signifies the great subconscious flow of life and substance in the organism of man. Until recent years little has been known of the source or sources of the Nile. Even so, man has known but little of the real source of the substance and life within him, though from this substance and life he receives his vitality and strength (*leading, drawing, flowing, possessing, inheriting*). But man is gradually awakening to the truth of his being, and is becoming acquainted with the one true source of all life and sustenance, which is God, Spirit.

This great river of life and substance, in flowing through the Egyptian, or darkened, ignorant, sensual phase of consciousness in man, apparently becomes material and corrupt, wild, turbulent, and destructive (*black, dark, turbid, torrent, flood;* see SIHOR).

Nimrah, nĭm'-răh (Heb.)—*variegated; spotted; speckled; a leopard; limpid; pure; crystal; clear; sweet water.*

A city of Gad, on the east of the Jordan (Num. 32:3). In the 36th verse it is called Beth–nimrah.

Meta. See BETH–NIMRAH.

Nimrod, nĭm'-rŏd (Heb.)—*self-ruling will; arbitrary sway; fallen from allegiance; insubordination; rebellion; revolution; anarchy; despotism; misrule; impiety.*

a Son of Cush. "He was a mighty hunter before Jehovah" (Gen. 10:8, 9). **b** The land of Nimrod (Mic. 5:6).

Meta. Nimrod ("a mighty one in the earth," also, "a mighty hunter before Jehovah," and meaning *self-ruling will, arbitrary sway, rebellion, despotism, misrule*) pertains to the rule of personal will in the animal forces of the organism; also to a material belief in courage and might. The adverse phase of the ruling personal will of man is under the observation of Jehovah, the true Christ self of the individual, since the will, in the process of unfoldment spiritually, must be cleansed of its adverseness and be made subject to and unified with the divine will.

Nimrod brought forth in the material, as is evidenced by Genesis 10:10: "And the beginning of his kingdom was Babel, and Erech, and Accad, and Calneh, in the land of Shinar." (See the metaphysical interpretations of these names.)

Nimshi, nĭm'-shī (Heb.)—*drawn out; extricated; extracted; chosen; rescued; saved; revealed; Jah reveals.*

Jehu, either the son or the grandson of Nimshi, was anointed king over Israel (I Kings 19:16; II Kings 9:2).

Meta. The awakening of the individual to the understanding that error rule must be denied away and Truth must be affirmed and restored to its rightful dominion throughout the consciousness (*drawn out, extricated, extracted, rescued, saved, Jah reveals*). Jehu is the executive power of the I AM, or Jehovah, acting upon this new understanding that Nimshi signifies. Jehu means *the self-existent One is He; Jehovah is He.* Jehu, upon his being anointed king in place of Joram son of Ahab, destroyed the whole house of the wicked King Ahab and took the throne of Israel for himself (II Kings 9 and 10).

Nineveh (in A. V., Luke 11:32, Nineve), nĭn'-ĕ-vĕh (Heb.)—*abode of Ninus; exterior growth; growing vigor; colonization; coördination; education of youth; handsome; agreeable.*

A city of Assyria that was built by Asshur (Gen. 10:11, see margin). Jonah was sent to prophesy against this city (Jon. 1:2).

Meta. Asshur typifies mental recognition that the entire man—spirit, soul, and body—is free, of spiritual origin, and is not bound by limitations of matter. Nineveh, a city built by Asshur, signifies the first natural outcome, in the outer thoughts and organism of man, of that for which Asshur stands. This outcome is *exterior growth, growing vigor,* and an outer sense of order, unity, harmony, and intellectual understanding (*colonization, coördination, education of youth, handsome, agreeable*). Unless really centered in spiritual thought this outer development may result in increased materiality.

Nineveh also represents the seat of the natural, animal forces in man's body consciousness. The people of Nineveh were not willfully wicked; they only awaited spiritual instruction that would turn their attention away from the outer and material, to God.

Jonah's condemnation of Nineveh symbolizes the unwise use that one sometimes makes of one's power of discernment. Jonah foresaw the coming effects of living without the knowledge of God, and he fled from the city till he might see what would become of it. This is symbolical of inattention or willful neglect in handling an error thought. What one's attitude should be toward the natural forces and emotions and functions is described as follows:

Discernment of more of Truth, which makes shortcomings apparent, should make one obedient to the instruction of Spirit, and there should be praise and rejoicing that the people (thoughts) of the city are being directed by infinite wisdom and love, and saved from sin and destruction.

Ninevites, nĭn'-ĕ-vītes (fr. Heb.)—*of* or *belonging to Nineveh.*

Inhabitants of the city of Nineveh.

Meta. Thoughts springing from and belonging to that in consciousness which Nineveh signifies. (See NINEVEH.)

Nisan, nī'-săn (Heb.)—*new day; newness; glittering; sparkling; verdant; blooming; month of flowers; month of green ears.*

The first month of the Jewish ecclesiastical year (Neh. 2:1; Esth. 3:7). It is called Abib in the books of Exodus and Deuteronomy (see Exod. 13:4 and Deut. 16:1).

Meta. The springing forth of new ideas into consciousness; also their coming into expression and manifestation (*new day, verdant, blooming, month of green ears*). The sprouting, budding, growing, and coming to fruition of vegetable life on the earth is always a miracle to us; much more marvelous are the resurrection of new ideas in our mind and their development, expression, and ultimate manifestation in our organism and in our outer affairs.

Nisroch, nĭs'-rŏch (Heb. fr. Pers.)—*great eagle; roc; eagle; hawk.*

An Assyrian god; Sennacherib, king of Assyria, was killed by his sons while worshiping in the house of this god (II Kings 19:37). This god is supposed to have been in the form of a man, with the head and wings of an eagle.

Meta. Exalting the intellect, and attributing power and dominion to it.

An *eagle* is a bird of prey; it is noted for its strength, size, keenness of vision, power of flight, and for its fighting, destructive, conquering propensities, all of which tend to make it a very powerful bird. The conquering king of Assyria is likened to an eagle, in Hosea 8:1.

Intellectual thought and reason, without true spiritual vision and love, are very hard, tyrannical, and devouring, when worshiped, or given highest place, by carnal man in his ignorance of spiritual understanding; this worship of the intellect is well represented by Nisroch, an Assyrian god, meaning *great eagle.*

No, nō, or **No–amon**, nō–ā'-mŏn (Heb. fr. Egypt.)—*measure of Amon; portion or possession of Amon; place of Amon; place of the grand artificer; portion of the master craftsman.*

A city of Egypt—Thebes. It was named after the Egyptian god Amon, and was a very large and celebrated city (Jer. 46:25; Nah. 3:8).

Meta. The Egyptian god Amon signifies the darkened belief of carnal man that his inheritance is of the flesh, that his body is material, and that the substance and life that sustain it are material. (See AMON.) No, a very populous and celebrated city of Egypt, was named after the god Amon, and means *place* or *portion of Amon.* No signifies the multitude of thoughts in the Egyptian, or darkened, obscure, carnal consciousness of man that go to make up the error belief for which Amon stands, and that give their substance to it.

In its spiritual aspect No–amon refers to God, Spirit, as the creator and builder of the universe (*place of the grand artificer, portion of the master craftsman;* see AMON also).

Thebes, another name for the Egyptian city of No, or No–amon, is derived from "thebah," which is the word used to designate the ark that Noah built, and in which he and his family were preserved (see ARK for its significance).

Noadiah, nō-ā-dī'-ăh (Heb.)—*Jehovah points out; Jehovah convenes; with whom Jehovah meets; Jah assembles; met by Jehovah.*

a Son of Binnui, a Levite, one of those who were given charge of the gold and silver and vessels of the house of God that were brought back to Jerusalem from Babylon (Ezra 8:33). **b** A prophetess who sought to hinder Nehemiah from proceeding with the rebuilding of Jerusalem's wall (Neh. 6:14).

Meta. The attracting, unifying power of the Christ love (*Jah assembles, Jehovah convenes, with whom Jehovah meets*) as expressing in the religious consciousness of man. (The first Noadiah mentioned was of the Levites, and was one of those who were given charge of the silver, gold, and vessels of the house of God.)

The other Noadiah, a false prophetess who sought to intimidate Nehemiah, and so to hinder the rebuilding of Jerusalem's wall, is this same unifying power of love, but expressing in the carnal phase of the soul consciousness in the individual. Because of the self-condemnation that exists in the human, unredeemed soul, it takes on fear thoughts that work destructively instead of constructively in the regeneration of soul and body. Any great outpouring of Spirit into the consciousness of man always exposes lesser, error thoughts that are ripe for being put out of consciousness entirely, and gives new life and strength to true ideals and their activities.

Noah (in A. V., Matthew 24:37, Noe), nō'-ah (Heb.)—*rest; calm; quiet; peace; tranquillity; equilibrium.*

a Son of Lamech. "And he called his name Noah, saying, This same shall comfort us in our work and in the toil of our hands, *which cometh* because of the ground which Jehovah hath cursed" (Gen. 5:29). Noah built the ark in which he and his family were later saved during the Flood (Gen. 6:8—9:29). **b** Noah was also the name of one of the daughters of Zelophehad, a Manassite who had no sons, and whose inheritance went to his five daughters (Num. 26:33; 27:7; 36:11).

Meta. The Noah of Genesis 6 to 9 was the son of Lamech. Lamech means *a strong young man,* and signifies the strength of youth, and Noah means *rest.* Thus it is in the strength of our youth that we idealize the material and attach our spiritual enthusiasm to the things of sense. But the law of reaction sets in: Noah (*rest*) finds "favor in the eyes of Jehovah." If in the strength of your youth you have indulged in the things of sense, the law of spiritual equilibrium, the Lord, Jehovah, is now working itself out in a *rest*, and you may have bodily ills. This is where the race of wicked thoughts drowns, and your earth is cleansed.

Noah can also be said to be the obedience through which seed for a new state of consciousness is saved.

Again, Noah typifies the consciousness at rest in God (Gen. 6:9). In Genesis 6:10 the three sons of Noah represent states of mind. Shem, meaning *renown*, typifies the spiritual; Ham, meaning *warm*, typifies the physical; and Japheth, meaning *extender*, typifies the intellect or reason.

The interpretation of Genesis 6:11 is that, when the faculties of mind have been used in wrong relation to Truth, certain destructive processes set in and the "earth" (the man-made realm of thought) is in a state of corruption.

Genesis 6:12: The law of the Lord begins to regulate the consciousness of man. The flood is representative of the baptism of Spirit, and is necessary in order to establish equilibrium in the three planes of mental activity.

Genesis 7:11-13: When the whole man (Noah and his wife and his sons and his sons' wives) has been washed in the regeneration, he takes refuge in the "ark" of the Lord. Man rests in the spiritual part of his consciousness, even in the midst of a flood of error.

Genesis 7:14, 15: Man takes into the ark all the ideas inherent in Being. The positive and the negative (the "two and two") activities of the organism are never separated.

Genesis 7:16, 17: By laying hold of spiritual ideas as the only reality, and declaring Spirit to be all in all, one is lifted "above the earth" and "shut . . . in" with Jehovah in perfect safety.

Genesis 7:18-20: Water represents unexpressed capacity. The whole "earth" (realm of manifestation) is filled with potential ideas, waiting for words of Truth to move upon the intelligence of the "waters" and bring forth spiritual realities.

Genesis 7:21, 22: When the faculties of mind find their poise in Truth, all lesser ideas die or disappear through a process of transmutation. Even the ideas that seem to contain the "breath of the spirit of life" are lost sight of in the fuller realization of Spirit as the only presence and power.

Genesis 7:23: When man lets go of his false sense of things and discerns God to be the one source of all good, he rests in spiritual consciousness (Noah) with his pure ideas of Being ("they that were with him in the ark").

Verse 24: The waters prevail so long as it is necessary to cleanse the "earth," thus making ready for the expression of purer and truer ideas.

In Genesis 9:8-17 Noah (the consciousness), with his sons (states of mind), after his purification (the flood) is very closely related to God. God covenants or agrees to bless the purified consciousness and its realm of ideas (seed). Every idea (living creature) that is illumined of Spirit—even ideas related to the body consciousness (earth)—is blessed when man knows the creative law and coöperates with it.

Once the consciousness has been cleansed and man has awakened to his spiritual nature, he is saved through obedience to divine law and is no longer subject to dissolution through negative means. This "covenant," which is eternal, is to those who give up mind and body into the keeping of divine law. The "bow" signifies the orderly arrangement of ideas in Divine Mind, and their perfect manifestation. One who is poised in Truth rests in the consciousness of God's presence, even in the midst of error (the cloud).

When man is obedient to the guidance of God he will never be flooded by negative conditions. The rainbow is a sign in the heavens symbolizing the perfect blending of the race into obedience to one harmonious Christ principle—the endless circle of natural perfection coming out of obedience to divine law.

The woman named Noah pertains to the establishment of poise and equilibrium in the soul of the unfolding individual.

Nob, nŏb (Heb.)—*height; prominence; sublimity; sprouting; germinating; flourishing; discourse; prophecy.*

A city of the priests, near Jerusalem. Saul caused this city, the priests, and all the people, children, flocks, and herds in it to be destroyed, because Ahimelech the high priest had befriended David (I Sam. 21:1; 22:9-19).

Meta. A group of high, spiritual thoughts in man (*height, sublimity,* a city of the priests) whereby he is consciously inspired by Spirit (*prophecy, discourse*). The individual who through personal will (Saul) fights against divine love (David) and refuses to recognize his higher spiritual thoughts and ideals because they sustain divine love (Saul caused the priests to be killed because they befriended David) cannot be directly inspired by Spirit, nor can he keep in conscious touch with the light that is of the one Mind, God.

Nobah, nō'-băh (Heb.)—*barking; striking; pulsating; prominent; vehement of voice.*

a A man of Manasseh. **b** A city, or district. "And Nobah went and took Kenath, and the villages thereof, and called it Nobah, after his own name (Num. 32:42). **c** A city near which Gideon smote the host of Zebah and Zalmunna, kings of Midian (Judg. 8:11).

Meta. Positive affirmations of Truth (*vehement of voice*). While these affirmations and thoughts of Truth are of a high character (*prominent*), there is something of personal force, or a fighting attitude of mind, in declaring them, as is signified by *barking* and *striking*.

Nod, nŏd (Heb.)—*staggering with fear; agitated with apprehension; raving with fright; wandering with uncertainty; agitated flight; banishment; exile.*

The land on the east of Eden, or in front of Eden, where Cain went out from the presence of Jehovah and dwelt, after he had killed Abel (Gen. 4:16).

Meta. After any positive action of the mind there is always an apparent negative reaction. The "land of Nod," as we know it today, is the condition called sleep. Thus Nod, meaning *agitated flight, wandering with uncertainty,* suggests the seemingly unguided activity of man's subconscious phase of mind during periods of sleep, or relaxation, or apparently negative reactions. The fundamental idea in Nod is that of uncertainty of mind, bewilderment.

Nodab, nō'-dăb (Heb.)—*nobility; willingness; spontaneous; liberal; abundant; free-willed; wandering of a father.*

A people against whom the Reubenites, Gadites, and the half tribe of Manasseh made war (I Chron. 5:19); an Arab tribe.

Meta. Thoughts holding a high place in man's outer consciousness because of their professions of greatness, broadness, abundance, liberality, and freedom (*nobility, liberal, willingness, abundant, free-willed*). These thoughts, however, are not stable (an Arab tribe, *wandering of a father*) but are of the changeable, personal mind in the individual. They are discerned in their right light and are overcome by the higher ideals suggested by Reuben (sight, discernment), Gad (power), and Manasseh (understanding).

Nogah, nō'-găh (Heb.)—*shining; giving light; dawn; morning light; brightness; illuminating; enlightening; clarifying.*

A son of David, who was born to him in Jerusalem (I Chron. 3:7).

Meta. Love ruling in consciousness does away with hate, prejudice, fear, narrow-mindedness, and the like, which darken and obscure the understanding. Thus the understanding becomes brighter and clearer, and shines with a truer, finer, purer light. David, king of Israel and father of Nogah, represents love as ruling in consciousness. Nogah is the clear, bright, shining, and unobstructed light of understanding.

Nohah, nō'-hăh (Heb.)—*gentleness; rest; quiet; calm; peace; equilibrium.*

Fourth son of Benjamin (I Chron. 8:2).

Meta. A state of mental rest, peace, quietness, poise, and assurance, which is the result of an active faith in God, the good. (Benjamin, father of Nohah, signifies an active, accomplishing faith.)

Nophah, nō'-phăh (Heb.)—*puffing; blowing; blustering; breathing out; expiring; inspiring; breathing; a windy place.*

A place in Moab (Num. 21:30).

Meta. The personal mind (Moab), which is often boastful, noisy, showy, explosive, tempestuous, yet is empty of real Truth and power (*puffing, blowing, blustering, a windy place*). Back of this phase of the carnal mind that Nophah represents is the very breath of life (Nophah comes from the same root as that used in Genesis 2:7, in connection with the "breath of life"). Under spiritual understanding and direction the expression will take on a very different aspect.

Nun (in A. V., I Chronicles 7:27, Non), nŭn (Heb.)—*spreading abroad; becoming extended; prolific; continuous; posterity; eternal increase; interpenetrating all; fish.*

Father of Joshua (Exod. 33:11).

Meta. Nun, father of Joshua (Josh. 1:1), belongs to the tribe of Ephraim (will). The name Joshua, identical with the name Jesus, signifies "I am savior."

Joshua is the directive general of the law. The I AM asserts its leadership based upon its understanding of divine law. Nun signifies the great and continuous increase of Truth, of spiritual ideas (*spreading abroad, prolific, continuous posterity, eternal increase, interpenetrating all, fish*), in the consciousness of the individual who opens his heart and mind to the Truth and wills to do the will of God, to keep the divine law.

Nymphas, nȳm'-phăs (Gk.)—*a betrothed woman; recently espoused; young married woman; nymph-given.*

A Christian of Laodicea to whom Paul sent salutation in his letter to the Colossians (Col. 4:15); evidently a woman. In the margin *"her"* is suggested in place of "their," which is used in the text.

Meta. Laodicea refers to a phase of the judgment faculty in individual consciousness. Nymphas (*young married woman, nymph-given*), a Christian of Laodicea, signifies a union of the Laodicea phase of the judgment faculty with the Christ, or, an introduction of the elements of divine love and mercy into one's intellectual conception of justice.

O

oak trees.

Meta. An oak tree in itself stands for something very strong and protective; but in Hebrew it has a deeper significance than this. The word comes from the root from which is derived the word *Elohim;* so we are reminded of the truth that those who trust God as their defense, as their refuge and their fortress, and dwell in the secret place of the Most High, shall abide under the shadow of the Almighty, and shall not only be kept from all evil and its results but also shall continue to grow and unfold in understanding, in spirituality, in every good.

The Hebrew words Ail, Elah, Allon, and Allah all refer to the oak or terebinth, derived from the ideas of power, elevation, and expansion. The prefix Al or El that begins the name Elohim, or better Ælohim, comes from the same root, which characterizes the power of expansive movement, the power of extension, and is also the personal pronoun He, which stands for the Absolute.

Obadiah, ō-bă-dī'-ăh (Heb.)—*servant of Jehovah; service of Jah; worshiper of Jehovah.*

a One who was "over the household" of King Ahab. Obadiah feared the Lord, and so he hid five hundred prophets in caves and fed them, when Jezebel "cut off the prophets of Jehovah" (I Kings 18:3, 4). **b** There were several other Israelites by this name also (I Chron. 7:3; 8:38; 9:16; 12:9; 27:19; II Chron. 17:7; 34:12; Ezra 8:9).

Meta. The higher thoughts in man that serve and worship God through the I AM, Jehovah, indwelling Christ. They are faithful and true. They are thoughts that are obedient to spiritual ideals, that hear and heed the voice of Spirit.

Obal, ō'-băl (Heb.)—*extreme attenuation of matter; uncovered; stripped; bare; naked; barren.*

Son of Joktan (Gen. 10:28). In I Chronicles 1:22 he is called Ebal.

Meta. The bareness, nakedness, nothingness of all that is not founded in Truth. Those who hold to material beliefs and do not enter into understanding and practice of spiritual Truth must experience age, decay, deterioration of consciousness and body; they enter into a seemingly very barren state of existence. (See EBAL.)

Obed, ō'-bĕd (Heb.)—*laboring; working; making; serving; worshiping.*

a Son of Boaz and Ruth, and grandfather of David (Ruth 4:21). **b** There were other Israelites by this name, also (I Chron. 2:37; 11:47; 26:7; II Chron. 23:1).

Meta. An active thought, in the spiritual consciousness of man, that pertains to service and worship. "God is spirit: and they that worship him must worship in spirit and truth" (John 4:24; first clause, as given in margin). In other words, God is Mind; and they that worship Him must worship through thinking, by their thoughts. Mind, in its highest aspect, and Spirit are synonymous.

Obed–edom, ō'-bĕd–ē'-dŏm (Heb.)—*servant of Edom; servant of Esau.*

a "The ark of Jehovah remained in the house of Obed–edom the Gittite three months" (II Sam. 6:10-12). **b** There are others named Obed–edom, also (I Chron. 15:18; 16:5, 38; II Chron. 25:24).

Meta. That which believes in serving others, especially that which pertains to looking after the physical comfort of others (*servant of Edom* or *Esau*, and pertaining to the outer, earthly, physical phase of man).

Because the Ark rested in the house of Obed–edom, great blessings were poured out on all that dwelt therein. This proves that working with the divine law always brings good.

Obil, ō'-bĭl (Heb.)—*chief of the camels; keeper of camels.*

Obil the Ishmaelite was "over the camels" in David's reign (I Chron. 27:30).

Meta. The camel, in its native country, is a beast of burden.

As pertaining to the individual, hard work, the bearing of burdens, are known only by the physical and seemingly mortal phase of his being. An Ishmaelite is a thought that is the fruit of the thoughts of the natural man at work in the flesh, Obil the Ishmaelite, meaning *keeper of camels,* is a thought activity belonging to the outer consciousness of man. Having joined itself to the ruling love (David) faculty of the individual, it comes into dominion over such of his forces and tendencies as are symbolized by the camel—the bearing of burdens, also great steadfastness and endurance—which are traits peculiar to camels and at times seem to develop into obstinacy. (See CAMEL.)

Oboth, ō'-bŏth (Heb.)—*waterskins; leather bottles; hollow skins; ventriloquists; divining spirits; necromancers.*

A place where the Children of Israel camped when in the wilderness (Num. 21:10).

Meta. A realization by the higher ideals of the individual (Israelites) that the cleansing water of denial, or the power to cleanse the consciousness and the body through denials, lies within his organism. In other words, cleansing comes from within, and not from without (*waterskins, leather bottles;* the skins and bottles referring to the body, and water to the cleansing quality of denials of error).

Oboth also seems to convey the idea of deception, of psychic development and expression instead of that truly spiritual, and a seeking to counterfeit the work of Spirit (*hollow skins, ventriloquists, divining spirits, necromancers*).

Ochran (A. V., Ocran), ŏch'-răn (Heb.)—*troubled; confused; muddled; disturbed; afflicted.*

Father of Pagiel, who was a chief or prince of the tribe of Asher, in the wilderness (Num. 1:13; 2:27).

Meta. A thought that belongs to the religious thoughts of man but is out of harmony (*troubled, disturbed, afflicted*) with Truth; it is not clear (*muddled, confused*).

Oded, ō'-dĕd (Heb.)—*turning back;*

returning; repeating; continuing without interruption; enduring; surrounding; aiding; sustaining; affirming; exhorting; setting up again; erecting; restoring to a former state.

a Father of Azariah, who was a prophet in the reign of Asa, king of Judah (II Chron. 15:1). The 8th verse of this chapter reads as if Oded himself were the prophet, but this is believed to be a mistranslation. **b** Another Oded was a prophet of Jehovah in the kingdom of Israel (II Chron. 28:9).

Meta. Continuously active, constructive, restoring, renewing, and sustaining thoughts in the higher phase of consciousness in the individual (*continuing without interruption, aiding, sustaining, enduring, affirming, erecting, restoring to a former state*, a prophet of Israel, and the father of a prophet of Judah). Oded could also be said to symbolize the waking of the Spirit of God in man and the universe, which will never cease until man returns fully to his original oneness with God, and all is perfect, complete.

offerings.

Meta. The burnt offerings of bullocks and sheep on the altar (I Kings 3:4; II Chron. 30:24) represent the transmutation of the physical forces to the next higher plane of action. This is a process of body refinement to be accomplished by those who follow Jesus in the regeneration.

Og, ŏg (Heb.)—*long-necked; giant.*

King of Bashan. He was defeated by the Israelites at Edrei, and his land was apportioned by Moses to the children of Gad, and of Reuben, and of the half tribe of Manasseh (Num. 21:33; 32:33).

Meta. The seeming immensity of the strength that has been given by the race thought to that in consciousness which the Amorites represent; or, the apparently very great and powerful hold that this Amorite belief has on the outer, personal man (*long-necked*, the neck being the seat of the power faculty in man; *giant*, a king of the Amorites).

Ohad, ō′-hăd (Heb.)—*one; becoming united; unity; union; indivisible; immutable; power; strength; stability; sanctity; purity; sole; only; principle.*

Son of Simeon (Gen. 46:10).

Meta. Simeon means one who listens and obeys. He refers to the spiritually receptive, attentive, and obedient attitude in man. Ohad, son of Simeon (meaning *one, becoming united, unity, immutable, power, strength, stability, sanctity, purity, sole, only, principle*), signifies unity with God, the principle of Truth, and the conscious increase of power, stability, strength, wholeness, purity, and completeness that is the result of this union between the divine and the individual who exercises the Simeon attitude of mind.

Ohel, ō′-hĕl (Heb.)—*tent; tabernacle; temple; habitation; dwelling; house; family; tribe; race; nation.*

Son of Zerubbabel (I Chron. 3:20).

Meta. A tent, tabernacle, or temple in the Bible refers to the body of man. Family indicates a group of thoughts like and springing from some certain idea. The word "race" often pertains to the whole race of mankind on the earth, and not just to certain types and nations of people taken separately; here, however, it signifies all the thoughts of the individual. Zerubbabel typifies a thought activity in the higher consciousness of man, whose work is to restore worship of God. Ohel, son of Zerubbabel (meaning *family, race, tent, tabernacle, house, temple, habitation*), signifies the truth that the worship of God, or the thinking and knowing of spiritual things, is to be established throughout the consciousness and the organism of the individual.

Oholah (A. V., Aholah), ŏ-hō′-läh (Heb.)—*she has her own tent; her own tabernacle; her temple; her own habitation; her tent.*

A symbolical name given to Samaria, because of her adultery in departing from Jehovah (Ezek. 23:4).

Meta. Samaria (*watch, watchtower* or *mountain*) refers to the department of the objective consciousness of man that functions through the head. Oholah (meaning *she has her own tent*, and being a symbolical name given to Samaria because of her adultery in departing from Jehovah) signifies the seemingly corruptible body that is the result of the mixed material ideas of the outer, intellectual man regarding himself. He sees in his organism only a physical machine that is brought forth by physical man; he does not recognize Divine Mind, God, or its perfect idea, Jehovah, the Christ, in his body. Thus he has departed from Jehovah, who is the real maker of the organism, and has caused his body to manifest according to his own material thought of it (a *tent* refers to the body).

Oholiab (A. V., Aholiab), ŏ-hō'-lĭ-ăb (Heb.)—*his father's tent; tent of the father; my father's tabernacle; temple of the father.*

Son of Ahisamach, of the tribe of Dan, a wise and skillful man who was chosen by Jehovah to help do the fine work in building the tabernacle with its furniture, vessels, and the like (Exod. 31:6).

Meta. An idea in the judgment faculty of the individual (a man of the tribe of Dan) that has been quickened by divine wisdom, and so recognizes that the whole organism of man is of God, belongs to God, and is not material but is divine in its origin (*his father's tent, my father's tabernacle, temple of the father*). Thus this idea becomes a builder, or one that aids in bringing into expression and manifestation a truer, purer, and more stable consciousness and body.

Oholibah (A. V., Aholibah), ŏ-hŏl'-ĭ-băh (Heb.)—*tent in her; my tabernacle is in her; her tabernacle; temple in her.*

A symbolical name given to Jerusalem (kingdom of Judah, here) by Jehovah because she played the harlot in departing from the true God and worshiping the idols of the heathen nations about her (Ezek. 23:4). In margin, "*My tent is in her.*"

Meta. A letting in of worldly thoughts by the inner, higher consciousness of the individual, that has known and loved and worshiped God (Jerusalem; *my tabernacle is in her, temple in her*). Thus error ideas become mixed with the true ones, and so the individual in his inner consciousness departs from the purity of spiritual understanding and comes into an adulterous state of mind, a state of mind partly true and partly false.

Oholibamah (A. V., Aholibamah), ŏ-hŏl'-ĭ-bā'-măh (Heb.)—*tent of the high place; tent of the height; my tabernacle is exalted; my dwelling is on high.*

"Daughter of Anah, the daughter of Zibeon the Hivite," and wife of Esau (Gen. 36:2). In verses 24 and 25 the inference is that Anah was a son of Zibeon, instead of a daughter.

Meta. Zibeon means *wild robber*, and the Hivites are thoughts belonging to the carnal consciousness in man. Esau, husband of Oholibamah, also pertains to the outer or the body. Oholibamah (granddaughter of Zibeon, a Hivite, and wife of Esau, and meaning *tent of the high place, my tabernacle is exalted*) signifies the lifting up and exalting of materiality, of the seemingly material phase of the organism of the individual, by the carnal phase of the soul.

Olivet, ŏl'-ĭ-vĕt (fr. Heb.)—*Mount of Olives; height yielding illuminating oil; high luminous principle; shining mount; exalted enlightenment.*

A mountain, or ridge of hills, near Jerusalem, to the east of the city. The ascension of Jesus Christ took place there (Acts 1:12; see also Zechariah 14:4). Jesus often went to the Mount of Olives (Matt. 21:1; 24:3; 26:30; John 8:1). David went up the Mount of Olives when he was fleeing from Absalom; it seems that this mount was a place where "he was wont to worship God" (II Sam. 15:30, 32, see margin). "The mountain which is on the east side of the city" (Ezek. 11:23) refers to the Mount of Olives.

Meta. The exalting of divine wisdom and love in consciousness (*Mount of Olives, height yielding illuminating oil, high luminous principle*).

A mountain always signifies an exalted state of mind, a high place in consciousness, while *olives* and olive trees signify the Spirit of love (the Mount of Olives was so named because of the many olive trees that grew on it), and *illumination* bespeaks light, understanding. Olive oil is symbolical of the Holy Spirit; also of peace and love. The "dove" returned to Noah in the ark with an olive leaf in her mouth (Gen. 8:11). In Psalms 52:8 David (love) said, "I am like a green olive-tree in the house of God: I trust in the lovingkindness of God for ever and ever." In Romans 11:17 we read of "the fatness of the olive tree," and it is a well-known fact that love is a great attracter of substance, of true riches. The "beauty" of the olive tree is mentioned in Hosea 14:6; love is a great beautifier. The two witnesses of Revelation 11 are said to be "the two olive trees and the two candlesticks, standing before the Lord of the earth," or in other words, love and wisdom.

Olympas, ō-lўm′-păs (Gk.)—*elysian; celestial; heavenly.*

A Christian at Rome whom Paul saluted in his letter to the Romans (Rom. 16:15).

Meta. A high thought activity of the intellect and will (a man of Rome) that has been illumined by the Holy Spirit and converted to the real Christ understanding. Thus it becomes truly spiritual, *heavenly,* filled with peace, love, justice, and perfection, as well as being high and sublime.

Omar, ō′-mär (Heb.)—*bringing forth; bearing into the light; top; summit; speaking; saying; talkative; eloquent; mountaineer; very elevated.*

Son of Eliphaz, who was one of Esau's sons (Gen. 36:11).

Meta. The ability of the outer man to receive the higher Truth ideals (*mountaineer, very elevated, summit*) and to express them (*bringing forth, eloquent, bearing into the light*). (See ELIPHAZ and ESAU, in regard to Omar as referring to the outer man.)

Omega, ō-mē′-gȧ (Gk.)—*the last; the end; the objective; the fulfillment; the consummation; perfection; restitution.*

The last letter of the Greek alphabet, "I am the Alpha and the Omega, the first and the last, the beginning and the end" (Rev. 22:13).

Meta. *The last, the end,* or the fulfillment. Christ, being the Alpha and the Omega, the first and the last, the beginning and the end, signifies the allness of Truth; through Christ, the ideal creation of God, or Divine Mind, all things came into existence in the first place and all things will finally come to the Christ likeness, which is the goal of perfection toward which the whole creation is unfolding. Christ is the fulfillment of all good to everybody and to everything.

Omri, ŏm′-rī (Heb.)—*pupil of Jehovah; taught of Jah; measure of Jah; my measure; Jah apportions; Jah's sheaf; untaught; inexperienced; my pupil.*

a Captain of the host of Israel, and later king (I Kings 16:16). There were other Israelites by this name (I Chron. 7:8; 9:4; 27:18).

Meta. The definitions of the name Omri signify that in man which is open to and receives true spiritual instruction (*pupil of Jehovah, taught of Jah*); that recognizes substance and supply as coming from Jehovah (*Jah apportions, Jah's sheaf*).

The Omri who became king of Israel and who was the father of Ahab, however, represents an external movement of the mind in a whirl of discord, caused largely by a lack of spiritual development, a lack of recognition of the spiritual source of life. This leads to a separation of intellect from the inner mind, and finally draws the vital forces of the organism so far from the center of life that the life currents run low and a drought sets in. This is the condition that the Omri and Ahab thoughts have brought upon the system when the spiritual I AM of man's consciousness (Elijah) appears on the scene (I Kings 17).

Omri, king of Israel, symbolizes the phase of consciousness in which the ruling thought is not in Truth, but outside of it. When the center of identity drops from Spirit to a recognition of form as the real, an entire change of character ensues—the thoughts of the outer world become the basis of action and life becomes a kind of fool's paradise.

In the beginning this reign has its pleasant aspects. "Six years reigned he in Tirzah." Tirzah means *delight.* But, the foundation being outside of Truth, the thoughts and acts wander farther and farther into error. Omri bought the hill Samaria, which means an exaltation of personality, and there set up a city, or center. He walked in the way of Jeroboam, who symbolizes that which his name implies: *adverse people, hostile people, contentious people.* This all illustrates a phase of intellectual rulership in which the one true God of reality is ignored, and secondary deities are substituted. Baal means *lord*, and it was the besetting sin of the ancient Hebrews to apply the name of the Lord to things formed instead of to the formless. All concepts of God as less than universal Mind are Baal. Whoever believes in a personal God tends toward a materialization of religion in all its aspects. When the mind is centered in the outer realm of consciousness, where the thoughts (people) are adverse to God, it retrogrades until that whole state of consciousness goes to pieces. This retrogression is by stages, from bad to worse. Omri was a little worse than any who had preceded him, but he was followed by Ahab, his son, who provoked more opposition or "anger" of the true law (Jehovah) than all the kings of Israel who were before him.

The reign of these error states of consciousness is temporary, however; there is an undercurrent of Truth constantly at work, deep in the man, that finally brings him to his senses. Omri and Ahab passed away; Jezebel met a violent death. The prophets of Baal were destroyed in a group by Elijah (the fiery word of God), and Israel was redeemed. So the higher principle in man erases the thoughts of error, and harmony in mind and body is restored.

On, ŏn (Heb. fr. Egypt.)—*Beth-shemesh; Heliopolis; city of the sun; embodiment of light; luminous corporeity; radiating brilliance; the sun; faculty; ability; strength; power of radiation; wealth; substance.*

a A city in Lower Egypt, one of the oldest known cities in the world. It is also called Heliopolis and Beth-shemesh. Heliopolis was devoted to the pure, monotheistic worship of a god that was symbolized in the sun. In its sanctuaries Moses was educated as the foster son of Pharaoh's daughter as a prince and priest of Egypt. Homer, Plato, Pliny, and other sages of the Western world went to this city to obtain initiation into philosophy and cosmic mystery. Joseph's wife was the daughter of Poti-phera, the priest of On (Gen. 41:45). (See Jeremiah 43:13, with margin.) Aven, in Ezekiel 30:17, is said to refer to the city of On in Egypt. **b** Another On was a

Reubenite; he was one of those who rebelled against Moses and Aaron; he was destroyed by the earth's opening up and closing over him (Num. 16:1).

Meta. In its purity, On refers to Spirit and to true spiritual understanding, substance, and power. As it appears in our Bible, however, the outer symbol (the sun) is worshiped and the truth back of the symbol has been lost sight of to a great degree. This worshiping of the outer symbol, or form, and looking to the outer for understanding and all good is idolatry and must come to an end. (See BETH–SHEMESH and AVEN.)

Onam, ō'-năm (Heb.)—*able; strong; stout; vigorous; powerful; wealthy; substantial; luminous; brilliant.*

a Son of Shobal and descendant of Seir the Horite (Gen. 36:23). **b** Son of Jerahmeel and his wife Atarah, of the tribe of Judah (I Chron. 2:26).

Meta. Thoughts pertaining to strength and vigor; also to understanding and substance. The Onam who was a Horite signifies a material belief in purely physical strength and power, outer possessions, and the carnal thought of understanding. This would lead to inharmony and error experiences instead of to the good that comes from knowing Spirit as the one true source of all. (See ATARAH.)

Onan, ō'-năn (Heb.)—*able-bodied; strong; stout; virile; vigorous; substantiated; wealthy; luminous; bright.*

Son of Judah by the daughter of Shua, a Canaanite (Gen. 38:4).

Meta. The significance of Onan is virtually the same as that of Onam, which see. While this thought is of a higher nature than that of Onam the Horite (Onan was a son of Judah), yet it is not spiritual but is of the intellect. It is influenced too, by lower, carnal soul emotions and tendencies (Onan's mother was a Canaanitish woman); therefore it is liable to bring about inharmony and error, because of the misdirection of energy. Yet in itself it is good and if directed by spiritual understanding yields great blessing.

Onesimus, ō-nĕs'-ĭ-mŭs (Gk.)—*useful; profitable; helpful.*

A servant, or slave, of Philemon's. He accepted the Christ message through

Paul at Rome, and returned to Philemon bearing a letter from Paul (Philem. 10; Col. 4:9).

Meta. Onesimus was a slave who had escaped from his master and was protected by Paul. His name in the Greek means *profitable, useful, helpful.* The significance here is that the industry, usefulness, and activity of man are hampered by his slavery to ignorance and error. (See PHILEMON.)

Ono, ō'-nŏ (Heb.)—*ability; strength; virility; vigor; substance; wealth; riches; brilliance.*

A city of Benjamin that was built by the sons of Elpaal, Eber, Misham, and Shemed (I Chron. 8:12). Nehemiah 6:2 mentions "the plain of Ono," where Sanballat and Geshem wanted to meet Nehemiah in order to do him mischief.

Meta. A consciousness of vigor and strength, and of understanding and substance, that is the result of an active faith, and the fruits of this faith at work in the individual (a city of Benjamin, Benjamin symbolizing an active faith; see ELPAAL, EBER, MISHAM, and SHEMED). The plain of Ono, where Sanballat and Geshem wanted to meet Nehemiah in order to injure him and put a stop to his work of rebuilding Jerusalem's wall, indicates a phase of consciousness wherein error thoughts seek to divert the strength and power of activity and growth and increase of substance to an unwise use, thus hindering the renewing of the organism.

Ophel, ō'-phĕl (Heb.)—*tumulus; protuberance; hill; mound; inflated; presumptuous; proud; elated; elevated place; high place.*

A high place in Jerusalem, in the eastern part of the city (II Chron. 27:3), where the Nethinim dwelt (Neh. 3:26, 27). See II Kings 5:24 with marginal note, also.

Meta. A lifting up of man's thought about himself. This may be a true elevating and building of his whole being into a more abiding and spiritual manifestation, or it may refer to a lifting up in pride because of one's seeming spiritual attainments (*tumulus, protuberance, inflated, presumptuous, proud, elated, elevated place, high place;* a swelling always denotes pride, and that which the Nethinim represent is not deeply established in Truth; see NETHINIM). One must be truly spiritual in order to stay humble in the midst of great achievement, success, and attainment.

Ophir, ō'-phīr (Heb.)—*a final state; fulfillment of an elementary principle; purity; nobility; riches; refined gold; pure gold; gold coast; land of gold; ashes; baseness.*

a Son of Joktan. The descendants of the sons of Joktan are supposed to have been Arab tribes (Gen. 10:29). **b** A land or district that was noted for its fine, pure, and abundant gold (I Kings 9:28; Job 22:24; Psalms 45:9; Isa. 13:12).

Meta. That which remains after the deeper purification by fire has taken place (*a final state, fulfillment of an elementary principle*—the principle here being fire; see Malachi 3:1-3 and Matthew 3:11, 12). By this purifying action of the Christ Spirit, of the fire baptism, all that is true (*pure gold*) is refined, purified, and elevated to its rightful place in the kingdom, while the dross, or error, of the carnal, adverse mind is reduced to dust and *ashes.*

Ophni, ŏph'-nī (Heb.) — *panting; aspiring; ardently desiring; pining; hunger; thirst; weariness; famine; folding together; rolling; writhing; pain; soreness.*

A city of Benjamin (Josh. 18:24).

Meta. A group of thoughts in man that really aspires to a higher, spiritual consciousness (*aspiring, ardently desiring*). It has, however, through error, or Canaanitish rule, exerted great personal effort in seeking to attain the fulfillment of its desire. The result is seeming weariness, lack, and inharmony. Great spiritual attainment is accomplished only by complete consecration to Spirit, and not by striving in the intellectual and personal to bring about one's good.

Ophrah, ŏph'-răh (Heb.)—*female fawn; dusty; ashen; blown by the wind; reduced to an essence; spiritous.*

a A city of Benjamin (Josh. 18:23). **b** The home of Gideon the Manassite, who delivered Israel from the Midianites and became judge of Israel (Judg. 6:11, 24). **c** Either a son of or a city founded by Meonothai, of the tribe of Judah (I Chron. 4:14).

Meta. Gideon the Manassite, a judge of Israel whose home was in Ophrah, represents denial of error. Benjamin is the active faith quality in man. Meonothai, parent or founder of the Ophrah of the tribe of Judah, signifies a thought in the praise-and-prayer consciousness of the individual that perceives or acknowledges the habitations of man—the consciousness and organism of each person—to be the abode of Jehovah. (See MEONOTHAI.) Ophrah therefore (a city of Benjamin, also a city that was the home of Gideon, and the name of a man or city of Judah, and meaning *female fawn*) stands for groups of thoughts of a very active, yet gentle, peaceable, and coöperative nature—thoughts that love and are zealous for the good. The other definitions of Ophrah point to a great degree of refinement, purification, spiritualization, as opposed to the dense and material.

Oreb, ō'-rĕb (Heb.)—*jet blackness; western darkness; rapacious; voracious; ravenous; raven.*

a A prince of Midian, and **b** the name of a rock where this prince was slain by the Ephraimites under Gideon (Judg. 7:25).

Meta. A greedy, rapacious ruling thought in unredeemed man (*raven,* meaning rapine, rapacity; and a prince of Midian, Midian meaning *strife, contention*). If the individual gives this thought a place it robs him of his peace of mind and consciousness of good. It must therefore be overcome by denial of the error (Gideon) backed up by the individual will (Ephraimites).

Oren, ō'-rĕn (Heb.)—*strength; power; enlightened; pine tree; fir tree; ash tree.*

Son of Jerahmeel, of the tribe of Judah (I Chron. 2:25).

Meta. A thought of abiding life and strength established in the nervous system of the individual (*strength, power;* also *fir tree* and *pine tree,* both being evergreen trees, and relating therefore to abiding, ever renewing life, while trees represent the nerves in the organism of

man). Trees signify a connecting link between the heaven and the earth, the formless and the formed, even as the nervous system in man is the connecting link between his unformed thoughts and his formed organism—the heavens (mind) and the earth (body). Nerves also connect thought centers; they are expressions of thoughts of unity.

Orion, ō-rī'-ŏn (Gk.)—*blooming; beautiful; strong; a mighty hunter; virtuous; lusty; loin; inward strength; confidence; hope; impiety; folly; foolishness; sluggish.*

A group of stars (Job 9:9). A brilliant constellation on the equator, pictured as a great hunter, or as a huge giant who had warred against God and had been bound with chains to the firmament of heaven (Job 38:31).

Meta. The seeming strength and desirability of the animal forces in man (*beautiful, blooming, strong, a mighty hunter*) and the apparent bondage of the individual to these forces ("Canst thou . . . loose the bands of Orion?"). Man has a very dim comprehension that back of even his apparently animal forces and propensities that seem to bind him so tightly to the flesh there is something that is divine, there is some wonderful truth. Yet, like the stars that represent truths apparently far beyond man's present conception, his inner forces and powers, with their origin and possibilities, are just beginning to be faintly understood by him.

Ornan, ŏr'-năn (Heb.)—*strong; active; nimble; tumultuous noise; joyous shout; rejoicing.*

It was by the threshing floor of Ornan the Jebusite that the angel of Jehovah stood when David saw him, and when the angel stopped from destroying Jerusalem, at the command of Jehovah. It was there that David offered sacrifices for the Children of Israel. David bought the threshing floor from Ornan (I Chron. 21:15-25). In II Samuel 24:16-24 Ornan is called Araunah.

Meta. See ARAUNAH. Then add the thought of the spiritual activity that accompanies the separating of error from good in consciousness (*active*), and the *rejoicing* that follows the revealing of the good. This will give you the significance of Ornan.

Orpah. ôr'-păh (Heb.) — *pulled; plucked; mane; forelock; nape of the neck; poll; top; vertex; fawn; youthful freshness.*

A Moabitish woman, daughter-in-law of Naomi. She stayed in Moab instead of going with Naomi to Beth–lehem–judah as Ruth did (Ruth 1:4, 14).

Meta. A youthfulness, grace, and activity (*youthful freshness, fawn*) in the natural soul (a woman always refers to some phase of the soul, or of the feminine element, in the individual); and zeal (*nape of the neck, mane, poll*), but more for the things of self than the things of spirit. *Nape of the neck, mane, top, forelock,* here also bespeak a lifting up in personal dignity and pride. This phase of the soul is too much in love with the outer man, the sense or carnal self, to give itself over to the real love for Spirit and Truth that would induce it to leave its native country (Moab) and accompany the higher aspects of the soul in its search for unity with God (go with Naomi back to her home, Beth–lehem–judah).

Othni, ŏth'-nī (Heb.)—*lion of Jehovah; Jehovah is strength; force of Jehovah.*

A son of Shemaiah, and a doorkeeper in the tabernacle (I Chron. 26:7).

Meta. A thought that is established in the realization of Jehovah—I AM, Christ—as one's unfailing courage, strength, and overcoming power (*lion of Jehovah, Jehovah is strength, force of Jehovah*).

Othniel, ŏth'-nĭ-ĕl (Heb.)—*lion of God; God is strength; force of God.*

Son of Kenaz, Caleb's younger brother. Othniel was a judge and a deliverer of Israel (Judg. 3:9, 11). It was to him that Caleb gave his daughter Achsah for a wife, as a reward for his bravery (Judg. 1:13; see I Chronicles 27:15 also).

Meta. A consciousness of divine life, strength, courage, and conquering power (*God is strength, force of God, lion of God*).

Ozem, ō'-zĕm (Heb.)—*growing might; power of growth; strength; might; power; numerous; multitude; bones; body.*

a Brother of David, and sixth son of Jesse (I Chron. 2:15). **b** A son of Jerahmeel of the tribe of Judah (I Chron. 2:25).

Meta. I AM *strength,* growing or increasing thoughts of I AM *power* or of the eternal existence of strength and power as fundamental principles of Being—of God and of man (Jesse, the father of the first-named Ozem, represents I AM, or eternal existence; see JESSE). There is also a thought of compassion and love closely associated with this idea of increasing strength and might, since David, brother of the one Ozem, means love; and Jerahmeel, father of the other man named Ozem, symbolizes the true idea of God as a loving, merciful, kind, compassionate Father, friend, and almighty resource. All this falls directly in line with our understanding that love, joy, and a constant holding to the good in all ways greatly increase man's consciousness of abiding power and strength, and aid their righteous expression in and through his organism.

Ozni, ŏz'-nī (Heb.)—*Jah hears; giving ear; hearkening; hearing; weighing; attending; pondering; considering; sharp; acute; pointed.*

Son of Gad, and founder of the family of the Oznites (Num. 26:16). In Genesis 46:16 he is called Ezbon.

Meta. An influential thought, belonging to the power faculty in man (Gad being the son of Jacob, and of the tribe of Israel that symbolizes the faculty of power in the individual), that is of an attentive, obedient, hearing attitude of mind (*giving ear, hearkening, hearing*). When man considers and lends his power toward making himself attentive and obedient to the things of Spirit, he will be heard of Jehovah (*Jah hears*) and his consciousness of power will be greatly increased.

Oznites, ŏz'-nītes (fr. Heb.)—*of or belonging to Ozni.*

Descendants of Ozni son of Gad (Num. 26:16).

Meta. Thoughts springing from and belonging to that in consciousness which Ozni signifies. (See OZNI.)

P

Paarai, pā'-ă-rāi (Heb.)—*opening wide; gaping; yawning; hiatus; cleft; revealing; revelation of Jah.*

"The Arbite," one of David's mighty warriors (II Sam. 23:35). In I Chronicles 11:37 he is called Naarai.

Meta. One of the higher religious thoughts of man's mind (a warrior of King David's) becoming awakened to divine revelation, inspiration, understanding (*opening wide, yawning, revelation of Jah*). (See NAARAI.)

Paddan (A. V., Padan), pād'-dăn (Heb.)—*field; open plain; table-land.*

The same place as PADDAN–ARAM, which see (Gen. 48:7).

Meta. A place of substance in the consciousness and the organism of the individual (a *field*, field relating to ground, substance).

Paddan–aram (A. V., Padan-aram), pād'-dăn-ā'-răm (Heb.)—*plain of Aram; a plain of Syria; plateau of Syria; table-land of Aram.*

The name of the country where Laban lived, and where Isaac and Jacob obtained their wives. It refers to the plain or tillable part of Aram-naharaim or Mesopotamia, in distinction from the mountainous part (Gen. 25:20; 28:2-7).

Meta. Substance lifted to a broad, level place (*plain of Aram, plain of Syria*) in the intellectual thought of the individual. (Land refers to substance, and Aram symbolizes the intellect. A plain or table-land is a level tract of land. See PADDAN and MESOPOTAMIA.)

Padon, pā'-dŏn (Heb.)—*ransom; deliverance; liberation; freedom; escape; redemption; preservation.*

His "children" were among the Nethinim who returned to Jerusalem from the Babylonian captivity (Ezra 2:44).

Meta. A thought of *redemption, freedom, liberation* from error; it leads to escape from sense bondage but is not yet free from the idea of serving God by keeping outer commandments and ordinances, and is still ruled to a certain extent by the outer elements and the inner animal forces—a bond servant under the law (one of the Nethinim). This Padon thought has not yet come into the true liberty of sonship with God (see Gal. 4:1-7), though it has brought forth fruit (ideas springing from it) that has become freed from the sense confusion that Babylon symbolizes (*escape, deliverance,* his descendants returned from the Babylonian captivity) and if continued in it will lead to the perfect liberty of the sons of God. "For freedom did Christ set us free: stand fast therefore, and be not entangled again in a yoke of bondage" (Gal. 5:1).

Pagiel, pā'-ḡĭ-ĕl (Heb.)—*event of God; peace of God; visitation of God; God meets; covenant of God; petition of God; prayer of God.*

Son of Ochran, and chief, or prince, of the tribe of Asher, in the wilderness (Num. 2:27).

Meta. A place in consciousness where *God meets* with the individual; where the individual enters into conscious unity with the Divine and is assured of his inheritance of good. This meeting place is in the devotional thought, or attitude, of true prayer (*prayer of God*).

Pahath–moab, pā'-hăth-mō'-ăb (Heb.)—*prefect of Moab; governor of Moab.*

a One whose "children" returned from the Babylonian captivity with Zerubbabel (Ezra 2:6). **b** One who joined Nehemiah in sealing the covenant (Neh. 10:14).

Meta. While the land of Moab represents the body and the most external conditions of life, there is good in Moab, or a great possibility of good. (See MOAB.) Pahath–moab (meaning *prefect of Moab, governor of Moab,* an Israelite who returned from the Babylonian captivity, and one who joined Nehemiah in sealing the covenant) is symbolical of thoughts in the higher religious consciousness of man that have a degree of dominion over that which Moab represents.

Pai, pā'-ī (Heb.)—*crying out; screaming; bleating; bellowing; sighing; hiss-*

ing; blowing; howling.

The city of Hadad, king of Edom (I Chron. 1:50). It is called Pau in Genesis 36:39.

Meta. See PAU.

Palal, pā'-lăl (Heb.)—*evening out; judging; coloring; thinking; supposing; interceding; praying; a judge; an umpire; a referee; mediator.*

Son of Uzai, one who helped to rebuild Jerusalem's wall (Neh. 3:25).

Meta. We look upon a thinking person as one who is reasonable, rational, capable of viewing a matter from every angle, or from several angles at least, and can therefore form a fairly just and unbiased opinion. Palal (an Israelite who returned from the Babylonian captivity and helped to rebuild Jerusalem's wall, and meaning *evening out, judging, a judge, thinking*) signifies a thought in the higher religious nature of man that is established in good judgment. This would make it a positive, upbuilding element in the consciousness and the organism of the individual (the rebuilding of the wall of Jerusalem refers metaphysically to the rebuilding and transmuting of the soul and the body of man from personal, corruptible expression to that which is spiritual and immortal).

Pallu (in A. V., Genesis 46:9, Phallu), păl'-lū (Heb.)—*separated; distinguished; set apart; great; famous; distinctive; wonderful; marvelous; extraordinary.*

Son of Reuben (I Chron. 5:3).

Meta. Reuben, the first-born of the sons of Jacob, represents the first bringing forth of sight, discernment, faith. The meaning of the name is *"behold a son!"* The idea is that of seeing. "And Leah conceived, and bare a son, and she called his name Reuben: for she said, Because Jehovah hath looked upon my affliction" (Gen. 29:32). This first bringing forth of sight, of the ability to see or discern higher and more interior things pertaining to Truth, is not really spiritual but is more of the outer man. However, it is a big step in advance of anything that the individual has known before, and it bears fruit (Pallu, meaning *set apart, distinguished, great, wonderful, marvelous, famous*). Pallu signifies the great general uplift that comes

to the consciousness that has begun to awaken out of the purely sense, carnal, animal phase of thought to a higher and truer concept of God and of life.

Palluites, păl'-lū-ītes (fr. Heb.)—*of or belonging to Pallu.*

Descendants of Pallu, son of Reuben (Num. 26:5).

Meta. Thoughts springing from that in consciousness which Pallu symbolizes. (See PALLU.)

Palti (in A. V., I Samuel 25:44, Phalti), păl'-tī (Heb.)—*Jehovah makes smooth; Jah is the way of escape; Jah brings forth; deliverance of Jehovah; Jah fully delivers; Jehovah makes free.*

a Son of Raphu; the man chosen from the tribe of Benjamin to help spy out the land of Canaan preparatory to the Israelites' going over and possessing the land (Num. 13:9). b The son of Laish, of Gallim, to whom Saul, king of Israel, gave Michal his daughter for a wife, after she had first been given to David (I Sam. 25:44). This latter Palti is called Paltiel in II Samuel 3:15.

Meta. A belief in or thoughts of deliverance through faith. (*Jah fully delivers* is one meaning of Palti. Both these men named Palti were Benjamites; a Benjamite signifies an active faith thought in consciousness. The second-mentioned Palti was from Gallim, and Gallim is thought to have been a town of Benjamin.)

Paltiel (in A. V., II Samuel 3:15, Phaltiel), păl'-tĭ-ĕl (Heb.)—*God makes smooth; deliverance of God; God is the way of escape; freedom of God.*

a Son of Azzan. A prince of the tribe of Issachar, who was chosen from that tribe to help divide the land of Canaan among the Israelites (Num. 34:26). b The husband of Michal, daughter of Saul. David took her from Paltiel, since had been given to David first (II Sam. 3:15; see PALTI).

Meta. Thoughts of divine protection and deliverance through the exercise of active faith and zeal by the individual. (Paltiel means *God makes smooth, deliverance of God, God is the way of escape.* The first man named Paltiel was of the tribe of Issachar; Issachar signifies active zeal. The second Paltiel was a native of Gallim, a town of Benjamin; Benjamin signifies faith.)

Paltite, păl'-tīte (fr. Heb.)—*of or belonging to Palti.*

"Helez the Paltite" was one of David's mighty warriors, and a member of his guard (II Sam. 23:26). In I Chronicles 11:27 he is called "the Pelonite."

Meta. "The Pelonite" is thought to be the correct rendering. (See PELONITE.)

Pamphylia, păm-phÿl'-ĭ-à (Heb.)—*heterogeneous peoples; of every race; mixture of nations.*

A seacoast district in Asia Minor. Paul preached in Perga, a city in Pamphylia (Acts 13:13; 14:24, 25). It was in Pamphylia that Mark left Paul and Barnabas on his first trip with them (Acts 15:38).

Meta. A mixed state of thought (*mixture of nations, of every race*).

Paphos, pā'-phŏs (Gk.)—*heated; boiling; amorous; passionate; affectionate; friendly; pretext; cozening; fraud.*

A city on the western part of the island of Cyprus. There Barnabas and Paul found Bar–Jesus, a false prophet and sorcerer, who tried to turn the proconsul Sergius Paulus away from the Christian faith (Acts 13:6-13).

Meta. A very zealous state of mind (*heated, boiling*), tending to deception and to animality (*cozening, fraud, amorous*). When the word of Truth (Paul) is declared in this attitude of great fervor and zeal, both good and seemingly error activities are brought to light (they found Sergius Paulus the proconsul, a man of understanding, who willingly accepted the Truth; and with him was Elymas the sorcerer, who signifies the carnal thought that tries to counterfeit the working of Spirit and thus turn the true understanding away from the true faith). Thus at Paphos an adjustment takes place in the consciousness, and the way is opened to a higher understanding.

paradise.

Meta. Paradise means *pleasure grounds, Elysium, region of surpassing beauty, Garden of Eden.* It is a place in which all the elemental forces of Being are at the disposal of the soul that believes in the supremacy of the good.

When we affirm the good to be all and in all, the pure elementals of mind begin to form in us and we bring forth good according to our word (Luke 23:43; see EDEN).

Parah, pā'-räh (Heb.)—*bearing; bringing forth; increasing; fruitful; voluptuous; being born; heifer; place of heifers.*

A city of Benjamin (Josh. 18:23).

Meta. A *bringing forth* of thoughts on the animal plane of the soul consciousness (*bearing, increasing, being born, place of heifers, voluptuous*).

Paran, pā'-răn (Heb.)—*region of caverns; places of caves; region of lurking places; place of much digging; region of searching.*

The wilderness, or desert, between Sinai and Canaan. Ishmael dwelt there (Gen. 21:21). Paran was the scene of much of the wanderings of the Children of Israel while they were on their way to the Promised Land (Num. 10:12; 12:16). In Deuteronomy 33:2 and Habakkuk 3:3 we read of "mount Paran."

Meta. The multitude of seemingly confused and undisciplined thoughts of the subconscious mind (*place of caves, region of caverns*); also a place or period of much earnest searching after Truth. This searching occurs when one is becoming sufficiently established in the good, or is entering into the conscious understanding and dominion that are necessary, to possess the land—begin the real upliftment and redemption of the organism (*place of much digging, region of searching;* the great wilderness in which the Israelites wandered for thirty-eight years after leaving Sinai and before passing over into Canaan).

Parbar, pär'-băr (Heb.)—*open portico; piazza; canopied; open summer house, i. e., open on all sides to light and air; colonnade.*

A place close to the Temple, probably within its outer walls; a precinct or *colonnade* on the west side of the Temple inclosure, that contained rooms for officials and divisions for stock (I Chron. 26:18, margin, the *precinct*). In II Kings 23:11 it is translated "the precincts," in the American Standard Version, and "the suburbs," in the Authorized Version. It is said to be the place where Nathan–melech the chamberlain had his room.

Meta. A phase of the higher consciousness of man (Jerusalem) that lies very close to the inner spiritual place of worship and the meeting place between God and the individual, yet is outside the real, true, inner spiritual realm (*open summer house, piazza, open portico, a precinct* close to and really a portion of the Temple; it was on the west side, west always referring to the without). This phase of consciousness might be said to be one that helps connect our inner spiritual thoughts and ideals with our more outer states of mind.

Parmashta, pär-măsh'-tà (Heb. fr. Skr.)—*superior; stronger; strong in fight; a yearling bull.*

One of Haman's ten sons; he was slain with his brothers (Esth. 9:9).

Meta. A seemingly strong warring thought, in the adverse consciousness of the individual, which Haman and his father signify.

Parmenas, pär'-mě-năs (Gk.)—*steadfast; constant; abiding; enduring; permanent; faithful.*

One of the seven men who were chosen to attend to the distribution of supply among the Christians in Jerusalem, that none might be overlooked (Acts 6:5).

Meta. A faithful, steadfast, abiding thought in the higher, spiritual consciousness of the individual—a thought that is resolute and firm in the Truth (*steadfast, faithful, permanent, enduring*; see Acts 6:3 for an insight into the character of the man Parmenas).

Parnach, pär'-năch (Heb. or Chald.)—*swift; agile; nimble; (or) to live delicately; to delight oneself; to weaken with tenderness.* The foregoing definitions of this name are drawn from two entirely different sources.

Father of Elizaphan, a prince of the tribe of Zebulun who was chosen to help divide the land of Canaan amongst the Israelites (Num. 34:25).

Meta. A thought belonging to the order faculty in individual consciousness (Zebulun symbolizes the faculty of order) that is alert and active (*swift, agile, nimble*). If the other definitions of

Parnach are considered, then the reference is to a thought tendency that is very loving and refined but needs to become established in strong, positive unselfishness, that the seeming weakness may be overcome.

Parosh (in A. V., Ezra 8:3, Pharosh), pä'-rŏsh (Heb.)—*jumping; leaping; springing; nimble; fleeing; a flea; a fugitive.*

a Two thousand one hundred and seventy-two of the descendants of Parosh returned from the Babylonian captivity with Zerubbabel (Ezra 2:3). **b** The name of a chief of the people who joined Nehemiah in sealing the covenant (Neh. 10:14).

Meta. Thoughts belonging to the higher and more religious phase of man's consciousness (Israelites) that are very quick, swift, and active (*jumping, leaping, springing, nimble*). They are somewhat lacking, however, in the stability and the sureness that enable the individual to take a positive stand for Truth (*fleeing, a fugitive*), though they lead to freedom and good (the "children" of the one man named Parosh, to the number of two thousand one hundred and seventy-two, returned from the Babylonian captivity, while the other Parosh joined Nehemiah in sealing the covenant).

Parshandatha, pär-shăn'-dă-thà (Heb. from Pers.)—*given to Persia; interpreter of the law; revelation of the law.*

One of Haman's ten sons. He was put to death with his brothers (Esth. 9:7).

Meta. Persia means *cutting, dividing.* One of the results of the rule of the Adversary in man (signified by Haman and his father Hammedatha, the Jews' enemy) is a divided mind, a lack of peace, poise, and unity. This phase of mind is typified by Parshandatha, Haman's son.

Parthians, pär'-thĭ-ăṇṣ (fr. Gk.)—*wounding as they fly; fighting backward; rapid flight; exiles; horsemen.* The Parthians practiced discharging their arrows backward over their shoulders while apparently riding from the enemy. Thus the enemy was never sure whether they were retreating or preparing to discharge an avalanche of arrows. They were expert horsemen also. and the name is coined from the combined ideas.

Inhabitants of Parthia, a country or mountainous district to the north of Media and Persia (Acts 2:9). They were among those who heard the gospel taught in their own language at Pentecost.

Meta. Very active thoughts of power (*horsemen, rapid flight*, horses referring to the vital force in man, or power), though with a warring and deceptive tendency of expression (*fighting backward, wounding as they fly*). In this instance they belong to the religious thoughts of the individual, since the Parthians of Acts 2:9 are supposed to have been Jews who had settled in Parthia.

Paruah, pă-ru̧'-ăh (Heb.)—*breaking forth; budding; blossoming; hatching; being born; flourishing; increase; progeny.*

His son Jehoshaphat was the officer of King Solomon's who gathered provisions out of Issachar sufficient to keep the king's household for one month in each year (I Kings 4:17).

Meta. The idea of spiritual substance and supply coming forth from within and increasing and abounding in the consciousness (*breaking forth, budding, blossoming, being born, flourishing, increase, progeny*). Paruah's son Jehoshaphat signifies judgment's being developed in consciousness; thus a right distribution and handling of this substance and supply would be made possible.

Parvaim, pär-vā'-ĭm (Heb.)—*eastern; original; primal; prior; anterior; virgin purity; pure virgin gold.*

A place that produced the very finest quality of gold (II Chron. 3:6). Solomon used gold from Parvaim in building the Temple. Parvaim is thought to be the same place as Ophir.

Meta. In Scripture symbology east always signifies the within. Parvaim therefore (meaning *eastern,* and being a country that produced the very finest quality of gold) would refer to the inner Christ mind or consciousness, whence comes our very highest and purest comprehension of divine wisdom and substance. (See OPHIR.)

Pasach, pā'-săch (Heb.)—*cutting up; cutting off; dividing; considering decisively; part; piece; halting; limping; lame.*

Son of Japhlet and descendant of Asher (I Chron. 7:33).

Meta. A deeply analytical and positive tendency of thought (*cutting up, considering decisively, dividing*), but more from a human or intellectual than from a spiritual standpoint. The result therefore is not a perfect deduction, or perfect understanding. (*Halting, limping,* a lameness in walking, signifies some kind of flaw in the phase of one's understanding that comes into contact with the outer conditions of life.)

Pas–dammim, păs–dăm'-mĭm (Heb.)—*end of bloodshed; boundary of blood; limit of blood.*

A place in Judah where the Philistines gathered to battle against Israel, and were defeated (I Chron. 11:13). In I Samuel 17:1 it is called Ephes–dammim.

Meta. See EPHES–DAMMIM.

Paseah (in A. V., Nehemiah 7:51, Phaseah), pă-sē'-ăh (Heb.)—*leaping over; passing over; sparing; delivering; halting; pausing; hesitating; limping; lame.*

a Son of Eshton, of the tribe of Judah (I Chron. 4:12). **b** Father of Joiada, who helped to rebuild Jerusalem's wall (Neh. 3:6).

Meta. Paseah (*passing over, sparing, delivering*) signifies thoughts of a freeing, overcoming character. We see also in this word a tendency to hesitate between two opinions, and to jump to conclusions, to decide matters without properly considering the details involved (*halting, pausing, hesitating, leaping over*). Thus a truer understanding is needed (*limping, lame,* bespeak a defect in that phase of the understanding which contacts outer conditions). The inner understanding and ideals of the individual who is in the Paseah consciousness must be made more practical; they must be used daily in thought, word, and deed for meeting and adjusting outer conditions and affairs.

Pashhur (A. V., Pashur), păsh'-hŭr (Heb.)—*encompassed by plenty; prosperity round about; surrounded by nobil-*

ity; liberty; freedom; liberation.

a Son of Immer the priest. He smote Jeremiah and put him in the stocks (Jer. 20:1). **b** A son of Malchijah and an officer of King Zedekiah. He was sent by the king to Jeremiah to inquire of Jehovah (Jer. 21:1). **c** In Nehemiah 7: 41 we read that a thousand two hundred and forty-seven of the descendants of Pashhur returned from the Babylonian captivity.

Meta. Freeing thoughts in consciousness, thoughts that are activated and surrounded by ideas of substance, of plenty, and of nobility (*encompassed by plenty, surrounded by nobility, liberty, freedom, liberation*). The first two of these men named Pashhur, however, worked against Jeremiah because he prophesied against Jerusalem. This shows that the thoughts that they symbolize need, at this stage of the unfoldment of the individual, a better comprehension of the divine law and of the necessity of working in harmony with it in order to bring about the true freedom from error and its results, and the true good, for which they stand.

In the case of the third man named Pashhur, who may have been one of the first two, the fact that so many of his descendants returned from the Babylonian captivity indicates that this lesson of conformity to divine law has been learned, or at least has been taken into consideration, and good is being realized (*prosperity round about*).

There are many persons today who see the wonderful good that is in store for God's children, and who claim this good, but do not like to hear anything about the law of sowing and reaping. They apparently do not wish to make the right adjustment in their life that is necessary to keep them from reaping inharmonies and to establish them in the good that is their inheritance.

Passover (fr. Heb.)—*passing over, i. e., a stream or obstruction; overcoming; sparing; protecting; delivering.*

Meta. "The passover" was an annual festival of the Israelites, and still is kept by the Jews, in commemoration of their escape from the Egyptians. It was used by Jesus to represent the freeing of the spiritual man from the dominion of sense. It is part of the regenerative process that goes on in the body under the inspiration of the Christ mind. It is the passing over or out of one state of consciousness into another.

In order to get the esoteric interpretation of the Passover, it is necessary to analyze the descent of Spirit into the subjective consciousness and follow it step by step in its many manifestations. Physically speaking, Egypt represents the part of the body below the diaphragm. The various plagues brought upon the Egyptians by the Lord through Moses are symbolical representations of appearances that ensue in this part of the organism when the presiding intelligence (Pharaoh) opposes the influx of the higher life.

A parallel to the bloody waters, frogs, lice, flies, murrain, boils, hail, locusts, darkness, and death of first-born may be found in the various diseases of bowels, kidneys, and other organs of the body, as named by doctors. A very large portion of these ills is the result of human resistance to spiritual consciousness, which is working widely in humanity.

A concept of Truth in the head will eventually find its way through the whole body; and when its vibrations penetrate into the centers established in materiality, great resistance and pain sometimes follow. This sets up a chronic irritation and gives rise to a local condition to which the physician gives a name. Did the patient only know that it was Spirit at work, and fearlessly affirm the presence and power of the divine life, the opposition of the physical would pass away and a new and more enduring life flow would follow.

There is a physical basis of life through which the natural world manifests. Physical generation is its law, and its seed is the material cell. In Exodus the natural world is called Egypt; Jesus spoke of it as "this world." Then there is the true world, whose foundation is Spirit. This is the "heaven" of Jesus, and the "house not made with hands, eternal, in the heavens," referred to by Paul. These are both in evidence in man's soul and body, and in regeneration there is a breaking up and passing away of the physical basis and an ushering in of the spiritual.

The "first-born" of the Egyptians is the highest concept of life perpetuation that the physical man possesses. When the divine word, or angel of the Lord, passes through consciousness, a transformation takes place in this life thought. If the consciousness is established in materiality and has no expectation or thought of spiritual life, the germ is destroyed by the high vibration and passes away through the kidneys or bowels, and a general physical weakness follows.

This is the death of the first-born of the Egyptians. If the mind is set on higher things, on the understanding that the enduring life is spiritual both within and without (blood on the doorposts), then the germ is saved from destruction; it is retained in the organism, goes through a regenerating process, is multiplied, and eventually strengthens the whole man.

We may mentally have made our truest statements and seemingly complied with all the law, yet Pharaoh does not let our people go—there is no realization of freedom in the body consciousness. Another step is necessary, which is typified in the feast of the Passover.

In every change of consciousness on the physical plane there is a breaking down of cells and a building up of other cells to take their place. Mentally this is denial and affirmation, and this process in the body is the result of these two movements in the mind. We let go the animal life and take hold of the spiritual life by giving up consciously to this "passing over" process, which takes place when the old cells are replaced by the new. The lamb that is killed and eaten in the night represents this giving up of the animal life in the obscurity of the carnal body. The command is that the lamb shall be without spot or blemish, and be wholly eaten after being roasted with fire. This refers to the complete surrender of the human life after it has been purified by the fires of regeneration. Fire represents the positive, affirmative state of mind, as opposed to the negative or watery state. The Children of Israel were commanded not to let the lamb be "boiled" (in the A. V., "sodden," which is the Old English present tense of seethe). We are not to allow the life in our organism to simmer and stew with the worries and negative words of carnality, but we must set it afire with strong words of Truth.

This is to show us that there must be a physical sacrifice as well as a mental, and that "all the congregation of Israel" shall join in it; that is, the whole consciousness of spiritual desire shall acquiesce. Many metaphysicians think that it is not necessary to change the habits of the sense man—that one has only to keep his thoughts right and the flesh will thereby be wholly regulated—but the Scripture teaches that there must be a conscious physical change before the complete demonstration in mind and body is manifest. Thoughts work themselves out in things, and we get the full result of this work only when we follow them consciously every step of the way and help them along. So watch your thoughts as they consecutively work their way through your organism; and if you find that some pure thought of spiritual life is striving to free the life in the appetites and passions of your physical Egypt, help it by consciously elevating that life to the open door of your mind. This is typified by putting the blood of the lamb on the two side posts and the lintel of the door of the house. Do not be afraid to expose your inner life to the sight of the Lord, for only in perfect candor and childlike innocence can man come under the protection of divine law.

So long as there is a hidden, secret use of God's life in our habits and ways that we are not willing that all should know, just so long will the bondage of Egypt's Pharaoh hold us in its clutches. The whole man must be pure, and his inner life must be made so open and free that he will not be afraid to blazon it upon the very doors of his house where all who pass may read. Then the Lord will execute His judgment, and those who have purified the life of the lamb (or the body) will escape the messenger (or thought) of death.

Patara, păt'-ă-rà (Gk.) — *trodden*

down; trampled under foot; desecration; contempt; insult; outrage.

A seaport city in Asia Minor (Acts 21:1).

Meta. A group of thoughts in the sense consciousness of man that are the result of suppression. These thoughts are of a browbeaten, subdued nature, and work toward bondage (*trodden down, trampled under foot*).

Pathros, păth'-rŏs (Heb. fr. Egypt.)—
—*Upper Egypt, i. e., distinguished from Mizraim, or Lower Egypt; region of the south; broken into fragments; reduced to impalpable particles; dust; ruptured; ruined.*

A district in Upper Egypt (Isa. 11:11; Ezek. 30:14).

Meta. A phase of the subconscious mind that, though there is good in it, is still in darkness so far as the individual is consciously or subconsciously concerned (*region of the south*, a district in Upper Egypt, *south* referring to that which is below). The fact that Pathros was in the upper or higher ground of Egypt bespeaks thoughts of a higher nature than those commonly attributed to Egypt. The other definitions of Pathros, with its history as given in Ezekiel and Isaiah (one prophesies of its destruction, and the other mentions it as one of the places whence the Lord will "recover the remnant of his people"), suggest a time of judgment, or a thorough looking into, breaking up, and analyzing of this phase of the subconsciousness to the end that the error in it shall be eliminated. Thus the good only will remain and be lifted into the light.

Pathrusim, păth-ru̧'-sĭm (Heb. fr. Egypt.)—*Egyptians of the upper kingdom.*

Descendants of Mizraim son of Ham, and the inhabitants of Pathros in Egypt (Gen. 10:14).

Meta. Thoughts belonging to the state of consciousness in man that Pathros signifies. (See PATHROS.)

Patmos, păt'-mŏs (Gk.)—*mortal.*

The island to which John was banished. It is a rocky island in the Ægean Sea (Rev. 1:9). This was where John received his vision recorded in The Book of Revelation.

Meta. A place in consciousness where we realize through Spirit that the fleshly or carnal man produces nothing. When we are in Spirit the body is physically quiet; all sensation is primarily from the Spirit. So far as the I AM or spiritual is concerned, the physical is as a rock, void of sensation or activity. When we still the outer we get the inspiration of Spirit within us.

Patmos means *mortal,* and isle suggests an isolated body of earth. This refers to the subjective body separated from its environment in the world and lifted in Spirit to the Lord's day, or degree of unfoldment where the higher law becomes operative. The voice that John heard behind him (Rev. 1:10) refers to the unseen or subjective consciousness, whose base of action in the body is the spinal cord and the medulla oblongata. It is there that divine law stores all the words and thoughts that we have ever entertained. "The word of God and the testimony of Jesus" is thus recorded in this "isle that is called Patmos."

Patrobas, păt'-rŏ-băs (Gk.)—*life of his father; according to the father's life; the father's substance; paternal resource; patrimony.*

A Christian at Rome to whom Paul sent salutation (Rom. 16:14).

Meta. The belief that man's inheritance, divine sonship, can be and should be demonstrated here and now (*life of his father, according to the father's life, the father's substance, paternal resource, patrimony*).

Pau, pā'-ū (Heb.)—*crying out; screaming; howling; bellowing; bleating; lowing; hissing; blowing.*

The city of Hadar king of Edom (Gen. 36:39). It is called Pai in I Chronicles 1:50.

Meta. The great effort and outer show, the commotion and unrest in expressing life and power, that attend the efforts of the animal or carnal nature in the individual (*crying out, screaming, howling,* and so forth). Especially does this become apparent to one who is awakening to the truth of his being and is beginning to develop the inner peace, poise, and quietness of Spirit, wherein the consciousness of true, abiding, unfailing energy and might is generated.

Paul, paul (fr. Lat.)—*restrained; constrained; reduced; lessened; made small; little.*

A Jewish man of Tarsus, who persecuted the Christians for a time but was converted to Christ by means of a vision. He became one of the greatest of the apostles, and he wrote many of the books of our New Testament. His name was Saul before he became a Christian (Acts 9:1-22; 13:9).

Meta. Different symbolisms and shades of meaning are given to Paul and to his life and ministry, all bearing on the important work of overcoming in the individual. Some of them are as follows:

In the early history of Paul we behold two states of mind: first, the pharisaical state of mind, which may be found in one who is intellectually educated and may inherit his religious bias or get it by association; second, the spiritual state of mind, which is found in one who attains real spiritual understanding through illumination by the Christ mind. Paul experienced both of these states.

When one has been associated with and has zealously defended the doctrines of some sect, and afterward changes one's mind and preaches differently, one is persecuted by those who are still loyal to the old faith. Under these circumstances one should make a simple statement of the facts in the case, and then go about defending the new doctrine that one has espoused, by demonstrating in one's life that which it teaches.

Paul represents the word of the Spirit of truth. The converted Paul (formerly Saul, the will) becomes, by the power of the word, the most active thought in the establishment of good throughout our being.

The will is the very essence of self-consciousness. The story of the conversion and work of Saul of Tarsus fills a large place in Biblical history. In this symbology Saul represents the human will. In all permanent character building the action of the will is based on understanding. Will and understanding go hand in hand. They are the Ephraim and Manasseh of Scripture, whose allotment in the Promised Land was in joint ownership.

The conversion of Saul was preceded by a great light of spiritual understanding. The word Saul typifies the will in its personal dominance. After the discovery that there is a wisdom greater than the personal will, the name is changed to Paul, which means *little, restrained, lessened, made small,* and its character is converted from that of the violent and oppressive persecutor of things spiritual to the devout and obedient champion of the humble Christ, the spiritual I AM.

It should not be inferred that the will is weakened by conversion; it is made stronger in every respect. When the will is acting in harmony with divine law, its work is gentle, and to the superficial onlooker the will seems *little.* Saul was a prominent figure in the work of suppressing the early Christians; he carried the authority of the mighty Sanhedrin with a zealous and cruel hand, because of lack of real spiritual understanding. But when conversion came he went forth with a price on his head. He was a very small figure in that day. It has taken the centuries to prove how great was that quiet but steady and persistent planting of the gospel among the Gentiles (Acts 22:3, 6-10).

Paul and Silas (Acts 16:25-40) represent the will and the understanding in their work of clearing up the consciousness. Paul's fearlessness was the strong point of his character. To him, Truth came first and the things of the world second. This is what made him the great apostle—he was will personified in conjunction with understanding. When these are joined in consciousness, man is equal to any emergency.

The entrance of Paul and his companions into Europe (Acts 16:6-15) is symbolical of opening up the word of Truth in parts of the consciousness where it has never before been realized.

The body is pervaded by a life and an intelligence that have formed a little world of their own. It has no knowledge of the higher life of Spirit. It has to be regenerated—born from above. The spiritual spark is carried by the converted will, Paul, and it has to meet obstacles of various kinds. The lands and towns in which Paul was "forbidden of the Holy Spirit to speak the word" (see Acts 16:6, 7) represent some of these. When guided by Spirit we are led to develop along the lines of least resistance and where the conditions are most favorable. We should not be discouraged when we strike seemingly barren places within our own consciousness and body, nor waste our time in trying to quicken the localities that at present apparently are too negative to respond. The experience of those who regenerate the body is that a certain fiery element is necessary to give action to the watery, negative parts. This need is referred to in this passage. Macedonia, where Paul worked for a time, means *burning adoration* and is representative of the enthusiasm and the energy of Spirit that set the whole man aflame. It is necessary that this phase of the consciousness be cultivated, because without it a certain passivity sets in that is content with the battle as only half won.

Philippi, where Paul spent some time preaching, means *lover of horses, warlike*, horses referring to the vital forces, or power. It is necessary to stir up this fiery power in the man when he gets into barren states of consciousness. The vision of the man in Macedonia crying, "Come over . . . and help us," is the discernment of this inner fervor that needs stirring up. One can do this stirring up by affirming that all obstacles and barriers to the supremacy of Spirit are now cleared away; then, like Paul, making a straight course to Neapolis, the *new city*, or center of action. This means that he who concentrates all his energies upon the accomplishment of his purpose will surely succeed.

Paul (the word of Truth, not the whole Truth) is a tentmaker (Acts 18:1-4). Truth always builds up; it never tears down. When this realization enters our mind it joins itself to all the upbuilding forces there at work. But Truth is not content with mere physical upbuilding (tentmaking). It would instruct the man how to build his own tent or body, symbolized by Paul's reasoning with both Jews and Greeks in the synagogue every Sabbath (the synagogue is the center of spiritual thought in individual consciousness, and the Sabbath signifies a time of rest or meditation).

Paul is also a tremendous outpicturing of ambition or zeal; first active on the intellectual plane as champion of the law and the prophets, afterward swift to carry out the freeing doctrine of the Christ consciousness.

Following are two lessons to be learned from Paul's going "bound in the spirit" to Jerusalem (Acts 20:22, 23):

Because Paul was a very great apostle, and wise in spiritual things far beyond us in many ways, it does not follow that he was perfect or that we should accept as gospel truth all that he wrote. He had his weak points. In this place he proclaims that he is going to Jerusalem "bound in the spirit." This is not a wise affirmation for one who is preaching freedom from bonds; neither is the one that he is going to Jerusalem regardless of the warnings of the Holy Spirit that "bonds and afflictions" await him there. It seems that he was told by Spirit not to go to Jerusalem, but his obstinacy and persistence, which he had so long held in abeyance, broke forth on this occasion, and he was determined to have his own way regardless of divine warnings.

So we find in our spiritual ongoing that old states of mind that we have thought wholly overcome will crop out again and have to be demonstrated over. Spiritual obedience will save us from hard experiences. Had Paul been obedient he would have avoided the years of imprisonment in Jerusalem and in Rome. The Lord does not put trials upon us nor are we bound in doing His work. "Where the Spirit of the Lord is, *there* is liberty" (II Cor. 3:17).

On the other hand, Paul's going to Jerusalem represents the word of Truth as going into the spiritual consciousness, proclaiming the I AM doctrine of Jesus Christ, just as Paul in all his missionary trips represents the word of Truth going into the various parts of the consciousness proclaiming this I AM doctrine of the Christ. The spiritual center (Jerusalem) is under the dominance of the

Jews who cling to the Mosaic law and make a great religious outcry against the new kingdom that the I AM or Christ proposes to set up. We are not to let the old religious convictions and teachings deter us from proclaiming that which we know to be true. Jesus Christ is King of the Jews (our religious ideas), and this Paul, with his true words, must go without fear of results into the most holy parts and there plant the seeds of the new church, or new state of consciousness.

It may seem for the time being that our words have borne no fruit, that we have been put in prison by these narrow religious thoughts that the Jews signify here; but if we are faithful to God we shall be swiftly and safely delivered from them.

If we turn to material law in our extremity the fruit of our words will be slow in coming to ripeness. This seems to be the lesson we are to learn in the appeal of Paul to Cæsar. In his extremity he claimed his Roman citizenship and asked the protection of manmade law (Acts 22:25-28; 25:11, 12; 26:32). He was put in chains and sent to Rome. Had he adhered to spiritual ways and sung songs of praise and given thanks to God for his speedy deliverance, he would doubtless have received such divine help as he and Silas had received on a former occasion.

Yet the true word finally bore its fruit, and the trip to Jerusalem and imprisonment in Rome brought forth abundantly in after years. So every word of Truth that we speak will surely make itself manifest; that manifestation will be swift or slow, according to our loyalty to spiritual ways under every trial.

Cæsar represents the tyrannical rule of the personal will unmodified by spiritual love, mercy, and justice. Paul (signifying the word of Truth), imprisoned at Cæsarea (Acts 23:23—25:4), indicates that the dominating force of the will had confined the expression of Truth to the intellectual, or sense, realm in consciousness.

The idea of Truth is inspired in man from the higher self and conceived by him in the heart, of which Jerusalem is the symbol, but because of intellectual dominance it is attracted to the head, of which Rome is the symbol. When one is dominated by his intellect in his religious ideas, he is given to form and ceremony without perceiving the spiritual Truth back of them; such a one still has Rome as his center. If he were truly spiritual, Jerusalem would be his center. Paul's being taken to Rome in chains (Acts 27:1; 28:16) is a fitting symbol of the word or expression of Truth that Paul symbolizes captured by the intellect in conjunction with the dominant personal will, and confined to the bonds of sense that it has placed upon itself.

Paul was a teacher, preacher, orator. He represents the expresser of the word. Christ is the word invisible; Paul is an avenue through which the word is outwardly expressed.

The reason why Paul symbolizes the will in some lessons, and the word of Truth in others, is that the faculties play many parts in the manifestations of the mind. Matthew represents the will in the individual development of the man Jesus. Paul represents the will in a universal sense. Before Paul's conversion took place he was called Saul. Saul is the name, in the Old Testament, of the king, or the will. When Saul changed his mind he became Paul (*little*); in other words, the large personal will was converted into the obedient servant of the Christ.

Paulus, pạu'-lŭs (Lat.)—*restrained; constrained; reduced; lessened; made small; little.*

The surname of Sergius, the proconsul at Paphos on the island of Cyprus (Acts 13:7).

Meta. See SERGIUS PAULUS.

Pedahel, pĕd'-ă-hĕl (Heb.) — *whom God delivers; ransomed of God; God redeems; preserved of God; whom God saves; whom God frees from servitude.*

Son of Ammihud and prince of the tribe of Naphtali. He was chosen to help divide Canaan among the Israelitish tribes (Num. 34:28).

Meta. A very influential thought in the strength faculty of man (a prince of Naphtali) that is established in the idea of divine deliverance from bondage to limitation and error (*whom God delivers, God redeems, God frees from servitude*).

Pedahzur, pĕ-däh'-zŭr (Heb.)—*the rock has redeemed; the rock of deliverance; stone of redemption.*

Father of Gamaliel, a prince of the tribe of Manasseh (Num. 2:20).

Meta. Faith in Christ as the redeeming, saving power of the individual (*the rock has redeemed, rock of deliverance, stone of redemption*, suggesting Christ and faith). Jesus said to Peter, "Thou art Peter, and upon this rock I will build my church." Peter means *a stone*, and symbolizes the faith faculty in man; "this rock" is the indwelling Christ, and the "church" is spiritual consciousness. In I Corinthians 10:4 we read, "and the rock was Christ"; this was the rock that supplied water to the Children of Israel during their journeyings in the wilderness.

Pedaiah, pĕ-dā'-ĭăh (Heb.)—*whom Jehovah delivers; Jah has ransomed; Jah delivers; redemption of the Lord; whom Jah saves.*

There were several Israelitish men by this name (II Kings 23:36; I Chron. 3:18; 27:20; Neh. 3:25; 8:4; 11:7).

Meta. The symbolism here is that of redemption, overcoming power, salvation, from error and its effects to manifest Christlikeness, by means of Jehovah, I AM, the indwelling Christ.

Pekah, pē'-kăh (Heb.)—*open-eyed; seeing; perceiving; watchful; restored to sight.*

Son of Remaliah and captain for Pekahiah, king of Israel. He conspired against the king, killed him, and became king in his stead (II Kings 15:25, 27-30).

Meta. The executive power of the will (captain of the king's army), very observant and attentive (*open-eyed, watchful*), but in an intellectual or outer reasoning way rather than in true spiritual understanding. Therefore it sees the evil in the will that is ruling in personal willfulness and ignorance (the wicked King Pekahiah) and seeks to put the evil away by violently destroying the function through which it is expressing (Pekah killed the king, in Samaria. Samaria means *watch mountain,* and signifies the objective consciousness as functioning through the head.) He also killed Argob and Arieh, who had helped kill Pekahiah, which shows that in violently opposing anything, even that which appears to be evil, one is sure to hinder the expression of much that is good also. (See ARGOB, ARIEH, and GILEAD.) Violence, being evil itself, must come to an end, and it will in time bring into deep trouble, even to the disintegration of soul and body, those who persist in holding to it and expressing it.

The lesson here is that we need to be watchful of good rather than of apparent error, and must seek always to overcome evil with good. Since we grow to be like that which we behold, that on which we keep our mind centered, we should by all means magnify only the good in our thoughts and in our life by seeing and thinking about it, both as relating to ourselves and to other persons. We should deny error appearances whenever they present themselves to our vision, then cease to give them our further attention, by turning persistently to the good.

Pekahiah, pĕk-ă-hī'-ăh (Heb.)—*Jehovah has opened his eyes; Jah perceives; Jah watches; Jehovah restores the sight.*

Son of Menahem and king of Israel. "He did that which was evil in the sight of Jehovah," and was slain by his captain, Pekah (II Kings 15:22-26).

Meta. The ruling will of the objective consciousness of man (king of Israel, in Samaria), reigning in willfulness and ignorance (Pekahiah was a wicked king), but watched over by Jehovah and being taught, or gaining, understanding by the way of experience (*Jehovah has opened his eyes, Jehovah restores the sight, Jah watches*, eyes relating to sight —understanding). Until we are able to learn by direct revelation from God, and by being obedient to our higher ideals and spiritual guidance, we have to learn our lessons by means of the harder way, experience, since the law is that we must continue to learn and grow.

Pekod, pē'-kŏd (Heb.)—*visitation;*

punishment.

A place in Babylonia (or a name that stands for Babylon) against which both Jeremiah and Ezekiel prophesied (Jer. 50:21; Ezek. 23:23).

Meta. The harvest time of error. There is a law of sowing and reaping. When error thoughts, fears, and beliefs have been sown in our consciousness they must—unless we discern the Truth and root out the errors by means of our true thoughts, words, and acts—come to fruition, and the harvest time will bring inharmonious experiences of some kind. Under the old thought this harvest time of error ·was looked upon as a *visitation* or *punishment* from the Lord. We now understand it to be but the outworking of some phase of divine law that we ourselves have set into action destructively, through our ignorance, and have left to work out into inharmony in our life.

Pelaiah, pĕ-lā'-iặh (Heb.)—*whom Jehovah makes distinguished; the Lord has distinguished; Jah is wonderful; marvel of Jah; whom Jehovah strengthens.*

a Son of Elioenai, of Judah, of the line of David and Solomon (I Chron. 3:24). **b** One who helped Ezra to cause the people to understand the law (Neh. 8:7). **c** Named among those who joined Nehemiah in sealing the covenant (Neh. 10:10).

Meta. A great sense of upliftment and strength, of Truth and might, that is the result of exalting and magnifying the I AM, Christ, or Jehovah in consciousness (*whom Jehovah makes distinguished, the Lord has distinguished, Jah is wonderful, whom Jehovah strengthens*).

Pelaliah, pĕl-ă-lī'-ăh (Heb.)—*Jah judges; Jehovah makes even; Jah is thinker; Jah intercedes; Jehovah is mediator; entreating the Lord; thinking on Jehovah.*

An Israelitish priest, son of Amzi (Neh. 11:12).

Meta. The significance of this name is that true judgment, inspiration, and prayer are spiritual, are of Jehovah, the Christ (*Jah judges; Jah is thinker; Jah intercedes*). By earnest desire (*entreat-ing the Lord*) and by *thinking on Jehovah,* man becomes spiritually discerning, discriminative, and divinely just in his judgment.

Pelatiah, pĕl-ă-tī'-ăh (Heb.)—*Jehovah makes smooth; Jah is way of escape; Jah delivers; deliverance of the Lord; safety of Jah.*

a Son of Hananiah, in line of descent from David and Solomon (I Chron. 3:21). **b** A captain of the Simeonites when they defeated and destroyed the Amalekites (I Chron. 4:42). **c** One who joined Nehemiah in sealing the covenant (Neh. 10:22). **d** A son of Benaiah and prince of the people of Israel, one whom Ezekiel prophesied against (Ezek. 11:1-13).

Meta. Freeing, delivering thoughts in consciousness, based on a degree of understanding of divine law (*Jehovah makes smooth, Jah is way of escape, Jah delivers, deliverance of the Lord,* Lord referring to divine law).

The Pelatiah whom Ezekiel was told to prophesy against was one of those "that give wicked counsel in this city; that say, *The time* is not near to build houses: this *city* is the caldron, and we are the flesh" (Ezek. 11:2, 3). He symbolizes the thoughts in us that lay hold of the idea of divine deliverance from error and its results but, when it comes to really taking the saving Truth into our body, begin to fear and try to make us believe that the time has not come yet when our outer man can really be delivered out of its seemingly mortal, corruptible state. Thus such thoughts become false prophets and must be denied away.

Peleg, pē'-lĕg (Heb.)—*moral distinction; separation through grace; distinction of principle; cleaving; cutting in two; dividing; separating; a watercourse; a channel; a canal.*

Son of Eber and descended from Shem, one of Noah's three sons; he was called Peleg (that is, *Division,* margin) "for in his days was the earth divided" (Gen. 10:25).

Meta. Eber, father of Peleg, and meaning *a shoot,* signifies the germination of the spiritual in man's consciousness. (Shem, from whom Eber was descended, was the son of Noah who represents the spiritual in man. From Eber, through Peleg, Abraham, Isaac, and Jacob, the Hebrew race later came into existence.)

Peleg, son of Eber, and meaning *dividing* ("in his days was the earth divided"), signifies man's first realization of the difference and seeming separation between his apparently material organism and his inner spiritual ideals. Before this he knew only the physical, the material, but here he began to distinguish between the earthly in his consciousness and make-up, and his higher ideals—the spiritual; thus "was the earth divided," and the individual began to recognize his higher nature.

Pelet, pē'-lĕt (Heb.)—*smooth; escape; deliverance; freedom; safety.*

a Son of Jahdai, of the tribe of Judah (I Chron. 2:47). b A son of Azmaveth, a Benjamite, who came to David at Ziklag when David was in hiding from Saul (I Chron. 12:3).

Meta. Freeing, delivering thoughts in consciousness (*smooth, escape, deliverance, freedom, safety*), based on an active faith (a Benjamite) and praise and prayer (a Judahite).

Peleth, pē'-lĕth (Heb.)—*swiftness; speed; dispatch; haste; flight; escape; freedom; separation; distinction.*

a Father of On of the tribe of Reuben (Num. 16:1). b A son of Jonathan of the tribe of Judah (I Chron. 2:33).

Meta. Swift, active, separating, discriminating, freeing thoughts (*swiftness, speed, haste, freedom, escape, separation, distinction,* a Reubenite, Reuben referring to inspiration, sight, but more of the outer man, and a man of Judah) that tend to eliminate error. These thoughts, however, must become more redemptive in their activities, that they may really serve to establish the individual in Truth. (A son of one of the men named Peleth joined in the rebellion against Moses; see Numbers, 16th chapter.)

Pelethites, pĕl'-ĕ-thītes (Heb.)—*public runners; messengers; couriers; swift horses.*

Members of David's bodyguard, and among his most brave and valiant attendants, *messengers,* and warriors (II Sam. 8:18).

Meta. Love's messengers—swift, vital, spiritual thoughts that are in attendance upon our inner love (David) faculty when it is ruling in consciousness (*public runners, couriers, swift horses;* attendants, *messengers,* and warriors of David).

Pelonite, pĕl'-ŏ-nīte (fr. Heb.)—*a separation; a distinction; definite; distinct.*

Designation of Helez and Ahijah, two of David's warriors and members of his "guard" or "council" (I Chron. 11:27, 36). In II Samuel 23:26 Helez is called "the Paltite." Helez the Pelonite· was the seventh captain for the seventh month, over the Ephraimites (I Chron. 27:10).

Meta. The thought activities that are symbolized by Helez and Ahijah set apart to do a specific work in the consciousness in behalf of the rule of divine love—David (*a separation, a distinction, a certain one, definite, distinct;* see HELEZ and AHIJAH).

Peniel, pĕ-nī'-ĕl (Heb.)—*turned toward God; face of God; within the presence of God; countenance of God; vision of God; recognition of God; beholden of God; understanding of God.*

The place where Jacob wrestled with the angel and prevailed, where his name was changed to Israel. "And Jacob called the name of the place Peniel: for, *said he,* I have seen God face to face, and my life is preserved" (Gen. 32:30; see margin also).

Meta. The inner realization of the divine presence, of having met God face to face, and of having succeeded through prayer in attaining the divine favor and blessing that have been sought (*turned toward God, face of God, within the presence of God, vision of God, recognition of God, beholden of God*). At Peniel Jacob's name was changed to Israel because, as it was explained to him, "thou hast striven with God and with men, and hast prevailed," *had power with,* margin (Gen. 32:28).

Peninnah, pĕ-nĭn'-näh (Heb.)—*pearl; red coral; precious stone; gem; jewel.*

One of the wives of Elkanah the Ephraimite. His other wife was Hannah, mother of Samuel the prophet (I Sam. 1:2).

Meta. The soul lifted up in individual consciousness and unified with the understanding that man's inheritance is from God; that while he does not own anything selfishly, yet all that the Father has is his (Elkanah). The union of the soul with this understanding makes of the soul, or causes the individual to realize that the soul is, a precious *jewel* (*pearl, precious stone*); thus there is brought forth increase of good in thoughts and ideas (Peninnah had sons and daughters).

Pentecost, pĕn'-tĕ-cŏst (Gk.)—*the fiftieth* (*day*). The day of Pentecost is the Greek rendering of the Hebrew "Hagha–Katzir" or festival of reaping, harvest of grain.

The "day of Pentecost" was with the Israelites the great feast of the harvest, or "day of the first fruits" (Exod. 23: 16; Num. 28:26). It was celebrated on the fiftieth day after the Passover. The first Pentecost after Jesus Christ's ascension was the time of the first recorded coming of the Holy Spirit baptism upon His disciples and immediate followers (Acts 2:1-4).

Meta. The metaphysical meaning of the "day of Pentecost" is that in the unfoldment of the spiritual mind there are periods when the ideas that we have meditated on, and accepted as true, spring forth into consciousness, becoming living realities in our life instead of mere mental concepts. In this awakening we get the fruits of the ideas that we have planted in our mind; we have escaped from darkness (Egypt) and have entered into light (Promised Land).

When we fill our mind with true ideas about God and man we should gather our thoughts to one point or "place." That point or place is: "I am that which I conceive myself to be in Spirit." If we proceed in an orderly manner, there will be an inrush of spiritual force from the higher realms of consciousness that will fill the whole body, as described in Acts 2:2.

To the one who is awakened to spiritual reality, the "day of Pentecost" signifies the degree of mind action that brings to consciousness the presence of Spirit as substance.

"They were all together in one place" means the concentration of all the faculties and activities of mind and body in acknowledgment and praise of Spirit. The result of this concentration is that the ordinary thinking mind (conscious mind) and the superconscious mind (perfect Christ mind) blend and there is a descent of spiritual energies into the body—"it filled all the house."

"The multitude came together, and were confounded." Man's devotional nature often lifts him in consciousness until he realizes within himself the urge of Spirit for expression. His conscious, reasoning mind does not understand what is taking place, and he may feel that the condition is the work of evil; but faith (Peter), cultivated through religious effort, gives assurance that all is well and that the new experience is really a greater activity of Spirit in body consciousness.

Christian experience shows that a habit of praying and giving thanks to the Lord daily will finally lead to a state of exhilaration of the whole man similar to that produced by wine. On the day of Pentecost the spiritually exhilarated disciples were thought to be "filled with new wine." This stimulant of Spirit builds up the mind and the body instead of tearing them down, however, and each day adds some new joy.

The ultimate result of this outpouring of Spirit is that the disciples (faculties of mind) receive new power to express Truth ("speak with other tongues"), and go forth proclaiming the salvation of God through Christ, until the whole man is renewed and regenerated.

"The day of Pentecost" signifies a gathering of spiritual powers for the purpose of harvesting the first fruits of Spirit; otherwise, a dedicating of these new forces of Spirit to unselfish service in the vineyard of the Lord.

Spirit always manifests according to the measure of our faith and trust. When our people (thoughts) are gathered in the upper chamber (a place of high spiritual understanding) and are unified in thought and purpose (prayer), the way of the Lord is made straight. We receive the gift of gifts—the baptism of the Holy Spirit.

Penuel, pĕ-nū'-ĕl (Heb.)—*turned toward God; face of God; within the presence of God.*

a The same place as Peniel (Gen. 32:31). **b** A man of the tribe of Judah (I Chron. 4:4). **c** A son of Shashak of the tribe of Benjamin (I Chron. 8:25).

Meta. See PENIEL.

people.

Meta. Our thoughts.

Peor, pē'-ôr (Heb.)—*hiatus; yawning chasm; cleft; opening wide; gaping; ravenous beasts; insatiable longings; an idol of prostitution.*

a A mountain in Moab. Balak, king of Moab, took Balaam to the top of this mountain in an effort to induce him to curse Israel, but Balaam was forced to bless Israel instead (Num. 23:28—24:9). **b** A Moabitish idol (Num. 25:18; Josh. 22:17).

Meta. See BAAL–PEOR.

Perazim, pĕr'-ă-zĭm (Heb.)—*breaches; rents; ruptures; dispersions; assaults; defeats.*

A mount, mentioned in Isaiah 28:21. *Meta.* "For Jehovah will rise up as in mount Perazim." The reference here is to Baal–perazim, a place where David gained a victory over the Philistines (II Sam. 5:20). The significance therefore is the same as that of BAAL–PERAZIM, which see.

peres, pē'-rĕṣ (Heb.)—*cloven; parted; divided; hoofed; horse; Persia.*

A word that appeared in the handwriting on the wall that Daniel interpreted for King Belshazzar of Babylon: "PERES; thy kingdom is divided, and given to the Medes and Persians" (Dan. 5:28).

Meta. Here, PERES refers to the dividing or breaking up of sense confusion (Babylon).

Peresh, pē'-rĕsh (Heb.)—*cleaning; separating; dividing; distinguishing; specifying; excrement; dung,* so called from being thrown off, divided, separated.

Son of Machir by his wife Maacah, of the tribe of Manasseh (I Chron. 7:16).

Meta. That which has served its purpose in the consciousness and organism, and is no longer needed, but is due to pass away (*separating, specifying, excrement*) as a result of the activity of Machir, father of Peresh (meaning *sold, purchased, acquired,* and signifying the right balance that must exist between that which is accepted into the consciousness of the individual and that which is ready to be separated and cast out).

Perez (in A. V., Genesis 38:29, Pharez; in Luke, 3:33, Phares), pē'-rĕz (Heb.)—*broken through; breached; torn asunder; demolished; rent; assaulted; defeated; dispersed; scattered; spread abroad; increased; abundant; redundant.*

A son of Judah by his daughter-in-law Tamar (Gen. 38:29; see I Chronicles 27:3 also).

Meta. Victory through praise, or making a way out of apparent limitation and error and predominating over them by means of prayer and praise. Perez means *broken through, torn asunder, dispersed.* Judah, father of Perez, signifies praise; his mother, Tamar, meaning *palm tree, erect,* represents uprightness and victory. Judah said of her, "She is more righteous than I" (Gen. 38:26).

Perezites (A. V., Pharzites), pĕr'-ĕ-zītes (fr. Heb.)—*of* or *belonging to Perez.*

Descendants of Perez, son of Judah (Num. 26:20).

Meta. Thoughts springing from and belonging to that in consciousness which Perez signifies. (See PEREZ.)

Perez–uzza, pē'-rĕz–ŭz'-zȧ (Heb.)—*breaking of Uzzah; breach of Uzza; defeat of strength; dispersion of strength.*

The place where Uzza was smitten by Jehovah because he put out his hand to steady the Ark (I Chron. 13:11). "And David was displeased, because Jehovah had broken forth upon Uzza: and he called that place Perez–uzza, unto this day."

Meta. Uzza, or Uzzah, means strength. Perez–uzza (meaning *breaking of Uzzah, breach of Uzza, dispersion of strength*), the place where Uzza was smitten by Jehovah because he put forth his hand to steady the Ark, signifies a dividing, and therefore diminishing, of one's consciousness of strength, because of one's acting on the mistaken idea that one can and should support Truth in outer, sense ways, as if Truth needed the help of man to uphold it.

Man should abide in Truth; if he does so, it will support and greatly strengthen him. But if he seeks in human ways to uphold Truth he enters into strife and contention and he reaps the inharmonious result of these errors in a breaking up of his own inner consciousness of strength and poise.

A common mistake among religious people is the idea that the human, fighting, warring spirit is justified in any one if he is seeking by his warlike methods to further the right, if he is seeking to establish and sustain what he believes to be the Christ Truth. This is not true, however. The fighting, contentious attitude is of the Adversary; it is from the adverse consciousness in man and it always results in inharmony to those who indulge in it, regardless of what their purpose is. Thus Uzza was smitten by Jehovah; that is, by divine law. We should not do evil that good may come. Real, true, abiding good is never brought about except by ways that are in accord with the law of love and Truth.

Perez–uzzah, pē'-rĕz–ŭz'-zăh (Heb.)— *breaking of Uzza; breach of Uzza; defeat of strength; dispersion of strength.*

See II Sam. 6:8; I Chron. 13:11.

Meta. See PEREZ–UZZA.

Perga, pĕr'-gȧ (Gk.)—*very earthy.*

A city of Pamphylia, in Asia Minor, where Mark parted from Paul and his company, and returned to Jerusalem (Acts 13:13). Later Paul preached there (Acts 14:25).

Meta. Very earthy, material thoughts. (See PAMPHYLIA.)

Pergamum (A. V., Pergamos), pĕr'-gă-mŭm (Gk.)—*strongly united; closely knit; tough texture; elevated; height; citadel; burg; parchment; skin.*

A town of Mysia in Asia Minor. It was the seat of one of the seven churches that John mentioned in Revelation (Rev. 2:12).

Meta. The intellectual consciousness in man (*strongly united, closely knit, tough texture, elevated, height, citadel*); Pergamum is intelligence.

"I know where thou dwellest, *even* where Satan's throne is" (Rev. 2:13). Satan is the adverse consciousness and Satan's throne, the place where the Ad-versary locates himself, takes his seat, is in the front brain. Adverse reason and thought begin there, in the sense reasoning of man. The Adversary, or Satan, is the adverse mind, or self mind, that which thinks and acts independently of God mind.

Antipas means *against one's native country, against all.* He represents faithfulness to Truth ideals, even to the point of standing against all that does not measure up to those ideals.

Idols (Rev. 2:14) are false beliefs about God. To sacrifice to idols is to give our substance to building up false beliefs. To eat food that has been sacrificed to idols is to appropriate the seeming substance of these false ideas. To commit fornication is to mix our thoughts with error.

The "sword of my mouth" (Rev. 2:16) is the word of Truth. The word of Truth sets the law into action, and thus makes war against the Nicolaitans— mixed thoughts.

The "hidden manna" (Rev. 2:17) is the inner substance, that which comes down out of heaven. We eat of it by affirmation. We affirm that we are fed by the one living substance, and so forth. A "white stone" is faith—Peter. Our consciousness is established in faith in God—a rock foundation, a sure, everlasting place.

The "new name" is the individual's concept of himself. His concept of God and of himself is a little different from that of any other person's. No other knows it, for it is peculiar to the individual. It would mean nothing to any one else. It is changing daily, as the individual's concept of God and of himself changes.

Perida, pĕ-rī'-dȧ (Heb.)—*broken off; separated; dispersed; divided; scattered; seed; grain; kernel; germ.*

A servant of Solomon's, whose "children" returned from the Babylonian captivity (Neh. 7:57). He is called Peruda in Ezra 2:55.

Meta. The main point, or central, vital idea existing in any matter that might come before our inner wisdom for adjustment (*kernel, separated,* a servant of Solomon's; Solomon signifies the reign of peace, and he was noted for his wisdom, for his ability to get at the very heart of any matter and discern the real truth, to judge righteously). The thought of analysis enters into the significance of Perida, and a scattering or sowing abroad, throughout the consciousness, of the central idea that has been gleaned by the analysis of the matter or situation in question.

Perizzite (Perizzites), pĕr'-ĭz-zīte (fr. Heb.)—*countryman; rustic; dweller in the country.*

The Perizzites were ancient inhabitants of Canaan (Gen. 13:7). They lived in the hill country (Josh. 11:3). They were defeated by Judah and Simeon (Judg. 1:3, 4), and the remainder of them were made bond servants by Solomon (I Kings 9:20, 21).

Meta. The Perizzites, like the Canaanites, refer to the elemental life forces in the organism, only elevated to a more exalted plane by the outer, personal man, and more strongly intrenched in the sense consciousness of the individual. (The Perizzites lived in the hill country; they are named with the Canaanites. Adoni–bezek was a king of the Perizzites and the Canaanites. See ADONI–BEZEK.)

Persia, pĕr'-si-à (fr. Skr.—same in Chald. and Heb.)—*cutting; cleaving; dividing; cloven-hoofed; a horse; a horseman; pure; splendid; Aryan; Iran.*

An ancient kingdom in Asia that still exists as a country. The Medes and Persians conquered Babylonia, and Cyrus king of Persia allowed all the captive Jews who wished to do so to return to their own land (II Chron. 36:20-23; Ezra 1:1-8).

Meta. The Medes and Persians are usually, if not always, mentioned together in the Bible. They were one kingdom, and their symbolism is virtually the same: the middle land, or psychic realm; that which lies between the outer and the true inner spiritual consciousness. (See MEDIA and MADAI.) *A horse,* as a meaning of Persia, bespeaks a degree of vital force or power; *cutting* and *dividing* reier to separation. This latter is directly the opposite of the prevailing tendency of the spiritual in man, the tendency to unity; Spirit is

the harmonizing, unifying principle of life. When the psychic dominates in an individual it separates him from, or hinders him from coming into, consciousness of the true peace, unity, and joy that are results of the spiritual life. The psychic, apart from true spiritual understanding and dominion, leads to piercing, cutting, inharmonious experiences.

Persian, pĕr'-si-ăn (fr. Skr.)—*of or belonging to Persia.*

An inhabitant of Persia (Dan. 5:28; Dan. 6:28).

Meta. A thought springing from and belonging to that in consciousness which Persia signifies. (See PERSIA.)

Persis, pĕr'-sĭs (Gk. fr. Pers.)—*Persian; cleaving; cutting; dividing; cloven-hoofed; a horse; a horseman; pure; splendid; Aryan; Iran.*

A Christian at Rome, to whom Paul sent salutation (Rom. 16:12).

Meta. A thought activity in consciousness that is of a separating nature (*cleaving, cutting, dividing*). Its work is to separate good from apparent error in the earth life of man, that the error may be cast out. The first work of Spirit in an individual is always a separating work, since before one can become established in spiritual love, peace, and unity a breaking up of old material ideas and habits must take place; hence the words of Jesus, "Think not that I came to send peace on the earth: I came not to send peace, but a sword" (Matt. 10:34).

Persis is thought to have been a woman; therefore the thought activity that she symbolizes is of the soul. She was a Christian to whom Paul sent salutation: "Salute Persis the beloved, who labored much in the Lord." The definitions, *pure, splendid,* are a result of the separating work that Persis signifies.

Peruda, pĕ-rṳ'-dà (Heb.)—*broken off; separated; dispersed; divided; scattered; seed; grain; kernel; germ.*

The same person as Perida, of Nehemiah 7:57 (Ezra 2:55).

Meta. See PERIDA. The thought of separation that is given in the meaning of these names suggests the ability to analyze a matter, to separate or disunite the parts of it, for the purpose of looking into it from different angles.

Peter, pē'-ter (Gk.)—*hard; compact; strong; firm; unyielding; a large stone; a rock; a cliff.*

Simon Peter, son of Jonas, a disciple of Jesus Christ (Matt. 16:18; Mark 3: 16).

Meta. The spiritual faculty of faith. This disciple's name, Simon (*hearing*), signifying his receptivity and ability to discern Truth, was changed by Jesus to Peter, or Cephas, which is the Greek for the word *rock*. This represents faith in God, strong, unwavering, and enduring. This faith is a necessary foundation for the building up of spiritual consciousness, the church of Christ, in the individual.

Peter (faith) was one of the first disciples that Jesus called. Faith is one of the first spiritual faculties to be called into expression by every one who would follow Jesus in the overcoming life.

The leading characteristic of Peter (faith) before he is firmly established in spiritual consciousness is changeableness. He typifies that state of unsteadiness which fluctuates from the high spiritual to the material, yet with an ever recurring desire for Spirit and for the things of Spirit, which is bound to lead into the light.

Peter, the wavering, denying one, is in reality faith, a rock. When faith works through the intellect it is subject to all the winds and waves of sense thought; but when it lays hold of life and substance, "the gates of Hades shall not prevail against it."

Simon (*hearing*) represents the spiritual receptivity of the mind. Peter (*stone, rock*) represents the ability of the mind to lay hold of and establish ideas in consciousness.

The spiritual import of Peter's repeated affirmations of love, as given in John 21:15-17, is that steadfastness of faith is developed through love. Peter wavered in his faith many times because he was not established in love. He cut off the ear of the servant of the high priest. Jesus had him affirm love three times, that is in spirit, soul, and body. Then he was prepared to serve—to "feed my sheep."

Peter is the impetuous, fiery enthusiasm of the soul, which finds a balance wheel in Andrew, the sturdy strength and endurance of integrity.

Faith is the central faculty in the consciousness of a master. Jesus said that upon it He would build His church, or ecclesia, an aggregation of spiritual ideas.

If Peter (faith) had been allowed to continue to concentrate his energy on the limited ideas of carnality, would he ever have become more than a common fisherman? In other words, if your faith is never exercised on a higher ideal than carnal man manifests, will it ever become spiritually strong?

To walk on the water of troubled thought without sinking requires the established faith of Jesus in the saving power of Spirit. Peter represents faith in its various stages of development (Matt. 14:27-31).

The world is full of ambitious people who seem to have success before them. They start out bravely, but they disappear in the boisterous waves of adversity. If they could but know the mighty power right at hand and could cry out with the Peter faith when they begin to sink, "Lord, save me," they would be raised up and made superior to the seemingly adverse conditions about them.

In the original Greek there is much metaphysical meaning hidden in Matthew 16:18. "Thou art Peter, and upon this rock," reads in the Greek, "Thou art Petros and upon this Petra." Petros is *rock*, masculine, and Petra is *rock*, feminine. The character of man must therefore be masculine and feminine in one. Jesus of Nazareth demonstrated this in His spiritualized body.

The "keys" to this "kingdom of heaven" are in binding (affirmations) and loosing (denials). The "earth" represents the fixed, or concrete, state of consciousness resting in this rock substance of faith. All affirmations and denials made by man from this plane of consciousness control the realm of free ideas or heavens ("heaven" is a mistranslation, and should be "heavens").

Get clearly into your understanding that you are not the faith-thinker, Peter.

You are Jesus; Peter is one of your twelve powers. Before this truth dawns on you you are a carpenter, a builder in the realm of matter. Peter is a fisherman, one who draws his thoughts from the changeable, unstable sea of sense.

When you realize that you are Mind, and that all things are originally generated in the laboratory of Mind, you leave your carpenter's bench and go forth proclaiming the Truth that is revealed to you. You find that your tools in this new field of labor are your untrained faculties. One of the first of these faculties to be brought under your dominion is Peter, the thinking power.

That Peter today stands at the gate of heaven is no mere figure of speech; he always stands there when you have acknowledged the Christ, and he has the "keys of the kingdom of heaven." The keys are the thoughts that he forms, the words that he speaks. He then stands porter at the door of thought and freely exercises that power which the Christ declares: "Whatsoever thou shalt bind on earth shall be bound in heaven; and whatsoever thou shalt loose on earth shall be loosed in heaven."

You can see readily why this faith-thinker, Peter, is the foundation; why the faith faculty should be guarded, directed, and trained. His words are operative on many planes of consciousness, and he will bind you to conditions of servitude if you do not guard his acts closely.

Persons who let their thinking faculty attach itself to the things of earth are limiting or binding their free ideas, or "heaven," and they thereby become slaves to hard, material conditions, gradually shutting out any desire for higher things.

Those who look right through the apparent hardships of earthly environments and persistently declare them not material, but spiritual, are loosing them in the ideal or "heaven," and such conditions must, through the creative power vested in the thinker, eventually rearrange themselves according to his word.

This is especially true of bodily conditions. If you allow Peter to speak of erroneous states of consciousness as true conditions you will be bound to them and you will suffer; but if you see to it that he pronounces them free from errors of sense, they will be "loosed."

Until faith is thoroughly identified with the Christ you will find that the Peter faculty in you is a regular weathercock. It will in all sincerity affirm its allegiance to Spirit, and then in the hour of adversity will deny that it ever knew Spirit. This, however, is in its probationary period. When you have trained it to look to Christ for all things, under all circumstances, it becomes the stanchest defender of the faith.

How necessary it is that you know the important place in your consciousness that this faculty, Peter, occupies! You are the free will, the directive ego, Jesus. You have the problem of life before you—the bringing forth of the Grand Man with His twelve powers.

This is your "church." You are the high priest without beginning of years or end of days, the alpha and the omega; but you cannot do what the Father has set before you, without disciplining your powers. Your thinking faculty is the first to be considered. It is the inlet and the outlet of all your ideas. It is always active, zealous, impulsive, but not always wise. Its nature is to think, and think it will. If you are ignorant of your office —a prince in the house of David—and stand meekly by and let it think unsifted thoughts, your thinking faculty will prove an unruly servant and will produce all sorts of discord.

Its food is ideas—symbolized in the Gospels as fishes—and it is forever casting its net on the right, or the left, for a draft. You alone can direct where its net shall be cast. You are he who says, "Cast the net on the right side." The "right side" is always on the side of Truth, the side of power. Whenever you, the master, are there, the nets are filled with ideas, because you are in touch with the infinite storehouse of wisdom.

You must stay very close to Peter— you must always be certain of his allegiance and love. Test him often. Say to him, "Lovest thou me more than these?" You want his undivided attention. He is inclined to wander; you say that your mind wanders. This is an error. Divine Mind never wanders. The faith-thinker, Peter, wanders; he looks in many directions. He stands at the door of heaven, the harmony within you; the same door is the entrance to the world of sense.

Peter looks within; he also looks without. This is his office, and it is right that he should look both ways; but he must be equalized, balanced. He must look within for his sustenance; he must recognize the Christ before he can draw his net full of fishes.

Keep your eye on Peter. Make him toe the mark every moment. Teach him to affirm Truth over and over again. Say to him "the third time, Simon, *son* of John, lovest thou me?" He may say, "Lord, thou knowest all things; thou knowest that I love thee." This is a very common protest. We hear, in this day of modern metaphysics, that concentration is not necessary; that if one only perceives spiritual Truth the demonstrations will follow.

Jesus Christ gave us many lessons on this point. He knew Peter like a book. He knew that a faculty whose office was so versatile was apt frequently to change its base. When in the exuberance of his allegiance Peter protested that he would lay down his life for Jesus, the Master said, "Verily, verily, I say unto thee, The cock shall not crow, till thou hast denied me thrice."

You must teach Peter to concentrate. Teach him to center on true words. It is through him that you feed your sheep, your other faculties. Keep him right at his task. He is inquisitive, impulsive, and dictatorial, when not firmly directed. When he questions your dominion and tries to dictate the movements of your other powers, put him into line with, "What *is that* to thee? follow thou me."

Descartes said, "I think, therefore I am." This is precisely as if Jesus had said, "I am Peter, therefore I am." This is I AM losing itself in its own creation. Exactly the converse of this statement is true: I am, therefore I think. Thinking is a faculty of the Ego, the omnipotent I AM of each of us. It is a process in mind, the formulating process of

mind, and is under our dominion.

The I AM does not think unless it wills to do so. You can stop all thought action when you have learned to separate your I AM from the thinking faculty. Know this and live in Christ.

Be no longer a slave to the thinking faculty; command it to be still and know. Stand at the center of your being and say, "I and the Father are one." "I am meek and lowly in heart." "All authority hath been given unto me in heaven and on earth." "I AM THAT I AM"—"there is none besides me."

Pethahiah, pĕth-ă-hī'-ăh (Heb.)—*Jehovah has opened; Jah is the open (door); whom Jehovah unbinds; whom Jah sets free; freed by Jehovah.*

a A priest in David's reign (I Chron. 24:16). **b** Other Levites by this name are mentioned in Ezra 10:23 and in Nehemiah 9:5 and 11:24.

Meta. The "way" out of every human, material limitation and apparent error, or inharmony. This "way" is made by Jehovah, I AM, Christ within the individual, acting in conjunction with the universal law of Truth (*Jehovah has opened, Jah is the open door, freed by Jehovah*). "God is faithful, who will not suffer you to be tempted above that ye are able; but will with the temptation make also the way of escape" (I Cor. 10:13).

We should always remember that no temptation comes from God. "Let no man say when he is tempted, I am tempted of God; for God cannot be tempted with evil, and he himself tempteth no man: but each man is tempted, when he is drawn away by his own lust, and enticed" (James 1:13, 14). The true way of deliverance out of every temptation or seeming error, however, is by means of Spirit, Truth; and it is because of his true, inner, abiding spiritual nature that man cannot be overcome of error to the point of annihilation, but is sure to triumph in the end. Truth must endure and must prevail over all.

Pethor, pē'-thôr (Heb. and Chald.)—*extension; table; tablet; interpreting of dreams; prophetic utterances; prophecies.*

A town in Mesopotamia, the home of Balaam the prophet, to whom Balak king of Moab sent messengers to get him to come and curse Israel (Num. 22:5; Deut. 23:4).

Meta. A certain broadening of mental vision (*extension*), and a degree of insight into the power of thoughts and their working out into expression (*prophecies*); also an understanding of thought forms and the ideas back of them (*interpreting of dreams*), but more under the dominion of the sense man than of the spiritual (a town in Mesopotamia, and the home of Balaam; see MESOPOTAMIA and BALAAM).

Pethuel, pĕ-thū'-ĕl (Heb.)—*opened toward God; enlarged of God; open-minded toward God; open expanse of God; open mouth of God; God delivers.*

Father of Joel the prophet (Joel 1:1).

Meta. The understanding of the individual *opened toward God*, and thus broadened and deepened (*enlarged of God*) into a comprehension of man as being a spiritual being, a divine creation, through which God, the Father-Mind, expresses and works (*open mouth of God*). This enlarged understanding brings about deliverance from lesser error ideas and their limited results (*God delivers*).

Peullethai (A. V., Peulthai), pĕ-ŭl-lē'-thāi (Heb.)—*wages of Jehovah; acquisitions of Jah; works of Jah; products of Jehovah; my wages; my works.*

Son of Obed–edom, and a doorkeeper in the tabernacle, in David's reign (I Chron. 26:5).

Meta. Love serving, and guarding the door of one's thoughts (Peullethai was a doorkeeper in the tabernacle, in David's reign. David represents love, and a doorkeeper suggests that which guards one's thoughts. *Wages* and *works* signify service too, as does Obed–edom the father of Peullethai.) *Wages of Jehovah, works of Jah, my wages, my works*, reveal two things: the fact that this idea of loving service is still mixed with personal, carnal beliefs and tendencies that give to service the feeling of burden and labor; and a deep sense of unity in consciousness, a realization by the individual that he and Jehovah are one.

Phanuel, phăn'-ū-ĕl (Gk. fr. Heb.)—*turned toward God; face of God; within*

the presence of God; countenance of God; vision of God; beholden of God; understanding of God.

A man of the tribe of Asher, and father of Anna, a prophetess (Luke 2:36). Penuel is the same name.

Meta. Spiritual understanding, divine insight into spiritual Truth (*face of God, vision of God, understanding of God*); also the inner realization of the divine presence, of having met God face to face and of having succeeded, through prayer, in attaining the divine favor and blessing that has been sought (*turned toward God, within the presence of God, beholden of God*). (See PENUEL and PENIEL.)

Pharaoh, phā'-raōh (Heb. fr. Egypt.)—*the king; the Ra; the sun.*

King of Egypt; the name, or title, of Egyptian kings as mentioned in the Bible (Gen. 12:15; 41; Exod. 1 to 14:30; I Kings 3:1).

Meta. Pharaoh means *the sun*. He is ruler of the solar plexus, the sun center in the subconscious mind. This is obscurity, or Egypt, to the conscious mind. Pharaoh's (*the sun's*) being in Egypt shows us that the light of the sun of righteousness is veiled by our life on the lower or sense plane. Joseph's being sold into Egypt signifies that our spiritual consciousness is being bartered away that we may enjoy the things of sense, and that the life forces are being spent in their gratification.

Pharaoh also signifies the whole house, or whole body consciousness; he is the force that rules the body under the material regime. His being ruler of Egypt means that he rules in obscurity. Thus we understand that this one to whom Joseph comes is not in divine understanding, yet is receptive. When the Lord shows him coming events in his dreams he seeks to know the true interpretation, and when he is convinced he makes the new state of consciousness ruler next to him over his whole kingdom.

Pharaoh can also be said to represent the conservator of the substance and life in the organism, but his consciousness covers the activities of the natural man only. His dreams of the seven full ears of corn and seven thin and blasted ears, and of the seven well-favored and fat-fleshed kine, and the seven ill-favored and lean-fleshed kine, point to this. The following is the significance of his dream:

Egypt has a specific significance in the body consciousness, and refers here to the subjective mind. There flows into the body functions an energy that especially stimulates the generative center when the subconsciousness is quickened by Truth (when Joseph goes down into Egypt). This lasts about seven years, or has seven degrees of activity. There is a great increase of vitality. This is the symbolism of the seven fat kine and the seven full ears. Those who are wise conserve this energy and store it in the consciousness, because there is always a reaction proportionate to the action. This is a law that holds good in all forms of energy. When the generated force of action is properly conserved, however, the reaction is not felt. When we let this higher or Joseph state of consciousness rule in our members the Lord shows us just how to handle the situation, and we make a storage battery of the "cities" or ganglion centers throughout the consciousness.

Moses and Pharaoh represent two forces at work in the consciousness—especially that part pertaining to the body. Moses represents the evolutionary force of new ideas that have grown in the subconscious mind, that are tugging at the old states of limitation and material ignorance and trying to rise into a higher life expression. Pharaoh represents the force that rules the body under the material *régime*. The Lord (Jehovah, as given in the American Standard Version) is here the universal law, the impulse of which is always upward and onward, yet seeking always to preserve equilibrium.

It is found by those who are undergoing the regenerative process, which the Scriptures symbolically illustrate, that these two forces are constantly at work in consciousness, one holding to old ideas and striving to perpetuate them in form, and the other idealizing the new and bending every effort to break away from material bondage and rise above its limitations. Paul says, "The flesh lusteth against the Spirit, and the Spirit against the flesh." Looking at it from the personal standpoint, we are likely to cry out in this struggle, "Who shall deliver me out of the body of this death?" But as philosophers in the understanding of the law of change we balance ourselves between these two forces and let them work out under the equilibrium of the universal preserver of all forms, which is the Lord, or Jehovah.

Here is consolation for those who chafe under the whips and the bonds of the regenerative law. They think that the defeats that they suffer and the snail's pace at which they apparently creep along are indications that they are off the track. This is not true; they have only to persevere and wait patiently upon the Lord. If the spiritual could have the ascendancy in you instantly it would destroy your body entirely and you would be left without a working vehicle. The purpose of the spiritual thoughts in the body (Children of Israel down in Egypt) is to raise it up, gradually to infuse into it a more enduring life and substance.

When you affirm the spirituality of the body and yearn for release from the bondage of materiality you are making demands on Pharaoh. Then, in fear that he will all at once lose his hold upon life, he hardens his heart—and sometimes the Lord, or Jehovah, the universal law of equilibrium, hardens it for him (Exod. 8:15; 9:12). Then there seems a failure to attain that which you have tried to demonstrate; but a step has been taken in the all-round evolution of the body and you will find that you are gradually becoming stronger both physically and spiritually. (See EGYPT, JOSEPH, and MOSES in studying the symbology of Pharaoh.)

Pharaoh Hophra, phā'-raōh hŏph'-rå (Heb. fr. Egypt.)—*priest of the sun; priest of Ra.*

A king of Egypt, whom Jeremiah prophesied against (Jer. 44:30).

Meta. A ruling religious thought of the Egyptian phase of consciousness in man. (See EGYPT and PHARAOH.)

Pharaoh–neco (A. V., Pharaoh–necho), phā'-raōh–nē'-eð (Heb. fr. Egypt.) —*Pharaoh the smitten; stricken with the* *sun; Pharaoh the lame.*

The same person as Neco, a king of Egypt when Josiah was king of Judah. Josiah was killed in waging battle against this king (Jer. 46:2).

Meta. See PHARAOH and NECO.

Pharaoh–necoh (A. V., Pharaoh–nechoh), phā'-raōh–nē'-cŏh (Heb. fr. Egypt.)—*Pharaoh the smitten; stricken with the sun; Pharaoh the lame.*

The same person as Pharaoh–neco and Neco (II Kings 23:29).

Meta. See PHARAOH and NECO.

Pharisees, phăr'-ĭ-sēeş (Gk. fr. Heb.) —*separatists; separated; distinct; accurate; literalist,* i. e., *separating word for word.*

A Jewish sect that flourished at the time of Jesus Christ and His apostles. They were opposed to Jesus and His teaching (Matt. 5:20).

Meta. The Pharisees (Matt. 12:24) were the religiously educated of Jesus' day, and to their minds all who claimed to do the works of the Lord were spurious unless they were members of the Pharisee cult. No matter how good the work of the outsider, the Pharisee always attributed it to an evil power.

In individual consciousness Pharisees represent thoughts that arise out of the subconsciousness, binding man to external forms of religion without giving him understanding of their real meaning (John 3:1).

The Pharisees, the religious thoughts pertaining to the realm of form, do not know that Truth comes into expression in the consciousness through understanding; they seek a "sign" in the external realm. No sign of the presence of Christ can be given to the pharisaical state of mind, for the things of Spirit are spiritually discerned (Mark 8:11, 12).

In Mark 7:1, the Pharisees represent the state of consciousness that is concerned with the formalities and customs of the external realm. The scribes represent fixed ideas built up in consciousness through one's adhering to tradition and superstition.

Mark 7:2: The disciples of Christ—that is, the thoughts that have been established in the Christ consciousness—become a law to themselves.

Mark 7:3, 4: Excessive thought relating to the realm of form leads to narrowness, bondage, and enslavement. "The letter killeth, but the Spirit giveth life."

Mark 7:5: The unillumined thoughts in consciousness must look to the Christ mind for guidance and instruction.

Mark 7:6: Isaiah means salvation and is the freeing principle in mind that foreshadows the coming of the Christ and discerns the thoughts that are not established in living substance.

Mark 7:7: The doctrines and precepts of men that have their foundation in personal opinion or traditional custom are profitless. To worship God is to conform to an entirely new principle and teaching. God is Spirit and must be worshiped "in spirit and truth."

Mark 7:8: The commandments of God embody living, harmonious ideas. The traditions of men are only symbols of the real principles, and lack the substance of Spirit.

Mark 7:9: The adverse consciousness in man rejects the Christ; man, in a degree, recognizes that this is so. Jesus imparted a life principle direct to the people through His teaching, and only by keeping His words can the adverse consciousness be overthrown.

Mark 7:10: Moses represents the phase of consciousness that is concerned with the moral law. This serves a purpose in disciplining the thoughts, but is only a preparation for the advent of spiritual law.

Mark 7:11, 12: The pharisaical state of mind casts all responsibility on God and refuses to "do aught" for the creative Father-Mother principle, through which spiritual growth is set into activity.

Mark 7:13: The word is the seed through which increase is rendered to God. When man fails to use the word, believing that divine law will adjust his consciousness, he renders "void the word of God."

In Luke 18:9-14 the "Pharisee" in consciousness is a selfish state of mind produced by the intellect. It is this self-satisfied mental attitude that causes man to lose sight of the real needs of soul and body, and finally results in dissolution of its own false structure, often at the expense of man's body.

The "publican" is the spirit of meekness that opens man to the inflow of cleansing, illuminating Truth. "He that humbleth himself," has reference to the crucifixion of personality. One who has crucified or humbled himself is "afar off," but empty and receptive to the love and wisdom of God, while the consciousness is being illumined and the Christ exalted.

Pharisees are religionists who have become unbalanced through giving undue attention to the forms of religious rites. Such persons lose sight of the principle back of the symbols. They go through the motions of one living a spiritual life, but the living substance is not present.

There are more Pharisees today than in the time of Jesus, but they have changed their symbols. Standards of life and action for Christian people have gone through many transformations, but the crystallizations in the realm of forms are found on every side. The omnipresent God of Abraham, Isaac, and Jacob is forgotten and ten thousand symbols of Him are worshiped instead (Mark 7:1-13).

Denial of the world of forms, specifically and as a whole, is the remedy for the Pharisee.

The Pharisee of Luke 7:36-39 and 14:1-13 is the good that is seen of men.

A Pharisee observes the forms but neglects the spirit of religion. Henry Ward Beecher said: "A Pharisee is one who worships instruments. Whoever believes that churches, or books, or institutions, or customs, are more valuable than men is a Pharisee."

You will have more trouble with your sectarian thoughts (Pharisees and chief priests) than with all others. They are very close to the spiritual realm in your consciousness, and therefore more powerful than the more material thoughts (John 7:32).

The old-established religious thoughts belonging to the intellectual domain never miss an opportunity to reason with and to dispute every true, spiritual idea that is presented to the consciousness. This is symbolized by the Pharisees, who would keep only the letter of the law. When the spirit of the law is taught it overthrows the outer forms and ceremonies that belong to the letter; so they who are strict in observing the letter usually oppose the spirit of the law. The Truth that the higher self is always bringing to every part of the individual is missed by the pharisaical phase of consciousness.

The Pharisees are exact in performing every little detail of religious acts, but they lack love and mercy, the deeper and higher consciousness of Truth. The intellect must be enlightened by the Christ mind, in order that it may be saved from the woes that are brought upon it by the reaction of the condemnation that it has bestowed upon others. When this enlightenment comes, the spirit of mercy and forgiveness enters into the religious ideas of the intellectual man and the reason will then no longer be inclined to condemn; neither will it lie in wait to assail the Spirit of truth at every point.

Those who interpret the Scriptures literally, those who personalize God, Christ, Devil, and localize heaven and hell, are the Pharisees of the present time.

It is the Pharisee in us that causes us to love the forms and ceremonies of religion. It is the Pharisee in us that refuses to go deep into the consciousness and cleanse the inner man. It is the Pharisee in us that is ambitious for temporal honors and loves to be saluted with high-sounding titles. It is the pharisaical thought that exalts and sustains personality.

We can overcome the Pharisee in ourselves by receiving continuously new inspiration from the original fount of being within us, and by refusing to be bound by old, effete, religious thoughts (Luke 11:42-54).

Jesus taught that the kingdom of God would not come in a form whereby it could be observed externally; that men should not look here or there in the outer for it, because it is within. But the old established religious thoughts that belong solely to the intellectual consciousness, the Pharisees, cannot comprehend the inner overcoming, and the establishing of Truth in consciousness that causes one to become aware of the kingdom. As soon as a person attains a certain degree of intellectual understanding of Truth he becomes self-righteous, pharisaical; he is inclined to think that he has all of Truth and should demonstrate at once the fullness of the kingdom in his outer life. However, he must learn to use aright the beginning of Truth that has been revealed to him, that he may become worthy of a place in the kingdom.

Those who come into the spiritual understanding and practice of Truth outgrow their old pharisaical beliefs that forms and ceremonies are fundamental in religious worship. As the scribes and the chief priests and the Pharisees of the Jewish people ever sought to trap and destroy Jesus, however, so the old established religious thoughts of the intellect are always trying to find some discrepancy in the inspirations of the great Teacher. The coldness and the hardness of formal religion would kill out the understanding of divine love and wisdom, if they could (Luke 20:19-26).

Pharpar, phär'-par (Heb.)—*borne rapidly; running swiftly; swift fruition; swift.*

A river of Damascus. Naaman thought that he might as well wash in this river to be healed of his leprosy, instead of washing in the Jordan (II Kings 5:12).

Meta. A current of thought in the intellectual realm of man's consciousness (a river symbolizes a current of thought, and Damascus in Syria is of the intellect guided by the senses). Outer, intellectual ideas and activities—apart from the real life current in the organism, which is signified here by the river Jordan, in which Naaman bathed and was healed, and the spiritual power of the I AM (Elisha)—have no real healing virtue. They cannot cleanse the soul and restore the body to wholeness. To think thoughts and speak words that will produce *swift fruition* in abiding health, the intellect must be quickened and directed by the inner Spirit of truth, since in that is the healing power. The outer man always wants to reap good results very quickly, and he does not see why the conditions

that must be met are necessary.

Phicol (A. V., Phichol), phī'-cŏl (Heb.)—*mouth of all; spokesman for all; all-commanding; every tongue; the whole speech.*

The captain of the host of Abimelech king of Gerar (Gen. 21:22). He was a Philistine.

Meta. The seeming all-sufficiency of the sense consciousness in man at a certain stage of his unfoldment or evolution (*mouth of all, spokesman for all, all-commanding, every tongue, the whole speech,* captain of the host of Abimelech king of Gerar, of the Philistines, Philistines signifying sense consciousness). At this stage of his unfoldment the individual seems to live wholly in the outer sense realm and to understand, perceive, and judge entirely according to the seeing of his outer eyes and the hearing of his physical ears. Thus the senses are *all-commanding* in his life; he gives all his thoughts and faculties over to the extension and support of the senses, and taboos everything of a higher, spiritual nature.

Philadelphia, phĭl-ă-dĕl'-phĭ-a (Gk.)—*brotherly love; loving as brethren; love of brothers (or sisters); fraternal love.*

The church in Philadelphia was one of the seven churches mentioned by John in Revelation. Philadelphia was a city of Lydia in Asia Minor (Rev. 3:7).

Meta. The love center in consciousness, or love expressing (*brotherly love*).

The church in Philadelphia is the love faculty, or the assembly of love thoughts in consciousness that make up the love faculty. He who has the "key of David" (Rev. 3:7) is the I AM. This I AM in its highest aspect is Christ; it has more or less of the personal element in those who are not fully lifted into the Christ consciousness. If the I AM love thoughts (or assembly) are dominated by selfishness they become "the synagogue of Satan" (Rev. 3:9). In the same text the statement, "them that say they are Jews, and they are not," means the selfish dominance of love that thinks itself to be the real thing, but that is not.

Lack of love causes the "trial" that is coming upon the inhabited earth (Rev. 3:10). From the synagogue of Satan come strife, hatred, and warring thoughts. Out of the heart proceed evil thoughts. Love will harmonize the warring conditions in our own consciousness and in all the earth. Harmony through love begins in the individual.

The "name of my God" (Rev. 3:12) is love. "The name of the city of my God, the new Jerusalem, which cometh down out of heaven from my God," is peace, the consciousness of peace, which comes about through love—I AM peace.

Philemon, phī-lē′-mŏn (Gk.)—*loving; affectionate.*

A wealthy man of Colossæ, a city of Phrygia in Asia Minor. He was the owner of Onesimus, a slave, and both of them became converted to Christianity. One of Paul's epistles was written to Philemon (Philem. 1).

Meta. A thought that belongs to the love nature in man, and becomes deeply attached to the Christ Truth (*loving, affectionate,* a convert to Christianity). This thought is established in substance and power (Philemon was a wealthy man, and a man of position).

The lesson that is being worked out through Paul's appeal to Philemon for clemency toward Onesimus the slave is the truth that, in spite of certain limitations in its activity, the word can, through the forgiving love of God, bring about freedom in some planes of consciousness.

The greatest slavery in the world today is the ignorant slavery to sin. "Every one that committeth sin is the bondservant of sin." True freedom comes through love guided by the reconciling power of the word. Paul's letter to Philemon is the word expressed in love, justice, and righteousness, which always bring forth fruit after their kind.

Philetus, phī-lē′-tŭs (Gk.)—*amiable; lovable; beloved.*

Evidently a Christian convert. Paul warned Timothy against him because of his erroneous teaching about the resurrection (II Tim. 2:17).

Meta. A thought in the higher, religious consciousness of man that is agreeable, lovable, harmonious, and pleasing (*amiable, lovable, beloved*). It is established in love, but has not unified itself with wisdom. It has not, therefore, as yet acquired true understanding of the resurrection and life in Christ. Thus it is in error; it misses the mark and is a hindrance to faith in the teaching that resurrection and life are now demonstrable.

Philip, phĭl′-ip (Gk.)—*lover of horses.*

a One of the twelve apostles of Jesus Christ (John 1:43); Philip the evangelist (Acts 6:5; 8:5). b Two other men by this name are also mentioned (Matt. 14: 3; Luke 3:1).

Meta. The power faculty in man. It functions through the power center in the body, at the root of the tongue. Through Philip the word is charged with power (John 6:7).

Philip means a *lover of horses.* We gather from this that he represents the faculty in us that, through love, masters the vital forces; hence we identify Philip as power. Philip exercises his power through the spiritual word, which is outwardly made manifest in speech (Acts 8:4-8); he represents the power of the home missionary movement.

Power is one branch of the great tree named "life" in Genesis. The body of the life tree is the spinal cord, over which the motor system, with branches to every part of the organism, exercises its nervous energy.

The power center in the throat controls all the vibratory energies of the organism. It is the open door between the formless and the formed worlds of vibrations pertaining to the expression of sound. Every word that goes forth receives its specific character from the power faculty. When Jesus said, "The words that I have spoken unto you are spirit, and are life," He meant that through the spoken word He conveyed an inner spiritual quickening quality that would enter the mind of the recipient and awaken the inactive spirit and life. When the voice has united with the life of the soul it takes on a sweetness and a depth that one feels and remembers; the voice that lacks this union is unpleasing and superficial. Voice culture may give one tone brilliancy, but there never was a great singer who lacked the soul contact. More attractive still is the voice of one who has made union with Spirit and can say with Jesus, "Heaven and earth shall pass away, but my words shall not pass away."

When we understand this power of the word, we have the key to the perpetuity of sacred writings. According to tradition, all the writings of the Hebrew Bible were destroyed; but they were restored by Esdras, who remembered in his heart and rewrote them. Modern discoveries in the realm of mind explain in a measure this mystical statement. We know now that every word that man utters makes an imprint in the astral ethers, and where there is consciousness of God life in the mind of the speaker his words become living identities and are preserved throughout the ages. Any one who develops sufficient spiritual power may enter this book of life within the cosmic mind and read out of its pages.

In the kingdom of God within man's consciousness the power disciple (Philip) plays an important part in controlling the expression of the many emotions, inspirations, and thoughts of the soul. The voice is the most direct avenue of this expression, when man has dominion over the emotions and feelings from which the original impulse has arisen. The power of love makes the voice rich, warm, and mellow. One can set love free in the soul by cultivating a loving attitude toward everybody and everything. One may gain strength by silently speaking words of strength to each of the disciples sitting on the twelve thrones within one. Power swings open all the doors of soul and body. When one feels vital and energetic the voice is strong and vibrant and brilliant. When the soul is sorrowful the body weakens and the voice betrays its lack by its mournful intonation. One can feel the power of unity with the higher self through the vibrations of power in the throat more quickly than in any other way. This reveals that ideas rule the man. Jesus affirmed that all power, or authority, was given to Him in heaven (mind) and on earth (body). When Jesus made this affirmation He undoubtedly realized His innate spiritual dominion.

When He consciously attuned His spiritual identity to soul and body He was conscious of an influx of power and His hearers said that He taught them as one having authority, and not as their scribes.

In the process of regeneration the consciousness of power ebbs and flows, because the old and the new tides of thought act and react in the conscious and the subconscious realms of mind. However, when a disciple realizes his unity with Omnipotence he is but little disturbed by the changes that go on in his mind and his body. He knows that his spiritual dominion is established, and this firm conviction expresses itself in firm words. He realizes,

"Men may come and men may go,
But I go on forever."

Jesus said, "Heaven and earth shall pass away, but my words shall not pass away." Here is evidence of spiritual power united with the idea of eternity. This union destroys the thought of years and of declining power; when awakened in those who have believed in age it will transform them.

No great vocalist ever lived but had inner spiritual power as an abiding conviction. This is strikingly illustrated today in the indomitable persistency and power with which a very famous opera star overcame big obstacles. In the early stages of her career she was discouraged by opera managers. They told her that she could never make a success, but she persevered in her unconquerable spirit; she never gave up, and so she finally mastered every defect of her voice. This is a wonderful lesson to those who apparently are meeting discouragements in their ongoing, those who are tempted to succumb to circumstances and conditions in body and environment. Take the words of Paul, "None of these things move me," and make affirmations of your spiritual supremacy mountain high.

Some metaphysical schools warn their students against the development of power because they fear that it will be used in selfish ways. It doubtless is true that the personal ego sometimes lays hold of the power faculty and uses it for selfish aggrandizement, and we can readily see how what is called the Devil had origin. To be successful in the use of the power of Being, one must be obedient in exercising all the ideas that make man. If there is an assumption of personal power, Satan falls "as lightning from heaven," and the adverse or carnal mind goes to and fro in the earth. Casting out these demons of personality formed a large part of the work of Jesus; those who follow Him in the regeneration are confronted with similar states of mind, and find it necessary to cast out the great demon selfishness, which claims to have power but "is a liar, and the father thereof."

No great overcoming work can be done by the disciple without a realization of spiritual power, dominion, mastery. Then do not fear to develop your power and mastery. They are not to be exercised on other people, but on yourself. "He that ruleth his spirit" is more powerful "than he that taketh a city." Alexander the Great cried because there were no more worlds to conquer, yet he had not conquered his own appetite, and died a drunkard at the age of thirty-two. Today men are striving to acquire power through money, legislation, and manmade government, and are falling short at every turn because they have not mastered themselves.

Man is the power of God in action. To man is given the highest power in the universe, the conscious power of thought. There is a universal creative force that urges man forward to the place where he recognizes the creative power of his individual thought. This force is elemental and all its attributes come under the dominion of man. When he cooperates with divine principle man sits on the throne of his authority and the elemental force is subject to him.

The power and the authority that are to rule in the kingdom of heaven are dependent on man's authority and his rule in the earth. Jesus said to Peter, "Whatsoever thou shalt bind on earth shall be bound in heaven; and whatsoever thou shalt loose on earth shall be loosed in heaven." If man binds or controls the appetites, passions, and emotions in the body (earth) he establishes an ability and power to control the same forces in the realms universal, out of which the heavens are formed. When he attains freedom in the expression of the qualities inherent in soul and body he expands in power and can set free the elements universal and restore equilibrium between heaven and earth, or between Spirit and seeming matter. When enough people have attained this power the "new heaven and . . . new earth," described in the 21st chapter of Revelation, will appear.

Each individual who complies with the law of overcoming may enter into power and sit at the right hand with Jesus on His throne. It should not be overlooked by the elect that the Scripture reads, "He that overcometh shall inherit these things." To overcome and sit with Jesus on His throne means that man shall overcome as He overcame. Jesus overcame the world, the flesh, and the Devil. To overcome the world one must be proof against all its false allurements of riches and honor. To overcome the flesh one must spiritualize the five-sense man until material consciousness is raised to spiritual consciousness in feeling, tasting, seeing, hearing, and smelling. This will result in complete mastery of the body and in its final redemption from death. The Devil is the personal ego that has in its freedom formed a state of consciousness peculiarly its own. When man lives wholly in the consciousness that personality has built up, he is ruled by the "mind of the flesh," which is the Adversary, or Satan. The mystery of the cross is hid in the overcoming of Satan. When the I AM identity that is man becomes so involved in its personal affairs that it ignores God, it lays hold of the body and rules all the bodily functions. When this rule is broken by the power of the Christ there is a crucifixion. It may seem that Jesus is being crucified, but this is seeming, only. Death comes to the Judas consciousness, which has a devil. The body, being closely connected with this usurping mind, passes through suffering and apparent death. This is no more than appearance, because the higher principle, the Christ, resurrects the body and transmutes it to higher spiritual substance, and it enters into harmony, or heaven.

The climax of man's power and dominion is set forth in the resurrection and ascension of the type-man, Jesus.

Philippi, phĭ-lĭp'-pī (Gk.)—*city of Philip,* i. e., Philip I of Macedon; *city of the lover of horses.*

A city of Macedonia (Acts 16:12).

Meta. Philip symbolizes power. Philippi (*city of Philip, city of the lover of horses*) signifies a thought center of power and vigor in consciousness.

Philippi was a city in Macedonia where the proconsul or governor of Macedonia lived. It is therefore the center of the executive faculty of that in us signified by Macedonia: *burning adoration.* It is necessary to stir up this fiery power in the man when he gets into negative states of consciousness. The vision of the man imploring, "Come over into Macedonia, and help us," is the discernment of this inner fervor, which needs stirring up. A certain fiery fervor is necessary in order to establish faith and persistency in barren, weak states of consciousness, such as those suggested by Phrygia, Galatia, and Asia. (See Acts 16:6-10.)

Another metaphysical interpretation of Philippi and Macedonia is given as follows: Philippi was the chief city in Macedonia. Macedonia represents the business mind, and Philippi means getting gain, which is the chief motive of business. It is very natural that in this place (state of consciousness) there is "no man likeminded, who will care truly for your state. For they all seek their own, not the things of Jesus Christ" (Phil. 2:20-21). And so Timothy was sent to the assembly of believers at Philippi. The thoughts wherein love of gain is uppermost need Timothy (inspired reason united with faith) to instruct them concerning spiritual substance and life (the true riches) and their use.

Philippians, phĭ-lĭp'-pĭ-ăns (fr. Gk.). People who lived in Philippi (Phil. 4:15). It was to the Christians at Philippi that Paul wrote his Epistle to the Philippians.

Meta. Thoughts springing from and belonging to that in consciousness signified by the city of Philippi. (See PHILIPPI.)

Philistia, phĭ-lĭs'-tĭ-à (fr. Heb.)—*rolling about; transition; migration; emigration; wandering; deviating from a true course; rejected; infidel.*

The land of the Philistines (Psalms 60:8; 83:7).

Meta. The sense realm in man. *Rolling about, transition, migration, wandering, deviating from a true course, rejected, infidel,* definitions of Philistia, reveal the changeableness, the transitoriness, the error, of the understanding that is founded on the perception of the senses functioning in the outer and established in material belief. The manifestations of the understanding that is based on the senses are just as temporary as the ideas back of them.

Philistines (in A. V., Genesis 10:14, Philistim; this form is the correct one), phĭ-lĭs'-tĭneş (fr. Heb.)—*rolling about; transitory; migrating; emigrating; moving to and fro; wandering; deviating from a true course; rejected; infidels.*

Inhabitants of Philistia; a tribe or nation of people in Palestine that was always at enmity with the Israelites, and against whom the Israelites were almost continually warring (Gen. 21:32; 26:1-18; Ex. 13:17; Josh. 13:2, 3).

Meta. Strangers, emigrants, foreigners; forces foreign to Spirit. The five great cities of the Philistines ruled by "lords" mean the five senses under the dominion of thoughts foreign to Spirit. The Philistines were opposed to all true spiritual discipline; they worshiped strange gods in the form of animals, and resorted to all kinds of sorcery and soothsaying.

When the five-sense man gives himself up to sense desires and makes no attempt to live in spiritual consciousness he is ruled by Philistine thoughts. This is a suppression of the real man, and if such living is continued the soul will finally be crowded out of its rightful domain, the land of Israel.

The two armies of I Samuel 17, the Israelites and the Philistines, represent two aggregations of thoughts in the mind of every individual: those that know and strive to follow the Truth, and those that are in open enmity and violent opposition to everything Godlike. In metaphysics we call these armies Truth and error. The error army sometimes seems the larger and stronger, because it is principally in the visible or outer expression, while the army of Truth is made up of spiritual, invisible forces.

We are often scared, even terrified, at the giant proportions of some leading thought on the error side, represented by Goliath. Our Goliath may be different from that of our neighbor, but it boasts and brags daily of its strength, and intimidates us with its show of power. People who depend on the resources of materiality, as Saul had come to do, often give up in despair when these thoughts of sense continue their bullying methods day and night. There is but one way to meet and subdue them, and that is through the power of love (represented by David, the little, ruddy-faced shepherd boy). When he suggested that he could, single-handed, vanquish the giant of the Philistines, he was ridiculed by his companions. Saul was grasping at straws and was willing to try anything. He put his own armor on David, but it did not fit, and was evidently cumbersome. David refused to wear it, saying that he had not "proved it." This illustrates the necessity of our doing things in our own natural, original way. People who try to fight their battles by using the methods of others usually fail.

David, unlike Saul, did not depend on the army, but proclaimed the hosts of the Lord as his resource. He evidently understood the power of the word, and met with strong denials and with affirmations of efficiency every boast of the giant. He was fearless, and his assurance led him to victory. An open, verbal statement of Truth will often demonstrate, where the silent thought will fail. The Philistines represent the most external thoughts, and they respond most quickly to the spoken word.

The smooth stone that David used is the rock of faith, and the sling is the assurance and force with which the mind sends it forth to do its perfect work of destroying error in the stronghold of error thought, the forehead.

The lesson may be summed up as an illustration of the necessity for having boldness, courage, and fearlessness in demonstrating Truth. Some metaphysicians think that sympathetic love will bring results, but they are often disappointed. Love must have the assurance of Truth, and must send Truth forth with confidence, courage, and power in both thought and word.

The meaning of I Samuel 7:7, "And when the Philistines heard that the children of Israel were gathered together to Mizpah, the lords of the Philistines went up against Israel," is that whenever the Children of Israel (spiritual thoughts) determine to be loyal to Jehovah and make a stand for Truth they have to meet the onslaught of the Philistines (sense consciousness).

Ferrar Fenton gives this translation of I Samuel 7:8: "The Children of Israel consequently said to Samuel, Word for us with a cry to the Ever-living our God, that He may save us from the hand of the Philishtim!" The wording of this is almost identical with that which a modern metaphysician would use in asking a teacher to work for him against error.

"Jehovah thundered with a great thunder on that day upon the Philistines, and discomfited them; and they were smitten down before Israel" (I Samuel 7:10). This means that while Samuel was mentally working and calling on the Jehovistic power, the vibratory energies became so strong that they dissolved the aggregation of error thoughts, which then passed away.

Philologus, phĭ-lŏl′-ŏ-gŭs (Gk.)—*lover of the word; lover of speech; erudite; learned; fond of talk; talkative; argumentative.*

A Roman Christian to whom Paul sent salutation (Rom. 16:15).

Meta. The tendency of the intellectual thought in one to reason things out and to argue, even after one has been spiritually quickened and awakened in some degree. The intellect loves and holds to the outer expression of ideas in words rather than to the inner ideas themselves, and to their source: Spirit (*lover of the word, lover of speech, erudite, learned, talkative, argumentative,* a Roman Christian, Rome referring to the head and the will, and a Christian referring to a thought awakened to the Christ Truth).

Phinehas, phĭn'-ĕ-hăs (Heb.)—*oracle; mouth of prophecy; mouth of the serpent; mouth of brass; brazen-faced; bold; unabashed.*

a Son of Eleazar and grandson of Aaron (Exod. 6:25). **b** Son of Eli the priest (I Sam. 1:3). **c** Father of Eleazar, a Levite, who returned from the Babylonian captivity (Ezra 8:33).

Meta. Spiritual revelation and power (*oracle, mouth of prophecy*). It is necessary for the thoughts that are awakening to spiritual revelation and power to be disciplined and directed intelligently in all their ways. If they become lifted up in spiritual pride, or become selfish and act on a purely material plane because of listening to outer sense wisdom (*mouth of the serpent*), they become all that is signified by *mouth of brass, brazen-faced, bold, unabashed,* harsh, shameless, insolent, presumptuous. (See HOPHNI, brother of the Phinehas who was Eli's son.)

Phlegon, phlē'-gŏn (Gk.)—*burning; fired; zealous.*

A Christian at Rome to whom Paul sent salutation (Rom. 16:14).

Meta. Ardent zeal, expressing in behalf of Truth (*burning, fired, zealous,* a Christian to whom Paul sent salutation).

Phœbe (A. V., Phebe), phœ'-bê (Gk.) —*bright; shining; brilliant; radiant; pure.*

A "servant" or "deaconess" (margin) of the church at Cenchreæ in Corinth, to whom Paul sent salutation in his letter to the Romans (Rom. 16:1).

Meta. The pure Christ light and love radiating throughout the consciousness (*bright, shining, radiant, pure,* a Christian of the church at Cenchreæ in Corinth. (See CENCHREÆ and CORINTH.)

Phœnicia (in A. V., Acts 21:2, Phenicia; in Acts 11:19 and 15:3, Phenice), phœ-nĭ'-ci-à (Gk.)—*land of the phœnix; land of palms; land of palm trees; blood-red; purple.*

Phœnix relates to the palm branch or the palm tree as an emblem of resurrection, from the ancient phœnix of Egyptian mythology that arose triumphant from its own ashes. The Greeks called the red and purple dye introduced from Phœnicia "phœnis," which holds to the same root. The phœnix was regarded as a manifestation of Ra and so became the symbol of resurrection, continuing to serve the early Christians as a symbol of the risen Lord.

A country to the north of Palestine and bordering on the Mediterranean Sea. Tyre and Sidon were its chief cities (Acts 11:19).

Meta. Conquering power, also resurrection into newness of life. (*Land of palm trees, blood-red, purple,* palm trees denote conquest and victory over error, even to the fullness of the resurrection life. Purple denotes power, and red denotes life activity; both enter into the idea and manifestation of resurrection.) This resurrecting power and dominion in Phœnicia, however, is hid under and suppressed by sense thought and belief. It must be lifted to a higher plane of understanding, realization, and use before it can become abiding in the consciousness of the individual and work for harmony and true upbuilding in his mind, body, and affairs. (See TYRE and SIDON, the chief cities of Phœnicia.)

Phœnix (A. V., Phenice), phœ'-nĭx (Gk.)—*the bennu bird; palm branch; palm tree; purple; blood-red.*

"A haven of Crete" that the master of the ship in which Paul was being taken to Rome tried to reach in order that they might winter there; but they were driven out of their course by a storm that arose, and were shipwrecked (Acts 27:12).

Meta. Crete (*carnal, fleshly*) signifies the material, sensual, worldly consciousness in man as opposed to the spiritual. Phœnix, a haven of Crete (*palm tree, purple, blood-red*), would signify a degree of conquest and power, also of renewal of life activity, expressing in the carnal consciousness of the individual. (See PHŒNICIA.)

Phrygia, phrȳg'-ĭ-à (Gk.)—*dried; parched; barren; lifeless; stubble; brush.*

A district, or province, in Asia Minor. Men from this place heard the Gospel taught in their own language at Pentecost (Acts 2:10). Paul was at first forbidden of Spirit to preach in Asia; therefore he simply passed through

Phrygia, but later he taught of Christ there (Acts 16:6; 18:23).

Meta. A dry, barren, fruitless state of thought. The central idea of this realm of the sense consciousness that Phrygia signifies is a belief in lack, lack of vitality, of substance, of strength, of power, and of increase of good (*dried, parched, barren, lifeless, stubble, brush*).

Phygelus (A. V., Phygellus), phў-ġĕl'-ŭs (Gk.)—*one in flight; a fugitive.*

A Christian of Asia who forsook Paul when Paul was a prisoner at Rome (II Tim. 1:15).

Meta. A thought that believes in the good and tends to good, but is as yet not stable, is not established. It is fearful, and lacks the staying, abiding qualities of Spirit. Therefore it backs down and disappears when seeming bondage and error arise in consciousness to oppose the word of Truth (Paul), when it is needed most (*one in flight, a fugitive,* a Christian of Asia who forsook Paul when he was in bonds at Rome).

Pi-beseth, pī-bē'-sĕth (Heb. fr. Egypt.)—*Pe-Ubastet; Bubastis; house of Ubastet; city of Bast or Past; place of the cat goddess Bast; place of fertility; place of vitality; place of Diana.*

A city of Egypt against which Ezekiel prophesied (Ezek. 30:17).

Meta. The worship of the vital force, of life activity, increase, and continuity, by the Egyptian, or darkened, sensate, carnal consciousness in the spiritually unawakened man.

The name Pi-beseth was derived from the Egyptian goddess Past or Bast, who was represented in the image of a woman with a cat's head and was dedicated to fertility and pleasure. The Greeks identified it with their Artemis. Artemis is another name for the goddess Diana of the Ephesians. This, with the meaning of the name, *place of the cat goddess Bast, place of fertility, place of vitality, place of Diana,* refers to life and fruitfulness, but on a carnal plane. Diana was the goddess of vitality. (See DIANA.) A cat has been said to have nine lives, and we understand cats to signify tenacity of life. We are told too that Pi-beseth was the Bubastis of the Greeks,

noted for its temple of Bast, goddess of fire. Fire, under the carnal thought, refers to life activity directed by carnal lusts and desires; these burn up the very cells of the body, to the degree that they are allowed to rule the individual. Under the spiritual thought, fire suggests the activity of the spiritual or Christ life in consciousness, which purifies and refines the whole being.

Pilate, pī'-lăte (Lat.)—*armed with a pilum; armed with a javelin; spear-armed; wearing the pileus; wearing the felt cap, i. e., emblem of liberty.*

The Roman governor of Judea in the time of Jesus Christ's ministry and crucifixion (Matt. 27:2).

Meta. The ruling principle of the sense plane, the carnal will.

Pilate questioned the I AM, Jesus (John 18:33), "Art thou the King of the Jews?" Applying this to the individual man, one would say to oneself, "Is there a ruling will over my religious nature?" The personal will has no concept of the factors of that inner higher realm, and believes that it is the ruler of the whole man. It is jealous of any attempt to usurp its power, but when it is assured that the kingdom that the higher self would rule is "not of this world," it finds in that self "no fault."

Pildash, pĭl'-dăsh (Heb.)—*flame of fire; consuming flame; devouring ardor; destruction; ruin.*

Son of Nahor, Abraham's brother (Gen. 22:22).

Meta. Zeal, ardor (*flame of fire*), the result of a quickening that has taken place in consciousness. (See NAHOR and MILCAH, the parents of Pildash.) This zeal may use its force either in tearing down old ideas and cells in the organism or in building up the consciousness and body in Truth, according to the degree of light, understanding, that actuates it. *Consuming flame, devouring ardor, destruction, ruin,* suggest the use of this zeal in a negative or destructive way.

Pilha (A. V., Pileha), pĭl'-há (Heb.) —*cleaving; breaking out; breaking forth; bringing forth; dividing; a slice; a fragment; a rider; a husbandman; labor; work; service; worship.*

One who joined Nehemiah in sealing

the covenant, a chief of the people (Neh. 10:24).

Meta. A *breaking out* of, away from, error, sense confusion (Babylon), by *bringing forth* a degree (*a slice, a fragment*) of dominion over one's vital thoughts and forces (*a rider*). Thus that which Pilha signifies becomes a server and worshiper of God, the divine principle of life and good, in the body temple (*a husbandman, labor, work, service, worship;* one who joined Nehemiah in sealing the covenant after the return from Babylon).

Piltai, pĭl'-tāi (Heb.)—*deliverance of Jah; Jah causes to escape; Jehovah is salvation; Jah saves.*

An Israelitish priest in the days of Joiakim (Neh. 12:17). He was of the house of Moadiah.

Meta. When man becomes established in the Christ righteousness—in grace, mercy, and Truth—and learns to affirm, meditate on, and realize divine life and substance, spiritual ideas, words of Truth (Moadiah), he is set free from all error and its results, as is signified by Piltai (*deliverance of Jah, Jah causes to escape, Jah saves*).

Pinon, pī'-nŏn (Heb.)—*darkness; perplexity; distraction; hopelessness.*

A chief of Edom. He was descended from Esau (Gen. 36:41).

Meta. The great anxiety, confusion, and hopelessness that often come over the purely mortal, darkened consciousness of man in times of error reaping (*darkness, perplexity, distraction, hopelessness;* a chief of Edom, Edom referring to Esau and signifying the seemingly physical and carnal phase of man's being).

Piram, pī-răm (Heb.)—*swift-running; fleet; indomitable; wild ass.*

King of Jarmuth, who with four other Amoritish kings was conquered and slain by the Israelites under Joshua (Josh. 10:3).

Meta. The Amorites are amorous, lustful thoughts; their seat of action is the generative function. Piram, a king of the Amorites (*swift, fleet, indomitable, wild ass*), signifies a ruling thought or tendency in this Amoritish consciousness that is very quick to be aroused to action

and is apparently unconquerable, in so far as the natural or animal man is concerned. It is only overcome and put out of consciousness by one's true, spiritual thoughts (Israelites) under the I AM or ruling Christ dominion, which is represented here by Joshua.

Pirathon, pĭr'-ă-thŏn (Heb.)—*leader; prince; chief; head of a family; surpassing; highest; peak; top; loosened; absolved; freed; dismissed; unbridled; unruly; naked; uncovered.*

A city of Ephraim, where Abdon, one of Israel's judges, was buried (Judg. 12:15).

Meta. A group of thoughts belonging to the will faculty in man (a city of Ephraim), that is of a very high, noble, ruling, freeing character, victorious over error. It works to uncover error and to put it out of the consciousness of the individual.

Pirathonite, pĭr'-ă-thŏn-īte (fr. Heb.) —*of* or *belonging to Pirathon.*

An inhabitant of Pirathon (Judg. 12:13; II Sam. 23:30). Abdon the son of Hillel, a judge of Israel, and Benaiah, one of David's mighty men, were Pirathonites.

Meta. A thought belonging to that in consciousness that Pirathon signifies. (See PIRATHON.)

Pisgah, pĭṣ'găh (Heb.)—*cut up; divided; cleft; hill; peak; point.*

A mountain or range of mountains in Moab, across the Jordan directly opposite Jericho. From the top of Pisgah Moses was given a view of the Promised Land (Deut. 34:1).

Meta. A very high, exalted state of mind in that phase of the consciousness signified by Moab (*peak, hill,* a mountain in Moab; see MOAB). From this elevated place in thought the spiritually developing phase of man's consciousness that is represented by Moses perceives the Promised Land, has a vision of the redeemed body. Henceforth a dividing line is drawn, in the thoughts of the individual who has reached this phase of development, between the old material ideas regarding his organism and the high possibilities that have been revealed to him (*cut up, divided, cleft*).

Pishon (A. V., Pison), pī'-shŏn (Heb.)

—great outpouring; full flowing; fully diffused; spread out; real existence; perfect substantiality; being, carried to its highest degree.

One of the four rivers of Eden (Gen. 2:11).

Meta. Pishon is defined as *fully diffused, carried to its highest degree.* This is descriptive of Spirit at work in man's consciousness, Spirit diffusing its ideas of intelligence and light, the activity of divine ideas in their fullness.

The river Pishon is described as encompassing "the whole land of Havilah." Havilah represents the struggle of elemental life, virtue born of trial. There is gold in this land, which means that locked up in our body temple are all the treasures of Spirit. These are released by the inflow of spiritual Pishon.

Pisidia, pĭ-sĭd'-ĭ-à (Gk.)—*pitchy; tenacious; clinging; a channel of water.*

A province in Asia Minor. One of the two Antiochs of the New Testament was a city of Pisidia (Acts 13:14).

Meta. One significance of Asia is that it refers to a state of consciousness impregnated by old, decayed, worn out, material ideas that should be left behind by the individual who would progress spiritually. Pisidia, a province in Asia Minor (*pitchy, tenacious, clinging*), signifies the apparent tenacity with which the old ideas represented by Asia stick to one. However, there is cleansing at hand (*a channel of water;* Paul taught the Truth in Pisidia).

Pispa (A. V., Pispah), pĭs'-pà (Heb.) —*expansion; swelling; diffusion; dispersion; profusion; abundance.*

A son of Jether, of the Israelitish tribe of Asher (I Chron. 7:38).

Meta. Jether, father of Pispa, represents an exalted thought and a thought of abundance. Asher means *happy,* and the significance points both to understanding and substance. Pispa (*expansion, swelling, dispersion, profusion, abundance*) bespeaks the enlarging, increasing, and spreading of the Jether and Asher phases of thought in consciousness.

Pithom, pī'-thŏm (Heb. fr. Egypt.)— *city or place of Tum; narrow place; narrow pass.*

One of the "store-cities" that the Israelites, as slaves in the land of Egypt, built there for Pharaoh, king of Egypt (Exod. 1:11).

Meta. A group of thoughts pertaining to conservation of substance, built up in the subjective consciousness of man (Egypt) by his higher ideals (Israelites) while they are in bondage to the darkened, sense thoughts that the Egyptians represent (a treasure city, "store-city," built in Egypt by the Israelites when in slavery to the Egyptians).

This conservation of substance in the subconsciousness is built in sorrow and bondage, and seemingly is hemmed in on every side by sense thoughts (*narrow place, narrow pass*). Yet the time must come when the darkened, sense rule is removed from the whole consciousness of man. Then all the substance in his organism will be used joyously to his true upbuilding in spirituality and perfection. (Some authorities find *opening of the mouth, very great space,* in the meanings of Pithom. This makes one think of II Samuel 22:20:

"He brought me forth also into a large place;

He delivered me, because he delighted in me").

Pithon, pī'-thŏn (Heb.)—*opened; enlarged; expanded; open-faced; open-mouthed; open-minded; ingenuous; childlike; harmless; persuaded; enticed; deluded; deceived; seduced.*

Son of Micah, a Benjamite, and descended from Saul through Jonathan (I Chron. 8:35; 9:41).

Meta. An open-minded, receptive, childlike phase of thought. If guided by Spirit and thus led unresistingly into Truth, it is good. If guided by personal willfulness and selfishness, however, (Pithon was descended from Saul, who represents the personal will), delusion and error will be the result.

plagues of Egypt.

Meta. It is right and proper to recognize the vital center in the organism, the generative or life center, as having a place in the divine economy, but spiritual man should never become involved in the mere animal processes of life generation through sex. This is what brings the plagues of Egypt (disease) upon the human family.

Pleiades, plē'-ĭă-dĕş (Gk.)—*the seven stars; seven daughters of Atlas; heap; cluster; bound together; family; much more; abundance; increase; multitude; superior; more excellent; perfect.*

A group of seven stars (only six are now visible) in the shoulder of Taurus, the Bull (Job 9:9). This constellation appears at the beginning of spring, and indicates the coming of spring. To the Greeks, with the rising of this group of stars in the early spring, navigation began, and was supposed to close when the Pleiades disappeared late in the autumn. According to the margin Job 38:31 would read, "Canst thou chain the *sweet influences* of the Pleiades?"

In Greek legends, too, the stars of the Pleiades were said to be the companions of Artemis, or Diana, who stood to them for the goddess of vitality, or of reproduction of life on the earth, and for the sustenance of all forms of life.

Meta. A star represents a truth, light, that apparently is beyond man's present conception, something that is but dimly understood by him; and seven is the number of fulfillment in the natural man. The Pleiades, the group of seven stars that indicate spring, with the "sweet influences" that bring the warm weather and the growth of vegetation for the nourishment of man, signify man's present faint comprehension of the one life and intelligence, the one love and guiding power, that is ever working for the eternal progress and good of the race—the Mother-God, the Holy Spirit, the Oversoul, that is always brooding over the earth and the human race, bringing about the fulfilling of the natural processes and lifting all to spiritual understanding, consciousness, and expression.

Pochereth–hazzebaim (A. V., Pochereth of Zebaim, pŏch'-ĕ-rĕth-hăz-zĕ-bā'-ĭm (Heb.)—*binding the roes; fettering the gazelles; beguiling the beauties; hindering the glories.*

His "children" returned from the Babylonian captivity (Ezra 2:57).

Meta. A limiting thought in the higher or religious phase of man's consciousness that for a time hinders Spirit from consciously expressing and demonstrating in his life, or at least hinders the individual from becoming conscious of the beauty and glory and splendor of his true self, his true being.

poise.

Meta. A state of balance of all man's faculties and the forces of his being. It is attained through recognition of God as supreme, all-powerful good, and of man's true relation to Him. The result of poise is perfect expression of all the faculties and powers.

Loss of poise is caused by lack of confidence in the all-sustaining power of Divine Mind. This lack of confidence disturbs poise because personality strives to build upon its own insufficiency and the result is failure and weakness. This affects the whole system, and every faculty is involved.

The relation of poise to mastery and dominion is this: the consciousness of dominion through divine principle gives a state of poise, and a poised state of mind adds to the realization of dominion and mastery. The realization of mastery is attained by unifying the consciousness with Divine Mind as its one source, by prayer and meditation, thus attaining the Christ consciousness.

Pontius, pŏn'-ti-ŭs (Lat.)—*of or belonging to the sea; mariner; fisherman.*

Pontius Pilate, governor of Judea at the time of Jesus' ministry and crucifixion (Luke 3:1).

Meta. See PILATE.

Pontus, pŏn'-tŭs (Gk.)—*deep; sea; wave.*

A district in the northeastern part of Asia Minor, and bordering on the sea, whence it received its name (Acts 2:9).

Meta. Universal mind (*deep, sea;* see AQUILLA, who was a man of Pontus).

Poratha, pŏr'-ă-thà (Heb. fr. Pers.) —*given by lot; divided by chance; mandate of fate.*

One of the ten sons of Haman. He was slain by the Jews in Shushan (Esth. 9:8).

Meta. The error belief of the outer, sense man that good comes to one by "luck," "fate," and not as a sure result of right and wise thinking and doing, of living in harmony with divine law and using one's faculties and powers in loving, faithful service to God, to one's fellow men, and to one's own highest spiritual welfare. This error belief in luck and fate (*given by lot, divided by chance, mandate of fate*) is in favor in the adverse consciousness of man, and bears fruit accordingly, but its fruit is not for life and good.

porches, five, of the pool of Bethesda (John 5:2).

Meta. The five-sense limitations. The great "multitude of them that were sick," or depleted life corpuscles, lie here near the pool in the five porches, or five-sense limitations. The five-sense consciousness does not realize the power of I AM to quicken the inner functions of man's organism, but lets the weak, depleted life cells accumulate and burden the system. A thought of the activity of life would, through divine law, set them free from their helplessness.

It is not necessary that all the purification and renewing of the depleted corpuscles shall take place through the lungs when man understands the power of I AM to declare the word of activity. Jesus Christ, the I AM of Spirit, did not tell the man to go down into the pool and be healed, but said, "Arise, take up thy bed, and walk." Thus we see that the work of Spirit is not confined to physical processes, although it does not ignore them. If your lung capacity is not equal to the purification of your blood, increase it by declaring the law of active life. Anæmic blood may be made vigorous and virile by one's daily centering the attention in the lungs and affirming them to be spiritual and under the perpetual inflow of new life and the outflow of old life. Command these life centers to do your will.

Do not be limited by the so-called established law of nature or of man's carnal thought that if one has reached the age of thirty-eight the life current is beginning to wane—that one's "sabbath" or day of rest is setting in. It is "lawful" in Spirit to declare the perpetual activity of life anywhere, at any time, and under all circumstances. Divine life takes no cognizance of the laws that the intellect has set up for its gov-

erning. Life is ever active. It is constantly present in all its fullness and power, and it has no day of rest, or "sabbath."

Porcius Festus, pôr'-ci-ŭs fĕs'-tŭs (Lat.)—*merry pig; swinish festival.*

The same person as Festus (Acts 24: 27).

Meta. Add to the significance of Festus the idea of hoggishness and swinishness, and you will have the significance of Porcius Festus.

Potiphar, pŏt'-ĭ-phär (Heb. fr. Egypt.) —*dedicated to Ra; belonging to the sun.*

An officer of Pharaoh, king of Egypt, and captain of his guard; the man to whom Joseph was sold (Gen. 37:36).

Meta. An executive thought or quality in that consciousness which Pharaoh indicates. (See PHARAOH.)

The understanding and the will should be especially active in one who would master the sensations of the body. Potiphar's wife (Gen. 39:7-20) represents the sense consciousness of the soul that tempts us to meet its desires and, when we deny her, has us put into jail. This means that when a habit in the sense consciousness is refused expression it reacts and for a time seems to lock up even the expression of the good through us. But let us patiently bide our time; the higher will yet show its God-given power.

Poti–phera (A. V., Poti–pherah), pŏt'-ĭ-phē'-rȧ (Heb. fr. Egypt.)—*belonging to Ra; dedicated to the sun.*

The "priest of On," an Egyptian priest whose daughter Asenath became the wife of Joseph and the mother of Ephraim and Manasseh (Gen. 41:45, 50).

Meta. Potiphera, an Egyptian priest of On (*belonging to Ra, dedicated to the sun*), indicates a natural religious tendency in the individual that gives the force of its influence to the worship and building up of that in consciousness which the Egyptian city of On signifies. (See ON.)

pounds (Luke 19:13-26).

Meta. Capacities of mind.

prayer.

Meta. Communion between man and God.

In true prayer we take with us words

of Truth, a statement of Truth, or an affirmation, and turn our attention within to the very center of our being, where the Father dwells. We affirm these words of Truth and meditate on them, then get very still and wait in the silence for God to make them real to us.

Prayer can be defined in many ways. It can be said to be "the taking hold of God's willingness." Jesus Christ forbade all prayers of doubt, but said, "All things whatsoever ye pray and ask for, believe that ye receive [*received*, margin] them, and ye shall have them" (Mark 11: 24); and "Your Father knoweth what things ye have need of, before ye ask him" (Matt. 6:8).

To one in understanding of Truth, prayer is an affirmation of that which is in Being. Then, why the necessity of the prayer, or affirmation, if the desired condition already is? In order that the creative law of the word may be fulfilled, we must pray. All things are in God as potentialities. It is man's share in the creative process to bring the unmanifest to manifestation. Everybody should pray. Through prayer we develop the highest phase of character and it softens and refines the whole man.

Prayer is not supplication, or begging, but a simple asking for and affirmation of that which we know is waiting for us at the hands of our Father. The prayer that Jesus gave as a model (Luke 11:1-4) is simplicity itself. There is in it none of that awe-inspiring "Oh, Thou!" which some ministers affect in public prayer, but the informal request of a son to his father for things needed.

"Father, Hallowed be thy name." Here is recognition of the all-inclusiveness and completeness of Divine Mind. Everything has its sustenance from this one source, therefore "the earth is Jehovah's, and the fulness thereof."

We need supplies for the day only. Hoarding for future necessities breeds selfishness. The children of Israel tried to save the manna, but it spoiled.

The law, "Whatsoever a man soweth, that shall he also reap," is here shorn of its terrors. If we forgive others we shall be forgiven and the penalty of suffering for sins will be eliminated.

It does not seem possible that God would lead us into temptation; in fact, in James 1:13 we are told plainly that God cannot be tempted of evil and that He tempts no man. This clause in the Lord's Prayer, "And bring us not into temptation," follows closely that concerning the forgiveness of sin, and it is evidently a part of it. Let not temptation lead us, is a permissible interpretation.

Jesus advised asking for what we want, and being steadfast in our demands. People ignorant of the relation in which man stands to God wonder why we should ask, and even importune, a Father who has provided all things for us. This is explained when we perceive that God is a great reservoir of mind that has to be tapped by man's mind, and through his thought or word poured into visibility. If the mind of man is clogged with doubt, lethargy, or fear, he must, through his faithful knocking and asking, open the way. We should "pray without ceasing." We should continue "steadfastly in prayer." We should acquire in prayer a facility in asking equal to the expert mathematician's swiftness in handling numbers; having done that, we shall get responses in like proportion.

We give our children what we consider good gifts, from our limited and transitory store, but when the gifts of God are put into our mind we have possessions that are eternal, that will go on producing for all time.

priests.

Meta. See LEVITES.

Prisca, pris'-ea (Lat.)—*ancient; old; of former times.*

The same person as Priscilla (II Tim. 4:19).

Meta. See PRISCILLA.

Priscilla, pris-çil'-la (Lat.)—*diminutive form of Prisca; ancient; old; of former times; little old (woman).*

Wife of Aquila, of Pontus and "lately come from Italy." The two were Christians, and tentmakers by trade. Paul abode and worked with them in Corinth (Acts 18:2).

Meta. The feminine or receptive phase of the healing forces of nature that are always at work rebuilding the body and repairing the ravages of ignorant man.

Aquila, husband of Priscilla, is the positive phase of these forces. (See AQUILLA.)

Ancient and *old,* given as the meaning of Priscilla and of Prisca, reveal the fact that these healing forces of nature are very old, in so far as man's idea of time refers to age. They have been present and active since manifest creation began. God has ever been in every atom of His universe as unifying, constructive life, energy, love, intelligence, power, substance, and progressive influence.

Prochorus, prŏch'-ŏ-rŭs (Gk.)—*before the singers; before the dancers; choir leader; choir master; leader of the dance.*

One of the seven men who were chosen from among the Christians in Jerusalem to look after the distribution of provisions among the disciples, that none might be overlooked (Acts 6:5).

Meta. An active thought in the higher, spiritual consciousness of man, whose central idea is joy, harmony, and unity (*choir leader, leader of the dance*).

prophet.

Meta. A teacher, one who receives the inspiration of Spirit, an understanding of spiritual law, and imparts it to others. A prophet, in individual consciousness, is a thought that is in contact with Spirit, that receives revelations direct from the Holy Spirit; it knows and understands divine law and its working, therefore it warns and instructs the other thoughts. (The prophets of old seemed to stand between God and the people; it was through them that the people received divine guidance.)

A prophet (Matt. 21:4) is one who states the spiritual law.

The prophets of Luke 16:29 represent divine law.

The prophet of John 6:14 is the promise of God.

prosperity.

Meta. The consciousness that Divine Mind is inexhaustible support and supply. The difference between spiritual prosperity and the material idea of prosperity is that spiritual prosperity is founded on understanding of the inexhaustible, omnipresent substance of Spirit as the source of supply; the material idea is that the possession of things constitutes prosperity. Man lays

hold of the one substance with his mind, through understanding and faith.

"Uncertainty of riches" indicates putting one's trust in the possession of things apart from the consciousness of the one substance as the source of all. Anxiety about supply can be overcome by a recognition of the omnipresence of Spirit substance and a centering of faith in it as the one source of supply.

The one substance is magnified and increased by thanksgiving and praise. One's conversation should ever magnify the Spirit of plenty.

It is necessary to give as freely as we receive, because there is a law of giving and receiving. Giving opens the way to a greater inflow of substance. We should give cheerfully, freely, out of the consciousness that supply is inexhaustible.

Ptolemais, ptŏl-ĕ-mā'-ĭs (Gk.)—*warlike; terrifying.*

A city in Palestine, on the Mediterranean coast, a place that Paul went to from Tyre (Acts 21:7). It is the same place as the Acco of the Israelitish tribe of Asher, mentioned in Judges 1:31.

Meta. An aggregation of thoughts of an opposing, hostile character (*warlike, terrifying*). (See ACCO.)

Puah, pū'-ăh (Heb.)—*mouth; orifice; aperture; puff; breath; blast; utterance; command.*

a Father of Tola and son of Dodo. He was a man of Issachar (Judg. 10:1). **b** Son of Issachar (I Chronicles 7:1). He is called Puvah in Genesis 46:13.

Meta. Giving one's true thoughts, one's zeal, to establishing the activity of Truth throughout the consciousness, that it may be declared aloud and expressed (*mouth, orifice, breath, utterance, command*). Thinking Truth zealously and affirming it aloud by word of mouth will cause strong vibrations (*a blast*) throughout one's being, and act destructively on the error in consciousness while building up the true (Israelites).

Puah was a son of Issachar, and Issachar, son of Jacob, represents the active zeal faculty in individual consciousness.

Puah, pū'-ăh (Heb.)—*shining; brightness; giving light; splendor; beauty.*

An Israelitish woman (Exod. 1:15).

Meta. The higher or spiritual phase of the soul aiding in bringing to birth, protecting, and actively radiating the light, joy, and beauty of new positive ideas in consciousness (*shining, brightness, giving light, splendor, beauty*). Puah was a midwife who was commanded by Pharaoh, king of Egypt, to kill all male Hebrew children at birth; this would mean, in symbol, to deny out of consciousness every new, positive spiritual idea that comes to mind. She did not do this, however, but trusted in God and obeyed Him rather than man. So she saved the children alive, to the increasing power of the Israelites and to the great fear of the Egyptians that they would become outnumbered and overthrown.

Publius, pŭb′-lĭ-ŭs (Lat.)—*public; common; of the people; popular.*

The "chief man" or governor of the island of Melita, upon which Paul and his companions were cast when they were shipwrecked while on their way to Rome. Paul was instrumental in healing the father of Publius, and so Publius received and entertained Paul while he was on the island (Acts 28:7, 8).

Meta. The central ruling idea in the Melita state of mind in the individual consciousness. Melita (*flowing with honey, sweetened with honey*) refers to the sweetness, the joy, and the pleasant, agreeable feeling that are sensed so deeply by the individual when in his overcoming he has experienced some great deliverance from error and has entered for the time being into the peace, content, and satisfaction that follow such an overcoming experience. In this state of mind all thought of high and low, all thought of great and small, all thought of inferiority and superiority, and all thought of separation or apartness are laid aside, and the idea that rules is one of unity with all, a thought of a common good, to be enjoyed and used by the whole consciousness and by all people (*public, of the people, common*).

Pudens, pū′-dĕnṣ (Lat.)—*shamefaced; bashful; modest; decent; virtuous.*

One who sent salutation to Timothy in Paul's letter written to Timothy from Rome (II Tim. 4:21).

Meta. Virtue and humility, the latter possibly carried somewhat to an extreme (*modest, bashful, shamefaced, virtuous*). True humility, as well as virtue and single-mindedness as to the good, is needed very much in the professing Christian. The true Christian is humble and true, since he knows the nothingness of the lesser self in man and the allness of the Christ; to the spiritual man he attributes all praise, all greatness, all capability, all glory.

Pul, pŭl (Heb. from Skr.)—*lofty; highest; lord; king; large; strong; elephant.*

A king of Assyria, who came against Israel in the reign of Menahem, king of Israel, in Samaria. He was given a thousand talents of silver by Menahem to insure his support (II Kings 15:19).

Meta. The exalting of the intellect, guided by the senses, to the highest ruling place in individual consciousness (*lofty, highest, lord, king, strong, elephant;* Assyria refers to the intellectual in man). The meanings of this word show clearly the great capacity, substance, strength, and power with which intellectual ability is endowed by those who see in and through it the source of man's highest attainments.

Pul, pŭl (Heb. fr. Egypt.)—*extremity; border; far country; breathed out; expired.*

A place and people (Isa. 66:19).

Meta. The very *extremity, border,* or end (*far country, breathed out, expired*) of carnal consciousness in man.

Punites, pū′-nītes (fr. Heb.)—*the Puni.*

Descendants of Puah, or Puvah, of Issachar (Num. 26:23).

Meta. Thoughts springing from and belonging to that in consciousness which Puah signifies. (See PUAH.)

Punon, pū′-nŏn (Heb.)—*darkness; perplexity; distraction; hopelessness.*

A place where the Israelites camped while in the wilderness (Num. 33:42).

Meta. A darkened, confused, agitated, almost hopeless phase of mind (*darkness, perplexity, distraction, hopelessness*) that sometimes seems to exist in the wilderness, or multitude of wild, uncultivated, and untrained thoughts that the individual becomes conscious of when he begins to awaken to spiritual understanding and to the necessity of overcoming limitations and error by gaining dominion over his thinking. This wilderness of thought may be partly, or at times wholly, subconscious; but the true spiritual thoughts (Israelites) must travel through it, camp in it, and bring order out of seeming chaos. These wilderness thoughts of man must be raised to the Christ light and cleansed by the water of denials and the refining fires of Spirit, in order to remove all of the darkness and its negative results, and to purify the good for use.

Pur, pûr, **Purim,** pū'-rĭm (Heb. fr. Pers.)—*part; portion; lot; die; oracle.*

Pur refers to the casting of lots and the consulting of astrologers by Haman the Agagite, the Jews' enemy, against the Jews to destroy them (Esth. 3:7; 9:24).

Purim is the name of a Jewish festival instituted by the Jews in remembrance of their deliverance from the destructive devices of the wicked Haman. Purim is the plural of Pur (Esth. 9:26-28).

Meta. Pur refers to superstitious belief in and fear of fate, luck, and astrological and psychic influences as having power for evil in one's life. Such error ideas and fears belong to the adverse consciousness, and if indulged in are destructive to one's true spiritual upbuilding and unfoldment.

Purim symbolizes the great joy and the new hold on spiritual life and substance that the overcomer realizes by means of his deliverance from the superstitious fears that Pur represents.

Put (in A. V., Genesis 10:6, Phut), pŭt (Heb.)—*state of being stifled; suffocation; asphyxiation; affliction; sorrow; sadness; breathing out of the spirit; despised.*

a Son of Ham (Gen. 10:6). b A people descended from Put, son of Ham (Ezek. 27:10). The Lubim or Libyans of Africa are thought to have been descendants of Put (see Nah. 3:9).

Meta. The darkened, troublous, sorrowful, and very material dying state of mind and body that results from a lack of spiritual inspiration, of the inbreath-ing and understanding of Spirit (*suffocation, affliction, sorrow, breathing out of the spirit, despised*).

Puteoli, pŭ-tē'-ŏ-lī (Lat.)—*wells; mineral springs; stinking wells; sulphur springs; putrid water.*

A seaport town on the north shore of the Bay of Naples. It was there that Paul left the boat when on a journey to Rome; he found "brethren" at this place and stayed with them seven days (Acts 28:13).

Meta. A thought center in consciousness, close to universal Mind, pertaining to one's receiving into consciousness a continuous flow of vitality, of life (*wells* and *springs* denote the welling up of life into consciousness). This conscious flow of vitality and energy that Puteoli signifies, however, is adulterated by the intellectual belief that strength and vital force are material, that they belong to the outer man entirely and should be exercised in selfish, personal dominion and in oppression of all that does not pertain specifically to the building up and strengthening of the outer, personal man. This vital flow therefore becomes distasteful (*stinking wells, putrid water*) to the finer, perceptive qualities of the individual. With "brethren" at this place, however (spiritual and Truth thoughts), and Paul, the word of Truth, staying there seven days, a cleansing and uplifting are sure to take place. Italy, as referred to in the Bible, signifies an outer consciousness of or a belief in strength, especially strength of the head (the intellect and will).

Puthites (A. V., Puhites), pū'-thītes (fr. Heb.)—*apart; separated; divided; hinged; deceptive; seductive.*

A family of Kiriath–jearim (I Chron. 2:53).

Meta. Divided thoughts, thoughts of a deceptive character, that have found a place in the phase of consciousness signified by Kiriath–jearim. (See KIRIATH–JEARIM.)

Putiel, pū'-tĭ-ĕl (Heb.)—*afflicted of God; stifled of God.*

Father-in-law of Eleazar who was Aaron's son (Exod. 6:25).

Meta. The mistaken belief that God limits His people, withholds good from them, and afflicts them, for some purpose of His own—presumably for their higher good (*afflicted of God, stifled of God*). This belief exists in the old-established religious thoughts of man, but is not of the Spirit of truth (Putiel evidently was an Israelite).

Puvah (in A. V., Numbers 26:23, Pua), pū'-văh (Heb.)—*mouth; orifice; aperture; puff; breath; blast; utterance; command.*

Son of Issachar (Gen. 46:13). He is called Puah in I Chronicles 7:1.

Meta. See PUAH.

Pyrrhus, pўr'-rhŭs (Gk.)—*fiery red; firelike; kindled; inflamed.*

Father of Sopater, the latter a companion of Paul's on one of his missionary journeys (Acts 20:4).

Meta. A thought of great vitality, of abundant life, but not expressing so harmoniously as is needful if one is to keep in poise and health (*fiery red, firelike, kindled, inflamed*).

Q

Quartus, quâr'-tŭs (Lat.)—*fourth.*

A Christian at Corinth who sent salutation by Paul to the Romans (Rom. 16:23). From his name he is thought to have been a Roman.

Meta. A positive, spiritually enlightened thought that relates to the foursquare (*fourth*) or perfectly rounded consciousness of the individual. "And the city lieth foursquare, . . . the length and the breadth and the height thereof are equal" (Rev. 21:16).

This thought that Quartus signifies is of the head, the reasoning faculty in man unified with the personal will (he is thought to have been a Roman), and is now established in love (a dweller in Corinth, Corinth referring to the love center in consciousness). Quartus therefore bespeaks the elevating of these two phases of man, the head and the heart, understanding and affection, to the plane of spiritual wisdom and love, and the unifying of them in consciousness. This is what makes a perfect balance in the individual, makes him "foursquare."

Quartus, meaning *fourth* and being a Christian at Corinth, also suggests the bringing of the fourth dimension, omnipresence, into man's comprehension.

queen of the south (Matt. 12:42).

Meta. The subconscious mind, which is awakened when the wisdom of Spirit begins its work in the consciousness. This awakening stirs up both the good and the evil thoughts in man, and he must choose or judge them, not by intellectual wisdom (Solomon) but by that "greater than Solomon," the Son of God in him.

Quirinius (A. V., Cyrenius), quī-rĭn'-ĭ-ŭs (Lat.)—*civil government; interior rule; spearman; armed peace.*

Governor of Syria at the time of the world enrollment by Cæsar Augustus, and at the time of the birth of Jesus (Luke 2:2).

Meta. A phase of the executive power of the personal will established in the mistaken belief that peace can be obtained and maintained by force (*civil government, interior rule, spearman, armed peace,* a governor of Syria).

This ruling thought, or executive power of the personal will in conjunction with intellectual reasoning guided by the senses (Syria), has a firm belief that all the world—every thought, faculty, force, and activity in the whole organism and consciousness of man—should acknowledge and pay tribute to Rome and Cæsar, should give of its substance to sustain the dominance of the selfish, personal will and reason in consciousness. This is signified by the fact that all the Jewish nation and all the other nations that were ruled by Rome were called together for enrollment and taxation. "And all went to enrol themselves, every one to his own city" (Luke 2:3).

R

Raama (A. V., Raamah), rā'-ă-mȧ (Heb.)—*moved with agitation; trembling; quaking; troubles;· tossed with rage; thundering.*

Son of Cush, and grandson of Ham, who was Noah's son (I Chron. 1:9). The name is also spelled Raamah in the same verse and in Genesis 10:7.

Meta. See RAAMAH.

Raamah, rā'-ă-măh (Heb.)—*moved with agitation; trembling; quaking; troubled; tossed with rage; thundering.*

a Son of Cush and grandson of Ham (Gen. 10:7). **b** A place or a people (Ezek. 27:22).

Meta. Ham represents the physical in man. Cush (meaning *blackened*) signifies the darkened, ignorant thought in which man has held his body and its activities—the physical, seemingly mortal part of himself. Raamah, son of Cush, is the result or fruit of the ignorant thought of the sense man regarding his body. This result takes the shape of the nameless fears, inner tremblings, quakings, and ungodlike emotions that the sense man experiences (*moved with agitation, trembling, quaking, tossed with rage, troubled*). Raamah also represents the human attempt to exalt the personal by a great show of power (*thundering*) instead of realizing that all true power is in Spirit.

Raamiah, rā-ă-mī'-ăh (Heb.)—*agitation of Jehovah; thunder of Jah; Jah moves with agitation; who fears Jehovah; anger of Jah; evil from the Lord.*

A chief or noble of the Jewish people who returned with Zerubbabel from the Babylonian captivity (Neh. 7:7). He is called Reelaiah in Ezra 2:2.

Meta. A prominent, influential thought in our higher, religious consciousness (a chief or noble of the Jewish people) that comes out of the Babylonian state of mind (sense confusion) and back to Jerusalem (spiritual consciousness) with Zerubbabel (one who restores the worship of God). This high, religious thought that Raamiah signifies has a degree of comprehension of the activity and power of God, but fears Him instead of approaching the Father in loving, confident assurance that only good emanates from Spirit to man. This is because the Raamiah thought still believes God to be the author of evil as well as of good (*who fears Jehovah, thunder of Jah, Jah moves with agitation, anger of Jah, evil from the Lord*); it does not understand the working of divine law and the need for man to harmonize his life with the divine law, in order that he may reap only the good.

Man pictures God according to his own ideas. One must come into very advanced spiritual understanding and realization in order to know God as "good only," to be reverenced and loved and worshiped with all the heart and soul, but with no element of fear.

Raamses, ră-ăm'-sĕṣ (Heb. fr. Egypt.)—*son of Ra; son of the sun; sun's emanation.*

A city that was built, or at least fortified, for Pharaoh king of Egypt by the Hebrews when they were in slavery in Egypt. It was one of his "store-cities" (Exod. 1:11). Raamses seems to be identical with RAMESES, which see.

Meta. A thought center of substance ("store-cities") in the domain of Pharaoh, king of Egypt, the sun center in the subconsciousness of the individual. This "sun" or "light" consciousness, which in Pharaoh and Egypt is obscured or veiled by our life on the lower, sense plane, works in conjunction with our higher religious thoughts (Hebrews) that are in servitude to the darkened sense consciousness that Egypt signifies, and so this reserve substance (Raamses) is built up in Egypt.

Raamses, so called by Pharaoh, means *son of the sun,* sun here referring to Pharaoh, who is the ruling ego of the Egypt realm of thought. The sun really refers to the true light, the Christ, but Pharaoh takes to himself, for his own exaltation and use, that which belongs to

Spirit only and should be used for the renewing and spiritualizing of the individual. This wrong appropriation of substance brings about disease in man—the plagues that came upon Egypt.

Rabbah, răb'-băh (Heb.)—*multiplied; numerous; accumulation; growth; increase; abundance; great; exalted; a great city; a metropolis.*

a A city of Ammon (Deut. 3:11). b A city in the hill country of Judah (Josh. 15:60).

Meta. Groups of thoughts whose central idea is greatness through numbers; the idea that anything becomes great by reason of its becoming increased in numbers (*numerous, multiplied, accumulation, growth, increase, abundance, great, exalted, a great city, a metropolis*).

Rabbi, răb'-bī (Heb.)—*my great one; my lord; my master; my teacher; my leader; my chief.*

a A title of respect and honor applied by the ancient Hebrews to their doctors and teachers. Jesus warned against thus receiving honor from men (Matt. 23:7). b A title given to Jesus, and meaning "Teacher" (John 1:38).

Meta. A guiding, teaching thought in consciousness, of great prominence and influence, and belonging to the understanding faculty in man. One must be watchful that the thoughts belonging to the understanding faculty always recognize the true spiritual source of all wisdom and do not look to human intellectual reasonings for light on the various problems that are ever confronting one. The outer intellectual realm in man ever tends to take to itself the honor that belongs to the spiritual only.

Rabbith, răb'-bĭth (Heb.)—*great place; great many; multitude; myriad; a metropolis,* i. e., *at least ten thousand.*

A border city of Issachar (Josh. 19:20).

Meta. A thought center belonging to the active zeal faculty in man (a city of Issachar) and pertaining to a great increase of ideas, ideas that tend to enlarge and elevate the consciousness (*great place, multitude, myriad, a metropolis*).

Rabboni, răb-bō'-nī (Gk. fr. Heb.)—*my lord; my master; my teacher; my leader; my chief; my prince.*

A title of great honor applied by the Hebrews to their doctors and lawyers—teachers. It was applied by Mary Magdalene to the risen Jesus (John 20:16).

Meta. See RABBI.

In the foregoing text Rabboni refers to the risen Jesus, spiritual I AM in consciousness, as the great demonstrating teacher and ruling power. Teaching of Truth is done most effectively by living Truth and by demonstrating it in one's life; one must realize one's inherent I AM dominion in order to demonstrate fully the good that one is idealizing in mind. Mary used the word Rabboni as a term of endearment, in addition to the respect and honor that were due to Jesus as a great teacher and demonstrator.

Rab–mag, răb'–măg (Heb. and Chald.)—*prince Magus; chief of the Magi; mighty multitude; high priest; chief priest.*

The title of an important officer of the king of Babylon (Jer. 39:3).

Meta. An executive phase of the will ruling in sense confusion (an officer of the king of Babylon), or an active belief in the psychic realm in man as the realm of guidance and power (*chief of the Magi, high priest, chief priest*).

A magician, metaphysically interpreted, is material thought's trying to counterfeit the working of Spirit. This phase of thought knows nothing of true, spiritual understanding and power, but its field of activity is in the psychic realm and the phenomena of that realm. Thus it falls short of making any real, abiding demonstration, and usually succeeds only in bringing the individual into greater and greater confusion (Babylon).

Rab–saris, răb'–sā-rĭs (Heb.)—*chief eunuch.*

a Title of one of the officers of the Assyrian army that came up against Jerusalem in the reign of Hezekiah king of Judah (II Kings 18:17). b The title of an officer of the king of Babylon (Jer. 39:3).

Meta. That which stands highest in rank, next to the will (king), in the phases of man's consciousness represented by Assyria and Babylon (*chief eunuch*). This idea, however, though of very high rank in the sense, intellectual, reasoning realm (Assyria) and in the realm of sense confusion (Babylon), has no creative power within itself, no capacity to increase life and its forms (it is a eunuch; see EUNUCH).

Rabshakeh, răb'-shă-kēh (Heb.)—*chief water bearer; chief cupbearer; head of irrigation; overwhelmed by the multitude.*

The title of an officer of the Assyrian army that came up against Hezekiah, king of Judah (II Kings 18:17).

Meta. A greatly exalted executive thought activity in the Assyria or intellectual, sense-reasoning realm of consciousness in man (*chief water bearer, chief cupbearer, head of irrigation*, an officer that the king of Assyria sent up against Hezekiah, king of Judah).

In olden times a cupbearer was a royal officer connected with the supplying of wine for the royal household. In this highly executive thought activity that Rabshakeh signifies, the idea of constantly instilling renewed fervor, life, spirit, into the ruling power of the sense-intellectual realm in man is emphasized (wine represents spirit, life). *Overwhelmed by the multitude* suggests a belief in power through numbers alone, instead of knowing that when indued with true spiritual power one can "chase a thousand" and two can put two thousand to flight.

Racal (A. V., Rachal), rā'-căl (Heb.) —*going about; trade; traffic; trader; merchant; commerce.*

A city of Judah. David sent a portion of the spoil to his friends in this city when he returned to Ziklag from destroying the Amalekites who had raided and burned Ziklag during his temporary absence from that place (I Sam. 30:29).

Meta. A thought center in the Judah, the praise-and-prayer or acquisitive, faculty in man, whose burden is one of commerce, an exchange of ideas of substance (*trade, traffic, merchant, trader*).

When kept on a high plane the acquisitive tendency in man is good. By its exercise man attracts to his consciousness great spiritual understanding and realization of spiritual substance, power, and the like; but when man lets the accumulative instinct function through the sense mind it takes the form of bartering and trading in outer goods, even to the acquiring of possessions by deceptive and dishonest means. It leads to the worship of money; and "the love of money," when allowed to rule the man, becomes "a root of all kinds of evil" (I Tim. 6:10).

Rachel (in A. V., Jeremiah 31:15, Rahel), rā'-chĕl (Heb.)—*migrating; journeying in droves; ewe; sheep; lamb.*

The younger daughter of Laban, and one of Jacob's two wives (Gen. 29:28). She was the mother of Joseph and Benjamin (Gen. 30:24; 35:18).

Meta. The feminine, receptive, or soul phase of the pure natural life in the organism of man (*ewe, lamb*). This phase of life that Rachel signifies is as yet in a transitory state (*migrating*). It is fruitful only on the higher, spiritual plane of ideas. (Rachel was for a time barren; her two sons, Joseph and Benjamin, were the result of prayer, and they represent the faculties of imagination and active faith. They, especially Joseph, were accepted above their brothers, the other sons of Jacob who were the offspring of Leah—the human soul— and the two handmaids. Jacob loved Joseph and Benjamin more dearly than his other sons.)

Raddai, răd'-dāi (Heb.)—*treading down; trampling; treading out; walking; expanding; overlaying; subduing; dominating; ruling.*

Fifth son of Jesse, and brother of David (I Chron. 2:14).

Meta. A belief in expansion and dominion (*walking, expanding, subduing, ruling*), but mixed with the sense idea of rulership, in which a domineering, oppressing tendency exists (*treading down, trampling, overlaying, dominating*).

Rahab (in A. V., Matt. 1:5, Rachab), rā'-hăb (Heb.)—*large; wide; broad; ample; spacious; breadth; freedom; unrestraint; liberty; license.*

A woman of Jericho, a harlot. She received the two spies that Joshua sent to Jericho, and aided them in getting away safely. For this act she and her household were saved alive when the Israelites took the town. Afterward she married Salmon, a Jewish man. Their son was Boaz, the husband of Ruth, so David and Jesus were descended from her (Josh. 2:1-24; 6:23, 25).

Meta. Rahab the harlot, Ruth the Moabitess (see The Book of Ruth), and Mary Magdalene all represent the natural love in man, with the fidelity and faithfulness of that love, which, becoming centered on spiritual things, opens the way for man to enter into the Promised Land, the kingdom of heaven, or spiritual consciousness.

Ruth was of a heathen race; yet because she loved Naomi and Naomi's people, the Israelites (spiritual thoughts and activities), better than the outer things of the physical world, she became the wife of Boaz, who was one of the foremost men of Israel (his name means *alacrity, in strength, in power*), and both David and Jesus were descended from her. So the love of the natural man in us, when turned to the things of Spirit, opens the way in our consciousness for the new birth into the realization and demonstration of our divine sonship.

Out of Mary Magdalene Jesus cast seven devils, which shows that she must have been under great bondage to sense thinking; yet, because she loved the Christ, she was made free. She lingered longest at the cross when Jesus was crucified, and she was first at the tomb on the morning of the resurrection; she served and worshiped much because she loved much, and she was greatly blessed.

Rahab the harlot gives another lesson along the same line. She lived in Jericho, the first city taken by the Israelites when they entered the Promised Land. She befriended the Israelitish spies, and she and her household were saved when the city was captured. Jericho (*his moon*) represents reflected thoughts about life in the subconsciousness. Rahab the harlot signifies the depths of sense into which the natural love had fallen. Yet when the city was approached by the spies (the first thoughts of Truth sent to the life center in the organism where sense had been exercising dominion so long), this natural love at once recognized the superiority of spiritual ideas over the old carnal beliefs, and so received gladly the new light. This love therefore is preserved and is lifted to higher expression. Rahab and her relatives not only dwelt among the Israelites in the Promised Land, but Rahab married Salmon and they were the parents of Boaz, who became Ruth's husband, and all four of them are named in the genealogy of Jesus (Matt. 1:5).

There is in reality but one love, and that is God. So this phase of, the one love that has been expressing in natural and even fallen ways is lifted, when purified of the error thoughts that have been woven about it by man in his ignorance and limitation, to its true expression; thus it becomes a part of man's spiritual, or Christ, consciousness. (Do not confuse this Rahab with the one that follows.)

Rahab, rā'-hăb (Heb.)—*outrageous; violent; tumult; fierce; courageous; proud; vain; insolent; a sea monster; crocodile.*

A symbolical name for Egypt (Psalms 89:10; Isa. 51:9).

Meta. The meanings of this name (*outrageous, violent, tumult, fierce, proud, vain, insolent, a sea monster, crocodile*) all point to error ideas and activities that exist in the darkened, ignorant, sense consciousness in man. (Do not confuse this Rahab with the preceding one.)

Raham, rā'-hăm (Heb.)—*to soften; to soothe; to be fond; to cherish; to love; pity; mercy; compassion; tenderness; inwards; belly; bowels; womb.*

Son of Shema and "father" of Jorkeam, of the tribe of Judah (I Chron. 2:44).

Meta. The tender, merciful, compassionate, brooding, mother phase of love active in the high, somewhat spiritual thoughts of man (*to soften, to soothe, to cherish, to love, pity, mercy, compassion, tenderness, inwards, belly, bowels, womb,* a man of Judah). In the Authorized Version, we read of "bowels of compassion" and "bowels of mercies" (I John 3:17; Col. 3:12).

rainbow.

Meta. The "rainbow" as a "token of a covenant between me and the earth" (Gen. 9:13-15) involves the law of obedience (Noah). The rainbow is formed of many drops of water, each of which acts as a prism receiving and transmitting the sunlight. Each drop represents a human being and the whole the race. The seven colors of the solar spectrum are produced by different rates of vibration in a universal energy, which in its myriad activities makes the visible universe.

When man is like Noah, obedient to the guidance of God, he will never be flooded by negative conditions; and when the whole race enters into this obedience the perfect principles will be forever established. The rainbow is a sign of this state in which we all shall form, with our obedient minds, a circle of natural perfection.

Rakem, rā'-kĕm (Heb.)—*decked with colors; variegated; versicolored; embroidered; curiously shaped; elaborately patterned; marvelously wrought; flower culture; princely raiment.*

Grandson of Machir, a Manassite (I Chron. 7:16).

Meta. A thought belonging to the understanding faculty in individual consciousness (a man of the tribe of Manasseh), and pertaining to the cultivation of that which is beautiful, Godlike, spiritual (*decked with colors, marvelously wrought, princely raiment, flower culture,* flowers representing spiritual ideas).

Rakkath, răk'-kăth (Heb.)—*pouring out; flowing; bank; shore; coast.*

A fortified city of Naphtali (Josh. 19:35).

Meta. Ideas of universal strength, *flowing* into individual consciousness and becoming established in substance. (*Bank, shore,* and *coast* relate to earth, or substance, lying alongside a stream or body of water. Rakkath is thought to have been situated on the shore of the Sea of Galilee. The Sea of Galilee represents life activity, soul energy, power, force, acting in conjunction with substance. Rakkath was a city of Naphtali, and Naphtali signifies the strength faculty in man.)

Rakkon, răk'-kŏn (Heb.)—*beaten out; thinness; overlaid; well-watered; extreme boundary; furthermost shore.*

A city of Dan (Josh. 19:46).

Meta. In I Corinthians 3:6 Paul says, "I planted, Apollos watered; but God gave the increase." Paul signifies the converted will sowing the word of Truth (seed) in all parts of the body; Apollos, who waters the growing Truth in consciousness, signifies understanding. Thus Rakkon, a city of Dan, and meaning *well-watered*, signifies a thought center, belonging to the judgment faculty in man, that is well supplied with understanding, discernment, discrimination.

Beaten out, thinness, overlaid, extreme boundary show that this group of discriminative, discerning thoughts has become established in substance in some degree; its influence has spread throughout the consciousness, acting as a covering or protection.

Ram, răm (Heb.)—*lifted up; raised; elevated; made high; exalted; extolled; elated.*

a Son of Hezron and father of Amminadab, of the direct descendants of Judah, from whom David was descended (Ruth 4:19). **b** Son of Jerahmeel, of the tribe of Judah (I Chron. 2:25). Elihu the son of Barachel the Buzzite, of the book of Job, was of the family of Ram (Job 32:2).

Meta. Exalted spiritual understanding in consciousness, exalting God as the source of all true intelligence and wisdom (*made high, elevated, lifted up, exalted, extolled,* Israelites). Elihu of The Book of Job, who was of the family of Ram, symbolizes the Holy Spirit's entering the consciousness of the individual, or the individual's becoming conscious of the Holy Spirit within him, and being taught by Spirit.

ram, caught in thicket by Abraham, for sacrifice (Gen. 22:13).

Meta. Animal strength in generation. The Hebrew word used in Genesis 22:13 is *ajil* or *ail,* and is applied to the ram because of his twisted horns, as an emblem of animal strength, might, power, and nobility, on the physical plane.

Ramah (in A. V., Matthew 2:18, Rama), rā'-măh (Heb.)—*a high place; height; an elevation; an exaltation; a sublimity.*

a A city of Benjamin (Josh. 18:25). **b** A city on the border of Asher (Josh.

19:29). **c** A fortified city of Naphtali (Josh. 19:36). **d** A city of Ephraim (I Sam. 1:1, 19). "Baasha king of Israel went up against Judah, and built Ramah, that he might not suffer any one to go out or come in to Asa king of Judah"; but Asa had his men destroy this Ramah that Baasha had built (I Kings 15:17, 22). Deborah the prophetess dwelt "between Ramah and Beth–el in the hill-country of Ephraim" (Judg. 4:5). Samuel the prophet lived in Ramah (I Sam. 7:17).

Meta. A very high place in consciousness, or an exalted state of mind (*a high place, height, an elevation, a sublimity*).

Ramathaim–zophim, rā-măth-ā'-ĭm-zō'-phĭm (Heb.)—*watchers of the heights; double watchtowers; double height of watchers; overcomers of the heights.*

A place in the hill country of Ephraim. There lived Elkanah and Hannah, the parents of Samuel, and there Samuel was born (I Sam. 1:1).

Meta. Doubly watchful, or doubly receptive to the inflow of high, spiritual understanding (*watchers of the heights, double watchtowers, double height of watchers, overcomers of the heights*, a place in the hill country of Ephraim). The idea of overcoming, of expressing and demonstrating Truth, is also contained in Ramathaim–zophim.

Ramathite, rā'-măth-īte (fr. Heb.)—*of* or *belonging to Ramah.*

An inhabitant of Ramah. Shimei the Ramathite was in charge of the vineyards, in David's reign (I Chron. 27:27).

Meta. A thought belonging to that in consciousness which Ramah signifies. (See RAMAH and SHIMEI.)

Ramath–lehi, rā'-măth-lē'-hī (fr. Heb.)—*the height of Lehi; throwing of the jawbone; raising up the jawbone; height of vigorous strength; height of virility.*

The place where Samson cast from his hand the jawbone of the ass with which he had just killed a thousand Philistines (Judg. 15:17, in margin, "*The hill of the jawbone*").

Meta. A lifting up, in consciousness, of the qualities that the jawbone of the ass signifies: determination, endurance, vigorous strength, and so forth. (See LEHI.)

Ramath–mizpeh, rā'-măth-mĭz'-pĕh (Heb.)—*height of Mizpeh; height of the watchtower; height for seeing far and wide; elevation of the watcher; high watch.*

A border city of Gad (Josh. 13:26).

Meta. Mizpah (*watchtower*) signifies spiritual watching, one's being on guard against the encroachment of error, keeping one's attention fixed steadfastly on the perfect good to which one aspires. "Take ye heed, watch and pray," was the admonition of Jesus.

Ramath–mizpeh (*height of Mizpeh*) refers to the very high phase of thought or of mind from which this spiritual watching is done, even the spiritual or Christ consciousness.

Rameses, răm'-ĕ-sĕs (fr. Egypt.)—*son of Ra; son of the sun; emanation of the sun; born of the sun; production of the sun.*

A place in Egypt where Joseph placed his father and his brothers, and gave them possessions (Gen. 47:11). It was a city in the land of Goshen, and the name was sometimes given to the whole province.

Meta. See RAAMSES.

Ramiah, rā-mī'-äh (Heb.)—*Jehovah is high; exalted by Jehovah; Jehovah exalts; Jah raises up on high.*

Son of Parosh, one who had taken a foreign wife during the Babylonian captivity (Ezra 10:25).

Meta. A thought activity in the higher religious ideals of man (Israelites) that exalts the Christ in consciousness (*Jehovah is high*), and is in turn lifted to a high plane of light and Truth (*exalted by Jehovah*). "And I, if I be lifted up from the earth, will draw all men unto myself," said the Christ in Jesus. The rendering of this text as given in the Emphatic Diaglott is, "And I, if I be raised on high from the EARTH, will draw All to myself." Even so, if one exalts the Christ —one's true, spiritual I AM—in one's life and keeps the mind's eye centered on seeing the Son in oneself and in all people, all of one's thoughts and all that is in one will be raised to spiritual expression and manifestation.

Ramoth – gilead, rā'-mŏth – gĭl'-ĕ-ăd (Heb.)—*heights of Gilead; high mound of witnesses; high perpetual testimony.*

A fortified city of Gad. It is identical with Ramoth in Gilead, or Ramoth, a city of Gad, and is thought to be the same city as Ramath–mizpeh (Deut. 4:43; I Kings 22:3-29). Ramoth-gilead was a Levitical city and a city of refuge (Josh. 21:38).

Meta. Ramoth–gilead (*heights of Gilead, high mound of witnesses, high perpetual testimony*) signifies a very high place in consciousness, that place, or phase of spiritual consciousness, in us wherein Spirit unceasingly discerns and witnesses to the Truth and to our thoughts and acts, that adjustment may be made throughout mind and body. (See RAMATH–MIZPEH.)

Rapha, rā'-phà. See REPHAIAH.

Raphah (A. V., Rapha), rā'-phăh (Heb.)—*high; tall; heroic; gigantic; repaired; mended; restored to a former state; healed; made whole; wholesome; allayed; quiet; calmed; consoled; comforted; relaxed; let go; slackened; feeble; slothful.*

a Son of Benjamin. The name here is spelled Rapha (I Chron. 8:2). **b** Son of Binea, a Benjamite descended from Saul through Jonathan (I Chron. 8:37). This latter Raphah is called Rephaiah in I Chronicles 9:43. **c** In the margin of II Samuel 21:16, 20, 22, the "giant" of the Philistines is called Raphah.

Meta. For the significance of the Benjamites named Rapha and Raphah, see REPHAIAH.

Raphah, the Philistine giant (*high, tall, heroic, gigantic*), refers to the apparent power and greatness of the thoughts and forces in us that are opposed to the rule of the Holy Spirit. These errors are the Philistines; we are often scared, even terrified, at the giant-like proportions of some leading thought on the error side, represented by Goliath and the other sons of this Raphah, the giant. Our "giant" of error may be different from that of other individuals, but it daily makes a great show of strength and intimidates us with its seeming power.

Persons who do not understand the conquering power of love (David) centered in I AM, Jehovah, see no way of overcoming the sense thoughts that continually defy with their show of strength. But they can be overcome and slain through the Christ in us raised to dominion, and we can enjoy the peace and good results of victory over all that is unlike our perfect model—spiritual man, who was created in God's image and likeness, who is the true self of each of us and has been manifested to us in the person of Jesus Christ.

Relaxed, slackened, feeble, slothful, meanings of Raphah, show the natural reaction from sense expressions of force and power through personal intellect and will.

Raphu, rā'-phū (Heb.)—*repaired; mended; healed; restored; made whole; wholesome.*

Father of Palti, of the tribe of Benjamin. Palti was chosen to assist in spying out the land of Canaan preparatory to the Israelites' going over and possessing it (Num. 13:9).

Meta. Faith in a high curative power —a power that works for healing and for good to man (*repaired, mended, healed, restored, made whole, wholesome, a Benjamite*).

ravens, the, that fed Elijah flesh and bread (I Kings 17:6).

Meta. Natural forces moving with the freedom of birds, or thoughts in objective consciousness.

In the Ferrar Fenton translation of the Bible the word "Arabs" is used in I Kings 17:4-6, instead of "ravens." The root from which this word is drawn is vocalized "arab." It relates to the natural, outer, or physical world. Thus we have Arbi, of the outer, westerner, from the region of darkness, an Arab; and Ereb, deprived of light, black, voracious appetites, a raven. The words in the plural as written in the original Hebrew, without vowel or vocalization points, are identical in appearance.

It is evident that in the story of I Kings 17:1-6 we can choose between ravens or Arabs. The reasoning intellect would be better satisfied with Arabs as the most logical. Whether ravens or Arabs, however, the spiritual interpretation would be the same, since both words rest on the same elements.

The ravens, or Arabs, here stand for the natural forces of the outer man, which apart from a consciousness of Spirit do not give lasting sustenance. Elijah had to move his headquarters because the brook, the very stream of life, eventually dried up. The bread and oil that became inexhaustible refer to the light and substance of Spirit.

Reaiah (in A. V., I Chronicles 5:5, Reaia), rê-ā'-ĭăh (Heb.)—*Jah sees; Jehovah looks upon; Jehovah approves; Jah chooses; Jehovah provides; Jah cares for.*

a Son of Shobal, a descendant of Judah (I Chron. 4:2). **b** A Reubenite (I Chron. 5:5). **c** One of the Nethinim whose "children" returned from the Babylonian captivity with Zerubbabel (Ezra 2:47).

Meta. Thoughts relating to spiritual sight, to the knowledge of God, through the indwelling Christ, Jehovah, as the source of man's understanding, judgment, protection, and supply (*Jah sees, Jehovah looks upon, Jah chooses, Jehovah provides, Jah cares for*).

Reba, rē'-bȧ (Heb.)—*four; quarter; fourth part; quadrated; quartered; side of a square; encouch; lie down with; gender; sprout; offspring; bestiality.*

One of the five kings of Midian, slain by the Israelites under Moses at the same time that Balaam, son of Beor, was killed (Num. 31:8).

Meta. A ruling thought in the judging and discerning yet very contentious state of mind in man that the Midianites signify (a king of Midian; see MIDIAN and MIDIANITES).

This thought has a fraction of Truth (*quarter, fourth part*), but expresses this Truth to the building up of sense. Thus it becomes one-sided, unbalanced, in its judgment, and bestial in its activity; it must be put away as error by the real, all-round true thoughts of one's consciousness (Israelites).

Rebekah, rê-bĕk'-ăh (Heb.)—*tying firmly; fastening; binding; noosed cord; captivating; snare; beauty that ensnares; grace that enraptures.*

Daughter of Bethuel, wife of Isaac, and mother of Jacob and Esau (Gen. 24:15-67). The name is spelled Rebecca in Romans 9:10.

Meta. The soul's natural delight in beauty. This essence of the soul is continually going forth and making attachments with the harmonious and beautiful (interpretation of Gen. 24:59).

Genesis 24:60: Through the inherent love of the harmonious, thousands are blessed and many hearts of "hate" are directed into other channels of expression.

Genesis 24:61: Faith in God and obedience to the urge of Spirit brings into expression a serene peace and joy.

Genesis 24:62: Isaac, meaning *laughter,* dwelt in the land of the South (subconsciousness). Spiritual living fills one with an inner satisfaction that radiates as a joyous expression of life and love.

Genesis 24:63: In the joy of spiritual realization the thoughts are lifted up in exaltation and praise.

Genesis 24:64: The devout, joyous soul readily makes union with the natural, harmonious expression of Spirit.

Genesis 24:65: The joyous soul is screened from contact with inharmonies, when established in spiritual faith and poise: "and she took her veil and covered herself."

Genesis 24:66, 67: Here is portrayed the union of the joyous soul and the divine, natural beauty. The happy Isaac consciousness claims its counterpart in Rebekah, whose name signifies *fastening, noosed cord, captivating, beauty that ensnares;* that is, a young woman whose beauty ensnares men. Faith and obedience bring joy, and spiritual joy links man with the beauty of nature.

Recah (A. V., Rechah) rē'-eăh (Heb.) —*softness; thigh; ham; haunch; side; hinder part; inner part; hidden part; inaccessible part; recess; declivity; uttermost part; most remote region; extremity.*

A city, or place, in Judah (I Chron. 4:12).

Meta. A very innermost state of thought that is sacred to the individual. In the meaning of Recah, *thigh* is considered in opposition to the loin and refers to that which is secret and sacred.

When Moses saw the "back" of Jehovah, it is to say that he had penetrated into the most sacred recesses of divine mystery (see Exod. 33:23, also I Kings 7: 25, in connection with this). The idea of *softness* is also associated with that which is the most *inaccessible*.

Rechab, rē'-ehăb (Heb.)—*rider*, i. e., of *horse, ass,* or *camel; driver,* i. e., of *wagon* or *chariot; band of riders on camels; horseman; troops; wagon; chariot; charioteer.*

a Son of Rimmon. With his brother Baanah he killed Ish–bosheth, Saul's son who had been proclaimed king by Abner after Saul was slain. Rechab and Baanah were captains under Ish–bosheth (II Sam. 4:2-12). **b** The father of Jehonadab, or Jonadab. Jehonadab joined Jehu in killing the remainder of the house of Ahab and in destroying the Baal worshipers out of Israel (II Kings 10:15, 23). This Rechab was the founder of the Rechabites of Jeremiah 35:6-19; see also I Chronicles 2:55 and Nehemiah 3:14.

Meta. The power to control and direct (*horseman, rider*) the vital thoughts and forces with their resultant body activities (*horses* relating to the vital forces in man, and *wagon, chariot,* to the body activities). The central thought in Rechab is that of riding and driving, or the power to control and direct.

Rechab, the father of Jonadab and founder of the Rechabites, symbolizes more particularly the power (*horseman*) of thoughts that are moved by sound logic. These thoughts (Rechabites) stand out clearly in their obedient, faithful nature. They do not respond to the mixed, confused ideas of the material consciousness, Babylonians, and the like.

The Rechabites would not drink wine because their ancestor Jonadab (*whom Jehovah impels*) had said that they should not. The power of understanding —even if this understanding is of the intellect—existing in companionship with divine wisdom is not influenced by the ignorant belief that material stimulation of any kind is needed. It knows that the life of Spirit is ever present in abundance to strengthen, support, and invigorate the entire system; there is

therefore no need of wine (false material stimulants) to revivify and sustain the mind and the body.

The Rechabites did not build houses; they dwelt in tents. This means that true reason in man would not bar man's spiritual ongoing and good by settling down to crystallized rules and forms of thought. It is ever progressive, ready to move on to higher and more perfect ideas and methods of thinking.

Rechabites, rē'-ehăb-ītes (fr. Heb.)— *of* or *belonging to Rechab.*

Descendants of Jonadab, son of Rechab. They were a Kenite tribe, or family, who adhered to certain principles or habits of life because they had been charged to do so by Jonadab (Jer. 35: 2-18).

Meta. That in consciousness which stands for logical reasoning, level-headedness, faithfulness, and good judgment.

Jehovah caused Jeremiah to tempt the Rechabites because Jehovah counted the Rechabites (logical reasoning) worthy of a test. Through trial of our spiritual strength our real worth is established. Sometimes when man is in an exalted state of consciousness he will for the time being lay aside his better judgment and do (in a spirit of jollity) that which he would not do otherwise; hence the need of being tested.

An explanation of the words of Jonadab, as given in Jeremiah 35:6, 7, is that this was Jehovah's way of working to keep these thoughts of logical reasoning from settling down into a crystallized, fixed state of consciousness. It was Jehovah's way of keeping these thoughts of level-headedness in a quickened, alert, energizing state of activity, where they would move about from place to place in the soul consciousness, yet retain their substantiality and reliableness.

Jeremiah 35:19 means that, through obedience to the things of Spirit, new strength, new power, and new courage are added. Logical reasoning stands the test, and thereafter operates from the eternal spiritual plane of consciousness, the kingdom of heaven within man.

The Rechabites can also be explained as representing the faithfulness of the intellect to ancestral laws and habits of thought.

History says that the Rechabites were a religious order in ancient Israel, whose rule in some respects was like that of the Nazirites to which John the Baptist belonged. Like the Nazirites, they were bound by vow to abstain from the use of wine. They lived in tents and refused to plant vineyards or sow seed. Their ideal was the nomadic, patriarchal life amid their flocks.

The object of these rules of life was to prevent the Rechabites from becoming attached to things of sense.

Jeremiah was appealing to the Children of Israel (who represent our spiritual thoughts, or our understanding of Truth) that they should be as faithful and obedient in following the commands of Jehovah as the Rechabites had been in following their father Jonadab.

Red Sea.

A long, narrow sea that lies between Asia and Africa (Josh. 24:6); it is called "the sea" in most places in the Bible wherein it is mentioned. It was through this sea that the Israelites passed on dry land, while the Egyptians who followed them were drowned (Exod. 14:2-28).

Meta. A fixed sea of universal thought that has become part of the very world in which we live. We find it as the race belief in life separate from God, and it has taken up its abode in the sense man and forms a part of his physical existence. The human concept that the life in the body is mortal must be set aside, and the God dominion declared. There is but one life, God.

There is a universal life force, which moves upon a universal substance. This combination of life and substance is the matrix in which all mind force works; symbolically it is the Red Sea or life sea. Human thoughts, which form part of the race consciousness, have impregnated this sea. The Red Sea represents the sum of all the thoughts about life with which the race has impregnated the universal ether. In the mythology of the Greeks and the Romans this is symbolized by the river Styx, over which souls were ferried by Charon. It is familiar to metaphysicians as the psychic realm or race thought, which has to be overcome by the progressive soul.

Reelaiah, rē-ĕl-ā′-ĭ̯ah (Heb.)—*shaken of Jehovah; whom Jehovah makes tremble; brandishing of Jah; shaking of the Lord.*

One who returned from the Babylonian captivity with Zerubbabel (Ezra 2:2). He is called Raamiah in Nehemiah 7:7.

Meta. See RAAMIAH.

Regem, rē′-ğĕm (Heb.)—*heaping up; piling up; accumulating; heap of stones; cairn; monument; laying on colors; writing; throng; band; associate; friend.*

Son of Jahdai, of the tribe of Judah (I Chron. 2:47).

Meta. A thought of accumulation of true ideas, coöperation, fellowship, in the Judah or praise consciousness in the individual (*heaping up, accumulating, laying on colors, writing, band, associate, friend*). *Heap of stones,* a definition of this name, may refer to the faith steps that have brought this Judah thought to its present basis of good (stones here make one think of Peter—a rock or stone, and symbolizing faith).

Regem – melech, rē′-ğĕm – mē′-lĕch (Heb.)—*friend of Melech; associate of the king; royal friend; regal color, i. e., purple.*

One who was sent by the captive Jews in Babylon to Jerusalem to inquire of the priests there concerning fasting, and other things (Zech. 7:2).

Meta. A thought of power that is related to and in association with the will faculty in the individual (*friend of Melech, associate of the king, regal color, i. e., purple,* purple representing power and the king representing the will). This thought perceives a higher ruling power for man than the human will, even the divine law, and it seeks association with that also (*royal friend,* one who was sent to Jerusalem from the Jews in Babylon to find out more about the statutes of Jehovah).

Rehabiah, rē-hă-bī′-ăh (Heb.)—*Jehovah is wide; Jah is a widener; whom Jehovah enlarges, i. e., liberates and makes happy; Jah is broad; Jehovah is ample.*

The only son of Eliezer son of Moses (I Chron. 23:17).

Meta.—

"There's a wideness in God's mercy,
    Like the wideness of the sea;
There's a kindness in His justice,
    Which is more than liberty.

"For the love of God is broader
    Than the measure of man's mind;
And the heart of the Eternal
    Is most wonderfully kind."

By contemplating this "wideness" and "broadness" of the divine love, mercy, justice, and Truth, the individual consciousness is lifted out of narrow, prejudiced, preconceived ideas and beliefs, and becomes enlarged so as to receive a true comprehension of God: this is Rehabiah (*Jehovah is wide, Jah is broad, Jah is a widener, whom Jehovah enlarges,* i. e., *liberates and makes happy*), a man of the tribe of Levi (love), and grandson of Moses, who represents the evolutionary law, or upward trend of all things, which is constantly working within each individual to lead him onward to higher and more perfect understanding and development.

Rehob, rē'-hŏb (Heb.) — *width; breadth; largeness; spacious; comprehensive; great understanding,* i. e., *broad-minded; broad-visioned; open place; market place; forum.*

a A city in Palestine (Num. 13:21). It was allotted to Asher (Josh. 19:30). **b** Father of Hadadezer king of Zobah, who was smitten by David and his men (II Sam. 8:3). **c** One who joined Nehemiah in sealing the covenant (Neh. 10:11).

Meta. Thoughts, and a group of thoughts, in individual consciousness that are broad and open, receptive and comprehensive.

The city of Asher, named Rehob, and the man who joined Nehemiah in sealing the covenant, being of Israel, would be thoughts receptive to a higher and broader understanding of God and of Truth. On the other hand, Rehob father of Hadadezer, king of Zobah, of Syria, indicates a sense or intellectual belief in broadness of vision that opens one to a multitude of intellectual reasonings and controversies. These do not lead to a real understanding of Truth, but are de-

structive. (See ZOBAH, the city of this latter Rehob and his son.)

Rehoboam, rē-hŏ-bō'-ăm (Heb.)—*the people are enlarged; comprehending the people; freer of the people; he enlarges the people.*

Son of Solomon by Naamah the Ammonitess. He became king when Solomon died, and during his reign the Israelites were divided into two kingdoms (I Kings 11:43; 14:21).

Meta. That in man's consciousness which exalts the senses, that which is receptive to and comprehensive of the selfish demands of the sense thoughts and desires only (*comprehending the people, the people are enlarged, he enlarges the people*):

The reason why Solomon (wisdom) brought forth a son who was considered evil and a fool was that Solomon (wisdom), one who was mighty in his understanding and use of God-given riches, appropriated the wealth of Israel (body consciousness) for his own selfish and sensuous pleasures. Rehoboam is the fruit of many sensuous and insane thought habits. Solomon had a thousand wives, but only one son—and that one was a fool.

The result in Israel (body consciousness) during the reign of Rehoboam (sense side of mind) is that, when sense thoughts and personal will dominate, the kingdom is divided. This results in various forms of insanity, weakness, and inharmony throughout the mind and the body. (See JEROBOAM, about the dividing of the kingdom.)

Rehoboam is the selfish ignoramus that a thousand sensuous thoughts have brought forth in a man. Give yourself up to the sense side of your mind wholly and you will eventually find your kingdom divided. No man can divorce himself from God and be sane. He will sooner or later develop some phase of mental aberration.

When man has centralized his kingdom in God he becomes true, pure, honest, righteous in all ways, and just in thought and deed. Solomon in his early reign was all this, but he did not stand up under prosperity. The sensuous nature became dominant and he had to levy heavy taxes on his people to keep up the expenditure of substance. When man revels in the sensuous nature, as did Solomon, the vitality of the whole organism is drawn upon. Thus all the people of the kingdom are taxed. This is carried to a point where the God-loving man loses his original character and becomes a conceited profligate: Solomon died and his son Rehoboam reigned in his stead.

Rehoboth (in A. V., Rehoboth–Ir of Genesis 10:11 is called the city Rehoboth), rĕ-hō'-bŏth (Heb.)—*broad places; enlargements; broad lands; wide streets; market places; forums.*

a A city built by Asshur (Gen. 10:11). **b** A well dug by Isaac's herdsmen, and for which the herdsmen of Gerar did not strive. "And he called the name of it Rehoboth; and he said, For now Jehovah hath made room for us, and we shall be fruitful in the land" (Gen. 26:22). Shaul of Rehoboth was a king of Edom (Gen. 36:37).

Meta. Thoughts of a broadening, increasing, enlarging nature (*broad places, enlargements*), principally in the intellectual or mental reasoning plane in the individual. (Asshur, who built the one city of Rehoboth, was of Assyria, and typifies the outer reasoning plane of thought in man; while Shaul, king of Edom, who was of Rehoboth, refers to the desire, longing, and eagerness of the outer consciousness for greater expression.) The place that Isaac named Rehoboth signifies a more interior expansion of thought.

Rehum, rē'-hŭm (Heb.)—*soothing; glowing with an inward warmth; compassionate; having pity; loving; tender; affectionate.*

a One who returned from the captivity with Zerubbabel (Ezra 2:2); in Nehemiah 7:7, he is called Nehum. **b** Other men by this name are mentioned in Nehemiah 3:17, 10:25, and 12:3.

Meta. Rehum suggests the tender, brooding, mother love of God, which soothes the whole being of man and through which new understanding and realization of Truth are germinated in consciousness and grow and increase to perfect expression and demonstration.

Rei, rē'-ī (Heb.)—*friendly; compan-ionable; sociable; lovable; inclination; thought; desire; will; nourishing; feeding; shepherding.*

One of David's mighty men. He remained friendly to David and would not join Adonijah in his conspiracy against David, to take the throne (I Kings 1:8).

Meta. The inner assurance of the individual. that Jehovah is a friend and a shepherd to him. This in turn begets a feeling of good will and kindly interest in the individual toward others (*friendly, companionable, lovable, nourishing, shepherding*). "We love, because he first loved us" (I John 4:19). This kindly, friendly, good-will attitude of mind belongs to and is a strong asset of the love (David) quality in man (Rei was one of David's mighty men, one who stayed with David at a time when he needed help).

Rekem, rē'-kĕm (Heb.)—*decking with colors; variegation; embroidering; shaping after an elaborate pattern; floriculture; artistic coloring; decking with princely raiment.*

a One of the five kings of Midian that the Israelites, under Moses, overcame and slew (Num. 31:8). **b** A city of Benjamin (Josh. 18:27). **c** Son of Hebron and father of Shammai, descendant of Caleb, of the tribe of Judah (I Chron. 2:43).

Meta. Rekem, like Rakem, pertains to the cultivation of ideas of Truth, of that which is beautiful, spiritual, Godlike, of that which belongs to the bringing into manifestation of the image-and-likeness-of-God man (*decking with colors, embroidering, shaping after an elaborate pattern, floriculture, artistic coloring, decking with princely raiment*). In a king of Midian this cultivation of beauty and Truth would be from a personal, carnal standpoint, and therefore would be defective; in a city of Benjamin and a man of Judah, it would take on a truer, higher aspect.

Remaliah, rĕm-ă-lī'-ăh (Heb.)—*Jah increases; whom Jehovah hath adorned; whom Jah bedecks; Jah has bedecked.*

Father of Pekah, who slew King Pekahiah of Israel and ruled in his stead (II Kings 15:25; see Isaiah 7:4, 5; 8:6, also).

Meta. A thought in the higher, more

real and true phase of mind in man (an Israelite of note, father of Pekah) that is established in at least a degree of righteousness (*whom Jah bedecks, whom Jehovah hath adorned*). "I will greatly rejoice in Jehovah, my soul shall be joyful in my God; for he hath clothed me with the garments of salvation, he hath covered me with the robe of righteousness, as a bridegroom decketh himself with a garland, and as a bride adorneth herself with her jewels" (Isa. 61:10). This attitude brings an increase of good to the consciousness (*Jah increases*).

While this Remaliah thought is in its highest aspect truly spiritual, in the person of Remaliah it must belong more to the intellectual or outer man than to the inner, and so partakes of limitation and error; the history of the son Pekah proves this. (See PEKAH.) Then too, Remaliah was of the kingdom of Israel and not of Judah. After the division of Israel into two kingdoms, Israel represents the outer and more intellectual religious thoughts of man, while Judah refers to the inner and more truly spiritual consciousness.

Remeth, rē'-měth (Heb.) — *height; high place.*

A city of Issachar (Josh. 19:21); called Ramoth in I Chronicles 6:73.

Meta. See RAMAH and RAMOTH.

rent, the veil of the temple was (Luke 23:45). (See VEIL.)

Meta. A letting go of belief in the reality of material consciousness, and an awakening to the light of Spirit. The final relinquishment of the soul to God is the final giving up of all human ambitions and aims. When this point is reached the soul enters into glory.

repentance.

Meta. The Greek word *metanoia* is translated "repentance," which has been interpreted to mean an admission to God of sorrow for past sin and a resolve to be good in the future. The field of action for that which has been assumed to be goodness in the sight of God has nearly always been in conduct. The whole Christian world has in a measure failed to discern the teaching of the New Testament about mental laws. A proper translation of the mission of John the Baptist is: He came into all the region round about Jordan preaching immersion in mentation for the doing away with shortcoming. *Metanoia* means *change of mind, middle mind, transformation of the mind, change of thought and purpose.*

Baptism means to *immerse in an element* (any element) *to a complete saturation;* one can be immersed in a transformed mind as well as in water. Therefore it is plain that the mission of John was to bring about a change of mind. The fundamental idea is not so much sorrow as a change—a change, however, be it observed, not merely of conduct, but of the thinking and mortal part of man. (In connection with this, see BAPTISM, and especially the baptism of John the Baptist.)

Repent is, in the original Greek, "change your mind."

Rephael, rē'-phă-ĕl (Heb.)—*God mends; God restores to a former state; whom God heals; God cures; God makes whole; consolation of God; God renders wholesome.*

Son of Shemaiah and grandson of Obed–edom, a doorkeeper in the house of Jehovah (I Chron. 26:7).

Meta. A natural religious tendency that is a guarding thought to the door of man's inner consciousness (a Levite, a doorkeeper in the Temple). This thought is established in the idea of divine health, wholeness, in God as healer, restorer, perfecter (*God restores to a former state, whom God heals, God makes whole, God renders wholesome*).

Rephah, rē'-phăh (Heb.)—*riches; wealth; abundance.*

Son of Beriah, an Ephraimite from whom Joshua was descended (I Chron. 7:25).

Meta. The will in man laying hold of the idea of abundant substance (*riches, wealth, abundance,* a man of Ephraim—Ephraim representing the will faculty in individual consciousness).

Rephaiah, rē-phā'-ĭăh (Heb.)—*Jah heals; whom Jehovah has healed; Jah restores; Jehovah makes whole; Jah makes wholesome.*

a A man of Judah (I Chron. 3:21).
b A captain of the Simeonites who went

to Mount Seir and smote the remaining Amalekites (I Chron. 4:42). **c** A man of Issachar (I Chron. 7:2). **d** A Benjamite, called Raphah in I Chronicles 8:37 (I Chron. 9:43). **e** One who helped repair the wall of Jerusalem under Nehemiah (Neh. 3:9).

Meta. The various men by this name, belonging to different Israelitish tribes or different faculties of mind, signify the growth—in man's consciousness—of knowledge of God, through his indwelling Christ, or I AM, as his healing, restoring power (*Jah heals, Jehovah makes whole*).

Rephaim, rĕph'-å-ĭm (Heb.)—*bonds; glooms; terrors; fears; fearful ones; giants; strong ones.*

a A people in Palestine that were to be driven out by the Israelites (Gen. 15:20). They were a people of great stature. Og, king of Bashan, was the only one left at the time Deuteronomy 3:11 was written. **b** A valley where the Philistines gathered to fight against Israel (II Sam. 5:18).

Meta. The seeming strength of binding, fear-producing, opposing thoughts in consciousness, at a certain stage of man's unfoldment into Truth (*bonds, terrors, giants, strong ones,* enemies in the Promised Land; also a place where the Philistines gathered against Israel).

Rephidim, rĕph'-ĭ-dĭm (Heb.)—*stays; supports; cushions; beds; refreshments; places of rest.*

A place where the children of Israel camped when in the wilderness (Exod. 17:1, 8).

Meta. Peace after victory over temptation (*places of rest*). We always enter a period of peace and rest after every inner conquest over error—this is Rephidim. Then comes the urge to press on to greater overcomings. The necessity of doing this is sometimes revealed to us in the form of an enemy that arises in our thoughts and reflects itself in our environment and affairs, or in a great need to be met (the Israelites had to demonstrate water to drink, in Rephidim, and Amalek came and fought them there).

Resen, rē'-sĕn (Heb.)—*executive power; reins of government; control from above; restraint; curbed; a bridle with bit; fountainhead.*

A city between Nineveh and Calah, an Assyrian city built by Asshur (Gen. 10:12).

Meta. Calah signifies a state of consciousness that is built about the belief that age (as it relates to time) and experience bring balanced judgment and all-round fullness or perfection. (See CALAH.)

Nineveh signifies exterior growth, an outer sense of growing vigor, order, unity, harmony, and intellectual understanding that, because of not being always conscious of Spirit, develops into increased materiality. (See NINEVEH.)

Resen (*executive power, reins of government, control from above, restraint, curbed, a bridle with bit, a fountainhead*), a great city that Asshur built between Nineveh and Calah, indicates a recognition by the natural man that there is a higher guiding, ruling, judging, restraining power in his life than that of the purely human and material.

Resheph, rē'-shĕph (Heb.)—*inflamed; flame; kindled; fire; lightning; fever; burning plague; arrows,* i. e., *lightning of the bow; sparks.*

Son of Beriah, a man of Ephraim (I Chron. 7:25).

Meta. The definitions of this name point to an unwise expenditure of energy in the fiery executiveness of an active will. (Ephraim refers to the will faculty in man; *lightning, flame, fire,* bespeak fiery executiveness and activity of the will; *inflamed, fever, burning plague,* reveal a lack of peace and poise, also cross currents in the organism, thus an unwise and destructive expenditure of energy.) A balance should be brought about by a calling of some of the other faculties, such as love, wisdom, good judgment, into expression.

resurrection.

Meta. The raising of man's mind and body from sense to spiritual consciousness. This is accomplished by the quickening power of the Holy Spirit. "If the Spirit of him that raised up Jesus from the dead dwelleth in you, he that raised up Christ Jesus from the dead shall give life also to your mortal bodies through his Spirit that dwelleth in you" (Rom. 8:11).

Jesus was raised from the dead. He overcame death in the body. "By man *came* death, by man *came* also the resurrection of the dead." Physical death is not necessary. "We all shall not sleep, but we shall all be changed" (I Cor. 15:21, 51).

The resurrection is not for the soul alone. "Who shall fashion anew the body of our humiliation, *that it may be* conformed to the body of his glory" (Phil. 3:21). Now is the time of the resurrection. "The hour cometh, and now is, when the dead shall hear the voice of the Son of God" (John 5:25).

The power of the resurrection is the Christ. "I am the resurrection, and the life" (John 11:25). This resurrection is not of the future, "but hath now been manifested by . . . our Saviour Christ Jesus, who abolished death, and brought life and immortality to light" (II Tim. 1:10).

The resurrection is the lifting up of the whole man into the Christ consciousness. The whole man is spirit, soul, and body. The resurrection lifts up all the faculties of mind until they conform to the absolute ideas of Divine Mind, and this renewal of the mind makes a complete transformation of the body so that every function works in divine order and every cell becomes incorruptible and immortal. The resurrection is an organic change that takes place daily in all who are conforming their lives to the regenerating Truth of Jesus Christ. The resurrection takes place here and now in all who conform their lives to the spiritual law under which it works.

Death does not change man and bring him into the resurrection and eternal life. Death has no place in the Absolute. It is the result of sin, and has no uplifting power. Every one who has reaped sin's wages must be restored to his place in the race, that he may have a body through which to work out his salvation under divine law.

Old limited personal relationships do not continue in the resurrection. Those who are being raised into the Christ consciousness will gradually, as their growth in understanding makes it possible, let go all that is personal and selfish in their relationships and come into the larger love, the love universal, where all who do the will of God are fathers and mothers and brothers and sisters. The divine law is fulfilled by the love universal.

Reu, rē'-ū (Heb.)—*leading to pasture; feeding a flock; shepherd; friend; companion.*

Son of Peleg and father of Serug, descended from Shem (Gen. 11:18).

Meta. The coöperative feeling, the feeling of fellowship (*friend, companion*), unfolding in individual consciousness to a sense of loving, active responsibility for the welfare of others (*leading to pasture, feeding a flock, shepherd*).

Reuben, reu'-bĕn (Heb.)—*behold a son; vision of the son; behold ye, a son; a son seen.*

Eldest son of Jacob, by Leah (Gen. 29:32).

Meta. Faith, in its aspect of discernment, sight, in the outer. (See PALLU, son of Reuben.) Reuben, like Simeon, bespeaks understanding.

A faculty takes on the tincture and tone of some associate faculty. We must understand the relation of that faculty, since any faculty can take on the character of another faculty or perform its office. And so we find in the sons of Jacob that the faculties that they signify are interblending and acting in various capacities under varying circumstances.

The twelve sons of Jacob represent the twelve foundation faculties of man. The name of each of these sons, correctly interpreted, gives the development and office of its particular faculty in spirit, soul, and body. For example, when the sons of Jacob were born their mothers revealed the character of the faculties that they represented as set forth in the 29th and 30th chapters of Genesis. "And Leah conceived, and bare a son, and she called his name Reuben: for she said, Because Jehovah hath looked upon my affliction." The emphasis is on the word *looked*, and by referring to the concordance we find that the meaning of the name Reuben is, "a son seen; behold, a son!" It is clear that this refers to the bringing forth of sight. "And she conceived again, and bare a son: and said,

Because Jehovah hath heard that I am hated." Here the emphasis is on the word *heard*, and referring to the concordance we find that Simeon means *who hears, obeys, hearing*. "And she conceived again, and bare a son; and said, Now this time will my husband be joined unto me." In this case the emphasis is on the word *joined*. Levi means *joined to, attached*, or unity, which in body is feeling; in soul, sympathy; and in spirit, love. So each of these twelve faculties in the complete man functions in this threefold degree.

What is here described as the twelve sons of Jacob is the first or natural bringing forth of the faculties, which arrive at a higher expression in the twelve disciples of Jesus Christ. Simon Peter is hearing and faith united. John is feeling and love joined. When we believe what we hear it forms in us the substance of the word, which is Peter, a rock, a sure foundation. "So belief *cometh* of hearing, and hearing by the word of Christ."

Reubenites, reṳ'-bĕn-ītes (fr. Heb.)— *of or belonging to Reuben.*

Descendants of Reuben, the eldest son of Jacob, members of the tribe of Reuben (Num. 26:7).

Meta. Thoughts springing from and belonging to that in consciousness which Reuben signifies. (See REUBEN.)

Reuel, reṳ'-ĕl (Heb.)—*led of God; shepherded of God; friendship of God; companion of God.*

a Son of Esau by Basemath (Gen. 36: 4). b Priest of Midian and father-in-law of Moses (Exod. 2:18). He is called Jethro in Exodus 3:1. c Father of Eliasaph, who was prince of the children of Gad, in the wilderness (Num. 2:14). In Numbers 1:14 he is called Deuel. d A Benjamite mentioned in I Chronicles 9:8.

Meta. A thought of divine guidance and care; also a sense of mutual understanding, comradeship, fellowship, existing between God and man (*led of God, shepherded of God, friendship of God, companion of God*). "Ye are my friends, if ye do the things which I command you. No longer do I call you servants; for the servant knoweth not what his lord doeth: but I have called you friends; for all things that I heard from my Fa-

ther I have made known unto you" (John 15:14, 15).

Reumah, reṳ'-măh (Heb.)—*high; raised; elevated; lofty; sublime; high-priced; red coral; pearl.*

A concubine of Nahor, brother of Abraham (Gen. 22:24).

Meta. The soul or feminine principle in man elevated to a high place of appreciation in consciousness, highly esteemed (*high, raised, lofty, high-priced, pearl*).

Rezeph, rē'-zĕph (Heb.)—*masonry; a pavement; stone mosaics; hearthstone; heated stone, i. e., for heating or baking; live coals.*

Evidently a city or place that was destroyed by the Assyrians. It was mentioned by Rabshakeh in his message from the king of Assyria to Hezekiah, king of Judah (II Kings 19:12).

Meta. A state of thought that has been built up by elaborate reasoning of the intellect, therefore is believed by the outer man to be permanent and sure (*masonry, a pavement, stone mosaics, hearthstone*). The ideas of heat and baking suggest zeal and crystallization of thought (*heated stone, i. e., for heating or baking, live coals*).

Rezin, rē'-zĭn (Heb.)—*delight; approbation; good will; favor; grace; will; pleasure; wicked pleasure; wantonness; ill will; firm; stable; dominion.*

a The king of Syria, whom Jehovah sent against Judah (II Kings 15:37). He was slain by Tiglath–pileser, king of Assyria, at the request of Ahaz, king of Judah, after Ahaz hired the king of Assyria with a large sum of money to fight for him (II Kings 16:7-9). b One of the Nethinim, whose descendants returned from the Captivity with Zerubbabel (Ezra 2:48).

Meta. A ruling thought in the phase of the intellectual realm that has no understanding of the real (a king of Syria who fought against Judah). It has a semblance of good (*pleasure, delight, good will*), which it uses in its reasoning against the inner religious thoughts of the individual that have given themselves over to material beliefs and loves (the people of Judah who had taken up Baal worship) instead of remaining true to omnipresent Spirit. (See BAAL and AHAZ.)

The Rezin who was one of the Nethinim signifies a thought tendency in the serving phase of mind in the Israelitish or true thoughts of man that has learned to *delight* in service, and to serve from a standpoint of *good will* and so to find *pleasure* in serving. Thus it brings forth thoughts that become free from bondage to sense confusion (descendants of Rezin returned to Judah from the Babylonian captivity).

Rezon, rē'-zŏn (Heb.) — *heavy; weighty; august; important; reputed; honored; prince; king.*

Son of Eliada, and an officer of Hadadezer, king of Zobah. He had revolted from Hadadezer and had set up a little kingdom of his own in Damascus. This man became an adversary to Solomon (I Kings 11:23).

Meta. A phase of intellectual thought that aspires to rulership in the consciousness of the individual (*weighty, august, important, prince, king;* Zobah was a portion of Syria, and Zobah, Syria, Hadadezer, and Damascus refer to phases of the intellect when it is guided by the senses).

The text says that God raised Rezon up against Solomon because Solomon had allowed his many foreign wives to turn his heart away from the one true God. This means that when the inner wisdom, represented here by Solomon, unifies itself with the many sensuous emotions and false desires of the animal nature and becomes enamored with them, its power to understand and guide and instruct the true Israelitish phase of mind in the individual becomes dulled. Thus it makes itself a prey to the material reasonings of the sense intellect.

Rhegium, rhē'-ġĭ-ŭm (Gk.) — *rent away; broken off; sundered; fractured; broken; ruptured; breached.*

A seaport of southern Italy. The boat on which Paul was being taken a prisoner to Rome stopped at this place (Acts 28:13).

Meta. A breaking through (*breached*) from one phase of thought to another.

Rhesa, rhē'-så (Gk. fr. Heb.)—*principle; head; chief; first; foremost; elder; former; sum; amount; metropolis; inclination; will; affection.*

Mentioned in the genealogy of Jesus Christ (Luke 3:27).

Meta. The will taking the lead, or first place, in consciousness (*will, head, chief, first, foremost*).

Rhesa expresses that which rules or enjoys by virtue of its own inherent movement; hence, the will. Taken in a negative sense this same independent movement will also characterize a venomous principle, evil, insidious desire, the source of evil, venom. Rhesa, taken in its negative sense, is the head of the serpent of Genesis 3:15.

Rhoda, rhŏ'-då (Gk.)—*rose; rosebush.*

A maid in the home of Mary, the mother of John Mark. She came to the door in answer to Peter's knocking after he had been delivered from prison by the angel in response to those who were praying for him (Acts 12:13-16).

Meta. Love, active in the feminine, intuitive, serving, receptive phase of consciousness in the individual (*rose;* a maid or servant in the home of Mary, the mother of John Mark).

Rhodes, rhōdeṣ (Gk.)—*rose; roses; a place of rosebushes.*

a An island in the Mediterranean Sea. **b** A city on the island. Paul stopped at Rhodes on his way to Jerusalem (Acts 21:1).

Meta. The places mentioned in Acts 21:1-3,—places through which Paul passed on his way to Jerusalem, whence he was going against the repeated warnings of Spirit—with the exception of Patara, indicate pleasant phases of consciousness in the individual who is seeking the highest. These pleasant phases of consciousness are not, however, really on the spiritual plane. Rhodes (*roses*) symbolizes a phase of love or human affection, the rose being a flower that stands especially for the love thought in man.

Ribai, rī'-bāi (Heb.)—*contention; strife; pleading a cause; defending a suit; whom Jehovah defends; Jah contends.*

A man of Gibeah of Benjamin, father of Ittai one of David's mighty men (II Sam. 23:29).

Meta. A high spiritual aspiration in the active faith faculty in man (a man of

Gibeah of Benjamin). This aspiration pertains to an inner perception (faith—Benjamin—being a perceptive quality of mind) of protection, and of overcoming power through Jehovah, I AM (*whom Jehovah defends, Jah contends*). There remains in this perception of protection and of overcoming power much of the old error idea of contention, of the necessity for continued entreaty and for resistance and argument in order to gain the fulfillment of that which one has perceived to be true for one. (This is shown by the definitions of the name, *contention, strife, pleading a cause, defending a suit, Jah contends*.)

We are now coming into the truer understanding that reveals to us that personal contention, strife, and argument are never needed. All that is necessary in overcoming apparent error is to know its unreality, since it is not founded in God, and then to take our stand in Truth —because God is, I AM. Truth is God, and exists eternally; it does not need to fight or strive.

Riblah, rĭb'-lăh (Heb.)—*very much, i. e., in number or volume; fertility; fruitful; abundance; multitude of people.*

a A city on the eastern boundary of the land of Canaan (Num. 34:11). **b** A city in the land of Hamath, where Pharaohnecoh put Jehoahaz, king of Judah, in bonds (II Kings 23:33). **c** The place where Zedekiah was taken as a captive before the king of Babylon. There his sons were slain, and his eyes were put out, and he was bound to be taken to Babylon (II Kings 25:6).

Meta. The belief of the outer man that riches and good, results of true fruitfulness of thought and act, are measured by outer possessions and seeming greatness in the outer; also the belief that strength and power lie in numbers and in outer display (*very much, i. e., in number or volume; fertility; fruitful; abundance; multitude of people*). At Riblah, in Hamath, great calamities befell Jehoahaz and Zedekiah, kings of Judah.

Hamath symbolizes confidence in material conditions rather than trust in God. When man comes into a degree of knowledge of Truth and then falls back into a belief in materiality, putting his trust in outer, seemingly material conditions and riches instead of God, destructive forces work in him to dull his spiritual insight into Truth and to destroy the ruling power of his high ideals. Of course, troubles in body and affairs follow, as a consequence. (See DIBLAH.)

rich man, the.

Meta. The "rich man" of Luke 16:19, who was "clothed in purple and fine linen, faring sumptuously every day," refers especially to the selfish gratification of the appetite and pride of the material man. The sense man hoards the substance of the Father and uses it continually for selfish, sensual gratification, without repentance or change of heart toward God.

rich young man (Mark 10:17-27).

Meta. Personality; the state of consciousness in man that lays hold of the world of form, seeking satisfaction in personal possessions and in fulfilling the letter of the law.

The real goal to be attained in dealing with the manifest world is spiritual understanding, to become conscious of the fact that the reality of anything is the idea underlying it. This goal is attained through the quickening of Spirit, by which man delves beyond intellectual knowledge into an understanding of his spiritual nature and his true relation to the world of manifestation.

Man's true relation to the manifest world may be explained as follows: Thought is the formative power of the mind. Through thought man has consciously or unconsciously laid hold of certain principles and brought into manifestation the world with its limitations. When man spiritualizes his thought he lifts himself and the race into a consciousness of reality and perfectness, which is vastly more important than moral law or external riches.

True prosperity is the being rich in spiritual ideas, out of which comes great abundance in the without, based on an understanding of God and His righteousness; then "all these things shall be added unto you." Spiritual man sees the "things . . . added" in their relation to the ideas that created them and as the expression of God substance. In this way he keeps his mind stayed on divine ideas and becomes a creator of every good thing necessary to the fulfillment of a perfect Christ life.

The promise to those who forsake all and follow the Christ is that those who live by the Christ principle, recognizing God as the source of supply and giving freely of all that they receive, "shall receive a hundredfold" and shall "inherit eternal life."

Personality (the rich young man) is that in us which lays store by the things of form and shape. Selfishness attaches personality to the things of sense, while unselfishness liberates it.

Personality is selfish for eternal life, and strives to attain it; but personality does not know the real good; it is disappointed because it cannot retain its belief in earthly possessions and at the same time have consciousness of spiritual things.

When personality attaches itself to material riches it really believes in another power than God. It trusts the resources of the visible instead of the invisible, and thus weakens its spiritual faculties. All the powers of the mind must be developed spiritward before man can rise to the higher consciousness called heaven. If we trust in riches, our trust in God is weakened; yet we are promised that we shall have all things when we have fulfilled the law of righteousness.

Rimmon, rĭm'-mŏn (Heb.)—*full of substance; marrowy; pomegranate; the exalted; very high.*

a A city of Judah (Josh. 15:32) that passed into the possession of the Simeonites (Josh. 19:7). **b** A border city of Zebulun (Josh. 19:13), given over to the Levites; called Rimmono in I Chronicles 6:77. **c** Father of Rechab and Baanah, captains under Ishbosheth, son of Saul (II Sam. 4:2). **d** A Syrian god (II Kings 5:18). **e** A rock in Benjamin near Gibeah, where six hundred Benjamites fled from the men of Israel and were saved (Judg. 20:47).

Meta. Fruitfulness, or the power to make fruitful (*full of substance, marrowy, pomegranate*). As a city of Judah it symbolizes the fructifying power of

praise. Passing into the possession of the Simeonites, Rimmon would indicate greater obedience and receptivity to Truth. As a border city of Zebulun it refers to an increasing idea of order in individual consciousness, and the good results that follow. As a Syrian god Rimmon denotes the attributing of increase of good, fruitfulness, to the intellect guided by the senses, instead of knowing that Spirit is the source of all increase of good.

Rimmon–perez (A. V., Rimmon–parez), rĭm'-mŏn–pē'-rĕz (Heb.)—*pomegranates of the breach; breaking up of substance; high cleft; substance of defeat; exalted wrath.*

A place where the Children of Israel camped when in the wilderness (Num. 33:19).

Meta. A breaking up of the substance idea in consciousness; breaking into its parts, or analyzing, the power to make fruitful (*pomegranates of the breach, breaking up of substance, high cleft*). This breaking up takes place so that true ideas of fruitfulness, of increase of substance and life, may find a lodging place in the mind. Taken in a negative sense this analysis would be of the outer thought and would bring about lack of success and supply (*substance of defeat*), but from a positive standpoint it leads to greater good.

Rinnah, rĭn'-näh (Heb.)—*tremulous vibration; strident sound; vibrant voice; song of praise; shout of joy; roaring torrent; mournful cry; wailing moan.*

Son of Shimon, a man of Judah (I Chron. 4:20).

Meta. Power expressing through the voice (*tremulous vibration, strident sound, vibrant voice, song of praise, shout of joy, roaring torrent*). Rinnah may also be said to signify an inner reaching after God. In the consciousness that is not yet poised in understanding, this inner urge and longing may take on characteristics either of positive affirmation and declaration of good as already received, or a negative form of prayer, that of sorrowful supplication (*mournful cry, wailing moan*).

Riphath, rī'-phăth (Heb.)—*centrifugal force; spoken word; rarefaction; slack-*

ening; remission; pardon; healing.

Son of Gomer who was a son of Japheth and grandson of Noah (Gen. 10:3). In I Chronicles 1:6, he is called Diphath.

Meta. Power expressing actively through the will and the word (*centrifugal force, spoken word*). This activity, though more mental than spiritual, is refining and healing (*rarefaction, healing*). Under a negative influence this same activity or movement becomes lassitude and weakness (*slackening*).

Rissah, rĭs'-săh (Heb.)—*breaking of bonds; disintegration; crushed; ruined; scattered; sprinkled; moistened; dew; distillation.*

A place where the Israelites camped when in the wilderness (Num. 33:21).

Meta. Upon the apparent *ruin* that is the result of a breaking up of old crystallized error or limited ideas and thoughts, there comes the refreshing *dew* of true understanding, of renewed peace, vigor, strength, and joy, from God, who is now being recognized by the individual as the one source of all that is necessary for his sustenance and upbuilding.

rites.

Meta. The rites and ceremonies of the priests in the tabernacle represent the action of spiritual forces in developing the body. The great object of man's existence in planetary consciousness is to build a body after the ideals given by the Lord. The physical body is the tabernacle or temporary structure in and through which the enduring body is formed, and regeneration is a combination of chemical, mental, and spiritual processes.

Digestion is the process of making utilizable the energy stored in material envelopes or cells. This energy may be used to vitalize the muscles or to aid in brain building, but it must get its life from Spirit. If it fails to do this the structure that it builds is lifeless.

It is evident from a reading of Leviticus 10:1-11 that Nadab and Abihu put alcohol (see verse 9) in their censers (stomachs) instead of the natural regenerative fire of Spirit. Alcohol is an attempt by man to make a substitute for the natural life energy that is imparted to him by the Lord. When this artificial fire is put into the stomach it clashes with the finer energies of the system; the result is destruction of the cells, similar to the burning out of a dynamo.

For this reason it is more dangerous for one who has entered the regeneration to drink wine, or anything else containing free alcohol, than for the unregenerate. In the latter the Spirit fire from on high has not been kindled, and after a period of stupor the nerves and temporarily excited cells are at peace. One who has started the soul life in his system, however, should beware how he attempts to stimulate that life from the material side of existence. It is sanctified to the Lord, and its only source of increase and glorification is Spirit.

Rithmah, rĭth'-măh (Heb.)—*bound; made fast; wound about; harnessed; Genista; broom; wild broom; juniper.*

A place where the Israelites camped when in the wilderness (Num. 33:18).

Meta. A degree of mind cleansing that results in a revivifying and energizing of the nervous system in the individual who has been wandering about in the wilderness of his undisciplined and confused thoughts, while on his way to a clear understanding and demonstrating of Truth (the Promised Land).

The "juniper" of the desert in which the Children of Israel wandered while on their way to the Promised Land is a bushlike tree belonging to the broom family. Rithmah (meaning *broom, juniper*) was no doubt so named because of the presence of large quantities of this shrub. There was doubtless no other kind of shelter at Rithmah, as is often the case in the deserts of Arabia, and especially of Sinai. Thus travelers are very thankful for this shelter. Elijah lay under a juniper tree and slept, after his day's journey into the wilderness to escape from Jezebel. A bush or tree represents the nervous system in man, and the *juniper* or *broom* here bespeaks a refreshing of the consciousness and organism by means of the cleansing of the thoughts and a renewing of the nervous system.

Discipline enters into the mind cleansing that Rithmah bespeaks, a binding or ceasing to give further expression to the error that is being put away (*bound, harnessed*).

river.

Meta. A current of thought or a current of vital forces, of life. The "river" of Genesis 2:10 symbolizes the current of life in the organism (garden).

Rizia (A. V., Rezia), rĭ-zī-'ȧ (Heb.)— *delight; pleasure; bliss; satisfaction; desire; love,* i. e., *to delight or take pleasure in anything.*

Son of Ulla, of the tribe of Asher (I Chron. 7:39).

Meta. A consciousness of Joy, satisfaction, because of fulfilled desire. The definitions of Rizia make us think of Psalms 37:4:

"Delight thyself also in Jehovah;
    And he will give thee the desires of thy
        heart."

Rizpah, rĭz'-păh (Heb.)—*hot stone* (for baking); *hearthstone; mosaic; variegated pavement; live coals.*

A concubine of Saul's (II Sam. 3:7).

Meta. The intense desire and very intricate, determined working of the human soul to preserve in consciousness the thoughts and activities resulting from adverse- or personal-will crystallization that Rizpah signifies (*hot stone, hearthstone, mosaic, variegated pavement, live coals*). Rizpah was a concubine of Saul's. She showed great love and endurance in watching over the bodies of her two sons and five grandsons of Saul's for a long time and under very trying circumstances in order to save their bodies from the indignity of being torn to pieces and eaten by vultures and wild animals, after these men had been hung by the Gideonites, with David's permission, and had been left exposed. (See II Samuel 21:8-11.)

robbers.

Meta. The two robbers who were crucified with Jesus (Matt. 27:38) symbolize the past and the future. These rob you of your consciousness of Omnipresence. The past, the one who railed against Jesus (Luke 23:39), did not enter into the paradise of God, the garden of Divine Mind; but the other was in a certain degree close to the mind of Jesus, and to him the way to enter was open.

All the past must be erased from memory and the aspirations and hopes of the future must be affirmed as now fulfilled. There is no future estate for man. Remember this. "Today shalt thou be with me in Paradise." This is the place of present fulfillment. Do not dream of anything as being in the future. Say to all your future thoughts, all your ideals and aspirations, "To-day shalt thou be with me in Paradise." (See THIEVES.)

The "robbers" of Luke 10:30 are the lusts of passion and appetite, that deplete the vitality of the consciousness and the body.

Rogelim, rȯ-gē'-lĭm (Heb.)—*fullers' place; fullers; washers; fulled cloths; footmen; cleansed by fullers.*

The home of Barzillai the Gileadite (II Sam. 17:27).

Meta. An orderly disciplining, cleansing, purifying, and adjusting in the character and consciousness of the individual, that he may be made a more fit abiding place for Spirit (*fullers' place, fullers, fulled cloths, footmen,* from treading with the feet, and carrying the idea of effort of an organized nature, *cleansed by fullers,* an Israelitish city). (See EN-ROGEL; it is virtually the same word.)

Rohgah, rōh'-găh (Heb.)—*outcry; cry of alarm; clamor; din of voices; outpouring; copious rain.*

Son of Shemer, or Shomer, of the tribe of Asher (I Chron. 7:34).

Meta. A very active expressing, or pouring out, of the thoughts and emotions. This activity is more personal (*outcry, cry of alarm, clamor, din of voices, outpouring, copious rain*) than spiritual.

Romamti - ezer, rȯ-măm'-tĭ - ē'-zẽr (Heb.)—*I have exalted his help; I have raised up (God's) help; succor of the Most High; my help is lifted up; highest help; exaltation of help.*

A son of Heman; a musician in the house of Jehovah in David's reign. He was over the 24th division of singers (I Chron. 25:4, 31).

Meta. Praising and exalting God by music and song, especially in His character as helper of man. This that Romamti–ezer signifies acknowledges and lauds the power and willingness of God, omnipresent Spirit, to heal, to inspire, to uplift, and to restore the individual to spiritual perfection (*I have exalted his help, I have raised up God's help, highest help, exaltation of help*, a musician and singer in the house of Jehovah, and the son of a musician and singer).

Romans, rō'-manṣ (Lat.).

Roman citizens (John 11:48).

Meta. Thoughts and their activities belonging to that in consciousness which Rome symbolizes. (See ROME.)

Rome, rōme (Lat.)—*lifted up; exalted; the head; height; strength; might; power.*

The capital of the Roman Empire; the ruling center of the Cæsars, the Roman emperors (Acts 18:2).

Meta. Rome represents the head, in contrast to Jerusalem, which represents the heart. The head is the seat of the dominating personal will, and also of the intellect in man; to the outer man these are the seat of all strength and power. Rome really refers more to the head as the seat of the will than it does to the intellect, though the latter may enter into consideration of the will's activities.

Paul was imprisoned in Rome. Paul represents the divine word; Rome is the center from which the will rules. When the will, guided by sense intellect and the personal idea of ruling power, imprisons the word, binds it in the realm of personal understanding and dictatorship, the activity of Spirit seems inhibited.

Rosh, rŏsh (Heb.)—*principle; head; chief; highest; top; first; foremost; elder; former; inclination; will; affection.*

A son of Benjamin (Gen. 46:21).

Meta. Benjamin (*son of the right hand*, one of Jacob's sons by Rachel) represents an active faith. Rosh (*principle, head, chief, first, highest, inclination, will*) relates to the will. Since Rosh was a son of Benjamin the significance is that the will, having been given first place in the consciousness of the individual, is acting through faith, or in conjunction with it. (See RHESA, which is the Greek form of Rosh.)

Rufus, rṳ'-fŭs (Lat.)—*red; reddish; ruddy.*

a Son of Simon of Cyrene. This Simon was compelled to bear Jesus' cross to Calvary (Mark 15:21). **b** A Christian at Rome to whom Paul sent salutation in his letter to the Romans (Rom. 16:13).

Meta. Life activity in body consciousness (*red, ruddy*).

Ruhamah, rṳ-hā'-măh (Heb.)—*softened; soothed; pitied; finding mercy; inner warmth; inner glowing; compassion; tenderness; love; bowels; womb.*

A symbolical name given to Israel (Hos. 2:1; margin, *"That hath obtained mercy"*).

Meta. A consciousness of forgiveness. True forgiveness includes the cleansing away of one's sins, or shortcomings (*that hath obtained mercy*). True forgiveness is more than just pitying some one and then letting him go on in his old bondage to error and inharmony. True, divine forgiveness releases one from his errors and hence saves him from further inharmonious results of previous error thinking, talking, and doing. In Ruhamah we find the activity of the brooding mother love that God bestows upon His children: mankind and the higher ideals of each individual consciousness.

rulership.

Meta. In personal rulership the great ones exercise authority; he who rules lords it over his subjects. In spiritual rulership he who serves best is greatest, and is therefore ruler through true merit (see Matthew 20:25-28).

Jesus Christ is the greatest ruler the world has ever known because He served humanity best, even to overcoming death itself; through His demonstration the way to eternal life was opened to humanity.

Rumah, rṳ'-măh (Heb.)—*elevation; uplifted head; height; exaltation; sublimity; elation; haughtiness; pride.*

The home of Pedaiah, father of Zebidah. This Zebidah was the mother of Jehoiakim, king of Judah (II Kings 23:36).

Meta. A group of thoughts in the Israel consciousness of man; they are of a lofty, sublime nature (*height, sublimity, exaltation*). To the extent that personality enters in, *haughtiness* and *pride* result from them.

Ruth, rųth (Heb.)—*female friend; sympathetic companion; desirable; delightful; friendship; pleasing; beautiful.*

A Moabitess who became the wife of Boaz, an Israelitish man of Beth–lehem–judah. David was descended from her. Ruth was the daughter-in-law of Naomi and returned with her from Moab to Beth–lehem–judah (Ruth 1 to 4).

Meta. The love of the soul in its natural state, or the love of the natural soul for God and for the things of Spirit.

Ruth is a type of the beautiful, the pure, and the loving characteristics of the natural man (*sympathetic companion, friendship, female friend, delightful, desirable, beautiful*). She was the one and only good that Naomi took with her back to Beth–lehem–judah (divnie substance, the real).

In Ruth's words in Ruth 1:16 is represented human love raised to divine love by its willingness to leave the love of the unreal, to follow after the real, to go wherever true love leads, to be steadfast in that love; in other words, to love in the highest and best degree and to acknowledge and worship always the God of love.

Ruth's loyalty to God and the spiritual life was rewarded, just as such loyalty always is. Boaz and Ruth were ancestors of King David and of David's greater son, Jesus the Christ. Here we have the progression of a thought from simple, loving obedience and devotion to a mighty ruler of worlds. Thus spiritual thought grows—very quietly and slowly at first, but gradually increasing—until it finally carries all before it.

S

sabachthani, sā-băch-thā′-nī (Gk. fr. Chald.)—*thou hast forsaken me; thou hast left me; (to what) hast thou surrendered me? (why) hast thou forsaken me?*

In *sabachthani* we find the root idea of loosening, setting free; letting alone and forsaking are secondary developments. The real root idea of the word expresses the cutting loose of bondage, or freeing from slavery.

On the cross Jesus cried, "Eli, Eli, lama sabachthani? that is, My God, my God, why hast thou forsaken me?" (Matt. 27:46).

Meta. The cry of the soul at the darkest hour of crucifixion. When the sensual is passing away it seems as though man were giving up all his life, including every good. The sensual looms so large at this hour that for the time being it shuts God from the consciousness of the individual who is going through the experience. But God never forsakes His children; there can be no real separation from the Divine, and a glorious resurrection into a greater degree of spiritual life than was ever realized before always follows each letting go of the old. "Even so reckon ye also yourselves to be dead unto sin, but alive unto God in Christ Jesus." "That like as Christ was raised from the dead through the glory of the Father, so we also might walk in newness of life."

Sabaoth, să-bā′-ŏth (Gk. fr. Heb.)—*armies; hosts.*

The Greek form of the Hebrew word for armies or hosts; generally used with Jehovah, as, Jehovah of hosts, and meaning Jehovah as ruler over the whole earth and heaven (Rom. 9:29).

Meta. The significance of "Lord of Sabaoth," or "Jehovah of hosts," in individual consciousness is that the Jehovah, Christ, true I AM in one, is Lord of—has dominion over—all the host of thoughts, forces, and activities in one's whole organism, in mind (heaven) and body (earth).

Sabbath (Heb.)—*the seventh; seventh (day); seventh (month); seventh (year); restoration; restitution; return to a former state; at-one-ment; atonement; completion; perfection; wholeness; repose; rest.*

The seventh day of the week. Under the old Jewish law, no one was allowed to do any work on that day (Exod. 20:8-11).

Meta. The Sabbath is the consciousness that we have fulfilled the divine law in both thought and act.

The Sabbath of the Lord has nothing to do with any day of the week. God did not make days and weeks, nor has He darkened His clear concepts of Truth by the time element. Time is an invention of the human.

The Sabbath is a very certain, definite thing. It is a state of mind that man enters or acquires when he goes into the silence of his own soul, into the realm of Spirit. There he finds true rest and peace. The seventh day means the seventh or perfect stage of one's spiritual unfoldment. Man had become so lost in the darkness of sense consciousness that he could not save himself, so a Savior came. When man lays hold of the indwelling Christ, the Savior, he is raised out of the Adam consciousness into the Christ consciousness. He then enters the seventh stage of his unfoldment, where he finds rest and peace. The Sabbath can be enjoyed at any hour. Man shows his ignorance and limits his happiness by confining the Sabbath to any one of the days of the week. He should learn to read the Bible in the spirit, and pay less attention to the letter of it.

The Sabbath as an institution was established by man. God does not rest from His works every seventh day, and there is no evidence that there ever has been a moment's cessation in the activity of the universe. Those who stickle most for Sabbath day observance are met on every hand by the evidence of perpetual activity on the part of Him whom they claim to champion.

We are cited to the trees, flowers, suns, and stars, as the work of God; we are told that it is God who sustains and governs, controls and directs, them in every minutia. Yet trees, flowers, suns, and stars are active the first day and the seventh day of the week just the same as on other days. Sacerdotalism has never yet found that the operations of nature on Sunday are in any way different from its operations on any other day of the week

It would seem that if God ordained a certain day for rest, and rested on that day Himself, He ought certainly to have left some evidence of it in His creations; but He has not, that anybody knows of. The fact is that Divine Mind rests in a perpetual Sabbath and that which seems work is not work at all. When man becomes so at one with the Father-Mind as to feel it consciously he also recognizes this eternal peace in which all things are accomplished. He then knows that he is not subject to any condition whatsoever, but is "lord of the sabbath."

It is your privilege to be as free as the birds, the trees, the flowers. "They toil not, neither do they spin," but are always obedient to the divine instinct, and their every day is a Sabbath. They stand in no fear of an angry God, though they build a nest, spread a leaf, or open a petal on the first or on the seventh day. All days are holy days to them. They live in the holy Omnipresence and do the will always of Him who sent them. It is our duty to do likewise. That which is instinct in them is in us conscious, loving obedience. When we have resolved to be attentive to the voice of the Father and to do His will at any cost, we are freed from the bondage of all man-made laws. What was a chain about our wrists, or a yoke about our neck, in the form of some fear of transgressing the divine law, slips away into the fathomless sea of nothingness and we sit on the shore and praise the loving Goodness that we are nevermore to be frightened by an accusing conscience or by the possibility of misunderstanding His law.

We are not to quarrel with our brother over observance of the Sabbath. If he insists that the Lord should be worshiped on the seventh day, let us joyfully join him on that day; and if he holds that the first day is the holy day, let us again acquiescce. Not only do we do God's service in praise, song, and thanksgiving on the seventh day and the first day, but every day. In the true Sabbath our souls are turned upward to God every moment, and we are ever ready to acknowledge His holy presence in our heart and life; we are ever praising the holy Omnipresence that burns its lamp of love perpetually in our heart and keeps the light of life before us on our way. This is the observance of God's holy day that the divinely wise soul always recognizes. The true church is the heaven within one, where one meets the Father face to face, where one goes to Him at will, in closest fellowship.

On the other hand, the observance of every seventh day as a day of rest, or Sabbath, has its source deep in the constitution of things. Among nearly all peoples similar rest days have been instituted, and history proves that Moses was not the originator of the system. The observance of a weekly rest day is now very widely held to prove a natural basis in the needs of man. The consistency with which such an institution has been maintained for many centuries among Jews, Christians, Mohammedans, and some of the so-called pagan nations amply supports this view. It has been found by experience that one day of rest in seven is the right proportion. During the French Revolution, when a ten-day period was substituted for the week, one day's rest in ten was found insufficient.

"And on the seventh day God finished his work which he had made; and he rested on the seventh day from all his work which he had made. And God blessed the seventh day, and hallowed it." This quotation from Genesis presents in concise words a law that pervades the universe. According to some geologists the rock-ribbed earth beneath our feet bears record of six great creative periods, with a seventh in process of completion. Seven movements of the creative law are found at the foundation of the world about us. The seven colors of the spectrum, the seven principal tones of music, the seven senses of man (two not yet universally used)—all point to these degrees or days of action and rest.

When man in his wisdom unites his thought with Divine Mind, as did Jesus, he has power to use the same creative law that God uses in bringing forth the universe. The seven elements of the body are found everywhere, and through understanding that they are not fixed, material things, but forms of thought, man gains entrance to a realm where he

can speak words that will give him the obedience of those elements, according to his power.

When you have gained power to still the stormy, undisciplined thoughts in your own mind you can speak to the winds and they will obey you. When you have arrested the scorching currents of anger that burn up your body cells you can quench the fire in a burning building. When you have ceased to drop into the weak, watery mental states called discouragement, despondency, and fear, you can command the waves and walk upon the waters, as did Jesus.

Before man can rise into his natural dominion, however, he must understand and realize that God's whole plan of creation is to bring forth the perfect man. This means that man is the supreme thing in creation and that all laws are for his convenience. The universal tendency of great men to manifest this inherent excellency proves that it is natural. Most of them miss the mark by seeking to dominate other men and nations before they have mastered themselves.

When men set up a law and make its observance burdensome they are slaves of their own creation. The Jews had become burdened with the observance of the letter of the Sabbath commandment, and had a multitude of ridiculous prohibitions and formalities, from which Jesus sought to rescue them by His example of bold freedom and disregard of certain man-made laws.

The Sabbath was instituted for man, not man for the Sabbath. It is lawful to do good on the Sabbath, whether it be preaching in a pulpit, healing the sick, or in any other way saving men from ignorance and its results. Luther said of the Sabbath: "Keep it holy for its use's sake both to body and soul. But if anywhere the day is made holy for the mere day's sake, if anywhere any one sets up its observance upon a Jewish foundation, then I order you to work on it, to ride on it, to dance on it, to feast on it, to do anything that shall reprove this encroachment on the Christian spirit and liberty."

To repeat, the true Sabbath is not

the observance of an outer day; the outer is but the symbol. The true Sabbath is that state of mind in which we rest from outer thought and doings, and give ourselves up to meditation or to the study of things spiritual; it is when we enter into the stillness of our inner consciousness, think about God and His law, and commune with Him.

Sabeans, să-bē'-ănş (fr. Heb.).

Descendants of Sheba, son of Joktan (Job 1:15; Joel 3:8); also of Seba, son of Cush (Isa. 45:14).

Meta. Thoughts springing from and belonging to that in consciousness which Sheba and Seba signify. (See SEBA and SHEBA.)

Sabtah, săb'-tăh (Heb.).—*determining motion; a turn; orbit; circuit; course of action; striking; stroke; rock.*

Son of Cush, who was a son of Ham and grandson of Noah (Gen. 10:7). In I Chronicles 1:9, the name is spelled Sabta.

Meta. The general cyclical trend of activity of the sensual in man (*orbit, circuit, course of action*). Led away by outer seeming, through exercise of personal will man has set up a course of action in sense consciousness that falls short of the divine ideal and is contentious and destructive (*determining motion, striking, stroke, rock; see* CUSH and HAM.)

Sabteca (in A. V., Genesis 10:7, Sabtechah; in I Chronicles 1:9, Sabtecha), săb'-tĕ-eà (Heb.)—*determined movement; enchaining; extreme oppression; compressive surroundings; great stroke.*

Son of Cush (Gen. 10:7).

Meta. The significance is the same as that of Sabtah, but greatly intensified. (See SABTAH.)

Sacar, sā'-eär (Heb.)—*hire; wages; rental; fare; stipend; reward; wage earners; laborers.*

a "The Hararite," father of Ahiam (I Chron. 11:35). In II Samuel 23:33, he is called Sharar the Ararite. **b** Fourth son of Obed–edom, doorkeeper in the house of Jehovah, in David's reign (I Chron. 26:4).

Meta. Sacar (*hire, wages, reward, wage earners, laborers,* the name of two Israelitish men) clearly points to the thought of spiritual life and service from a standpoint of earning one's salvation, one's good, eternal life, instead of accepting it as a free gift of God through the Son, the Christ, the true self of each individual. While there is truth in the belief that each one must work out his own salvation, yet in the knowledge of Sonship, which must take the place of the thought of labor, of working for wages, for reward, he realizes that he can do nothing of himself, but the Father within him expresses through him.

sacrifices to the Lord.

Meta. A refining process that is constantly going on in consciousness. Every thought and act of man sets free an energy that gravitates to its appointed place in the various realms of mind and body. The Lord is the one universal Mind, which is the receptacle of all thought. If you have a thought of love and good will, you set free invisible emanations that are impregnated with these ideas. These ascend to a higher realm and form part of your soul, and at the same time relate you to the Lord, who is the presiding Oversoul of the race. This is the inner meaning of offering sacrifices to the Lord. Everything in nature is going through this refining process and there is a constant ascension of matter to mind and mind to Spirit. We are taught that a period will finally come when the whole universe will be resolved back into its original essence in God.

We must purify our mind and body in order that Spirit may come in and do the regenerative work. Some people think it necessary to cleanse the mind only, and let the body take care of itself. Truth reveals, however, that we must in all ways fulfill the law of purity. Whoever defiles his body with impure thoughts, lustful passions, or decaying food will find his progress retarded.

The burnt offerings of bullocks and sheep on the altar represent the transmutation of the physical forces to the next higher plane of action. This is a process of body refinement that pertains to those who follow Jesus in the regeneration. The altar represents the place in consciousness where we are willing to give up the lower to the higher, the personal to the impersonal, the animal to the spiritual. The life forces of those living in generation flow to the generative center in the body and are spent in the material. This brings death to the body. When through a sincere desire for things spiritual man lifts his mind, there is a complete reversal of these life forces. Instead of a downward flow the currents start toward the heart and a process of body rejuvenation begins. Then there is rejoicing in the man and he sings praises to the Lord. This is represented by the *"singing* with loud instruments unto Jehovah."* (See II Chron. 30:13-27.) When this blessed realization of the regeneration comes to consciousness the voices of men are heard by the Lord and their prayers ascend "even unto heaven."

When we have faith in God and the ways of Spirit we are willing to give up all our material pleasures, if such be the instruction of the inner guide, the Holy Spirit. This is a point that is also symbolized by the sacrifices so often referred to in the history of the Children of Israel.

Sadducees, săd'-dū-çēeş (Gk. fr. Heb.) —*just; righteous; upright; good; vindicated; justified.*

A sect of Jews, at the time of Jesus and His disciples (Matt. 22:23). This sect was composed of descendants of Zadok (II Sam. 15:24) and their adherents, and was mentioned as "the sons of Zadok" in Ezekiel 40:46. They were the rationalists of their day, adhering to the Old Testament law only in matters of morals. They did not believe in the resurrection or in the immortality of the soul.

Meta. The Sadducees and the Pharisees represent the religious concepts of the intellect. The Sadducees were a religious sect of Jews with strong materialistic beliefs, and the Pharisees were formalists, without spiritual understanding. The fact is that the intellect cannot comprehend absolute Truth. Its religious beliefs are all built up from conclusions based on relative conditions, and are therefore of time and place.

The self-sufficiency of the religionist —the Pharisee; the self-sufficiency of the agnostic—the Sadducee; the Sadducees and Pharisees, mentioned in Matt. 22:34-46—these represent one's preconceived religious ideas. (See PHARISEES.)

Sadoc, sā'-dŏc (Gk. fr. Heb.)—*right; straight; just; righteous; upright; good; justified; vindicated.*

Named in the genealogy of Jesus Christ (Matt. 1:14). Zadok is the same name in the Hebrew.

Meta. The consciousness awakening to and laying hold of the true idea of righteousness and justice. True righteousness and justice measure up to the Christ standard of right, and that standard includes mercy; it involves the right relation of all one's thoughts, faculties, and powers to oneself as well as to people and the world without one.

Salamis, săl'-ă-mĭs (Gk.)—possibly, *tossing; shaking.* More likely, *salt; savor; fertility; arable land; concord; wisdom; grace of speech.*

A city on the island of Cyprus. Paul preached in the Jewish synagogues in Salamis (Acts 13:5).

Meta. A state of thought that is protective, preservative, uplifting, fertile, harmonious, and wise—or at least is receptive to these qualities (*salt, savor, fertility, concord, wisdom*).

Salecah (A. V., Salcah and Salchah), săl'-ĕ-căh (Heb.)—*moving along; going about; migration; wandering; a way; tract; extension.*

A city of the kingdom of Og in Bashan. It was conquered by the Israelites and was allotted to Gad (Josh. 13:11; I Chron. 5:11).

Meta. A group of thoughts of a migratory, changeable nature (*moving along, going about, migration, wandering, a city*). The tendency of this thought activity, however, is toward that which is broader and better (*a way, extension*); thus it passes into the hands of the Israelitish tribe of Gad, which represents the power faculty in individual consciousness. By its contact with this power a stability enters into it that will eventually change it to a higher and more steadfast nature.

Salem, sā'-lĕm (Heb.)—*whole; sound; complete; perfect; finished; summit; peace; concord; friendship.*

The city of Melchizedek. It is thought to have been the same city that was later called Jerusalem (Gen. 14:18; Heb. 7:1, 2).

Meta. A consciousness of spiritual peace, wholeness, and perfection (*whole, summit, peace, complete, perfect;* see JERUSALEM).

Salim, sā'-lĭm (Gk. fr. Heb.)—*whole; entire; perfect; complete; peace.*

A place near Ænon where John was baptizing (John 3:23).

Meta. A thought of peace, also of wholeness and perfection. (See SALEM and ÆNON.)

Sallai, săl'-lāi (Heb.)—*worker in reeds; basketmaker; wicker basket; lifting up; suspending; weighing; judging; exaltation.*

a A Benjamite who lived in Jerusalem after the return from the Babylonian captivity (Neh. 11:8). b A priest (Neh. 12:20). The name is spelled Sallu in Nehemiah 12:7.

Meta. The blending of thoughts that have a capacity for retaining that which the individual wishes to keep in mind; the ability to hold to accepted ideas until they become a part of the consciousness, instead of letting them slip away (*basketmaker,* one who weaves materials to make a basket, a basket being a vessel to hold or carry articles). Sallai signifies also the ability to discern and put away error, limited thoughts (*weighing, judging*) and to magnify ideas that are acceptable (*exaltation*). Thus is the consciousness elevated (*lifting up*).

Sallu, săl'-lū (Heb.)—*lifted up; exalted; weighed; compared; judged; valued; accepted; rejected; suspended.*

a A Benjamite (I Chron. 9:7). b A priest who returned from the Babylonian captivity (Neh. 12:7). The name is spelled Sallai in Nehemiah 12:20.

Meta. The exaltation of the faculty of good judgment; the ability to discern and decide between the true and the false or limited in consciousness, that the error may be rejected and the true may be rightly valued and retained.

Salma, săl'-má (Heb.)—*covering; garment; mantle; raiment; strength; firmness; peace; perfection.*

a Father of Boaz, from whom David

and Jesus were descended (I Chron. 2:11). In other Bible texts he is called Salmon. b A son of Caleb (I Chron. 2:51).

Meta. See SALMON.

Salmai (A. V., Shalmai), săl'-māi (Heb.)—*Jah is recompenser; my recompense; my thanks; my garment.*

One of the Nethinim whose descendants returned from the Babylonian captivity (Neh. 7:48). He is called Shamlai in Ezra 2:46.

Meta. The serving thought in consciousness that rejoices greatly, gives praise and thanksgiving to God, because it perceives that all good comes from or through Jehovah. It is learning that all service should be done as to the Lord and that He is the compensator, not man. (*Jah is recompenser, my thanks, my garment,* the garment here being the praise and thanksgiving with which one clothes himself. "Put on thy beautiful garments, O Jerusalem." "All thy garments *smell* of myrrh, and aloes, *and* cassia.")

Salmon, săl'-mŏn (Heb.)—*covered; enwrapped; garment; mantle; clothing; raiment; clothed; strong; firm; peaceable; perfect.*

Father of Boaz, from whom David and Jesus were descended (Ruth 4:20).

Meta. The idea of peace and perfection's becoming established in individual consciousness and clothing one with harmony, poise, steadfastness, strength, and Truth (*clothed, enwrapped, strong, firm, peaceable, perfect;* see SALMA).

Salmone, săl-mō'-nĕ (Gk.)—*agitated by the sea; tossing; billowy; commotion; of the sea.*

A high, rocky point on the eastern shore of the island of Crete. The boat in which Paul was being taken as a prisoner to Rome passed "over against Salmone" (Acts 27:7).

Meta. A very unrested state of thought (*agitated by the sea, tossing, commotion*).

Salome, să-lō'-mĕ (Gk. fr. Heb.)—*whole; sound; perfect; complete; finished; peaceful; friendly; enveloped; enveloping; clothed.*

a A woman disciple of Jesus (Mark 15:40); she is thought to have been the wife of Zebedee and mother of James and John. **b** Said to have been the name of Herodias' daughter (Matt. 14:6).

Meta. The soul clothed in the thought of wholeness, soundness, love, peace, and Truth.

Salome is said to have been the name of the daughter of Herodias, who danced before Herod and pleased him so much that he offered her anything that she desired, even to the half of his kingdom. At the instigation of her mother she asked for the head of John the Baptist. She represents the deceptive (because fleeting and destructive) pleasure of sex sensation. (See HERODIAS.)

Salu, sā′-lū (Heb.)—*lifted up; weighed; judged; exalted.*

A Simeonite. His son Zimri, a prince of his father's house, was slain with a Midianitish woman, by Phinehas (Num. 25:7-14).

Meta. A very exalted thought of judgment, discernment, in the higher, truer phase of man's consciousness (*lifted up, exalted, weighed, judged,* a man of the Israelitish tribe of Simeon). The fate of Salu's son Zimri shows the inharmonious and disastrous results that ensue when this high ideal attaches itself to or is overcome by the desires and emotions of the sense phase of the human soul.

Samaria, să-mā′-rĭ-à (Lat. fr. Heb.) —*watcher; guard; watch post; watch height; watch mountain.*

a A city in Palestine, built on **b** a mountain of the same name. It was the capitol of the kingdom of Israel, after the Israelites were divided into two kingdoms (I Kings 16:24). **c** The whole country of the kingdom of Israel, of which the city of Samaria was the metropolis. The king of Assyria carried the Israelites away captive from Samaria, and settled it with heathen tribes (II Kings 17:24). These heathen tribes were taught something of the Israelitish worship of God by a priest of Israel (II Kings 17:27-29), but they continued to worship their own gods, along with their worship of God. It was in this mixed state of understanding that the Samaritans existed in Jesus' day (John 4:4).

Meta. Intellectual perception, the department of the objective consciousness that functions through the head (*watch-*er, *watch mountain*). It signifies also a mixed state of consciousness.

Luke 9:51-53 signifies that when a great spiritual work is to be accomplished the mind is centered on the goal of attainment and progress is not to be hindered by the minor mind powers. Thus it is that the I AM is established in the city of peace within the soul (Jerusalem).

The buying of the hill of Samaria (I Kings 16:24) means the exaltation of personality.

Samaritan, să-măr′-ĭ-tăn (Lat. fr. Heb.).

An inhabitant of Samaria (II Kings 17:29; John 4:9).

Meta. The Samaritans signify mixed thoughts, partly worldly and partly religious. They were a mixture of Assyrian and Hebrew. They claimed to be direct descendants of Abraham, and taught the books of Moses, but they were not recognized by the Jews as followers of the Jewish religion. Metaphysically Samaria represents a state of consciousness in which Truth and error are mixed.

The woman at the well represents the psychic or soul nature. The psychical realm is not the true source of wisdom, although many searchers for Truth fail to distinguish the difference between its revelations and those of the spiritual. The Samaritans claimed to be the descendants of Jacob, and they used portions of the Hebrew Scriptures, but the Jews repudiated them. In the eyes of the Israelites the Samaritans were pretenders. Thus spiritually enlightened people see in psychic phenomena and the revelations of that phase of occultism an imitation of Truth, without its understanding.

The soul must have Truth, however, and it is recognized by the Christ as worthy, hence this wonderful lesson of John 4, to only one auditor. The soul in its natural state draws its life from the earthly side of existence (Jacob's well), but is destined to draw from a higher fount, omnipotent life. Jesus asked the woman for a drink—indicating the universality of Spirit.

"If thou knewest the gift of God." The "gift of God" to man is eternal life. The soul informed of this asks the Father to let it be the subject of a manifestation of that life, and there gushes forth a never failing stream. Where sense consciousness is dominant, however, the soul is slow to see the realities of ideas, thoughts, and words. The sight is fixed on material ways and means: "Thou hast nothing to draw with, . . . whence then hast thou that living water?" This is a fair setting forth of the questioning souls of this day who ask the explanation of spiritual things on a material or sense basis.

The husband of the woman represents the intellectual side of the soul, with its sense perceptions. She had been the wife of five husbands; that is, the soul had been attached to the five senses, and its present attachment, which was evidently sense perception of Truth, was not her true husband. The soul is easily led away from Truth, and often becomes attached to the phenomenal phases of the mysterious unknowable, under the delusion that it is good and in line with true doctrine.

The Christ is a discerner of thoughts, and from them the history of the soul is read like an open book. When Jesus displayed this ability to the woman He had her faith at once, and she accepted Him as a prophet, not because she understood His doctrine but because He told her past. "Come, see a man, who told me all things that *ever* I did."

The soul is in its natural state attached to localities, forms, and conditions in the world. It believes in the importance of places of worship and the observance of outward forms. The mind of Spirit puts all this aside and proclaims the universality of spiritual forces: "God is spirit." "Neither in this mountain, nor in Jerusalem, shall ye worship the Father." The soul falls into forms of worship, and thereby fails to get the true understanding, but the Christ-minded know Spirit; they enter the consciousness of the formless life and substance, and are satisfied.

The leading characteristics of the Samaritan cited in Luke 10:33 are kindheartedness, helpfulness, and generosity. He typifies the traits that make religion a living, spiritual, uplifting power. The activities of these spiritual qualities are the stepping-stones that lead to the great demonstration. They are the forces that throw wide open the doors of the inner kingdom, so that man's consciousness may be lifted up and merged with the God consciousness. "Go, and do thou likewise," the Master was saying to all who wish to triumph over the last enemy, to all who wish to attain eternal life.

Two principal lessons are set forth in Jesus' parable of the good Samaritan. One is that we keep the law of eternal life by loving God; the other is that we keep this law by expressing love for our neighbor.

Metaphysically a man's neighbor is his nearest and most intimate embodied thought. The body is our nearest and most intimate embodied thought; therefore the body is our neighbor.

The man who was stripped and beaten and left half dead symbolizes the physical body that is in a similar condition. The robbers are our lawless thoughts that rob our body of its energy and substance.

The priest and the Levite represent the ignorance and the indifference to Truth that are found in both formal religion and law.

The good Samaritan is "Christ in you, the hope of glory." Sacerdotalism disdains the inner Christ, but without His ministry the body would never be healed of its many wounds. The "beast" is the divine-natural substance; the "oil" is love, and the "wine" is life.

The parable of the good Samaritan teaches that the body is being robbed of its life by ignorant, lawless thoughts, and that that life will be restored by Christ if we exercise His merciful, healing love. Thus this parable helps one to attain eternal life.

Samgar-nebo, săm'-gär-nē'-bô (Heb. fr. Pers.)—*graciousness of Nebo; sword of Mercury; gracious interpreter.*

A prince or officer of the king of Babylon at the time when the king took Jerusalem (Jer. 39:3).

Meta. Nebo here refers to a Babylonian or Chaldean god. It represents a limited degree of discernment and understanding operative on the purely mental, psychic, or soul plane. Mercury refers to worship of the intellect.

Samgar–nebo (*graciousness of Nebo, sword of Mercury, gracious interpreter*), a prince and officer of the king of Babylon at the time when the king took Jerusalem, signifies giving service to and trusting in that which Nebo and Mercury represent, instead of looking to Spirit for understanding and conquering power. Thus the higher thoughts of one's consciousness, when one is untrue to spiritual ideals, give place to sense confusion (Babylon); one's peace is taken away (Jerusalem was captured by the king of Babylon) and one's understanding is darkened (the Jewish king's eyes were put out and he and his people were carried captive to Babylon).

Samlah, săm'-läh (Heb.)—*garment; raiment; outer garment; mantle; covered; wrapped; clothed.*

A king of Edom. He was of Masrekah (Gen. 36:36).

Meta. The general ruling characteristics of the outer, seemingly mortal phase of consciousness in man that Edom signifies (*garment, raiment, clothed*—clothing signifying characteristics—a king of Edom).

Samos, sā'-mŏs (Gk.)—*height; distinguished; prominent.*

An island in the Ægean Sea, near the coast of Lydia. The boat in which Paul traveled on his way to Jerusalem from one of his missionary trips "touched at Samos" (Acts 20:15).

Meta. A high, noble state of thought (*height, distinguished*; see SAMOTHRACE).

Samothrace (A. V., Samothracia), săm'-ŏ-thrāce (Gk.)—*Samos of Thrace; height of Thrace.*

An island in the northern part of the Ægean Sea. Paul came to this island on his first missionary journey into Europe (Acts 16:11).

Meta. The interpretation is virtually the same as that of Samos, which see. The state of thought that Samos and Samothrace symbolize is intellectual rather than spiritual, since their location is in the Grecian Archipelago and Greece refers to the intellect.

Samson, săm'-son (Heb.)—*sunlike; little sun; sunny; distinguished.*

Son of Manoah, of Zorah, of the tribe of Dan. He was noted for his great strength and for his victories over the Philistines. He was a judge of Israel and began to deliver Israel out of the hands of the Philistines (Judg. 13:2—16:31).

Meta. Physical strength under spiritual discipline, or consciousness of spiritual strength. The root, seat, or cause of this strength is understanding (*sunlike, distinguished*).

Samson, like John the Baptist, was a Nazirite. He was consecrated to God before his birth as one who should "begin to save Israel out of the hand of the Philistines" (Judges 13). As a Nazirite Samson vowed total abstinence from all intoxicating liquors; that his hair should go uncut and that all contamination with dead bodies should be avoided by him. It was usually a temporary vow, but Samson and John the Baptist were Nazirites for life. The meaning of the vow was *entire consecration to God.* (See NAZIRITE.)

When Samson first began his work the Israelites were under the dominion of the Philistines, vanquished and dispirited. The nation was in danger of extinction, and peace was purchased of the Philistines with deepest dishonor.

The life of Samson, as given in Judges, represents the different movements of strength in human consciousness, and its betrayal and end. Samson did all kinds of athletic stunts, but was finally robbed of his strength by Delilah, a Philistine woman, who had his head shaved while he slept on her knees. Hair represents vitality. When the vital principle is taken away the strength goes with it. This weakens the body and it finally perishes. Eve took away the strength of Adam in like manner, and every man who gives up the vital essence of his body for the pleasure of sensation commits suicide, as did Samson.

Great strength can be attained by one who trusts in Spirit, who awakens to true understanding of the light of Spirit and conserves his vital substance. The strength and the understanding of Spirit are necessary to the perpetuation of soul and body and to the overcoming of death.

Eyes represent light, or spiritual perception. Through spiritual strength (Samson) regeneration of the sense consciousness is begun, but the thoughts of the carnal mind (Philistines) resist the advent of Truth.

The destruction of Samson and his enemies pictures the activity of strength independent of divine law. Ideas of strength must be established in substance and expressed in judgment before they will act constructively in the organism and preserve the body.

Samuel, săm'-ū-ĕl (Heb.)—*name of God; sublimity of God; heard of God; instructed of God; God hath heard.*

A prophet and judge of Israel, the last one before Israel began to have kings to rule over it (I Sam. 1:20 to 10:25).

Meta. Spiritual discernment; that in man which has conscious contact with God and learns of God (*God hath heard, instructed of God*).

The boy Samuel represents the inner voice, through whose expression we come into a larger realization of ourselves.

Samuel also signifies judgment. He judged Israel forty years; he was brought forth in direct answer to prayer and his mother dedicated him to the Lord even before he was born in the flesh. At two years of age "the child Samuel ministered unto Jehovah before Eli," for it was recognized that he was to serve in the Temple, that he would unfold and become great in spiritual understanding. By listening to the voice of divine wisdom we bring forth the Son of God in our soul.

Samuel represents both judgment and the inner voice; he is the wisdom and the judgment that come often as a still, small voice at the heart center. It is deep within the stillness of the silence that our ears first become attuned to the rhythmic motions of Spirit, and that we are first enabled to catch the sound of the inner voice. Man makes connection with Jehovah by building up a consciousness of divine ideas. This is accomplished through thought, prayer, meditation, and realization. Receptivity to Spirit and obedience, fearlessness, and candor are essentials to the inviting of communion with the inner voice.

Hannah, mother of Samuel, earnestly petitioned God for a son. She made regular trips to the Temple, where she made known her desire; she listened attentively for the inner leadings, which showed her just what to do that she might comply with the law and have her prayers answered. This earnest seeking led her deep into the things of Spirit; therefore when her prayers were fulfilled the child that she bore possessed the faculty of spiritual hearing. Samuel was first conceived in Spirit, and by the sure law of Spirit the outer manifestation came into visibility.

Samuel was so quickened that he heard the word of Spirit. As you sit in the silence you no doubt often get the inner word through the still, small voice, yet you do not hear it; you do not feel it—you simply know it. When Samuel first heard it he went to Eli, the high priest, and said: "Here am I; for thou calledst me." A similar experience may come often to you. You hear, yet you do not understand; but as you go on in unfoldment you finally come to the place where you say, "This is Spirit talking to me." When you have once made union with Spirit you will understand and will get the messages, just as Samuel did.

I Samuel 7:2-12: The Spirit of God in man knows no defeat. Though it be kept for a time in bondage to man's material ideas, it sooner or later resumes its search for deliverance and free expression. Samuel, the inner spiritual perception that has the capacity for receiving spiritual inspiration, brings to the outer consciousness that which is necessary for this deliverance.

Samuel here tells the Children of Israel of the three great steps in spiritual progress. These are as applicable to man today as they were to the Children of Israel. First, if man is to serve the one true God he will put away all false gods. With a single standard in one's life there is a centralizing force at work, and wherever this centralizing influence becomes active, organization results. Thus all the scattered forces of man's being are brought together and are made capable of undertaking effectually the tasks of life.

The second step that Samuel took was

to have the Children of Israel assemble at Mizpah (*watchtower*). In order to maintain his unity with God and to keep his forces organized in singleness of thought and purpose, man must keep his attention steadily fixed in the direction of that to which he aspires. Samuel is here only carrying out that Scriptural injunction, "Look unto me, and be ye saved, all the ends of the earth." By looking away from the besetting forces of materiality and maintaining the high watch, one is enabled to discern the action of God, in meeting the various situations of life.

The third step for man in his spiritual progress is to conform his action to the action of God; when he has done that, the opposition of material forces becomes as nothing. The matter of importance is always to maintain one's perfect relationship with the movement of Principle, regardless of what may arise. Victory is inevitable when this unity with God is maintained; no adverse condition in the life of man can prevail against him, because there never has been and never can be any effective opposition to God. Victory is truly won the moment one establishes one's unity with God, because the adversity that appears is not in God, and when the situation is seen in God its aspects are entirely changed. When adversity appears the sure cure is to "cease not to cry unto Jehovah our God."

When man has succeeded in any overcoming after this manner of procedure, he reaches Beth–car (*house of the lamb*), that place where he consciously abides in the overcoming power of Spirit. This is a genuine milestone in the spiritual progress of man, and he has conquered all the ground that his consciousness grasps of that which is real in man and in the universe.

I Samuel 7:16, 17: In the high places in consciousness (represented by Beth–el, Gilgal, Mizpah, and Ramah, the places where Samuel went from year to year to judge Israel), spiritual judgment in us discerns the Truth and adjusts our life.

I Samuel 8: Samuel symbolizes that in man which keeps him in touch with the Source of wisdom. He stands for man's own higher judgment, and is active in consciousness so long as man depends on that judgment and trusts Spirit to direct him and to fight his battles. The Children of Israel were not willing to be guided by their own higher judgment (Samuel, the wise judge) because they lacked understanding and were mentally and spiritually lazy.

When man meekly goes with the crowd, uniting with some popular religious movement and trusting the authority of man-made creeds and doctrines for his salvation, he retires the wise judge Samuel. The king of man's consciousness is the will. When the will is given supreme control and the judgment ignored, the mind and the body are under autocratic rule.

Sanballat, săn-băl′-lăt (Heb. fr. Pers.) —*who strengthens the army; lauded by the army; muzzled hatred; hatred in secret; secret enemy.*

"The Horonite," one who opposed the Jews in their work of rebuilding the walls of Jerusalem and in resettling Judea with Jewish people from Babylon (Neh. 2:19; 4:1).

Meta. Enemies in secret (*secret enemy, hatred in secret*); error thoughts and fears of which we have not as yet really become conscious, but which are working with seemingly great strength (*who strengthens the army*) in our subconsciousness and out into our body consciousness and our body.

"Who can discern *his* errors?
Clear thou me from hidden *faults.*"

Sansannah, săn-săn′-năh (Heb.)— *palm branch; secret instruction.*

A city of southern Judah (Josh. 15: 31).

Meta. Victory, through knowledge of Truth (*palm branch, secret instruction;* palms denote victory, conquest, triumph, resurrection, life; secret instruction bespeaks the inspiration or inner teaching of Spirit). "Ye shall know the truth, and the truth shall make you free."

Saph, săph (Heb.)—*threshold; vestibule; dish; basin; doorkeeper; preserver; addition; extension; achievement; orbicular extent; gigantic.*

A son of the Philistine giant Raphah, who was slain by Sibbecai the Hushathite (II Sam. 21:18). In I Chronicles 20:4, he is called Sippai.

Meta. The seeming power, expansion, greatness, and influence that the intellect possesses when given first place in man's consciousness (*threshold, vestibule, dish, doorkeeper, extension, gigantic,* a Philistine giant). Saph refers to the rule of the intellect guided by the senses apart from or opposed to Spirit. It is the claim of the senses that outer, seemingly material appearances and manifestations are real; that the cause of all achievement is material. That which is symbolized by Saph, son of the Philistine giant Raphah, does not recognize Spirit as being back of and interpenetrating all that is. It believes not only in material causes for all manifestations, but it also believes that protection and preservation of life and good come from without (*preserver*).

Sapphira, săp-phī'-rȧ (Gk. fr. Heb.)— *beautiful; splendid; sapphire; precious stone; writer; enumerator; narrator.*

Wife of Ananias, and his partner in the deception that brought about the death of both of them (Acts 5:1-11).

Meta. See ANANIAS.

A sapphire is a stone of a pure, deep, transparent blue, and blue is the color of Truth. Truth is *beautiful,* but this for which Sapphira stands in the individual must be cleansed from its greed and deception before it can really represent Truth in all its purity and can testify (*narrator*) only to that which is wholly true.

Sarah (in A. V., Hebrews 11:11, Sara), sā'-rah (Heb.)—*princess; noble woman; noble lady.*

Wife of Abraham and mother of Isaac (Gen. 17:15-21).

Meta. The soul, the affectional, emotional part of the man. It is the daughter of the king (*princess*) and should never be allowed to unite in any way with matter or with material conditions. When Abraham, not in divine understanding, was drawn down into the vital processes of the organism for recuperation, he allowed his loves, affections, and emotions (Sarah) to become united with the ruling states of consciousness there, and brought plagues upon the house of Pha-

raoh in consequence (Gen. 12:11-19).

It is right and proper to recognize the vital center in the organism, which is the generative or sex center, as having a place in the divine economy; but man should never become involved in the mere animal processes of life generation, of which a coarse form of animal sensation is one phase. This is what brings the plagues of Egypt (disease) upon the human family.

Metaphysicians who are regenerating their bodies through the concentrated power of their I AM word should heed this lesson, and when quickening, cleansing, and readjusting the cells at this life center they should not forget to declare silently the Truth of Spirit. The following is a good affirmation to make: *"The sensation of the flesh cannot hold my love. My love is the daughter of God, and we are joined to purity and pure desire in our Father's house."* Thus shall they escape the plagues of Egypt and the rebuke of Pharaoh: "What is this that thou hast done unto me? why didst thou not tell me that she was thy wife?"

Sarai's name was changed to Sarah (*princess*). In spiritual symbology woman represents the soul, or intuitive phase of man. Sarah is the spiritual soul. Abraham did not doubt God's promise, but he felt it necessary that he help to bring it about in his own way instead of abiding God's time. So he took Sarah's maid, Hagar, and had a son by her. Hagar represents the natural soul, and God would not recognize as the heir the fruit of the union with the natural will and affection.

There is a very important lesson in this for every one who is growing in faith and seeking to bring forth the fruits of Spirit. No real spiritual demonstration is made unless the divine law is recognized and obeyed. If we try to demonstrate Truth through our personal will and effort, we shall find that we have fallen short.

Sarai, sā'-rāi (Heb.)—*bitter; contentious; dominative; quarrelsome.*

The name of Abraham's wife before the Lord changed it to Sarah (Gen. 17:15).

Meta. In Sarai the soul is contending

for its rightful place in consciousness; the individual is just recognizing the fact that his affections and emotions (his soul) are in essence divine and must not be united with material conditions, but with Spirit. In Sarah this is more fully realized and expressed.

Saraph, sā′-răph (Heb.)—*burning; fiery; poisonous; venomous; deadly; burned up; consumed with fire.*

A man named in the genealogy of Judah (I Chron. 4:22).

Meta. The thought that Saraph signifies belongs to the result of a wrong or unwise use of the life, or vital forces and powers, in the organism of the individual (*burning, fiery, poisonous, venomous, burned up*). The appetites and lusts of the flesh, when indulged in, poison the system, dull the ability to think and to accomplish, and finally burn up and destroy the body itself.

"At the last it biteth like a serpent,
And stingeth like an adder."

Judah, in its negative aspect, stands for the life center in the body, on the generative plane, while in its positive aspect it is praise and the upliftment of the life idea, consequently of the vital forces (Saraph was a man of Judah).

Sardis, sär′-dĭs (Gk.)—*precious stone; carnelian; sardonyx; sard; prince of joy.*

A city, the capital of ancient Lydia, and the site of one of the seven churches to which John wrote (Rev. 3:1-6).

Meta. The riches of power (*precious stone*); also joyous dominion (*prince of joy*, a prince belonging to the ruling family). Lydia, the country of which Sardis was the capital, refers to power. When we think of Lydia we think of purple, of the woman by this name who was a seller of purple; purple is the color that stands for power.

"He that hath the seven Spirits of God, and the seven stars" (Rev. 3:1) signifies the natural man redeemed or rounded out; seven is the number of fulfillment in the natural. The "stars" are faculties that we have not yet developed; they are remote, not clearly understood. The central point in regard to this church at Sardis seems to be: Are we where we think we are? (See Rev. 3:2.) Are we exercising power and dominion over all our thoughts? Theoretically we may be, but really are we? The natural man is reputed to have great power—he goes out and kills the animals—but when he gives up to his emotions, passions, appetites, and sense desires he is not exercising spiritual power over the beasts of the field—his own animal propensities. Nor has he perfect dominion over the fishes of the sea, birds of the air, and creeping things—the primal elements of life.

We are developing the sevenfold man of the stars. There is no limit to what we can become. Not only may we control and direct and use our own faculties, but we can use the spiritual powers and propensities. If we allow our thoughts of power to slow down, however, we lose the spiritual aspect of power. The static in radio is cross currents, discords. During electric storms the static is very great, so that at times we cannot hear the radio program. Even so, when we get angry, excited, or confused, cross currents enter our consciousness and we cannot get into the silence, we cannot get in touch with the spiritual. We should affirm power and dominion.

Revelation 3:3: Remember the foundation principles, your first instructions: man is spiritual. If you are watching you will not let yourself get confused and congested when Spirit comes to you in greater power. Do not think that because you may be having some seemingly adverse experience it is really adverse. Go apart from others and get hold of Spirit, and you can handle the problem. Beware of persons who offer remedies. Affirm more spiritual power, more steadfastness, more understanding.

"White" (Rev. 3:4) represents purity, and also the aura of Spirit. Your aura has become purified, whitened. We are clothed with this white aura, with this garment of life (Rev. 3:5), by overcoming.

Sargon, sär′-gŏn (Heb. fr. Pers.)—*sun prince; prince of the sun.*

A king of Assyria. He sent his commander in chief, Tartan, to take Ashdod (Isa. 20:1).

Meta. The exaltation of the will functioning through sense intellect, as though it were the rightful ruling power in the individual (*sun prince*, a king of Assyria).

Sarid, sā'-rĭd (Heb.)—*a sole survivor; one left; a survivor; a remnant; a refuge.*

A border city of Zebulun (Josh. 19: 12).

Meta. The divine idea of man, the Word of God, that abides forever, even though all outer seemings may fail. Heaven and earth may pass away, yet the true Word, the spiritual idea underlying all existence, remains (*a survivor, one left*), and retains its protecting, sustaining, working power (*a refuge*). This divine idea, or Word, enters into man's life and consciousness with greatly increased power when man begins to bring his order faculty into expression (Sarid was a boundary city of Zebulun, and Zebulun, son of Jacob, represents the faculty of order in the individual).

Sarsechim, sär-sē'-chĭm (Heb.)— *prince of the eunuchs; chief eunuch.*

A prince of the king of Babylon, evidently one of the commanders of his army that came up against Jerusalem and conquered the city (Jer. 39:3).

Meta. The significance is virtually the same as that of RAB–SARIS, which see. It is thought that the two are identical.

Satan, sā'-tan (Heb.)—*lier in wait; an adversary; an enemy; hater; accuser; opposer; contradictor.*

The same as the Devil, the Adversary, the Evil One, and the like (Job. 1:6-12; Matt. 4:10).

Meta. The deceiving phase of mind in man that has fixed ideas in opposition to Truth (*adversary, lier in wait, accuser, opposer, hater, an enemy*). Satan assumes various forms in man's consciousness, among which may be mentioned egotism, a puffing up of the personality; and the opposite of this, self-depreciation, which admits the "accuser" into the consciousness. This "accuser" makes man believe that he is inherently evil.

Satan is the "Devil," a state of mind formed by man's personal ideas of his power and completeness and sufficiency apart from God. Besides at times puffing up the personality, this satanic thought often turns about and, after having tempted one to do evil, discourages the soul by accusing it of sin. Summed up, it is the state of mind in man that believes in its own sufficiency independent of its creative Source.

Rebellion against God under hard experiences is another form of this *"hater."* The personality that disbelieves in God and acknowledges no law save that of man is satanic.

When the seventy returned, saying, "Lord, even the demons are subject unto us in thy name," Jesus said, "I beheld Satan fallen as lightning from heaven" (Luke 10:17, 18).

Heaven is conscious harmony. When this harmony is invaded by a thought adverse to the divine law, there is Satan, and "war in heaven." When the Christ declares the Truth, error thought falls away; that is, Satan falls from heaven as lightning.

Lightning is a force that gathers and explodes and wastes its energy because it is not in harmony with the universal equilibrium. This well illustrates the mind that believes itself an independent and unrelated creation. When this kind of thought is allowed full sway in a man's consciousness, he becomes so egotistical and self-opinionated that he destroys himself. Thus error is its own destruction.

The Greek word that is translated "devil" in Luke 4:1-13 means *accuser* or *the critical one. Personality* describes the meaning more fully than any other word in the English language.

Saul, saul (Heb.)—*asked for; desired; demanded; wished.*

a A Benjamite, son of Kish. He was the first king of Israel (I Sam. 9:2). **b** The former name of Paul (Acts 9:1-18).

Meta. The action of the will in attaining that which it desires.

Saul, the first king of Israel, represents the will functioning in the limitations of personality. The will should be anointed or inspired by judgment, but in its development it often asserts its own initiative and is thereby defeated in its leadership.

Saul was a child of nature. Had he lived in this country he would have been called a cowboy. He was hunting his father's drove of asses and, not finding them, dropped in to consult Samuel, a prophet, who was also evidently a finder of lost property. Samuel was impressed with the young man and, being informed by the Lord that Saul should be made king, the prophet anointed him.

Saul signifies personal will. He represents the consciousness in its natural estate. It is willful and stubborn, shy and impulsive, yet very brave under great stress. When first chosen as king Saul was very humble; and true humility is one of the first qualifications for spiritual leadership. The will is a very complex phase of the mind, however, and its paradoxes often perplex the most acute. The character of Saul has always been a puzzle to Bible students and ministers.

A study of one's own personality will reveal the character of Saul. He is that in us which lies very close to sense consciousness.

When the personal will is wholly given to sense life it is a Gentile. When it recognizes Jehovah and has a semblance of spiritual understanding it is an Israelite. Saul was recognized by the Lord and selected by Him to be king; yet Saul did not adhere strictly to the spiritual law. He consulted soothsayers and mediums, when he could not at once get a response from the Lord.

People who are under the dominion of personality are very liable to be led away from Truth, through a desire to know temporal things instead of eternal. When we are very anxious to know the future, and slyly seek the so-called wisdom of a medium or clairvoyant, we are under the dominion of wavering human will. When we are sure of our premise in God we do not fear the outcome, and we always know that we shall succeed in every good work; there is then no temptation to go to a fortune teller for advice.

The conflict between Saul and David represents the war in man between the head and the heart, personal will and divine love, for control. The will functioning in sense consciousness would destroy its own soul (Jonathan) and innate love (David).

Everything in man that does not recog-

nize and acknowledge its source in God must finally die to things spiritual. Such was the death of Saul and Jonathan.

Neither Saul nor Jonathan was wholly dedicated to the Lord. They stood alone in personal consciousness, and Saul's insanity was the epilepsy that accompanies excessive personality. Jonathan's love for David was personal—he was not in spiritual understanding. Not having the resource of Spirit, personal will and personal consciousness grow weaker and weaker until the Philistines, representing thoughts in open rebellion against all spiritual law, destroy them.

On one side Saul was open to Spirit and was often guided by Jehovah. But he was not loyal to Jehovah. When his error thoughts obscured his inspiration and the Almighty answered him not "by dreams, nor by Urim, nor by prophets," Saul disguised himself and went to the woman at Endor that had "a familiar spirit" (see I Sam. 28). Saul had the woman call up Samuel, just as mediums do in this day, and she told Saul what the prophet said. Had Saul followed the law he would have waited patiently on the Lord until he got his answer direct. When we place anybody or anything between ourselves and our indwelling Lord we weaken our power, and adverse thoughts overwhelm us just as they did Saul.

Saul, in the individual consciousness, means the executive power of the mind, that in us which directs and leads our spiritual thoughts into a larger degree of freedom. Saul represents divine will only as man apprehends and uses it in personal leadership.

David represents love. He was the well-beloved of the Lord. His constancy, his faithfulness to his friends, his universal kindness and charity, all prove the predominance of the love quality in his nature. But David was not able to manifest the unselfish love of our Savior, Jesus Christ. David demonstrated up to the point where he could say of the Lord, "my shepherd"; Jesus came to the place in consciousness where His unselfish love reached out and encompassed all people, where He could say, "our Father."

Solomon represents the wisdom of

Spirit; he typifies that in us which is able to turn within and make conscious at-one-ment with the light of Spirit. Solomon was not able, however, to express the full light of Spirit. By allying himself with heathenish tribes, for the sake of peace, he opened the way for the inflow of the unenlightened forces that eventually divided his kingdom.

The great lesson to be gleaned from a close study of the lives of Saul, David, and Solomon is that to continue to unfold spiritually and to be successful one must live very close to Spirit and must be always humble and obedient before the Lord. Outer success and personal glory tend to make one all-sufficient to himself, and this mental attitude shuts off the light of Spirit. Knowing that all power is from the Lord, and being always willing to do the unselfish act for the good of all, one insures for oneself an eternal kingdom of peace and happiness that can never be divided against itself.

Saul of Tarsus, who was later called Paul and was an apostle of Jesus Christ, signifies the will. By the power of the will we plant in every part of the consciousness a spiritual potency that has within it all the possibilities of its God source. This divine seed is the word of Truth, which will spring up after many days.

Saul, before his conversion (Acts 9:1, 2), represents one who is zealous in his search for God but is so filled with the religious ideas that have been inculcated by his previous training that he resists the true Christ understanding.

Saul on his way to Damascus (sack of blood) to persecute the Christians represents the fanatical will filled with zeal to destroy everything that opposes its traditional religion. In Acts 22:3, 6:10, and Philippians 3:7-14, Saul represents the obedience of the will and its acceptance of the word of Truth.

The will must be dealt with in every movement, because it is the very essence of self-consciousness. The conversion and the work of Saul of Tarsus fill a large place in Bible history. Saul represents in this symbology the human will. In all permanent character building the action of the will is based on understanding. Will and understanding go hand in hand. They are the Ephraim and Manasseh of Scripture, whose allotment in the Promised Land was in joint ownership.

The conversion of Saul was preceded by a great light of spiritual understanding. Saul (asked for, wished, demanded) typifies the will in its personal dominance. In this unregenerate state it recognizes no master or guide save self-gratification, and it grows large in its own conceit. King Saul is a type of this unregenerate will. Mystics say that he was a former incarnation of Saul of Tarsus. After the discovery that there is a wisdom greater than that of the personal will, its name is changed to Paul, which means little, and it is converted from the violent and oppressive persecutor of things spiritual to the devout and obedient champion of the humble Christ.

Saul of Tarsus was sincere, and that sincerity was the open way to the Christ mind. (See PAUL, in your study of Saul of Tarsus.)

Sceva, sçē'-vȧ (Gk.)—covered; obscured; secret; the left side; left-handed; vessel; utensil; implement; instrument; armament; gear; fitting.

A Jewish priest at Ephesus. His seven sons undertook to cast the evil spirit out of a man, in imitation of the work of Paul, but with disastrous results (Acts 19:14).

Meta. A fixed state of mind that prevails in the physical consciousness. The "seven sons" are the seven centers of thought and action in the body.

The word of Truth cast out evil spirits and healed the sick at Ephesus, and this work was imitated by strolling Jewish exorcists. They used the same formulas that Paul used, but they had not been converted, or mentally purified, and the evil spirits turned on them and overpowered them so that they fled.

We find people who want to be healed without repentance; they want to be freed from the penalty of error but do not wish to do right. These ask for word formulas, magic, and they create a demand for the exorcists that imitate the Truth but are not in the understanding of the change of heart and thought that must accompany all true healing.

When we find that through the mere use of words and formulas there is no permanent casting out of the evil that besets us, fear falls upon us and the name of the Lord is magnified.

The burning of the books of those who practiced "magical arts" means the total denial of all formulas and aids that are not based on understanding of Truth.

scribes.

Meta. The scribes of Mark 1:22 represent the thoughts that come to us from other personalities or from books. The scribes of the 7th chapter of Mark are our external religious thoughts.

There is a faculty of the mind that receives and transcribes upon the tablets of memory every wave of thought that touches the consciousness, whether from the flesh or from Spirit. This faculty is Ezra the scribe; it may be exalted to a point where it will receive impressions from the spiritual side only.

Scythian, sçўth′-ĭ-ăn (Gk.)—*of or belonging to Scythia; cut off; rough; barbarous; immoderate; fierce-looking; rude; ignorant; degraded.*

A name generally applied to the wandering, barbarous tribes of people north of the Black and Caspian seas (Col. 3: 11).

Meta. Thoughts of a very low, ignorant, uncultivated, and seemingly warring character (*rough, barbarous, rude, ignorant, fierce-looking, degraded*). When the "old man" has been put off, however, and the "new man" fully put on, there will be no more Scythians in consciousness, because all one's thoughts will then have been raised to the Christ standard.

sea.

Meta. The "sea," in Revelation 21:1, that is "no more," is the universal sensate thought of the race, which is to be dissolved and cast into the bottomless pit of nothingness.

The sea also signifies universal Mind, that great realm of unexpressed and unformed thoughts and ideas that contains all-potentiality.

We sometimes think of a "sea," too, as a state of unrest.

seamless robe of Jesus (John 19:23, 24).

Meta. See COAT of Jesus, without seam.

Seba, sē′-bà (Heb.)—*radical moisture; vital fluid; condensation; sap; sucking up saturation; drinking to excess; drunken; intoxicated; turning; reeling.*

a Son of Cush (Gen. 10:7). **b** A nation (Isa. 43:3).

Meta. Intemperate desire expressing in the body consciousness. The Seba thought and state of thought are not poised, moderate, or well balanced about anything; they go to the extreme, especially in indulgence of the appetites and desires of the flesh when the "mind of the flesh" is in the ascendancy in the individual. Yet at the back of all desire there is good; there is that which in the end works for the uplift and enrichment of the consciousness. Thus we have the assurance that "the kings of Sheba and Seba shall offer gifts" to the Christ, who is the righteous king in man and in the whole earth.

Sebam (A. V., Shebam), sē′-băm (Heb.)—*cool; fragrant; aromatic; spicy; odorous; sweet; pleasant; kind; balsam; balsam plant; cinnamon.*

Sebam (Num. 32:3) is the same place as Sibmah (Josh. 13:19).

Meta. See SIBMAH.

Secacah, sĕc′-ă-căh (Heb.)—*interwoven; interlaced; entwined; hedge; thicket; inclosure; cover; protection; envelopment; shade; shadow; defense; secret.*

A city of Judah, in the wilderness (Josh. 15:61).

Meta. A consciousness of security, of protection, that is built up in the soul by the unifying and interweaving action of high spiritual aspiration coupled with abundant praise of God—the good, perfect, true, and all-powerful source of all that really is (*interwoven, entwined, protection, envelopment, shade, defense,* a city of Judah—Judah representing the life faculty in man, which, in its highest aspect, expresses as spiritual aspiration, praise).

Secu (A. V., Sechu), sē′-cū (Heb.)—*cutting; separating; discerning; viewing; looking; watching; overseeing; watch place; watchtower.*

A place in Palestine, at or near Ramah, where there is a great well (I Sam. 19: 22).

Meta. A consciousness of spiritual discernment, of judgment or separating and cutting off of error; a watchful attitude of mind (*cutting, separating, discerning, looking, watching, watch place*; a place at Ramah).

Ramah was the home of Samuel, and signifies a very exalted state of mind. Naioth (*habitations, dwellings*), a place in Ramah where Samuel had his "company of prophets," signifies the abiding place of the Most High, or a conscious abiding in the higher things of Spirit. David (love) fled to that place for protection from Saul (the will functioning in the selfishness of personality), and when Saul came there seeking David to slay him, all his power to harm David departed from him and he also began to prophesy; he was for the time being inspired by the Spirit of truth.

Secundus, se-cŭn′-dŭs (Lat.)—*second; following; the next; secondary; inferior; favorable; similar; favoring.*

One who accompanied Paul on one of his missionary journeys (Acts 20:4). He was a Christian of Thessalonica.

Meta. A secondary attitude of thought (*second*) that is necessary to promote the acceptance and growth of Truth in the whole being of man. It is an attitude of thought that approves of Truth and is willing to do all in its power to further the activity of the word of Truth (Paul) in the consciousness (*favorable*, a Christian man who accompanied Paul as far as Asia on one of his missionary journeys).

Segub, se′-gŭb (Heb.)—*high; elevated; exalted; raised up; set on high; supreme; secure; protected; inaccessible; difficult to assail; strong; fortified.*

a Youngest son of Hiel the Bethelite, who rebuilt Jericho (I Kings 16:34). **b** Son of Hezron of the tribe of Judah, and father of Jair (I Chron. 2:21).

Meta. High, powerful, protective thoughts belonging to the Israelite or truer spiritual realm of consciousness (*elevated, raised up, supreme, secure, protected, strong, fortified*, two Israelitish men of the tribe of Judah).

See HIEL, father of the first-named Segub, for an explanation of I Kings 16:34.

Seir, se′-ĭr (Heb.)—*standing on end; bristling; shaggy; hairy; rough; shrinking; shaking; shuddering; stormy; tempestuous; horror; fearful; he-goat; satyr; wood demon.*

a A mountainous land or country, near the Dead Sea, that was occupied first by the Horites and later by Esau and his descendants (Gen. 14:6; 36:8, 9). Edom and Seir are the same land, Edom referring to Esau and Seir to the Horites. **b** The name of a Horite chief (Gen. 36:20).

Meta. The significance is virtually the same as that of Edom, the physical or sense consciousness in man (*bristling, shaggy, hairy, rough, tempestuous, fearful, he-goat*, and so forth; Seir apparently refers especially to the very emotional and stormy, yet deep-seated, carnal tendencies in the physical). (See EDOM, ESAU, and HORITES.)

Seirah (A. V., Seirath), se′-ĭ-răh (Heb.)—*standing on end; bristling; hairy; rough; shrinking; shaking; shuddering; fearful; stormy; tempestuous; she-goat; wood nymph.*

Ehud escaped to this place after he had killed Eglon, king of Moab, and there Ehud gathered the Children of Israel to fight against Moab (Judg. 3:26).

Meta. Seirah, being the feminine form of Seir, refers to the soul, receptive, or feminine phase of that which Seir signifies.

Sela, se′-là (Heb.)—*rock; large rock; cliff; firm; solid; elevated; lofty; fortress; stronghold.*

The capital of Edom (II Kings 14:7, "*the rock*," margin). It is called Selah in Isaiah 16:1; in margin, *Petra.*

Meta. Sense man's trust centered in physical strength and power (*rock, cliff, firm, elevated, fortress*, the capital of Edom and a stronghold in Edom). Sela is the Hebrew equivalent of the Greek word *petra* (rock), that Jesus used in regard to Peter (faith) in Matthew 16: 18. (See JOKTHEEL for the significance of this city's being conquered by the king of Judah and renamed *Joktheel*.)

Selah, se′-lăh (Heb.)—*tranquil; secure; at rest; silence; pause; quiet;*

peaceful; serene; prosperous.

A word that occurs many times in the Psalms.

Meta. The state of mind in prayer in which we relax from our affirmation of Truth and thanksgiving for good received and to be received, and "wait" on God in the stillness, that the Holy Spirit may reveal more of its inspirations to us and that it may establish our thoughts and our heart more firmly in the divine harmony and good.

Sela–hammahlekoth, sē'lȧ–hăm'-măh-lē'-kŏth (Heb.)—*rock of the escapes; rock of the separations; cliff of the divisions.*

The place where Saul ceased pursuing David and went against the Philistines (I Sam. 23:28).

Meta. The will functioning in personal selfishness and egotism (Saul) has been seeking to destroy love (David), which is gradually rising in the individual consciousness to the place of rulership. Thus the sense mind, against which the will should have been exercising itself, has grown stronger and stronger until its error, fearing, self-exalting, opposing thoughts and beliefs (Philistines) are about to take possession of the whole man, to his undoing.

Sela–hammahlekoth (*rock of the escapes, rock of the separations, cliff of the divisions*) is the phase of thought or dividing line in the will's activities where it suddenly realizes the real need of the man, and so for the time being leaves off opposing its own good and begins to act executively, in union with the higher, and truer, religious ideals (Israelites) against the hordes of sense thoughts that have come up in seemingly conquering power against the kingdom of Israel.

Seled, sē'-lĕd (Heb.)—*springing up; leaping up; exulting; burning; roasting; consuming; torment; affliction.*

Son of Nadab, descended from Jerahmeel, named in the genealogy of Judah. Seled died without sons (I Chron. 2:30).

Meta. A very emotional, changeable state of thought, and like experiences (*springing up, leaping up, exulting, burning, consuming, torment;* the idea in the name is that of jumping up and down in excess of emotion, whether joy or pain). This changeable, emotional, unpoised state of thought that is not established in the one omnipresent good does not bring forth any positive results for good. (Seled died without sons).

Seleucia, sẻ-leū'-cȧ-ȧ (Gk.)—*beaten by waves; troubled; tossed; afflicted; white with brightness; moonstruck.*

Paul and Barnabas, "being sent forth by the Holy Spirit, went down to Seleucia; and from thence they sailed to Cyprus" (Acts 13:4). Seleucia was a Syrian seaport, west of Antioch.

Meta. Seleucia means *beaten by waves, troubled, tossed,* and Cyprus means *fairness.* Being shaken (Seleucia) is a common experience of those who send Spirit down into the body. Some are afraid that this disturbed condition is wrong. Spirit does not do the shaking; the experience is simply the revealment by Spirit (*white with brightness*) of a shaky subconsciousness that is not established in the good, which already existed and of which the individual was but vaguely aware. Fear not; but clear away the clouds of doubt and you will sail to the island of Cyprus, *fairness.*

Semachiah, sĕm-ȧ-ehī'-ăh (Heb.)—*Jehovah sustains him; whom Jah upholds; who leans upon the Lord; joined to Jehovah.*

Son of Shemaiah, and grandson of Obed–edom (I Chron. 26:7).

Meta. One who is consciously *joined to Jehovah* and *leans upon the Lord;* who is supported and sustained by Jehovah, the indwelling Christ or Father (*Jehovah sustains him, whom Jah upholds*).

Semein (A. V., Semei), sĕm'-ĕ-ĭn (Gk. fr. Heb.)—*heard distinctly; understood; hearkening; obeying; reported; reputed; famed; distinguished.*

Father of Mattathias, and son of Josech, in the genealogy of Jesus Christ (Luke 3:26).

Meta. The understanding that attention and obedience to Spirit increase one's power of spiritual perception and discrimination, and truly exalt and ennoble the character (*heard distinctly, understood, hearkening, obeying, famed*).

Senaah, sẻ-nā'-ăh (Heb.)—*thorny; bristling; thorn bush; thorn hedge; brambly.*

The name of either a city or a man, whose inhabitants or "children" returned from the Babylonian captivity (Ezra 2: 35).

Meta. An enemy to error (*thorny, brambly,* the name of a city or a man of Judah, whose inhabitants or "children" returned from the Babylonian captivity). Some authorities connect this name with Hassenaah. (See HASSENAAH.)

Seneh, sē'-nĕh (Heb.)—*thorny; bristling; thorn bush; pointed (thorny) rock; bramble bush; thorn rock.*

A rocky crag that was on one side of the pass by which Jonathan and his armor-bearer went over into the garrison of the Philistines and killed many of them (I Sam. 14:4).

Meta. The fear that causes one to think that he dare not undertake to overcome and to drive out of his consciousness those error, sense thoughts of opposition to Spirit that the Philistines signify. Two rocky crags, Seneh and Bozez, separated Jonathan from the Philistines; Jonathan had to pass them in order to enter the Philistine camp and smite the Philistine host. Even so the fear that one cannot and dare not lay hold fearlessly of all the good that is in Christ for one, and deny away every error, opposing thought and activity in mind, body, and affairs, must be dealt with and overcome before one can gain a real victory over one's lesser self and enter conscious union with one's higher self, the Christ.

Senir, sē'-nĭr (Heb.)—*interwoven; entwined; connected; coat of mail; corselet; glistening; peak; snowy mountain.*

The Amoritish name for Mount Hermon (Deut. 3:9).

Meta. Mount Hermon represents a high, sublime state of mind. Senir (*peak, snowy mountain, glistening,* the Amoritish name for Mount Hermon) symbolizes the highest thought of Truth that the Amorite phase of consciousness in man can perceive. (See AMORITES.) This high ideal is to this consciousness more or less a mixture of sense thoughts about Truth (*interwoven, entwined*), and takes on an aggressive or defensive attitude (*coat of mail*).

Sennacherib, sĕn-năch'-ĕ-rĭb (Heb. fr. Pers.)—*conqueror of armies; Sin (moon*

god) has increased the brothers; bramble of destruction; devastation by the enemy.

King of Assyria. He came up against Hezekiah, king of Judah, and Hezekiah paid tribute. Later the Assyrians were overcome by divine help rendered the Jewish people, and Sennacherib was killed by his sons while he was worshiping in the house of the god Nisroch (II Kings 18:13; 19:37).

Meta. A ruling thought in the sense-reasoning plane of consciousness in man. This is not the true source of understanding; it is head of the realm of thought represented by the Assyrians (a king of the Assyrians; see ASSYRIA). Though this ruling thought multiplies error in the consciousness that gives it place (*Sin, moon god, has increased the brothers*), it comes to an end (*bramble of destruction;* the king was killed and the Assyrians were overcome).

Seorim, sĕ-ō'-rĭm (Heb.)—*hairy; bristling; bearded; barley; barleycorn; fears; distresses; terrors.*

A priest to whom was allotted the fourth course in Temple service, in David's reign (I Chron. 24:8).

Meta. Seorim is a form of the words SEIR and SEIRAH, which see. Since Seorim was the name of an Israelitish priest who served in the Temple in David's reign, we see in it a suggestion of elevation and transmutation of the sense or physical consciousness to higher and more spiritual expression.

Sephar, sē'-phär (Heb.)—*spiritual travail; meditation; numbering; recounting; remembering; narrating; engraving; writing; scroll; sacred writing; book; scribe.*

Concerning the "sons" or descendants of Joktan, descendant of Shem, the text says: "And their dwelling was from Mesha, as thou goest toward Sephar, the mountain of the east" (Gen. 10:30).

Meta. The east always represents the within, while a mountain signifies a high plane of thought. Sephar, "the mountain of the east" (meaning *remembering, engraving, numbering, book, scribe*), is, in consciousness of the individual, that high place within the spiritual realm of his being where a record is kept of all the thoughts, ideals, tendencies, desires, and activities to which he has given place, even those that belong to the seemingly changeable and unestablished phase of his consciousness (the Arabian tribes that were descended from Joktan).

Sepharad, sĕph'-ă-răd (Heb.)—*divided number; severed; boundary; limit.*

A place where captive Jews from Jerusalem were taken (Obad. 20).

Meta. There is always a *limit* to any seeming separation or wandering away from God, Spirit, Truth. When this *limit* or *boundary* is reached, a reaction sets in and the soul begins to swing back toward its center. Sepharad indicates this boundary or termination of the separation of the Jews from their native land —the higher religious and spiritual thoughts of the individual from his inner heart center, or Jerusalem (spiritual consciousness); a coming back to their own rightful high place of dominion is begun.

The prophet Obadiah—the high spiritual ideal that remains faithful and true to the things of Spirit and is ever attentive and obedient—prophesied that "the captives of Jerusalem, that are in Sepharad," shall return to the Promised Land of their inheritance. They are to "possess the cities of the South." This means that higher ideals will be freed in consciousness and are to enter into the thought centers of the subconscious realm of mind to do a redeeming, regenerating work there.

Sepharvaim, sĕph-ăr-vā'-ĭm (Heb.)— *dual meditations; two inscriptions; two letters; two books; two scribes.*

A city in Syria. The king of Assyria took people from this place and settled them in Samaria after he had carried the Israelites away captive (II Kings 17:24; 19:13). The "gods of Sepharvaim" are mentioned in II Kings 17:31.

Meta. A dual state of consciousness— partly good, partly evil (*dual meditations, two inscriptions*). This dual habit of thinking is the result of reasoning according to the senses, or outer appearances (a city of Syria, and Syria signifies the thoughts of the intellectual realm that have no understanding of the

real but draw their conclusions from the reasonings of the outer or sense man).

Sepharvites, sĕ'-phär-vītes (fr. Heb.). Natives of the city of Sepharvaim. "And the Sepharvites burnt their children in the fire to Adrammelech and Anammelech, the gods of Sepharvaim" (II Kings 17:31).

Meta. Thoughts springing from and belonging to that in consciousness which Sepharvaim signifies. (See SEPHARVAIM and ADRAMMELECH.)

Serah, sē'-răh (Heb.)—*poured forth; diffused; spread out; extension; redundance; abundance; excess.*

Daughter of Asher (Num. 26:46).

Meta. While Serah bespeaks a rich, broad, extensive phase of soul quality (*extension, abundance, spread out*), there is also a strong suggestion of waste of substance, lack of conservation (*poured forth, diffused, excess*).

Seraiah, sĕ-rā'-ĭăh (Heb.)—*Jehovah hath prevailed; Jah strives; Jah is prince; whom Jehovah leads; warrior of Jehovah.*

There were several Israelites by this name (II Sam. 8:17; II Kings 25:18, 23; I Chron. 4:13, 35; Ezra 2:2, and others).

Meta. Thoughts of dominion, of conquest and victory, based on the overcoming power of the indwelling Christ, I AM, Jehovah (*Jehovah hath prevailed, Jah is prince, warrior of Jehovah,* Israelitish men).

seraphim (A. V., seraphims), sĕr'-ă-phĭm (Heb.)—*the burning; fiery ones; consuming with fire; nobility; eminence; glorious; princely.*

Heavenly beings that Isaiah saw in his vision, described in the 6th chapter of Isaiah.

Meta. Ideas of purity, or the cleansing power of exalted ideas (*the burning, fiery ones, glorious, princely*).

Wings symbolize freedom from material limitations. Six wings indicate that the purification must go through the six avenues of consciousness in the body. Those who are spiritually quickened have a partial development of intuition, in addition to the five senses. The intelligence, represented by the face, is concealed, because the work to be done is too deep for human inderstanding; the flying shows the divine action. The "Holy, holy, holy, is Jehovah of hosts" is the word of Truth, the statement of wholeness in the whole body—"the whole earth is full of his glory." This spiritual perception of the all-pervading glory of the divine perfection is well understood by those who have had visions of the heavenly law.

The consciousness of personal impurity is taken away through the realization of divine purity in thought and word (Isa. 6:5-7).

The mystery of this hard message of the Lord to the people who so greatly needed help has often been commented on and generally misunderstood because taken in its literal sense. This is a treatise on body rejuvenation after a great depletion. The body must be built up in strength and flesh before the mental and spiritual forces can be expressed through it; hence, "Make the heart of this people fat, and make their ears heavy, and shut their eyes" (Isa. 6:10). Give the natural man opportunity to rebuild his wasted forces before you pour in upon him the high voltage of Spirit.

Regeneration begins its work in the conscious mind and completes it in the subconscious mind. The body is the substance side of the subconscious mind. In Scripture it is called "earth" and "land"; its brain centers are "cities" and its specific functions are "houses" (Isa. 6:11).

When the regenerative process sets in, the poison in the system is starved out by a withdrawing of the consciousness from certain centers. The Lord has "removed men far away, and the forsaken places be many in the midst of the land" (Isa. 6:12). A parallel to this is observed when the body has been excessively weakened by sickness; the functions are dormant for a time, but as the strength returns they gradually resume their normal action. If there is even a "tenth" (Isa. 6:13) of the normal life left in the body it will serve as "holy seed" and the fruit thereof will be eaten again.

A most holy and wonderful thing is man's body. The whole universe is epitomized in it, and through a right study of its laws man may gain full knowledge of the cosmos. The greatest of the prophets, Isaiah, could have chosen no higher theme for his inspired messages. "Why will ye be still stricken, that ye revolt more and more? the whole head is sick, and the whole heart faint. From the sole of the foot even unto the head there is no soundness in it" (Isa. 1:5, 6).

Sered, sē'-rĕd (Heb.)—*fear; trembling; flight; escape.*

A son of Zebulun (Gen. 46:14).

Meta. Fearfulness, extreme unrest (*fear, trembling*) existing in the order faculty in the individual consciousness (Sered was a son of Zebulun, and Zebulun represents order). Back of this fearful, seemingly unstable thought that Sered signifies, however, deep within the truth that the order faculty is of spiritual origin and is abidingly perfect, there is that to which this thought can flee for refuge and escape from all sense of fear and its results (*flight, escape*).

Seredites (A. V., Sardites), sē'-rĕd-ītes (fr. Heb.)—*of* or *belonging to Sered.*

Descendants of Sered, son of Zebulun (Num. 26:26).

Meta. Thoughts springing from that in consciousness which Sered signifies. (See SERED.)

Sergius Paulus, sēr'-ġĭ-ŭs pạu'-lŭs (Lat.)—*little net; little searcher; small sieve.*

The "proconsul" of the island of Cyprus. He was "a man of understanding. The same called unto him Barnabas and Saul, and sought to hear the word of God" (Acts 13:7).

Meta. The reasoning faculty searching into the things of Spirit. In Acts 13:7-12 we find the proconsul, Sergius Paulus, a man of understanding, observing the effect of Spirit, being astonished at its power, and believing the Truth. In other words the reasoning faculty in man, unified with a certain executive power (Sergius Paulus was the governor of Cyprus, under the Roman emperor), looks into the work of Spirit through the word of Truth (Paul) in the consciousness, and accepts the Christ as its guiding light and as its power of action. The reasoning faculty in man is all right when it is based on Spirit, and receives its conclusions by working from a spiritual premise. "Come now, and let us reason together, saith Jehovah" (Isa. 1: 18).

serpent.

Meta. The "serpent" of the garden of Eden is sense consciousness. It may also be called desire, and sensation, or the activity of life in an external expression, apart from the Source of life. When the life is lifted to the realization that it is Spirit, it becomes healing, as illustrated by Moses' lifting up the serpent in the wilderness. Those who had been bitten by the fiery serpents (lustful expressions of life) were healed when they looked upon the serpent that was lifted up by Moses at the command of God. They looked up, or perceived the truth about divine life, and their minds and bodies were cleansed.

Bitterness always has back of it a bite for some one. When man rebels against life's conditions and curses God he sets up fiery forces in his thoughts that react on his body like poison. This is the condition illustrated in the allegory of Numbers 21:5-9. God does not directly send serpents upon man, but man's rebellious thoughts set up cross currents in his consciousness, and the burning and the biting seem a divine visitation. The original Hebrew does not imply that these were real serpents, but state that they were "the seraphim," "the burning ones."

The serpent is a form of elemental life. The Oriental symbol of eternal life is the serpent with tail in mouth. When this elemental form is "lifted up," or spiritualized, it adds glory and radiance to the whole man. The brazen serpent that Moses caused to be put up where all could see it, and so be healed, represents this elevation of the sense man to a higher consciousness.

Moses prayed for the people, and they confessed their sins and repented; there was a complete change of thought and especially a concentration on the one life (represented by the brazen serpent) to which all must look to be healed. When we turn our attention within and concentrate all our thoughts of life on divine life as manifest in Christ, a har-

monizing and uplifting process sets in throughout the organism. The life force is no longer dissipated in sense sensation, but is conserved and concentrated at the various nerve centers. Through the action of the mind in prayer, faith, and meditation, the life force is transmuted to higher forms of energy and the whole man is lifted up. This is the way in which the body is spiritualized, and through this method man will finally make an immortal body.

"As Moses lifted up the serpent in the wilderness [of sense], even so must the Son of man [personal consciousness] be lifted up." Taking up serpents represents lifting up sense consciousness without being hurt by its reaction. Laying hands on the sick represents pouring out the healing power of Spirit. (See Mark 16:18.)

Serug, sĕ'-rŭg (Heb.)—*woven together; interwoven; braided; shoot; branch; tendril; braid; strength.*

Son of Reu and father of Nahor, who was the grandfather of Abraham (Gen. 11:20-23).

Meta. The budding, sprouting, growing, and developing (*shoot, tendril*) of spiritual seed, or Truth ideas, deep down in the subconsciousness, preparatory to extending the saving work to the body. At the Serug phase of man's unfoldment the work is done mostly in secret, with just a ray of light extending here and there above the horizon of man's conscious comprehension. This spiritual seed is a *branch* of the one true vine, Christ; by the interweaving of the higher thoughts and impulses that it generates, it is strengthening its hold in the individual to the end that his entire being may be raised to spiritual perfection.

servants, of John 2:5-9.

Meta. The elemental forces of Being, ever at hand to carry out one's demands.

Seth, sĕth (Heb.)—*settled; determined; founded; set; placed; disposed; constituted; substituted; compensation.*

Son of Adam and Eve, who "called his name Seth: For, *said she,* God hath appointed me another seed instead of Abel; for Cain slew him" (Gen. 4:25).

Meta. The root idea of this name is that of a surrounding sympathetic movement that envelops a thing and defines its limits, places it, founds it, disposes of it. Some mystics have seen in the name Seth a law of destiny, that which predetermines a thing and settles its order.

While man is in a sense a creature of free will, yet in a larger sense he is a son of God, made in the image and likeness of God, and is destined to express and demonstrate spiritual perfection. There is in all the universe, including man, a balancing power of good, of perfection, which causes a readjustment, a healing, to set in after every transgression of the law, every wandering away from that which is wholesome and true. We find this set forth very clearly in Bible history and symbology. Man seems ever to have wandered away to the limit; then a great reaction has set in, and he has been led back to a saner level. Thus he evolves, grows; and finally he shall come into a full consciousness of his perfect good. His growth into Christlikeness is accelerated greatly as he comes into a knowledge of the Truth that makes free, and thinks and acts consciously, voluntarily, in harmony with it.

"And to Seth, to him also there was born a son; and he called his name Enosh. Then began men to call upon the name of Jehovah" (Gen. 4:26). Enosh means *a miserable man, mortal man;* it is when man comes to the end of his personal resources and sees the nothingness of all his efforts in the outer, apart from Spirit, that he begins to look for a higher power to express in his life—he calls upon the name of Jehovah. It is the activity of the awakening spiritual ideals within him (Seth) that causes him first to realize the futility of his human efforts to better himself, and then to recognize the one Source of all true uplift and good.

Sethur, sē'-thŭr (Heb.)—*covered; veiled; secreted; hidden; protected; covert; hidden sin; deceitful; self-defilement.*

The man chosen from the tribe of Asher to help spy out the land of Canaan (Num. 13:13).

Meta. A degree of understanding of Truth, but kept in the background and not acted upon (*covered, veiled, hidden,*

secreted). Thus deceptive errors are developed in the inner consciousness of the individual (*covert, deceitful, hidden sin, self-defilement*), errors that are harmful to him and greatly hinder his spiritual development. (Sethur was one of the ten spies who brought back an evil report of the land of Canaan. These spies acknowledged that the land was good, and greatly to be desired, but they magnified the size and strength of the enemies in it, and minimized their own strength, not counting on the power of God, which was to win their battles; thus they discouraged the people of Israel and were the cause of many more years of wandering in the wilderness than was necessary.)

seven.

Meta. The number representing fullness in the world of phenomena; seven always refers to the divine law of perfection for the divine-natural man. Adam was a divinely natural man, and had he conformed to the divine law he would not have died. He would have just naturally slipped over into the spiritual man. In the spiritual, twelve is the number of fulfillment, instead of seven.

Elisha told Naaman to bathe in the Jordan seven times.

Seven is so universally used as a mystical number that its basis must be in some fundamental arrangement of the natural world. The golden candlestick that was made expressly for use in the tabernacle in the wilderness had seven lamps (see Exod. 25:31-39). This candlestick of gold, with its lamps, was also used later in the Temple that Solomon built at Jerusalem; it is mentioned in II Chronicles 13:11. We know that the tabernacle and the Temple represented the body of man, and the seven lamps were symbols of seven centers in the organism, through which intelligence is expressed. Everybody knows of five of these avenues: seeing, hearing, tasting, smelling, feeling. There are two in addition to these: intuition and telepathy. The solar plexus is the organ of intuition, and the brain is the organ of telepathy.

These lights have been dimmed by seven sins. These sins have also been given a sevenfold classification: pride, anger, lust, covetousness, envy, gluttony, sloth. The great purifying river of life must wash away these sins and their leprosy from the body. To bring this to pass man must deny in sevenfold measure the darkness of error that obscures the inner light and life.

The meaning of the sending out of the seventy by Jesus (Luke 10:1) is that the seven avenues of expression in man, the seven senses or seven centers in the organism, are to be trained in spiritual ways and their efficiency is to be multiplied tenfold.

"Seventy times seven" (Matt. 18:22) implies unlimited forgiveness.

Shaalabbin, shā-ăl-ăb'-bĭn (Heb.)—*place of foxes; place of jackals; place of hollows; son of a fox; fox holes.*

A border city of Dan (Josh. 19:42). It is called Shaalbim in Judges 1:35 and I Kings 4:9.

Meta. The wisdom, slyness, and cunning of the senses (*place of foxes, place of jackals, son of a fox*). The chief characteristic of the fox is craftiness, and that which is of a sly, deceptive nature is not easy to adjust according to Truth. This city of Shaalabbin was allotted to Dan, but the Danites failed to drive out its Amoritish inhabitants.

Shaalbim. See SHAALABBIN.

Shaalbonite, shă-ăl'-bŏ-nīte (fr. Heb.).

A native of Shaalbim, or Shaalabbin (II Sam. 23:32). Eliahba the Shaalbonite was one of David's mighty men. (See SHAALABBIN.)

Meta. A thought springing from that in consciousness which Shaalabbin signifies. There is but one real understanding. Whatever of true wisdom is gained, even by the senses, must be spiritual in its original essence. This is suggested in the fact that one of David's mighty men was a Shaalbonite.

Shaalim (A. V., Shalim), shā'-ă-lĭm (Heb.)—*burrows; burrowers; foxes; jackals; foxes' region; land of jackals.*

A land through which Saul son of Kish passed while hunting for his father's asses (I Sam. 9:4). It is thought to have been the district in which the city of Shaalabbin, or Shaalbim, was located.

Meta. The wisdom, slyness, and cunning of the senses, which exist secretly in the consciousness. There must be a substance of good in this wisdom, even if it does seem to be of the outer senses instead of originating in Spirit, since Shaalbim provided some of the provisions for Solomon's household (I Kings 4:9; see SHAALBONITE also).

Shaaph, shā'-ăph (Heb.)—*cutting off; separating; division; divided mind; doubtful; skeptical; divided opinions; branches.*

a Son of Jahdai, of the tribe of Judah (I Chron. 2:47). **b** Son of Caleb and his concubine, Maacah, and founder of Madmannah, of the land of Judah (I Chron. 2:49).

Meta. In its most positive or extreme sense Shaaph signifies denial, denial of error (*cutting off, separating, division*). Preceding this comes a division of thought in the mind, a certain discernment between good and seeming error. If this discernment is applied negatively double-mindedness might enter in: doubt, skepticism, *divided opinions*. (See JAHDAI, CALEB, and MADMANNAH.)

Shaaraim, shā'-ă-rā'-ĭm (Heb.) — *double cleft; double apertures; two gates; two sluices; double measures; two assemblages; two forums.*

a A city in the lowland of Judah (Josh. 15:36). **b** A city of Simeon (I Chron. 4:31).

Meta. "And the wounded of the Philistines fell down by the way to Shaaraim, even unto Gath, and unto Ekron" (I Sam. 17:52). Shaaraim (*double cleft, two gates, double apertures*), a city in the lowland of Judah, and also a city of Simeon, through which the Philistines were driven by the Israelites to Gath (*wine press,* trial) and Ekron (*extermination*), signifies the double way that is opened up by the attentive and obedient attitude of mind (Simeon) and by prayer and praise (Judah), to eliminate from the consciousness and the organism the error sense beliefs and thoughts for which the Philistines stand.

Shaashgaz, shă-ăsh'-găz (Heb. fr. Pers.)—*beauty's keeper; servant of the beautiful; devotee of beauty.*

A chamberlain of King Ahasuerus of Persia and Media. He kept the king's concubines (Esth. 2:14).

Meta. An inherent devotion to that which is beautiful and refined, that serves as a connecting link between the dominion of the puffed-up personal will in the individual and his feminine or soul qualities (*servant of the beautiful, devotee of beauty*, a chamberlain to King Ahasuerus, one who kept the concubines of the king).

Shabbethai, shăb'-bĕ-thāi (Heb.)—*Sabbath-born; seventh birth; my restoration; my rest.*

a A Levite who helped Ezra in the matter of those who had taken foreign wives (Ezra 10:15). **b** One of those who helped Ezra to cause the people to understand the law, after the return from the Babylonian captivity (Neh. 8:7; 11:16).

Meta. Abiding thoughts of peace and Truth, or an abiding consciousness of Truth, born of the silence, prayer, of the giving up of one's personal desires and workings, and an entering into conscious unity with Spirit, that God may work in and through one to will and to do according to His good pleasure (*my rest, Sabbath-born*).

Shachia, shă-chī'-ă (Heb.)—*appeased with Jah; fame of Jehovah; Jah protected.*

Son of Shaharaim, of the Benjamites (I Chron. 8:10).

Meta. A sense of quietness, peace, harmony, protection, through one's indwelling Christ, I AM, Jehovah (*appeased with Jah, Jah protected*). This does much to acquaint one with one's inner divine presence and power, and so honors the indwelling Christ (*fame of Jah*), through whom all dominion and good become expressed and manifested in one.

Shadrach, shā'-drăch (Heb. fr. Pers.)—*command of the moon god; rejoicing in the way; zealously striving; royal.*

Hananiah, one of Daniel's three captive Jewish friends, whose name was changed to Shadrach by the prince of the eunuchs of the king of Babylon (Dan. 1:7). He was one of the three who were cast into the fiery furnace and came out alive (Dan. 3:12-30).

Meta. Meekness. True understanding and power always give meekness to one's character. (*Royal* signifies princely power and Truth. It is true understanding in one that has *command of the moon god*, or the reflected light of the intellect. Besides, Hananiah, the former name of Shadrach, signifies knowledge of Jehovah, the indwelling Christ, as love, mercy, goodness, and the channel of all power, wisdom, Truth to the manifest man; hence the true spirit of meekness, which causes its possessors to "inherit the land.")

The "fiery furnace" into which Shadrach, Meshach, and Abed-nego were cast is the testing that proves whether one will follow God or mammon—the "golden image" represents mammon. The fourth man in the fiery furnace is the consciousness of one's I AM in its spiritual unity with God.

Shagee (A. V., Shage), shā'-ġēe (Heb.)—*wandering; straying; going astray; reeling; staggering; erring; transgressing; mistaking; sinning.*

"The Hararite." His son Jonathan was one of David's mighty men (I Chron. 11:34).

Meta. A tendency to go astray, or a fear of going astray, in one's first blind groping for greater light, truer understanding. A Hararite (*mountaineer*) signifies a high aspiration, a strong, noble, uplifting thought; and this Shagee thought is groping for a truer light and a more efficient power that will enable the individual to reach a higher standard, even that of spiritual understanding. It brings forth Jonathan, who symbolizes human affection set upon spiritual things. This affection (Jonathan), becoming attached to divine love (David), helps to establish love more fully and perfectly in the consciousness (Jonathan, son of Shagee the Hararite, was one of King David's guard or council of mighty men).

Shaharaim, shă-hă-rā'-ĭm (Heb.)—*two cleavings; double breaking forth; two dawns; double aurora; double morning.*

A Benjamite, husband of Hodesh, and by her the father of seven sons, all "heads of fathers' *houses*" (I Chron. 8:8-10).

Meta. The breaking of new light, understanding, in consciousness, doubly strong or doubly great and effective (*two dawns, double morning*, a Benjamite).

Shahazumah (A. V., Shahazimah), shä-häz'-ū-măh (Heb.)—*heights; elevations; elations; sublimities; prides.*

A border city of Issachar (Josh. 19: 22).

Meta. A group of thoughts of a high character, or that aspire to higher, more spiritual expression and attainment (*heights, elevations*), in the active zeal faculty in individual consciousness (a city of Issachar, Issachar signifying the zeal faculty in man). In its negative aspect Shahazumah refers to a lifting up of the personal, of pride (*prides, elations*).

Shalishah (A. V., Shalisha), shäl'-ĭ-shäh (Heb.)—*third; threefold; trinity; triad; triune; triangular.*

A land near the hill country of Ephraim that Saul son of Kish passed through while hunting his father's asses (I Sam. 9:4). Baal–shalishah, of II Kings 4:42, was a city in the district of Shalishah.

Meta. The three-dimensional or outer man (*third, triangular*). *Threefold, triad, triune*, also denote a trinity; and man is the *third* in the trinity composed of mind, idea, expression, or God, Christ, man. This man, however, is manifest man in his perfect state, and not sense man subject to corruption, as he so generally appears today. Yet back of even the sense or material man there ever remains the perfect-man idea, which in time will come forth into the fullness of spiritual perfection. The individual will then manifest what he really is in Truth—oneness with God in the divine trinity.

Shallecheth, shäl'-lĕ-chĕth (Heb.)—*felling; overthrowing; casting out; thrown down.*

A gate of the house of God, in Jerusalem, in David's reign (I Chron. 26: 16, "Casting forth," margin).

Meta. The word of denial; putting away out of consciousness that which is not acceptable to it; the *casting forth* of error by denial (*casting out, felling, overthrowing, thrown down*).

Shallecheth, the gate at the west of the Temple (west signifying the without), is "at the causeway that goeth up, watch against watch." This symbolizes a raised way or highway that has been built by the individual, by means of true thoughts and words; it leads step by step to higher realms of expression and manifestation in the outer, to the west. Shuppim and Hosah, who were given charge of this gate, bespeak a degree of wisdom in the outer man and a trustful, hopeful spirit that becomes a real haven to him while he is passing through his overcoming experiences.

Shallum, shäl'-lŭm (Heb.)—*completion; perfection; restoration; peace; prosperity; gift; reward; restitution; recompense; requital; retribution; punishment.*

There were several Israelites by this name (II Kings 15:10; 22:14; and others).

Meta. Thoughts belonging to the real in man (Israelites), that pertain to the law of cause and effect, giving and receiving, sowing and reaping (*recompense, perfection, peace, reward, retribution, punishment*). "Be not deceived; God is not mocked: for whatsoever a man soweth, that shall he also reap. For he that soweth unto his own flesh shall of the flesh reap corruption; but he that soweth unto the Spirit shall of the Spirit reap eternal life" (Gal. 6:7, 8).

Shallun, shäl'-lŭn (Heb.)—*completed; perfected; restored; peaceful; prosperous; restitution; retribution; recompense; punishment.*

Son of Colhozeh. He helped repair the gates and the wall of Jerusalem (Neh. 3:15). Shallun is a form of Shallum.

Meta. See SHALLUM.

Shalman, shäl'-măn (Heb. fr. Pers.)—*fire worshiper; modesty opposed to vehemence.*

King of Assyria (Hos. 10:14). Shalman is a contracted form of Shalmaneser.

Meta. Fire, in the Scriptures, as it relates to God and to the sacrifices of the Hebrews, signifies a purifying, refining, transmuting process. In Shalman, a king of Assyria (the ruling idea in the intellectual realm in man that is directed by the outer senses and opposed to Truth), the idea of *fire* would take on an especially destructive nature. The significance here is a strong belief in evil, in destruction, as being from God (*fire worshiper*).

The definition, *modesty opposed to vehemence,* belongs to the negative aspect of that which Shalman signifies, a degree of personal humility and lack of aggressiveness. But this does not put away belief in evil and the destructive tendency of the Shalman characteristic. Only in spiritual understanding does one perceive God as all and in all; only in spiritual understanding does one comprehend the purifying, refining, transmuting process of Spirit and know that it leads to eternal life, peace, and joy, and not to death, destruction, or evil of any other kind.

Shalmaneser, shăl-mă-nē′-şēr (Heb. fr. Pers.)—*fire worshiper; modesty opposed to vehemence.*

An Assyrian king who came up against Israel, took Samaria, and carried the Israelites away captive (II Kings 18:9-11).

Meta. See SHALMAN.

Shama, shā′-mà (Heb.)—*hearing; hearkening; obedient; dutiful; understanding.*

Son of Hotham the Aroerite, and one of David's mighty men (I Chron. 11:44).

Meta. An obedient attitude of mind, one attentive to the higher things of Spirit (*obedient, hearing, dutiful,* an Israelite).

Shamgar, shăm′-gär (Heb.)—*cupbearer; most careful keeping; fleer; sword.*

A deliverer of Israel. He smote six hundred Philistines with an oxgoad, and "saved Israel" (Judg. 3:31).

Meta. Anath, father of Shamgar, and meaning *answering,* signifies the Spirit's response to the cry of the soul for deliverance from opposing error thoughts. Shamgar represents the affirmations or words of Truth (*sword*) by whose power the opposing thoughts (Philistines) are overcome. The oxgoad signifies the strength and force of the thought back of one's true words. *Cupbearer* and *most careful keeping* bespeak the watchful attention and service that the individual gives to Truth when he desires with all his heart to become established in it.

Shamhuth, shăm′-hŭth (Heb.)—*astonishment; awesome; laying waste; desolation; destruction; ruin; rumor; report; repute; fame; renown.* The two lines of thought given in the definitions

of this name come from opposing ideas in different roots. The most probable are the ones given first.

"The Izrahite," the fifth captain for the fifth month over twenty-four thousand men, in David's army (I Chron. 27:8); the same name as Shammah and Shammoth.

Meta. An influential thought in man's higher consciousness that is very active in destroying error (*laying waste, destruction, desolation*). In some of the men named Shammah, especially the one who was of Edom, the name signifies a destructive, fearful tendency in consciousness that leads to inharmonies of mind and body. The outer man, apart from the dominion of Spirit, is very likely to swing from one extreme to the other—from the height of noble thinking and feeling (*fame, renown*) to the depth of fear, *desolation,* emptiness, and error. He must, by consciously laying hold of the Christ Truth and making it practical in his life, come into a better balance, greater stability and poise.

Shamir, shā′-mĭr (Heb.)—*stiff; rigid; bristling; hard; thorn; sharp point; adamant; diamond; fixed stare; hard look; close watch; observation; keeping a commandment; regard; approval; honor; worship; preservation.*

a A city in the hill country of Judah (Josh. 15:48). **b** A city in the hill country of Ephraim, where Tola, a deliverer of Israel, lived (Judg. 10:1). **c** A Levite, son of Micah (I Chron. 24:24). **d** According to Fallows the same word is translated "diamond" in Jeremiah 17:1 and "adamant" in Ezekiel 3:9 and Zechariah 7:12.

Meta. A sharp, piercing, perceiving, unyielding phase of consciousness, in the faculties in man that are represented by Judah, Ephraim, and Levi (*stiff, rigid, hard, thorn, hard look, close watch,* cities in the hill country of Judah and of Ephraim, and a Levite). These thoughts are always to the point, and do not prevaricate (*sharp point*); hence when they take sides with Truth they are approved by our higher consciousness and are very useful in overcoming error.

Shamlai (A. V., Shalmai), shăm′-lāi (Heb.)—*my thanks; my reward; Jah is* *recompenser; Jehovah makes whole; my garment.*

His descendants were among the Nethinim who returned with Zerubbabel from the Babylonian captivity (Ezra 2:46). In Nehemiah 7:48, he is called Salmai.

Meta. See SALMAI.

Shamma, shăm'-mȧ (Heb.)—*astonishment; amazement; awesome; laid waste; desolation; destruction; ruin; rumor; report; repute; fame; renown.*

Son of Zophah, of the tribe of Asher (I Chron. 7:37).

Meta. See SHAMHUTH, the significance of which is virtually the same. The balance that these thoughts need will be brought about by a steadfast belief in good only. So long as one believes in both Truth and error, good and evil, true poise cannot be established firmly in one's consciousness.

Shammah, shăm'-măh (Heb.)—*astonishment; amazement; awe; laid waste; desolation; destruction; ruin; rumor; report; repute; fame; renown.*

a Son of Reuel, one of Esau's sons, and a chief of Edom (Gen. 36:13). **b** A son of Jesse and brother of David (I Sam. 16:9). Shammah, son of Jesse, is called Shimeah in II Samuel 13:3, and Shimea in I Chronicles 2:13. **c** There were others by this name also (II Sam. 23:11, 25, 33).

Meta. See SHAMHUTH.

Shammai, shăm'-māi (Heb.)—*astonishment; awe; laid waste; desolation; destruction; ruin; rumor; report; repute; fame; renown.*

a Son of Onam, and father of Nadab and Abishur, of the tribe of Judah (I Chron. 2:28). **b** Two other men named among the descendants of Judah (I Chron. 2:44; 4:17).

Meta. See SHAMHUTH.

Shammoth, shăm'-mŏth (Heb.)—*amazement; awe; laid waste; desolation; destruction; ruin; rumor; report; repute; fame; renown.*

One of David's mighty men (I Chron. 11:27). In II Samuel 23:25, he is called Shammah. Shamhuth of I Chronicles 27:8 is thought to be the same man.

Meta. See SHAMHUTH.

Shammua, shăm-mū'-ȧ (Heb.)—*what is heard; report; rumor; obedience; understanding; reputation; fame; whisper; jeer; mockery; derision.*

a Son of Zaccur, the man who was chosen from the tribe of Reuben to help spy out the land of Canaan preparatory to the Israelites' going over to possess it (Num. 13:4). **b** A son of David (II Sam. 5:14); he is called Shimea in I Chronicles 3:5. **c** A Levite and a priest (Neh. 11:17; 12:18).

Meta. Common truth; thoughts of man's higher religious state of mind that are attentive and receptive to only such truth as is commonly and widely known and accepted (*what is heard, report, fame, obedience*). They would tend to make light of and scorn the deep inspirations of Spirit, or anything not generally understood as Truth.

Shamsherai, shăm'-shĕ-rāi (Heb.)—*keeper of brilliance; hero; heroic; keeper of the sun; sunlike; sunny; radiance.*

A Benjamite, son of Jeroham, and a chief man who lived in Jerusalem (I Chron. 8:26).

Meta. An understanding faith, strong, joyous, fearless, which retains and radiates the light of Spirit (*keeper of brilliance, hero, heroic, radiance,* a Benjamite, Benjamin representing the active faith faculty in man).

Shapham, shā'-phăm (Heb.)—*polished; smoothed; bright; youthful; vigorous; bold; worn away; bare; bald; wasted; pining away; disappearing.*

A Gadite and second in rank, a chief (I Chron. 5:12).

Meta. A ruling or strongly influencing thought of splendid courage, energy, and youthfulness (*polished, bright, youthful, bold, vigorous*), the result of power active in life and substance (a chief of Gad, who lived in Bashan, Gad referring to the power faculty in man, and Bashan referring to abundant life and substance). *Worn away, wasted, bald, bare* infer a putting away of the belief in purely physical and material strength and life, that the spiritual and true may be established.

Shaphan, shā'-phăn (Heb.)—*covered; hidden; underground; sly; cunning; prudent; small ruminant; rabbit; cony; bearded; covered lip.*

a Son of Azaliah, a scribe at the time

of Josiah, king of Jerusalem, and Hilkiah, the high priest (II Kings 22:3-14). **b** There were other Israelites by this name (II Kings 22:12; Jer. 29:3; Ezek. 8:11).

Meta. The subjective memory, or recurring consciousness of the law, which brings out the inner rule of action that leads on to higher and better things through mental and physical evolution.

In II Chronicles 34:14-28 the subjective memory (Shaphan the scribe) receives through the religious tendencies (Hilkiah the priest) the impression of the higher standards of life, as man consecrates himself to God and begins to use the energies of his mind and body (money in the house of Jehovah) in the restoration of his body temple.

Shaphat, shā'-phăt (Heb.)—*to set upright; to judge; true judgment; condemnation; punishment; prosecution; defense; vindication; rule; government.*

a Son of Hori of the tribe of Simeon, one of the twelve spies (Num. 13:5). **b** Father of Elisha the prophet (I Kings 19:16). **c** Others of the same name (I Chron. 3:22; 5:12; 27:29).

Meta. These men by the name of Shaphat (*to judge*) signify the development of the discerning, judging faculty throughout the consciousness, or the judgment idea's becoming operative throughout the various faculties of mind that are represented by the tribes of Israel to whom the men by this name belonged.

Shaphir (A. V., Saphir), shā'-phīr (Heb.)—*scratched; scraped; rubbed to a polish; fair; brilliant; bright; shining; beautiful; pleasing; delightful; clear-toned; sonorous.*

A city of Judah, that was prophesied against by Micah (Mic. 1:11).

Meta. The beauty and glory and joy of spiritual ideals (*bright, shining, beautiful, fair, delightful,* a city of Israel), destroyed out of consciousness by willful disobedience to Truth. "Pass away, O inhabitant of Shaphir, in nakedness and shame."

Sharai, shā'-rāi (Heb.)—*Jehovah loosens; Jah is deliverer; whom Jah sets free; beginning, i. e., opening up; solution.*

An Israelite. He had taken a foreign wife after the return from the Babylonian captivity, but gave her up at the command of Ezra (Ezra 10:40).

Meta. An awakening to understanding that from the inner Christ comes the solution to all life's problems and deliverance from all error (*Jah is deliverer, beginning,* i. e., *opening up, solution,* an Israelite).

Sharar, shā'-rär (Heb.)—*turning about; twisting together; cord; sinew; muscle; navel; strong; hard; firm; pressed together; oppression; affliction; treating as an enemy; hostile.*

"The Ararite," father of Ahiam. This Ahiam was one of David's mighty men, and a member of his guard or council (II Sam. 23:33). He is called Sacar the Hararite in I Chronicles 11:35.

Meta. An active thought of strength, firmness, and order (*strong, hard, firm, navel;* the order faculty in the individual is located at the navel). The definitions of Sharar, as a whole, bespeak a great need of more love, coöperation, and harmony. These seem to be attained in the son Ahiam. (See AHIAM.)

Sharezer, shā-rē'-zĕr (Heb. fr. Pers.) —*prince of fire; ruler of the treasury; chief of stores.*

Son of Sennacherib, king of Assyria (II Kings 19:37).

Meta. Error brings about its own destruction. Sennacherib (*bramble of destruction*)—the ruling thought of the Assyria state of consciousness in man, and therefore actively engaged in the promotion of error—sets into operation a devouring, fiery element that destroys him: he was slain by his son Sharezer (*prince of fire*) and another of his sons.

Sharon, shâr'-ŏn (Heb.)—*even; level; plain; straight; right; tranquil; harmonious; composed; straightforward; upright; fruitful; prosperous; righteous; just.*

a A level tract of country in Palestine, bordering on the Mediterranean Sea, and extending from Joppa to Cæsarea (I Chron. 27:29; Isa. 35:2; 65:10). **b** A place mentioned as being in the inheritance of Gad, on the east of the Jordan (I Chron. 5:16).

Meta. The rich substance of Spirit established in body consciousness (*fruit-*

ful, prosperous a tract of country in Palestine that was noted for its rich pasture lands). See LASSHARON for the significance of *plain*. The thoughts of justice, honor, poise, and harmony are also symbolized in this name.

Sharonite, shâr'-ŏn-īte (fr. Heb.).

A native of Sharon (I Chron. 27:29). The name is applied here to Shitrai, who had charge of David's herds that fed in Sharon.

Meta. A thought activity springing from and belonging to that in consciousness which Sharon signifies. (See SHARON and LASSHARON.)

Sharuhen, shă-ru̧'-hĕn (Heb.)—*loosening of kindness; unbinding of compassion; dwelling of grace; abode of pleasure; gracious house; freedom of beauty.*

A city of Simeon that had first been allotted to Judah (Josh. 19:6). The children of Simeon received their inheritance "in the midst of the inheritance of the children of Judah." In Joshua 15:32, this city is called Shilhim, and in I Chronicles 4:31, Shaaraim.

Meta. Loosening or awakening of love and Truth within one, this bringing one into an abiding consciousness of grace and joy and all good—a sense of satisfaction such as is suggested in Psalms 37:4: "Delight thyself also in Jehovah; And he will give thee the desire of thy heart."

Shashai, shā'-shāi (Heb.)—*whiteness; fine white linen; noble; free; harmonious; proportional measure; mastery; overcoming.*

A son or descendant of Bani. He had married a foreign woman after the return from the Babylonian captivity, but put her away at the command of Ezra (Ezra 10:40).

Meta. The thought of *overcoming*, with its results, is borne out in this name. "He that overcometh shall . . . be arrayed in white garments"; "They shall walk with me in white; for they are worthy"; "The fine linen is the righteous acts of the saints."

Shashak, shā'-shăk (Heb.)—*running to and fro; pedestrian; seeker; prayer; assaulter; eagerness; vehement desire; ravenous appetite; longing; yearning; thirst.*

Son of Beriah of the tribe of Benjamin (I Chron. 8:14).

Meta. An intense desire for good, but unfulfilled because of *running to and fro* in the outer, because of seeking in the outer only. That which Shashak signifies lacks poise, self-mastery, concentration. It does not seek the Spirit of truth in quietness and confidence. Violence enters into the activity of this great desire in its efforts to attain the fulfillment of the good that it is seeking; understanding is needed.

Shaul, shā'-ŭl (Heb.)—*asked for; desired; wished; demanded; searching; inquiring; digging; hollowing out; excavating.*

a Son of Simeon. His mother was a Canaanitish woman (Gen. 46:10). b A king of Edom, Shaul of Rehoboth (Gen. 36:37). c Son of Uzziah, a Levite (I Chron. 6:24).

Meta. Shaul is a form of the name Saul, and its meaning is the same as that of Saul. It relates to the will in individual consciousness, the personal will. (See SAUL.)

The men by this name, one a king of Edom, one a son of Simeon, and one a Levite, refer to the will or executive faculty in man, active at different times through the various phases of consciousness that Simeon, Edom, and Levi signify, to draw to or work out for the individual that which he desires for his personal advancement.

Shaulites, shā'-ŭl-ītes (fr. Heb.)—*of* or *pertaining to Shaul.*

Descendants of Shaul the son af Simeon (Num. 26:13).

Meta. Thoughts springing from that in consciousness which Shaul the son of Simeon signifies. (See SHAUL.)

Shaveh, shā'-vĕh (Heb.)—*compared; likened; equalized; placed in order; composed; calm; balanced; harmonious; plain; level; even.*

A valley in Palestine, near Jerusalem, or Salem (Gen. 14:17); also called the "King's Vale."

Meta. An equalization of the thoughts, forces, and powers in the organism—a reestablishment on a true basis: poise, peace, equilibrium, wholeness. Shaveh (*plain, level, even, equalized, balanced, placed in order, composed, calm*) was the place near Jerusalem where Melchizedek, king of Salem, and the king of Sodom, met Abraham on his return from the slaughter of the kings who had taken Lot captive. (Melchizedek was priest of God, and he brought forth bread and wine, and blessed Abraham.) In the Shaveh thought the organism is built up in renewed substance and life, and peace is restored to the whole man.

Shaveh–kiriathaim, shā'-vĕh–kĭr-ĭ-ă-thā'-ĭm (Heb.)—*plain of Kiriathaim; plain of the twin cities; plain of the double meetings.*

A plain near Kiriathaim, a city that later came into possession of the tribe of Reuben. It was a place where lived the Emim who were smitten in the time of Abraham (Gen. 14:5).

Meta. Shaveh means a *plain,* an equalized, poised state of mind and body; Kiriathaim means *double city* and signifies a twofold strength or supply of whatever the central idea of the group of thoughts may be. In Shaveh–kiriathaim, the significance is poise and equalization in the consciousness and the organism, doubly established and sure. (See SHAVEH and KIRIATHAIM.)

Shavsha, shăv'-shà (Heb.)—*bright; shining; white; nobility; splendor; purity.*

David's scribe, or secretary (I Chron. 18:16). He is called Seraiah in II Samuel 8:17, and Sheva in II Samuel 20:25. In I Kings 4:3 two sons of Shisha are mentioned as being Solomon's scribes, or secretaries; Shisha is a form of Shavsha.

Meta. That which impresses Truth indelibly upon or within the consciousness (a scribe), and exalts and radiates the light and purity of Truth (*bright, shining, white, splendor, nobility, purity*). (See SCRIBES and EZRA the scribe.)

Sheal, shē'-ăl (Heb.)—*digging out; searching; inquiring; asking; requesting; desiring; praying.*

A son of Bani. He had married a foreign woman after the return from the Babylonian captivity, but he gave her up at the command of Ezra (Ezra 10: 29).

Meta. A thought activity in the higher consciousness of man (an Israelite) that is seeking earnestly after more of God (*searching, inquiring, desiring, praying*).

Shealtiel, shĕ-ăl'-tĭ-ĕl (Heb.)—*I have asked of God; having asked of God.*

Father of Zerubbabel (Ezra 3:2; Hag. 1:1; 2:23).

Meta. Zerubbabel is the activity in the higher consciousness of the individual that restores the worship of God. Shealtiel, father of Zerubbabel (*I have asked of God*), signifies the *I* in man appealing to the divine in him and making conscious union with Spirit.

Sheariah, shē-ă-rī'-ăh (Heb.)—*whom Jehovah estimates; Jah decides; judgment of Jah; Jehovah hath esteemed; appraised of Jah; prized of Jehovah; Jah hath opened; gate of Jah; assemblage of Jah; Jah is gatekeeper.*

Son of Azel, a Benjamite, in descent from Saul (I Chron. 8:38).

Meta. Azel, father of Sheariah, signifies the uplifting and ennobling influence that the recognition of one's divine origin—sonship with God—has on one's character.

Sheariah (*Jehovah hath esteemed, whom Jehovah estimates, prized of Jehovah*) is that high appreciation and estimation in which the Father regards us, His offspring. We have thought that we were so inferior to God that He must look upon us as of little worth; we have felt that we must of necessity be more or less despised by God because of the great contrast between what we have looked upon as our inborn limitations or sins and His perfection and greatness. This is a mistake. God, the Father of all, sees only His perfection in His creation; in us He sees the man whom He made in the beginning in His image and likeness, the only begotten Son, the Christ.

If we could but know ourselves in the high, perfect light in which the Father beholds us, we should be lifted at once out of all error and limited seemings, into the manifestation of the perfect, spiritual beings that God created us to be.

Jah decides and *judgment of Jah* reveal the fact that the Father in us really decides our course after all. He becomes our judgment; hence we shall come into the fullness of our divine inheritance as sons of God, because He wills it so. The definitions, *Jah hath opened, gate of Jah*, suggest the open door to this fulfillment of perfection in us, which door or way is a recognition of what we are in Truth: sons of God, made in His image and likeness; sons, not by adoption, but by reason of birth; sons because of the Christ who dwells ever in us as the real inner self of each of us.

Shear–jashub, shē'-är-jăsh'-ŭb (Heb.) —*the remnant shall return; what is left behind shall be brought back; the residue shall be recovered; the remainder shall be recalled.*

Son of the prophet Isaiah. He went with his father to King Ahaz of Judah when Isaiah went to encourage the king concerning the final redemption of Judah and the restoration of the land, through the Christ (Isa. 7, especially the 3d verse).

Meta. The inspiration or assurance of man's ultimate return in spirit, soul, and body to that spiritual perfection in which he was created. This return is brought about by a recognition of the "remnant" of divine seed, or true spiritual ideas, that has remained in man's real inner self, even when he has apparently been farthest away from God (*the remnant shall return;* see also the prophecy of Isaiah 7, and note in verse 3 that God told Isaiah to take his son, Shear–jashub, with him when he went to meet King Ahaz). This inner assurance of man's ultimate return to his innate perfection comes to the spiritually awakening individual by means of his higher self, which Isaiah the father of Shear–jashub signifies.

Sheba, shē'-bȧ (Heb.)—*seven; cyclic fullness; completeness; fullness of times; fulfillment; an oath; a covenant.*

Name of a famous well that gave its name to Beer–sheba (Gen. 21:31-33).

Meta. See BEER–SHEBA.

Sheba, shē'-bȧ (Heb.)—*rest; repose; stability; equilibrium; reintegration; return to an original state; restoration; redemption.*

a Son of Raamah, descended from Ham (Gen. 10:7). **b** Son of Joktan, descended from Shem (Gen. 10:28). **c** Son of Jokshan and grandson of Abraham by Keturah (Gen. 25:3). **d** A city of Simeon (Josh. 19:2). **e** Son of Bichri, a Benjamite. This Sheba was a base fellow who revolted from David (II Sam. 20:1-22). **f** The country of Sheba, or Seba, whence the queen of Sheba came to prove Solomon with hard questions (I Kings 10:1). **g** A man of Gad (I Chron. 5:13).

Meta. Sheba pertains to wholeness or fullness on some plane of existence (*return to an original state, rest, repose, equilibrium, reintegration, restoration*). Whether or not this thought of wholeness, of bringing to fullness and stabilization, belongs to the inner or outer man, to good or to seeming ill, depends on who the persons in the Bible named Sheba were, and on their history. Those who were of Israel and were constructive in their activities would refer to higher and more spiritual thoughts than those who were descended from Ham and from others who were not of Israel.

The queen of Sheba indicates the ruling intuitive intelligence of the whole consciousness pertaining to that part of being which has to do with nature. We are to understand that Solomon, in meeting and entertaining the queen of Sheba, had to meet and impart to his body consciousness an intuitive wisdom that it had not previously possessed.

Solomon, in the wisdom of Spirit, comes in touch with his unillumined natural being, the queen of Sheba. When the illumination from Spirit is first received we are for a time so absorbed in it and in its revelations that we are almost wholly unconscious of our body; but a thought is formed in us that presides over that domain called the body substance. Its outer aspect is termed flesh, blood, and bone, but the real substance is mental, and when we have been illuminated by Spirit the body will come to us in its true light and ask for our higher wisdom; it will bring to us many presents, or valuable substances.

The queen of Sheba "came to prove him with hard questions." "She communed with him of all that was in her heart." Here is indicated the questioning tendency of the natural side of being. There is implanted in the substance side of our consciousness a degree of intelligence, but it is not the source of wisdom; hence it is not a safe guide for man. This is illustrated in the Eden allegory by the serpent, symbolic of the sensuous intelligence that pervades nature.

The sense consciousness constantly asks an explanation of the riddle of phenomena. Those who do not seek the Solomon within themselves are constantly seeking without for answers to their many questions as to the origin and character of material things. Never can these questions be answered satisfactorily except by the supreme wisdom of that state of mind which is, in the Bible, named Solomon. Matter has no real substance; it is the result of a darkened state of consciousness and it passes away when the light is turned on. Therefore all matter will disappear when man enters into the real substance of Being. Within the corruptible forms of flesh are real life and imperishable flesh. This inner life is represented by the camels and the imperishable flesh is represented by the spices that the queen brought to Solomon. The substance idea rejoices when it sees or perceives the Truth of Spirit. We thus see the importance of spiritualizing the body consciousness by declaring for it the wisdom of the Lord.

Whenever a question is presented about the character of matter and the many points pertaining to the overcoming of physical decay, we may know that the queen of Sheba has come and is seeking to prove our spiritual wisdom with some of her "hard questions."

Solomon (wisdom) recognizes that the body consciousness is his own unillumined being, which needs the light. Therefore nothing is withheld, but every questioning of the queen of Sheba, the power that rules over this part of being, is fully answered.

It is a spiritual law that when the natural forces of being express the desire to learn the way of Spirit, and are willing to pay the price for it, the desire and the willingness are in themselves full compensation; therefore the gifts are returned with abundant increase. This law is set forth in II Chronicles 9:12: "And King Solomon gave to the queen of Sheba all her desire, whatsoever she

asked, besides that which she had brought unto the king."

The queen of Sheba (ruler over the natural plane) was able to take back to her kingdom the knowledge that there is a higher understanding or a brighter light that, when laid hold of by the body consciousness, will transmute and lift that consciousness to incorruptible spiritual substance. This is the beginning of the process by which the mortal puts on immortality.

Shebaniah, shĕb-ă-nī'-ăh (Heb.)—*Jehovah has made grow up; Jehovah increases; whom Jehovah makes youthful; Jah is powerful.*

a One of the priests who blew the trumpets before the Ark of God when David had the Ark brought up to Jerusalem out of the house of Obed–edom (I Chron. 15:24). **b** A Levite who, with some others, exhorted the people to bless Jehovah and give thanks to Him who is the source of all (Neh. 9:4). **c** Two Israelites, a priest and a Levite, who joined Nehemiah in sealing the covenant (Neh. 10:4, 12).

Meta. Our natural religious tendencies (priests and Levites) recognizing, rejoicing in, and seeking to inspire the whole consciousness with the realization that the Father in us, our indwelling Christ, Jehovah, is our power to unfold and to grow spiritually; that the healing, restoring, constructive, uplifting impetus in us is Spirit (*Jehovah has made grow up, Jah is powerful, whom Jehovah makes youthful, Jehovah increases*).

By reading about these priests and Levites named Shebaniah one will see that they all were actively engaged in service to God and to the people in a spiritual way; they were doing things to bring about a better understanding of God's law on the part of the people, and a stronger conscious union between the people and God.

Shebarim, shĕb'-ă-rĭm (Heb.) — *breaks; breaches; pieces; fragments; fractures; ruins; destructions.*

A place not far from Ai. It was there that the men of Ai stopped pursuing the Israelites who had attempted to take their city. In the margin, *"the quarries"* is given instead of Shebarim (Josh. 7:5).

Meta. Shattered hopes (*breaks, ruins, breaches*).

The Israelites, after their entrance into the Promised Land and their great victory at Jericho, had given room to a covetous thought (in the person of Achan; see Josh. 7). Thus they experienced defeat at Ai (*the heap, a heap of rubbish*, and signifying egotism and self-confidence without recognition of Spirit) and were very much discouraged. Their way out was to admit their error and put it away from their midst. The same lesson holds good to us individually. If we allow covetousness, a too strong seeking after outer demonstrations of wisdom and substance, to enter into our higher, truer consciousness (Israelites), our spiritual vision will become dimmed and we shall be conscious of defeat until we cleanse our thoughts and desires of the error and put God first in our life.

Sheber, shē'-bĕr (Heb.)—*breach; fracture; broken in pieces; fragment; ruin; destruction; piece; portion; allotment; allowance; infant*, i. e., *who has broken the womb.*

Son of Caleb by his concubine, Maacah (I Chron. 2:48).

Meta. Caleb signifies spiritual faith and enthusiasm; Maacah suggests a negative, depressed state of thought or feeling that exists in the natural soul in man. Sheber and Tirhanah, the first two sons of Caleb by Maacah (notice that these two sons are named as though they belonged together), indicate a breaking up of the depressed condition and its results in consciousness that Maacah signifies (*fracture, breach, broken in pieces*), and the establishment in its place of the assurance of divine favor (*inclination, favor, kindness*). Notice that Sheber is named first and Tirhanah follows; even so the putting away of an error always precedes an establishment of Truth in consciousness.

Shebna, shĕb'-nà (Heb.)—*growth; increase; youth; youthfulness; freshness; tenderness; delicacy; strength; fullness; completeness.*

An Israelite, scribe to King Hezekiah of Judah (II Kings 18:37).

Meta. A phase of the subjective memory (a scribe to King Hezekiah of Judah) that receives and transcribes thoughts that tend to *growth*, fruitfulness, *youthfulness, strength*, love, and *completeness* as they enter the consciousness; thus the expression of spiritual strength in the executive power of the mind is aided.

The mind that Shebna typifies does not accept anything of error, but brings all suggestions and fears of failure and weakness to the executive faculty (Hezekiah) that they may be dealt with according to Truth. (Shebna was one of those who brought the words of Rabshakeh, an officer of the king of Assyria, to Hezekiah, who prayed to Jehovah and was given the assurance through Isaiah that God would fight for the Israelites and the Assyrians would be defeated.) Thus fear of failure and defeat is overcome.

Shebuel, shĕb'-ū-ĕl (Heb.)—*captive of God; God's leading back; restored to a former state by God; restoration of prosperity by God.*

a Son of Gershom of the descendants of Levi, a chief (I Chron. 23:16). **b** Son of Heman, a musician in the house of God, in David's reign (I Chron. 25:4). The name is spelled Shubael in I Chronicles 24:20 and 25:20.

Meta. True, spiritually inclined thoughts and activities in the religious phase of man's consciousness (Israelites, a chief of Levi, and a musician in the house of God, in David's reign) that have become irresistibly attracted to the real things of Spirit and wish to gain full spiritual guidance and direction (*captive of God*). These God-captivated thoughts and activities in the individual, which the men named Shebuel signify, become a restorative power within him (*God's leading back, restored by God*).

Shecaniah (in A. V., all places but I Chron. 24:11 and II Chron. 31:15, Shechaniah), shĕc-ă-nī'-ăh (Heb.)—*Jehovah hath dwelt; abiding place of Jehovah; abiding with Jehovah; familiar with Jah; Jah is a neighbor.*

There are several Israelites by this name (I Chron. 24:11; II Chron. 31:15; Ezra 8:3, 5; 10:2; Neh. 3:29; 6:18).

Meta. The higher and more real and true thoughts of the individual consciousness (Israelites) abiding in conscious oneness with Spirit (*abiding with Jehovah, abiding place of Jehovah, Jah is a neighbor, familiar with Jah*).

Shechem, shĕ'-chĕm (Heb.)—*inclining; bending down; shoulder; ridge; upper part of the back; a burden.*

a Son of Hamor the Hivite, who was killed by the sons of Jacob (Gen. 33:19 to 34:26). **b** An ancient town of Palestine (Gen. 12:6; Josh. 24:32). It was in the hill country of Ephraim, in the Promised Land (Josh. 20:7; see also Judg. 9:1-49; I Kings 12:1). **c** Son of Gilead, from whom the family of the Shechemites was descended (Num. 26:31). **d** Son of Shemida of the tribe of Manasseh (I Chron. 7:19).

Meta. A burden-bearing attitude of thought (*shoulder, a burden*). Of Issachar we read:

"And he bowed his shoulder to bear,

And became a servant under taskwork."

Persons who are constantly bowed down with the thought of burdens and responsibilities and hard work become round-shouldered and stooped. On the other hand ideas of freedom and dominion always cause one involuntarily to throw one's shoulders back and stand erect.

Shechemites, shĕ'-chĕm-ītes (fr. Heb.) —*of* or *belonging to Shechem.*

The family and descendants of Shechem son of Gilead, of Manasseh (Num. 26:31).

Meta. Thoughts springing from and partaking of the character of that in consciousness which Shechem signifies. (See SHECHEM.)

Shedeur, shĕd'-ĕ-ŭr (Heb.)—*shedder of light; sender of revelation; shooting forth of flame; pouring out of fire; flood of light.*

Father of Elizur of the tribe of Reuben (Num. 2:10).

Meta. Divine intelligence, inspiration, active in the consciousness of the spiritually awakening individual (*shedder of light, sender of revelation, flood of light*).

sheep.

Meta. Sheep are the most harmless and innocent of animals. They represent the natural life that flows into man's consciousness from Spirit. It is pure, innocent, guileless, and when we open our

mind to this realization of Spirit life we open the gate by the sheep market (John 5:2; also see this text in the A. V.).

Shehariah, shē-hă-rī'-ăh (Heb.)— *breaking forth of Jehovah; Jehovah hath sought carefully; morning of Jah; Jehovah is the dawn (good after evil); aurora of Jehovah.*

Son of Jeroham, a Benjamite (I Chron. 8:26).

Meta. The following gives the significance of Shehariah, as applied to us individually:

Jehovah, the Christ or Father in us, ever seeks to express more of God in and through us (*Jehovah hath sought carefully*). Our response to the attempts of Spirit to bring greater good into our life appears first in our consciousness in the nature of desire—desire for something higher and better than we have been experiencing. This desire moves us to seek greater understanding of Truth, of God. Then, in answer to this conscious seeking on our part, the light, the revelation of spiritual truths, comes to us (*breaking forth of Jehovah, Jehovah is the dawn, morning of Jah*).

Shelah, shē'-lăh (Heb.)—*tranquillity; security; rest; peace; inquiry; petition; prayer; request; demand.*

a Son of Judah, by the daughter of Shua the Canaanite. He was born at Chezib (Gen. 38:5). **b** Son of Arpachshad and grandson of Shem, who was one of Noah's three sons (I Chron. 1:18).

Meta. A sense of *peace*, harmony, *security*, that has come about by prayer, affirmation, desire, centered in that which is good and true (*prayer, petition, request, demand*).

Shelanites, shē'-lăn-ītes (fr. Heb.).

The "family" of Shelah, the son of Judah (Num. 26:20).

Meta. Thoughts springing from and like to that in consciousness which is signified by Shelah. (See SHELAH.)

Shelemiah, shĕl-ĕ-mī'-ăh (Heb.)—*Jehovah makes secure; completion of Jehovah; Jah finishes; Jehovah renders; Jehovah hath repaid; Jah is recompense; whom Jehovah repays.*

There were several Israelites by this name (I Chron. 26:14; Ezra 10:39; Neh. 3:30; 13:13; Jer. 37:3, 13). The Shelemiah of I Chronicles 26:14 is called Meshelemiah in the 1st verse.

Meta. Thoughts belonging to the real and true in man (Israelites); that recognize the law of sowing and reaping, giving and receiving, as being a spiritual law (*Jehovah hath repaid, Jah is recompense*); that work in harmony with divine law and therefore bring about a sense of security and wholeness in the consciousness of the individual in whom these thoughts are active (*Jehovah makes secure, completion of Jehovah*). (See MESHELEMIAH.)

Sheleph, shē'-lĕph (Heb.)—*reaction; reflection; refraction; emission; extraction; drawing out; drawn out; plucking; gathering.*

The second of the sons of Joktan (Gen. 10:26).

Meta. A working out, from within, of the spiritual in man, or at least a striving of Spirit within man for greater expression in and through the individual (*reaction, refraction, extraction, drawing out, drawn out*). At the Sheleph stage of one's unfoldment, however, the spiritual does not gain much headway, apparently, in finding a place in one's consciousness and practical living. Further general evolution, or unfoldment and growth, is needed.

Shelesh, shē'-lĕsh (Heb.)—*three; third; triad; threefold; triplet; triune; triangular; solidarity; strength; might; fulfillment; realization; holiness; salvation; preservation.*

Son of Helem of the tribe of Asher (I Chron. 7:35).

Meta. A consciousness of strength, power, wholeness, and fulfillment of all good, multiplied threefold (*strength, might, fulfillment, realization, holiness, solidarity, salvation, preservation, threefold*).

Shelomi, shĕl'-ŏ-mī (Heb.)—*pacific; tranquil; completed; my peace; Jah is peace; friendly with Jehovah.*

Father of Ahihud, a prince of Asher who helped divide the Promised Land among the Israelites (Num. 34:27).

Meta. Satisfaction, an inner sense of peace, of fulfillment of one's good (*pacific, completed*); also an awakening in the higher consciousness of man to the understanding that the Christ Spirit is one of peace and that man enters into peace through realizing his oneness with Christ (*Jah is peace, my peace, friendly with Jehovah*).

Shelomith, shĕl'-ŏ-mĭth (Heb.)—*pacific; tranquil; whole; peacefulness; love of peace; reward; recompense.*

There are two Israelitish women and several Israelitish men by this name (Lev. 24:11; I Chron. 3:19; 23:18; II Chron. 11:20; Ezra 8:10).

Meta. Peace and wholeness are established throughout the whole being of man as a result of the love of peace and Truth that exists in his higher consciousness and the expression of these higher thoughts in his life (*pacific, whole, love of peace, reward,* the name of both men and women of Israel).

Shelomoth, shĕl'-ŏ-mŏth (Heb.)—*pacifications; peacemaking; peacefulness; love of peace.*

a A descendant of Levi (I Chron. 24:22). He is called Shelomith in I Chronicles 23:18. **b** Other Levites (I Chron. 23:9; 26:25).

Meta. The same as Shelomith: the love for and establishment of peace in consciousness; at least the awakening to an understanding of the value of peace. "And the work of righteousness shall be peace; and the effect of righteousness, quietness and confidence for ever" (Isa. 32:17).

Shelumiel, shĕ-lū'-mĭ-ĕl (Heb.)—*peace of God; God's peace; friend of God; God makes complete; God is wholeness.*

Son of Zurishaddai and prince of the tribe of Simeon. He was chosen to be head over this tribe during its journeyings in the wilderness (Num. 1:6; 2:12).

Meta. A sense of companionship with God (*friend of God*) and of spiritual peace and wholeness (*peace of God, God makes complete*). This comes about by attentiveness and obedience, or consecration, to higher ideals (Simeon, meaning *hearing*) and by becoming established in the staying qualities of Spirit (Zurishaddai, father of Shelumiel, meaning *my rock is the Almighty*).

Shem, shĕm (Heb.)—*upright; righteous; renowned; brilliant; shining;*

splendor; dignity; sign; monument; memorial; name.

Son of Noah (Gen. 5:32).

Meta. The spiritual in man (*upright, renowned, splendor, name*).

Shema, shē'-mȧ (Heb.)—*sound; music; a hearing; hearkening; obeying; report; rumor; repute; fame.*

a A southern city of Judah (Josh. 15:26). **b** A man of Judah (I Chron. 2:43). **c** A Reubenite (I Chron. 5:8). **d** A Benjamite (I Chron. 8:13). **e** One who stood at the right hand of Ezra when he read the law to the people (Neh. 8:4).

Meta. Ideas of Truth becoming generally known and accepted throughout one's consciousness, especially by the phase of it that is signified by Judah and Israel (*rumor, fame, repute, hearing, obeying*).

Shemaah, shḗ-mā'-ăh (Heb.)—*hearing; hearkening; obeying; understanding; rumor; report; fame; annunciation.*

A Gibeathite of the tribe of Benjamin, and father of Ahiezer and Joash who joined David at Ziklag while he was in hiding from Saul (I Chron. 12:3).

Meta. An attentive, receptive, obedient attitude (*hearing, hearkening, obeying*) in the active faith faculty in individual consciousness (Benjamin signifies active faith); also the *understanding,* the inspirations, of Truth that become current throughout the consciousness of one who is receptive and attentive to the things of Spirit (*understanding, report, rumor, fame, annunciation*).

Shemaiah, shḗ-mā'-ĭah (Heb.)—*Jehovah has heard; hearkening unto Jah; Jehovah hears; obedience to Jehovah; fame of Jehovah.*

Between twenty and thirty Israelitish men by this name are mentioned in the Bible (I Kings 12:22, and so forth). The Shemaiah of I Chronicles 9:16 is called Shammua in Nehemiah 11:17.

Meta. The attentive, receptive, obedient (to Spirit) attitude of thought greatly multiplied throughout one's whole Israelite consciousness—or one's higher and more religious and true thoughts and beliefs—and throughout one's being; also the increased understanding, the conscious fellowship between one and one's inner Christ, the assurance that one is heard of Spirit, that is the result of the obedient, attentive (to Spirit) attitude of mind (*Jehovah has heard, hearkening unto Jah, obedience to Jehovah, fame of Jehovah*). There were many Israelites by this name, showing that many thoughts of this nature have place in the consciousness. (See SHAMMUA.)

Shemariah, shĕm-ȧ-rī'-ăh (Heb.)—*Jehovah has kept; whom Jehovah keeps; Jehovah keeps guard; Jah watches; Jehovah is the shepherd; safe-keeping of the Lord.*

a One of "Saul's brethren of Benjamin" who came to David at Ziklag (I Chron. 12:5). **b** Son of Rehoboam (II Chron. 11:19). **c** Two men of Israel who had married foreign women, but put them away at the command of Ezra (Ezra 10:32, 41).

Meta. Faith in the keeping, protecting, sustaining power of God, through Jehovah, the indwelling Christ (*Jehovah keeps guard, whom Jehovah keeps, safe-keeping of the Lord*), being awakened and established in the phases or faculties of man's being that are represented by the different tribes of Israel (Benjamin and Judah) to which the men named Shemariah belonged.

Shemeber, shĕm-ē'-bĕr (Heb.)—*splendor of heroism; superior brilliance; striving upward to the height; high flight; superior name.*

King of Zeboiim (Gen. 14:2).

Meta. The innate spiritual ideal, implanted in man from the beginning, that causes him to grow, unfold, and unceasingly to desire and seek to attain higher and better understanding and expression (*superior brilliance, superior name, striving upward to the height*). The fact that Shemeber was king of Zeboiim shows that the perfect-man idea of God is implanted in the seemingly physical being of man as well as in his more inner and spiritual consciousness. Because of ignorance, however, the spiritual impetus within him is misunderstood by the sense mind in man, and to the extent that sense mind rules an individual the inner urge of Spirit apparently serves only to. stimulate sense activity in him. (See ZEBOIIM.)

Shemed (A. V., Shamed), shē'-mĕd

(Heb.)—*astonishment; cut off; cast down; persecuted; laid waste; extinct; destroyed.*

Son of Elpaal. He and his brothers, Eber and Misham, "built Ono and Lod, with the towns thereof" (I Chron. 8:12).

Meta. Shemed refers to one's putting away error by denial. There is in the sense of this name a tendency to magnify the seeming evil (*astonishment*) and to make denials very emphatic, with the thought of utterly destroying the evil (*cut off, cast down, laid waste, extinct, destroyed*).

Shemer (in A. V., I Chronicles 6:46; 7:34, Shamer), shē'-mẽr (Heb.)—*stiff; erect; rigid; hard; adamant; thorn; watch; guard; shepherding; preserving; heeding; worshiping; that which is left standing; lees; dregs.*

a The man from whom Omri, king of Israel, bought the hill Samaria. On the hill Omri built the city of Samaria and named it after Shemer (I Kings 16:24). b Father of Bani, a Levite (I Chron. 6:46). c A man of Asher (I Chron. 7:34). He is called Shomer in the 32d verse.

Meta. Crystallization of thought. At their root the ideals contained in Shemer are good, are spiritual, but they have been worked over by the intellect until the finer love essence of Spirit has been forced out of them (*stiff, erect, rigid, hard, thorn, watch,* and so forth).

Shemida (in A. V., I Chronicles 7:19, Shemidah), shĕ-mī'-dȧ (Heb.)—*upright sight; righteous perception; brilliant discernment; renowned knowledge; splendor of wisdom; comprehension of the name.*

Son of Gilead of the tribe of Manasseh (Josh. 17:2).

Meta. Spiritual understanding, discernment, a perceiving, knowing attitude of thought, true knowledge and wisdom (*upright sight, righteous perception, brilliant discernment, renowned knowledge, splendor of wisdom, comprehension of the name*).

Shemidaites, shĕ-mī'-dȧ-ītes (fr. Heb.). Descendants of Shemida, son of Gilead of the Israelitish tribe of Manasseh (Num. 26:32).

Meta. Thoughts springing from that in consciousness which Shemida signifies. (See SHEMIDA.)

Sheminith, shĕm'-ĭ-nĭth (Heb.)—*eight; the eighth; octave; aggregation; accretion; increased; fattened; enlarged; excelling; an eight-stringed musical instrument.*

According to Gesenius, a technical musical term denoting the lowest tones sung by men, the modern basso, in opposition to female or boys' voices. A musical instrument of eight strings (I Chron. 15:21; Psalms 6 and 12, titles).

Meta. The organism of man attuned to the Infinite; the individual living, acting, being, in harmony with Spirit—complete in Him (*eight, the eighth, octave, an eight-stringed musical instrument*); also the great good that results from such living (*increased, enlarged, excelling*). Eight is double four, and the city that "lieth foursquare," the New Jerusalem, refers to man perfected, fully rounded out on every side and in every way. Man's body is a musical instrument, meant to give forth the harmony of Divine Mind; therefore it must be kept in tune with the Infinite.

Shemiramoth, shĕ-mĭr'-ȧ-mŏth (Heb.) —*name of the Most High; fame of the highest; brilliant exaltation; heights of the heavens.*

a A Levite, a musician at the time that David had the Ark brought to Jerusalem from the house of Obed–edom (I Chron. 15:18). b A Levite, one of those whom Jehoshaphat, king of Judah, sent throughout the cities of Judah to teach the people from the book of the law (II Chron. 17:8).

Meta. Very high spiritual illumination and realization (*name of the Most High, fame of the highest, heights of the heavens*—the heavens here being the highest realms of consciousness in man), spiritual consciousness, the Christ mind. Paul tells of a man (presumably himself) who was caught up to the third heaven, "into Paradise," where he heard unspeakable words; he was shown things beyond the possibility of description by one person to another, because, as Paul tells us in another place, the things of God are revealed by Spirit; that is, they must come from the Holy Spirit within man, direct to the soul or consciousness of the individual who receives them.

Shemuel, shĕm'-ū-ĕl (Heb.)—*name of God; sublimity of God; heard of God; instructed of God; asked of God; God has heard.* In Hebrew Shemuel is identical with Samuel.

a The man who was chosen from the tribe of Simeon to help divide the Promised Land among the Israelites. He was the son of Ammihud (Num. 34:20). **b** A son of Tola of the tribe of Issachar, a chief man and mighty in valor (I Chron. 7:2).

Meta. The significance is the same as that of Samuel: the inner voice, or inner, spiritual wisdom and judgment (*heard of God, instructed of God*). Here this wisdom and judgment, by conscious contact with God, Spirit, is expressing in and through the attentive, obedient faculty of mind in the individual (Simeon), and through his active zeal (Issachar).

Shen, shĕn (Heb.)—*tooth; tusk; ivory; tine; prong; comb; sharp rock; peak; summit; dividing in twain; change; mutation.*

A place in Palestine near which Samuel set up the stone Ebenezer, in memory of Jehovah's helping the Israelites to defeat the Philistines (I Sam. 7:12).

Meta. The analyzing and assimilating of the true ideas that are gained through prayer. (*Tooth* and *peak* are meanings of Shen. Teeth are used for the breaking up and masticating of food, and in consciousness they refer to the analyzing and assimilating of ideas, preparatory to their use in sustaining the organism. "Man shall not live by bread alone, but by every word that proceedeth out of the mouth of God," said Jesus; thus we understand that everybody needs the strength and sustaining power of true words if he is to abide in life and wholeness.)

Shenazzar (A. V., Shenazar), shē-năz'-zär (Heb.)—*store of ivory; treasurer of ivory; fiery tooth; cleaving brightness.*

A son of "Jeconiah the captive" (I Chron. 3:18). He was descended from Solomon through Rehoboam.

Meta. Light, understanding, from the bright shining of the I AM in the consciousness, breaking up old thoughts and conditions, that new ideas and realizations of substance, of prosperity and sup-ply, may be established (*cleaving brightness, fiery tooth, store of ivory, treasurer of ivory;* in olden times ivory was a medium of exchange just as money is today, therefore it would represent substance, supply). It would be well to look up the significance of the name of each of Shenazzar's brothers, and study them together, with the name of the father, Jeconiah or Jehoiachin. Jeconiah or Jehoiachin signifies the I AM at work to establish the will in spiritual understanding, strength, assurance, faith, all good. Each of the sons of Jeconiah signifies some phase or result of this activity of the I AM, Jehovah.

Shepham, shē'-phăm (Heb.)—*cold; bare; bald; shaven; naked; stripped; denuded of flesh; bare of trees; smoothed; polished; bright; brilliant.*

A place on the eastern boundary of the Israelitish inheritance in the land of Canaan (Num. 34:10).

Meta. East represents the within. Shepham (*bare, cold, naked, stripped*) reveals the little esteem in which the unspiritualized thoughts and states of consciousness in man hold his body, as related to his true inner self. When Israel (the real and true thoughts in the individual) takes possession of the Promised Land, however, the lifting up of the body begins. Then this that has been regarded as barren and naked of spirituality begins to manifest what it is in Truth: spiritual, fruitful for good, and abiding; it brings forth abundantly of glad, joyous life, substance, peace, and wholeness.

Shephatiah (in A. V., I Chron. 9:8, Shephathiah), shĕph-ă-tī'-ăh (Heb.)—*Jehovah sets upright; Jehovah has judged; judgment of Jah; whom Jehovah defends; whose cause Jah pleads.*

The name of several Israelitish men (II Sam. 3:4; I Chron. 12:5; 27:16; II Chron. 21:2; Ezra 2:4, 57; Jer. 38:1).

Meta. Divine judgment and adjustment active throughout the higher, truer thoughts and states of consciousness (Israelites) in the individual. The judgments of the Lord (ordinances of Jehovah) are not evil, but they are "true and righteous," and they abound in mercy and goodness (*Jehovah sets upright, judg-*

ment of Jah, whom Jehovah defends).

Shepher (A. V., Shapher), shē'-phĕr (Heb.)—*smooth; polished; bright; shining; brilliant; fair; pleasant; beautiful; splendid; pleasing; acceptable; clear; sonorous.*

Mount Shepher was a place where the Children of Israel camped while in the wilderness, on their way to the Promised Land (Num. 33:23).

Meta. Shepher bespeaks the refining, transforming work of Spirit that goes on when man gives it place in consciousness. "By his Spirit the heavens are garnished" (Job 26:13), i. e., are rendered *bright, splendid, beautiful.* Jesus' prayer, "Thy will be done, as in heaven, so on earth" (Matt. 6:10), bespeaks the restoration of the earth also.

Shephi, shē'-phī (Heb.)—*wearing away; nakedness; naked hill; barren; destitute; wasted away; pining; apathetic; unconcerned.*

Son of Shobal, a descendant of Seir (I Chron. 1:40). He is called Shepho in Genesis 36:23.

Meta. A thought activity in body consciousness that is wholly without interest in the things of Spirit (*unconcerned*), hence is unfruitful and naked in so far as real life, strength, wholeness, substance, and good are concerned (*nakedness, barren, wasted away*). "And knowest not that thou art . . . poor and blind and naked: I counsel thee to buy of me gold refined by fire, that thou mayest become rich; and white garments, that thou mayest clothe thyself, and *that* the shame of thy nakedness be not made .manifest" (Rev. 3:17, 18).

Shepho, shē'-phô (Heb.)—*wearing away; nakedness; naked of flesh; barren; destitute; wasted away; pining; apathetic; unconcerned.*

Shepho of Genesis 26:23 is the same person as Shephi of I Chronicles 1:40. See SHEPHI.

Shephuphan, shē-phū'-phăn (Heb.)—*creeping along; smoothly gliding; serpent; reptile.*

Son of Bela, one of Benjamin's sons (I Chron. 8:5). This name is written Shephupham in Numbers 26:39, Shuppim in I Chronicles 7:12, 15, and Muppim in Genesis 46:21.

Meta. A human or sense wisdom (*serpent*). See MUPPIM.

Sherebiah, shĕr-ĕ-bī'-ăh (Heb.)—*heat of Jehovah; Jehovah hath glowed; Jah glimmers; Jah is originator*

a A Levite who came to Ezra at the river Ahava, preparatory to leaving Babylon and returning to Jerusalem (Ezra 8:18). **b** One who joined Nehemiah in sealing the covenant (Neh. 10: 12).

Meta. One's natural religious tendencies (priests and Levites) awakening to the fact that through the indwelling Christ one becomes conscious of the activity of all true light, or understanding, life, love, and purification within one. (Some of the meanings of Sherebiah are *Jehovah hath glowed, heat of Jehovah, Jah is originator.* Glowing suggests both light and fire, or heat; light refers to understanding; and heat refers to life, love, and the refining, purifying fire of Spirit.)

The word declared in the I AM consciousness sets spiritual qualities into activity for good throughout one's being. The word may be declared somewhat as follows: "I am light; I am wisdom; I am love; I am the pure substance of Spirit."

Sheresh, shē'-rĕsh (Heb.)—*scraping the ground; creeping; germ; sprout; shoot; root; germination; trunk; branch; lowest part; bottom; base; seat; abode; stock; race; genus.*

Son of Machir, and grandson of Manasseh (I Chron. 7:16).

Meta. Sheresh, in its highest sense, signifies the fact that the *root*, the beginning, or foundation (*base, seat*) of all understanding, of all expression and manifestation, is Spirit. In Isaiah 11: 10 this same word is used figuratively of the Messiah, as the "root" of Jesse.

Sheshach, shē'-shăch (derivation unknown)—*Babel; gate fastened with iron; secure habitation; pride; arrogance; warlike pursuits.*

A name relating to Babylon, given by Jeremiah (Jer. 25:26; 51:41).

Meta. The seemingly established state (*gate fastened with iron, secure habitation*) of unredeemed man in that which Babylon or Babel signifies. (See BABEL and BABYLON.) Error, however, is not true; it is due to be overthrown in consciousness, according to the prophecies of Jeremiah (spiritual faith in us that demands that our every religious thought must be true to the observance of divine law, thus bringing about true understanding, peace, poise, and harmony in place of the confusion and sense of Babylon).

Sheshai, shē′-shāi (Heb.)—*whitish; wearer of fine linen; free; noble; princely.*

A son of Anak the giant. He was driven from Hebron and was killed by Caleb and the men of Judah (Josh. 15: 14; Judg. 1:10).

Meta. The high esteem in which the reasonings of the intellect functioning in sensate thought are held by the individual who is unawakened spiritually (*free, noble, princely, whitish*). (See ANAK, AHIMAN, and TALMAI.)

Sheshan, shē′-shăn (Heb.)—*whitish; bright-colored; oriental lily; brilliant; shining; free; noble; princely.*

A descendant of Jerahmeel of the tribe of Judah (I Chron. 2:31-35).

Meta. A freeing, ennobling thought activity (*whitish, shining, free, noble*) in the phase of the high, true, religious consciousness of man that Judah signifies. This thought activity is of a very high, honorable character and is in line for rulership (*princely*). But it brings results at first only on the soul plane (Sheshan had no sons, but he had daughters), and from there it continues its work in the individual in a more definite and positive way. (Sheshan's lineage was preserved through his daughter Ahlai, who married his Egyptian servant Jarha. Attai was their son. See AHLAI, JARHA, and ATTAI.)

Sheshbazzar, shĕsh-băz′-zär (Heb. fr. Pers.)—*fire worshiper; joyous vintager; joy of the vintage; unassailable joy; joy in tribulation.*

The name of Zerubbabel in Persia. He was a prince of Judah and was made governor over Judah by Cyrus, king of Persia (Ezra 1:8; 5:14).

Meta. The inner assurance of faith, which rejoices and triumphs even in the midst of trial because it knows that new realizations of life and understanding,

power and glory, are at hand (*joy in tribulation, joy of the vintage, unassailable joy*). "We also rejoice in our tribulations: knowing that tribulation worketh stedfastness; and stedfastness, approvedness; and approvedness, hope" (Rom. 5:3, 4). "Wherein ye greatly rejoice, though now for a little while, if need be, ye have been put to grief in manifold trials, that the proof of your faith, *being* more precious than gold that perisheth though-it is proved by fire, may be found unto praise and glory and honor at the revelation of Jesus Christ: whom not having seen ye love; on whom, though now ye see him not, yet believing, ye rejoice greatly with joy unspeakable and full of glory: receiving the end of your faith, *even* the salvation of *your* souls (I Pet. 1:6-9). (See ZERUBBABEL.)

Shethar, shē′-thär (Heb. fr. Pers.)—*star; a star; commanding; commander.*

One of the seven princes of Media and Persia. These men ranked next to the king (Esth. 1:14).

Meta. A star signifies something that is of a lofty character, but as yet only faintly understood by man; still, the light that stars represent has a degree of guiding illumination for man. Jesus Christ is likened to "the bright, the morning star."

Shethar (*a star, commanding, commander*), one of the seven princes of Media and Persia, who sat with the king, bespeaks the very dim comprehension of higher spiritual truths that the natural man is capable of receiving apart from spiritual quickening and awakening; yet this comprehension of Truth, lacking in clearness as it is, adds to the strength and executive power of the will (Ahasuerus; see CARSHENA, MARSENA, MEMUCAN, and MERES, others of these seven princes).

A star, in the meaning of this name, may refer to the reflected and very uncertain, fragmentary bits of understanding that seem to be obtained at times through the psychic realm, apart from true divine understanding and dominion.

Shethar–bozenai (A. V., Shethar–boznai), shē′-thär–bŏz′-ĕ-nāi (Heb. fr. Pers.) —*shining star; stellar splendor; brilliant commander.*

A Persian officer or governor. With Tattenai and others he wrote to the king of Persia to find out whether or not it was that monarch's will for Zerubbabel and the Jews to rebuild Jerusalem (Ezra 5:3, 6; 6:6, 13).

Meta. Persia and Media refer to the *middle land,* or psychic realm in individual consciousness, guided by the senses. Shethar–bozenai (meaning *shining star, stellar splendor, brilliant commander*), who doubted the right of the Jews to rebuild Jerusalem, denotes the purely mental, psychic, reflected comprehension in man that does not recognize the true source and channels of wisdom—Spirit, and spiritual inspiration and ideas—but takes to itself all the glory of unlimited understanding. It goes to the central ruling idea of the psychical sense realm (Darius, king of Persia) for its guidance even in matters pertaining to the upbuilding and spiritualizing of the body. To the extent that the true light is shining throughout one's consciousness will this comprehension that Shethar–bozenai signifies be of aid in bringing about one's good.

Sheva, shē'-vȧ (Heb.)—*self-will; covetous desire; self-satisfaction; emptiness; vanity; fallacy; evil; wickedness; nothingness; void.*

a A scribe, or secretary, to King David of Israel (II Sam. 20:25). He is called Seraiah in II Samuel 8:17; Shisha in I Kings 4:3, and Shavsha in I Chronicles 18:16. **b** Son of Caleb by Maacah his concubine, and father or founder of Machbena (I Chron. 2:49).

Meta. A scribe is the faculty of the mind that receives and transcribes upon the tablets of memory every wave of thought that touches the consciousness, whether from the flesh or from Spirit. This faculty, which is the subjective memory, may be exalted to a point where it will receive impressions from the spiritual side only. However, the scribe who is variously named Sheva, Seraiah, Shisha, and Shavsha has not yet reached this high place. This faculty takes account of both good and seeming error at different phases of the unfoldment of the individual.

In Sheva we have that phase of the subjective memory which receives and holds to error ideas that tend to build up and give false satisfaction to the personal or lesser self in the individual (*self-will, covetous desire, fallacy, evil*). This brings about inharmony, unrest, and vexation of spirit (*emptiness, vanity, void*). Concerning the works and strivings of the outer personal man, apart from a consciousness of Spirit, we read, "Vanity of vanities, all is vanity . . . I have seen all the works that are done under the sun; and, behold, all is vanity and a striving after wind" (*vexation of spirit,* margin, Eccl. 1:2, 14; see SHISHA).

Shibboleth, shĭb'-bȯ-lĕth (Heb.)—*an ear of grain; copiously flowing; stream; flood; channel of a stream; heavy downpour; cloudburst.*

A word that the Gileadites under Jephthah, after taking the fords of the Jordan, asked each man to say who desired to pass over. The Ephraimites, who had just been defeated by the Gileadites, could not pronounce the "sh," but said "Sibboleth." Thus they were detected and slain (Judg. 12:6).

Meta. A great inflow of new life into consciousness (*stream, flood, copiously flowing*) and a renewed consciousness of substance (*an ear of grain*) that cannot be comprehended, assimilated, or withstood by the will established in intellectual thought (the Ephraimites in this instance).

The human will is not able of itself to deliver the individual from all his inner enemies, yet it does not seem to understand that there are spiritual qualities within one with which it should work, qualities that can go ahead and gain victories over error without the conscious coöperation of the will (see Judges 12: 2, 3).

Shiggaion, shĭg-gā'-ion (Heb.)—*wandering; reeling; staggering; erring; transgression; erratic; wild; enthusiastic; seductive; a dithyrambic ode; boisterous speech.*

A song, ode, or poem that David "sang unto Jehovah, concerning the words of Cush a Benjamite" (Psalms 7, title). It is of a wild, irregular nature.

Meta. The tendency of the "feelings" in man, when aroused and given control, to run on wildly, changing from one point of view or from one emotion to another (*wandering, reeling, erring, erratic, wild, enthusiastic, seductive, boisterous speech, a dithyrambic ode*). Note the many different strains of thought that are brought out by David in the 7th Psalm, and how quickly he changes from one strain to another and then back again, and so on.

Shigionoth, shĭg-ĭ-ō′-nŏth (Heb.)— *wanderings; reelings; errors; erratic; wild; enthusiasms; dithyrambic odes; boisterous speeches.*

"A prayer of Habakkuk the prophet, set to Shigionoth" (Hab. 3:1).

Meta. Expressive of feeling, apart from conscious order and guidance; the same as SHIGGAION, which see.

Shihor (in A. V., Josh. 13:3; Isa. 23:3; Jer. 2:18, Sihor), shĭ′-hôr (Heb.)— *black; blackness; dark; swarthy; turbid; disturbed; clouded; misty.*

a The river Nile (Isa. 23:3; Jer. 2:18).
b "*The brook* of Egypt" (I Chron. 13:5; Josh. 13:3, see margin) may also refer to the Nile, though some think it to be the present *Wady el Arish*.

Meta. The great subconscious current of life, but seemingly dark and corrupt with ignorant, material thought (the river Nile of Egypt, *dark, turbid, clouded, blackness*).

Shihor – libnath, shĭ′-hôr – lĭb′-năth (Heb.)—*blackness made white; turbid made transparent; cloudiness clarified; darkness bleached white.*

A boundary of Asher, in Canaan (Josh. 19:26).

Meta. Shihor means *black, dark, turbid;* Libnath means *to be white, to make white, cleanse, purify, clarify, transparent.* The former signifies impure and ignorant thoughts and beliefs; the latter, purity and clearness of thought expressing. The two together, Shihor–libnath, the name of a small river on the border of Asher in the land of Canaan, bespeak a purifying current of thought that is doing a cleansing work in the body consciousness.

Shilhi, shĭl′-hī (Heb.)—*one sent out; courier; messenger; warrior; armed with spears or arrows; spearman; lancer; bowman.*

Father of Azubah, who was the mother of King Jehoshaphat, of Judah (I Kings 22:42).

Meta. A thought, belonging to the higher, truer consciousness in man (an Israelite), that perceives the Christian life to be a warfare until the lesser self is overcome and everything in one is adjusted according to Truth (*courier, messenger, warrior, armed with spears or arrows*).

This is true, yet our weapons are not carnal but spiritual; they are true thoughts and words pertaining to our own inner Christ dominion and power, and not thoughts, words, or acts of a resistant, personally aggressive nature. That the thought that Shilhi signifies has something of a warring and oppressive character, and is not wholly established in the spiritual method of overcoming, is suggested by the deserted, forsaken attitude of the soul that Shilhi's daughter Azubah signifies.

Shilhim, shĭl′-hĭm (Heb.)—*messengers; couriers; sprouts; shoots; darts; javelins; swords; armed men; warriors.*

A southern city of Judah (Josh. 15:32). This city is called Sharuhen in Joshua 19:6, and Shaaraim in I Chronicles 4:31.

Meta. A phase of thought in the subconsciousness, close to the body consciousness (one of the uttermost cities of Judah toward the border of Edom in the south), that tends to look to the without for good and for ill; that resists outward expressions and manifestations of error, instead of looking within. This phase of thought needs to know that one's good comes from one's inner Christ self and that all of one's overcoming is to be done within. It might be termed a phase of thought that is very active in outer reform, in setting persons and conditions right in the outer.

Shillem, shĭl′-lĕm (Heb.)—*restoration; restitution; requital; recompense; retribution; made whole; in the way of salvation; peace.*

Son of Naphtali (Gen. 46:24). He is called Shallum in I Chronicles 7:13.

Meta. See SHALLUM. In the significance of both of these names the thought that *restoration, salvation, peace,* perfection, are the result of sowing to Spirit is in the ascendancy. This thought that Shillem represents belongs particularly to the strength faculty in the individual, and so gives the substance of its strength to the working out of the law of cause and effect in consciousness, for good.

Shillemites, shĭl'-lĕm-ītes (fr. Heb.)—*of* or *belonging to Shillem.*

The "family" or descendants of Shillem, son of Naphtali (Num. 26:49).

Meta. Thoughts springing from and like that in consciousness which is signified by Shillem, son of Naphtali. (See SHILLEM.)

Shiloah, shĭ-lō'-ăh (Heb.)—*a sending forth; emission; a ray; inspiration; luminous flash; emissary; messenger; sending of water; conduit; aqueduct; pool; reservoir; fountain.*

The same place as Siloam. Isaiah 8:6 tells of "the waters of Shiloah that go softly."

Meta. The flowing forth of peace throughout the consciousness (*a sending forth*) by a putting away of error and a giving of attention to Spirit ("that go softly" bespeaks attentiveness and obedience, also quietness; see SILOAM). This word is related to every emission of good, whether it be a ray of light, a flash of illumination, an inspiration, or anything else that moves along in peace and order.

Shiloh, shī'-lōh (Heb.)—*whole; sound; safe; integral; rest; peace; quiet; security; tranquillity; health; weal; abundance; prosperity; place of rest; pacificator; harmonizer; tranquilizer; Prince of Peace; Savior; Messiah.*

a It is thought that in Genesis 49:10 Jacob referred to the coming of the Messiah, which prophecy we believe to have been fulfilled outwardly in Jesus Christ. **b** A city of Ephraim, and a central city in the time of Joshua (Josh. 18:1-10). Until the time of Eli the tabernacle and the Ark were at this place (Judg. 18:31; I Sam. 4:3); after this, Shiloh seems to have been forsaken, and we find its downfall mentioned (Jer. 7:12-14).

Meta. Peace of mind, wholeness, security, abundant good. In *Messiah, Prince of Peace,* the significance is that of becoming conscious of the Christ presence, which brings abiding peace, health,

and good, "Peace I leave with you; my peace I give unto you: not as the world giveth, give I unto you. Let not your heart be troubled, neither let it be fearful."

The city of Shiloh, which was a central city in the time of Joshua, signifies the first establishment of that which Shiloh represents in consciousness, through the activity of the will (Ephraim). A certain self-control, which gives a degree of peace and poise, is thus brought about. This peace, however, cannot be lasting because it is of the outer personal or intellectual, like John the Baptist, seeking the attainment of peace and good. True peace has its place of abode in Jerusalem, the heart, or love center in man, and not in the head, or will center. It is from the heart center that it radiates throughout the being of the individual; and it is the result not of control through will power, but of the entrance of the Christ or spiritual consciousness into the consciousness of the individual.

Shilonite (in A. V., Nehemiah 11:5, Shiloni), shĭ'-lō-nīte (fr. Heb.).

a Descendants of Judah who reoccupied Jerusalem after the return from the Babylonian captivity (I Chron. 9:5). These are thought to be the same as the Shelanites, descendants of Shelah, Judah's son (Num. 26:20). **b** Ahijah the Shilonite (I Kings 11:29) was a native of the city of Shiloh.

Meta. Thoughts springing from and of like character to that in consciousness which Shelah and Shiloh signify. (See SHELAH, SHILOH, and AHIJAH.

Shilshah, shĭl'-shăh (Heb.)—*third; threefold; triplet; triplication; third part; third time; solidarity; might; dominion; welfare; perfection; extraction; subtraction; trial.*

Son of Zophah, an Asherite (I Chron. 7:37).

Meta. The threefold man—spirit, soul, and body (*triplication, triplet*)—but with the *third* phase of his being, that which pertains to the body and outer consciousness, occupying the most prominent place. Thus the individual experiences *trial* and inharmony, since his higher ideas of *dominion* and *might* and his *welfare* as yet pertain more to personal force and greatness than they do to the true inner Christ rule of love.

Shimea (in A. V., I Chronicles 2:13, Shimma), shĭm′-ĕ-à (Heb.)—*sound; song; music; hearing; hearkening; report; rumor; fame; announcement; declaration; obedience; understanding.*

a Son of Jesse and brother of David (I Chron. 2:13). **b** Son of David, born to him in Jerusalem of Bathshua, or Bathsheba, who was also the mother of Solomon (I Chron. 3:5). **c** A Levite, descended from Merari (I Chron. 6:30). **d** Another Levite, grandfather of Asaph, a chief musician and singer in David's reign (I Chron. 6:39). Shimea, the brother of David, is called Shammah in I Samuel 16:9, Shimeah in II Samuel 13:3, and Shimei in II Samuel 21:21.

Meta. High ideas of Truth becoming generally received and accepted throughout one's truer and more real thoughts (Israelites), though as yet the origin of these ideas is but little known or understood (*rumor, fame, hearing*).

Shimeah, shĭm′-ĕ-äh (Heb.)—*hearing; report; rumor; intelligence; news; fame.*

a David's brother (II Sam. 13:3); called Shammah, Shimea, and Shimei, in other places. **b** A Benjamite, descendant of Jeiel who was the "father" of Gibeon (I Chron. 8:32); called Shimeam in I Chronicles 9:38.

Meta. See SHIMEA for the significance of this name; in Shimeah the ideas of Truth received are more specific and localized.

Shimeam, shĭm′-ĕ-ăm (Heb.)—*hearing; report; rumor; fame.*

Son of Mikloth; descended from Jeiel the "father" of Gibeon, a Benjamite who lived in Jerusalem (I Chron. 9:38). He is called Shimeah in I Chronicles 8:32.

Meta. See SHIMEA.

In this name the ideas of Truth are of a general and universal nature.

Shimeath, shĭm′-ĕ-ăth (Heb.)—*hearing; report; rumor; intelligence; news; fame.*

The feminine construction of Shimeah. Shimeath was an Ammonitess, mother of Jozacar, or Zabad, who with Jehozabad conspired against and slew Joash, king of Judah (II Chron. 24:26).

Meta. The animal phase of the soul

(an Ammonitess) becoming open to and affected by the higher ideas (*hearing, fame, report, rumor*) that are becoming current in man's more real and true state of consciousness (Israelites), as is signified by Shimea, the masculine of Shimeath. (See SHIMEA.)

Shimeathites, shĭm′-ĕ-ăth-ītes (fr. Heb.).

A family of scribes that lived at Jabez. They were of the tribe of Judah (I Chron. 2:55). They may have been descendants of Shimea, David's brother.

Meta. Thoughts springing from and of like character to that which Shimea signifies, being inscribed in the memory of the individual (scribes, descendants of Shimea, David's brother; see SHIMEA).

Shimei (in A. V., Exod. 6:17, Shimi; I Chron. 8:21, Shimhi; II Sam. 21:21, Shimeah), shĭm′-ĕ-ī (Heb.)—*famous; renowned; reputed; Jah is famed; who hears; who hearkens; who obeys.*

There are several Israelites by this name mentioned in the Bible (Num. 3:18; II Sam. 16:5-14). The Shimei of I Chronicles 8:21 is called Shema in I Chronicles 8:13.

Meta. Ideas of Truth becoming current throughout the phases of consciousness in the individual that the Israelites represent. In Shimei, however, these higher Truth ideals are getting past the place of being like a "rumor" (see SHEMA), suggestions whose origin is not known; the Christ or spiritual consciousness is now being understood to be their source (*Jah is famed*). The obedient, receptive attitude is marked in these names.

Shimeites (A. V., Shimites), shĭm′-ĕ-ītes (fr. Heb.)—*of or belonging to Shimei.*

Descendants of Shimei son of Gershon, of the Levites (Num. 3:21).

Meta. Thoughts springing from and in close relation to that in consciousness signified by Shimei. (See SHIMEI.)

Shimeon, shĭm′-ĕ-ŏn (Heb.)—*a hearkening; a famous one; obedient.*

"*Of* the sons of Harim," an Israelite. He had married a foreign woman, but gave her up at the command of Ezra (Ezra 10:31).

Meta. A lifting up of the Christ in

consciousness (*a famous one*) by means of an attitude that is attentive and obedient to Spirit (*a hearkening, obedient*).

Shimon, shĭ'-mŏn (Heb.)—*astonishment; amazement; desert; waste; solitary; ruin; desolation; extinction.*

A man named in the genealogy of Judah as being the father of four sons (I Chron. 4:20).

Meta. The seemingly amazed, dazed, lonely, lost feeling that comes over a person when, because of his new conception of Truth, he can no longer believe in the reality or security of outer seemings; when he has had to let go of old limited ideas and beliefs but has not yet become established in Truth, in the reality of things spiritual. By ever turning within to Spirit, however, one gradually becomes centered and poised in that which is real and true, and brings forth qualities such as Shimon's four sons signify. Four sons here bespeak a certain fullness or all-around realization and expression of Truth.

Shimrath, shĭm'-răth (Heb.)—*standing erect; watch; guard; keeper; protector; preserver; vigilant; alert; watchful; watcher; observer; worshiper.*

Son of Shimei, or Shema, of the tribe of Benjamin (I Chron. 8:21).

Meta. Active faith, on guard against error (*watch, watcher, guard, protector, a Benjamite*). Jesus very earnestly admonished His followers to watch and pray, that they might not be overtaken and overcome by temptation, by the carnal desires of the "mind of the flesh" within themselves. In every one of the twelve faculties of mind in us, therefore, there should be awakened a watchful and attentive attitude toward Spirit.

Shimri (in A. V., I Chron. 26:10, Simri), shĭm'-rī (Heb.)—*standing erect; watchful; observing; vigilant; Jah is watcher; keeping of the Lord; Jah keeps vigil.*

a A prince or head of a family of Simeonites (I Chron. 4:37). **b** Father of Jediael, one of David's mighty men who belonged to his guard, or council (I Chron. 11:45). **c** "Chief" son of Hosah of the Merari Levites (I Chron. 26:10). **d** Son of Elizaphan of the Levites (II Chron. 29:13).

Meta. A degree of awakening to the fact that the Spirit of the Christ is ever *vigilant* in keeping watch in our consciousness, to our eternal protection and good (*Jah keeps vigil*).
"He that keepeth thee will not slumber.
Behold, he that keepeth Israel
Will neither slumber nor sleep.
Jehovah is thy keeper" (Psalms 121:3).

Shimrith, shĭm'-rĭth (Heb.)—*watcher; guard; vigilante; keeper; protector;* feminine form of *Shamer*, the root word.

A Moabitish woman, mother of Jehozabad who was one of the servants who helped to kill Joash, king of Judah (II Chron. 24:26). She is called Shomer in II Kings 12:21.

Meta. A watchful, attentive attitude in the soul of the spiritually awakening individual (*vigilante, watcher, keeper,* a Moabitish woman whose son was a servant of Joash king of Judah, and who aided in bringing about the death of Joash after he had forsaken God and ceased ruling according to God's law).

Shimron (in A. V., I Chron. 7:1, Shimrom), shĭm'-rŏn (Heb.)—*extended; watch; watch place; extreme vigilance; careful keeping; watch height.*

a Son of Issachar (Gen. 46:13). **b** A city of Zebulun (Josh. 19:15). Shimron-meron of Joshua 12:20 is thought to be the same city.

Meta. A watchful, observant, attentive attitude being raised to a high plane in the faculties of mind in the individual that Issachar and Zebulun represent (*watch height, watch place, extended watch*).

Shimronites, shĭm'-rŏn-ītes (fr. Heb.).

The family and descendants of Shimron, son of Issachar (Num. 26:24).

Meta. Thoughts springing from and of like character to that in consciousness represented by Shimron, son of Issachar. (See SHIMRON.)

Shimron-meron, shĭm'-rŏn-mē'-rŏn (Heb.)—*watch place of rebellion; guard of lashing; careful keeping of rebellion; watch height of the lord.*

One of the towns of ancient Canaan whose kings were defeated by Joshua (Josh. 12:20). It is thought to be the same city as Shimron of Joshua 11:1 and 19:15.

Meta. A watchful, observant state of thought. This attitude of mind is at first under the dominion and guidance of the destructive thoughts and beliefs that exist in the "mind of the flesh" (*guard of the lashing, watch place of rebellion*). Coming under the influence of Truth (this city came into the possession of the Israelites), the analysis and the assimilation of spiritual ideas enter in; thus the individual is nourished and sustained, and becomes truly rich within and without.

Shimshai, shĭm'-shāi (Heb.)—*sunny; bright; glowing; astonishment; wonder; reverence; Jah is splendor.* Another idea developed from this word is *stupor, dread, terror,* from gazing upon the full-orbed sun.

A scribe who, with Rehum the chancellor, wrote to Artaxerxes, king of Persia, against the rebuilding of Jerusalem by the Jews. This caused the work on the house of God in Jerusalem to be discontinued until the second year of the reign of Darius, king of Persia (Ezra 4:8-24).

Meta. A degree of light, understanding, based on belief in Jehovah (*sunny, bright, Jah is splendor*), but more of a carnal or sense intellectual understanding. The spiritually unawakened intellect of the sense man cannot contain the full light of spiritual understanding. It cannot perceive and will not accept spiritual Truth relating to the actual renewing and spiritualizing of the body (the renewing and spiritualizing of the body is symbolized by the rebuilding of the wall of Jerusalem and the Temple by the Jews after their return from the Babylonian captivity); therefore the phase of thought that Shimshai signifies works to hinder the individual in the immortalizing of his entire being—which includes his outer organism.

Shinab, shĭ'-năb (Heb.)—*father's tooth; sharpened desire; father of change; father of mutation; father of transgression.*

King of Admah, who rebelled against Chedorlaomer, king of Elam, and the kings who were with him, and was defeated (Gen. 14:2).

Meta. The presiding thought of the state of consciousness that Admah signifies. (See ADMAH.) In Shinab we find a thought of assimilation of substance (*father's tooth*), which may easily apply to a gluttonous desire for food (*sharpened desire*). In this name we also find that which tends to destructiveness and error (*father of mutation, father of transgression*) and to a changeable, unreliable nature (*father of changing*). "Father," in the meaning of this name, does not refer to God but to the adverse thought or consciousness from which all fleshly and sense desires and activities spring.

Shinar, shĭ'-när (Heb.)—*two rivers; divided stream; wholly severed; wholly cast off; divided mind; overthrow of restraint; revolution.*

The ancient name of Babylonia, the country through which the rivers Tigris and Euphrates flow. It includes Babylon and the country round about, with probably Mesopotamia, but not Assyria (Gen. 10:10; Dan. 1:2).

Meta. A divided mind, a belief in two powers, evil as well as good, and the error results. The basis of this word Shinar is two, duality, change, division, and separation. To this is united the idea of that which moves out of its place, with violence and vehemence: a heated mind, ardent passion, enmity, anxiety, terror.

Shiphi, shĭ'-phī (Heb.)—*abundant; copious; overflowing; superabundant; wealth; multitude; myriad; Jah is fullness; multitude of Jehovah.*

Father of Ziza and son of Allon, chiefs of the Simeonites (I Chron. 4:37).

Meta. A prosperity idea; a rich, influential thought of great increase, founded in Spirit (*Jah is fullness, abundant, wealth, multitude of Jehovah*), the result of an attentive, obedient attitude (Shiphi was a chief of the Simeonites, and Simeon the son of Jacob, from whom the Simeonites were descended, means *hearing*; hearing relates to attentiveness and obedience).

Shiphmite, shĭph'-mīte (fr. Heb.)—*of or pertaining to Shepham.*

Thought to be a native of Shepham. "Zabdi the Shiphmite" was "over the increase of the vineyards for the wine-cellars" in David's reign (I Chron. 27: 27).

Meta. A thought that brings forth abundantly of glad, joyous life and good. (See SHEPHAM.)

Shiphrah, shĭph'-răh (Heb.)—*polished; bright; shining; brilliant; splendid; beautiful; pleasing; a sonorous tone; trumpet-clear.*

One of the Hebrew midwives whom Pharaoh commanded to kill all the male children of the Hebrew women at birth. However, like the others, she saved them alive because she "feared God"; she was therefore blessed by the Lord (Exod. 1: 15-21).

Meta. A spiritual phase of the soul in the individual that refers very specifically to the receiving into consciousness of new ideas, or to their care as they enter the consciousness. Pharaoh, the ruling thought of the darkened, ignorant state of consciousness that Egypt signifies, would have these new positive Truth ideas for which the Hebrew male infants stand denied away at once (slain at birth). Shiphrath, however, the light, wholesomeness, justice, trueness, and purity of the spiritual soul character (*bright, splendid, beautiful, trumpet-clear*), does not obey Pharaoh, even though the Hebrews are seemingly in bondage to him at the time. Because her trust is in God and not in man, Shiphrath saves the children (new ideas of Truth) alive; thus these ideas grow stronger in consciousness and multiply greatly to the outworking of deliverance from darkness and bondage and to wonderful growth of the real and true in the individual (Israelites).

Shiphtan, shĭph'-tăn (Heb.)—*judge; judicial; judgment; rectitude; righteous judgment.*

Father of Kemuel, who was the prince chosen from the tribe of Ephraim to help divide the land of Canaan among the Israelitish tribes (Num. 34:24).

Meta. The development of good judgment, in relation to the will (*judge, judicial, righteous judgment,* father of a prince of Ephraim, Ephraim referring to the will).

Shisha, shĭ'-shȧ (Heb.)—*whiteness; purity; distinction; nobility.*

Father of Elihoreph and Ahijah, who were scribes or secretaries to King Solomon of Israel (I Kings 4:3). He is thought to be the same person as Shavsha of I Chronicles 18:16, Seraiah of II Samuel 8:17, and Sheva of II Samuel 20:25.

Meta. See SERAIAH and SHEVA. In Shisha the phase of the subjective memory that transcribes thoughts of a high, noble, and pure nature is in evidence (*whiteness, purity, distinction, nobility*).

Shishak, shĭ'-shăk (Heb. fr. Egypt.)—*present of a bag or pot; like a river.*

King of Egypt, to whom Jeroboam fled from King Solomon of Israel (I Kings 11:40). Later, in the reign of Rehoboam, Solomon's son, this king came against Jerusalem and "took away the treasures of the house of Jehovah" (I Kings 14:25, 26).

Meta. A ruling thought over the phase of darkened, ignorant, sense consciousness that Egypt signifies.

Shitrai, shĭt'-rāi (Heb.)—*engraver; scribe; writer; magistrate; prefect; director; inspector; extractor; gatherer of money; Jah is deciding; the Lord is administrator.*

"The Sharonite" who was over the herds of King David that fed in Sharon (I Chron. 27:29).

Meta. The appropriation of substance ideas in consciousness (*scribe, gatherer of money*), through the attracting power of divine love (David); also a trust in Jehovah, the inner Christ, for direction, guidance, and sound judgment (*director, Jah is deciding, the Lord is administrator*). The herds for which Shitrai cared are the animal forces in man, or substance and life in the body consciousness. Sharon represents the rich substance of Spirit established in body consciousness.

Shittim, shĭt'-tĭm (Heb.)—*acacias; acacia wood; thorny.*

a A place in Moab; the last place in which the Israelites encamped before passing over the Jordan to possess the land of Canaan (Num. 25:1; Josh. 3:1). b A valley mentioned in Joel 3:18 ("*the valley of acacias*," margin).

Meta. Abel-shittim, of Numbers 33: 49, is believed to be the same place. See ABEL-SHITTIM and BETH-SHITTAH. Shittim (*acacias*) refers to resurrection life. When there has been a resurrection experienced in consciousness—an inflow of new life, with the corresponding quickening, awakening, and vitalizing in mind and body—if the Moab or earthly mind in one is in evidence there are sure to be some troublous conditions to adjust (*thorny*).

Shiza, shī'-zà (Heb.)—*splendor; lifting up; captivating; loving.*

Father of Adina, who was a chief of the Reubenites and one of David's mighty men (I Chron. 11:42).

Meta. The glory of true understanding working through love to the elevating of the consciousness (*splendor, loving, lifting up,* a Reubenite, Reuben referring to the seeing quality of the mind).

Shoa, shō'-à (Heb.)—*broad; ample; rich; opulent; wealthy; powerful; liberal; noble; magnanimous; freedom; prosperity.*

A place named with Pekod and Koa, and the Babylonians, Chaldeans, and Assyrians, with whom Oholibah, or Jerusalem, had defiled herself; it was prophesied that these places were to be raised up against her, "because thou art polluted with their idols" (Ezek. 23:23, 30).

Meta. This must refer to outer ideas of and trust in worldly riches, in manifest substance, without an understanding of or a real love for the true, inner, spiritual riches that must stand back of every manifestation that is to be abiding (*rich, broad, noble, opulent,* a place wherein Jerusalem defiled herself, and by which she was to be assailed). "Because thou sayest, I am rich, and have gotten riches, and have need of nothing; and knowest not that thou art the wretched one and miserable and poor and blind and naked: I counsel thee to buy of me gold refined by fire, that thou mayest become rich; and white garments, that thou mayest clothe thyself, and *that* the shame of thy nakedness be not made manifest; and eyesalve to anoint thine eyes, that thou mayest see" (Rev. 3:17, 18; see Luke 12:16-21 also).

Shobab, shō'-băb (Heb.)—*turned away; turned back; apostate; rebellious; hostile; impious; backsliding.*

a Son of David, born in Jerusalem (II Sam. 5:14). **b** Son of Caleb, by Azubah (I Chron. 2:18).

Meta. An apparent falling away from the consciousness of love, divine enthusiasm, and faith, that in their highest sense are signified by David and Caleb (*turned away, apostate; rebellious, hostile, impious, backsliding*).

Shobach, shō'-băch (Heb.)—*poured out; profusely expended; copiously extended; exhausted; weakened.*

Captain of the host of Hadarezer, king of Syria. David defeated this host at Helam, and Shobach was killed (II Sam. 10:16, 18). He is called Shophach in I Chronicles 19:16.

Meta. The dissipation of one's mental and bodily forces by unwise and riotous expression in thinking, talking, and acting (*poured out, profusely expended, copiously extended*); also the result of this dissipation or lack of righteous conservation. This result is exhaustion, lack of strength, lack of substance, lack of executive ability (*exhausted, weakened*).

Shobai, shō'-bāi (Heb.)—*taking captive; captivating; returning; returning of Jah; Jah is glorious.*

His descendants were among the "porters" in the Temple, Levites who returned from the Babylonian captivity with Zerubbabel (Ezra 2:42).

Meta. A guarding thought activity (a porter or doorkeeper in the Temple) that, being lifted to a higher understanding and realization of Spirit (*Jah is glorious, returning of Jah*), sees the wonderful possibilities of the individual, or causes the individual to see his wonderful possibilities, through his indwelling Christ mind. Thus freedom is brought about by one's refusing to give further place or expression to the error, limited ideas that have heretofore held one in bondage (*taking captive, captivating, returning,* one whose descendants returned from the Babylonian captivity). That which Shobai signifies reminds one of the words in Ephesians 4:8:

"When he ascended on high, he led captivity captive,

And gave gifts unto men."

Even so when we lift up the Christ in ourselves we obtain power and dominion to restrain, take captive, and cast out of our life limited ideas and conditions. "Casting down imaginations, and every high thing that is exalted against the knowledge of God, and bringing every thought into captivity to the obedience of Christ" (II Cor. 10:5).

Shobal, shō'-băl (Heb.)—*way; path; going away; wandering; traveling; going up; growing; producing ears; sprouting; shoot; flowing copiously; rain; current.*

a Son of Seir the Horite, and a chief in the land of Seir or Edom (Gen. 36:20). **b** Son of Caleb, and founder of Kiriath-jearim (I Chron. 2:50). **c** Son of Judah (I Chron. 4:1).

Meta. Each individual is *traveling* the pathway of life. To a great extent the race has been—and still is—*wandering* about in ignorance and darkness as to the true source of man's being. The *way* that each one takes in his thoughts, beliefs, and expressions determines whether that which he brings forth, the results in his world of mind, body, and affairs, shall be the fruit of the "mind of the flesh" or the fruit of Spirit (*growing, producing ears, sprouting, shoot, flowing copiously, rain, current;* see Galatians 6:7, 8).

Shobal's being the name of a son of Seir the Horite and of a chief of Edom, as well as the name of two Israelites, shows that that which the name signifies may take place either in the higher, truer thoughts of the individual or in the sense or material phase of his consciousness.

Shobek, shō'-bĕk (Heb.)—*freeing; leaving; forsaking; left; forsaken.*

One who joined Nehemiah in sealing the covenant (Neh. 10:24).

Meta. The renunciation (*leaving, forsaking*) of lesser, limited ideas and conditions that always accompanies a determination to adhere more closely to the divine law, to serve and obey God more perfectly (Shobek joined Nehemiah in sealing the covenant). By letting go the lesser thoughts and beliefs of the outer personal man and laying hold of the greater, or divine ideals, one becomes truly free (*freeing*).

Shobi, shō'-bī (Heb.)—*taking captive; captive; captivity; carrying off; driving into exile; one who captures; Jah is glorious; returning of the Lord.*

"Son of Nahash of Rabbah of the children of Ammon" (II Sam. 17:27).

Meta. A thought activity in the seemingly outer, sense consciousness (Shobi was of the children of Ammon) that has become awakened to and captivated by the splendid, all-conquering qualities of Spirit (*Jah is glorious*). At Mahanaim (meaning *two hosts,* or *two companies*), signifying spiritual ideas and the error thoughts of man as coming together through the medium of man's consciousness, this thought activity (Shobi) comes into direct contact with the fleeing love idea (David) and succeeds in getting its attention lifted again to the infinite possibilities of Spirit (*one who captures, returning of the Lord*). Thus divine love feeds on true ideas of substance and life and Truth, and is refreshed thereby (Shobi brought provisions to David and his men at Mahanaim).

Shoham, shō'-hăm (Heb.)—*universally sublimated; quickened; pale; flesh-colored; sardonyx; onyx; beryl.*

a The name of a very precious stone. It is thought to be either the beryl or the onyx, and is translated as such in various places in the Bible (see Gen. 2:12; Exod. 28:9; 35:9, 27; Job 28:16; Rev. 21:20; see both text and margin). **b** Son of Jaaziah, of the Merari Levites, in the time that David was king of Israel (I Chron. 24:27).

Meta. A very highly refined idea and expression of substance in individual consciousness, or spiritual substance being revealed in all its purity, beauty, and priceless value to the consciousness of the spiritually awakened individual (*universally sublimated, quickened, sardonyx, onyx, beryl,* the precious stones here bespeaking substance).

Shomer, shō'-mĕr (Heb.)—*watchman; guard; keeper.*

a Parent of Jehozabad, one of the two servants of King Joash of Judah who conspired against the king and killed him (II Kings 12:21). This person is called Shimrith in II Chronicles 24:26); **b** Son of Heber, who was a grandson of Asher, according to I Chronicles 7:32.

In I Chronicles 7:34 he is called Shemer.

Meta. Watchful, vigilant, guarding, protecting thought attitudes (*watchman, guard, keeper*), in the higher, more religious and true phase of being in the individual and in his outer or seemingly mortal state of consciousness (an Israelite, and a Moabitish person. See SHIMRITH and SHEMER.)

Shophach, shō'-phäch (Heb.)—*poured out; poured forth; expended with profusion; copiously shed; extended to excess; exhausted; weakened.*

Captain of the host of Hadarezer, king of Syria (I Chron. 19:16). He is called Shobach in II Samuel 10:16.

Meta. See SHOBACH.

Shoshannim, sho-shǎn'-nim (Heb.)—*lilies; lilylike; ornamental; trumpets; cymbals; bright, colorful music.*

A title, introductory to the 45th and 69th Psalms. A marginal note says of this word, "that is, *Lilies.*" The indication is that Shoshannim was a formal direction to the choirmaster or leader of the music, as to the tune, tempo, quality, or the instruments to be used as accompaniments.

Meta. The idea here is beauty and purity of thought and feeling (*lilies*) as a factor in bringing about harmony, music, orderly and melodious ideas, and their expression in mind and in body (*trumpets* bespeak giving expression to).

Shoshannim Eduth, sho-shǎn'-nim ē'-duth (Heb.)—*lilies of the law; lilies of the covenant; lilies of the testimony; trumpets of revelation; ornaments of the psalm; with trumpet and lute; ornamental lyric song.*

The manner or melody after which the psalm was to be sung (Psalms 80, title; "that is, *Lilies, a testimony,*" margin.)

Meta. Purity of thought; also the beauty of high spiritual thought, actively expressing in the consciousness and in the very depths of the soul, thus proving that pure thinking, desiring, and feeling are strong factors in establishing harmony and music—orderly, melodious activities of mind and body, and their resultant conditions (*lilies of the testimony, ornamental lyric song, lilies of the covenant, trumpets of revelation*).

Shua (in A. V., Gen. 38:2, 12, Shuah), shu̯'-à (Heb.)—*broad; ample; riches; wealth; prosperity; saving; set free; delivered, i. e., out of straits and danger; a cry for help; prayer; supplication; invocation.*

a Father of Judah's wife, a Canaanite (I Chron. 2:3). **b** Daughter of Heber, of the tribe of Asher (I Chron. 7:32).

Meta. Broad, rich thoughts of abundant substance, in the depths of the subconscious mind (*ample, riches, wealth, prosperity,* a Canaanitish man and an Israelitish woman; the Canaanites refer to the elemental life forces in the depths of the subconsciousness, and a woman signifies some phase of the soul). Shua signifies also a strong desire for the uplifting power of God, for something higher and better, emanating from the soul and from the subconscious elemental life forces (*a cry for help, prayer, supplication*), with the sure response of Spirit to the cry (*saving, set free, delivered*).

Shuah, shu̯'-ăh (Heb.)—*a sinking down,* i. e., as in the mud; *settling down; bowed down,* i. e., the mind or soul; *despair; depressed; depression; pit.*

Sixth son of Abraham by Keturah (Gen. 25:2).

Meta. An exceedingly depressed, downcast state of thought (*bowed down, despair, depression, pit*).

Shual, shu̯'-ăl (Heb.)—*digging; burrowing; sly; difficult to capture; howling; coughing; fox; jackal.*

a A place in Palestine into which one of the three companies of Philistine spoilers came when fighting against Israel (I Sam. 13:17). **b** Son of Zophah of the tribe of Asher (I Chron. 7:36).

Meta. The wisdom and cunning of the outer senses (*fox, jackal*); also the seeming ability of that which is of sense to hide itself (*digging, burrowing*) from the higher understanding of the individual and thus avoid being truly understood and transmuted into higher spiritual expression (*difficult to capture*). Shual, the son of Zophah, of the Israelitish tribe of Asher, shows one's lifting up this wisdom and cunning of the outer senses (as they refer to the animal nature in the individual) to higher expression and transforming them into truer skill and wisdom. (See HAZAR-SHUAL.)

Shubael, shu'-bå-ĕl (Heb.)—*captive of God; God's captive; return of God; turning to God; response to God; tribute to God; restored of God.*

a A Levite, son of Amram and father of Jehdeiah (I Chron. 24:20). In I Chronicles 23:16 the name is Shebuel. **b** Another Levite, a singer in the house of God in David's reign (I Chron. 25:20).

Meta. See SHEBUEL.

Shuhah (A. V., Shuah), shu'-hăh (Heb.)—*sinking down; bowed down; depressed; desperate; depression; pit.*

Brother of Chelub, of the tribe of Judah (I Chron. 4:11).

Meta. This is virtually the same name as Shuah, and the significance is the same. (See SHUAH.)

Shuham, shu'-hăm (Heb.)—*sinking; bowing down; depression; humility; desperation; well digger; pit digger.*

Son of Dan (Num. 26:42). In Genesis 46:23, he is called Hushim.

Meta. A very lowly, depressed tendency in the judgment faculty in individual consciousness (*bowing down, humility, depression, pit digger,* a man of Dan, Dan meaning *a judge* and signifying the judgment faculty in man). In Shuham we find the natural reaction to the great acceleration of thought activity that Hushim signifies. (See HUSHIM.)

Shuhamites, shu'-hăm-ītes (fr. Heb.).

Descendants of Shuham, son of Dan (Num. 26:42).

Meta. Thoughts springing from and in character like that in consciousness which Shuham signifies. (See SHUHAM.) Man in his unredeemed state swings from one extreme to another. In his overcoming and adjustment according to Truth, he will find a balance.

Shuhite, shu'-hīte (fr. Heb.).

A descendant of Shuah, son of Abraham and Keturah. Bildad the Shuhite (Job. 2:11) was one of Job's "three friends."

Meta. A thought springing from and of character similar to that in consciousness signified by Shuah, son of Abraham and Keturah. (See SHUAH.)

Bildad stands for the intellect's love

for reasoning, contending, and striving for that which appears right to it—its judgments and decisions being founded, for the greater part at least, in appearances. This striving naturally depletes the vital forces, and after the lowering of the vitality a depressed and downcast state of mind is almost sure to be in evidence. (See BILDAD.)

Shulammite (A. V., Shulamite), shu'-läm-mīte (fr. Heb.)—*pacific; peace-loving; peaceful; restful; perfect.*

Supposed to be an inhabitant of Shunem, of Issachar (Song of Sol. 6:13); here the name refers to the bride.

Meta. A soul quality relating to that which Shunem signifies. The central thought in that which Shulammite represents is peace and perfection.

Shumathites, shu'-măth-ītes (fr. Heb.) —*fragment; odorous; pungent; acrid; smelling.*

A family of Kiriath–jearim, descended from Shobal, son of Caleb (I Chron. 2: 53).

Meta. A group of thoughts of a discriminative, intuitive character (*fragrant, odorous, pungent, smelling*), and belonging to or located in the thought and nerve center that Kiriath–jearim represents. (See SHOBAL and KIRIATH–JEARIM.)

Shunammite, shu'-năm-mīte (fr. Heb.).

a A native of Shunem. Here the reference is to Abishag, who was brought to King David to care for him in his old age (I Kings 1:3). **b** The woman whose son was restored to life by Elisha (II Kings 4:8-37).

Meta. See ABISHAG and SHUNEM for the significance of Abishag the Shunammite.

The Shunammite woman whose son was restored to life by Elisha represents that loving, faithful attitude of mind which entertains and gives substance to the spiritual side of life.

The Shunammite's husband represents the more materialistic side of the consciousness, dealing with the manifest realm. It has its place in the soul's development, but is apt to give way to weak sympathy when confronted with negative conditions, unless it is unified with spiritual forces of faith and love. The husband receives the assurance that "it shall be well." The child, the sensitive offspring of these two qualities, cannot yet cope with the seeming powers of material conditions. While with "the reapers" he was overcome by sunstroke.

The Shunammite's coming to Elisha has this symbolism: During a trial of faith, when darkness of death seems to have overcome some faculty or activity in consciousness, one must turn in loving trust to God, through the center of spirituality (Elisha).

It was necessary for Elisha to go with the Shunammite woman into the presence of the dead child, because intellectual perception (Gehazi) is not enough to restore life. The servant, Gehazi, was sent with Elisha's staff, but returned reporting failure. In restoring order and life in any part of the organism it is necessary first to make union with the spiritual I AM (Elisha), then to go in a consciousness of power, faith, love, and life to the place needing attention and there to set up new activity through the positive force thus engendered and breathed forth.

Elisha went into the room with the child and shut out mortal sympathy, represented by the mother and the servant, because in true prayer all the attention is turned to Spirit and one for the time ceases to function in relative qualities. I AM (Elisha) in the silence receives the inflow of pure spiritual life and distributes it through the seven life centers: "The child sneezed seven times." Thus the natural man's organism is quickened, revitalized, and restored to health.

Shunem, shụ'-nĕm (Heb.)—*two resting places; double supports; doubly reposed; two tranquil dwellings.*

A border city of Issachar (Josh. 19: 18), where the Philistines encamped against Israel (I Sam. 28:4). It was the home of the Shunammite woman whose son Elisha raised to life (II Kings 4:8); also of Abishag the Shunammite (I Kings 1:3).

Meta. The meaning of this name, with the significance of Abishag (see ABISHAG; also the story of the Shunammite woman's son who died), point to a very

great need of the activity of the resurrecting Christ life in this Shunem thought and nerve center. Shunem signifies a doubly restful, peaceful (because of inactivity) state of being, in what should be the very active zeal faculty in man (a city of Issachar, and Issachar represents active zeal). Elisha's work with the Shunammite woman and her son reveals a quickening and stirring of the Shunem thought to new life and enthusiasm.

Shuni, shụ'-nī (Heb.)—*rest; quiet; calm; peace; tranquillity; ease.*

Son of Gad (Gen. 46:16).

Meta. A tranquil, poised, peaceful attitude of thought (*rest, calm, peace, quiet*) existing in the power faculty in the individual (Gad, son of Jacob, signifies the power faculty in man, and Shuni was a son of Gad).

This restful attitude that Shuni represents can be carried so far, because of the love of *ease,* as to bring about inertia or deadness, which is anything but good.

Shunites, shụ'-nītes (fr. Heb.).

Descendants of Shuni, son of Gad (Num. 26:15).

Meta. Thoughts springing from and in character like that in consciousness which Shuni signifies. (See SHUNI.)

Shuphamites, shụ'-phăm-ītes (fr. Heb.).

The descendants of Shephupham, son or grandson of Benjamin (Num. 26:39).

Meta. Thoughts springing from and of a character like that in consciousness which Shephuphan signifies. (See SHEPHUPHAN.)

Shuppim, shŭp'-pĭm (Heb.)—*creepers; gliders; crawlers; serpents.*

A Benjamite (I Chron. 7:12). He is also called Shephuphan and Muppim.

Meta. See SHEPHUPHAN and MUPPIM.

Shur, shûr (Heb.)—*going round about; traversing; journeying; surrounding; inclosing; looking around; spying; observing; surveying; considering; regarding; beholding; wall; fortification; lier-in-wait; enemy,* i. e., *between the walls; ox; bullock.* Most of the foregoing are developed from the one idea of *going round about. Ox* is developed from the idea of going round and round in plowing a field.

A wilderness and a city between Palestine and Egypt (Exod. 15:22; I Sam. 15:7). In Numbers 33:8 "the wilderness of Shur" is called "the wilderness of Etham."

Meta. The never ceasing progress, unfoldment, and development of man (*going round about, journeying, looking around, surveying, considering,* and so forth). Man has ever moved in cycles, apparently, in his evolution (history repeats itself); but each time that he seems to come again to his starting place he is a little in advance of his former state. When he begins to awaken spiritually his progress is more rapid. There is also a thought of strength and might in this that Shur signifies (*wall, fortification, ox*). Abraham "dwelt between Kadesh and Shur; and he sojourned in Gerar" (Gen. 20:1), Gerar signifying subjective substance and life. Thus Abraham had on one hand Kadesh—the inherently pure, sinless, ideal state that exists in the depths of the consciousness of every individual—and on the other hand Shur (unceasing progress) while he had his existence in life and substance. Thus does faith (typified by Abraham) develop in the spiritually awakening individual.

Shushan, shụ'-shăn (Heb.) — *lily; bright-colored; white; red; purple; colorful; joyous; bright; ornamental; trumpet; cymbal.*

a The palace or castle of the king of Persia and Media. **b** The capital of Elam, where the kings had their winter palace. Later the kingdom of Persia included what was formerly called Elam (Esth. 1:2; Dan. 8:2). The same word is translated *lily* and *lilies* in other places in the Bible (I Kings 7:19-26; Song of Sol. 2:1, 2, 16).

Meta. Pure thoughts (*lily*). The orientals associate white with any brilliant color. The different colors, in their highest sense, bespeak spiritual qualities, and these all enter into true spiritual light and purity. (See ELAM.)

Shushan Eduth, shụ'-shan ē'-duth (Heb.)—*lily of the covenant; lily of testimony; trumpet of revelation; ornament of the psalm; with trumpet and lute; colorful lyric song.*

Instruction to the choirmaster or leader of the Temple music, as to the tune, tempo, quality, or instruments to be used as accompaniments (Psalms 60, title).

Meta. See SHOSHANNIM EDUTH.

Shuthelah, shụ'-thĕ-lăh (Heb.)—*noise of breaking; crash of rupture; tumult of the breach; roar of frenzy; rabid tumult.*

Son of Ephraim (I Chron. 7:20).

Meta. The confusion, tumult, and inharmony in consciousness that attend the breaking up and passing away of any seemingly strongly established error, by means of the activity of the will (*crash of rupture, noise of breaking,* a son of Ephraim, Ephraim referring to the will faculty in man). When personal will is brought to bear on the disrupting and dissolving of error, the inner conflict is much greater than when the word of Truth is declared in I AM, or in the Christ consciousness of the allness of God, the good.

Shuthelahites (A. V., Shuthalhites), shụ'-thĕl-a̱'-hītes (fr. Heb.).

The descendants of Shuthelah, son of Ephraim (Num. 26:35).

Meta. The thoughts in consciousness belonging to that which Shuthelah signifies. (See SHUTHELAH.)

Sia, sī'-à, or **Siaha,** sī'-à-hȧ (Heb.)—*coming together; conversing; convocation; congregation; assembly; multitude; a troop.*

One whose descendants were among the returned Nethinim (Neh. 7:47; Ezra 2:44).

Meta. A unifying, gathering, thought activity (*coming together, congregation, assembly*) in the phase of consciousness in the individual that is signified by the Nethinim. (See NETHINIM.)

Sibbecai (in A. V., II Sam. 21:18 and I Chron. 20:4, Sibbechai), sĭb'-bĕ-cāi (Heb.)—*interweaving of Jehovah; Jah is intervening; thicketlike; thicket of Jah; weaver; four-stringed musical instrument; harp; lyre; latticework.*

The Hushathite who slew Saph, or Sippai, one of the sons of the giant Raphah (II Sam. 21:18). He was one of David's mighty men, and was the eighth captain for the eighth month, over the Zerahites (I Chron. 11:29; 27:11). In II Samuel 23:27, he is called Mebunnai.

Meta. A quick, strong, harmonious thought activity in the higher, truer phase of man's consciousness (an Israelite, one of David's valiant men) that is of a true, character-weaving, constructive nature (*weaver, harp, lyre*). It is based on the overcoming power of the Christ or I AM, which is working in its behalf (*interweaving of Jehovah, Jah is intervening*). *Thicketlike* and *thicket of Jah* pertain to the ideas or inspirations of Spirit, which cannot be penetrated by the sense reasonings that the giant Raphah and his sons represent, but easily reveal the limitations of these sense reasonings and put them out of consciousness. (See HUSHATHITE and MEBUNNAI.)

Sibboleth, sĭb'-bŏ-lĕth (Heb.)—See SHIBBOLETH.

A form of Shibboleth (Judg. 12:6).

Meta. See SHIBBOLETH.

Sibmah (in A. V., Numbers 32:38, Shibmah), sĭb'-măh (Heb.)—*coolness; sweet-smelling; fragrant; sweet; pleasant; spicy; balsam; balsam plant.*

A city of Moab, on the east side of the Jordan, allotted to Reuben (Josh. 13:19). In Isaiah 16:8, 9 and in Jeremiah 48:32 the "vine of Sibmah" is mentioned, in telling of the destruction of Moab. This city is called Sebam in Numbers 32:3.

Meta. A thought group or center (a city) in the sense or material consciousness of man (Moab), that comes under the influence of that which the Israelitish tribe of Reuben signifies (*beholding, seeing*). In this thought center healing is perceived to the extent of changing the outer, apparently physical body of man into pure, immortal, spiritual substance by the abundant cleansing and redeeming qualities of the Christ life. (According to our interpretation of the queen of Sheba, the spices that she brought to Solomon represent the imperishable flesh that lies within the seemingly perishable forms of flesh; and *spicy, balsam plant,* are definitions of Sibmah.) *Fragrant, pleasant, sweet-smelling, balsam,* bespeak a perception of something exceedingly pleasing and good and healing. The same word that is translated "balsam" is also translated "balm" in places in the Bible, as in "balm in Gilead," and points to

healing. The balsam shrub or tree was prized for healing purposes as well as for its fragrance. The "vine of Sibmah" suggests grapes and wine, and they signify abundant life.

Sibraim, sĭb-rā'-ĭm (Heb. fr. Chald.) *twofold hope; double hope; doubly thoughtful; twofold understanding.*

A northern border of Palestine (Ezek. 47:15), "between the border of Damascus and the border of Hamath."

Meta. Damascus is a state of consciousness that is founded on a material concept of life in the body; Hamath signifies confidence in material conditions rather than trust in God. Sibraim, a northern border of Palestine, situated between Damascus and Hamath, in Syria (Sibraim means *twofold hope, double hope, doubly thoughtful, twofold understanding*), represents understanding of Truth and trust in God becoming awakened in the outer intellectual and physical phases of man's being. This understanding of Truth and its consequent trust in God, or "hope" of perfection of life and good, become doubly exalted and strengthened in one when accepted and championed by the outer man, in addition to the inner consciousness that has already been awakened to the Truth.

Siddim, sĭd'-dĭm (Heb.)—*extensions; fields; open country; plowed fields; stony land; rough grounds; pitted fields; difficult passages.*

A valley full of bitumen pits, in which the kings mentioned in Genesis 14 fought (Gen. 14:3, 8). Afterward this valley became the bed of the Dead (Salt) Sea.

Meta. The very lowest material idea and manifestation of substance in the sense subconsciousness and the body consciousness of the individual (*fields, stony land, pitted fields, rough grounds,* a valley). "Now the vale of Siddim was full of slime pits; and the kings of Sodom and Gomorrah fled, and they fell there" (Gen. 14:10; "bitumen pits," margin). *Extensions, open country,* definitions of this name, reveal the apparent extent to which sensuality and materiality have gained expression in the individual when he is at the place in his growth and experience that is signified by this Valley of Siddim and by the battle fought there by the kings mentioned in Genesis 14. (See CHEDORLAOMER, who was seemingly the leading king.)

Sidon (in some places in the A. V., Zidon), sī'-dŏn (Heb.)—*lier-in-wait; providing*, i. e., as for a journey; *catching of fish; fishery; fishing; hunter; trapper; beast of prey.*

a Son of Canaan (Gen. 10:15). b A city of the Canaanites (Gen. 10:19), afterward allotted to Asher. The Asherites failed to drive out the Canaanitish inhabitants (Judg. 1:31). Sidon and Tyre are mentioned together in Joel 3:4, and in the New Testament (see Matthew 11:21; 15:21).

Meta. The signification here is a great increase of ideas in the animal phase of thought or of being in the individual (*lier-in-wait, fishery, fishing, hunter, trapper, beast of prey*). (See TYRE for a further explanation of Sidon.)

Sidonians (in some places in the A. V., Zidonians), sī-dō'-nĭ-ănṣ (fr. Heb.).

Natives or inhabitants of Sidon (Josh. 13:6).

Meta. Thoughts belonging to that in consciousness signified by Sidon. (See SIDON and TYRE.)

Sihon, sī'-hŏn (Heb.)—*wiping out; uprooting; eradicating; exterminating; sweeping away,* i. e., *as a warrior sweeping all before him; great; extreme boldness.*

A king of the Amorites who refused to let the Israelites pass through the borders of his country. He went out to fight against Israel, but was smitten by the Israelites and his land was taken from him (Num. 21:21-35).

Meta. The strong, seemingly unconquerable desire of the animal nature of man for sex sensation; also the almost ferocious determination with which he carries this desire into activity when the "mind of the flesh" rules in him, and its destructive tendencies (*great, extreme boldness, sweeping away,* i. e., *a warrior sweeping all before him, wiping out, uprooting, exterminating*). This sense desire that Sihon signifies is the central ruling thought of the Amorite state of consciousness while man is under the dominion of the carnal mind. (See AMO-

RITES; also HESHBON, the city of Sihon.)

Silas, sī'-lăs (Gk. fr. Lat.)—*abounding in trees; abundant growth; forestlike; wooded; woody.*

A chief man among the believers in Jerusalem, who accompanied Paul on some of his missionary journeys (Acts 15:22). Paul chose Silas to go with him in place of Barnabas after Paul's disagreement with Barnabas (Acts 15:40). Silas is a contracted form of the name Silvanus.

Meta. The rugged state of mind (*woody*) that goes well with the Paul consciousness (Acts 15:40).

In Acts 16:25 Paul and Silas represent the will and the understanding in their work of clearing up the consciousness.

The verse, "But when Silas and Timothy came down from Macedonia, Paul was constrained by the word, testifying to the Jews that Jesus was the Christ" (Acts 18:5), is explained metaphysically as follows: When fired with perception (Silas) from on high, and with zeal (Timothy), and the fervor of the soul (Macedonia), Truth is pressed by the word to proclaim that Jesus (I AM) is the Christ (the saving power).

Silla, sĭl'-là (Heb.)—*lifted up; raised; cast up; highway; causeway; elevated; exalted; high; tall; slender; flexible; pendulous; twig; branch; osier; willow; basket; broom.*

Joash, king of Judah, was killed by two of his servants "at the house of Millo, *on the way* that goeth down to Silla" (II Kings 12:20).

Meta. The *highway* to victory—a putting away of error by denial, and a lifting up of Truth (*elevated, exalted, branch*), thus converting the consciousness from the likeness of "broken cisterns, that can hold no water," into a container of substance and Truth (*basket*). In *broom* we also see a thought of cleansing, of putting away error. Joash was a good king at the beginning of his reign over Judah, but after Jehoiada the high priest died Joash became very wicked and worshiped other gods (II Chron. 24:15 to end of chapter. See the metaphysical interpretations of JOZACAR and JEHOZABAD, the servants who conspired against Joash and killed him.)

Siloam, sĭ-lō′-ăm (Gk. fr. Heb.)—*sending forth; one sent; messenger.*

a Luke 13:4 tells of "the tower in Siloam." **b** A pool, in which Jesus told the blind man to wash after He put clay on his eyes (John 9:7-11). It is called Shiloah in Isaiah 8:6, and Shelah in Nehemiah 3:15.

Meta. One sent, sending forth, or putting away. "Go, wash in the pool of Siloam" means to deny away the false idea. We are to deny the universal race belief in the reality and power of matter, and to affirm the spirituality of all substance.

Silvanus, sĭl-vā′-nŭs (Gk. fr. Lat.)—*wood dwelling; living in woods; genius of the trees; wood nymph; rural deity of fields and flocks; abundant growth; abounding in trees; wooded; woody.*

Thought to be the same person as Silas (II Cor. 1:19).

Meta. A rugged state of mind (*wood dwelling, woody*); also perception, understanding, working in conjunction with the will or the word of Truth (Paul), and zeal or the inspired reason united with faith (Timothy). (See SILAS, a form of this name.)

Simeon, sĭm′-ĕ-ŏn (Heb.)—*hearing; hearkening; obeying; obedient; understanding; announced; reported; reputed; famous.*

Second son of Jacob, by Leah. "And she conceived again, and bare a son: and said, Because Jehovah hath heard that I am hated, he hath therefore given me this *son* also: and she called his name Simeon" (Gen. 29:33). Jacob's blessing of this son is as follows:
"Simeon and Levi are brethren;
Weapons of violence are their swords.
O my soul, come not thou into their council;
Unto their assembly, my glory, be not thou united;
For in their anger they slew a man,
And in their self-will they hocked an ox.
Cursed be their anger, for it was fierce;
And their wrath, for it was cruel:
I will divide them in Jacob,
And scatter them in Israel"
(Gen. 49:5-7).

In Moses' blessing of the tribes of Israel, Simeon is not mentioned. In the Promised Land "their inheritance was in the midst of the inheritance of the children of Judah" (Josh. 19:1).

Meta. The bringing forth of hearing. This son of Jacob did not, according to his history, fulfill that which the name implies. (See REUBEN for further light on the import of Jacob's sons.)

Simeon means one who listens and obeys. *Hearing,* in its higher aspect, refers to the state of mind in the devout Christian that looks for and expects spiritual guidance and instruction direct from God. It may be summed up in the word "receptivity." (See Luke 2:25.) In Luke 2:29 this new consciousness of the indwelling immortal life takes the place of hope, expectancy, obedience (Simeon).

Simon, sī′-mŏn (Gk. fr. Heb.)—*hearing; hearkening; obeying; understanding; announced; reported; reputed; famous.*

a The apostle of Jesus Christ who was called Peter (Matt. 4:18). **b** A brother of Jesus' (Matt. 13:55). **c** Simon the leper (Matt. 26:6). **d** Another apostle of Jesus Christ, Simon the Zealot (Luke 6:15). **e** The father of Judas Iscariot (John 6:71). **f** A sorcerer who believed in Christ, through Philip's teaching (Acts 8:9-24). Simon is the same name as Simeon.

Meta. For the general significance of Simon, see SIMEON. Strength (Andrew) is clearly related to substance (Simon), which in spirit we call faith (Peter; John 1:40, 41). "Faith is the giving substance to *things* hoped for" (Heb. 11:1, with marginal note). What we hope for and mentally see as a possibility in our life comes into visibility, and we call it substance.

In Mark 1:29-34 Jesus' coming "into the house of Simon and Andrew, with James and John," in individual consciousness signifies the coming of the spiritual I AM into a firm, unyielding, enduring consciousness of faith and strength (typified by Simon and Andrew), supported by the faculties of judgment and love (James and John).

The results are a positive activity of these spiritual forces, directed by the I AM, which brings about a healing, redeeming work within the soul (represented by Simon's mother-in-law who was healed by Jesus).

This living demonstration of the power of Spirit in the soul consciousness awakens the soul to the knowledge of the power of Spirit to free and to make whole. All that are sick, all thoughts of a demoniac character, are brought to Simon's door (the door of faith) and are healed.

Simon the Canaanite, or Simon the Zealot, another of Jesus' apostles, represents the zeal faculty in man. In the body this faculty is located at the base of the brain.

The house of Simon the leper represents a state of body consciousness in which vital substance has been vitiated.

Simon the sorcerer is the ambition of personality to handle the power of Spirit without paying the price through faith and love. The offer of money for spiritual power entails the thought of man's putting a price on the works of God.

The power of the Holy Spirit is obtained only by unselfish service; therefore personal power and glorification have "neither part nor lot" in the spiritual realm, the kingdom of heaven.

The only way to loose the bonds of personality, to make the heart right toward God, is through repentance, diligent prayer, and meditation, which transmute selfishness into unselfishness, personality into individuality. The law is: "As I live, saith the Lord, to me every
knee shall bow,
And every tongue shall confess to God."

Sin, sĭn (Heb.)—*clayey; muddy; marshy; miry; hateful passion; bloody disposition; rage; combat.*

a A wilderness between Elim and Sinai, which the Israelites entered after they passed through the Red Sea out of Egypt and were on their way to Canaan (Exod. 16:1). **b** An Egyptian city (Ezek. 30: 15).

Meta. Evidently very material, combative, destructive states of thought (*muddy, marshy, clayey, rage, combat*).

sin.

Meta. Missing the mark; falling short of the divine law. The divine law is the law of God, the law of Being; it is the underlying principle of every man's being and of the universe.

Sin is a departure from the law of our being. The command of God to man is, "Be fruitful, and multiply, and replenish the earth, and subdue it; and have dominion over the fish of the sea, and over the birds of the heavens, and over every living thing that moveth upon the earth." The creatures of land and sea represent states of mind and they all are contained in the consciousness of every man. Any failure on our part to exercise this dominion is a falling short, or a "sin."

The "eternal sin," or unpardonable sin, referred to by Jesus in Mark 3:28-30, is the belief that God is the creator of disease or inharmony of any nature. This belief is called an "eternal sin" because that which is eternal is abiding. So long as man abides in the conviction that God causes him to suffer, he closes his mind against the inflow of God's gifts of health, peace, and harmony. Man's sins are forgiven when he ceases to sin and opens his mind to the fact that he is heir only to the good.

Sinai, sī'-nāi (Heb.)—*cliff; deep ravine; precipitous; sharp; jagged; cleft with ravines.*

a A wilderness into which the Israelites came the third month after they left Egypt. **b** A mount, or chain of mountains, on which Moses received the law (Exod. 19:1-25). The northern part of this chain was called Horeb, and the southern, Sinai.

Meta. The Children of Israel went from Rephidim to Sinai, or Horeb, the mount where God revealed Himself to Moses in the burning bush when the first impulse was given Moses to lead his people out of Egypt, and where God later met and talked to Moses, and gave him the Ten Commandments. This mount symbolizes, in us, a high place in consciousness where we come into conscious communion with the Divine.

The wilderness or desert of Sinai signifies the state of consciousness in which we find the exalted place in mind that the mountains called Sinai and Horeb represent. It may seem rugged and thorny to the sense man, but God is there. (See HOREB.)

Sinim, sĭ'-nĭm (Heb.)—*far East; Chinese; eastern extremity (of the earth); southern country.*

A place mentioned in Isaiah 49:12. It is supposed to have been a very distant country, possibly China.

Meta. Thoughts very remote, little known.

In Isaiah 49:8-13 the lifting up of the whole consciousness and body of man is taught in symbol. In verse 12 we read, "Lo, these shall come from far; and, lo, these from the north and from the west; and these from the land of Sinim." The inference is that the thoughts and states of consciousness from every part of one's being, even those most remote and unknown, will be gathered together to the light of Truth to be made free from error and to be redeemed. (See verse 13.)

Sinite, sĭn'-īte (Heb.) — *clayey; muddy; miry; hateful passions; bloody dispositions; bloodshed; rage; combat.*

A people descended from Canaan, son of Ham (Gen. 10:17).

Meta. Thoughts springing from and in character like that which Canaan, the son of Ham, and the Canaanites signify. (See CANAAN and CANAANITES.) See SIN (a wilderness and a city) for the specific characteristics of these thoughts.

Sion, sĭ'-ŏn (Heb.)—*elevation of power; lifting up of being; lofty virtue; high courage; exaltation of strength; elevated; projecting; very high.*

A mount "(the same is Hermon)" (Deut. 4:48). It is the peak of Hermon.

Meta. A great uplifting of the whole man. (See HERMON.)

Siphmoth, sĭph'-mŏth (Heb.)—*fertile; fruitful; fruitful places.*

A city of Judah; to his friends in this place David sent some of the "spoil" that he had taken from the Amalekites (I Sam. 30:28).

Meta. A rich consciousness of substance and of increase (*fruitful, fruitful places, fertile*).

Sippai, sĭp'-pāi (Heb.)—*lipped; sill; threshold; dish; basin; bowl; edge; rim; border; margin.*

Another name for Saph, son of Raphah the giant (I Chron. 20:4).

Meta. The meaning of this name bespeaks an outer expression, a surface understanding, rather than the inner Truth of Spirit. (See SAPH.)

Sirah, sĭ'-răh (Heb.)—*going off; turning aside; departure; retreat; deflection; apostasy; transgression; turning away; cessation; avoidance.*

A well, or cistern, near Hebron (II Sam. 3:26).

Meta. A *turning aside, departure,* from the real and the true—*apostasy.*

Joab called Abner back to Hebron from Sirah, and slew him at Hebron. Hebron signifies the front brain, the seat of conscious thought. Abner signifies the intellect, illumined in degree. He was Saul's commander-in-chief. He served and defended the selfish, egotistical, personal will (Saul) against the rightful ruler, love (David). After Saul was slain Abner stood by Saul's son, Ishbosheth, against David, until Ishbosheth reproached him for an unlawful act that he had done. Then he turned to David and made peace with him. This all shows how the outer reasoning faculty in man, the intellect, even when partially illumined, is still selfish, is of the personal.

Joab, the captain of the hosts of David, who represents the executive power of love, the pivotal center within man, which preserves the unity and integrity of soul and body, remembered the slaying of Asahel his brother by Abner, and killed Abner because of this act. Asahel signifies the activity of the word in man's consciousness, which the intellect (Abner) had caused to cease expressing for the time being. The intellect therefore must be overthrown; that is, its dominant place in consciousness must be taken away from it, that the true inspiration of the word may guide the thoughts of the individual. True guidance and understanding come through inspiration of Spirit, and not by means of the intellect; the intellect must take a subordinate place. It is necessary as a servant, but it must not be in command.

Sirion, sĭr'-ĭ-ŏn (Heb.)—*coat of mail; breastplate; corselet; covered with armor; connected; interwoven.*

The Sidonian name for Mount Hermon (Deut. 3:9).

Meta. Hermon (*lofty, prominent, sacred mountain*) signifies a high, sublime state of mind. The Sidonian thoughts in man would perceive in this high, spiritual consciousness something strongly defensive and impregnable in an outer way. This is denoted by their name for Hermon, which is Sirion and means *breastplate, coat of mail, covered with armor.*

Sisera, sĭs'-ĕ-rȧ (Heb.)—*fermenting; boiling; battle array; springing to onset; ready for war; enraged; a pot boiling over.*

a Captain of the host of Jabin, king of Canaan. "And the children of Israel cried unto Jehovah: for he had nine hundred chariots of iron; and twenty years he mightily oppressed the children of Israel." He was defeated by Barak, and was slain by Jael, the wife of Heber the Kenite (Judg. 4:2-22). **b** There was another Sisera, whose "children" were among the Nethinim who returned with Zerubbabel from the Babylonian captivity (Ezra 2:53).

Meta. The great aggressiveness, passion, inner unrest, and lack of poise and dominion that exist in the life forces of man while he is under the dominion of carnal thought (*fermenting, boiling, battle array, ready for war, springing to onset, enraged*). Sisera is really the executive power of that which Jabin signifies. It is significant that Sisera was killed by having a tent pin driven through his "temples."

Jabin (*intelligent, discerning, understanding*) represents a degree of discernment and intelligence that is inherent in the elemental life forces of the organism (Canaanites). In Jabin this intelligence is not subject to spiritual thought; it is centered in and actuated by the carnal mind. It takes Barak (the fiery executiveness of an active will), in coöperation with Deborah (a fine spiritual sense of discrimination), with ten thousand men of Naphtali and Zebulun (strength and order), to defeat Sisera, captain of the hosts of Jabin, king of Canaan, who reigned in Hazor. Hazor symbolizes a fortified state of thought in the subconsciousness of man, of which Jabin is the dominating ego.

Sithri (A. V., Zithri), sĭth'-rī (Heb.) —*Jehovah conceals; hidden by Jah; protection of Jehovah; Jehovah's shelter.*

Son of Uzziel, and grandson of Kohath, a son of Levi (Exod. 6:22).

Meta. A thought of divine care and protection (*Jehovah conceals, protection of Jehovah*). "Hide me under the shadow of thy wings" (Psalms 17:8; 91:4).

Sitnah, sĭt'-näh (Heb.)—*lier-in-wait; adversary; enemy; opponent; opposer; persecutor; enmity; accusation; strife; hatred.*

A well that was dug by Isaac's herdsmen in Gerar of the Philistines, for which the herdsmen of Gerar strove with Isaac's herdsmen (Gen. 26:21; "that is, *Enmity*," margin).

Meta. Gerar signifies subjective substance and life. In the beginning of man's journey toward Spirit this substance and life are utilized and activated by the sense nature (Philistines). However, the awakening intellectual and spiritual man must draw on this substance and life for sustenance; this is signified in the digging of wells by Isaac's herdsmen.

Sitnah (*adversary, opposer, strife, enmity, accusation, hatred*), the name that Isaac gave to the well for the possession of which the herdsmen of Gerar strove with his herdsmen, signifies the contention or striving for supremacy that takes place between the higher and the lower natures of the individual at a certain phase of his spiritual unfoldment. Paul, in the 7th chapter of Romans, describes this inner warfare very graphically. (See ESEK, the name of another well that Isaac's herdsmen dug and the Philistine herdsmen contended for.)

Sivan, sī'-văn (Heb.)—*opening; key; rejoicing; pleasure month; clothed with verdure; appearing externally; clayey; muddy; miry.*

The third month of the Hebrew sacred or ecclesiastical year, and the ninth month of their civil year: from the new moon in June to the new moon in July (Esth. 8:9).

Meta. Divisions of time represent steps or degrees of unfoldment in individual consciousness. The third month, or third division of time, as relating to the Jewish sacred year (meaning *opening, key, rejoicing, clothed with verdure, appearing externally*), refers to an awakening in the consciousness of man, pertaining to demonstration, manifestation. Manifestation is third in the Trinity as expressed in metaphysical terms: mind, idea, manifestation.

Smyrna, smy̆r′-nȧ (Gk. fr. Heb.)—*myrrh; flowing; distilling; sweet; fragrant; aromatic; spirituous; gall; sorrow; lamentation; bitterness; rebellion.*

A city of Ionia in Asia Minor, about forty to fifty miles north of Ephesus. In it was one of the Christian churches, or assemblies, that John addressed (Rev. 2:8-11).

Meta. Substance (*myrrh*, "but thou art rich")—the substance center in the body, located at the pit of the stomach. They "that say they are Jews, and they are not," 9th verse, are false thoughts. The ten days of tribulation, 10th verse, refer to degrees or steps in the perfecting of the individual, a work that will go on until a complete letting go of the lesser, or personal, self is fulfilled.

sneeze (II Kings 4:35).

Meta. When we sneeze, the life current is animating some nerve center; to sneeze "seven times" means the animation of all the life centers in the physical organism.

So, sō (Heb. fr. Egypt.)—*chief; prince; rulership; crocodile; Saturn; a measure,* i. e., one third ephah, about one and one half pecks; *measuring; measured.*

A king of Egypt, to whom Hoshea, king of Israel, sent messengers, in conspiring against the king of Assyria (II Kings 17:4).

Meta. A limited idea of judgment, discrimination (*a measure, measuring*), ruling in the darkened phase of consciousness that Egypt signifies (*chief, prince, rulership,* a king of Egypt).

Soco (in A. V., I Chron. 4:18, Socho; II Chron. 11:7, Shoco; II Chron. 28:18, Shocho), sō′-cȯ (Heb.)—*interwoven; entwined; inclosed; covered; hedged with thorns; protected; branches; sinews; tendons; tents; tabernacles.*

A city of Judah that was founded by Heber (I Chron. 4:18). Rehoboam forti-

fied this city (II Chron. 11:7). It is the same city as the Socoh of Joshua 15: 35. In II Chronicles 28:18 it is mentioned as one of the places that the Philistines invaded and took, in the time of Ahaz.

Meta. Heber signifies a passing over from the purely physical earthly thought to a higher concept of Truth. This is the beginning of a conscious alliance of the individual consciousness with the mind of Spirit, and it will culminate in man and God's becoming companions, associates. (See HEBER.)

Soco, a city founded in Judah by Heber, refers to thoughts of Truth, or spiritual qualities (*branches*) as growing and developing in the consciousness and organism of the individual (*interwoven, entwined, inclosed, sinews, tents*); also to a dividing line in thought that they bring about between the higher true ideals (Israelites) and the lower sense activities (Philistines), with a pricking and disturbing of these sense activities (*hedged with thorns*), and a certain degree of protection to the higher ideals (*protected*). Jesus referred to Himself as the "true vine," and to His disciples as the "branches" of that vine. Jesus here signifies the I AM, or perfect, ideal man, which is the true higher self of every individual; the disciples are inner, unfolding spiritual faculties, or qualities of mind.

Socoh (in A. V., I Kings 4:10, Sochoh; I Sam. 17:1, Shochoh), sō′-cȯh (Heb.) —*interwoven; entwined; inclosed; covered; hedged with thorns; protected; branches; sinews; tendons; tents; tabernacles.*

The name of two cities of Judah, **a** one in the lowlands, and **b** the other in the hill country (Josh. 15:35, 48). It was at Socoh in the lowlands of Judah that the Philistines gathered for battle against the Israelites under Saul (I Sam. 17:1). Socoh is also named in the district whence Benhesed obtained victuals for King Solomon's household for one month in each year (I Kings 4:10).

Meta. The significance is the same as that of SOCO, which see.

Sodi, sō′-dī (Heb.)—*circular divan; circle; common consultation; familiar*

converse; intimacy; secrecy; deliberation; confidants; familiar friends; confidant of Jehovah; intimacy of Jehovah;
Jah deliberates.

Father of Gaddiel, the man chosen
from the tribe of Zebulun to help spy out
the land of Canaan preparatory to the Israelites' going over and possessing it
(Num. 13:10).

Meta. An influential thought belonging to the order faculty in man (a man
of the Israelitish tribe of Zebulun) that
is in close fellowship with the spiritual
I AM of the consciousness (*intimacy of
Jehovah, familiar friends*); that is open
to divine inspiration (*confidant of Jehovah, common consultation, secrecy*) and
is guided in its activities by I AM (*Jah
deliberates*).

Sodom (in A. V., Romans 9:29, Sod-
oma), sŏd'-ŏm (Heb.)—*burning; consuming with fire; conflagration; secret intrigues; hidden wiles; covered conspira-
cies; place of bitumen or lime.*

One of the "cities of the Plain," in
which Lot lived for a time. It was destroyed later by fire because of its
wickedness (Gen. 13:12; 18:20—19:29).

Meta. Sodom (*secret intrigues, hidden wiles*) represents a concealed or obscure thought or habit of man. Gomorrah (*tyranny, material force*) signifies
a state of mind that is adverse to the
law of Spirit. These wicked "cities of
the Plain" are located within man, and
before he can come into a realization of
the promised "son," or "Christ," he must
consent to the thorough purification of
his consciousness from the sins that Sodom and Gomorrah represent. This purification is by fire, and it must be complete.

We try hard to save some of our sense
thoughts and secret habits. We have indulged them so long, and our ancestors
before us did likewise beyond the memory
of man, that we cannot help thinking
that there is some good in them. "And
Abraham drew near, and said, Wilt thou
consume the righteous with the wicked?
Peradventure there are fifty righteous
within the city: wilt thou consume and
not spare the place for the fifty righteous
that are therein?" The Lord agreed to
spare the place for the fifty righteous to
be found in it. Then Abraham begged
that it be spared if forty-five righteous
be found, which was consented to; then
forty, then thirty, then twenty—until he
got down to ten, but there were not even
ten righteous, and the city had to be destroyed.

Sodom symbolizes the lowest form of
sense desire in the procreative center.
(Sodom was the southernmost of the four
cities in the vale of Siddim that were destroyed by fire. The Dead Sea exists
where they were). Sodomy is to this
day an almost unmentionable sin; yet the
spiritual-minded Abraham maintained to
the last that there was some good in it.

The tendency to plead for the good in
sense habits is characteristic of man's
development. We cannot conceive why
these functions that seem so necessary
to the reproduction of the race should
not be under the divine law. We have
not yet awakened to the fact that they
are, in the external expression, a degenerate imitation of the divine law of reproduction.

We do not quickly see spiritual Truth,
and we protest that there is good in sense
functions. In the early stages of the
work of regeneration we believe that we
perceive a very large proportion of good,
but as we go on in spiritual discernment
it grows gradually less until it is cut
down to almost nothing. Only Lot and
his wife and their two daughters were
found righteous in that city. They
were helped to escape and the city was
destroyed.

Error must be wholly wiped out of
consciousness, and the sooner we accept
the divine law in full, the sooner shall
we arrive at the door of the kingdom.
Do not hold to your so-called natural
functions as divine. There are great
mysteries in human consciousness. The
race has gone through strange experiences, and wonderful revelations come
to those who get beneath the surface of
things. Turn your back resolutely on
all forms of sense thought, and you will
gradually discern the light that shines
within the light.

Under divine guidance the demoraliza-
tion that mere animalism has produced
must be purified through the descent

of the fires of Spirit. This is what happened to Sodom and Gomorrah.

Sodomites, sŏd'-om-ītes (fr. Heb.)— *sacred; set apart; consecrated; devotee; a male prostitute; a catamite.*

"Sodomites" as used in the Bible does not refer to the inhabitants of Sodom, but to men who committed the sins of which Sodom was guilty and for which it was destroyed (Deut. 23:17; I Kings 14:24). When women thus debased themselves they were called prostitutes.

Meta. Demoralizing, sensual thoughts and desires. (See SODOM.)

sole of your foot, the (Josh. 1:3).

Meta. The firm impression of the understanding upon divine substance. This establishes the unity between divine substance and understanding, giving man the concept of his unlimited possibilities.

Solomon, sŏl'-ŏ-mŏn (Heb.)—*whole; entire; complete; integral; peace; concord; integrity; rectitude; soundness; peaceful; pacific.*

A son of David by Bathsheba, and king of Israel after David (II Sam. 12:24; I Kings 1:30; 2:12).

Meta. The state of mind that is established in consciousness when the soul is unified with wisdom and love (*whole, complete, concord, peaceful*).

That Solomon stands for more than a great Hebrew king and a wise man is quite evident to those who have searched deeply in religious and mythological history.

As students who look especially for information about the individual man, we discern in Solomon a development of the presiding genius at the heart center. In Scripture, brain and nerve centers— or, more strictly speaking, thought centers—are designated as cities, and the presiding or ruling intelligence that controls or directs the work of any center, as a personality. Jerusalem (city of peace) stands for the heart center, and Solomon (*peaceful* man) stands for the presiding intelligence.

When the ruling intelligence is in harmony with the fundamental character of the center, rapid construction of the spiritual body goes on. We are told that David could not build the great Temple because he was a "man of war." When

violent and resistant emotions hold sway in the mind, the turmoil is such as to prevent any permanent construction of the new body on the higher planes of consciousness. So we see the importance of cultivating peace instead of war, nonresistance instead of resistance, harmony and love instead of discord and hate.

Solomon was also a great judge. When asked by the Lord what He should give him, Solomon chose wisdom above riches and honor. Then all the other things were added. Solomon was given a rare intuition, and he used it freely in arriving at his judgments. He did not rest his investigations on visible facts, but sought out the inner motives. In the case of the two women who claimed the same infant, he commanded an attendant to bring a sword and cut the child in two and give a half to each woman. Of course the real mother begged him not to do this, and he knew at once that she was the mother.

The symbolic object of Solomon's assembling the head men of Israel (I Kings 8:1-11) is to construct, under the guiding light of divine wisdom, an imperishable body. All constructive processes must be under the guidance of divine wisdom. The "elders," the "heads of the tribes," and the "princes" represent the directive powers to which the various aggregations of thoughts in the subconsciousness look for instruction.

For an interpretation of the inner meaning of the feast of the seventh month (I Kings 8:2) see ETHANIM.

The Ark of the Covenant is the sum total of man's conscious understanding of Truth, combined with faith affirmations and loyalty within and without to the principles of Truth. This covenant was written on tablets of stone, showing that the spiritual law is expressed not only in mind but in body also.

The tent of meeting symbolizes the spiritual-body idea, which has not yet taken permanent form and substance in consciousness. The holy vessels are the true thoughts that lie back of the body organs.

The sacrificing of sheep and oxen means that we must transmute to higher planes of consciousness our animal propensities and the body substance through which they express.

The cherubim represent divine protection, and the spreading wings symbolize the thought of freedom.

The meaning of the cloud that so filled the house of Jehovah' that the priests could not stand to minister is that in a realization of the true spiritual principles of life there is no necessity for ritualism or outside worship. The living Christ is all, in all, and through all.

Another interpretation of I Kings 8: 1-11, the dedication of the Temple by Solomon, is given as follows:

A "tent" or tabernacle represents a transitory or perishable body built by man before he has brought forth his inherent spiritual faculties sufficiently to enable him to demonstrate eternal life. The "house of Jehovah" is the abiding, spiritualized body of man, the temple of God. This temple is the result of man's bringing forth all his spiritual powers; when man abides in it he can say with Jesus Christ, "He that hath seen me hath seen the Father."

"The city of David" (Zion) is the subjective consciousness of the individual.

The "ark of Jehovah" represents the inner results of the thoughts that have been harmonized with Principle. The "ark of Jehovah," or of the covenant, was brought up out of the city of David (subconsciousness) because in building the abiding, spiritual body temple it is necessary that all of the accumulated good of the inner consciousness be brought into expression.

The center in consciousness from which this accumulated good radiates and expresses is the heart center, Jerusalem, the city of peace and harmony. The ruling factors in this center are peace and wisdom, represented by King Solomon.

The "holy vessels" in consciousness are the thoughts that lie back of and form the various organs of the body.

The "cherubim," in consciousness, represent the attributes and the majesty of God. They stand for the unfettered truths of Being that must always be present in the holy of holies within us.

son, nobleman's, healing of (John 4: 46-54).

Meta. In the healing of the nobleman's son, the nobleman, representing exalted thoughts, makes more direct contact with Divine Mind, and so seeks to have the healing power brought to bear upon that activity in the subconsciousness (son, at Capernaum) which is apparently dying, in other words, losing sight of the life and substance necessary for its perfect expression.

Jesus did not go down to the sick child, because in doing its quickening, healing work the spiritual I AM does not direct its force into the realm of effects or give weight to adverse appearances, but calmly and deliberately declares the Truth. The subconsciousness receives the word and is comforted, healed. The bodily activities (servants) bear witness to the fact that harmony and order are restored; "the father knew . . . himself believed, and his whole house."

Son of God—Son of man—Christ.

Jesus is referred to as both the Son of God (Luke 1:35; Mark 1:11) and the Son of man (Matt. 12:8, 40).

Meta. Jesus represents God's idea of man in expression (Son of man); Christ is that idea in the absolute (Son of God). The Christ is the man that God created in His image and likeness, the perfect-idea man, and is the real self of all men.

Christ is the one and only complete, ideal man in the mind of the everywhere present God; the "only begotten Son of God" and "hid with Christ in God." The "Son of man" is the thought of this spiritual man, or idea of God, and like all thoughts is subject to the limitations of its own identity. By voluntarily casting off these limitations the man identity may come into realization of its own universality as the only begotten of God. So we find Jesus referring to Himself as both the "Son of God" and the "Son of man," because He had reached a place in understanding where He realized His relation to Being. In John 7:29 Jesus explains this realization when He says, "I know him; because I am from him, and he sent me."

Son of man. See SON OF GOD; CHRIST.

son, prodigal.

Meta. The "two sons" of Luke 15:11 are the two departments of the soul or consciousness. The son who stayed at home is the religious or moral nature; the son who went into the far country is the human phase of the soul, in which are the appetites and passions. Going into a "far country" is separating the consciousness from its parent source. The first step in complying with the law of return to the Father's house is repentance and confession. Confession should be made to God. If we are truly repentant the Father will forgive; He will have compassion, and the bounty of Divine Mind will be poured out upon us.

When we make unity between the outer sense and the inner Spirit (the return of the younger son to his father's house), there is great rejoicing; the outer is flooded with vitality (robe), unending power is put into his hand (ring), and his understanding (feet) is strengthened. The "fatted calf" is the richness of strength always awaiting the needy soul. When all these relations have been established between the within and the without there is rejoicing. The dead man of sense is made alive in the consciousness of Spirit—the lost is found.

Sopater, sŏp'-ă-tĕr (Gk.)—*the father who saves; saving father; savior of the father; father saved; defender of father.*

A Christian of Berœa, and son of Pyrrhus; he accompanied Paul as far as Asia on one of Paul's missionary trips (Acts 20:4).

Meta. The spiritually awakened or illumined understanding, that perceives the saving power of Spirit and defends the cause (as by argument, reasoning) of the true Source of all (*the father who saves, savior* or *defender of the father*).

Sophereth, sŏph'-ĕ-rĕth (Heb.)—*military scribe; tribune; muster master; enumerator; narrator; writer; scribe; satrap; governor; learned; lettered.*

A servant of Solomon's, or a descendant of one of Solomon's servants. His descendants returned from the Babylonian captivity (Neh. 7:57). He is called Hassophereth in Ezra 2:55.

Meta. See HASSOPHERETH.

In the significance of this name we find also the idea of an orderly gathering together, a directing and instructing of thoughts stressed (*military scribe, muster master, governor, learned*).

Sorek, sō'-rĕk (Heb.)—*reddish; fox-colored; purple; vine bearing cerulean grapes; choice vine; noble vine; vineyard.*

A valley where lived Delilah, the Philistine woman whom Samson loved and who was the direct cause of his downfall (Judg. 16:4).

Meta. A very material aspect of life (*reddish, vine*). This life is really of the true *choice vine,* or Christ life; but by the exercise of the phase of the soul that Delilah here signifies (sensuality, sense thought, belief, and desire) the life expression takes on a very material and corrupt appearance.

Sosipater, sŏ-sĭp'-ă-tĕr (Gk. fr. Lat.) —*the father who saves; saving father; savior of the father; father saved; defender of the father.*

A kinsman of Paul's (Rom. 16:21), a form of Sopater, and thought to be the same person as Sopater.

Meta. See SOPATER.

Sosthenes, sŏs'-thĕ-nĕṣ (Gk.)—*of sound strength; strong savior; secure in strength.*

A ruler of the synagogue in Corinth, who was beaten by the Jews before the judgment seat (Acts 18:17).

Meta. A strong, healthful, saving, redeeming thought activity in the higher consciousness of man (*of sound strength, sound* suggesting health, wholeness, *strong savior*), or the idea of Christ as the saving, redeeming principle in man and as the unfailing strength of one's life (*secure in strength*). The Jews (old, established formal, religious thoughts) do not accept the true concept and presence of the Christ consciousness, but denounce and seek to destroy it.

Sotai, sō'-tāi (Heb.)—*turning aside; turning away; deviating from a true course; fickle; adulterous; apostate; revolting; transgressing.*

His descendants were among those who returned from the Babylonian captivity (Ezra 2:55).

Meta. Changeableness and inconstancy of thought; voluntary transgression and turning away from the right and true.

soul.

Meta. The Scriptures give spirit, soul, and body as constituting all of man. Spirit is I AM, the same in character as Divine Mind, or God. Soul is man's consciousness—that which he has apprehended or developed out of Spirit; also the impressions that he has received from the outer world. Soul is both conscious and subconscious. Body is the form of expression of both spirit and soul. In its invisible forces it expresses Spirit, and in its seeming materiality it pictures the limitations of soul. When man puts out of consciousness all limitations and realizes the perfection of Spirit, his body will be perfect; in other words the salvation of the soul results in the redemption or spiritualization of the body.

The ether, the astral, and the soul are virtually one. It is in this realm of the soul that ideas first take form. The soul is not the realm of God ideas, but is the second emanation in the creative law. This is the "garden" of Genesis 2:8, in which are all possibilities. But the Supreme Being lies deeper than soul. The mind must grasp ideas in their absolute, unrelated, and unlimited degree before God can be comprehended.

Man is eternally one with the Father in His divine essence as the divine will, but when that will is sent forth to carry out the ideals of the Father, wisdom, a condition is set up, a state of consciousness called the soul, and its outer court called the body.

This realm of things made, or consciousness of condition, is termed the soul. The body is the outer court of the soul, and an exact representative, in form, of the ideals that are revolving in the inner realms of its domain.

The planet on which we live is a type of every man's soul. The solid part represents the body; the electrical currents that permeate it from center to circumference, and far beyond, represent the passions and emotions of man; the clouds are a fit symbol of human thoughts that have been thrown out by the discords of unwise thinking.

All these are things, and are under-

going constant change. They appear to progress from lower to higher forms; men have observed this progression and called it evolution. This perpetual change is symbolic of man's consciousness—which is going through just such an evolutionary process as is observed in the planet.

The ego is building, and these states and conditions are the evidence of its handiwork.

The difference between soul and spirit—also the difference between the Spirit of God and the indwelling Christ—is as follows:

The soul touches both the inner realm of Spirit, from which it receives direct inspiration, and the external world, from which it receives impressions. But as man brings into expression the original purity of the divine consciousness his soul is purified and established in its primitive innocence.

The spirit is the divine center in man and is always in the Absolute; it does not become involved in effects but stands as the creative Cause of the absolute good.

The indwelling Christ is the Son of God or spiritual nucleus within each individual, about which all our thoughts must harmonize before we can bring into expression the divine consciousness. The Spirit of God is the divine consciousness carrying out the Christ ideas.

Spain, spāin (Lat. fr. Gk.)—*Hispania; the Iberian peninsula; rare; precious; abounding with conies; land of rabbits.*

A country in Europe. In Paul's time it was a Roman province. Paul planned to make a visit there, since many Jews lived in Spain; we have no record, however, that he ever carried out his desire to take the gospel of Christ to Spain (Rom. 15:24, 28).

Meta. A state of thought relating to the animal phase of life in the individual consciousness (*abounding with conies, land of rabbits;* conies being small animals, a species of rabbit, that make their homes in the clefts of rocks).

This life consciousness, therefore, though seemingly animal and limited in its expression, is really founded in something that is very strong, even in Christ

—a rock—and it has its impetus there. Hence when the individual awakens to the Truth about life he will perceive it to be very *precious;* he will look on it as something *rare,* of great excellence and worth, and will seek diligently to preserve it.

Spirit.

Meta. A name for God. Spirit and Mind are synonymous; therefore we know God—Spirit—as Mind, the one Mind, or Intelligence, of the universe. (See SOUL.)

Spirit, Holy.

The source of all manifestation is in mind. This is exactly like the Father—is the Father in degree.

An idea arises in a man's mind of something that he wants to do; this idea is the Son.

He expresses that idea in definite thought—that is the Spirit going forth to accomplish that whereto he has sent it.

The Father is Principle. The Son is that Principle revealed in a creative plan. The Holy Spirit is the executive power of both Father and Son carrying out the creative plan.

Thus we might also say, Father is Being in the absolute, the unlimited, the unrelated. Son is I AM identity of Being. Holy Spirit is the personality of Being.

The Holy Spirit is not all of Being, nor the fullness of Christ, but an emanation, or "breath," sent forth to do a definite work. Thus circumscribed it may in a sense be said to take on the characteristics of personality, a personality transcending in its capacity the concepts of the intellectual man.

The Holy Ghost, or Holy Spirit, is the law of God in action; and in that action it appears as having individuality. From this the Hebrews got their concept of the personal, tribal God, Jehovah.

The function of the Holy Ghost, or Spirit of truth, implies distinct personal subsistence: he speaks, searches, selects, reveals, reproves, testifies, leads, comforts, distributes to every man, knows the deep things of God, and so forth (Acts 13:2; I Cor. 2:10, 11; 12:11).

The Holy Ghost, or Holy Spirit, may also be defined as the whole Spirit of God, and can be known by man only through his spiritual nature. The prayer of the soul alone in its upper room (state of high spiritual aspiration) brings down the Holy Ghost.

spirit, unclean.

"A man with an unclean spirit" is a fixed state of mind in which the thought of impurity is dominant. The man with the "unclean spirit" (Mark 1:23) may also be said to represent sense consciousness possessed with the thought that it can find satisfaction in the sensations of the flesh.

The "unclean spirit" or sense consciousness recognizes one who speaks with the authority of the I AM, recognizes him as the Holy One of God because it is approached on the side of the subconsciousness, in the silence, and recognizes that it is dealing with the Master.

The rebuke of Jesus (Mark 1:25) signifies a denial of sense power and an affirmation of peace, followed by a command, "Come out of him." The "tearing" ("convulsing," margin) and "crying" are signs of the resistance of the sense thought to Truth. The cause of so-called epileptic fits is the spiritual ego's trying to put out a false sense ego that has been built up in consciousness. An obsession is the control of a person's mind by a false state of consciousness.

Stachys, stā'-chўs (Gk.)—*standing; an ear of grain; an ear of corn.*

A Christian at Rome, whom Paul saluted in his Epistle to the Romans. It is thought from his name that he was a Greek (Rom. 16:9).

Meta. A positive, illumined, intellectual thought of substance, subject to spiritual direction and use (*standing, an ear of grain,* a Christian).

stars.

Meta. Revelations of Truth that are as yet remote. The human mind cannot conceive the wonders and immensity of the universe of stars in the heavens.

Stars are sometimes likened to psychic thoughts.

The star that pointed the way for the Wise Men to find Jesus was in the east. It symbolizes our inner conviction of our divine sonship. This is developed in some people so strongly that they actually see it reflected in the atmosphere and, like Napoleon, believe that a destiny is theirs that cannot be defeated so long as this star is in its ascendancy. This inner conviction of our ability to accomplish whatever we undertake calls forth the very best in us, and helps us to succeed where others of equal ability fail. The accumulated wisdom and experience of the soul (Wise Men from the East) rejoice when this faith in one's destiny to do the will of God begins to rise within, and all the riches of wise experience, such as gifts of gold, frankincense, and myrrh, are bestowed on the young child. These gifts represent the subconscious reserve forces of the organism that enter into and form the new body of Jesus.

When the Jesus ego first appears in the subconsciousness it is a mere speck of light, a "star in the east."

Stephanas, stĕph'-ă-năs (Gk.)—*surround; encompass; encircle with a crown; royal diadem; victor's wreath; crowned.*

A Christian at Corinth. The members of his household were baptized by Paul and were the first in Achaia to accept Christ (I Cor. 1:16; 16:15).

Meta. Like Stephen, the highest point of intelligent expression in the body, the head (*crowned*). The head is the seat of reason, and when he who is strong in this part of the consciousness receives the Christ power he is quickened in all that pertains to that realm. (Achaia pertains to the intellect.)

Stephen, stē'-phĕn (fr. Gk.)—*surround; encompass; encircle with a crown; royal diadem; victor's wreath; crowned.*

"A man full of faith and of the Holy Spirit," one of the seven men chosen in the assembly of Christians at Jerusalem to look after the distribution of food among the believers there (Acts 6:5); the first Christian martyr (Acts 7:59).

Meta. The word "Stephen" means *encircle with a crown, crowned, victor's wreath.* Crowns are worn on the head, and the head is the seat of the intellect. Therefore Acts 6:8 means that the intellect has been illumined and has received power to demonstrate in the outer realms of consciousness.

Stephen really represents the man who is baptized of the Holy Spirit and gets intellectually a clear understanding of the truth of man. The heavens are opened to him; he sees the Son of man standing at the right hand of God. The Son of man is God's idea of man expressed. When the illumination of the Holy Spirit comes to one, there is a discernment, a perception, a prophecy of man, given to the one who is illumined. One who has had this experience can see the possibilities of man, far beyond what has been demonstrated. These possibilities seem so real that they become a moving factor in life and the illumined one goes forth preaching them, talking about them as if they had really come to pass, as if all had been demonstrated.

Stephen was in that illumined state of mind, and in that state of mind he is typical of the students today who receive the Truth, who perceive it, not with full understanding, not with demonstration yet, but with an illumination so strong that they become enthusiasts. They are what we call our "newly illuminated" students, and they do wonderfully effective work in those early stages —but their work is done in the enthusiasm of the intellect. The full regeneration has not yet been established in them.

When the enthusiasm of the intellect begins to adjust itself to the regenerate states of consciousness in man there is apt to be friction. We must remember that there are two great states of consciousness—the spiritual and the material. These work in mind and body, concurrently; they are interpenetrating, and when illumination comes a great energy is generated. The activity of mind is increased at a tremendous rate. The thoughts become swift, and they can be felt moving here and there in the organism.

The thoughts in the heaven of man's mind must, sooner or later, find their placés in the body. Mind works through brain cells, and the brain cells are made more active or inactive according to the character of the ideas. Thinking about the omnipotence of the power of God sets up in the body a force, a power, a swiftness, that it never had before. The effect on the organism is that some of the thoughts, which have crystallized in cells, respond. There is increased activity; healing and harmony on inner planes of consciousness take place, but the outer crust does not at once respond. That requires what we call time, and adjustment. In the story of Stephen the delay represents the opposition of the Jews. Formal religion resists spiritual consciousness. It does not receive and adjust itself to the high understanding.

Stephen was argumentative: he wanted to prove to the whole world that the Scripture was true; that Jesus Christ was the Messiah, prophesied from the earliest teaching. He showed and proved that, all the way down from Moses, Jesus was the fulfillment of prophecy; the King for whom they were looking. Stephen became so enthusiastic that he suffered a reaction. The people, because of lack of understanding, could not receive those truths all at once.

Similarly we find in our mind that we can receive such high statements of Truth that the brain cells do not respond to them. Our ideas have been so different that there is no receptivity. If we would avoid a chemicalization such as Stephen had, it is necessary that we go slow in the beginning, that we use caution about setting up opposition. We should listen to Spirit and adjust ourselves to the new ideas that are being poured into the mind. Where there is no receptivity we should not talk to people about Truth. As Jesus said, do not "cast your pearls before the swine."

The Spirit of truth within one is judge as to where one shall express Truth and where one shall not. It is a guide and an equalizer. It will put us in touch with the universal Spirit. When trusting it we know just where to sow the seed; we know just when to be very enthusiastic and under what circumstances to be silent.

Those who observe these points are as "wise as serpents, and harmless as doves." We can escape the hard conditions that make martyrs of Christians, if we know the divine law, if we know when to be still and when to let Spirit work in the silence.

There is a silent force that we carry deep into our mind and can manifest in our daily living. In the end it will result in a larger expression of Spirit than can be had by talking, by proving in an argument to unbelievers that we have found Truth. The enthusiastic believer should not stop all conversation with unbelievers, but he should be wise; he should be discreet; he should listen to Spirit, and drop a word of wisdom here and there. This manner of working will harmonize the within and the without.

Many of us suffer from bodily ills through unbridled enthusiasm. The power of Spirit is thrown upon the organism with such force that there is resistance between the inner and the outer. The outer man must be dealt with as we deal with an unbelieving and material-minded person. Besides the spiritual mind we have a material mind that deals with seemingly material things—it believes that it is body, a material body. We must adjust ourselves to that state of consciousness. If we do not, the little cells of the organism begin to react and we feel the pounding of the stones of material thought. After a high illumination some persons feel a stiffness and soreness all through the organism, as if they had been pounded. The explanation is that there has been the precipitation of a spiritual force into the body and the material cells have resisted.

Spiritual thoughts are real. The body can appear and disappear, but the thought abides. If an arm is cut off the sensation of the hurt and the arm temporarily remains in consciousness. This shows that the thought is the source of sensation and the source of consciousness. Then it must be the real thing; in this instance it is the real arm. In all our work of regeneration there must be a wise adjustment of Spirit and of so-called matter.

The Scriptures portray the Jews and the Gentiles. The Jews, in their highest sense, represent the regenerate. They are those who come into consciousness of the power of the spiritual man. They are the "chosen of God"; they are the people who are coming out of generation, who are coming out of the material, carnal, animal man, into a higher man. The Gentiles are those who are in generation. They are under the law of the man of flesh.

We set spiritual ideas working with just one object in view: the introduction of the regenerate consciousness. When we have received the full baptism of Spirit and have come into the Jew consciousness, we are conscious of a new spiritual formation within us. This is the new creature in Christ Jesus, and the carnal man is transformed, readjusted, and lifted up into unity therewith.

When Jesus spoke of salvation's being from the Jews He meant that salvation is of or from the regenerate man. There is no salvation without regeneration. One must put on a new mind; one must take the ideas that are presented by Truth, and adjust the whole man to them. Every department of man must be lifted up. There must be a new man in Christ Jesus and the old man must pass away.

Metaphysically interpreted, this change is what took place in Stephen. The old state of consciousness passed away. We are told that he fell asleep, but the language expresses an important metaphysical fact: everything of a material character crystallizes, falls asleep; it passes from the positive to the negative pole.

The positive pole of mind is spirituality; the negative pole is materiality. The first is I AM; the second is *I am not*. When the I-am-not thought gets possession of a life, that life goes down into negation, or falls asleep. The word *cemetery* means "sleeping chamber." Everything that relaxes its I AM energy, I AM power, I AM life, falls asleep. If in our daily experiences we relax our hold upon the high spiritual ideas, some part of our life is falling asleep. It may be that the eyes are the "sleeping chambers" of the thought; perhaps it is the ears. But if, with Stephen, we keep making conscious affirmation of the I AM Spirit— I AM life, I AM that I AM, I AM the Son of God sitting at the right hand of the Father and exercising the power of God—we shall see what he beheld. He saw the real man, and saw that man in himself.

Let us see this divine man in ourselves. Let us rise to the standard of the regenerate man, not questioning what is going to become of the race if all people are regenerated. God will take care of that. All that we have to do is to know that there is a new possibility for man, a new possibility for you and for me, if we will accept Spirit and the law of Spirit as laid down by Jesus Christ.

Let us agree to enter the new race, become one with Spirit, and reap the reward of Spirit in a new state of consciousness, a new possibility that includes health of mind, health of body, spiritual understanding, and all other things that we have desired.

The stoning of Stephen (Acts 7:54-60) also shows that the final outcome of exercising arguments and zeal continually is to bring about resistance. Stephen is extolled as the first Christian martyr, and thousands have made themselves martyrs by taking his life as a literal example, instead of learning from it that violent martyrdom for Truth's sake is the result of zeal without wisdom. It is not necessary to be a martyr in the cause of Truth. To obviate martyrdom, or useless persecution, do not argue, do not dispute, do not let your zeal run away with your love and consideration for those who do not see things from the same standpoint that you do. Even though one sees the error of others, he should not be too ready to condemn. If it is necessary to quote Scripture to fortify your cause, do so without heat; then the hard, material thoughts of those with whom you are talking will not fly at you like stones ("they stoned Stephen").

Stoic philosophers (Acts 17:18).

Meta. The opposite of the Epicureans. The Stoics believe that indifference to both pleasure and pain is the highest attainment of man.

stone, that the builders rejected.

Meta. In Luke 20:17 it is recorded that Jesus told the scribes and Pharisees that

"The stone which the builders rejected, The same was made the head of the corner."

This stone refers to the indwelling

Christ, which is the keystone of man's character.

strange fire (Lev. 10:1).

Meta. See RITES.

stumblingblock (Rom. 14:13).

Meta. Stumblingblocks at first sight seem to be in the environment, but a closer discernment reveals that they are primarily in the mind. Then we should not put additional weight into the already existing stumblingblocks by filling them with the thought stuff of condemnation.

Do not judge others, but strive to remove their limitations.

We should beware how we let our zeal to help others interfere with their liberty of choice.

Suah, sū'-ăh (Heb.)—*sweep away; wipe off; wash away; sweepings; filth; dung; sweeping everything before one; eradicating; going afield; meditation; thought; discourse; speech.*

Son of Zophah, of the Israelitish tribe of Asher (I Chron. 7:36).

Meta. A cleansing away of error by the word of denial (*sweep away, eradicating, filth, dung, discourse, speech*). Greater discrimination and true understanding are needed in this activity, that only error may be put away, since the tendency is to *sweep everything before one* in the intensity of the denials. Also, the sons of Zophah show a state of thought that is illumined by Spirit, or is awakened to a conception of Truth but is not yet fully established in the good, since some of these sons stand for that which includes error, limited ideals, while others symbolize high spiritual truths.

substance.

Meta. An idea in Divine Mind; an attribute of Being. It is the spiritual essence out of which all things are made. It is visible and comprehensible to mind, but the five senses of man cannot apprehend it.

One forms a consciousness of substance by dwelling in mind on the idea of the substantial abidingness of Being and the eternal reality of all true substance.

Substance is made visible to the sense man by man's thought. However, he does not see it as it is in Being, but as it appears to his limited understanding.

Men have not recognized substance, because their minds have been centered on effect instead of cause, on manifestation in matter instead of the idea back of manifestation.

"The true bread out of heaven" is spiritual substance.

Heaven is the realm of divine ideas, omnipresent, eternal, and substance is one of these divine ideas.

Sucathites (A. V., Suchathites), sū'-căth-ītes (fr. Heb.)—*entwined; interwoven; hedged in.*

A family of scribes who lived at Jabez. They are named in the genealogy of Caleb of Judah (I Chron. 2:55).

Meta. A phase of the subjective memory of man; it receives the awakened understanding and realization that Jabez signifies, and carries them into activity in the subconscious mind and the body consciousness of the individual (a family of scribes dwelling at Jabez; see JABEZ; also, SCRIBES).

Succoth, sŭc'-cŏth (Heb.)—*interwoven; interlaced; coverts; shelters; protections; hedges; booths; tents; tabernacles.*

a A place in Egypt where the Israelites first camped after leaving Rameses and before crossing the Red Sea (Exod. 12:37). **b** A city of Gad at the east of the Jordan (Josh. 13:27). **c** The "valley of Succoth" is mentioned in Psalms 60:6. "Jacob journeyed to Succoth, and built him a house, and made booths for his cattle: therefore the name of the place is called Succoth" ("booths," margin; Gen. 33:17).

Meta. *Booths* represent temporary abiding places, as compared with permanent houses. Succoth (*interwoven, booths, tents*) refers to the seeming temporary, carnal, material organism of man; this is the fruit or manifestation of the belief that the man who is unawakened spiritually holds concerning his physical body.

The abiding, spiritual body will come into manifestation when man learns and affirms and knows that he is wholly spiritual and that no part of him, not even his body, is material and subject to corruption. Spiritual, true thinking will transform the present material seeming and will bring forth immortality, eternal life, throughout the whole of man's being.

Succoth–benoth, sŭc′-cŏth–bē′-nŏth (Heb.)—*booths of the daughters; booths for the daughters; daughters' tents.*

Some think it is a Babylonian idol, and others think that it refers to tents or booths where the Babylonian daughters prostituted themselves in the worship of their god (II Kings 17:30).

Meta. The apparently physical body of man, in its temporary, corruptible state of manifestation, given over to the carrying out of the lustful, animal desires and emotions of the sense phase of the soul, and believing these to be of divine origin—many people think that God gave man his lustful desires (*booths for the daughters, daughters' tents,* either a Babylonian idol or booths, tents, where Babylonian women prostituted themselves in the worship of their god).

Sukkiim (A. V., Sukkiims), sŭk′-kĭ-ĭm (Heb.)—*dwelling in booths; coverings; shelters; protections.*

Supposedly an African people who came up against Jerusalem with Shishak, king of Egypt (II Chron. 12:3).

Meta. Dark, ignorant, material thoughts and beliefs pertaining to the body, existing in the subconscious mind of man. These thoughts help to keep the body manifesting materially when it should be immortal and abiding (*dwelling in booths, coverings,* an African people who were connected with the Egyptians).

Suph (A. V., the Red Sea), sūph (Heb. fr. Egypt.)—*rush; reed; sedge; seaweed; bulrush; sword grass; (I am—Suph) sea of weeds; Red Sea.*

A part (the Gulf of Arabia, because it abounds in seaweed), if not all, of the Red Sea (Deut. 1:1).

Meta. See the RED SEA for the significance of this name.

Seaweed here gives the idea of obstruction of the pure life flow in the organism of man because of material thoughts, *weeds,* tares.

Suphah (A. V., the Red Sea), sū′-phăh (Heb.)—*sweeping away; coming to an end; whirlwind; hurricane; tempest,* i. e., *which sweeps away all before it; destruction.*

Some authorities have thought Suphah to be a name standing for the Red Sea, but this supposition is very doubtful (Num. 21:14; in margin, "in storm").

Meta. A very great commotion that has been set up in the consciousness and the organism of man. This is a result of introducing new ideas of life and Truth into the mind and the body, breaking up old, material, darkened phases of thought and their resultant corruptible body cells (*sweeping away, whirlwind, tempest,* i. e., *which sweeps away all before it, destruction;* "Wherefore it is said in the book of the Wars of Jehovah, Vaheb in Suphah"). Jesus said, "Think not that I came to send peace on the earth: I came not to send peace, but a sword." Old-established errors and limitations must be broken up and destroyed, that the new ideas, which result in life and peace, may be established. Great commotion often attends this first breaking up and *destruction* of the old limited thoughts and conditions.

supper, great, of Luke 14:15-24.

Meta. The feast of the pure substance of Spirit ever accessible to the individual. Before one can partake fully of the substance of Spirit there must be a willingness to turn the attention to the ideas of Spirit, to the exclusion of all outer attractions.

Having turned our attention to the invisible substance, we move upon it with our thoughts and words of Truth, in faith believing that our words are instantly fulfilled (filled full) in Spirit.

The "servants" (Luke 14:17) that are sent forth are desires. They bid us come to the ever ready fullness of Spirit mind.

The "field" of Luke 14:18 is the belief in the reality of matter and material things, which keeps one from the consciousness of the real substance, which is spiritual.

The "five yoke of oxen" (Luke 14:19) symbolize the dependence of man on the strength of the five senses for his satisfaction.

Marrying a wife (Luke 14:20) is to center the affections on the things of the without, thus becoming lost in personal love.

We may excuse ourselves from the

spiritual feast by pleading the pressing demands of the outer world, but this will not relieve us from the effects of our failure to observe the law. We are spiritual beings first, last, and always. If we do not feed our soul we must not be surprised if it absorbs the medley of thoughts nearest at hand in the subconsciousness. If we do not invite the flow of the pure substance of Spirit into consciousness, the discordant thoughts of the subconsciousness or race thought come in and feast on the natural life and substance of the organism, thus depleting the vitality.

Soul starvation and nerve prostration go hand in hand. When you feel a nervous tension, you may know that your soul is starving, and if you do not feed it the poor and the lame and the blind will be your portion. There must be a constant communion with Spirit, through true ideas, prayer, meditation, and words. In this way union is made with the indwelling substance and the soul is fed and satisfied with the abundance of good.

Sur, sûr (Heb.)—*going off; exit; turning aside; departing; leaving; removing; deflecting; removed; driven out; recession; deteriorated; degenerated.*

A gate of the Temple (II Kings 11:6).

Meta. Elimination, as it pertains to the consciousness and the organism of man (*going off, exit, removing, removed*).

Susanna, sū-săn'-nȧ (Heb.)—*white; shining; brilliant; bright-colored; lily; lilylike; ornamental; beautiful; pure.*

One of the women who went with Jesus and His disciples and "ministered unto them of their substance" (Luke 8:3).

Meta. Purity of soul (*white, shining, lily, pure*, a woman follower of Jesus, one of those who ministered to His needs).

Susi, sū'-sī (Heb.)—*leaping; bounding; springing; swiftly flying; horseman; swallow* (so called from its swift and cheerful flight); *Jah is swift; rejoicing of Jehovah.*

Father of Gaddi. Gaddi was the man chosen from the tribe of Manasseh to help spy out the land of Canaan preparatory to the Israelites' going over and possessing it (Num. 13:11).

Meta. A quick, swift, free power thought, working in the understanding faculty in man (*horseman, Jah is swift, rejoicing of Jehovah, swallow*—so called from its swift and cheerful flight; a man of the Israelitish tribe of Manasseh, Manasseh referring to the faculty of understanding in individual consciousness, and *horseman* indicating vital energy, and power).

swaddling clothes (Luke 2:7, 12).

Meta. "Swaddling clothes" were bands of cloth in which it was customary to wrap newly born children. They represent confinement to the limitations of the physical nature (manger) of this first emanation of divine life, "because there was no room for them in the inn" (outer consciousness).

The helplessness of man's thoughts about the new life can also be said to be represented by the "swaddling clothes."

Sychar, sȳ'-ehär (Heb.)—*drunken; hilarious; merry; deeply drunk; madness; falsehood; deceit; deception; disappointment; foolish; impious; ungodly.*

A city of Samaria (John 4:5).

Meta. Sychar (*drunken*) signifies a confused state of mind or a mixed state of consciousness, idolatry. Sychar is located near the parcel of ground that Jacob gave to his son Joseph; this ground symbolizes the forehead, the seat of intellectual perception. Here was Jacob's well—inspiration through the intellect alone. (See SAMARIA; Sychar was a city of Samaria.)

synagogue (Mark 1:21).

Meta. A Jewish synagogue was a little chapel, where any one could hear the law read out of the Hebrew Scriptures; or if he was a Rabbi he could read out of the law himself. There was a constant stream of people going and coming in the synagogue, and it fitly represents the mind of man, or the phase of man's mind that is given over to religious thought. In the new birth, or regeneration, the rebuilding of your consciousness begins in this synagogue or religious mentality.

The synagogues of the Jews can also be said to represent aggregations of religious ideas based on Truth, thoughts that have not yet received the inspiration of the whole Truth. They are what might be called fixed religious states of consciousness.

The synagogue of Acts 17:1, 2, in which Paul "for three sabbath days reasoned with them from the scriptures," is the established religious thought bred in us by tradition, education, and inheritance. It is part of the very tissue of our brain cells, and holds its sway even after we have fully accepted the new revelation.

Syntyche, sўn'-tў-chē (Gk.)—*to meet; come in contact; accident; fortunate; chance; fate.*

A Christian woman at Philippi. Paul exhorts her and Euodia "to be of the same mind in the Lord" (Phil. 4:2).

Meta. Euodia signifies aspiration, the soul's aspiring after that which is spiritual and good. Syntyche (*fortunate, accident, fate*) is a phase of the soul that is in close touch with the Euodia state of thought, which is aspiring after the highest and best but has not yet become fully awakened to the fact that everything comes about according to divine law, that we all make our own *fate*, and that nothing just "happens."

Syracuse, sўr'-ǎ-eūse (Gk. fr. Phoenician)—*Tyre hidden; hidden rock; luxurious living; secret; violent drawing.*

A very wealthy commercial city on the southeastern coast of the island of Sicily; Paul and his companions tarried there for three days while he was being taken a prisoner to Rome (Acts 28:12).

Meta. Tyre (*rock, strength, compressed*) signifies the realm of sensation in man's consciousness. Tyre and Sidon refer to the region of man that may be termed bodily sensation.

Syracuse (*Tyre hidden, luxurious living, secret, violent drawing*) symbolizes the tendency to hide, to keep secret, the thoughts and habits and knowledge that pertain to this phase of the physical and sensual in man that is typified by Tyre. Thus we find that there is much false prudery in the world and that it tends to keep people in ignorance of facts regarding bodily sensation as it relates to sex. Especially are young people kept from knowledge that they should have in order to protect themselves and to learn to direct their thoughts and desires

aright, so as to avoid much error and inharmony. Paul's tarrying there three days while on his way to Rome bespeaks a work of Truth as being done in the Syracuse phase of consciousness.

Violent drawing suggests the unnatural and turbulent push and pull, the unrest in consciousness, that results from the action and reaction of sense desire and sense habits. Syracuse, being a very wealthy commercial city, signifies the vast amount of thought and substance that man gives to the sustaining of the carnal and sense phase of his being, and the commerce that is carried on there.

Syria, sўr'-ĭ-ȧ (Gk.)—*Aram; Aramaic; highland; high; swelling up; increasing.*

The country called Aram, north of Palestine, sometimes associated with Assyria and Babylon. Its capital was Damascus (Judg. 10:6; see margin also; II Sam. 8:6).

Meta. The intellect, intellectual pride (*highland, swelling up, increasing*, the same country as Aram; see ARAM). The king of Syria is the ruling power in the egotistic, purely intellectual thought.

The Syria thoughts of the intellectual realm that have no understanding of the real (Israel) come down and seek to kill the spiritual thoughts of the heart (II Kings 6:8-14).

Syrian (in A. V., Daniel 2:4, Syriack), sўr'-ĭ-ăn (fr. Heb.).

The language used by the Syrians (II Kings 18:26). It is the Aramaic language, and was used at times by the Chaldeans.

Meta. The Syrians, or error thoughts of the intellect, expressing themselves in consciousness (a language denotes expression).

Syrians, sўr'-ĭ-ăns (fr. Gk.)—*Aramæans*, i. e., those speaking the Aramaic tongue.

Natives of Syria, or Aram (II Sam. 8:6).

Meta. Thoughts of the intellect that resist or war against spiritual consciousness, or Israel. It is best not to engage in open warfare with resisting thoughts. As a rule it is better to apply the law of nonresistance and by spiritual discernment to avoid open conflict (II Kings 6:8-23).

The warring of the Syrians (intellectual thoughts) against Israel signifies the tendency of the intellect that has not been spiritually quickened to kill out spiritual truths that are developing at the heart center in body consciousness.

The meaning of Elisha's taking the Syrians into Samaria is: Samaria symbolizes the intellectual realm, which has its foundation in Truth. It is not wholly reliable but when used as an instrument of Spirit is an aid in casting out alien thoughts and conditions. The intellect receives words of Truth and establishes them in consciousness by affirmation.

The Syrians (intellectual activities) are not to be destroyed; they are to be redeemed, but they must first be denied any power or authority in themselves (blinded). Then Elisha commanded that great provision be made for the Syrian hosts, "that they may eat and drink, and go to their master" (be absolved in the mind that had given them birth).

This transformation is the result of a making of, and acting on, I AM affirmations of divine love, wisdom, substance, life, power. Each demonstration of this kind results in increased consciousness of spiritual power and freedom in mind and in body.

When we have cleansed ourselves of false thoughts we affirm that the true spiritual understanding is restored (this opens the eyes of the Syrians in Samaria). Samaritans were an offshoot of the Israelites that had mixed with the Syrians and other pagan races. They represent an intellectual realm in us that has its foundation in Truth.

Syrophœnician (A. V., Syrophenician), sȳ-rŏ-phœ-nĭ'-çĭän (Gk.)—*Syrian Phœnicia; heights of Phœnicia; high palms; rising up of the phœnix; high redness; high purple.*

A native of Phœnicia at the time when it was a portion of the Roman province of Syria. There it was that the woman came to Jesus to get Him to "cast forth the demon out of her daughter" (Mark 7:26).

Meta. The Syrophœnician woman signifies the intuitive perception of Truth reflected into the intellect from within the soul. Her daughter symbolizes affection, which had an "unclean spirit." This "demon" was evidently love centered on the outer things of the "mind of the flesh"—mixed thoughts, family selfishness, fear, and the like. These are what we find in persons of Gentile consciousness, and in the regeneration they must be eliminated. Thus are victory and health realized through renewed vitality and power (*high palms, high redness, high purple*).

T

Taanach (in A. V., Joshua 21:25, Tanach), tā'-ă-năch (Heb.)—*deep; hard to pass; sandy soil; sandy; battlement; shut up; a gate.*

A city of the Canaanites (Josh. 12:21). It was allotted to the Israelitish tribe of Manasseh (Judg. 1:27).

Meta. The seemingly deep and strong establishment of error in the life forces (*deep, hard to pass, battlement, shut up; a city of the Canaanites*, the Canaanites representing the elemental life forces of man, under sense dominion).

"In Taanach by the waters of Megiddo" Sisera was overthrown and the river Kishon swept away his hosts, according to Judges 5:19-21. The "waters of Megiddo" signify a place of cleansing, a great washing away of error by denial. (See MEGIDDO.) Thus the unreality of error is revealed and is put away (*sandy, sandy soil*). "And every one that heareth these words of mine, and doeth them not, shall be likened unto a foolish man, who built his house upon the sand," said Jesus. Such a house is sure to fall in times of proving, because it is not built on a rock. All error is unreal and will pass away ultimately, since it is not of Spirit.

Taanath – shiloh, tā'-ă-năth – shī'-lōh (Heb.)—*approach to Shiloh; threshold of Shiloh; pass to Shiloh.*

A place mentioned as being on the

border of Ephraim, in Palestine (Joshua 16:6).

Meta. Shiloh signifies acquisition of peace of mind by entering into the consciousness of the Christ presence. Taanath–shiloh (*approach to Shiloh, threshold of Shiloh, pass to Shiloh*) signifies a state of thought that is entering into this peace, or that is at least on the way to the peace that Shiloh represents.

Tabbaoth, tăb'-bă-ŏth (Heb.)—*impressions; indentures; marks; signatures; spots; signets; signet rings; rings.*

His descendants were among the Nethinim who returned from the Babylonian captivity with Zerubbabel (Ezra 2: 43).

Meta. The man named Tabbaoth signifies a thought activity that is still in bondage to the elements of the world—a "bondservant" (see Galatians 4:1, 3)—but is getting hold of the idea of sonship as to God, of the Truth that is eternal and is on the .way to true deliverance: his "children" returned to Jerusalem from the Babylonian captivity.

The word Tabbaoth (*impressions, indentures, marks, signatures, spots, signets, signet rings*) bespeaks the central idea, ideas, or characteristics that identify a thought, state of consciousness, or even the individual in his entirety, making known its or his standing in relation to Truth, to Spirit.

Tabbath, tăb'-băth (Heb.)—*spreading out; extending; extension; good report; famous; celebrated.*

A place mentioned in the account of the fleeing of the hosts of Midian from Gideon and his three hundred picked men (Judg. 7:22).

Meta. The broadening and deepening of peace, joy, and good thoughts in consciousness (*extension, good report*) and of spiritual excellence and true worth (*famous, celebrated*) that result from the overcoming of contention and strife. (The Midianites who fled from Gideon and his men signify strife and contention).

Tabeel (in A. V., Isaiah 7:6, Tabeal), tă'-bĕ-ĕl (Heb.)—*God is good; goodness of God; good God.*

a One of those who wrote a letter to the king of Persia in an attempt to influence him against Jerusalem and the Jews (Ezra 4:7). **b** One whose son the king of Syria and the king of Israel purposed to make king of Judah upon their defeating Ahaz, Judah's king (Isa. 7:6).

Meta. Thoughts in the outer consciousness of man taking advantage of the *goodness of God,* or of the understanding that *God is good.* When the personal man lays hold of the idea of the *goodness of God,* or the allness of good, he uses it for building up and gratifying the lesser self, unless he has been thoroughly purified by the word of Truth and is under the dominion of the I AM.

Some persons who believe in and partly understand good as being the only reality still do not seek to lift themselves to the absolute good in all their thoughts and ways; they pronounce good every relative thing that pleases their selfish personal and fleshly man, and go on living in error and the pleasing of self. Such persons are fitting examples of the kind of thought activities that the men named Tabeel signify. They do not believe in really doing any overcoming of self, but work against the true lifting up of the individual.

Taberah, tăb'-ĕ-răh (Heb.)—*feeding; consuming; burning; kindling; inflaming; place of feeding; place of burning.*

A place in the wilderness, where the fire of Jehovah burned among the people of Israel because of their murmurings (Num. 11:3).

Meta. A day of judgment, or a time and place in consciousness wherein the individual meets the results of the error thoughts that he has been sowing, and a purification sets in (*burning, place of burning;* the "fire of Jehovah" is the purifying aspect of the divine presence of light and love, wherein much error and dross are consumed). *Feeding* and *place of feeding* suggest the entrance of thoughts of substance and Truth into consciousness to take the place of the errors that have been put away.

tabernacle (Exod. 40:2).

Meta. The temporal body of man. The tabernacle represents the temporal body, as the Temple built by Solomon in Jerusalem represents the regenerated, permanent body. In the wilderness of sense, man worships God in a tent, or a temporary, transitory state of mind, which makes a perishable body. Yet in this flimsy structure are all the furnishings of the great temple that is to be built. The outer structure was of cloth, but the altar, laver, candlestick, Ark of the Covenant, and all the inner utensils were of gold and silver and precious woods. This means that the central functions of the body are enduring and that it is the fleshly covering that is so perishable. When the Lord commanded the building of this temporary structure there was a promise of a permanent one. So the body of every man is the promise of an imperishable one, even the body of Christ.

The setting up of the tabernacle means the establishing of a new state of consciousness. Man builds his own mind, his character, and his body—God furnishes the design. The tabernacle was built after the pattern that was shown to Moses in the mount.

The first step toward the building was the giving of gifts (Exod. 25:1-9). A great variety was called for. The gifts included jewels, gold, silver, brass, spices, oil, skins, linen, acacia wood, and help in preparing the materials for the tabernacle and its furnishings, and in erecting it. The gifts had to be willing ones from the heart (Exod. 25:2). We are here shown that we must give up the material ideas of value before we can build the spiritual. Back of these material ideas, however, is the substance that is converted into the new. Nothing is lost in the divine economy. Every experience leaves its form in the soul, and in the divine alchemy may be converted into gold for the tabernacle.

"The first day of the first month" means that you shall begin right where you are now.

"The tabernacle of the tent of meeting" means that a definite point shall be established in consciousness where we shall dwell in the universal substance of Being, which moves as a tent wherever we go.

"The ark of the testimony" is the remembrance of God's promises, which are sacred and are peculiar to each soul. No human hand is allowed to touch this "ark of the covenant." In it we have stored

that indefinable spark which links us to God. No human thought should enter its sacred precincts, which should be kept veiled from all eyes.

"The ark of the testimony" can also be said to symbolize the innate potentialities of Spirit in man. These are kept veiled until man comes into the consciousness of his divine self.

The "table . . . set in order" represents a definite arrangement of thought in communing with Spirit. Upon this table were twelve loaves or cakes of bread. This means that we should realize that the substance of Spirit perpetually supplies the twelve faculties of mind. The candlestick and its seven lights are symbolical of the divine intelligence, inherent in man, which lights the seeming darkness within him.

This "temple" was the inheritance of those who were faithful. Faith must also become substance. Before we can enter into the consciousness of an eternal body we must vitalize with our concentrated thought every part of the temporal body in its inner processes. The table that was to be set up represents the orderly appropriation of the daily needs, and the bringing in of the candlestick and lighting of the lamps thereof is the establishing of the divine intelligence in the inner consciousness.

"The golden altar for incense," "the altar of burnt-offering," and so forth, are the establishing of permanent resolutions of purity, and covenants with the higher law of obedience and conformity thereto, though daily sacrifices are entailed thereby.

The "laver" with "water therein" is the word of denial ever at hand ready to cleanse every impure thought that comes into consciousness. "The court round about" is the outer realm of thoughts that have not yet been spiritualized.

"The anointing oil" is the thought of love, which is poured over all, making it holy or a perfect whole. "Love . . . is the fulfillment of the law."

The bringing of Aaron and his sons to the door and washing them with water means that we shall declare spiritual strength to be the presiding, directive power of this new state of consciousness —not a mere animal strength but a strength washed clean and purified from all the grossness of sense. This declaration of strength is absolutely necessary to the permanency of our tabernacle. Through it is set up an abiding thought action that continues while our attention is elsewhere. Aaron continues to "minister . . . in the priest's office."

Tabitha, tăb'-ĭ-thá (Gk. fr. Aram.)— *beautiful; splendid; glorious; gazelle; antelope; roe.*

The same person as Dorcas (Acts 9: 36).

Meta. Tabitha and Dorcas both mean *gazelle, antelope, doe, roe,* which signify a grace, lightness, and symmetry of soul and body that are of Spirit.

When faith (Peter), the spiritual quality that realizes the reality of the inner life forces, begins its work in consciousness and joins the saints (consecrated thought forces) dwelling in Lydda, there is a renewing of the life consciousness in both mind and body (Acts 9:32-34). Then Æneas is healed. (See ÆNEAS.)

Next, neighboring states of consciousness hear of the works of faith (Peter), and believe (Acts 9:35). Joppa (*beauty*) is the dwelling place of Tabitha, signifying here an awakened soul-opulence in Christ, or spiritual benevolence. When this spiritual force works too much in the outer consciousness it loses connection with the one life, falls sick, and dies (Acts 9:36, 37).

Acts 9:39-42: The "widows" who stand round weeping typify mixed thoughts, only half established in Truth—half truths; they therefore waste their substance in the without. But when the radiant light of faith penetrates the darkness, all is changed. The grace and the beauty of Spirit are again awakened, and Tabitha (spiritual benevolence) is made alive.

The raising of Tabitha from the dead by Peter teaches us to deny away and put out of mind the belief in failures and lost opportunities.

Tabor, tā'-bôr (Heb.)—*heaped up; highest part; height; summit; umbilicus; navel, i. e., height of the belly; mound; hill; mountain.*

a A mountain in Palestine, on the border of Issachar (Josh. 19:22). It was from this mountain that Barak went to defeat Sisera and the army of Jabin, king of Canaan (Judg. 4:6, 12, 14). **b** The name of a Levitical city of Zebulun (I Chron. 6:77). **c** "The oak of Tabor" is mentioned in I Samuel 10:3. The reference here is believed to be to a grove of oak trees on or near the border of Benjamin.

Meta. A high place in consciousness, a very exalted group of thoughts, or thought center (*heaped up, highest part, height, summit, mountain;* a mountain in Palestine, a Levitical city, and a grove of oak trees, oaks denoting great strength and protection). "Tabor and Hermon rejoice in thy name." Mountains always stand for thoughts of a lofty character.

Tabrimmon (A. V., Tabrimon), tăb'-rĭm-mŏn (Heb.)—*Rimmon the good; Rimmon is good; pleasing to Rimmon; exalted good.*

Father of Benhadad, a king of Syria (I Kings 15:18).

Meta. A ruling thought in the sense intellect of man that believes in the power of and works in harmony with that which the Syrian god Rimmon denotes. (See RIMMON.)

Tadmor, tăd'-môr (Heb.)—*Tamar; Palmyra; palms; city of palms.*

A city built in the wilderness by King Solomon (II Chron. 8:4). In I Kings 9:18 it is called Tamar.

Meta. A consciousness of victory (*palms,* which denote victory).

Tahan, tā'-hăn (Heb.)—*bent down; bowed down; inclined; settling down; pitching one's tent; tent place; encampment; graciousness; entreaty; supplication; prayer.*

a A descendant of Ephraim, perhaps a son (Num. 26:35). **b** A son of Telah an Ephraimite (I Chron. 7:25).

Meta. Humble, gracious, prayerful, earnestly desirous of good, abiding thoughts relating to the will faculty in man (*bowed down, graciousness, encampment, settling down, entreaty, prayer,* men of the Israelitish tribe of Ephraim, which represents the will in individual consciousness).

Tahanites, tā'-hăn-ītes (fr. Heb.).

The "family" of Tahan of the "sons" of Ephraim (Num. 26:35).

Meta. Thoughts springing from and of a character like that in consciousness which is signified by Tahan. (See TAHAN.)

Tahash (A. V., Thahash), tā'-hăsh (Heb.)—*thrusting in; breaking; burrowing; diving; badger; seal; ram; reddish.*

Nahor's son by his concubine Reumah (Gen. 22:24). Nahor was Abraham's brother.

Meta. An increase of life activity in the organism. At this phase of individual unfoldment this life activity is more animal than spiritual (commentators agree that the name Tahash refers to the skin of some animal, dyed red; red bespeaks the life activity).

Tahath, tā'-hăth (Heb.)—*sunk down; settled; inclined backward; low; depressed; immersed; underneath; low condition; humility; in place of; substitution; place; station.*

a A place where the Children of Israel camped when in the wilderness (Num. 33:26). **b** Son of Assir in descent from Kohath son of Levi (I Chron. 6:24). **c** Two men named in descent from Ephraim (I Chron. 7:20).

Meta. A lowly, humble, established, basic state of consciousness in which the higher, and truer, and more spiritual thoughts of the individual may rest when needful, while they are becoming positive enough and strongly enough established in Truth to enter upon the decided overcoming of error that is necessary in the redemption of the body (*sunk down, low,* like a corner stone or that which is underneath, *settled, humility, station*).

Tahchemonite (A. V., Tachmonite), tăh-chē'-mō-nīte (Heb.)—*wise; knowing; intelligent; judicious; acute judgment; discrimination; indued with reason; sagacious; learned; reverent; pious.*

Josheb–basshebeth a Tahchemonite was one of David's mighty men, and "chief of the captains" (II Sam. 23:8). In I Chronicles 11:11 he is called "Jashobeam, the son of a Hachmonite."

Meta. A very wise, keen, discerning thought belonging to the wisdom center in consciousness (*wise, knowing, judicious, sagacious*). (See HACHMONITE and

HACHMONI for further signification.)

Tahpanhes (in A. V., Jer. 2:16, Tahapanes), täh'-păn-hēṣ (Heb. fr. Egypt.)—*principle of bringing forth; principle of beginnings; beginning of the world; source of the race; the goddess Taphnæ (Greek Daphne); laurel.*

An Egyptian city (Jer. 44:1). Jeremiah was taken to this city, along with the remnant of Judah that Nebuchadrezzar left behind in Judea when he took the people captive to Babylon (Jer. 43:7-9). This city is called Tehaphnehes in Ezekiel 30:18.

Meta. Jeremiah's being taken to Tahpanhes, along with the remnant of Judah that was left in Judea by Nebuchadrezzar when he took the people of Judah captive to Babylon (Jer. 43:4-7), bespeaks a falling in consciousness from faith in the higher spiritual Truth regarding the source of wholeness and of all good (which source is spiritual ideas) to the darkened Egyptian or carnal belief in human means of healing and of bringing forth (*principle of bringing forth, laurel,* an Egyptian city). This belief breaks down one's confidence in divine wisdom and understanding (see Jeremiah 2:16). The higher spiritual wisdom center is located in the top or crown of the head.

Jeremiah 43 states that the Israelites who were left behind in Judea by the king of Babylon would not listen to Jeremiah, who warned them to stay where they were in order to be safe. Instead of obeying Jeremiah's warning they went to Egypt, to Tahpanhes, and forced Jeremiah to accompany them. The result was that what they had feared in Judea overtook them in Egypt. The inference is clear: when one will not listen to the higher wisdom (the word of the Lord by Jeremiah), but goes to the darkened sense mind for guidance, one is sure to come to grief; the thing that one fears will come to pass.

Tahrea, täh-rē'-å (Heb.)—*quick; fleet; flight; adroitness; adroit; crafty; cunning.*

Son of Micah, who was a grandson of Jonathan son of Saul (I Chron. 9:41). He is called Tarea in I Chronicles 8:35.

Meta. The quickness of movement in consciousness, and very great skill, perception, and judgment, of spiritual faith (*quick, fleet, adroit, cunning, a Benjamite*). To the extent that this thought belongs to the outer consciousness and partakes of guile (*crafty, cunning*), its results will be unsatisfactory and inharmonious.

Tahtim – hodshi, täh'-tĭm – hŏd'-shī (Heb.) — *lowlands newly inhabited; nether lands newly inhabited; new depths; new foundation; under the new moon.*

A land now unknown, mentioned as being between Gilead and Dan–jaan, through which "Joab and the captains of the host" went when numbering Israel (II Samuel 24:6).

Meta. A phase of subconscious substance. (*Nether lands* infers substance that is beneath; and the fact that this land is now unknown indicates a phase of thought substance in man that he knows little or nothing about. Both suggest the subconsciousness, which lies under or back of the outer consciousness and is virtually unknown to the ordinary individual.) These *nether lands'* being *newly inhabited* shows that new and higher thoughts are being introduced into this phase of substance in the subconsciousness (Israelites lived in this land, and Joab, David's captain, went through it with his men while numbering Israel).

talents (Matt. 25:14-30).

Meta. Spiritual gifts—life, love, Truth, substance, intelligence, faith, power, judgment, will, in fact, every inherent attribute of man's being—have their roots in God. All the gifts of Spirit are to be used to man's fullest ability. The confident one uses that which is given him, and meets with the commendation of the divine law, or Lord, and is led into greater possibilities: "Enter thou into the joy of thy lord." The "joy of thy lord" is the consciousness of having done one's best.

The too cautious one buries his talent, because of fear that he will not meet the requirements of the law, which he discerns is very exact. In his caution he does nothing, and meets with condemnation in consequence. The world is full of persons who have a talent that they are afraid to use because it seems so insignificant. The fact is that the one includes all the others, and he who boldly launches out into the activity of spiritual gifts with a single perception of Truth soon finds that there is a steady increase, and in due season he enters into the joy of the Lord.

Industry, activity, boldness, should be the motto of those who lack confidence in their ability to do things spiritually. Cultivate your spiritual nature with the same industry that you do your art or music or business. Be bold and fearless in making the highest claims for yourself as a spiritual being.

Too cautious metaphysicians say, "Be careful of high statements, because you will have to prove your words and it may be hard on you." They are the slothful servants who are fearful and spiritually lazy and accuse the Lord of hardness. They say, "I knew thee that thou art a hard man, reaping where thou didst not sow, and gathering where thou didst not scatter." The reply of the Lord is according to the law of manifestation, from the formless in Being to the formed in man: "Thou oughtest therefore to have put my money to the bankers." Man sows, or makes God manifest. The crop is a perfected humanity, which is finally gathered back to the Father. Thus God reaps where He has not sown, but man gets the credit for activity, for work well done, and is made ruler "over many things."

If any function of your organism is slow and sluggish, some talent is buried in your subconsciousness. Find out what it is and bring it into expression. Do not allow yourself to come under bondage to the "I can't" man. He is the one who believes in limitations and wraps his talent in them. No increase is possible to him. Be positive in Spirit and you will succeed.

Appetite, lust, passion, and the various secret sins of mankind are buried talents. They are returning no increase, because they are held in the bondage of material thought. It is this thought that digs in the earth and covers up many a good quality. Uncover the buried talent and return it to the Lord, with the increase of right use. Affirm that God's will is being done in all your thoughts and acts, and the higher law will resurrect the buried talents.

Talitha, tăl'-ĭ-thá (Gk. fr. Aram.)—*fresh; young; new; tender; maiden; damsel.* Talitha cumi—*damsel, arise;* (*maiden, stand up; little girl, come forth; arising of newness*).

The words that Jesus spoke to the daughter of the ruler of the synagogue when He restored her to life. "And taking the child by the hand, he saith unto her, Talitha cumi; which is, being interpreted, Damsel, I say unto thee, Arise" (Mark 5:41).

Meta. Talitha (*fresh, young, new, damsel, maiden*) refers here to the soul, which is being awakened to a new, higher, and fuller realization of life by the I AM or Christ consciousness in the individual.

Talmai, tăl'-māi (Heb.)—*broken up; scattered; sown; furrowed; brave; bold; spirited.*

a One of the three sons of Anak the giant, who dwelt at Hebron (Num. 13:22) but was driven out by Caleb and the men of Judah (Josh. 15:14; Judg. 1:10). **b** King of Geshur, father of one of David's wives (II Sam. 3:3).

Meta. The deeply established thought habits of sense reasoning in individual consciousness; also the seemingly forceful, daring, confident, yet impatient and intolerant manner in which these thought habits and reasonings assert themselves (*furrowed, broken up, sown, bold, spirited, brave*).

We are told that, as we use our brains more and more in thinking and reasoning, furrows or indentations develop in the gray matter that constitutes the brain cells in the human body. *Furrowed,* therefore, in the meaning of Talmai, son of Anak the giant, bespeaks thought habits of the character that these giants of the Anakim signify. (See ANAK, AHIMAN, and SHESHAI.)

Talmon, tăl'-mŏn (Heb.)—*oppressor; oppressed; wronged; violent oppression; violated; despoiled; captive.*

A porter in the house of God (I Chron. 9:17). Some of his descendants returned with him from the Babylonian captivity (Ezra 2:42). He kept watch at the gates (Neh. 11:19).

Meta. A thought activity on guard at the gate or door of the consciousness (a porter in the house of God, who kept watch at the gates). This thought activity is of the old-established religious thoughts (one significance of the Jews) and is not open to the real Christ Truth, since it is of a tyrannical and violent character. This tends to keep the individual in bondage to old ideas and conditions (*oppressor, violent oppression, oppressed, captive*) instead of aiding him to become truly free from limited beliefs and their results in the outer world. "Where the Spirit of the Lord is, *there* is liberty."

While the porters, or thought activities within us that guard the door of our consciousness, must be of a positive character to keep out error thoughts and invite true ideas, there should be nothing of personal force, anger, or tyranny about them. The word spoken in love, faith, and the true Christ power suffices.

Tamar (in A. V., I Kings 9:18, Tadmor), tā'-mär (Heb.)—*standing forth; ascending; high; lofty; erect; upright; mast; spire; column of smoke; landmark; date palm; palm tree; phœnix.*

a The wife of the two elder sons of Judah. These sons both died childless, and because Judah did not give her to his third son she deceived him and had two sons, twins, by her father-in-law, Judah (Gen. 38:6-30). **b** Daughter of David and sister of Absalom (II Sam. 13). **c** Daughter of Absalom (II Sam. 14:27). **d** A city that Solomon built in the wilderness (I Kings 9:18); called Tadmor in II Chronicles 8:4. **e** Either the same city as mentioned in I Kings 9:18 or another place in the southern part of Judah (Ezek. 47:19).

Meta. Victory and conquest (*palm tree, palm*) through uprightness (*high, lofty, erect, upright*); "And Judah . . . said, She is more righteous than I, forasmuch as I gave her not to Shelah my son" (Gen. 38:26). In the cases of the women named Tamar this consciousness of victory, or conquest, and overcoming power is of the soul in the individual.

Tammuz, tăm'-mŭz (Heb.)—*summer solstice; fullness; waning; departing.*

A Syrian god; the same as the Babylonian sun god. It also corresponded to the Greek Adonis. This god was worshiped in the month Tammuz of each year, which month began with the new moon in July. A great festival was held, wherein the people mourned the disappearance of Tammuz (the sun) in winter, and joyfully celebrated his return in spring. Many myths and legends were connected with this sun worship. Hebrew women were weeping for Tammuz, according to Ezekiel 8:14, this being a great abomination.

Meta. The outer, sense, and intellectual man's worship of the Giver of life, light, and supply. The sense man does not comprehend the true Source of light, understanding, energy, substance, and all growth and unfoldment to fruition and perfection. He perceives only outer channels and activities, and worships them; that is, he gives them the whole of his attention and thought. Therefore, he does not experience abiding, unchanging, unlimited Spirit as the ever present source and substance of his good. He believes that the blessings of life, as well as that which gives them to him, come and go, and so he lacks poise in himself; he gives himself over to the emotions that sway his soul. (See BAAL.) This is suggested by the women who were mourning the departure of the sun in the winter time, when its rays fail to keep the earth warm in every part and so stop vegetation's growing. Later they would express great gladness over the return of the sun in the spring. This all shows how the spiritually unawakened individual is bound in outer appearances of changeableness, uncertainty, and lack; he is not sure of the continuation of his health, supply, life, or of any other blessing, and he is emotional and changeable in his own nature and expressions of life.

Tanhumeth, tăn'-hū-mĕth (Heb.)— *rest; quiet; comfort; consolation.*

Father of Seraiah, who came to Gedaliah to Mizpah. In II Kings 25:23 he is called "the Netophathite," but according to Jeremiah 40:8 this appellative belongs to Ephai instead of Tanhumeth.

Meta. A peaceful, helpful, cheering, strengthening thought activity in the higher, more spiritual phase of man's consciousness (*rest, quiet, comfort, consolation,* an Israelite).

Taphath, tā'-phăth (Heb.)—*drop; pendant; ornament; eardrop; distillation; dew.*

Daughter of Solomon and wife of Ben-abinadab (I Kings 4:11).

Meta. A spiritually receptive, attentive, obedient attitude of the soul in man. This is indeed a priceless ornament, or adornment, to the individual (*drop, pendant, ornament, eardrop,* an ear ornament relating to the blessing of true hearing, which is receptivity, obedience, and attentiveness to Spirit, to Truth). *Distillation, dew,* bespeak the refreshing grace of Spirit that renews and strengthens the spiritually receptive and attentive soul.

Tappuah, tăp'-pū-ăh (Heb.)—*exhaled fragrance; aromatic breath; apple; fragrant fruit; apple region; fruitful place.*

a A city of Canaan whose king was conquered by Joshua and the Children of Israel (Josh. 12:17). **b** A city in the lowland of Judah (Josh. 15:34). **c** A city on the border of Ephraim (Josh. 16:8). **d** A land belonging to Manasseh (Josh. 17:8). **e** Another Tappuah was a son of Hebron, of the tribe of Judah (I Chron. 2:43).

Meta. Perception, discrimination, discernment expressing in different phases of consciousness and faculties in the spiritually awakening and unfolding individual, to abundant fruitfulness and good (*exhaled fragrance, apple, fragrant fruit, aromatic breath, fruitful place,* smell bespeaks perception and discrimination, while the different cities named Tappuah, and the tribes of Israel connected with this name, point to states of consciousness and to faculties).

Taralah, tăr'-ă-läh (Heb.)—*agitating; brandishing; trembling; reeling; fluttering; staggering; drunkenness.*

A city of Benjamin (Josh. 18:27).

Meta. The desire for a greater realization of the divine presence and power has gone forth from the innermost being of the individual. Taralah signifies a result of the beginnings of the fulfillment of this desire. When the divine presence and power begins its activity in the consciousness and the organism, one is likely to sense great inner agitation because of the human, which fears and resists the spiritual, the—to it—unknown (*agitating, trembling, fluttering, reeling, staggering, drunkenness;* when the disciples received the spiritual baptism at Pentecost, some who saw and heard them accused them of being drunk).

Tarea, tă-rē'-à (Heb.)—*quick; fleet; flight; adroitness, adroit; crafty; cunning.*

Son of Micah, of the tribe of Benjamin (I Chron. 8:35). He is called Tahrea in I Chronicles 9:41.

Meta. See TAHREA.

Tarpelites, tär'-pĕl-ītes (fr. Heb.)—*plunderers; ravishers; despoilers.*

Assyrian colonists in Samaria (Ezra 4:9).

Meta. The violent and destructive tendency (*ravishers*) of the phase of intellectual thought that is represented by the Assyrians. (See ASSYRIA and ASSYRIANS.)

Tarshish, tär'-shĭsh (Heb.)—*gravitational energy; precipitant force; hard; hardness; severity; breaking; broken; subdued; subjected; place of the stone; chrysolite; topaz; beryl; amber.*

a Son of Javan, who was a son of Japheth and grandson of Noah (Gen. 10:4). **b** Son of Bilhan, a Benjamite (I Chron. 7:10). **c** One of the seven princes of Persia (Esth. 1:14). **d** A commercial city, or a district, that is supposed to have been in Spain (II Chron. 9:21).

Meta. The *hard,* unyielding, argumentative, battering, demolishing tendency that is characteristic of the purely intellectual and reasoning nature in man when unmixed with divine love and the softening influence of spiritual wisdom. (Tarshish means *precipitant force, hard, hardness, severity, breaking.* Japheth, grandfather of the first Tarshish mentioned in the Bible, represents the intellectual phase of being in man. Javan was an original name for Greece. The ancient Grecians were descended from Javan, son of Japheth and father of Tarshish, and Greece also refers to the intellect in man.)

Intellectual reasoning, with its seemingly hard, intolerant attitude, can enter into the various faculties of mind in the individual, such as faith (the second Tarshish was a Benjamite and Benjamin represents faith). But the aspect of intellectual thought that Tarshish signifies belongs especially to the outer, personal man (the third-mentioned Tarshish was one of the seven princes of King Ahasuerus of Persia, and the number seven refers to fulfillment in the outer). The intellect is very active in the trading, trafficking state of thought that the commercial city of Tarshish signifies.

Yet, regardless of its seeming *hardness* while in its purely carnal state, the intellectual capacity in man is really a precious stone, a rare treasure (*place of the stone, chrysolite, topaz, beryl, amber*). Under the influence of the Holy Spirit of truth and love it becomes softened and mellowed, and it is in time brought into complete subjection (*subdued*) to the higher spiritual understanding and inspiration. The intellect is a very valuable servant, but it should not rule in consciousness; "the wisdom that is from above" should always be given the precedence. This higher wisdom, we are told, "is first pure, then peaceable, gentle, easy to be entreated, full of mercy and good fruits, without variance, without hypocrisy" (Jas. 3:17).

Tarsus, tär'-sŭs (Gk.)—*flat broad surface; flat of the foot; wing; wing of Pegasus; blade; oar; flat basket; mat of reeds; tranquillity; pleasantness.*

A very celebrated city of Cilicia, in Asia Minor. It was the birthplace of Paul (Acts 21:39), and was classed with Athens and Alexandria as a seat of learning and art.

Meta. A group of thoughts in man's consciousness of an intellectual character and bordering on, becoming blended with, the more deeply inspirational phase of understanding that we recognize as being spiritual. These thoughts, though intellectual, are of an even, peaceful, broad, pleasing nature. (Tarsus means *flat broad surface, wing, blade, oar, flat basket, tranquillity, pleasantness.* It was a metropolitan city, noted for its schools and learned men. Tarsus was a seat of Greek philosophy and literature; it is also noted for being the birthplace of

Paul, who in much of his symbology suggests the truly inspired intellect.)

Tartak, tär'-tăk (Heb. fr. Pers.)—*hero of darkness; prince of darkness; deep of darkness.*

A god of the Avvites in Samaria (II Kings 17:31).

Meta. A demoniac thought or condition of ignorance, error, limitation (*hero of darkness, prince of darkness, deep of darkness*) to which the carnal beliefs and activities that the Avvites signify in consciousness give their substance and homage (a god of the Avvites; see AVVIM; also NIBHAZ, who was another god of the Avvites, or Avvim).

Tartan, tär'-tăn (Heb. fr. Pers.)—*embodiment of the law; extended preceptor; greatest extension; commander in chief; general.*

Tartan is not a proper name, but is the title of an Assyrian officer who was sent by the king of Assyria with a great army against Jerusalem (II Kings 18:17).

Meta. The executive activity, or seeming power of execution, that belongs to the ruling sense-reasoning phase of the will in man that is signified by Sennacherib, king of Assyria. (Tartan was a *commander in chief* or *general* of this king, and was sent with the Assyrian army against Jerusalem. See SENNACHERIB and ASSYRIA.)

Tattenai (A. V., Tatnai), tăt'-tĕ-nāi (Heb. fr. Pers.)—*dispenser of gifts; overseer of gifts; gift; reward; rewarder.*

A Persian governor "beyond the River" near Judea (Ezra 5:3).

Meta. A ruling thought in the sense phase of man's being that, becoming awakened to the understanding that right adjustment, balance, poise, and equilibrium are obtained through Spirit and not in outer ways, acts in conjunction with the true spiritual thoughts in their work of rebuilding and spiritualizing the consciousness and the body. Tattenai means *gift, reward, rewarder,* reminding one of the law of sowing and reaping, giving and receiving, which is the law of right adjustment, balance in individual consciousness. Tattenai wrote to Darius, king of Persia, concerning the right of the Jews

to rebuild the Temple in Jerusalem, and after being assured that they were acting in accord with the decree of the king he aided them in their work. (See SHETHAR-BOZENAI, who is named with Tattenai; also PERSIA, DARIUS, and CYRUS.)

Tebah, tē'-băh (Heb.)—*slaughter,* i. e., of animals or of human beings; *killing; slaying; execution; life guard; bodyguard; cooking; butchering.*

Nahor's son by his concubine, Reumah (Gen. 22:24).

Meta. An active thought of or strong belief in self-defense (*life guard, bodyguard*) that is very destructive (*slaughter,* i. e., of animals or of persons, *killing, slaying, execution, butchering*).

Tebaliah, tĕb-ă-lī'-ăh (Heb.)—*dipping of Jehovah; Jehovah immerses; Jah purifies; cleansing of Jah.*

Third son of "Hosah, of the children of Merari" (I Chron. 26:11).

Meta. A thought activity of inner spiritual cleansing and purifying through Christ, Jehovah, or spiritual I AM (*Jehovah immerses, Jah purifies, cleansing of Jah*).

Tebeth, tē'-bĕth (Heb.)—*goodness; returning good; good.*

Tenth month of the Jewish sacred year and the fourth month of their civil year, beginning with the new moon in January. It was the month in which Esther was taken to King Ahasuerus (Esth. 2:16).

Meta. A belief in divine, omnipresent *goodness,* in the allness of *good,* even when the seemingly cold, blighting, barren experience of winter is being felt in consciousness.

Tehaphnehes, tĕ-hăph'-nĕ-hĕṣ (Heb. fr. Egypt.)—*principle of bringing forth; principle of beginnings; beginning of the world; source of the race; laurel.*

a A city of Egypt (Ezek. 30:18). b A form of Tahpanhes (Jer. 2:16).

Meta. See TAHPANHES.

Tehinnah, tĕ-hĭn'-năh (Heb.)—*inclination; disposed with favor; mercy; compassion; graciousness; grace; imploring mercy; entreaty; supplication; prayer.*

Son of Eshton of the tribe of Judah, and the father of Ir-nahash (I Chron. 4:12).

Meta. One's praying earnestly but in a supplicating, entreating manner, as though mercy and grace would come from without, instead of having confidence in the inner Source of all overcoming power and positively affirming one's good until it comes into manifestation (*prayer, entreaty, supplication, imploring mercy, disposed with favor, mercy, compassion*).

Tekel, tē'-kĕl (Chald.)—*poised; held suspended; examined; tried; weighed.*

A word of the handwriting on the wall (Dan. 5:25, 27). "TEKEL; thou art weighed in the balances, and art found wanting."

Meta. The inner feeling of inefficiency, defeat, lack of power to meet the problems at hand, and failure to be what one should be, that takes possession of the very soul of an individual in whom sense consciousness, the outer life with its desires for pleasure in sensation, has been allowed to rule until he has become depleted in substance and strength, both in mind and body, to the point where a great reaction sets in (*held suspended, weighed*—"thou art weighed in the balances, and art found wanting").

Tekoa (in A. V., II Sam. 14:2, Tekoah), tĕ-kō'-à (Heb.)—*striking; driving; pitching a tent; fixing (of tents); fastening; securing; settling; pledging; confirming; trumpet blast; alarm; signal; clapping the hands,* i. e., *rejoicing.*

A city of Judah, founded by Ashhur (I Chron. 2:24). It was fortified by Rehoboam (II Chron. 11:6). Amos was "among the herdsmen of Tekoa" (Amos 1:1). The "wise woman" whom Joab sent to David to intercede for Absalom lived in Tekoa (II Sam. 14:2).

Meta. The establishing in the individual of a more firm and abiding idea regarding his body (*pitching a tent, fixing (of tents), fastening, securing, confirming*).

Tekoite, tĕ-kō'-īte (fr. Heb.).

A native of Tekoa. Here the reference is to "Ira the son of Ikkesh the Tekoite" (II Sam. 23:26).

Meta. A thought like and belonging to the group of thoughts that Tekoa signifies. (See TEKOA; also IRA and IKKESH.)

Tel–abib, tĕl–ā'-bĭb (Heb.)—*hill of corn; hill of green ears; hill of verdure; green hill; hill of eager desire; hill of young fruits.*

A city of Babylonia, or Chaldea, on the river Chebar, where Ezekiel and many of the captive Jews lived (Ezek. 3:15).

Meta. The river Chebar signifies a current of vital thought force that strengthens the religious thoughts of man (Jews) that have been reaching out for spiritual Truth but have become entangled in psychic forces (Chaldeans) and have fallen into sense confusion (Babylon). Spiritual revelation also comes to them here (in the person of Ezekiel the prophet), and tends to join them to the one true Source of all inspiration and strength (Spirit).

Tel–abib (on the river Chebar, where Ezekiel and many of the captive Jews in Babylon lived, and meaning *hill of green ears, hill of verdure, green hill, hill of eager desire, hill of young fruits*) bespeaks groups of thoughts whose ardent desire for good, for God, for Truth, becomes fruitful in bringing about a renewed consciousness of spiritual substance and life, to manifestation of abundant good.

Telah, tē'-läh (Heb.)—*breach; rupture; cleft; fracture; break.*

A descendant of Ephraim's from whom Joshua was descended (I Chron. 7:25).

Meta. A breaking-up, separating, putting-away tendency of the will (*breach, rupture, cleft*). This may pertain to a putting off of error or a breaking up of harmony and peace, according to whether the will is exercised in union with Truth or in personal consciousness. Ephraim refers to the will.

Telaim, tĕ-lā'-ĭm (Heb.) — *young lambs; lambs; infants; youths.*

The place where Saul, king of Israel, gathered his people together and numbered them, preparatory to going to war against the Amalekites (I Sam. 15:4).

Meta. A thought center in consciousness that is of the nature of active life, youth, freshness, and newness (*young lambs, infants, youths*). In other words; fresh, new, alive ideas.

Telassar (in A. V., II Kings 19:12, Thelasar), tĕ-lăs'-sär (Heb.)—*hill of Asshur; Assyrian hill.*

A city of Mesopotamia, in which "the children of Eden" lived. (Isa. 37:12).

Meta. A lifting, exalting, of the sense reasoning or intellectual plane of thought in individual consciousness (*hill of Asshur, Assyrian hill*, Asshur and Assyria typify the mental, reasoning plane in man).

Telem, tē'-lĕm (Heb.)—*overshadowing; oppression; wrongdoing.*

a A southern city of Judah (Josh. 15: 24). **b** A porter in the Temple. He had married a foreign woman, but gave her up at the command of Ezra (Ezra 10:24).

Meta. The higher thought and life obscured, overshadowed for the time being, by the seeming reality and power of some carnal belief in error (*overshadowing, oppression, wrongdoing*).

Tel–harsha (in A. V., Nehemiah 7:61, Tel–haresha; Ezra 2:59, Tel–harsa), tĕl–här'–shå (Heb.)—*forest hill; wooded hill; hill of Magus; artificial hill; mound of workmanship; hill of magic.*

A place in Babylonia (Ezra 2:59).

Meta. A place in consciousness wherein the apparent wisdom and skill of the psychic in man are exalted (*hill of Magus, wooded hill, artificial hill, hill of magic, mound of workmanship*, a city of Babylonia).

The Jews of the priesthood who returned to Jerusalem from Tel–harsha could not prove their lineage, and so were unqualified for service in the Temple. Even so, there is a difference between the psychic and the spiritual realms in man. Spiritual thoughts and activities alone belong to the real and the true, though many persons who are on the psychic plane mistakenly think that they are dealing in spiritual Truth.

Tel–melah, tĕl–mē'–läh (Heb.)—*hill of salt; hill of the covenant; oath hill.*

A Babylonian city from which some of the Jews who could not prove their lineage returned to Jerusalem with Zerubbabel (Ezra 2:59).

Meta. A lifting, in consciousness, of the thought of preservation of life and of the sureness, the inviolability, of Truth, but a failure to cleanse oneself from the errors of sense (*hill of salt, hill of the covenant, oath hill,* a city of Babylonia from which there returned to Jerusalem Levites who were unable to prove their lineage).

Salt represents a preservative quality. "Ye are the salt of the earth," Jesus said to His disciples. By some of the Eastern peoples a covenant sealed by an exchange of salt was considered very binding.

The mind of Spirit expressing in and through man tends toward lengthened life, and God omnipresent in the universe keeps life in existence. Lot's wife looked back and became a pillar of salt. This teaches us that if we continue to long for and keep the mind's eye fixed on the things of sense, which we should leave behind after we have turned consciously to God and Truth, we shall become like salt that has "lost its savor" and is "good for nothing"—we shall be of little worth in either the old life or the new (see Matt. 5:13). Adam and Eve were driven out of the Garden of Eden lest they should partake of the tree of life and live forever in their limitations and errors. So we should be faithful in holding for the cleansing, purifying presence of the Christ to put away every. thought of and desire for that which belongs to the worldly, carnal, and adverse in us; thus we shall become new vessels and shall be able to contain aright the wondrous and abundant life that Jesus Christ came to bring to light.

Tema, tē'-må (Heb.)—*south; southern quarter; on the right side,* i. e., when facing east; *sunny; good fortune; prosperity; abundance; good faith; firm; faithful.*

a One of Ishmael's twelve sons (Gen. 25:15). **b** A people. **c** A land (Job 6: 19).

Meta. Abundant substance and life, firmness, faithfulness, and Truth, stored in the subconsciousness (*south, southern quarter, on the right side,* i. e., when facing east, *sunny, good fortune, prosperity, abundance, good faith, firm, faithful,* a person, a people, and a land). "The inhabitants of the land of Tema did meet the fugitives with their bread" (Isaiah 21:14).

Teman, tē'-măn (Heb.)—*south; southern quarter; on the right side,* i. e., when facing east; *sunny; good fortune; prosperity; abundance; good faith; firm; faithful.*

a Son of Eliphaz who was a son of Esau (Gen. 36:11). **b** A place in Edom (Jer. 49:7).

Meta. Teman, like Tema, refers to the realm of the subconsciousness with its inherently rich stores of substance and good. Here this realm is under the influence of the Esau-and-Edom phase of mind in the individual; in other words, under material thought. (See ESAU and EDOM.)

Temanites (in A. V., Genesis 36:34, Temani), tĕ'-măn-ītes (fr. Heb.).

Descendants of Teman, or inhabitants of the place named Teman (Gen. 36:34). In Job 2:11 the reference is to one of Job's three friends, Eliphaz the Temanite.

Meta. Thoughts springing from and belonging to that in consciousness which Teman signifies. (See ELIPHAZ the Temanite; also TEMAN.)

Temeni, tĕm'-ĕ-nī (Heb.)—*right side; south; south quarter; sunny; happy; prosperous; fortunate; firm; faithful.*

Son of Ashhur, of the tribe of Judah (I Chron. 4:6).

Meta. A subconscious belief in good, in success, happiness, prosperity, integrity (*south, sunny, prosperous, faithful, fortunate,* a son of Ashhur, of the tribe of Judah).

temperance.

Meta. Temperance is the control and satisfaction, under the divine law, of the desires of the soul. It is established in consciousness through a harmonious adjustment of all the faculties of man to the law of Being.

Spiritual understanding is a clear, living, inner knowing of Truth of Being.

Temperance depends on spiritual understanding. Without understanding the soul seeks satisfaction in external things, and this looking to the outer throws the faculties out of balance. The man becomes deluded with the idea that there is satisfaction outside himself, and he gives up to the gratification of the senses. Intemperance is not confined to drinking. Every form of sensation is intoxicating.

The real character of the desires of the soul is spiritual. To be demonstrated as spiritual they should be given expression in spiritual ways. The desire for stimulants is a desire for more life. The only true stimulant is spiritual life, and the soul craves it. Man, not understanding the source and meaning of his desire, fails to direct it into proper channels and thereby misses the mark of satisfaction.

When Jesus said, "There is nothing from without the man, that going into him can defile him," He was talking about the tradition of the elders, and He was showing the people that they should not be in bondage to it. In this connection He also taught them that power is in thought.

You may ask, "If nothing from without a man entering into him can defile him, how is it that intoxicants degrade and defile him so?" The explanation is that the defiling power is not in the thing, but in the error thought of the mind that reaches out to the intoxicant as having power to stimulate and satisfy, thus making a god of it and putting it in the place of Spirit, which alone can give life and satisfaction.

There is little reason for one's calling drink defiling while accepting stimulating solid foods, such as animal flesh. It is illogical and inconsistent to hold that the things that are swallowed without chewing are defiling while anything that must be chewed is accepted and eaten without question. The same good judgment should be used in the choice of solid foods as in the choice of liquid foods.

This common erroneous distinction between food and drink is caused by lack of spiritual understanding, by the illogical thinking of the natural man and by his narrow concept of his world.

His thoughts that consciously or unconsciously breathe out cruelty, injustice, and murder, and a general violation of the law of the whole creation—which law is love—make meat eating defiling to man. Men should follow the precept of Paul: "Whether therefore ye eat, or drink, . . . do all to the glory of God." God is love.

Temple, Solomon's, or "house of Jehovah" (I Kings 6).

Meta. Solomon's Temple is a symbol of the regenerated body of man, which, when he attains it, he will never again leave. This enduring temple is built in the understanding of Spirit as the one and only cause of all things. In I Corinthians 6:19 and in II Corinthians 6:16 we learn that man's body is the temple or house of God.

History says that for magnificence, splendor, and cost Solomon's Temple has never been equaled. It occupied three fourths of a square mile, and cost a billion dollars; yet not a vestige of it remains. Several Temples have since been built on the spot where it stood. So we see that the enduring temple that man is to build is not the outer symbol, but the body temple of Jesus Christ.

When Jesus came teaching that the body is the temple He brought to man the revelation of the enduring temple. We as a race are educated through symbols. The Temple of Solomon and the tabernacle that preceded it were object lessons, symbols of the true tabernacle that God pitched, but not man; of the temple "not made with hands, eternal in the heavens." The heavens represent the consciousness of the ideal in each of us. The real temple idea is a permanent abiding place for the ego. The ego must be clothed upon. Man is a series of conscious projections from center (ego) to circumference (body). This clothing is made of thoughts.

We are told by physiologists that the whole organism is built cell by cell and destroyed cell by cell. The builder of a house uses brick and mortar, and to this we have a correspondence in body building and in character building. There must be pigeonholes where all the different thoughts, feelings, and memories can be filed away, that they may be found readily when wanted. This is the object of the divine body temple, and it is a wonderful structure. It is not only substance, but life, intelligence, power. It is fitted to express Divine Mind perfectly.

All that preceded Jesus Christ was transitory. He came as the enduring man, and His body was "a temple of the living God" because He made it alive. He said, "Follow me"—"ye who have followed me, in the regeneration . . . "

In its courts, furnishings, and observances, the Temple of Solomon represents regeneration. It shows the various steps through which man passes in order to come to completeness in universal Mind, where he is indeed "a temple of the living God."

In the Temple there was first the court of the Gentiles, the outer court where all people of every nation could gather and be in touch with spiritual life; but the Gentiles were not allowed to enter the inner court. Only those were permitted there who took religious vows. These two courts are representative of two states of mind. In orderly process of man's development there are certain conditions to be observed. The rabble from the outer court cannot enter the inner without purification. People who strive to enter without a mental cleansing, a change of mind, meet conditions worse than they had before. In the inner court was the altar for sacrificial offering. It was thirty feet square, and seven and a half feet high. On this altar "burnt-offerings" of all kinds were made. Every person who came to worship was expected to bring an offering: a goat, a kid, a dove, or the like. Here is a representation of the giving up of all animal proclivities in the regeneration. In the religious life those who seek God must live differently from those who are in sense consciousness. There must be a change of mind and a relinquishment of all that pertains to sense ways.

Still further in the second court was the brazen sea, held up by twelve brazen oxen. There were ten lavers also. The brazen sea represents the soul. It is necessary to have a certain cleansing of the whole consciousness from the idea of sin. He who enters "the temple" must realize his innate purity, and if he observes the various steps in purification through denial, he will have this consciousness.

The next step after sacrifice and cleansing is the entrance into the holy of holies. There were the seven-pronged candlestick, and the shewbread, and the incense. The candlestick represents the light of Spirit—which light cannot be explained to outer consciousness. What was within the Temple was invisible from without. The shewbread was the symbol of the invisible substance of consciousness, the manna of God. There is a spiritual substance in the body itself, but only those who can lay hold of it and make it theirs enter the holy of holies.

Incense is a symbol of prayer. There must be a constant going forth of the word of Spirit, proclaiming Truth. This spiritual essence should radiate from center to circumference, and permeate the whole consciousness.

After man has dwelt in the holy of holies he can go still further into the holy place. Here the high priest entered once a year, and in it was the divine Shekinah, a pillar of light, symbol of the Holy One, formless, absolute, without limitation of any kind. In the play "Ben Hur," Christ is represented by a beam of light. He is never seen in the personal; His presence is merely suggested by the light. So is the ray of God, the divine-man ego, in the holy place within every man.

The high priest is I AM. Every one of us is a high priest in his own temple. When we enter the absolute we sacrifice the personal upon the altar, that we may realize the Christ way into the secret place of the Most High.

By observation we see that man was and is being educated by symbols. Our temples become more magnificent as consciousness broadens and we go deeper into the mysteries of Being. Spiritual thought and spiritual meditations are constantly carrying us to the place of ascension, where form is resolved into its divine idea. This was the supreme victory of Jesus Christ. When He came proclaiming that the Spirit of the Lord was upon Him, anointing Him to open the eyes of the blind, a new consciousness came to the race. He opened the eyes of men, and showed them the way into their body temple. We must follow Him in this eternal temple building. He is the only man that ever created a permanent body. If we make the proper sacrifice and enter in absolute purity the way will be easy. But we must have courage and boldness to enter the absolute as Jesus did, and proclaim with Him, "I and the Father are one."

Jesus Christ taught the beauty and continuity of the body temple. This was one object of His ministry. He first proclaimed that His mission was to preach and to heal, and all of His work was to demonstrate perfection of the temple, to establish the true worship of the living God throughout the body, which is God's temple.

Every person is a high priest in his own consciousness. When you say, "Jehovah is in his holy temple," do you think of God as dwelling in externals? If you do, have the fearlessness to say to every tumultuous thought, "Be still, and know that I am God." "Jehovah is in his holy temple: let all the earth keep silence before him" and know that your own God-given ego is speaking.

tents, in which the Children of Israel lived in the wilderness.

Meta. The flesh bodies of man that he puts on and off again and again. (See TABERNACLE.)

Terah (in A. V., Numbers 33:27, 28, Tarah), tē'-răh (Heb.)—*lagging behind; loitering; delaying; waiting; stopping; waiting place; station.*

a Son of Nahor and father of Abraham (Gen. 11:24-32). **b** A camping place of the Israelites in the wilderness (Num. 33:27).

Meta. The movement in consciousness that is represented by Terah the father of Abraham is that of one who has been inactive spiritually—has been a laggard or loiterer (*delaying, lagging behind, loitering, waiting, stopping, station, waiting place*). To the extent that an individual lives in and is guided by the senses, his spiritual development is delayed; but the Lord, or his spiritual inner impulse, presses forth to religious activity. In the case of Abram, son of the man named Terah, this spiritual impulse virtually says, "Get thee out of thy country, and from thy kindred, and from thy father's house, unto the land that I will show thee." Then lofty ideals begin to possess the mind: Abram, or Abraham, *the lofty one is father.* (See ABRAM and ABRAHAM.)

teraphim, tĕr'-ă-phĭm (Heb.)—*givers of prosperity; guardians of comforts; household gods; domestic idols; nourish-*

ers; the Lares and Penates of the early Hebrews.

The teraphim were household gods of the eastern peoples. They were images, supposed to have been made in the form of a man, that were used for purposes of worship in the homes of the people. They were supposed to bring prosperity and health and general domestic good. Even the Israelites used these images much of the time, though the practice was of heathen origin (Gen. 31:34, Judg. 17:5).

Meta. Thoughts tending to the outer only for supply, protection, and all good (*givers of prosperity, guardians of comforts, nourishers, domestic idols*); centering one's trust in the many outer channels through which one's good comes to one, instead of knowing God as one's sustenance and power of development; also the many thoughts and desires that man entertains and gives expression to in outer ways, that should be first of all centered in the one Presence within him.

Man should remember always that he does not live by bread alone, by outer ways and means, but by every word that proceeds out of the mouth of God—by the inner creative, sustaining, energizing life, love, power, strength, and intelligence of Spirit.

Teresh, tē'-rĕsh (Heb.)—*hard; severe; austere; strict; unyielding; stony.*

A chamberlain of King Ahasuerus of Persia (Esth. 2:21).

Meta. A harsh, rigidly methodical thought (*hard, austere, strict, severe, unyielding, stony*) belonging to the outer, sense consciousness of man, that serves the puffed-up personal will (King Ahasuerus) but would put in bonds and destroy the dominance of this will if it did not conform in every particular to the very exact rules that this thought seeks to promote (Teresh was one of the two chamberlains who became angry with the king and attempted to kill him).

Tertius, tẽr'-ti-ŭs (Lat.)—*third; third part; threefold; three parts; triune.*

The man who wrote The Epistle to the Romans for Paul (Rom. 16:22).

The Holy Spirit, or Word in expression (*third*, the man who wrote for Paul his letter to the Romans). Expression is the *third* in the divine Trinity, as metaphysically understood—mind, idea, expression, mind referring to the Father-God, idea to the Son, Christ, or creative Word, and expression to the action of the Word, or Holy Spirit, in bringing forth into the outer that which has been idealized in Divine Mind.

Tertullus, tĕr-tŭl'-lŭs (Lat.)—*diminutive of Tertius; little third; minor third.*

An "orator" who came with Ananias and certain elders of the Jews to inform the Roman governor at Cæsarea against Paul (Acts 24:1).

Meta. Expression in an outer, sense way, and incited by the outer, established religious ideas of the intellect in man (*diminutive of Tertius, little third, minor third*, one who came with the elders of the Jews to testify against Paul; see TERTIUS).

Tetrarch, tē'-trärch (Gk.)—*ruler of the fourth; chief of the fourth part.*

A Roman governor or ruler of the fourth part of a kingdom (Matt. 14:1).

Meta. A tetrarch (*ruler of the fourth part*, and referring here to a Roman governor) indicates the very carnal thought that guides and directs the outer, manifest man, or body of man in its seemingly physical, corruptible state.

The first three steps in bringing forth are purely spiritual—Father, Son, and Holy Spirit, or, mind, idea, and expression—but the fourth step, the outer manifestation, becomes very physical and material, apparently, whenever material thoughts and beliefs are given first place in the body-building consciousness of the individual.

Thaddæus, thăd-dæ'-ŭs (Gk. fr. Heb.)—*of the breast; of the heart; large-hearted; warm-hearted; courageous.*

One of the twelve apostles of Jesus Christ (Matt. 10:3). In Luke 6:16 and Acts 1:13 he is called "Judas *the son* [*brother,* margin] of James." Jude, who wrote The Epistle of Jude, is the same person, the surname being Thaddæus and the given name Jude, or Judas.

Meta. Thaddæus represents the faculty of elimination in man. In the body the eliminative center is situated in the lower part of the back.

It is just as necessary that one should

learn to let go of thoughts, conditions, and substances in consciousness, body, and affairs, when they have served their purpose and one no longer needs them, as it is that one should lay hold of new ideas and new substances to meet one's daily requirements. Therefore it is very necessary that the eliminative faculty be quickened in one, and a right balance between receiving and giving, laying hold and letting go, be established.

Love, tenderness, and fearlessness (*of the breast, of the heart, large-hearted, warm-hearted, courageous*) seem to be the dominating characteristics back of proper elimination for mind and body. Fear, hate, revenge, and the like cause resistance and tension in the consciousness and the organism, thus shutting off elimination, while love puts away fear, and is of a softening, releasing, freeing, balancing nature.

Thebez, thē'-bĕz (Heb.)—*shining; brightness; conspicuous; prominent; seen afar.*

A city of Ephraim in Palestine, near Shechem, where Abimelech was killed (Judg. 9:50). Joab mentioned this place when instructing his messenger to tell David of the death of Uriah the Hittite (II Sam. 11:21).

Meta. The bright *shining* of the light of Truth into and through the will faculty in man (*brightness, seen afar,* a city of Ephraim, Ephraim representing the will faculty in individual consciousness). When the will accepts the Christ light and becomes subject to spiritual I AM, a great change takes place in the individual, a change that is clearly manifest to all (*conspicuous, prominent*). Then Abimelech, a phase of the unregenerate will, is killed—is denied rulership in the person whose will has become unified with the divine will and so no longer functions in personality, selfishness, and materiality.

Theophilus, thē-ŏph'-ĭ-lŭs (Gk.)—*lover of Theos; lover of God; loved of God; love of God; longing for the divine; delight in God; friend of God.*

The person to whom Luke wrote his letters that later became our New Testament books of Luke and The Acts (Luke 1:3; Acts 1:1).

Meta. Divine love—spiritual unity.

Thessalonica, thĕs-să-lô-nī'-eȧ (Gk.)—*billowy; tossed by the waves.* Its ancient name was Thermæ, because of the many hot springs that were there.

A city of Macedonia. Paul visited the city and formed a church there (Acts 17:1); his two Epistles to the Thessalonians were written to the Christians at that place.

Meta. Macedonia is representative of the enthusiasm and energy of Spirit that set the whole man aflame. (See MACEDONIA.) Thessalonica (its ancient name, Thermæ, meaning *hot springs*), a city of Macedonia from which Paul was driven by persecution by the Jews there, represents the burning or heated zeal of the soul in its desire for Truth, but at this phase of unfoldment it is without a sufficient thinking balance to give tolerance and wisdom (*billowy, tossed by the waves;* see BERŒA). Of the Berœans we read: "Now these were more noble than those in Thessalonica, in that they received the word with all readiness of mind, examining the scriptures daily, whether these things were so. Many of them therefore believed; also of the Greek women of honorable estate, and of men, not a few" (Acts 17:11, 12).

Theudas, theū'-dăs (Gk.)—*God-given; God's gift; gratuitously given of God; God's benefaction.*

A man whom Gamaliel mentioned in defense of Peter and the apostles, to show that if their teaching was not of Truth it would come to naught (Acts 5:36). The Theudas of whom Gamaliel made mention is thought to have been a man sometimes called Matthias, a renowned Jewish teacher. This man had gathered together a band of men to destroy a large eagle of gold that had been placed above the Temple gate contrary to the Jewish law that forbade images; but his followers were dispersed by the Roman soldiers and Matthias was killed.

Meta. A belief in the goodness of God (*God's benefaction*), in the truth that life and all good are *God's gift* to man; but carried to the extent of refusal to recognize that these *God-given* qualities and their manifestations can be attained consciously by man only on condition that he conform in thought, word, and deed to the divine law of life and being. (All that God is and has was given freely and fully to man in the beginning, for all time. On man's side of the proposition, however, we find conditions to be met that he may receive into consciousness and utilize God—the unlimited good—to his eternal perfection, abidingness, and well-being.)

thieves, two, crucified with Jesus (Matt. 27:38, "robbers").

Meta. The two thieves who were crucified with Jesus represent the human belief in duality, good and evil, past and future. "Jesus in the midst" represents the steady poise of the I AM. The past is full of regrets and accusations, but the future is hopeful and sees good ahead in spite of the great trial at hand. Jesus tells one—the good, the future—that he shall be with Him in Paradise; but the evil, the dead past, dies cursing. This is to show that after the carnal has thoroughly given up there is no further necessity for an opposite; it is lost in its own nothingness or negation. (See ROBBERS.)

Thomas, thŏm'-as (Gk. fr. Heb.)—*joined; conjoined; doubled; twain; twin.*

One of the twelve apostles of Jesus Christ. This disciple is also called Didymus (John 14:5; 21:2).

Meta. Thomas is the disciple of Jesus Christ who represents the understanding faculty in man. Understanding and will function, or should function, in unison; each has its center of activity in the front brain, the forehead.

Among the disciples of Jesus, Thomas stood for the head, representing reason and intellectual perception. Jesus did not ignore Thomas's demand for physical evidence of His identity, but respected it. He convinced Thomas by corporeal evidence that there had been a body resurrection and that it was not a ghost body that he saw, but the same body that had been crucified, as was evidenced by the wounds that Thomas saw and felt.

In John 14:5 Thomas represents reason functioning in the realm of sense, seeking to discern the things of Spirit through outer signs. The truth contained in Jesus' answer to Thomas, "I am the way, and the truth, and the life: no one cometh unto the Father, but by me," is that the I AM in man, or the Christ, is the open door to the kingdom of God.

thought.

Meta. Thought is the process in mind by which substance is acted on by energy, directed by intelligence. Thought is the movement of ideas in mind.

Thought control is established by aligning the thoughts with the mind of Christ, bringing every thought into a harmonious relation to eternal, unchangeable principles.

The healing balm for every inharmony in consciousness is understanding of the creative power of thought and its relation to God-Mind and to manifestation.

Adverse conditions are built into mind and body by the law of mind action. Ignorant thinking forms the substance of mind and body into inharmonious states.

Thummim, thŭm'-mĭm (Heb.)—*whole; entire; complete; perfect; sound; without blemish; whole-minded; upright; blameless; good; true; virtuous; verity; Truth.*

See URIM (Exod. 28:30; Ezra 2:63).

Meta. See URIM.

Thyatira, thȳ-à-tī'-rà (Gk.)—*burning incense; rushing headlong; inspired; frantic; aromatic wood; perfume.*

A city of Asia Minor. Lydia, the woman who was a seller of purple, was of the city of Thyatira (Acts 16:14). One of the seven Christian assemblies to which John wrote was in Thyatira (Rev. 2:18-24).

Meta. The intense desire of the soul for the higher expressions of life (*burning incense, inspired, perfume*). Zeal is the central thought represented by this church; it is also connected with power and faith.

The following interpretations are based on Revelation 2:19-29.

"Thy last works are more than the first" (verse 19) means that the expression and demonstration, or outer working out, of the ideal, is greater in this Thyatira phase of thought, or shows up greater, than the inner ideal itself.

"Jezebel" (verse 20) is the animal soul

that has control of the animal nature. Zeal acts through the soul quality.

To commit fornication or adultery is to mix thoughts, to get two lines of thought into action. The animal soul is connected with the animal nature; it also becomes connected with the spiritual, and the individual becomes zealous for both the sense and the spiritual. This is adultery.

To "repent" (verse 22) is to change one's mind. One must store only true, spiritual thoughts and desires, and put away sense thoughts.

"Her children" (verse 23) are the errors, sicknesses, pains, and the thousand and one inharmonies and discords that come about because of our zealous desire to do things apart from wisdom (*rushing headlong*). Thus we eat the very substance of our body, and weaknesses result. We must see that all our zeal is spiritual and is used wisely, to build up the spiritual nature only. In this way we can overcome and put away sense thoughts, desires, and activities.

If you overcome, you will raise yourself to the consciousness of power (verses 26 and 27).

"The morning star" is the ideal that is given to us, the Christ ideal, and we must attain it, make it ours.

"He that hath an ear" (verse 29) means he who is in a receptive attitude of mind.

Tiberias, tĭ-bē'-rĭ-ăs (Lat.)—*good vision; observance; ostium,* i. e., pertaining to the mouth; *an opening.*

A city on the western shore of Lake Gennesaret, or the Sea of Galilee. This lake was called *"the sea* of Tiberias," also (John 6:1, 23).

Meta. Spiritual insight into things, discernment (*good vision, observance*), and its orderly expression in thought and word (*ostium,* i. e., pertaining to the mouth, *an opening*).

In the feeding of the multitude (John 6:1-14) Jesus represents the I AM identity in every one. Galilee signifies action, which is the first step in every demonstration. Do not expect results unless you act with promptness and order (Tiberias). The "great multitude" is composed of your own hungry thoughts. They

want the influx of the truths of Spirit into consciousness. Man does not live by bread alone, but by every word proceeding out of the mouth of God. You go up into "the mountain" (state of spiritual realization) and there rest with your disciples (faculties). You are then near a consciousness of divine ideas (Jews) and their fullness of supply (feast).

(See GENNESARET and GALILEE, for the significance of the Sea of Tiberias.)

Tiberius Cæsar, tĭ-bē'-rĭ-ŭs çæ'-şär (Lat.)—*pertaining to the Tiber; son of the Tiber; clear-visioned; observant; mouth; opening.*

A Roman emperor in the time of Jesus Christ (Luke 3:1; in other places he is called Cæsar).

Meta. Tiberius Cæsar refers mainly to the reasoning-activity or sense-understanding side of that which Cæsar signifies. (See CÆSAR.)

Tibhath, tĭb'-hăth (Heb.)—*extensive level; security; tranquillity; confidence; safety.*

A city of Hadarezer, king of Zobah (I Chron. 18:8). This city is called Betah in II Samuel 8:8.

Meta. An enlarging of one's consciousness of equity, of fairness, of justice, or order (*extensive level*); also peace, confidence, and trust (*security, tranquillity, confidence, safety*), but especially on the material plane at first. Later this consciousness comes under the direct influence of Spirit, thereby yielding substance to the upbuilding and establishing of the body temple in abiding, enduring spirituality and life. (See BETAH.)

Tibni, tĭb'-nī (Heb.)—*structure; model; figure; pattern; likeness; similitude; building of Jehovah; similitude of Jah; insight; intelligence; understanding; knowing.*

Son of Ginath (I Kings 16:21).

Meta. An *intelligent, knowing* thought in the higher consciousness of man that receives spiritual *insight* into the truth that the divine-ideal man, the Christ, in each individual, is the divine *pattern, model,* or *likeness;* and that man's perfect inner, spiritual organism is the *structure* or *building of Jehovah.* Part of the true thoughts seek to lift this Tibni thought to active expression in the consciousness (half the Israelites followed Tibni and tried to make him king). At this stage of his unfoldment the carnal is still in the ascendancy, however, so the spiritual is forced back into apparent inactivity in the subconscious mind until a further spiritual unfolding of the individual takes place (Tibni was defeated and killed, and Omri reigned).

Tidal, tī'-dăl (Heb.)—*splendor; renown; veneration; awe; fear.*

King of Goiim. He joined Chedorlaomer, king of Elam, in battle against the five kings of the plain, in the vale of Siddim (Gen. 14:1, 9).

Meta. The very large and prominent place (*splendor, renown, veneration*) that sensuality has in the sense, material, and carnal states of consciousness that belong to the outer, animal man; also the fearfulness that results from sense expression (*fear*). (See GOIIM and CHEDORLAOMER.)

Tiglath - pileser, tĭg'-lăth–pī-lē'-ṣĕr (Assyr.)—*my confidence is the son of Eshara,* i. e., Ninib; *lord of the Tigris; swift, mighty king.*

A king of Assyria who defeated Pekah, king of Israel, and took many of the Israelites, including all of Naphtali, captive to Assyria. Ahaz, king of Judah, also became subject to him (II Kings 15: 29; 16:7, 10). In I Chronicles 5:6, 26 and II Chronicles 28:20 he is called Tilgath–pilneser, and he is thought to have been the same person as Pul of II Kings 15:19.

Meta. The significance is virtually the same as that of Pul. (See PUL.)

Tikvah, tĭk'-văh (Heb.)—*twisted together; cord; strong; robust; expectation; hoping strongly; mental constancy; wound together; assembly; congregation.*

Father of Shallum, who was the husband of the prophetess Huldah (II Kings 22:14). He is called Tokhath in II Chronicles 34:22. Another Tikvah is mentioned in Ezra 10:15; his son Jahzeiah helped Ezra to induce Jewish men who had married foreign wives to put them away.

Meta. Strong desire for higher, truer attainment and development, with the expectation of receiving (*hoping*

strongly, expectation; Israelites, and fathers of men who were closely associated with and actively engaged in attempts to put away evils from among the Israelitish and Jewish people). These thought attitudes that the two men named Tikvah signify become a *cord* (*twisted together, wound together*) that helps to link the individual with God. They also attract other ideals of like character (*assembly, congregation*), thus adding to their strength and executive power.

Tilon, tī'-lŏn (Heb.)—*hung up; suspended; pendulous; balanced; obstinate; stubborn; murmuring; scorning; mocking; gift.* The foregoing definitions come from three different Hebrew roots. The definitions that are most likely to be correct are those from *obstinate* to *mocking.*

Son of Shimon, of the tribe of Judah (I Chron. 4:20).

Meta. The almost universal tendency of individuals to grumble and complain (*murmuring*) because of things as they appear. The tendency also to resist inwardly (*obstinate, stubborn*) the Spirit that holds sway in one, even after one has accepted Truth to some degree. Thus one's realization and manifestation of good are delayed (*hung up, suspended*). We must all learn to put away complaining and doubting; we must ever praise God for the good that we desire, that is ours all the time in Spirit. Thus do we make ourselves open and receptive to the things of Spirit, to the good that will become manifest to us as we lay hold of it with thanksgiving.

Timæus, tī-mæ'-ŭs (Gk. fr. Heb.)—*contaminated; defiled; unclean; impure; polluted; infamous; profaned.*

Father of Bartimæus, a blind beggar who was healed by Jesus (Mark 10:46).

Meta. A phase of consciousness that is *contaminated* with error (*defiled, polluted, infamous, profaned*), which is the result of the race habit of attributing honor and precedence to old-established religious beliefs and customs to the exclusion of present spiritual inspiration (a Jewish man, the father of the blind beggar, Bartimæus; see BARTIMÆUS).

time.

Meta. Outer divisions of time into minutes, hours, days, weeks, and so forth are man-made. From the spiritual viewpoint there is no such thing as time in the way that man has come to regard it. With God a thousand years are as one day and one day is as a thousand years.

Time signifies the measure of events. The events are the main thing and they should always be so recognized, else the measure of them assumes undue importance. Divisions of time signify degrees of unfoldment.

Men have gone insane working with Daniel's "time and times and half a time" and other prophecies, such as the 24th chapter of Matthew, trying to calculate by literal interpretation of Scripture the date on which the world would come to an end, not discerning the spiritual meaning of these writings. All this comes from believing man's idea of time to be a reality. Eternity is not an endless number of years, and things that are spiritual and eternal cannot be measured by days and months and years.

One can overcome the spirit of hurry by quietly declaring: *"I am not in bondage to any false idea of time. I, with God, inhabit eternity, and the divine order of God's universe is manifest in my mind and in all my affairs."*

Timna (in A. V., Genesis 36:40 and I Chronicles 1:51, Timnah), tĭm′-nȧ (Heb.)—*withheld; restrained; forbidden.*

a Concubine to Eliphaz, Esau's son, and mother of Amalek (Gen. 36:12, 22). **b** A chief of Esau, or of Edom (Gen. 36:40).

Meta. A restricting, curbing influence (*withheld, restrained, forbidden*) that is ever at work even in the soul of man and in his body consciousness. This influence is the result of the power and the perfection of Spirit that are inherent in every desire of man, no matter how materially these desires may be interpreted by man's carnal thoughts and tendencies. This restricting influence is good; it is very necessary until man has really entered into the regeneration and has lifted his desires, thoughts, and expressions to the Christ standard. If there were no restraint to the carnal mind in man, and to its activities, man would destroy himself utterly.

Timnah (in A. V., Genesis 38:12 and Judges 14:1-5, Timnath; Joshua, 19:43, Thimnathah), tĭm′-näh (Heb.)—*part; portion; number; lot; allotment; assignment.*

a A Canaanitish city. Judah went up to Timnah to his sheep shearers (Gen. 38:12). **b** A city of Judah (Josh. 15:10, 57). **c** A city of Dan (Josh. 19:43); however, this city evidently remained in the hands of the Philistines, for some years at least; it was the home of the Philistine woman whom Samson loved and desired to marry (Judg. 14:1, 2).

Meta. The error race belief that a share of the life forces in man rightly belongs to the use of the purely animal, physical, and sense phase of his being. (Timnah means *portion, allotment;* it was a Canaanitish city, where Judah kept his sheep. Sheep refer to the pure, natural life of the organism, and Canaanites represent the elemental life forces in man.)

While two of the cities by this name are mentioned as belonging to the Israelites (the tribes of Judah and Dan), the one in Dan (judgment) remained for a long time at least in possession of the Philistines (the outer senses). In Judges 14:5, the "vineyards of Timnah" are mentioned. Vineyards and grapes refer to life. The Philistine women to whom Samson attached himself, and who were the cause of his downfall, signify sensuality.

Timnath – heres, tĭm′-năth – hē′-rĕṣ (Heb.)—*portion of Heres; portion of the sun.*

A city in the hill country of Ephraim. It was the home and burial place of Joshua (Judg. 2:9).

Meta. As an individual, under the leadership of some central ideal such as Joshua signifies, succeeds in bringing all his faculties and forces into subservience to this central ideal, the ideal itself seems to die or to be merged into the general activity of his being as a whole (Joshua died and was buried at Timnath–heres). Thus light is diffused to a greater degree throughout one's being. This is the *portion of the sun,* or *portion of Heres.*

When the central idea is absorbed by the being the individual becomes *doubly fruitful* (a meaning of Ephraim; Joshua was an Ephraimite, and Timnath–heres was in the hill country of Ephraim) and his consciousness of creative power is greatly increased. (Timnath–serah, the more correct name of this city, and meaning *fruitful, productive, a multiplying portion, portion of redundancy,* carries out this same idea.) In this state of greatly increased consciousness of creative power it is not long before there is a great accumulation of new forces, and unless they are definitely directed the individual encounters difficulties and is likely to be drawn back into materiality. One should be very watchful to avoid the condition that later overcame the Israelites, who drifted into idolatry and worshiped Baal and other heathen gods.

Timnath – serah, tĭm'–năth – sē'–răh (Heb.)—*remaining portion; part; part that runs over; part of redundancy; portion of excess; fruitful, productive,* or *multiplying portion.*

The same city as Timnath–heres. It was the inheritance of Joshua, in the mountains of Ephraim, in the land of Canaan or Palestine (Josh. 19:50).

Meta. See TIMNATH–HERES.

Timnite, tĭm'–nīte (fr. Heb.).

A native of Timnah. Here the reference is to Samson's father-in-law, who lived in Timnah (Judg. 15:6).

Meta. A thought that springs from and belongs to that in consciousness which Timnah signifies. (See TIMNAH.)

Timon, tī'–mŏn (Gk. fr. Heb.)—*upright; honorable; sound; whole; valuable; precious.*

A Christian man at Jerusalem (Acts 6:5).

Meta. Soundness and uprightness of thought, integrity; also understanding of the great worth of spiritual substance and life, of words of Truth as the sustenance and strength of the true thoughts and activities of one's consciousness (*upright, sound, valuable, whole, honorable, precious*). Timon was a man full of wisdom and of the Spirit, who was chosen to help distribute provisions among the believers in Jerusalem, to see that none was overlooked in the daily ministration. It is by words of Truth that one's consciousness is fed with spiritual food—spiritual life and substance.

Timothy, tĭm'–ŏ–thў (Gk.)—*worshiping God; honored of God; honoring God; veneration of God; prized of God; valued of God.*

A Christian convert, who helped Paul much in his ministry (Acts 16:1; I Tim. 1:2).

Meta. Inspired reason united with faith; also zeal.

The word Timothy means *worshiping God, honoring God, honored of God, prized of God.* He was "the son of a Jewess that believed; but his father was a Greek." A Greek symbolizes intellectual reasoning. The Jews often called any Gentile by the term "Greek." Gentiles signify the outer sense consciousness in man. "A Jewess that believed" would have reference here to our faith in God and to our love for Him. Timothy therefore represents an idea in us that has its inception in a union between our intellectual reasoning and our inner spiritual qualities of faith and love. So we understand Timothy to symbolize inspired reason united with faith and zeal (Paul, in II Timothy 1:5, writes of the unfeigned faith that was in Timothy, and that dwelt first in his grandmother Lois, and in his mother Eunice).

Tiphsah, tĭph'–săh (Heb.)—*crossing over; passage; ford; crossing; fording place.*

A city on the western shore of the Euphrates River, at a fording place that was under Solomon's command (I Kings 4:24). Later this city was captured and its inhabitants were destroyed by Menahem, son of Gadi, who killed Shallum, king of Israel, and reigned in his stead (II Kings 15:16).

Meta. A consciousness of peace, which protects the true and harmonious *passage,* or transition, of thoughts to and fro across the network of nerves in the organism of man (*ford;* the Euphrates River signifies the nervous system in man, and Tiphsah was a city at a very prominent fording place of this river; it was owned by Solomon, who represents peace).

Later Tiphsah was captured and its inhabitants were destroyed by Menahem, king of Israel, because they would not accept him in place of the former king whom he had killed. This indicates the great inharmony that occurs when the will guided by ambitious human desire alone, without the consciousness of love and wisdom, attempts to control the nervous system and to direct the thoughts (Menahem, son of Gadi, signifies the will ruling by ambitious human desire alone, with the idea of and belief in personal force, and not guided by wisdom).

Tiras, tī'-răs (Heb.)—*formative faculty; determination of forms; thought; imagination; conception; desire; longing.*

Youngest of the seven sons of Japheth, son of Noah (Gen. 10:2).

Meta. The *formative faculty* of man, the *imagination*, made active in the mind of the individual by the inner *longing* of the soul (*desire*), which ever leads to unfoldment Godward. As the seventh son of Japheth, Tiras signifies a certain fullness or completeness of that for which Japheth stands, the mental phase of man's being. The power to think, to image in the mind, is the formative power in man. In its highest aspect the formative faculty or imagination is a spiritual quality.

Tirathites, tī'-răth-ītes (fr. Heb.)——*openings; cleavages; gates; doors; courts; porters; gatekeepers.*

A family of scribes that lived at Jabez (I Chron. 2:55).

Meta. Thoughts that stand at the entrance to the inner consciousness (*openings, doors, gatekeepers*) to receive and transcribe upon the memory, the subconscious mind, all ideas relating to that which Jabez signifies (a family of scribes that lived in Jabez. See SCRIBES and JABEZ.)

Tirhakah, tīr'-hă-kăh (Heb. fr. Ethiop.)—*exalted; searcher; inquirer; beholder.*

An Ethiopian king who fought against Sennacherib, king of Assyria, at the time that Sennacherib was warring against Hezekiah, king of Judah (II Kings 19:9).

Meta. A ruling thought over the phase of man's being that has been looked on as purely physical and material (king of Ethiopia). But this ruling thought perceives, and is aspiring to, higher and more spiritual understanding and realization for the body (*exalted, searcher,*

inquirer, beholder). Therefore it wars against the ruling sense intellect (king of Assyria) that continues to hold the seemingly physical consciousness and organism of man under the old error, material thought as long as it can.

Tirhanah, tīr'-hă-năh (Heb.)—*bending; inclination; kindness; favor; condescension.*

Son of Caleb, by Maacah his concubine (I Chron. 2:48).

Meta. A humble, kindly thought tendency, not stiff or unbending, in the enthusiastic, faith faculty of mind that Caleb signifies (*bending, kindness, inclination, favor, condescension*; a son of Caleb).

Tiria, tīr'-ĭ-à (Heb.)—*agitation; trembling; excitement; reverence; worship; piety; awe; fear; dread.*

Son of Jehallelel, of the tribe of Judah (I Chron. 4:16).

Meta. An undefined *fear* or *dread*, an inner *agitation, trembling,* or *excitement,* that sometimes comes over the personal in us when by means of prayer and praise (see JUDAH and JEHALLELEL) we have entered a very strong realization of the presence of God. We have not known that we are in truth spiritual; therefore we stand in awe, at times amounting to fear and dread, of God. Especially is this so when we come "face to face" with Him at the center of our being.

Tirzah, tīr'-zăh (Heb.) — *delight; pleasure; pleasantness; pleasing; favorable; loving; kindness; graciousness; approbation; conciliation; benevolence; inclination; desire; will.*

a One of the five daughters of Zelophehad son of Hepher, of the tribe of Manasseh (Num. 26:33). **b** A Canaanitish city whose king was defeated by Joshua and the Children of Israel (Josh. 12:24). Baasha, king of Israel, lived and was buried in Tirzah (I Kings 15:21; 16:6); and Omri, king of Israel, reigned six years in Tirzah (I Kings 16:23; see Song of Sol. 6:4).

Meta. A very delightful aspect of thought and of soul (*delight, pleasantness, pleasing, benevolence;* the name of an Israelitish woman, and of a Canaanitish city that was taken by the Israelites under Joshua).

The foundation of the delightful phase of thought that the city of Tirzah signifies is outside of Truth; therefore the thoughts and acts of one who dwells in it wander farther and farther into error. Omri bought the hill Samaria (I Kings 16:23, 24), which means an exaltation of personality, and set up a city or center there. In the beginning this reign of Omri has its pleasant aspects. "Six years reigned he in Tirzah."

Tishbite, tĭsh'-bīte (fr. Heb.)—*carrying off; appropriating; captivating; capturing; leading away; making a prisoner; leading captive.*

A native of the town of Tishbi, or Thisbe, of Naphtali; Elijah the prophet is called a Tishbite (I Kings 17:1).

Meta. Elijah the prophet signifies the spiritual I AM of man's consciousness. This I AM, when in activity in one's higher thoughts (Israel), is a Tishbite, one that makes captive, brings into subjection to Spirit (*appropriating, captivating, leading captive*), and in time brings to the Christ standard, all one's thoughts and activities.

Titus, tī'-tŭs (Gk. fr. Lat.)—*titled; honorable; renowned; glorious; pretext; pleasant; pleasing.*

A Grecian man who was converted to the Christian faith by Paul (Gal. 2:1, 3; Tit. 1:4).

Meta. A *pleasing*, agreeable, and *honorable* attitude of mind (*pleasant, honorable, titled, renowned*) that accompanies the word of Truth in its restoring work throughout the organism and the consciousness of man (Titus was a fellow worker with Paul in the ministry).

In Acts 18:7 Paul, the word of Truth, goes into the house or body consciousness, typified here by Titus Justus, and speaks the word to many Gentiles—outer worldly thoughts.

In II Timothy 4:10 it is not clear whether Titus forsook Paul and went to Dalmatia or Paul sent him there to preach. Dalmatia means *deceitful.* Unless it is established in a very strong sense of honor the attitude of mind that seeks always to please others (Titus) is likely to become deceptive (*pretext*), in its attempts.

Tizite, tī'-zīte (fr. Heb.)—*coming forth; springing up; germinating; sprouting; going forth; extending; spreading; broadcasting; scattering; publishing.*

Joha, one of David's mighty men, was called "the Tizite" (I Chron. 11:45).

Meta. A spreading and enlarging of the idea of the omnipresence and abidingness of divine life and love throughout the consciousness (*germinating, scattering, going forth, extending, publishing;* see JOHA).

Toah, tō'-ăh (Heb.)—*sunk down; immersed; depressed; humble; lowly; underneath; prostrated; bowed down; downcast; inferior; declining; weakness.*

A Levite, an ancestor of Samuel (I Chron. 6:34). He is called Nahath in I Chronicles 6:26. Tohu of I Samuel 1:1, is the same name, apparently, and the same lineage; here the men given in the lineage are said to be of the hill country of Ephraim.

Meta. A *lowly, humble* attitude of thought, to the point of negativeness and dejection (*sunk down, bowed down, depressed, prostrated, downcast*). The meek, humble attitude of mind is good. One must abide in the divine qualities of joy, strength, power, and assurance also, however, that one may avoid negative tendencies that are deteriorative (*inferior, declining, weakness*) instead of upbuilding and vitalizing.

Tob, tŏb (Heb.)—*good; whole; in good health; healthy; wholesome; fair; pleasant; beautiful; much; great; abundant; benign; benevolent; kind; well-disposed; upright; honest; joyous; happy; fruitful.*

The name of the land to which Jephthah fled when his brothers drove him from home, and the land where he lived until his people came to ask him to lead them in battle against the Ammonites (Judg. 11:3, 5).

Meta. A consciousness of that which is *good, wholesome,* honorable, *upright, joyous,* and true; also a consciousness of abundance. Everything that is good is contained in that which Tob signifies. (See JEPHTHAH.) In the significance of the Tob that is mentioned in II Samuel 10:6, 8, at least, the consciousness of good must be centered in outer seeming instead of Truth.

Tob–adonijah, tŏb–ăd-ŏ-nī'-jäh (Heb.) —*my Lord Jehovah is good; the Lord Jehovah is good; goodness of the Lord Jah.*

One of the Levites whom Jehoshaphat sent throughout Judah to teach the book of the law to the people (II Chron. 17:8).

Meta. An acknowledgment of God as good. Especially does this refer to God in His character as I AM and as divine law—the working out of the divine idea of man into manifestation (*my Lord Jehovah is good, goodness of the Lord Jah;* "Lord" refers to God as law, while "Jehovah" is the Christ, or perfect-man idea in Divine Mind, and exists as the true self, the spiritual I AM, of every individual).

Tobiah, tŏ-bī'-äh (Heb.)—*Jehovah is good; Jah is good; goodness of Jehovah.*

An Ammonite, a servant of Sanballat the Horonite, who hindered Nehemiah and the Jews in their work of rebuilding Jerusalem's wall and in reëstablishing the worship of God in the Temple (Neh. 2:10, 19). It seems that because of intermarriage some of the chief Jewish men were allied to Tobiah, and he was given a chamber in the Temple; but Nehemiah cast him and his goods out (Neh. 6:17-19; 13:4-9). "The children of Tobiah" were among those who returned from the Babylonian captivity with Zerubbabel, but were unable to prove their lineage as Jews (Ezra 2:60).

Meta. The Ammonites are a wild, uncultivated state of consciousness, which thoughts of sensuality, sin, and ignorance have formed in the outer, worldly phase of man's being. Tobiah is one of the ruling thoughts in the Ammonitish phase of mind. This Tobiah thought is very deceptive, and is sometimes believed to be of a true spiritual character; but it is not. While it acknowledges the Christ Truth to be good, and professes to believe in the law of God and in the divine goodness (*Jehovah is good, goodness of Jehovah*), it does not seek to lift itself to the spiritual plane. It continues to express in its old error ways and thus hinders the true overcoming of the individual— the true rebuilding of the body temple. It must be discovered for what it is and must be cast out of the Temple (man's consciousness and body) completely with all its goods—all the thought substance that it has gathered about it.

Tobijah, tŏ-bī'-jäh (Heb.)—*Jehovah is good; goodness of Jehovah; Jah's goodness; pleasing unto Jah.*

a One of the Levites whom Jehoshaphat sent throughout Judah to teach the law to the people (II Chron. 17:8). **b** A Jewish captive from whom Zechariah was to take silver and gold to make a crown for Joshua the son of Jehozadak, the high priest (Zech. 6:10, 14).

Meta. Thoughts, belonging to the high and spiritual phase of man, that, having laid hold of the idea of divine goodness, aid in establishing the consciousness of the individual in wisdom and substance (*Jehovah is good, goodness of Jah, Jah's goodness*).

Tochen, tō'-chĕn (Heb.)—*made even; leveled; poised; weighed out; meted; proved; tried; set up; established; adjusted by plumb or level; made equal; task; portion.*

A city of Simeon (I Chron. 4:32).

Meta. A group of thoughts in the attentive, obedient quality of mind that the Israelitish tribe of Simeon signifies (a city of Simeon), which is of an examining, weighing, discriminating, adjusting, evening character (*made even, leveled, poised, weighed out, proved, tried, adjusted by plumb or level, meted, made equal*). *Established* and *set up* point to something made firm and stable. This is good, so long as the thought of limitation is not allowed to enter (limitation may be suggested in *portion*).

Togarmah, tŏ-gär'-mäh (Heb.)—*universal centripetal force; centralizing energy; density; gravitation; precipitation; compactness; bony; hard; strong.*

a A son of Gomer and grandson of Japheth, son of Noah (Gen. 10:3); **b** his descendants (Ezek. 38:6).

Meta. Strength and a drawing, centralizing force and energy, but of the outer man rather than of the inner spiritual understanding and therefore carried to the point of very great hardness and selfishness (*centralizing energy, gravitation, density, compactness, bony, hard, strong*). The statement, "They of the house of Togarmah" traded for the wares of Tyre "with horses and war-horses and mules" (Ezek. 27:14), signifies that this strong, drawing, concentrating energy lays hold of the vital forces of man's being and uses them for the keeping up of that in consciousness which Tyre represents. (See TYRE.)

Tohu, tō'-hū (Heb.)—*sunk down; immersed; depressed; humble; lowly; underneath; prostrated; bowed down; downcast; inferior; declining; weakness.*

An ancestor of Samuel (I Sam. 1:1). Toah of I Chronicles 6:34, is the same name.

Meta. See TOAH.

Toi, tō'-ī (Heb.)—*wandering; straying from a path; error; impiety; idolatry; ungodliness.*

King of Hamath. He sent his son Joram to David with blessings and with gifts—vessels of gold and silver—because David had defeated Hadadezer, king of Zobah, who had also been at war with Toi (II Sam. 8:9).

Meta. The indefinite, unsettled, vacillating, and seemingly untrue phase of thought that is the central characteristic of the Hamath state of consciousness (*straying from a path, error, wandering, impiety,* king of Hamath; Hamath signifies confidence in material conditions rather than trust in God). However, this Toi thought recognizes and gives substance to divine love (David) when it triumphs over the false reasoning of the intellect guided by the senses (Syrians).

Tola, tō'-là (Heb.)—*licking; swallowing; a worm; coccus worm; coccus color; crimson; scarlet; very red; crimson cloth.*

a Son of Issachar and grandson of Jacob (Gen. 46:13). **b** The son of Puah of the Israelitish tribe of Issachar. This Tola was a judge of Israel for twenty-three years (Judg. 10:1).

Meta. Life activity (*crimson, scarlet, very red*) on a seemingly low plane but in process of unfoldment to higher and greater expressions (*a worm, coccus worm*).

Tolad, tō'-làd (Heb.)—*birth; nativity; generation; propagation; posterity; begetting,* as a father; *conceiving,* as a mother; *bringing forth; producing; creating; originating.*

A city of Simeon (I Chron. 4:29). It is called Eltolad in Joshua 15:30, where it is named as a city of Judah (see the latter half of Joshua 19:1).

Meta. The originating, forming, and bringing into expression of a new state of consciousness (*generation, begetting, conceiving, bringing forth, birth,* a city of Simeon; see ELTOLAD).

Tolaites, tō'-là-ītes (fr. Heb.). Descendants of Tola, son of Issachar (Num. 26:23).

Meta. Thoughts springing from that in man which Tola signifies. (See TOLA.)

Tophel, tō'-phel (Heb.)—*sticking; adhering; cement; lime; mortar; whitewash; patching up; falsehood; foolishness; fetid; ill-seasoned; unsavory; insipid; vile; quagmire; decay.*

A place in the wilderness near Paran (Deut. 1:1).

Meta. Thoughts of an adhesive nature (*sticking, adhering, cement, lime, mortar*). These adhesive thoughts in one's consciousness, if not balanced by a proper releasing attitude of mind, will cause one to hold fast to old thoughts and habits that are no longer of use in the consciousness, and so will lead to error and deterioration (*falsehood, unsavory, vile, fetid, decay, foolishness, quagmire*).

Topheth (in A. V., Isaiah 30:33; Jeremiah 7:31, 32; 19:6, 11-14, Tophet), tō'-phĕt (Heb.)—*spittle; spat upon; vile; contemned; abhorred; abomination.*

A place in the Valley of Hinnom, near Jerusalem, where the Canaanitish inhabitants and later the Jewish people worshiped Baal and made their children pass through the fire to Molech. Later this place became a dumping ground for the refuse of the city of Jerusalem and fires were kept going continually to burn up the filth. Thus Topheth, or Hinnom, became a type of what has been known in the Christian world as "hell fire" (II Kings 23:10).

Meta. A phase of consciousness in the spiritually unfolding individual where a continual purification is going on—where lesser thoughts and tendencies belonging to the man of sense are given up to God, that a transmutation may take place. Topheth refers more specifically to the very little esteem (*spat upon, vile, contemned*) in which the errors that are being cleansed away are held by the spiritually enlightened individual. (See HINNOM.)

Tormah, tôr'-mah (Heb.)—*deception; fraud; betrayal.*

A place that is mentioned in the margin of Judges 9:31. There the messengers of Zebul found Abimelech.

Meta. A crafty, treacherous, deceptive state of thought (*deception, fraud;* "craftily" is used in the text, in place of "in Tormah").

Tou, tŏ'-ū (Heb.)—*wandering; straying from a path; error; impiety; idolatry; ungodliness.*

King of Hamath (I Chron. 18:9). He is the same person as Toi of II Samuel 8:9.

Meta. See TOI.

Trachonitis, trăch-ŏ-nī'-tĭs (Gk.)—*rough; rocky; precipitous; stony; cruel.*

A rocky territory that was ruled by Philip, brother of Herod, at the time of the ministry of John the Baptist (Luke 3:1). It is associated with Argob of the Old Testament. Argob was a district of the kingdom of Og in Bashan (Deut. 3:4).

Meta. A very strong, hard, defensive, resistant state of thought in man, whose central ruling idea is power exercised in selfish, personal reason and will, unmodified by spiritual understanding and love (*rocky, rough, stony, cruel;* a district ruled by Philip, brother of Herod, of the Romans). (See ARGOB.)

trees.

Meta. "Trees" represent nerves, and nerves are expressions of thoughts of unity; they connect thought centers. In Ezekiel 47:7 the trees growing on both sides of the river represent the nerves radiating from the spinal column, and connecting and unifying the whole organism through the nerve fluid.

The "tree" (Gen. 2:9) signifies the connecting link between earth and heaven —between body and mind, the formless and the formed. "Every tree that is pleasant to the sight" pertains to the perceptive faculty of mind. It is always pleasant to perceive Truth. The substance of spiritual thought is the "food" that is good. The "tree of life also in the midst of the garden" represents the absolute life principle established in man consciousness by Divine Mind. The roots of the tree of life are centered in the solar plexus region, and they are symbolized in the physical organism by the nerves.

The generative center in the loins of man is the point at which the physical man contacts life, but when the consciousness has been redeemed and man has placed himself in the "garden" through I AM, Jehovah God, he contacts the "tree of life" at the solar plexus region, or heart center, and from this center exercises authority and dominion over the whole current of life in the organism.

The "tree of the knowledge of good and evil" represents the discerning capacity of mind. Man first perceives Truth; then he must discern the relation of ideas before perfect activity is set up within him.

Jehovah God told Adam to avoid the tree whose fruit was a knowledge of good and evil, "for in the day that thou eatest thereof thou shalt surely die." It is evident that this tree is closely related to individual free will, which is in direct touch with the "serpent" or selfhood. In that state of consciousness, or day, the individual shall surely die.

The branch that separates itself from the tree withers away and dies. So a belief by the ego that its life, substance, and intelligence are self-derived cuts off the source of supply, and the ego begins to revolve in a mental vortex whose dominant tones are good and evil, birth and death—duality.

It is through the affections, the feminine in us, that we partake of both good and evil. The soul, or woman, was given to man by Jehovah God, and is the avenue through which the inspirations of Spirit come. When the I AM assumes mastery over the soul it brings forth only good.

If man could lay hold of the tree of life while thinking both good and evil to be real, he would go on living in the negative part of his being and would bring destruction upon himself.

Man lost consciousness of his divine nature in Spirit, and so must begin again to lay hold of the potential ideas in substance and must "till the ground from whence he was taken."

The spiritual life is protected from the coarser consciousness by the "flame of a sword which turned every way," or the word of God and "the Cherubim," sacred wisdom. Man can regain entrance into Eden only by being "born anew" of Spirit.

The "tree of life, bearing twelve *manner of* fruits, yielding its fruit every month" (Rev. 22:2) is explained as follows:

The "tree of life" is the inherent life of the organism; it is symbolized in the physical by the nerves and the spinal column. The spinal column represents the tree; the nerves, which carry the living waters, are the branches and the leaves of the tree. Every month a transmutation of the living waters takes place, under divine order; thus are the "twelve *manner of* fruits" produced by the "tree of life . . . in the midst of the garden," the spiritualized body. (This latter text reverts to Gen. 2:9.) Man is kept from partaking of this precious, healing, lifegiving fruit only by thoughts of sensuality. When this phase of sense consciousness is taken up in Truth and eliminated, and the idea of purity is built in, man's body begins to express its original holiness and perfection. We eat of the fruit of the "tree of life" when we appropriate ideas of divine life, ceasing to dwell on life as something that comes and goes, or something that is governed by birth and death.

Trinity.

God, threefold in Being.

Meta. The divine Trinity is known as Father, Son, and Holy Spirit. Metaphysically we understand these to refer to mind, idea, and expression, or thinker, thought, and action.

Man is also threefold—spirit, soul, and body; spirit relating to I AM, soul to consciousness (I am conscious), and body to manifestation (I appear).

Troas, trō'-ăs (Gk.)—*bored through; penetrated; perforated.*

A city of Asia Minor (Acts 16:8-11).

Meta. A phase of thought by which Spirit can find its way into consciousness more easily than by other ways (*pene-*

trated, bored through). It was while in this city, after having been forbidden by the Holy Spirit to preach in some other places, that Paul received his vision of the man of Macedonia crying to him to come over and help the Macedonian people.

Trogyllium, tro-ġy̆l'-li-ŭm (Gk.)— *eating place; place of fruits, nuts, vegetables.*

A city on the western coast of Asia Minor. It is mentioned in the margin of Acts 20:15 as being a tarrying place of Paul's while he was on one of his missionary journeys.

Meta. An analyzing and assimilating of ideas; a conscious taking on of substance (*eating place, place of fruits, nuts, vegetables*), by means of the word of Truth, represented here by Paul. (See the significance of the other cities mentioned in Acts 20:14 and 15, wherein Paul stopped while on this missionary trip.)

Trophimus, trŏph'-ĭ-mŭs (Gk.)—*feeding; nourishing; instructing; fostering; educating; a foster child; nursing; anxious and tender care.*

A Christian of Asia who accompanied Paul to Jerusalem and worked with him in the ministry (Acts 20:4). He was an Ephesian, and at the Temple in Jerusalem caused trouble for Paul in that the Jews thought that Paul defiled the Temple by bringing Greeks into it to worship (Acts 21:29). In II Timothy 4:20 Paul writes that he left Trophimus at Miletus sick.

Meta. A thought or expression of desire (Trophimus was an Ephesian, and Ephesus signifies desire) in individual consciousness. Desire, which often becomes recognized only by the outer, carnal phase of man's consciousness as it seeks expression in sense ways—especially is this the case in those who have not been really awakened to spiritual understanding—is believed by one's old-established and formally religious ideas (Jews) not to be spiritual, and therefore to have no place in one's being (the Temple). But desire in man is fundamentally spiritual; it is the foundation quality of all growth and unfoldment, and when it expresses in the higher, spiritual understanding it is fed and supported by true spiritual life and substance. This is the significance of Trophimus (*feeding, nourishing, a foster child, instructing, fostering, nursing, tender care*).

trumpets, and cymbals (Ezra 3:10).

Meta. The trumpets and cymbals in the hands of the priests and Levites are the thrills and waves of harmonious energy that go to every part of our mind and our body when we rejoice in spirit and our heart is filled with gratitude and we express ourselves in thanksgiving to the Author of our being.

Tryphæna (A. V., Tryphena), trȳ-phæ'-nȧ (Gk.)—*living delicately; luxurious; softness; effeminacy; luxurious living.*

A Christian worker, a woman, whom Paul saluted in his letter to the Romans (Rom. 16:12).

Meta. A very highly refined, rich soul quality, in the spiritually awakening individual, that ministers to the consciousness (a woman at Rome who labored for the Lord). The definitions of Tryphæna, however (*living delicately, luxurious living, softness, effeminacy*), bespeak a certain yielding to sense and a weakness and negativeness that need correcting.

Tryphosa, trȳ-phō'-sȧ (Gk.)—*living delicately; luxurious; softness; effeminacy; luxurious living.*

A Christian woman named with Tryphæna, whom Paul saluted in his letter to the Romans (Rom. 16:12).

Meta. The significance is the same as that of Tryphæna. (See TRYPHÆNA.)

Tubal, tū'-bȧl (Heb.)—*diffusibility; diffusive motion; flowing forth; welling; flowing copiously; leading; conducting; bringing forth; jubilation; shout of joy; triumphal song.*

a A son of Japheth and grandson of Noah (Gen. 10:2); also **b** a people descended from him (Ezek. 27:13).

Meta. Noah's three sons, Shem, Ham, and Japheth, represent the threefold being of man: the spiritual, the physical, and the mental. Japheth signifies the intellect or reason, the mental realm. Tubal, a son of Japheth (meaning *diffusibility, flowing forth, welling, flowing copiously, leading, conducting, bringing forth, jubilation, triumphal song*), be-

speaks the expanding possibilities of the consciousness of man, with the joy and the good that result from increased understanding. (See JAPHETH.)

Tubal–cain, tū'-bȧl–eāin (Heb.)—*diffusion of Cain; diffusion of worldly possessions; central diffusion; flowing of centralized might; mineral principle; physical power; mercury; metals and the instruments made from them.*

Son of Lamech by Zillah. He was "the forger of every cutting instrument of brass and iron" (Gen. 4:22).

Meta. Cain (*centralization, acquisition, that which draws to itself*) signifies the sense selfishness of an individual centralized in his own physical being. Tubal–cain, a descendant of Cain (meaning *diffusion of Cain, diffusion of worldly possessions, flowing of centralized might*), bespeaks a broadening out of that which Cain signifies, or the same selfish thought removed to a broader, more universal base. For instance, a person's care and ambition for his children, for the community or city in which he lives, or even for his country, may be just as selfish and unreasonable and far removed from the true Christ love as is the selfishness in an individual that seeks to draw all good to himself. However, a broader base for one's centralization of love and ambition does lead to a larger life and to undertakings and successes on a much larger and broader scale than can ever be attained so long as one's whole thought is of oneself alone. Tubal–cain was supposed to be the inventor of the art of forging metals into cutting instruments.

twelve, the number.

Meta. Twelve always refers to spiritual fulfillment.

The twelve stones, in I Kings 18:31, represent the twelve most important nerve centers in the body. All material things represent spiritual realities. The I AM (Elijah) in this demonstration must understand and affirm the spiritual reality of all seemingly material organs and functions.

Tychicus, tỹeh'-ĭ-eŭs (Gk.)—*casualty; fortuitous; fortunate; fateful; fate; chance.*

A Christian, and a fellow worker of

Paul's, "faithful minister" (Eph. 6:21).

Meta. A belief in fate (*fortuitous, fateful, chance, fortunate*). Converted to Christian faith, this belief would take on a strong assurance of good as being ever present and demonstrable. One who learns the divine law is not subject to *fate*. He makes his own destiny by his use of divine law.

Tyrannus, tȳ-răn'-nŭs (Gk.)—*tyrant; sovereign; ruling prince.*

A man of Ephesus, in whose school Paul was "reasoning daily" for two years after they of the synagogue turned away from the Truth (Acts 19:9, 10).

Meta. The absolute ruling power of desire in the individual. Desire knows no restraint by law or custom; it works irresistibly toward expression (*tyrant, sovereign, ruling prince,* a man of Ephesus). Ephesus signifies desire, which is the central building faculty of the consciousness.

After Paul was forced to leave off preaching in the synagogue because of the resistance of the Jews, he continued for two years to reason daily in the school of Tyrannus. This signifies that the word of Truth continues to work in the spiritually awakening individual through his inner desires that truly long for the things of Spirit, even though the individual may for a time outwardly repudiate the higher messages of Truth because of his preconceived, formal, established religious beliefs' still holding so great a place in his thought.

Tyre (in A. V., Jeremiah 25:22, Tyrus), tȳre (Gk.)—*compressed; pressed together; strength; rock; refuge; shelter; stone; pebble; stone knife; cutting; carving; forming; fashioning.*

A city on the eastern coast of the Mediterranean Sea, near the northwestern border of Palestine (Joel 3:4; Matt. 15:21).

Meta. Tyre (*compressed, rock, strength, shelter, cutting, carving*) and Sidon (*lier in wait, catching of fish, hunter, trapper, beast of prey, fishery*) refer to the realm of sensation in man's consciousness, with its numberless thoughts and tendencies. This realm must be consciously entered and spiritualized by the Christ. It has not heretofore been illumined by Spirit, and has been considered too material to be worthy of spiritualization.

The "king of Tyre" (Ezek. 28:12) is the personal ego, the ruling power in the sense man. In connection with him, the precious stones (Ezek. 28:13) evidently refer to the spiritual man. The picture of Tyre given by Ezekiel shows it to be sense consciousness puffed up with pride and self-sufficiency. The prophet describes the overthrow of the sinful consciousness, at the same time giving a most remarkable declaration of the innate perfection of man. "Thus saith the Lord Jehovah: Thou sealest up the sum, full of wisdom, and perfect in beauty." (See Ezek. 28:12-17.)

The cities referred to in Matthew 11: 20-24 are symbols of fixed states of thought in the individual. Tyre and Sidon represent the state of mind that makes no excuse for wrongdoing, but when brought to judgment under the law is willing to admit its error and repent.

U

Ucal, ū'-căl (Heb.)—*I am strong; I shall be nourished; I am power; I am mighty; I shall prevail.*

One of the two men to whom Agur seems to have addressed his words of the 30th chapter of Proverbs (Prov. 30:1).

Meta. An inner consciousness of strength, power, and might. This consciousness is the result of feeding upon, receiving, affirming, realizing, assimilating, and being nourished by words of Truth (*I am strong, I shall be nourished, I am power, I am mighty, I shall prevail*).

Uel, ū'-ĕl (Heb.)—*will of God; desire of God; wish of God; desiring of God; God's will.*

One of the sons of Bani. He had taken a foreign wife, but gave her up at the command of Ezra (Ezra 10:34).

Meta. An awakening in man to his

true desire, which is for God and is caused by God's seeking greater expression in him. (Uel means *will of God, desire of God, wish of God, God's will.* At its root every desire of man is God's seeking greater and truer expression in and through him, though by the time these desires reach man's outer consciousness he often interprets them falsely, and according to the ignorance of his sense or carnal mind.

Ulai, ū'-lāi (Heb.)—*twisted together; strong; stout; robust; powerful; first; foremost; ram's horn; leather bottle.*

A river near Shushan the palace, in Persia. It was there that Daniel saw his vision of a ram and a he-goat (Dan. 8 :2).

Meta. A current of thought in the individual (a river), of a firm, strong, powerful, pushing, aggressive character, more material than spiritual (*twisted together, strong, robust, powerful, foremost, ram's horn, leather bottle*). This current of thought may be one concerning the seemingly physical organism (*leather bottle* suggests this interpretation).

Ulam, ū'-lăm (Heb.)—*anterior; beforehand; in front; first of all; apposition; opposition; contrary; porch; portico; vestibule; piazza; covered walk.*

a An Israelite, of the tribe of Manasseh (I Chron. 7:16). b Son of Eshek, descended from Saul of the tribe of Benjamin (I Chron. 8:39).

Meta. Pioneer thoughts of understanding (a man of Manasseh) and of faith (a man of Benjamin) that go ahead, that enter first into new ideals and states of consciousness (*anterior, beforehand, first of all, porch, vestibule*).

Ulla, ŭl'-là (Heb.)—*above; lifted up; overhead; bound on; made fast; thrust with the head; yoke; burden; servitude; bondage; service.*

A chief man of the Israelitish tribe of Asher (I Chron. 7:39).

Meta. Since the blessed Asher state of mind does not harmonize with the burden-bearing thought, this name, Ulla, with its meaning (*bound on, made fast, yoke, servitude, bondage, service, burden*), calls to mind the words of Jesus as recorded in Matthew 11:29, 30: "Take

my yoke upon you, and learn of me . . . For my yoke is easy, and my burden is light." *Yoke* here refers to a union with Christ, or with the high ideals of Spirit. *Burden* refers to the taking on of a right degree of responsibility: "For each man shall bear his own burden," meaning his own proper load. Service then becomes spiritual.

Above, lifted up, overhead, bespeak a change from a carnal plane of thought and activity to a higher or more nearly spiritual plane. *Thrust with the head* suggests the exercise of will, as well as reason or understanding.

Ummah, ŭm'-măh (Heb.)—*brought together; conjoined; united; gathering; community; equality; alike; communion; a people; family; society; fraternity.*

A city of Asher (Josh. 19:30).

Meta. A group of thoughts or a thought center that is of a unifying, gathering, and coöperative character (*brought together, united, gathering, community, family, a people, fraternity, a city*).

Unni, ŭn'-nī (Heb.)—*labor; suffering; affliction; oppression; brought low; depressed; humiliated; humbled; exhausted; impoverished; poor.*

a A Levite, a doorkeeper in the tabernacle, who was appointed one of the musicians to assist in bringing the Ark to Jerusalem, in the reign of David (I Chron. 15 :18, 20).

Meta. Unni (*labor, affliction, oppression, humbled, impoverished*) refers to the result, in man's consciousness and world, of the very human belief in hard work, labor, instead of expression in joyous, loving service. In other words it would typify the "bondservant" type of Christian service instead of the "son" type (see the 4th chapter of Galatians).

Unno (in A. V., Unni), ŭn'-nō (Heb.) —same as Unni.

A Levite who returned from the Babylonian captivity with Zerubbabel (Neh. 12:9).

Meta. See UNNI.

upharsin, ū-phär'-sĭn (Heb.)—*and shall be divided; and they divide; and shall be broken in fragments; and shall be sundered.* It is a significant fact that *parsi,* by a simple vocal change without any change in characters, means a Persian. So it seems that not only what was to take place, but also the force destined to accomplish it, is contained in the word UPHARSIN.

One of the words of the handwriting that appeared on the wall during Belshazzar's feast (Dan. 5:25).

Meta. The significance is virtually the same as that of PERES. See PERES; see also the other words belonging to this handwriting on the wall: MENE and TEKEL.

Uphaz, ū'-phăz (Heb.)—*radiating light; pure gold; gold region.*

A place from which pure gold was obtained (Jer. 10:9; Dan. 10:5). The word is thought to be a corruption of Ophir.

Meta. Pure substance as it is in the mind of God, and set apart from the adulterated thoughts of the carnal in man (*gold region, pure gold*). When this substance is appropriated to meet the needs of the outer man it carries the consciousness of riches, or opulence, and it manifests abundantly in apparently material ways. It is no longer purely spiritual, however, since more or less of the limited, personal, selfish, material thoughts and beliefs of the outer consciousness of the individual has been introduced into it. (See OPHIR.) The idea of spiritual understanding, actively expressing, is also contained in this word (*radiating light*).

upper chamber, Acts 1:13.

Meta. The "upper chamber" to which the disciples went for the baptism of the Holy Spirit is the high state of mind that we assume in thinking about spiritual things. It may be attained through prayer, or going into the silence with true words, or in spiritual meditation. There are various methods for making this attainment, but in order to have this Holy Spirit baptism we must be looking for it; that is, our attention must be toward things spiritual.

When the earnest Christian has such unusual experiences the thought comes into his mind, "It must be that I am coming into an abiding spiritual state of consciousness." The disciples asked, "Lord, dost thou at this time restore the kingdom to Israel? And he said unto them, It is not for you to know times or seasons, which the Father hath set within his own authority" (Acts 1:6, 7). The Christian does not know when the final change will come, when "this corruptible shall have put on incorruption." He does find, however, that he gets the consciousness of the descent of spiritual power, which is witnessed in "the uttermost part of the earth," or his body.

After a great spiritual illumination we find our mind and heart reaching out for heavenly things until we almost forget our practical life. We continue to look steadfastly into heaven until the "two men . . . in white apparel" (consciousness of Spirit within and about us) call our attention to the fact that this new man in Christ has not left us but will return in the same manner in which he went—that is, in consciousness.

Ur, ûr (Heb.)—*light; region of light; East; Orient; brightness; brilliance; splendor; fire; flame; blaze.*

a "Ur of the Chaldees" was the place of Abraham's nativity (Gen. 11:28-31). b Father of Eliphal, who was one of David's mighty men (I Chron. 11:35).

Meta. Understanding, intelligence, active in man, or the inner spiritual phase of man's being, whence true light shines throughout the consciousness (*light, region of light, East, brightness, splendor, fire, blaze*); also the shining of that light.

Urbanus, ûr-bā'-nŭs (Lat.)—*of the city; urbane; cultivated; refined; polite.*

A Christian whom Paul saluted in his letter to the Christians at Rome (Rom. 16:9).

Meta. A very highly refined thought activity that has been awakened to and is actively expressing spiritual ideals (*of the city, urbane, cultivated, refined, polite,* a Christian at Rome who was one of Paul's fellow workers in Christ).

Uri, ū'-rī (Heb.)—*filled with light; brilliant; shining; illumined; enlightened; inflamed; fiery; burning; light of Jehovah; my light.*

a Son of Hur, of the tribe of Judah (Exod. 31:2). b Father of Geber, who was the officer appointed by Solomon to gather provisions for his household for one month in each year from the land of Gilead (I Kings 4:19). **c** A porter in the Temple. He had taken a foreign wife, but gave her up at the command of Ezra (Ezra 10:24).

Meta. Purified understanding (*filled with light, fiery, enlightened, light of Jehovah, my light*).

Uriah, ū-rī'-ăh (Heb.)—*my light is Jehovah; whose light Jah is; Jah is light; the Lord is my light; fire of Jehovah; flame of Jehovah.*

a "The Hittite," the husband of Bathsheba. David caused Uriah to be placed in the front of a battle with the Ammonites, where the hottest fighting was done, that he might be killed; then after Uriah's death David took Bathsheba for his wife. Solomon was their second son, the first one having died (II Sam. 11:3–12:24). **b** There were noted Israelitish priests by this name (Ezra 8:33; Neh. 8:4; Isa. 8:2).

Meta. Spiritual illumination, which is purifying in character (*my light is Jehovah, Jah is light, the Lord is my light, flame of Jehovah, fire of Jehovah*). The activity of the cleansing, refining process of Spirit is hindered in man when he lets lustful desires enter the love consciousness: David (love) was instrumental in having Uriah the Hittite killed that he might have Uriah's wife, Bathsheba.

Uriel, ū-rī'-ĕl (Heb.)—*light of God; God is light; fire of God; radiation of God; God is the radiating principle of light.*

a A Levite (I Chron. 6:24). **b** A Kohathite Levite, a chief (I Chron. 15:5). **c** A man of Gibeah and father of Micaiah, who was wife of Rehoboam, and mother of Abijah. This Abijah succeeded Rehoboam on the throne of Judah (II Chron. 13:2).

Meta. The truth that *God is the radiating principle of light.* A recognition of this truth opens the consciousness to spiritual understanding and purification (Uriel means *light of God, fire of God, radiation of God;* light signifies understanding, and fire denotes a purifying element that exists in true understanding. The fact that these are "of God" shows that they are spiritual.)

Urijah, ū-rī'-jăh (Heb.)—*my light is Jehovah; whose light Jah is; the Lord is my light; Jah is light; fire of Jehovah; flame of Jehovah.*

A priest in the time of King Ahaz of Judah (II Kings 16:10). Urijah is the same name as Uriah.

Meta. Uriel, Uriah, and Urijah have virtually the same meaning. (See URIAH and URIEL.)

Urim, ū'-rĭm (Heb.)—*radiating principles; lights; illuminations; revelations; shining brilliances; understanding; enlightenments.*

The Urim and Thummim are correctly rendered "lights" and "truth," or "revelations" and "truth." The Urim and Thummim (Exod. 28:30; *the Lights and the Perfections,* margin) were placed in the breastplate of the high priest of the Israelites; by them, in some way, the high priest obtained divine guidance for the people, especially in difficult cases (Exod. 28:30; Lev. 8:8; Num. 27:21).

Fallows says that there are two principal opinions respecting the Urim and Thummim. One is that these words simply denote the four rows of precious stones in the breastplate of the high priest, and are so called from their brilliancy and perfection; which stones, in answer to an appeal to God in difficult cases, indicated His mind and will by some supernatural appearance. Thus, as we know that upon each of the stones was to be engraved the name of one of the sons of Jacob, it has been conjectured that the letters forming the divine response became, in some way or other, distinguished from the other letters. It has been conjectured by others that the response was given by an audible voice to the high priest arrayed in full pontificals, and standing in the holy place with his face turned toward the Ark. The other principal opinion is that the Urim and Thummim were two small oracular images, similar to the teraphim, typifying "revelations" and "truth," which were placed in the cavity or pouch formed by the folds of the breastplate, and which uttered oracles by a voice. The latter view is corroborated by the authority of Philo, and seems to be best supported by external evidence.

Meta. The consciousness of divine guidance in any specific matter, when this guidance is sought in prayer; the inner illuminating experiences that one realizes when one seeks God earnestly and with pure, holy, unselfish intent, in the sacred meeting place between God and man, the holy of holies within the innermost of one's being (*radiating principles, illuminations, lights, enlightenments, revelations, whole, perfect, sound, verity, truth;* devices by which the will of God regarding the Israelitish tribes and people was learned in special cases, by their high priests).

Uthai, ū'-thāi (Heb.)—*to whom Jehovah hastens; whom Jehovah sustains; Jehovah succors; comfort of Jah; Jah is help.*

a Son of Ammihud, descended from Perez, son of Judah (I Chron. 9:4). **b** Son of Bigvai, who returned from the Babylonian captivity with Ezra (Ezra 8: 14).

Meta. Thoughts of divine helpfulness, of divine aid in all the affairs of one's daily life (*whom Jehovah sustains, Jah is help, comfort of Jah, Jehovah succors*). The significance of this name is quite clearly revealed in Psalms 46:1 and in Philippians 4:13: "God is our refuge and strength, a very present help in trouble." "I can do all things in him that strengtheneth me." Divine assistance is realized by words of Truth declared in I AM, or Jehovah.

Uz, ŭz (Heb.)—*substantiation; growing might; formative power; concentration; purpose; plan; impression; imagination; fertility; counsel; advising; consulting; making firm; fixing; hardness.*

a Son of Aram, who was a son of Shem and grandson of Noah (Gen. 10:23). **b** Son of Nahor the brother of Abraham (Gen. 22:21). **c** Son of Dishan of the descendants of Seir the Horite (Gen. 36:28). **d** The native land of Job (Job 1:1). **e** The land of Uz is mentioned in Jeremiah 25:20 and in Lamentations 4:21, and from the latter text it is evident that this land was inhabited by Edomites.

Meta. The process of thought by which man arrives at a conclusion (be it Truth or error) and establishes it in consciousness (*substantiation, growing might, formative power, concentration, purpose, plan, impression, imagination, fertility, counsel, advising, consulting, making firm, fixing, hardness;* the native land of Job).

The significance of Uz fits perfectly with the lesson that the experience of Job teaches. (See JOB.) Job's arguments with his three friends, and his finally getting at the Truth, which wrought such a great change in his life, picture the inner controversies that the spiritually awakening individual is very likely to experience with various phases of his own consciousness before he arrives at true spiritual understanding. Especially is this the case if he is more or less established in outer forms of righteousness, and is the intellectual, reasoning type of person.

Uzai, ū'-zāi (Heb.)—*hasting of Jehovah; Jah is refuge; strong; robust; powerful; mighty.*

Father of Palal, who helped in repairing Jerusalem's wall after the Babylonian captivity (Neh. 3:25).

Meta. Uzai bespeaks strength, health, power, might, divine protection, and earnest, zealous, spiritual activity toward perfection (*hasting of Jehovah, Jah is refuge, strong, robust, powerful, mighty*).

Uzal, ū'-zăl (Heb.)—*sympathetic communication; carried rapidly to an object; constant progression; continual going forth; divine spark; purifying fire; purified air.*

A son of Joktan, who was descended from Shem (Gen. 10:27).

Meta. The continual unfoldment that takes place in the progressively inclined individual because of his natural conformity to the divine ideal or *divine spark* within him, which is ever urging him on to higher light, new understanding, purer thoughts and ways (*sympathetic communication, carried rapidly to an object, constant progression, continual going forth, divine spark, purifying fire, purified air;* a son of Joktan, who was descended from Shem).

Uzza, ŭz'-zȧ (Heb.)—*strength; might; power; firmness; splendor; majesty; glory.*

a The name of the man who owned the garden in which Manasseh and Amon, kings of Judah, were buried (II Kings 21:18, 26). b A Benjamite, brother of Ahihud (I Chron. 8:7). c An ancestor of some of the Nethinim who returned with Zerubbabel from the Babylonian captivity (Ezra 2:49).

Meta. See UZZAH.

Uzzah (in A. V., I Chron. 6:29, Uzza), ŭz′-zàh (Heb.) — *strength; might; power; firmness; splendor; majesty; glory.*

Son of Abinadab. He was slain by Jehovah for touching the Ark of God in trying to steady it (II Sam. 6:3-8). Uzza is the same name.

Meta. Strength. In II Samuel 6 Uzzah means human strength. When the oxen (also representing strength) stumbled, the effort from the human side to steady Spirit met with a quick reaction from the divine law. Natural strength may be called into activity to sustain and uphold that which is sublimely exalted; the attitude of mind that makes the contact successfully is reverence, honor mingled with love. When reverence is missing, the natural strength will not fuse with the spiritual. This failure is portrayed as "the anger of Jehovah," to bring out forcibly the resistance of Spirit to human intervention. When a matter has been intrusted to Spirit it should not be touched by sense thought. Put your entire trust in the Lord and He will bring it to pass.

When man allows the carnal part of himself to act in place of the spiritual, and is defeated, he often rebels or is "displeased." He cannot see why strength of muscle is not just as good as strength of Spirit, and in his confusion he says, "How shall the ark of Jehovah come unto me?"

Uzzen–sheerah (A. V., Uzzen–sherah), ŭz′-zĕn-shē′-ĕ-răh (Heb.)—*point; summit of Sheerah; acuteness of the flesh; ear of the flesh; hearing of blood relative.*

A city that was built by Sheerah the daughter of Ephraim (I Chron. 7:24).

Meta. A high idea of relationship, or the human idea of kinship raised to its highest standard (*summit of Sheerah, acuteness of the flesh, ear of the flesh, hearing of blood relative*). In Sheerah we find the thought of *blood relatives, kindred, of the same flesh. Ear* and *hearing* denote that this belief in flesh kinship is becoming attentive to some higher and more nearly spiritual idea, while *summit of Sheerah* signifies the lifting up of the Sheerah idea to its highest point of understanding.

Uzzi, ŭz′-zī (Heb.)—*Jehovah is strength; Jah is strong; Jehovah is my strength; mighty is Jehovah; power of Jah; glory of the Lord.*

a Son of Bukki, and descended from Aaron, of the Kohathite Levites (I Chron. 6:5). b Son of Tola and grandson of Issachar (I Chron. 7:2). c Son of Bela and grandson of Benjamin (I Chron. 7:7). d There were also others of the same name. The name is a contraction of UZZIAH, which see.

Meta. A realization of strength and power as coming from or through Jehovah, Christ, I AM (*Jehovah is my strength, Jah is strong, mighty is Jehovah, power of Jah*).

Uzzia, ŭz-zī′-å (Heb.)—*Jehovah is strength; Jehovah is my strength; Jah is strong; mighty is Jehovah; power of Jah; glory of the Lord.*

Uzzia the Ashterathite is named among David's mighty men (I Chron. 11:44).

Meta. See UZZI.

Uzziah, ŭz-zī′-ăh (Heb.)—*Jehovah is strength; Jah is strong; Jehovah is my strength; mighty is Jehovah; power of Jah; glory of the Lord.*

a A king of Judah (II Kings 15:13). He is sometimes called Azariah (II Kings 14:21; see margin also). b Other men by this name are mentioned in I Chronicles 27:25; Ezra 10:21; Nehemiah 11:4. Uzzi, Uzzia, and Uzziah are forms of the same name.

Meta. Kings represent ruling faculties of mind in the body consciousness.

Uzziah means *Jehovah is strength.* Azariah means *whom Jehovah hath helped.* These two names are happily associated, for so long as man recognizes that his strength is divine and comes from Jehovah he is marvelously helped by the Lord.

In connection with the following discussion of Uzziah, king of Judah, study carefully II Chronicles 26:8-21.

Judah represents the inner life in the organism. Different kings (qualities of mind) reign in Judah (life forces) because changes in consciousness bring about changes in dominant ideas active there. When wisdom dominates, Solomon is king. When health dominates, Asa is king. When judgment dominates, Jehoshaphat is king. When strength is dominant, Uzziah is king.

The strength center in the body is located at the small of the back. The strength of the natural man is not a permanent quality until it is transmuted. This transmutation is accomplished by affirming that one's strength is divine, and by consecrating it to the Lord, to be used in spiritual ways.

The transmutation of strength is symbolized in the story of Uzziah by the burning of incense upon the altar.

Uzziah failed to abide in the exalted state of consciousness that is represented by the priesthood, because he represents the more physical side of strength. Azariah is the spiritual quality of strength. Uzziah cannot do the work of Azariah, because he lacks understanding; when he attempts it he brings about disastrous results. When strength is developed in the organism it must be used in spiritual ways; man cannot appropriate divine qualities for dominant personal expression and be protected under divine law.

Man can have divine protection and guidance by daily consecrating all his faculties to the realization and expression of Truth. When he follows the directions of Spirit he harmonizes all his faculties and gives them righteous expression, without experiencing the inharmonies and the waste that result from an unbalanced consciousness.

When man gives attention to physical strength and exercises it for the purpose of combating all opposition, physical strength is increased. Uzziah "was marvellously helped, till he was strong."

When physical strength is exalted, it is made to supersede spiritual strength; but the physical man must be transmuted or refined through spiritual consciousness before he is acceptable to Jehovah. "Flesh and blood cannot inherit the kingdom of God."

When physical strength is cultivated without the refining influence of the spiritual idea (priest), deterioration sets in and the breaking up of the whole body begins. This is symbolized by the leprosy of the king. The remedy is understanding, and a repetition of some such affirmation as this: "*My strength is not material, but spiritual.*"

Isaiah 6:1-8 shows a certain movement of the healing processes, which are always working out the salvation of those who are trusting in divine help. Uzziah, the dominating physical strength, has lost his hold on the organism. "King Uzziah died." Then the higher self, Isaiah (*salvation of Jehovah*), begins the purification of the body.

Uzziel, ŭz-zī'-ĕl (Heb.)—*God is my strength; strength of God; whom God strengthens; power of God; glory of God.*

a A son of Kohath, and grandson of Levi (Exod. 6:18). **b** Son of Ishi, and a captain of the tribe of Simeon (I Chron. 4:42). **c** Son of Bela, and grandson of Benjamin (I Chron. 7:7). **d** There were others of this name.

Meta. Thoughts in the higher, more spiritual consciousness of man (Israelites) that recognize the qualities of strength and power as being not of material, but of divine, origin (*God is my strength, whom God strengthens, power of God, glory of God*).

Uzzielites, ŭz-zī'-ĕl-ītes (fr. Heb.)—*of or belonging to Uzziel.*

Descendants of Uzziel, son of Kohath, of the Israelitish tribe of Levi (Num. 3:27).

Meta. Thoughts springing from and of character like that in consciousness which Uzziel signifies. (See UZZIEL.)

V

Vaizatha (A. V., Vajezatha), vă-ĭz'-ă-thà (Pers.)—*white; whitened; white-robed; born of Ized; strong as the wind.*

One of the ten sons of Haman the son of Hammedatha, "the Jews' enemy" (Esth. 9:9).

Meta. The seeming strength of adverse thoughts and appearances (*strong as the wind*). Adversity appears to be very blusterous and to have great power at times, but it has no foundation in Spirit. It passes away into nothingness when the light of Truth is turned upon it, when the one Power and the one Intelligence are declared and realized.

The definitions *white, whitened, white-robed,* call to mind II Corinthians 11:13-15. Verse 14 reads: "And no marvel; for even Satan fashioneth himself into an angel of light."

Vaniah, vă-nī'-ăh (Heb.)—*distress; oppression; weapon of Jehovah; Jah is praise.*

A son of Bani. He had taken a foreign wife, but agreed to give her up at the command of Ezra (Ezra 10:36).

Meta. Vaniah bespeaks the demonstrating power of the word, or of thoughts and words, perhaps more in a negative than in a constructive way. The *weapon of Jehovah* is the divine thought or word in expression; "for the word of God is living, and active, and sharper than any two-edged sword" (Heb. 4:12). When man thinks thoughts and speaks words that are destructive he brings trouble to himself (*distress, oppression*). A word can act in two ways, for good or for ill. "Death and life are in the power of the tongue" (Prov. 18:21). To praise and magnify Jehovah (*Jah is praise*), the divine ideal, in our thoughts and words brings good results.

Vashti, văsh'-tī (Pers.) — *beauty; belle; beautiful; fair; lovely.*

The Persian queen of Ahasuerus. She was deposed because of her refusal to obey the king's order that she should appear unveiled before the princes and the people that they might see her beauty—

"she was fair to look on" (Esth. 1:9-19).

Meta. The emotions of the human soul in their most pleasing aspect, or personal love, which is very beautiful and good to the outer consciousness (*beauty, belle, beautiful, fair, lovely,* the queen of King Ahasuerus of the Medes and Persians). The egotistic, personal, dictatorial will (King Ahasuerus) thinks that even the affections and emotions of the soul should be wholly subject to its every whim and command. But this cannot be; soul expressions are activated by a more inner cause than that of the outer personal will.

veil, of the temple, rent in the midst.

Meta. "The veil of the temple was rent in the midst" (Luke 23:45) means that the last step in regeneration is the giving up of the thought of the corporeal existence of the body temple. Then the veil of sense thought that conceals the spiritual body is rent, and man comes into consciousness of the body imperishable and eternal. (See RENT.)

vessels, holy.

Meta. The "holy vessels" (I Kings 8:4) are the thoughts that lie back of and form the various organs of the body.

The vessels that had been taken from the Temple by Nebuchadnezzar and returned by Cyrus (Ezra 1:6-8) represent our capacity to comprehend and our ability to measure or appreciate life, love, and Truth.

vesture, of Jesus.

Meta. The "vesture" or "coat" (*tunic,* margin) of Jesus (John 19:24) that was "without seam, woven from the top throughout," symbolizes the consciousness of unity, which is the inner conviction of all things; without it even error could not retain a semblance of permanency. Hence in the final relinquishment of the carnal thought realm one lets go the belief that it has a diversity of causes or elements, and one soldier gets the vestment, which is an admission of the one Cause, the one unbroken life, running through all manifestation. The four soldiers who received Jesus' outer garments represent the powers of the four elements—earth, air, fire, and water.

vine, and branches. (John 15).

Meta. The I AM within us is the vine, our faculties are the branches, and the perfect body is the fruit (John 15). The life current as it comes from the Universal is one in vine, branches, and fruit, and it is on this free-flowing inner force that we fix our attention when we demonstrate the power of Spirit. Material symbols are likely to be misleading unless we remember always to get the spiritual import in its I AM application.

virgins, ten.

Meta. The ten virgins (Matt. 25:1-13) represent the senses. They are five in number, but have a twofold action—five in the inner realm, and five in the outer world. The way to supply oil for the lamps of the virgins, even of the foolish ones, is to affirm that the life source, Spirit, from which comes the power of hearing, smelling, feeling, seeing, and tasting, is not material but spiritual.

Vophsi, vŏph'-sī (Heb.)—*my increase; added unto me; additional; riches; gain; profit; addition of Jehovah.*

Father of Nahbi, who was the spy chosen from the tribe of Naphtali to help search out the land of Canaan preparatory to the Israelites' going over and possessing it (Num. 13:14).

Meta. An acquisitive, accumulative thought belonging to the strength faculty in individual consciousness (*my increase, added unto me, additional, riches, gain, profit;* a prominent man of Naphtali, Naphtali referring to the faculty of strength in man). This thought can be carried to the extreme and all the substance of one's strength can be used for the purpose of getting for self, rather than for the rendering of strong, loving service to others. *Addition of Jehovah,* a definition of Vophsi, gives the idea of a righteous increase of strength and might, under the direction of I AM, the inner Christ of God.

W

wandering, of Israelites in the wilderness.

Meta. The Israelites' leaving Egypt, wandering through the wilderness, entering Canaan, and taking possession of the Promised Land are symbolical of the unfoldment and growth of the individual from material to spiritual consciousness.

According to the record the Children of Israel wandered in the wilderness for forty years on their way to the Promised Land, although the journey might have been accomplished in forty weeks. The reason is given in Deuteronomy 8: 2, 3:

"And thou shalt remember all the way which Jehovah thy God hath led thee these forty years in the wilderness, that he might humble thee, to prove thee, to know what was in thy heart, whether thou wouldest keep his commandments, or not. And he humbled thee, and suffered thee to hunger, and fed thee with manna, which thou knewest not, neither did thy fathers know; that he might make thee know that man doth not live by bread only, but by everything that proceedeth out of the mouth of Jehovah doth man live."

When under spiritual discipline, we should accept without murmuring whatever comes to us, and try to find the mental cause. We do not go direct to the Promised Land, because we are ignorant of the law of existence; we attribute to life a physical instead of a metaphysical basis. We try to solve the problem of life in material ways instead of spiritual, and thus continually fall short. We wander to and fro, searching for a way out of our difficulties, yet ignoring the only way, which is an adjustment of our thoughts to Divine Mind. The soul of man is a mental thing, and its growth depends on spiritual food—thoughts and words of Truth.

The Lord is striving to make Himself known to our confused thoughts (the wilderness experience in our mind), and when we cry out in our sense of lack there is an invisible outpouring and temporary satisfaction. We are not always aware of the source, but we know that we have in some unseen way been fed inwardly. People who have had this spiritual refreshing after a period of darkness often exclaim: "What an outpouring of the blessed Spirit we have had! Oh, if it would only stay with us always!"

When we are obedient to the divine law, having cast all error out of our mind, we shall consciously have the heavenly substance all the time. But we shall not attain this condition by murmuring against the law or by calling blindly on the Lord. We must strive patiently and earnestly to overcome our errors, our sins, our shortcomings. Then the word of God will create in us a new man, and we shall know that there are flesh, blood, and substance of an abiding nature, which Jesus Christ manifested and of which we can partake through Him. Thus shall we enter into and begin to take possession of the Promised Land, which symbolizes the lifting up of both soul and body to spiritual expression and manifestation.

water.

Meta. Water in its different aspects represents weakness and negativeness, cleansing, mental potentiality, and in some cases life, or vital energy.

The waters of Genesis 1:6, 7 represent unexpressed possibilities in mind. There must be a firm starting point established. This point or "firmament" is faith moving on the unformed capacities of Spirit consciousness.

In every mental proposition we have an above and a below. Above the firmament are the unexpressed capacities (waters) of the conscious mind resting in faith in Divine Mind. Below the firmament are the unexpressed capacities (waters) of the subconscious mind.

The "Seas" of Genesis 1:10 represent the unformed state of mind. We say that a man is "at sea" when he is in doubt about a mental process; in other words he has not established his thoughts in line with the principle involved, he is unstable. The sea is capable of production, but must come under the dominion of the formative power of mind, the imagination.

Water ("the sea"), in Mark 6:47-51, represents mental potentiality; it can also be understood as negation. The race thoughts have formed a sea of thought, and to walk over it safely requires that one have faith in oneself. Faith necessary to accomplish so great a work comes from understanding—understanding of God and man and the law of mastery given to man.

God is substance: *sub,* under; *stare,* to stand. He is the underlying principle of the universe, upholding all things by His word of power, by the omnipresent energy that permeates all creation. An understanding of God in His true character establishes the mind firmly in faith and causes the feet to walk safely over the sea of the mixed, negative thoughts of the race.

It is not necessary to walk on material water to follow Jesus. His walking on the water is a lesson in spiritual overcoming. When we have found the spirit of the law the material expression adjusts itself. We live constantly in a sea of thought that is moved on by every impulse of the mind. There are greater storms on land than on sea, and they are far more destructive because of the many minds reached by the psychic waves. Men need every day the saving call, "Be of good cheer: it is I; be not afraid."

The majority of men try to sail the ocean of life without the sustaining power of Spirit, but eventually they always go down in a troubled sea. Even those who have been taught of the Master are still filled with doubts and fears when storms arise, and instead of a reality they see an apparition. But the Christ mind is not an apparition; it is a mighty power, and when we have faith in it all the discordant elements of our life are quieted and we reduce to harmony and wholeness everything that our peace-giving thoughts touch.

Water, in one of its phases, represents negativeness. The individual who allows himself to become negative to the good finds himself uncertain and unstable in his mind, and often his body becomes so submerged in the waters of negation that his physical condition is low. Weak sympathy with error and the results of error helps to produce this condition. To be positive in the good it is very necessary that one have right ideas of God, that one know Him as good. The mind and the body are often toned up by one's thinking of God as divine law. One's understanding Him to be divine law frees the mind from sentimental ideas of God solely as love. It is these sentimental ideas that make weak human sympathy.

God is our Father, and it is His place to instruct and discipline us in righteousness. Those who will not learn their lessons in easy ways will have to learn them in hard ways, and we should not be sentimentally sympathetic with those who make severe corrections necessary. Weak, teary sympathy is just one of the ways in which we bring floods upon ourselves. Water often breaks up and dissolves old error states of consciousness in the individual, just as the Flood dissolved and washed away from the race the old conditions that the combined error force of individuals had formed.

Water is symbolical of weakness, lack of stability: "Unstable as water, thou shalt not excel" (Gen. 49:4, A. V.). In Mark 14:13 it is stated that the disciples were to recognize the man in whose home they were to eat the Passover by his carrying a pitcher of water. The meaning is that we should meet the error thought at the weakest point in consciousness. The error thought to be met in this case was designated as Judas, one of the disciples, who was possessed of a devil. This means that Jesus had discovered that He had one point in His character that was not yet cleansed and spiritualized by the power of the word, or the regenerating thought given by the Father. He said on a former occasion that His disciples (faculties) were all clean through the power of the word, save this one. So Jesus had to meet in the Judas faculty the reaction of an error thought that was working there from the personal or adverse side of existence.

Water also represents material cleansing, and fire represents spiritual cleansing. When John the Baptist baptized with water, he washed away the sins of an external character. He did not enter into the subconsciousness. It takes something more powerful than water to purify the error conditions accumulated by the soul in its many incarnations. The presence of God through Christ is necessary to purify this part of man. (See BAPTISM.)

Water also represents the great mass of thoughts that conform to environment. Every thought leaves its form in the consciousness, and all the weak, characterless words and expressions gather in the subconscious mind as water gathers in holes. When we get discouraged or disappointed and "give up," the undertow of life sweeps this flood of negative thought over us, and we are conscious of bodily weakness of some sort. Then, if we get scared, there is trouble ahead. When we know the Truth, and "brace up," however, the waters are confined to their natural channels again and our strength is restored.

It is the Lord that responds under the divine law to our thought and word. Those who "believe . . . through their word" are the ones that demonstrate. When one is so attached to property or to position that its loss takes away courage and ambition, the functions of the body sympathize with the negative thought and express in like manner.

"Living water" (John 4:10) signifies the inspiration of Spirit, also life. In Revelation 22:17 we read, "He that will, let him take the water of life freely."

waterpots.

Meta. The "six waterpots of stone" (John 2:6, 7) are the six nerve centers in the body, which are filled with the water of life, or nerve fluid.

The symbol represents the abundance of vital energy that may be generated from a union of I AM spiritual thought with the water of life, or nerve fluid, in the various centers of the organism. With every thought we are setting this nerve fluid into a state of action, and it rushes to any part of the body to which our attention draws it.

wedding–garment.

Meta. Garments represent the outer clothing of the mind. The "wedding-garment" (Matt. 22:11) is symbolical of a state of consciousness in which there is special preparation for the union unique; in other words, our external thinking must be in harmony with the inner revelation before we can make complete union with the Christ.

well, Jacob's (John 4:6).

Meta. Inspiration through the intellect alone.

wellbeloved.

"My wellbeloved" (Isa. 5:1) is the Christ, the ideal man. The theme of the song in Isaiah 5:1, 2 is life. The fruit of the vine is a symbol of life, the wine of life. Jesus said, "I am the vine." The vineyard is manifest man, humanity. It was planted in perfection, and perfection was its destiny. "He looked that it should bring forth grapes, and it brought forth wild grapes."

wells.

Meta. The wells that were dug by Isaac's herdsmen (Gen. 26:15-25) are inward sources of life that are opened up by joy (Isaac means laughter).

The well of living water (see John 4:10-14) in man is the fount of inspiration within his consciousness, which, when the seal is broken, flows forth peacefully, majestically—vitalizing and renewing mind and body. In this clear light of Truth we are conscious that life is never changing, eternal.

widow.

Meta. The "widows" of Acts 9:39 represent half truths. These half truths see the external of Truth but they reject the real or inner spirit of it; thus they are in lack.

The "widow" in Luke 18:1-5 typifies a belief in lack. It is not good in itself, but it serves to call man's attention to the law (judge). Dependence on the judgments of the law, without consciousness of love, subjects one to hard experiences and laborious expression.

In this lesson of Luke 18:1-5 Jesus also portrays the power of affirmative prayer, or repeated silent demands for justice, as a widow, one bereft of worldly protection and power. Under her persistence even the seemingly ungodly judge succumbs. The unceasing prayer of faith is commanded in the Scriptures, in various places.

The widow of Zarephath, to whom Elijah was sent for sustenance, represents love bereft of wisdom. She represents the divine feminine, while Elijah, here, is the divine masculine, or wisdom. Separated, they are both in a state of semi-starvation; but when they are joined in consciousness, increase at once begins and lack ceases. "The jar of meal wasted not, neither did the cruse of oil fail" (I Kings 17:9-16).

wilderness.

Meta. The wilderness (Josh. 1:4) represents in individual consciousness the multitude of undisciplined and uncultivated thoughts.

wine.

Meta. The "wine" (John 2:1-11) symbolizes the vitality that forms the connecting link between soul and body. It is an all-pervading free essence that is generated from the nerve substance, or water of life. This wine of life or free vitality of the organism must be present in large quantities before a blending of thoughts, or of soul and body (wedding), can be made successfully.

Wise–men, from the east (Matt. 2:1).

Meta. The stored-up resources of the soul, which rise to the surface when its depths are stirred by a great spiritual revelation. They are the inner realms of consciousness that, like books of life, have kept the records of past lives and held them in reserve for the great day when the soul would receive the supreme ego, Jesus. These "Wise-men" represent the wisdom that is carried within the soul from previous incarnations. The east represents the within, man's inner consciousness.

They bring gifts to the Christ Child, the inner resources of Spirit, which are open to the Christ mind. Gold represents the riches of Spirit; frankincense, the beauty of Spirit; myrrh, the eternity of Spirit.

The star that the "Wise-men" saw in the east represents intuition; the "Wise-men" were guided by intuition. Stars represent subjective and not fully understood guiding lights.

witnesses, two, of Revelation 11:3, and the "two anointed ones" of Zechariah 4:14.

Meta. While we believe that there is an outer interpretation to all prophecy, we know that there is also an inner interpretation, and since this is the more necessary in our overcoming we always seek to give the Scriptures an individual meaning or explanation. According to the 1st chapter of Revelation the whole book is the picture of a redeemed man; therefore there is no doubt that the 11th chapter is representative of an inner work, something that will take place in each one as he is being transformed into the perfect image and likeness of God.

Revelation 21:15 reads, "And he that spake with me had for a measure a golden reed to measure the city." The 17th verse, giving the measurements, states that they were *"according to* the measure of a man, that is, of an angel." In the 11th chapter we read, "And there was given me a reed like unto a rod: and one said, Rise, and measure the temple of God, and the altar, and them that worship therein." Things are sometimes measured to find out not their size, but their true value.

The Temple was in Jerusalem and represents the place of worship in the heart center (Jerusalem being symbolical of this center in consciousness). The altar would be the consciousness of full consecration that takes place first in the Temple of worship. "Present your bodies a living sacrifice, holy, acceptable to God, *which is* your spiritual service." "Them that worship therein" are the true spiritual thoughts in man, that love and worship God.

Those who are in the process of overcoming realize that (as Paul tells us in Romans) within them are the carnal mind, or the outer, personal self, and the inner or Christ consciousness of Truth. The putting off of the personal is a gradual work, which begins after a full consecration to God on the part of the individual, and until it is entirely overcome there is often "war in heaven" within him. So the "court which is without the temple" that "hath been given unto the nations," and was not to be measured, represents the carnal thoughts or states of consciousness, conscious and subconscious, that have not yet been redeemed. Until they are lifted up and redeemed they to a certain extent "tread under foot," or keep from perfect expression and demonstration, the spirituality or God consciousness within man.

The two witnesses (Rev. 11:3), or two olive trees (read carefully the 4th chapter of Zechariah), seem to be avenues by which the oil of life of the Spirit is brought into the body consciousness. In Zechariah 4:14 we are told of "the two anointed ones" ("sons of oil," margin, A. V.) "that stand by the Lord of the whole earth." In Zechariah 4:4 the question is asked, "What are these, my lord?" The 6th verse gives the answer: "This is the word of Jehovah unto Zerubbabel, saying, Not by might, nor by power, but by my Spirit, saith Jehovah of hosts." Zerubbabel is one who restores the worship of God. So these two witnesses or anointed ones keep declaring the word of God in faith and power, from the heart center (Jerusalem) into the whole earth —the uttermost parts of our body.

Just below the heart is the seat of judgment; so these witnesses have power to discern and judge the thoughts and intents of the heart, and to cause a drought to come into the earth or carnal consciousness, and plagues of different kinds, as well as fire to purify and put away error thoughts that oppose the Truth.

"The beast that cometh up out of the abyss" (Rev. 11:7) must be some race error thought that has gained great ascendancy through the power of people's belief in it. This thought for a time keeps the witnesses from continuing their work, and they remain seemingly inactive. "They that dwell on the earth" (the carnal mind) rejoice, for they think that they are free to go on in their old error, sense ways, and not be brought into judgment for them; but in a very short time the word comes into greater activity than ever, with renewed power.

The remainder of this chapter, together with the 12th chapter, shows the great final struggle that occurs when error, the Adversary, is cast out of heaven (the kingdom of Truth within man) into the earth. The succeeding chapters tell of the overcoming in the earth or outer man, until in the 21st and 22d chapters, which show forth complete redemption, the "holy city" comes down from God out of heaven to dwell in the earth. There shall be no more death, neither sorrow nor crying, neither shall there be any more pain, for the former things will have passed away. All things will have been made new.

We go through all these experiences, to the very highest and best, even the perfect renewal of the whole man—spirit, soul, and body. It all takes place right here on earth. Then that which takes place in us as individuals will be fulfilled in the earth also, and it will be redeemed. "For we know that the whole creation groaneth and travaileth in pain together until now. And not only so, but ourselves also, who have the first-fruits of the Spirit, even we ourselves groan within ourselves, waiting for *our* adoption, *to wit*, the redemption of our body."

woman, Greek, of Mark 7:25-30; also the woman with the alabaster cruse of ointment (Matt. 26:7).

Meta. Besides the interpretation given under SYROPHŒNICIAN (which see), the Greek woman of Tyre and Sidon may also be said to represent the unspiritualized love that is natural to the body. Her daughter is physical sensation, which has been sensualized by impure thought.

Whenever the illumined I AM (Jesus) centers its attention anywhere in the body there is at once a quickening of intelligence and a reaching out for higher things by the consciousness functioning there. Every part of the organism is under the control of a set of thoughts that direct and care for that particular function. The nerves are under the control of a thought that thinks about nerves; the muscles, bones, blood—every department of the man has its distinct thought center. So we are made up of many men and many women, because the masculine and feminine qualities are equally distributed and they all work together in harmony when divine order is established.

We use all these different parts of our being, but not understandingly. In our ignorance we dissipate the natural purity and strength of these obedient people who form our soul and our body; but when we become illumined by Spirit a reform sets in, and they all reflect the new light that has come to us, especially so when we concentrate our mind on the life centers, or "enter into a house" (Mark 7:24).

There lingers in the mind that old idea, borrowed from the limited vision of the Jew, that Spirit does not include the body in its redemptive process, but the body cries out for cleansing and purification. "Even the dogs under the table eat of the children's crumbs." Good common sense should teach us that life is always present throughout nature, a stream proceeding from the highest to the lowest.

This understanding of the unity and purity of the one life brings healing to the demonized sense consciousness. "She . . . found the child laid upon the bed, and the demon gone out."

The woman with the "alabaster cruse of exceeding precious ointment" (Matt. 26:7) signifies the forgiving love of Spirit, and her ointment is the conserved nerve fluid that is stored up in the secret recesses of the body.

The disciples thought that this precious ointment should be sold and the proceeds given to the poor, because they were in the outer consciousness where there is a seeming lack of vitality at times, and, not understanding the law of conservation, they thought that their "poor" needs should be supplied first.

Jesus was passing through the regeneration, and the sense consciousness of the flesh body was being crucified. The precious substance of love was consumed to the end that it might be brought forth as the vitalizing element of His resurrected body. This is what Jesus meant when He said that the ointment that the woman poured upon His body was preparation for His burial.

Word, of God.

Meta. John gives us the following concerning the Word of God: "In the beginning was the Word, and the Word was with God, and the Word was God." The Word of God is the divine Logos, God in His capacity as creative power, and includes all the potentialities of Being. It is the idea of God, the image and likeness of God, spiritual man. In it are all the possibilities, all the qualities, of God.

Being, the original fount, is an impersonal principle; but in its work of creation it puts forth an idea that contains all ideas: the Logos, Word, Christ, the Son of God, or spiritual man. This spiritual man or Christ, the Word of God, is the true inner self of every individual. Man therefore contains within himself the capacities of Being, and through his words uses the creative principle of Divine Mind to create.

The Greek *logos*, which has been translated Word, literally means reasonable speech, or, as we may say, the reasonable thought or word. That is, all things that God, or Mind, made in the beginning were perfect results of the power of Mind at work through thought, along lines of accurate reason based on the perfect, ideal conceptions inherent in infinite Mind.

The orthodox Christian says that the 1st chapter of John refers directly to Christ, which from our standpoint of universal Mind is admissible, for Christ and the Son of God, or the Thought or Word of Mind, are interchangeable.

The man Jesus became so transparent by purification that the universal Christ or God thought expressed itself through Him more clearly than through any other man of whom we have record; yet this Son of God, or perfect thought of infinite Mind, is shining in degree through every man, woman, and child in the universe. All life, all love, all Truth, are the expressions of the one great Cause. It is the ever present principle of good that shows forth in man in proportion to the purity of his thoughts.

The only expression of Divine Mind is the Logos, or Word, the one universal Man-God. This is the Christ or anointed one. It is Mind manifest, and he who lets the "mind . . . which was also in Christ Jesus" be in him becomes the Son of God. As thought is the only mode of manifestation of Mind, it follows that the only way to accomplish such manifestation is to think the thoughts that we know correspond in purity and truth to the thought of God. Thoughts are things,

which can be controlled and regulated. The thoughts of men ultimate in their bodies and environments. When men know this they will proceed to cultivate their thoughts more carefully than they do their fields. By casting out by denial all undesirable thoughts and planting by affirmation all good thoughts, man will soon find himself surrounded by a universe of beauty and harmony only. All sin, sickness, poverty, and death will disappear. He will have a new body as light as air and as indestructible as electricity. This training of the mind results in habitual thinking of pure thoughts until finally the thinker slips like a crystal dewdrop into the flowing sea of pure thinking, the Logos or Word of God.

Absent healing is done through the power of the spoken word of God. The Word of God is His creative power. It includes all the potentialities of Being: life, love, wisdom, substance, power, strength, and all God's other attributes.

All who have faith in its power to accomplish that whereto it is sent may speak the word with effect.

All who open their minds to the Word by faith may receive it into consciousness.

Every word of man has back of it an idea, and the power of the word is primarily in that idea. Added power is given by the speaker according to his realization of oneness with the idea and the force of his thought.

The two fundamental attitudes of mind are the positive and the negative, or affirmation and denial. "Let your speech be, Yea, yea; Nay, nay."

The character of the idea that a word conveys determines whether it is constructive or destructive.

Man makes his world by his word, either silently or audibly expressed.

The ideas that make words constructive are life, love, wisdom, substance, power, strength, and all other ideas that express divine attributes. Words carrying the life idea produce a vitalizing and life-giving effect. Words that express divine love are harmonizing and unifying in their effect.

Words are made active in the body

through their being received by the mind and carried into the body through the subconsciousness by one's thought. Constructive words that renew the body are made a part of the body consciousness by prayer and meditation.

wrath, of God.

Meta. Some Bible authorities claim that the "wrath of God," or of the Lord (Rom. 1:18), might with equal propriety be translated the "blessings" of the Lord. We know that after the destruction of limited and inferior thoughts and forms of life, other and higher thoughts and forms take their place, and the change is actually a blessing in the end. So even the "wrath" that comes to our fleshly tabernacles, when we persist in holding them in material thought, is a blessing ultimately. When we are loving and nonresistant we do not suffer under the transformations that go on when the Mosaic law is being carried out.

The "wrath of God" is really the working out of the law of Being destructively or inharmoniously for the individual who does not conform to the law but thinks and acts in opposition to it.

Z

Zaanan, zā'-ă-năn (Heb.) — *going forth; migrating; rich in flocks; place of flocks; flocking place.*

A town of Judah (Mic. 1:11). Zenan is thought to be the same place.

Meta. A thought center, deep within the consciousness, changing from belief in lack of life and of substance to belief in abundant substance and vitality (*going forth, migrating, rich in flocks, place of flocks, flocking place,* a town in the lowlands of Judah).

Zaanannim (in A. V., Judg. 4:11, plain of Zaanaim), zā-ă-năn'-nĭm (Heb.) —*complete changes; removals; migrations; double migratory tent; great migration; exodus.*

A place near Kedesh. In Joshua 19: 33 and Judges 4:11 we read of the "oak in Zaanannim." It was on the border of Naphtali.

Meta. Great and complete changes for the better, taking place in consciousness.

In bringing about higher and better ideals and experiences in one's consciousness, there must be first a dissatisfaction with present apparent thoughts and conditions, and a willingness to alter one's views. In this name a very great desire for a change is indicated; also an activity tending toward that change (*complete changes, double migratory tent, great migration, removals, exodus*). Then too, there are the staying qualities that are needed to balance the unsettled, changing attitude of mind. These quali-ties are signified in "oak," which stands for something very strong and protective; also the nearness of Naphtali (strength) and Kedesh (the divine presence within the individual consciousness) is significant. It was by the oak in Zaanannim that Sisera, captain of the host of Jabin, king of Canaan, fled from Barak to the tent of Heber the Kenite and was killed by Jael, the wife of Heber. This brought great victory and deliverance to the Israelites. In man's consciousness this experience signifies deliverance from error and advancement into greater realization of Truth.

Zaavan (in A. V., I Chron. 1:42, Zavan), zā'-ă-văn (Heb.) — *disquieted; shaken; disturbed; agitated; trembling; quaking; terrified; fearful.*

Son of Ezer. Ezer was a Horite chief and a son of Seir (Gen. 36:27).

Meta. A confused, fearful, unstable thought tendency in the outer or body consciousness in the individual (*disquieted, disturbed, trembling;* a man of Seir, or Edom).

Zabad, zā'-băd (Heb.)—*whom God gave; gift; present; donation; endowment; dowry.*

a Son of Ahlai; one of David's mighty men (I Chron. 11:41). **b** Other men by this name are mentioned in II Chronicles 24:26; Ezra 10:27, 33, 43.

Meta. In giving His Son, the Christ, spiritual man, or Jehovah, to be the true inner self or spiritual I AM of each individual, God gave His whole gift to man. In the Son there is all-possibility; in embryo there is all that the Father is and has. This is suggested in the name Zabad, which means *whom God gave, gift, endowment, dowry.* One authority gives as the meaning of the name, "my gift is Jehovah."

It is interesting, in conjunction with this name, to look up the significance of ZATTU, HASHUM, and NEBO, the fathers of the men named Zabad that are mentioned in the 10th chapter of Ezra.

Zabbai, zăb'-bāi (Heb.)—*washed; cleansed; clean; clear; limpid; pure; innocent.*

a One of the sons of Bebai. He had taken a foreign wife, but agreed to give her up when his error was made clear to him by Ezra (Ezra 10:28). **b** The father of a Jewish man named Baruch, who helped to repair the wall of Jerusalem after the return from the Babylonian captivity (Neh. 3:20).

Meta. Thoughts belonging to the high, spiritual phase of consciousness in man (Israelites), which tend to purity and Truth (*washed, cleansed, clean, pure*) and to clearness of comprehension (*limpid, clear*).

Zabbud, zăb'-bŭd (Heb.)—*given; donated; bestowed; endowed; dowered.*

Son of Bigvai. He returned from the Babylonian captivity with Ezra (Ezra 8:14). The margin says, "Another reading is, *Zaccur.*"

Meta. An awakening to the fact that man is furnished with a permanent, inexhaustible source of life, love, wisdom, intelligence, power, strength — every good that he can need or desire (*endowed, given, bestowed*). This source is God Himself, who in the ideal Man, the Son, Christ, is the true self of everybody and expresses in and through each individual just to the extent that the individual gives Him coöperation.

Zabdi, zăb'-dī (Heb.)—*gift of Jehovah; Jah is endower; Jehovah gave; my dowry.*

a Grandfather of Achan of the tribe of Judah (Josh. 7:1). **b** A son of Shimei of the tribe of Benjamin (I Chron. 8:19). **c** Zabdi the Shiphmite was "over the increase of the vineyards for the wine-

cellars" in David's reign (I Chron. 27:27). **d** A Levite (Neh. 11:17).

Meta. Thoughts recognizing fullness of life, of vitality, as being possible of continuous expression in and through man, by means of his indwelling Christ, Jehovah, I AM (*gift of Jehovah, Jah is endower, Jehovah gave, my dowry*). "I came that they may have life, and may have *it* abundantly" (John 10:10).

Zabdiel, zăb'-dĭ-ĕl (Heb.)—*God is my gift; gift of God; God endows; dowry of God.*

a Father of Jashobeam, who was the officer over the first course of twenty-four thousand men who served King David in the first month of each year (I Chron. 27:2). **b** A son of Haggedolim. This Zabdiel was overseer of a number of the priests who returned from the Babylonian captivity (Neh. 11:14).

Meta. The idea signified here is that God, Spirit, being omnipresent in man and in all creation, has given man, or is to man, all-life, all-intelligence, all-substance, all-power, all-Truth—everything that man can need and use in his unfoldment and growth into the full manifestation of the perfect image and likeness of God in which he was created in the beginning (*God is my gift, God endows, gift of God, dowry of God*). See ZABAD.

Zabud, zā'-bŭd (Heb.)—*given; presented; bestowed; endowed; dowered.*

Son of Nathan. He was "chief minister, *and* the king's friend," in the reign of Solomon (I Kings 4:5). Zabad, Zabud, and Zabbud are virtually the same name.

Meta. See ZABBUD and ZABAD.

Zaccai, zăc'-cāi (Heb.)—*washed; cleansed; purified; clean; clear; limpid; guileless; innocent; virtuous; just; righteous.*

Seven hundred and sixty of his descendants returned from the Babylonian captivity with Zerubbabel (Ezra 2:9).

Meta. A very influential, or fruitful, thought belonging to the spiritual phase of consciousness in man (an Israelite, who had numerous descendants who returned to Judea from the Captivity) that is true, honest, upright, and unadulterated by materiality or by error (*cleansed, purified, just, guileless, righteous*).   .

Zacchæus, zăc-chæ'-ŭs (Gk. fr. Heb.) —*washed; cleansed; cleaned; clean; purified; clear; limpid; guileless; innocent; virtuous; just; righteous.*

"A chief publican," a taxgatherer, who lived in Jericho. He climbed a tree to see Jesus, because he was small of stature. He received Jesus into his house, accepted the Truth that Jesus taught, and made a more than right adjustment in his life (Luke 19:1-10).

Meta. Conservatism degenerated to avarice. Zacchæus means *just,* or *clean, purified.* In the Truth of Being, conservatism, or the power to accumulate, is legitimate; but Zacchæus wrongfully had exacted more than his share of goods. This represents the tendency of race thought to reflect into consciousness selfish ideas of accumulation.

The methods of avarice are known to all as unjust, and are under universal condemnation. Zacchæus (conservatism) becomes a publican and a sinner (avarice, injustice, withholding). When Jesus went to lodge with him the bystanders murmured; but the I AM must deal fearlessly with all its thoughts, and must bring them to repentance. In telling Zacchæus that he also was a son of Abraham, Jesus recognized the good as the central substance of every thought. The center around which avarice accumulates is "justice." The accumulative faculty starts out with the *just* thought of getting only its own, but in the reflected world's hurry to get rich it loses sight of justice and adopts methods that bring it under condemnation. When its attention is called to its inner substance of goodness and Truth it remembers its true nature, and cries, "The half of my goods I give to the poor; and if I have wrongfully exacted aught of any man, I restore fourfold." The I AM puts its seal of approval on this just resolve, with the words of assurance, "To-day is salvation come to this house."

Avarice expresses in body consciousness as a tendency of the mind to deplete one center in the effort to sustain normal activity in another center. For example, the whole organism may be depleted by a too intense activity of the intellectual powers, without the direction of spiritual I AM.

The "sycomore tree" is the fig mulberry, which produces fruit of little value. It represents a false standard of expression. The ego must "come down" from its false standard before justice and harmony can be established. Zacchæus was commanded to come down from the tree.

Another interpretation of this lesson in Luke 19:1-10 is as follows:

The Hebrew meaning of Zacchæus is *purified, just, righteous.* One authority says that Zacchæus means "justice."

Zacchæus is described as being little of stature, a chief publican, and rich. This description of him represents the limitations of a good thought that is steeped in materiality.

The "sycomore tree" that Zacchæus climbed to see Jesus is the fig mulberry, which produces a figlike fruit of little value. His climbing this tree represents the tendency of small thoughts to elevate themselves to high places on false foundations.

It is possible for an inherently just and pure faculty to degenerate until, in its small perspective, it becomes avaricious and unjust. Justice is a divine quality, but the selfish grasping for temporal things has created a race consciousness called Mammon, which seems to be gripping men and nations with avarice and hate.

The remedy for shortsighted selfishness and avarice is obedience to the Christ command: "Zacchæus, make haste, and come down; for to-day I must abide at thy house." We all must come down from assumed standards of right, and abide with the Christ in divine justice and righteousness.

When we awaken spiritually and discern the Truth we become like Zacchæus; we are willing to give up our unlawfully acquired possessions of every kind, and to restore fourfold to those whom we have cheated.

The meaning of Luke 19:9, 10 is that Jesus, who represents man's demonstration of Christ, redeems every sinning or lost faculty. Every true faculty of the mind has its origin in spiritual faith (represented by Abraham—*father of a multitude*), the one source of all the faculties of man.

Zaccur, zăc'-cŭr (Heb.)—*pricking; piercing; penetrating; calling to mind; remembering; mindful; considering; reflecting; testimony; renown; praise; a male; bearing a male child.*

a Father of Shammua, who was the spy chosen from the tribe of Reuben (Num. 13:4). **b** Other Israelites by this name are mentioned in I Chronicles 4:26; 24:27; 25:2; Nehemiah 3:2; 10:12; 13: 13.

Meta. The action that an idea sets up in entering the consciousness of an individual, producing thought, reflection, due consideration, and bringing forth a positive conclusion (*pricking, penetrating, remembering, considering, reflecting, bearing a male child*).

Zachariah (A. V., Zacharias), zăch-ă-rī'-ăh (Heb.)—*Jehovah has penetrated; Jah is mindful; Jehovah has remembered; concentrating on Jehovah; memory of Jah; Jah is renowned; praise the Lord.*

Son of Barachiah, a righteous man whom Jesus accused the Jewish people of having slain (Matt. 23:35). Zechariah is the same name.

Meta. The significance is the same as that of Zacharias and Zechariah, spiritual consciousness (*Jehovah has penetrated, Jehovah has remembered, concentrating on Jehovah, memory of Jah, Jah is renowned*), or the entrance of spiritual thought into man's consciousness and a lifting up of spiritual understanding.

Zacharias, zăch-ă-rī'-ăs (Gk. fr. Heb.) —*Jehovah has penetrated; Jah is mindful; Jehovah has remembered; concentrating on Jehovah; memory of Jah; Jah is renowned; praise the Lord.*

Father of John the Baptist (Luke 1:5-67). Zechariah and Zachariah are the same name.

Meta. Spiritual consciousness (*Jehovah has penetrated, Jehovah has remembered*).

Zadok, zā'-dŏk (Heb.)—*righteous; just; true.*

a Son of Ahitub, a priest in David's reign (II Sam. 8:17); also in Solomon's reign (I Kings 4:4). **b** Other men by this name are mentioned in II Kings 15: 33; Nehemiah 3:4, 29; 13:13.

Meta. Thoughts that are right and true and just (*righteous, just*). Zadok the priest and Nathan the prophet (I Kings 1:34, 38, 39) are representatives of the spiritual kingdom, which is the real source of all enduring power.

Zaham, zā'-hăm (Heb.)—*offensive; stinking; rancid; impure; unwholesome; unclean; leprous; loathsome; hateful.*

One of Rehoboam's sons (II Chron. 11:19).

Meta. Rehoboam represents that in man's consciousness which exalts the senses; it is the fruit of many sensuous and insane thought habits. (See REHOBOAM.) Zaham (*offensive, impure, unclean, leprous, loathsome, hateful*), son of Rehoboam, signifies the offensiveness of extreme uncleanness of thought and habit.

Zair, zā'-ĭr (Heb.)—*small; little; minor; reduced; made few; petty; ignoble; mean; despised; contemned; dishonored; worthless.*

A place, evidently in Edom, where Joram, king of Judah, defeated the Edomites (II Kings 8:21).

Meta. The inferiority of the "mind of the flesh" in man, in comparison with the phase of his being that is established in spiritual understanding and expression (*little, small, made few, petty, ignoble, worthless*; a place in Edom, Edom referring to the sense consciousness in man). Jesus said, "It is the spirit that giveth life; the flesh profiteth nothing" (John 6:63).

Zalaph, zā'-lăph (Heb.)—*breaking; breaking forth; breaking up; fracturing; bruising; wounding; hurting.*

Father of Hanun, who helped to repair the wall of Jerusalem after the return from the Babylonian captivity (Neh. 3:30).

Meta. A *breaking forth* from, or *breaking up* of, errors in consciousness, that good may be established. Seeming sorrow and travail in one's being often accompany a breaking up and passing away of established error thoughts, habits, and conditions (*fracturing, bruising, wounding, hurting*), but the outcome is always joy, peace, and greater good: "A woman when she is in travail hath sorrow, because her hour is come: but when she is delivered of the child, she remembereth no more the anguish, for the joy that a man is born into the world."

Zalmon, zăl'-mŏn (Heb.)—*shade; shadow; overcast; shadowy; shady; darkness; shadowed forth; apposition; projected image; reflection; making like; likeness; image; idol.*

a "The Ahohite," one of David's mighty men and a member of his guard, or council (II Sam. 23:28). He is called Ilai in I Chronicles 11:29. **b** A mountain near Shechem (Judg. 9:48).

Meta. A going up to a higher plane of thought (a mountain; also the man named Zalmon is called Ilai in I Chronicles 11:29, Ilai meaning *elevated, supreme*), but with the understanding of Truth as yet obscure. Because of man's seeing more from the standpoint of the outer senses than from the inner Spirit, the light and the presence of that which is divine are not yet fully revealed to the consciousness (*shady, shadowy, darkness, projected image, making like*). "For now we see in a mirror, darkly; but then face to face: now I know in part; but then shall I know fully even as also I was fully known." (See ZALMONAH.)

Zalmonah, zăl-mō'-năh (Heb.)—*giving shade; shady; shaded; sheltered; canopied; overcast.*

A camping place of the Israelites in the wilderness (Num. 33:41).

Meta. Divine protection from more intense light and heat, or spiritual illumination and inflow of life and energy, than the individual at this stage of his unfoldment Godward is able to apprehend, to assimilate, and to use rightly (*giving shade, shaded, sheltered, canopied*; a shade here signifying something that casts a shadow, a tree for instance, and under which one can gain protection from the direct rays of the sun when its heat and light are so intense as to cause discomfort).

The flaming sword that turned every way was placed, with the cherubim, at the east of the Garden of Eden to keep the way of the tree of life, so that Adam might not eat of it in his sinful state and so live forever in that condition; even so it is necessary that we go through a purification and a putting away of our sense beliefs so that we may attain fullness of life and understanding. This is good, because, if it were possible for us to attain to the fullness of Truth while clinging to the fleshly consciousness with its activities, we should bring upon ourselves utter destruction. While we are living in error thought, the very material is a protection to us in that only as we put it away and rise out of it is our consciousness opened to more light, to spiritual understanding. This illumination in turn enables us to overcome more negation; then a greater realization of the abundant Christ life comes to us, and so on, all the way to the complete putting on of the Christ. It is better, therefore, that we "grow" out of the old and into the new, out of the material and into the spiritual, than that we go the whole way in one great step, as many of us feel like doing.

Zalmunna, zăl-mŭn'-nà (Heb.)—*withdrawn from protection; deprived of shade; coming out from the shadow.*

One of the two kings of Midian who were defeated and slain by Gideon (Judg. 8:5-21).

Meta. A certain belief in evil or a contentious thought, with its activity, upon which the light of Truth has been turned; this belief or thought has occupied a ruling place in the phase of consciousness in the individual that Midian signifies. All the protection of error thought has been removed from it and it is overcome, put out of consciousness (*withdrawn from protection, deprived of shade*, a king of Midian who was defeated and slain by Gideon, who signifies denial).

Zamzummim (A. V., Zamzummims), zăm-zŭm'-mĭm (Heb.)—*buzzes; hubbub; noises; noisy multitude; swarming rabble; barbarians.*

An ancient race of giants. They were called Zamzummim by the Ammonites (Deut. 2:20); they are thought to have been the Zuzim of Genesis 14:5.

Meta. Disorder, confusion, worries, fears, inharmony, the result of the rule of physical force, of vitality, of strength, in individual consciousness, without any restraining or refining influences whatever. (The meaning of Zamzummim is *buzzes, hubbub, noises, noisy multitude, swarming rabble, barbarians.* These people were an ancient race of giants, who disappeared before the time of the Israelites. They gave place to the Ammonites, who dwelt in their land until they in turn were conquered by Israel.)

The Ammonites were enemies of the Israelites; they represent, among other things, "popular opinion." This is a very active restraining influence over brute force and strength. Man first begins to restrain himself, and to act in a more civilized manner, to a great extent because of what others may think and say, since he learns early to desire the good will of his friends and associates. Then as he gains a degree of refinement because of this and other human reasons (Ammonites), higher ideals come to him, until sooner or later he unfolds to the place wherein he is ready for true spiritual understanding and expression, which are here represented by the Israelites.

Zanoah, ză-nō′-ăh (Heb.)—*spit out; spittle; foul; rancid; stinking; vile; cast out; rejected; deserted; stagnant stream; marsh; bog; swamp.*

The name of two cities of Judah, one in the lowland and the other in the hill country (Josh. 15:34, 56). One of these cities evidently was founded by Jekuthiel (I Chron. 4:18).

Meta. Groups of thoughts that belong to or are associated with the high, spiritual phase of consciousness in man (cities of Judah), but have corrupted themselves by centering in personality instead of Spirit. Thus stagnation ensues (*spit out, foul, rancid, cast out,* and so forth). "If a man abide not in me, he is cast forth as a branch, and is withered." "If the salt have lost its savor, . . . it is thenceforth good for nothing, but to be cast out and trodden under foot of men."

Zaphenath–paneah (A. V., Zaphnath-paaneah), zăph-ē′-năth-pā-nē′-ăh (Heb. fr. Egypt.)—*the savior speaks and lives; health of world; savior of the universe; salvation of the age; savior of the dynasty; sustainer of the life of the world.*

The name that Pharaoh gave to Joseph (Gen. 41:45).

Meta. Pharaoh called Joseph Zaphenath-paneah (*the savior speaks and lives, savior of the universe, salvation of the age, sustainer of the life of the world,* or, as Charles Fillmore defines it, "governor of the district of the place of life"), which indicates clearly that the generative center is to be ruled by the state of consciousness in which God, through the indwelling Christ, is the directive power.

We understand that Joseph down in Egypt portrays the involution of a high spiritual idea. The several visits of his brothers to Egypt for corn, and the final reconciliation, are a symbolical representation of the manner in which we make connection with the obscured vitality in the organism and finally bring all our faculties into conjunction with it.

Zaphon, ză′-phŏn (Heb.)—*covered; protected; concealed; secret; private; unknown; unmanifest; hidden powers; not to be revealed; boreal; the left side,* i. e., when facing east; *north; north quarter; northern; north wind.*

A city in Gad, in Palestine (Josh. 13:27).

Meta. Zaphon refers to the *north*, to that which is above in consciousness, or in this case, we might say, to that which is above the consciousness of man—the spiritual or God wisdom and intelligence. Its center or seat in man is in the very top of the head. From this higher wisdom—which is *secret* and hidden, and *not to be revealed,* so far as the human or sensate is concerned—come all the clear, keen revelations of Truth that often seem so hard, cold, and cutting (signified by *north wind*) to the sense mind of the individual. Truth discloses and puts away error, without sympathy or compromise. Thus Truth teachers and healers are sometimes called hardhearted by patients and students, especially by those who want help but are loath to let go of cherished error beliefs and practices.

Zarephath, zăr′-ĕ-phăth (Heb.)—*place of refinement; smelter; smelting place;*

place of purification with fire; place of purity; place of trial.

The place where lived the widow who fed Elijah during the famine. According to the story she gave him the last of the supply of food that she had on hand, whereupon there continued to be sufficient food for them throughout the whole period of the famine (I Kings 17:9; Luke 4:26).

Meta. The purifying fires of the inner subjective life centers.

Zarephath means *place of refinement, smelting place, place of purification with fire,* and smelting is the extracting of precious metals by heat. This refining work is literally what takes place in the man who has let sense expression deplete him until he is forced to give up and turn to the purifying fires of Spirit for renewal; thus the error is separated from the true, it is put away, and the true strength, substance, power, life, and other spiritual qualities come forth in renewed expression. It is at Zarephath that the widow (love bereft of wisdom), in a state of partial starvation, gives her little supply of substance and joy to the sustenance of spiritual life and wisdom, and receives an all-sufficient supply in return.

The widow in Zarephath represents the divine feminine, or the love principle, in individual consciousness. Elijah is the divine masculine, or wisdom. Separated, these are both in a state of lack, but when they are joined in consciousness, increase at once begins and there is abundant good. "The jar of meal wasted not, neither did the cruse of oil fail."

Zarethan (in A. V., Joshua 3:16, Zaretan; I Kings 4:12, Zartanah; I Kings 7:46, Zarthan), zăr'-ĕ-thăn (Heb.)—*piercing; penetrating; cooling.*

A place near which the Israelites crossed the river Jordan when they entered the Promised Land (Josh. 3:16). In the clay ground between Succoth and Zarethan the vessels that were made by Hiram, king of Tyre, for Solomon's Temple were "cast" or formed, as in a mold (see I Kings 7:46).

Meta. The process of an idea's finding entrance into the consciousness or into

substance, and taking on form and shape; or, substance emerging from the invisible and purely spiritual realm into outer or seemingly material expression and manifestation (*piercing, penetrating, cooling,* a place near which the vessels, basins, and many of the various parts and furnishings of the Temple were cast; also a place beside which the waters of the Jordan rose in a heap so that the Children of Israel crossed the river on dry ground).

Zattu (in A. V., Neh. 10:14, Zatthu), zăt'-tu (Heb.)—*sprout; shoot; branch; green; fresh; lovely; pleasant; tender; young; olive branch.*

His descendants returned with Zerubbabel from the Babylonian captivity (Ezra 2:8).

Meta. A sprouting, growing consciousness and realization of peace and prosperity, under direction of the indwelling Christ Spirit (*sprout, shoot, branch, green, fresh, lovely, pleasant, olive branch.*)

Zaza, zā'-zȧ (Heb.)—*glittering; sparkling; projecting rays; emitting splendor; flowering; sprouting; spouting forth.*

Son of Jonathan, and brother of Peleth, of the tribe of Judah (I Chron. 2:33).

Meta. The love of God for mankind, as revealed in Christ. This love, when understood even in faintest degree by the individual, shines out above and beyond all else in his life and brings forth fruit (*glittering, sparkling, projecting rays, emitting splendor, flowering, sprouting;* a son of Jonathan, of the tribe of Judah, Jonathan suggesting the idea of love).

Zebadiah, zĕb-ȧ-dī'-ăh (Heb.)—*Jehovah has given; Jah is endower; dowry of Jah; presentation of Jehovah.*

The name of several Israelites; some of them were prominent men (I Chron. 8:15; 12:7; II Chron. 19:11; Ezra 8:8).

Meta. "I came that they may have life, and may have *it* abundantly," were the words of Jesus. "The free gift of God is eternal life in Christ Jesus our Lord." That which Jehovah gives to man is Godlikeness, and this includes continuity of fullness of life, as well as love, wisdom, substance, power, everything that man can possibly need and use for his unfoldment and growth into spiritual perfection, into the eternal consciousness of life, of every good (*Jehovah has given, Jah is endower, dowry of Jah, presentation of Jehovah*).

Zebah, zē'-băh (Heb.) — *slaying; slaughtering; killing; sacrificing; immolation of victims; victim; sacrifice.*

One of the two Midianite kings who were defeated and killed by Gideon (Judg. 8:5-21).

Meta. The offering to God of the phase of thought that stands back of the strife and contention, or Midianite state of mind, in the individual (*sacrifice*, a king of Midian who was pursued and slain by Gideon and his men).

When any error thought or state of consciousness is put on the altar, is sacrificed to God definitely and consciously, a transmutation takes place: the power, energy, and good that are in and back of the error activity are raised to higher expression, while the ignorance and darkness that made possible the former unwise and inharmonious expression disappear before the light of Truth.

Zebedee, zĕb'-ĕ-dēe (Gk. fr. Heb.)— *Jehovah has given; Jah is endower; dowry of Jah; presentation of Jehovah; my dowry.*

Father of James and John, who were two of the disciples of Jesus Christ (Matt. 4:21). This name is taken from Zabdi; Zebadiah is a form of the same name.

Meta. See ZABDI and ZEBADIAH for the significance of Zebedee.

Personal ambition trying to enter the kingdom is represented in Matthew 20: 20, 21 by the attempt of the wife of Zebedee to gain the promise that her two sons, James and John (wisdom and love), should sit, one at Jesus' right hand and the other at Jesus' left, in the kingdom of heaven.

Ambition should not be killed out. It should be exalted. When thus transformed it becomes purely spiritual aspiration, or the desire for spiritual excellence.

Zebidah (A. V., Zebudah), zĕ-bī'-dăh (Heb.)—*gift outright; bestowal; dowry; endowment.*

Daughter of Pedaiah of Rumah, and mother of Jehoiakim, king of Judah (II Kings 23:36).

Meta. The soul of man's recognizing the Truth that is signified by Zabbud (the masculine form of Zebidah). Zebidah, being the name of a woman, signifies the soul or feminine phase of that for which the masculine form of the name stands. (See ZABBUD.)

Zebina, zĕ-bī'-nȧ (Heb.)—*getting for oneself; purchase; bought; gain; profit; acquisition; precious possession.*

Son of Nebo, an Israelite. He had taken a foreign wife after the return from the Babylonian captivity, but gave her up at Ezra's command (Ezra 10:43).

Meta. Acquisition, *getting for oneself.* This is good, so long as one does not let the spirit of acquisition degenerate into selfishness and dishonesty, so long as one exercises it in acquiring that which tends to Christlikeness, to one's eternal good (*precious possession*), and does not draw to oneself error, limitation, bondage.

Zeboiim (in A. V., all but Genesis 14: 2, 8, Zeboim), zĕ-boi'-ĭm (Heb.)—*wars; waging of wars; plunderings; preyings; rending with the teeth; beasts of prey; ravenous appetites; bestiality; carnivorous wild beasts generally.*

A Canaanitish city. Its king was Shemeber, one of the five kings who joined forces in the vale of Siddim to war against Chedorlaomer, king of Elam, whom they had been serving (Gen. 10: 19; 14:2). This city was overthrown along with Sodom and Gomorrah (Deut. 29:23). Zeboim is the same name.

Meta. Zeboiim pertains to *ravenous appetites*, sensual passions, the wild-beast nature, holding sway in the subconsciousness (*wars, plunderings, preyings, rending with the teeth, beasts of prey, bestiality, carnivorous wild beasts*; a city whose king was subject to Chedorlaomer, rebelled against him, and was overcome. Zeboiim was destroyed with Sodom and Gomorrah, therefore was in the same class with those wicked cities). (See ZEBOIM.)

Zeboim, zĕ-bō'-ĭm (Heb.)—*wild place; place of ravenous beasts; hyenas; carnivorous wild beasts generally; ravenous appetites; bestiality.*

a A valley in Benjamin (I Sam. 13:18).
b A town that was occupied by Benjamites after the return from the Captivity (Neh. 11:34).

Meta. A group of thoughts, deep within the life forces of man, that is given over to the expression of his beastly and sensual nature, appetite, and passion (*place of ravenous beasts, ravenous appetites, bestiality;* see ZEBOIIM). This thought center, at the stage of individual unfoldment signified in I Samuel 13:18 and Nehemiah 11:34, has come under the directive power of man's active faith in God (Benjamin), for upliftment.

Zebul, zē'-bŭl (Heb.)—*making round; surrounding; habitation; dwelling; dwelling together; abiding; cohabiting.*

The ruler of the city of Shechem. He joined Abimelech against Gaal, son of Ebed, and against the people of the city, who were rebelling against Abimelech's rule (Judg. 9:28-41).

Meta. A ruling thought in the burden-bearing attitude of mind that Shechem signifies, which persists in holding to things as they appear; is content to abide in present beliefs and conditions; goes with the crowd; joins forces with the present seeming prevailing power, whatever it may be (*habitation, dwelling, abiding, cohabiting*). This thought activity is always opposed to any change that would in any way disturb its settled ways; it is not progressive.

Zebulun (in A. V., Matthew 4:13, 15 and Rev. 7:8, Zabulon), zĕb'-ū-lŭn (Heb.)—*surrounded; habitation; dwelling; abiding; neighbor; of one's household.*

a Jacob's tenth son, and the sixth by Leah. "And Leah conceived again, and bare a sixth son to Jacob. And Leah said, God hath endowed me with a good dowry; now will my husband dwell with me, because I have borne him six sons: and she called his name Zebulun" (Gen. 30:20). **b** One of the Israelitish tribes, descendants of Zebulun (Num. 1:30, 31). Jacob's blessing on his son Zebulun was: "Zebulun shall dwell at the haven of the sea;

And he shall be for a haven of ships;
And his border shall be upon Sidon"
(Gen. 49:13). The blessing of Moses on the tribe of Zebulun is given in conjunc-

tion with that of Issachar (Deut. 33:18, 19).

"And of Zebulun he said,
Rejoice, Zebulun, in thy going out;
And, Issachar, in thy tents.
They shall call the peoples unto the mountain;
There shall they offer sacrifices of righteousness:
For they shall suck the abundance of the seas,
And the hidden treasures of the sand."

Meta. Order, static (*habitation, dwelling;* "the abundance of the seas," universal Mind). In the organism of man the faculty of order is located in the center of the abdomen, at the navel.

Zebulun may also be said to represent the intelligence in the stomach that directs the digestion, and presides over the chemistry of the organism, separating and apportioning to each part its needed and correct share of the food taken into the system.

Zebulunite (A. V., Zebulonite), zĕb'-ū-lŭn-īte (fr. Heb.).

A descendant of Zebulun. Here the reference is to Elon the Zebulunite, a judge of Israel (Judg. 12:11).

Meta. A discriminating, ruling thought in consciousness that belongs to that which Zebulun signifies. (See ZEBULUN.)

Zebulunites, zĕb'-ū-lŭn-ītes (fr. Heb.).

Descendants of Zebulun, son of Jacob (Num. 26:27).

Meta. Thoughts belonging to the order faculty in man. (See ZEBULUN.)

Zechariah, zĕch-ȧ-rī'-ah (Heb.)—*whom Jehovah has remembered; Jehovah has remembered; whom Jah calls to mind; memorial of Jah; memory of Jehovah; the Lord is remembered.*

Name of twenty-eight Israelites (II Chron. 24:20; 26:5; Ezra 8:16; Zech. 1:1, and so forth). Zachariah and Zacharias are forms of the same name.

Meta. See ZACHARIAH and ZACHARIAS.

Zecher (A. V., Zacher), zē'-chĕr (Heb.)—*called to mind; remembrance; recollection; memory; memorial; testimony; renown; praise; male; bearing a male child.*

Son of Jeiel of Gibeon (I Chron. 8:31). In I Chronicles 9:37, he is called Zechariah.

Meta. Zaccur has virtually the same meaning and significance. (See ZACCUR; see ZECHARIAH also.)

Zedad, zē'-dăd (Heb.)—*a side; turning aside; turning one's side to another; opposition; aversion; steep place; hillside; mountain side; coast; border.*

A place on the north border of Israel's inheritance in the Promised Land, as mapped out by Moses (Num. 34:8).

Meta. A phase of consciousness in man wherein he can go no further in his human-reasoning processes. He must accept divine inspiration and ideas consciously, and so be raised to spiritual understanding, the mountain top, or else degenerate into purely material thinking, which will lead him down into chaos and confusion (*a side, turning aside, opposition, mountain side, steep place, hillside, coast, border*). It is a place in mind where one can either go up, or go down with the downward tendency that is the result of limited, material reasoning and belief.

Zedekiah (in A. V., Neh. 10:1, Zidkijah), zĕd-ĕ-kī'-ăh (Heb.)—*uprightness of Jehovah; righteousness of Jehovah; justice of Jah; Jah is innocent; justification of Jehovah; Jah vindicates.*

a A false prophet. He made horns of iron and said to King Ahab of Israel: "Thus saith Jehovah, With these shalt thou push the Syrians, until they be consumed" (I Kings 22:11). **b** The last king of Judah before the Babylonian captivity. This king's name was Mattaniah, but was changed to Zedekiah by the king of Babylon, who placed him on the throne of Judah in place of Jehoiachin (II Kings 24:17). **c** A son of Hananiah, a prince of Judah (Jer. 36:12).

Meta. Zedekiah the false prophet symbolizes a belief in the uprightness and power of the Christ Truth, but with no understanding of the necessity for conforming to divine law in order to realize the victories that come to one when Jehovah fights one's battles.

Zedekiah, king of Judah, is the ruling thought of the spiritual consciousness at a certain phase of man's unfoldment. In the Bible story of Zedekiah we have an illustration of the relation that the will (king) bears to divine justice (one

definition of Zedekiah is *justice of Jah*).

Back of physical man is an idea. This idea is in God-Mind. God created man in His own image and likeness, a perfect spiritual being. The perfect-man idea is held in the mind of God, much as an idea is held in a human mind. The man idea found expression in physical man, who has freedom of will and freedom of thought.

God continually holds the perfect ideal before every man, but every man is not discerning enough to see this ideal. Every man feels the divine urge, however, and, whether he realizes it or not, he is continually striving to copy the divine ideal. The small boy in school tries to copy the perfect letters formed by the writing master, and makes crude characters that in some respects resemble the original copy. Thus do men try to copy the perfect man.

Man is also a creator. His thoughts are the pattern by which he shapes his character, his body, and his affairs. As he realizes the nature of his true sonship he becomes more Godlike; his realization of sonship shows forth in greater love, more life, harmony, happiness, and wisdom.

Man seems to have a dual nature. Part of the time he thinks of himself as a child of God, and part of the time he thinks of himself as a child of the flesh. When he turns his mind Godward he knows the reality of Spirit; then he masters mere things by the spiritual law, which transcends materiality. When he acts upon the idea that he is a physical being apart from God, he becomes involved in the labyrinth of appearances, and subject to discordant ideas, which he calls evil. The false and the true states of consciousness are continually warring against each other. The Bible, in symbols, tells of this struggle.

In II Kings 25:1-12 we find a warning of what may happen to the spiritual ideals that we have cultivated, if we allow our attention to become wholly taken up with the intellectual, the psychical, and the physical.

Jerusalem means *dwelling place of peace;* Judah, *praise;* Zedekiah, *justice of Jehovah;* Jericho, *fragrance.* Here we have a group of spiritual ideals. Contrast them with the group that overcame them: Babylon means *confusion*; Nebuchadnezzar means *may Nebo protect*. Nebo was a god of learning. Nebuzaradan means *whom Nebo favors*. The Chaldeans were the wise men, astrologers, magicians, of that time. Outside of Israel, the true, they refer to the psychic realm in man.

The king of Judah represents the will, although his name, Zedekiah, means *uprightness of Jehovah*, or *justice of Jah*. He turned his life away from God and directed it into the maze of selfish living and thinking. He trusted in the wisdom of men and in the idols made by men. He put his trust in Egypt for his deliverance, instead of putting his trust in God. He had terrible reverses because he was not loyal to Principle. He knew the divine law but he did not depend on it for his defense. He made an alliance with Egypt (darkness), which weakened his hold on spiritual resources.

When faith is placed in the power of material things the finer spiritual ideals of the mind are destroyed. Spiritual consciousness is necessary to the well-being and happiness of the race.

Many people today are suffering all kinds of sorrow and inharmony because they are trying to build a foundation upon the changing things that appear, instead of building upon unchanging Principle. Man is not happy unless he is making progress. The only true progress is the putting on of the perfect, spiritual ideal.

When our thoughts and acts do not conform to the law of Spirit, the judgment, or the exact result of our thoughts, is finally expressed in disaster of some kind. The siege and the final destruction of Jerusalem symbolize the various movements that sense consciousness (Babylon) makes in battering down the walls of spiritual consciousness (Jerusalem) when the will (King Zedekiah) has not called on God for protection.

When the will no longer perceives the Truth (puts out the eyes of the king) its spiritual dominion is ended (is bound in fetters and is carried to Babylon). This does not, however, represent the end of spiritual consciousness (the Jews and Jerusalem). History tells of the return, after seventy years, of a remnant of the Children of Israel, and of the slow rehabilitation of Jerusalem. The superior faculties (the priests and the prophets), which are loyal to the principles of justice and righteousness, restore the rule of Spirit (the priests inspired the people to return to Judah).

Zeeb, zē'-ĕb (Heb.)—*golden; yellow; yellowish; tawny; brazen; bold; wolf*.

A prince of Midian. He was slain by Gideon and his men at the wine press of Zeeb (Judg. 7:25).

Meta. A thought activity that has its inception in wisdom (*golden, yellow*). Because of the errors and limitations of the Midian phase of consciousness, with which this wisdom thought activity is associated, it has become tainted with error (*tawny*) and has taken on the attributes that are expressed in *brazen, bold, wolf*. This prince of Midian's being slain by Gideon at the wine press of Zeeb signifies that error thoughts and tendencies destroy themselves when the light of understanding and the word of denial are turned upon them.

Zela (in A. V., Zelah), zē'-lȧ (Heb.)—*sheltering involutions; outer coverings; exterior envelope; protective shelter; sheltering wings; side; sides of a room; walls of a tabernacle; quarter of the heavens; a rib*.

A city in Benjamin, in which Saul and Jonathan were buried in the sepulcher of Kish, Saul's father (II Sam. 21: 14). In Joshua 18:28, the name is spelled Zelah.

Meta. Zela is the same word that is translated "rib" in Genesis 2:21; it signifies the female principle in man, the soul, which is not only within but also infolds, envelops, and protects (see the foregoing definitions). When that which Saul and Jonathan signify comes to the end of outer dominance and expression, it is received by the soul and gives place to the rule of a higher and more spiritual phase of love and will (David). The sepulcher of Kish, in which Saul and Jonathan were buried, indicates that which holds a remembrance only of former power and dominion. (See KISH.)

Zelek, zē'-lĕk (Heb.)—*cleaving; splitting; rending; rent; fissure; chasm.*

An Ammonite, one of David's guard of mighty men (II Sam. 23:37).

Meta. A breaking up, taking place in the outer consciousness (*cleaving, splitting, rending, fissure, chasm,* an Ammonite who was one of David's guard of mighty men). This breaking up results when the effects of the rule of divine love (David) in the individual reach the outer man (the Ammonites belong to man's outer, sense thoughts).

When any phase of Truth begins to work in the outer phase of man's being, an upheaval, a division of thought, an inharmony and unrest, takes place before the harmony and peace of Spirit are finally established. This is what Jesus meant when He said, "Think not that I came to send peace on the earth: I came not to send peace, but a sword." Zelek represents this breaking up in the outer consciousness that is a result of the activity of the word of love and Truth.

Zelophehad, zĕ-lō'-phĕ-hăd (Heb.)— *first breaking out; first fracture; first opening; first-born.*

Son of Hepher, of the Israelitish tribe of Manasseh (Josh. 17:3-6).

Meta. The phase of understanding that perceives the falsity of error and so goes ahead opening up the consciousness to Truth, by means of denial of error (*first breaking out, first-born, first opening*). Established error thoughts must be overthrown, to a certain extent at least, before one can come into positive understanding. Zelophehad signifies this negative, or denial, letting-go-of-error side of the faculty of understanding (he was a man of Manasseh, and Manasseh signifies understanding). This that Zelophehad represents in the individual consciousness does not express in positive knowledge; it brings forth fruit in the inner, soul phase of being, however (he had no sons, but he had five daughters, who received his inheritance as if they had been sons). These daughters must in some way refer to the five senses as they relate inwardly to the soul.

Zelzah, zĕl'-zăh (Heb.)—*protection from dazzling brightness; sun-protected; shade from the sun; shade at noontide.*

A place on the border of Benjamin, by Rachel's sepulcher (I Sam. 10:2). It was there that Saul, in going from Samuel, met two men who told him that his father's asses, which he had been seeking, were found, and that now his father was troubled about him instead.

Meta. In Zelzah and the persons connected with the incident recorded in I Samuel 10 we find a union of faith and will with the animal and life forces in the organism. Samuel the prophet signifies the inner voice of Spirit, or the inner spiritual understanding expressing itself to the individual. He was of the Levites who were settled in Ephraim, Ephraim referring to the will faculty. Saul, too, represents the will; here, it had not yet come into dominion, but was on the way to rulership. Saul was of the tribe of Benjamin, and Benjamin signifies active faith. Zelzah signifies the bright shining of the inner discernment, reaching to a more outer phase of consciousness in the individual in such a way that the outer can receive the needed Truth and profit by it instead of being blinded by its dazzling brightness (*protection from dazzling brightness, sun-protected, shade at noontide; a place on the border of Benjamin*).

This expression of light or understanding that we find in Zelzah is a protection to the individual also, in that it gives him conscious unification of his faith and his will (Saul, of the tribe of Benjamin) with his animal life, with a much needed dominion over the animal phase of his consciousness. Saul was to be told at Zelzah that his father's asses had been found and that his father's attention was now turned toward him. Saul's father, Kish, signifies power and authority. Rachel's sepulcher was near Zelzah, and this has significance, since Rachel—*ewe, lamb*—refers to the soul phase of the pure natural life in the organism of man. The asses that Saul was hunting pertain to a phase of one's animal life and forces.

Zemaraim, zĕm-ă-rā'-ĭm (Heb.)— *double shearings; second shearing; double fleece; two coats of wool; double pruning.*

a A city of Benjamin (Josh. 18:22). **b** A mount in the hill country of Ephraim (II Chron. 13:4). Abijah, king of Judah, stood on this mountain and talked to the Israelites who had come up, a great army, to fight against Judah.

Meta. Thoughts of substance multiplied and strengthened in consciousness (*double shearings, double fleece, two coats of wool, double pruning*). *Pruning* and *shearing* give the idea of cutting off; even so thoughts of lack must be put away, that thoughts of substance may be established.

The Zemaraim that was a mountain in the hill country of Ephraim, upon which Abijah stood and talked to the Israelitish army, also signifies the exalting of the will in the individual, by recognition of God as the one guiding, overcoming power.

Zemarite, zĕm′-ă-rīte (fr. Heb.)—*that which exceeds the limits of moral authority; hunger for dominion; thirst for power; despot; tyrant; rebel.*

A tribe of people who were descended from Canaan, son of Ham (Gen. 10:18).

Meta. Rebellious, tyrannical, despotic thoughts and desires belonging to the "mind of the flesh" phase of consciousness in unredeemed man; the outer man seeking the dominion that belongs alone to the inner, or spiritual, man. (See HAM and CANAAN.)

Zemirah (A. V., Zemira), zĕ-mī′-răh (Heb.)—*striking the harp; music; song; chant; hymn of praise; song of triumph; singing birds; pruning vines.*

First-named son of Becher, who was one of Benjamin's sons (I Chron. 7:8).

Meta. Harmonious expression in joy, praise, and triumph over error (*striking the harp, music, hymn of praise, song of triumph*). This comes about by means of an active faith (Benjamin).

Zenan, zē′-năn (Heb.)—*rich in flocks; place of the flocks.*

A town in the lowland of Judah (Josh. 15:37). It is thought to be the same place as Zaanan of Micah 1:11.

Meta. Abundant substance and vitality (*rich in flocks, place of flocks*; see ZAANAN).

Zenas, zē′-năs (Gk.)—*Zeus-given; gift of Jove; living.*

A "lawyer," presumably one skilled in the Mosaic law, who had been converted to Christianity (Tit. 3:13).

Meta. The belief that the understanding and the power of life come from some material source (*Zeus-given, gift of Jove, living*). Zeus and Jove are names of Jupiter, who was worshiped as the supreme god by the ancient Greeks. Metaphysically Jupiter represents the great value that the spiritually unawakened man puts on that which he can see with his outer eyes and conceive with his outer mind, intellect, as force, power, strength. (See JUPITER.) In Zenas' being converted to Christianity this error thought is changed to coincide with the Truth as it concerns man's being.

Zephaniah, zĕph-ă-nī′-ăh (Heb.)—*Jehovah has hidden; protected of Jehovah; Jah is secret; secret place of Jehovah; Jah is secreted; mystery of Jehovah.*

a A priest of Judah (Jer. 21:1) who was put to death at Riblah in the land of Hamath, by the king of Babylon (II Kings 25:18, 21). **b** An ancestor of Heman, who was one of the singers in the tabernacle in David's reign (I Chron. 6:36). **c** A prophet who prophesied in the days of Josiah, king of Judah (Zeph. 1:1).

Meta. Truth active in the consciousness of the individual but hidden from the outer, sense phase of his being (*Jehovah has hidden, Jah is secret, secret place of Jehovah*). That the Truth of man's real being is hidden from his outer, personal, or carnal self is really a protection to him (*protected of Jehovah*), since the outer man in his unredeemed state is very likely to put to unwise use the power, understanding, and other divine qualities that he apprehends, thus increasing inharmony and sorrow in his life instead of realizing greater good.

Zephath, zē′-phăth (Heb.)—*looking about; viewing from a distance; bending forward to behold; attending; broad vision; high watch; watchtower; mountain watch; seen afar; beacon.*

A city of the Canaanites. It was captured by Judah and Simeon and its name was changed to Hormah (Judg. 1:17).

Meta. A group of thoughts of a high, wide-awake, watchful character (*looking* about, attending, mountain watch, watchtower, bending forward to behold) that has become a bearer of light (beacon) to the phase of consciousness in which the city of Zephath belongs (Canaanites, Canaan, lowland, signifying the body consciousness). The Canaanites signify the elemental life forces in the subconscious realm of mind in man. Therefore Zephath, a city of the Canaanites, would pertain to the seemingly mortal or physical phase of man's being, which is apparently far removed from that which is really true of man (viewing from a distance).

Because of its high, watchful, awakened character, however, this group of thoughts that Zephath signifies passes into the possession of the more spiritual qualities in the individual (Zephath was captured by Judah and Simeon) and it becomes a fortress and a sanctuary for many inner thoughts and ideals during times of adjustment in consciousness— the name of this city was changed to Hormah. (See HORMAH.)

Zephathah, zĕph'-ă-thăh (Heb.)— place of the watchtower; high watch; beholding; awaiting; attending.

At Mareshah (in the Valley of Zephathah) Asa, king of Judah, met Zerah the Ethiopian in battle, and the Ethiopians were defeated and put to rout (II Chron. 14:10).

Meta. Spiritual watch being kept in the lower or more subconscious phase of thought in the individual (place of the watchtower, high watch, a valley in the lowlands of Judah; see MARESHAH and ZERAH).

The Ethiopians here are the undisciplined and undeveloped thought forces in the subconscious mind. They are destructive. Zerah, as a leader of the Ethiopian army that came up against Judah, signifies the result of the first shining of new light into this darkened (Ethiopian) phase of thought, which result is that these ignorant and destructive thoughts are stirred to greater activity and so must be met and dealt with by Asa, king of Judah. Asa means *physician, healing, curing,* and represents the will directing constructively. Thus dark and destructive tendencies are put away

and the light of Truth shines in one's consciousness.

Zephi, zē'-phī (Heb.) — outlook; watcher; watchtower; high watch; awaiting; expectation; attention; observation.

A son of Eliphaz, and grandson of Esau (I Chron. 1:36). In Genesis 36: 11, 15, he is called Zepho.

Meta. A watchful, seeing, expectant thought, or attitude of mind, with an upward tendency, that belongs seemingly to the outer or physical man (outlook, watchtower, high watch, attention, expectation, observation, son of Eliphaz, and grandson of Esau; see ELIPHAZ and ESAU).

Zephon, zē'-phŏn (Heb.)—watchman; observer; attender; waiter; expecter; keeper of the high watch.

The first-named of the sons of Gad (Num. 26:15). In Genesis 46:16, he is called Ziphion.

Meta. A realization of power (Gad, a son of Jacob, represents the power faculty in man), which is the result of a desire for, and a seeking after, power (watchman, observer, expecter, keeper of the high watch; the latter definition suggests prayer, an earnest desire for and expectation of something higher and better than that which relates purely to the mental and physical aspect of power and might).

Zephonites, zē'-phŏn-ītes (fr. Heb.). Descendants of Zephon, son of Gad (Num. 26:15).

Meta. Thoughts springing from and like that in consciousness which Zephon signifies. (See ZEPHON.)

Zer, zēr (Heb.)—strait; narrow; pent up; compressed; cleavage; fissure; straits; distress; affliction; tribulation; perplexity; rock; stone pebble; flint.

A fortified city of Naphtali (Josh. 19: 35).

Meta. A group of thoughts of a very strong, established character (rock, a fortified city of Naphtali, Naphtali representing the strength faculty in individual consciousness). This consciousness of great strength lacks the spiritual quality as yet. It is narrow, hard, and unyielding (flint), and has not learned to express in union with love and true understanding, because it is more physical and personal than spiritual. Therefore it leads to confusion, limitation, anxiety, and conflict (*perplexity, pent up, compressed, straits, tribulation*).

Zerah (in A. V., Genesis 38:30; 46:12, Zarah; Matt. 1:3, Zara), zē'-răh (Heb.) —*rising of light; beginning of light; breaking forth of the sun; sunrise; appearing; birth of a child; germination of a seed; scattering rays; brightness; brilliance; splendor; glory.*

a Son of Judah and Tamar, and twin brother of Perez (Gen. 38:30). **b** Son of Simeon (I Chron. 4:24). In Genesis 46:10 this Zerah is called Zohar. **c** A son of Reuel, and grandson of Esau (Gen. 36:13). **d** An Ethiopian king who came with his army to fight against Asa, king of Judah, and was defeated (II Chron. 14:9).

Meta. Zerah (*rising of light, sunrise, birth of a child, germination of a seed, beginning of light, brightness, splendor*) denotes the rise of new light, understanding, in the consciousness. It is the first conscious awakening to the presence of this new inner light, or understanding (the sun rises in the east, and the east signifies the within).

The Zerah who was leader of the Ethiopian army that came up against Judah signifies a result of the rising of this new light into the darkened (Ethiopian) phase of thought in man; which result is that these ignorant thoughts and beliefs are stirred to greater activity and expression and so must be dealt with by the people of Judah, under Asa, who represents the will directing constructively. (See ZEPHATHAH, where the conflict between Asa, king of Judah, and Zerah took place.)

Zerahiah, zĕr-ă-hī'-ăh (Heb.) —*Jehovah has arisen; Jah shines forth with glory; brilliance of Jehovah; Jah is appearing; birth of Jehovah.*

a A priest who was descended from Aaron, through Eleazar, and was an ancestor of Ezra (Ezra 7:4). **b** Father of Eliehoenai "of the sons of Pahath–moab." Descendants of his returned from the Babylonian captivity with Ezra (Ezra 8:4).

Meta. The individual awakening to the conscious recognition of his own indwelling Christ or I AM understanding and might (*Jehovah has arisen, Jah shines forth with glory, Jah is appearing, brilliance of Jehovah, birth of Jehovah*), and expressing this light and power constructively.

Zerahites (A. V., Zarhites), zē'-răh-ītes (fr. Heb.).

Descendants of Zerah, son of Simeon (Num. 26:13).

Meta. Thoughts and activities springing from and in character like that in consciousness which is signified by Zerah, son of Simeon. (See ZERAH.)

Zered (in A. V., Num. 21:12, Zared), zē'-rĕd (Heb.) —*power to spread abroad; exuberant growth; luxuriant foliage; willow bush; willow brook.*

a A brook. **b** A valley. The brook empties into the Dead Sea, and in the valley was one of the places where the Israelites camped while journeying through the wilderness on their way to the Promised Land (Num. 21:12; Deut. 2:13).

Meta. An abundant increase and growth in consciousness of the substance of one's thoughts and words; also the ability to radiate and express to the outer that which is being established so abundantly within one (*power to spread abroad, exuberant growth, luxuriant foliage, willow bush, willow brook*).

Zeredah (A. V., Zereda, Zeredathah), zĕr'-ĕ-dăh (Heb.) —*sharp; cutting; penetrating; piercing; cold; cool; cooling.*

A city in Palestine that was the birthplace of Jeroboam.

Meta. As a city of Ephraim, Zeredah bespeaks the *sharp, cold, piercing, penetrating* nature of the will as expressing in personal consciousness, apart from the very needful balancing faculties of love and wisdom.

The Zeredah of II Chronicles 4:17 has virtually the same significance as the Zarethan of I Kings 7:46. (See ZARETHAN.)

Zererah (A. V., Zererath), zĕr'-ĕ-răh

(Heb.)—*cutting; sharp; penetrating; piercing; cold; cool; cooling.*

A place named in the account of the defeat of the Midianites by Gideon (Judg. 7:22). It is thought to be the same place as Zarethan and Zeredah.

Meta. The significance is virtually the same as that of ZARETHAN, which see. Then look up the significance of BETH-SHITTAH, ABEL–MEHOLAH, and TABBATH, places that are named in conjunction with Zererah. Thus you will perceive how Zererah represents the "expression" of the overcoming ideas that are suggested by these other cities, and by Gideon's defeating the Midianites and putting them to rout.

No real victory over error can be gained in the thoughts of an individual without a corresponding manifestation in his body and affairs.

Zeresh, zē'-rĕsh (Heb.)—*gold.*

Wife of Haman (Esth. 5:10).

Meta. A degree of soul wisdom (*gold,* a woman) that is of the carnal, adverse phase of consciousness in man.

Zereth, zē'-rĕth (Heb.)—*appearing; coming into manifestation; light; brilliance; brightness; splendor; oil.*

Son of Ashhur and his wife Helah, of the tribe of Judah (I Chron. 4:7).

Meta. The bright shining of spiritual understanding into and through the consciousness of the spiritually awakening individual (*light, oil, splendor, brightness*); this is the result of the freeing activity of prayer and praise (Judah). This name also bespeaks the manifestation of Truth in the outer life and affairs (*appearing, coming into manifestation*).

Zereth–shahar (A. V., Zareth–shahar), zē'-rĕth-shā'-här (Heb.) — *breaking forth of light; brilliance of the dawn; aurora's splendor; brightness of the morning.*

A city of Reuben, east of the Jordan (Josh. 13:19).

Meta. The wonderful illumination and glory, the spiritual uplift, the ecstasy, that so often accompany the inflow of new spiritual understanding, or light, into the consciousness of man after a period of trial or seeming darkness. (Zereth–shahar means *breaking forth of light, aurora's splendor, brilliance of the dawn, brightness of the morning,* and was a city of Reuben, east of the Jordan. Reuben refers to the "seeing" faculty in man; east signifies the within, whence the light of Spirit comes.)

Zeri, zē'-rī (Heb.)—*running; flowing; distilling; mastic; balsam; balm.*

A son of Jeduthun, who played the harp in the Temple worship during David's reign (I Chron. 25:3). In I Chronicles 25:11, he is called Izri.

Meta. The very essence of Spirit entering into the consciousness and organism of man as a harmonizing, healing, renewing energy and power (*running, flowing, distilling, mastic, balsam, balm,* an Israelitish musician in David's reign). (See IZRI.)

Zeror, zē'-rôr (Heb.)—*pressing; compressing; binding; oppressing; tied; a bundle; a packet; bundle of money; purse; bag; small stone; pebble; grain; kernel; particle.*

A Benjamite, the great-grandfather of Saul (I Sam. 9:1).

Meta. Concentrated thought, bringing one's thoughts together, and centering the attention on one central idea (*bundle, particle, tied, binding, compressing, bag, pebble, grain, kernel*).

Zeruah, zĕ-rụ'-ăh (Heb.)—*heavily smitten; stricken; prostrated; scourged; leprous; hornets; wasps,* i. e., striking as they sting; *terror; panic.*

A widow, the mother of Jeroboam (I Kings 11:26).

Meta. A phase of the soul consciousness in man that is unclean and impure in thought and desire (*leprous*); also the troublous, fearful, stinging, error experiences that are the result of this condition of the soul (*heavily smitten, stricken, hornets, terror*).

Zerubbabel (A. V., Matt. 1:12, Zorobabel), zĕ-rŭb'-bă-bĕl (Heb.)—*sown in Babylon; conceived in Babel; born in Babylon; begotten of confusion; dispersion of illusions.*

Son of Shealtiel. He was of the royal line of David, a prince, and was at the head of a large company of Jews who returned to Jerusalem and Judea from Babylon (Ezra 2:2; 3:2). He is called Sheshbazzar in Ezra 1:8, 11; 5:14-16.

Meta. A very strong and influential thought activity belonging to the spiritual phase of man. It comes to light in the consciousness of the unfolding individual in the midst of the stress and sorrow of the sense confusion and bondage (Babylon) into which he has drifted because of not understanding the true nature of Spirit, and so persisting in looking to the outer senses as the source of that which is real and true and worth while. This spiritual thought activity becomes a leading factor in putting away error illusions and restoring the worship of God, with its resultant good (*sown, conceived, born, in Babylon, dispersion of illusions;* a prince of the royal line of David, who was at the head of a large company of Jewish people who returned to Judea from Babylon; see SHESHBAZ-ZAR).

Zeruiah, zĕ-rụ'-ịăh (Heb.)—*cleft; wounded; flowing; running; distilling; balsam; balm.*

A sister of David's, and mother of Joab, Abishai, and Asahel (I Chron. 2:16).

Meta. Zeruiah and Abigail, sisters of David and daughters of Jesse, signify two attitudes of the soul in the spiritually awakening individual who is in the overcoming phase of his development. Abigail bespeaks the great joy and gladness that one feels because of the entrance of new light and Truth into consciousness, with their uplifting and strengthening power. Zeruiah signifies the phase of the soul consciousness that is cleansing and healing, yet experiences sorrow in letting go of human loves and desires that are dear to the material consciousness (*cleft, wounded, flowing, running, distilling, balsam, balm*).

Zetham, zĕ'-thăm (Heb.)—*luminous essence; giving light; shining; brightness; oil; oil tree; olive tree; olive branch; an olive.*

Son of Ladan, of the Gershonite Levites (I Chron. 23:8). I Chronicles 26:22 states that he is the son of Jehieli, in descent from Ladan, or Libni.

Meta. A thought belonging to the love faculty in the individual (a man of the tribe of Levi) that radiates the spirit of peace and prosperity (*luminous essence, giving light, oil, shining, olive tree, olive,* olives being representative of peace and of great abundance, while oil symbolizes the Holy Spirit).

Zethan, zĕ'-thăn (Heb.)—*giving light; shining; brightness; olive; olive tree.*

Son of Bilhan, a Benjamite (I Chron. 7:10).

Meta. A thought in the active faith faculty of the individual (a man of Benjamin) that is radiating the spirit of peace and bounty (*shining, olive, olive tree;* see ZETHAM for the significance of olives).

Zethar, zĕ'-thär (Heb. fr. Pers.)—*splendor; brilliance; star; conqueror.*

One of the seven chamberlains, or eunuchs, "that ministered in the presence of Ahasuerus the king" (Esth. 1:10).

Meta. A purely mental perception and amplification of conquest and dominion (*splendor, brilliance, star, conqueror*) that helps to sustain the puffed-up personal will (a chamberlain who ministered to King Ahasuerus of Media and Persia).

Zia, zī'-ȧ (Heb.)—*motion; movement; agitation; commotion; disquiet; trembling; shaking; quaking; fear; terror.*

A man of Gad (I Chron. 5:13).

Meta. A step in the unfolding of dominion and power in the individual consciousness, wherein fearfulness and instability seemingly prevail (*motion, movement, disquiet, trembling, fear,* a man of the Israelitish tribe of Gad, Gad referring to the power faculty). We find in Peter (faith), at a certain stage of his history, a changeable and seemingly unfaithful tendency. This is shown in his denial of Jesus and in other incidents. Later he became very steadfast and reliable. Even so, when the power idea is moving toward expression in man there may be a period wherein the individual feels, and perhaps acts, very unlike the possessor of power and dominion over himself and over every phase of his life and affairs. But when he enters fully enough into the consciousness of established power, the power that works in union with love and understanding, every trace of fear and unrest will be a thing of the past.

Ziba, zī'-bȧ (Heb.)—*placed; stationed; left standing; statue; plantation; fixed;*

settled; determined; firmness; strength.

A servant of Saul's. He enabled David to get into touch with Mephibosheth, Saul's grandson, and Jonathan's son, to whom David restored the land that had belonged to Saul. Ziba and his sons and servants were appointed to till this land for Mephibosheth (II Sam. 9:2-11). Later Ziba testified falsely against Mephibosheth to David and was given the property for himself (II Sam. 16:1-4). When Mephibosheth explained the matter to David, David gave him back half the land (II Sam. 19:24-29).

Meta. After Saul's household was destroyed, only Ziba, a servant, and Mephibosheth, a grandson who was crippled, were left. Ziba means a *statue*. This shows that the old-time fire that animated the will has burned itself out, leaving nothing but a form. Ziba represents only a remembrance of former experiences after the personal will has yielded to the divine will.

Zibeon, zĭb'-ĕ-ŏn (Heb.)—*immersed; dipped in; dyed; tinged; variegated; ravenous preyer; wild robber.*

a A Hivite. His granddaughter, Oholibamah, was one of Esau's wives (Gen. 36:2). b A son of Seir the Horite, and probably the same person as the former (Gen. 36:20).

Meta. Hivites represent thoughts of opposition and resistance in the carnal phase of consciousness in unredeemed man. Zibeon (*wild robber, ravenous preyer, immersed, dipped in, variegated, dyed*) symbolizes a wild, lawless sense thought that has the capacity of adapting itself to the varying ideas and moods of the individual; thus it remains in his consciousness (until it is cast forth by Truth) and robs his body of its energy and substance.

Zibia, zĭb'-ĭ-à (Heb.)—*beauty; gracefulness; antelope; gazelle; roe; deer.*

a A Benjamite, son of Shaharaim and Hodesh (I Chron. 8:9). b A woman of Beersheba. She was the mother of Jehoash, king of Judah, and her name is spelled Zibiah (II Kings 12:1).

Meta. A swift, graceful, harmonious thought activity in the faith faculty in consciousness (*beauty, gracefulness, gazelle, roe, deer;* a man of Benjamin), also

in the spiritual phase of the soul (a woman of Beersheba, and mother of Jehoash, king of Judah).

Zibiah. (See ZIBIA, b.)

Zichri, zĭch'-rī (Heb.)—*called to mind; remembered; memorial; remembrance; recollected; renowned.*

There were several Israelites by this name. They were of the tribes of Levi, Benjamin, Judah, and Ephraim (Exod. 6:21; I Chron. 8:19; II Chron. 17:16). Zichri of the tribe of Ephraim (II Chron. 28:7) is thought to be the same person as "the son of Tabeel" (Isa. 7:6).

Meta. Thoughts in man's higher, religious and spiritual consciousness (Israelites, some of them men of note) that keep calling his attention to the outworking of the law of Being, and to the importance of taking cognizance of this law (*called to mind, remembered, recollected, remembrance, renowned*).

Ziddim, zĭd'-dĭm (Heb.) — *sides; walls; steeps; declivities; oppositions; adversaries; enemies; oppressions; destructions.*

A fortified city of Naphtali (Josh. 19:35).

Meta. Strength, exalted very highly in the consciousness of the spiritually awakening individual, but expressed in a downward, destructive way because of the outer, material beliefs that he still holds regarding this important faculty of mind (*sides, declivities, steeps, oppressions, destructions,* a fortified city of Naphtali).

Ziha, zī'-hà (Heb.)—*dazzling white; brightness; bright; sunny; clear; plain; manifest; serene; warm; dry; clear heat; dried; thirsty; drought.*

a The "children" of Ziha were among the Nethinim who returned with Zerubbabel from the Babylonian captivity (Ezra 2:43). b An overseer of the Nethinim who dwelt in Ophel (Neh. 11:21).

Meta. Serving thoughts in consciousness (men who were of the Nethinim, or bond servants in the Temple) that are pure and radiant (*dazzling white, brightness*) and that desire greatly, but have not as yet appropriated as their own, the real joy, energy, substance, and soul satisfaction that are the result of one's realizing one's spiritual sonship (*thirsty*).

It is only by knowing oneself to be the son of God, and therefore the rightful heir to all that the Father is and has, that one becomes free from bondage of every kind and realizes abundance of every good.

Ziklag, zĭk'-lăg (Heb.) — *winding; bending; flowing; outpouring of a fountain; pouring out of water.*

A southern city of Judah (Josh. 15: 31). It is mentioned as being a city of Simeon, in Joshua 19:5. This city seems to have remained in the possession of the Philistines until Achish, king of Gath, gave it to David (I Sam. 27:6). David lived in Ziklag until after Saul's death, when he became king of Israel. In the 12th chapter of I Chronicles we read of many chief and mighty men of Israel who joined David at Ziklag while Saul was still king.

Meta. Adaptability (*winding, bending, flowing*), to which love (David) has to resort in order to protect itself from the onslaughts of the selfish, personal will (Saul) that is determined to retain its rulership in consciousness, even if divine love has to be killed out in consequence. But love cannot be destroyed, since it is not stiff and unbending but is adaptable even to seemingly adverse conditions, when necessary. By being able to adjust oneself to existing conditions and circumstances, and by continually radiating love and Truth (suggested in *outpouring of a fountain, pouring out of water*), one realizes the strength and uplift needed to carry one through any adverse experience (many mighty men of Benjamin joined David at Ziklag; they represent high, active, powerful, spiritual, faith ideals).

Zillah, zĭl'-lăh (Heb.)—*deep; darkness; gloom; shadow; screened; veiled; protected.*

A wife of Lamech who was descended from Cain. She was the mother of Tubal–cain and of his sister Naamah (Gen. 4:19).

Meta. A very great or dense obscurity of thought, regarding his true spiritual nature and capabilities, that exists in the soul of the individual who is still living wholly in the outer or sense consciousness (*deep, darkness,*

gloom, shadow, wife of Lamech, of the line of Cain). Lack of true and clear understanding, at this phase of unfoldment, is a protection to the individual (*protected*) in that it shields or screens him (*screened*) from experiences that he is not yet able to meet, yet would have to face were it possible for the full light of Truth to enter his consciousness at this time. (See ZALMONAH for a more detailed explanation of this line of thought.)

Zillethai (A. V., Zilthai), zĭl'-lē-thāi (Heb.)—*shadow of Jehovah; Jehovah's inaccessible depth; unassailable protection of Jehovah.*

a Son of Shimei, and a chief man of Benjamin (I Chron. 8:20). **b** A man of Manasseh, one of those who fell away from Saul and joined David at Ziklag (I Chron. 12:20).

Meta. The secret place of the Most High, deep within the inner consciousness and organism of man (*shadow of Jehovah, Jehovah's inaccessible depth*), or the deep things of Spirit that cannot be understood by the carnal mind because they must be spiritually discerned. This name suggests the 91st Psalm, "He that dwelleth in the secret place of the Most High shall abide under the shadow of the Almighty" (*unassailable protection of Jehovah*).

Zilpah, zĭl'-păh (Heb.)—*distilling; extracting an essence; dropping; dripping; trickling; leaking; exuding myrrh; tears; bitterness.*

Leah's handmaid. Leah gave her to Jacob as his wife, and she bore Jacob two sons, Gad and Asher (Gen. 30:9-13).

Meta. The unfolding soul of man. Little by little, drop by drop, as it were, the soul becomes awakened to spiritual thought (*distilling, extracting an essence, dropping*, the essence here relating to Spirit as the fundamental principle of being). But in the Zilpah phase of the unfolding soul we do not find sufficient staying qualities; too much of the human is still in evidence and much of the good is dissipated (*leaking, exuding myrrh, tears, bitterness*).

Zimmah, zĭm'-măh (Heb.)—*having in mind; thought; meditation; purpose; consideration; counsel; plan; device;*

plot; mischief; wickedness; crime; unchastity; rape; incest.

a A Gershonite Levite (I Chronicles 6:20, 42). **b** Another Levite by this name is mentioned in II Chronicles 29:12.

Meta. Love, degenerated into wickedness and lasciviousness because of the prevalence of sense desires in the consciousness, owing to the influence of the carnal mind (*having in mind, thought, device, plot, wickedness, unchastity*, men of the Israelitish tribe of Levi, Levi referring to the love faculty in individual consciousness).

Zimran, zĭm'-răn (Heb.)—*celebrated in song; sung; song; music; chant; jubilee; singer; dancer; leaper; mountain sheep; gazelle.*

Eldest son of Abraham by Keturah (Gen. 25:2).

Meta. A positive expression of joy, harmony, and grace (*celebrated in song, sung, jubilee, dancer, gazelle*); the first conscious result of a union of the awakening faith in the individual (Abraham) with the aspiration of the soul for higher bodily attainment (Keturah).

Zimri, zĭm'-rī (Heb.)—*celebrated in song; singing; music; praise; jubilation; dancing; leaping; mountain sheep; gazelle.*

a Son of Zerah, and grandson of Judah (I Chron. 2:6). In Joshua 7:1, he is called Zabdi. **b** Son of Salu, a prince of the Simeonites. He was slain by Phinehas (Num. 25:14). **c** A servant of Elah, king of Israel, who killed Elah and reigned in his stead (I Kings 16:9). **d** Others of the same name.

Meta. An inner sense of harmony; also an inner lauding and praising, thus a lifting up, of the activity-of-life idea in individual consciousness (*celebrated in song, singing, dancing, music, mountain sheep, gazelle*). In this way a new and increased realization of life becomes vibrant throughout the consciousness. Unless established in understanding and spiritual dominion it is likely to contribute to just such conditions and situations as are expressed in the histories of the persons named Zimri that are mentioned in Numbers 25:14, I Kings 16:9-20, and in the immediate descend-

ants of the one who is called Zabdi in the 7th chapter of Joshua. The Achan of the tribe of Judah, who committed the trespass that is told about in this chapter, was a grandson of this Zimri, or Zabdi. (See ZABDI.)

Zin, zĭn (Heb.)—*sharp; pointed; piercing; coldness; thorn; covering; protection; preservation; shield; buckler; target; depression; lowland; shrub; low palm.*

A wilderness on the southern boundary of Palestine and of Judah (Josh. 15:1).

Meta. A seemingly very small beginning of a comprehension of Truth, of preservation, salvation, and of victory, working in the subconsciousness of the individual toward the body consciousness (*lowland, low palm, piercing, covering, preservation, buckler*). In this phase of thought the way to possession of the Promised Land (the renewal and spiritualization of the body of man) still appears very thorny (*sharp, thorn*), and there is not the necessary fervor to carry one through to complete victory (*coldness*).

Zina, zĭ'-nà (Heb.)—*throwing out rays; glittering; sparkling; brilliant; ornamental; flowing with milk; full-breasted; abundant; fruitful; productive; cheerfulness; contentment.*

Son of Shimei of the Gershonite Levites (I Chron. 23:10). He is called Zizah in I Chronicles 23:11.

Meta. Love, radiating the thought of understanding, satisfaction, richness, opulence (*throwing out rays, brilliant, flowing with milk, abundant, fruitful, productive, contentment*, a man of the Israelitish tribe of Levi).

Zion, zĭ'-ŏn (Heb.)—*sunny; very dry; clear, i. e., unobstructed, sunshine; set up; placed; established; constituted; fortress; monument; column; landmark.*

a A fortified hill that David took from the Jebusites. David built his palace there (II Sam. 5:7), and the place was called the city of David. The tent of meeting and the Ark of the Covenant were on Zion during David's reign (I Kings 8:1); this is why it was called the "holy hill" (Psalms 2:6). Later Zion became a part of the city of Jerusalem. **b** Zion as mentioned in many places in the Bible refers to the whole city of Jerusalem (as in Isa. 33:20). **c** Zion is sometimes used as figurative of the Holy City, the New Jerusalem (Heb. 12:22).

Meta. Love's abode in the phase of the subjective consciousness where high, holy thoughts and ideals abide (*clear,* i. e., *unobstructed, sunshine, sunny, set up, monument, fortress, landmark,* a fortified hill, which later became a part of Jerusalem).

In referring to the Holy City, the New Jerusalem, Zion symbolizes spiritual consciousness.

Zior, zī′-ôr (Heb.)—*reduced; brought low; littleness; smallness; contemned; dishonored.*

A city in the hill country of Judah (Josh. 15:54).

Meta. The inferiority of material thought and belief, in the light of the higher, truer understanding of Spirit (*reduced, brought low, littleness, smallness, contemned, dishonored,* a city in the hill country of Judah).

Ziph, zĭph (Heb.)—*flowing; overflowing; overwhelming; becoming liquid; liquefaction; refining; purifying; cleansing.*

a A southern city of Judah. **b** A city in the hill country of Judah (Josh. 15:24, 55). **c** A wilderness, in the hill country of Judah, where David was in hiding from Saul (I Sam. 23:14). **d** The name of a man of Judah (I Chron. 4:16).

Meta. Cleansing, purifying thoughts and groups of thoughts in the prayer-and-praise (Judah) consciousness of man (*flowing, refining, purifying, cleansing;* two cities, a wilderness, and a man, of Judah).

Ziphah, zī′-phăh (Heb.)—*flux; fluidity; liquid; flowing; pure; refined; clean.*

A brother of Ziph, and son of Jehallelel of the Israelitish tribe of Judah (I Chron. 4:16).

Meta. The significance of Ziphah is the same as that of Ziph, a cleansing, purifying, refining thought in action in the consciousness. In Ziphah we also see established the effect of this thought in cleanliness and purity of thought (*flux, flowing, clean, pure, refined*).

Ziphion, zĭph′-ĭ-ŏn (Heb.)—*looking out; outlook; looking about; watcher; watchman; high watch; watchtower; observer; waiter; expecter.*

A son of Gad, and grandson of Jacob (Gen. 46:16). He is called Zephon in Numbers 26:15.

Meta. See ZEPHON.

Ziphites, zĭph′-ītes (fr. Heb.).

Inhabitants of the city of Ziph, or of the wilderness of Ziph in which this city was located. Twice they went to Saul at Gibeah and told him where David was hiding (I Sam. 23:19; 26:1).

Meta. Thoughts belonging to the cleansing, purifying state of mind that Ziph signifies. The wilderness of Ziph denotes a lack of discipline, understanding, and cultivation in these thoughts. Hence in their cleansing, purifying activities they are liable to become destructive, in that, for the sake of establishing harmony, they would purge out even the spiritual and good if these seemed to be standing in the way of the ruling personal will (the Ziphites sought to help Saul—the ruling personal will—to destroy David, divine love working toward rulership in the consciousness).

Ziphron, zĭph′-rŏn (Heb.)—*emitting sweet odor; fragrance; perfume; pleasantness; a flower garden.*

A place on the northern border of the Promised Land (Num. 34:9).

Meta. Spiritual perception (*emitting sweet odor, fragrance, perfume*).

Zippor, zĭp′-pôr (Heb.) — *chirper; peeper; twitterer; hopper; small bird; sparrow; anything that moves swiftly.*

Father of Balak, king of Moab (Num. 22:2, 4). Balak was the king who tried to get Balaam, son of Beor, to curse Israel.

Meta. The thought here, while free, unattached (*bird*), is of that which is not clear in its utterances. Isaiah writes of "them that have familiar spirits," and of "wizards, that chirp and that mutter" (Isa. 8:19); this suggests the nature of that which Zippor signifies (*chirper, peeper, twitterer,* and so forth).

Zipporah, zĭp-pō′-răh (Heb.)—*little bird; sparrow; chirper; twitterer.*

Daughter of Reuel, or Jethro, priest of Midian, and wife of Moses (Exod. 2:21; 18:2).

Meta. Zipporah is the feminine of Zippor, and one definition of both names is *little bird.* In our study of the involution of the soul we learn that birds signify, or should signify, free, swift thoughts, thoughts that unite heaven and earth. Moses, the one drawn forth to deliver the spiritual consciousness (Israel) out of bondage to the darkened phase of the subconsciousness that Egypt represents, is now associated with free, winged thoughts, though these are still somewhat limited (Moses married Zipporah, and the definitions *little bird, chirper, twitterer,* relating to this name bespeak limitation). Fear is losing some of its power over the soul, however, and the preparations for the deliverance of Israel prosper.

Ziv (A. V., Zif), zĭv (Heb.)—*radiant; shining; brightness; splendor; beauty,* especially of flowers; *blooming; flowering; flower month; month of the brightness of flowers.*

The second month of the Hebrew sacred year, and the eighth month of the Hebrew civil year (I Kings 6:1, 37). It was during this month, in the four hundred and eightieth year after the Israelites left Egypt, that Solomon began to build the "house of Jehovah," or Temple, in Jerusalem. This month was called Iyar also.

Meta. The phase of individual unfoldment wherein one expresses the Truth of Being in one's words (*blooming, flower month, brightness, splendor*).

A month, in fact any division of time, signifies a step in unfoldment. The meaning of Ziv calls to mind the third line of the little stanza:

"Kind hearts are the gardens;
  Kind thoughts are the roots;
Kind words are the blossoms;
Kind deeds are the fruits."

And this brings to mind such texts as: "A word fitly spoken is *like* apples of gold in network of silver" (Prov. 25:11); "The tongue of the wise is health" (Prov. 12:18); "Death and life are in the power of the tongue" (Prov. 18:21);

"What man is he that desireth life,
  And loveth *many* days, that he may see good?
Keep thy tongue from evil,

And thy lips from speaking guile" (Psalms 34:12, 13). True words are blossoms of the heart and soul that bring forth fruit to eternal life; they radiate the *brightness* and *splendor* of Spirit in the life of the individual.

Ziz, zĭz (Heb.)—*reflecting light; emitting splendor; glowing; brilliant; a brightness; a burnished plate of gold,* i. e., on the forehead of the high priest; *a flower; a wing; a lock of hair.*

It was by the "ascent of Ziz" that the Moabites and the Ammonites came up to battle against Jehoshaphat, king of Israel (II Chron. 20:16).

Meta. The "ascent of Ziz," by which the Moabites and the Ammonites came up against Jehoshaphat, king of Israel, to battle, signifies the reflected understanding of purely intellectual thought guided by sense reason (*reflecting light,* and so forth). The carnal in man lays great store by the intellect; only by true spiritual understanding can man rise above its errors and limitations.

Ziza, zī'-zȧ (Heb.)—*throwing out rays; shining; glittering; sparkling; brilliant; ornamental; living; moving; active; full-breasted; flowing with milk; abundant; productive; nourishment; cheerfulness; contentment.*

a Son of Shiphi, a Simeonite (I Chron. 4:37). **b** A Son of Rehoboam (II Chron. 11:20).

Meta. Thoughts that radiate understanding, satisfaction, and substance—rich, bountiful, wise, radiant thoughts (*throwing out rays, shining, abundant, productive, contentment*) that belong to the attentive, obedient attitude in man (a Simeonite) and to the prayer-and-praise consciousness, or consciousness of accumulation (a man of the royal line of Judah, a son of Rehoboam, who was Solomon's son and the first king of Judah).

Zizah, zī'-zäh (Heb.)—*radiant; brilliant; shining; full breast; flowing with milk; abundance; production; nutriment; cheerfulness; contentment.*

Son of Shimei of the Gershonite Levites (I Chron. 23:11). In I Chronicles 23:10, he is called Zina.

Meta. See ZINA.

Zoan, zō'-ăn (Heb. fr. Egypt.)—*de-*

pressed region; low region; loading beasts for a journey; departure; removal; migration.

A very prominent city of ancient Egypt, built seven years later than Hebron (Num. 13:22). It was a dwelling place of some of the kings or princes of Egypt (Isa. 19:11; 30:4). Its destruction is prophesied in Ezekiel 30:14. The "field of Zoan" (Psalms 78:12) no doubt refers to the plain that was about the city.

Meta. A lowered state of vitality, a depressed, dejected, unstable center of thought activity in the subconscious phase of mind in man (*depressed region, low region, migration,* a city and a plain in Egypt). This state of thought is due to the belief that man, and especially the substance of which his body is composed, is material and is separate from the one ever present Source of unlimited, never ending life, vitality, substance, strength, and joy.

Zoar, zō'-är (Heb.)—*reduced; made small; lessened; smallness; littleness; brought low; despised; contemned; dishonored.*

One of the cities of the plain, to which Lot escaped when Sodom and Gomorrah were destroyed (Gen. 13:10; 19:22). It was the same city as Bela (Gen. 14:2). In Isaiah 15:5 and Jeremiah 48:34 Zoar is mentioned as being a city of Moab.

Meta. Inferiority (*smallness, littleness;* one of the wicked cities of the plain, and belonging to Moab, or carnal mind).

Zobah, zō'-bäh (Heb.) — *settled; placed; appointed; caused to stand; station; encampment; fixed; set in bounds; prefect; director.*

A Syrian kingdom that Saul and David both fought against (I Sam. 14:47; II Sam. 10:6).

Meta. A *fixed* error state of thought belonging to the sense intellectual realm of mind in man (*settled, station, encampment,* a Syrian kingdom in the time of Saul and David).

Zobebah, zŏ-bē'-bäh (Heb.)—*the slow moving; the gentle moving; gently flowing along; softly moving; the slow coming; the affable; litter; sedan; caravan.*

Son of Hakkoz of the tribe of Judah

(I Chron. 4:8).

Meta. The poise, the harmony, the quiet, gentle, peaceful assurance and rhythm of the inner or spiritual consciousness and life (*the slow moving, the gentle moving, gently flowing along, softly moving, the affable,* a man of Judah).

Zohar, zō'-här (Heb.)—*dazzling brilliance; brightness; whiteness; white; nobility; distinction; purity.*

a Father of Ephron, from whom Abraham bought the cave of Machpelah in which he buried Sarah (Gen. 23:8). **b** A son of Simeon (Gen. 46:10; Exod. 6:15). In Numbers 26:13 and I Chronicles 4:24, Zohar the son of Simeon is called Zerah.

Meta. Thoughts of a pure, clear, lofty, discriminating character (*whiteness, brightness, nobility, distinction,* the name of two men, one of them being of the Israelitish tribe of Simeon).

Zoheleth, zō'-hĕ-lĕth (Heb.)—*creeping; crawling; slippery; sliding; serpent; timidity; fearfulness.*

A stone just outside Jerusalem, near the well of En–rogel, where the men who followed Adonijah gathered, and Adonijah sacrificed, sheep, oxen, and fatlings. This was when Adonijah attempted to make himself king of Israel in the place of his father David (I Kings 1:9).

Meta. The sense life, with its wisdom, which is of the outer man of carnality (*creeping, crawling, slippery, serpent*). Adonijah's sacrificing sheep, oxen, and fatlings by this stone denotes the using of one's vitality, strength, and body substance to the furtherance of the sense life, or to the furtherance of the rule of the senses.

Zoheth, zō'-hĕth (Heb.)—*corpulence; strength.*

Son of Ishi, of the tribe of Judah (I Chron. 4:20).

Meta. See BEN–ZOHETH.

Zophah, zō'-phăh (Heb.)—*extending; drawing out; spreading out; expanding; cruse; flask; vial or phial; oil container; dish; platter.*

Son of Helem, of the Israelitish tribe of Asher (I Chron. 7:35).

Meta. A *cruse,* or *vial,* in the meaning of this name, points to the body of man, which is a vessel to hold the water and the wine of life and the oil of Spirit. In Matthew 9:17 (A. V.) we read of putting new wine into new bottles, which means that the body must be renewed and spiritualized that it may contain safely the fullness of spiritual vitality and life.

The significance of Zophah, son of Helem, is the great increase and extending of ideas of vitality, health, strength, and Truth (which Helem signifies; see HELEM) throughout the body consciousness (*spreading out, expanding, extending, cruse, flask, vial, oil container*). This is accomplished by prayer, by keeping one's attention fixed on Spirit, perfection.

Zophai, zō'-phāi (Heb.)—*a flowing; an overflowing; honeycomb; honeycombed; floater; swimmer.*

Son of Elkanah, of the Israelitish tribe of Levi (I Chron. 6:26). In I Chronicles 6:35, he is called Zuph.

Meta. A very orderly, true-to-principle, loving thought of the higher and more spiritual phase of individual consciousness in expression (*a flowing, an overflowing, honeycomb;* a man of Levi; the little cells in a piece of honeycomb are built in a most exact way, each one virtually perfect). *Honeycomb, honeycombed,* refer specifically to Truth, both to true words and to the ordinances of God, which are true and lovely. The significance of Zophai is very beautifully expressed in Proverbs 16:24 and Psalms 19:10.

Zophar, zō'-phär (Heb.)—*chirping; peeping; twittering; hopping; moving swiftly; small bird; sparrow.*

"The Naamathite," one of Job's three friends (Job 2:11).

Meta. Job's three friends represent phases of intellectual and mental thought and reason; that which is less than spiritual understanding. This is why they could not help him to find any remedy for his afflictions. They could show him to be wrong, but could not reveal to him the right way. Intellect only points out evil appearances and condemns the sinner. Spiritual understanding alone gives the remedy and leads the individual into life and peace. The world today is full

of people who continually find fault with and call attention to the limitations and errors of present seeming conditions, but only the spiritually enlightened can point out a way really to make people and conditions better. Jesus Christ came not to condemn the world but to save it; even so the true Christian will seek always to lift up a right standard for those whom he wishes to help, instead of calling attention to, and thereby magnifying, apparent evil.

Zophar signifies a plane of darkened, limited thought or reason such as is suggested in Isaiah 8:19. (See ZIPPOR, in relation to this.) The understanding that God gives, spiritual understanding, is alive, alert, progressive; when man holds to old, obsolete ideas, and reasons from their standpoint, he is seeking "unto the dead."

Zophim, zō'-phĭm (Heb.)—*watchers; watchmen; viewers; lookers from afar; honeycombs; flowing sweetnesses; fertilities.*

a A field at the top of Pisgah (Num. 23:14). **b** The latter part of the name of a place in the hill country of Ephraim (I Sam. 1:1).

Meta. An attentive, vigilant attitude, but more from a standpoint of looking on from the outside than laying hold of and becoming one with that which is perceived (*watchers, watchmen, viewers, lookers from afar;* a field at the top of Pisgah, where Balak, king of Moab, took Balaam to try to induce him to curse Israel).

Zorah (in A. V., Neh. 11:29, Zareah; Joshua 15:33, Zoreah), zō'-răh (Heb.)—*stricken; smitten; scourged; prostrated; terrified; panic; hornet; place of hornets; hornets' town; leprosy.*

A city in the lowland of Judah (Josh. 15:33), and also mentioned as being on the border of Dan (Josh. 19:41). It was inhabited evidently by the Danites, since it was the home of Manoah, the father of Samson (Judg. 13:2). It was resettled by some of the children of Judah after the return from the Babylonian captivity (Neh. 11:29).

Meta. A thought center in the subconsciousness (a city in the lowland of Judah) that is bowed under fear of oppression and affliction (*stricken, smitten, prostrated, terrified*), that is of a stinging, petulant nature (*hornet, place of hornets*), and that is in need of purifying (*leprosy*).

Zorathites (in A. V., I Chron. 2:53, Zareathites), zō'-răth-ītes (fr. Heb.).

Descendants of Shobal, of the tribe of Judah, and inhabitants of the city of Zorah (I Chron. 4:2).

Meta. Thoughts that are the result of new, high ideas' springing into consciousness and being energized by a realization of abundant life. These thoughts take root in substance (see SHOBAL) but are lacking in purity and in the harmonizing influence of divine love; therefore they have taken on more or less of the sharp, stinging, fearful character that Zorah suggests. (See ZORAH.) It may be, however, that, although these thoughts have entered into the Zorah state of consciousness in order to lift it up, they have not necessarily partaken of its characteristics.

Zorites, zō'-rītes (fr. Heb.).

Descendants of Salma, of the tribe of Judah, and thought to have been inhabitants of Zorah (I Chron. 2:54).

Meta. Thoughts that tend to perfection and Truth (descendants of Salma; see SALMA), though still expressing something of the character that Zorah signifies. (See ZORAH.)

Zuar, zū'-är (Heb.)—*reduced; lessened; made little; smallness; littleness; brought low.*

Father of Nethanel, a prince of the tribe of Issachar, who was chosen from that tribe to help Moses number the Children of Israel in the wilderness of Sinai, by command of Jehovah (Num. 1:8).

Meta. Humility (*made little, smallness*). Nethanel, son of Zuar, signifies the grace that God imparts to His children. This grace is realized by those who are small in their own eyes, in so far as the lesser self is concerned. "God . . . giveth grace to the humble" (James 4:6; I Pet. 5:5); "whosoever shall humble himself shall be exalted" (Matt. 23:12); "Blessed are the meek: for they shall inherit the earth" (Matt. 5:5). (See NETHANEL.)

Zuph, zŭph (Heb.)—*flowing; overflowing; flowing honey; honeycomb.*

a An Ephraimite Levite from whom Samuel the prophet and seer was descended (I Sam. 1:1). In I Chronicles 6:26, 35, he is called both Zuph and Zophai. **b** A land to which Saul and his servant came when they were hunting for some asses that had gone astray (I Sam. 9:5).

Meta. The significance is the same as that of Zophai, the sweetness and orderliness of Truth. (See ZOPHAI.)

Zur, zûr (Heb.)—*rock; stone; acute; sharp; precipitous; refuge; shelter; protection; founder of a people; bound; compressed; beset; assailed; besieged.*

a Father of Cozbi, the Midianitish woman who was slain by Phinehas (Num. 25:15). He was a king or prince of Midian, and was killed by the Israelites in the wilderness when they were warring against Midian (Num. 31:8). **b** A son of Jeiel of Gibeon, a Benjamite (I Chron. 8:30).

Meta. Faith, as referring to the man of Benjamin (*rock, refuge*), and a very hard, aggressive, besieging, warring thought activity, as it pertains to the prince of Midian (*rock, stone, precipitous, beset, assailed, besieged*).

Zuriel, zū'-rĭ-ĕl (Heb.)—*God is my rock; whose protection is God; God is my defense; God is a refuge; strength of God.*

Son of Abihail, and a prince of the Merari Levites, in the wilderness (Num. 3:35).

Meta. A realization of God, the indwelling Spirit of truth, as one's firm, unwavering faith, as one's steadfastness and defense (*God is my rock, God is a refuge, strength of God*; a Levite).

Zurishaddai, zū-rĭ-shăd'-dāi (Heb.)—*the Almighty is a rock; my rock is the Almighty; the Omnipotent is a rock of refuge.*

Father of Shelumiel, who was the prince chosen from the tribe of Simeon to stand with Moses and Aaron in numbering the Children of Israel in the wilderness of Sinai (Num. 1:6).

Meta. Like Zuriel, the knowledge or realization of God as unchanging principle, as one's staying power, defense, the sure foundation of one's abiding perfection and good (*the Almighty is a rock, my rock is the Almighty*).

Zuzim (A. V., Zuzims), zū'-zĭm (Heb.) —*emitting rays; sparkling; glittering; flowing out like rays; spouting; sprouting; flowing; flowering; flourishing; budding; fertile; moving about; restless.*

A tribe of people, "in Ham," that was defeated by King Chedorlaomer and the other kings that were with him (Gen. 14:5). These people are thought to be the same as the Zamzummim of Deuteronomy 2:20.

Meta. The confusions, fears, unrestrained emotions, and general terrors of the physical consciousness, or "mind of the flesh," seemingly very prominent and flourishing at a certain stage in the evolution, or unfoldment, of the individual (*sparkling, glittering, flowing out like rays, spouting, sprouting, flowering, flourishing, restless, moving about*). (See ZAMZUMMIM.)

ADDENDA

ADDENDA

Aaron's rod. See rod (in Addenda).

ascension.

Meta. The ascension is the final step in the attainment of the Christ consciousness. In the ascended state the individual attains the cosmic consciousness of oneness with the Father. His body loses its limitations and takes on the livingness of the substance of God; he transcends the limitations of space and time; he acquires full control over his body (the earth) and over all the faculties of his mind (the heavens); he takes on the divine powers and attributes.

"Lo, I am with you always," said Jesus. This is literally true because the ascended one rises to a level of oneness with the father and puts on the omnipresence and omnipotence, the universal body and mind, of God.

Avvites. See Avvim.

body.

Meta. The word body is used in the English Bible to translate many Hebrew words, from carcass to soul. The body is the material manifestation of the life principle. It can seem to be merely a carcass or it can be an incorruptible habitation of the Spirit, depending on the spiritual unfoldment of the individual whose body it is.

Man is a threefold being: spirit, soul, and body. Body is the projection of the soul on the material plane, and it expresses the ideas and state of consciousness of the soul embodied in it.

Body is just as essential a part of man as soul or spirit. Creation is not complete until it becomes manifest in the outer, and man must have a body through which to express his ideas. Jesus' resurrection was bodily as well as spiritual.

In order to be complete and perfect man must incorporate the divine ideas of perfection into his body and redeem it just as Jesus did.

Comforter.

Meta. The Comforter is spiritual understanding, the realization of man's inherent God character. The Comforter, the Holy Spirit, the inner presence are all synonymous terms. When we have taken the external steps toward a renewed consciousness, we begin to feel that we are not left alone in our effort to behold and express ourselves spiritually. We feel that we are being companioned, guarded, and guided by the light of love; being taught in Truth through feeling and through thoughts that were formerly beyond us. This teaching, this light, this love comes from within. Jesus called it the Comforter because it is soothing, strengthening, something we can depend on.

covenant.

Meta. A covenant is an agreement. The covenant of the Bible represents the principles or rules by which men are able to gain their true spiritual heritage and possess the riches of the kingdom of God.

Man must be true to the Spirit within him. If a man follows false gods, that is, material things, he will find these to be powerless to satisfy him, and he will fail to enter into the spiritual state that God has promised him. A man must be true to his I AM nature if he would reap the benefits of the I AM consciousness.

God has promised all His children perfect health, prosperity, peace, light, and happiness, but it is necessary for us to abide by the spiritual law if we would gain the blessings of Spirit. We must keep faith in God and seek Him diligently. Then His good will be ours. We must not follow after lesser goods or gods. We must keep faith in our own spirituality if we hope to use our spiritual powers and handle spiritual substance.

cymbals. See trumpets.

I

death. See dying.

Divine Mind. See Mind.

Euphrates. The fourth river, Euphrates, means "fructifying," or "that which is the fructifying cause." Metaphysically, it represents the blood stream. The circulatory system receives and distributes the nutrients contained in the food we eat. The blood stream is charged with the food substance for bone, muscle, brain, teeth, and hair. Every part of the organism is supplied with substance through this wonderful river Euphrates.

Father.

Meta. A father is one who has begotten a child; one who gives origin to; a generator. God as Father is the great cause, the cause of all life, all being. There is only one source from which all living ideas and all living objects proceed. We call this source the Father. God is Father of all that is. He is the cause.

As cause God is the seed idea of life present in every unmanifest or manifest creation. As source He continually sustains and supplies each expression of Himself with all that is necessary for its development.

God as Father is the cause and source of the mind and life that is being expressed everywhere, whether this is known to the senses or unknown to them.

There is also another sense in which we think of God as Father. Jesus would not have chosen the word father to describe God had He wished simply to describe a cause or principle.

There is a relationship with God into which we can enter where He seems "closer . . . than breathing, and nearer than hands and feet." When we enter into this relationship, we become acutely aware of God as a living presence and we are lifted up by His love. In this consciousness we are able to say as Jesus did, "Father."

God. See Jehovah.

Holy Spirit. See Spirit, Holy.

idea.

Meta. An idea is the mode of expression of the mind. Ideas may be thought of as offspring or children of the mind. Since all minds are part of the one Divine Mind, ideas are children of God.

God expresses Himself through ideas. Ideas, timeless and spaceless agents of the divine will, mold and form all outer manifestation.

It is through ideas that we know God. They might be thought of as a kind of bridge by which we can unite ourselves with Him, or as divine messengers sent from Him to us to inform us of His nature and of the nature of the world.

The world is God's idea. The creation of God was in the form of ideas. It was ideal. Man works with divine ideas to mold and shape the substance of God.

Lord.

Meta. In the Old Testament Jehovah, in the New Testament Christ, is referred to as Lord. Jehovah and Christ both represent spiritual man. Lord then is another name for spiritual man. It represents one of the aspects of his being.

As Lord spiritual man is ruler of himself, of his faculties, and of the world. The Lord consciousness is one of dominion. When we enter into our lordship we rule. We rule over ourselves, our thoughts, our body, our environment, and all the creatures and creations of the earth.

old man.

Meta. The old man is the sense man, the Adam man, the personal man. This is the man who sees himself as an imperfect, limited, mortal being rather than as perfect spirit, soul, and body. This is man before he receives the new life that is in Christ.

The old man is subject to death and to all the ills of the flesh. He is separate in consciousness from God.

We must lift up this man and wipe him out of our consciousness so that the Christ may be resurrected in us. This we do by the renewing of our mind.

Promised Land. See Canaan.

Queen of Sheba. See Sheba.

rod.

Meta. The rod represents spiritual power. Men have always considered a rod to be a symbol of power. The wizard waves a wand and the king carries a scepter to show his power. The staff or club is probably man's earliest tool. Through the ages it has assisted him in his rise to mastery.

In the Bible the rod also represents life. In this connection note that Aaron's rod burst into bloom and also turned into a serpent (an Oriental symbol of life). Aaron symbolizes the executive function of divine law. This power expressed itself through his rod. So the rod may rightly be considered a symbol of the power of divine life.

The rod is a symbol of mastery, a symbol of our Christ dominion. When we have gained the Christ mastery, it is expressed in our thoughts as order and strength and in our body as life.

sun.

Meta. The sun represents spiritual intelligence. Light is always a symbol of intelligence, and the sun, the supreme source of light in man's world, represents the highest form of intelligence, spiritual intelligence. The moon, which symbolizes the intellect, receives all its light from the spiritual intelligence. This is the true source of all light. Our individual mind is quickened to the extent that we make it receptive to the inflooding of the light of Spirit.

transfiguration.

Meta. The transfiguration of Jesus described in Matthew and Mark took place when Jesus went with three apostles up into a mountain. There the three beheld Him transfigured.

The Christ body is a transfigured one. We perceive it when we ascend into a high place spiritually, into the secret place of the Most High; when we lift up our thoughts. The apostles of Jesus represent the faculties of the spiritual man. When we lift up our faculties, we behold spiritual reality and we see the body as it is in Truth, refined and vitalized in every cell, quickened and harmonized in every function, transformed into a body of living, luminiferous energy, beautiful, strong, whole, young, eternal, incorruptible, a true center of the divine energy.

III

CPSIA information can be obtained
at www.ICGtesting.com
Printed in the USA
LVHW061039210922
728925LV00008B/195

9 781163 140222